CONTEMPORARY LITERARY CRITICISM

Longman English and Humanities Series

Series Editor: Lee A. Jacobus
University of Connecticut, Storrs

CONTEMPORARY LITERARY CRITICISM

LITERARY AND CULTURAL STUDIES

Second Edition

Robert Con Davis
University of Oklahoma

Ronald Schleifer
University of Oklahoma

Longman
New York & London

Contemporary Literary Criticism: Literary and Cultural Studies, Second Edition

Longman Inc., 95 Church Street, White Plains, N.Y. 10601

Associated companies:
Longman Group Ltd., London
Longman Cheshire Pty., Melbourne
Longman Paul Pty., Auckland
Copp. Clark Pitman, Toronto
Pitman Publishing Inc., New York

Executive editor: Gordon T. R. Anderson
Production editor: Louise M. Kahan
Text and cover design: Steven A. Krastin
Production supervisor: Eduardo Castillo

Library of Congress Cataloging-in-Publication Data

Contemporary literary criticism.

(Longman English and humanities series)
Includes bibliographies.
1. Criticism–History–20th century. I. Davis, Robert Con, 1948– . II. Schleifer, Ronald. III. Series.
PN94.C67 1989 801′.95′0904 88-6780

ISBN 0-8013-0154-8

89 90 91 92 93 94 9 8 7 6 5 4 3

Acknowledgments

"Tradition and the Individual Talent," by T.S. Eliot from *Selected Essays*, pp. 3–11. Copyright © 1950 by Harcourt Brace Jovanovich, Inc.; renewed 1978 by Esme Valerie Eliot. Reprinted by permission of Harcourt Brace Jovanovich and Faber and Faber Ltd.

"The Language of Paradox" by Cleanth Brooks from *The Well Wrought Urn*, pp. 3–21. Copyright © 1947, 1975 by Cleanth Brooks. Reprinted by permission of Harcourt Brace Jovanovich and Dobson Books Ltd.

"The Intentional Fallacy," by W.K. Wimsatt, Jr., and Monroe C. Beardsley from *The Verbal Icon*, pp. 3–18. Copyright © 1946 by The University Press of Kentucky. Reprinted by permission of The University Press of Kentucky.

"Art as Technique," by Viktor Shklovsky from *Russian Formalist Criticism: Four Essays*, translated with an introduction by Lee T. Lemon and Marion J. Reis, pp. 5–24, by permission of University of Nebraska Press. Copyright © 1965 by the University of Nebraska Press.

"Literature as Equipment for Living," by Kenneth Burke from *The Philosophy of Literary Form*, 3rd revised edition, pp. 293–304. Copyright © 1973 by The Regents of the University of California. Reprinted by permission of the University of California Press.

"The Writer's Audience Is Always a Fiction," by Walter J. Ong from *PMLA* 90, pp. 9–21. Copyright © 1975 by the Modern Language Association. Reprinted by permission of the Modern Language Association.

"Interpreting the *Variorum*," by Stanley E. Fish from *Critical Inquiry*, 2, No. 3., pp. 465–486. Copyright © 1980 by The University of Chicago Press. Reprinted by permission of The University of Chicago Press.

"Reading Ourselves: Toward a Feminist Theory of Reading," by Elizabeth A. Flynn and Patrocinio P. Schweickart from *Gender and Reading: Essays on Readers, Texts, and Contexts*, pp. 31–62. Copyright © 1986 by the Johns Hopkins University Press. Reprinted by permission of the Johns Hopkins University Press.

"The Object of Linguistics," "Nature of the Linguistic Sign," "The Concrete Entities of Language," and "Identities, Realities, Values," by Ferdinand de Saussure from *Course in General Linguistics*, pp. 7–17, 65–70, and 102–111. Copyright © 1959 by The Philosophical Library. Reprinted by permission of The Philosophical Library.

"The Structuralist Activity" by Roland Barthes from *Critical Essays*, pp. 213–220. Copyright © 1972 by Northwestern University Press. Reprinted by permission of the publisher.

"The Uncanny and the Marvelous," by Tzvetan Todorov from *The Fantastic*, pp. 40–57, translated by Richard Howard. Copyright ©

Editions du Seuil 1970. Reprinted by permission of Georges Borchardt, Inc.

"Stabat Mater," by Julia Kristeva from *The Kristeva Reader*, pp. 160–186. Copyright © 1986 Columbia University Press. Reprinted by permission of the Columbia University Press.

"Convention and Meaning: Derrida and Austin," by Jonathan Culler from *New Literary History* 13.1, pp. 15–30. Copyright © 1981 by New Literary History. Reprinted by permission of New Literary History.

"Structure, Sign, and Play in the Discourse of the Human Sciences," by Jacques Derrida from *The Structuralist Controversy*, pp. 247–272, edited by Richard Macksey and Eugenio Donato. Copyright © 1972 by the Johns Hopkins University Press. Reprinted by permission of the Johns Hopkins University Press.

"Semiology and Rhetoric," by Paul de Man from *Allegories of Reading*, pp. 3–20. Copyright © 1979 by Yale University Press. Reprinted by permission of the Yale University Press.

"What Is an Author?" by Michel Foucault from *Textual Strategies: Perspectives in Post-Structuralist Criticism*, pp. 141–160, translated from the French and edited by Josue V. Harari. Copyright © 1979 by Cornell University. Reprinted by permission of Cornell University Press and Schmidt Periodicals GmbH.

"Freud's Masterplot," by Peter Brooks from *Yale French Studies*, No. 55/56, pp. 280–300. Copyright © 1977 by Yale French Studies. Reprinted by permission of Yale French Studies.

"Seminar on 'The Purloined Letter,'" by Jacques Lacan from *Yale French Studies*, No. 48, pp. 38–72. Copyright © 1972 by Yale French Studies. Reprinted by permission of Yale French Studies.

"The Frame of Reference: Poe, Lacan, Derrida," by Barbara Johnson from *The Critical Difference*, pp. 110–146. Copyright © 1980 by Johns Hopkins University Press. Reprinted by permission of Johns Hopkins University Press.

"The Purloined Punchline: Joke as Textual Paradigm," by Jerry Flieger from *MLN*, Vol. 98, No. 5, pp. 941–967. Copyright © 1983 by Johns Hopkins University Press. Reprinted by permission of Johns Hopkins University Press.

"Base and Superstructure in Marxist Cultural Theory" by Raymond Williams from *Problems in Materialism and Culture*, pp. 31–49. Copyright © 1980 by Verso. Reprinted by permission of Verso.

"Discourse in Life and Discourse in Art," by V.N. Vološinov from *Freudianism: A Marxist Critique*, pp. 93–116, translated by I.R. Titunik. Copyright © 1976 by Academic Press, Inc. Reprinted by permission of Academic Press, Inc.

(*Continued on page 659*)

Contents

Preface

READING LITERARY CRITICISM

This book derives largely from our experience teaching literary criticism in undergraduate and graduate courses at the University of Oklahoma, the University of Tulsa, and Knox College. Additionally, we were enriched, and this book has benefited, from discussions about contemporary criticism with faculty and students at the University of Hawaii, Kenyon College, Marquette University, Hobart and William Smith Colleges, the Southern Illinois University at Edwardsville, as well as a few other institutions. Finally, this second edition has been greatly improved by the help and good advice of a host of people who have used the first edition. Many of these people were friends and colleagues, but at least equal in number were the many who simply wrote to discuss their experiences using the book in class. In all of these ways, then, the book has been designed and shaped by more or less formal teaching situations.

All of us who have attempted to teach contemporary criticism have repeatedly watched some students struggle with this "exotic" and "difficult" subject. Many other students, however, have few difficulties from the beginning, do well in class and on papers, and clearly enjoy studying criticism. We are convinced that the second group knows something the first does not—namely, how to study this subject, or, better, how to do things with criticism. For literary criticism is not intrinsically a discipline to isolate and study. It is, by definition, always related to something else, and as such it is an activity, a doing in the human sciences, which, as we argue in the introduction, opens onto the largest questions about the relationship of people to culture. "Doing" criticism, in this way, is one of the more important things a literate person can do.

Students who do well with this material not only recognize criticism as essentially an activity to be performed but also see it as important. Other students tend to regard criticism as simply a body of knowledge to be learned, in which failure is always lurking so that each new critical position or school they encounter could be something to confuse and confound them. They imagine that successful completion of the course means getting through it unscathed, "mastering" criticism, but basically remaining untouched by the critical positions they have examined, their own views on literature still intact. In "Psychoanalysis and Education" in Section VIII Shoshana Felman discusses these two versions of "learning." They are related, as she demonstrates, to Jonathan Culler's discussion of "Convention and Meaning" in Section IV, and tutored by the recent turn in psychology and psychoanalysis discussed by Jacques Lacan, Barbara Johnson, and Jerry Flieger in Section V. The "performative" version of learning encourages students to view a course in criticism as a tour on which they will explore a number of worlds from the "inside." When students read the New Critics, for example, as much as possible they should "become" New Critics and see a text held in tension by irony and paradox—

organized, as Cleanth Brooks says, by the structure of the imagination. When they read poststructuralism, they should come to know a text as decentered by the play of difference and learn to read while undoing the fixation of hierarchical authority. As Marxist critics, they should try to understand a text as situated within an ideological superstructure in relation to an historical and "material" base, while as feminist critics, they should (whether they are men or women) self-consciously read, in Elaine Showalter's words, "as a woman."

In other words, "becoming" a critic is making the assumptions particular critics make about literature and culture in their reading and understanding. Learning (and "doing") criticism, like learning to play the piano, is something one practices to do, that one does by *doing*. Students may eventually reject some or all of the critical schools covered. But while studying each school, they can try to see it as one of its adherents might view it. Becoming a "member" of the critical school we are studying constitutes a methodological wager that valuable insight can be gained from a sympathetic entry into a critical system, as opposed to an "objective" scrutiny of a foreign object—or a wary tiptoeing around a danger. At the end of this book, essays will examine the most fundamental assumptions of these schools themselves and situate the practice of criticism in larger social contexts of the classroom, the profession, and society at large. But even these macrocosmic approaches to criticism—these broad "stances"—are positions to be assumed by students.

Seeing criticism not as a set of monuments—or dangers to avoid, as the case may be—but as a set of activities undertaken with others who have made a record of their explorations in literary studies makes a critical stance something that one tries out, tries on, lives in, lives through, and digests. It is an experience that one actively engages in rather than a difficulty that one avoids or fends off. In short, doing things with criticism makes it possible to understand and to enact criticism rather than merely to know it.

READING *CONTEMPORARY LITERARY CRITICISM*

This book is intended to help readers to do things with—to explore and interrogate—contemporary literary criticism and theory. To that end, it provides the immediate background for current criticism with essays from the Modernist and Formalist movements. The book then presents criticism from six major paradigms, or large systems of thought—rhetorical, structuralist, poststructuralist, psychological, historical, and gender-based—and a final section (the longest in the book) examines the ways that contemporary criticism has taught us to reexamine and "critique" (a concept explicitly discussed in the introduction to Section IV) the practice of literary studies themselves in terms of the "ethics" of criticism, the profession of teaching, and the formation of literary canons, of what comprises "literature." This is not an inclusive listing of contemporary approaches to reading literature—it presents little that deals with traditional literary history or, at another extreme, the homosexual dimensions in literature. And it touches too little on the rich, recent work demonstrating the relationship between reading and writing. But the eight areas covered are arguably major developments that suggest and connect with many of the others and are likely to spawn other developments in this century and beyond.

THE STRUCTURE OF THE SECTIONS

A significant feature of this book is the manner in which each section is structured. First of all, we have chosen the first essay of each section to provide a relatively clear and basic description of the school or approach of the whole section. Burke, Culler, Williams, Brooks, and Showalter each provide a lucid introduction to a way of thinking about literature—a way of performing, enacting, criticism—which helps to situate the essays that follow in each section. Even in Section III we have attempted to introduce the interdisciplinary work of structuralism with Saussure's technical but illuminating attempt to reorient students to language study. In the first and last sections, the opening essays have a conspicuous function. T. S. Eliot's famous "Tradition and the Individual Talent" begins *Contemporary Literary Criticism* by reminding us that "criticism is as inevitable as breathing." Northrop Frye's equally famous essay then begins the last section by attempting to define the "function" of criticism at the present time. Both of these essays help to situate the activity of criticism in general in relation to wider areas of concern addressed in the book as a whole.

Moreover, the essays of each section were not chosen for their harmony with one another. While the essays in Section V dealing with what is perhaps the most formidable language of contemporary approaches to literature, that of recent French psychoanalysis, build upon one another to reinforce understanding through reading and rereading, every other section is designed to include in its last selection a work within its particular paradigm that raises important questions about the approach of that section. Viktor Shklovsky's essay in Section I, for instance, offers a version of formalism that participates in and yet transforms the Western Formalisms of T. S. Eliot, Cleanth Brooks, and Wimsatt and Beardsley. Patrocinio Schweickart, in Section II, offers a feminist overview and critique of the versions of rhetorical criticism described in that section. Julia Kristeva's haunting essay in Section III both presents and undermines the scientific semiotics examined in that section. Perhaps most striking is Stephen Greenblatt's "new historicism" in Section VI that subtly transforms the "base/superstructure" model of Marxist criticism into a more "textual" model—a "superstructure/superstructure" model as it were—of the new historicism. Michel Foucault offers a similar "reorienting" of deconstructive criticism in Section IV, and Gayatri Spivak, in Section VII, brings the kind of social critique that feminist studies have incorporated within their critical practice to alter the practice of Western feminism itself. Even the difficulties of Section V that we attempted to mitigate with more "harmonious" selections are subject to the scrutiny of Jerry Flieger's overview of Freudian and Lacanian readings in relation to feminism. It is our conviction—supported by our and others' experience—that these conflicts and the diversity they represent will enable students to explore contemporary criticism productively beyond the eight paradigms represented.

THE STRUCTURE OF THE BOOK

Like the other sections, the essays of Section VIII, "Ethics, Profession, Canon," are designed to raise questions about one another, and in this section we have included a version of the Miller/Abrams debate discussed in the introduction as well as Edward Said's critical look at the nature of contemporary critical "debate" altogether. But we have also designed this section to answer, in the wider context of the "cultural studies" discussed in the introduction, the various approaches *Contemporary Literary Criticism* presents, and to engage in "debate" with many of the essays from other sections. Here again, Frye's introductory essay addresses, among other things (including the "pluralism" of M. H. Abrams's approach in this section), the formalism of Section I and the "textual rhetoric" of Section II, and it offers a rationale for the systematization of structuralism in Section III. J. Hillis Miller's essay catalogues the various "grounds" represented by various schools of criticism (Sections III, IV, V, VI, and VII), even while it attempts to argue with the Arnoldian premises of literary historians like Abrams (Section VIII) and rhetoricians like Ong (Section II). Said examines the debates of criticism from an "historical" view that, implicitly and explicitly, examines the historical approaches of Section VI, and Felman expands the view of psychoanalysis (Section V) to include teaching. Gates offers a social–historical reading—in relation to Afro-American culture—of the "signifying" of structuralism and poststructualism (Sections III and IV), and Robinson examines feminist studies (Section VII) in relation to the literary canon.

In other words, the essays of this book are closely interrelated, and the last section attempts to make that interrelationship clear. There are two other ways we have attempted to clarify this. The introduction to each section provides a list of "related" readings at its end. These alternative readings address the concerns defined by the paradigm of that section from a different vantage point. Further, each section provides cross references to essays in other sections as well as to a variety of readings not contained in the book. In this way, students and instructors can choose to follow a thematic rather than paradigmatic exploration of contemporary literary studies. But more than this, the introduction to each section also offers an overview of the paradigm governing the essays contained in it, which aims, as far as possible, to relate that section to the others. Just as, earlier in the preface, we attempted to relate our discussion of ways of reading criticism to the two definitions of teaching Felman examines in Section VIII—and then offered a short list of essays in the book that help define her approach—so the introduction to each section offers discursive relationships among the sections themselves.

We have substantially redesigned *Contemporary Literary Criticism*—substantially changing the essays from the first edition—so that there are twenty-five new essays, and only nine remain from the first edition. We have also substantially redefined and reordered the section headings. The most striking addition, we feel, is the expansion of the general introduction and the eight section introductions. We have attempted, in these introductions, to offer a short overview of contemporary literary and cultural criticism, and we believe that one possible way of reading this text is to begin with the introductions, as one integrated discussion and as a kind of intellectual history of contemporary thought about literature and discourse in general. To this end we have extensively interrelated the discussions across sections. The general introduction examines contemporary criticism and the "humanities" in relation to the concept of the "human sciences" and in relation to cultural studies. Later, the introduction to Section IV, drawing on essays from throughout the book, attempts to define the crucial term "critique" in ways that shed light on all the modes of contemporary literary criticism. And the central introduction, that of Section V (the longest sectional introduction), attempts to offer a wide discussion of literary studies before and after the advent of "poststructuralism" in the context of psychological approaches to literature: it discusses the introduction of archetypal criticism in the 1950s and the earlier "genetic" criticism of ego-psychology before introducing the specifics of its section. In this, it attempts to situate not only psychoanalytical criticism but all the various forms of criticism "post" structuralism—deconstruction, Marxism, feminism, and the wider cultural critique of Section VIII, including, of course, the "semiotic" Freud of recent psychological criticism. The last introduction in many ways sums up all the other sectional introductions, and the introductions together comprise a history—a coherent narrative and survey—of contemporary critical thought.

Thus, *Contemporary Literary Criticism* offers alternative tables of contents in the cross-referenced essays in the introductions, and it offers, as well, a text-survey of the field of criticism and theory as a whole. Many who offered suggestions and criticism based on using the first edition expressed a need for such guides for students and classes, and we hope that these innovations will prove to be useful.

ACKNOWLEDGMENTS

As we mentioned, a large number of people assisted us in redesigning the second edition of *Contemporary Literary Criticism*. As in the first edition, Gordon T. R. Anderson of Longman helped us immensely and gave much encouragement. Many colleagues and friends at the University of Oklahoma lent books, read material, made suggestions, and endlessly discussed this collection with us. They include James Comas, David S. Gross, Nancy Mergler, and Alan R. Velie. Also, several colleagues and graduate students wrote some of the biographical headnotes for the critics represented in the book, as follows: John C. Orr—*W. K. Wimsatt, Monroe C. Beardsley*, and *Cleanth Brooks;* David S. Gross—*Fredric Jameson, Raymond Williams*, and *Terry Eagleton;* Thomas Elliott—*Peter Brooks* and *Tzvetan Todorov;* Jeannie Rhodes—*Elaine Showalter* and *Julia Kristeva;* Joyce Zonana—*Sandra M. Gilbert;* Suzanne Rose—*Gayatri Chakravorty Spivak* and *Hélène Cixous;* Tom Argiro—*Walter Ong, S. J.;* James Comas—*Kenneth Burke* and *Michel Foucault*; Susan Williams—*Jonathan Culler* and *Edward Said;* Elizabeth Hinds—*Jacques Lacan* and (with Thomas Bowden) *Mikhail Bakhtin;* Pamela Liggett—*Ferdinand de Saussure;* Dorie Glickman—*T. S. Eliot;* Kate Meyers—*Patrocinio Schweickart* and *Shoshana Felman;* Betty Neal—*Barbara Johnson* and *Lillian Robinson;* Justin Everett—*Northrop Frye;* T. Roring—*Stephen Greenblatt*. Our greatest debt, however, is to Thaïs Morgan of Arizona State University who, as in the first edition, offered superb general advice and helpful specific suggestions beyond what we could have hoped for. In addition to all of this help, we received much encouragement and practical advice from Nina Baym, Shari Benstock, Paul Bové, Peter Brooks, Régis Durand, Stanley Fish, Barbara Foley, Sandra M. Gilbert, Norman N. Holland, Juliet McCannell, Patrick McGee, J. Hillis Miller, James C. Raymond, Russell Reising, Edward Said, and Elaine Showalter.

Dr. Kenneth Hoving, Vice Provost for Research, and Dr. Robert Hemenway, Dean of the College of Arts and Sciences, kindly supplied two research assistants, Christy Leiter and Jeannie Rhodes—wonderful and tireless helpers without whom there would be no second edition of this book. Also, we wish to thank Dr. George D. Economou, our department chair, for continued support including the valuable assistance of Paula Stacy and Resa Masopust, who did much work and solved many problems for us—we still owe them lunch.

We are profoundly grateful to all of these many friends for their help.

Robert Con Davis
Ronald Schleifer

INTRODUCTION: THE STUDY OF CRITICISM AT THE PRESENT TIME

AN APOLOGY FOR CRITICISM

It should not surprise any reader of an introduction to literary criticism to encounter defensiveness and apology. Matthew Arnold established the genre of the *apologia critica* when he began "The Function of Criticism at the Present Time" (1864) by mentioning the "many objections" to a previous "proposition about criticism, and its importance for the present day." He had erred, he quoted his detractors as saying, in that the "importance . . . [he] assigned to criticism . . . was excessive." Arnold then pointed out that there is creativity in criticism as well as in literature: "If it were not so," he said, "all but a very few men would be shut out from the true happiness of all men." Northrop Frye also took this apologetic stance in the introduction to *Anatomy of Criticism* (1957), an introduction first published in 1949, and reprinted in Section VIII of this book, as "The Function of Criticism at the Present Time." In that essay Frye worried that the critic was being viewed as an "artist manqué" and that criticism was taken as a "parasite form of literary expression," a "second-hand imitation of creative power." Appearing fifteen years after this text and apparently confirming Frye's fear, Susan Sontag in *Against Interpretation* (1966) scolded all critics for their interpretation of literary texts, for their claims, in particular, that "X is really—or really means—A. . . . That Y is really B. . . . That Z is really C." More valuable than this misleading activity, in Sontag's view, was "transparence," "the highest, most liberating value in art"—that is, "experiencing the luminousness of the thing itself, of things being what they are." Interpretation, she concluded rather sharply, is simply pointless. David Lodge disputed this attitude in his foreward to *Twentieth-Century Literary Criticism* (1972) and imagined a cadre of "teachers of literature who believe that students should be discouraged from reading criticism, on the grounds that such reading blunts their capacity for independent response and judgment."

More recently, Geoffrey Hartman wrote his own version of the *apologia critica* in *Criticism in the Wilderness* (1980), the epigraph for which he took from Arnold's "Function of Criticism" essay. Beginning with T. S. Eliot's assurance that "criticism is as inevitable as breathing," Hartman explores "the gulf between philosophic criticism [in Continental Europe] and *practical criticism* [in England and the United States]," repeatedly assuring us that "criticism" must be accorded its status as "a genre, or a primary text," too. In this Hartman is shifting the grounds of anxiety associated with criticism—or at least making them more apparent. This anxiety is occasioned by the possibility that criticism might be more than just commentary, more, in fact, than "just" literary. Along this same line, J. Hillis Miller in "The Search for Grounds in Literary Study" (Section VIII) focuses his discussion around Arnold and contemporary understandings of his critical practice in order to isolate an "imperial" element in literary criticism. Beginning in the eighteenth century at least, Miller argues, literary criticism—as well as "contemplating" and "explaining" literary works—has attempted to address wider areas of cultural practice beyond literature. The study of literature, Miller says, "has been weighted down in our culture with the burden of carrying from generation to generation the whole freight of the values of that culture, what Matthew Arnold called 'the best that is known and thought in the world.' " Miller explicitly raises the questions of why this should be—what historical events in the eighteenth or nineteenth centuries might have contributed to this practice, and what implications it has for the study of literature. But whatever its implications, this phenomenon has occasioned repeated apologies for criticism, repeated discussions and much anxiety about the nature and goals of literary study.

THE CONTRARIETY OF CRITICISM

In this context undergraduate and graduate literature students could well have their own anxiety about the *apologia critica*. They may wonder what they are getting into when the critics themselves are unsure about what they are doing. Is this *apologia* a gesture of modesty cloaking the grand—perhaps presumptuous—ambitions of traditional literary study? Is it an indication that critics are simply nervous about the usefulness of what they are doing? It is historically true that from Dante's time on, writers also have been critics. The coupling of poetry and poetics, therefore, should not be startling to anyone. Why, then, should critics—at least since the time of Arnold—be nervous or even unclear about what they do, especially now, when so many "do" criticism during what can legitimately be called "the critical age"? Indeed, most of the "literary theorists" in world history, those who actually try to formulate the principles of literary study, are probably alive at the present time.

Despite the wide practice of criticism and formulation of theory, the conflict within critical practice that Arnold articulates and Miller describes gives rise to great anxiety and great intellectual debate. This conflict is the contradiction between the modest activity of creating a situation in which the best that is known and thought can have wide currency (Sontag's "transparency" or Frye's description of the job of criticism "to get as many people in contact with the best that has been and is being thought and said") and the imperial "burden" of maintaining cultural values in general (Frye's description of the "verbal universe, in which life and reality are inside literature" and which only the methods of criticism can help us to understand). In fact, the very *function* of criticism has changed or become more self-reflective in recent time. Contemporary criticism has expanded its horizon to include a vast array of questions (Miller's "freight") that heretofore seemed outside, or only implicit within, its purview. This includes questions of politics, semantics, the philosophy of language, sexual and social relations, and probing concerning the nature of literary study—its responsibilities and its very objects of study.

Such expansion has occasioned much controversy and debate, exacerbating rather than resolving the contradiction within criticism and the anxiety of its practice. The exploration of wider cultural questions has come in recent times to be called literary "theory," and while literary theory is not always explicitly apologetic, it often meets tremendous opposition, especially within the academy, since it has tended to make explicit the very contradiction in criticism that occasioned Arnold's anxiety. Moreover, the apologies for criticism we have examined are forms of self-consciousness in critical practice, and in one sense literary "theory" is always apologetic precisely because it self-consciously explores and situates what it is doing. Thus, from the first articulations of modern literary theory in the early nineteenth century when Friedrich Schlegel imagined criticism to be a "reconstructive" process whereby a critic enhances the development of art, it has self-consciously explored its practice and social situation. In so doing, as Schlegel imagined (and Hartman later claimed), the critic actually elevates criticism as a genre to the level of art. Schlegel's romantic view of criticism as an organic outgrowth of art survives in the poetics of the English Romantics and in the theory of such neoclassicists as T. S. Eliot and Ezra Pound, as well as in much current thinking.

The contrary view, however, also present in the early nineteenth century, says that criticism merely supplements art and, at worst, is a parasite draining away its lifeblood. At best it is a "hermeneutics" whose aim is to recover the intentional meanings of the artist and then, mission accomplished, quietly disappear. Only on occasion, in this view, does criticism marginally increase our appreciation of artistic form, thereby giving support to art in a limited way. This separation of criticism from art is also implicit in Frank Kermode's idea of genre as a "consensus, a set of foreunderstandings exterior to a text which enable us to follow that text." Kermode, thus, believes that criticism is totally dependent on literature, and he therefore has little sympathy for the conflicts, and convolutions, of current theory. Criticism is merely an adjunct to literature, and the two—as Kermode believes—belong in different areas of culture anyway.

Current theory, lacking Schlegel's belief in unity and Kermode's in separation, has intensified this debate. Contemporary criticism, in fact, is stranded between these two views—"nervous" about criticism's having a separate identity, and yet it constantly undermines distinctions separating fiction and poetry, or prose fiction and expository prose, and even (despite what Kermode says) the basic distinction between criticism and literature. Certainty about the discreteness of critical and literary texts has been vanishing for some time, and we are left with a hybrid critical "thing," which Henry James's term for the novel as a genre could describe—a baggy monster, that is, criticism and literature intertwined and intermixed, and mutually implicated. In other words, we consistently find it more difficult than Kermode suggests to place the implicit "and" between criticism/literature and cannot say precisely how the two relate, either merging or forming a relationship. As we have been asking, why does it make critics nervous to formulate the relationship of criticism and literature?

THE CONTEMPORARY DEBATE

We can focus on these questions by looking at a specific dispute, the recent controversy over the criticism/literature relationship between M. H. Abrams and J. Hillis Miller. In a review of Abrams's *Natural Supernaturalism: Tradition and Revolution in Romantic Literature* (1971), Miller—who genuinely appreciates Abrams's work—grants the fundamental claim of Abrams's historical scholarship, namely that "Blake, Hölderlin, Wordsworth, and the rest have 'translated' the supernaturalism of the Platonic and Christian tradition into a humanism" and that what followed this "translation" is the fact of Romanticism itself. But Miller goes on to add the qualification that "Abrams' presuppositions [in such a study] . . . are themselves a version of Western metaphysics, even a version which might be defined as romantic. *Natural Supernaturalism* therefore presents the familiar spectacle of a book about Romanticism which is permeated through and through with Romantic assumptions." Miller is arguing that Abrams, unconsciously drawing upon Romantic assumptions in his work, unwittingly blurs the distinction between criticism and literature, even though it is this distinction upon which his "criticism" is based.

In a description of his work Abrams says that "in retrospect, I think I was right to compose *Natural Supernaturalism* . . . by relying [almost solely] on taste, tact, and intuition rather than on a controlling method," because the rules of Romantic discourse "are complex, elusive, unsystematic, and subject to innovative modification; they manifest themselves in the intuitive expertise of the historian; and the specification of these rules should not precede, but follow practice." Thus, whereas Miller demonstrated that Abrams wrote a Romantic (though "critical") fiction in *Natural Supernaturalism*—a "fiction" in the genre of "criticism," a fiction that reiterates the characteristics of other Romantic fictions—Abrams, like Kermode, claims that he was simply working intuitively to discover the threads of Romantic influence that are located with objective validity "out there," actually in poetry. Abrams saw no such Romantic stance in his own work, no mixing, or contamination, of poetry with criticism. Literature and Criticism, for Abrams, like "life" and "art," are intelligible only as distinct entities, the "and" in this coupling indicating total separation.

Further, Abrams also sees criticism as a fundamentally derivative pursuit that draws its life (parasitically) from literature's body. Criticism, if the world were a little better place, would not be needed. In contrast, for Miller the "and" implicit in "criticism/literature" is a moment of "aporia" designating varying and reversible priorities wherein we may see—upsetting Abrams's schema—the "critic as host" to literary texts. This is a reversal, as Miller writes, in which "both word and counterword ["host" and "guest"] subdivide. Each reveals itself to be fissured already within itself, to be" in Miller's term borrowed from Freud, "uncanny." In other words, literature is the host, as Abrams claims, or criticism and literature participate in a "literary" discourse where "host" and "guest" are significant and reversible alternatives—phases, so to speak, in the process of reading. In sum, for Miller, criticism (nurture) is inherently "fictional," and fiction (nature) is deeply "critical." For Abrams, on the other side, the two clearly are not interchangeable in any way that challenges their distinctness or intelligibility as categories.

The Abrams/Miller debate points up, among other things, the range of possibilities in current theory for positioning criticism in relation to literature. If we use Abrams and Miller to mark extremes, we can further divide contemporary critical strategies into four major areas. First, according to Kermode and Abrams, the criticism/literature relationship is broadly *exegetical*. Criticism here—either a full "interpretation" or a narrow judgment about generic classification—finds the external constraints on a text, a dimension not part of the text but a "formal" ordering of otherwise polymorphous textual "content." Suggesting a brace or prosthetic limb, criticism in this regard is the undesirable and yet unavoidable thing, useful but embarrassing. This is a variant of Sontag's anti-interpretation stance and close to the "textual rhetoric" presented in Section II of this book. In that section, Walter Ong, for example, examines how the language of literature—its rhetoric—creates roles for readers to assume in relation to a text.

Second, positing a less rigid division between criticism and literary text is the *hermeneutic* approach. Most pointedly in phenomenological interpretation (as in the Geneva School), this criticism attempts to discover literary "form" in the sympathetic and imaginative probing of a text, the intimate interrogation of the textual "interior." This approach, as practiced by Georges Poulet, Gaston Bachelard, and (at one time) J. Hillis Miller, entails believing that a text constitutes its own interior "world," which can be entered directly by the reader through an imaginative experience of the text. This is close to the rhetorical analysis of Kenneth Burke (Section II), but unlike that analysis this approach posits less distance between the manipulated reader and the manipulating text.

A third approach, positing a smaller separation of criticism from literary texts, is that of *Reader-Response*. Here, the relationship is an "affective," or psychological one in criticism that attempts to describe the text's "affect" (or emotional contour) and "effect" on the reader. This kind of criticism may also, as in Stanley Fish's work (Section II), suggest a less "personal" and more "social" and conventional context in which to understand the workings of the text within the reader. (Fish's conventional interpretation of Reader-Response criticism can be traced to the "ordinary language" philosophy of J. L. Austin—discussed in Section IV—and, ultimately, to the late philosophy of Ludwig Wittgenstein, an approach sharply opposed to Ong's "personal" rhetoric.)

Finally, when the barrier between criticism and literature dissolves altogether, the *semiotic* (see Julia Kristeva, Section III) and *deconstructive* (Paul de Man, Section IV, and Henry Louis Gates, Section VIII) approaches suggest that the criticism/literature relationship involves multiple influences among both critical and literary texts and among, more broadly, textual "systems"—that is, "chains" of signifiers that move freely through every order of text. In the semiotic and deconstructive views, each "text," whether critical or literary, is a localized but always indeterminate inscription of an "intertext." Thus, at one extreme, represented by Abrams and Kermode, we find the essentially rhetorical theory wherein genre is an extratextual "context of expectation," precisely "a set of foreunderstandings" present in readers' and writers' minds. At the other extreme, with semiotics and deconstruction, criticism is positioned problematically as an indeterminate fold (or twist) in reading. The critical text slips in and out of sight as it merges into and then comes out of the literary text.

Another important view of the criticism/literature relationship is implied in this collection's many practical and interpretive essays. Each such essay addresses issues of reading, textuality, narrativity, influence, history, or cultural reference and, thereby, stages an encounter between literature and current theory. Each such essay brings theoretical discourse into contact with literary texts and finds insights in the careful reading of a text. Like other critical/literary encounters—Abram's *The Mirror and the Lamp* (1953), Michael

Ryan's *Marxism and Deconstruction* (1982), and Jane Gallop's *The Daughter's Seduction* (1982)—these essays argue for critical connections that have previously gone unnoticed or have been strategically ignored.

Perhaps closer to the Miller pole than the Abrams, many of these "practical" essays indicate the intervention of history in criticism. The reader interprets a text from a defined viewpoint and produces a unique "reading" in that encounter, and this reading is a radically historical concern, an unrepeatable event in literary history, happening each time as if for the first time. Gerald Graff, in his study of criticism at the present time, notes this contemporary historical sense in the coupling of "postmodern . . . literature and literary criticism," the reading of one with the other marking a particular historical moment. The same assumption holds in Raymond Federman's *Surfiction: Fiction Now and Tomorrow* (1981), an impassioned promotion of the connection, and the inseparability, of contemporary theory and postmodern literature. In this work, Federman predicted that "the primary focus" of fiction in the future will be not to "pretend any longer to pass for reality, for truth, or for beauty. Consequently, fiction will no longer be regarded as a mirror to life, as a pseudorealistic document that informs us about life, nor will it be judged on the basis of its social, moral, psychological, metaphorical, commercial value." In Federman's view, tomorrow's fiction will "unmask its own fictionality" and "expose the metaphor of its own fraudulence." This prediction divides into four propositions for "the future of fiction": (1) the typography of traditional novels, which has become "boring and restrictive," will be changed so as "to give the reader an element of choice . . . [and] discovery"; (2) the advent of this new typography will mean that "linear and orderly narration," "no longer possible," will be broken up and refracted; (3) these developments will then lead to the realization that "there cannot be any truth nor any reality exterior to fiction," to the extent that "writing fiction will be a process of inventing, on the spot, the material of fiction"; and (4) future fiction "will be seemingly devoid of any meaning, it will be deliberately illogical, irrational, unrealistic, non sequitur, and incoherent."

These avant-garde propositions—intended to expose "the fictionality of reality" and to show that "reality as such does not exist, or rather it exists only in its fictionalized version"—seem distant from current concerns with ethics and politics in criticism. Even so, Federman's propositions constitute not merely "criticism," in this case a prediction for the future, but a fundamentally literary text situated within the genre of "criticism of prose fiction." This genre, whether the "predictions" are correct or not, must be taken precisely as a fictional construct, a piece of "surfiction" and, thus, aimed at no "truth" and touching no "reality exterior to fiction." Federman's overtly "critical" text, thus, provides its own case in point, being neither merely a critical commentary (nurture) on literature conceived as a host nor purely a fictional text (nature). Federman's text, a kind of "aliterature" (in Ihab Hassan's term), is simultaneously critical and literary, the very sort of "fiction" Federman predicted.

We have examined Federman's work because, in making no gesture toward apology the way others (even self-proclaimed radical departures) often do, his text helps us to distinguish the important features of a transitional phase in literary criticism, or the movement from the New Criticism of Cleanth Brooks and Wimsatt and Beardsley, as well as the historical criticism of Abrams, to contemporary developments of reader-centered approaches. Moreover, Federman is describing in "surfiction" the critical practice with which we end this volume, Henry Louis Gates, Jr.'s "The Blackness of Blackness: A Critique of the Sign and the Signifying Monkey." In that essay, Gates follows the traditional black practice of "signify'n"—as it is designated in what Ralph Ellison calls "the unwritten dictionary of American Negro usage"—through colloquial "practices" in black cultures and reconceives "signify'n" as a "critical" tool that Gates "discovers" in the postmodern fiction of Ishmael Reed. In this essay—disarmingly "traditional" in its critical presentation—Gates situates himself at the intersection of the "transitional phase" of criticism, semiotic studies, and social and cultural history. That is, he situates himself between an old paradigm strongly akin to existentialism, archetypal interpretation, and Kantian esthetics—which flourished during what may be called the Age of the Critic, an age of "expert" critical strategies formulated under the authority of T. S. Eliot, the southern Fugitives, I. A. Richards, and Northrop Frye—and the new paradigm influenced by Ferdinand de Saussure, Martin Heidegger, Claude Lévi-Strauss, and Maurice Merleau-Ponty. The latter paradigm, as Gates's work shows, has connections with deconstruction, Reader-Response criticism, and the social consciousness of feminism, under the strong sway of Jacques Derrida, Geoffrey Hartman, J. Hillis Miller, Paul de Man, Stanley Fish, Julia Kristeva, and Jacques Lacan.

This new paradigm develops in what may be called the Age of the Reader, a period of nonspecialized reading strategies, or "ordinary" reading. Whereas in the earlier paradigm critic and criticism were thought (though unconsciously) to be vampirizing literature's vital body, in today's paradigm the critical parasite is also a host, or a "primary text," as Geoffrey Hartman claims, that gives rise to interpretation, too. This shift from text to reader—really from text-as-product to reading activity—entails a new view of the criticism/literature relationship. While criticism in the New Critical paradigm was a useful but artificial addition to the literary experience conceived as a transparent experience—as Sontag said—of "the luminousness of the thing itself, of things being what they are," in the contemporary paradigm criticism is a species of literature, another way to read and write, the parasite/host relationship becoming a paradigm of multiple possibilities and not a fixed orientation. In Gates, however, a third dimension can be seen, what we will call a sense of the social or "cultural" place of contemporary criticism.

THE HUMAN SCIENCES AND CULTURAL CRITICISM

Another form the contemporary debate in criticism has taken—in a sense, an essential debate—revolves around the question of the nature of humanistic study and the "disciplinary" practice of literary criticism. The traditional view is that the "humanities" have been areas of knowledge that examined unique human events. Every "object" of humanistic study—Chaucer's *Canterbury Tales*, the battle of Waterloo, Locke's *Treatise on Human Nature*, Picasso's *Guernica*, Mozart's *Hunt Quartet*, even Newton's *Principia* and Darwin's *Origin of Species*—is a unique event that occurred only once and, consequently, can only be studied through description and paraphrase. As the linguist Louis Hjelmslev noted, according to this traditional view "humanistic, as opposed to natural phenomena are nonrecurrent and for that very reason cannot, like natural phenomena, be subjected to exact and generalizing treatment. . . . In the field of the humanities," he goes on, "consequently, there would have to be a different method [from science]—namely, mere description, which would be nearer to poetry than to exact science—or, at any event, a method that restricts itself to a discursive form of presentation in which the phenomena pass by, one by one, without being interpreted through a system." This "method," Hjelmslev suggests, is "history" in its most chronological manifestation. Since the "objects" of humanistic study are unique, they can be catalogued only in chronological order, and so the humanities have traditionally been "historical" studies: the history of philosophy, the history of art, history itself, the history of science, literary history, and so forth. Frye said the same thing about critical practice in 1949: "literature being as yet unorganized by criticism, it still appears as a huge aggregate or miscellaneous pile of creative efforts. The only organizing principle so far discovered in it is chronology, and when we see the miscellaneous pile strung out along a chronological line, some coherence is given to it by tradition [chronologically conceived]."

Implicit in Frye and Hjelmslev is the possibility that the humanities could "reorient" themselves and adopt a more scientific model for their study. Instead of following what Frye calls "naive induction," the humanities could attempt, as Hjelmslev says, "to rise above the level of mere primitive description to that of a systematic, exact, and generalizing science, in the theory of which all events (possible combinations of elements) are foreseen and the conditions for their realization established." Such a discipline would attempt to account for the objects of the humanistic study in terms of systematic relationships among them (e.g., Frye's discussion of genre) or among the elements that combine to constitute those objects (e.g., Paul de Man's discussion of grammar and tropes in Section IV) rather than their chronological description. In this case, the "humanities" could be conceived as the "human sciences."

In such a conception, as Frye notes, criticism would take its place among the social sciences rather than the natural sciences. In fact, such a division can be seen in the social sciences themselves. In the *Course in General Linguistics*, for instance, Saussure specifically distinguishes between two methods of studying economics—economic history and the "synchronic" study of the economic system at any particular moment. Most of the social sciences, in contemporary practice, are divided in this fashion. Psychology, for instance, encompasses the analysis of unique case histories of "clinical" psychology, and experimental psychology attempts to articulate the "general" functioning of mental activity. Anthropology encompasses both the study of unique cultures and, as in Claude Lévi-Strauss's work, the "general" functioning of aspects of culture. Even an earth science such as geology studies both the historical development and the synchronic composition of geological formations.

In this way, literary study also can be seen to offer two "methods" of study—in Frye's terms, literary history and more or less systematizing criticism. What allows the systemization of criticism, however, is the common and "recurrent" element of traditional humanistic study, the fact that, as Hjelmslev notes, all the humanities deal in the study of language and discourse. Discourse, moreover, is common to the social sciences in general, and consequently a systematic criticism could be a more general theory of discourse, a more general study of cultural (i.e., discursive) formations. In this way, criticism can transform itself into being the "human science" which would study the functioning and creation of a host of "discourses" within society (including, of course, "literary" discourse). Such a human science would attempt to describe what distinguishes literature from other language uses and what literature shares with them. It would attempt, as many have already attempted, to situate literary practice within other cultural practices (including linguistics, teaching, politics, psychology, philosophy, ideology, sociology—and even the "professional" debates within literary studies themselves), all areas, intersecting with the study of literature, that are examined in various essays of this book.

In a way, then, we are suggesting that the study of criticism can profitably be situated as a part—and a leading part—of the study of culture. A more complete justification for this expansion would necessarily involve a discussion of the definition of the term "culture" beyond what we have offered. "Culture," Raymond Williams notes in *Keywords,* is "one of the two or three most complicated words in the English Language." In another book, *Culture,* Williams says that " 'cultural practice' and 'cultural production' are not simply derived from an otherwise constituted social order but are themselves major elements in its constitution." In this conception, culture is not some "informing spirit" within society; rather, Williams says, it is "the *signifying system* through which necessarily . . . a social system is communicated, reproduced, experienced and explored."

Williams's definitions, of course, are not the only valid description of culture, but it is clear from his ideas that literary studies conceived as a systematized critical activity—a criticism that studies "signifying systems" in a more or less systematic, exact, and generalizing way—is in a position to direct its methods and observations to the widest area of the production of meanings—to cultural activities as specific signifying practices and as a general area of inquiry. In fact, a strong argument can be made that the texts we customarily call "literature" constitute a privileged site where the most important social, psychological, and cultural forces combine and contend. In this way, the attention to discourse, to language in all its manifestations, in its production and in its reception, is a "natural" focus of literary studies and a "natural" outgrowth of criticism. One result of such a possibility has been the recent turn, in critical activity, to the examination of the institution of literary study in the academy. In books like Robert Scholes's *Textual Power,* Richard Ohmann's *English in America,* Gerald Graff's *Professing Literature,* Jonathan Culler's *Framing the Sign: Criticism and its Institutions,* Frank Lentricchia's *Criticism and Social Change,* as well as a host of feminist and black studies, the very nature of the study of literature is being examined in relation to other cultural practices. We have attempted in this book—and especially in the last section—to include as much as possible this wider conception of critical practice as cultural critique as an important informing force within contemporary literary criticism.

THE DIFFICULTY OF CRITICISM

A central paradox—given the widened scope and ambition of criticism we are describing, and given, as we have suggested, the reorientation of recent critical work toward the reader—is that many critical texts in this book should be "writerly" (as Roland Barthes said), or obscure in their density and generally difficult to read. Yet such is the case. It is a commonplace of contemporary thought that so much contemporary criticism and cultural critique—de Man's literary studies, Kristeva's semiotics, Derrida's "deconstructive" philosophy, the psychoanalysis of Lacan, Jameson's Marxist analyses, and Cixous's feminist discourse—should be difficult to follow. But what does it mean exactly for a critical text to be difficult? For one thing, since they did not write in the tradition of *explication de texte,* or "close reading," or in the formalist mode that dominated modern interpretation, these critics are frequently maddeningly elliptical, especially in word play. As George Steiner remarks about such "difficult" writers, it can seem as though "at certain levels, we are not meant to understand at all, and our interpretation, indeed our reading itself, is an intrusion. . . . For whom"—and here Steiner could be referring to many contemporary critical texts—are they "composing [their] cryptograms?" Why should the reading of contemporary criticism be this difficult?

Steiner sheds light on four different types of difficulty—*contingent, modal, tactical*, and above all, *ontological*—that are relevant to the task of reading contemporary criticism. In brief, he describes *contingent* difficulties as those problems we have with the obscurity of a particular text—its exotic or unclear allusions or its use of deconstructive, psychoanalytic, linguistic, and philosophical terms that we, as Steiner said, "need to look up." Either we look up "trace," "aporia," "aphanisis," "metonymy," and "metaphor" and understand them, or we fail to understand. Since current criticism is interdisciplinary and steeped in the debates of philosophy, psychoanalysis, linguistics, and twentieth-century thought generally, the difficulty here can be formidable. Next, *model* difficulty, rather than being an obscurity in the text, is the reader's resistance to a text's presentation and the reader's misunderstanding, or possibly dislike of its mode (its genre or form). Much contemporary criticism, for instance, is polemical—written in a restricted dialogue with other theorists who diligently pursue theoretical debates and ongoing commentaries. This magisterial mode—wherein the writer proclaims and argues, and the audience may be restricted to readers already knowledgeable as critics—can block all understanding by others. (Derrida's, Kristeva's, de Man's, and Lacan's essays are most notorious in this regard.) Third, *tactical* difficulty is created by a writer's strategies for dislocating the reader and inhibiting any usual or conventional response to a text. Steiner identifies this difficulty (and the next) with the strategies of modernist literature—the difficulty, for instance, in simply following the "narrative line" of *The Waste Land*, or the play of ideas and sounds in Wallace Stevens's poetry. But similar difficulties are encountered in criticism. When Kristeva, for example, splits her voice into competing double columns in "Stabat Mater" in Section III, the reader is prevented from following a linear reading pattern. The text, in effect, intentionally dislocates a customary orientation in order to establish a "deconstructive" one, and the competition within the text for the reader's attention helps to accomplish this end. Likewise, Lacan's constant word play and his refusal to spell out and pursue a clear analysis of either Poe's story or the analytic practice he is simultaneously describing in "Seminar on 'The Purloined Letter' " (Section V) present the same tactical difficulty. The reader is intentionally dislocated, just as, one could argue, psychoanalysis itself strategically attempts to dislocate and disorient the patient/reader.

These difficulties—even though they are enough to sabotage a single reading—in time are "naturalized," as the Structuralists say, and become formal and familiar aspects of a text's structure and orientation. In short, in time they become less *difficult*—less a part of textual obscurity, just as, in Jameson's argument in Section VI, the difficulties of modernism themselves have become "canonical" and "reified." The fourth difficulty in reading contemporary criticism—the greatest and by far the most interesting—is *ontological*: the difficulty, as Steiner wrote, that breaks "the contract of ultimate or preponderant intelligibility between poet and reader, between text and meaning. . . . Difficulties of this category cannot be looked up," he continues, because "they confront us with blank questions about the nature of human speech [and] about the status of significance."

An *ontological* difficulty, in other words, arises when the contract is breached between writer and reader, or text and meaning, because the text is positing a new ontology, a new paradigm of understanding. This shift requires a new grasp of phenomena, of their relations, and of the horizon of human possibility behind them. This difficulty is insurmountable except through a transformation of understanding into the mode of the new paradigm—through a change in the sense of what is "real." Miller, in "The Search for Grounds" in Section VIII, begins his essay with literary presentations of such "ontological" difficulties—presentations of what seems to be a sort of breach within "reality" in Maurice Blanchot, George Eliot, and Wallace Stevens, all texts that he says seem "irreducibly strange, inexplicable, perhaps even mad." He goes on, in this essay, to describe the ways criticism has attempted to account for and tame such uncanny experiences.

The scandal presented by contemporary criticism, which goes to the heart of the ontological difficulty, can be described as a radical division, a *split*—the "devasting experience," Miller describes, "of a transformation of the scene which leaves it nevertheless exactly the same." The pervasive figure of the split indicates a sense in contemporary theory of a fundamental division within texts, specifically as regards their involvement in time. Most current theories of textuality, for example, do not emphasize criticism as attempting a unified "reading," or even see a text as defined by "meaning" or "content." They see, instead, a process, a "split" twofold process, that swings like a metronome from side to side—back and forth between textual "product" and "production," between meaning/content and reading activity—and never reaches stability or wholeness. This interpretive model, encompassing order and a large measure of disorder, poses a serious threat to the empirically based tradition of interpretation as a transparent (in Sontag's term) and focusable lens, an open subjectivity through which a detached critical investigator peers into a stable text.

From the viewpoint of much contemporary criticism, in fact, the notion of a detached observer—an epistemological innocent bystander—no longer exists. Rather, contemporary criticism posits complete involvement between critic and text and believes that an ontological fault line, time itself, runs through and creates a radical split in all knowledge, making "subjectivity" (both what we know and how we know it) irremediably problematic. Contemporary criticism, in this regard, is "difficult" because it promotes a new paradigm and a radically new mode of comprehension that fundamentally alters the nature/nurture relationship of literary studies. The greatest difficulty of current criticism, then, has to do with a new paradigm's emergence and the reorientation it necessitates. What the New Critics were accustomed to calling "unity" and "wholeness" in form, as concepts central to interpretation, are unceremoniously marginalized. "Unity" and "wholeness" in literature are now relegated to the periphery of critical concern and are no longer regarded as formative. Changes in contemporary theory have gone that far.

In global shifts such as these—dislocating and potentially painful shifts in which sense and nonsense, the central and the marginal, culture and literature, are seen to switch places—we witness outselves moving from one paradigm to the other, from a world that already made sense to a world that is just now making sense. This revolution in criticism, and the resultant shift in the way we understand literature, poses an ontological difficulty of the highest order. This difficulty, more than any other, explains both the challenge and the excitement of (and also the occasional hostility toward) contemporary literary theory and criticism.

APOLOGIA

Finally, this introductory discussion, too, is a version of the *apologia critica* and implicitly enters the conversation with Matthew Arnold, Northrop Frye, Susan Sontag, Geoffrey Hartman, David Lodge, J. Hillis Miller, and others. But it is an *apologia critica* with an historical difference. The relationship with literature has evolved so that criticism now is no longer automatically cast as nurture, as the poor relation of literature. Instead, contemporary discourse ventures to reconceive this relationship in a variety of ways, and the *apologia critica*—no longer merely a defense of criticism—looks increasingly like a (critical/literary) genre as well, one that could usefully be studied in the context of contemporary criticism that this book attempts to establish. In other words, we may see the *apologia critica* more clearly as a genre once we stop feeling awkward about needing to study and write criticism, which, as we have been arguing, is becoming as *natural* as the reading and writing of literature.

REFERENCES

Abrams, M. H., *The Mirror and the Lamp: Romantic Theory and the Critical Tradition* (New York: Oxford University Press, 1953).

______, *Natural Supernaturalism: Tradition and Revolution in Romantic Literature* (New York: W.W. Norton, 1971).

______, "Rationality and Imagination in Cultural History: A Reply to Wayne Booth," in *Critical Inquiry*, 2 (1976), 447–64.

Arnold, Matthew, *Arnold: Poetry and Prose*, John Bryson, ed. (London: Rupert Hart-Davis, 1954).

Barthes, Roland, *S/Z*, Richard Miller, trans. (New York: Hill and Wang, 1974).

Bloom, Harold, et al., *Deconstruction and Criticism* (New York: Continuum, 1979).

Culler, Jonathan, *Framing the Sign: Criticism and Its Institutions* (Norman, Okla.: University of Oklahoma Press, 1988).

Federman, Raymond, ed., *Surfiction: Fiction Now and Tomorrow*, 2nd ed. (Chicago: Swallow Press, 1981).

Frye, Northrop, *Anatomy of Criticism: Four Essays* (Princeton, N.J.: Princeton University Press, 1957).

Gallop, Jane, *The Daughter's Seduction* (Ithaca: Cornell University Press, 1982).

Graff, Gerald, *Literature Against Itself: Literary Ideas in Modern Society* (Chicago: University of Chicago Press, 1979).

______, *Professing Literature* (Chicago: University of Chicago Press, 1987).

Hartman, Geoffrey H., *Criticism in the Wilderness* (New Haven: Yale University Press, 1980).

Hjelmslev, Louis, *Prolegomena to a Theory of Language*, Francis Whitfield, trans. (Madison: University of Wisconsin Press, 1961).

Kermode, Frank, *Genesis of Secrecy* (Cambridge: Harvard University Press, 1979).

Lentricchia, Frank, *Criticism and Social Change* (Chicago: University of Chicago Press, 1983).

Lodge, David, ed., *Twentieth-Century Literary Criticism: A Reader* (White Plains, N.Y.: Longman, 1972).

Miller, J. Hillis, "The Critic as Host," in his *Deconstruction and Criticism* (New York: Continuum, 1979), 217–53.

———, "Tradition and Difference," *Diacritics*, 2, No. 4 (1972), 6–13.

Ohmann, Richard, *English in America* (New York: Oxford University Press, 1976).

Ryan, Michael, *Marxism and Deconstruction: A Critical Articulation* (Baltimore: Johns Hopkins University Press, 1982).

Schleifer, Ronald, "The Poison of Ink: Post-War Literary Criticism," in *New Orleans Review*, 8 (1981), 241–49.

Scholes, Robert, *Textual Power* (New Haven: Yale University Press, 1985).

Sontag, Susan, *Against Interpretation* (New York: Dell, 1966).

Steiner, George, *On Difficulty and Other Essays* (New York: Oxford University Press, 1978).

Williams, Raymond, *Keywords* (New York: Oxford University Press, 1976).

———, *Culture* (London: Fantana, 1984).

I

MODERNISM AND FORMALISM

It is appropriate to begin *Contemporary Literary Criticism* with essays written at the beginning of the twentieth century representing the "modernist" movement in the arts. At the beginning of the modern era writers and artists from throughout Europe and America were conceiving of themselves and their intellectual life in terms of an ending and a new beginning. Ezra Pound's call to "make it new" became the rallying cry of many in the arts as they sought both to recover the past and to break with it. This book begins with an essay of one of Pound's "students," T. S. Eliot. In his famous essay, "Tradition and the Individual Talent," Eliot virtually begins by asserting that "criticism is as inevitable as breathing and that we should be none the worse for articulating what passes in our minds when we read a book and feel an emotion about it." In this statement Eliot captures the double sense of formalism presented in this section, the exploration of linguistic and literary form as a way of creating the so-called "objective" sense that literature presents and the exploration of that form to examine the subjective "effects" such literary forms give rise to. In the next section we will examine this same dichotomy in terms of conflicting conceptions of rhetoric as the study of formal linguistic figures and of the persuasive power of language. But here we want to offer examples of the modernist sense of literature and culture and the formal treatments of literature that develop from this movement.

MODERNISM

Modernism as a literary movement in the Anglo-American world dates from the early twentieth century and the influence of the French Symbolist poetry of Baudelaire, Mallarmé, Valery, and others. Modernism is a body of literature and criticism as well as a critical perspective—or, rather, several related perspectives—that produced some of the greatest writers and critics of our age. Sometimes the movement is said to have begun at the turn of the century with Conrad and Yeats, but others claim that it is most clearly delineated as a post-World War I phenomenon, best represented by the publications of James Joyce's *Ulysses* and T. S. Eliot's *The Waste Land* in 1922. By some accounts, the movement ended in the mid-1930s; others say it went on until World War II, and some note, as Fredric Jameson points out in Section VI, that contemporary postmodernism is simply another version of modernism. In any case, the height of Modernist fervor was surely Virginia Woolf's assurance in 1924 that "in or about December, 1910, human character changed." Woolf explained that "all human relations have shifted—those between masters and servants, husbands and wives, parents and children. And when human relations change there is at the same time a change in religion, conduct, politics, and literature." A decade earlier D. H. Lawrence had described a similarly radical reconception of human character in a letter to his editor describing the heroine of *The Rainbow:* "I don't so much care about what the woman *feels*—in the ordinary usage of the word. That presumes an *ego* to feel with. I only care about what the woman *is* . . . as a phenomenon (or as representing some greater, inhuman will), instead of what she feels according to the human conception." Like Woolf—and like Eliot in the essay included here—Lawrence is presenting an antiromantic, antiexpressionist conception of human character in literature—a conception of the subject which, as Eliot says, is "impersonal" and a conception of literature as something other than "expressive." It is one that focuses on the *forms* of literature and experience rather than on the narrowest sense of their "personal," "human" significance.

Such an "impersonal" and "formal" conception of literature led many of the Modernists—though not all: Joyce and Auden are notable exceptions—to approve of authoritarian politics to one degree or another. Pound, for instance, thought Italian fascism an important social movement; Eliot proclaimed himself a royalist and conservative and, in some of his published writings, made ethnic (particularly anti-Semitic) remarks he later publicly regretted; Yeats flirted with a right-wing authoritarian Irish party. It has been argued that the kind of "impersonality" that formalism suggests might lead—or at least be conducive—to a disregard for human rights of one kind or another. Some critics, in fact (such as Frank Lentricchia in *After the New Criticism*), have suggested that certain proponents of structuralist and poststructuralist literary criticism share some of these attitudes with their modernist forbears. It is not clear exactly how much structuralism and formalism share as intellectual movements—Lévi-Strauss published an important essay distinguishing structuralism and formalism in 1960 entitled "Structure and Form"—and even if it could be shown that both are species of "formalism," it is clearly not the case that structuralism and poststructuralism attract people with homogenous political views. But recent evidence that Paul de Man—whose work presents one of the most rigorous and "formal" articulations of poststructuralism—voiced pro-Nazi sentiments in articles and book reviews in Belgium during World War II adds support to the contention that there is a correlation between the "formal" sense of esthetic experience and devaluation of the ties between art and social responsibility.

Another aspect of modernism that could lead to such politics is the sense of impending end—the sense of enormous radical changes in society—that many felt in the early part of the century. It is here, in fact, that art and politics seem to come together. The claims of the essays in this section are generally not so dramatic as Woolf's or Lawrence's sense of a modern apocalypse—or as dramatic as Yeats's in 1922 when he wrote in his *Autobiography*: "After us the Savage God"—yet such an apocalyptic sense of the twentieth century as a new beginning accurately reflects the idea of new beginning that runs through most Modernist criticism. The newness consists in what Frank Kermode calls an "open breach with the past," "a reaction against the crushing weight of an artistic past which cannot be surveyed any longer by any one person." Like Pound in the ambiguity of "make it new," Kermode describes a double vision of the twentieth century as empowered to step free of the past and simultaneously as suffering in its failure to encompass or even to survey that past—both of which visions suggest, as Woolf says, some shift in what it means to be human. From this shift, as the essays by Eliot and Shklovsky in this section testify, comes the anxiety embedded throughout modernism. If "modernism strongly implies some sort of historical discontinuity . . . a liberation from inherited patterns," as Richard Ellmann and Charles Feidelson claim, then it simultaneously means "deprivation and disinheritance"—being set free and also broken off from the values of the past.

Notwithstanding the rhetoric of loss, apocalypse, and new beginnings (the rhetoric typical of modernism and the commentary about it)—and notwithstanding questionable politics—the Modernists were involved in a serious reevaluation of the limits of literary form and of the possibilities for a new esthetic in the arts generally—if not exactly new ways of being human, then at least a new paradigm of presentation for the products of twentieth-century culture. Henceforth, as Irving Babbitt said most forcefully, any romantic or sentimental tendencies in literature must be viewed as mere "emotional naturalism," a dissolving of real-world distinctions and a glossing over of important cultural demarcations. In place of nineteenth-century romantic "sloppiness," Babbitt said, is the emergent "modern spirit . . . the positive and critical spirit, the spirit that refuses to take things on authority." Babbitt even called for a further movement away from supposedly "soft" and "uncritical" romanticism to "tough," "critical" modernism, a shift, as T. E. Hulme argued, into a contemporary version of the neoclassic sensibility and its modes of precise expression and carefully modulated sentiments. In short, Babbitt and Hulme called for a complete abandonment of romanticism and for the development of an emergent modern, antiromantic, *formal* sensibility.

This sensibility, as the essays in this section show, most immediately calls for a movement away from the irrationality of what British romantic poets called *imagination*. (Wimsatt and Beardsley are most explicitly "antiromantic" in these essays, but such an impulse can be seen in Eliot's description of the "impersonality" of art.) Rather, the modernists chose *fancy*, Coleridge's term for the human capacity to reason and to make demonstrable (in this sense, "critical") connections within and among experiences, an endless endeavor but finite in that precise forms (distinct images and the like) are used to accomplish it. The Modernists made this choice for epistemological reasons, particularly the belief that superior art comes out of the knowledge born of reasoned discriminations and a rational perspective. They were not trying for dryness and banality in poetry, but for the "hard, dry" presentation of precise images and a modulated use of language. Such imagery, like Eliot's "pair of ragged claws/ Scuttling across the floors of silent seas," aims at a "hard," or direct and detailed, presentation of sensory information; it is "dry" in being free of dependence on predetermined emotions that could be brought to or imposed on the text.

Further, the "hard, dry" language of modernism, as an ideal, does not need to impose emotions on the text because the text provides its own in the *form* of its progression, that is, in its discourse. Eliot calls these "structural emotions" and says that they are generated out of the text itself. By this he means that in reading poetry particular "feelings" are elicited from the reader by the formal arrangement of the poem's images. These images, in turn, are arranged in the text as an "objective correlative," or a particular image sequence in the poem that corresponds to a human emotion. It follows that the act of reading draws forth all the "feelings" that combine to make up a particular "emotion," which can be said to be "in" the text insofar as the text, by means of its form, specifically elicits that emotion. In short, this entire operation, from the deployment of images as an objective correlative through the received effect of a "structural emotion," takes place as a "textual" operation, a poetic experience that is not brought to the text as a personal experience but is generated precisely out of the text's particular patterning or structure. The Modernist preference for fancy, in this way, means valuing the esthetic structure of a text as conveyed in imagery—actually produced "in" the text—over the more personal responses that less rigorous reading (or a less "rigorous" poem) might produce.

Modernist poetics, then, as a "formal" explanation of poetry's function, is a scheme for art that fits into the twentieth century's broader picture of cultural discontinuity and irrationality. That is, the rational process whereby images in poetry call forth "structural emotions" in the reader happens against the modern background of lost connections between the cultural past and present, a world that is made over with each new work of art. For modernism, there are no ordained or natural lines of order in the world, no cultural backdrop that gives automatic meaning to a text; there is no providential plan according to which history and its outcomes are meaningfully situated. On the contrary, the disinheritance of modern culture is precisely the loss of belief in such traditional schemes as the Great Chain of Being. Pound and Eliot, in particular, do speak of grand cultural orders ("the mind of Europe," "tradition," "the past," and so on), but these are always distinctly human artifacts that must be reimagined for each poet and each culture. Eliot describes a kind of creative surrender whereby the poet's interactions with conventional possibilities may emerge as poetry—so that, in short, "new" culture will exist.

Eliot elaborates this process in "Tradition and the Individual Talent" when he argues that "past," "present," and "future" are not given facts or simple realities of experience but a *formal* arrangement of areas of disturbance and discontinuity in the midst of which the poet constructs art and culture like a collage. Similarly, in this period the semiotician Ferdinand de Saussure—Eliot's contemporary (see Section III)—proposes that reality itself is a linguistic arrangement of "signified" and potential meanings, a rational and formal arrangement situated within a context of arbitrariness. Thus, cut off from the past, disinherited from it, the poet, artist, or even any user of language can choose to accept the imperative and responsibility "to make it new" or else remain without any operative sense of past or present culture at all. This Modernist version of poetry suggests a highly rational (almost Augustan) practice, but its poetic logic is shown to exist in the wasteland of modern culture, where the poet toils to make (actually *create*) cultural connections that otherwise would not exist. In other words, poetry introduces form into a cultural flux (the modern world) that by definition cannot be well formed, or "finished," because it remains in transition.

A call for form, therefore, is a distinctly Modernist gesture wherein the Modernists promoted the emergence of a new esthetic to compensate for the lost connections with the past that Kermode spoke of, the Modernists believing themselves, as Patricia Tobin has said, to be "living in the temporal belatedness of a cultural aftermath." They promoted a reconstituted version of neoclassic poetics, with some important differences. The Modernists believed that through new poetic forms they were creating new worlds; whereas for prior ages there was only one world, given to humanity by one God. In the call for form the Modernists argued for the necessity of a modern cultural and artistic sensibility adequate to the felt quality of living in the aftermath of post-enlightenment culture. This Modernist perception of a contemporary crisis in values and artistic form is surely a concern for the history of ideas, and the Modernist program for a new understanding of poetic and literary form has a direct bearing on Anglo-American and Continental criticism.

RUSSIAN FORMALISM

In fact, Russian formalism, even though it was long unknown in Anglo-American criticism, is itself a significant part of the movement of modernism, as is—more clearly—the American "New Criticism" of the 1930s and 1940s. These movements took the Modernist esthetic and epistemology to heart and attempted to analyze literature not by its identifiable or "natural" (or "representational") content but consistently by its form—how it is constructed and how it functions so as to have meaning in the first place. This emphasis on form in literary criticism has two general applications: (1) an understanding of a text's interior patterning, or how it works; and (2) the recognition that form marks a work as belonging to a particular genre—a novel, lyric, drama, and so on. Thus, formalism in the broadest sense views literature as a complex system of forms that may be analyzed in relation to one another at different levels of generality—from the specifics of a poetic image or line through that poem's genre. Formalism, in short, attempts to view literature not as constituted by its intrinsic ("natural") meaning, as an imitation of reality, but by relational patterns that are meaningful in a particular work and genre.

Russian formalism was the work of two groups of critics, the Moscow Linguistic Circle, begun in 1915, and OPOYAZ (Society for the Study of Poetic Language), started in 1916. Both groups were disbanded in 1930 in response to official Soviet condemnation of their willingness to depart from the ideological and esthetic standards of Soviet socialist realism. Their influence continued strongly in the work of the Prague Linguistic Circle (founded in 1926), of which Roman Jakobson is perhaps the best-known figure, and in a few key works such as Vladimir Propp's *Morphology of the Folktale* (1928). It is an oddity of the modern history of ideas, however, that after 1930 the Russian formalists had almost no impact on Western criticism and theory but resurfaced thirty years later with the advent of literary structuralism in France and the United States in the 1960s.

Like Eliot and the Modernists in general, the Russian Formalists sought to move away from nineteenth-century romantic attitudes in criticism and to avoid all romantic notions about poetic inspiration, genius, or esthetic organicism. Instead, the Formalists adopted a deliberately mechanistic view of poetry and other literary art as the products of *craft*. Considered as *fancy*, poetry-as-craft may be investigated according to immediately analyzable literary functions. Thus, while the Formalists believed that no particular deployment of words, images, or other language effects is intrinsically literary (there being no such thing as literary language), they saw that literature, like other usages of language, could have a particular *function*, could "work" to accomplish particular ends, an assumption shared with Kenneth Burke (see Section II). Yet they are more linguistic rather than "sociological" (as Burke calls his work); they want to see language deployed as *language* and highlight its linguistic functioning as the object of criticism. Linguistic properties then become the primary concern—instead of "inspiration," "poetic genius," or "poetic organicism"—as a poem's meaning and effect are sought. The Formalists attempted to maintain and extend this view at every step of analysis by identifying formal properties as *effective* properties through detailed dissections of poetic (and narrative) technique.

This impulse in theory toward a literary formalism can be seen most clearly in Viktor Shklovsky's definition of literary "device" aimed at effecting some end (a concept analogous to Saussure's "functional" definition of linguistic entities). Central to formalism, for example, is Shklovsky's argument against the esthetic notion of "art as thinking in images" and his promotion, instead, of the importance of literary (and nonimagistic) devices. A concentration on images, Shklovsky maintained, leads one to view a poem as having actual "content," and this assumption inhibits any truly formal or relational analysis. What may appear as "content" needs to be considered as "device," or any operation in language that promotes "defamiliarization." That is, since language is a medium of communication before it is used in art, its expressions and conventions inevitably will be overly familiar to the reader and too feeble to have a fresh or significant impact in a poem. To be made new and poetically useful, such language must be "defamiliarized" and "made strange" through linguistic displacement, which means deploying language in an unusual context or effecting its presentation in a novel way. Rhyme schemes (or lack of rhyme), chiasmus (rhetorical balance and reversal), catachresis (the straining of a word or figure beyond its usual meaning), conceits, mixed metaphors, and so on—all these devices for producing particular effects in literature can be used to defamiliarize language and to awaken readers to the intricacy and texture of verbal structure. Such defamiliarization is, therefore, the manner in which poetry functions to rejuvenate and revivify language. All this is quite different from romantic criticism's view of what happens in a poem as the expressive channel for transcendent (or divine) feelings or poetic (or personal) genius.

THE NEW CRITICISM

The principal American version of formalism, the New Criticism, shares some general precepts with Russian Formalism, but there is historically only a negligible influence of one on the other. (René Wellek, for example, was associated with both schools but did little to "introduce" Russian Formalist ideas into American criticism.) A single orthodoxy for the New Criticism as a broad movement does not exist, but we can isolate several of the key tenets articulated by major Anglo-American critics from the late 1920s through the 1950s, the period of the New Criticism's active development. In particular, like Russian Formalism, the New Criticism tried to displace content in literary analysis and, therein, to treat a work's form in a manner analogous to empirical research. Also like Russian Formalism, the New Criticism tried to organize the larger, generic forms of literature in accord with the inner ordering of works as revealed in specific analyses or "close readings."

These general similarities point up the Modernist and Formalist leanings of both movements, but the New Criticism departed from Russian Formalism on the key issue of the *function* of forms. (It is true, though, that there are moments in New Criticism—as when Cleanth Brooks asserts in "The Language of Paradox" that Donne's effect "is to cleanse and revivify metaphor"—that are close to Shklovsky's definition of "defamiliarization.") Rather than conceive of the formal properties of literature as a means of achieving particular effects, the New Critics conceived literature to be a self-sustaining "artifact," a "spatial form" in Joseph Frank's term, and form as a self-contained "autonomous" entity, what Brooks meant by a "well-wrought urn." Perhaps most important was the New Critical reliance on "imagery" as a concept with which to define form. Drawing heavily on the work of the Modernist critics, New Critics like Brooks made the literary image the primary material or constituent of form itself. A New-Critical "close reading" of John Donne's poem "The Canonization," for instance, involves a preliminary identification of key images in a recurring pattern of opposition, or as Brooks says, "tension." Only once this pattern of imagery is established do the New Critics attend to any interpretive considerations of form. Thus, while the Russian Formalists successfully avoided any focus on literary content, the New Critics posited paradox and irony (which themselves could be seen as particular *effects* of literature) as controlling figures and, in effect, turned them into content. As Brooks says in his discussion of "The Canonization" in this section, paradox and irony actually reflect the structure of the imagination itself. His reasoning, based on Kantian esthetics, is simply that since poetry is produced by the imagination, it must reflect the imagination's own structure. That structure, or "form," is opposition, as seen rhetorically in the figures of paradox and irony. These figures, then, although they are intended to be poetry's form, virtually become its *content*, in that they are the ultimate referents for all the indications (largely imagistic) of meaning. From this standpoint, all poems are about, or "contain," these patterns.

In this is the largest difference between the "substantial" formalism of the New Criticism and the "functional" formalism of Russian Formalism. Whereas the Russian Formalists attempted merely to lay bare the operation of local devices, rejecting any authoritative and final interpretation of a work, the New Critics believed that a work can be read objectively and accurately in light of its actual structure or form. A work can, thus, have a single, or "correct," interpretation. W. K. Wimsatt and Monroe C. Beardsley in "The Intentional Fallacy," for example, stipulate the manner of reading a work the "right" way. They explain the interference and inaccuracies possible when authorial intentions become a consideration in close reading—the "wrong" way. In "The Affective Fallacy," further, they show how at the other extreme a reader's undisciplined "affective" responses to a text—the very *effects* that Shklovsky attempts to account for—may distort the correct apprehension and interpretation of images. So, whereas the Formalists concentrated on form as a plurality of literary devices and on interpretation as an activity (see Fish, Barthes, Culler, Bakhtin, and Felman for other versions of this "active" or "performative" conception of understanding throughout this book), the New Critics retrieved from romanticism the concept of esthetic wholeness and unity as well as a unified or single interpretation of a work. They argued that a work, properly read, will always be unified by a set of preconceived tensions, as expressed in paradox and irony. In short, the New Critics assumed total coherence in a work; the Russian Formalists (like a significant portion of contemporary criticism) did not.

These differences represent two main lines of formalist development in the twentieth century and two aspects of contemporary literary criticism that will appear in this book. The Russian Formalists examined literary form as an important constituent of a work's operation but saw it as enmeshed in an ongoing process. This effort, more fully realized, became structuralism and some versions of poststructuralism. The New Critics, drawing heavily from the Modernists' ideas about imagery, created a formalism that viewed literary form as arrestable, with a content that may be examined more or less directly. This tendency, as we will see, informed the psychological readings of Freudian ego psychology, Northrop Frye's archetypal criticism in the late 1950s, and the "pluralism" of the 1960s (represented in this collection in M. H. Abrams's argument with deconstruction in Section VIII).

RELATED TEXTS IN *CONTEMPORARY LITERARY CRITICISM*

Roland Barthes, "The Structuralist Activity"
Bakhtin/Vološinov, "Discourse in Life and Discourse in Art"
Northrop Frye, "Function of Criticism at the Present Time"
M. H. Abrams, "The Deconstructive Angel"

FURTHER READING

Babbitt, Irving, *Rousseau and Romanticism* (Boston and New York: Houghton Mifflin, 1919).

Bakhtin, Mikhail, *Problems of Dostoevsky's Poetics*, trans. Caryl Emerson (Minneapolis: University of Minnesota Press, 1984).

Bann, Stephen, and John E. Bowlt, eds., *Russian Formalism* (Edinburgh: Scottish Academic Press, 1973).

Bennett, Tony, *Formalism and Marxism* (London: Methuen, 1979).

Berman, Marshall, *All That Is Solid Melts into Air: The Experience of Modernity* (New York: Simon & Schuster, 1982).

Bradbury, Malcolm, and James McFarlane, *Modernism: 1890–1930* (New York: Penguin, 1976).

Brooks, Cleanth, "My Credo: Formalist Critics," in *Kenyon Review*, 13 (1951), 72–81.

———, "The Poet's Fancy," in *New Republic*, 85 (November 13, 1935), 26–27.

———, and Robert Penn Warren, eds., *Understanding Poetry* (New York: Holt, 1938).

Conroy, Mark, *Modernism and Authority: Strategies of Legitimation in Flaubert and Conrad* (Baltimore: Johns Hopkins University Press, 1985).

Crane, R. S., et al., eds., *Critics and Criticism: Ancient and Modern* (Chicago: University of Chicago Press, 1957).

Eliot, T. S., *The Sacred Wood* (London: Methuen, 1920).

Ellmann, Richard, and Charles Feidelson, Jr., *The Modern Tradition: Backgrounds of Modern Literature* (New York: Oxford University Press, 1965).

Empson, William, *Seven Types of Ambiguity* (New York: New Directions, 1947).

Erlich, Victor, *Russian Formalism: History and Doctrine*, 3rd ed. (New Haven: Yale University Press, 1981).

Frank, Joseph, *The Widening Gyre: Crisis and Mastery in Modern Literature* (New Brunswick, N.J.: Rutgers University Press, 1963).

Howe, Irving, ed., *Literary Modernism* (New York: Fawcett, 1967).

Hulme, T. E., *Speculations* (London: Routledge, 1924).

Jefferson, Ann, "Russian Formalism," in *Modern Literary theory*, Ann Jefferson and David Robey, eds. (Totowa, N.J.: Barnes and Noble, 1982), 16–37.

Kenner, Hugh, *A Homemade World: The American Modernist Writers* (New York: Morrow, 1975).

_____, *The Pound Era* (Berkeley: University of California Press, 1971).

Kermode, Frank, and John Hollander, eds., *Modern British Literature* (New York: Oxford University Press, 1973).

Langbaum, Robert, *The Modern Spirit: Essays on the Continuity of Nineteenth- and Twentieth-Century Literature* (London: Chatto and Windus, 1970).

Lemon, Lee T., and Marion J. Reis, eds., *Russian Formalist Criticism: Four Essays* (Lincoln: University of Nebraska Press, 1965).

Lentricchia, Frank, *After the New Criticism* (Chicago: University of Chicago Press, 1980).

Lévi-Strauss, Claude, "Structure and Form: Reflections of a Work by Vladimir Propp," trans. Monique Layton, rev. by Anatoly Liberman. In Vladimir Propp, *Theory and History of Folklore* (Minneapolis: University of Minnesota Press, 1984).

Matejka, Ladislav, and Krystyna Pomorska, *Readings in Russian Poetics: Formalist and Structuralist Views* (Cambridge: MIT Press, 1971).

Miller, J. Hillis, *Poets of Reality* (Cambridge: Harvard University Press, 1965).

North, Michael, *The Final Sculpture: Public Monuments and Modern Poets* (Ithaca: Cornell University Press, 1985).

Ortega y Gasset, José, *The Dehumanization of Art and Other Writings of Art and Culture* (1948); reprint Garden City, N.Y.: Doubleday, 1956.

Pound, Ezra, *The ABC of Reading* (New Haven: Yale University Press, 1934).

Ransom, John Crowe, *The New Criticism* (New York: New Directions, 1941).

Read, Herbert, *Icon and Idea* (Cambridge: Harvard University Press, 1956).

Richards, I. A., *Practical Criticism* (New York: Harcourt, Brace, 1929).

_____, *Principles of Literary Criticism* (New York: Harcourt, Brace, 1925).

Scholes, Robert, and Robert Kellog, *The Nature of Narrative* (New York: Oxford University Press, 1966).

Spears, Monroe K., *Dionysus and the City: Modernism in Twentieth-Century Poetry* (New York: Oxford University Press, 1970).

Spender, Stephen, *The Struggle of the Modern* (Berkeley: University of California Press, 1963).

Steiner, Peter, *Russian Formalism: A Metapoetics* (Ithaca: Cornell University Press, 1984).

Symons, Arthur, *The Symbolist Movement in Literature* (1899); reprint New York: Dutton, 1958.

Thompson, E. M., *Russian Formalism and Anglo-American New Criticism* (The Hague: Mouton, 1971).

Tindall, William York, *Forces in Modern British Literature: 1885–1956* (New York: Knopf, 1947).

Wellek, René, and Austin Warren, *Theory of Literature* (New York: Harcourt, Brace, 1949).

Wimsatt, W. K., Jr., "The Chicago Critics," in *Comparative Literature*, 5 (1953), 50–74.

———, *The Verbal Icon* (Lexington: University of Kentucky Press, 1954).

Winters, Yvor, *In Defense of Reason* (Denver: Swallow Press, 1947).

Woolf, Virginia, "Mr. Bennett and Mrs. Brown," in *The Captain's Death Bed and Other Essays* (New York: Harcourt, Brace and Co., 1950).

1

T. S. Eliot
1888–1965

T. S. (Thomas Stearns) Eliot is best known as a poet, but he is arguably a central modern critic writing in English because of his vast influence in several areas: he almost singlehandedly brought about the reappraisal of sixteenth- and seventeenth-century drama and metaphysical poetry; he demonstrated the necessity of reading American and English literature in relation to European and non-European (especially Oriental) traditions; he helped to formulate a modern way of reading and writing that eschewed romantic values and furthered an esthetic of "hard, dry" images and sentiments. Eliot thus directed modern readers in what and how to read and how to understand literary texts. These achievements, along with the critical revolution signaled by his own poetry, mark Eliot as a modern critic of the first rank. His major works of criticism include *The Sacred Wood* (1920), *The Use of Poetry and the Use of Criticism* (1933), *Christianity and Culture* (1940), *Notes Towards a Definition of Culture* (1949), *Selected Essays* (1953), and *On Poetry and Poets* (1957).

Eliot directed his criticism as much toward professional literary critics as he did towards the general public. In "Tradition and the Individual Talent" (1919), an essay which could easily borrow Pope's title *Essay on Criticism,* Eliot emphasizes the necessity of critical thinking—"criticism is as inevitable as breathing." This essay shows some of the furthest reaches of Eliot's theories and literary philosophy. He asserts the value of poetic creation as the process by which a whole culture locates itself in the present in relation to an acquired sense of the past. The past is an active force in the present, constituting "the presentness of the past," and is a channel of access to a cultural "mind" larger than any single poet's and ultimately decisive in determining the direction and import of all "significant" art in any age. These ideas had a direct influence on modernist criticism and literature, but—to a greater extent than is sometimes recognized—they also underlie some contemporary cultural theories, such as Reader-Response criticism and various approaches to audience-reception theory. Noteworthy for its coherence and cogency, this essay is perhaps Eliot's most important critical statement.

Tradition and the Individual Talent

I

In English writing we seldom speak of tradition, though we occasionally apply its name in deploring its absence. We cannot refer to "the tradition" or to "a tradition"; at most, we employ that adjective in saying that the poetry of So-and-so is "traditional" or even "too traditional." Seldom, perhaps, does the word appear except in a phrase of censure. If otherwise, it is vaguely approbative, with the implication, as to the work approved, of some pleasing archaeological reconstruction. You can hardly make the word agreeable to English ears without this comfortable reference to the reassuring science of archaeology.

Certainly the word is not likely to appear in our appreciations of living or dead writers. Every nation, every race, has not only its own creative, but its own critical turn of mind; and is even more oblivious of the shortcomings and limitations of its critical habits than of those of its creative genius. We know, or think we know, from the enormous mass of critical writing that has appeared in the French language the critical method or habit of the French; we only conclude (we are such unconscious people) that the French are "more critical" than we, and sometimes even plume ourselves a little with the fact, as if the French were the less spontaneous. Perhaps they are; but we might remind ourselves that criticism is as inevitable as breathing, and that we should be none the worse for articulating what passes in our minds when we read a book and feel an emotion about it, for criticizing our own minds in their work of criticism. One of the facts that might come to light in this process is our tendency to insist, when we praise a poet, upon those aspects of his work in which he least resembles anyone else. In these aspects or parts of his work we pretend to find what is individual, what is the peculiar essence of the man. We dwell with satisfaction upon the poet's difference from his predecessors, especially his immediate predecessors; we endeavour to find something that can be isolated in order to be enjoyed. Whereas if we approach a poet without this prejudice we shall often find that not only the best, but the most individual parts of his work may be those in which the dead poets, his ancestors, assert their immortality most vigorously. And I do not mean the impressionable period of adolescence, but the period of full maturity.

Yet if the only form of tradition, of handing down, consisted in following the ways of the immediate generation before us in a blind or timid adherence to its successes, "tradition" should positively be discouraged. We have seen many such simple currents soon lost in the sand; and novelty is better than repetition. Tradition is a matter of much wider significance. It cannot be inherited, and if you want it you must obtain it by great labour. It involves, in the first place, the historical sense, which we may call nearly indispensable to anyone who would continue to be a poet beyond his twenty-fifth year; and the historical sense involves a perception, not only of the pastness of the past, but of its presence; the historical sense compels a man to write not merely with his own generation in his bones, but with a feeling that the whole of the literature of Europe from Homer and within it the whole of the literature of his own country has a simultaneous existence and composes a simultaneous order. This historical sense, which is a sense of the timeless as well as of the temporal and of the timeless and of the temporal together, is what makes a writer traditional. And it is at the same time what makes a writer most acutely conscious of his place in time, of his own contemporaneity.

No poet, no artist of any art, has his complete meaning alone. His significance, his appreciation is the appreciation of his relation to the dead poets and artists. You cannot value him alone; you must set him, for contrast and comparison, among the dead. I mean this as a principle of aesthetic, not merely historical, criticism. Then necessity that he shall conform, that he shall cohere, is not onesided; what happens when a new work of art is created is something that happens simultaneously to all the works of art which preceded it. The existing monuments form an ideal order among themselves, which is modified by the introduction of the new (the really new) work of art among them. The existing order is complete before the new work arrives; for order to persist after the supervention of novelty, the whole existing order must be, if ever so slightly altered; and so the relations, proportions, values of each work of art towards the whole are readjusted; and this is conformity between the old and the new. Whoever has approved this idea of order, of the form of European, of English literature will not find it preposterous that the past should be altered by the present as much as the present is directed by the past. And the poet who is aware of this will be aware of great difficulties and responsibilities.

In a peculiar sense he will be aware also that he must inevitably be judged by the standards of the past. I say judged, not amputated, by them; not judged to be as good as, or worse or better than, the dead; and certainly not judged by the canons of dead critics. It is a judgment, a comparison, in which two things are measured by each other. To conform merely would be for the new work not really to conform at all; it would not be new, and would therefore not be a work of art. And we do not quite say that the new is more valuable because it fits in; but its fitting in is a test of its value—a test, it is true, which can only be slowly and cautiously applied, for we are none of us infallible judges of conformity. We say: it appears to conform, and is perhaps individual, or it appears individual, and may conform; but we are hardly likely to find that it is one and not the other.

To proceed to a more intelligible exposition of the relation of the poet to the past: he can neither take the past as a lump, an indiscriminate bolus, nor can he form himself wholly on one or two private admirations, nor can he form himself wholly upon one preferred period. The first course is inadmissible, the second is an important experience of youth, and the third is a pleasant and highly desirable supplement. The poet must be very conscious of the main current, which does not at all flow invariably through the most distinguished reputations. He must be quite aware of the obvious fact that art never improves, but that the material of art is never quite the same. He must be aware that the mind of Europe—the mind of his own country—a mind which he learns in time to be much more important than his own private mind—is a mind which changes, and that this change is a development which abandons nothing *en route*, which does not superannuate either Shakespeare, or Homer, or the rock drawing of the Magdalenian draughtsmen. That this development, refinement perhaps, complication certainly, is not from the point of view of the artist, any improvement. Perhaps not even an improvement from the point of view of the psychologist or not to the extent which we imagine; perhaps only in the end based upon a complication in economics and machinery. But the difference between the present and the past is that the conscious present is an awareness of the past in a way and to an extent which the past's awareness of itself cannot show.

Someone said: "The dead writers are remote from us because we know so much more than they did." Precisely, and they are that which we know.

I am alive to a usual objection to what is clearly part of my programme for the *métier* of poetry. The objection is that the doctrine requires a ridiculous amount of erudition (pedantry), a claim which can be rejected by appeal to the lives of poets in any pantheon. It will even be affirmed that much learning deadens or perverts poetic sensibility. While, however, we persist in believing that a poet ought to know as much as will not encroach upon his necessary receptivity and necessary laziness, it is not desirable to confine knowledge to whatever can be put into a useful shape for examinations, drawing-rooms, or the still more pretentious modes of publicity. Some can absorb knowledge, the more tardy must sweat for it. Shakespeare acquired more essential history from Plutarch than most men could from the whole British Museum. What is to be insisted upon is that the poet must develop or procure the consciousness of the past and that he should continue to develop this consciousness throughout his career.

What happens is a continual surrender of himself as he is at the moment to something which is more valuable. The progress of an artist is a continual self-sacrifice, a continual extinction of personality.

There remains to define this process of depersonalization and its relation to the sense of tradition. It is in this depersonalization that art may be said to approach the condition of science. I therefore invite you to consider, as a suggestive analogy, the action which takes place when a bit of finely filiated platinum is introduced into a chamber containing oxygen and sulphur dioxide.

II

Honest criticism and sensitive appreciation are directed not upon the poet but upon the poetry. If we attend to the confused cries of the newspaper critics and the susurrus of popular repetition that follows, we shall hear the names of poets in great numbers; if we seek not Blue-book knowledge but the enjoyment of poetry, and ask for a poem, we shall seldom find it. I have tried to point out the importance of the relation of the poem to other poems by other authors, and suggested the conception of poetry as a living whole of all the poetry that has ever been written. The other aspect of this Impersonal theory of poetry is the relation of the poem to its author. And I hinted, by an analogy, that the mind of the mature poet differs from that of the immature one not precisely in any valuation of "personality," not being necessarily more interesting, or having "more to say," but rather by being a more finely perfected medium in which special, or varied, feelings are at liberty to enter into new combinations.

The analogy was that of the catalyst. When the two gases previously mentioned are mixed in the presence of a filament of platinum, they form sulphurous acid. This combination takes place only if the platinum is present; nevertheless the newly formed acid contains no trace of platinum, and the platinum itself is apparently unaffected: has remained inert, neutral, and unchanged. The mind of the poet is the shred of platinum. It may partly or exclusively operate upon the experience of the man himself; but, the more perfect the artist, the more completely separate in him will be the man who suffers and the mind which creates; the more perfectly will the mind digest and transmute the passions which are its material.

The experience, you will notice, the elements which enter the presence of the transforming catalyst, are of two kinds:

emotions and feelings. The effect of a work of art upon the person who enjoys it is an experience different in kind from any experience not of art. It may be formed out of one emotion, or may be a combination of several; and various feelings, inhering for the writer in particular words or phrases or images, may be added to compose the final result. Or great poetry may be made without the direct use of any emotion whatever: composed out of feelings solely. Canto XV of the *Inferno* (Brunetto Latini) is a working up of the emotion evident in the situation; but the effect, though single as that of any work of art, is obtained by considerable complexity of detail. The last quatrain[1] gives an image, a feeling attaching to an image, which "came" which did not develop simply out of what precedes, but which was probably in suspension in the poet's mind until the proper combination arrived for it to add itself to. The poet's mind is in fact a receptacle for seizing and storing up numberless feelings, phrases, images, which remain there until all the particles which can unite to form a new compound are present together.

If you compare several representative passages of the greatest poetry you see how great is the variety of types of combination, and also how completely any semi-ethical criterion of "sublimity" misses the mark. For it is not the "greatness," the intensity, of the emotions, the components, but the intensity of the artistic process, the pressure, so to speak, under which the fusion takes place, that counts. The episode of Paolo and Francesca employs a definite emotion, but the intensity of the poetry is something quite different from whatever intensity in the supposed experience it may give the impression of. It is not more intense, furthermore, than Canto XXVI, the voyage of Ulysses, which has not the direct dependence upon an emotion. Great variety is possible in the process of transmutation of emotion: the murder of Agamemnon, or the agony of Othello, gives an artistic effect apparently closer to a possible original than the scenes from Dante. In the *Agamemnon*, the artistic emotion approximates to the emotion of an actual spectator; in *Othello* to the emotion of the protagonist himself. But the difference between art and the event is always absolute; the combination which is the murder of Agamemnon is probably as complex as that which is the voyage of Ulysses. In either case there has been a fusion of elements. The ode of Keats contains a number of feelings which have nothing particular to do with the nightingale, but which the nightingale, partly perhaps because of its reputation, served to bring together.

The point of view which I am struggling to attack is perhaps related to the metaphysical theory of the substantial unity of the soul: for my meaning is, that the poet has, not a "personality" to express, but a particular medium, which is only a medium and not a personality, in which impressions and experiences combine in peculiar and unexpected ways. Impressions and experiences which are important for the man may take no place in the poetry, and those which become important in the poetry may play quite a negligible part in the man, the personality.

I will quote a passage which is unfamiliar enough to be regarded with fresh attention in the light—or darkness—of these observations:

> And now methinks I could e'en chide myself
> For doating on her beauty, though her death
> Shall be revenged after no common action.
> Does the silkworm expend her yellow labours
> For thee? For thee does she undo herself?
> Are lordships sold to maintain ladyships
> For the poor benefit of a bewildering minute?

> Why does yon fellow falsify highways,
> And put his life between the judge's lips,
> To refine such a thing—keeps horse and
> men
> To beat their valours for her? . . .[2]

In this passage (as is evident if it is taken in its context) there is a combination of positive and negative emotions: an intensely strong attraction towards beauty and an equally intense fascination by the ugliness which is contrasted with it and which destroys it. This balance of contrasted emotion is in the dramatic situation to which the speech is pertinent, but that situation alone is inadequate to it. This is, so to speak, the structural emotion, provided by the drama. But the whole effect, the dominant tone, is due to the fact that a number of floating feelings, having an affinity to this emotion by no means superficially evident, have combined with it to give us a new art emotion.

It is not in his personal emotions, the emotions provoked by particular events in his life, that the poet is in any way remarkable or interesting. His particular emotions may be simple, or crude, or flat. The emotion in his poetry will be a very complex thing, but not with the complexity of the emotions of people who have very complex or unusual emotions in life. One error, in fact, of eccentricity in poetry is to seek for new human emotions to express; and in this search for novelty in the wrong place it discovers the perverse. The business of the poet is not to find new emotions, but the use of ordinary ones and, in working them up into poetry, to express feelings which are not in actual emotions at all. And emotions which he has never experienced will serve his turn as well as those familiar to him. Consequently, we must believe that "emotion recollected in tranquility"[3] is an inexact formula. For it is neither emotion, nor recollection, nor, without distortion of meaning, tranquillity. It is a concentration, and a new thing resulting from the concentration, of a very great number of experiences which to the practical and active person would not seem to be experiences at all; it is a concentration which does not happen consciously or of deliberation. These experiences are not "recollected," and they finally unite in an atmosphere which is "tranquil" only in that it is a passive attending upon the event. Of course this is not quite the whole story. There is a great deal, in the writing of poetry, which must be conscious and deliberate. In fact, the bad poet is usually unconscious where he ought to be conscious, and conscious where he ought to be unconscious. Both errors tend to make him "personal." Poetry is not a turning loose of emotion, but an escape from emotion; it is not the expression of personality, but an escape from personality. But, of course, only those who have personality and emotions know what it means to want to escape from these things.

III

> *ὁ δὲ νοῦς ἴυως θειότερόν τι καὶ ἀπαθές ἐστιν.*[4]

This essay proposes to halt at the frontier of metaphysics or mysticism, and confine itself to such practical conclusions as can be applied by the responsible person interested in poetry. To divert interest from the poet to the poetry is a laudable aim: for it would conduce to a juster estimation of actual poetry, good and bad. There are many people who appreciate the expression of sincere emotion in verse, and there is a smaller number of people who can appreciate technical excellence. But very few know when there is an expression of *significant* emotion, emotion which has its life in the poem and not in the history of the poet. The emotion of art is impersonal. And the poet cannot reach this impersonality without surrendering himself wholly to the work to be done. And he is not likely to know what is to be done unless he believes in what is not merely the present, but the present moment of the past, unless he is conscious, not of what is dead, but of what is already living.

NOTES

1. In the translation of Dorothy L. Sayers:

Then he turned round,
And seemed like one of those who over the flat
  And open course in the fields beside Verona
  Run for the green cloth; and he seemed, at that,
Not like a loser, but the winning runner.

2. Cyril Tourneur, *The Revenger's Tragedy* (1607), III, iv.

3. "Poetry is the spontaneous overflow of powerful feelings: it takes its origins from emotion recollected in tranquility." Wordsworth, Preface to *Lyrical Ballads* (1800).

4. "While the intellect is doubtless a thing more divine and is impassive." Aristotle, *De Anima*.

2

Cleanth Brooks
1906–

Cleanth Brooks remains the quintessential New Critic. In him the theories of Eliot, Richards, Empson, Leavis, and even Winters find practical application. Although his best-known work is *The Well-Wrought Urn* (1947), Brooks and Robert Penn Warren coauthored *Understanding Poetry* (1938) and *Understanding Fiction* (1943); and Brooks and W. K. Wimsatt wrote *Literary Criticism: A Short History* (1957). All three are firmly entrenched in the New Critical canon. Along with Warren, John Crowe Ransom, and Allen Tate, Brooks was a central figure in the Southern Agrarians, or Fugitives, organized at Vanderbilt University. From 1935 to 1942 Brooks and Warren edited *Southern Review*, the chief outlet for the Agrarians. Counting Cleanth Brooks, Allen Tate, and Robert Penn Warren among its members, the Agrarians were drawn together by shared traditional, conservative values as well as an affinity for the South. They likewise held common ideas about the nature of literary criticism, ideas that ultimately became the tenets of the New Criticism. Brooks's major work spanned the 1930s and 1940s, the height of the New Criticism. His *Literary Criticism* of 1957 signaled the close of the movement. Educated at Vanderbilt, Tulane, and Oxford universities, Brooks taught at Louisiana State University before settling at Yale University, where he is now professor emeritus.

Taken from *The Well-Wrought Urn*, "The Language of Paradox" (1942) exemplifies the type of close reading that the New Critics valued. The essay echoes I. A. Richards's distinction between referential and emotive language, as Brooks carefully points out that scientific language contains no trace of paradox, while paradox is "appropriate and inevitable to poetry." Brooks argues that science desires stable terms—terms that are strictly denotative. Poetry, however, relies on connotations and meanings derived from the careful juxtaposition of terms. After all, poetry is built on metaphor, and "the poet has to work by analogies." Brooks demonstrates the language of paradox in Donne's "The Canonization" by showing how Donne combines several metaphors to create a meaning that transcends any single one. The paradox arises because "the metaphors do not lie in the same plane or fit neatly edge to edge." This paradoxical juxtaposition of images is what generates the poem's richness. Like Winters, Brooks sees the paradoxical nature of the poem as creating a meaning that cannot be paraphrased, that cannot be translated into scientific or referential language. Like most of the New Critics, Brooks believes that literature has a language all its own. In "The Language of Paradox" (1942) he presents the clearest explanation of that special language.

The Language of Paradox

Few of use are prepared to accept the statement that the language of poetry is the language of paradox. Paradox is the language of sophistry, hard, bright, witty; it is hardly the language of the soul. We are willing to allow that paradox is a permissible weapon which a Chesterton may on occasion exploit. We may permit it in epigram, a special subvariety of poetry; and in satire, which though useful, we are hardly willing to allow to be poetry at all. Our prejudices force us to regard paradox as intellectual rather than emotional, clever rather than profound, rational rather than divinely irrational.

Yet there is a sense in which paradox is the language appropriate and inevitable to poetry. It is the scientist whose truth requires a language purged of every trace of paradox; apparently the truth which the poet utters can be approached only in terms of paradox. I overstate the case, to be sure; it is possible that the title of this chapter is itself to be treated as merely a paradox. But there are reasons for thinking that the overstatement which I propose may light up some elements in the nature of poetry which tend to be overlooked.

The case of William Wordsworth, for instance, is instructive on this point. His poetry would not appear to promise many examples of the language of paradox. He usually prefers the direct attack. He insists on simplicity; he distrusts whatever seems sophistical. And yet the typical Wordsworth poem is based upon a paradoxical situation. Consider his celebrated

> It is a beauteous evening, calm and free
> The holy time is quiet as a Nun
> Breathless with adoration. . . .

The poet is filled with worship, but the girl who walks beside him is not worshipping. The implication is that she should respond to the holy time, and become like the evening itself, nunlike; but she seems less worshipful than inanimate nature itself. Yet

> If thou appear untouched by solemn thought,
> Thy nature is not therefore less divine:
> Thou liest in Abraham's bosom all the year;
> And worhip'st at the Temple's inner shrine,
> God being with thee when we know it not.

The underlying paradox (of which the enthusiastic reader may well be unconscious) is nevertheless thoroughly necessary, even for the reader. Why does the innocent girl worship more deeply than the self-conscious poet who walks beside her? Because she is filled with an unconscious sympathy for *all* of nature, not merely the grandiose and solemn. One remembers the lines from Wordsworth's friend, Coleridge:

> He prayeth best, who loveth best
> All things both great and small.[1]

Her unconscious sympathy is the unconscious worship. She is in communion with nature "all the year," and her devotion is continual whereas that of the poet is sporadic and momentary. But we have not done with the paradox yet. It not only underlies the poem, but something of the paradox informs the poem, though, since this is Wordsworth, rather timidly. The comparison of the evening to the nun actually has more than one dimension. The calm of the evening obviously means "worship," even to the dull-witted and insensitive. It corresponds to the trappings of the nun, visible to everyone. Thus, it suggests not merely holiness, but, in the total poem, even a hint of Pharisaical holiness, with which the girl's careless innocence, itself a symbol of her continual secret worship, stands in contrast.

Or consider Wordsworth's sonnet, *Composed upon Westminster Bridge.* I believe that most readers will agree that it is one of Wordsworth's most successful poems; yet most students have the greatest difficulty in accounting for its goodness. The attempt to account for it on the grounds of nobility of sentiment soon breaks down. On this level, the poem merely says: that the city in the morning light presents a picture which is majestic and touching to all but the most dull of souls; but the poem says very little more about the sight: the city is beautiful in the morning light and it is awfully still. The attempt to make a case for the poem in terms of the brilliance of its images also quickly breaks down: the student searches for graphic details in vain: there are next to no realistic touches. In fact, the poet simply huddles the details together:

> . . . silent, bare,
> Ships, towers, domes, theatres, and temples
> lie
> Open unto the fields . . .

We get a blurred impression—points of roofs and pinnacles along the skyline, all twinkling in the morning light. More than that, the sonnet as a whole contains some very flat writing and some well-worn comparisons.

The reader may ask: Where, then, does the poem get its power? It gets it, it seems to me, from the paradoxical situation out of which the poem arises. The speaker is honestly surprised, and he manages to get some sense of awed surprise into the poem. It is odd to the poet that the city should be able to "wear the beauty of the morning" at all. Mount Snowdon, Skiddaw, Mont Blanc—these wear it by natural right, but surely not grimy, feverish London. This is the point of the almost shocked exclamation:

> Never did sun more beautifully steep
> In his first splendour, *valley, rock,*
> or *hill* . . .

The "smokeless air" reveals a city which the poet did not know existed: man-made London is a part of nature too, is lighted by the sun of nature, and lighted to as beautiful effect.

> The river glideth at his own sweet
> will . . .

A river is the most "natural" thing that one can imagine; it has the elasticity, the curved line of nature itself. The poet had never been able to regard this one as a real river—now, uncluttered by barges, the river reveals itself as a natural thing, not at all disciplined into a rigid and mechanical pattern: it is like the daffodils, or the mountain brooks, artless, and whimsical, and "natural" as they. The poem closes, you will remember, as follows:

> Dear God! the very houses seem asleep;
> And all that mighty heart is lying still!

The city, in the poet's insight of the morning, has earned its right to be considered organic, not merely mechanical. That is why the stale metaphor of the sleeping houses is strangely renewed. The most exciting thing that the poet can say about the houses is that they are *asleep.* He has been in the habit of counting them dead—as just mechanical and inanimate; to say they are "asleep" is to say that they are alive, that they participate in the life of nature. In the same way, the tired old metaphor which sees a great city as a pulsating heart of empire becomes revivified. It is only when the poet sees the city under the semblance of death that he can see it as actually alive—quick with the only life which he can accept, the organic life of "nature."

It is not my intention to exaggerate Wordsworth's own consciousness of the paradox involved. In this poem, he prefers, as is usual with him, the frontal attack. But the situation is paradoxical here as in so many of his poems. In his preface to the second edition of the *Lyrical Ballads* Wordsworth stated that his general purpose was "to choose incidents and situations from common life" but so to treat them that "ordinary things should be preserved to the mind in an unusual aspect." Coleridge was to state the purpose for him later, in terms which make ever more evident Wordsworth's exploitation of the paradoxical: "Mr. Wordsworth . . . was to propose to himself as his object, to give the charm of novelty to things of every day, and to excite a feeling analogous to the supernatural, by awakening the mind's attention from the lethargy of custom, and directing it to the loveliness and the wonders of the word before us. . . " Wordsworth, in short, was consciously attempting to show his audience that the common was really uncommon, the prosaic was really poetic.

Coleridge's terms, "the charm of novelty to things of every day," "awakening the mind," suggest the Romantic preoccupation with wonder—the surprise, the revelation which puts the tarnished familiar world in a new light. This may well be the *raison d'être* of most Romantic paradoxes; and yet the neo-classic poets use paradox for much the same reason. Consider Pope's lines from *The Essay on Man*:

In doubt his Mind or Body to prefer;
Born but to die, and reas'ning but to err;
Alike in ignorance, his Reason such,
Whether he thinks too little, or too
much. . .

Created half to rise, and half to fall;
Great Lord of all things, yet a Prey to all;
Sole Judge of Truth, in endless Error
hurl'd;
The Glory, Jest, and Riddle of the world!

Here it is true, the paradoxes insist on the irony, rather than the wonder. But Pope too might have claimed that he was treating the things of every day, man himself, and awakening his mind so that he would view himself in a new and blinding light. Thus, there is a certain awed wonder in Pope just as there is a certain trace of irony implicit in the Wordsworth sonnets. There is, of course, no reason why they should not occur together, and they do. Wonder and irony merge in many of the lyrics of Blake; they merge in Coleridge's *Ancient Mariner*. The variations in emphasis are numerous. Gray's *Elegy* uses a typical Wordsworth "situation" with the rural scene and with peasants contemplated in the light of their "betters." But in the *Elegy* the balance is heavily tilted in the direction of irony, the revelation an ironic rather than a startling one:

Can storied urn or animated bust
Back to its mansion call the fleeting
breath?
Can Honour's voice provoke the silent
dust?
Or Flatt'ry sooth the dull cold ear of
Death?

But I am not here interested in enumerating the possible variations; I am interested rather in our seeing that the paradoxes spring from the very nature of the poet's language: it is a language in which the connotations play as great a part as the denotations. And I do not mean that the connotations are important as supplying some sort of frill or trimming, something external to the real matter in hand. I mean that the poet does not use a notation at all—as the scientist may properly be said to do so. The poet, within limits, has to make up his language as he goes.

T. S. Eliot has commented upon "that perpetual slight alteration of language, words perpetually juxtaposed in new and sudden combinations," which occurs in poetry. It *is* perpetual; it cannot be kept out of the poem; it can only be directed and controlled. The tendency of science is necessarily to stabilize terms, to freeze them into strict denotations; the poet's tendency is by contrast disruptive. The terms are continually modifying each other, and thus violating their dictionary meanings. To take a very simple example, consider the adjectives in the first lines of Wordsworth's evening sonnet: *beauteous, calm, free, holy, quiet, breathless*. The juxtapositions are hardly startling; and yet notice this: the evening is like a nun breathless with adoration. The adjective "breathless" suggests tremendous excitement; and yet the evening is not only quiet but *calm*. There is no final contradiction, to be sure: it is *that* kind of calm and *that* kind of excitement, and the two states may well occur together. But the poet has no one term. Even if he had a polysyllabic technical term, the term would not provide the solution for his problem. He must work by contradiction and qualification.

We may approach the problem in this way: the poet has to work by analogies. All of the subtler states of emotion, as I. A. Richards has pointed out, necessarily demand metaphor for their expression. The poet must work by analogies, but the metaphors do not lie in the same plane or fit neatly edge to edge. There is a continual tilting of the planes; necessary overlappings, discrepancies, contradictions. Even the most direct and simple poet is forced into paradoxes far more often than we think, if we are sufficiently alive to what he is doing.

But in dilating on the difficulties of the poet's task, I do not want to leave the impression that it is a task which necessarily defeats him, or even that with his method he may not win to a fine precision. To use Shakespeare's figure, he can

> . . . with assays of bias
> By indirections find directions
> out.

Shakespeare had in mind the game of lawn bowls in which the bowl is distorted, a distortion which allows the skillful player to bowl a curve. To elaborate the figure, science makes use of the perfect sphere and its attack can be direct. The method of art can, I believe, never be direct—is always indirect. But that does not mean that the master of the game cannot place the bowl where he wants it. The serious difficulties will only occur when he confuses his game with that of science and mistakes the nature of his appropriate instrument. Mr. Stuart Chase a few years ago, with a touching naïveté, urged us to take the distortion out of the bowl—to treat language like notation.

I have said that even the apparently simple and straightforward poet is forced into paradoxes by the nature of his instrument. Seeing this, we should not be surprised to find poets who consciously employ it to gain a compression and precision otherwise unobtainable. Such a method, like any other, carries with it its own perils. But the dangers are not overpowering: the poem is not predetermined to a shallow and glittering sophistry. The method is an extension of the normal language of poetry, not a perversion of it.

I should like to refer the reader to a concrete case. Donne's *Canonization* ought to provide a sufficiently extreme instance. The basic metaphor which underlies the poem (and which is reflected in the title) involves a sort of paradox. For the poet daringly treats profane love as if it were divine love. The canonization is not that of a pair of holy anchorites who have renounced the world and the flesh.

The hermitage of each is the other's body; but they do renounce the world, and so their title to sainthood is cunningly argued. The poem then is a parody of Christian sainthood; but it is an intensely serious parody of a sort that modern man, habituated as he is to an easy yes or no, can hardly understand. He refuses to accept the paradox as a serious rhetorical device; and since he is able to accept it only as a cheap trick, he is forced into this dilemma. Either: Donne does not take love seriously; here he is merely sharpening his wit as a sort of mechanical exercise. Or: Donne does not take sainthood seriously; here he is merely indulging in a cynical and bawdy parody.

Neither account is true; a reading of the poem will show that Donne takes both love and religion seriously; it will show, further, that the paradox is here his inevitable instrument. But to see this plainly will require a closer reading than most of us give to poetry.

The poem opens dramatically on a note of exasperation. The "you" whom the speaker addresses is not identified. We can imagine that it is a person, perhaps a friend, who is objecting to the speaker's love affair. At any rate, the person represents the practical world which regards love as a silly affectation. To use the metaphor on which the poem is built, the friend represents the secular world which the lovers have renounced.

Donne begins to suggest this metaphor in the first stanza by the contemptuous alternatives which he suggests to the friend:

> . . . chide my palsie, or my gout,
> My five gray hairs, or ruin'd fortune
> flout. . . .

The implications are: (1) All right, consider my love as an infirmity, as a disease, if you will, but confine yourself to my other infirmities, my palsy, my approaching old age, my ruined fortune. You stand a better chance of curing those; in chiding me for this one, you are simply wasting your time as well as mine. Why don't you pay attention to your own welfare—go on and get wealth and honour for yourself. What should you care if I do give these up in pursuing my love.

The two main categories of secular success are neatly, and contemptuously epitomized in the line:

> Or the Kings reall, or his stamped
> face . . .

Cultivate the court and gaze at the king's face there, or, if you prefer, get into business and look at his face stamped on coins. But let me alone.

This conflict between the "real" world and the lover absorbed in the world of love runs through the poem; it dominates the second stanza in which the torments of love, so vivid to the lover, affect the real world not at all—

> What merchants ships have my sighs
> drown'd?

It is touched on in the fourth stanza in the contrast between the word "Chronicle" which suggests secular history with its pomp and magnificence, the history of kings of princes, and the word "sonnets" with its suggestions of trivial and precious intricacy. The conflict appears again in the last stanza, only to be resolved when the unworldly lovers, love's saints who have given up the world, paradoxically achieve a more intense world. But here the paradox is still contained in, and supported by, the dominant metaphor: so does the holy anchorite win a better world by giving up this one.

But before going on to discuss this development of the theme, it is important to see what else the second stanza does. For it is in this second stanza and the third, that the poet shifts the tone of the poem, modulating from the note of irritation with which the poem opens into the quite different tone with which it closes.

Donne accomplishes the modulation of tone by what may be called an analysis of love-metaphor. Here, as in many of his poems, he shows that he is thoroughly self-conscious about what he is doing. This second stanza he fills with the conventionalized figures of the Petrarchan tradition: the wind of lovers' sighs, the floods of lovers' tears, etc.—extravagant figures with which the contemptuous secular friend might be expected to tease the lover. The implication is that the poet himself recognizes the absurdity of the Petrarchan love metaphors. But what of it? The very absurdity of the jargon which lovers are expected to talk makes for his argument: their love, however absurd it may appear to the world, does no harm to the world. The practical friend need have no fears: there will still be wars to fight and lawsuits to argue.

The opening of the third stanza suggests that this vein of irony is to be maintained. The poet points out to his friend the infinite fund of such absurdities which can be applied to lovers:

> Call her one, mee another flye,
> We'are Tapers too, and at our owne
>   cost die. . . .

For the matter, the lovers can conjure up for themselves plenty of such fantastic comparisons: *they* know what the world thinks of them. But these figures of the third stanza are no longer the threadbare Petrarchan conventionalities; they have sharpness and bite. The last one, the likening of the lovers to the phoenix, is fully serious, and with it, the tone has shifted from ironic banter into a defiant but controlled tenderness.

The effect of the poet's implied awareness of the lovers' apparent madness is to cleanse and revivify metaphor; to indicate the sense in which the poet accepts it, and thus to prepare us for accepting seriously the fine and seriously intended metaphors which dominate the last two stanzas of the poem.

The opening line of the fourth stanza,

> Wee can dye by it, if not live by love,

achieves an effect of tenderness and deliberate resolution. The lovers are ready to die to the world; they are committed; they are not callow but confident. (The basic metaphor of the saint, one notices, is being carried on; the lovers, in their renunciation of the world, have something of the confident resolution of the saint. By the bye, the word "legend"—

> . . . if unfit for tombes and hearse
> Our legend bee—

in Donne's time meant "the life of a saint.") The lovers are willing to forego the ponderous and stately chronicle and to accept the trifling and insubstantial "sonnet" instead; but then if the urn be well wrought, it provides a finer memorial for one's ashes than does the pompous and grotesque monument. With the finely contemptuous, yet quiet phrase, "halfe-acre tombes," the world which the lovers reject expands into something gross and vulgar. But the figure works further; the pretty sonnets will not merely hold their ashes as a decent earthly memorial. Their legend, their story, will gain them canonization; and approved as love's saints, other lovers will invoke them.

In the last stanza, the theme receives a final complication. The lovers in rejecting life actually win to the most intense life. This paradox has been hinted at earlier in the phoenix metaphor. Here it receives a powerful dramatization. The lovers in becoming hermits, find that they have not lost the world, but have gained the world in each other, now a more intense, more meaningful world. Donne is not content to treat the lovers' discovery as something which comes to them passsively, but rather as something which they actively achieve. They are like the saint, God's athlete:

> Who did the whole worlds soule *contract*,
> and drove
> Into the glasses of your eyes. . . .

The image is that of a violent squeezing as of a powerful hand. And what do the lovers "drive" into each other's eyes? The "Countries, Townes," and "Courts," which they renounced in the first stanza of the poem. The unworldly lovers thus become the most "worldly" of all.

The tone with which the poem closes is one of triumphant achievement, but the tone is a development contributed to by various earlier elements. One of the more important elements which works towards our acceptance of the final paradox is the figure of the phoenix, which will bear a little further analysis.

The comparison of the lovers to the phoenix is very skillfully related to the two earlier comparisons, that in which the lovers are like burning tapers, and that in which they are like the eagle and the dove. The phoenix comparison gathers up both: the phoenix is a bird, and like the tapers, it burns. We have a selected series of items: the phoenix figure seems to come in a natural stream of association. "Call us what you will," the lover says, and rattles off in his desperation the first comparisons that occur to him. The comparison to the phoenix seems thus merely another outlandish one, the most outrageous of all. But it is this most fantastic one, stumbled over apparently in his haste, that the poet goes on to develop. It really describes the lovers best and justifies their renunciation. For the phoenix is not two but one, "we two being one, are it"; and it burns, not like the taper at its own cost, but to live again. Its death is life: "Wee dye and rise the same . . ." The poet literally justifies the fantastic assertion. In the sixteenth and seventeenth centuries to "die" means to experience the consummation of the act of love. The lovers after the act are the same. Their love is not exhausted in mere lust. This is their title to canonization. Their love is like the phoenix.

I hope that I do not seem to juggle that meaning of *die*. The meaning that I have cited can be abundantly justified in the literature of the period; Shakespeare uses "die" in this sense; so does Dryden. Moreover, I do not think that I give it undue emphasis. The word is in a crucial position. On it is pivoted the transition to the next stanza,

> Wee can dye by it, if not live by love,
> And if unfit for tombes . . .

Most important of all, the sexual submeaning of "die" does not contradict the other meanings: the poet is saying: "Our death is really a more intense life"; "We can afford to trade life (the world) for death (love), for that death is the consummation of life"; "After all, one does not expect to live *by* love, one expects, and wants, to die *by* it." But in the total passage he is also saying: "Because our love is not mundane, we can give up the world"; "Because our love is not merely lust, we can give up the other lusts, the lust for wealth and power"; "because," and this is said with an inflection of irony as by one who knows the world too well, "because our love can outlast its consummation, we are a minor miracle, we are love's saints." This passage with its ironical tenderness and its realism feeds and supports the brilliant paradox with which the poem closes.

There is one more factor in developing and sustaining the final effect. The poem is an instance of the doctrine which it asserts; it is both the assertion and the realization of the assertion. The poet has actually before our eyes built within the song the "pretty room" with which he says the lovers can be content. The poem itself is the well-wrought urn which can hold the lovers' ashes and which will not suffer in comparison with the prince's "halfe-acre tomb."

And how necessary are the paradoxes? Donne might have said directly, "Love in a cottage is enough." *The Canonization* contains this admirable thesis, but it contains a great deal more. He might have been as forthright as a later lyricist who wrote, "We'll build a sweet little nest, / Somewhere out in the West, / And let the rest of the world go by." He might even have imitated that more metaphysical lyric, which maintains, "You're the cream in my coffee." *The Canonization* touches on all these observations, but it goes beyond them, not merely in dignity, but in precision.

I submit that the only way by which the poet could say what *The Canonization* says is by paradox. More direct methods may be tempting, but all of them enfeeble and distort what is to be said. This statement may seem the less surprising when we reflect on how many of the important things which the poet has to say have to be said by means of paradox: most of the languages of lovers is such—*The Canonization* is a good example; so is most of the language of religion—"He who would save his life, must lose it"; "The last shall be first." Indeed, almost any insight important enough to warrant a great poem apparently has to be stated in such terms. Deprived of the character of paradox with its twin concomitants of irony and wonder, the matter of Donne's poem unravels into "facts," biological, sociological, and economic. What happens to Donne's lovers if we consider them "scientifically," without benefit of the supernaturalism which the poet confers upon them? Well, what happens to Shakespeare's lovers, for Shakespeare uses the basic metaphor of *The Canonization* in his *Romeo and Juliet?* In their first conversation, the lovers play with the analogy between the lover and the pilgrim to the Holy Land. Juliet says:

> For saints have hands, that pilgrims'
> hands do touch
> And palm to palm is holy palmers' kiss.

Considered scientifically, the lovers become Mr. Aldous Huxley's animals, "quietly sweating, palm to palm."

For us today, Donne's imagination seems obsessed with the problem of unity; the sense in which the lovers become one—the sense in which the soul is united with God. Frequently, as we have seen one type of union becomes a metaphor for the other. It may not be too far-fetched to see both as instances of, and metaphors for, the union which the creative imagination itself effects. For that fusion is not logical; it apparently violates science and common sense; it welds together the discordant and the contradictory. Coleridge has of course given us the classic description of its nature and power. It

> reveals itself in the balance or reconcilement of opposite or discordant qualities: of sameness, with difference; of the general, with the concrete; the idea, with the image; the individual, with the representative; the sense of novelty and freshness, with old and familiar objects; a more than usual state of emotion, with more than usual order . . .[2]

It is a great and illuminating statement, but is a series of paradoxes. Apparently Coleridge could describe the effect of the imagination in no other way.

Shakespeare, in one of his poems, has given a description that oddly parallels that of Coleridge.

Reason in it selfe confounded,
Saw Division grow together,
To themselves yet either neither,
Simple were so well compounded.

I do not know what his *The Phoenix and the Turtle* celebrates. Perhaps it *was* written to honour the marriage of Sir John Salisbury and Ursula Stanley; or perhaps the Phoenix is Lucy, Countess of Bedford; or perhaps the poem is merely an essay on Platonic love. But the scholars themselves are so uncertain, that I think we will do little violence to established habits of thinking, if we boldly pre-empt the poem for our own purposes. Certainly the poem is an instance of that magic power which Coleridge sought to describe. I propose that we take it for a moment as a poem about that power;

So they loved as love in twaine,
Had the essence but in one,
Two distincts, Division none,
Number there in love was slaine.

Hearts remote, yet not asunder,
Distance and no space was seene,
Twixt his *Turtle* and his Queene;
But in them it were a wonder. . . .

Propertie was thus appalled,
That the selfe was not the same;
Single Natures double name,
Neither two nor one was called.

Precisely! The nature is single, one, unified. But the name is double, and today with our multiplication of sciences, it is multiple. If the poet is to be true to his poetry, he must call it neither two nor one: the paradox is his only solution. The difficulty has intensified since Shakespeare's day: the timid poet, when confronted with the problem of "Single Nature's double name," has too often funked it. A history of poetry from Dryden's time to our own might bear as its subtitle "The Half-Hearted Phoenix."

In Shakespeare's poem, Reason is "in it selfe confounded" at the union of the Phoenix and the Turtle; but it recovers to admit its own bankruptcy:

Love hath Reason, Reason none,
If what parts, can so remaine. . . .

and it is Reason which goes on to utter the beautiful threnos with which the poem concludes:

Beautie, Truth, and Raritie,
Grace in all simplicitie,
Here enclosde, in cinders lie.

Death is now the *Phoenix* nest,
And the *Turtles* loyall brest,
To eternitie doth rest. . . .

Truth may seeme, but cannot be,
Beautie bragge, but tis not she,
Truth and Beautie buried be.

To this urne let those repaire,
That are either true or faire,
For these dead Birds, sigh a prayer.

Having pre-empted the poem for our own purposes, it may not be too outrageous to go on to make one further observation. The urn to which we are summoned, the urn which holds the ashes of the phoenix, is like the well-wrought urn of Donne's *Canonization* which holds the phoenix-lovers' ashes; it is the poem itself. One is reminded of still another urn, Keats's Grecian urn, which contained for Keats, Truth and Beauty, as Shakespeare's urn encloses "Beautie, Truth, and Raritie." But there is a sense in which all such well-wrought urns contain the ashes of a phoenix. The urns are not meant for memorial purposes only, though that often seems to be their chief significance to the professors of literature. The phoenix rises from its ashes; or ought to rise; but it will not arise for all our mere sifting and measuring the ashes, or testing them for their chemical content. We must be prepared to accept the paradox of the imagination itself; else "Beautie, Truth, and Raritie" remain enclosed in their cinders and we shall end with essential cinders, for all our pains.

APPENDIX

THE CANONIZATION

For Godsake hold your tongue, and let me
    love,
  Or chide my palsie, or my gout,
My five gray haires, or ruin'd fortune flout,
  With wealth your state, your minde with
    Arts improve,
  Take you a course, get you a place,
  Observe his honour, or his grace,
Or the Kings reall, or his stamped face
  Contemplate, what you will, approve,
  So you will let me love.

Alas, alas, who's injur'd by my love?
  What merchants ships have my sighs
  drown'd?
Who saies my teares have overflow'd his
    ground?
  When did my colds a forward spring
    remove?
  When did the heats which my veines fill
  Adde one more to the plaguie Bill?
Soldiers finde warres, and Lawyers finde out
    still
  Litigious men, which quarrels move,
  Though she and I do love.

Call us what you will, wee are made such by
    love;
  Call her one, mee another flye,
We'are tapers too, and at our owne cost die,
  And wee in us finde the Eagle and the
    Dove.
  The phoenix ridle hath more wit
  By us, we two being one, are it.
So to one neutrall thing both sexes fit,
  We dye and rise the same, and prove
  Mysterious by this love.

Wee can dye by it, if not live by love,
  And if unfit for tombes and hearse
Our legend bee, it will be fit for verse;
  And if no peece of Chronicle wee prove,
  We'll build in sonnets pretty roomes;
  As well a well wrought urne becomes
The greatest ashes, as halfe-acre tombes,
  And by these hymnes, all shall approve
  Us Canoniz'd for Love:

And thus invoke us; You whom reverend
    love
  Made one anothers hermitage;
You, to whom love was peace, that now is
    rage;
  Who did the whole worlds soule contract,
    and drove
  Into the glasses of your eyes
  (So made such mirrors, and such spies,
That they did all to you epitomize,)
  Countries, Townes, Courts: Beg from
    above
  A patterne of your love!

NOTES

1. *The Rime of the Ancient Mariner.*
2. *Biographia Literaria* (1817), chap. xiv.

3

W. K. Wimsatt, Jr.
1907–1975

Monroe Beardsley
1915–

One of the preeminent representatives of the New Criticism, W. K. Wimsatt, Jr., taught at Yale University from 1939 until his death. His works include *The Prose Style of Samuel Johnson* (1941), *Literary Criticism* (with Cleanth Brooks, 1957), and *Hateful Contraries* (1965). In his most important book, *The Verbal Icon* (1954), Wimsatt outlined an "objective" criticism in which the critic disregards both the intentions of the poet and the emotional reactions of the reader. Monroe Beardsley has taught philosophy at Yale University, Mount Holyoke College, Swarthmore College, and Temple University. His works include *Aesthetics* (1958) and *Aesthetics from Classical Greece to the Present* (1966). In "The Intentional Fallacy" (1946) and "The Affective Fallacy" (1949) Wimsatt and Beardsley defined the parameters of the critic's concern: the poem itself. With these essays, the so-called "scientific objectivity" of the New Criticism reached an extreme it would not go beyond.

In "The Intentional Fallacy" (1946) Wimsatt and Beardsley argue that because the poem is no longer the poet's but "belongs to the public," any serious consideration of the poet's intention as an avenue for understanding the poem is misplaced. Instead, the poem's meaning is found in its internal patterns, its existence as an esthetic phenomenon. The external, "private or idiosyncratic," aspects of the poem provide information about the poem's creation, which may be of interest in another context but which in literary criticism contributes nothing to the meaning of "the work as a linguistic fact." This strict adherence to a "close reading" of the text, in practice isolated from biographical or historical information, is a relatively late and definitive formulation of the New Criticism.

The Intentional Fallacy

I

The claim of the author's "intention" upon the critic's judgment has been challenged in a number of recent discussions, notably in the debate entitled *The Personal Heresy* (1939), between Professor Lewis and Tillyard. But it seems doubtful if this claim and most of its romantic corollaries are as yet subject to any widespread questioning. The present writers, in a short article entitled "Intention" for a *Dictionary*[1] of literary criticism, raised the issue but were unable to pursue its implications at any length. We argued that the design or intention of the author is neither available nor desirable as a standard for judging the success of a work of literary art, and it seems to us that this is a principle which goes deep into some differences in the history of critical attitudes. It is a principle which accepted or rejected points to the polar opposites of classical "imitation" and romantic expression. It entails many specific truths about inspiration, authenticity, biography, literary history and scholarship, and about some trends of contemporary poetry, especially its allusiveness. There is hardly a problem of literary criticism in which the critic's approach will not be qualified by his view of "intention."

"Intention," as we shall use the term, corresponds to *what he intended* in a formula which more or less explicitly has had wide acceptance. "In order to judge the poet's performance, we must know *what he intended.*" Intention is design or plan in the author's mind. Intention has obvious affinities for the author's attitude towards his work, the way he felt, what made him write.

We begin our discussion with a series of propositions summarized and abstracted to a degree where they seem to us axiomatic.

1. A poem does not come into existence by accident. The words of a poem, as Professor Stoll has remarked, come out of a head, not out of a hat. Yet to insist on the designing intellect as a *cause* of a poem is not to grant the design or intention as a *standard* by which the critic is to judge the worth of the poet's performance.
2. One must ask how a critic expects to get an answer to the question about intention. How is he to find out what the poet tried to do? If the poet succeeded in doing it, then the poem itself shows what he was trying to do. And if the poet did not succeed, then the poem is not adequate evidence, and the critic must go outside the poem—for evidence of an intention that did not become effective in the poem. "Only one *caveat* must be borne in mind," says an eminent intentionalist[2] in a moment when his theory repudiates itself; "the poet's aim must be judged at the moment of the creative act, that is to say, by the art of the poem itself."
3. Judging a poem is like judging a pudding or a machine. One demands that it work. It is only because an artifact works that we infer the intention of an artificer. "A poem should not mean but be." A poem can *be* only through its meaning—since its medium is words—yet it is, simply is, in the sense that we have no excuse for inquiring what part is intended or meant. Poetry is a feat of style by which a complex of meaning is handled all at once. Poetry

succeeds because all or most of what is said or implied is relevant: what is irrelevant has been excluded, like lumps from pudding and "bugs" from machinery. In this respect poetry differs from practical messages, which are successful if and only if we correctly infer the intention. They are more abstract than poetry.

4. The meaning of a poem may certainly be a personal one, in the sense that a poem expresses a personality or state of soul rather than a physical object like an apple. But even a short lyric poem is dramatic, the response of a speaker (no matter how abstractly conceived) to a situation (no matter how universalized). We ought to impute the thoughts and attitudes of the poem immediately to the dramatic *speaker,* and if to the author at all, only by an act of biographical inference.
5. There is a sense in which an author, by revision, may better achieve his original intention. But it is a very abstract sense. He intended to write a better work, or a better work of a certain kind, and now has done it. But it follows that his former concrete intention was not his intention. "He's the man we were in search of, that's true," says Hardy's rustic constable, "and yet he's not the man we were in search of. For the man we were in search of was not the man we wanted."

"Is not a critic," asks Professor Stoll, "a judge, who does not explore his own consciousness, but determines the author's meaning or intention, as if the poem were a will, a contract, or the constitution? The poem is not the critic's own." He has accurately diagnosed two forms of irresponsibility, one of which he prefers. Our view is yet different. The poem is not the critic's own and not the author's (it is detached from the author at birth and goes about the world beyond his power to intend about it or control it). The poem belongs to the public. It is embodied in language, the peculiar possession of the public, and it is about the human being, an object of public knowledge. What is said about the poem is subject to the same scrutiny as any statement in linguistics or in the general science of psychology.

A critic of our *Dictionary* article, Ananda K. Coomaraswamy, has argued[3] that there are two kinds of inquiry about a work of art: (1) whether the artist achieved his intentions; (2) whether the work of art "ought ever to have been undertaken at all" and so "whether it is worth preserving." Number (2), Coomaraswamy maintains, is not "criticism of any work of art *qua* work of art," but is rather moral criticism; number (1) is artistic criticism. But we maintain that (2) need not be moral criticism: that there is another way of deciding whether works of art are worth preserving and whether, in a sense, they "ought" to have been undertaken, and this is the way of objective criticism of works of art as such, the way which enables us to distinguish between a skilful murder and a skilful poem. A skilful murder is an example which Coomaraswamy uses, and in his system the difference between murder and the poem is simply a "moral" one, not an "artistic" one, since each if carried out according to plan is "artistically" successful. We maintain that (2) is an inquiry of more worth than (1), and since (2) and not (1) is capable of distinguishing poetry from murder, the name "artistic criticism" is properly given to (2).

II

It is not so much a historical statement as a definition to say that the intentional fallacy is a romantic one. When a rhetorician of the first century A.D. writes: "Sublimity is the echo of a great soul," or when he tells us that "Homer enters into the sublime actions of his heroes" and "shares the full inspiration of the combat," we shall not be surprised to find this rhetorician considered as a distant harbinger of romanticism and greeted in the warmest terms by Saintsbury. One may wish to argue whether Longinus should be called romantic, but there can hardly be a doubt that in one important way he is.

Goethe's three questions for "constructive criticism" are "What did the author set out to do? Was his plan reasonable and sensible, and how far did he succeed in carrying it out?" If one leaves out the middle question, one has in effect the system of Croce—the culmination and crowning philosophic expression of romanticism. The beautiful is the successful intuition-expression, and the ugly is the unsuccessful; the intuition or private part of art is *the* aesthetic fact, and the medium or public part is not the subject of aesthetic at all.

> The Madonna of Cimabue is still in the Church of Santa Maria Novella; but does she speak to the visitor of today as to the Florentines of the thirteenth century?
> *Historical interpretation* labours . . . to reintegrate in us the psychological conditions which have changed in the course of history. It . . . enables us to see a work of art (a physical object) as its *author saw it* in the moment of production.[4]

The first italics are Croce's, the second ours. The upshot of Croce's system is an ambiguous emphasis on history. With such passages as a point of departure a critic may write a nice analysis of the meaning or "spirit" of a play by Shakespeare or Corneille—a process that involves close historical study but remains aesthetic criticism—or he may, with equal plausibility, produce an essay in sociology, biography, or other kinds of non-aesthetic history.

III

> I went to the poets; tragic, dithyrambic, and all sorts. . . . I took them some of the most elaborate passages in their own writings, and asked what was the meaning of them. . . . Will you believe me? . . . there is hardly a person present who would not have talked better about their poetry than they did themselves. Then I knew that not by wisdom do poets write poetry, but by a sort of genius and inspiration.

That reiterated mistrust of the poets which we hear from Socrates may have been part of a rigorously ascetic view in which we hardly wish to participate, yet Plato's Socrates saw a truth about the poetic mind which the world no longer commonly sees—so much criticism, and that the most inspirational and most affectionately remembered, has proceeded from the poets themselves.

Certainly the poets have had something to say that the critic and professor could not say; their message has been more exciting: that poetry should come as naturally as leaves to a tree, that poetry is the lava of the imagination, or that it is emotion recollected in tranquillity. But it is necessary that we realize the character and authority of such testimony. There is only a fine shade of difference between such expressions and a kind of earnest advice that authors often give. Thus Edward Young, Carlyle, Walter Pater:

> I know two golden rules from *ethics*, which are no less golden in Composition, than in life. 1. *Know thyself*; 2dly, *Reverence thyself*. This is the grand secret for finding readers and retaining them: let him who would move and convince others, be first moved and convinced himself. Horace's rule, *Si vis me flere*, is applicable in a wider sense than the literal one. To every poet, to every writer, we might say: Be true, if you would be believed.
>
> Truth! there can be no merit, no craft at all, without that. And further, all beauty is

> in the long run only *fineness* of truth, or what we call expression, the finer accommodation of speech to that vision within.

And Housman's little handbook to the poetic mind yields this illustration:

> Having drunk a pint of beer at luncheon—beer is a sedative to the brain, and my afternoons are the least intellectual portion of my life—I would go out for a walk of two or three hours. As I went along, thinking of nothing in particular, only looking at things around me and following the progress of the seasons, there would flow into my mind, with sudden and unaccountable emotion, sometimes a line or two of verse, sometimes a whole stanza at once.

This is the logical terminus of the series already quoted. Here is a confession of how poems were written which would do as a definition of poetry just as well as "emotion recollected in tranquillity"—and which the young poet might equally well take to heart as a practical rule. Drink a pint of beer, relax, go walking, think on nothing in particular, look at things, surrender yourself to yourself, search for the truth in your own soul, listen to the sound of your own inside voice, discover and express the *vraie vérité* ["true truth"].

It is probably true that all this is excellent advice for poets. The young imagination fired by Wordsworth and Carlyle is probably closer to the verge of producing a poem than the mind of the student who has been sobered by Aristotle or Richards. The art of inspiring poets, or at least of inciting something like poetry in young persons, has probably gone further in our day than ever before. Books of creative writing such as those issued from the Lincoln School are interesting evidence of what a child can do.[5] All this, however, would appear to belong to an art separate from criticism—to a psychological discipline, a system of self-development, a yoga, which the young poet perhaps does well to notice, but which is something different from the public art of evaluating poems.

Coleridge and Arnold were better critics than most poets have been, and if the critical tendency dried up the poetry in Arnold and perhaps in Coleridge, it is not inconsistent with our argument, which is that judgment of poems is different from the art of producing them. Coleridge has given us the classic "anodyne" story, and tells what he can about the genesis of a poem which he calls a "psychological curiosity," but his definitions of poetry and of the poetic quality "imagination" are to be found elsewhere and in quite other terms.

It would be convenient if the passwords of the intentional school, "sincerity," "fidelity," "spontaneity," "authenticity," "genuineness," "originality," could be equated with terms such as "integrity," "relevance," "unity," "function," "maturity," "subtlety," "adequacy," and other more precise terms of evaluation—in short, if "expression" always meant aesthetic achievement. But this is not so.

"Aesthetic" art, says Professor Curt Ducasse, an ingenious theorist of expression, is the conscious objectification of feelings, in which an intrinsic part is the critical moment. The artist corrects the objectification when it is not adequate. But this may mean that the earlier attempt was not successful in objectifying the self, or "it may also mean that it was a successful objectification of a self which, when it confronted us clearly, we disowned and repudiated in favour of another."[6] What is the standard by which we disown or accept the self? Professor Ducasse does not say. Whatever it may be, however, this standard is an element in the definition of art which will not reduce to terms of objectification. The evaluation of the work of art remains public; the work is measured against something outside the author.

IV

There is criticism of poetry and there is author psychology, which when applied to the present or future takes the form of inspirational promotion; but author psychology can be historical too, and then we have literary biography, a legitimate and attractive study in itself, one approach, as Professor Tillyard would argue, to personality, the poem being only a parallel approach. Certainly it need not be with a derogatory purpose that one points out personal studies, as distinct from poetic studies, in the realm of literary scholarship. Yet there is danger of confusing personal and poetic studies; and there is the fault of writing the personal as if it were poetic.

There is a difference between internal and external evidence for the meaning of a poem. And the paradox is only verbal and superficial that what is (1) internal is also public: it is discovered through the semantics and syntax of a poem, through our habitual knowledge of the language, through grammars, dictionaries, and all the literature which is the source of dictionaries, in general through all that makes a language and culture; while what is (2) external is private or idiosyncratic; not a part of the work as a linguistic fact: it consists of revelations (in journals, for example, or letters or reported conversations) about how or why the poet wrote the poem—to what lady, while sitting on what lawn, or at the death of what friend or brother. There is (3) an intermediate kind of evidence about the character of the author or about private or semi-private meanings attached to words or topics by an author or by a coterie of which he is a member. The meaning of words is the history of words, and the biography of an author, his use of a word, and the associations which the word had for *him*, are part of the word's history and meaning.[7] But the three types of evidence, especially (2) and (3), shade into one another so subtly that it is not always easy to draw a line between examples, and hence arises the difficulty for criticism. The use of biographical evidence need not involve intentionalism, because while it may be evidence of what the author intended, it may also be evidence of the meaning of his words and the dramatic character of his utterance. On the other hand, it may not be all this. And a critic who is concerned with evidence of type (1) and moderately with that of type (3) will in the long run produce a different sort of comment from that of the critic who is concerned with (2) and with (3) where it shades into (2).

The whole glittering parade of Professor Lowes' *Road to Xanadu*, for instance, runs along the border between types (2) and (3) or boldly traverses the romantic region of (2). " 'Kubla Khan,' " says Professor Lowes, "is a fabric of a vision, but every image that rose up in its weaving had passed that way before. And it would seem that there is nothing haphazard or fortuitous in their return." This is not quite clear—not even when Professor Lowes explains that there were clusters of associations, like hooked atoms, which were drawn into complex relation with other clusters in the deep well of Coleridge's memory, and which then coalesced and issued forth as poems. If there was nothing "haphazard or fortuitous" in the way the images returned to the surface, that may mean (1) that Coleridge could not produce what he did not have, that he was limited in his creation by what he had read or otherwise experienced, or (2) that having received certain clusters of associations, he was bound to return them in just the way he did, and that the value of the poem may be described in terms of the experiences on which he had to draw. The latter pair of propositions (a sort of Hartleyan associationism which Coleridge himself repudiated in the *Biographia*) may not be assented to. There were certainly other combinations, other poems, worse or better, that might have been written by men who had read Bartram and Purchas and Bruce and Milton. And this will be true no matter how many times we are able to add to the brilliant complex of Coleridge's reading. In certain flourishes (such as the sentence we have quoted) and in chapter headings like "The Shaping Spirit," "The Magical Synthesis," "Imagination Creatrix," it may be that Professor Lowes pretends to say more about the actual poems than he does. There is a certain deceptive variation in these fancy chapter titles; one expects to pass on to a new stage in the argument, and one finds—more and more sources, more and more about "the streamy nature of association."[8]

"Wohin der Weg?" quotes Professor Lowes for the motto of his book. "Kein Weg! Ins Unbetretene." Precisely because the way is *unbetreten*, we should say, it leads away from the poem. Bartram's *Travels* contain a good deal of the history of certain words and of certain romantic Floridian conceptions that appear in "Kubla Khan." And a good deal of that history has passed and was then passing into the very stuff of our language. Perhaps a person who has read Bartram appreciates the poem more than one who has not. Or, by looking up the vocabulary of "Kubla Khan" in the *Oxford English Dictionary*, or by reading some of the other books there quoted, a person may know the poem better. But it would seem to pertain little to the poem to know that *Coleridge* has read Bartram. There is a gross body of life, of sensory and mental experience, which lies behind and in some sense causes every poem, but can never be and need not be known in the verbal and hence intellectual composition which is the poem. For all the objects of our manifold experience, for every unity, there is an action of the mind which cuts off roots, melts away context—or indeed we should never have objects or ideas or anything to talk about.

It is probable that there is nothing in Professor Lowes' vast book which could detract from anyone's appreciation of either *The Ancient Mariner* or "Kubla Khan." We next present a case where preoccupation with evidence of type (3) has gone so far as to distort a critic's view of a poem (yet a case not so obvious as those that abound in our critical journals).

In a well-known poem by John Donne ["A Valediction: Forbidding Mourning"] appears this quatrain:

> Moving of th' earth brings harmes and
> feares,
> Men reckon what it did and meant,
> But trepidation of the spheares,
> Though greater farre, is innocent.

A recent critic in an elaborate treatment of Donne's learning has written of this quatrain as follows:

> He touches the emotional pulse of the situation by a skilful allusion to the new and the old astronomy. . . . Of the new astronomy, and "moving of the earth" is the most radical principle; of the old, the "trepidation of the spheres" is the motion of the greatest complexity. . . . The poet must exhort his love to quietness and calm upon his departure; and for this purpose the figure based upon the latter motion (trepidation), long absorbed into the traditional astronomy, fittingly suggests the tension of the moment without arousing the "harmes and feares" implicit in the figure of the moving earth.[9]

The argument is plausible and rests on a well substantiated thesis that Donne was deeply interested in the new astronomy and its repercussions in the theological realm. In various works Donne shows his familiarity with Kepler's *De Stella Nova*, with Galileo's *Siderius Nuncius*, with William Gilbert's *De Magnete*, and with Clavius' commentary on the *De Sphaera* of Sacrobosco. He refers to the new science in his Sermon at Paul's Cross and in a letter to Sir Henry Goodyer. In the *First Anniversary* he says the "new philosophy calls in doubt." In the *Elegy on Prince Henry* he says that the "least moving of the centre" makes "the world to shake."

It is difficult to answer argument like this, and impossible to answer it with evidence of like nature. There is no reason why Donne might not have written a stanza in which the two kinds of celestial motion stood for two sorts of emotion at parting. And if we become full of astronomical ideas and see Donne only against the background of the new science, we may believe that he did. But the text itself remains to be dealt with, the analysable vehicle of a complicated metaphor. And one may observe: (1) that the movement of the earth according to the Copernican theory is a celestial motion, smooth and regular, and while it might cause religious or philosophic fears, it could not be associated with the crudity and earthiness of the kind of commotion which the speaker in the poem wishes to discourage; (2) that there is another moving of the earth, an earthquake, which has just these qualities and is to be associated with the tear-floods and sigh-tempests of the second stanza of the poem; (3) that "trepidation" is an appropriate opposite of earthquake, because each is a shaking or vibratory motion; and "trepidation of the spheres" is "greater far" than an earthquake, but not much greater (if two such motions can be compared as to greatness) than the annual motion of the earth; (4) that reckoning what it "did and meant" shows that the event has passed, like an earthquake, not like the incessant celestial movement of the earth. Perhaps a knowledge of Donne's interest in the new science may add another shade of meaning, an overtone to the stanza in question, though to say even this runs against the words. To make the geocentric and heliocentric antithesis the core of the metaphor is to disregard the English language, to prefer private evidence to public, external to internal.

V

If the distinction between kinds of evidence has implications for the historical critic, it has them no less for the contemporary poet and his critic. Or, since every rule for a poet is but another side of a judgment by a critic, and since the past is the realm of the scholar and critic, and the future and present that of the poet and the critical leaders of taste, we may say that the problems arising in literary scholarship from the intentional fallacy are matched by others, which arise in the world or progressive experiment.

The question of "allusiveness," for example, as acutely posed by the poetry of Eliot, is certainly one where a false judgment is likely to involve the intentional fallacy. The frequency and depth of literary allusion in the poetry of Eliot and others has driven so many in pursuit of full meanings to the *Golden Bough* and the Elizabethan drama that it has become a kind of commonplace to suppose that we do not know what a poet means unless we have traced him in his reading—a supposition redolent with intentional implications. The stand taken by F. O. Matthiessen is a sound one and partially forestalls the difficulty.

> If one reads these with an attentive ear and is sensitive to their sudden shifts in movement, the contrast between the actual Thames and the idealized vision of it during an age before it flowed through a megalopolis is sharply conveyed by that movement itself, whether or not one recognizes the refrain to be from Spenser.

Eliot's allusions work when we know them—and to a great extent even when we do not know them, through their suggestive power.

But sometimes we find allusions supported by notes, and it is a nice question whether the notes function more as guides to send us where we may be educated, or more as indications in themselves about the character of the allusions. "Nearly everything of importance . . . . that is apposite to an appreciation of 'The Waste Land,' " writes Matthiessen of Miss Weston's book [*From Ritual to Romance*], "has been incorporated into the structure of the poem itself, or into Eliot's notes." And with such an admission it may begin to appear that it would not much matter if Eliot invented his sources (as Sir Walter Scott invented chapter epigraphs from "old plays" and "anonymous" authors, or as Coleridge wrote marginal glosses for *The Ancient Mariner*). Allusions to Dante, Webster, Marvell, or Baudelaire doubtless gain something because these writers existed, but it is doubtful whether the same can be said for an allusion to an obscure Elizabethan:

> The sound of horns and motors, which
> shall bring
> Sweeney to Mrs Porter in the spring.

"Cf. Day, *Parliament of Bees:*" says Eliot,

> When of a sudden, listening, you shall
> hear,
> A noise of horns and hunting, which
> shall bring
> Actaeon to Diana in the spring,
> Where all shall see her naked skin.

The irony is completed by the quotation itself; had Eliot, as is quite conceivable, composed these lines to furnish his own background, there would be no loss of validity. The conviction may grow as one reads Eliot's next note: "I do not know the origin of the ballad from which these lines are taken: it was reported to me from Sydney, Australia." The important word in this note—on Mrs Porter and her daughter who washed their feet in soda water—is "ballad." And if one should feel from the lines themselves their "ballad" quality, there would be little need for the note. Ultimately, the inquiry must focus on the integrity of such notes as parts of the poem, for where they constitute special information about the meaning of phrases in the poem, they ought to be subject to the same scrutiny as any of the other words in which it is written. Matthiessen believes the notes were the price Eliot "had to pay in order to avoid what he would have considered muffling the energy of his poem by extended connecting links in the text itself." But it may be questioned whether the notes and the need for them are not equally muffling. F. W. Bateson has plausibly argued that Tennyson's "The Sailor Boy" would be better if half the stanzas were omitted, and the best versions of ballads like "Sir Patrick Spens" owe their power to the very audacity with which the minstrel has taken for granted the story upon which he comments. What then if a poet find he cannot take so much for granted in a more recondite context and rather than write informatively, supplies notes? It can be said in favour of this plan that at least the notes do not pretend to be dramatic, as they would if written in verse. On the other hand, the notes may look like unassimilated material lying loose beside the poem, necessary for the meaning of the verbal context, but not integrated, so that the symbol stands incomplete.

We mean to suggest by the above analysis that whereas notes tend to seem to justify themselves as external indexes to the author's *intention*, yet they ought to be judged like any other parts of a composition (verbal arrangement special to a particular context), and when so judged their reality as parts of the poem, or their imaginative integration with the rest of the poem, may come into question. Matthiessen, for instance, sees that Eliot's titles for poems and his epigraphs are informative apparatus, like the notes. But while he is worried by some of the notes and thinks that Eliot "appears to be mocking himself for writing the note at the same time that he wants to convey something by it," Matthiessen believes that "the device" of epigraphs "is not at all open to the objection of not being sufficiently structural." "The intention," he says, "is to enable the poet to secure a condensed expression in the poem itself." "In each case the epigraph is *designed* to form an integral part of the effect of the poem." And Eliot himself, in his notes, has justified his poetic practice in terms of intention.

> The Hanged Man, a member of the traditional pack, fits my purpose in two ways: because he is associated in my mind with the Hanged God of Frazer, and because I associate him with the hooded figure in the passage of the disciples to Emmaus in Part V. . . . The man with Three Staves (an authentic member of the Tarot pack) I associate, quite arbitrarily, with the Fisher King himself.

And perhaps he is to be taken more seriously here, when off guard in a note, than when in his Norton Lectures he comments on the difficulty of saying what a poem means and adds playfully that he thinks of prefixing to a second edition of *Ash Wednesday* some lines from *Don Juan:*

> I don't pretend that I quite understand
> My own meaning when I would be very
> fine;
> But the fact is that I have nothing
> planned
> Unless it were to be a moment merry.

If Eliot and other contemporary poets have any characteristic fault, it may be in *planning* too much.

Allusiveness in poetry is one of several critical issues by which we have illustrated the more abstract issue of intentionalism, but it may be for today the most important illustration. As a poetic practice allusiveness would appear to be in some recent poems an extreme corollary of the romantic intentionalist assumption, and as a critical issue it challenges and brings to light in a special way the basic premise of intentionalism. The following instance from the poetry of Eliot may serve to epitomize the practical implications of what we have been saying. In Eliot's "Love Song of J. Alfred Prufrock," towards the end, occurs the line: "I have heard the mermaids singing, each to each," and this bears a certain resemblance to a line in a Song by John Donne, "Teach me to heare Mermaides singing," so that for the reader acquainted to a certain degree with Donne's poetry, the critical question arises: Is Eliot's line an allusion to Donne's? Is Prufrock thinking about Donne? Is Eliot thinking about Donne? We suggest that there are two radically different ways of looking for an answer to this question. There is (1) the way of poetic analysis and exegesis, which inquires whether it makes any sense if Eliot-Prufrock is thinking about Donne. In an earlier part of the poem, when Prufrock asks, "Would it have been worth while, . . . To have squeezed the universe into a ball," his words take half their sadness and irony from certain energetic and passionate lines of Marvell's "To His Coy Mistress." But the exegetical inquirer may wonder whether mermaids considered as "strange sights" (to hear them is in Donne's poem analogous to getting with child a mandrake root) have much to do with Prufrock's mermaids, which seem to be symbols of romance and dynamism, and which incidentally have literary authentication, if they need it, in a line of a sonnet by Gérard de Nerval. This method of inquiry may lead to the conclusion that the given resemblance between Eliot and Donne is without significance and is better not thought of, or the method may have the disadvantage of providing no certain conclusion. Nevertheless, we submit that this is the true and objective way of criticism, as contrasted to what the very uncertainty of exegesis might tempt a second kind of critic to undertake: (2) the way of biographical or genetic inquiry, in which, taking advantage of the fact that Eliot is still alive, and in the spirit of a man who would settle a bet, the critic writes to Eliot and asks what he meant, or if he had Donne in mind. We shall not here weigh the probabilities—whether Eliot would answer that he meant nothing at all, had nothing at all in mind—a sufficiently good answer to such a question—or in an unguarded moment might furnish a clear and, within its limit, irrefutable answer. Our point is that such an answer to such an inquiry would have nothing to do with the poem "Prufrock"; it would not be a critical inquiry. Critical inquiries, unlike bets, are not settled in this way. Critical inquiries are not settled by consulting the oracle.

NOTES

1. *Dictionary of World Literature*, Joseph T. Shipley, ed. (New York, 1942), 326–9.

2. J. E. Spingarn, "The New Criticism," in *Criticism in America* (New York, 1924), 24–5.

3. Ananda K. Coomaraswamy, "Intention," in *American Bookman*, i (1944), 42–8.

4. It is true that Croce himself in his *Ariosto, Shakespeare, and Corneille* (London, 1920), chap. vii, "The Practical Personality and the Poetical Personality," and in his *Defence of Poetry* (Oxford, 1933), 24, and elsewhere, early and late, has delivered telling attacks on emotive geneticism, but the main drive of the *Aesthetic* is surely towards a kind of cognitive intentionalism.

5. See Hughes Mearns, *Creative Youth* (Garden City, (1925), esp. 10, 27–9. The technique of inspiring poems has apparently been outdone more recently by the study of inspiration in successful poets and other artists. See, for instance, Rosamond E. M. Harding, *An Anatomy of Inspiration* (Cambridge, 1940); Julius Portnoy, *A Psychology of Art Creation* (Philadelphia, 1942); Rudolf Arnheim and others, *Poets at Work* (New York, 1947); Phyllis Bartlett, *Poems in Process* (New York, 1951); Brewster Ghiselin, ed., *The Creative Process: a symposium* (Berkeley and Los Angeles, 1952).

6. Curt Ducasse, *The Philosophy of Art* (New York, 1929), 116.

7. And the history of words *after* a poem is written may contribute meanings which if relevant to the original pattern should not be ruled out by a scruple about intention.

8. Chaps. viii, "The Pattern," and xvi, "The Known and Familiar Landscape," will be found of most help to the student of the poem.

9. Charles M. Coffin, *John Donne and the New Philosophy* (New York, 1927), 97–8.

4

Viktor Shklovsky
1893–1984

Viktor Borisovich Shklovsky was one of the leaders of the Russian Formalists, a group of literati (officially called OPOYAZ, Society for the Study of Poetic Languages) that thrived in Moscow from 1916 until 1930. Shklovsky, Boris Eichenbaum, Yary Tynyanov, and other Formalists sought to put literary theory on a par with the natural sciences through rigorous consistency in their systematic elaboration of primary and defensible tenets about literature. At their most expansive, they offered a theory of literary function and critical interpretation as well as a theory of art's purpose. They are most famous for demonstrating and defending the need to emphasize form and structure in literature over content and the fact that social conditions may be said to produce literary works. They tended to view literary works not as monolithic esthetic wholes with prescribed effects, but as collections of devices that interact in a textual field; the result may or may not produce an overall esthetic effect. The ultimate purpose of literary art is estrangement, or "making strange," displacing language out of its usual, workaday meaning and freeing it to stimulate and produce fresh linguistic apprehensions—of language itself and of the world. These goals, however, tended to conflict with the governmental aims of socialist realism, and in 1930 the Formalists were officially suppressed.

"Art as Technique" (1917) is Shklovsky's central theoretical statement and one of the primary documents of Russian Formalism. In it Shklovsky attacks then-current esthetic theories (especially Potebnyaism) about the essence of art being a "thinking in images." The imagist approach to literary art, of course, is highlighted in Anglo-American poetic imagism and in New Criticism. Shklovsky, however, argues against the centrality of "images" and, instead, defines a field of literary activity in which linguistically based devices (such as metaphor and metonymy) create an experience more complex, and possibly less coherent, than the examination of images can suggest. In *On the Theory of Prose* (1925) and *The Technique of the Writer's Craft* (1928) he elaborated these notions in theoretical and practical criticism. In 1928, though, he began to recant formalist theory—especially in "*War and Peace* of Leo Tolstoy" (1928)—and tried to include sociological material in his interpretations. Both his earlier formalist and later socialist criticism are influential, as we will see later, in structuralism—which in many ways is the extension of work done by the Formalists in their brief but productive fifteen years.

Art as Technique

"Art is thinking in images." This maxim, which even high school students parrot, is nevertheless the starting point for the erudite philologist who is beginning to put together some kind of systematic literary theory. The idea, originated in part by Potebnya, has spread. "Without imagery there is no art, and in particular no poetry," Potebnya writes.[1] And elsewhere, "Poetry, as well as prose, is first and foremost a special way of thinking and knowing."[2]

Poetry is a special way of thinking; it is, precisely, a way of thinking in images, a way which permits what is generally called "economy of mental effort," a way which makes for "a sensation of the relative ease of the process." Aesthetic feeling is the reaction to this economy. This is how the academician Ovsyaniko-Kulikovsky[3] who undoubtedly read the works of Potebnya attentively, almost certainly understood and faithfully summarized the ideas of his teacher. Potebnya and his numerous disciples consider poetry a special kind of thinking—thinking by means of images; they feel that the purpose of imagery is to help channel various objects and activities into groups and to clarify the unknown by means of the known. Or, as Potebnya wrote:

> The relationship of the image to what is being clarified is that: (a) the image is the fixed predicate of that which undergoes change—the unchanging means of attracting what is perceived as changeable. . . . (b) the image is far clearer and simpler than what it clarifies.[4]

In other words:

> Since the purpose of imagery is to remind us, by approximation, of those meanings for which the image stands, and since, apart from this, imagery is unnecessary for thought, we must be more familiar with the image than with what it clarifies.[5]

It would be instructive to try to apply this principle to Tyutchev's comparison of summer lightning to deaf and dumb demons or to Gogol's comparison of the sky to the garment of God.[6]

"Without imagery there is no art"—"Art is thinking in images." These maxims have led to far-fetched interpretations of individual works of art. Attempts have been made to evaluate even music, architecture, and lyric poetry as imagistic thought. After a quarter of a century of such attempts Ovsyaniko-Kulikovsky finally had to assign lyric poetry, architecture, and music to a special category of imageless art and to define them as lyric arts appealing directly to the emotions. And thus he admitted an enormous area of art which is not a mode of thought. A part of this area, lyric poetry (narrowly considered), is quite like the visual arts: it is also verbal. But, much more important, visual art passes quite imperceptibly into nonvisual art; yet our perceptions of both are similar.

Nevertheless, the definition "Art is thinking in images," which means (I omit the usual middle terms of the argument) that art is the making of symbols, has survived the downfall of the theory which supported it. It survives chiefly in the wake of Symbolism, especially among the theorists of the Symbolist movement.

Many still believe, then, that thinking in images—thinking in specific scenes of "roads and landscape" and "furrows and boundaries"[7]—is the chief characteristic of poetry. Consequently, they should have expected the history of "imagistic art," as they call it, to consist of a history of changes in imagery. But we find that images change little; from century to century, from nation to nation, from poet to poet, they flow on without changing. Images belong to no one: they are "the Lord's." The more you understand an age, the more convinced you become that the images a given poet used and which you thought his own were taken almost unchanged from another poet. The works of poets are classified or grouped according to the new techniques that poets discover and share, and according to their arrangement and development of the resources of language; poets are much more concerned with arranging images than with creating them. Images are given to poets; the ability to remember them is far more important than the ability to create them.

Imagistic thought does not, in any case, include all the aspects of art nor even all the aspects of verbal art. A change in imagery is not essential to the development of poetry. We know that frequently an expression is thought to be poetic, to be created for aesthetic pleasure, although actually it was created without such intent—e.g., Annensky's opinion that the Slavic languages are especially poetic and Andrey Bely's ecstasy over the technique of placing adjectives after nouns, a technique used by eighteenth-century Russian poets. Bely joyfully accepts the technique as something artistic, or more exactly, as intended, if we consider intention as art. Actually, this reversal of the usual adjective-noun order is a peculiarity of the language (which had been influenced by Church Slavonic). Thus a work may be (1) intended as prosaic and accepted as poetic, or (2) intended as poetic and accepted as prosaic. This suggests that the artistry attributed to a given work results from the way we perceive it. By "works of art," in the narrow sense, we mean works created by special techniques designed to make the works as obviously artistic as possible.

Potebnya's conclusion, which can be formulated "poetry equals imagery," gave rise to the whole theory that "imagery equals symbolism," that the image may serve as the invariable predicate of various subjects. (This conclusion, because it expressed ideas similar to the theories of the Symbolists, intrigued some of their leading representatives—Andrey Bely, Merezhkovsky and his "eternal companions"—and, in fact, formed the basis of the theory of Symbolism.) The conclusion stems partly from the fact that Potebnya did not distinguish between the language of poetry and the language of prose. Consequently, he ignored the fact that there are two aspects of imagery: imagery as a practical means of thinking, as a means of placing objects within categories; and imagery as poetic, as a means of reinforcing an impression. I shall clarify with an example. I want to attract the attention of a young child who is eating bread and butter and getting the butter on her fingers. I call, "Hey, butterfingers!" This is a figure of speech, a clearly prosaic trope. Now a different example. The child is playing with my glasses and drops them. I call, "Hey, butterfingers!"[8] This figure of speech is a poetic trope. (In the first example, "butterfingers" is metonymic; in the second, metaphoric—but this is not what I want to stress.)

Poetic imagery is a means of creating the strongest possible impression. As a method it is, depending upon its purpose, neither more nor less effective than other poetic techniques; it is neither more nor less effective than ordinary or negative parallelism, comparison, repetition, balanced structure, hyperbole, the commonly accepted rhetorical figures, and all those methods which emphasize the emotional effect of an expression (including words or even articulated sounds).[9] But poetic imagery only externally resembles either the stock imagery of fables and ballads or thinking in images—e.g., the example in Ovsyaniko-Kulikovsky's *Language and Art* in which a little girl calls a ball a little watermelon. Poetic imagery is but one of the devices of poetic language. Prose imagery is a means of abstraction: a little watermelon instead of a lampshade, or a little watermelon instead of a head, is only the abstraction of one of the object's characteristics, that of roundness. It is no different from saying that the head and the melon are both round. This is what is meant, but it has nothing to do with poetry.

The law of the economy of creative effort is also generally accepted. [Herbert] Spencer wrote:

> On seeking for some clue to the law underlying these current maxims, we may see shadowed forth in many of them, the importance of economizing the reader's or the hearer's attention. To so present ideas that they may be apprehended with the least possible mental effort, is the desideratum towards which most of the rules above quoted point. . . . Hence, carrying out the metaphor that language is the vehicle of thought, there seems reason to think that in all cases the friction and inertia of the vehicle deduct from its efficiency; and that in composition, the chief, if not the sole thing to be done, is to reduce the friction and inertia to the smallest possible amount.[10]

And R[ichard] Avenarius:

> If a soul possess inexhaustible strength, then, of course, it would be indifferent to know how much might be spent from this inexhaustible source; only the necessarily expended time would be important. But since its forces are limited, one is led to expect that the soul hastens to carry out the apperceptive process as expediently as possible—that is, with comparatively the least expenditure of energy, and, hence, with comparatively the best result.

Petrazhitsky, with only one reference to the general law of mental effort, rejects [William] James's theory of the physical basis of emotion, a theory which contradicts his own. Even Alexander Veselovsky acknowledged the principle of the economy of creative effort, a theory especially appealing in the study of rhythm, and agreed with Spencer: "A satisfactory style is precisely that style which delivers the greatest amount of thought in the fewest words." And Andrey Bely, despite the fact that in his better pages he gave numerous examples of "roughened" rhythm[11] and (particularly in the examples from Baratynsky) showed the difficulties inherent in poetic epithets, also thought it necessary to speak of the law of the economy of creative effort in his book[12]—a heroic effort to create a theory of art based on unverified facts from antiquated sources, on his vast knowledge of the techniques of poetic creativity, and on Krayevich's high school physics text.

These ideas about the economy of energy, as well as about the law and aim of creativity, are perhaps true in their application to "practical" language; they were, however, extended to poetic language. Hence they do not distinguish properly between the laws of practical language and the laws of poetic language. The fact that Japanese poetry has sounds not found in conversational Japanese was hardly the first factual indication of the differences between poetic and everyday language. Leo Jakubinsky has observed that the law of the dissimilation of liquid sounds does not apply to poetic language.[13] This suggested to him that poetic language tolerated the admission of hard-to-pronounce conglomerations of similar sounds. In his article, one of the first examples of scientific criticism, he indicates inductively the contrast (I shall say more about this point later) between the laws of poetic language and the laws of practical language.[14]

We must, then, speak about the laws of expenditure and economy in poetic language not on the basis of an analogy with prose, but on the basis of the laws of poetic language.

If we start to examine the general laws of perception, we see that as perception becomes habitual, it becomes automatic. Thus, for example, all of our habits retreat into the area of the unconsciously automatic; if one remembers the sensations of holding a pen or of speaking in a foreign language for the first time and compares that with his feeling at performing the action for the ten thousandth time, he will agree with us. Such habituation explains the principles by which, in ordinary speech, we leave phrases unfinished and words half expressed. In this process, ideally realized in algebra, things are replaced by symbols. Complete words are not expressed in rapid speech: their initial sounds are barely perceived. Alexander Pogodin offers the example of a boy considering the sentence "The Swiss mountains are beautiful" in the form of a series of letters: *T, S, m, a, b.*[15]

This characteristic of thought not only suggests the method of algebra, but even prompts the choice of symbols (letters, especially initial letters). By this "algebraic" method of thought we apprehend objects only as shapes with imprecise extensions; we do not see them in their entirety but rather recognize them by their main characteristics. We see the object as though it were enveloped in a sack. We know what it is by its configuration, but we see only its silhouette. The object, perceived thus in the manner of prose perception, fades and does not leave even a first impression; ultimately even the essence of what it was is forgotten. Such perception explains why we fail to hear the prose word in its entirety (see Leo Jakubinsky's article[16]) and, hence, why (along with other slips of the tongue) we fail to pronounce it. The process of "algebrization," the overautomatization of an object, permits the greatest economy of perceptive effort. Either objects are assigned only one proper feature—a number, for example—or else they function as though by formula and do not even appear in cognition:

> I was cleaning a room and, meandering about, approached the divan and couldn't remember whether or not I had dusted it. Since these movements are habitual and unconscious, I could not remember and felt that it was impossible to remember—so that if I had dusted it and forgot—that is, had acted unconsciously, then it was the same as if I had not. If some conscious person had been watching, then the fact could be established. If, however, no one was looking, or looking on unconsciously, if the whole complex lives of many people go on unconsciously, then such lives are as if they had never been.[17]

And so life is reckoned as nothing. Habitualization devours works, clothes, furniture, one's wife, and the fear of war. "If the whole complex lives of many people go on unconsciously, then such lives are as if they had never been." And art exists that one may recover the sensation of life; it exists to make one feel things, to make the stone stony. The purpose of art is to impart the sensation of things as they are perceived and not as they are known. The technique of art is to make objects "unfamiliar," to make forms difficult, to increase the difficulty and length of perception because the process of perception is an aesthetic end in itself and must be prolonged. *Art is a way of experiencing the artfulness of an object; the object is not important.*

The range of poetic (artistic) work extends from the sensory to the cognitive, from poetry to prose, from the concrete to the abstract: from Cervantes' Don Quixote—scholastic and poor nobleman, half consciously bearing his humiliation in the court of the duke—to the broad but empty Don Quixote of Turgenev; from Charlemagne to the name "king" [in Russian "Charles" and "king" obviously derive from the same root, *korol*]. The meaning of a work broadens to the extent that artfulness and artistry diminish; thus a fable symbolizes more than a poem, and a proverb more than a fable. Consequently, the least self-contradictory part of Potebnya's theory is his treatment of the fable, which, from his point of view, he investigated thoroughly. But since his theory did not provide for "expressive" works of art, he could not finish his book. As we know, *Notes on the Theory of Literature* was published in 1905, thirteen years after Potebnya's death. Potebnya himself completed only the section on the fable.[18]

After we see an object several times, we begin to recognize it. The object is in front of us and we know about it, but we do not see it[19]—hence we cannot say anything significant about it. Art removes objects from the automatism of perception in several ways. Here I want to illustrate a way used repeatedly by Leo Tolstoy, that writer who, for Merezhkovsky at least, seems to present things as if he himself saw them, saw them in their entirety, and did not alter them.

Tolstoy makes the familiar seem strange by not naming the familiar object. He describes an object as if he were seeing it for the first time, an event as if it were happening for the first time. In describing something he avoids the accepted names of its parts and instead names corresponding parts of other objects. For example, in "Shame" Tolstoy "defamiliarizes" the idea of flogging in this way: "to strip people who have broken the law, to hurl them to the floor, and to rap on their bottoms with switches," and, after a few lines, "to lash about on the naked buttocks." Then he remarks:

> Just why precisely this stupid, savage means of causing pain and not any other—why not prick the shoulders or any part of the body with needles, squeeze the hands or the feet in a vise, or anything like that?

I apologize for this harsh example, but it is typical of Tolstoy's way of pricking the conscience. The familiar act of flogging is made unfamiliar both by the description and by the proposal to change its form without changing its nature. Tolstoy uses this technique of "defamiliarization" constantly. The narrator of "Kholstomer," for example, is a horse, and it is the horse's point of view (rather than a person's) that makes the content of the story seem unfamiliar. Here is how the horse regards the institution of private property:

> I understood well what they said about whipping and Christianity. But then I was absolutely in the dark. What's the meaning of "his own," "his colt"? From these phrases I saw that people thought there was some sort of connection between me and the stable. At that time I simply could not understand the connection. Only much later, when they separated me from the other horses, did I begin to understand. But even then I simply could not see what it meant when they called me "man's property." The words "my horse" referred to me, a living horse, and seemed as strange to me as the words "my land," "my air," "my water."
>
> But the words made a strong impression on me. I thought about them constantly, and only after the most diverse experiences with people did I understand, finally, what they meant. They meant this: In life people are guided by words, not by deeds. It's not so much that they love the possibility of doing or not doing something as it is the possibility of speaking with words, agreed on among themselves, about various topics. Such are the words "my" and "mine," which they apply to different things, creatures, objects, and even to land, people, and horses. They agree that only one may say "mine" about this, that, or the other thing. And the one who says "mine" about the greatest number of things is, according to the game which they've agreed to among themselves, the one they consider the most happy. I don't know the point of all this, but it's true. For a long time I tried to explain it to myself in terms of some kind of real gain, but I had to reject that explanation because it was wrong.
>
> Many of those, for instance, who called me their own never rode on me—although others did. And so with those who fed me. Then again, the coachman, the veterinari-

> ans, and the outsiders in general treated me kindly, yet those who called me their own did not. In due time, having widened the scope of my observations, I satisfied myself that the notion "my," not only in relation to us horses, has no other basis than a narrow human instinct which is called a sense of or right to private property. A man says "this house is mine" and never lives in it; he only worries about its construction and upkeep. A merchant says "my shop," "my dry goods shop," for instance, and does not even wear clothes made from the better cloth he keeps in his own shop.
>
> There are people who call a tract of land their own, but they never set eyes on it and never take a stroll on it. There are people who call others their own, yet never see them. And the whole relationship between them is that the so-called "owners" treat the others unjustly.
>
> There are people who call women their own, or their "wives," but their women live with other men. And people strive not for the good in life, but for goods they can call their own.
>
> I am now convinced that this is the essential difference between people and ourselves. And therefore, not even considering the other ways in which we are superior, but considering just this one virtue, we can bravely claim to stand higher than men on the ladder of living creatures. The actions of men, at least those with whom I have had dealings, are guided by *words*—ours, by deeds.

The horse is killed before the end of the story, but the manner of the narrative, its technique, does not change:

> Much later they put Serpukhovsky's body, which had experienced the world, which had eaten and drunk, into the ground. They could profitably send neither his hide, nor his flesh, nor his bones anywhere.
>
> But since his dead body, which had gone about in the world for twenty years, was a great burden to everyone, its burial was only a superfluous embarrassment for the people. For a long time no one had needed him; for a long time he had been a burden on all. But nevertheless, the dead who buried the dead found it necessary to dress this bloated body, which immediately began to rot, in a good uniform and good boots; to lay it in a good new coffin with new tassels at the four corners, then to place this new coffin in another of lead and ship it to Moscow; there to exhume ancient bones and at just that spot, to hide this putrefying body, swarming with maggots, in its new uniform and clean boots, and to cover it over completely with dirt.

Thus we see that at the end of the story Tolstoy continues to use the technique even though the motivation for it [the reason for its use] is gone.

In *War and Peace* Tolstoy uses the same technique in describing whole battles as if battles were something new. These descriptions are too long to quote; it would be necessary to extract a considerable part of the four-volume novel. But Tolstoy uses the same method in describing the drawing room and the theater:

> The middle of the stage consisted of flat boards; by the sides stood painted pictures representing trees, and at the back a linen cloth was stretched down to the floor boards. Maidens in red bodices and white skirts sat on the middle of the stage. One, very fat, in a white silk dress, sat apart on a narrow bench to which a green pasteboard box was glued from behind. They were all singing something. When they had finished, the maiden in white approached the prompter's box. A man in silk with tight-fitting pants on his fat legs approached her with a plume and began to sing and spread his arms in dismay. The man in the tight pants finished his song alone; then the girl sang. After that both remained silent as the music resounded; and the man, obviously waiting to begin singing his part with her again, began to run his fingers over the hand of the girl in the white dress. They finished their song together, and everyone in the theater began to clap and shout. But the men and women on stage, who represented lovers, started to bow, smiling and raising their hands.
>
> In the second act there were pictures representing monuments and openings in the linen cloth representing the moonlight, and they raised lamp shades on a frame. As the musicians started to play the bass horn and counter-bass, a large number of people

> in black mantles poured onto the stage from right and left. The people, with something like daggers in their hands, started to wave their arms. Then still more people came running out and began to drag away the maiden who had been wearing a white dress but who now wore one of sky blue. They did not drag her off immediately, but sang with her for a long time before dragging her away. Three times they struck on something metallic behind the side scenes, and everyone got down on his knees and began to chant a prayer. Several times all of this activity was interrupted by enthusiastic shouts from the spectators.

The third act is described:

> . . . But suddenly a storm blew up. Chromatic scales and chords of diminished sevenths were heard in the orchestra. Everyone ran about and again they dragged one of the bystanders behind the scenes as the curtain fell.

In the fourth act, "There was some sort of devil who sang, waving his hands, until the boards were moved out from under him and he dropped down."[20]

In *Resurrection* Tolstoy describes the city and the court in the same way; he uses a similar technique in "Kreutzer Sonata" when he describes marriage—"Why, if people have an affinity of souls, must they sleep together?" But he did not defamiliarize only those things he sneered at:

> Pierre stood up from his new comrades and made his way between the campfires to the other side of the road where, it seemed, the captive soldiers were held. He wanted to talk with them. The French sentry stopped him on the road and ordered him to return. Pierre did so, but not to the campfire, not to his comrades, but to an abandoned, unharnessed carriage. On the ground, near the wheel of the carriage, he sat cross-legged in the Turkish fashion, and lowered his head. He sat motionless for a long time, thinking. More than an hour passed. No one disturbed him. Suddenly he burst out laughing with his robust, good natured laugh—so loudly that the men near him looked around, surprised at his conspicuously strange laughter.
>
> "Ha, ha, ha," laughed Pierre. And he began to talk to himself. "The soldier didn't allow me to pass. They caught me, barred me. Me—me—my immortal soul. Ha, ha, ha," he laughed with tears starting in his eyes.
>
> Pierre glanced at the sky, into the depths of the departing, playing stars. "And all this is mine, all this is in me, and all this is I," thought Pierre. "And all this they caught and put in a planked enclosure." He smiled and went off to his comrades to lie down to sleep.[21]

Anyone who knows Tolstoy can find several hundred such passages in his work. His method of seeing things out of their normal context is also apparent in his last works. Tolstoy described the dogmas and rituals he attacked as if they were unfamiliar, substituting everyday meanings for the customarily religious meanings of the words common in church ritual. Many persons were painfully wounded; they considered it blasphemy to present as strange and monstrous what they accepted as sacred. Their reaction was due chiefly to the technique through which Tolstoy perceived and reported his environment. And after turning to what he had long avoided, Tolstoy found that his perceptions had unsettled his faith.

The technique of defamiliarization is not Tolstoy's alone. I cited Tolstoy because his work is generally known.

Now, having explained the nature of this technique, let us try to determine the approximate limits of its application. I personally feel that defamiliarization is found almost everywhere form is found. In other words, the difference between Potebnya's point of view and ours is this: An image is not a permanent referent for those mutable complexities of life which are revealed through it; its purpose is not to make us perceive meaning, but to create a special perception of the object—*it creates a "vision" of the object instead of serving as a means for knowing it.*

The purpose of imagery in erotic art can be studied even more accurately; an erotic object is usually presented as if it were seen for the first time. Gogol, in "Christmas Eve," provided the following example:

> Here he approached her more closely, coughed, smiled at her, touched her plump, bare arm with his fingers, and expressed himself in a way that showed both his cunning and his conceit.
> "And what is this you have, magnificent Solokha?" and having said this, he jumped back a little.
> "What? An arm, Osip Nikiforovich!" she answered.
> "Hmm, an arm! *He, he, he!*" said the secretary cordially, satisfied with his beginning. He wandered about the room.
> "And what is this you have, dearest Solokha?" he said in the same way, having approached her again and grasped her lightly by the neck, and in the very same way he jumped back.
> "As if you don't see, Osip Nikoforovich!" answered Solokha, "a neck, and on my neck a necklace."
> "Hmm! On the neck a necklace! *He, he, he!*" and the secretary again wandered about the room, rubbing his hands.
> "And what is this you have, incomparable Solokha?" . . . It is not known to what the secretary would stretch his long fingers now.

And Knut Hamsum has the following in "Hunger": "Two white prodigies appeared from beneath her blouse."

Erotic subjects may also be presented figuratively with the obvious purpose of leading us away from their "recognition." Hence sexual organs are referred to in terms of lock and key[22] or quilting tools[23] or bow and arrow, or rings and marlinspikes, as in the legend of Stavyor, in which a married man does not recognize his wife, who is disguised as a warrior. She proposes a riddle:

> "Remember, Stavyor, do you recall
> How we little ones walked to and fro in the street?
> You and I together sometimes played with a marlinspike—
> You had a silver marlinspike,
> But I had a gilded ring?
> I found myself at it just now and then,
> But you fell in with it ever and always."
> Says Stavyor, son of Godinovich,
> "What! I didn't play with you at marlinspikes!"
> Then Vasilisa Mikulichna: "So he says.
> Do you remember, Stavyor, do you recall,
> Now must you know, you and I together learned to read and write;
> Mine was an ink-well of silver,
> And yours a pen of gold?
> But I just moistened it a little now and then,
> And I just moistened it ever and always."[24]

In a different version of the legend we find a key to the riddle:

> Here the formidable envoy Vasilyushka
> Raised her skirts to the very naval,
> And then the young Stavyor, son of Godinovich,
> Recognized her gilded ring. . . .[25]

But defamiliarization is not only a technique of the erotic riddle—a technique of euphemism—it is also the basis and point of all riddles. Every riddle pretends to show its subject either by words which specify or describe it but which, during the telling, do not seem applicable (the type: "black and white and 'red'—read—all over") or by means of odd but imitative sounds ("'Twas brillig, and the slithy toves/Did gyre and gimble in the wabe").[26]

Even erotic images not intended as riddles are defamiliarized ("boobies," "tarts," "piece," etc.). In popular imagery there is generally something equivalent to "trampling the grass" and "breaking the guelder-rose." The technique of defamiliarization is absolutely clear in the widespread image—a motif of erotic affectation—in which a bear and other wild beasts (or a devil, with a different reason for nonrecognition) do not recognize a man.[27]

The lack of recognition in the following tale is quite typical:

> A peasant was plowing a field with a piebald mare. A bear approached him and asked, "Uncle, what's made this mare piebald for you?"
>
> "I did the piebalding myself."
>
> "But how?"
>
> "Let me, and I'll do the same for you."
>
> The bear agreed. The peasant tied his feet together with a rope, took the ploughshare from the two-wheeled plough, heated it on the fire, and applied it to his flanks. He made the bear piebald by scorching his fur down to the hide with the hot ploughshare. The man untied the bear, which went off and lay down under a tree.
>
> A magpie flew at the peasant to pick at the meat on his shirt. He caught her and broke one of her legs. The magpie flew off to perch in the same tree under which the bear was lying. Then, after the magpie, a horsefly landed on the mare, sat down, and began to bite. The peasant caught the fly, took a stick, shoved it up its rear, and let it go. The fly went to the tree where the bear and the magpie were. There all three sat.
>
> The peasant's wife came to bring his dinner to the field. The man and his wife finished their dinner in the fresh air, and he began to wrestle with her on the ground.
>
> The bear saw this and said to the magpie and the fly, "Holy priests! The peasant wants to piebald someone again."
>
> The magpie said, "No, he wants to break someone's legs."
>
> The fly said, "No, he wants to shove a stick up someone's rump."[28]

The similarity of technique here and in Tolstoy's "Kholstomer," is, I think, obvious.

Quite often in literature the sexual act itself is defamiliarized; for example, the Decameron refers to "scraping out a barrel," "catching nightingales," "gay wool-beating work" (the last is not developed in the plot). Defamiliarization is often used in describing the sexual organs.

A whole series of plots is based on such a lack of recognition; for example, in Afanasyev's *Intimate Tales* the entire story of "The Shy Mistress" is based on the fact that an object is not called by its proper name—or, in other words, on a game of nonrecognition. So too in Onchukov's "Spotted Petticoats," tale no. 525, and also in "The Bear and the Hare" from *Intimate Tales*, in which the bear and the hare make a "wound."

Such constructions as "the pestle and the mortar," or "Old Nick and the infernal regions" (*Decameron*), are also examples of the technique of defamiliarization. And in my article on plot construction I write about defamiliarization in psychological parallelism. Here, then, I repeat that the perception of disharmony in a harmonious context is important in parallelism. The purpose of parallelism, like the general purpose of imagery, is to transfer the usual perception of an object into the sphere of a new perception—that is, to make a unique semantic modification.

In studying poetic speech in its phonetic and lexical structure as well as in its characteristic distribution of words and in the characteristic thought structures compounded from the words, we find everywhere the artistic trademark—that is, we find material obviously created to remove the automatism of perception; the author's purpose is to create the vision which results from that deautomatized perception. A work is created "artistically" so that its perception is impeded and the greatest possible effect is produced through the slowness of the perception. As a result of this lingering, the object is perceived not in its extension in space, but, so to speak, in its continuity. Thus "poetic language" gives satisfaction. According to Aristotle, poetic language must appear strange and wonderful; and, in fact, it is often actually foreign: the Sumerian used by the Assyrians, the Latin of Europe during the Middle Ages, the Arabisms of the Persians, the Old Bulgarian of Russian literature, or the elevated, almost literary language of folk songs. The common archaisms of poetic language, the intricacy of the sweet new style [*dolce stil nuovo*],[29] the obscure style of the language of Arnaut Daniel with the "roughened" [harte] forms *which make pronunciation difficult*—these are used in much the same way. Leo Jakubinsky has demonstrated the principle of phonetic "roughening" of poetic language in the particular case of the repetition of identical sounds. The language of poetry is, then, a difficult, roughened, impeded language. In a few special instances the language of poetry approximates the language of prose, but this does not violate the principle of "roughened" form.

> Her sister was called Tatyana.
> For the first time we shall
> Wilfully brighten the delicate
> Pages of a novel with such a name.

wrote Pushkin. The usual poetic language for Pushkin's contemporaries was the elegant style of Derzhavin; but Pushkin's style, because it seemed trivial then, was unexpectedly difficult for them. We should remember the consternation of Pushkin's contemporaries over the vulgarity of his expressions. He used the popular language as a special device for prolonging attention, just as his contemporaries generally used Russian words in their usually French speech (see Tolstoy's examples in *War and Peace*).

Just now a still more characteristic phenomenon is under way. Russian literary language, which was originally foreign to Russia, has so permeated the language of the people that it has blended with their conversation. On the other hand, literature has now begun to show a tendency towards the use of dialects (Remizov, Klyuyev, Essenin, and others,[30] so unequal in talent and so alike in language, are intentionally provincial) and of barbarisms (which gave rise to the Severyanin group[31]). And currently Maxim Gorky is changing his diction from the old literary language to the new literary colloquialism of Leskov.[32] Ordinary speech and literary language have thereby changed places (see the work of Vyacheslav Ivanov and many others). And finally, a strong tendency, led by Khlebnikov, to create a new and properly poetic language has emerged. In the light of these developments we can define poetry as *attenuated, tortuous* speech. Poetic speech is formed speech. Prose is ordinary speech—economical, easy, proper, the goddess of prose [*dea prosae*] is a goddess of the accurate, facile type, of the "direct" expression of a child. I shall discuss roughened form and retardation as the general law of art at greater length in an article on plot construction.[33]

Nevertheless, the position of those who urge the idea of the economy of artistic energy as something which exists in and even distinguishes poetic language seems, at first glance, tenable for the problem of rhythm. Spencer's description of rhythm would seem to be absolutely incontestable:

> Just as the body in receiving a series of varying concussions, must keep the muscles ready to meet the most violent of them, as not knowing when such may come: so, the mind in receiving unarranged articulations, must keep its perspectives active enough to recognize the least easily caught sounds. And as, if the concussions recur in definite order, the body may husband its forces by adjusting the resistance needful for each concussion; so, if the syllables be rhythmically arranged, the mind may economize its energies by anticipating the attention required for each syllable.[34]

This apparently conclusive observation suffers from the common fallacy, the confusion of the laws of poetic and prosaic language. In *The Philosophy of Style* Spencer failed utterly to distinguish between them. But rhythm of prose, or of a work song like "Dubinushka," permits the members of the work crew to do their necessary "groaning together" and also eases the work by making it automatic. And, in fact, it is easier to march with music than without it, and to march during an animated conversation is even easier, for the walking is done unconsciously. Thus the rhythm of prose is an important automatizing element; the rhythm of poetry is not. There is "order" in art, yet not a single column of a Greek temple stands exactly in its proper order; poetic rhythm is similarly disordered rhythm. Attempts to systematize the irregularities have been made, and such attempts are part of the current problem in the theory of rhythm. It is obvious that the systematization will not work, for in reality the problem is not one of complicating the rhythm but of disordering the rhythm—a disordering which cannot be predicted. Should the disordering of rhythm became a convention, it would be ineffective as a device for the roughening of language. But I will not discuss rhythm in more detail since I intend to write a book about it.[35]

Translated by Lee T. Lemon and Marion J. Reis

NOTES

1. Alexander Potebnya, *Iz zapisok po teorii slovesnosti* [*Notes on the theory of Language*] (Kharkov, 1905), 83.

2. Ibid., p. 97.

3. Dmitry Ovsyaniko-Kulikovsky (1835–1920), a leading Russian scholar, was an early contributor to Marxist periodicals and a literary conservative, antagonistic towards the deliberately meaningless poems of the Futurists. *Trans. note.*

4. Potebnya, *Iz zapisok po teorii slovesnosti*, p. 314.

5. Ibid., p. 291.

6. Fyodor Tyutchev (1803–1873), a poet, and Nicholas Gogol (1809–1852), a master of prose fiction and satire, are mentioned here because their bold use of imagery cannot be accounted for by Potebnya's theory. Shklovsky is arguing that writers frequently gain their effects by comparing the commonplace to the exceptional rather than vice versa. *Trans. note.*

7. This is an allusion to Vyacheslav Ivanov's *Borozdy i mezhi* [*Furrows and Boundaries*] (Moscow, 1916), a major statement of Symbolist theory. *Trans. note.*

8. The Russian text involves a play on the word for "hat," colloquial for "clod," "duffer," etc. *Trans. note.*

9. Shklovsky is here doing two things of major theoretical importance: (1) he argues that different techniques serve a single function, and that (2) no single technique is all-important. The second permits the Formalists to be concerned with any and all literary devices; the first permits them to discuss the devices from a single consistent theoretical position. *Trans. note.*

10. Herbert Spencer, *The Philosophy of Style* [(Humboldt Library, Vol. XXXIV; New York, 1882), 2–3. Shklovsky's quoted reference, in Russian, preserves the idea of the original but shortens it].

11. The Russian *zatrudyonny* means "made difficult." The suggestion is that poems with "easy" or smooth rhythms slip by unnoticed; poems that are difficult or "roughened" force the reader to attend to them. *Trans. note.*

12. *Simvolizm*, probably. *Trans. note.*

13. Leo Jakubinsky, "O zvukakh poeticheskovo yazyka" ["On the Sounds of Poetic Language"], *Sborniki*, I (1916), 38.

14. Leo Jakubinsky, "Skopleniye odinakovykh plavnykh v prakticheskom i poeticheskom yazykakh" ["The Accumulation of Identical Liquids in Practical and Poetic language"], *Sborniki*, II (1917), 13–21.

15. Alexander Pogodin, *Yazyk, kak tvorchestvo* [*Language as Art*] (Kharkov, 1913), 42. [The original sentence was in French, "*Les montaignes de la Suisse sont belles*," with the appropriate initials.]

16. Jakubinsky, *Sborniki*, I (1916).

17. Leo Tolstoy's *Diary*, entry dated February 29, 1897. [The date is transcribed incorrectly; it should read March 1, 1897.]

18. Alexander Potebnya, *Iz lektsy po teorii slovesnosti* [Lectures on the Theory of Language] (Kharkov, 1914).

19. Victor Shklovsky, *Voskresheniye slova* [*The Ressurrection of the Word*] (Petersburg, 1914).

20. The Tolstoy and Gogol translations are ours. The passage occurs in Vol. II, Part 8, Chap. 9 of the edition of *War and Peace* published in Boston by the Dana Estes Co. in 1904–1912. *Trans. note.*

21. Leo Tolstoy, *War and Peace*, IV, Part 13. Chap. 14. *Trans. note.*

22. [Dimitry] Savodnikov, *Zagadki russkovo naroda* [*Riddles of the Russian People*] (St. Petersburg, 1901), Nos. 102–107.

23. Ibid., Nos. 588–591.

24. A. E. Gruzinsky, ed., *Pesni, sobrannye P[avel]N. Rybnikovym* [*Songs Collected by P. N. Rybnikov*] (Moscow, 1909–1910), No. 30.

25. Ibid., No. 171.

26. We have supplied familiar English examples in place of Shklovsky's wordplay. Shklovsky is saying that we create words with no referents or with ambiguous referents in order to force attention to the objects represented by the similar-sounding words. By making the reader go through the extra step of interpreting the nonsense word, the painter prevents an automatic response. A toad is a toad, but "tove" forces one to pause and think about the beast. *Trans. note.*

27. E. R. Romanov, "Besstrashny barin," *Velikoruskiye skazki* (*Zapiski Imperskovo Russkovo Geograficheskovo Obschestva*, XLII, No. 52). Belorussky sbornik, "Spravyadlivy soldat" ["The Intrepid Gentleman," *Great Russian Tales* (*Notes of the Imperial Russian Geographical Society*, XLII, No. 52). *White Russian Anthology*, "The Upright Soldier" (1886–1912)].

28. D[mitry] S. Zelenin, *Velikorusskiye skazki Permskoy gubernii* [*Great Russian Tales of the Permian Province* (St. Petersburg, 1913)], No. 70.

29. Dante, *Purgatorio*, 24:56. Dante refers to the new lyric style of his contemporaries. *Trans. note.*

30. Alexy Remizov (1877–1957) is best known as a novelist and satirist: Nicholas Klyuyev (1885–1937) and Sergey Essenin (1895–1925) were "peasant poets." All three were noted for their faithful reproduction of Russian dialects and coloquial language. *Trans. note.*

31. A group noted for its opulent and sensuous verse style. *Trans. note.*

32. Nicholas Leskov (1831–1895), novelist and short story writer, helped popularize the *skaz*, or yarn, and hence, because of the part dialect peculiarities play in the *skaz*, also altered Russian literary language. *Trans. note.*

33. Shklovsky is probably referring to his *Razvyortyvaniye syuzheta* [*Plot Development*] (Petrograd, 1921). *Trans. note.*

34. Spencer, [p. 169. Again the Russian text is shortened from Spencer's original].

35. We have been unable to discover the book Shklovsky promised. *Trans. note.*

II

RHETORIC AND READER RESPONSE

The oldest form of literary criticism in Western culture—the oldest rigorous study of verbal activity—is rhetoric. In the ancient world and throughout the Middle Ages, rhetoric—the method of teaching the practical uses of language—was the avenue to reading, speaking, and writing in areas such as politics, law, and even theology. Rhetoric studies the *effects* of language—effects of persuasion, emotional affect, and clarity—and attempts to understand how language creates those effects. Rhetoric, thus, emphasizes the essentially *social* aspect of language and literature, its intersubjective affects—its impact in particular situations, what Kenneth Burke calls its function as "equipment" for living. As such, rhetoric—from at least one viewpoint—is as far from the formalist approaches to language and literature described in Section I (and, in a different way, in Section III) as possible. Yet in another sense, rhetoric is part and parcel of all the "schools" of contemporary criticism examined in this book because all criticism examines the "effects" of language—even when these "effects" are, as contemporary linguistics describes it, "meaning-effects," meaning conceived as particular effects or results particular uses of language give rise to.

In other words, as we have already suggested, there are—and, traditionally, there have always been—two distinct conceptions of the nature of rhetoric. On the one hand, rhetoric examines how language persuades and uses so-called "ornaments" to say what could have been said differently ("in other words") in actual language use, what philosophers call "speech acts." On the other hand, rhetoric studies the nature of language itself, the possibilities of figures and tropes that govern rather than ornament meaning. Paul de Man, in his essay in Section IV, "Semiology and Rhetoric," emphasizes the latter understanding of rhetoric—rhetoric as, he argues, "the study of tropes and of figures (which is how the term *rhetoric* is used here, and not in the derived sense of comment or of eloquence or persuasion)." Terry Eagleton, in "Brecht and Rhetoric" (in Section VI) more fully uses the first sense: " 'Rhetoric' here means grasping language and action in the context of the politico-discursive conditions inscribed within them." In another essay, Eagleton, describing the global, dual sense of rhetoric, examines "the ways discourses are constructed in order to achieve certain effects." Rhetoric, in this view, looks at the "concrete performance . . . and at people's responses to discourse in terms of linguistic structures and the material situations in which they functioned. . . . Rhetoric, or discourse theory," he goes on,

> shares with Formalism, structuralism and semiotics an interest in the formal devices of language, but like reception theory it is also concerned with how these devices are actually effective at the point of "consumption"; its preoccupation with discourse as a form of power and desire can

> learn much from deconstruction and psychoanalytical theory, and its belief that discourse can be a humanly transformative affair shares a good deal with liberal humanism.

In this sense, then, rhetoric encompasses all contemporary literary criticism, all the schools that are implicated in the rhetorical effects of language.

TEXTUAL RHETORIC

The two definitions of rhetoric we have offered create a useful distinction beyond the narrow conception of rhetoric as the study of the interpersonal effectiveness of language, a distinction that corresponds to the two modes of formalism examined in our last section introduction. On the one hand, rhetoric focuses on the text itself by examining the formal arrangement of the figures and tropes (whether or not it conceives such arrangements as ornamenting or constituting meaning), much as Eliot's modernism and the New Criticism focus on the "impersonality" of literary texts. On the other hand, rhetoric focuses on the actual effects of texts in readers, the "functions" of formal arrangements the modernism of Russian Formalism describes. In this section we see this division in the study of the rhetoric of particular texts, what Burke calls "the attempt to treat literature from the standpoint of situations and strategies." Burke examines such strategies in terms of the sociology of literature, and in this he shares much with the Marxist approach of Bakhtin/Vološinov's "Discourse in Life and Discourse in Art (Concerning Sociological Poetics)"; they even share the "sociological" version of rhetoric. For Burke, finally, literature is essentially "functional"; it does not aim at articulating transcendental truths or human nature or a vision of "reality" or anything else "for its own sake." Literature, rather, is a form of social activity, a rhetorical gesture, that accomplishes an end.

Walter Ong pursues a similar rhetorical conception of literature—though more conservatively than the "sociological" descriptions of Burke and Bakhtin—when he attempts to describe literary history in terms of the different "roles" that literature creates for its "readers" throughout literary history. Ong examines how literature creates particular responses in its audience. In this account the responses are fully determined by the text, and Ong's approach is, as Patrocinio Schweickart says, fully "text dominant." In this analysis, the "fiction" of the audience's role is determined by textual rhetoric: the language of the text constructs particular roles for the reader, and Ong studies both those roles and the language creating them. Equally evident in Ong's essay is that within a discussion of literary history—within the history of rhetoric—is a second important feature of contemporary textual ɪhetoric, the relationship between rhetoric and writing. Accordingly, Ong traces the history of writing as well as literature—most globally, he traces (based on work by Eric Havelock) the difference between the rhetoric of oral and print cultures, and his discussion casts rhetoric as "equipment" for writing. That is, this essay implies the important relationship between textal rhetoric and composition. It marks the place where contemporary literary criticism and practical and theoretical discussions of composition intersect by examining the particular rhetorical practices necessitated by an imagined, but absent, audience.

RHETORIC AS READER RESPONSE

Whereas textual rhetoric examines the relationship between rhetoric and writing, another version of rhetoric focuses on the reader's responses, the relationship between rhetoric and reading. Criticism that focuses on a reader's response to a text has existed as long as rhetoric itself, at least since Aristotle. In the *Poetics*, for example, Aristotle spoke of the cathartic, purging effect of tragedy, thus defining a major component of that genre in terms of a reader's reaction. Coleridge emphasized the importance of a reader's "response" when he developed the romantic theory of esemplastic power, or a reader's sympathetic response to natural forms in literature and in nature. In the 1920s the modern British critic I. A. Richards proposed to catalogue readers' strategies for understanding and interpreting poetry. Unlike other New Critics, he discussed the practical steps readers go through and the assumptions they make while they read. Kenneth Burke, too, in work only recently being appreciated, attempted to chart what readers actually do, the strategies by which they adopt "terministic screens" and "dramatistic" poses in reading literature. These critics and others have found the reading activity itself to be a primary channel for understanding literary experience.

Modern Reader-Response theory, from the late 1960s through the present, concentrates exclusively on what readers do and how they do it. This movement derives some of its inspiration from psychoanalysis, but one major formulation of Reader-Response theory, found in the work of Wolfgang Iser and Hans Robert Jauss, is phenomenological. Phenomenology, as defined by Edmund Husserl and Martin Heidegger, is a philosophical view that posits a continuous field of experience between the perceiver (subject) and the object of experience. A phenomenologist believes that objects-in-the-world cannot be the valid focus of a rigorous philosophical investigation. Rather, the contents of consciousness itself—"objects" as constituted by consciousness—should be investigated. As elaborated by Maurice Merleau-Ponty, Ludwig Binswanger, Hans-Georg Gadamer, and others, this view defines literary experience holistically, with a minimal sense of separation between text and its reception—with a recognition, rather, of the inseparability of the two.

Georges Poulet's "Phenomenology of Reading," to which Schweickart alludes in her essay included here, is a primary document of Reader-Response theory. It argues that the dynamics of the reading process are centered on the reader, producing, paradoxically, an experience of "otherness." By this Poulet means that a reader reading always confronts something strange within a familiar context. The reader may begin a text presumably at one with, in possession of, his or her own thoughts, "thinking one's own thought," as Poulet says. However, because the text necessarily leads the reader to discover new information and experience that are *not* the reader's own, the reader, when reading is informative, is soon "thinking the thoughts of another." These "alien" thoughts then elicit a kind of alternative consciousness, again *not* the reader's own. The result of this step is that "my consciousness [as a reader] behaves as though it were the consciousness of another." This alien consciousness, as Poulet reasons, must be thought by someone, a subject. It follows that "this *thought* which is alien to me and yet in me, must also have in me a *subject* which is alien to me."

Poulet here describes the process of discovering "otherness" in reading as culminating in a direct confrontation with a kind of transcendental subjectivity, or "being." Poulet describes this phase of reading when he says that "when reading a literary work, there is a moment when it seems to me that the subject *present* in this work disengages itself from all that surrounds it, and stands alone." This confrontation with "being" is such that "no object can any longer express it, no structure can any longer define it; it is exposed in its ineffability and in its fundamental indeterminancy." Reading, in other words, begins with the personal recognition of "otherness" but then opens upon an experience wherein the difference, or gap, separating subjects from objects, or reader from text, is transcended altogether. In reading, thus, subject and object ultimately merge in a continuous field of experience.

On this basis, Poulet's literary criticism explores not just the dynamics of individual texts but the dynamics of each author's "world," a particular staging of the process that opens upon the disengaged subject. The philosopher Ludwig Binswanger, similarly, has explored Henrik Ibsen's dramatic "world," and J. Hillis Miller—in the phenomenological phase of his work—investigated the fictional "world" of Charles Dickens just as he explored the "experience" (the "world") of modernity in *Poets of Reality* (1965) and *The Disappearance of God* (1963). In each case, the emphasis is on a "descriptive" approach that gradually, and painstakingly, isolates the text's presentation of subject/object relations. Out of these connections, usually made for several works or for a writer's whole corpus, emerges the "consciousness" that constitutes the authorial world. The descriptive technique of this phenomenological criticism appears to link it with formalism, but phenomenology's aim is to capture "experience," not form, and to disregard formal limits—particularly a work's chronology, the functions of language, and the like—in characterizing the essential aspects of that work.

Contemporary reader-oriented criticism is carried out against the background of this earlier work—as well as the background of textual rhetoric—but tends, as Steven Mailloux notes, to divide into three separate strains: phenomenology, subjectivism, and structuralism. For instance, the lineal descendants of the earlier phenomenology are studies by Hans-Georg Gadamer, Hans Robert Jauss, and Wolfgang Iser. Particularly important theoretically is Gadamer's *Truth and Method* (translated in 1975), which attempts to rethink the confluence of phenomenology and literary criticism by returning to Heidegger's discussion of consciousness as always *situated* culturally, what Heidegger called *Dasein*—"being there," or "being-in-the-world." Gadamer's work brought about a minor revival of interest in phenomenological reading, not least because of his influence on Hans Robert Jauss, also a phenomenologist, who examines a work's reception (what Jauss calls "reception esthetic") within a cultural milieu and attempts to establish a "horizon of expectation," or a "paradigm" accounting for that culture's responses to literature at a certain moment. His work, especially in medieval studies, has stimulated a new kind of "historical" criticism and has even been useful to the "New Historicism" examined in Section VI.

Still in the phenomenological camp, but intensely concerned with practice—the dynamics of practical interpretation—Wolfgang Iser (whose work on the reading process Schweickart also examines) builds a reader-oriented theory around the concept of narrative "gaps." By "gaps," Iser means the details or connections—the vaguenesses—within a story that a reader must fill in or make up. No story, no matter how "realistic," can avoid such gaps, and the structural need to fill them is the text's way of completing itself through the reader's experience. Ambiguous in Iser's thinking, however, is the question of whether the text orchestrates the reader's participation or whether the reader virtually writes the text by filling the gaps without external constraint. This dilemma—is the text (author) in charge, or is the reader—is, as Schweickart notes, a recurrent and as yet unanswered question in Reader-Response criticism.

In the related school that Mailloux calls subjectivism, this same problem concerning the text's-versus-the-reader's authority is intensified. Drawing from psychoanalytic theory, David Bleich, for instance, practices a "subjective criticism," which assumes that literary interpretation is never more than an elaboration of a person's most personal motivations and desires, which are projected or "discovered"—perhaps even "disavowed"—in the literary text. Bleich's method involves establishing the connection between literary interpretation, the esthetic effect of a text, and the individual search for self-knowledge. In short, by psychologizing the reading process in this way, Bleich resolves the text/reader question in the reader's favor. The reader is in charge. This strategy, however, as some believe, leaves the text virtually undefined and without intrinsic meaning—"blank," so to speak.

Initially, Norman N. Holland, also a Freudian, seemed to resolve the text/reader question without losing the text, but the result of his criticism (with some differences) is very like Bleich's. In books such as *5 Readers Reading* and *Poems in Persons*, Holland attempts "to understand the combination of text and personal association," an approach suggesting evenhandedness. But for Holland, as Mailloux points out, while "the reader makes sense of the text by creating a meaningful unity out of its elements," there is no unity "in the text [itself] but [only] in the mind of the reader." More pointedly, concerning the text's authority, in *5 Readers Reading* Holland says that "the reader is surely responding to *something*. The literary text may be only so many marks on a page—at most a matrix of psychological possibilities for its readers." This minimalist sense of the literary text as "marks on a page," much like Bleich's subjective criticism, again leaves little sense of the text as anything more than a reflection, a mirroring, of the reader's personal concerns. Again, the text/reader question is resolved completely in the reader's favor, leaving the literary text in the role of mere stimulus (again, a virtually "blank" text) for the reader's response. (M. H. Abrams articulates the extreme opposite to this view in "The Deconstructive Angel" in Section VIII.)

Stanley E. Fish and Jonathan Culler try to avoid the ambiguities of Bleich's and Holland's subjectivism through a third approach to reading, one that Mailloux calls structuralism. They begin by imagining, as do Bleich and Holland, that reading and interpretation are "free" activities virtually ungoverned by the texts being read. However, while assuming the initial polymorphous perversity of reading, Fish and Culler then place constraints on reading to account for what may be considered a "valid" interpretation of a particular text. In "Interpreting the *Variorum*" (reprinted here), for example, Fish explains how the stylistic economy of a text initially elicits multiple and conflicting responses. Any one text, though, will not finally be read in a multiplicity of ways because the reader belongs to an "interpretive community" of other readers, and this community will allow certain readings and reject others. Out of this community's censoring activity, in other words, will emerge "valid," or normative, readings of a text. In a similar way, drawing on Noam Chomsky's distinction between competence and performance, Culler posits a set of reading conventions, or strategies for understanding written texts, that a qualified reader in a culture will learn and employ. A person's measurable ability to implement these conventions constitutes reading "competence," which for Fish and Culler—under different names—becomes nearly the whole of the reading activity, even virtually obliterating any "text."

Thus, Fish and Culler place "common-sense" restrictions on an activity that most readers feel to be, in some way, bounded or constrained. Readers do not generally report reading from every conceivable perspective. Rather, they argue, readers experience only an indeterminacy of interpretation in a first stage of reading, that is, before external constraints of the interpretive community are applied to the text. But unlike Bleich and Holland, Fish and Culler—most explicitly in Culler's *Structuralist Poetics*—attempt to articulate a conception of the "facts" in literature in a way that grows out of Saussure's description of the nature of linguistic fact (see Section III). Fish also describes the contextual and conventional nature of literary "facts" when he says that "phonological 'facts' are no more uninterpreted (or less conventional) than the 'facts' of orthography; the distinctive features that make articulation and reception possible are the product of a system of differences that must be *imposed* before it can be recognized. . . . The patterns the ear hears (like the patterns the eye sees)," Fish goes on, "are the patterns its perceptual habits make available."

It does seem eminently reasonable to assume, with Fish and Culler, that constraints on reading do exist that are analogous to the constraints language produces. However, the hypothesis about the implementation of an interpretive community's constraints is a difficult one. One grants that meaning, or the authority of a single interpretation, is difficult to locate or prove within a text. It is not easy to see that a text can exercise textual or interpretive judgments for itself to support such a reading. Can an inanimate text possess an intention? Whatever the answer to this may be—and there are different answers possible—the simple removal of interpretive authority from the text to the community may not solve the problem. Who will be "competent" enough to determine the proper communal interpretation of a text? And how is the "interpretive community" any more of a decidable, unambiguous concept than "textual" authority? A moment's reflection suggests that Fish and Culler may have "solved" the problem of interpretation only by deferring it, the "interpretive community" and "competence" being themselves indeterminate and problematic concepts. The text/reader question remains as difficult for Fish and Culler as for Bleich and Holland.

While current Reader-Response criticism is unable to lay to rest primary questions its thinking has generated, it has been a productive movement. Like many critical schools since World War II, Reader-Response has argued against formalist approaches to literature by emphasizing reading or interpretation as an *activity*, as an ongoing rather than static or contained event. Still, there is a sense in which Reader-Response criticism participates in the generalizing practices of formalism against which Burke, among others, argues. Schweickart addresses this issue in the feminist critique in the last essay of this section, "Reading Ourselves: Toward a Feminist Theory of Reading." (For a discussion of the nature of "critique," see the introduction to Section IV.) This essay, which offers a helpful overview of various practices of Reader-Response criticism, also explores the "utopian" impulse within contemporary criticism. It does so, as Schweickart notes, by overlooking "the issues of race, class, and sex," and, thus, it gives "no hint of the conflicts, sufferings, and passions that attend these realities. . . . The relative tranquility of the tone of these theories," she concludes, "testifies to the privileged position of the theorists."

In this way, more than Burke—and in a fashion quite different from Bakhtin/Vološinov—Schweickart attempts to situate the rhetorical reading (and the act of *criticism*) as a social and political activity. While Burke describes the role of literature as strategically situated (and analyzable by rhetoric) and Ong describes the role of the reader as an imposed fiction governed by the discourse of literature (which is similarly analyzable by rhetoric), Schweickart describes the role of the critic as politically and socially situated.

After surveying the various schools of Reader-Response criticism, Schweickart then discusses the gender-based aspects of reading and describes two different *kinds* of reader response. The first is carried out "under the sign of the 'Resisting Reader,'" wherein the goal is to *resist* the "fiction" that the audience is male and expose "the androcentricity of what has customarily passed for the universal." The second kind of reader response is to create a new role for the reader, a feminine role for the reader of women's writing, which—eschewing "mainstream reader-response theories [which are] preoccupied with issues of control and partition"—seeks to discover "the dialectic of communication informing the relationship between the feminist reader and the female author/text." In this, Schweickart is attempting to articulate a rhetoric of reading—functioning "equipment"—that is both textual and reader-oriented, a description of "rhetoric," once again, attempting to connect reader and text. In other words, in her feminist critique, Schweickart is describing ways in which contemporary rhetorical analyses of literature can create new ways of reading and understanding.

RELATED READING IN *CONTEMPORARY LITERARY CRITICISM*

Jonathan Culler, "Convention and Meaning"
Paul de Man, "Semiology and Rhetoric"
Terry Eagleton, "Brecht and Rhetoric"
Bakhtin/Vološinov, "Discourse in Life and Discourse in Art"
J. Hillis Miller, "The Search for Grounds in Literary Study"
Lillian Robinson, "Treason Our Text"
Shoshana Felman, "Psychoanalysis and Education"

FURTHER READING

Bleich, David, *Readings and Feelings: An Introduction to Subjective Criticism* (New York: Harper & Row, 1977).

_____, *Subjective Criticism* (Baltimore: Johns Hopkins University Press, 1978).

Booth, Wayne C., *The Rhetoric of Fiction* (Chicago: University of Chicago Press, 1961).

Chabot, Barry C., ". . . Reading Readers Reading Readers Reading . . ." in *Diacritics*, 5, No. 3 (1975), 24–38.

Chatman, Seymour, *Narrative Structure in Fiction and Film* (Ithaca: Cornell University Press, 1978).

Culler, Jonathan, "Stanley Fish and the Righting of the Reader," in *Diacritics*, 5, No. 1 (1975), 26–31.

_____, *Structuralist Poetics* (Ithaca: Cornell University Press, 1975).

Fish, Stanley, *Is There a Text in This Class?* (Cambridge: Harvard University Press, 1980).

———, *Self-Consuming Artifacts: The Experience of Seventeenth-Century Literature* (Berkeley: University of California Press, 1972).

———, *Surprised by Sin: The Reader in Paradise Lost* (Berkeley: University of California Press, 1967).

———, "Why No One's Afraid of Wolfgang Iser," in *Diacritics*, 11, No. 1 (1981), 2–13.

Havelock, Eric, *Preface to Plato* (Cambridge: Harvard University Press, 1963).

Holland, Norman N., *The Dynamics of Literary Response* (New York: Oxford University Press, 1968).

———, *5 Readers Reading* (New Haven: Yale University Press, 1975).

———, *Poems in Persons* (New York: Norton, 1973).

Ingarden, Roman, *The Cognition of the Literary Work of Art* (Evanston, Ill.: Northwestern University Press, 1973).

Iser, Wolfgang, *The Act of Reading* (Baltimore: Johns Hopkins University Press, 1978).

———, *The Implied Reader: Patterns of Communication in Prose Fiction from Bunyan to Beckett* (Baltimore: Johns Hopkins University Press, 1974).

Jauss, Hans Robert, "Literary History as a Challenge to Literary Theory," in *New Directions in Literary History*, Ralph Cohen, ed. (Baltimore: Johns Hopkins University Press, 1974), 11–41.

———, *Toward an Aesthetic of Reception*, trans. Timothy Bahti (Minneapolis: University of Minnesota Press, 1982).

Mailloux, Steven, *Interpretive Conventions: The Reader in the Study of American Fiction* (Ithaca: Cornell University Press, 1982).

Ong, Walter, S. J., *Orality and Literacy* (New York: Methuen, 1982).

Pratt, Mary Louise, *Toward a Speech Act Theory of Literary Discourse* (Bloomington: Indiana University Press, 1977).

Prince, Gerald, "Introduction à l'étude de narrataire," in *Poetique*, 14 (1973), 178–96.

"Reading, Interpretation, Response," special section of *Genre*, 10 (1977), 363–453.

Roudiez, Leon, "Notes on the Reader as Subject," in *Semiotext(e)*, 1, No. 3 (1975), 69–80.

Starobinski, Jean, *Word Upon Words* (New Haven: Yale University Press, 1979).

Suleiman, Susan, and Inge Corsman, eds., *The Reader in the Text: Essays on Audience and Interpretation* (Princeton, N.J.: Princeton University Press, 1980).

Tompkins, Jane, ed., *Reader-Response Criticism* (Baltimore: Johns Hopkins University Press, 1980).

5

Kenneth Burke
1897–

In an era of critical thought that understands itself increasingly in terms of movements and schools, Kenneth Burke has produced over sixty years of criticism and theory that distances itself from any single approach to literature. This antinomian attitude is captured in one of Burke's mottoes: "When in Rome, do as the Greeks"; and it is this role of gadfly within the critical establishment that makes Burke a central figure in the development of American criticism. But to say that Burke continually opposed himself to prevailing critical schools is not to say that he disdained critical method; quite the contrary. In fact, one might characterize the trajectory of his thought as a search for a method adequate not only to an understanding of literature but adequate to an understanding of all aspects of human behavior. This broader concern with human behavior begins to develop after the publication of his first book, *Counter-Statement* (1931), when he turns his attention to the question of human motivation, focusing on the nature of perspective, or what he often calls "attitude." The major publications from this early concern are *Permanence and Change* (1935) and *Attitudes Toward History* (1937). It is during this transitional period that "Literature as Equipment for Living" is written. During the following years, Burke writes his best known works: *A Grammar of Motives* (1945), *A Rhetoric of Motives* (1950), and the essays collected in *Language as Symbolic Action* (1966). Interest in these works, as in Burke's thought in general, has increased over the past ten years, as American critics influenced by Continental theories of language have rediscovered Burke's concern with the relationship of language, knowledge, and social structures.

"Literature as Equipment for Living" was published initially in 1937, in the first volume of the American leftist journal *Direction*, which Burke later joined as an associate editor. In this essay, Burke positions his critical method, more or less explicitly, in relation to three currents in American criticism, all of which, according to Burke, neutralize the vitality of literature. The first is the idea that literature is detached from everyday life and, consequently, more "pure" than the practicalities of living; but in opposition to this idea, Burke asserts that we use literature to deal with recurrent situations in our lives. The second current, which Burke discusses toward the end of the essay, is the drive toward specialization that is encouraged by academic criticism; the tendency of academic criticism, because it excludes other areas of learning, is to reify older literary classifications and thereby to stifle the development of literary criticism. In opposition to these first two currents, Burke calls for a "sociological criticism," but, as he suggests in his opening paragraph, his idea of a sociological criticism has an emphasis different from traditional sociological criticism. Burke appears to be referring to Marxist critics like Van Wyck Brooks, Granville Hicks, and V. F. Calverton, whose work he had reviewed unfavorably as positing a simplistic economic determinism between literary work and social context. In opposition to this determinism, Burke suggests a broader range of motivations that could affect the production of a literary work and redefines sociological criticism as the codifying of "the various strategies which artists have developed with relation to the naming of situations."

Literature as Equipment for Living

Here I shall put down, as briefly as possible, a statement in behalf of what might be catalogued, with a fair degree of accuracy, as a *sociological* criticism of literature. Sociological criticism in itself is certainly not new. I shall here try to suggest what partially new elements or emphasis I think should be added to this old approach. And to make the "way in" as easy as possible. I shall begin with a discussion of proverbs.

1

Examine random specimens in *The Oxford Dictionary of English Proverbs.* You will note, I think, that there is no "pure" literature here. Everything is "medicine." Proverbs are designed for consolation or vengeance, for admonition or exhortation, for foretelling.

Or they name typical, recurrent situations. That is, people find a certain social relationship recurring so frequently that they must "have a word for it." The Eskimos have special names for many different kinds of snow (fifteen, if I remember rightly) because variations in the quality of snow greatly affect their living. Hence, they must "size up" snow much more accurately than we do. And the same is true of social phenomena. Social structures give rise to "type" situations, subtle subdivisions of the relationships involved in competitive and cooperative acts. Many proverbs seek to chart, in more or less homey and picturesque ways, these "type" situations. I submit that such naming is done, not for the sheer glory of the thing, but because of its bearing upon human welfare. A different name for snow implies a different kind of hunt. Some names for snow imply that one should not hunt at all. And similarly, the names for typical, recurrent social situations are not developed out of "disinterested curiosity," but because the names imply a command (what to expect, what to look out for).

To illustrate with a few representative examples:

Proverbs designed for consolation: "The sun does not shine on both sides of the hedge at once." "Think of ease, but work on." "Little troubles the eye, but far less the soul." "The worst luck now, the better another time." "The wind in one's face makes one wise." "He that hath lands hath quarrels." "He knows how to carry the dead cock home." "He is not poor that hath little, but he that desireth much."

For vengeance: "At length the fox is brought to the furrier." "Shod in the cradle, barefoot in the stubble." "Sue a beggar and get a louse." "The higher the ape goes, the more he shows his tail." "The moon does not heed the barking of dogs." "He measures another's corn by his own bushel." "He shuns the man who knows him well." "Fools tie knots and wise men loose them."

Proverbs that have to do with foretelling: (The most obvious are those to do with the weather.) "Sow peas and beans in the wane of the moon, Who soweth them sooner, he soweth too soon." "When the wind's in the north, the skilful fisher goes not forth." "When the sloe tree is as white as a sheet, sow your barley whether it be dry or wet." "When the sun sets bright and clear, An easterly wind you need not fear. When the sun sets in a bank, A westerly wind we shall not want."

In short: "Keep your weather eye open": be realistic about sizing up today's weather, because your accuracy has bearing upon tomorrow's weather. And forecast not only the meteorological weather, but also the social weather: "When the moon's in the full, then wit's in the wane." "Straws show which way the wind blows." "When the fish is caught, the net is laid aside." "Remove an old tree, and it will wither to death." "The wolf may lose his teeth, but never his nature." "He that bites on every weed must needs light on poison." "Whether the pitcher strikes the stone, or the stone the pitcher, it is bad for the pitcher." "Eagles catch no flies." "The more laws, the more offenders."

In this foretelling category we might also include the recipes for wise living, sometimes moral, sometimes technical: "First thrive, and then wive." "Think with the wise but talk with the vulgar." "When the fox preacheth, then beware your geese." "Venture a small fish to catch a great one." "Respect a man, he will do the more."

In the class of "typical, recurrent situations" we might put such proverbs and proverbial expressions as: "Sweet appears sour when we pay." "The treason is loved but the traitor is hated." "The wine in the bottle does not quench thirst." "The sun is never the worse for shining on a dunghill." "The lion kicked by an ass." "The lion's share." "To catch one napping." "To smell a rat." "To cool one's heels."

By all means, I do not wish to suggest that this is the only way in which the proverbs could be classified. For instance, I have listed in the "foretelling" group the proverb, "When the fox preacheth, then beware your geese." But it could obviously be "taken over" for vindictive purposes. Or consider a proverb like, "Virtue flies from the heart of a mercenary man." A poor man might obviously use it either to console himself for being poor (the implication being, "Because I am poor in money I am rich in virtue") or to strike at another (the implication being, "When he got money, what else could you expect of him but deterioration?"). In fact, we could even say that such symbolic vengeance would itself be an aspect of solace. And a proverb like "The sun is never the worse for shining on a dunghill" (which I have listed under "typical recurrent situations") might as well be put in the vindictive category.

The point of issue is not to find categories that "place" the proverbs once and for all. What I want is categories that suggest their active nature. Here there is no "realism for its own sake." There is realism for promise, admonition, solace, vengeance, foretelling, instruction, charting, all for the direct bearing that such acts have upon matters of welfare.

2

Step two: Why not extend such analysis of proverbs to encompass the whole field of literature? Could the most complex and sophisticated works of art legitimately be considered somewhat as "proverbs writ large"? Such leads, if held admissible, should help us to discover important facts about literary organization (thus satisfying the requirements of technical criticism). And the kind of observation from this perspective should apply beyond literature to life in general (thus helping to take literature out of its separate bin and give it a place in a general "sociological" picture).

The point of view might be phrased in this way: Proverbs are *strategies* for dealing with *situations*. In so far as situations are typical and recurrent in a given social structure, people develop names for them and strategies for handling them. Another name for strategies might be *attitudes*.

People have often commented on the fact that there are contrary *proverbs*. But I believe that the above approach to proverbs suggests a necessary modification of that comment. The apparent contradictions depend upon differences in *attitude*, involving a correspondingly different choice of *strategy*. Consider, for instance, the *apparently* opposite pair: "Repentance comes too late" and "Never too late to mend." The first is admonitory. It says in effect: "You'd better look out, or you'll get yourself too far into this business." The second is consolatory, saying in effect: "Buck up, old man, you can still pull out of this."

Some critics have quarreled with me about my selection of the word "strategy" as the name for this process. I have asked them to suggest an alternative term, so far without profit. The only one I can think of is "method." But if "strategy" errs in suggesting to some people an overly *conscious* procedure, "method" errs in suggesting an overly "*methodical*" one. Anyhow, let's look at the documents:

Concise Oxford Dictionary: "Strategy: Movement of an army or armies in a compaign, art of so moving or disposing troops or ships as to impose upon the enemy the place and time and conditions for fighting preferred by oneself" (from a Greek word that refers to the leading of an army).

New English Dictionary: "Strategy: The art of projecting and directing the larger military movements and operations of a campaign."

André Cheron, *Traité Complet d'Echecs: "On entend par stratégie les manoeuvres qui ont pour but la sortie et le bon arrangement des pièces."*

Looking at these definitions, I gain courage. For surely, the most highly alembicated and sophisticated work of art, arising in complex civilizations, could be considered as designed to organize and command the army of one's thoughts and images, and to so organize them that one "imposes upon the enemy the time and place and conditions for fighting preferred by oneself." One seeks to "direct the larger movements and operations" in one's campaign of living. One "maneuvers," and the maneuvering is an "art."

Are not the final results one's "strategy"? One tries, as far as possible, to develop a strategy whereby one "can't lose." One tries to change the rules of the game until they fit his own necessities. Does the artist encounter disaster? He will "make capital" of it. If one is a victim of competition, for instance, if one is elbowed out, if one is willy-nilly more jockeyed against than jockeying, one can by the solace and vengeance of art convert this very "liability" into an "asset." One tries to fight on his own terms, developing a strategy for imposing the proper "time, place, and conditions."

But one must also, to develop a full

strategy, be *realistic*. One must *size things up* properly. One cannot accurately know how things *will be*, what is promising and what is menacing, unless he accurately knows how things are. So the wise strategist will not be content with strategies of merely a self-gratifying sort. He will "keep his weather eye open." He will not too eagerly "read into" a scene an attitude that is irrelevant to it. He won't sit on the side of an active volcano and "see" it as a dormant plain.

Often, alas, he will. The great allurement in our present popular "inspirational literature," for instance, may be largely of this sort. It is a strategy for easy consolation. It "fills a need," since there is always a need for easy consolation—and in an era of confusion like our own the need is especially keen. So people are only too willing to "meet a man halfway" who will *play down* the realistic naming of our situation and *play up* such strategies as make solace cheap. However, I should propose a reservation here. We usually take it for granted that people who consume our current output of books on "How to Buy Friends and Bamboozle Oneself and Other People" are reading as *students* who will attempt applying the recipes given. Nothing of the sort. *The reading of a book on the attaining of success is in itself the symbolic attaining of that success.* It is *while they read* that these readers are "succeeding." I'll wager that, in by far the great majority of cases, such readers made no serious attempt to apply the book's recipes. The lure of the book resides in the fact that the reader, while reading it, is then living in the aura of success. What he wants is *easy* success; and he gets it in symbolic form by the mere reading itself. To attempt applying such stuff in real life would be very difficult, full of many disillusioning difficulties.

Sometimes a different strategy may arise. The author may remain realistic, avoiding too easy a form of solace—yet he may get as far off the track in his own way. Forgetting that realism is an aspect for foretelling, he may take it as an end in itself. He is tempted to do this by two factors: (1) an *ill-digested* philosophy of science, leading him mistakenly to assume that "relentless" naturalistic "truthfulness" is a proper end in itself, and (2) a merely *competitive* desire to outstrip other writers by being "more realistic" than they. Works thus made "efficient" by tests of competition internal to the book trade are a kind of academicism not so named (the writer usually thinks of it as the *opposite* of academicism). Realism thus stepped up competitively might be distinguished from the proper sort by the name of "naturalism." As a way of "sizing things up," the naturalistic tradition tends to become as inaccurate as the "inspirational" strategy, though at the opposite extreme.

Anyhow, the main point is this: A work like *Madame Bovary* (or its homely American translation, *Babbitt*) is the strategic naming of a situation. It singles out a pattern of experience that is sufficiently often *mutandis mutatis*, for people to "need a word for it" and to adopt an attitude towards it. Each work of art is the addition of a word to an informal dictionary (or, in the case of purely derivative artists, the addition of a subsidiary meaning to a word already given by some originating artist). As for *Madame Bovary*, the French critic Jules de Gaultier proposed to add it to our formal dictionary by coining the word "Bovarysme" and writing a whole book to say what he meant by it.

Mencken's book on *The American Language*, I hate to say, is splendid. I console myself with the reminder that Mencken didn't write it. Many millions of people wrote it, and Mencken was merely the amanuensis who took it down from their dictation. He found a true "vehicle" (that is, a book that could be greater than the author who wrote it). He gets the royalties, but the job was done by a collectivity. As you read that book, you see a people who were up against a new set of typical recurrent situations, situations typical of their business, their politics, their criminal organizations, their sports. Either there were no words for these in standard English, or people didn't know them, or they didn't "sound right." So a new vocabulary arose, to "give us a word for it." I see no reason for believing that Americans are unusually fertile in word-coinage. American slang was not developed out of some exceptional gift. It was developed out of the fact that new typical situations had arisen and people needed names for them. They had to "size things up." They had to console and strike, to promise and admonish. They had to describe for purposes of forecasting. And "slang" was the result. It is, by this analysis, simple *proverbs not so named*, a kind of "folk criticism."

3

With what, then, would "sociological criticism" along these lines be concerned? It would seek to codify the various strategies which artists have developed with relation to the naming of situations. In a sense, much of it would even be "timeless," for many of the "typical, recurrent situations" are not peculiar to our own civilization at all. The situations and strategies framed in Aesop's Fables, for instance, apply to human relations now just as fully as they applied in ancient Greece. They are, like philosophy, sufficiently "generalized" to extend far beyond the particular combination of events named by them in any one instance. They name an "essence." Or, as Korzybski might say, they are on a "high level of abstraction." One doesn't usually think of them as "abstract," since they are usually so concrete in their stylistic expression. But they invariably aim to discern the "general behind the particular" (which would suggest that they are good Goethe).

The attempt to treat literature from the standpoint of situations and strategies suggests a variant of Spengler's notion of the "contemporaneous." By "contemporaneity" he meant corresponding stages of different cultures. For instance, if modern New York is much like decadent Rome, then we are "contemporaneous" with decadent Rome, or with some corresponding decadent city among the Mayas, etc. It is in this sense that situations are "timeless," "nonhistorical," "contemporaneous." A given human relationship may be at one time named in terms of foxes and lions, if there are foxes and lions about; or it may now be named in terms of salesmanship, advertising, the tactics of politicians, etc. But beneath the change in particulars, we may often discern the naming of the one situation.

So sociological criticism, as here understood, would seek to assemble and codify this lore. It might occasionally lead us to outrage good taste, as we sometimes found exemplified in some great sermon or tragedy or abstruse work of philosophy the same strategy as we found exemplified in a dirty joke. At this point, we'd put the sermon and the dirty joke together, thus "grouping by situation" and showing the range of possible particularizations. In his exceptionally discerning essay, "A Critic's Job of Work," R. P. Blackmur says, "I think on the whole his (Burke's) method could be applied with equal fruitfulness to Shakespeare, Dashiell Hammett, or Marie Corelli." When I got through wincing, I had to admit that Blackmur was right. This article is an attempt to say for the method what can be said. As a matter of fact, I'll go a step further and maintain: You can't properly put Marie Corelli and Shakespeare apart until you have first put them together. First genus, then differentia. The strategy in common is the genus. The *range* or *scale* of *spectrum* of particularizations is the differentia.

Anyhow, that's what I'm driving at. And that's why reviewers sometime find in my work "intuitive" leaps that are dubious as "science." They are not "leaps" at all. They are classifications, groupings, made on the basis of some strategic element common to the items grouped. They are neither more nor less "intuitive" than *any* grouping or classification of social events. Apples can be grouped with bananas as fruits, and they can be grouped with tennis balls as round. I am simply proposing, in the social sphere, a method of classification with reference to *strategies*.

The method of these things to be said in its favor: It gives definite insight into the organization of literary works; and it automatically breaks down the barriers erected about literature as a specialized pursuit. People can classify novels by reference to three kinds, eight kinds, seventeen kinds. It doesn't matter. Students patiently copy down the professor's classification and pass examinations on it, because the range of possible academic classifications is endless. Sociological classification, as herein suggested, would derive its relevance from the fact that it should apply both to works of art and to social situations outside of art.

It would, I admit, violate current pieties, break down current categories, and thereby "outrage good taste." But "good taste" has become *inert*. The classifications I am proposing would be *active*. I think that what we need is active categories.

These categories will lie on the bias across the categories of modern specialization. The new alignment will outrage in particular those persons who take the division of faculties in our universities to be an exact replica of the way in which God himself divided up the universe. We have had the Philosophy of the Being; and we have had the Philosophy of the Becoming. In contemporary specialization, we have been getting the Philosophy of the Bin. Each of these mental localities has had its own peculiar way of life, its own values, even its own special idiom for seeing, thinking, and "proving." Among other things, a sociological approach should attempt to provide a reintegrative point of view, a broader empire of investigation encompassing the lot.

What would such sociological categories be like? They would consider works of art, I think, as strategies for selecting enemies and allies, for socializing losses, for warding off evil eye, for purification, propitiation, and desanctification, consolation and vengeance, admonition and exhortation, implicit commands or instructions of one sort or another. Art forms like "tragedy" or "comedy" or "satire" would be treated as *equipments for living*, that size up situations in various ways and in keeping with correspondingly various attitudes. The typical ingredients of such forms would be sought. Their relation to typical situations would be stressed. Their comparative values would be considered, with the intention of formulating a "strategy of strategies," the "over-all" strategy obtained by inspection of the lot.

6

Walter J. Ong, S. J.
1912–

Educated in both the secular academy and the Jesuit priesthood Walter Ong received his Ph.D. from Harvard in 1955. He then went on to teach at Regis College (Denver) and later at St. Louis University, where he now resides as William E. Haren Professor of English and professor of humanities in psychiatry in the School of Medicine. Ong has lectured at the University of Poitiers, and was Terry Lecturer at Yale (1963–64). He also has lectured at N.Y.U., the University of Chicago, Indiana University, and McGill University. Ong served as vice-chairman of the National Council on the Humanities (1971–74) and was president of the Modern Language Association (1978). Numerous awards include a Guggenheim fellowship (1949–52) and the Chevaliers of L'Ordre des Palmes (France). Ong's major publications embrace a wide field of disciplines dealing with language, cultural studies, theology, and pedagogy. *The Presence of the Word* (1967); *Rhetoric, Romance and Technology* (1971); *Interfaces of the Word* (1971); and *Orality and Literacy* (1982) are all investigations into how modern language and writing reflect a recapitulation to earlier patterns of discourse, notably traceable to primary oral cultures. In addition to his books, Ong has contributed articles to literary publications edited by such well-known critics as M. H. Abrams, Geoffrey Hartman, Paul R. Sullivan, Nathan A. Scott Jr., James L. Calderwood, and Harold E. Toliver. Ong has written on such diverse figures as Gerard Manley Hopkins and Marshall McLuhan, as well as on the intersecting fields of rhetoric, religion, pedagogy, poetry, and social science.

Walter J. Ong has enjoyed an exemplary career as a scholar and theologian. Having developed a body of scholarly works whose expositions encompass the history of rhetoric and pedagogy from beginnings to the present, Ong's ambitious tasks have reawakened interests in the relationship of writing to its oral heritage in all phases of language arts disciplines. Ong's scholarship centers on the investigation of rhetoric as a critical axis for understanding writing's relationship to orality. His selection here, reprinted in *The Presence of the Word,* is concerned with the reader–writer relationship as an example of how classical rhetorical practices reemerge through the writer's projection of an expected audience. In order to communicate, the writer must envision a reader (real or imaginary), then conceive of the possible audience response of this "fictionalized" figure. The reader is in turn clued to this rhetorical game through certain semantic devices in the text, for example, Hemingway's use of demonstrative pronouns to imply a familiarity with the reader. From the realization that this reader as a fictionalized projection is a double game, present to a degree in all modern narrative, Ong offers that "the relationship of audience fictionalizing to modern narrative prose is very mysterious, and I do not pretend to explain it all here, but only to point to some of the strange problems often so largely ignored in the relationship." As one of the major factors "overlooked in the relationship," Ong considers the way "Script culture has preserved a heavy oral residue signaled by its continual fascination with rhetoric, which has always been orally grounded." Ong's theories are important to the study of Reader-Response theory and criticism, which attempts to uncover the complex relationships of how the reader is moved (or not) to participate in the very rhetorical devices meant to engage his/her role. While Ong is concerned here with the "fictionalizing" of an audience as a kind of "masking," his goal is to mitigate the supposed difference between speech and writing by utilizing classical rhetorical devices, developed for an oral culture, in the context of modern "print" media.

The Writer's Audience Is Always a Fiction[1]

Epistola . . . non erubescit.

—Cicero *Epistolae ad familiares* v.12.1.

Ubi nihil erit quae scribas, id ipsum scribes.

—Cicero *Epistolae ad Atticum* iv.8.4.

I

Although there is a large and growing literature on the differences beween oral and written verbalization, many aspects of the differences have not been looked into at all, and many others, although well known, have not been examined in their full implications. Among these latter is the relationship, of the so-called "audience" to writing as such, to the situation that inscribed communication establishes and to the roles that readers as readers are consequently called on to play. Some studies in literary history and criticism at times touch near this subject, but none, it appears, take it up in any detail.

The standard locus in Western intellectual tradition for study of audience responses has been rhetoric. But rhetoric originally concerned oral communication, as is indicated by its name, which comes from the Greek word for public speaking. Over two millennia, rhetoric has been gradually extended to include writing more and more, until today, in highly technological cultures, this is its principal concern. But the extension has come gradually and has advanced pari passu with the slow and largely unnoticed emergence of markedly chirographic and typographic styles out of those originating in oral performance, with the result that the differentiation between speech and writing has never become a matter of urgent concern for the rhetoric of any given age: when orality was in the ascendancy, rhetoric was oral-focused; as orality yielded to writing, the focus of rhetoric was slowly shifted, unreflectively for the most part, and without notice.

Histories of the relationship between literature and culture have something to say about the status and behavior of readers, before and after reading given materials, as do mass media studies, readership surveys, liberation programs for minorities or various other classes of persons, books on reading skills, works of literary criticism, and works on linguistics, especially those addressing differences between hearing and reading. But most of these studies, except perhaps literary criticism and linguistic studies, treat only perfunctorily, if at all, the roles imposed on the reader by a written or printed text not imposed by spoken utterance. Formalist or structuralist critics, including French theorists such as Paul Ricoeur as well as Roland Barthes, Jacques Derrida, Michel Foucault, Philippe Sollers, and Tzvetan Todorov, variously advert to the immediacy of the oral as against writing and print and occasionally study differences between speech and writing, as Louis Lavelle did much earlier in *La Parole et l'écriture* (1942). In treating of masks and "shadows" in his *Sociologie du théâtre* (1965), Jean Duvignaud brilliantly discusses the projections of a kind of collective consciousness on the part of theater audiences. But none of these appear to broach directly the question of readers' roles called for by a written text, either synchronically as such roles stand at present or diachronically as they have developed through history. Linguistic theorists such as John R. Searle and John L. Austin treat "illocutionary acts" (denoted by "warn," "command," "state," etc.), but these regard the speaker's or writer's need in certain instances to secure a special hold on those he addresses[2] not any special role imposed by writing.

Wayne Booth in *The Rhetoric of Fiction* and Walker Gibson, whom Booth quotes, come quite close to the concerns of the present study in their treatment of the "mock reader," as does Henry James, whom Booth also cites, in his discussion of the way an author makes "his reader very much as he makes his character."[3] But this hint of James is not developed—there is no reason why it should be—and neither Booth nor Gibson discusses in any detail the history of the ways in which readers have been called on to relate to texts before them. Neither do Robert Scholes and Robert Kellogg in their invaluable work, *The Nature of Narrative:* they skirt the subject in their chapter on "The Oral Heritage of Written Narrative,"[4] but remain chiefly concerned with the oral performer, the writer, and techniques, rather than with the recipient of the message. Yet a great many of the studies noted here as well as many others, among which might be mentioned Norman N. Holland's *The Dynamics of Literary Response* (1968), suggest the time is ripe for a study of the history of readers and their enforced roles, for they show that we have ample phenomenological and literary sophistication to manage many of the complications involved.

So long as verbal communication is reduced to a simplistic mechanistic model which supposedly moves corpuscular units of something labeled "information" back and forth along tracks between two termini, there is of course no special problem with those who assimilate the written or printed word. For the speaker, the audience is in front of him. For the writer, the audience is simply further away, in time or space or both. A surface inscribed with information can neutralize time by preserving the information and conquer space by moving the information to its recipient over distances that sound cannot traverse. If, however, we put aside this alluring but deceptively neat and mechanistic mock-up and look at verbal communication in its human actuality, noting that words consist not of corpuscular units but of evanescent sound and that, as Maurice Merleau-Ponty has pointed out,[5] words are never fully determined in their abstract signification but have meaning only with relation to man's body and to its interaction with its surroundings, problems with the writer's audience begin to show themselves. Writing calls for difficult, and often quite mysterious, skills. Except for a small corps of highly trained writers, most persons could get into written form few if any of the complicated and nuanced meanings they regularly convey orally. One reason is evident: the spoken word is part of present actuality and has its meaning established by the total situation in which it comes into being. Context for the spoken word is simply present, centered in the person speaking and the one or ones to whom he addresses himself and to whom he is related existentially in terms of the circumambient actuality.[6] But the meaning caught in writing comes provided with no such present circumambient actuality, at least normally. (One might except special cases of written exchanges between persons present to one another physically but with oral channels blocked: two deaf persons, for example, or two persons who use different variants of Chinese and are orally incomprehensible to one another but can communicate through the same written characters, which carry virtually the same meaning though they are sounded differently in the different varieties of Chinese.)

Such special cases apart, the person to whom the writer addresses himself normally is not present at all. Moreover, with certain special exceptions such as those just suggested, he must not be present. I am writing a book which will be read by thousands, or, I modestly hope, by tens of thousands. So, please, get out of the room. I want to be alone. Writing normally calls for some kind of withdrawal.

How does the writer give body to the audience for whom he writes? It would be fatuous to think that the writer addressing a so-called "general audience" tries to imagine his readers individually. A well-known novelist friend of mine only laughed when I asked him if, as he was writing a novel, he imagined his real readers—the woman on the subway deep in his book, the student in his room, the businessman on a vacation, the scholar in his study. There is no need for a novelist to feel his "audience" this way at all. It may be, of course, that at one time or another he imagines himself addressing one or another real person. But not all his readers in their particularities. Practically speaking, of course, and under the insistent urging of editors and publishers, he does have to take into consideration the real social, economic, and psychological state of possible readers. He has to write a book that real persons will buy and read. But I am speaking—or writing—here of the "audience" that fires the writer's imagination. If it consists of the real persons who he hopes will buy his book, they are not these persons in an untransmuted state.[7]

Although I have thus far followed the common practice in using the term "audience," it is really quite misleading to think of a writer as dealing with an "audience," even though certain considerations may at times oblige us to think this way. More properly, a writer addresses readers—only, he does not quite "address" them either: he writes to or for them. The orator has before him an audience which is a true audience, a collectivity. "Audience" is a collective noun. There is no such collective noun for readers, nor, so far as I am able to puzzle out, can there be. "Readers" is a plural. Readers do not form a collectivity, acting here and now on one another and on the speaker as members of an audience do. We can devise a singularized concept for them, it is true, such as "readership." We can say that the *Reader's Digest* has a readership of I don't know how many millions—more than it is comfortable to think about, at any rate. But "readership" is not a collective noun. It is an abstraction in a way that "audience" is not.

The contrast between hearing and reading (running the eye over signals that encode sound) can be caught if we imagine a speaker addressing an audience equipped with texts. At one point, the speaker asks the members of the audience all to read silently a paragraph out of the text. The audience immediately fragments. It is no longer a unit. Each individual retires into his own microcosm. When the readers look up again, the speaker has to gather them into a collectivity once more. This is true even if he is the author of the text they are reading.

To sense more fully the writer's problem with his so-called audience let us envision a class of students asked to write on the subject to which schoolteachers, jaded by summer, return compulsively every autumn: "How I Spent My Summer Vacation." The teacher makes the easy assumption, inviting and plausible but false, that the chief problem of a boy and a girl in writing is finding a subject actually part of his or her real life. In-close subject matter is supposed to solve the problem of invention. Of course it does not. The problem is not simply what to say but also whom to say it to. Say? The student is not talking. He is writing. No one is listening. There is no feedback. Where does he find his "audience"? He has to make his readers up, fictionalize them.

If the student knew what he was up against better than the teacher giving the assignment seemingly does, he might ask, "Who wants to know?" The answer is not easy. Grandmother? He never tells grandmother. His father or mother? There's a lot he would not want to tell them, that's sure. His classmates? Imagine the reception if he suggested they sit down and listen quietly while he told them how he spent his summer vacation. The teacher? There is no conceivable setting in which he could imagine telling his teacher how he spent his summer vacation other than in writing this paper, so that writing for the teacher does not solve his problems but only restates them. In fact, most young people do not tell anybody how they spent their summer vacation, much less write down how they spent it. The subject may be in-close; the use it is to be put to remains unfamiliar, strained, bizarre.

How does the student solve the problem? In many cases, in a way somewhat like the following. He has read, let us say, *The Adventures of Tom Sawyer*. He knows what this book felt like, how the voice in it addressed its readers, how the narrator hinted to his readers that they were related to him and he to them, whoever they may actually have been or may be. Why not pick up that voice and, with it, its audience? Why not make like Samuel Clemens and write for whomever Samuel Clemens was writing for? This even makes it possible to write for his teacher—itself likely to be a productive ploy—whom he certainly has never been quite able to figure out. But he knows his teacher has read *Tom Sawyer*, has heard the voice in the book, and could therefore obviously make like a *Tom Sawyer* reader. His problem is solved, and he goes ahead. The subject matter now makes little difference, provided that it is something like Mark Twain's and that it interests him on some grounds or other. Material in-close to his real life is not essential, though, of course, it might be welcome now that he has a way to process it.

If the writer succeeds in writing, it is generally because he can fictionalize in his imagination an audience he has learned to know not from daily life but from earlier writers who were fictionalizing in their imagination audiences they had learned to know in still earlier writers, and so on back to the dawn of written narrative. If and when he becomes truly adept, an "original writer," he can alter it. Thus it was that Samuel Clemens in *Life on the Mississippi* could not merely project the audience that the many journalistic writers about the Midwestern rivers had brought into being, but could also shape it to his own demands. If you had read Isaiah Sellers, you could read Mark Twain, but with a difference. You had to assume a part in a less owlish, more boisterous setting, in which Clemens' caustic humor masks the uncertainty of his seriousness. Mark Twain's reader is asked to take a special kind of hold on himself and on life.

II

These reflections suggest, or are meant to suggest, that there exists a tradition in fictionalizing audiences that is a component part of literary tradition in the sense in which literary tradition is discussed in T. S. Eliot's "Tradition and the Individual Talent." A history of the ways audiences have been called on to fictionalize themselves would be a correlative of the history of literary genres and literary works, and indeed of culture itself.

What do we mean by saying the audience is a fiction? Two things at least. First, that the writer must construct in his imagination, clearly or vaguely, an audience cast in some sort of role—entertainment seekers, reflective sharers of experience (as those who listen to Conrad's Marlow), inhabitants of a lost and remembered world of prepubertal latency (readers of Tolkien's hobbit stories), and so on. Second, we mean that the audience must correspondingly fictionalize itself. A reader has to play the role in which the author has cast him, which seldom coincides with his role in the rest of actual life. An office worker on a bus reading a novel of Thomas Hardy is listening to a voice which is not that of any real person in the real setting around him. He is playing the role demanded of him by this person speaking in a quite special way from the book, which is not the subway and is not quite "Wessex" either, though it speaks of Wessex. Readers over the ages have had to learn this game of literacy, how to conform themselves to the projections of the writers they read, or at least how to operate in terms of these projections. They have to know how to play the game of being a member of an audience that "really" does not exist. And they have to adjust when the rules change, even though no rules thus far have ever been published and even though the changes in the unpublished rules are themselves for the most part only implied.

A history of literature could be written in terms of the ways in which audiences have successively been fictionalized from the time when writing broke away from oral performance, for, just as each genre grows out of what went before it, so each new role that readers are made to assume is related to previous roles. Putting aside for the moment the question of what fictionalizing may be called for in the case of the audience for oral performance, we can note that when script first came on the scene, the fictionalizing of readers was relatively simple. Written narrative at first was merely a transcription of oral narrative, or what was imagined as oral narrative, and it assumed some kind of oral singer's audience, even when being read. The transcribers of the *Iliad* and the *Odyssey* presumably imagined an audience of real listeners in attendance on an oral singer, and readers of those works to this day do well if they can imagine themselves hearing a singer of tales.[8] How these texts and other oral performances were in fact originally set down in writing remains puzzling, but the transcribers certainly were not composing in writing, but rather recording with minimal alteration what a singer was singing or was imagined to be singing.

Even so, a scribe had to fictionalize in a way a singer did not, for a real audience was not really present before the scribe, so it would seem, although it is just possible that at times one may have been (Lord, pp. 125–128). But, as transcription of oral performance or imagined oral performance gave way gradually to composition in writing, the situation changed. No reader today imagines *Second Skin* as a work that John Hawkes is reciting extempore to a group of auditors, even though passages from it may be impressive when read aloud.

III

We have noted that the roles readers are called on to play evolve without any explicit rules or directives. How readers pick up the implicit signals and how writers change the rules can be illustrated by examining a passage from a specialist in unpublished directives for readers, Ernest Hemingway. The passage is the opening of *A Farewell to Arms*. At the start of my comment on the passage, it will be clear that I am borrowing a good deal from Walker Gibson's highly discerning book on modern American prose styles, *Tough, Sweet, and Stuffy*.[9] The Hemingway passage follows:

> In the late summer of that year we lived in a house in a village that looked across the river and the plain to the mountains. In the bed of the river there were pebbles and boulders, dry and white in the sun, and the water was clear and swiftly moving and blue in the channels.

Hemingway's style is often characterized as straightforward, unadorned, terse, lacking in qualifiers, close-lipped; and it is all these things. But none of them were peculiar to Hemingway when his writing began to command attention. A feature more distinctive of Hemingway here and elsewhere is the way he fictionalizes the reader, and this fictionalizing is often signaled largely by his use of the definite article as a special kind of qualifier or of the demonstrative pronoun "that," of which the definite article is simply an attenuation.

"The late summer of that year," the reader begins. What year? The reader gathers that there is no need to say. "Across the river." What river? The reader apparently is supposed to know. "And the plain." What plain? "*The* plain"—remember? "To the mountains." What mountains? Do I have to tell you? Of course not. *The* mountains—*those* mountains we know. We have somehow been there together. Who? You, my reader, and I. The reader—every reader—is being cast in the role of a close companion of the writer. This is the game he must play here with Hemingway, not always exclusively or totally, but generally, to a greater or lesser extent. It is one reason why the writer is tight-lipped. Description as such would bore a boon companion. What description there is comes in the guise of pointing, in verbal gestures, recalling humdrum, familiar details. "In the bed of the river there were pebbles and boulders, dry and white in the sun." The known world, accepted and accepting. Not presentation, but recall. The writer needs only to point, for what he wants to tell you about is not the scene at all but his feelings. These, too, he treats as something you really had somehow shared, though you might not have been quite aware of it at the time. He can tell you what was going on inside him and count on sympathy, for you were there. You *know*. The reader here has a well-marked role assigned him. He is a companion-in-arms, somewhat later become a confidant. It is a flattering role. Hemingway readers are encouraged to cultivate high self-esteem.

The effect of the definite article in Hemingway here is quite standard and readily explicable. Normally, in English, we are likely to make an initial reference to an individual object by means of the indefinite article and to bring in the definite only subsequently. "Yesterday on the street *a* man came up to me, and when I stopped in my stride *the* man said. . . ." "A" is a modified form of the term "one," a kind of singular of "some." "A man" means "one man" (of many real or possible men). The indefinite article tacitly acknowledges the existence or possibility of a number of individuals beyond the immediate range of reference and indicates that from among them one is selected. Once we have indicated that we are concerned not with all but with one-out-of-many, we train the definite article or pointer article on the object of our attention.[10] The definite article thus commonly signals some previous, less definite acquaintanceship. Hemingway's exclusion of indefinite in favor of definite articles signals the reader that he is from the first on familiar ground. He shares the author's familiarity with the subject matter. The reader must pretend he has known much of it before.

Hemingway's concomitant use of the demonstrative distancing pronoun "that" parallels his use of "the." For "the" is only an attenuated "that." It is a modified form of the demonstrative pronoun that replaced the original Old English definite article "seo." Both hold their referents at a distance, "that" typically at a somewhat greater distance than "the." *That* mountain you see ten miles away is indicated there on *the* map on *the* wall. If we wish to think of the map as close, we would say, "*This* map on this wall." In distancing their objects, both "that" and "the" can tend to bring together the speaker and the one spoken to. "That" commonly means that-over-there at a distance from you-and-me here, and "the" commonly means much the same. These terms thus can easily implement the Hemingway relationship: you-and-me.

This you-and-me effect of the distancing demonstrative pronoun and the definite article can be seen perhaps more spectacularly in romance etymology. The words for "the" in the romance languages come from the Latin word *ille, illa, illud*, which yields in various romance tongues, *il, le, la, el, lo*, and their cognates. *Ille* is a distancing demonstrative in Latin: it means "that-over-there-away-from-you-and-me" and stands in contrastive opposition to another Latin demonstrative which has no counterpart in English, *iste, ista, istud*, which means "that-over-there-by-you" (and thus can readily become pejorative—"that-little-no-account-thing-of-yours"). *Ille* brings together the speaker and the one spoken to by contrast with the distanced object; *iste* distances from the speaker the one spoken to as well as the object. *Ille* yields the romance definite articles, which correspond quite closely in function to the English "the," and thus advertises the close tie between "the" and "that."

Could readers of an earlier age have managed the Hemingway relationship, the you-and-me relationship, marked by tight-lipped empathy based on shared experience? Certainly from antiquity the reader or hearer of an epic was plunged in medias res. But this does not mean he was cast as the author's boon companion. It means rather that he was plunged into the middle of a narrative sequence and told about antecedent events only later. A feeling of camaraderie between companions-in-arms is conveyed in epics, but the companions-in-arms are fictional characters; they are not the reader or hearer and the narrator. "*Forsan et haec olim meminisse iuvabit*"—these words in the *Aeneid*, "perhaps some day it will help to recall these very things," are spoken by Aeneas to his companions when they are undergoing a period of hardships. They are one character's words to other characters, not Virgil's words to his hearer or reader. One might urge further that, like Hemingway's reader, the reader or hearer of an epic—most typically, of an oral folk epic—was hearing stories with which he was already acquainted, that he was thus on familiar ground. He was, but not in the sense that he was forced to pretend he had somehow lived as an alter ego of the narrator. His familiarity with the material was not a pretense at all, not a role, but a simple fact. Typically, the epic audience had heard the story, or something very much like it, before.

The role in which Hemingway casts the reader is somewhat different not only from anything these situations in early literature demand but also from anything in the time immediately before Hemingway. This is what makes Hemingway's writing interesting to literary historians. But Hemingway's demands on the reader are by no means entirely without antecedents. The existence of antecedents is indicated by the fact that Hemingway was assimilated by relatively unskilled readers with very little fuss. He does not recast the reader in a disturbingly novel role. By contrast, the role in which Faulkner casts the reader is a far greater departure from preceding roles than is Hemingway's. Faulkner demands more skilled and daring readers, and consequently had far fewer at first, and has relatively fewer even today when the Faulkner role for readers is actually taught in school. (Perhaps we should say the Faulkner roles.)

No one, so far as I know, has worked up a history of the readers' roles that prepared for that prescribed by Hemingway. But one can discern significantly similar demands on readers beginning as early as Addison and Steele, who assume a new fashionable intimacy among readers themselves and between all readers and the writer, achieved largely by casting readers as well as writer in the role of coffeehouse habitués. Defoe develops in his own way comparable author-reader intimacy. The roots of these eighteenth-century intimacies are journalistic, and from earlier journalism they push out later in Hemingway's own day into the world of sportswriters and war correspondents, of whom Hemingway himself was one. With the help of print and the near instantaneousness implemented by electronic media (the telegraph first, later radio teletype and electronic transmission of photography), the newspaper writer could bring his reader into his own on-the-spot experience, availing himself in both sports and war of the male's strong sense of camaraderie based on shared hardships. Virgil's *forsan et haec olim meminisse iuvabit* once more. But Virgil was telling a story of the days of old and, as has been seen, the camaraderie was among characters in the story, Aeneas and his men. Sports and war journalism are about the here and now, and, if the story can be got to the reader quickly, the camaraderie can be easily projected between the narrator and the reader. The reader is close enough temporally and photographically to the event for him to feel like a vicarious participant. In journalism Hemingway had an established foundation on which to build, if not one highly esteemed in snobbish literary circles. And he in turn has been built upon by those who have come later. Gibson has shown how much the style of *Time* magazine is an adaptation of Hemingway (pp. 48–54). To Hemingway's writer-reader camaraderie *Time* adds omniscience, solemnly "reporting," for example, in eyewitness style, the behavior and feelings of a chief of state in his own bedroom as he answers an emergency night telephone call and afterward returns to sleep. Hemingway encouraged his readers in high self-esteem. *Time* provides its readers, on a regular weekly basis, companionship with the all-knowing gods.

When we look the other way down the corridors of time to the period before the coffeehouses and the beginnings of intimate journalism, we find that readers have had to be trained gradually to play the game Hemingway engages them in. What if, *per impossibile*, a Hemingway story projecting the reader's role we have attended to here had turned up in Elizabethan England? It would probably have been laughed out of court by readers totally unable to adapt to its demands upon them. It would certainly have collided with representative literary theory, as propounded for example by Sir Philip Sidney in *The Defense of Poesie*. For Sidney and most of his age, poetry—that is to say, literature generally—had as its aim to please, but even more basically to teach, at least in the sense that it gave the reader to know what he did not know before. The Hemingway convention that the reader had somehow been through it all before with the writer would have been to Sidney's age at best confusing and at worst wrongheaded. One could argue that the Hemingway narrator would be telling the reader at least something he did not know before—that is, largely, the feelings of the narrator. But even this revelation, as we have seen, implies in Hemingway a covert awareness on the part of the reader, a deep sympathy or empathy of a basically romantic, nonpublic sort, grounded in intimacy. Sidney would have sent Hemingway back to his writing table to find something newer to write about, or to find a way of casting his material in a fresher-sounding form.

Another, and related, feature of the Hemingway style would have repelled sixteenth-century readers: the addiction to the "the" and "that" to the calculated exclusion of most descriptive qualifiers. There is a deep irony here. For in the rhetorical world that persisted from prehistoric times to the age of romanticism, descriptive qualifiers were commonly epithetic, expected qualifiers. The first chapter of Sidney's *Arcadia* (1590) presents the reader with "the hopeless shepheard," the "friendly rival," "the necessary food," "natural rest," "flowery fields," "the extreme heat of summer," and countless other souvenirs of a country every rhetorician had trod many times before. Is this not making the reader a recaller of shared experience much as Hemingway's use of "the" and "that" does? Not at all in the same way. The sixteenth-century reader recalls the familiar accouterments of literature, which are the familiar accouterments or commonplaces also of sculpture, painting, and all art. These are matters of shared public acquaintanceship, not of private experience. The sixteenth-century reader is walking through land all educated men know. He is not made to pretend he knows these familiar objects because he once shared their presence with this particular author, as a Hemingway reader is made to pretend. In Sidney, there is none of the you-and-I-know-even-if-others-don't ploy.

IV

To say that earlier readers would have been nonplussed at Hemingway's demands on them is not to say that earlier readers did not have special roles to play or that authors did not have their own problems in devising and signaling what the roles were. A few cases might be instanced here.

First of all, it is only honest to admit that even an oral narrator calls on his audience to fictionalize itself to some extent. The invocation to the Muse is a signal to the audience to put on the epic-listener's cap. No Greek, after all, ever talked the kind of language that Homer sang, although Homer's contemporaries could understand it well enough. Even today we do not talk in other contexts quite the kind of language in which we tell fairy stories to children. "Once upon a time," we begin. The phrase lifts you out of the real world. Homer's language is "once upon a time" language. It establishes a fictional world. But the fictionalizating in oral epic is directly limited by live interaction, as real conversation is. A real audience controls the narrator's behavior immediately. Students of mine from Ghana and from western Ireland have reported to me what I have read and heard from many other sources: a given story may take a skilled or "professional" storyteller anywhere from ten minutes to an hour and a half, depending on how he finds the audience relates to him on a given occasion. "You always knew ahead of time what he was going to say, but you never knew how long it would take him to say it," my Irish informant reported. The teller reacts directly to audience response. Oral storytelling is a two-way street.

Written or printed narrative is not two-way, at least in the short run. Readers' reactions are remote and initially conjectural, however great their ultimate effects on sales. We should think more about the problems that the need to fictionalize audiences creates for writers. Chaucer, for example, had a problem with the conjectural readers of the *Canterbury Tales*. There was no established tradition in English for many of the stories, and certainly none at all for a collection of such stories. What does Chaucer do? He sets the stories in what, from a literary-structural point of view, is styled a frame. A group of pilgrims going to Canterbury tell stories to one another: the pilgrimage frames the individual narratives. In terms of signals to his readers, we could put it another way: Chaucer simply tells his readers how they are to fictionalize themselves. He starts by telling them that there is a group of pilgrims doing what real people do, going to a real place, Canterbury. The reader is to imagine himself in their company and join the fun. Of course this means fictionalizing himself as a member of a nonexistent group. But the fictionalizing is facilitated by Chaucer's clear frame-story directives. And to minimize the fiction by maximizing real life, Chaucer installs himself, the narrator, as one of the pilgrims. His reader-role problem is effectively solved. Of course, he got the idea pretty much from antecedent writers faced with similar problems, notably Boccaccio. But he naturalizes the frame in the geography of southeast England.

The frame story was in fact quite common around Europe at this period. Audience readjustment was a major feature of mature medieval culture, a culture more focused on reading than any earlier culture had been. Would it not be helpful to discuss the frame device as a contrivance all but demanded by the literary economy of the time rather than to expatiate on it as a singular stroke of genius? For this it certainly was not, unless we define genius as the ability to make the most of an awkward situation. The frame is really a rather clumsy gambit, although a good narrator can bring it off pretty well when he has to. It hardly has widespread immediate appeal for ordinary readers today.

In the next period of major audience readjustment, John Lyly's *Euphues* and even more Thomas Nashe's *The Unfortunate Traveler* can be viewed as attempts to work out a credible role in which Elizabethan readers could cast themselves for the new medium of print. Script culture had preserved a heavy oral residue signaled by its continued fascination with rhetoric, which had always been orally grounded, a fascination that script culture passed on to early print culture. But the new medium was changing the noetic economy, and, while rhetoric remained strong in the curriculum, strain was developing. Lyly reacts by hyperrhetoricizing his text, tongue-in-cheek, drowning the audience and himself in the highly controlled gush being purveyed by the schools. The signals to the reader are unmistakable, if unconsciously conveyed: play the role of the rhetorician's listener for all you are worth (*Euphues* is mostly speeches), remembering that the response the rhetorician commands is a serious and difficult one—it takes hard work to assimilate the baroque complexity of Lyly's text—but also that there is something awry in all the isocola, apophonemata, and antisagogai, now that the reader is so very much more a reader than a listener. Such aural iconographic equipment had been functional in oral management of knowledge, implementing storage and recall, but with print it was becoming incidental—which is, paradoxically, why it could be so fantastically elaborated.

Nashe shows the same uneasiness, and more, regarding the reader's role. For in the phantasmagoria of styles in *The Unfortunate Traveler* he tries out his reader in every role he can think of: whoever takes on Nashe's story must become a listener bending his ear to political orations, a participant in scholastic disputations, a hanger-on at goliardic Woodstocks, a camp follower fascinated by merry tales, a simpering reader of Italian revenge stories and sixteenth-century true confessions, a fellow conspirator in a world of picaresque cheats, and much more.

Nashe gives a foretaste of other trial-and-error procedures by which recipes were to be developed for the reader of the narrative prose works we now call novels. Such recipes were being worked out in other languages, too: in French notably by Rabelais, whose calls for strenuous shifts in the reader's stance Nashe emulated, and in Spanish by Cervantes, who explores all sorts of ironic possibilties in the reader's relationship to the text, incorporating into the second part of *Don Quixote* the purported reactions of readers and of the tale's characters to the first part of the work. Apuleius' *Golden Ass*, multiplied, with major audience adjustments, in English down through *Tom Jones:* the unsettled role of the reader was mirrored and made acceptable by keeping the hero himself on the move. Samuel Richardson has his readers pretend they have access to other persons' letters, out of which a story emerges. Journals and diaries also multiplied as narrative devices: the reader becoming a snooper or a collector of seeming trivia that turn out not to be trivia at all. Ultimately, Laurence Sterne is able to involve his reader not only in the procreation of his hero Tristram Shandy but also in the hero's writing of his autobiography, in which pages are left blank for the reader to put his "own fancy in." The audience-speaker interaction of oral narrative here shows the reader in a new ironic guise—somewhat destructive of the printed book, toward which, as an object obtruding in the person-to-person world of human communication, the eighteenth century was feeling some ambiguous hostilities, as Swift's work also shows.

The problem of reader adjustment in prose narrative was in great part due to the difficulty that narrators long had in feeling themselves as other than oral performers. It is significant that, although the drama had been tightly plotted from classical antiquity (the drama is the first genre controlled by writing, and by the same token, paradoxically, the first to make deliberate use of colloquial speech), until the late eighteenth century there is in the whole Western world (and I suspect in the East as well) no sizable prose narrative, so far as I know, with a tidy structure comparable to that known for two millennia in the drama, moving through closely controlled tensions to a climax, with reversal and denouement. This is not to say that until the modern novel emerged narrative was not organized, or that earlier narrators were trying to write modern novels but regularly fell short of their aims. (Scholes and Kellogg have warned in *The Nature of Narrative* against this retroactive analysis of literary history.) But it is to say that narrative had not fully accommodated itself to print or, for that matter, to writing, which drama had long before learned to exploit. *Tom Jones* is highly programmed, but in plot it is still episodic, as all prose narrative had been all the way back through the Hellenic romances. With Jane Austen we are over the hurdle: but Jane Austen was a woman and women were not normally trained in the Latin-based, academic, rhetorical, oral tradition. They were not trained speechmakers who had turned belatedly to chirography and print.

Even by Jane Austen's time, however, the problem of the reader's role in prose narrative was by no means entirely solved. Nervousness regarding the role of the reader registers everywhere in the "dear reader" regularly invoked in fiction well through the nineteenth century. The reader had to be reminded (and the narrator, too) that the recipient of the story was indeed a reader—not a listener, not one of the crowd, but an individual isolated with a text. The relationship of audience-fictionalizing to modern narrative prose is very mysterious, and I do not pretend to explain it all here, but only to point to some of the strange problems often so largely overlooked in the relationship. Tightly plotted prose narrative is the correlative of the audiences fictionalized for the first time with the aid of print, and the demands of such narrative on readers were new.

V

The present reflections have focused on written fictional narrative as a kind of paradigm for the fictionalizing of writers' "audiences" or readers. But what has been said about fictional narrative applies ceteris paribus to all writing. With the possible[11] exception noted above of persons in the presence of one another communicating by writing because of inability to communicate orally, the writer's audience is always a fiction. The historian, the scholar or scientist, and the simple letter writer all fictionalize their audiences, casting them in a made-up role and calling on them to play the role assigned.

Because history is always a selection and interpretation of those incidents the individual historian believes will account better than other incidents for some explanation of a totality, history partakes quite evidently of the nature of poetry. It is a making. The historian does not make the elements out of which he constructs history, in the sense that he must build with events that have come about independently of him, but his selection of events and his way of verbalizing them so that they can be dealt with as "facts," and consequently the overall pattern he reports, are all his own creation, a making. No two historians say exactly the same thing about the same given events, even though they are both telling the truth. There is no *one* thing to say about anything; there are many things that can be said.

The oral "historian" captures events in terms of themes (the challenge, the duel, the arming of the hero, the battle, and so on), and formulas (the brave soldier, the faithful wife, the courageous people, the suffering people), which are provided to him by tradition and are the only ways he knows to talk about what is going on among men. Processed through these conventions, events become assimilable by his auditors and "interesting" to them. The writer of history is less reliant on formulas (or it may be he has such a variety of them that it is hard to tell that is what they are). But he comes to his material laden with themes in much vaster quantity than can be available to any oral culture. Without themes, there would be no way to deal with events. It is impossible to tell everything that went on in the Pentagon even in one day: how many stenographers dropped how many sheets of paper into how many wastebaskets when and where, what they all said to each other, and so on ad infinitum. These are not the themes historians normally use to write what really "happened." They write about material by exploiting it in terms of themes that are "significant" or "interesting." But what is "significant" depends on what kind of history you are writing—national political history, military history, social history, economic history, personal biography, global history. What is significant and, perhaps even more, what is "interesting" also depends on the readers and their interaction with the historian. This interaction in turn depends on the role in which the historian casts his readers. Although so far as I know we have no history of readers of history, we do know enough about historiography to be aware that one could well be worked out. The open-faced way the reader figures in Samuel Eliot Morison's writings is different from the more conspiratorial way he figures in Perry Miller's and both are quite different from the way the reader figures in Herodotus.

Scholarly works show comparable evolution in the roles they enforce on their readers. Aristotle's works, as has often been pointed out, are an agglomerate of texts whose relationship to his own holographs, to his student's notes, and to the work of later editors will remain always more or less a puzzle. Much of Aristotle consists of school logia or sayings, comparable to the logia or sayings of Jesus to his followers of which the Gospels chiefly consist. Aristotle's logia were addressed to specific individuals whom he knew, rather than simply to the wide world. Even his more patently written compositions retain a personal orientation: his work on ethics is the *Nicomachean Ethics*, named for his son. This means that the reader of Aristotle, if he wants to understand his text, will do well to cast himself in the role of one of Aristotle's actual listeners.

The practice of orienting a work, and thereby its readers, by writing it at least purportedly for a specific person or persons continues well through the Renaissance. The first edition of Peter Ramus' *Dialectic* was the French *Dialectique de Pierre de la Ramée à Charles de Lorraine Cardinal, son Mécène* (Paris, 1555), and the first edition of the far more widely used Latin version preserved the same personal address: *Dialectici Libri Duo . . . ad Carolum Lotharingum Cardinalem* (Paris, 1556). Sidney's famous romance or epic is *The Countess of Pembroke's Arcadia*. Often in Renaissance printed editions a galaxy of prefaces and dedicatory epistles and poems establishes a whole cosmos of discourse which, among other things, signals the reader what roles he is to assume. Sidney's, Spenser's, and Milton's works, for example, are heavily laden with introductory material—whole books have been devoted to the study of Sidney's introductory matter alone.

Until recent times the rhetorical tradition, which, with the allied dialectical or logical tradition, dominated most written as well as oral expression, helped in the fictionalizing of the audience of learned works in a generic but quite real way. Rhetoric fixed knowledge in agonistic structures.

For this reason, the roles of the reader of learned works until fairly recent times were regularly more polemic than those demanded of the reader today. Until the age of romanticism reconstituted psychological structures, academic teaching of all subjects had been more or less polemic dominated by the ubiquitous rhetorical culture, and proceeding typically by proposing and attacking theses in highly partisan fashion. (The academic world today preserves much of the nomenclature, such as "thesis" and "defense" of theses, but less of the programed fighting spirit, which its members let loose on the social order more than on their subject matter or colleagues.) From Augustine through St. Thomas Aquinas and Christian Wolff, writers of treatises generally proceeded in adversary fashion, their readers being cast as participants in rhetorical contests or in dialectical scholastic disputations.

Today the academic reader's role is harder to describe. Some of its complexities can be hinted at by attending to certain fictions which writers of learned articles and books generally observe and which have to do with reader status. There are some things the writer must assume that every reader knows because virtually every reader does. It would be intolerable to write, "Shakespeare, a well-known Elizabethan playwright," not only in a study on Renaissance drama but even in one on marine ecology. Otherwise the reader's role would be confused. There are other things that established fiction holds all readers must know, even though everyone is sure all readers do not know them: these are handled by writing, "as everyone knows," and then inserting what it is that not quite everyone really does know. Other things the reader can safely be assumed not to know without threatening the role he is playing. These gradations of admissible ignorance vary from one level of scholarly writing to another, and since individual readers vary in knowledge and competence, the degree to which they must fictionalize themselves to match the level of this or that reading will vary. Knowledge of the degrees of admissible ignorance for readers is absolutely essential if one is to publish successfully. This knowledge is one of the things that separates the beginning graduate student or even the brilliant undergraduate from the mature scholar. It takes time to get a feel for the roles that readers can be expected comfortably to play in the modern academic world.

Other kinds of writing without end could be examined in our reflections here on the fictionalizing of readers' roles. For want of time and, frankly, for want of wider reflection, I shall mention only two others. These are genres that do not seem to fall under the rule that the writer's audience is always a fiction since the "audience" appears to be simply one clearly determined person, who hardly need fictionalize himself. The first of the genres is the familiar letter and the second the diary.

The case of the letter reader is really simple enough. Although by writing a letter you are somehow pretending the reader is present while you are writing, you cannot address him as you do in oral speech. You must fictionalize him, make him into a special construct. Whoever saluted a friend on the street with "Dear John"? And if you try the informal horrors, "Hi!" or "Greetings!" or whatever else, the effect is not less but more artificial. You are reminding him that you wish you were not writing him a letter, but, then, why are you? There is no way out. The writer has to set up another relationship to the reader and has to set the reader in a relationship to the writer different from that of nonchirographical personal contact.

The dimensions of fiction in a letter are many. First, you have no way of adjusting to the friend's real mood as you would be able to adjust in oral conversation. You have to conjecture or confect a mood that he is likely to be in or can assume when the letter comes. And, when it does come, he has to put on the mood that you have fictionalized for him. Some of this sort of adjustment goes on in oral communication, too, but it develops in a series of exchanges: a tentative guess at another's mood, a reaction from him, another from yourself, another from him, and you know about where you are. Letters do not have this normal give-and-take: they are one-way movements. Moreover, the precise relationships of writer to reader in letters vary tremendously from age to age even in intensively role-playing correspondence. No one today can capture exactly the fiction in Swift's *Journal to Stella*, though it is informative to try to reconstruct it as fully as possible, for the relationships of children to oldsters and even of man to woman have subtly altered, as have also a vast mesh of other social relationships which the *Journal to Stella* involves.

The epistolary situation is made tolerable by conventions, and learning to write letters is largely a matter of learning what the writer-reader conventions are. The paradoxes they involve were well caught some years ago in a Marx Brothers movie—if I recall correctly where the incident occurred. Letters start with "Dear Sir." An owlish, bemused businessman calls his secretary in. "Take this letter to Joseph Smithers," he directs."You know his address. 'Dear Sir: You dirty rat . . . .' " The fiction of the exordium designed to create the *lector benevolens* is first honored and then immediately wiped out.

The audience of the diarist is even more encased in fictions. What is easier, one might argue, than addressing oneself? As those who first begin a diary often find out, a great many things are easier. The reasons why are not hard to unearth. First of all, we do not normally talk to ourselves—certainly not in long, involved sentences and paragraphs. Second, the diarist pretending to be talking to himself has also, since he is writing, to pretend he is somehow not there. And to what self is he talking? To the self he imagines he is? Or would like to be? Or really thinks he is? Or thinks other people think he is? To himself as he is now? Or as he will probably or ideally be twenty years hence? If he addresses not himself but "Dear Diary," who in the world is "Dear Diary"? What role does this imply? And why do more women than men keep diaries? Or if they don't (they really do—or did), why do people think they do? When did the diary start? The history of diaries, I believe, has yet to be written. Possibly more than the history of any other genre, it will have to be history of the fictionalizing of readers.

The case of the diary, which at first blush would seem to fictionalize the reader least but in many ways probably fictionalizes him or her most, brings into full view the fundamental deep paradox of the activity we call writing, at least when writing moves from its initial account-keeping purposes to other more elaborate concerns more directly and complexly involving human persons in their manifold dealings with one another. We are familiar enough today with talk about masks—in literary criticism, psychology, phenomenology, and elsewhere. Personae, earlier generally thought of as applying to characters in a play or other fiction (dramatis personae), are imputed with full justification to narrators and, since all discourse has roots in narrative, to everyone who uses language. Often in the complexities of present-day fiction, with its "unreliable narrator" encased in layer after layer of persiflage and irony, the masks within masks defy complete identification. This is a game fiction writers play, harder now than ever.

But the masks of the narrator are

matched, if not one-for-one, in equally complex fashion by the masks that readers must learn to wear. To whom is *Finnegans Wake* addressed? Who is the reader supposed to be? We hesitate to say—certainly I hesitate to say—because we have thought so little about the reader's role as such, about his masks, which are as manifold in their own way as those of the writer.

Masks are inevitable in all human communication, even oral. Role playing is both different from actuality and an entry into actuality: play and actuality (the world of "work") are dialectically related to one another. From the very beginning, an infant becomes an actual speaker by playing at being a speaker, much as a person who cannot swim, after developing some ancillary skills, one day plays at swimming and finds that he is swimming in truth. But oral communication, which is built into existential actuality more directly than written, has within it a momentum that works for the removal of masks. Lovers try to strip off all masks. And in all communication, insofar as it is related to actual experience, there must be a movement of love. Those who have loved over many years may reach a point where almost all masks are gone. But never all. The lover's plight is tied to the fact that every one of us puts on a mask to address himself, too. Such masks to relate ourselves to ourselves we also try to put aside, and with wisdom and grace we to some extent succeed in casting them off. When the last mask comes off, sainthood is achieved, and the vision of God. But this can only be with death.

No matter what pitch of frankness, directness, or authenticity he may strive for, the writer's mask and the reader's are less removable than those of the oral communicator and his hearer. For writing is itself an indirection. Direct communication by script is impossible. This makes writing not less but more interesting, although perhaps less noble than speech. For man lives largely by indirection, and only beneath the indirections that sustain him is his true nature to be found. Writing, alone, however, will never bring us truly beneath to the actuality. Present-day confessional writing—and it is characteristic of our present age that virtually all serious writing tends to the confessional, even drama—likes to make an issue of stripping off all masks. Observant literary critics and psychiatrists, however, do not need to be told that confessional literature is likely to wear the most masks of all. It is hard to bare your soul in any literary genre. And it is hard to write outside a genre. T. S. Eliot has made the point that so far as he knows, great love poetry is never written solely for the ear of the beloved (p. 97), although what a lover speaks with his lips is often indeed for the ear of the beloved and of no other. The point is well made, even though it was made in writing.

NOTES

1. In a briefer adaptation, this paper was read at Cambridge University, 24 Aug. 1972, at the Twelfth International Congress of the International Federation for Modern Languages and Literatures. At the Center for Advanced Study in the Behavioral Sciences at Stanford, California, I have profited from conversations with Albert Cook of the State University of New York, Buffalo, and Robert Darnton of Princeton University, concerning matters in this final version.

2. See, e.g., J. R. Searle, *The Philosophy of Language* (London: Oxford University Press, 1971), 24–28, where Austin is cited, and Searle's bibliography, pp. 146–48.

3. *The Rhetoric of Fiction* (Chicago: University of Chicago Press, 1961), pp. 49–52, 138, 363–64.

4. *The Nature of Narrative* (New York: Oxford University Press, 1966), 17–56. Among recent short studies exhibiting concerns tangent to but not the same as those of the present article might be mentioned three from *New Literary History:* Georges Poulet, "Phenomenology of Reading," 1 (1969–70). 53–68; Geoffrey H. Hartman, "History-Writing

as Answerable Style," 2 (1970–71), 73–84; and J. Hillis Miller, "The Still Heart: Poetic Form in Wordsworth," 2 (1970–71), 297–310, esp. p. 310, as well as Gerald Prince, "Introduction à l'étude du narrataire," *Poétique*, No. 14 (1973), 178–96, which is concerned with the "narrataire" only in novels ("narratee" in a related English-language study by the same author as noted by him here) and with literary taxonomy more than history. See also Paul Ricoeur, "What Is a Text? Explanation and Interpretation," Appendix, pp. 135–50, in David Rasmussen, *Mythic-Symbolic Language and Philosophical Anthropology: A Constructive Interpretation of the Thought of Paul Ricoeur* (The Hague: Martinus Nijhoff, 1971).

5. *Phenomenology of Perception*, trans. Colin Smith (London: Routledge, 1962), 181–84.

6. See my *The Presence of the Word* (New Haven and London: Yale University Press, 1967), 116-17.

7. T. S. Eliot suggests some of the complexities of the writer-and-audience problem in his essay on "The Three Voices of Poetry," by which he means (1) "the voice of the poet talking to himself—or to nobody," (2) "the voice of the poet addressing an audience," and (3) "the voice of the poet when he attempts to create a dramatic character speaking" (*On Poetry and Poets*, New York: Noonday Press, 1961, p. 96). Eliot, in the same work, states that these voices often mingle and indeed, for him, "are most often found together" (p. 108). The approach I am here taking cuts across Eliot's way of enunciating the problem and, I believe, brings out some of the built-in relationships among the three voices which help account for their intermingling. The "audience" addressed by Eliot's second voice not only is elusively constituted but also, even in its elusiveness, can determine the voice of the poet talking to himself or to nobody (Eliot's first sense of "voice"), because in talking to oneself one has to objectify oneself, and one does so in ways learned from addressing others. A practiced writer talking "to himself" in a poem has a quite different feeling for "himself" than does a complete illiterate.

8. See Albert B. Lord, *The Singer of Tales*, Harvard Studies in Comparative Literature, No. 24 (Cambridge, Mass.: Harvard University Press, 1964), 124–38.

9. *Tough, Sweet, and Stuffy*, (Bloomington and London: Indiana University Press, 1966), 28–54. In these pages, Gibson gets very close to the concern of the present article with readers' roles.

10. The present inclination to begin a story without the initial indefinite article, which tacitly acknowledges a range of existence beyond that of the immediate reference, and to substitute for the indefinite article a demonstrative pronoun of proximity, "this," is one of many indications of the tendency of present-day man to feel his lifeworld—which is now more than ever the whole world—as in-close to him, and to mute any references to distance. It is not uncommon to hear a conversation begin, "Yesterday on the street this man came up to me, and. . . ." A few decades ago, the equivalent would very likely have been, "Yesterday on the street a man came up to me, and. . . ." This widespread preference, which Hemingway probably influenced little if at all, does show that Hemingway's imposition of fellowship on the reader was an indication, perhaps moderately precocious, of a sweeping trend.

11. "Possible," because there is probably a trace of fictionalizing even when notes are being exchanged by persons in one another's presence. It appears unlikely that what is written in such script "conversations" is exactly the same as what it would be were voices used. The interlocutors are, after all, to some extent pretending to be talking, when in fact they are not talking but writing.

7

Stanley E. Fish
1938–

Stanley Fish has taught at the University of California at Berkeley, Johns Hopkins University, and Duke. His training was in seventeenth-century British literature, but as a critic he has been identified with the development of Reader-Response criticism since the publication of *Surprised by Sin: The Reader in "Paradise Lost"* (1967). His approach to reading is fiercely pragmatic, and he tends to shun philosophical or abstract formulation of his methods. The temperament and tone of his work place it close to that of Ordinary Language philosophers (especially John L. Austin). His method consists largely of anticipating the direction of narrative development and then discussing in detail how closely actual development coincides with or frustrates what was expected. He tends to think of interpretive strategies as guided by a reader's "interpretive community." His work, in addition to many essays, includes: *John Skelton's Poetry* (1965); *Self-Consuming Artifacts: The Experience of Seventeenth-Century Literature* (1972); and *Is There a Text in This Class?* (1980).

Fish's "Interpreting the *Variorum*" (1980) is a critical document remarkable for its insight into reading and for its candor. Fish looks at the problems of interpretation raised by publication of the first two volumes of the Milton *Variorum Commentary*, noting that again and again the *Variorum* gives evidence for multiple readings of key passages in Milton's work. Fish then does two things. First, he demonstrates how a reader transforms an interpretive dispute by making it "signify, first by regarding it as evidence of an experience and then by specifying for that experience a meaning." This reader-oriented approach, however, is marked by its "inability to say how it is that one ever begins" to read and interpret. Fish's answer is that readers are guided by "interpretive communities" of readers. Second, Fish asks, "how can any one of us know whether or not he is a member of the same interpretive community as any other of us?" His answer is that we can never be sure, but that our common-sense experience tends to confirm the existence of such reading communities.

Interpreting the *Variorum*

THE CASE FOR READER-RESPONSE ANALYSIS

The first two volumes of the Milton *Variorum Commentary* have now appeared, and I find them endlessly fascinating. My interest, however, is not in the questions they manage to resolve (although these are many) but in the theoretical assumptions which are responsible for their occasional failures. These failures constitute a pattern, one in which a host of commentators—separated by as much as two hundred and seventy years but contemporaries in their shared concerns—are lined up on either side of an interpretive crux. Some of these are famous, even infamous: what is the two-handed engine in *Lycidas*? what is the meaning of Haemony in *Comus*? Others, like the identity of whoever or whatever comes to the window in *L'Allegro*, line 46, are only slightly less notorious. Still others are of interest largely to those who make editions: matters of pronoun referents, lexical ambiguities, punctuation. In each instance, however, the pattern is consistent: every position taken is supported by wholly convincing evidence—in the case of *L'Allegro* and the coming to the window there is a persuasive champion for every proper noun within a radius of ten lines—and the editorial procedure always ends either in the graceful throwing up of hands or in the recording of a disagreement between the two editors themselves. In short, these are problems that apparently cannot be solved, at least not by the methods traditionally brought to bear on them. What I would like to argue is that they are not meant to be solved but to be experienced (they signify), and that consequently any procedure that attempts to determine which of a number of readings is correct will necessarily fail. What this means is that the commentators and editors have been asking the wrong questions and that a new set of questions based on new assumptions must be formulated. I would like at least to make a beginning in that direction by examining some of the points in dispute in Milton's sonnets. I choose the sonnets because they are brief and because one can move easily from them to the theoretical issues with which this paper is finally concerned.

Milton's twentieth sonnet—"Lawrence of virtuous father virtuous son"—has been the subject of relatively little commentary. In it the poet invites a friend to join him in some distinctly Horatian pleasures—a neat repast intermixed with conversation, wine, and song, a respite from labor all the more enjoyable because outside the earth is frozen and the day sullen. The only controversy the sonnet has inspired concerns its final two lines:

Lawrence of virtuous father virtuous son,
Now that the fields are dank, and ways are mire,
Where shall we sometimes meet, and by the fire
Help waste a sullen day; what may be won

From the hard season gaining; time will run
On smoother, till Favonius reinspire
The frozen earth: and clothe in fresh attire
The lily and rose, that neither sowed nor spun.

What neat repast shall feast us, light and choice,
Of Attic taste, with wine, whence we may rise
To hear the lute well touched, or artful voice

Warble immortal notes and Tuscan air?
He who of those delights can judge, and spare
To interpose them oft, is not unwise.[1]

The focus of the controversy is the word "spare," for which two readings have been proposed: leave time for and refrain from. Obviously the point is crucial if one is to resolve the sense of the lines. In one reading "those delights" are being recommended—he who can leave time for them is not unwise; in the other, they are the subject of a warning—he who knows when to refrain from them is not unwise. The proponents of the two interpretations cite as evidence both English and Latin syntax, various sources and analogues, Milton's "known attitudes" as they are found in his other writings, and the unambiguously expressed sentiments of the following sonnet on the same question. Surveying these arguments, A. S. P. Woodhouse roundly declares: "It is plain that all the honours rest with" the meaning "refrain from" or "forbear to." This declaration is followed immediately by a bracketed paragraph initialled D. B. for Douglas Bush, who, writing presumably after Woodhouse has died, begins "In spite of the array of scholarly names the case for 'forbear to' may be thought much weaker, and the case for 'spare time for' much stronger, than Woodhouse found them."[2] Bush then proceeds to review much of the evidence marshaled by Woodhouse and to draw from it exactly the opposite conclusion. If it does nothing else, this curious performance anticipates a point I shall make in a few moments: evidence brought to bear in the course of formalist analyses—that is, analyses generated by the assumption that meaning is embedded in the artifact—will always point in as many directions as there are interpreters; that is, not only will it prove something, it will prove anything.

It would appear then that we are back at square one, with a controversy that cannot be settled because the evidence is inconclusive. But what if that controversy is *itself* regarded as evidence, not of an ambiguity that must be removed, but of an ambiguity that readers have always experienced? What, in other words, if for the question "what does 'spare' mean?" we substitute the question "what does the fact that the meaning of 'spare' has always been an issue mean?" The advantage of this question is that it can be answered. Indeed it has already been answered by the readers who are cited in the *Variorum Commentary*. What these readers debate is the judgment the poem makes on the delights of recreation; what their debate indicates is that the judgment is blurred by a verb that can be made to participate in contradictory readings. (Thus the important thing about the evidence surveyed in the *Variorum* is not how it is marshaled but that it could be marshaled at all, because it then becomes evidence of the equal availability of both interpretations.) In other words, the lines first generate a pressure for judgment—"he who of those delights can judge"—and then decline to deliver it; the pressure, however, still exists, and it is transferred from the words on the page to the reader (the reader is "he who"), who comes away from the poem not with a statement but with a responsibility, the responsibility of deciding when and how often—if at all—to indulge in "those delights" (they remain delights in either case). This transferring of responsibility from the text to its readers is what the lines ask us to do—it is the essence of their experience—and in my terms it is therefore what the lines *mean*. It is a meaning the *Variorum* critics attest to even as they resist it, for what they are laboring so mightily to do by fixing the sense of the lines is to give the responsibility back. The text, however, will not accept it and remains determinedly evasive, even in its last two words, "not unwise." In their position these words confirm the impossibility of extracting from the poem a moral formula, for the assertion (certainly too strong a word) they complete is of the form, "He who does such and such, of him it cannot be said that he is unwise"; but of course neither can it be said that he is wise. Thus what Bush correctly terms the "defensive" "not unwise" operates to prevent us from attaching the label "wise" to any action, including *either* of the actions—leaving time for or refraining from—represented by the ambiguity of "spare." Not only is the pressure of judgment taken off the poem, it is taken off the activity the poem at first pretended to judge. The issue is finally not the moral status of "those delights"—they become in seventeenth-century terms "things indifferent"—but on the good or bad uses to which they can be put by readers who are left, as Milton always leaves them, to choose and manage by themselves.

Let us step back for a moment and see how far we've come. We began with an apparently insoluble problem and proceeded not to solve it, but to make it signify, first by regarding it as evidence of an experience and then by specifying for that experience a meaning. Moreover, the configurations of that experience, when they are made available by a reader-oriented analysis, serve as a check against the endlessly inconclusive adducing of evidence which characterizes formalist analysis. This is to say, any determination of what "spare" means (in a positivist or literal sense) is liable to be upset by the bringing forward of another analogue, or by a more complete computation of statistical frequencies, or by the discovery of new biographical information, or by anything else; but if we first determine that everything in the line before "spare" creates the expectation of an imminent judgment then the ambiguity of "spare" can be assigned a significance in the context of that expectation. (It disappoints it and transfers the pressure of judgment to us.) That context is experiential, and it is within its contours and constraints that significances are established (both in the act of reading and in the analysis of that act). In formalist analyses the only constraints are the notoriously open-ended possibilities and combination of possibilities that emerge when one begins to consult dictionaries and grammars and histories; to consult dictionaries, grammars, and histories is to assume that meanings can be specified independently of the activity of reading; what the example of "spare" shows is that it is in and by that activity that meanings—experiential, not positivist—are created.

In other words, it is the structure of the reader's experience rather than any structures available on the page that should be the object of description. In the case of Sonnet 20, that experiential structure was uncovered when an examination of formal structures led to an impasse; and the pressure to remove that impasse led to the substitution of one set of questions for another. It will more often be the case that the pressure of a spectacular failure will be absent. The sins of formalist-positivist analysis are primarily sins of omission, not an inability to explain phenomena but an inability to see that they are there because its assumptions make it inevitable that they will be overlooked or suppressed. Consider, for example, the concluding lines of another of Milton's sonnets, "Avenge O Lord thy slaughtered saints."

> Avenge O Lord they slaughtered saints,
> whose bones
> Lie scattered on the Alpine mountains
> cold,
> Even them who kept thy truth so pure
> of old
> When all our fathers worshipped
> stocks and stones,

Forget not: in thy book record their groans
Who were thy sheep and in their ancient fold
Slain by the bloody Piedmontese that rolled
Mother with infant down the rocks. Their moans
The vales redoubled to the hills, and they
To heaven. Their martyred blood and ashes sow
O'er all the Italian fields where still doth sway
The triple Tyrant: that from these may grow
A hundredfold, who having learnt thy way
Early may fly the Babylonian woe.

In this sonnet, the poet simultaneously petitions God and wonders aloud about the justice of allowing the faithful—"Even them who kept thy truth"—to be so brutally slaughtered. The note struck is alternately one of plea and complaint, and there is more than a hint that God is being called to account for what has happened to the Waldensians. It is generally agreed, however, that the note of complaint is less and less sounded and that the poem ends with an affirmation of faith in the ultimate operation of God's justice. In this reading, the final lines are taken to be saying something like this: From the blood of these martyred, O God, raise up a new and more numerous people, who, by virtue of an early education in thy law, will escape destruction by fleeing the Babylonian woe. Babylonian woe has been variously glossed;[3] but whatever it is taken to mean it is always read as part of a statement that specifies a set of conditions for the escaping of destruction or punishment; it is a warning to the reader as well as a petition to God. As a warning, however, it is oddly situated since the conditions it seems to specify were in fact met by the Waldensians, who of all men most followed God's laws. In other words, the details of their story would seem to undercut the affirmative moral the speaker proposes to draw from it. It is further undercut by a reading that is fleetingly available, although no one has acknowledged it because it is a function not of the words on the page but of the experience of the reader. In that experience, line 13 will for a moment be accepted as a complete sense unit and the emphasis of the line will fall on "thy way" (a phrase that has received absolutely no attention in the commentaries). At this point "thy way" can refer only to the way in which God has dealt with the Waldensians. That is, "thy way" seems to pick up the note of outrage with which the poem began, and if we continue to so interpret it, the conclusion of the poem will be a grim one indeed: since by this example it appears that God rains down punishment indiscriminately, it would be best perhaps to withdraw from the arena of his service, and thereby hope at least to be safely out of the line of fire. This is not the conclusion we carry away, because as line 14 unfolds, another reading of "thy way" becomes available, a reading in which "early" qualifies "learnt" and refers to something the faithful should do (learn thy way at an early age) rather than to something God has failed to do (save the Waldensians). These two readings are answerable to the pulls exerted by the beginning and ending of the poem: the outrage expressed in the opening lines generates a pressure for an explanation, and the grimmer reading is answerable to that pressure (even if it is also disturbing); the ending of the poem, the forward and upward movement of lines 10–14, creates the expectation of an affirmation, and the second reading fulfills that expectation. The criticism shows that in the end we settle on the more optimistic reading—it feels better—but even so the other has been a part of our experience, and because it has been a part of our experience, it *means*. What it means is that while we may be able to extract from the poem a statement affirming God's justice, we are not allowed to forget the evidence (of things seen) that makes the extraction so difficult (both for the speaker and for us). It is a difficulty we experience in the act of reading, even though a criticism which takes no account of that act has, as we have seen, suppressed it.

In each of the sonnets we have considered, the significant word or phrase occurs at a line break where a reader is invited to place it first in one and then in another structure of syntax and sense. This moment of hesitation, of semantic or syntactic slide, is crucial to the experience the verse provides, but in a formalist analysis that moment will disappear, either because it has been flattened out and made into an (insoluble) interpretive crux or because it has been eliminated in the course of a procedure that is incapable of finding value in temporal phenomena. In the case of "When I consider how my light is spent," these two failures are combined.

When I consider how my light is spent,
  Ere half my days, in this dark world and wide,
  And that one talent which is death to hide,
  Lodged with me useless, though my soul more bent
To serve therewith my maker, and present
  My true account, lest he returning chide,
  Doth God exact day-labour, light denied,
  I fondly ask; but Patience to prevent
That murmur, soon replies, God doth not need
  Either man's work or his own gifts, who best
  Bear his mild yoke, they serve him best, his state
Is kingly. Thousands at his bidding speed
  And post o'er land and ocean without rest:
They also serve who only stand and wait.

The interpretive crux once again concerns the final line: "They also serve who only stand and wait." For some this is an unqualified acceptance of God's will, while for others the note of affirmation is muted or even forced. The usual kinds of evidence are marshaled by the opposing parties, and the usual inconclusiveness is the result. There are some areas of agreement. "All the interpretations," Woodhouse remarks, "recognize that the sonnet commences from a mood of depression, frustration [and] impatience."[4] The object of impatience is a God who would first demand service and then take away the means of serving, and the oft noted allusion to the parable of the talents lends scriptural support to the accusation the poet is implicitly making; you have cast the wrong servant into unprofitable darkness. It has also been observed that the syntax and rhythm of these early lines, and especially of lines 6–8, are rough and uncertain; the speaker is struggling with his agitated thoughts and he changes directions abruptly, with no regard for the line as a unit of sense. The poem, says one critic, "seems almost out of control."[5]

The question I would ask is "whose control?" For what these formal descriptions point to (but do not acknowledge) is the extraordinary number of adjustments required of readers who would negotiate these lines. The first adjustment is the result of the expectations created by the second half of line 6—"lest he returning chide." Since there is no full stop after "chide," it is natural to assume that this will be an introduction to reported speech, and to assume further that what will be reported is the poet's anticipation of the voice of God as it calls him, to an unfair accounting. This assumption does not survive line 7—"Doth God exact day-labour, light denied"—which, rather than chiding the poet for his inactivity, seems to rebuke him for having expected that chiding. The accents are precisely those heard so often in the Old Testament when God answers a reluctant Gideon, or a disputatious Moses, or a self-justifying Job: do you presume to judge my ways or to appoint my motives? Do you think I would exact day labor, light denied? In other words, the poem seems to turn at this point from a questioning of God to a questioning of that questioning; or, rather, the reader turns from the one to the other in the act of revising his projection of what line 7 will say and do. As it turns out, however, that revision must itself be revised because it had been made within the assumption that what we are hearing is the voice of God. This assumption falls before the very next phrase. "I fondly ask," which requires not one but two adjustments. Since the speaker of line 7 is firmly identified as the poet, the line must be reinterpreted as a continuation of his complaint—Is that the way you operate, God, denying light, but exacting labor?—but even as that interpretation emerges, the poet withdraws from it by inserting the adverb "fondly," and once again the line slips out of the reader's control.

In a matter of seconds, then, line 7 has led four experiential lives, one as we anticipate it, another as that anticipation is revised, a third when we retroactively identify its speaker, and a fourth when that speaker disclaims it. What changes in each of these lives is the status of the poet's murmurings—they are alternately expressed, rejected, reinstated, and qualified—and as the sequence ends, the reader is without a firm perspective on the question of record: does God deal justly with his servants?

A firm perspective appears to be provided by Patience, whose entrance into the poem, the critics tell us, gives it both argumentative and metrical stability. But in fact the presence of Patience in the poem finally assures its continuing instability by making it impossible to specify the degree to which the speaker approves, or even participates in, the affirmation of the final line: "They also serve who only stand and wait." We know that Patience to prevent the poet's murmur soon replies (not soon enough however to prevent the murmur from registering), but we do not know when that reply ends. Does Patience fall silent in line 12, after "kingly"? or at the conclusion of line 13? or not at all? Does the poet appropriate these lines or share them or simply listen to them, as we do? These questions are unanswerable, and it is because they remain unanswerable that the poem ends uncertainly. The uncertainty is not in the statement it makes—in isolation line 14 is unequivocal—but in our inability to assign that statement to either the poet or to Patience. Were the final line marked unambiguously for the poet, then we would receive it as a resolution of his earlier doubts; and were it marked for Patience, it would be a sign that those doubts were still very much in force. It is marked for neither, and therefore we are without the satisfaction that a firmly conclusive ending (in *any* direction) would have provided. In short, we leave the poem unsure, and our unsureness is the realization (in our experience) of the unsureness with which the affirmation of the final line is, or is not, made. (This unsureness also operates to actualize the two possible readings of "wait": wait in the sense of expecting, that is waiting for an opportunity to serve actively; or wait in the sense of waiting *in* service, a waiting that is itself fully satisfying because the impulse to self-glorifying action has been stilled.)

The question debated in the *Variorum Commentary* is, how far from the mood of frustration and impatience does the poem finally move? The answer given by an experiential analysis is that you can't tell, and the fact that you can't tell is responsible for the uneasiness the poem has always inspired. It is that uneasiness which the critics inadvertently acknowledge when they argue about the force of the last line, but they are unable to make analytical use of what they acknowledge because they have no way of dealing with or even recognizing experiential (that is, temporal) structures. In fact, more than one editor has eliminated those structures by punctuating them out of existence: first by putting a full stop at the end of line 6 and thereby making it unlikely that the reader will assign line 7 to God (there will no longer be an expectation of reported speech), and then by supplying quotation marks for the sestet in order to remove any doubts one might have as to who is speaking. There is of course no warrant for these emendations, and in 1791 Thomas Warton had the grace and honesty to admit as much. "I have," he said, "introduced the turned commas both in the question and answer, not from any authority, but because they seem absolutely necessary to the sense."[6]

UNDOING THE CASE FOR READER-RESPONSE ANALYSIS

Editorial practices like these are only the most obvious manifestations of the assumptions to which I stand opposed: the assumption that there *is* a sense, that it is embedded or encoded in the text, and that it can be taken in at a single glance. These assumptions are, in order, positivist, holistic, and spatial, and to have them is to be committed both to a goal and to a procedure. The goal is to settle on a meaning, and the procedure involves first stepping back from the text, and then putting together or otherwise calculating the discrete units of significance it contains. My quarrel with this procedure (and with the assumptions that generate it) is that in the course of following it through the reader's activities are at once ignored and devalued. They are ignored because the text is taken to be self-sufficient—everything is *in* it—and they are devalued because when they are thought of at all, they are thought of as the disposable machinery of extraction. In the procedures I would urge, the reader's activities are at the center of attention, where they are regarded not as leading to meaning but as *having* meaning. The meaning they have is a consequence of their not being empty; for they include the making and revising of assumptions, the rendering and regretting of judgments, the coming to and abandoning of conclusions, the giving and withdrawing of approval, the specifying of causes, the asking of questions, the supplying of answers, the solving of puzzles. In a word, these activities are interpretive—rather than being preliminary to questions of value, they are at every moment settling and resettling questions of value—and because they are interpretive, a description of them will also be, and without any additional step, an interpretation, not after the fact but of the fact (of experiencing). It will be a description of a moving field of concerns, at once wholly present (not waiting for meaning but constituting meaning) and continually in the act of reconstituting itself.

As a project such a description presents enormous difficulties, and there is hardly time to consider them here;[7] but it should be obvious from my brief examples how different it is from the positivist-formalist project. Everything depends on the temporal dimension, and as a consequence the notion of a mistake, at least as something to be avoided, disappears. In a sequence where a reader first structures the field he inhabits and then is asked to restructure it (by changing an assignment of speaker or realigning attitudes and positions) there is no question of priority among his structurings; no one of them, even if it is the last, has privilege; each is equally legitimate, each equally the proper object of analysis, because each is equally an event in his experience.

The firm assertiveness of this paragraph only calls attention to the questions it avoids. Who is this reader? How can I presume to describe his experiences, and what do I say to readers who report that they do not have the experiences I describe? Let me answer these questions or rather make a beginning at answering them in the context of another example, this time from Milton's Comus. In line 46 of Comus we are introduced to the villain by way of a genealogy:

> Bacchus that first from out the purple grape,
> Crushed the sweet poison of misused wine.

In almost any edition of this poem, a footnote will tell you that Bacchus is the god of wine. Of course most readers already know that, and because they know it, they will be anticipating the appearance of "wine" long before they come upon it in the final position. Moreover, they will also be anticipating a negative judgment on it, in part because of the association of Bacchus with revelry and excess, and especially because the phrase "sweet poison" suggests that the judgment has already been made. At an early point then, we will have both filled in the form of the assertion and made a decision about its moral content. That decision is upset by the word "misused"; for what "misused" asks us to do is transfer the pressure of judgment from wine (where we have already placed it) to the abusers of wine, and therefore when "wine" finally appears, we must declare it innocent of the charges we have ourselves made.

This, then, is the structure of the reader's experience—the transferring of a moral label from a thing to those who appropriate it. It is an experience that depends on a reader for whom the name Bacchus has precise and immediate associations; another reader, a reader for whom those associations are less precise will not have that experience because he will not have rushed to a conclusion in relation to which the word "misused" will stand as a challenge. Obviously I am discriminating between these two readers and between the two equally real experiences they will have. It is not a discrimination based simply on information, because what is important is not the information itself, but the action of the mind which its possession makes possible for one reader and impossible for the other. One might discriminate further between them by noting that the point at issue—whether value is a function of objects and actions or of intentions—is at the heart of the seventeenth-century debate over "things indifferent." A reader who is aware of that debate will not only *have* the experience I describe; he will recognize at the end of it that he has been asked to take a position on one side of a continuing controversy; and that recognition (also a part of his experience) will be part of the disposition with which he moves into the lines that follow.

It would be possible to continue with this profile of the optimal reader, but I would not get very far before someone would point out that what I am really describing is the intended reader, the reader whose education, opinions, concerns, linguistic competences, and so on make him capable of having the experience the author wished to provide. I would not resist this characterization because it seems obvious that the efforts of readers are always efforts to discern and therefore to realize (in the sense of becoming) an author's intention. I would only object if that realization were conceived narrowly, as the single act of comprehending an author's purpose, rather than (as I would conceive it) as the succession of acts readers perform in the continuing assumption that they are dealing with intentional beings. In this view discerning an intention is no more or less than understanding, and understanding includes (is constituted by) all the activities which make up what I call the structure of the reader's experience. To describe that experience is therefore to describe the reader's efforts at understanding, and to describe the reader's efforts at understanding is to describe his realization (in two senses) of an author's intention. Or to put it another way, what my analyses amount to are descriptions of a succession of decisions made by readers about an author's intention—decisions that are not limited to the specifying of purpose but include the specifying of every aspect of successively intended worlds, decisions that are precisely the shape, because they are the content, of the reader's activities.

Having said this, however, it would appear that I am open to two objections. The first is that the procedure is a circular one. I describe the experience of a reader who in his strategies is answerable to an author's intention, and I specify the author's intention by pointing to the strategies employed by that same reader. But this objection would have force only if it were possible to specify one independently of the other. What is being specified from either perspective are the conditions of utterance, of what could have been understood to have been meant by what was said. That is, intention and understanding are two ends of a conventional act, each of which necessarily stipulates (includes, defines, specifies) the other. To construct the profile of the informed of at-home reader is at the same time to characterize the author's intention and vice versa, because to do either is to specify the contemporary conditions of utterance, to identify, by becoming a member of, a community made up of those who share interpretive strategies.

The second objection is another version of the first: if the content of the reader's experience is the succession of acts he performs in search of an author's intentions, and if he performs those acts at the bidding of the text, does not the text then produce or contain everything—intention *and* experience—and have I not compromised my antiformalist position? This objection will have force only if the formal patterns of the text are assumed to exist independently of the reader's experience, for only then can priority be claimed for them. Indeed, the claims of independence and priority are one and the same; when they are separated it is so that they can give circular and illegitimate support to each other. The question "do formal features exist independently?" is usually answered by pointing to their priority: they are "in" the text before the reader comes to it. The question "are formal features prior?" is usually answered by pointing to their independent status: they are "in" the text before the reader comes to it. What looks like a step in an argument is actually the spectacle of an assertion supporting itself. It follows then that an attack on the independence of formal features will also be an attack on their priority (and vice versa), and I would like to mount such an attack in the context of two short passages from *Lycidas*.

The first passage (actually the second in the poem's sequence) begins at line 42:

> The willows and the hazel copses green
> Shall now no more be seen,
> Fanning their joyous leaves to thy soft
> lays.

It is my thesis that the reader is always making sense (I intend "making" to have its literal force), and in the case of these lines the sense he makes will involve the assumption (and therefore the creation) of a completed assertion after the word "seen," to wit, the death of Lycidas has so affected the willows and the hazel copses green that, in sympathy, they will wither and die (will no more be seen by *anyone*). In other words, at the end of line 43 the reader will have hazarded an interpretation, or performed an act of perceptual closure, or made a decision as to what is being asserted. I do not mean that he has done four things, but that he has done one thing the description of which might take any one of four forms—making sense, interpreting, performing perceptual closure, deciding about what is intended. (The importance of this point will become clear later.) Whatever he has done (that is, however we characterize it), he will undo it in the act of reading the next line, for here he discovers that his closure, or making of sense, was premature and that he must make a new one in which the relationship between man and nature is exactly the reverse of what was first assumed. The willows and the hazel copses green will in fact be seen, but they will not be seen by Lycidas. It is he who will be no more, while they go on as before, fanning their joyous leaves to someone else's soft lays (the whole of line 44 is now perceived as modifying and removing the absoluteness of "seen"). Nature is not sympathetic, but indifferent, and the notion of her sympathy is one of those "false surmises" that the poem is continually encouraging and then disallowing.

The previous sentence shows how easy it is to surrender to the bias of our critical language and begin to talk as if poems, not readers or interpreters, did things. Words like "encourage" and "disallow" (and others I have used in this essay) imply agents, and it is only "natural" to assign agency first to an author's intentions and then to the forms that assumedly embody them. What really happens, I think, is something quite different: rather than intention and its formal realization producing interpretation (the "normal" picture), interpretation creates intention and its formal realization by creating the conditions in which it becomes possible to pick them out. In other words, in the analysis of these lines from *Lycidas* I did what critics always do: I "saw" what my interpretive principles permitted or directed me to see, and then I turned around and attributed what I had "seen" to a text and an intention. What my principles direct me to "see" are readers performing acts: the points at which I find (or to be more precise, declare) those acts to have been performed become (by a sleight of hand) demarcations *in* the text; those demarcations are then available for the designation "formal features," and as formal features they can be (illegitimately) assigned the responsibility for producing the interpretation which in fact produced them. In this case, the demarcation my interpretation calls into being is placed at the end of line 42; but of course the end of that (or any other) line is worth noticing or pointing out only because my model *demands* (the word is not too strong) perceptual closures and therefore locations at which they occur; in that model this point will be one of those locations, although (1) it need not have been (not every line ending occasions a closure) and (2) in another model, one that does not give value to the activities of readers, the possibility of its being one would not have arisen.

What am I suggesting is that formal units are always a function of the interpretative model one brings to bear; they are not "in" the text, and I would make the same argument for intentions. That is, intention is no more embodied "in" the text than are formal units; rather an intention, like a formal unit, is made when perceptual or interpretive closure is hazarded: it is verified by an interpretive act, and I would add, it is not verifiable in any other way. This last assertion is too large to be fully considered here, but I can sketch out the argumentative sequence I would follow were I to consider it: intention is known when and only when it is recognized; it is recognized as soon as you decide about it; you decide about it as soon as you make a sense: and you make a sense (or so my model claims) as soon as you can.

Let me tie up the threads of my argument with a final example from *Lycidas*:

> He must not float upon his wat'ry bier
> Unwept . . .
>
> (13–14)

Here the reader's experience has much the same career as it does in lines 42–44: at the end of line 13 perceptual closure is hazarded, and a sense is made in which the line is taken to be a resolution bordering on a promise: that is, there is now an expectation that something will be done about this unfortunate situation, and the reader anticipates a call to action, perhaps even a program for the undertaking of a rescue mission. With "Unwept," however, that expectation and anticipation are disappointed, and the realization of that disappointment will be inseparable from the making of a new (and less comforting) sense: nothing will be done; Lycidas will continue to float upon his wat'ry bier, and the only action taken will be the lamenting of the fact that no action will be efficacious, including the actions of speaking and listening to this lament (which in line 15 will receive the meretricious and self-mocking designation "melodious tear"). Three "structures" come into view at precisely the same moment, the moment when the reader having resolved a sense unresolves it and makes a new one; that moment will also be the moment of picking out a formal pattern or unit, end of line beginning of line, and it will also be the moment at which the reader, having decided about the speaker's intention, about what is meant by what has been said, will make the decision again and in so doing will make another intention.

This, then, is my thesis: that the form of the reader's experience, formal units, and the structure of intention are one, that they come into view simultaneously, and that therefore the questions of priority and independence do not arise. What does arise is another question: what produces them? That is, if intention, form, and the shape of the reader's experience are simply different ways of referring to (different perspectives on) the same interpretive act, what is that act an interpretation *of*? I cannot answer that question, but neither, I would claim, can anyone else, although formalists try to answer it by pointing to patterns and claiming that they are available independently of (prior to) interpretation. These patterns vary according to the procedures that yield them: they may be statistical (number of two-syllable words per hundred words), grammatical (ratio of passive to active constructions, or of right-branching to left-branching sentences, or of anything else); but whatever they are I would argue that they do not lie innocently in the world but are themselves constituted by an interpretive act, even if, as is often the case, that act is unacknowledged. Of course, this is as true of my analyses as it is of anyone else's. In the examples offered here I appropriate the notion "line ending" and treat it as a fact of nature; and one might conclude that as a fact it is responsible for the reading experience I describe. The truth I think is exactly the reverse: line endings exist by virtue of perceptual strategies rather than the other way around. Historically, the strategy that we know as "reading (or hearing) poetry" has included paying attention to the line as a unit, but it is precisely that attention which has made the line as a unit (either of print or of aural duration) available. A reader so practiced in paying that attention that he regards the line as a brute fact rather than as a convention will have a great deal of difficulty with concrete poetry; if he overcomes that difficulty, it will not be because he has learned to ignore the line as a unit but because he will have acquired a new set of interpretive strategies (the strategies constitutive of "concrete poetry reading") in the context of which the line as a unit no longer exists. In short, what is noticed is what has been *made* noticeable, not by a clear and undistorting glass, but by an interpretive strategy.

This may be hard to see when the strategy has become so habitual that the forms it yields seem part of the world. We find it easy to assume that alliteration as an effect depends on a "fact" that exists independently of any interpretive "use" one might make of it, the fact that words in proximity begin with the same letter. But it takes only a moment's reflection to realize that the sameness, far from being natural, is enforced by an orthographic convention; that is to say, it is the product of an interpretation. Were we to substitute phonetic conventions for orthographic ones (a "reform" traditionally urged by purists), the supposedly "objective" basis for alliteration would disappear because a phonetic transcription would require that we distinguish between the initial sounds of those very words that enter into alliterative relationships; rather than conforming to those relationships, the rules of spelling make them. One might reply that, since alliteration is an aural rather than a visual phenomenon when poetry is heard, we have unmediated access to the physical sounds themselves and hear "real" similarities. But phonological "facts" are no more uninterpreted (or less conventional) than the "facts" of orthography; the distinctive features that make articulation and reception possible are the product of a system of differences that must be imposed before it can be recognized: the patterns the ear hears (like the patterns the eye sees) are the patterns its perceptual habits make available.

One can extend this analysis forever, even to the "facts" of grammar. The history of linguistics is the history of competing paradigms, each of which offers a different account of the constituents of language. Verbs, nouns, cleft sentences, transformations, deep and surface structures, semes, rhemes, tagmemes—now you see them, now you don't, depending on the descriptive apparatus you employ. The critic who confidently rests his analyses on the bedrock of syntactic descriptions is resting on an interpretation; the facts he points to *are* there, but only as a consequence of the interpretive (man-made) model that has called them into being.

The moral is clear: the choice is never between objectivity and interpretation but between an interpretation that is unacknowledged as such and an interpretation that is at least aware of itself. It is this awareness that I am claiming for myself, although in doing so I must give up the claims implicitly made in the first part of this essay. There I argue that a bad (because spatial) model had suppressed what was really happening, but by my own declared principles the notion "really happening" is just one more interpretation.

INTERPRETIVE COMMUNITIES

It seems then that the price one pays for denying the priority of either forms or intentions is an inability to say how it is that one ever begins. Yet we do begin, and we continue, and because we do there arises an immediate counterobjection to the preceding pages. If interpretive acts are the source of forms rather than the other way around, why isn't it the case that readers are always performing the same acts of a sequence of random acts, and therefore creating the same forms or a random succession of forms? How, in short, does one explain these two "facts" of reading? (1) The same reader will perform differently when reading two "different" (the word is in quotation marks because its status is precisely what is at issue) texts; and (2) different readers will perform similarly when reading the "same" (in quotes for the same reason) text. That is to say, both the stability of interpretation among readers and the variety of interpretation in the career of a single reader would seem to argue for the existence of something independent of and prior to interpretive acts, something which produces them. I will answer this challenge by asserting that both the stability and the variety are functions of interpretive strategies rather than of texts.

Let us suppose that I am reading *Lycidas*. What is it that I am doing? First of all, what I am not doing is "simply reading," an activity in which I do not believe because it implies the possibility of pure (that is, disinterested) perception. Rather, I am proceeding on the basis of (at least) two interpretive decisions: (1) that *Lycidas* is a pastoral and (2) that it was written by Milton. (I should add that the notions "pastoral" and "Milton" are also interpretations; that is, they do not stand for a set of indisputable, objective facts; if they did, a great many books would not now be getting written.) Once these decisions have been made (and if I had not made these I would have made others, and they would be consequential in the same way), I am immediately predisposed to perform certain acts, to "find," by looking for, themes (the relationship between natural processes and the careers of men, the efficacy of poetry or of any other action), to confer significances (on flowers, streams, shepherds, pagan deities), to mark out "formal" units (the lament, the consolation, the turn, the affirmation of faith, and so on). My disposition to perform these acts (and others; the list is not meant to be exhaustive) consitutes a set of interpretive strategies, which, when they are put into execution, become the large act of reading. That is to say, interpretive strategies are not put into execution after reading (the pure act of perception in which I do not believe); they are the shape of reading, and because they are the shape of reading, they give texts their shape, making them rather than, as it is usually assumed, arising from them. Several important things follow from this account:

1. I did not have to execute this particular set of interpretive strategies because I did not have to make those particular interpretive (pre-reading) decisions. I could have decided, for example, that *Lycidas* was a text in which a set of fantasies and defenses find expression. These decisions would have entailed the assumption of another set of interpretive strategies (perhaps like that put forward by Norman Holland in *The Dynamics of Literary Response*), and the execution of that set would have made another text.
2. I could execute this same set of strategies when presented with texts that did not bear the title (again a notion which is itself an interpretation) *Lycidas, A Pastoral Monody*. I could decide (it is a decision some have made) that *Adam Bede* is a pastoral written by an author who consciously modeled herself on Milton (still remembering that "pastoral" and "Milton" are interpretations, not facts in the public domain): or I could decide, as Empson did, that a great many things not usually considered pastoral were in fact to be so read; and either decision would give rise to a set of interpretive strategies, which, when put into action, would write the text I

write when reading *Lycidas*. (Are you with me?)

3. A reader other than myself who, when presented with *Lycidas*, proceeds to put into execution a set of interpretive strategies similar to mine (how he could do so is a question I will take up later), will perform the same (or at least a similar) succession of interpretive acts. He and I then might be tempted to say that we agree about the poem (thereby assuming that the poem exists independently of the acts either of us performs); but what we really would agree about is the way to write it.
4. A reader other than myself who, when presented with *Lycidas* (please keep in mind that the status of *Lycidas* is what is at issue), puts into execution a different set of interpretive strategies will perform a different succession of interpretive acts. (I am assuming, it is the article of my faith, that a reader will always execute some set of interpretive strageties and therefore perform some succession of interpretive acts.) One of us might then be tempted to complain to the other that we could not possibly be reading the same poem (literary criticism is full of such complaints) and he would be right; for each of us would be reading the poem he had made.

The large conclusion that follows from these four smaller ones is that the notions of the "same" or "different" texts are fictions. If I read *Lycidas* and *The Waste Land* differently (in fact I do not), it will not be because the formal structures of the two poems (to term them such is also an interpretive decision) call forth different interpretive strategies but because my predisposition to execute different interpretive strategies will *produce* different formal structures. That is, the two poems are different because I have decided that they will be. The proof of this is the possibility of doing the reverse (that is why point 2 is so important). That is to say, the answer to the question "why do different texts give rise to different sequences of interpretive acts?" is that *they don't have to*, an answer which implies strongly that "they" don't exist. Indeed, it has always been possible to put into action interpretive strategies designed to make all texts one, or to put it more accurately, to be forever making the same text. Augustine urges just such a strategy, for example, in *On Christian Doctrine* where he delivers the "rule of faith" which is of course a rule of interpretation. It is dazzlingly simple: everything in the Scriptures, and indeed in the world when it is properly read, points to (bears the meaning of) God's love for us and our answering responsibility to love our fellow creatures for His sake. If only you should come upon something which does not at first seem to bear this meaning, that "does not literally pertain to virtuous behavior or to the truth of faith," you are then to take it "to be figurative" and proceed to scrutinize it "until an interpretation contributing to the reign of charity is produced." This then is both a stipulation of what meaning there is and a set of directions for finding it, which is of course a set of directions—of interpretive strategies—for making it, that is, for the endless reproduction of the same text. Whatever one may think of this interpretive program, its success and ease of execution are attested to by centuries of Christian exegesis. It is my contention that any interpretive program, any set of interpretive strategies, can have a similar success, although few have been as spectacularly successful as this one. (For some time now, for at least three hundred years, the most successful interpretive program has gone under the name "ordinary language.") In our own discipline programs with the same characteristic of always reproducing one text include psychoanalytic criticism, Robertsonianism (always threatening to extend its sway into later and later periods), numerology (a sameness based on the assumption of innumerable fixed differences).

The other challenging question—"why will different readers execute the same interpretive strategy when faced with the 'same' text?"—can be handled in the same way. The answer is again that *they don't have to,* and my evidence is the entire history of literary criticism. And again this answer implies that the notion "same text" is the product of the possession by two or more readers of similar interpretive strategies.

But why should this ever happen? Why should two or more readers ever agree, and why should regular, that is, habitual, differences in the career of a single reader ever occur? What is the explanation on the one hand of the stability of interpretation (at least among certain groups at certain times) and on the other of the orderly variety of interpretation if it is not the stability and variety of texts? The answer to all of these questions is to be found in a notion that has been implicit in my augment, the notion of *interpretive communities.* Interpretive communities are made up of those who share interpretive strategies not for reading (in the conventional sense) but for writing texts, for constituting their properties and assigning their intentions. In other words, these strategies exist prior to the act of reading and therefore determine the shape of what is read rather than, as is usually assumed, the other way around. If it is an article of faith in a particular community that there are a variety of texts, its members will boast a repertoire of strategies for making them. And if a community believes in the existence of only one text; then the single strategy its members employ will be forever writing it. The first community will accuse the members of the second of being reductive, and they in turn will call their accusers superficial. The assumption in each community will be that the other is not correctly perceiving the "true text," but the truth will be that each perceives the text (or texts) its interpretive strategies demand and call into being. This, then, is the explanation both for the stability of interpretation among different readers (they belong to the same community) and for the regularity with which a single reader will employ different interpretive strategies and thus make different texts (he belongs to different communities). It also explains why there are disagreements and why they can be debated in a principled way: not because of a stability in texts, but because of a stability in the makeup of interpretive communities and therefore in the opposing positions they make possible. Of course this stability is always temporary (unlike the longed for and timeless stability of the text). Interpretive communities grow larger and decline, and individuals move from one to another; thus, while the alignments are not permanent, they are always there, providing just enough stability for the interpretive battles to go on, and just enough shift and slippage to assure that they will never be settled. The notion of interpretive communities thus stands between an impossible ideal and the fear which leads so many to maintain it. The ideal is of perfect agreement and it would require texts to have a status independent of interpretation. The fear is of interpretive anarchy, but it would only be realized if interpretation (text making) were completely random. It is the fragile but real consolidation of interpretive communities that allows us to talk to one another, but with no hope or fear of ever being able to stop.

In other words interpretive communities are no more stable than texts because interpretive strategies are not natural or universal, but learned. This does not mean that there is a point at which an individual has not yet learned any. The ability to interpret is not acquired; it is constitutive of being human. What is acquired are the ways of interpreting and those same ways can also be forgotten or supplanted, or complicated or dropped from favor ("no one reads that way anymore"). When any of these things happens, there is a corresponding change in texts, not because they are being read differently, but because they are being written differently.

The only stability, then, inheres in the fact (at least in my model) that interpretive strategies are always being deployed, and this means that communication is a much more chancy affair than we are accustomed to think it. For if there are no fixed texts, but only interpretive strategies making them, and if interpretive strategies are not natural, but learned (and are therefore unavailable to a finite description), what is it that utterers (speakers, authors, critics, me, you) do? In the old model utterers are in the business of handing over ready-made or prefabricated meanings. These meanings are said to be encoded, and the code is assumed to be in the world independently of the individuals who are obliged to attach themselves to it (if they do not they run the danger of being declared deviant). In my model, however, meanings are not extracted but made and made not by encoded forms but by interpretive strategies that call forms into being. It follows then that what utterers do is give hearers and readers the opportunity to make meanings (and texts) by inviting them to put into execution a set of strategies. It is presumed that the presumption rests on a projection on the part of a speaker or author of the moves he would make if confronted by the sounds or marks he is uttering or setting down.

It would seem at first that this account of things simply reintroduces the old objection; for isn't this an admission that there is after all a formal encoding, not perhaps of meanings, but of the directions for making them, for executing interpretive strategies? The answer is that they will only *be* directions to those who already have the interpretive strategies in the first place. Rather than producing interpretive acts, they are the product of one. An author hazards his projection, not because of something "in" the marks, but because of something he assumes to be in his reader. The very existence of the "marks" is a function of an interpretive community, for they will be recognized (that is, made) only by its members. Those outside that community will be deploying a different set of interpretive strategies (interpretation cannot be withheld) and will therefore be making different marks.

So once again I have made the text disappear, but unfortunately the problems do not disappear with it. If everyone is continually executing interpretive strategies and in that act constituting texts, intentions, speakers, and authors, how can any one of us know whether or not he is a member of the same interpretive community as any other of us? The answer is that he can't, since any evidence brought forward to support the claim would itself be an interpretation (especially if the "other" were an author long dead). The only "proof" of membership is fellowship, the nod of recognition from someone in the same community, someone who says to you what neither of us could ever prove to a third party: "we know." I say it to you now, knowing full well that you will agree with me (that is, understand) only if you already agree with me.

NOTES

1. All references are to *The Poems of John Milton*, ed. John Carey and Alastair Fowler (London: Longman, Green, 1968).

2. *A Variorum Commentary on the Poems of John Milton*, Vol. 2, pt. 2, ed. A. S. P. Woodhouse and

Douglas Bush (New York: Columbia University Press, 1972), 475.

3. It is first of all a reference to the city of iniquity from which the Hebrews are urged to flee in Isaiah and Jeremiah. In Protestant polemics Babylon is identified with the Roman Church whose destruction is prophesied in the book of Revelation. And in some Puritan tracts Babylon is the name for Augustine's earthly city, from which the faithful are to flee inwardly in order to escape the fate awaiting the unregenerate. See *Variorum Commentary*, pp. 440–441.

4. *Variorum Commentary*, p. 469.

5. Ibid., p. 457.

6. *Poems upon Several Occasions, English, Italian, and Latin, with Translations, by John Milton*, ed, Thomas Warton (London, 1791), 352.

7. See my *Surprised by Sin: The Reader in "Paradise Lost"* (London and New York: Macmillan, 1967); *Self-Consuming Artifacts: The Experience of Seventeenth-Century Literature* (Berkeley: University of California Press, 1972); "What Is Stylistics and Why Are They Saying Such Terrible Things About It?" (chap. 2, in *Is There a Text in This Class?*); "How Ordinary Is Ordinary Language?" (chap. 3, *Is There a Text in This Class?*); "Facts and Fictions: A Reply to Ralph Rader" (chap. 5, *Is There a Text in This Class?*).

8

Patrocinio Schweickart
1942–

Patrocinio Schweickart is a leader in the development of new theories of feminist Reader-Response criticism. She has published articles on literary theory and women's literature in *Reader, Modern Fiction Studies, Signs,* and the *Canadian Journal of Social and Political Theory.* With Elizabeth A. Flynn she edited *Gender and Reading* (1986), and her essay "Engendering Critical Discourse" is included in *The Current in Criticism: Essays on the Present and Future of Literary Theory* (1987). Schweickart is associate professor of English at the University of New Hampshire.

Schweickart's "Reading Ourselves: Toward a Feminist Theory of Reading" won the 1984 Florence Howe Award for Outstanding Feminist Scholarship. In this essay Schweickart calls for a change in the "utopian" nature of standard forms of Reader-Response criticism (both the text-oriented and reader-oriented varieties) to include considerations of gender. She asserts that if it is possible to locate the "difference" in women's writing, then it must be possible to locate the "difference" in women's reading. Feminist critics and Reader-Response theorists must develop "reading strategies consonant with the concerns, experiences, and formal devices" that inform women's reading. Women, especially women in the academy, have been "immasculated" by their training; they have been taught to read as men, therefore denying meaning that a text may have for them as women. Rather than accepting a traditional interpretation women must learn to read a text as it was "not meant to be read," to read it "against itself." In doing so, Schweickart hopes, women readers may be able to reverse the process of immasculation. Such a reversal may lead not only to a reevaluation of texts by male writers but to a reevaluation of women writers whose works have been devalued by years of misreading.

Reading Ourselves: Toward a Feminist Theory of Reading

THREE STORIES OF READING

A. Wayne Booth begins his Presidential Address to the 1982 MLA Convention by considering and rejecting several plausible myths that might enable us "to dramatize not just our inescapable plurality but the validity of our sense that [as teachers and scholars of literature and composition] we belong together, somehow working on common ground." At last he settles on one story that is "perhaps close enough to our shared experience to justify the telling."[1]

Once upon a time there was a boy who fell in love with books. When he was very young he heard over and over the legend of his great-grandfather, a hard-working weaver who so desired knowledge that he figured out a way of working the loom with one hand, his legs, and his feet, leaving the other hand free to hold a book, and worked so steadily in that crooked position that he became permanently crippled. The boy heard other stories about the importance of reading. Salvation, he came to believe, was to be found in books. When he was six years old, he read *The Wizard of Oz*—his first *real* book—and was rewarded by his Great-Aunt Manda with a dollar.

When the boy grew up, he decided to become a teacher of "litcomp." His initiation into the profession was rigorous, and there were moments when he nearly gave up. But gradually, "there emerged from the trudging a new and surprising love, a love that with all my previous reading I had not dreamed of: the love of skill, of craft, of getting clear in my mind and then in my writing what a great writer had got right in his work" (Booth, p. 315). Eventually, the boy, now grown, got his doctorate, and after teaching for thirteen years in small colleges, he returned to his graduate institution to become one of its eminent professors.

Booth caps his narration by quoting from *The Autobiography of Malcolm X*. It was in prison that Malcolm learned to read:

> For the first time I could pick up a book and now begin to understand what the book was saying. Anyone who has read a great deal can imagine the new world that opened. Let me tell you something: from then until I left that prison, in every free moment I had, if I was not reading in the library, I was reading on my bunk. . . . [M]onths passed without my even thinking about being imprisoned. In fact, up to then, I never had been so truly free in my life. (As quoted by Booth, p. 317)

"Perhaps," says Booth, "when you think back now on my family's story about great-grandfather Booth, you will understand why reading about Malcolm X's awakening speaks to the question of where I got my 'insane love' [for books]" (p. 317).

B. When I read the Malcolm X passage quoted in Booth's address, the ellipsis roused my curiosity. What, exactly, I wondered, had been deleted? What in the original exceeded the requirements of a Presidential Address to the MLA? Checking, I found the complete sentence to read: "Between Mr. Muhammad's teachings, my correspondence, my visitors—usually Ella and Reginald—and my reading, months passed without my even thinking about being imprisoned."[2] Clearly, the first phrase is the dissonant one. The reference to the leader of the notorious Black Muslims suggests a story of reading very different from Booth's. Here is how Malcolm X tells it. While serving time in the Norfolk Prison Colony, he hit on the idea of teaching himself to read by copying the dictionary.

> In my slow, painstaking, ragged handwriting, I copied into my tablet every thing on the first page, down to the punctuation marks. . . . Then, aloud, to myself, I read back everything I'd written on the tablet. . . . I woke up the next morning thinking about these words—immensely proud to realize that not only had I written so much at one time, but I'd written words that I never knew were in the world. . . . That was the way I started copying what eventually became the entire dictionary. (P. 172)

After copying the dictionary, Malcolm X began reading the books in the prison library. "No university would ask any student to devour literature as I did when this new world opened to me, of being able to read and *understand*" (p. 173). Reading had changed the course of his life. Years later, he would reflect on how "the ability to read awoke inside me some long dormant craving to be mentally alive" (p. 179).

What did he read? What did he understand? He read Gregor Mendel's *Findings in Genetics* and it helped him to understand "that if you started with a black man, a white man could be produced; but starting with a white man, you never could produce a black man—because the white chromosome is recessive. And since no one disputes that there was but one Original Man, the conclusion is clear" (p. 175). He read histories, books by Will Durant and Arnold Toynbee, by W. E. B. du Bois and Carter G. Woodson, and he saw how "the glorious history of the black man" had been "bleached" out of the history books written by white men.

> [His] eyes opened gradually, then wider and wider, to how the world's white men had indeed acted like devils, pillaging and raping and bleeding and draining the whole world's non-white people. . . . I will never forget how shocked I was when I began reading about slavery's total horror. . . . The world's most monstrous crime, the sin and the blood on the white man's hands, are almost impossible to believe. (P. 175)

He read philosophy—the works of Schopenhauer, Kant, Nietzsche, and Spinoza—and he concluded that the "whole stream of Western Philosophy was now wound up in a cul-de-sac" as a result of the white man's "elaborate, neurotic necessity to hide the black man's true role in history" (p. 180). Malcolm X read voraciously, and book after book confirmed the truth of Elijah Muhammad's teachings. "It's a crime, the lie that has been told to generations of black men and white both. . . . Innocent black children growing up, living out their lives, dying of old age—and all of their lives ashamed of being black. But the truth is pouring out of the bag now" (p. 181).

Wayne Booth's story leads to the Crystal Ballroom of the Biltmore Hotel in Los Angeles, where we attend the protagonist as he delivers his Presidential Address to the members of the Modern Language Association. Malcolm X's love of books took him in a different direction, to the stage of the Audubon Ballroom in Harlem, where, as he was about to address a mass meeting of the Organization of Afro-American Unity, he was murdered.

C. As we have seen, an ellipsis links Wayne Booth's story of reading to Malcolm X's. Another ellipsis, this time not graphically marked, signals the existence of a third story. Malcolm X's startling reading of Mendel's genetics overlooks the most rudimentary fact of human reproduction: whether you start with a black man or a white man, without a woman, you get *nothing*. An excerpt from Virginia Woolf's *A Room of One's Own* restores this deleted perspective.[3]

The heroine, call her Mary, says Woolf, goes to the British Museum in search of information about women. There she discovers to her chagrin that woman is, "perhaps, the most discussed animal in the universe?"

> Why does Samuel Butler say, "Wise men never say what they think of women"? Wise men never say anything else apparently. . . . Are they capable of education? Napoleon thought them incapable. Dr. Johnson thought the opposite. Have they souls or have they not souls? Some savages say they have none. Others, on the contrary, say women are half divine and worship them on that account. Some sages hold that they are shallower in the brain; others that they are deeper in consciousness. Goethe honoured them; Mussolini despises them. Wherever one looked men thought about women and thought differently. (Pp. 29–30)

Distressed and confused, Mary notices that she has unconsciously drawn a picture in her notebook, the face and figure of Professor von X, engaged in writing his monumental work, *The Mental, Moral, and Physical Inferiority of the Female* Sex. "His expression suggested that he was labouring under some emotion that made him jab his pen on the paper as if he were killing some noxious insect as he wrote, but even when he had killed it that did not satisfy him; he must go on killing it. . . . A very elementary exercise in psychology . . . showed me . . . that the sketch had been made in anger" (pp. 31–32).

Nothing remarkable in that, she reflects, given the provocation. But "How explain the anger of the professor? . . . For when it came to analysing the impression left by these books, . . . there was [an] element which was often present and could not be immediately identified. Anger, I called it. . . . To judge from its effects, it was anger disguised and complex, not anger simple and open" (p. 32).

Disappointed with essayists and professors, Mary turns to historians. But apparently women played no significant role in history. What little information Mary finds is disturbing: "Wife-beating, I read, was a recognized right of a man, and was practiced without shame by high as well as low" (p. 44). Oddly enough, literature presents a contradictory picture.

> If women had not existence save in fiction written by men, we would imagine her to be a person of utmost importance; very various; heroic and mean; splendid and sordid; infinitely beautiful and hideous in the extreme; as great as a man, some think even greater. But this is women in fiction. In fact, as Professor Trevelyan points out, she was locked up, beaten and flung about the room. (P. 45)

At last, Mary can draw but one conclusion from her reading. Male professors, male historians, and male poets can not be relied on for the truth about women. Woman herself must undertake the study of woman. Of course, to do so, she must secure enough money to live on and a room of her own.

Booth's story, we recall, is told within the framework of a professional ritual. It is intended to remind us of "the loves and fears that inform our daily work" and of "what we do when we are at our best," to show, if not a unity, then enough of a "center" "to shame us whenever we violate it." The principal motif of the myth is the hero's insane love for books, and the way this develops with education and maturity into "critical understanding," which Booth defines as that synthesis of thought and passion which should replace, "on the one hand, sentimental and uncritical identifications that leave minds undisturbed, and on the other, hypercritical negations that freeze or alienate" (pp. 317–18). Booth is confident that the experience celebrated by the myth is archetypal. "Whatever our terms for it, whatever our theories about how it happens or why it fails to happen more often, can we reasonably doubt the importance of the moment, at any level of study, when any of us—you, me, Malcolm X, my great-grandfather—succeeds in entering other minds, or 'taking them in,' as nourishment for our own?" (p. 318).

Now, while it is certainly true that something one might call "critical understanding" informs the stories told by Malcolm X and Virginia Woolf, these authors fill this term with thoughts and passions that one would never suspect from Booth's definition. From the standpoint of the second and third stories of reading, Booth's story is utopian. The powers and resources of his hero are equal to the challenges he encounters. At each stage he finds suitable mentors. He is assured by the people around him, by the books he reads, by the entire culture, that he is right for the part. His talents and accomplishments are acknowledged and justly rewarded. In short, from the perspective of Malcolm X's and Woolf's stories, Booth's hero is fantastically privileged.

Utopian has a second meaning, one that

is by no means pejorative, and Booth's story is utopian in this sense as well. In overlooking the realities highlighted by the stories of Malcolm X and Virginia Woolf, Booth's story anticipates what might be possible, what "critical understanding" might mean for *everyone*, if only we could overcome the pervasive systemic injustices of our time.

READER-RESPONSE THEORY AND FEMINIST CRITICISM

Reader-response criticism, as currently constituted, is utopian in the same two senses. The different accounts of the reading experience that have been put forth overlook the issues of race, class, and sex, and give no hint of the conflicts, sufferings, and passions that attend these realities. The relative tranquility of the tone of these theories testifies to the privileged position of the theorists. Perhaps, someday, when privileges have withered away or at least become equitably distributed, some of these theories will ring true. Surely we ought to be able to talk about reading without worrying about injustice. But for now, reader-response criticism must confront the disturbing implications of our historical reality. Paradoxically, utopian theories that elide these realities betray the utopian impulses that inform them.

To put the matter plainly, reader-response criticism needs feminist criticism. The two have yet to engage each other in a sustained and serious way, but if the promise of the former is to be fulfilled, such an encounter must soon occur. Interestingly, the obvious question of the significance of gender has already been explicitly raised, and—this testifies to the increasing impact of feminist criticism as well as to the direct ideological bearing of the issue of gender on reader-response criticism—not by a feminist critic, but by Jonathan Culler, a leading theorist of reading: "If the experience of literature depends upon the qualities of a reading self, one can ask what difference it would make to the experience of literature and thus to the meaning of literature if this self were, for example, female rather than male. If the meaning of a work is the experience of a reader, what difference does it make if the reader is a woman?"[4]

Until very recently this question has not occurred to reader-response critics. They have been preoccupied with other issues. Culler's survey of the field is instructive here, for it enables us to anticipate the direction reader-response theory might take when it is shaken from its slumber by feminist criticism. According to Culler, the different models (or "stories") of reading that have been proposed are all organized around three problems. The first is the issue of control: Does the text control the reader, or vice versa? For David Bleich, Normal Holland, and Stanley Fish, the reader holds controlling interest. Readers read the poems they have made. Bleich asserts this point most strongly: the constraints imposed by the words on the page are "trivial," since their meaning can always be altered by "subjective action." To claim that the text supports this or that reading is only to "moralistically claim . . . that one's own objectification is more authoritative than someone else's."[5]

At the other pole are Michael Riffaterre, Georges Poulet, and Wolfgang Iser, who acknowledge the creative role of the reader, but ultimately take the text to be the dominant force. To read, from this point of view, is to create the text according to *its* own promptings. As Poulet puts it, a text, when invested with a reader's subjectivity, becomes a "subjectified object," a "second self" that depends on the reader, but is not, strictly speaking, identical with him. Thus, reading "is a way of giving way not only to a host of alien words, images and ideas, but also to the very alien principle which utters and shelters them. . . . I am on loan to another, and this other thinks, feels, suffers and acts within me."[6] Culler argues persuasively that, regardless of their ostensible theoretical commitments, the prevailing stories of reading generally vacillate between these reader-dominant and text-dominant poles. In fact, those who stress the subjectivity of the reader as against the objectivity of the text ultimately portray the text as determining the responses of the reader. "The more active, projective, or creative the reader is, the more she is manipulated by the sentence or by the author" (p. 71).

The second question prominent in theories of reading is closely related to the first. Reading always involves a subject and an object, a reader and a text. But what constitutes the objectivity of the text? What is "in" the text? What is supplied by the reader? Again, the answers have been equivocal. On the face of it, the situation seems to call for a dualistic theory that credits the contributions of both text and reader. However, Culler argues, a dualistic theory eventually gives way to a monistic theory, in which one or the other pole supplies everything. One might say, for instance, that Iser's theory ultimately implies the determinacy of the text and the authority of the author: "The author guarantees the unity of the work, requires the reader's creative participation, and through his text, prestructures the shape of the aesthetic object to be produced by the reader."[7] At the same time, one can also argue that the "gaps" that structure the reader's response are not built into the text, but appear (or not) as a result of the particular interpretive strategy employed by the reader. Thus, "there is no distinction between what the text gives and what the reader supplies; he supplies *everything*."[8] Depending on which aspects of the theory one takes seriously, Iser's theory collapses either into a monism of the text or a monism of the reader.

The third problem identified by Culler concerns the ending of the story. Most of the time stories of reading end happily. "Readers may be manipulated and misled, but when they finish the book their experience turns into knowledge . . . as though finishing the book took them outside the experience of reading and gave them mastery of it" (p. 79). However, some critics—Harold Bloom, Paul de Man, and Culler himself—find these optimistic endings questionable, and prefer instead stories that stress the impossibility of reading. If, as de Man says, rhetoric puts "an insurmountable obstacle in the way of any reading or understanding," then the reader "may be placed in impossible situations where there is no happy issue, but only the possibility of playing out the roles dramatized in the text" (Culler, p. 81).

Such have been the predominant preoccupations of reader-response criticism during the past decade and a half. Before indicating how feminist critics could affect the conversation, let me consider an objection. A recent and influential essay by Elaine Showalter suggests that we should not enter the conversation at all. She observes that during its early phases, the principal mode of feminist criticism was "feminist critique," which was counter-ideological in intent and concerned with the feminist as *reader*. Happily, we have outgrown this necessary but theoretically unpromising approach. Today, the dominant mode of feminist criticism is "gynocritics," the study of woman as *writer*, of the "history, styles, themes, genres, and structures of writing by women; the psychodynamics of female creativity; the trajectory of the individual or collective female career; and the evolution and laws of a female literary tradition." The shift from "feminist critique" to "gynocritics"—from emphasis on woman as reader to emphasis on woman as writer—has put us in the position of developing a feminist criticism that is "genuinely woman-centered, independent, and intellectually coherent."

> To see women's writing as our primary subject forces us to make the leap to a new conceptual vantage point and to redefine the nature of the theoretical problem before us. It is no longer the ideological dilemma of reconciling revisionary pluralisms but the essential question of difference. How can we constitute women as a distinct literary group? What is the *difference* of women's writing?[9]

But why should the activity of the woman writer be more conducive to theory than the activity of the woman reader is? If it is possible to formulate a basic conceptual framework for disclosing the "difference" of women's writing, surely it is no less possible to do so for women's reading. The same difference, be it linguistic, biological, psychological, or cultural, should apply in either case. In addition, what Showalter calls "gynocritics" is in fact constituted by feminist *criticism*—that is, *readings*—of female texts. Thus, the relevant distinction is not between woman as reader and woman as writer, but between feminist readings of male texts and feminist readings of female texts, and there is no reason why the former could not be as theoretically coherent (or irreducibly pluralistic) as the latter.

On the other hand, there are good reasons for feminist criticism to engage reader-response criticism. Both dispute the fetishized art object, the "Verbal Icon," of New Criticism, and both seek to dispel the objectivist illusion that buttresses the authority of the dominant critical tradition. Feminist criticism can have considerable impact on reader-response criticism, since, as Culler has noticed, it is but a small step from the thesis that the reader is an active producer of meaning to the recognition that there are many different kinds of readers, and that women—because of their numbers if because of nothing else—constitute an essential class. Reader-response critics cannot take refuge in the objectivity of the text, or even in the idea that a gender-neutral criticism is possible. Today they can continue to ignore the implications of feminist criticism only at the cost of incoherence or intellectual dishonesty.

It is equally true that feminist critics need to question their allegiance to text- and author-centered paradigms of criticism. Feminist criticism, we should remember, is a mode of *praxis*. The point is not merely to interpret literature in various ways; the point is to *change the world*. We cannot afford to ignore the activity of reading, for it is here that literature is realized as *praxis*. Literature acts on the world by acting on its readers.

To return to our earlier question: What will happen to reader-response criticism if feminists enter the conversation? It is useful to recall the contrast between Booth's story and those of Malcolm X and Virginia Woolf. Like Booth's story, the "stories of reading" that currently make up reader-response theory are mythically abstract, and appear, from a different vantage point, to be by and about readers who are fantastically privileged. Booth's story had a happy ending; Malcolm's and Mary's did not. For Mary, reading meant encountering a tissue of lies and silences; for Malcolm it meant the verification of Elijah Muhammad's shocking doctrines.

Two factors—gender and politics—which are suppressed in the dominant models of reading gain prominence with the advent of a feminist perspective. The feminist story will have *at least* two chapters: one concerned with feminist readings of male texts, and another with feminist readings of female texts. In addition, in this story, gender will have a prominent role as the locus of political struggle.

The story will speak of the difference between men and women, of the way the experience and perspective of women have been systematically and fallaciously assimilated into the generic masculine, and of the need to correct this error. Finally, it will identify literature—the activities of reading and writing—as an important arena of political struggle, a crucial component of the project of interpreting the world in order to change it.

Feminist criticism does not approach reader-response criticism without preconceptions. Actually, feminist criticism has always included substantial reader-centered interests. In the next two sections of this paper, I will review these interests, first with respect to male texts, then with respect to female texts. In the process, I will uncover some of the issues that might be addressed and clarified by a feminist theory of reading.

THE FEMALE READER AND THE LITERARY CANON

Although reader-response critics propose different and often conflicting models, by and large the emphasis is on features of the process of reading that do not vary with the nature of the reading material. The feminist entry into the conversation brings the nature of the text back into the foreground. For feminists, the question of *how* we read is inextricably linked with the question of *what* we read. More specifically, the feminist inquiry into the activity of reading begins with the realization that the literary canon is androcentric, and that this has a profoundly damaging effect on women readers. The documentation of this realization was one of the earliest tasks undertaken by feminist critics. Elaine Showalter's 1971 critique of the literary curriculum is exemplary of this work.

> [In her freshman year a female student] . . . might be assigned an anthology of essays, perhaps such as *The Responsible Man,* . . . or *Conditions of Man,* or *Man in Crisis,* or again, *Representative Man: Cult Heroes of Our Time,* in which thirty-three men represent such categories of heroism as the writer, the poet, the dramatist, the artist, and the guru, and the only two women included are the actress Elizabeth Taylor, and the existential Heroine Jacqueline Onassis.
>
> Perhaps the student would read a collection of stories like *The Young Man in American Literature: The Initiation Theme,* or sociological literature like *The Black Man and the Promise of America.* In a more orthodox literary program she might study eternally relevant classics, such as *Oedipus;* as a professor remarked in a recent issue of *College English,* all of us want to kill our fathers and marry our mothers. And whatever else she might read, she would inevitably arrive at the favorite book of all Freshman English courses, the classic of adolescent rebellion, *The Portrait of the Artist as a Young Man.*
>
> By the end of her freshman year, a woman student would have learned something about intellectual neutrality; she would be learning, in fact, how to think like a man. And so she would go on, increasingly with male professors to guide her.[10]

The more personal accounts of other critics reinforce Showalter's critique.

> The first result of my reading was a feeling that male characters were at the very least more interesting than women to the authors who invented them. Thus if, reading their books as it seemed their authors intended them, I naively identified with a character, I repeatedly chose men; I would rather have been Hamlet than Ophelia, Tom Jones instead of Sophia Western, and, perhaps, despite Dostoevsky's intention, Raskolnikov not Sonia.
>
> More peculiar perhaps, but sadly unsurprising, were the assessments I accepted about fictional women. For example, I quickly learned that power was unfeminine and powerful women were, quite literally, monstrous. . . . Bitches all, they must be eliminated, reformed, or at the very least, condemned. . . . Those rare women who are shown in fiction as both powerful and, in

> some sense, admirable are such because their power is based, if not on beauty, then at least on sexuality.[11]

For a woman, then, books do not necessarily spell salvation. In fact, a literary education may very well cause her grave psychic damage: schizophrenia "is the bizarre but logical conclusion of our education. Imagining myself male, I attempted to create myself male. Although I knew the case was otherwise, it seemed I could do nothing to make this other critically real."[12]

To put the matter theoretically, androcentric literature structures the reading experience differently depending on the gender of the reader. For the male reader, the text serves as the meeting ground of the personal and the universal. Whether or not the text approximates the particularities of his own experience, he is invited to validate the equation of maleness with humanity. The male reader feels his affinity with the universal, with the paradigmatic human being, precisely because he is male. Consider the famous scene of Stephen's epiphany in *The Portrait of the Artist as a Young Man.*

> A girl stood before him in midstream, alone and still, gazing out to sea. She seemed like one whom magic had changed into the likeness of a strange and beautiful seabird. Her long slender bare legs were delicate as a crane's and pure save where an emerald trail of seaweed had fashioned itself as a sign upon the flesh. Her thighs, fuller and softhued as ivory, were bared almost to the hips, where the white fringes of her drawers were like feathering of soft white down. Her slateblue skirts were kilted boldly about her waist and dovetailed behind her. Her bosom was a bird's, soft and slight, slight and soft, as the breast of some dark plummaged dove. But her long fair hair was girlish: and touched with the wonder of mortal beauty, her face.[13]

A man reading this passage invited to identify with Stephen, to feel "the riot in his blood," and, thus, to ratify the alleged universality of the experience. Whether or not the sight of a girl on the beach has ever provoked similar emotions in him, the male reader is invited to feel his *difference* (concretely, *from the girl*) and to equate that with the universal. Relevant here is Lévi-Strauss's theory that woman functions as currency exchanged between men. The woman in the text converts the text into a woman, and the circulation of this text/woman becomes the central ritual that establishes the bond between the author and his male readers.[14]

The same text affects a woman reader differently. Judith Fetterley gives the most explicit theory to date about the dynamics of the woman reader's encounter with androcentric literature. According to Fetterley, notwithstanding the prevalence of the castrating bitch stereotype, "the cultural reality is not the emasculation of men by women, but the *immasculation* of women by men. As readers and teachers and scholars, women are taught to think as men, to identify with a male point of view, and to accept as normal and legitimate a male system of values, one of whose central principles is misogyny."[15]

The process of immasculation does not impart virile power to the woman reader. On the contrary, it doubles her oppression. She suffers "not simply the powerlessness which derives from not seeing one's experience articulated, clarified, and legitimized in art, but more significantly, the powerlessness which results from the endless division of self against self, the consequence of the invocation to identify as male while being reminded that to be male—to be universal— . . . is to be *not female*."[16]

A woman reading Joyce's novel of artistic awakening, and in particular the passage quoted above, will, like her male counterpart, be invited to identify with Stephen and therefore to ratify the equation of maleness with the universal. Androcentric literature is all the more efficient as an instrument of sexual politics because it does not allow the woman reader to seek refuge in her difference. Instead, it draws her into a process that uses her against herself. It solicits her complicity in the elevation of male difference into universality and, accordingly, the denigration of female difference into otherness without reciprocity. To be sure, misogyny is abundant in the literary canon.[17] It is important, however, that Fetterley's argument can stand on a weaker premise. Androcentricity is a sufficient condition for the process of immasculation.

Feminist critics of male texts, from Kate Millett to Judith Fetterley, have worked under the sign of the "Resisting Reader." Their goal is to disrupt the process of immasculation by exposing it to consciousness, by disclosing the androcentricity of what has customarily passed for the universal. However, feminist criticism written under the aegis of the resisting reader leaves certain questions unanswered, questions that are becoming ripe for feminist analysis: Where does the text get its power to draw us into its designs? Why do some (not all) demonstrably sexist texts remain appealing even after they have been subjected to thorough feminist critique? The usual answer—that the power of male texts is the power of the false consciousness into which women as well as men have been socialized—oversimplifies the problem and prevents us from comprehending both the force of literature and the complexity of our responses to it.

Fredric Jameson advances a thesis that seems to me to be a good starting point for the feminist reconsideration of male texts: "The effectively ideological is also at the same time necessarily utopian."[18] This thesis implies that the male text draws its power over the female reader from authentic desires, which it rouses and then harnesses to the process of immasculation.

A concrete example is in order. Consider Lawrence's *Women in Love*, and for the sake of simplicity, concentrate on Birkin and Ursula. Simone de Beauvoir and Kate Millet have convinced me that this novel is sexist. Why does it remain appealing to me? Jameson's thesis prompts me to answer this question by examining how the text plays not only on my false consciousness but also on my authentic liberatory aspirations—that is to say, on the very impulses that drew me to the feminist movement.

The trick of reversal comes in handy here. If we reverse the roles of Birkin and Ursula, the ideological components (or at least the most egregious of these, e.g., the analogy between women and horses) stand out as absurdities. Now, if we delete these absurd components while keeping the roles reversed, we have left the story of a woman struggling to combine her passionate desire for autonomous conscious being with an equally passionate desire for love and for other human bonds. This residual story is not far from one we would welcome as expressive of a feminist sensibility. Interestingly enough, it also intimates a novel Lawrence might have written, namely, the proper sequel to *The Rainbow*.

My affective response to the novel Lawrence did write is bifurcated. On the one hand, because I am a woman, I am implicated in the representation of Ursula and in the destiny Lawrence has prepared for her: man is the son of god, but woman is the daugher of man. Her vocation is to witness his transcendence in rapt silence. On the other hand, Fetterley is correct that I am also induced to identify with Birkin, and in so doing, I am drawn into complicity with the reduction of Ursula, and therefore of myself, to the role of the other.

However, the process of immasculation

is more complicated than Fetterley allows. When I identify with Birkin, I unconsciously perform the two-stage rereading described above. I reverse the roles of Birkin and Ursula and I suppress the obviously ideological components that in the process show up as absurdities. The identification with Birkin is emotionally effective because, stripped of its patriarchal trappings, Birkin's struggle and his utopian vision conform to my own. To the extent that I perform this feminist rereading *unconsciously*, I am captivated by the text. The stronger my desire for autonomous selfhood and for love, the stronger my identification with Birkin, and the more intense the experience of bifurcation characteristic of the process of immasculation.

The full argument is beyond the scope of this essay. My point is that *certain* (not all) male texts merit a dual hermeneutic: a negative hermeneutic that discloses their complicity with patriarchal ideology, and a positive hermeneutic that recuperates the utopian moment—the authentic kernel—from which they draw a significant portion of their emotional power.[19]

READING WOMEN'S WRITING

Showalter is correct that feminist criticism has shifted emphasis in recent years from "critique" (primarily) of male texts to "gynocritics," or the study of women's writing. Of course, it is worth remembering that the latter has always been on the feminist agenda. *Sexual Politics*, for example, contains not only the critique of Lawrence, Miller, and Mailer that won Millett such notoriety, but also her memorable rereading of *Villette*.[20] It is equally true that interest in women's writing has not entirely supplanted the critical study of patriarchal texts. In a sense "critique" has provided the bridge from the study of male texts to the study of female texts. As feminist criticism shifted from the first to the second, "feminist critique" turned its attention from androcentric texts per se to the androcentric critical strategies that pushed women's writing to the margins of the literary canon. The earliest examples of this genre (for instance, Showalter's "The Double Critical Standard," and Carol Ohmann's "Emily Brontë in the Hands of Male Critics") were concerned primarily with describing and documenting the prejudice against women writers that clouded the judgment of well-placed readers, that is, reviewers and critics.[21] Today we have more sophisticated and more comprehensive analyses of the androcentric critical tradition.

One of the most cogent of these is Nina Baym's analysis of American literature.[22] Baym observes that, as late as 1977, the American canon of major writers did not include a single woman novelist. And yet, in terms of numbers and commercial success, women novelists have probably dominated American literature since the middle of the nineteenth century. How to explain this anomaly?

One explanation is simple bias of the sort documented by Showalter, Ohmann, and others. A second is that women writers lived and worked under social conditions that were not particularly conducive to the production of "excellent" literature: "There tended to be a sort of immediacy in the ambitions of literary women leading them to professionalism rather than artistry, by choice as well as by social pressure and opportunity."[23] Baym adduces a third, more subtle, and perhaps more important reason. There are, she argues, "gender-related restrictions that do not arise out of the cultural realities contemporary with the writing woman, but out of later critical theories . . . which impose their concerns anachronistically, after the fact, on an earlier period."[24] If one reads the critics most instrumental in forming the current theories about American literature (Matthiessen, Chase, Feidelson, Trilling, etc.), one finds that the theoretical model for the canonical American novel is the "melodrama of beset manhood." To accept this model is also to accept as a consequence the exclusion from the canon of "melodramas of beset womanhood," as well as virtually all fiction centering on the experience of women.[25]

The deep symbiotic relationship between the androcentric canon and androcentric modes of reading is well summarized by Kolodny.

> *Insofar as we are taught to read, what we engage are not texts, but paradigms.* . . . Insofar as literature is itself a social institution, so, too, reading is a highly socialized—or learned—activity. . . . We read well, and with pleasure, what we already know how to read; and what we know how to read is to a large extent dependent on what we have already read [works from which we have developed our expectations and learned our interpretive strategies]. What we then choose to read—and, by extension, teach and thereby "canonize"—usually follows upon our previous reading.[26]

We are caught, in other words, in a rather vicious circle. An androcentric canon generates androcentric interpretive strategies, which in turn favor the canonization of androcentric texts and the marginalization of gynocentric ones. To break this circle, feminist critics must fight on two fronts: for the revision of the canon to include a significant body of works by women, and for the development of the reading strategies consonant with the concerns, experiences, and formal devices that constitute these texts. Of course, to succeed, we also need a community of women readers who are qualified by experience, commitment, and training, and who will enlist the personal and institutional resources at their disposal in the struggle.[27]

The critique of androcentric reading strategies is essential, for it opens up some ideological space for the recuperation of women's writing. Turning now to this project, we observe, first, that a large volume of work has been done, and, second, that this endeavor is coming to look even more complicated and more diverse than the criticism of male texts. Certainly, it is impossible in the space of a few pages to do justice to the wide range of concerns, strategies, and positions associated with feminist readings of female texts. Nevertheless, certain things can be said. For the remainder of this section, I focus on an exemplary essay: "Vesuvius at Home: The Power of Emily Dickinson," by Adrienne Rich.[28] My commentary anticipates the articulation of a paradigm that illuminates certain features of feminist reading of women's writing.

I am principally interested in the rhetoric of Rich's essay, for it represents an implicit commentary on the process of reading women's writing. Feminist readings of male texts are, as we have seen, primarily resisting. The reader assumes an adversarial or at least a detached attitude toward the material at hand. In the opening pages of her essay, Rich introduces three metaphors that proclaim a very different attitude toward her subject.

> The methods, the exclusions, of Emily Dickinson's existence could not have been my own; yet more and more, as a woman poet finding my own methods, I have come to understand her necessities, could have served as witness in her defense. (P. 158)
>
> I am traveling at the speed of time, along the Massachusetts Turnpike. . . . "Home is not where the heart is," she wrote in a letter, "but the house and adjacent buildings." . . . I am traveling at the speed of time, in the direction of the house and buildings. . . . For years, I have been not so much envisioning Emily Dickinson as trying to visit, to enter her mind through her poems and letters, and through my own intimations of what it could have meant to be one of the two mid-nineteenth century American ge-

> niuses, and a woman, living in Amherst, Massachusetts. (Pp. 158–59)
>
> For months, for most of my life, I have been hovering like an insect against the screens of an existence which inhabited Amherst, Massachusetts between 1830 and 1886. (P. 158) . . . Here [in Dickinson's bedroom] I become again, an insect, vibrating at the frames of windows, clinging to the panes of glass, trying to connect. (P. 161)

A commentary on the process of reading is carried on silently and unobtrusively through the use of these metaphors. The first is a judicial metaphor: the feminist reader speaks as a witness in defense of the woman writer. Here we see clearly that gender is crucial. The feminist reader takes the part of the woman writer against patriarchal misreadings that trivialize or distort her work.[29] The second metaphor refers to a principal tenet of feminist criticism: a literary work cannot be understood apart from the social, historical, and cultural context within which it was written. As if to acquiesce to the condition Dickinson had imposed on her friends, Rich travels through space and time to visit the poet on her own *premises*. She goes to Amherst, to the house where Dickinson lived. She rings the bell, she goes in, then upstairs, then into the bedroom that had been "freedom" for the poet. Her destination, ultimately, is Dickinson's mind. But it is not enough to read the poet's poems and letters. To reach her heart and mind, one must take a detour through "the house and adjacent buildings."

Why did Dickinson go into seclusion? Why did she write poems she would not publish? What mean these poems about queens, volcanoes, deserts, eternity, passion, suicide, wild beasts, rape, power, madness, the daemon, the grave? For Rich, these are related questions. The revisionary re-reading of Dickinson's work is of a piece with the revisionary re-reading of her life. "I have a notion genius knows itself; that Dickinson chose her seclusion, knowing what she needed. . . . She carefully selected her society and controlled the disposal of her time. . . . Given her vocation, she was neither eccentric nor quaint; she was determined to survive, to use her powers, to practice necessary economies" (p. 160).

> To write [the poetry that she needed to write] she had to enter chambers of
> the self in which
>
> Ourself, concealed—
> Should startle most—
>
> and to relinquish control there, to take those risks, she had to create a relationship to the outer world where she could feel in control. (P. 175)

The metaphor of visiting points to another feature of feminist readings of women's writing, namely, the tendency to construe the text not as an object, but as the manifestation of the subjectivity of the absent author—the "voice" of another woman. Rich is not content to revel in the textuality of Dickinson's poems and letters. For her, these are doorways to the "mind" of a "woman of genius." Rich deploys her imagination and her considerable rhetorical skill to evoke "the figure of powerful will" who lives at the heart of the text. To read Dickinson, then, is to try to visit with her, to hear her voice, to make her live *in* oneself, and to feel her impressive "personal dimensions."[30]

At the same time, Rich is keenly aware that visiting with Dickinson is *only* a metaphor for reading her poetry, and an inaccurate one at that. She signals this awareness with the third metaphor. It is no longer possible to visit with Dickinson; one can only enter her mind through her poems and letters as one can enter her house—through the backdoor out of which her coffin was carried. In reading, one encounters only a text, the trail of an absent author. Upstairs, at last, in the very room where Dickinson exercised her astonishing craft, Rich finds herself again "an insect, vibrating at the frames of windows, clinging to panes of glass, trying to connect." But though "the scent is very powerful," Dickinson herself is absent.

Perhaps the most obvious rhetorical device employed by Rich in this essay, more obvious even than her striking metaphors, is her use of the personal voice. Her approach to Dickinson is self-consciously and unabashedly subjective. She clearly describes her point of view—what she saw as she drove across the Connecticut Valley toward Amherst (ARCO stations, McDonald's, shopping plazas, as well as "light-green spring softening the hills, dogwood and wild fruit trees blossoming in the hollows"), and what she thought about (the history of the valley, "scene of Indian uprisings, religious revivals, spiritual confrontations, the blazing-up of the lunatic fringe of the Puritan coal," and her memories of college weekends in Amherst). Some elements of her perspective—ARCO and McDonald's—would have been alien to Dickinson; others—the sight of dogwood and wild fruit trees in the spring, and most of all, the experience of being a woman poet in a patriarchal culture—would establish their affinity.

Rich's metaphors together with her use of the personal voice indicate some key issues underlying feminist readings of female texts. On the one hand, reading is necessarily subjective. On the other hand, it must not be wholly so. One must respect the autonomy of the text. The reader is a visitor and, as such, must observe the necessary courtesies. She must avoid unwarranted intrusions—she must be careful not to appropriate what belongs to her host, not to impose herself on the other woman. Furthermore, reading is at once an intersubjective encounter and something less than that. In reading Dickinson, Rich seeks to enter her mind, to feel her presence. But the text is a screen, an inanimate object. Its subjectivity is only a projection of the subjectivity of the reader.

Rich suggests the central motivation, the regulative ideal, that shapes the feminist reader's approach to these issues. If feminist readings of male texts are motivated by the need to disrupt the process of immasculation, feminist readings of female texts are motivated by the need "to connect," to recuperate, or to formulate—they come to the same thing—the context, the tradition, that would link women writers to one another, to women readers and critics, and to the larger community of women. Of course, the recuperation of such a context is a necessary basis for the nonrepressive integration of women's point of view and culture into the study of a Humanities that is worthy of its name.[31]

FEMINIST MODELS OF READING: A SUMMARY

As I noted in the second section, mainstream reader-response theory is preoccupied with two closely related questions: (1) Does the text manipulate the reader, or does the reader manipulate the text to produce the meaning that suits her own interests? and (2) What is "in" the text? How can we distinguish what it supplies from what the reader supplies? Both of these questions refer to the subject-object relation that is established between reader and text during the process of reading. A feminist theory of reading also elaborates this relationship, but for feminists, gender—the gender inscribed in the text as well as the gender of the reader—is crucial. Hence, the feminist story has two chapters, one concerned with male texts and the other with female texts.

The focus of the first chapter is the experience of the woman reader. What do male texts *do* to her? The feminist story takes the subject-object relation of reading through three moments. The phrasing of the basic question signals the first moment. Control is conferred on the text: the woman reader is immasculated by the text. The feminist story fits well at this point in Iser's framework. Feminists insist that the androcentricity of the text and its damaging effects on women readers are not figments of their imagination. These are implicit in the "schematized aspects" of the text. The second movement, which is similarly consonant with the plot of Iser's story, involves the recognition of the crucial role played by the subjectivity of the woman reader. Without her, the text is *no-thing*. The process of immasculation is latent in the text, but it finds its actualization only through the reader's activity. In effect, the woman reader is the agent of her own immasculation.[32]

Here we seem to have a corroboration of Culler's contention that dualistic models of reading inevitably disintegrate into one of two monisms. Either the text (and, by implication, the author) or the woman reader is responsible for the process of immasculation. The third moment of the subject-object relation—ushered in by the transfiguration of the heroine into a feminist—breaks through this dilemma. The woman reader, now a feminist, embarks on a critical analysis of the reading process, and she realizes that the text has power to structure her experience. Without androcentric texts she will not suffer immasculation. However, her recognition of the power of the text is matched by her awareness of her essential role in the process of reading. Without her, the text is nothing—it is inert and harmless. The advent of feminist consciousness and the accompanying commitment to emancipatory *praxis* reconstitutes the subject-object relationship within a dialectical rather than a dualistic framework, thus averting the impasse described by Culler between the "dualism of narrative" and the "monism of theory." In the feminist story, the breakdown of Iser's dualism does not indicate a mistake or an irreducible impasse, but the necessity of *choosing* between two modes of reading. The reader can submit to the power of the text, or she can take control of the reading experience. The recognition of the existence of a choice suddenly makes visible the normative dimension of the feminist story: She *should* choose the second alternative.

But what does it mean for a reader to take control of the reading experience? First of all, she must do so without forgetting the androcentricity of the text or its power to structure her experience. In addition, the reader taking control of the text is not, as in Iser's model, simply a matter of selecting among the concretizations allowed by the text. Recall that a crucial feature of the process of immasculation is the woman reader's bifurcated response. She reads the text both as a man and as a woman. But in either case, the result is the same: she confirms her position as other. Taking control of the reading experience means reading the text as it was *not* meant to be read, in fact, reading it against itself. Specifically, one must identify the nature of the choices proffered by the text and, equally important, what the text precludes—namely, the possibility of reading as a woman *without* putting one's self in the position of the other, of reading so as to affirm womanhood as another, equally valid, paradigm of human existence.

All this is easier said than done. It is important to realize that reading a male text, no matter how virulently misogynous, could do little damage if it were an isolated event. The problem is that within patriarchal culture, the experience of immasculation is paradigmatic of women's encounters with the dominant literary and critical traditions. A feminist cannot simply refuse to read patriarchal texts, for they are everywhere, and they condition her participation in the literary and critical enterprise. In fact, by the time she becomes a feminist critic, a woman has already read numerous male texts—in particular, the most authoritative texts of the literary and critical canons. She has introjected not only androcentric texts, but also androcentric reading strategies and values. By the time she becomes a feminist, the bifurcated response characteristic of immasculation has become second nature to her. The feminist story stresses that patriarchal constructs have objective as well as subjective reality; they are inside and outside the text, inside and outside the reader.

The pervasiveness of androcentricity drives feminist theory beyond the individualistic models of Iser and of most reader-response critics. The feminist reader agrees with Stanley Fish that the production of the meaning of a text is mediated by the interpretive community in which the activity of reading is situated: the meaning of the text depends on the interpretive strategy one applies to it, and the choice of strategy is regulated (explicitly or implicitly) by the canons of acceptability that govern the interpretive community.[33] However, unlike Fish, the feminist reader is also aware that the ruling interpretive communities are androcentric, and that this androcentricity is deeply etched in the strategies and modes of thought that have been introjected by all readers, women as well as men.

Because patriarchal constructs have psychological correlates, taking control of the reading process means taking control of one's reactions and inclinations. Thus, a feminist reading—actually a rereading—is a kind of therapeutic analysis. The reader recalls and examines how she would "naturally" read a male text in order to understand and therefore undermine the subjective predispositions that had rendered her vulnerable to its designs. Beyond this, the pervasiveness of immasculation necessitates a collective remedy. The feminist reader hopes that other women will recognize themselves in her story, and join her in her struggle to transform the culture.[34]

"Feminism affirms women's point of view by revealing, criticizing and examining its impossibility."[35] Had we nothing but male texts, this sentence from Catherine MacKinnon's brilliant essay on jurisprudence could serve as the definition of the project of the feminist reader. The significant body of literature written by women presents feminist critics with another, more heartwarming, task: that of recovering, articulating, and elaborating positive expressions of women's point of view, of celebrating the survival of this point of view in spite of the formidable forces that have been ranged against it.

The shift to women's writing brings with it a shift in emphasis from the negative hermeneutic of ideological unmasking to a positive hermeneutic whose aim is the recovery and cultivation of women's culture. As Showalter has noted, feminist criticism of women's writing proposes to articulate woman's difference: What does it mean for a woman to express herself in writing? How does a woman write as a woman? It is a central contention of this essay that feminist criticism should also inquire into the correlative process of *reading:* What does it mean for a woman to read without condemning herself to the position of other? What does it mean for a woman, reading as a woman, to read literature written by a woman writing as a woman?[36]

The Adrienne Rich essay discussed in the preceding section illustrates a contrast between feminist readings of male texts and feminist readings of female texts. In the former, the object of the critique, whether it is regarded as an enemy or as symptom of a malignant condition, is the text itself, *not* the reputation or the character of the author.[37] This impersonal approach contrasts sharply with the strong personal interest in Dickinson exhibited by Rich. Furthermore, it is not merely a question of friendliness toward the text. Rich's reading aims beyond "the unfolding of the text as a living event," the goal of aesthetic reading set by Iser. Much of the rhetorical energy of Rich's essay is directed toward evoking the personality of Dickinson, toward making *her* live as the substantial, palpable presence animating her works.

Unlike the first chapter of the feminist story of reading, which is centered around a single heroine—the woman reader battling her way out of a maze of patriarchal constructs—the second chapter features two protagonists—the woman reader and the woman writer—in the context of two settings. The first setting is judicial: one woman is standing witness in defense of the other; the second is dialogic: the two women are engaged in intimate conversation. The judicial setting points to the larger political and cultural dimension of the project of the feminist reader. Feminist critics may well say with Harold Bloom that reading always involves the "art of defensive warfare."[38] What they mean by this, however, would not be Bloom's individualistic, agonistic encounter between "strong poet" and "strong reader," but something more akin to "class struggle." Whether concerned with male or female texts, feminist criticism is situated in the larger struggle against patriarchy.

The importance of this battle cannot be overestimated. However, feminist reading of women's writing opens up space for another, equally important, critical project, namely, the articulation of a model of reading that is centered on a female paradigm. While it is still too early to present a full-blown theory, the dialogic aspect of the relationship between the feminist reader and the woman writer suggests the direction that such a theory might take. As in all stories of reading, the drama revolves around the subject-object relationship between text and reader. The feminist story—exemplified by the Adrienne Rich essay discussed earlier—features an intersubjective construction of this relationship. The reader encounters not simply a text, but a "subjectified object": the "heart and mind" of another woman. She comes into close contact with an interiority—a power, a creativity, a suffering, a vision—that is *not* identical with her own. The feminist interest in construing reading as an intersubjective encounter suggests an affinity with Poulet's (rather than Iser's) theory, and, as in Poulet's model, the subject of the literary work is its author, *not* the reader: "A book is not only a book; it is a means by which an author actually preserves [her] ideas, [her] feelings, [her] modes of dreaming and living. It is a means of saving [her] identity from death . . . . To understand a literary work, then, is to let the individual who wrote it reveal [herself] to us *in* us."[39]

For all this initial agreement, however, the dialogic relationship the feminist reader establishes with the female subjectivity brought to life in the process of reading is finally at odds with Poulet's model. For the interiorized author is "alien" to Poulet's reader. When he reads, he delivers himself "bound hand and foot, to the omnipotence of fiction." He becomes the "prey" of what he reads. "There is no escaping this takeover." His consciousness is "invaded," "annexed," "usurped." He is "dispossessed" of his rightful place on the "center stage" of his own mind. In the final analysis, the process of reading leaves room for only one subjectivity. The work becomes "a sort of human being" at "the expense of the reader whose life it suspends."[40] It is significant that the metaphors of mastery and submission, of violation and control, so prominent in Poulet's essay, are en-

tirely absent in Rich's essay on Dickinson. In the paradigm of reading implicit in her essay, the dialectic of control (which shapes feminist readings of male texts) gives way to the dialectic of communication. For Rich, reading is a matter of "trying to connect" with the existence behind the text.

This dialectic also has three moments. The first involves the recognition that genuine intersubjective communication demands the duality of reader and author (the subject of the work). Because reading removes the barrier between subject and object, the division takes place *within* the reader. Reading induces a doubling of the reader's subjectivity, so that one can be placed at the disposal of the text while the other remains with the reader. Now, this doubling presents a problem, for in fact there is only one subject present—the reader. The text—the words on the page—has been written by the writer, but meaning is always a matter of interpretation. The subjectivity roused to life by reading, while it may be attributed to the author, is nevertheless not a separate subjectivity but a projection of the subjectivity of the reader. How can the duality of subjects be maintained in the absence of the author? In an actual conversation, the presence of another person preserves the duality. Because each party must assimilate and interpret the utterances of the other, we still have the introjection of the subject-object division, as well as the possibility of hearing only what one wants to hear. But in a real conversation, the other person can interrupt, object to an erroneous interpretation, provide further explanations, change her mind, change the topic, or cut off conversation altogether. In reading, there are no comparable safeguards against the appropriation of the text by the reader. This is the second moment of the dialectic—the recognition that reading is necessarily subjective. The need to keep it from being *totally* subjective ushers in the third moment of the dialectic.

In the feminist story, the key to the problem is the awareness of the double context of reading and writing. Rich's essay is wonderfully illustrative. To avoid imposing an alien perspective on Dickinson's poetry, Rich informs her reading with the knowledge of the circumstances in which Dickinson lived and worked. She repeatedly reminds herself and her readers that Dickinson must be read in light of her *own* premises, that the "exclusions" and "necessities" she endured, and, therefore, her choices, were conditioned by her own world. At the same time, Rich's sensitivity to the context of writing is matched by her sensitivity to the context of reading. She makes it clear throughout the essay that her reading of Dickinson is necessarily shaped by her experience and interests as a feminist poet living in the twentieth-century United States. The reader also has her own premises. To forget these is to run the risk of imposing them surreptitiously on the author.

To recapitulate, the first moment of the dialectic of reading is marked by the recognition of the necessary duality of subjects; the second, by the realization that this duality is threatened by the author's absence. In the third moment, the duality of subjects is referred to the duality of contexts. Reading becomes a mediation between author and reader, between the context of writings and the context of reading.

Although feminists have always believed that objectivity is an illusion, Rich's essay is the only one, as far as I know, to exhibit through its rhetoric the necessary subjectivity of reading coupled with the equally necessary commitment to reading the text as it was meant to be read.[41] The third moment of the dialectic is apparent in Rich's weaving—not blending—of the context of writing and the context of reading, the perspective of the author and that of the reader. The central rhetorical device effecting this mediation is her use of the personal voice. As in most critical essays, Rich alternates quotes from the texts in question with her own commentary, but her use of the personal voice makes a difference. In her hands, this rhetorical strategy serves two purposes. First, it serves as a reminder that her interpretation is informed by her own perspective. Second, it signifies her tactful approach to Dickinson; the personal voice serves as a gesture warding off any inclination to appropriate the authority of the text as a warrant for the validity of the interpretation. Because the interpretation is presented as an *interpretation*, its claim to validity rests on the cogency of the supporting arguments, *not* on the authorization of the text.

Rich accomplishes even more than this. She reaches out to Dickinson not by identifying with her, but by establishing their affinity. Both are American, both are women poets in a patriarchal culture. By playing this affinity against the differences, she produces a context that incorporates both reader and writer. In turn, this common ground becomes the basis for drawing the connections that, in her view, constitute the proper goal of reading.

One might ask: Is there something distinctively female (rather than "merely feminist") in this dialogic model? While it is difficult to specify what "distinctively female" might mean, there are currently very interesting speculations about differences in the way males and females conceive of themselves and of their relations with others. The works of Jean Baker Miller, Nancy Chodorow, and Carol Gilligan suggest that men define themselves through individuation and separation from others, while women have more flexible ego boundaries and define and experience themselves in terms of their affiliations and relationships with others.[42] Men value autonomy, and they think of their interactions with others principally in terms of procedures for arbitrating conflicts between individual rights. Women, on the other hand, value relationships, and they are most concerned in their dealings with others to negotiate between opposing needs so that the relationship can be maintained. This difference is consistent with the difference between mainstream models of reading and the dialogic model I am proposing for feminist readings of women's writing. Mainstream reader-response theories are preoccupied with issues of control and partition—how to distinguish the contribution of the author/text from the contribution of the reader. In the dialectic of communication informing the relationship between the feminist reader and the female author/text, the central issue is not of control or partition, but of managing the contradictory implications of the desire for relationship (one must maintain a minimal distance from the other) and the desire for intimacy, up to and including a symbiotic merger with the other. The problematic is defined by the drive "to connect," rather than that which is implicit in the mainstream preoccupation with partition and control—namely, the drive to get it right. It could also be argued that Poulet's model represents reading as an intimate, intersubjective encounter. However, it is significant that in his model, the prospect of close rapport with another provokes both excitement and anxiety. Intimacy, while desired, is also viewed as a threat to one's integrity. For Rich, on the other hand, the prospect of merging with another is problematical, but not threatening.

Let me end with a word about endings. Dialectical stories look forward to optimistic endings. Mine is no exception. In the first chapter the woman reader becomes a feminist, and in the end she succeeds in extricating herself from the androcentric logic of the literary and critical canons. In the second chapter the feminist reader succeeds in effecting a mediation between her perspective and that of the writer. These "victories" are part of the project of producing women's culture and literary tradition, which in turn is part of the project of overcoming patriarchy. It is in the nature of people working for revolutionary change to be optimistic about the prospect of redirecting the future.

Culler observes that optimistic endings have been challenged (successfully, he thinks) by deconstruction, a method radically at odds with the dialectic. It is worth noting that there is a deconstructive moment in Rich's reading of Dickinson. Recall her third metaphor: the reader is an insect "vibrating the frames of windows, clinging to the panes of glass, trying to connect." The suggestion of futility is unmistakable. At best, Rich's interpretation of Dickinson might be considered as a "strong misreading" whose value is in its capacity to provoke other misreadings.

We might say this—but must we? To answer this question, we must ask another: What is at stake in the proposition that reading is impossible? For one thing, if reading is impossible, then there is no way of deciding the validity of an interpretation—the very notion of validity becomes problematical. Certainly it is useful to be reminded that the validity of an interpretation cannot be decided by appealing to what the author "intended," to what is "in" the text, or to what is "in" the experience of the reader. However, there is another approach to the problem of validation, one that is consonant with the dialogic model of reading described above. We can think of validity not as a property inherent in an interpretation, but rather as a *claim* implicit in the *act* of propounding an interpretation. An interpretation, then, is not valid or invalid in itself. Its validity is contingent on the agreement of others. In this view, Rich's interpretation of Dickinson, which is frankly acknowledged as conditioned by her own experience as a twentieth-century feminist poet, is not necessarily a misreading. In advancing her interpretation, Rich implicitly claims its validity. That is to say, to read a text and then to write about it is to seek to connect not only with the author of the original text, but also with a community of readers. To the extent that she succeeds and to the extent that the community is potentially all-embracing, her interpretation has that degree of validity.[43]

Feminist reading and writing alike are grounded in the interest of producing a community of feminist readers and writers, and in the hope that ultimately this community will expand to include everyone. Of course, this project may fail. The feminist story may yet end with the recognition of the impossibility of reading. But this remains to be seen. At this stage I think it behooves us to *choose* the dialectical over the deconstructive plot. It is dangerous for feminists to be overly enamored with the theme of impossibility. Instead, we should strive to redeem the claim that it is possible for a woman, reading as a woman, to read literature written by women, for this is essential if we are to make the literary enterprise into a means for building and maintaining connections among women.

NOTES

I would like to acknowledge my debt to David Schweickart for the substantial editorial work he did on this essay.

1. Wayne Booth, Presidential Address, "Arts and Scandals 1982," *PMLA*, 98 (1983), 313. Subsequent references to this essay are cited parenthetically in the text.

2. *The Autobiography of Malcolm X*, written with Alex Haley (New York: Grove Press, 1964), 173.

Subsequent references are cited parenthetically in the text.

3. Virginia Woolf, *A Room of One's Own* (New York: Harcourt Brace Jovanovich, 1981). Subsequent references are cited parenthetically in the text.

4. Jonathan D. Culler, *On Deconstruction: Theory and Criticism after Structuralism* (Ithaca: Cornell University Press, 1982), 42. (Subsequent references are cited parenthetically in the text.) Wayne Booth's essay "Freedom of Interpretation: Bakhtin and the Challenge of Feminist Criticism," *Critical Inquiry*, 9 (1982), 45–76, is another good omen of the impact of feminist thought on literary criticism.

5. David Bleich, *Subjective Criticism* (Baltimore: Johns Hopkins University Press, 1978), 112.

6. Georges Poulet, "Criticism and the Experience of Interiority," trans. Catherine and Richard Macksey, in *Reader-Response Criticism: From Formalism to Structuralism*, ed. Jane Tompkins (Baltimore: Johns Hopkins University Press, 1980), 43. Poulet's theory is not among those discussed by Culler. However, since he will be useful to us later, I mention him here.

7. This argument was advanced by Samuel Weber in "The Struggle for Control: Wolfgang Iser's Third Dimension," cited by Culler in *On Deconstruction*, p. 75.

8. Stanley E. Fish, "Why No One's Afraid of Wolfgang Iser," *Diacritics*, 11 (1981), 7. Quoted by Culler in *On Deconstruction*, p. 75.

9. Elaine Showalter, "Feminist Criticism in the Wilderness," *Critical Inquiry*, 8 (1981), 182–85. [Reprinted below, essay #26.] Showalter argues that if we see feminist critique (focused on the reader) as our primary critical project, we must be content with the "playful pluralism" proposed by Annette Kolodny: first because no single conceptual model can comprehend so eclectic and wide-ranging an enterprise, and second because "in the free play of the interpretive field, feminist critique can only compete with alternative readings, all of which have the built-in obsolescence of Buicks, cast away as newer readings take their place" (p. 182). Although Showalter does not support Wimsatt and Beardsley's proscription of the "affective fallacy," she nevertheless subscribes to the logic of their argument. Kolodny's "playful pluralism" is more benign than Wimsatt and Beardsley's dreaded "relativism," but no less fatal, in Showalter's view, to theoretical coherence.

10. Elaine Showalter, "Women and the Literary Curriculum," *College English*, 32 (1971), 855. For an excellent example of recent work following in the spirit of Showalter's critique, see Paul Lauter, *Reconstructing American Literature* (Old Westbury, N.Y.: Feminist Press, 1983).

11. Lee Edwards, "Women, Energy, and *Middlemarch*," *Massachusetts Review*, 13 (1972), 226.

12. Ibid.

13. James Joyce, *The Portrait of the Artist as a Young Man* (London: Jonathan Cape, 1916), 195.

14. See also Florence Howe's analysis of the same passage, "Feminism and Literature," in *Images of Women in Fiction: Feminist Perspectives*, ed. Susan Koppelman Cornillon (Bowling Green, Ohio: Bowling Green State University Press, 1972), 262–63.

15. Judith Fetterley, *The Resisting Reader: A Feminist Approach to American Fiction* (Bloomington: Indiana University Press, 1978), p. xx. Although Fetterley's remarks refer specifically to American literature, they apply generally to the entire traditional canon.

16. Fetterley, *Resisting Reader*, p. xiii.

17. See Katharine M. Rogers, *The Troublesome Helpmate: A History of Misogyny in Literature* (Seattle: University of Washington Press, 1966).

18. Fredric Jameson, *The Political Unconscious: Narrative as a Socially Symbolic Act* (Ithaca: Cornell University Press, 1981), 286.

19. In *Woman and the Demon: The Life of a Victorian Myth* (Cambridge: Harvard University Press, 1982), Nina Auerbach employs a similar—though not identical—positive hermeneutic. She reviews the myths and images of women (as angels, demons, victims, whores, etc.) that feminist critics have "gleefully" unmasked as reflections and instruments of sexist ideology, and discovers in them an "unexpectedly empowering" mythos. Auerbach argues that the "most powerful, if least acknowledged creation [of the Victorian cultural imagination] is an explosively mobile, magic woman, who breaks the boundaries of family within which her society restricts her. The triumph of this overweening creature is a celebration of the corporate imagination that believed in her" (p. 1). See also idem, "Magi and Maidens: The Romance of the Victorian Freud," *Critical Inquiry*, 8 (1981), 281–300. The tension between the positive and negative feminist hermeneutics is perhaps most apparent when one is dealing with the "classics." See, for example, Carol Thomas Neely, "Feminist Modes of Shakespeare Criticism: Compensatory, Justificatory, Transformational," *Women's Studies*, 9 (1981), 3–15.

20. Kate Millett, *Sexual Politics* (New York: Avon Books, 1970).

21. Elaine Showalter, "The Double Critical Standard and the Feminine Novel," chap. 3 in *A Literature of Their Own: British Women Novelists from Brontë to Lessing* (Princeton: Princeton University

Press, 1977), 73–99; Carol Ohmann, "Emily Brontë in the Hands of Male Critics," *College English*, 32 (1971), 906–13.

22. Nina Baym, "Melodramas of Beset Manhood: How Theories of American Fiction Exclude Women Authors," *American Quarterly*, 33 (1981), 123–39.

23. Ibid., p. 125.

24. Ibid., p. 130. One of the founding works of American Literature is "The Legend of Sleepy Hollow," about which Leslie Fiedler writes: "It is fitting that our first successful homegrown legend would memorialize, however playfully, the flight of the dreamer from the shrew" (*Love and Death in the American Novel* [New York: Criterion, 1960], xx).

25. Nina Baym's *Women's Fiction: A Guide to Novels by and about Women in America, 1820–1870* (Ithaca: Cornell University Press, 1978) provides a good survey of what has been excluded from the canon.

26. Annette Kolodny, "Dancing through the Minefield: Some Observations on the Theory, Practice, and Politics of a Feminist Literary Criticism," *Feminist Studies*, 6 (1980), 10–12. Kolodny elaborates the same theme in "A Map for Rereading: Or, Gender and the Interpretation of Literary Texts," *New Literary History*, 11 (1980), 451–67.

27. For an excellent account of the way in which the feminist "interpretive community" has changed literary and critical conventions, see Jean E. Kennard, "Convention Coverage, or How to Read Your Own Life," *New Literary History*, 8 (1981), 69–88. The programs of the MLA Convention during the last twenty-five years offer more concrete evidence of the changes in the literary and critical canons, and of the ideological and political struggles effecting these changes.

28. In Adrienne Rich, *On Lies, Secrets, and Silence: Selected Prose, 1966–1978* (New York: W. W. Norton, 1979). Subsequent references are cited parenthetically in the text.

29. Susan Glaspell's story "A Jury of Her Peers" revolves around a variation of this judicial metaphor. The parable of reading implicit in this story has not been lost on feminist critics. Annette Kolodny, for example, discusses how it "explores the necessary gender marking which *must* constitute any definition of 'peers' in the complex process of unraveling truth or meaning." Although the story does not exclude male readers, it alerts us to the fact that "symbolic representations depend on a fund of shared recognitions and potential references," and in general, "female meaning" is inaccessible to "male interpretation." "However inadvertently, [the male reader] is a *different kind* of reader and . . . where women are concerned, he is often an inadequate reader" ("Map for Rereading," pp. 460–63).

30. There is a strong counter-tendency, inspired by French poststructuralism, which privileges the appreciation of textuality over the imaginative recovery of the woman writer as subject of the work. See, for example, Mary Jacobus, "Is There a Woman in This Text?" *New Literary History*, 14 (1982), 117–41, especially the concluding paragraph. The last sentence of the essay underscores the controversy: "Perhaps the question that feminist critics should be asking is not 'Is there a woman in this text?' but rather: 'Is there a text in this woman?' "

31. I must stress that although Rich's essay presents a significant paradigm of feminist readings of women's writing, it is not the only such paradigm. An alternative is proposed by Caren Greenberg, "Reading Reading: Echo's Abduction of Language," in *Women and Language in Literature and Society*, ed. Sally McConnell-Ginet, Ruth Borker, and Nelly Furman (New York: Praeger, 1980), 304–9.

Furthermore, there are many important issues that have been left out of my discussion. For example:

a. The relationship of her career as reader to the artistic development of the woman writer. In *Madwoman in the Attic* (New Haven: Yale University Press, 1980) Sandra Gilbert and Susan Gubar show that women writers had to struggle to overcome the "anxiety of authorship" which they contracted from the "sentences" of their predecessors, male as well as female. They also argue that the relationship women writers form with their female predecessors does not fit the model of oedipal combat proposed by Bloom. Rich's attitude toward Dickinson (as someone who "has been there," as a "foremother" to be recovered) corroborates Gilbert and Gubar's claim.

b. The relationship between women writers and their readers. We need actual reception studies as well as studies of the way women writers conceived of their readers and the way they inscribed them in their texts.

c. The relationship between the positive and the negative hermeneutic in feminist readings of women's writing. Rich's reading of Dickinson emphasizes the positive hermeneutic. One might ask, however, if this approach is applicable to *all* women's writing. Specifically, is this appropriate to the popular fiction written by women, e.g., Harlequin Romances? To what extent is women's writing itself a bearer of patriarchal ideology? Janice Radway addresses these issues in "Utopian Impulse in Popular Literature: Gothic Romances and 'Feminist Protest,' " *American Quarterly*, 33 (1981), 140–62, and "Women Read the Romance: The Interaction of Text and Context," *Feminist Studies*, 9 (1983), 53–78. See also Tania Modleski, *Loving with a Vengeance: Mass-Produced*

Fantasies for Women (New York: Methuen, 1982).

32. Iser writes:

> Text and reader no longer confront each other as object and subject, but instead the "division" takes place within the reader [herself] . . . . As we read, there occurs an artificial division of our personality, because we take as a theme for ourselves something we are not. Thus, in reading there are two levels—the alien "me" and the real, virtual "me"—which are never completely cut off from each other. Indeed, we can only make someone else's thoughts into an absorbing theme for ourselves provided the virtual background of our personality can adapt to it. ("The Reading Process: A Phenomenological Approach," in Tompkins, *Reader-Response Criticism*, p. 67)

Add the stipulation that the alien "me" is a male who has appropriated the universal into his maleness, and we have the process of immasculation described in the third section.

33. Stanley E. Fish, *Is There a Text in This Class? The Authority of Interpretive Communities* (Cambridge: Harvard University Press, 1980), especially pt. 2.

34. Although the woman reader is the "star" of the feminist story of reading, this does not mean that men are excluded from the audience. On the contrary, it is hoped that on hearing the feminist story they will be encouraged to revise their own stories to reflect the fact that they, too, are gendered beings, and that, ultimately, they will take control of their inclination to appropriate the universal at the expense of women.

35. Catherine A. MacKinnon, "Feminism, Marxism, Method, and the State: Toward Feminist Jurisprudence," *Signs*, 8 (1981), 637.

36. There is lively debate among feminists about whether it is better to emphasize the essential similarity of women and men, or their difference. There is much to be said intellectually and politically for both sides. However, in one sense, the argument centers on a false issue. It assumes that concern about women's "difference" is incompatible with concern about the essential humanity shared by the sexes. Surely, "difference" may be interpreted to refer to what is distinctive in women's lives and works, *including* what makes them essentially human; unless, of course, we remain captivated by the notion that the standard model for humanity is male.

37. Although opponents of feminist criticism often find it convenient to characterize such works as a personal attack on authors, for feminist critics themselves, the primary consideration is the function of the text as a carrier of patriarchal ideology, and its effect as such especially (but not exclusively) on women readers.The personal culpability of the author is a relatively minor issue.

38. Harold Bloom, *Kabbalah and Criticism* (New York: Seabury, 1975), 126.

39. Poulet, "Criticism and the Experience of Interiority," p. 46.

40. Ibid., p. 47. As Culler has pointed out, the theme of control is prominent in mainstream reader-response criticism. Poulet's story is no exception. The issue of control is important in another way. Behind the question of whether the text controls the reader or vice versa is the question of how to regulate literary criticism. If the text is controlling, then there is no problem. The text itself will regulate the process of reading. But if the text is not necessarily controlling, then, how do we constrain the activities of readers and critics? How can we rule out "off-the-wall" interpretations? Fish's answer is of interest to feminist critics. The constraints, he says, are exercised not by the text, but by the institutions within which literary criticism is situated. It is but a small step from this idea to the realization of the necessarily political character of literature and criticism.

41. The use of the personal conversational tone has been regarded as a hallmark of feminist criticism. However, as Jean E. Kennard has pointed out ("Personally Speaking: Feminist Critics and the Community of Readers," *College English*, 43 [1981], 140–45), this theoretical commitment is not apparent in the overwhelming majority of feminist critical essays. Kennard found only five articles in which the critic "overtly locates herself on the page." (To the five she found, I would add three works cited in this essay: "Women, Energy, and *Middlemarch*," by Lee Edwards; "Feminism and Literature," by Florence Howe; and "Vesuvius at Home," by Adrienne Rich.) Kennard observes further that, even in the handful of essays she found, the personal tone is confined to a few introductory paragraphs. She asks: "If feminist criticism has on the whole remained faithful to familiar methods and tone, why have the few articles with an overt personal voice loomed so large in our minds?" Kennard suggests that these personal introductions are invitations "to share a critical response which depends upon unstated, shared beliefs and, to a large extent, experience; that of being a female educated in a male tradition in which she is no longer comfortable." Thus, these introductory paragraphs do not indicate a "transformed critical methodology; they are devices for transforming the reader. I read the later portions of these essays—and by extension other feminist criticism—in a different way because I have been invited to participate in the

underground. . . . I am part of a community of feminist readers" (pp. 143–44).

I would offer another explanation, one that is not necessarily inconsistent with Kennard's. I think the use of a personal and conversational tone represents an overt gesture indicating the dialogic mode of discourse as the "regulative ideal" for all feminist discourse. The few essays—indeed, the few introductory paragraphs—that assert this regulative ideal are memorable because they strike a chord in a significant segment of the community of feminist critics. To the extent that we have been touched or transformed by this idea, it will be implicit in the way we read the works of others, in particular, the works of other women. Although the ideal must be overtly affirmed periodically, it is not necessary to do so in all of our essays. It remains potent as long as it is assumed by a significant portion of the community. I would argue with Kennard's distinction between indicators of a transformed critical methodology and devices for transforming the reader. To the extent that critical methodology is a function of the conventions implicitly or explicitly operating in an interpretive community—that is, of the way members of the community conceive of their work and of the way they read each other—devices for transforming readers are also devices for transforming critical methodology.

42. Jean Baker Miller, *Toward a New Psychology of Women* (Boston: Beacon Press, 1976); and Nancy Chodorow, *The Reproduction of Mothering: Psychoanalysis and the Sociology of Gender* (Berkeley and Los Angeles: University of California Press, 1978); and Carol Gilligan, *In a Different Voice: Psychological Theory and Women's Development* (Cambridge: Harvard University Press, 1982).

43. I am using here Jurgen Habermas's definition of truth or validity as a claim (implicit in the act of making assertions) that is redeemable through discourse—specifically, through the domination-free discourse of an "ideal speech situation." For Habermas, consensus attained through domination-free discourse is the warrant for truth. See "Wahrheitstheorien," in *Wirklichkeit und Reflexion: Walter Schulzzum, 60. Geburtstag* (Pfullingen: Nesge, 1973), 211–65. I am indebted to Alan Soble's unpublished translation of this essay.

III

STRUCTURALISM AND SEMIOTICS

In many ways structuralism and semiotics are the opposite of the rhetorical analysis of literature—the analysis of the usefulness and persuasiveness of language—described in the previous section. Instead of examining the effects or results of language—the *communicative* function of language—structural and semiotic analyses attempt to examine the *conditions* that allow language and meaning to arise in the first place; they seek to know what Roland Barthes calls in "The Structuralist Activity" in this section "how meaning is possible." Both structuralism and semiotics grow out of the great advances in twentieth-century linguistics initiated by Ferdinand de Saussure. Saussure reconceived the study of linguistics at the beginning of the century by reorienting the kinds of questions linguists asked. Instead of asking where particular linguistic formations came from—their history and cause in the etymological and "diachronic" linguistic methods of nineteenth-century linguistics—he asked how the elements of language are *configured* in order to produce the results or effects they had. In other words, Saussure replaced the "diachronic" study of language through time, the study of the *development* of language, with the "synchronic" study of the particular formation of language *at a particular moment.* In this it is clear that Saussure is related to the formalism of the Modernist movement we examined in the first section. As he notes himself in the *Course in General Linguistics*, the elements of linguistic science—and of language as well—are "*a form, not a substance.*"

From this assumption of the formal nature of linguistic elements comes the crucial, reorienting assumptions of Saussure's linguistic work: (1) the *relational* nature of linguistic elements; that is, the fact that the entities of language are a product of relationships—that, as Saussure says here, "it is the viewpoint that creates the object" of linguistic science; (2) the *arbitrary* nature of the linguistic sign—that all the elements of language could be different from what they are, and that implicit here is an essential aspect of the nature of language: namely, it takes whatever material is at hand in order to create its meanings and communication; (3) the *synchronic* method of study that refuses to seek explanations in terms of cause and effect but, rather, seeks understanding in terms of function and activity; (4) the *double nature* of language and linguistic elements, including, most significantly here, the double nature of the linguistic sign as the combination of a signified and a signifier; and the double nature of language itself (the French term Saussure uses is *langage*), its particular manifestations in speech (*parole*) and the system (or order or *structure* of its code), language as system (*la langue*). As Saussure says elsewhere, "the absolutely final law of language is, we dare say, that there is nothing which can ever reside in *one* term, as a direct consequence of the fact that linguistic symbols are unrelated to what they should designate."

These assumptions lead Saussure to posit, as he does here, the possibility of a new science for the twentieth century, "*a science that studies the life of signs within society*," what he calls "semiology." At the same time Saussure was working, in America Charles Sanders Peirce, philosopher and logician, suggested a similar new science, which he called "semiotics." As it is practiced today, semiotics examines *meaningful*, cultural phenomena from the viewpoint of the conditions that make such meaningful phenomena possible, including the structures that give rise to that meaning. That is, semiotics takes its methods from the structural linguistics Saussure initiated (and, sometimes, from the *pragmatics* Peirce initiated) in order to understand the conditions governing meaning in society. It does this whether that meaning is literary texts and the *system* of genres that constitute the literary canon (see Todorov's structural analysis of the genre of the fantastic, what we might call the gothic, in this section; and see also Northrop Frye's example of "genre" study as a systematic part of criticism in "The Function of Criticism at the Present Time" in Section VIII); or art objects, or general cultural concepts (such as the concept of the Virgin Mary Kristeva examines) or gestural communication, or even the myths of "primitive" societies.

The last example—the semiotic or structural study of myth and culture—has been the life work of the foremost practitioner of structuralism in the twentieth century, the French anthropologist Claude Lévi-Strauss. Lévi-Strauss has studied a wide range of myths, mostly Amerindian myths, and has attempted to discover the structure—or what might be called the grammar—of mythological narrative. In other words, Lévi-Strauss has attempted to apply the methods of structural linguistics to narrative so that, in just the way linguistics analyzes sentences, structural anthropology—as he calls it—can analyze narrative discourse. In this endeavor, he has articulated the highest ambition of structuralism and semiotics. In *The Raw and the Cooked* he says: "I have tried to transcend the contrast between the tangible and the intelligible by operating from the outset at the sign level. The function of signs, is, precisely, to express the one by means of the other." This, then, is the aim of semiotics and structuralism: to attempt to isolate and define the conditions of meaning in culture, to articulate the relationship between the tangible entities of nature and the intelligible meanings of culture.

STRUCTURALISM AND LITERARY CRITICISM

Structuralism—beginning with Lévi-Strauss's analyses of narrative discourse in the early 1950s in France—has had a huge impact on twentieth-century criticism. Anticipating the many developments of poststructuralism, this movement of the 1960s and early 1970s has proved to be a watershed in modern criticism, causing a major reorientation in literary studies. Prior to structuralism, literary studies often seemed insular and isolated even in the humanities. After it, literary criticism seemed more actively engaged in the discourse of the human sciences, a vital participant and in some areas a guide. In fact, by basing its methods on those of linguistics, structuralism helped to transform the traditional "humanities" into what has come to be called the "human sciences."

At first, the rise of structuralism was greeted with considerable hostility by critics in the United States and Europe. It was generally acknowledged that this movement was attempting an ambitious, "scientific" examination of literature in all its dimensions. To some, however, the supposed detachment of such an investigation appeared to be offensively antihumanistic and unrelated to the values of a Western liberal education. Anthropologist Alfred Kroeber argued that "structure" is a redundant concept that needs no articulation, and many literary critics judged this new movement to be an ephemeral fad. Not only was structuralism considered antihumanistic; to the Anglo-American world it was further suspect as a French import, merely an exotic dalliance for a few intellectuals who were arrogantly and blindly worshipping a foreignism. In 1975, however, the Modern Language Association awarded Jonathan Culler's *Structuralist Poetics* the annual James Russell Lowell prize for a literary study, and the Anglo-American academy (if not critics and readers generally) began to acknowledge that, for good or ill, structuralism was in place as a functioning critical system.

In retrospect, the rise of structuralism and semiotics in the 1960s vividly dramatizes—among other things—the extent to which modern theory has become an interdisciplinary phenomenon. Structuralism and semiotics virtually constitute a field in themselves, designatable simply as "theory" because, by taking meaning and the varying conditions of meaning as their "objects" of study, they cut through, without being confined to, traditional "humanities" and "social sciences" such as literary studies, philosophy, history, linguistics, psychology, and anthropology, all of which directly influenced literary theory since the late 1960s.

In literary criticism, structuralism is closely related to literary formalism, as represented by both American New Criticism and Russian formalism. The principal aim of these movements was to displace "content" in literary analysis and to focus, instead, on literary "form" in a detailed manner analogous to the methods of empirical research. Both movements also sought to organize the generic structures of literature into a system consistent with the inner ordering of works that close reading revealed. In each case, literature is viewed as a complex system of "forms" analyzable with considerable objectivity at different levels of generality—from the specific components of a poetic image or line through the poem's genre to that genre's place in the system of literature. The New Criticism and Russian formalism, in short, promoted the view of literature as a system and a general scientific approach to literary analysis. (Northrop Frye called for an analogous systematization of literary studies in "The Function of Criticism" in Section VIII.) This systematizing and scientistic impulse, especially as formulated in the linguistically oriented theories of Russian formalism, is a major link between early modern formalism and the structuralism of the 1960s.

As a school of literary criticism, structuralism is dedicated to explaining literature as a system of signs and codes and the conditions which allow that system to function, including relevant cultural frames. With its intense rationalism and sophisticated models, structuralism at its inception seemed without bounds in what it could "understand." Like the linguistic methodology it assumed, structuralism and semiotics—most importantly—have conceived of themselves as *scientific* projects, and they assume, as Lévi-Strauss says, the essential *intelligibility* of the phenomena they study. As A.-J. Greimas wrote in 1966, "It may be—it is a philosophic and not linguistic question—that the phenomenon of language as such is mysterious, but there are no mysteries in language." For literary structuralism the same assumption held: its aim was to "account for" literature as fully and objectively as possible, without recourse to such "mysterious" and unanalyzable concepts as "genius" or "inexhaustible richness" or "poetic language" unassimilable into general linguistics. Not since the Russian Formalists had literary theory aimed at such lofty theoretical goals and expected so much of itself as practical criticism. As the most ambitious movement in recent literary studies, structuralism in the 1960s seemed poised to explain literature in every respect.

Structuralism's strength as an analytical technique, however, was connected to what many conceive to be its major weakness. The power of structuralism derived, as Roland Barthes said, from its being "essentially an *activity*" that could "reconstruct an 'object' in such a way as to manifest thereby the rules of functioning." These rules are manifested as the "generally intelligible" *imitation* of a literary object. By this, Barthes meant that structuralism focused on the *synchronic* dimension of a text (*langue* as opposed to *parole*), the specific ways in which a text is like other texts. The structural comparison of texts is based on similarities of function (character development, plot, theme, ideology, and so on), relationships that Lévi-Strauss called *homologies*. The predominately synchronic analysis of homologies "recreates" the text as a "paradigm," a timeless system of structural possibilities. Following these precepts, Todorov, for example, attempts to *position* the fantastic as a genre within a configuration of other literary genres. The fantastic, in his analysis, like the linguistic elements in Saussure's discussion, is an "entity" of literature precisely because it relates to other so-called "entities" of literature (which are themselves a function of other relationships).

Thus, in a structural analysis, changes within and among texts or genres can be accounted for as "transformations" in the synchronic system. However, structuralism tended to focus on the fixity of relations within synchronic paradigms at the expense of temporality, or the "diachronic" dimension, which involves history. (Todorov offers no discussion of the development of the fantastic genre, for example; he simply wants to define the genre in relation to other, "synchronic" genres.) This tendency to avoid dealing with time and social change concerned many critics of structuralism from its beginning and ultimately became a main target of deconstruction's critique of the prior movement.

While the critique of structuralism is an important development (that will be discussed in more detail later), structuralism's achievement in practical criticism is undeniable and must be underlined. Roland Barthes's work, for example, charting a course through the early and late stages of structuralism, illuminated semiotic theory, the system of fashion, narrative structure, textuality, and many other topics. These stand as important achievements in modern criticism. Tzvetan Todorov, to give just one more example, has also contributed to the understanding of narrative structure, genre theory, and the theory of symbolism. Further, in semiotic approaches to semantic theory, closely allied to structuralism, there is significant work by Michael Riffaterre, Umberto Eco, A.-J. Greimas, and others.

Besides the structural analysis of the "system" of literature which, more or less rigorously, genre theory attempts, structuralism has more broadly attempted to analyze the structures (or grammar) of narrative. As already mentioned, Lévi-Strauss's work has been very important in this regard, leading to such diverse approaches as those of Greimas, Genette, Bremond, and others. A particularly influential example of structuralism's positive achievement is Claude Lévi-Strauss's early essay "The Structural Study of Myth" (1955), an anthropological study that heavily influenced subsequent literary studies. In this essay Lévi-Strauss presents a structural analysis of narrative wherein the diachronic dimension (the story line) is eclipsed in favor of a synchronic "reading" of "mythemes" (recurrent narrative structures) in several versions of the Oedipus story. While this structural analysis seemed quite bold at the time, similar structural connections are now routinely made and assumed to be literary common sense. Thus, Lévi-Strauss codified, extended, and even created structuralist possibilities for literary analysis. Objections arose about the "hidden" subjectivity or the bias of Lévi-Strauss's selection of mythemes for analysis, and even about the arbitrariness of what could be called a "mytheme." Nevertheless, "The Structural Study of Myth" and Lévi-Strauss's work as a whole had a tremendously stimulating effect on narrative study and induced Anglo-American criticism to reexamine its own formalistic and strongly descriptive tendencies.

THE CRITIQUE OF STRUCTURALISM

Structuralism's self-imposed limitations, especially its lack of concern with diachronic change and its focus on general systems rather than on individual cases, became increasingly evident, however, in the late 1960s. The French philosopher Jacques Derrida offered a particularly decisive critique, a central example of which is "Structure, Sign, and Play in the Discourse of the Human Sciences" (in Section IV), which focuses on the structural anthropology of Lévi-Strauss. Derrida connects structuralism with a traditional Western blindness to the "structurality" of structure, or an unwillingness to examine the theoretical and ideological implications of "structure" as a concept. Derrida points out that the attempt to investigate structure implies the ability to stand outside and apart from it—as if one could move outside of cultural understanding in order to take a detached view of culture. In specific terms, Derrida's critique of Lévi-Strauss (not only in "Structure, Sign and Play," but in his *Grammatology* and many other works) is a critique of the privileging of the opposition between "nature" and "culture"—what in a different context Lévi-Strauss calls the tangible and the intelligible. Derrida argues that since one never transcends culture, one can never examine it from the "outside"; there is no standing free of structure, no so-called "natural" state free of the structural interplay that, in the structuralist analysis, constitutes meaning. There is no objective examination of structure. Therefore, as Derrida shows, the attempt to "read" and "interpret" cultural structures cannot be adequately translated into exacting scientific models. If "structure," therefore, cannot be isolated and examined, then structuralism is seriously undermined as a method. Derrida, in fact, argues that in place of structuralism we should recognize the interplay of differences among texts, the activity that he and others call *structuration*.

While the importance of structuralism for current criticism is enormous, literary history will show that when structuralism was "packaged" for an Anglo-American audience in Jonathan Culler's *Structuralist Poetics: Structuralism, Linguistics, and the Study of Literature* (1975), Derrida's "deconstruction" had already brought the Structuralist movement to an end. This movement, newly arrived in the English speaking world, was effectively already finished in Europe. With Gayatri Chakravorty Spivak's translation of Jacques Derrida's *Of Grammatology* as a critical landmark in 1976, this young movement was pressed and sealed forever into history, to be known only retrospectively in the United States and England (as it is not known in Europe) in the shadow of its own aftermath—as *poststructuralism*.

Nevertheless, structuralism and semiotics have come to learn from that critique of the Structuralist enterprise and its enabling assumption of the opposition between the tangible and the intelligible, nature and culture. The last essay of this section, Julia Kristeva's "Stabat Mater," uses this critique in its semiotic analysis of the cultural concept of the Virgin Mary and, more generally, "motherhood" itself. Even the structure of Kristeva's essay—simultaneously addressing in one text the Virgin Mary's history in Western culture and (in boldface type) the "private," largely autobiographical, experience of motherhood—brings together nature and culture. Kristeva is attempting to articulate both "mother" as cultural concept and the biology of "primary narcissism"—that is, the cultural semiotics of the Virgin Mother and a discursive articulation of the private experience of motherhood. The "natural" discourse here is that of the "tangible" rather than the "intelligible" in that Motherhood is described as the birth of "pain," as "rhythmic" and essentially bodily: "a woman is neither nomadic nor a male body that considers itself earthly only in erotic passion." Instead, Kristeva implies, motherhood emphasizes the material, corporeal nature of human life, the (natural) "otherness" of intelligibility itself.

Against this "natural" reading of motherhood, Kristeva describes its most "cultural" manifestations in the Catholic Church. In this discussion, parallel to the "natural" articulation, Mary's "motherhood" is analyzed as a semiotic phenomenon. That is, the "position" of the Virgin, like that of the fantastic in Todorov's analysis, is therein "homologized" (shown to have a structural relationship) with the Father and the Son of the Trinity. The social function of the Virgin, then, is examined in different historical contexts, and the tradition itself is examined in relation to a mistranslation from the Greek (an example of the arbitrary nature of the sign with a vengeance). Finally, even the opposition between nature and culture is explored as a *determining condition* of the semiotic concepts of "mother" and "virgin mother" in that "a woman as mother . . . changes culture into nature, the speaking [mind] into biology."

Yet within this semiotic analysis the opposition between nature and culture becomes problematic in these two discourses in just the way Derrida suggests it does for structuralism generally. At the heart of the semiotics of motherhood—its analysis as a cultural phenomenon susceptible to rigorous structuration—Kristeva discusses the tears and milk of the mother. "They are," she writes, "the metaphors of nonspeech, of a 'semiotics' that linguistic communication does not account for." This "natural," "material" aspect of motherhood is "repressed," the essay claims, in the semiotic analysis, though it returns both in the analytical dimension of this text and in the autobiographical discourse "outside" (or alongside) it. Similarly, "semiotics" finds its way into the "natural" boldfaced discourse of motherhood when it creates a way of examining "the bipolar structure of belief," the opposition between the passionate "intelligibility" of the word and the proverbial "tangibility" of mother-love. In other words, Kristeva offers a structural/semiotic analysis that is informed by both structuralism and has a tendency toward poststructuralism, by the scientific method of semiotics and the deconstructive extension of that method. In so doing, her essay offers a semiotics that demonstrates the importance of structuralism to contemporary cultural and literary studies, a semiotic analysis that, even though it demonstrates how theory can be at odds with itself, nevertheless demonstrates the usefulness of structural and semiotic analyses to understanding.

RELATED ESSAYS IN *CONTEMPORARY LITERARY CRITICISM:*

Cleanth Brooks, "The Language of Paradox"
Viktor Shklovsky, "Art as Technique"
Jacques Derrida, "Structure, Sign, and Play in the Discourse of the Human Sciences"
Paul de Man, "Semiology and Rhetoric"
Northrop Frye, "Function of Criticism at the Present Time"
Henry Louis Gates, Jr., "The Signifying Monkey"

FURTHER READING

Barthes, Roland, *Critical Essays*, trans. Richard Howard (Evanston, Ill.: Northwestern University Press, 1972).

_____, *Elements of Semiology*, trans. A. Lavers and C. Smith (New York: Hill and Wang, 1977).

_____, *Writing Degree Zero*, trans. A. Lavers and C. Smith (New York: Hill and Wang, 1977).

Bloom, Harold, *The Anxiety of Influence: A Theory of Poetry* (New York: Oxford University Press, 1973).

Culler, Jonathan, *Ferdinand de Saussure* (Baltimore: Penguin Books, 1976).

_____, *Structuralist Poetics: Structuralism, Linguistics, and the Study of Literature* (Ithaca: Cornell University Press, 1975).

Derrida, Jacques, *On Grammatology*, trans. Gayatri Spivak (Baltimore: Johns Hopkins University Press, 1976).

Eco, Umberto, *L'Opera aperta* (Milan: Bompiani, 1962).

Ehrmann, Jacques, ed., *Structuralism* (Garden City, N.Y.: Doubleday, 1970).

Genette, Gerard, *Figures of Discourse*, trans. A. Sheridan (New York: Columbia University Press, 1982).

Greimas, A.-J., *Structural Semantics: An Attempt at a Method*, trans. Daniele McDowell, Ronald Schleifer, and Alan Velie, introduction by Ronald Schleifer (Lincoln: University of Nebraska Press, 1983).

Hawkes, Terence, *Structuralism and Semiotics* (Berkeley: University of California Press, 1977).

Jakobson, Roman, *Fundamentals of Language* (The Hague: Mouton, 1975).

_____, "Linguistics and Poetics," in *Style in Language*, ed. Thomas Sebeok (Cambridge: MIT Press, 1960).

Jameson, Fredric, *The Prison-House of Language: A Critical Account of Structuralism and Russian Formalism* (Princeton, N.J.: Princeton University Press, 1972).

Kristeva, Julia, *Desire in Language*, trans. Thomas Gora, Alice Jardine, and Leon S. Roudiez (New York: Columbia University Press, 1980).

Lentricchia, Frank, *After the New Criticism* (Chicago: University of Chicago Press, 1980).

Lévi-Strauss, Claude, *Structural Anthropology*, Vol. I, trans. Clair Jacobson and Brooke Schoepf (New York: Basic Books, 1963).

———, *Structural Anthropology*, Vol. II, trans. Monique Layton (New York: Basic Books, 1976).

———, *The Raw and the Cooked*, trans. John and Doreen Weightman (New York: Harper Books, 1975).

Macksey, Richard, and Eugenio Donato, eds., *The Structuralist Controversy* (Baltimore: Johns Hopkins University Press, 1970).

Peirce, Charles S., *Collected Papers*, ed. Charles Hartshorne and Paul Weiss (Cambridge: Harvard University Press, 1931–58).

Propp, Vladimir, *The Morphology of the Folktale*, trans. Laurence Scott (Austin: University of Texas Press, 1968).

Riffaterre, Michael, *Semiotics of Poetry* (Bloomington: Indiana University Press, 1978).

Saussure, Ferdinand de, *Course in General Linguistics*, trans. Wade Baskin (New York: McGraw-Hill, 1966).

Schleifer, Ronald, *A.-J. Greimas and the Nature of Meaning: Linguistics, Semiotics and Discourse Theory* (Lincoln: University of Nebraska Press, 1987).

Scholes, Robert, *Structuralism in Literature: An Introduction* (New Haven: Yale University Press, 1974).

Tatham, Campbell, "Beyond Structuralism," in *Genre*, 10, No. 1 (1977), 131–55.

Todorov, Tzvetan, *The Fantastic: A Structural Approach to a Literary Genre*, trans. R. Howard (Ithaca, N.Y.: Cornell University Press, 1975).

———, *Introduction to Poetics*, trans. R. Howard (Minneapolis: University of Minnesota Press, 1981).

9

Ferdinand de Saussure 1857–1913

Ferdinand de Saussure, Swiss linguist, is known as the founder of modern linguistics and structuralism. His intensive theories of language established new ways of studying human behavior and revealed strategies of Modernist thought. Speaking French, German, English, and Greek by the age of fifteen, Saussure achieved international fame at twenty-one with *Memoire sur le système primitif des voyelles dans les langues indo-européennes* (Memoir on the Primitive System of Vowels in Indo-European Languages). His value to modern literary theory, however, comes from his work in Paris at Ecole Pratique des hautes Etudes and University of Geneva. This work was only available after his death in 1913 when his students and colleagues published *Course in General Linguistics* (1915) from class notes.

The sections from the *Course* excerpted here present the substance of Saussure's thinking that influenced twentieth-century ideas of how language and texts operate. In the first section, Saussure distinguishes various levels of words and sounds and determines that what is fundamental to humans is not the ability to speak but the ability to construct a language or sign system. He details the nature of communication in terms of processes: concept and sound production and concept and sound reception. He also addresses the social relationship of mankind and language and asserts that the reality of language is found in an intellectual process (as opposed to a physical one). Most importantly, he predicts the development of semiotics, the study of all sign systems, as a discipline that could shed light on the basic nature of social life. In the second section, Saussure explains the arbitrary nature of the linguistic sign and establishes the duality of its nature as signified (concept) and signifier (sound-image). The third section explains Saussure's understanding of the planes on which language operates, especially those of synchronic (simultaneous) versus diachronic (chronological). He begins by asserting that language is a system based entirely on the opposition of units. He then states the need to determine the identity of those units which convey conventional meaning yet simultaneously convey new shades of meaning as well. Saussure is especially concerned with the notion of value in a system where the basic unit has meaning only in relation to another unit. Recent theorists see these processes and realms of study as having larger applications. In fact, Saussure's notions of relationships as a focus of study is fundamental to twentieth-century literary theory beginning with structuralism and continuing through deconstruction. Essentially, Saussure saw such complexity and chaos in language that he wished to organize and classify universal qualities. The work in discourse is so rich that the basic thoughts of modern theorists such as Derrida, Fish, de Man, Eagleton, and other Poststructuralists are easily traced back to Saussure.

from Course in General Linguistics

The Object of Linguistics

1. DEFINITION OF LANGUAGE

What is both the integral and concrete object of linguistics? The question is especially difficult; later we shall see why; here I wish merely to point up the difficulty.

Other sciences work with objects that are given in advance and that can then be considered from different viewpoints; but not linguistics. Someone pronounces the French word *nu* 'bare': a superficial observer would be tempted to call the word a concrete linguistic object; but a more careful examination would reveal successively three or four quite different things, depending on whether the word is considered as a sound, as the expression of an idea, as the equivalent of Latin *nudum*, etc. Far from it being the object that antedates the viewpoint, it would seem that it is the viewpoint that creates the object; besides, nothing tells us in advance that one way of considering the fact in question takes precedence over the others or is in any way superior to them.

Moreover, regardless of the viewpoint that we adopt, the linguistic phenomenon always has two related sides, each deriving its values from the other. For example:

1. Articulated syllables are acoustical impressions perceived by the ear, but the sounds would not exist without the vocal organs; an *n*, for example, exists only by virtue of the relation between the two sides. We simply cannot reduce language to sound or detach sound from oral articulation; reciprocally, we cannot define the movements of the vocal organs without taking into account the acoustical impression (see pp. 38 ff.).
2. But suppose that sound were a simple thing: would it constitute speech? No, it is only the instrument of thought; by itself, it has no existence. At this point a new and redoubtable relationship arises: a sound, a complex acoustical-vocal unit, combines in turn with an idea to form a complex physiological-psychological unit. But that is still not the complete picture.
3. Speech has both an individual and a social side, and we cannot conceive of one without the other. Besides:
4. Speech always implies both an established system and an evolution; at every moment it is an existing institution and a product of the past. To distinguish between the system and its history, between what it is and what it was, seems very simple at first glance; actually the two things are so closely related that we can scarcely keep them apart. Would we simplify the question

by studying the linguistic phenomenon in its earliest stages—if we began, for example, by studying the speech of children? No, for in dealing with speech, it is completely misleading to assume that the problem of early characteristics differs from the problem of permanent characteristics. We are left inside the vicious circle.

From whatever direction we approach the question, nowhere do we find the integral object of linguistics. Everywhere we are confronted with a dilemma: if we fix our attention on only one side of each problem, we run the risk of failing to perceive the dualities pointed out above; on the other hand, if we study speech from several viewpoints simultaneously, the object of linguistics appears to us as a confused mass of heterogeneous and unrelated things. Either procedure opens the door to several sciences—psychology, anthropology, normative grammar, philology, etc.—which are distinct from linguistics, but which might claim speech, in view of the faulty method of linguistics, as one of their objects.

As I see it there is only one solution to all the foregoing difficulties: *from the very outset we must put both feet on the ground of language and use language as the norm of all other manifestations of speech.* Actually, among so many dualities, language alone seems to lend itself to independent definition and provide a fulcrum that satisfies the mind.

But what is language [*langue*]? It is not to be confused with human speech [*langage*], of which it is only a definite part, though certainly an essential one. It is both a social product of the faculty of speech and a collection of necessary conventions that have been adopted by a social body to permit individuals to exercise that faculty. Taken as a whole, speech is many-sided and heterogeneous; straddling several areas simultaneously—physical, physiological, and psychological—it belongs both to the individual and to society; we cannot put it into any category of human facts, for we cannot discover its unity.

Language, on the contrary, is a self-contained whole and a principle of classification. As soon as we give language first place among the facts of speech, we introduce a natural order into a mass that lends itself to no other classification.

One might object to that principle of classification on the ground that since the use of speech is based on a natural faculty whereas language is something acquired and conventional, language should not take first place but should be subordinated to the natural instinct.

That objection is easily refuted.

First, no one has proved that speech, as it manifests itself when we speak, is entirely natural, i.e. that our vocal apparatus was designed for speaking just as our legs were designed for walking. Linguists are far from agreement on this point. For instance Whitney, to whom language is one of several social institutions, thinks that we use the vocal apparatus as the instrument of language purely through luck, for the sake of convenience: men might just as well have chosen gestures and used visual symbols instead of acoustical symbols. Doubtless his thesis is too dogmatic; language is not similar in all respects to other social institutions (see p. 73 f. and p. 75 f.); moreover, Whitney goes too far in saying that our choice happened to fall on the vocal organs; the choice was more or less imposed by nature. But on the essential point the American linguist is right: language is a convention, and the nature of the sign that is agreed upon does not matter. The question of the vocal apparatus obviously takes a secondary place in the problem of speech.

One definition of *articulated speech* might confirm that conclusion. In Latin, *articulus* means a member, part, or subdivision of a sequence; applied to speech, articulation designates either the subdivision of a spoken chain into syllables or the subdivision of the chain of meanings into significant units; *gegliederte Sprache* is used in the second sense in German. Using the second definition, we can say that what is natural to mankind is not oral speech but the faculty of constructing a language, i.e. a system of distinct signs corresponding to distinct ideas.

Broca discovered that the faculty of speech is localized in the third left frontal convolution; his discovery has been used to substantiate the attribution of a natural quality to speech. But we know that the same part of the brain is the center of *everything* that has to do with speech, including writing. The preceding statements, together with observations that have been made in different cases of aphasia resulting from lesion of the centers of localization, seem to indicate: (1) that the various disorders of oral speech are bound up in a hundred ways with those of written speech; and (2) that what is lost in all cases of aphasia or agraphia is less the faculty of producing a given sound or writing a given sign than the ability to evoke by means of an instrument, regardless of what it is, the signs of a regular system of speech. The obvious implication is that beyond the functioning of the various organs there exists a more general faculty which governs signs and which would be the linguistic faculty proper. And this brings us to the same conclusion as above.

To give language first place in the study of speech, we can advance a final argument: the faculty of articulating words—whether it is natural or not—is exercised only with the help of the instrument created by a collectivity and provided for its use; therefore, to say that language gives unity to speech is not fanciful.

2. PLACE OF LANGUAGE IN THE FACTS OF SPEECH

In order to separate from the whole of speech the part that belongs to language, we must examine the individual act from which the speaking-circuit can be reconstructed. The act requires the presence of at least two persons; that is the minimum number necessary to complete the circuit. Suppose that two people, A and B, are conversing with each other:

Suppose that the opening of the circuit is in A's brain, where mental facts (concepts) are associated with representations of the linguistic sounds (sound-images) that are used for their expression. A given concept unlocks a corresponding sound-image in the brain; this purely *psychological* phenomenon is followed in turn by a *physiological* process: the brain transmits an impulse corresponding to the image to the organs used in producing sounds. Then the sound waves travel from the mouth of A to the ear of B: a purely *physical* process. Next, the circuit continues in B, but the order is reversed: from the ear to the brain, the physiological transmission of the sound-image; in the brain, the psychological association of the image with the corresponding concept. If B then speaks, the new act will follow—from his brain to A's—exactly the same course as the first act and pass through the same successive phases, which I shall diagram as follows:

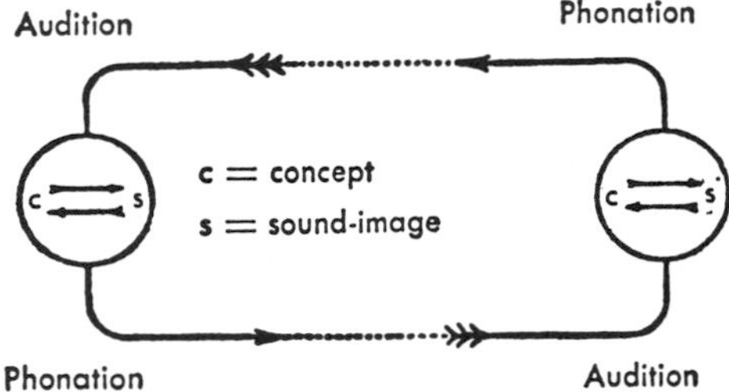

The preceding analysis does not purport to be complete. We might also single out the pure acoustical sensation, the identification of that sensation with the latent sound-image, the muscular image of phonation, etc. I have included only the elements thought to be essential, but the drawing brings out at a glance the distinction between the physical (sound waves), physiological (phonation and audition), and psychological parts (word-images and concepts). Indeed, we should not fail to note that the word-image stands apart from the sound itself and that it is just as psychological as the concept which is associated with it.

The circuit that I have outlined can be further divided into:

a. an outer part that includes the vibrations of the sounds which travel from the mouth to the ear, and an inner part that includes everything else;
b. a psychological and a nonpsychological part, the second including the physiological productions of the vocal organs as well as the physical facts that are outside the individual;
c. an active and a passive part: everything that goes from the associative center of the speaker to the ear of the listener is active, and everything that goes from the ear of the listener to his associative center is passive;
d. finally, everything that is active in the psychological part of the circuit is executive ($c \rightarrow s$), and everything that is passive is receptive ($s \rightarrow c$).

We should also add the associative and co-ordinating faculty that we find as soon as we leave isolated signs; this faculty plays the dominant role in the organization of language as a system (see pp. 122 ff.).

But to understand clearly the role of the associative and co-ordinating faculty, we must leave the individual act, which is only the embryo of speech, and approach the social fact.

Among all the individuals that are linked together by speech, some sort of average will be set up: all will reproduce—not exactly of course, but approximately—the same signs united with the same concepts.

How does the social crystallization of language come about? Which parts of the circuit are involved? For all parts probably do not participate equally in it.

The nonpsychological part can be rejected from the outset. When we hear people speaking a language that we do not know, we perceive the sounds but remain outside the social fact because we do not understand them.

Neither is the psychological part of the circuit wholly responsible: the executive side is missing, for execution is never carried out by the collectivity. Execution is always individual, and the individual is always its master: I shall call the executive side *speaking* [*parole*].

Through the functioning of the receptive and co-ordinating faculties, impressions that are perceptibly the same for all are made on the minds of speakers. How can that social product be pictured in such a way that language will stand apart from everything else? If we could embrace the sum of word-images stored in the minds of all individuals, we could identify the social bond that constitutes language. It is a storehouse filled by the members of a given community through their active use of speaking, a grammatical system that has a potential existence in each brain, or, more specifically, in the brains of a group of individuals. For language is not complete in any speaker; it exists perfectly only within a collectivity.

In separating language from speaking we are at the same time separating: (1) what is social from what is individual; and (2) what is essential from what is accessory and more or less accidental.

Language is not a function of the speaker; it is a product that is passively assimilated by the individual. It never requires premeditation, and reflection enters in only for the purpose of classification, which we shall take up later (pp. 122 ff.).

Speaking, on the contrary, is an individual act. It is wilful and intellectual. Within the act, we should distinguish between: (1) the combinations by which the speaker uses the language code for expressing his own thought; and (2) the psychophysical mechanism that allows him to exteriorize those combinations.

Note that I have defined things rather than words; these definitions are not endangered by certain ambiguous words that do not have identical meanings in different languages. For instance, German *Sprache* means both "language" and "speech"; *Rede* almost corresponds to "speaking" but adds the special connotation of "discourse." Latin *sermo* designates both "speech" and "speaking," while *lingua* means "language," etc. No word corresponds exactly to any of the notions specified above; that is why all definitions of words are made in vain; starting from words in defining things is a bad procedure.

To summarize, these are the characteristics of language:

1. Language is a well-defined object in the heterogeneous mass of speech facts. It can be localized in the limited segment of the speaking-circuit where an auditory image becomes associated with a concept. It is the social side of speech, outside the individual who can never create nor modify it by himself; it exists only by virtue of a sort of contract signed by the members of a community. Moreover, the individual must always serve an apprenticeship in order to learn the functioning of language; a child assimilates it only gradually. It is such a distinct thing that a man deprived of the use of speaking retains it provided that he understands the vocal signs that he hears.
2. Language, unlike speaking, is something that we can study separately. Although dead languages are no longer spoken, we can easily assimilate their linguistic organisms. We can dispense with the other elements of speech; indeed, the science of language is possible only if the other elements are excluded.
3. Whereas speech is heterogeneous, language, as defined, is homogeneous. It is a system of signs in which the only essential thing is the union of meanings and sound-images, and in which both parts of the sign are psychological.
4. Language is concrete, no less so than speaking; and this is a help in our study of it. Linguistic signs, though basically psychological, are not abstractions; associations which bear the stamp of collective approval—and which added together constitute language—are realities that have their

seat in the brain. Besides, linguistic signs are tangible; it is possible to reduce them to conventional written symbols, whereas it would be impossible to provide detailed photographs of acts of speaking [*actes de parole*]; the pronunciation of even the smallest words represents an infinite number of muscular movements that could be identified and put into graphic form only with great difficulty. In language, on the contrary, there is only the sound-image, and the latter can be translated into a fixed visual image. For if we disregard the vast number of movements necessary for the realization of sound-images in speaking, we see that each sound-image is nothing more than the sum of a limited number of elements or phonemes that can in turn be called up by a corresponding number of written symbols (see pp. 61 ff.). The very possibility of putting the things that relate to language into graphic form allows dictionaries and grammars to represent it accurately, for language is a storehouse of sound-images, and writing is the tangible form of those images.

3. PLACE OF LANGUAGE IN HUMAN FACTS: SEMIOLOGY

The foregoing characteristics of language reveal an even more important characteristic. Language, once its boundaries have been marked off within the speech data, can be classified among human phenomena, whereas speech cannot.

We have just seen that language is a social institution; but several features set it apart from other political, legal, etc. institutions. We must call in a new type of facts in order to illuminate the special nature of language.

Language is a system of signs that express ideas, and is therefore comparable to a system of writing, the alphabet of deaf-mutes, symbolic rites, polite formulas, military signals, etc. But it is the most important of all these systems.

A *science that studies the life of signs within society* is conceivable; it would be a part of social psychology and consequently of general psychology; I shall call it *semiology*[1] (from Greek *sēmeîon* 'sign'). Semiology would show what constitutes signs, what laws govern them. Since the science does not yet exist, no one can say what it would be; but it has a right to existence, a place staked out in advance. Linguistics is only a part of the general science of semiology; the laws discovered by semiology will be applicable to linguistics, and the latter will circumscribe a well-defined area within the mass of anthropological facts.

To determine the exact place of semiology is the task of the psychologist.[2] The task of the linguist is to find out what makes language a special system within the mass of semiological data. This issue will be taken up again later; here I wish merely to call attention to one thing: if I have succeeded in assigning linguistics a place among the sciences, it is because I have related it to semiology.

Why has semiology not yet been recognized as an independent science with its own object like all the other sciences? Linguists have been going around in circles: language, better than anything else, offers a basis for understanding the semiological problem; but language must, to put it correctly, be studied in itself; heretofore language has almost always been studied in connection with something else, from other viewpoints.

There is first of all the superficial notion of the general public: people see nothing more than a name-giving system in language (see p. 65), thereby prohibiting any research into its true nature.

Then there is the viewpoint of the psychologist, who studies the sign-mechanism in the individual; this is the easiest method, but it does not lead beyond individual execution and does not reach the sign, which is social.

Or even when signs are studied from a social viewpoint, only the traits that attach language to the other social institutions—those that are more or less voluntary—are emphasized; as a result, the goal is by-passed and the specific characteristics of semiological systems in general and of language in particular are completely ignored. For the distinguishing characteristic of the sign—but the one that is least apparent at first sight—is that in some way it always eludes the individual or social will.

In short, the characteristic that distinguishes semiological systems from all other institutions shows up clearly only in language where it manifests itself in the things which are studied least, and the necessity or specific value of a semiological science is therefore not clearly recognized. But to me the language problem is mainly semiological, and all developments derive their significance from that important fact. If we are to discover the true nature of language we must learn what it has in common with all other semiological systems; linguistic forces that seem very important at first glance (e.g., the role of the vocal apparatus) will receive only secondary consideration if they serve only to set language apart from the other systems. This procedure will do more than to clarify the linguistic problems. By studying rites, customs, etc. as signs, I believe that we shall throw new light on the facts and point up the need for including them in a science of semiology and explaining them by its laws.

NOTES

1. *Semiology* should not be confused with *semantics*, which studies changes in meaning, and which de Saussure did not treat methodically; the fundamental principle of semantics is formulated on page 75. *Original Ed. note.*

2. Cf. A. Naville, *Classification des Sciences*, (2nd. ed.), p. 104. *Original Ed. note.* The scope of semiology (or semiotics) is treated at length in Charles Morris' *Signs, Language and Behavior* (New York: Prentice-Hall, 1946). *Trans. note.*

Nature of the Linguistic Sign

1. SIGN, SIGNIFIED, SIGNIFIER

Some people regard language, when reduced to its elements, as a naming-process only—a list of words, each corresponding to the thing that it names. For example:

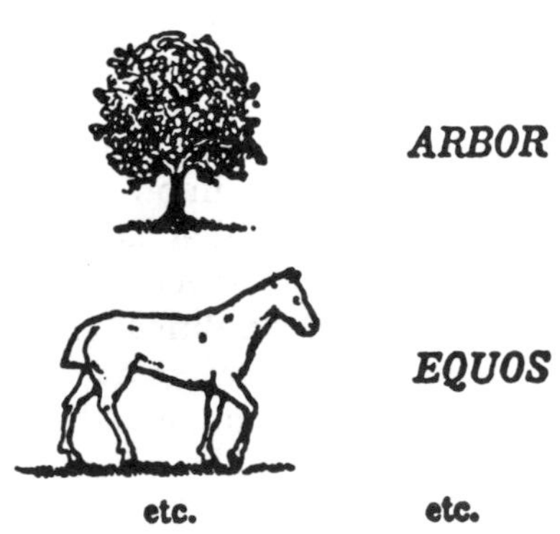

This conception is open to criticism at several points. It assumes that ready-made ideas exist before words (on this point, see below, p. 111); it does not tell us whether a name is vocal or psychological in nature (*arbor*, for instance, can be considered from either viewpoint); finally, it lets us assume that the linking of a name and a thing is a very simple operation—an assumption that is anything but true. But this rather naive approach can bring us near the truth by showing us that the linguistic unit is a double entity, one formed by the associating of two terms.

We have seen in considering the speaking-circuit (p. 11) that both terms involved in the linguistic sign are psychological and are united in the brain by an associative bond. This point must be emphasized.

The linguistic sign unites, not a thing and a name, but a concept and a sound-image.[1] The latter is not the material sound, a purely physical thing, but the psychological imprint of the sound, the impression that it makes on our senses. The sound-image is sensory, and if I happen to call it "material," it is only in that sense, and by way of opposing it to the other term of the association, the concept, which is generally more abstract.

The psychological character of our sound-images becomes apparent when we observe our own speech. Without moving our lips or tongue, we can talk to ourselves or recite mentally a selection of verse. Because we regard the words of our language as sound-images, we must avoid speaking of the "phonemes" that make up the words. This term, which suggests vocal activity, is applicable to the spoken word only, to the realization of the inner image in discourse. We can avoid that misunderstanding by speaking of the *sounds* and *syllables* of a word provided we remember that the names refer to the sound-image.

The linguistic sign is then a two-sided psychological entity that can be represented by the drawing:

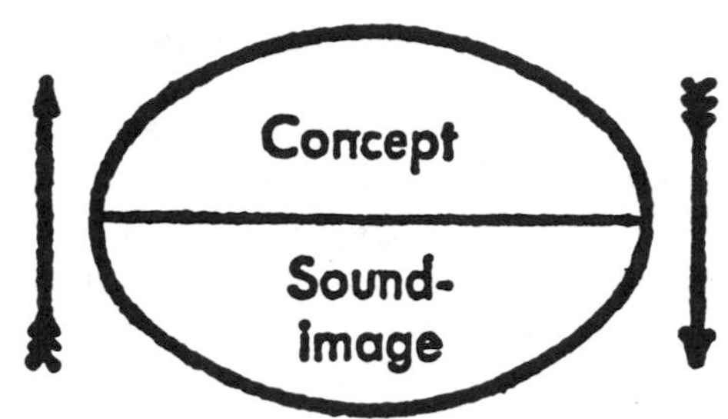

The two elements are intimately united, and each recalls the other. Whether we try to find the meaning of the Latin word *arbor* or the word that Latin uses to designate the concept "tree," it is clear that only the associations sanctioned by that language appear to us to conform to reality, and we disregard whatever others might be imagined.

Our definition of the linguistic sign poses an important question of terminology. I call the combination of a concept and a sound-image a *sign*, but in current usage the term generally designates only a sound-image, a word, for example (*arbor*, etc.). One tends to forget that *arbor* is called a sign only because it carries the concept "tree," with the result that the idea of the sensory part implies the idea of the whole.

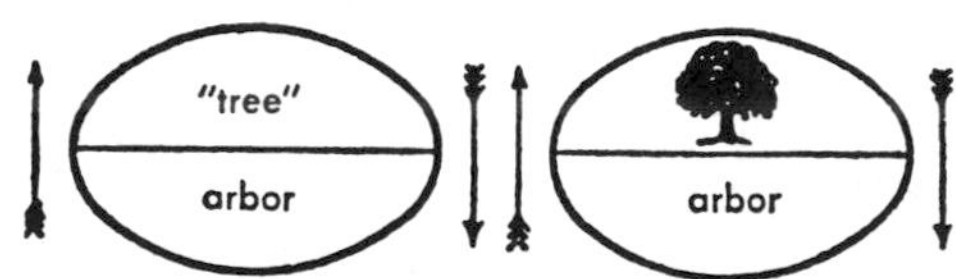

Ambiguity would disappear if the three notions involved here were designated by three names, each suggesting and opposing the others. I propose to retain the word *sign* [*signe*] to designate the whole and to replace *concept* and *sound-image* respectively by *signified* [*signifié*] and *signifier* [*signifiant*]; the last two terms have the advantage of indicating the opposition that separates them from each other and from the whole of which they are parts. As regards *sign*, if I am satisfied with it, this is simply because I do not know of any word to replace it, the ordinary language suggesting no other.

The linguistic sign, as defined, has two primordial characteristics. In enunciating them I am also positing the basic principles of any study of this type.

2. PRINCIPLE I: THE ARBITRARY NATURE OF THE SIGN

The bond between the signifier and the signified is arbitrary. Since I mean by sign the whole that results from the associating of the signifier with the signified, I can simply say: *the linguistic sign is arbitrary.*

The idea of "sister" is not linked by any inner relationship to the succession of sounds *s-ö-r* which serves as its signifier in French; that it could be represented equally by just any other sequence is proved by differences among languages and by the very existence of different languages: the signified "ox" has as its signifier *b-ö-f* on one side of the border and *o-k-s* (*Ochs*) on the other.

No one disputes the principle of the arbitrary nature of the sign, but it is often easier to discover a truth than to assign to it its proper place. Principle I dominates all the linguistics of language; its consequences are numberless. It is true that not all of them are equally obvious at first glance; only after many detours does one discover them, and with them the primordial importance of the principle.

One remark in passing: when semiology becomes organized as a science, the question will arise whether or not it properly includes modes of expression based on completely natural signs, such as pantomime. Supposing that the new science welcomes them, its main concern will still be the whole group of systems grounded on the arbitrariness of the sign. In fact, every means of expression used in society is based, in principle, on collective behavior or—what amounts to the same thing—on convention. Polite formulas, for instance, though often imbued with a certain natural expressiveness (as in the case of a Chinese who greets his emperor by bowing down to the ground nine times), are nonetheless fixed by rule; it is this rule and not the intrinsic value of the gestures that obliges one to use them. Signs that are wholly arbitrary realize better than the others the ideal of the semiological process; that is why language, the most complex and universal of all systems of expression, is also the most characteristic; in this sense linguistics can become the master-pattern for all branches of semiology although language is only one particular semiological system.

The word *symbol* has been used to designate the linguistic sign, or more specifically, what is here called the signifier. Principle I in particular weighs against the use of this term. One characteristic of the symbol is that it is never wholly arbitrary; it is not empty, for there is the rudiment of a natural bond between the signifier and the signified. The symbol of justice, a pair of scales, could not be replaced by just any other symbol, such as a chariot.

The word *arbitrary* also calls for comment. The term should not imply that the choice of the signifier is left entirely to the speaker (we shall see below that the individual does not have the power to change a sign in any way once it has become established in the linguistic community); I mean that it is unmotivated, i.e. arbitrary in that it actually has no natural connection with the signified.

In concluding let us consider two objections that might be raised to the establishment of Principle I:

1. *Onomatopoeia* might be used to prove that the choice of the signifier is not always arbitrary. But onomatopoeic formations are never organic elements of a linguistic system. Besides, their number is much smaller than is generally supposed. Words like French *fouet* 'whip' or *glas* 'knell' may strike certain ears with suggestive sonority, but to see that they have not always had this property we need only examine their Latin forms (*fouet* is derived from *fāgus* 'beech-tree,' *glas* from *classicum* 'sound of a trumpet'). The quality of their present sounds, or rather the quality that is attributed to them, is a fortuitous result of phonetic evolution.

   As for authentic onomatopoeic words (e.g. *glug-glug, tick-tock,* etc.), not only are they limited in number, but also they are chosen somewhat arbitrarily, for they are only approximate and more or less conventional imitations of certain sounds (cf. English *bow-bow* and French *ouaoua*). In addition, once these words have been introduced into the language, they are to a certain extent subjected to the same evolution—phonetic, morphological, etc.—that other words undergo (cf. *pigeon,* ultimately from Vulgar Latin *pīpiō,* derived in turn from an onomatopoeic formation): obvious proof that they lose something of their original character in order to assume that of the linguistic sign in general, which is unmotivated.
2. *Interjections,* closely related to onomatopoeia, can be attacked on the same grounds and come no closer to refuting our thesis. One is tempted to see in them spontaneous expressions of reality dictated, so to speak, by natural forces. But for most interjections we can show that there is no fixed bond between their signified and their signifier. We need only compare two languages on this point to see how much such expressions differ from one language to the next (e.g. the English equivalent of French *aïe!* is *ouch!*). We know, moreover, that many interjections were once words with specific meanings (cf. French *diable!* 'darn!' *mordieu!* 'golly!' from *mort Dieu* 'God's death,' etc.).[2]

Onomatopoeic formations and interjections are of secondary importance, and their symbolic origin is in part open to dispute.

3. PRINCIPLE II: THE LINEAR NATURE OF THE SIGNIFIER

The signifier, being auditory, is unfolded solely in time from which it gets the following characteristics: (a) it represents a span, and (b) the span is measurable in a single dimension; it is a line.

While Principle II is obvious, apparently linguists have always neglected to state it, doubtless because they found it too simple; nevertheless, it is fundamental, and its consequences are incalculable. Its importance equals that of Principle I; the whole mechanism of language depends upon it (see p. 122 f.). In contrast to visual signifiers (nautical signals, etc.) which can offer simultaneous groupings in several dimensions, auditory signifiers have at their command only the dimension of time. Their elements are presented in succession; they form a chain. This feature becomes readily apparent when they are represented in writing and the spatial line of graphic marks is substituted for succession in time.

Sometimes the linear nature of the signifier is not obvious. When I accent a syllable, for instance, it seems that I am concentrating more than one significant element on the same point. But this is an illusion; the syllable and its accent constitute only one phonational act. There is no duality within the act but only different oppositions to what precedes and what follows (on this subject, see p. 131).

NOTES

1. The term sound-image may seem to be too restricted inasmuch as beside the representation of the sounds of a word there is also that of its articulation, the muscular image of the phonational act. But for F. de Saussure language is essentially a depository, a thing received from without (see p. 13). The sound-image is par excellence the natural representation of the word as a fact of potential language, outside any actual use of it in speaking. The motor side is thus implied or, in any event, occupies only a subordinate role with respect to the sound-image. Original *ed. note.*

2. Cf. English *goodness!* and *zounds!* (from *God's wounds*). *Trans. note.*

The Concrete Entities of Language

1. DEFINITION: ENTITY AND UNIT

The signs that make up language are not abstractions but real objects (see p. 15); signs and their relations are what linguistics studies; they are the *concrete entities* of our science.

Let us first recall two principles that dominate the whole issue:

1. The linguistic entity exists only through the associating of the signifier with the signified (see p. 66 ff.). Whenever only one element is retained, the entity vanishes; instead of a concrete object, we are faced with a mere abstraction. We constantly risk grasping only a part of the entity and thinking that we are embracing it in its totality; this would happen, for example, if we divided the spoken chain into syllables, for the syllable has no value except in phonology. A succession of sounds is linguistic only if it supports an idea. Considered independently, it is material for a physiological study, and nothing more than that.

   The same is true of the signified as soon as it is separated from its signifier. Considered independently, concepts like "house," "white," "see," etc. belong to psychology. They become linguistic entities only when associated with sound-images; in language, a concept is a quality of its phonic substance just as a particular slice of sound is a quality of the concept.

   The two-sided linguistic unit has often been compared with the human person, made up of the body and the soul. The comparison is hardly satisfactory. A better choice would be a chemical compound like water, a combination of hydrogen and oxygen; taken separately, neither element has any of the properties of water.
2. The linguistic entity is not accurately defined until it is *delimited*, i.e. sepa-

rated from everything that surrounds it on the phonic chain. These delimited entities or units stand in opposition to each other in the mechanism of language.

One is at first tempted to liken linguistic signs to visual signs, which can exist in space without becoming confused, and to assume that separation of the significant elements can be accomplished in the same way, without recourse to any mental process. The word "form," which is often used to indicate them (cf. the expression "verbal form," "noun form") gives support to the mistake. But we know that the main characteristic of the sound-chain is that it is linear (see p. 70). Considered by itself, it is only a line, a continuous ribbon along which the ear perceives no self-sufficient and clear-cut division; to divide the chain, we must call in meanings. When we hear an unfamiliar language, we are at a loss to say how the succession of sounds should be analyzed, for analysis is impossible if only the phonic side of the linguistic phenomenon is considered. But when we know the meaning and function that must be attributed to each part of the chain, we see the parts detach themselves from each other and the shapeless ribbon break into segments. Yet there is nothing material in the analysis.

To summarize: language does not offer itself as a set of predelimited signs that need only be studied according to their meaning and arrangement; it is a confused mass, and only attentiveness and familiarization will reveal its particular elements. The unit has no special phonic character, and the only definition that we can give it is this: it *is a slice of sound which to the exclusion of everything that precedes and follows it in the spoken chain is the signifier of a certain concept.*

2. METHOD OF DELIMITATION

One who knows a language singles out its units by a very simple method—in theory, at any rate. His method consists of using speaking as the source material of language and picturing it as two parallel chains, one of concepts (*A*) and the other of sound-images (*B*).

In an accurate delimitation, the division along the chain of sound-images (*a*, *b*, *c*) will correspond to the division along the chain of concepts (*a′*, *b′*, *c′*):

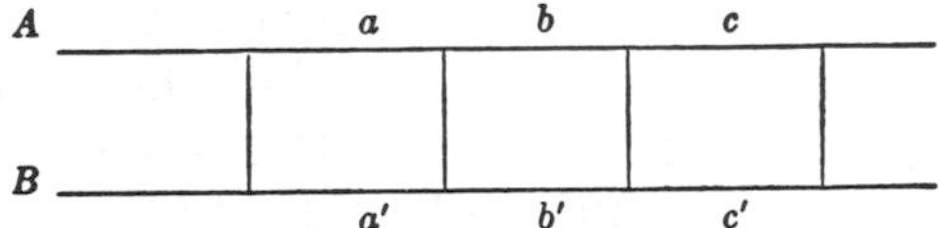

Take French *sižlaprã*. Can we cut the chain after *l* and make *sižl* a unit? No, we need only consider the concepts to see that the division is wrong. Neither is the syllabic division *siž-la-prã* to be taken for granted as having linguistic value. The only possible divisions are these: (1) *si-ž-la-prã (si je la prends* 'if I take it') and (2) *si-ž-l-aprã (si je l'apprends* 'if I learn it'), and they are determined by the meaning that is attached to the words.[1]

To verify the result of the procedure and be assured that we are really dealing with a unit, we must be able in comparing a series of sentences in which the same unit occurs to separate the unit from the rest of the context and find in each instance that meaning justifies the delimitation. Take the two French phrases *lafǫrsdüvã* (la *force* du vent 'the *force* of the wind'), and *abudfǫrs* (à bout de *force* 'exhausted'; *literally*: 'at the end of one's *force*'). In each phrase the same concept coincides with the same phonic slice, *fǫrs*, thus it is certainly a linguistic unit. But in *ilməfǫrsaparle* (il me *force* a parler 'he *forces* me to talk') *fǫrs* has an entirely different meaning: it is therefore another unit.

3. PRACTICAL DIFFICULTIES OF DELIMITATION

The method outlined above is very simple in theory, but is it easy to apply? We are tempted to think so if we start from the notion that the units to be isolated are words. For what is a sentence except a combination of words? And what can be grasped more readily than words? Going back to the example given above, we may say that the analysis of the spoken chain *sižlaprã* resulted in the delimiting of four units, and that the units are words: *si-je-l-apprends*. But we are immediately put on the defensive on noting that there has been much disagreement about the nature of the word, and a little reflection shows that the usual meaning of the term is incompatible with the notion of concrete unit.

To be conceived, we need only think of French *cheval* 'horse' and its plural from *chevaux*. People readily say that they are two forms of the same word; but considered as wholes, they are certainly two distinct things with respect to both meaning and sound. In *mwa (mois,* as in le *mois* de Septembre 'the *month* of September') and *mwaz (mois,* in un *mois* après 'a *month* later') there are also two forms of the same word, and there is no question of a concrete unit. The meaning is the same, but the slices of sound are different. As soon as we try to liken concrete units to words, we face a dilemma: we must either ignore the relation–which is nonetheless evident—that binds *cheval* and *chevaux*, the two sounds of *mwa* and *mwaz*, etc. and say that they are different words, or instead of concrete units be satisfied with the abstraction that links the different forms of the same word. The concrete unit must be sought, not in the word, but elsewhere. Besides, many words are complex units, and we can easily single out their subunits (suffixes, prefixes, radicals). Derivatives like *pain-ful* and *delight-ful* can be divided into distinct parts, each having an obvious meaning and function. Conversely, some units are larger than words: compounds (French *porte-plume* 'penholder'), locutions (*s'il vous plaît* 'please'), inflected forms (*il a été* 'he has been'), etc. But these units resist delimitation as strongly as do words proper, making it extremely difficult to disentangle the interplay of units that are found in a sound-chain and to specify the concrete elements on which a language functions.

Doubtless speakers are unaware of the practical difficulties of delimiting units. Anything that is of even the slightest significance seems like a concrete element to them and they never fail to single it out in discourse. But it is one thing to feel the quick, delicate interplay of units and quite another to account for them through methodical analysis.

A rather widely held theory makes sentences the concrete units of language: we speak only in sentences and subsequently single out the words. But to what extent does the sentence belong to language (see p. 124)? If it belongs to speaking, the sentence cannot pass for the linguistic unit. But let us suppose that this difficulty is set aside. If we picture to ourselves in their totality the sentences that could be uttered, their most striking characteristic is that in no way do they resemble each other. We are at first tempted to liken the immense diversity of sentences to the equal diversity of the individuals that make up a zoological species. But this is an illusion: the characteristics that animals of the same species have in common are much more significant than the differences that separate them. In sentences, on the contrary, diversity is dominant, and when we look for the link that bridges their diversity, again we find, without having looked for it, the word with its grammatical characteristics and thus fall back into the same difficulties as before.

4. CONCLUSION

In most sciences the question of units never even arises: the units are delimited from the outset. In zoology, the animal immediately presents itself. Astronomy works with units that are separated in space, the stars. The chemist can study the nature and composition of potassium bichromate without doubting for an instant that this is a well-defined object.

When a science has no concrete units that are immediately recognizable, it is because they are not necessary. In history, for example, is the unit the individual, the era, or the nation? We do not know. But what does it matter? We can study history without knowing the answer.

But just as the game of chess is entirely in the combination of the different chess-pieces, language is characterized as a system based entirely on the opposition of its concrete units. We can neither dispense with becoming acquainted with them nor take a single step without coming back to them; and still, delimiting them is such a delicate problem that we may wonder at first whether they really exist.

Language then has the strange, striking characteristic of not having entities that are perceptible at the outset and yet of not permitting us to doubt that they exist and that their functioning constitutes it. Doubtless we have here a trait that distinguishes language from all other semiological institutions.

NOTES

1. Cf. the sounds [jurmaın] in English: "your mine" or "you're mine." *Trans. note.*

Identities, Realities, Values

The statement just made brings us squarely up against a problem that is all the more important because any basic notion in static linguistics depends directly on our conception of the unit and even blends with it. This is what I should like successively to demonstrate with respect to the notions of synchronic identity, reality, and value.

A. What is a synchronic *identity*? Here it is not a question of the identity that links the French negation *pas* 'not' to Latin *passum*, a diachronic identity that will be dealt with elsewhere (see p. 181), but rather of the equally interesting identity by virtue of which we state that two sentences like je ne sais *pas* 'I *don't* know' and ne dîtes *pas* cela '*don't* say that' contain the same element. An idle question, one might say; there is identity because the same slice of sound carries the same meaning in the two sentences. But that explanation is unsatisfactory, for if the correspondence of slices of sound and concepts is proof of identity (see above, p. 105, la *force* du vent: à bout de *force*), the reverse is not true. There can be identity without this correspondence. When *Gentlemen!* is repeated several times during a lecture, the listener has the feeling that the same expression is being used each time, and yet variations in utterance and intonation make for appreciable phonic differences in diverse contexts—differences just as applicable as those that elsewhere separate different words (cf. French *pomme* 'apple' and *paume* 'palm,' *goutte* 'drop' and *je goute* 'I taste,' *fuir* 'flee,' and *fouir* 'stuff,' etc.),[1] besides, the feeling of identity persists even though there is no absolute identity between one *Gentlemen!* and the next from a semantic viewpoint either. In the same vein, a word can express quite different ideas without compromising its identity (cf. French *adopter* une mode '*adopt* a fashion' and *adopter* un enfant '*adopt* a child,' la *fleur* du pommier 'the *flower* of the apple tree' and la *fleur* de la noblesse 'the *flower* of nobility,' etc.).

The linguistic mechanism is geared to differences and identities, the former being only the counterpart of the latter. Everywhere then, the problem of identities appears; moreover, it blends partially with the problem of entities and units and is only a complication—illuminating at some points—of the larger problem. This characteristic stands out if we draw some comparisons with facts taken from outside speech. For instance, we speak of the identity of two "8:25 p.m. Geneva-to-Paris" trains that leave at twenty-four hour intervals. We feel that it is the same train each day, yet everything—the locomotive, coaches, personnel—is probably different. Or if a street is demolished, then rebuilt, we say that it is the same street even though in a material sense, perhaps nothing of the old one remains. Why can a street be completely rebuilt and still be the same? Because it does not constitute a purely material entity; it is based on certain conditions that are distinct from the materials that fit the conditions, e.g. its location with respect to other streets. Similarly, what makes the express is its hour of departure, its route, and in general every circumstance that sets it apart from other trains. Whenever the same conditions are fulfilled, the same entities are obtained. Still, the entities are not abstract since we cannot conceive of a street or train outside its material realization.

Let us contrast the preceding examples with the completely different case of a suit which has been stolen from me and which I find in the window of a secondhand store. Here we have a material entity that consists solely of the inert substance—the cloth, its lining, its trimmings, etc. Another suit would not be mine regardless of its similarity to it. But linguistic identity is not that of the garment; it is that of the train and the street. Each time I say the word *Gentlemen!* I renew its substance; each utterance is a new phonic act and a new psychological act. The bond between the two uses of the same word depends neither on material identity nor on sameness in meaning but on elements which must be sought after and which will point up the true nature of linguistic units.

B. What is a synchronic *reality*? To what concrete or abstract elements of language can the name be applied?

Take as an example the distinction between the parts of speech. What supports the classing of words as substantives, adjectives, etc.? Is it done in the name of a purely logical, extra-linguistic principle that is applied to grammar from without like the degrees of longitude and latitude on the globe? Or does it correspond to something that has its place in the system of language and is conditioned by it? In a word, is it a synchronic reality? The second supposition seems probable, but the first could also be defended. In the French sentence *ces gants sont bon marché* 'these gloves are cheap,' is *bon marché* an adjective? It is apparently an adjective from a logical viewpoint but not from the viewpoint of grammar, for *bon marché* fails to behave as an adjective (it is invariable, it never precedes its noun, etc.); in addition, it is composed of two words. Now the distinction between parts of speech is exactly what should serve to classify the words of language. How can a group of words be attributed to one of the "parts"? But to say that *bon* 'good' is an adjective and *marché* 'market' a substantive explains nothing. We are then dealing with a defective or incomplete classification; the division of words into substantives, verbs, adjectives, etc. is not an undeniable linguistic reality.[2]

Linguistics accordingly works continuously with concepts forged by grammarians without knowing whether or not the concepts actually correspond to the constituents of the system of language. But how can we find out? And if they are phantoms, what realities can we place in opposition to them?

To be rid of illusions we must first be convinced that the concrete entities of language are not directly accessible. If we try to grasp them, we come into contact with the true facts. Starting from there, we can set up all the classifications that linguistics needs for arranging all the facts at its disposal. On the other hand, to base the classifications on anything except concrete entities—to say, for example, that the parts of speech are the constituents of language simply because they correspond to categories of logic—is to forget that there are no linguistic facts apart from the phonic substance cut into significant elements.

C. Finally, not every idea touched upon in this chapter differs basically from what we have elsewhere called *values*. A new comparison with the set of chessmen will bring out this point (see pp. 88 ff.). Take a knight, for instance. By itself is it an element in the game? Certainly not, for by its material make-up—outside its square and the other conditions of the game—it means nothing to the player; it becomes a real, concrete element only when endowed with value and wedded to it. Suppose that the piece happens to be destroyed or lost during a game. Can it be replaced by an equivalent piece? Certainly. Not only another knight but even a figure shorn of any resemblance to a knight can be declared identical provided the same value is attributed to it. We see then that in semiological systems like language, where elements hold each other in equilibrium in accordance with fixed rules, the notion of identity blends with that of value and *vice versa*.

In a word, that is why the notion of value envelopes the notions of unit, concrete entity, and reality. But if there is no fundamental difference between these diverse notions, it follows that the problem can be stated successively in several ways. Whether we try to define the unit, reality, concrete entity, or value, we always come back to the central question that dominates all of static linguistics.

It would be interesting from a practical viewpoint to begin with units, to determine what they are and to account for their diversity by classifying them. It would be necessary to search for the reason for dividing language into words—for in spite of the difficulty of defining it, the word is a unit that strikes the mind, something central in the mechanism of language—but that is a subject which by itself would fill a volume. Next we would have to classify the subunits, then the larger units, etc. By determining in this way the elements that it manipulates, synchronic linguistics would completely fulfill its task, for it would relate all synchronic phenomena to their fundamental principle. It cannot be said that this basic problem has ever been faced squarely or that its scope and difficulty have been understood; in the matter of language, people have always been satisfied with ill-defined units.

Still, in spite of their capital importance, it is better to approach the problem of units through the study of value, for in my opinion value is of prime importance.

Translated by Wade Baskin

NOTES

1. Cf. English *bought: boat, naught: note, far: for: four* (for many speakers). *Trans. note.*

2. Form, function, and meaning combine to make the classing of the parts of speech even more difficult in English than in French. Cf. *ten-foot: ten feet in a ten-foot pole: the pole is ten feet long. Trans. note.*

10

Roland Barthes 1915–1980

Roland Barthes was born and grew up in Bayonne, France. At the time of his death he was a professor at the Collège de France, the highest position in the French academic system. In the course of a thirty-year career, wide-ranging enough to be characterized as that of a "man of letters," Barthes became a central force in French intellectual life, and—with a writing style that is at once sophisticated and accessible—a major force in the dissemination of postwar French thinking throughout the world. His major works include: *Writing Degree Zero* (1953, translated into English 1968); *Michelet par lui-meme* (1954); *Mythologies* (1957, trans. 1972); *On Racine* (1963, trans. 1964); *Elements of Semiology* (1964, trans. 1967); *Critique et vérité* (1966); *Système de la mode* (1967); *S/Z* (1970, trans. 1975); *Empire of Signs* (1970, trans. 1982); *Sade/Fourier/Loyola* (1971, trans. 1976); *The Pleasure of the Text* (1973, trans. 1976); *Roland Barthes by Roland Barthes* (1975, trans. 1977); *A Lover's Discourse: Fragments* (1977, trans. 1978); and *The Grain of the Voice: Interviews* 1962–1980 (1981, trans. 1985). "The Structuralist Activity" was first published in 1963; it is reprinted from *Critical Essays* (1964, trans. 1972).

In many ways Barthes's career recapitulates the intellectual life of postwar France. His first book, *Writing Degree Zero*, was an extended response to Jean-Paul Sartre's *What Is Literature?* and his work bears the influence of the linguistic studies of his early colleague, A.-J. Greimas, and of Émile Benveniste, Roman Jakobson, and, of course, Ferdinand de Saussure. Developing from such study, Barthes's work participated successively in structuralism and poststructuralism. More importantly, however, Barthes was able throughout his career to synthesize and articulate, without distortion, difficult theoretical concepts in ways that made them widely accessible. His *Mythologies*, for instance, applied Saussure's semiological principles to discover the underlying *langue* that governs such manifestations of popular culture as advertisements, wrestling matches, and photographic exhibitions. His defense of the avant-garde throughout the 1950s ultimately made possible the assimilation of the difficult works of Alain Robbe-Grillet, Bertolt Brecht, Philip Sollers, and others. In the same way, he aided the assimilation of Lévi-Strauss, Greimas, and, in essays such as "The Structuralist Activity," the structuralist movement in France.

This essay grounds structuralism in the linguistic "science" of Saussure, Greimas, and Roman Jakobson. More importantly—especially in relation to Barthes's own later work and that of the Poststructuralists—it reconceives of scholarship as an "activity," something whose significance is located in a process rather than a product. Thus, he writes here that "one might say that structuralism is essentially an *activity of imitation*, which is also why there is, strictly speaking, no *technical* difference between structuralism as an intellectual activity, on the one hand, and literature in particular, art in general, on the other: both derive from a *mimesis*, based not on the analogy of substances . . . , but on the analogy of functions. . . ." The examination of functions rather than substances is a defining characteristic of structuralism and locates the movement within similar redefinitions of the "objects" of study in the modern sciences. In fact, the crossing of discourse and science in linguistics, as Barthes suggests, opens the way to redefining humanistic studies as the "human sciences" and scholarship as an "activity." Such redefinitions are among the important contributions of structuralism and of Barthes's fruitful career.

The Structuralist Activity

What is structuralism? Not a school, nor even a movement (at least, not yet), for most of the authors ordinarily labeled with this word are unaware of being united by any solidarity of doctrine or commitment. Nor is it a vocabulary. *Structure* is already an old word (of anatomical and grammatical provenance), today quite overworked: all the social sciences resort to it abundantly, and the word's use can distinguish no one, except to engage in polemics about the content assigned to it; *functions, forms, signs* and *significations* are scarcely more pertinent: they are, today, words of common usage, from which one asks (and obtains) whatever one wants, notably the camouflage of the old determinist schema of cause and product; we must doubtless go back to pairings like those of *significans/significatum* and *synchronic/diachronic* in order to approach what distinguishes structuralism from other modes of thought: the first because it refers to the linguistic model as originated by Saussure, and because along with economics, linguistics is, in the present state of affairs, the true science of structure, the second, more decisively, because it seems to imply a certain revision of the notion of history, insofar as the notion of the synchronic (although in Saussure this is a preeminently *operational* concept) accredits a certain immobilization of time, and insofar as that of the diachronic tends to represent the historical process as a pure succession of forms. This second pairing is all the more distinctive in that the chief resistance to structuralism today seems to be of Marxist origin and that it focuses on the notion of history (and not of structure); whatever the case, it is probably the serious recourse to the nomenclature of signification (and not to the word itself, which is, paradoxically, not at all distinctive) which we must ultimately take as structuralism's *spoken sign*: watch who uses *signifier* and *signified*, *synchronic* and *diachronic*, and you will know whether the structuralist vision is constituted.

This is valid for the intellectual metalanguage, which explicitly employs methodological concepts. But since structuralism is neither a school nor a movement, there is no reason to reduce it a priori, even in a problematical way, to the activity of philosophers; it would be better to try and find its broadest description (if not its definition) on another level than that of reflexive language. We can in fact presume that there exist certain writers, painters, musicians, in whose eyes a certain *exercise* of structure (and not only its thought) represents a distinctive experience, and that both analysts and creators must be placed under the common sign of what we might call *structural man*, defined not by his ideas or his languages, but by his imagination—in other words, by the way in which he mentally experiences structure.

Hence the first thing to be said is that in relation to *all* its users, structuralism is essentially an *activity*, i.e., the controlled succession of a certain number of mental operations: we might speak of structuralist activity as we once spoke of surrealist activity (surrealism, moreover, may well have produced the first experience of structural literature, a possibility which must some day be explored). But before seeing what these operations are, we must say a word about their goal.

The goal of all structuralist activity, whether reflexive or poetic, is to reconstruct an "object" in such a way as to manifest thereby the rules of functioning (the "functions") of this object. Structure is therefore actually a *simulacrum* of the object, but a directed, *interested* simulacrum, since the imitated object makes something appear which remained invisible, or if one prefers, unintelligible in the natural object. Structural man takes the real, decomposes it, then recomposes it; this appears to be little enough (which makes some say that the structuralist enterprise is "meaningless," "uninteresting," "useless," etc.). Yet, from another point of view, this "little enough" is decisive: for between the two objects, or the two tenses, of structuralist activity, there occurs *something new*, and what is new is nothing less than the generally intelligible: the simulacrum is intellect added to object, and this addition has an anthropological value, in that it is man himself, his history, his situation, his freedom and the very resistance which nature offers to his mind.

We see, then, why we must speak of a structuralist *activity:* creation or reflection are not, here, an original "impression" of the world, but a veritable fabrication of a world which resembles the first one, not in order to copy it but to render it intelligible. Hence one might say that structuralism is essentially *an activity of imitation*, which is also why there is, strictly speaking, no *technical* difference between structuralism as an intellectual activity on the one hand and literature in particular, art in general on the other: both derive from a *mimesis* based not on the analogy of substances (as in so-called realist art), but on the analogy of functions (what Lévi-Strauss calls *homology*). When Troubetskoy reconstructs the phonetic object as a system of variations; when Dumézil elaborates a functional mythology; when Propp constructs a folktale resulting by structuration from all the Slavic tales he has previously decomposed; when Lévi-Strauss discovers the homologic functioning of the totemic imagination, or Granger the formal rules of economic thought, or Gardin the pertinent features of prehistoric bronzes; when Richard decomposes a poem by Mallarmé into its distinctive vibrations—they are all doing nothing different from what Mondrian, Boulez or Butor are doing when they articulate a certain object—what will be called, precisely, a composition—by the controlled manifestation of certain units and certain associations of these units. It is of little consequence whether the initial object liable to the simulacrum-activity is given by the world in an already assembled fashion (in the case of the structural analysis made of a constituted language or society or work) or is still scattered (in the case of the structural "composition"); whether this initial object is drawn from a social reality or an imaginary reality. It is not the nature of the copied object which defines an art (though this is a tenacious prejudice in all realism), it is the fact that man adds to it in reconstructing it: technique is the very being of all creation. It is therefore to the degree that the goals of structuralist activity are indissolubly linked to a certain technique that structuralism exists in a distinctive fashion in relation to other modes of analysis or creation: we recompose the object *in order* to make certain functions appear, and it is, so to speak, the way that makes the work; this is why we must speak of the structuralist activity rather than the structuralist work.

The structuralist activity involves two typical operations: dissection and articulation. To dissect the first object, the one which is given to the simulacrum-activity, is to find in it certain mobile fragments whose differential situation engenders a certain meaning; the fragment has no meaning in itself, but it is nonetheless such that the slightest variation wrought in its configuration produces a change in the whole; a *square* by Mondrian, a series by Pousseur, a *versicle* of Butor's *Mobile*, the "mytheme" in Lévi-Strauss, the phoneme in the work of the phonologists, the "theme" in certain literary criticism—all these units (whatever their inner structure and their extent, quite different according to cases) have no significant existence except by their frontiers: those which separate them from other actual units of the discourse (but this is a problem of articulation) and also those which distinguish them from other virtual units, with which they form a certain class (which linguistics calls a *paradigm*); this notion of a paradigm is essential, apparently, if we are to understand the structuralist vision: the paradigm is a group, a reservoir—as limited as possible—of objects (of units) from which one summons, by an act of citation, the object or unit one wishes to endow with an actual meaning; what characterizes the paradigmatic object is that it is, vis-à-vis other objects of its class, in a certain relation of affinity and dissimilarity: two units of the same paradigm must resemble each other somewhat *in order* that the difference which separates them be indeed evident: s and z must have both a common feature (dentality) and a distinctive feature (presence or absence of sonority) so that we cannot, in French, attribute the same meaning to *poisson* and *poison;* Mondrian's squares must have both certain affinities by their shape as squares, and certain dissimilarities by their proportion and color; the American automobiles (in Butor's *Mobile*) must be constantly regarded in the same way, yet they must differ each time by both their make and color; the episodes of the Oedipus myth (in Lévi-Strauss's analysis) must be both identical and varied—in order that all these languages, these works may be intelligible. The dissection-operation thus produces an initial dispersed state of the simulacrum, but the units of the structure are not at all anarchic: before being distributed and fixed in the continuity of the composition, each one forms with its own virtual group or reservoir an intelligent organism, subject to a sovereign motor principle: that of the smallest difference.

Once the units are posited, structural man must discover in them or establish for them certain rules of association: this is the activity of articulation, which succeeds the summoning activity. The syntax of the arts and of discourse is, as we know, extremely varied; but what we discover in each work of structural enterprise is the submission to regular constraints whose formalism, improperly indicted, is much less important than their stability; for what is happening, at this second stage of the simulacrum-activity, is a kind of battle against chance; this is why the constraint of recurrence of the units has an almost demiurgic value: it is by the regular return of the units and of the associations of units that the work appears constructed, i.e., endowed with meaning; linguistics calls these rules of combination forms, and it would be advantageous to retain this rigorous sense of an overtaxed word: form, it has been said, is what keeps the contiguity of units from appearing as a pure effect of chance: the work of art is what man wrests from chance. This perhaps allows us to understand on the one hand why so-called nonfigurative works are nonetheless to the highest degree works of art, human thought being established not on the analogy of copies and models but with the regularity of assemblages; and on the other hand why these same works appear, precisely, fortuitous and thereby useless to those who discern in them no form: in front of an abstract painting, Khrushchev was certainly wrong to see only the traces of a donkey's tail whisked across the canvas; at least he knew in his way, though, that art is a certain conquest of chance (he simply forgot that every rule must be learned, whether one wants to apply or interpret it).

The simulacrum, thus constructed, does not render the world as it has found it, and it is here that structuralism is important. First of all, it manifests a new category of the object, which is neither the real nor the rational, but the *functional*, thereby joining a whole scientific complex which is being developed around information theory and research. Subsequently and especially, it highlights the strictly human process by which men give meaning to things. Is this new? To a certain degree, yes; of course the world has never stopped looking for the meaning of what is given it and of what it produces; what is new is a mode of thought (or a "poetics") which seeks less to assign completed meanings to the objects it discovers than to know how meaning is possible, at what cost and by what means. Ultimately, one might say that the object of structuralism is not man endowed with meanings, but man fabricating meanings, as if it could not be the content of meanings which exhausted the semantic goals of humanity, but only the act by which these meanings, historical and contingent variables, are produced. *Homo significans:* such would be the new man of structural inquiry.

According to Hegel, the ancient Greek was amazed by the *natural* in nature; he constantly listened to it, questioned the meaning of mountains, springs, forests, storms; without knowing what all these objects were telling him by name, he perceived in the vegetal or cosmic order a tremendous *shudder* of meaning, to which he gave the name of a god: Pan. Subsequently, nature has changed, has become social: everything that is given to man is *already* human, down to the forest and the river which we cross when we travel. But confronted with this social nature, which is quite simply culture, structural man is no different from the ancient Greek: he too listens for the natural in culture, and constantly perceives in it not so much stable, finite, "true" meanings as the shudder of an enormous machine which is humanity tirelessly undertaking to create meaning, without which it would no longer be human. And it is because this fabrication of meaning is more important, to its view, than the meanings themselves, it is because the function is extensive with the works, that structuralism constitutes itself as an activity, and refers the exercise of the work and the work itself to a single identity: a serial composition or an analysis by Lévi-Strauss are not objects except insofar as they have been *made*: their present being is their past act: they are *having-been-mades;* the artist, the analyst recreates the course taken by meaning, he need not designate it: his function, to return to Hegel's example, is a *manteia;* like the ancient soothsayer, he *speaks* the locus of meaning but does not name it. And it is because literature, in particular, is a mantic activity that it is both intelligible and interrogating, speaking and silent, engaged in the world by the course of meaning which it remakes with the world, but disengaged from the contingent meanings which the world elaborates: an answer to the man who consumes it yet always a question to nature, an answer which questions and a question which answers.

How then does structural man deal with the accusation of unreality which is sometimes flung at him? Are not forms in the world, are not forms responsible? Was it really his Marxism that was revolutionary in Brecht? Was it not rather the decision to link to Marxism, in the theater, the placing of a spotlight or the deliberate fraying of a costume? Structuralism does not withdraw history from the world: it seeks to link to history not only certain contents (this has been done a thousand times) but also certain forms, not only the material but also the intelligible, not only the ideological but also the esthetic. And precisely because all thought about the historically intelligible is also a participation in that intelligibility, structural man is scarcely concerned to *last;* he knows that structuralism, too, is a certain *form* of the world, which will change with the world; and just as he experiences his validity (but not his truth) in his power to speak the old languages of the world in a new way, so he knows that it will suffice that a new language rise out of history, a new language which speaks him in his turn, for his task to be done.

Translated by Richard Howard

11

Tzvetan Todorov 1939–

Born in Sofia, Bulgaria, Tzvetan Todorov attended the University of Sofia (M.A., 1961) and the University of Paris (Doctorat de Troisième Cycle, 1966; Doctorat des Lettres, 1970). He has been on the staff of the Centre National de la Recherche Scientifique in Paris since 1968. Todorov has been a pioneer in structuralism and much of his work has been translated into English and other languages. His books include: *Literature et Signification* (1967); *The Fantastic: A Structural Approach to a Literary Genre* (1970; trans. 1973); *The Poetics of Prose* (1971; trans. 1977); *Introduction to Poetics* (1973; trans. 1981); *Theories of the Symbol* (1977; trans. 1982); and *The Conquest of America: The Question of the Other* (1982; trans. 1984).

Todorov's structuralist approach to literature is evident in "The Uncanny and the Marvelous," the second chapter of *The Fantastic*, where his thesis is that the fantastic is a frontier between two adjacent genres: the uncanny (the supernatural explained) and the marvelous (the supernatural accepted). In keeping with his belief that literature is a vehicle in which language creates an internal system through a large, complex system of signs that produces structure, Todorov examines the differences and similarities between the fantastic, the uncanny, and the marvelous. In this essay he *positions* the genres in relation to one another in much the same way Saussure positions the elements of language in relation to other elements of language. He states that these three genres emphasize the ambiguity of the supernatural but explains that the end of a work determines in which of the three categories that work falls. By defining each of the three categories and juxtaposing the canny and the marvelous with the fantastic, Todorov opens the door to further discussion of all three and also lays the foundation for his definition and discussion of the fantastic as a clearly defined genre based on structural criticism.

The Uncanny and the Marvelous

The fantastic, we have seen, lasts only as long as a certain hesitation: a hesitation common to reader and character, who must decide whether or not what they perceive derives from "reality" as it exists in the common opinion. At the story's end, the reader makes a decision even if the character does not; he opts for one solution or the other, and thereby emerges from the fantastic. If he decides that the laws of reality remain intact and permit an explanation of the phenomena described, we say that the work belongs to another genre: the uncanny. If, on the contrary, he decides that new laws of nature must be entertained to account for the phenomena, we enter the genre of the marvelous.

The fantastic therefore leads a life full of dangers, and may evaporate at any moment. It seems to be located on the frontier of two genres, the marvelous and the uncanny, rather than to be an autonomous genre. One of the great periods of supernatural literature, that of the Gothic novel, seems to confirm this observation. Indeed, we generally distinguish, within the literary Gothic, two tendencies: that of the supernatural explained (the "uncanny"), as it appears in the novels of Clara Reeves and Ann Radcliffe; and that of the supernatural accepted (the "marvelous"), which is characteristic of the works of Horace Walpole, M. G. Lewis, and Mathurin. Here we find not the fantastic in the strict sense, only genres adjacent to it. More precisely, the effect of the fantastic is certainly produced, but during only a portion of our reading: in Ann Radcliffe, up to the moment when we are sure that everything which has happened is susceptible of a rational explanation; in M. G. Lewis, up to the moment when we are sure that the supernatural events will receive *no* explanation. Once we have finished reading, we understand—in both cases—that what we call the fantastic has not existed.

We may ask how valid a definition of genre may be if it permits a work to "change genre" by a simple sentence like: "At this moment, he awakened and saw the walls of his room. . . ." But there is no reason not to think of the fantastic as an evanescent genre. Such a category, moreover, has nothing exceptional about it. The classic definition of the *present,* for example, describes it as a pure limit between the past and the future. The comparison is not gratuitous: the marvelous corresponds to an unknown phenomenon, never seen as yet, still to come—hence to a future; in the uncanny, on the other hand, we refer the inexplicable to known facts, to a previous experience, and thereby to the past. As for the fantastic itself, the hesitation which characterizes it cannot be situated, by and large, except in the present.

Here we also are faced with the problem of the work's unity. We take this unity as self-evident, and we assert that a sacrilege has been committed when cuts are made. But matters are probably more complicated; let us not forget that in school, where our first, and decisive, experience of literature occurred, we read only "selected passages" or "extracts" from most works. A certain fetishism of the book survives in our own day and age: the literary work is transformed both into a precious and motionless object and into a symbol of plenitude, and the act of cutting it becomes an equivalent of castration. How much freer was the attitude of a Khlebnikov, who composed his poems out of fragments of preceding poems and who urged his editors and even his printers to revise his text! Only an identification of the book with its author explains our horror of cuts.

If we do decide to proceed by examining certain parts of the work in isolation, we discover that by temporarily omitting the end of the narrative we are able to include a much larger number of texts within the genre of the fantastic. The modern (French or English) editions of *The Saragossa Manuscript* precisely confirm this: without its end, which resolves the hesitation, the book clearly belongs to the fantastic. Charles Nodier, one of the pioneers of the fantastic in France, thoroughly understood this, and deals with it in one of his tales, "Inès de las Sierras." This text consists of two apparently equal parts, and the end of the first part leaves us in utter perplexity: we are at a loss to explain the strange phenomena which occur; on the other hand, we are not as ready to admit the supernatural as we are to embrace the natural. The narrator hesitates between two procedures: to break off his narrative (and remain in the fantastic) or to continue (and abandon it). His own preference, he declares to his hearers, is to stop, with the following justification: "Any other outcome would be destructive to my story, for it would change its nature."

Yet it would be wrong to claim that the fantastic can exist only in a part of the work, for here are certain texts which sustain their ambiguity to the very end, i.e., even beyond the narrative itself. The book closed, the ambiguity persists. A remarkable example is supplied by Henry James' tale "The Turn of the Screw," which does not permit us to determine finally whether ghosts haunt the old estate, or whether we are confronted by the hallucinations of a hysterical governess victimized by the disturbing atmosphere which surrounds her. In French literature, Mérimée's tale "La Vénus d'Ille" affords a perfect example of this ambiguity. A statue seems to come alive and to kill the bridegroom; but we remain at the point of "seems," and never reach certainty.

Whatever the case, we cannot exclude from a scrutiny of the fantastic either the marvelous or the uncanny, genres which it overlaps. But we must not, on the one hand, forget Louis Vax's remark that "an ideal art of the fantastic must keep to indecision."

Let us take a closer look, then, at these two neighbors. We find that in each case, a transitory sub-genre appears: between the fantastic and the uncanny on the one hand, between the fantastic and the marvelous on the other. These sub-genres include works that sustain the hesitation characteristic of the true fantastic for a long period, but that ultimately end in the marvelous or in the uncanny. We may represent these sub-divisions with the help of the following diagram:

uncanny	*fantastic-uncanny*	*fantastic-marvelous*	*marvelous*

The fantastic in its pure state is represented here by the median line separating the fantastic-uncanny from the fantastic-marvelous. This line corresponds perfectly to the nature of the fantastic, a frontier between two adjacent realms.

Let us begin with the fantastic-uncanny. In this sub-genre events that seem supernatural throughout a story receive a rational explanation at its end. If these events have long led the character and the reader alike to believe in an intervention of the supernatural, it is because they have an unaccustomed character. Criticism has described, and often condemned, this type under the label of "the supernatural explained."

Let us take as an example of the fantastic-uncanny the same *Saragossa Manuscript*. All of the "miracles" are explained rationally at the end of the narrative. Alfonso meets in a cave the hermit who had sheltered him at the beginning, and who is the grand sheik of the Gomélez himself. This man reveals the machinery of all the foregoing events:

> Don Emmanuel de Sa, the Governor of Cadiz, is one of the initiates. He had sent you Lopez and Moschite, who abandoned you at the spring of Alcornoques. . . . By means of a sleeping potion you were made to waken the next day under the gallows of the Zoto brothers. Whence you came to my hermitage, where you encountered the dreadful Pascheco, who is in fact a Basque

> dancer. . . . The following day, you were subjected to a far crueler ordeal: the false inquisition which threatened you with horrible tortures but did not succeed in shaking your courage.

Doubt had been sustained up to this point, as we know, between two poles: the existence of the supernatural and a series of rational explanations. Let us now enumerate the types of explanation that erode the case for the supernatural: first, accident or coincidence—for in the supernatural world, instead of chance there prevails what we might call "pandeterminism" (an explanation in terms of chance is what works against the supernatural in "Inès de las Sierras"); next, dreams (a solution proposed in *Le Diable Amoureux*); then the influence of drugs (Alfonso's dreams during the first night); tricks and prearranged apparitions (an essential solution in *The Saragossa Manuscript*): illusion of the senses (we shall find examples of this in Théophile Gautier's "La Morte Amoureuse" and John Dickson Carr's *The Burning Court*); and lastly madness, as in Hoffmann's "Princess Brambilla." There are obviously two groups of "excuses" here which correspond to the oppositions real/imaginary and real/illusory. In the first group, there has been no supernatural occurrence, for nothing at all has actually occurred: what we imagined we saw was only the fruit of a deranged imagination (dream, madness, the influence of drugs). In the second group, the events indeed occurred, but they may be explained rationally (as coincidences, tricks, illusions).

We recall that in the definitions of the fantastic cited above, the rational solution was decided as "completely stripped of internal probability" (Solovyov) or as a loophole "small enough to be unusable" (M. R. James). Indeed, the realistic solutions given in *The Saragossa Manuscript* or "Inès de las Sierras" are altogether improbable; supernatural solutions would have been, on the contrary, quite probable. The coincidences are too artificial in Nodier's tale. As for *The Saragossa Manuscript*, its author does not even try to concoct a credible ending: the story of the treasure, of the hollow mountain, of the empire of the Gomélez is more incredible than that of the women transformed into corpses! The probable is therefore not necessarily opposed to the fantastic: the former is a category that deals with internal coherence, with submission to the genre; the *fantastic* refers to an ambiguous perception shared by the reader and one of the characters. Within the genre of the fantastic, it is *probable* that "fantastic" reactions will occur.

In addition to such cases as these, where we find ourselves in the uncanny rather in spite of ourselves—in order to explain the fantastic—there also exists the uncanny in the pure state. In works that belong to this genre, events are related which may be readily accounted for by the laws of reason, but which are, in one way or another, incredible, extraordinary, shocking, singular, disturbing or unexpected, and which thereby provoke in the character and in the reader a reaction similar to that which works of the fantastic have made familiar. The definition is, as we see, broad and vague, but so is the genre which it describes: the uncanny is not a clearly delimited genre, unlike the fantastic. More precisely, it is limited on just one side, that of the fantastic; on the other, it dissolves into the general field of literature (Dostoievsky's novels, for example, may be included in the category of the uncanny). According to Freud, the sense of the uncanny is linked to the appearance of an image which originates in the childhood of the individual or the race (a hypothesis still to be verified; there is not an entire coincidence between Freud's use of the term and our own). The literature of horror in its pure state belongs to the uncanny—many examples from the stories of Ambrose Bierce could serve as examples here.

The uncanny realizes, as we see, only one of the conditions of the fantastic: the description of certain reactions, especially of fear. It is uniquely linked to the sentiments of the characters and not to a material event defying reason. (The marvelous, by way of contrast, may be characterized by the mere presence of supernatural events, without implicating the reaction they provoke in the characters.)

Poe's tale "The Fall of the House of Usher" is an instance of the uncanny bordering on the fantastic. The narrator of this tale arrives at the house one evening summoned by his friend Roderick Usher, who asks him to stay for a time. Usher is a hypersensitive, nervous creature who adores his sister, now seriously ill. When she dies some days later, the two friends, instead of burying her, leave her body in one of the vaults under the house. Several days pass. On a stormy night the two men are sitting in a room together, the narrator reading aloud an ancient tale of chivalry. The sounds that are described in the chronicle seem to correspond to the noises they hear in the house itself. At the end, Roderick Usher stands up and says, in a scarcely audible voice: "We have put her living in the tomb!" And, indeed, the door opens, the sister is seen standing on the threshold. Brother and sister rush into each other's arms, and fall dead. The narrator flees the house just in time to see it crumble into the environing tarn.

Here the uncanny has two sources. The first is constituted by two coincidences (there are as many of these as in a work of the *supernatural explained*). Although the resurrection of Usher's sister and the fall of the house after the death of its inhabitants may appear supernatural, Poe has not failed to supply quite rational explanations for both events. Of the house, he writes: "Perhaps the eye of a scrutinizing observer might have discovered a barely perceptible fissure, which, extending from the roof of the building in front, made its way down the wall in a zig-zag direction, until it became lost in the sullen waters of the tarn." And of Lady Madeline: "Frequent although transient affections of a partially cataleptical character were the unusual diagnosis." Thus the supernatural explanation is merely suggested, and one need not accept it.

The other series of elements that provoke the sense of the uncanny is not linked to the fantastic but to what we might call "an experience of limits," which characterizes the whole of Poe's *oeuvre*. Indeed, Baudelaire wrote of Poe: "No man has more magically described the *exceptions* of human life and of nature." Likewise Dostoievsky: "He almost always chooses the most exceptional reality, puts his character in the most exceptional situation, on the external or psychological level. . . ." (Poe, moreover, wrote a tale on this theme, a "meta-uncanny" tale entitled "The Angel of the Odd.") In "The Fall of the House of Usher," it is the extremely morbid condition of the brother and sister which disturbs the reader. In other tales, scenes of cruelty, delight in evil, and murder will provoke the same effect. The sentiment of the uncanny originates, then, in certain themes linked to more or less ancient taboos. If we grant that primal experience is constituted by transgression, we can accept Freud's theory as to the origin of the uncanny.

Thus the fantastic is ultimately excluded from "The Fall of the House of Usher." As a rule, we do not find the fantastic in Poe's works, in the strict sense, with the exception perhaps of "The Black Cat." His tales almost all derive their effect from the uncanny, and several from the marvelous. Yet Poe remains very close to the authors of the fantastic both in his themes and in the techniques that he applies.

We also know that Poe originated the detective story or murder mystery, and this relationship is not a matter of chance. It has often been remarked, moreover, that for the reading public, detective stories have in our time replaced ghost stories. Let us consider the nature of this relationship. The murder mystery, in which we try to discover the identity of the criminal, is constructed in the following manner: on the one hand there are several easy solutions, initially tempting but turning out, one after another, to be false; on the other, there is an entirely improbable solution disclosed only at the end and turning out to be the only right one. Here we see what brings the detective story close to the fantastic tale. Recalling Solovyov's and James's definitions, we note that the fantastic narrative, too, involves two solutions, one probable and supernatural, the other improbable and rational. It suffices, therefore, that in the detective story this second solution be so inaccessible as to "defy reason" for us to accept the existence of the supernatural rather than to rest with the absence of any explanation at all. A classical example of this situation is Agatha Christie's *Ten Little Indians*. Ten characters are isolated on an island; they are told (by a recording) that they will all die, punished for a crime which the law cannot punish. The nature of each death, moreover, is described in the counting-rhyme "Ten Little Indians." The doomed characters—and the reader along with them—vainly try to discover who is carrying out the successive executions. They are alone on the island and dying one after another, each in a fashion announced by the rhyme; down to the last one, who—and it is this that arouses an aura of the supernatural—does not commit suicide but is killed in his turn. No rational explanation seems possible, we must admit the existence of invisible beings or spirits. Obviously this hypothesis is not really necessary: the rational explanation will be given. The murder mystery approaches the fantastic, but it is also the contrary of the fantastic: in fantastic texts, we tend to prefer the supernatural explanation; the detective story, once it is over, leaves no doubt as to the absence of supernatural events. This relationship, moreover, is valid only for a certain type of detective story (the "sealed room") and a certain type of uncanny narrative (the "supernatural explained"). Further, the emphasis differs in the two genres: in the detective story, the emphasis is placed on the solution to the mystery; in the texts linked to the uncanny (as in the fantastic narrative), the emphasis is on the reactions which this mystery provokes. This structural proximity nonetheless produces a resemblance which we must take into account.

An author who deserves a more extended scrutiny when we deal with the relation between detective stories and fantastic tales is John Dickson Carr. Among his books there is one in particular which raises the problem in an exemplary fashion, *The Burning Court*. As in *Ten Little Indians*, we are confronted with an apparently insoluble problem: four men open a crypt in which a corpse had been placed a few days before; the crypt is empty, but it is not possible that anyone could have opened it in the meantime. Throughout the story, moreover, ghosts and supernatural phenomena are evoked. There is a witness to the crime that had taken place, and this witness asserts he has seen the murderess leave the victim's room, passing through the wall at a place where a door existed two hundred years earlier. Furthermore, one of the persons implicated in the case, a young woman, believes herself to be a witch, or more precisely, a poisoner (the murder was the result of poison) who belongs to a particular type of human beings, *the non-dead:*

"Briefly, the non-dead are those persons—commonly women—who have been condemned to death for the crime of poisoning, and whose bodies have been burnt at the stake, whether alive or dead," we learn later on. While leafing through a manuscript he has received from the publishing house that he works for, Stevens, the young woman's husband, happens on a photograph whose caption reads: *Marie d'Aubray: Guillotined for Murder, 1861.* The text continues: "He was looking at a photograph of his own wife." How could this young woman, some seventy years later, be the same person as a famous nineteenth-century poisoner, guillotined into the bargain? Quite simply, according to Stevens' wife, who is ready to assume responsibility for the present murder. A series of further coincidences seems to confirm the presence of the supernatural. Finally, a detective arrives, and everything begins to be explained. The woman who had been seen passing through the wall was an optical illusion caused by a mirror. The corpse had not vanished after all, but was cunningly concealed. Young Marie Stevens had nothing in common with a long-dead poisoner, though an effort had been made to make her believe that she had. The entire supernatural atmosphere had been created by the murderer in order to confuse the case, to avert suspicion. The actual guilty parties are discovered, even if they are not successfully punished.

Then follows an epilogue, as a result of which *The Burning Court* emerges from the class of detective stories that simply evoke the supernatural, to join the ranks of the fantastic. We see Marie once again, in her house, thinking over the case; and the fantastic re-emerges. Marie asserts once again (to the reader) that she is indeed the poisoner, that the detective was in fact her friend (which is not untrue), and that he has provided the entire rational explanation in order to save her ("It was clever of him to pluck a physical explanation, a thing of sizes and dimensions and stone walls").

The world of the non-dead reclaims its rights, and the fantastic with it: we are thrown back on our hesitation as to which solution to choose. But it must be noted, finally, that we are less concerned here with a resemblance between two genres than with their synthesis.

If we move to the *other* side of that median line which we have called the fantastic, we find ourselves in the fantastic-marvelous, the class of narratives that are presented as fantastic and that end with an acceptance of the supernatural. These are the narratives closest to the pure fantastic, for the latter, by the very fact that it remains unexplained, unrationalized, suggests the existence of the supernatural. The frontier between the two will therefore be uncertain; nonetheless, the presence or absence of certain details will always allow us to decide.

Gautier's "La Morte Amoureuse" can serve as an example. This is the story of a monk (Romuald) who on the day of his ordination falls in love with the courtesan Clarimonde. After several fleeting encounters, Romuald attends Clarimonde's deathbed—whereupon she begins to appear in his dreams, dreams that have a strange property: instead of conforming to impressions of each passing day, they constitute a continuous narrative. In his dreams, Romuald no longer leads the austere life of a monk, but lives in Venice in continuous revelry. And at the same time he realizes that Clarimonde has been keeping herself alive by means of blood she sucks from him during the night. . . .

Up to this point, all the events are susceptible of rational explanations. The explanations are largely furnished by the dreams themselves ("May God grant that it is a dream!" Romuald exlaims, in this resembling Alvaro in *Le Diable Amou-*

reux). Illusions of the senses furnish another plausible explanation. Thus: "One evening, strolling along the box-lined paths of my little garden, I *seemed to see* through the hedgerow a woman's shape . . ."; "For a moment *I thought* I saw her foot move . . ."; "*I do not know if this was an illusion or a reflection of the lamp, but it seemed* that the blood began to circulate once more beneath that lustreless pallor," etc. (italics mine). Finally, a series of events can be considered as simply uncanny and due to chance. But Romuald himself is ready to regard the matter as a diabolic intervention:

> The strangeness of the episode. Clarimonde's supernatural [!] beauty, the phosphorescent lustre of her eyes, the burning touch of her hand, the confusion into which she had thrown me, the sudden change that had occurred in me—all of this clearly proved the presence of the Devil; and that silken hand was perhaps nothing but the glove in which he had clad his talons.

It might be the Devil, indeed, but it might also be chance and no more than that. We remain, then, up to this point in the fantastic in its pure state. At this moment there occurs an event which causes the narrative to swerve. Another monk, Sérapion, learns (we do not know how) of Romuald's adventure. He leads the latter to the graveyard in which Clarimonde lies buried, unearths the coffin, opens it, and Clarimonde appears, looking just as she did on the day of her death, a drop of blood on her lips. . . . Seized by pious rage, Abbé Sérapion flings holy water on the corpse. "The wretched Clarimonde had no sooner been touched by the holy dew than her lovely body turned to dust; nothing was left but a shapeless mass of ashes and half-consumed bones." This entire scene, and in particular the metamorphosis of the corpse, cannot be explained by the laws of nature as they are generally acknowledged. We are here in the realm of the fantastic-marvelous.

A similar example is to be found in Villiers de l'Isle-Adam's "Véra." Here again, throughout the tale, we may hesitate between believing in life-after-death or thinking that the count who so believes is mad. But at the end, the count discovers the key to Véra's tomb in his own room, though he himself had flung it into the grave; it must therefore be Véra, his dead wife, who has brought it to him.

There exists, finally, a form of the marvelous in the pure state which—just as in the case of the uncanny in the pure state—has no distinct frontiers (we have seen in the preceding chapter that extremely diverse works contain elements of the marvelous). In the case of the marvelous, supernatural elements provoke no particular reaction in either the characters or in the implicit reader. It is not an attitude toward the events described which characterizes the marvelous, but the nature of these events.

We note, in passing, how arbitrary the old distinction was between form and content: the event, which traditionally belonged to "content," here becomes a "formal" element. The converse is also true: the stylistic (hence "formal") procedure of modalization can have, as we have seen in connection with *Aurélia*, a precise content.

We generally link the genre of the marvelous to that of the fairy tale. But as a matter of fact, the fairy tale is only one of the varieties of the marvelous and the supernatural events in fairy tales provoke no surprise: neither a hundred years' sleep, nor a talking wolf, nor the magical gifts of the fairies (to cite only a few elements in Perrault's tales). What distinguishes the fairy tale is a certain kind of writing, not the status of the supernatural. Hoffmann's tales illustrate this difference perfectly: "The Nutcracker and the Mouse-King,"

"The Strange Child," and "The King's Bride" belong, by stylistic properties, to the fairy tale. "The Choice of a Bride," while preserving the same status with regard to the supernatural, is not a fairy tale at all. One would also have to characterize the *Arabian Nights* as marvelous tales rather than fairy tales (a subject which deserves a special study all its own).

In order to delimit the marvelous in the pure state, it is convenient to isolate it from several types of narrative in which the supernatural is somewhat justified.

1. We may speak first of all of *hyperbolic marvelous*. In it, phenomena are supernatural only by virtue of their dimensions, which are superior to those that are familiar to us. Thus in the *Arabian Nights* Sinbad the Sailor declares he has seen "fish one hundred and even two hundred ells long" or "serpents so great and so long that there was not one which could not have swallowed an elephant." But perhaps this is no more than a simple manner of speaking (we shall study this question when we deal with the poetic or allegorical interpretation of the text); one might even say, adapting a proverb, that "fear has big eyes." In any case, this form of the supernatural does not do excessive violence to reason.
2. Quite close to this first type of the marvelous is the *exotic marvelous*. In this type, supernatural events are reported without being presented as such. The implicit reader is supposed to be ignorant of the regions where the events take place, and consequently he has no reason for calling them into question. Sinbad's second voyage furnishes some excellent examples, such as the *roc*, a bird so tremendous that it concealed the sun and "one of whose legs . . . was as great as a great tree-trunk." Of course, this bird does not exist for contemporary zoology, but Sinbad's hearers were far from any such certainty and, five centuries later, Galland himself writes: "Marco Polo, in his travels, and Father Martini, in his *History of China*, speak of this bird," etc. A litter later, Sinbad similarly describes the rhinoceros, which however is well known to us:

> There is, on the same island, a rhinoceros, a creature smaller than the elephant and larger than the buffalo: it bears a single horn upon its snout, about one ell long; this horn is solid and severed through the center, from one end to the other. Upon it may be seen white lines which represent the face of a man. The rhinoceros attacks the elephant, pierces it with its horn through the belly, carries it off and bears it upon its head; but when the elephant's blood flows over its eyes and blinds it, the rhinoceros falls to the ground, and—what will amaze you [indeed], the roc comes and bears off both creatures in its talons, in order to feed its young upon their bodies.

This virtuoso passage shows, by its mixture of natural and supernatural elements, the special character of the *exotic marvelous*. The mixture exists, of course, only for the modern reader; the narrator implicit in the tale situates everything on the same level (that of the "natural").

3. A third type of the marvelous might be called the *instrumental marvelous*. Here we find the gadgets, technological developments unrealized in the period described but, after all, quite possible. In the "Tale of Prince Ahmed" in the Arabian Nights, for instance, the marvelous instruments are, at the beginning: a flying carpet, an apple that cures diseases, and a "pipe" for seeing great distances; today, the helicopter, antibiotics, and binoculars, endowed with the same qualities, do not belong in any way to the marvelous. The same is true of the flying horse in the "Tale

of the Magic Horse." Similarly in the case of the revolving stone in the "Tale of Ali Baba," we need only think of recent espionage films in which a safe opens only when its owner's voice utters certain words. We must distinguish these objects, products of human skill, from certain instruments that are often similar in appearance but whose origin is magical, and that serve to communicate with other worlds. Thus Aladdin's lamp and ring, or the horse in "The Third Calender's Tale," which belong to a different kind of marvelous.

4. The "instrumental marvelous" brings us very close to what in nineteenth-century France was called the *scientific marvelous,* which today we call *science fiction.* Here the supernatural is explained in a rational manner, but according to laws which contemporary science does not acknowledge. In the high period of fantastic narratives, stories involving magnetism are characteristic of the scientific marvelous: magnetism "scientifically" explains supernatural events, yet magnetism itself belongs to the supernatural. Examples are Hoffmann's "Spectre Bridegroom" or "The Magnetizer," and Poe's "The Facts in the Case of M. Valdemar" or Maupassant's "Un Fou?". Contemporary science fiction, when it does not slip into allegory, obeys the same mechanism: these narratives, starting from irrational premises, link the "facts" they contain in a perfectly logical manner. (Their plot structure also differs from that of the fantastic tale; we discuss science fiction plots in Chapter 10 of *The Fantastic.*)

All these varieties of the marvelous—"excused," justified, and imperfect—stand in opposition to the marvelous in its pure—unexplained—state. We shall not consider it here: first, because the elements of the marvelous, as themes, will be examined below in Chapters 7 and 8; and also because the aspiration to the marvelous, as an anthropological phenomenon, exceeds the context of a study limited to literary aspects. In any case, the marvelous has been, from this perspective, the object of several penetrating books; and in conclusion, I shall borrow from one of these, Pierre Mabille's *Miroir du Merveilleux,* a sentence which neatly defines the meaning of the marvelous:

> Beyond entertainment, beyond curiosity, beyond all the emotions such narratives and legends afford, beyond the need to divert, to forget, or to achieve delightful or terrifying sensations, the real goal of the marvelous journey is the total exploration of universal reality.

Translated by Richard Howard

12

Julia Kristeva 1941–

Julia Kristeva, a Parisienne born in Bulgaria, since 1966 has carried on a radical critique of what she calls the "signifying practice" of literature. During her years of teaching at the Université de Paris VII, she made signal contributions to the fields of narratology, poetics, theory of language, psychoanalysis, and political philosophy. Kristeva has also taught at Columbia University. Her major works include: *Semeiotiké: Recherches pour une semanalyse* (1969); *Le Texte du Roman* (1970); *Revolution in Poetic Language* (1973; trans. 1984); *About Chinese Women* (1974; trans. 1977); *Polylogue* (1977); *Soleil Noir* (1987); *Tales of Love* (1987; trans. 1987); and *The Kristeva Reader* (1986). Some of her essays appear in English translation under the title *Desire in Language* (1980). In 1974, Kristeva traveled to China and wrote her landmark study of sexual ideology, *About Chinese Women.*

However, Kristeva is perhaps best known for her work on literature and the theory of language. In *Semiotiké* Kristeva delivers a thorough critique of structuralism, especially its static notion of the sign and its bracketing of the so-called "extralinguistic" factors of history and psychology. In its place, she proposes "semanalysis," a poststructuralist approach to literature that redefines the text as a dynamic "working" of language through the desires of the speaking subject as he or she responds to the concrete socio-economic forces of history. Whether medieval or modern, the literary text now becomes a "productivity" in which the writer confronts the ideological givens of his or her culture's discourse and displaces or decenters them by deploying the linguistic signifier in forbidden or unanticipated ways. The result is a polyvalent "negativity" that undermines and suspends all oppressive, univocal oppositions (such as good vs. evil, true vs. false, male vs. female), thereby opening up not only the text but the cultural discourse that underlies it.

"Stabat Mater" (1974) stylistically displaces the reader's expectations of how a literary text should perform; Kristeva's essay juxtaposes—page by page—a critical analysis of Western culture's supra-mother, the Virgin Mary, with a lively description of her own responses to the activity of mothering. The Virgin Mary is a cultural construct, an abstraction, which removes the focus of maternity from the mother and places it on the relationship with the child: primary narcissism. By acknowledging the historical gaps and inconsistencies in the story of Mary's elevation to heavenly queen, Kristeva poses the question: "what are the aspects of the feminine psyche for which that representation of motherhood does not provide a solution or else provides one that is felt as too coercive by twentieth century women?" The essay itself responds by creating a dialogue between mother as an abstraction and mother as an individual woman. As the essay evolves, Kristeva's personal account becomes a woman's voice acknowledging not just the experiences of one mother; it recognizes the experience of all mothers by responding personally to the cultural issues involved in mothering. The two parts of the essay merge but do not meld. The specific is not subsumed by the universal; they remain in tension. Thus, the discourse is decentered and open.

Stabat Mater

THE PARADOX: MOTHER OR PRIMARY NARCISSISM

If it is not possible to say of a *woman* what she *is* (without running the risk of abolishing her difference), would it perhaps be different concerning the *mother*, since that is the only function of the "other sex" to which we can definitely attribute existence? And yet, there too, we are caught in a paradox. First, we live in a civilization where the *consecrated* (religious or secular) representation of femininity is absorbed by motherhood. If, however, one looks at it more closely, this motherhood is the *fantasy* that is nurtured by the adult, man or woman, of a lost territory; what is more, it involves less an idealized archaic mother than the idealization of the *relationship* that binds us to her, one that cannot be localized—an idealization of primary narcissism. Now, when feminism demands a new representation of femininity, it seems to identify motherhood with that idealized misconception and, because it rejects the image and its misuse, feminism circumvents the real experience that fantasy overshadows. The result?—a negation or rejection of motherhood by some avant-garde feminist groups. Or else an acceptance—conscious or not—of its traditional representations by the great mass of people, women and men.

FLASH—instant of time or of dream without time; inordinately swollen atoms of a bond, a vision, a shiver, a yet formless, unnamable embryo. Epiphanies. Photos of what is not yet visible and that language necessarily skims over from afar, allusively. Words that are always

Christianity is doubtless the most refined symbolic construct in which femininity, to the extent that it transpires through it—and it does so incessantly—is focused on *Maternality*.[1] Let us call "maternal" the ambivalent principle that is bound to the species, on the one hand,

too distant, too abstract for this underground swarming of seconds, folding in unimaginable spaces. Writing them down is an ordeal of discourse, like love. What is loving, for a woman, the same thing as writing. Laugh. Impossible. Flash on the unnamable, weavings of abstractions to be torn. Let a body venture at last out of its shelter, take a chance with meaning under a veil of words. WORD FLESH. From one to the other, eternally, broken up visions, metaphors of the invisible.

and on the other stems from an identity catastrophe that causes the Name to topple over into the unnamable that one imagines as femininity, nonlanguage, or body. Thus Christ, the Son of man, when all is said and done, is "human" only through his mother—as if Christly or Christian humanism could only be a maternalism (that is, besides, what some secularizing trends within its orbit do not cease claiming in their esotericism). And yet, the humanity of the Virgin mother is not always obvious, and we shall see how, in her being cleared of sin, for instance, Mary distinguishes herself from mankind. But at the same time the most intense revelation of God, which occurs in mysticism, is given only to a person who assumes himself as "maternal." Augustine, Bernard of Clairvaux, Meister Eckhart, to mention but a few, played the part of the Father's virgin spouses, or even, like Bernard, received drops of virginal milk directly on their lips. Freedom with respect to the maternal territory then becomes the pedestal upon which love of God is erected. As a consequence, mystics, those "happy Schrebers" (Sollers) throw a bizarre light on the psychotic sore of modernity: it appears as the incapability of contemporary codes to tame the maternal, that is, primary narcissism. Uncommon and "literary," their present-day counterparts are always somewhat oriental, if not tragical—Henry Miller, who says he is pregnant; Artaud, who sees himself as "his daughters" or "his mother" . . . It is the orthodox constituent of Christianity, through John Chrysostom's golden mouth, among others, that sanctioned the transitional function of the Maternal by calling the Virgin a "bond," a "medium," or an "interval," thus opening the door to more or less heretical identifications with the Holy Ghost.

This resorption of femininity within the Maternal is specific to many civilizations, but Christianity, in its own fashion, brings it to its peak. Could it be that such a reduction represents no more than a masculine appropriation of the Maternal, which, in line with our hypothesis, is only a fantasy masking primary narcissism? Or else, might one detect in it, in other respects, the workings of enigmatic sublimation? These are perhaps the workings of masculine sublimation, a sublimation just the same, if it be true that for Freud picturing Da Vinci, and even for Da Vinci himself, the taming of that economy (of the Maternal or of primary narcissism) is a requirement for artistic, literary, or painterly accomplishment?

Within that perspective, however, there are two questions, among others, that remain unanswered. What is there, in the portrayal of the Maternal in general and particularly in its Christian, virginal, one, that reduces social anguish and gratifies a male being; what is there that also satisfies a woman so that a commonality of the sexes is set up, beyond and in spite of their glaring incompatibility and permanent warfare? Moreover, is there something in that Maternal notion that ignores what a woman might say or want—as a result, when women speak out today it is in matters of conception and motherhood that their annoyance is basically centered. Beyond social and political demands, this takes the well-known "discontents" of our civilization to a level where Freud would not follow—the discontents of the species.

A TRIUMPH OF THE UNCONSCIOUS IN MONOTHEISM

It would seem that the "virgin" attribute for Mary is a translation error, the translator having substituted for the Semitic term that indicates the sociolegal status of a young unmarried woman the Greek word *parthenos,* which on the other hand specifies a physiological and psychological condition: virginity. One might read into this the Indo-European fascination (which Dumezil analyzed)[2] with the virgin daughter as guardian of paternal power; one might also detect an ambivalent conspiracy, through excessive spiritualization, of the mother-goddess and the underlying matriarchy with which Greek culture and Jewish monotheism kept struggling. The fact remains that western Christianity has organized that "translation error," projected its own fantasies into it, and produced one of the most powerful imaginary constructs known in the history of civilizations.

The story of the virginal cult in Christianity amounts in fact to the imposition of pagan-rooted beliefs in, and often against, dogmas of the official Church. It is true that the Gospels already posit Mary's existence. But they suggest only very discreetly the immaculate conception of Christ's mother, they say nothing concerning Mary's own background and speak of her only seldom at the side of her son or during crucifixion. Thus Matthew 1:20 (". . . the angel of the Lord appeared to him in a dream and said, 'Joseph, son of David, do not be afraid to take Mary home as your wife, because she has conceived what is in her by the Holy Spirit' "), and Luke 1:34 ("Mary said to the angel, 'But how can this come about since I do not know man?' ") open a door, a narrow opening for all that, but one that would soon widen thanks to apocryphal additions, on impregnation without sexuality; according to this notion a woman, preserved from masculine intervention, conceives alone with a "third party," a nonperson, the Spirit. In the rare instances when the Mother of Jesus appears in the Gospels, she is informed that filial relationship rests not with the flesh but with the name or, in other words, that any possible matrilinearism is to be repudiated and the symbolic link alone is to last. We thus have Luke 2:48–49 (". . . his mother said to him, 'My child, why have you done this to us? See how worried your father and I have been, looking for you.' 'Why were you looking for me?' he replied. 'Did you not know that I must be busy with my father's affairs?' "), and also John 2:3–5 (". . . the mother of Jesus said to him, 'They have no wine.' Jesus said, 'Woman, why turn to me?[3] My hour has not come yet.' ") and 19:26–27 ("Seeing his mother and the disciple he loved standing near her, Jesus said to his mother, 'Woman, this is your son.' Then to the disciple he said, 'This is your mother.' And from that moment the disciple made a place for her in his home.")

Starting from this programmatic material, rather skimpy nevertheless, a compelling imaginary construct proliferated in essentially three directions. In the first place, there was the matter of drawing a parallel between Mother and Son by expanding the theme of the immaculate conception, inventing a biography of Mary similar to that of Jesus, and, by depriving her of sin to deprive her of death. Mary leaves by way of Dormition or Assumption. Next, she needed letters patent of nobility, a power that, even though exercised in the beyond, is nonetheless political, since Mary was to be proclaimed queen, given the attributes and paraphernalia of royalty and, in parallel fashion, declared Mother of the divine institution on earth, the Church. Finally, the relationship with Mary and from Mary was to be revealed as the prototype of a love relationship and followed two fundamental aspects of western love: courtly love and child love, thus fitting the entire range that goes from sublimation to asceticism and masochism.

NEITHER SEX NOR DEATH

Mary's life, devised on the model of the life of Jesus, seems to be the fruit of apocryphal literature. The story of her own miraculous conception, called "immaculate conception," by Anne and Joachim, after a long, barren marriage, together with her biography as a pious maiden, show up in apocryphal sources as early as the end of the first century. Their entirety may be found in the *Secret Book of James* and also in one of the pseudoepigrapha, the Gospel according to the Hebrews (which inspired Giotto's frescoes, for instance). Those "facts" were quoted by Clement of Alexandria and Origen but not officially accepted; even though the Eastern Church tolerated them readily, they were translated into Latin only in the sixteenth century. Yet the West was not long before glorifying the life of Mary on its own but always under orthodox guidance. The first Latin poem, "Maria," on the birth of Mary was written by the nun Hrotswith von Gandersheim (who died before 1002), a playwright and poet.

Fourth-century asceticism, developed by the Fathers of the Church, was grafted on that apocryphal shoot in order to bring out and rationalize the immaculate conception postulate. The demonstration was based on a simple logical relation: the intertwining of sexuality and death. Since they are mutually implicated with each other, one cannot avoid the one without fleeing the other. This asceticism, applicable to both sexes, was vigorously expressed by John Chrysostom (*On Virginity*: "For where there is death there is also sexual copulation, and where there is no death there is no sexual copulation either"); even though he was attacked by Augustine and Aquinas, he nonetheless fueled Christian doctrine. Thus, Augustine condemned "concupiscence" (*epithumia*) and posited that Mary's virginity is in fact only a logical precondition of Christ's chastity. The Orthodox Church, heir no doubt to a matriarchy that was more intense in eastern European societies, emphasized Mary's virginity more boldly. Mary was contrasted with Eve, life with death (Jerome, *Letter* 22, "Death came through Eve but life came through Mary"; Irenaeus, "Through Mary the snake becomes a dove and we are freed from the chains of death"). People even got involved in tortuous arguments in order to demonstrate that Mary remained a virgin after childbirth (thus the second Constantinople council, in 381, under Arianistic influence, emphasized the Virgin's role in comparison to official dogma and asserted Mary's perpetual virginity; the 451 council called her *Aeiparthenos*—ever virgin). Once this was established, Mary, instead of being referred to as Mother of man or Mother of Christ, would be proclaimed Mother of God: *Theotokos*. Nestorius, patriarch of Constantinople, refused to go along; Nestorianism, however, for all practical purposes died with the patriarch's own death in 451, and the path that would lead to Mary's deification was then clear.

Head reclining, nape finally relaxed, skin, blood, nerves warmed up, luminous flow: stream of hair made of ebony, of nectar, smooth darkness through her

Very soon, within the complex relationship between Christ and his Mother where relations of God to mankind, man to woman, son to mother, etc., are

fingers, gleaming honey under the wings of bees, sparkling strands burning bright . . . silk, mercury, ductile copper: frozen light warmed under fingers. Mane of beast—squirrel, horse, and the happiness of a faceless head, Narcissuslike touching without eyes, sight dissolving in muscles, hair, deep, smooth, peaceful colors. Mamma: anamnesis.

Taut eardrum, tearing sound out of muted silence. Wind among grasses, a seagull's faraway call, echoes of waves, auto horns, voices, or nothing? Or his own tears, my newborn, spasm of syncopated void. I no longer hear anything, but the eardrum keeps transmitting this resonant vertigo to my skull, the hair. My body is no longer mine, it doubles up, suffers, bleeds, catches cold, puts its teeth in, slobbers, coughs, is covered with pimples, and it laughs. And yet when its own joy, my child's, returns, its smile washes only my eyes. But the pain, its pain—it comes from inside, never remains apart, other, it inflames me at once, without a second's respite. As if that was what I had given birth to and, not willing to part from me, insisted on coming back, dwelled in me permanently. One does not give birth in pain, one gives birth to pain: the child represents it and henceforth it settles in, it is continuous. Obviously you may close your eyes, cover up your ears, teach courses, run errands, tidy up the house, think about objects, subjects. But a mother is always branded by pain, she yields to it. "And a sword will pierce your own soul too . . ."

Dream without glow, without sound, dream of brawn. Dark twisting, pain in the back, the arms, the thighs—pincers

hatched, the problematics of *time* similar to that of cause loomed up. If Mary preceded Christ and he originated in her if only from the standpoint of his humanity, should not the conception of Mary herself have been immaculate? For, if that were not the case, how could a being conceived in sin and harboring it in herself produce a God? Some apocryphal writers had not hesitated, without too much caution, to suggest such an absence of sin in Mary's conception, but the Fathers of the Church were more careful. Bernard of Clairvaux is reluctant to extol the conception of Mary by Anne, and thus he tries to check the homologation of Mary with Christ. But it fell upon Duns Scotus to change the hesitation over the promotion of a mother goddess within Christianity into a logical problem, thus saving them both, the Great Mother as well as logic. He viewed Mary's birth as a *praeredemptio*, as a matter of congruency: if it be true that Christ alone saves us through his redemption on the cross, the Virgin who bore him can but be preserved from sin in "recursive" fashion, from the time of her own conception up to that redemption.

For or against, with dogma or logical shrewdness, the battle around the Virgin intensified between Jesuits and Dominicans, but the Counter-Reformation, as is well known, finally ended the resistance: henceforth, Catholics venerated Mary in herself. The Society of Jesus succeeded in completing a process of popular pressure distilled by patristic asceticism, and in reducing, with neither explicit hostility nor brutal rejection, the share of the Maternal (in the sense given above) useful to a certain balance between the two sexes. Curiously and necessarily, when that balance began to be seriously threatened in the nineteenth century, the Catholic Church—more dialectical and subtle here than the Protestants who were already

turned into fibers, infernos bursting veins, stones breaking bones: grinders of volumes, expanses, spaces, lines, points. All those words, now, ever visible things to register the roar of a silence that hurts all over. As if a geometry ghost could suffer when collapsing in a noiseless tumult . . . Yet the eye picked up nothing, the ear remained deaf. But everything swarmed, and crumbled, and twisted, and broke—the grinding continued . . . Then, slowly, a shadowy shape gathered, became detached, darkened, stood out: seen from what must be the true place of my head, it was the right side of my pelvis. Just bony, sleek, yellow, misshapen, a piece of my body jutting out unnaturally, asymmetrically, but slit: severed scaly surface, revealing under this disproportionate pointed limb the fibers of a marrow . . . Frozen placenta, live limb of a skeleton, monstrous graft of life on myself, a living dead. Life . . . death . . . undecidable. During delivery it went to the left with the afterbirth . . . My removed marrow, which nevertheless acts as a graft, which wounds but increases me. Paradox: deprivation and benefit of childbirth. But calm finally hovers over pain, over the terror of this dried branch that comes back to life, cut off, wounded, deprived of its sparkling bark. The calm of another life, the life of that other who wends his way while I remain henceforth like a framework. Still life. There is him, however, his own flesh, which was mine yesterday. Death, then, how could I yield to it?

spawning the first suffragettes—raised the Immaculate Conception to dogma status in 1854. It is often suggested that the blossoming of feminism in Protestant countries is due, among other things, to the greater initiative allowed women on the social and ritual plane. One might wonder if, in addition, such a flowering is not the result of a *lack* in the Protestant religious structure with respect to the Maternal, which, on the contrary, was elaborated within Catholicism with a refinement to which Jesuits gave the final touch, and which still makes Catholicism very difficult to analyze.

The fulfillment, under the name of Mary, of a totality made of woman and God is finally accomplished through the avoidance of death. The Virgin Mary experiences a fate more radiant than her son's: she undergoes no Calvary, she has no tomb, she doesn't die and hence has no need to rise from the dead. Mary doesn't die but, as if to echo oriental beliefs, Taoists' among others, according to which human bodies pass from one place to another in an eternal flow that constitutes a carbon copy of the maternal receptacle—she is transported.

Her transition is more passive in the Eastern Church: it is a Dormition (*Koimesis*) during which, according to a number of iconographic representations, Mary can be seen changed into a little girl in the arms of her son who henceforth becomes her father; she thus reverses her role as Mother into a Daughter's role for the greater pleasure of those who enjoy Freud's "Theme of the Three Caskets."

Indeed, *mother* of her son and his *daughter* as well, Mary is also, and besides, his *wife:* she therefore actualizes the threefold metamorphosis of a woman in the tightest parenthood structure. From 1135 on, transposing the Song of Songs, Bernard of Clairvaux glorifies Mary in her role of beloved and wife. But Catherine of Alexandria (said to have been martyred in 307) already pictured herself as receiving the wedding ring from Christ, with the Virgin's help, while Catherine of Siena (1347–80) goes through a mystical wedding with him. Is it the impact of mary's function as Christ's beloved and wife that is responsible for the blossoming out of the Marian cult in the West after Bernard and thanks to the Cistercians? "*Vergine Madre, figlia del tuo Figlio,*" Dante exclaims, thus probably best condensing the gathering of the three feminine functions (daughter-wife-mother) within a totality where they vanish as specific corporealities while retaining their psychological functions. Their bond makes up the basis of unchanging and timeless spirituality; "the set time limit of an eternal design" [*Termine fisso d'eterno consiglio*], as Dante masterfully points out in his *Divine Comedy.*

The transition is more active in the West, with Mary rising body and soul toward the other world in an *Assumption.* That feast, honored in Byzantium as early as the fourth century, reaches Gaul in the seventh under the influence of the Eastern Church; but the earliest Western visions of the Virgin's assumption, women's visions (particularly that of Elizabeth von Schönau who died in 1164) date only from the twelfth century. For the Vatican, the Assumption became dogma only in 1950. What death anguish was it intended to soothe after the conclusion of the deadliest of wars?

IMAGE OF POWER

On the side of "power," *Maria Regina* appears in imagery as early as the sixth century in the church of Santa Maria Antiqua in Rome. Interestingly enough, it is she, woman and mother, who is called upon to represent supreme earthly power. Christ is king but neither he nor his father are pictured wearing crowns, diadems, costly paraphernalia, and other external signs of abundant material goods. That opulent infringement to Christian idealism is centered on the Virgin Mother. Later, when she assumed the title of *Our Lady,* this would also be an analogy to the earthly power of the noble feudal lady of medieval courts. Mary's function as guardian of power, later checked when the Church became wary of it, nevertheless persisted in popular and pictorial representation, witness Piero della Francesca's impressive painting, *Madonna della Misericordia,* which was disavowed by Catholic authorities at the time. And yet, not only did the papacy revere more and more the Christly mother as the Vatican's power over cities and municipalities was strengthened, it also openly identified its own institution with the Virgin: Mary was officially proclaimed Queen by Pius XII in 1954 and *Mater Ecclesiae* in 1964.

EIA MATER, FONS AMORIS!

Fundamental aspects of Western love finally converged on Mary. In a first step, it indeed appears that the Marian cult homologizing Mary with Jesus and carrying asceticism to the extreme was opposed to courtly love for the noble lady, which, while representing social transgression, was not at all a physical or moral sin. And yet, at the very dawn of a "courtliness" that was still very carnal, Mary and the lady shared one common trait: they are the focal point of men's desires and aspirations. Moreover, because they were unique and thus excluded all other women, both the lady and the Virgin embodied an absolute authority the more attractive as it appeared removed from paternal sternness. This feminine power must have been experienced as denied power, more pleasant to seize because it was both archaic and secondary, a kind of substitute for effective power in the family and the city but no less authoritarian, the underhand double of explicit phallic power. As early as the thirteenth century, thanks to the implantation of ascetic Christianity and especially, as early as 1328, to the promulgation of Salic laws, which excluded daughters from the inheritance and thus made the loved one very vulnerable and colored one's love for her with all the hues of the impossible, the Marian and courtly streams came together. Around the time of Blanche of Castile (who died in 1252), the Virgin explicitly became the focus of courtly love, thus gathering the attributes of the desired woman and of the holy mother in a totality as accomplished as it was inaccessible. Enough to make any woman suffer, any man dream. One finds indeed in a *Miracle de Notre Dame* the story of a young man who abandons his fiancée for the Virgin: the latter came to him in a dream and reproached him for having left her for an "earthly woman."

Nevertheless, besides that ideal totality that no individual woman could possibly embody, the Virgin also became the fulcrum of the humanization of the West in general and of love in particular. It is again about the thirteenth century, with Francis of Assisi, that this tendency takes shape with the representation of Mary as poor, modest, and humble—madonna of humility at the same time as a devoted, fond mother. The famous nativity of Piero della Francesca in London, in which Simone de Beauvoir too hastily saw a feminine defeat because the mother kneeled before her barely born son, in fact consolidates the new cult of humanistic sensitivity. It replaces the high spirituality that assimilated the Virgin to Christ with an earthly conception of a wholly human mother. As a source for the most popularized pious images, such maternal humility comes closer to "lived" feminine experience than the earlier representations did. Beyond this, however, it is true that it integrates a certain feminine masochism but also displays its counterpart in gratification and jouissance. The truth of it is that the lowered head of the mother before her son is accompanied by the immeasurable pride of the one who knows she is also his wife and daughter. She knows she

Scent of milk, dewed greenery, acid and clear, recall of wind, air, seaweed (as if a body lived without waste): it slides under the skin, does not remain in the mouth or nose but fondles the veins, detaches skin from bones, inflates me like an ozone balloon, and I hover with feet firmly planted on the ground in order to carry him, sure, stable, ineradicable, while he dances in my neck, flutters with my hair, seeks a smooth shoulder on the right, on the left, slips on the breast, swingles, silver vivid blossom of my belly, and finally flies away on my navel in his dream carried by my hands. My son.

Nights of wakefulness, scattered sleep, sweetness of the child, warm mercury in my arms, cajolery, affection, defenseless body, his or mine, sheltered, protected. A wave swells again, when he goes to sleep, under my skin—tummy, thighs, legs: sleep of the muscles, not of the brain, sleep of the flesh. The wakeful tongue quietly remembers another withdrawal, mine: a blossoming heaviness in the mid-

dle of the bed, of a hollow, of the sea . . . Recovered childhood, dreamed peace restored, in sparks, flash of cells, instants of laughter, smiles in the blackness of dreams, at night, opaque joy that roots me in her bed, my mother's, and projects him, a son, a butterfly soaking up dew from her hand, there, nearby, in the night. Alone: she, I, and he.

He returns from the depths of the nose, the vocal chords, the lungs, the ears, pierces their smothering stopping sickness swab, and awakens in his eyes. Gentleness of the sleeping face, contours of pinkish jade—forehead, eyebrows, nostrils, cheeks, parted features of the mouth, delicate, hard, pointed chin. Without fold or shadow, neither being nor unborn, neither present nor absent, but real, real inaccessible innocence, engaging weight and seraphic lightness. A child?—An angel, a glow on an Italian painting, impassive, peaceful dream—dragnet of Mediterranean fishermen. And then, the mother-of-pearl bead awakens: quicksilver. Shiver of the eyelashes, imperceptible twitch of the eyebrows, quivering skin, anxious reflections, seeking, knowing, casting their knowledge aside in the face of my nonknowledge: fleeting irony of childhood gentleness that awakens to meaning, surpasses it, goes past it, causes me to soar in music, in dance. Impossible refinement, subtle rape of inherited genes: before what has been learned comes to pelt him, harden him, ripen him. Hard, mischievous gentleness of the first ailment overcome, innocent wisdom of the first ordeal undergone, yet hopeful blame on account of the suffering I put you through, by calling for you, desiring, creating . . . Gentleness, wisdom, blame: your face is already human, sickness has caused you to join our species, you speak without words but your throat no longer

is destined to that eternity (of the spirit or of the species), of which every mother is unconsciously aware, and with regard to which maternal devotion or even sacrifice is but an insignificant price to pay. A price that is borne all the more easily since, contrasted with the love that binds a mother to her son, all other "human relationships" burst like blatant shams. The Franciscan representation of the Mother conveys many essential aspects of maternal psychology, thus leading up to an influx of common people to the churches and also a tremendous increase in the Marian cult—witness the building of many churches dedicated to her ("Notre Dame"). Such a humanization of Christianity through the cult of the mother also led to an interest in the humanity of the father-man: the celebration of "family life" showed Joseph to advantage as early as the fifteenth century.

WHAT BODY?

We are entitled only to the ear of the virginal body, the tears, and the breast. With the female sexual organ changed into an innocent shell, holder of sound, there arises a possible tendency to eroticize hearing, voice, or even understanding. By the same token, however, sexuality is brought down to the level of innuendo. Feminine sexual experience is thus rooted in the universality of sound, since wit is distributed *equally* among all men, all women. A woman will only have the choice to live her life either *hyperabstractly* ("immediately universal," Hegel said) in order thus to earn divine grace and homologation with symbolic order; or merely *different*, other, fallen ("immediately particular," Hegel said). But she will not be able to accede to the complexity of being divided, of heterogeneity, of the

gurgles—it harkens with me to the silence of your born meaning that draws my tears toward a smile.

The lover gone, forgetfulness comes, but the pleasure of the sexes remains, and there is nothing lacking. No representation, sensation, or recall. Inferno of vice. Later, forgetfulness returns but this time as a fall—leaden—grey, dull, opaque. Forgetfulness: blinding, smothering foam, but on the quiet. Like the fog that devours the park, wolfs down the branches, erases the green rusty ground, and mists up my eyes.

Absence, inferno, forgetfulness. Rhythm of our loves.

A hunger remains, in place of the heart. A spasm that spreads, runs through the blood vessels to the tips of the breasts, to the tips of the fingers. It throbs, pierces the void, erases it, and gradually settles in. My heart: a tremendous pounding wound. A thirst.

Anguished, guilty. Freud's *Vaterkomplex* on the Acropolis? The impossibility of being without repeated legitimation (without books, man, family). Impossibilities—depressing possibility —of "transgression."

Either repression in which *I* hands the Other what I want from others.

Or this squalling of the void, open wound in my heart, which allows me to be only in purgatory.

I yearn for the Law. And since it is not made for me alone, I venture to desire outside the law. Then, narcissism thus awakened—the narcissism that wants to be sex—roams, astonished. In sensual rapture I am distraught. Nothing reassures, for only the law sets anything down. Who calls such a suffering jouissance? It is the pleasure of the damned.

catastrophic-fold-of-"being" ("never singular," Hegel said).

Under a full, blue gown, the maternal, virginal body allowed only the breast to show, while the face, with the stiffness of Byzantine icons gradually softened, was covered with tears. Milk and tears became the privileged signs of the *Mater Dolorosa* who invaded the West beginning with the eleventh century, reaching the peak of its influx in the fourteenth. But it never ceased to fill the Marian visions of those, men or women (often children), who were racked by the anguish of a maternal frustration. Even though orality—threshold of infantile regression—is displayed in the area of the breast, while the spasm at the slipping away of eroticism is translated into tears, this should not conceal what milk and tears have in common: they are the metaphors of nonspeech, of a "semiotics" that linguistic communication does not account for. The Mother and her attributes, evoking sorrowful humanity, thus become representatives of a "return of the repressed" in monotheism. They reestablish what is nonverbal and show up as the receptacle of a signifying disposition that is closer to so-called primary processes. Without them the complexity of the Holy Ghost would have been mutilated. On the other hand, as they return by way of the Virgin Mother, they find their outlet in the arts—painting and music—of which the Virgin necessarily becomes both patron saint and privileged object.

The function of this "Virginal Maternal" may thus be seen taking shape in the Western symbolic economy. Starting with the high Christly sublimation for which it yearns and occasionally exceeds, and extending to the extralinguistic regions of the unnamable, the Virgin Mother occupied the tremendous territory on this and that side of the parenthesis of language.

She adds to the Christian trinity and to the Word that delineates their coherence the heterogeneity they salvage.

The ordering of the maternal libido reached its apotheosis when centered in the theme of death. The *Mater Dolorosa* knows no masculine body save that of her dead son, and her only pathos (which contrasts with the somewhat vacant, gentle serenity of the nursing Madonnas) is her shedding tears over a corpse. Since resurrection there is, and, as Mother of God, she must know this, nothing justifies Mary's outburst of pain at the foot of the cross, unless it be the desire to experience within her own body the death of a human being, which her feminine fate of being the source of life spares her. Could it be that the love, as puzzling as it is ancient, of mourners for corpses relates to the same longing of a woman whom nothing fulfills—the longing to experience the wholly masculine pain of a man who expires at every moment on account of jouissance due to obsession with his own death? And yet, Marian pain is in no way connected with tragic outburst: joy and even a kind of triumph follow upon tears, as if the conviction that death does not exist were an irrational but unshakable maternal certainty, on which the principle of resurrection had to rest. The brilliant illustration of the wrenching between desire for the masculine corpse and negation of death, a wrenching whose paranoid logic cannot be overlooked, is masterfully presented by the famous *Stabat Mater*. It is likely that all beliefs in resurrections are rooted in mythologies marked by the strong dominance of a mother goddess. Christianity, it is true, finds its calling in the displacement of that bio-maternal determinism through the postulate that immortality is mainly that of the name of the Father. But it does not succeed in imposing *its* symbolic revolution without relying on the feminine representation of an immortal biology. Mary defying death is the theme that has been conveyed to us by the numerous variations of the *Stabat Mater*, which, in the text attributed to Jacopone da Todi, enthralls us today through the music of Palestrina, Pergolesi, Haydn, and Rossini.

Let us listen to the baroque style of the young Pergolesi (1710–36), who was dying of tuberculosis when he wrote his immortal *Stabat Mater*. His musical inventiveness, which, through Haydn, later reverberated in the work of Mozart, probably constitutes his one and only claim to immortality. But when this cry burst forth, referring to Mary facing her son's death, "*Eia Mater, fons amoris!*" ("Hail mother, source of love!")—was it merely a remnant of the period? Man overcomes

Belief in the mother is rooted in fear, fascinated with a weakness—the weakness of language. If language is powerless to locate myself for and state myself to the other, I assume—I want to believe—that there is someone who makes up for that weakness. Someone, of either sex, *before* the id speaks, before language, who might make me be by means of borders, separations, vertigoes. In asserting that "in the beginning was the Word," Christians must have found such a postulate sufficiently hard to believe and, for whatever it was worth, they added its compensation, its permanent lining: the maternal receptacle, purified as it might be by the virginal fantasy. Archaic maternal love would be an incorporation of my suffering that is unfailing, unlike what often happens with the lacunary network of signs. In that sense, any belief, anguished by definition, is upheld by the fascinated fear of language's impotence. Every God, even including the God of the Word, relies on a mother Goddess. Christianity is perhaps also the last of the religions to have displayed in broad daylight the bi-

polar structure of belief: on the one hand, the difficult experience of the Word—a passion; on the other, the reassuring wrapping in the proverbial mirage of the mother—a love. For that reason, it seems to me that there is only one way to go through the religion of the Word, or its counterpart, the more or less discreet cult of the Mother; it is the "artists' " way, those who make up for the vertigo of language weakness with the oversaturation of sign systems. By this token, all art is a kind of counter reformation, an accepted baroqueness. For is it not true that if the Jesuits finally did persuade the official Church to accept the cult of the Virgin, following the puritanical wave of the Reformation, that dogma was in fact no more than a pretext, and its efficacy lay elsewhere. It did not become the opposite of the cult of the mother but its inversion through expenditure in the wealth of signs that constitutes the baroque. The latter renders belief in the Mother useless by overwhelming the symbolic weakness where she takes refuge, withdrawn from history, with an overabundance of discourse.

The immeasurable, unconfinable maternal body.

First there is the separation, previous to pregnancy, but which pregnancy brings to light and imposes without remedy.

On the one hand—the pelvis: center of gravity, unchanging ground, solid pedestal, heaviness and weight to which the thighs adhere, with no promise of agility on that score. On the other—the torso, arms, neck, head, face, calves, feet: unbounded liveliness, rhythm and mask, which furiously attempt to compensate for the immutability of the central tree. We live on that border, crossroads beings, crucified beings. A woman is neither no-

the unthinkable of death by postulating maternal love in its place—in the place and stead of death and thought. This love, of which divine love is merely a not always convincing derivation, psychologically is perhaps a recall, on the near side of early identifications, of the primal shelter that insured the survival of the newborn. Such a love is in fact, logically speaking, a surge of anguish at the very moment when the identity of thought and living body collapses. The possibilities of communication having been swept away, only the subtle gamut of sound, touch, and visual traces, older than language and newly worked out, are preserved as an ultimate shield against death. It is only "normal" for a maternal representation to set itself up at the place of this subdued anguish called love. No one escapes it. Except perhaps the saint, the mystic, or the writer who, through the power of language, nevertheless succeeds in doing no better than to take apart the fiction of the mother as mainstay of love, and to identify with love itself and what he is in fact—*a fire of tongues*, an exit from representation. Might not modern art then be, for the few who are attached to it, the implementation of that maternal love—a veil over death, in death's very site and with full knowledge of the facts? A sublimated celebration of incest . . .

ALONE OF HER SEX

Freud collected, among other objects of art and archeology, countless statuettes representing mother goddesses. And yet his interest in them comes to light only in discreet fashion in his work. It shows up when Freud examines artistic creation and homosexuality in connection with Leonardo da Vinci and deciphers there the ascendancy of an archaic mother, seen therefore from the standpoint of her ef-

madic nor a male body that considers itself earthly only in erotic passion. A mother is a continuous separation, a division of the very flesh. And consequently a division of language—and it has always been so.

Then there is this other abyss that opens up between the body and what had been its inside: there is the abyss between the mother and the child. What connection is there between myself, or even more unassumingly between my body and this internal graft and fold, which, once the umbilical cord has been severed, is an inaccessible other? My body and . . . him. No connection. Nothing to do with it. And this, as early as the first gestures, cries, steps, long before *its* personality has become my opponent. The child, whether *he* or *she,* is irremediably an other. To say that there are no sexual relationships constitutes a skimpy assertion when confronting the flash that bedazzles me when I confront the abyss between what was mine and is henceforth but irreparably alien. Trying to think through that abyss: staggering vertigo. No identity holds up. A mother's identity is maintained only through the well-known closure of consciousness within the indolence of habit, when a woman protects herself from the borderline that severs her body and expatriates it from her child. Lucidity, on the contrary, would restore her as cut in half, alien to its other—and a ground favorable to delirium. But also and for that very reason, motherhood destines us to a demented jouissance that is answered, by chance, by the nursling's laughter in the sunny waters of the ocean. What connection is there between it and myself? No connection, except for that overflowing laughter where one senses the collapse of some ringing, subtle, fluid identity or other, softly buoyed by the waves.

fects on man and particularly on this strange function of his sometimes to change languages. Moreover, when Freud analyzes the advent and transformations of monotheism, he emphasizes that Christianity comes closer to pagan myths by integrating, through and against Judaic rigor, a preconscious acknowledgment of a maternal feminine. And yet, among the patients analyzed by Freud, one seeks in vain for mothers and their problems. One might be led to think that motherhood was a solution to neurosis and, by its very nature, ruled out psychoanalysis as a possible other solution. Or might psychoanalysis, at this point, make way for religion? In simplified fashion, the only thing Freud tells us concerning motherhood is that the desire for a child is a transformation of either penis envy or anal drive, and this allows her to discover the neurotic equation child-penis-feces. We are thus enlightened concerning an essential aspect of male phantasmatics with respect to childbirth, and female phantasmatics as well, to the extent that it embraces, in large part and in its hysterical labyrinths, the male one. The fact remains, as far as the complexities and pitfalls of maternal experience are involved, that Freud offers only a massive *nothing,* which, for those who might care to analyze it, is punctuated with this or that remark on the part of Freud's mother, proving to him in the kitchen that his own body is anything but immortal and will crumble away like dough; or the sour photograph of Marthe Freud, the wife, a whole mute story . . . There thus remained for his followers an entire continent to explore, a black one indeed, where Jung was the first to rush in, getting all his esoteric fingers burnt, but not without calling attention to some sore points of the imagination with regard to motherhood, points that are still resisting analytical rationality.[4]

Concerning that stage of my childhood, scented, warm, and soft to the touch, I have only a spatial memory. No time at all. Fragrance of honey, roundness of forms, silk and velvet under my fingers, on my cheeks. Mummy. Almost no sight—a shadow that darkens, soaks me up, or vanishes amid flashes. Almost no voice in her placid presence. Except, perhaps, and more belatedly, the echo of quarrels: her exasperation, her being fed up, her hatred. Never straightforward, always held back, as if, although the unmanageable child deserved it, the daughter could not accept the mother's hatred—it was not meant for her. A hatred without recipient or rather whose recipient was no "I" and which, perturbed by such a lack of recipience, was toned down into irony or collapsed into remorse before reaching its destination. With others, this maternal aversion may be worked up to a spasm that is held like a delayed orgasm. Women doubtless reproduce among themselves the strange gamut of forgotten body relationships with their mothers. Complicity in the unspoken, connivance of the inexpressible, of a wink, a tone of voice, a gesture, a tinge, a scent. We are in it, set free of our identification papers and names, on an ocean of preciseness, a computerization of the unnamable. No communication between individuals but connections between atoms, molecules, wisps of words, droplets of sentences. The community of women is a community of dolphins. Conversely, when the other woman posits herself as such, that is, as singular and inevitably in opposition, "I" am startled, so much that "I" no longer know what is going on. There are then two paths left open to the rejection that bespeaks the recognition of the other woman as such. Either, not wanting to experience her, I ignore her and, "alone of my sex," I turn my back on her in friendly fashion. It is a

There might doubtless be a way to approach the dark area that motherhood constitutes for a woman; one needs to listen, more carefully than ever, to what mothers are saying today, through their economic difficulties and, beyond the guilt that a too existentialist feminism handed down, through their discomforts, insomnias, joys, angers, desires, pains, and pleasures . . . One might, in similar fashion, try better to understand the incredible construct of the Maternal that the West elaborated by means of the Virgin, and of which I have just mentioned a few episodes in a never-ending history.

What is it then in this maternal representation that, alone of her sex, goes against both of the two sexes,[5] and was able to attract women's wishes for identification as well as the very precise interposition of those who assumed to keep watch over the symbolic and social order?

Let me suggest, by way of hypothesis, that the virginal maternal is a way (not among the less effective ones) of dealing with feminine paranoia.

—The Virgin assumes her feminine denial of the other sex (of man) but overcomes him by setting up a third person: I do not conceive with *you* but with *Him*. The result is an immaculate conception (therefore with neither man nor sex), conception of a God with whose existence a woman has indeed something to do, on condition that she acknowledge being subjected to it.

—The Virgin assumes the paranoid lust for power by changing a woman into a Queen in heaven and a Mother of the earthly institutions (of the Church). But she succeeds in stifling that megalomania by putting it on its knees before the child-god.

—The Virgin obstructs the desire for murder or devouring by means of a strong oral cathexis (the breast), valorization of pain (the sob), and incitement to replace

hatred that, lacking a recipient worthy enough of its power, changes to unconcerned complacency. Or else, outraged by her own stubbornness, by that other's belief that she is singular, I unrelentingly let go at her claim to address me and find respite only in the eternal return of power strokes, bursts of hatred—blind and dull but obstinate. I do not see her as herself but beyond her I aim at the claim to singularity, the unacceptable ambition to be something other than a child or a fold in the plasma that constitutes us, an echo of the cosmos that unifies us. What an inconceivable ambition it is to aspire to singularity, it is not natural, hence it is inhuman; the mania smitten with Oneness ("There is only One woman") can only impugn it by condemning it as "masculine" . . . Within this strange feminine see-saw that makes "me" swing from the unnamable community of women over to the war of individual singularities, it is unsettling to say "I." The languages of the great formerly matriarchal civilizations must avoid, do avoid, personal pronouns: they leave to the context the burden of distinguishing protagonists and take refuge in tones to recover an underwater, transverbal communication between bodies. It is a music from which so-called oriental civility tears away suddenly through violence, murder, blood baths. A woman's discourse, would that be it? Did not Christianity attempt, among other things, to freeze that seesaw? To stop it, tear women away from its rhythm, settle them permanently in the spirit? Too permanently . . .

the sexed body with the ear of understanding.

—The Virgin assumes the paranoid fantasy of being excluded from time and death through the very flattering representation of Dormition or Assumption.

—The Virgin especially agrees with the repudiation of the other woman (which doubtless amounts basically to a repudiation of the woman's mother) by suggesting the image of A woman as Unique: alone among women, alone among mothers, alone among humans since she is without sin. But the acknowledgment of a longing for uniqueness is immediately checked by the postulate according to which uniqueness is attained only through an exacerbated masochism: a concrete woman, worthy of the feminine ideal embodied by the Virgin as an inaccessible goal, could only be a nun, a martyr, or, if she is married, one who leads a life that would remove her from that "earthly" condition and dedicate her to the highest sublimation alien to her body. A bonus, however: the promised jouissance.

A skillful balance of concessions and constraints involving feminine paranoia, the representation of virgin motherhood appears to crown the efforts of a society to reconcile the social remnants of matrilinearism and the unconscious needs of primary narcissism on the one hand, and on the other the requirements of a new society based on exchange and before long on increased production, which require the contribution of the superego and rely on the symbolic paternal agency.

While that clever balanced architecture today appears to be crumbling, one is led to ask the following: what are the aspects of the feminine psyche for which that representation of motherhood does not provide a solution or else provides one that is felt as too coercive by twentieth-century women?

The unspoken doubtless weighs first on the maternal body: as no signifier can uplift it without leaving a remainder, for the signifier is always meaning, communication, or structure, whereas a woman as mother would be, instead, a strange fold that changes culture into nature, the speaking into biology. Although it concerns every woman's body, the heterogeneity that cannot be subsumed in the signifier nevertheless explodes violently with pregnancy (the threshold of culture and nature) and the child's arrival (which extracts woman out of her oneness and gives her the possibility—but not the certainty—of reaching out to the other, the ethical). Those particularities of the maternal body compose woman into a being of folds, a catastrophe of being that the dialectics of the trinity and its supplements would be unable to subsume.

Silence weighs heavily nonetheless on the corporeal and psychological suffering of childbirth and especially the self-sacrifice involved in becoming anonymous in order to pass on the social norm, which one might repudiate for one's own sake but within which *one must* include the child in order to educate it along the chain of generations. A suffering lined with jubilation—ambivalence of masochism—on account of which a woman, rather refractory to perversion, in fact allows herself a coded, fundamental, perverse behavior, ultimate guarantee of society, without which society will not reproduce and will not maintain a constancy of standardized household. Feminine perversion does not reside in the parcelling or the Don Juan-like multiplying of objects of desire; it is at once legalized, if not rendered paranoid, through the agency of masochism: all sexual "dissoluteness" will be accepted and hence become insignificant, provided a child seals up such outpourings. Feminine perversion [*père-version*] is coiled up in the desire for law as desire for reproduction and continuity, it promotes feminine masochism to the rank of structure stabilizer (against its deviations); by assuring the mother that she may thus enter into an order that is above humans' will it gives her her reward of pleasure. Such coded perversion, such close combat between maternal masochism and the law have been utilized by totalitarian powers of all times to bring women to their side, and, of course, they succeed easily. And yet, it is not enough to "declaim against" the reactionary role of mothers in the service of "male dominating power." One would need to examine to what extent that role corresponds to the biosymbolic latencies of motherhood and, on that basis, to try and understand, since the myth of the Virgin does not subsume them, or no longer does, how their surge lays women open to the most fearsome manipulations, not to mention blinding, or pure and simple rejection by progressive activists who refuse to take a close look.

Among things left out of the virginal myth there is the war between mother and daughter, a war masterfully but too quickly settled by promoting Mary as universal and particular, but never singular—as "alone of her sex." The relation to the other woman has presented our culture, in massive fashion during the past century, with the necessity to reformulate its representations of love and hatred—inherited from Plato's *Symposium*, the troubadours, or Our Lady. On that level, too, motherhood opens out a vista: a woman seldom (although not necessarily) experiences her passion (love and hatred) for another woman without having taken her own mother's place—without having herself become a mother, and especially without slowly learning to differentiate between same beings—as being face to face with her daughter forces her to do.

Finally, repudiation of the other sex (the masculine) no longer seems possible under the aegis of the third person, hypostatized in the child as go-between: "neither me, nor you, but him, the child, the third person, the nonperson, God, which I still am in the final analysis . . ." Since there is repudiation, and if the feminine being that struggles within it is to remain there, it henceforth calls for, not the deification of the third party, but countercathexes in strong values, in strong *equivalents of power*. Feminine psychosis today is sustained and absorbed through passion for politics, science, art . . . The variant that accompanies motherhood might be analyzed perhaps more readily than the others from the standpoint of the rejection of the other sex that it comprises.

The love of God and for God resides in a gap: the broken space made explicit by sin on the one side, the beyond on the other. Discontinuity, lack, and arbitrariness: topography of the sign, of the symbolic relation that posits my otherness as impossible. Love, here, is only for the impossible.

For a mother, on the other hand, strangely so, the other as arbitrary (the child) is taken for granted. As far as she is concerned—impossible, that is just the way it is: it is reduced to the implacable. The other is inevitable, she seems to say, turn it into a God if you wish, it is nevertheless natural, for such an other has come out of myself, which is yet not myself but a flow of unending germinations, an eternal cosmos. The other goes much without saying and without my saying that, at the limit, it does not exist for itself. The "just the same" of motherly peace of mind, more persistent than philosophical doubt, gnaws, on account of its basic disbelief, at the symbolic's allmightiness. It bypasses perverse negation ("I know, but just the same") and constitutes the basis of the social bond in its generality, in the sense of "resembling others and eventually the species." Such an attitude is frightening when one imagines that it can crush everything the other (the child) has that is specifically irreducible: rooted in that disposition of motherly love, besides, we find the leaden strap it can become, smothering any different individuality. But it is there, too, that the speaking being finds a refuge when his/her symbolic shell cracks and a crest emerges where speech causes biology to show through: I am thinking of the time of illness, of sexual-intellectual-physical passion, of death . . .

To allow what? Surely not some understanding or other on the part of "sexual partners" within the pre-established harmony of primal androgyny. Rather, to lead to an acknowledgment of what is irreducible, of the irreconcilable interest of both sexes in asserting their differences, in the quest of each one—and of women, after all—for an appropriate fulfillment.

These, then, are a few questions among others concerning a motherhood that today remains, after the Virgin, without a discourse. They suggest, all in all, the need of an ethics for this "second" sex, which, as one asserts it, is reawakening.

Nothing, however, suggests that a feminine ethics is possible, and Spinoza excluded women from his (along with children and the insane). Now, if a contemporary ethics is no longer seen as being the same as morality; if ethics amounts to not avoiding the embarrassing and inevitable problematics of the law but giving it flesh, language, and jouissance—in that case its reformulation demands the contribution of women. Of women who harbor the desire to reproduce (to have stability). Of women who are available so that our speaking species, which knows it is mortal, might withstand death. Of mothers. For an heretical ethics separated from morality, an *herethics*, is perhaps no more than that which in life makes bonds, thoughts, and therefore the thought of death, bearable: herethics is undeath [*a-mort*], love . . . *Eia mater, fons amoris* . . . So let us again listen to the *Stabat Mater*, and the music, all the music . . . it swallows up the goddesses and removes their necessity.

Translated by Leon S. Roudiez

NOTES

1. Between the lines of this section one should be able to detect the presence of Marina Warner, *Alone of All Her Sex: The Myth and Cult of the Virgin Mary* (New York: Knopf, 1976) and Ilse Barande, *Le Maternel singulier* (Paris: Aubier-Montaigne, 1977), which underlay my reflections.

2. Georges Dumezil, *La Religion romaine archaïque* (Paris: Payot, 1974).

3. The French version quoted by Kristeva ("Woman, what is there in common between you and me?") is even stronger than the King James translation, "Woman, what have I to do with thee?"—*Trans. note.*

4. Jung thus noted the "hierogamous" relationship between Mary and Christ as well as the overprotection given the Virgin with respect to original sin, which places her on the margin of mankind; finally, he insisted very much on the Vatican's adoption of the Assumption as dogma, seeing it as one of the considerable merits of Catholicism as opposed to Protestantism. C. G. Jung, *Answer to Job* (Princeton: Princeton University Press, 1969).

5. As Caelius Sedulius wrote, "She . . . had no peer/Either in our first mother or in all women/Who were to come. But alone of all her sex/She pleased the Lord" ("Paschalis Carminis," Book II, lines 68ff. of *Opera Omnia* [Vienna, 1885]). Epigraph to Marina Warner, *Alone of All Her Sex.*

IV

DECONSTRUCTION AND POSTSTRUCTURALISM

The introduction to the third section of this book, "Structuralism and Semiotics," ended with a discussion of Jacques Derrida's "deconstructive" critique of structuralism and a brief look at the Derrida essay reprinted here, "Structure, Sign, and Play in the Discourse of the Human Sciences." It also discussed how Julia Kristeva used that critique in her semiotic analysis of motherhood in the West, pointing out an important difference between structuralism and poststructuralism. Structuralism and semiotics, on the one hand, are firmly embedded in the tradition of Western thought and science; their aim, typical of most Western thought, is to find ways of "understanding" phenomena through models of explanation that offer *coherent* pictures of the order of things, a picture that embodies what Michel Foucault calls a "principle of unity." As Jonathan Culler says in his discussion of the relation between Derrida and the English philosopher J. L. Austin, the aim of understanding is to find a way to present and master the context of whatever is to be understood. "Meaning," Culler writes, "is context-bound." Kristeva treads closely to the limits of this project in her attempt to describe the materiality of motherhood—the creaturely (as opposed to intellectual or spiritual) nature of mothering—which she calls its "otherness" in her essay. There she multiplies contexts *almost* to the point of incoherence. Even there, however, can be seen the great project of structuralism and semiotics, to "account" for the existence of things and their "conditions" of existence.

On the other hand, the aim of deconstructive "critique" is different from this project. Instead of attempting to account for how things are, their order, such a critique aims at describing the limits of understanding. As J. Hillis Miller says in "The Search for Grounds in Literary Study" in Section VIII, "the fundamental sense of [a deconstructive] 'critique' [is] discriminating testing out." That is, a deconstructive critique examines and tests the assumptions supporting intellectual insight in order to interrogate the "self-evident" truths they are based on. It tests the legitimacy of the contextual "bounds" understanding both presents and requires. Rather than seeking a way of "understanding"—that is, a way of incorporating new phenomena into coherent (i.e., "bounded") existing or modified models—a deconstructive critique seeks to uncover the unexamined axioms that give rise to those models and their boundaries.

DECONSTRUCTION

"Deconstruction" is a mode of critique in this broad sense. It was named in the sixties by Jacques Derrida, who in 1967 began to describe certain events he saw taking place in the history of philosophy, that is, events in Western modes of conceiving and articulating knowledge. In sweeping analyses, Derrida noted that traditional embodiments of legitimate authority have traditionally been taken to be self-evident in their absolute "rightness," as is the case with concepts such as "goodness," "purity," "naturalness," and "truth." The same is true of more abstract versions of authority such as (in Derrida's examples) "*aletheia*, transcendentality, consciousness, or conscience, God, man, and so forth"—all assumed in the West to be self-evident givens of understanding and "correct." He also noted that such concepts are necessarily defined in relation to their opposites. Further, Derrida explained, authority in the West is generally conceived as existing in a structure and thought to be the precise *center* "at which the substitution of contents, elements, or terms is no longer possible." "It has always been thought," Derrida wrote, "that [this] center, which is by definition unique, constituted that very thing within a structure which governs the structure, while escaping structurality." Certain aspects of understanding, in other words, are themselves taken to be self-evidently "true." Thus, the concept of "center," or foundation of knowledge, is an epistemologically immovable mover, on which structures and hierarchies of belief or understanding have been thought to be based or securely "centered."

Most importantly, Derrida saw that this "center"—a conception which he says in a telling phrase is "contradictorily coherent"—has traditionally taken on two manifestations that correspond to the two definitions of rhetoric discussed in the Introduction to Section II. In each case, as Derrida says, "center" was understood to be an "origin"—"a truth or an origin that is free from freeplay and forms the order of the sign." In one case, the original is *structurally* conceived—that is, conceived as a *function* of structurality—and it corresponds to the grammatical structure (or what Paul de Man calls here the "semiology") of meaning. In a second case, the original is *humanly* (or referentially) conceived—that is, conceived as an *intention* of a person. For this reason Derrida's critique of Western philosophy has been twofold. On the one hand, he has subjected structuralism—especially the structuralism of Claude Lévi-Strauss (as in "Structure, Sign, and Play") and that of Saussure as well—to his "deconstructive" critique. On the other hand, he has subjected Continental phenomenology and Anglo-American speech-act philosophy to his "deconstructive" critique, and both forms of deconstruction here are presented in this book.

The word "deconstruction" is Derrida's coinage in response to the philosopher Martin Heidegger's idea of "destructive" analysis, the attempt to introduce "time" as a decisive element of the way we understand the world. In the same way that time inevitably upsets and reshapes any human scheme of understanding, so—as Derrida shows—meanings and values, by their very nature, are so mutually interdependent in systems of thought as to be continually destabilizing to each other and even to themselves. Deconstruction as a concept that focuses on this instability of meaning, then, rises out of Derrida's recognition that in modern conceptions of knowledge there is a temporal "decentering" or a "rupture" in the conventional order, a dramatic and decisive shift in traditional relations to authority, what might be termed a radical challenge to all authority. That is, the Western mind has learned to accept authority only by positing its underlying basis—what Derrida means by "center" and what Miller describes as its "ground" in Section VIII—around or upon which that "authority" is founded and beyond which one cannot go. But the investigation or "interrogation" of deconstructive critique reveals an underlying "authority" (or "center" or "ground") beneath the prior authority, and so on—in Derrida's critique of Lévi-Strauss, it is the seemingly unconscious valorization of "nature" over "culture" beneath Lévi-Strauss's attempt to demonstrate the relationship between the tangible and the intelligible—and at the same time it reveals, as de Man argues in "Semiology and Rhetoric," no coherent reason for choosing one or another as a ground. Thus, de Man describes "two entirely coherent but entirely incompatible readings" of Yeats's "Among School Children" that hinge upon one line that calls for both a "grammatical" and a "rhetorical" reading. In this regress of certainty and absolute reference points, modern thought—especially in the nineteenth and twentieth centuries—brings about a depreciation, or displacement, of conventional cultural references, of notions such as "truth," "objectivity," and so on. This "decentering," in other words, deeply undercuts or destroys all notions of self-evident and absolute grounds in knowledge. In short, as Nietzsche said, God, or any absolute reference point, really does "die" (does become "decentered") for the modern world. Accordingly, there is the recognition in modern thought of what Derrida calls the "structurality of structure," or Western culture's ironic ability to know and not know something at the same time—in effect, to *know* that knowledge *conceived as spatial structures*, conceived as ideal "form" beginning with Plato and Aristotle, is ultimately problematic and "undecidable."

As it bears on literary criticism, as our allusion to de Man suggests, deconstruction is a *strategy* of reading. Derrida describes deconstructive reading as starting from a philosophical hierarchy in which two opposed terms are presented as the "superior" general case and the "inferior" special case. These oppositions are Western culture's most important categories of thought, such as truth/error, health/disease, male/female, nature/culture, philosophy/literature, speech/writing, seriousness/play. De Man adds the certainties of grammar/the uncertainties of rhetoric to this list; and Jonathan Culler gives the example of language conceived as "constative" (i.e., as essentially a system of true or false meanings) versus language conceived as "performative" (i.e., the actual *activity* of using language). Another example, as much of the feminist criticism in this book suggests, is the generally accepted use of "man" to mean "human" and "woman" to mean only the special case of a female human being. Deconstruction then reverses such crucial hierarchies so as to elevate the "inferior" over the "superior"—making, as Culler says, "the constative a special case of the performative." A final example of a deconstructive reversal, as Derrida himself says, would be Lévi-Strauss's reversal of "nature" and "culture," making the once superior category of "nature" a special case (an "inferior" category) of "culture."

The purpose of these reversals, however, is not merely to invert value systems; doing such, Derrida says elsewhere, would only "confirm" the old system of opposition that is the object of analysis. Rather, deconstruction attempts to "explode" (in Derrida's metaphor) the original relationship of "superior" and "inferior" which gives rise to the semantic horizon—the possibility of any particular meaning—of a discourse. Deconstruction attempts, in Derrida's words, to confront one interpretation "of interpretation, of structure, of sign, of freeplay"—one that seeks "a truth or an origin which is free from freeplay and from the order of the sign"—with another interpretation of interpretation "which is no longer turned toward the origin, [but] affirms freeplay and tries to pass beyond man and humanism." In de Man's terms, this second interpretation refuses the specific meanings of grammar for the "suspended" logic and meanings of rhetoric, a "rhetorical model" that de Man chooses to call "literature." It refuses the propositional logic of language conceived as constative, information or knowledge as exclusively "true or false," for the open-ended "promises" of performative language. Such a confrontation, though, should not constitute itself into a new hierarchy. Rather, it presents an "undecidability," an inability to choose, an *aporia,* de Man's "vertiginous possibilities," and Derrida's "*affirmation*—the joyous affirmation of the freeplay of the world and without truth, without origin, offered to an active interpretation."

DECONSTRUCTIVE CRITICISM

Derrida's deconstructive critique of Western epistemology, the manner in which the West knows the world, has led him to deconstruct many institutions of Western culture—that is, to extend the epistemological analysis into areas of actual practice and, thus, to investigate at first hand the cultural changes he first described in general terms. He has done this extensively with psychoanalysis and literary criticism (especially theories of representation, or mimesis). From his general theories and specific commentaries, we can take three issues that have a direct bearing on literary theory and criticism: textuality, undecidability, and strategy. By textuality, Derrida means largely what the structuralists mean by that term: anything that can be known will be articulated *as a text* within a system of differences, in Saussure's description, *without positive terms.* Consequently, because it is a system without positive terms (i.e., without a "center"), textuality is subject to a certain instability, or undecidability. That is, texts of any sort (social or literary phenomena, for example) will produce meanings, but since the production of meaning cannot be arrested through a relationship with absolute referents (positive terms) or absolutely closed contexts (centers or grounds), textuality will always be in progress and unfinished—thus, undecidable. The notion of deconstructive textuality, as de Man, Henry Louis Gates, Jr., Barbara Johnson, Shoshana Felman, and others have shown, is easily applicable in practical criticism. Indeed, in practical criticism, the dimension of undecidability separates the structuralist from the deconstructionist version of the text.

Most decisive for deconstructive literary criticism, though, is the issue of deconstructive strategy we have described above, its two strategic "moves." A deconstructive analysis of literature involves reversing and reinscribing the terms of a hierarchy. Such reversal and reinscription are of course playful, but with a playfulness intended to be radically disruptive—in a way, as if to institute a kind of nonsense. But however innocuous such a strategy of "nonsense" may seem, Derrida is playful in the "serious" Nietzschean sense; that is, his play is intended to subvert the most fundamental strictures of seriousness and, thus, to displace and "contaminate" the very basis of (Western) authority. It is play, in other words, aimed at producing revolutionary changes in thought. In fact, deconstructive play offers a virtual model of continual revolution (political and cultural) in its drive to overturn the status quo and then to institute a new order. In this way, as Derrida and other deconstructionists have become more playful, rhetorically and conceptually, they have also become more intent about instituting new practices in writing and thinking.

Such a reading of literature can be seen in de Man's reading of Yeats and Proust, and de Man, probably more than most critics, takes the disruptions of deconstruction "seriously" indeed. De Man is interested primarily in the manner in which a text *says* one thing and *does* another. To show this, de Man (following Charles S. Peirce) opposes "rhetoric" to "grammar" in the essay ("Semiology and Rhetoric") reprinted in this section. For de Man, "pure rhetoric" is an interpretive swerving or "deflection" of meaning, a mode of error, whereas "pure grammar . . . postulates the possibility of unproblematic, dyadic meaning." De Man then deconstructs the opposition between rhetoric and grammar: first, a text has a "meaning," or a given and somewhat static significance; next, the text "asserts" or "performs" (as the reading continues) a quite different meaning, as if to constitute a different "text" inconsistent with the first. This "discrepancy between meaning and assertion" in the same "text"—the text as *information* and as *activity*—de Man shows to be "a constitutive part of their logic," of "textual" logic. The text, in this way, swerves from meaning to assertion, from "blindness" to "insight," from falsehood to truth, the gap between terms (which allows the swerving) in each case de Man calls irony or "error," not the "mere error" of a factual mistake, but a dynamic constituent of textuality. This irony, or error, is generated specifically because of a text's inability to *say* what it *does*, to unite saying and doing, because of its own (in Ortega y Gasset's term) "constitutive instability."

Other writers in this book offer similar deconstructive readings. Stanley Fish presents a deconstructive reading of "reading" in "Interpreting the *Variorum*," which is even more playful than de Man's discussion, and both Johnson and Jerry Aline Flieger offer deconstructive readings of Lacan and Freud. What these readings all do, to different extents, is confront the performances of authors/narrators/texts with their "constative" meanings in order to examine what is going on in literature. These critics make us confront the two senses of rhetoric discussed in the introduction to Section II, and the two approaches to formalism discussed in the introduction to Section I.

Along with this confrontation, deconstruction, as Derrida himself suggests, involves a reversal and reinscription of the usual patterns of interpretation—that is, it examines criticism as well as literature. In fact, one hierarchical opposition that it has brought into question is the opposition between literature/criticism, "primary" and "secondary" texts, and in this, perhaps more than anywhere else, deconstructive criticism has encountered resistance. Among others, critics who taught and wrote at Yale University during the seventies (J. Hillis Miller and Geoffrey Hartman along with de Man) attempted to challenge the "superiority" of literature over criticism. De Man, in particular, claims a "literary" status for critique itself—"the key to this critique of metaphysics," he writes, ". . . is the rhetorical model of the trope or, if one prefers to call it that, literature"—and claims the essentially "critical" nature of literature. All the Yale critics have focused their attention, similarly, on the changing hierarchy of "literature" and "criticism." (Perhaps the most striking example here is Gayatri Spivak's reading of three texts—a poem, a short story, and a discussion paper of the East India Company in her examination of feminist criticism in Section VII of this book.) Geoffrey Hartman, among the Yale critics, has experimented with deconstructive criticism to re-articulate a traditionally "literary" use of language (to "save" the text) while J. Hillis Miller has aimed at communicating deconstructive reading to an unusually wide audience. Most usefully, he has articulated in the relationship between deconstructive reading and more traditional humanistic concerns two extremes of interpretation that Miller calls "uncanny" and "canny" (irrational and rational) criticism.

Finally, it is the avant-garde, or "uncanny," atmosphere surrounding the work of the Yale critics that sets them apart in Anglo-American criticism. In a manner largely alien to the American tradition of philosophical pragmatism and temperamental optimism—against the native impulse to focus all of experience in the "light of common day," within the bounds of empiricism—the Yale critics have tried to "bring the plague" to American scholarship and teaching. The history of criticism, of course, is a history of such imports and exports, some more unsettling than others, but the Yale importation of deconstruction has produced an "uncanniness" calculated to decenter American formalism (whether New Critical, archetypal, or Rhetorical) with an irony and undecidability foreign and almost completely "other" to it. More than any other feature, it is this deliberate introduction of irony (of absolute loss, or death—not New Critical irony) that has alarmed many American academics and has prompted the charge that current theory "turns literature against itself." In an important sense, this charge is entirely accurate. As de Man shows (indeed, virtually *enacts* in his criticism), language/literature is irrevocably divided against itself—is at each moment different from itself, turned against itself in the temporal folds of error and irony.

POSTSTRUCTURALISM

The poststructuralist era that has followed from Derrida's work takes in a large area of literary criticism. Current psychoanalytic criticism, influenced by Jacques Lacan, decenters the traditional Freudian version of the "subject" and is distinctly deconstructive in its practice. Feminism, too, especially in the work of Hélène Cixous, Barbara Johnson, Jane Gallop, and Patrocinio Schweickart, uses deconstructive strategies for displacing maleness and "male" readings of literary texts (and Gayatri Spivak even used deconstructive critique to displace the universalized "female" in feminist criticism). Marxist critics, especially Louis Althusser, Fredric Jameson, John Ellis, and Rosalind Coward, and Michael Ryan have found deep affinities between the Marxist and deconstructive critiques of cultural production. All these critics have adopted a deconstructive approach to literary texts and have attempted from different angles to understand the forces that shape and "rupture" those texts. In one sense, poststructuralism can be said to cover all post-Derridean developments in criticism, including the contemporary rhetoric examined earlier in this book (though it could be plausibly argued—Newton Garver and Richard Rorty have made this argument—that Derrida is the latest example of a long tradition in philosophy which is quintessentially *rhetorical*). It is, in any event, difficult to find the limits of deconstruction's influence. More conservatively, the poststructuralist approach to the literary text arises from definitions of literature and criticism that have followed from Derrida's ideas about textuality, undecidability, and strategy.

But there is another sense of "poststructuralism" that is equally important, namely the articulation of a *critique* of deconstruction itself. For, as we have already suggested, the constant danger of deconstruction is that it falls into the same kinds of hierarchies it attempts to expose. Derrida himself is quite aware of this danger, and his response—really a *rhetorical* response—is recurrently to present "deconstruction" in relation to particular textual practices, those of Lévi-Strauss or Saussure or Austin, and recurrently to articulate that practice in terminology specific to those contexts ("writing" in discussing Saussure, "structure" in relation to Lévi-Strauss, "iteration" in relation to Austin, etc.). Nevertheless, if, like rhetoric, deconstruction aims at situating the concepts that are assumed in any particular discourse, then deconstruction can have its own focus on discourse also subject to examination.

In "What Is An Author? " Michel Foucault performs this very "poststructuralist" critique. In that essay Foucault examines the *function* of the author-role as a social function, a "position" (like the positions that structural analysis describes). It is not enough "to repeat the empty affirmation that the author has disappeared," Foucault writes. "Instead, we must locate the space left empty by the author's disappearance, follow the distribution of gaps and breaches, and watch for the openings that this disappearance uncovers." In this way Foucault attempts to describe the social and political "role" of the author, the ends its serves as a principle of unity, its links with juridical and institutional systems, its function within different classes, and, finally, its changing nature.

In this, Foucault's essay can be profitably contrasted with Roland Barthes's essay "The Death of the Author" (1968), which is more conventionally a "deconstructive," poststructuralist work. There Barthes argues that in discourse "it is language which speaks, not the author; to write is, through a prerequisite impersonality . . . , to reach that point where only language acts, 'performs,' and not 'me.' " In this discussion Barthes hypothesizes "language" rather than situating it; instead of examining the "death" of the author in situated terms—terms which examine what Foucault calls the "author function"—he reverses the opposition between author and reader and claims, in a deconstructive gesture of reversal, that it is in "the place of the reader, not . . . the author" that writing exists: "a text's unity lies not in its origin but in its destination." And in the second move of deconstruction Barthes explodes this opposition altogether by making the reader and the author *equally* unrecoverable; "this destination," he adds, "cannot any longer be personal: the reader is without history, biography, or psychology. He is simply that *someone* who holds together in a single field all the traces by which the written text is constituted." But what Barthes fails to do is precisely what constitutes Foucault's implicit critique: he fails to show what situated function the role of author—or even Barthes's role of reader—serves: how it *works* within the confines of particular discursive practices that are, also, practices of power.

In this Foucault is offering an implicit critique of deconstruction that is analogous to the critique of structuralism Kristeva offers or the critique of rhetoric Schweickart presents. Like deconstruction itself, Foucault's critique uses the categories of the object of critique to demonstrate its shortcomings. Yet Foucault—unlike Kristeva or Derrida—never makes that critique explicit. Instead, he offers a reading of a cultural and socially defined category, the "author," which Barthes "deconstructs" and both formalism and structuralism erase in their different ways (Eliot's in his talk of the "impersonality" of poetry and Todorov in his discussion of genre without any regard for authorial intention) in order to show the relationship between discursive social "categories" and practices and strategies of power within culture itself. Such an analysis, as we shall see, offers the possibility, articulated in Section VI by Stephen Greenblatt, of a "new historicism" in literary criticism.

RELATED READING IN *CONTEMPORARY LITERARY CRITICISM*

Stanley Fish, "Interpreting the *Variorum*"
Roland Barthes, "The Structuralist Activity"
Henry Louis Gates, Jr., "The Blackness of Blackness: A Critique of the Sign and the Signifying Monkey"
Julia Kristeva, "Stabat Mater"
Stephen Greenblatt, "Shakespeare and the Exorcists"
Barbara Johnson, "The Frame of Reference"
J. Hillis Miller, "The Search for Grounds in Literary Study"
Ferdinand de Saussure, Selections from *Course in General Linguistics*
Gayatri Spivak, "Imperialism and Sexual Difference"

FURTHER READING

Arac, Jonathan, et al., *The Yale Critics: Deconstruction in America* (Minneapolis: University of Minnesota Press, 1983).

Barthes, Roland, *S/Z*, trans. Richard Miller (New York: Hill and Wang, 1974).

———, "The Death of the Author," in *Image-Music-Text*, trans. Stephen Heath (New York: Hill and Wang, 1977).

Culler, Jonathan, *On Deconstruction: Theory and Criticism After Structuralism* (Ithaca: Cornell University Press, 1982).

———, *The Pursuit of Signs: Semiotics, Literature, Deconstruction* (Ithaca: Cornell University Press, 1981).

Davis, Robert Con, and Ronald Schleifer, eds., *Rhetoric and Form: Deconstruction at Yale* (Norman: University of Oklahoma Press, 1985).

de Man, Paul, *Allegories of Reading: Figural Language in Rosseau, Nietzsche, Rilke, and Proust* (New Haven: Yale University Press, 1979).

———, *Blindness and Insight: Essays in the Rhetoric of Contemporary Criticism* (Minneapolis: University of Minnesota Press, 1983).

Derrida, Jacques, "Difference," in *Speech and Phenomena, and Other Essays on Husserl's Theory of Signs*, trans. David B. Allison (Evanston, Ill.: Northwestern University Press, 1973).

———, *Dissemination*, trans. Barbara Johnson (Chicago: University of Chicago Press, 1981).

———, *Glas*, trans. John P. Leavy (Lincoln: University of Nebraska Press, 1987).

———, *Of Grammatology*, trans. Gayatri Spivak (Baltimore: Johns Hopkins University Press, 1976).

———, "La Loi du genre/The Law of Genre," in *Glyph*, 7 (1980), 176–232.

———, *Writing and Difference*, trans. Alan Bass (Chicago: University of Chicago Press, 1978).

Eco, Umberto, *A Theory of Semiotics* (Bloomington: Indiana University Press, 1976).

Felman, Shoshana, *The Literary Speech Act: Don Juan with J. L. Austin, or Seduction in Two Languages*, trans. Catherine Porter (Ithaca: Cornell University Press, 1983).

Garver, Newton, "Preface" to Jacques Derrida, *Speech and Phenomena* (cited above).

Gasché, Rodolphe, "Deconstruction as Criticism," *Glyph*, 6 (1979), 177–215.

Harari, Josué, ed., *Textual Strategies: Perspectives in Post-Structuralist Criticism*. (Ithaca: Cornell University Press, 1979).

Hartman, Geoffrey H., *Criticism in the Wilderness* (New Haven: Yale University Press, 1980).

_____, et al., *Deconstruction and Criticism* (New York: Continuum, 1979).

_____, *Saving the Text: Literature/Derrida/Philosophy* (Baltimore: Johns Hopkins University Press, 1981).

Irwin, John T., *American Hieroglyphics* (New Haven: Yale University Press, 1980).

Johnson, Barbara, *The Critical Difference: Essays in the Contemporary Rhetoric of Reading* (Baltimore: Johns Hopkins University Press, 1980).

_____, *Defigurations du langage poétique* (Paris: Flammarion, 1979).

Miller, J. Hillis, "Ariadne's Thread: Repetition and the Narrative Line," in *Critical Inquiry*, 3 (1976), 55–77.

_____, "Narrative Middles: A Preliminary Outline," in *Genre*, 11 (1978), 375–87.

_____, "Tradition and Difference," in *Diacritics*, 2, No. 4 (1972), 6–13.

Rorty, Richard, *Consequences of Pragmatism* (Minneapolis: University of Minnesota Press, 1982).

Ryan, Michael, *Marxism and Deconstruction* (Baltimore: Johns Hopkins University Press, 1982).

Schleifer, Ronald, "Deconstruction and Linguistic Analysis," *College English*, 49 (1987), 381–95.

13

Jonathan Culler 1944–

Born in Ohio in 1944, Jonathan Culler completed his undergraduate degree at Harvard in 1966 and was a Rhodes Scholar from 1966 until 1969. He completed his D.Phil. (the British equivalent of the Ph.D.) at Oxford in 1972, and until 1977, when he became professor of English and Comparative Literature at Cornell University, was a lecturer at Cambridge and Oxford. In 1975, while a visiting professor in French and comparative literature at Yale, Culler received the prestigious James Russell Lowell Prize from the Modern Language Association of America for his second book, *Structuralist Poetics* (1975). This book is a revised and expanded version of his doctoral dissertation, which was an investigation of contemporary French criticism's theoretical foundations and a discussion of the usefulness of the model of structural linguistics for literary criticism. Culler has also written *Flaubert: The Uses of Uncertainty* (1974), *Saussure* (1976), *Roland Barthes* (1983), *On Deconstruction* (1982), and *Framing the Sign: Criticism and Its Institutions* (1988).

The following article, "Convention and Meaning: Derrida and Austin," is an excerpt from *On Deconstruction*, where it appears in expanded form as the chapter "Meaning and Iterability." The article provides an account of the debate between the American philosopher and speech-act theorist John Searle and the French philosopher Jacques Derrida concerning their different readings of J. L. Austin's *How to Do Things with Words*, a seminal British work in ordinary language philosophy. Culler takes Derrida's part in the debate, discussing to what extent Searle's responses to Derrida miss the thrust of Derrida's critical approach to Austin and the conclusions to be drawn from that approach. The article is a significant contribution to literary criticism because it summarizes and clarifies a debate of much importance to both literary critics and philosophers studying the philosophy of language. Moreover, Culler's article makes an understanding of Derrida's deconstruction of texts accessible to a wide audience that might sometimes be overwhelmed by the rhetoric of Derrida's work in deconstruction.

Very briefly, Culler begins with Austin's attempt to address the meaning of utterances in terms of a system of speech acts, a system to provide conventional rules of meaning involving the contextual features of utterances. Austin's attempt purportedly provides an account of utterance and meaning that is independent of a speaker's intention—what the speaker has in mind to say when speaking. However, in providing his account in *How to Do Things with Words*,

Austin introduces a distinction between serious and nonserious speech acts. Derrida contends that this introduction provides the wedge by which the speaker's intention is reintroduced into the account of meaning, thus defeating Austin's project—a project with which Derrida is somewhat sympathetic. Searle's counter contention, in defense of Austin, is that Derrida misunderstands Austin's methodological use of "serious" and makes more of this use than is warranted. In the article, Culler discusses Searle's failure to address the issues Derrida raises in his criticism of Austin, as well as Searle's possible oversight on the scope of Austin's project: "The project of clarifying all possible ways and varieties of *not exactly doing things,*" Culler quotes Austin, ". . . has to be carried through if we are to understand properly what doing this is."

In reading Culler, one should pay particular attention to the account of supplementarity and iterability, key concepts to understanding the fundamentals of the Searle/Derrida debate. Supplementarity is a Derridean term that (in French) means both a supplement—an addition—to something and a substitution—a supplanting—of something. Iterability, the possibility of repeating discourse, is the notion of an infinite number of contexts for an utterance that make for the undecidability of meaning without reference to a code for the conventions of context. But it is Derrida's point, ultimately, that the possibility of an infinite number of conventions defeats the project of providing a systematic code for them.

Convention and Meaning: Derrida and Austin[1]

In the Saussurian perspective, meaning is the product of linguistic conventions, the effect of a system of differences. To account for meaning is to set forth the relations of contrast and the possibilities of combination that constitute a language. However, as many have observed, a theory that derives meaning from linguistic conventions does not account for it completely. If one conceives of meaning as the effect of linguistic relations manifested in an utterance, then one must contend with the fact that, as we say, a speaker can mean different things by the same linguistic sequence on different occasions. "Could you move that box?" may be a request, or a question about one's interlocutor's strength, or even, as rhetorical question, the resigned indication of an impossibility.

Such examples seem to reinstate a model in which the subject—the consciousness of the speaker—is made the source of meaning: despite the contribution of linguistic structure, the meaning of the utterance varies from case to case; its meaning is what the speaker means by it. Confronted with such a model, the partisan of structural explanation will ask what makes it possible for the speaker to mean these several things by the one utterance. Just as we account for the meaning of sentences by analyzing the linguistic system, so we should account for the meaning of utterances (or as Austin calls it; their illocutionary force) by analyzing another system; the system of speech acts. As the founder of speech act theory, Austin is, in fact, repeating at another level (though less explicitly) the crucial move made by Saussure: to account for signifying events (*parole*) one attempts to describe the system that makes them possible.

Thus Austin argues, for example, that to mean something by an utterance is not to perform an inner act of meaning that accompanies the utterance. The notion that I may mean different things by "Can you move this box?" seems to urge that we explain meaning by inquiring what the speaker has in mind, as though this were the determining factor, but this is what Austin denies. What makes an utterance a command or a promise or a request is not the speaker's state of mind at the moment of utterance but conventional rules involving features of the context. If in appropriate circumstances I say "I promise to return this to you," I have made a promise, whatever was running through my mind at the time; and conversely, when earlier in this sentence I wrote the words "I promise to return this to you," I did not succeed in making a promise, even if the thoughts in my mind were similar to those that occurred on an occasion when I did make a promise. Promising is an act governed by certain conventions which the theorist of speech acts attempts to make explicit.

Austin's project is thus an attempt at structural explanation which offers a pertinent critique of logocentric premises, but in his discussion he reintroduces precisely those assumptions that his project puts in question. Derrida outlines this self-deconstructive movement in a section of "Signature événement contexte" in *Marges de la philosophie*, but John Searle's egregious misunderstanding in his "Reiterating the Differences: A Reply to Derrida" indicates that it may be important to proceed more slowly than Derrida does, with fuller discussion of Austin's project and Derrida's observations.

Austin begins *How to Do Things with Words* with the observation that "it was for too long the assumption of philosophers that the business of a 'statement' can only be to 'describe' some state of affairs, or to 'state some fact,' which it must do either truly or falsely."[2] The normal sentence was conceived as a true or false representation of a state of affairs, and numerous sentences which failed to correspond to this model were treated either as unimportant exceptions or as deviant "pseudo-statements." "Yet we, that is, even philosophers, set some limits to the amount of nonsense that we are prepared to admit we talk; so that it was natural to go on to ask, as a second stage, whether many apparent pseudo-statements really set out to be 'statements' at all."

Austin thus proposes to attend to cases previously ignored as marginal and problematic and to treat them not as failed statements but as an independent type. He proposes a distinction between statements, or *constative* utterances, which describe a state of affairs and are true or false, and another class of utterances which are not true or false and which actually perform the action to which they refer (e.g., "I promise to pay you tomorrow" accomplishes the act of promising). These he calls *performatives*.

This distinction between *performative* and *constative* has proved very fruitful in the analysis of language, but as Austin presses further in his description of the distinctive features of the performative and the various forms it can take, he reaches a surprising conclusion. An utterance such as "I hereby affirm that the cat is on the mat" seems also to possess the crucial feature of accomplishing the act (of affirming) to which it refers. *I affirm X*, like *I promise X*, is neither true nor false but performs the act it denotes. It would thus seem to count as a performative. But another important feature of the performative, Austin has shown, is the possibility of deleting the explicit performative verb. Instead of saying "I promise to pay you tomorrow," one can in appropriate circumstances perform the act of promising by saying "I will pay you tomorrow"—a statement whose illocutionary force remains performative. Similarly, one can perform the act of affirming or stating while omitting "I hereby affirm that." "The cat is on the mat" may be seen as a shortened version of "I hereby state that the cat is on the mat" and thus a performative. But, of course, "The cat is on the mat" is the classic example of a constative utterance.

Austin's analysis provides a splendid instance of the logic of supplementarity at work. Starting from the philosophical hierarchy that makes true or false statements the norm of language and treats other utterances as flawed statements or as extra—supplementary—forms, Austin's investigation of the qualities of the marginal case leads to a deconstruction and inversion of the hierarchy: the performative is not a flawed constative; rather, the constative is a special case of the performative. The conclusion that a constative is a performative from which one of various performative verbs has been deleted has since been adopted by numerous linguists. John Lyons notes, "It is natural to consider the possibility of deriving all sentences from underlying structures with an optionally deletable main clause containing a first-person subject, a performative verb of saying and optionally an indirect-object expression referring to the addressee."[3]

This would be a way of extending grammar to account for part of the force of utterances. Instead of saying that speakers can mean different things by the sentence "This chair is broken," linguists can extend the linguistic system to account for certain variations in meaning. "This chair is broken" can have different meanings because it can be derived from any of several underlying strings—strings which could be expressed as "I warn you that this chair is broken," "I inform you that this chair is broken," "I concede to you that this chair is broken," "I proclaim to you that this chair is broken," "I complain to you that this chair is broken."

Austin does not cast his theory in this form and would be skeptical of such attempts to extend grammar. He cites relationships between such pairs as "I warn you that this chair is broken" and "This chair is broken" to show that illocutionary force does not necessarily follow from grammatical structure. Indeed, he proposes a distinction between locutionary and illocutionary acts. When I say "This chair is broken," I perform the *locutionary* act of uttering a particular English sentence and the *illocutionary* act of stating, warning, proclaiming, or complaining. (There is also what Austin calls a *perlocutionary* act, the act I may accomplish by my performance of the locutionary and illocutionary acts: by arguing I may *persuade* you, by proclaiming something I may *bring you to know* it.) The rules of the linguistic system account for the meaning of the locutionary act; the goal of speech act theory is to account for the meaning of the illocutionary act or, as Austin calls it, the illocutionary force of an utterance.

To explain illocutionary force is to set forth the conventions that make it possible to perform various illocutionary acts: what one has to do in order to promise, to warn, to complain, to command. "Besides the uttering of the words of the so-called performative," Austin writes, "a good many other things have as a general rule to be right and to go right if we are to be said to have happily brought off our action. What these are we may hope to discover by looking at and classifying types of case in which something *goes wrong* and the act—marrying, betting, bequeathing, christening, or what not—is therefore at least to some extent a failure" (*How to . . .* , p. 14). Austin thus does not treat failure as an external accident that befalls performatives and has no bearing on their nature. The possibility of failure is internal to the performative and a point of departure for investigating it. Something cannot be a performative unless it can go wrong.

This approach may seem unusual, but in fact it accords with the basic axioms of semiotics. "A sign," writes Umberto Eco in *A Theory of Semiotics*, "is everything which can be taken as significantly substituting for something else . . . . *Semiotics is in principle the discipline studying everything which can be used in order to lie.* If something cannot be used to tell a lie, conversely it cannot be used to tell the truth."[4] "The bat is on my hat" would not be a signifying sequence if it were not possible to utter it falsely. Similarly, "I now pronounce you man and wife" is not a performative unless it is possible for it to misfire, to be used in inappropriate circumstances and without the effect of performing a marriage.

For the smooth functioning of a performative, Austin says, "(A.1) There must exist an accepted conventional procedure having a certain conventional effect, that procedure to include the uttering of certain words by certain persons in certain circumstances, and further, (A.2) the particular persons and circumstances in a given case must be appropriate for the invocation of the particular procedure invoked. (B.1) The procedure must be executed by all participants both correctly and (B.2) completely" (*How to . . .* , pp. 14–15). As these formulations suggest, to promise is to utter one of the conventional formulae in appropriate circumstances. It would be wrong, Austin argues, to think of the utterance "as (merely) the outward and visible sign, for convenience or other record or for information, of an inward and spiritual act" (*How to . . .* , p. 9). For example, "the act of marrying, like, say, the act of betting, is at least *preferably* . . . to be described as *saying certain words*, rather than as performing a different, inward and spiritual, action of which these words are merely the outward and audible sign. That this is so can perhaps hardly be *proved*, but it is, I should claim, a fact" (*How to . . .* , p. 13).

Austin refuses to explain meaning in terms of a state of mind and proposes, rather, an analysis of the conventions of discourse. Can such an account be developed? Can Austin proceed without reinstating the notion of meaning as a signifying intention present to consciousness at the moment of utterance and thus treating the meaning of a speech act as ultimately determined by or grounded in a consciousness whose intention is fully present to itself? Derrida's reading focuses on the way in which this reintroduction occurs. An especially interesting moment in which the argument can be shown to involve such an appeal occurs in the opening pages of *How to Do Things with Words*, as Austin is staking out the ground for his enterprise. After chastizing philosophers for treating as marginal any utterances that are not true or false statements and thus leading us to suppose that he himself will be concerned with such things as fictional utterances which are neither true nor false, Austin proposes an objection to the notion of performative utterance: "Surely the words must be spoken 'seriously' and so as to be taken 'seriously'? This is, though vague, true enough in general—it is an important commonplace in discussing the purport of any utterance whatsoever. I must not be joking, for example, nor writing a poem" (*How to . . .* , p. 9).

The rhetorical structure of this passage is itself quite revealing. Although he proposes to exclude the nonserious, Austin offers no characterization of it, presumably because he is particularly anxious at this point to avoid the reference to an inner intention that such description would doubtless involve. Instead his text posits an anonymous objection which introduces "seriously" in quotation marks, as if it were itself not altogether serious. Doubling itself to produce this objection whose key term remains unanchored, the text can then grant the objection as something to be taken for granted.

Once, Austin has already told us, it was customary for philosophers to exclude—unjustifiably—utterances that were not true or false statements. Now his own text makes it appear customary to exclude utterances that are not serious. We have here, as the remark about the vagueness of the "serious" indicates, not a rigorous move within philosophy but a customary exclusion on which philosophy relies.

This exclusion is repeated in a longer passage which helps to indicate what is at stake. After listing various failures that may prevent the accomplishment of a performative, Austin notes that performatives are subject

> to certain other kinds of ill which infect *all* utterances. And these likewise, though again they might be brought into a more general account, we are deliberately at present excluding. I mean, for example, the following: a performative utterance will, for example, be *in a peculiar way* hollow or void if said by an actor on the stage, or if introduced in a poem, or spoken in soliloquy. This applies in a similar manner to any and every utterance—a sea-change in special circumstances. Language in such circumstances is in special ways—intelligibly—used not seriously, but in ways *parasitic* upon its normal use—way which fall under the doctrine of the *etiolations* of language. All this we are *excluding* from consideration. Our performative utterances, felicitous or not, are to be understood as issued in ordinary circumstances. [*How to . . .* , pp. 21–22]

As the image of the parasite suggests, we have here a familiar relationship of supplementarity: the nonserious use of language is something extra, added to ordinary language and wholly dependent upon it. It need not be taken into consideration in discussing ordinary language use since it is only a parasite.

John Searle argues in his reply to Derrida that this exclusion is of no importance but purely provisional.

> Austin's idea is simply this: if we want to know what it is to make a promise or make a statement we had better not *start* our investigation with promises made by actors on stage in the course of a play or statements made in a novel by novelists about characters in the novel, because in a fairly obvious way such utterances are not standard cases of promises and statements . . . . Austin correctly saw that it was necessary to hold in abeyance one set of questions, about parasitic discourse, until one has answered a logically prior set of questions about "serious" discourse.[5]

This may well have been "Austin's idea," but the appropriateness of such an idea is precisely what is in question. "What is at stake," Derrida writes, "is above all the structural impossibility and illegitimacy of such an 'idealization,' even one which is methodological and provisional."[6] Indeed, Austin himself, who begins his investigation of performatives by looking at ways in which they can go wrong, contests Searle's notion of simple logical priority: "The project of clarifying all possible ways and varieties of *not exactly doing things* . . . has to be carried through if we are to understand properly what doing things is" (Austin's italics).[7] To set aside as parasitic certain uses of language in order to base one's theory on other, "ordinary" uses of language is to beg precisely those questions about the essential nature of language that a theory of language ought to answer. Austin objected to such an exclusion by his predecessors: in assuming that the ordinary use of language was to make true or false statements, they excluded precisely those cases that enable him to conclude that statements are a particular case of performative. When Austin then performs a similar exclusion, his own example prompts us to ask whether it is not equally illicit, especially since both he and Searle, by putting "serious" in quotation marks, suggest the dubiousness of the hierarchical opposition serious/nonserious. The fact that Austin's own writing is often highly playful and seductive, or that he does not hesitate to undermine distinctions that he proposes, only emphasizes the inappropriateness of excluding nonserious discourse from consideration.[8]

Searle uses his "Reply to Derrida" not to explore this problem but dogmatically to reaffirm the structure in question. "The existence of the pretended form of the speech act is logically dependent on the possibility of the nonpretended speech act in the same way that any pretended form of behavior is dependent on nonpretended forms of behavior, and in that sense the pretended forms are *parasitical* on the nonpretended forms."[9]

In what sense is the pretended dependent upon the nonpretended? Searle gives an example: "There could not, for example, be promises made by actors in a play if there were not the possibility of promises made in real life." We are certainly accustomed to thinking in this way: a promise I make is real; a promise in a play is a fictional imitation of a real promise, an empty iteration of a formula used to make real promises. But in fact one can argue that the relation of dependency works the other way. If it were not possible for a character in a play to make a promise, there could be no promises in real life, for what makes it possible to promise, as Austin tells us, is the existence of a conventional procedure, of formulae one can repeat. For me to be able to make a promise in "real life," there must be iterable procedures or formulae, such as are used on stage.

"Could a performative utterance succeed," Derrida asks or pretends to ask, "if its formulation did not repeat a 'coded' or iterable utterance, or in other words, if the formula I pronounce in order to open a meeting, to launch a ship or a marriage were not identifiable as *conforming* with an iterable model, if it were not thus identifiable in some way as 'citation'?"[10] For the "standard case" of promising to occur, it must be recognizable as the repetition of conventional procedure, and the actor's performance on the stage is an excellent model of such repetition. The possibility of "serious" performatives depends upon the possibility of performances, because performatives depend upon the iterability that is most explicitly manifested in performances.[11] Just as Austin reversed his predecessors' hierarchical opposition by showing that constatives were a special case of performatives, so we can reverse Austin's opposition between the serious and the parasitic by showing that his so-called serious performatives are only a special case of performances.

Indeed, this is a principle of considerable breadth. Something can be a signifying sequence only if it is iterable, only if it can be repeated in various serious and nonserious contexts, cited, and parodied. Imitation is not an accident that befalls an original but its condition of possibility. There is such a thing as an original Hemingway style only if it can be cited, imitated, and parodied. For there to be such a style, there must be recognizable features that characterize it and produce its distinctive effects; for features to be recognizable, one must be able to isolate them as elements that could be repeated, and thus the iterability manifested in the inauthentic, the derivative, the imitative, the parodic is what makes possible the authentic or original.

A deconstructive reading of Austin focuses on the way he repeats the move that he identifies and criticizes in others and on the way in which the distinction between the serious and the parasitic, which makes it possible for him to undertake an analysis of speech acts, is undone by the implications of that analysis. Since any serious performative can be reproduced in various ways and is itself a repetition of a conventional procedure, the possibility of repetition is not something external that may afflict the serious performative. On the contrary, Derrida insists, the performative is from the outset structured by this possibility. "This *possibility* is part of the so-called 'standard case.' It is an essential, internal, and permanent part, and to exclude what Austin himself admits is a *constant* possibility from one's description is to describe something other than the so-called standard case."[12]

Nevertheless, Austin's exclusion of the parasitic is not simply an error, an error he might have avoided. It is a strategic part of his enterprise. As we saw above, for Austin an utterance can function as a performative and thus have a certain meaning or illocutionary force when there exists a conventional procedure involving "the utterance of certain words by certain persons in certain circumstances" and when these specified conditions are actually fulfilled. Illocutionary force is thus held to depend upon context, and the theorist must, in order to account for meaning, specify the necessary features of the context—the nature of the words, persons, and circumstances required. What happens when one attempts such specification? Marriage is an example Austin cites. When the minister says "I now pronounce you man and wife," his utterance successfully performs the act of uniting a couple in marriage if the context meets certain conditions. The speaker must be one authorized to perform weddings; the persons he addresses must be a man and a woman who are not married, who have obtained a license to marry, and who have uttered the required phrases in the preceding ceremony. But when one formulates such conditions regarding the words, persons, and circumstances that are necessary for an utterance to have a particular meaning or force, a listener or critic can usually without great difficulty imagine circumstances that fit these conditions but in which the utterance would not have the illocutionary force that is supposed to follow from them. Suppose that the requirements for a marriage ceremony were met but that one of the parties were under hypnosis, or again that the ceremony were impeccable in all respects but had been called a "rehearsal," or finally, that while the speaker was a minister licensed to perform weddings and the couple had obtained a license, the three of them were on this occasion acting in a play that, coincidentally, included a wedding ceremony.

When anyone proposes an example of a meaningless sentence, listeners can usually imagine a context in which it would in fact have meaning; by placing a frame around it, they can make it signify. This aspect of the functioning of language, the possibility of grafting a sequence onto a context that alters its functioning, is also at work in the case of performatives. For any specification of the circumstances under which an utterance counts as a promise, we can either imagine further details that would make a difference or else place a further frame around the circumstances. (We imagine that the conditions are fulfilled on a stage or in an example.)

In order to arrest or control this process, which threatens the possibility of a successful theory of speech acts, Austin is led to reintroduce the notion, previously rejected, that the meaning of an utterance depends on the presence of a signifying intention in the consciousness of the speaker. First, he sets aside the non-serious—a notion not explicitly defined but which clearly would involve reference to intention: a "serious" speech act is one in which the speaker consciously assents to the act he appears to be performing. Second, he introduces intention as one feature of the circumstances by setting aside speech acts performed unintentionally—"done under duress, or by accident, or owing to this or that variety of mistake, say, or otherwise unintentionally" (*How to . . .* , p. 21).

However, this reintroduction does not solve the problem; intention cannot serve as the decisive determinant or the ultimate foundation of a theory of speech acts. To see this, one need only consider what would happen if, after apparently completing a marriage ceremony, one of the parties said that he had been joking when he uttered his lines—only pretending, just rehearsing, or acting under duress. Assuming that the others believe his report of his intention, it will not in itself be decisive. What he had in mind at the moment of utterance does not determine what speech act his utterance performed. On the contrary, the question of whether a marriage did indeed take place will depend upon further discussion of the circumstances. If the minister had said that there would be a full dress rehearsal immediately before the real ceremony, or if the groom can sustain his claim that throughout the ceremony the bride's father was threatening him with a pistol, then one might reach a different conclusion about the illocutionary force of their utterances. What counts is the plausibility of the description of the circumstances: whether the features of the context adduced create a frame that alters the illocutionary force of the utterances.

Thus the possibility of grafting an utterance upon a new context, of repeating a formula in different circumstances, does not discredit the principle that illocutionary force is determined by context rather than by intention. On the contrary, it confirms this principle: in citation, iteration, or framing, it is new contextual features that alter illocutionary force. We are here approaching a general principle of considerable importance. What the indissociability of performative and performance puts in question is not the determination of illocutionary force by context but the possibility of mastering the domain of speech acts by exhaustively specifying the contextual determinants of illocutionary force. A theory of speech acts must in principle be able to specify every feature of context that might affect the success or failure of a given speech act or that might affect what particular speech act an utterance effectively performed. This would require, as Austin recognizes, a mastery of the total context: "The total speech act in the total speech situation is the *only actual* phenomenon which, in the last resort, we are engaged in elucidating" (*How to . . .* , p. 148). But total context is unmasterable, both in principle and in practice. Meaning is context-bound, but context is boundless.[13]

This is true in two senses. First, any given context is always open to further description. There is no limit in principle to what might be included in a given context, to what might be shown relevant to the interpretation of a particular speech act. This structural openness of context is essential to all disciplines: the scientist discovers that factors previously disregarded are relevant to the behavior of particular objects; the historian brings new or reinterpreted data to bear on a particular event; the critic relates a particular passage or text to contexts that make it appear in a new light. A striking instance of the possibilities of further specification of context, Derrida notes, is the question of the unconscious. In his *Speech Acts* Searle proposes, as one of the conditions of promising, that "if a purported promise is to be non-defective, the thing promised must be something the hearer wants done, or considers to be in his interest."[14] An utterance that promised to do what the listener apparently wants but unconsciously dreads might thus cease to be a promise and become instead a threat; conversely, an utterance that seemed a defective promise—a threat to do what the listener claims not to want—may become a well-formed promise, should unconscious desire be specified as part of the total context.[15] This example illustrates very well how meaning is determined by context and for that very reason open to further possibilities.

Context is also unmasterable in a second sense: any attempt to codify context can always be grafted onto the context it sought to describe, yielding a new context which escapes the previous formulation. Attempts to describe limits always make possible a displacement of those limits, so that Wittgenstein's suggestion that one cannot say "bububu" and mean "if it does not rain I shall go out for a walk" has, paradoxically, made it possible to do just that. Its denial establishes a connection that can be exploited. Adepts of speech act theory, interested in excluding nonserious utterances from the corpus they are attempting to master, might admire the principle at work in a sign displayed in certain American airports at the spot where passengers and hand luggage are searched: "All remarks concerning bombs and weapons will be taken seriously." Designed to master signification by specifying the illocutionary force of certain statements in this context, it attempts to preclude the possibility of saying in jest "I have a bomb in my shoe" by identifying such utterances as serious statements. But this codification fails to arrest the play of meaning, nor is its failure an accident. The structure of language grafts this codification onto the context it attempts to master, and the new context creates new opportunities for obnoxious behavior. "If I were to remark that I had a bomb in my shoe, you would have to take it seriously, wouldn't you?" is only one of numerous remarks whose force is a function of context but which escape the prior attempt to codify contextual force. A metasign, "All remarks about bombs and weapons, including remarks about remarks about bombs and weapons, will be taken seriously," would escalate the struggle without arresting it, engendering the possibility of obnoxious remarks about this sign about remarks.

But if this seems a nonserious example, let us consider a more serious instance. What speech act is more serious than the act of signing a document, a performance whose legal, financial, and political implications may be enormous? Austin cites the act of signature as the equivalent in writing of explicit performative utterances with the form "I hereby . . . ," and indeed it is in appending a signature that one can in our culture most authoritatively take responsibility for an utterance. By signing a document, one intends its meaning and seriously performs the signifying act it accomplishes.

Derrida concludes "Signature événement contexte" with what he calls an "improbable signature," the "reproduction" of a "J. Derrida" in script above a printed "J. Derrida," accompanied by the following "Remark": "(Remark: the—written—text of this—oral—communication should have been sent to the Association des sociétés de philosophie de langue française before the meeting. That dispatch should thus have been signed. Which I do, and counterfeit, here. Where? There. J.D.)."[16] Is the cursive "J. Derrida" a signature even if it is a citation of the signature appended to the copy of this text sent through the mails? Is it still a signature when the supposed signatory calls it counterfeit? Can one counterfeit one's own signature? What, in sum, is a signature?

Traditionally, as Austin's remarks suggest, a signature is supposed to attest to the presence to consciousness of a signifying intention at a particular moment. Whatever my thoughts before or after, there was a moment when I fully intended a particular meaning. The notion of signature thus seems to imply a moment of presence to consciousness which is the origin of subsequent obligations or other effects. But if we ask what enables a signature to function in this way, we find that effects of signature depend on iterability. As Derrida writes, "The condition of possibility of those effects is simultaneously, once again, the condition of their impossibility, of the impossibility of their rigorous purity. In order to function, that is, to be readable, a signature must have a repeatable, iterable, imitable form; it must be able to be detached from the present and singular intention of its production. It is its sameness which, by corrupting its identity and its singularity, divides its seal."[17]

A proper signature, one that will validate a check or some other document, is one that conforms to a model and can be recognized as a repetition. This iterability, an essential feature of the structure of the signature, introduces as part of its structure an independence from any signifying intention. If the signature on a check corresponds to the model, the check can be cashed whatever my intentions at the moment of signature. So true is this that the empirical presence of the signatory is not even an essential feature of the signature. It is part of the structure of the signature that it can be produced by a stamp or by a machine. We can, fortunately, cash checks signed by a machine and receive a salary even though the signatory never saw the check nor entertained a specific intention to pay us the sum in question.

It is tempting to think of checks signed by a machine as a perverse exception irrelevant to the fundamental nature of signatures. Logocentric idealization sets aside such cases as accidents, "supplements," or "parasites" in its attempt to preserve a model predicated upon the presence of a full intention to consciousness at the moment of signature. But such cases could not occur if they did not belong to the structure of the phenomenon in question, and far from being a perverse exception, the check signed by machine is a logical and explicit example of the fundamental iterability of signatures. The requirement that a signature be recognizable as a repetition introduces the possibility of a machine as part of the structure of the signature at the same time as it eliminates the need for any particular intention at the point of signature.

Signatures thus ought to be included in what Derrida calls "a typology of forms of iteration":

> In such a typology the category of intention will not disappear: it will have its place, but from that place it will no longer be able to govern the entire scene and system of utterance. Above all, we will then be dealing with different kinds of marks or chains of iterable marks and not with an opposition between citational utterances on the one hand and singular and original event-utterances on the other. The first consequence of this will be the following: given that structure of iteration, the intention animating the utterance will never be through and through present to itself and to its content. The iteration structuring it introduces into it *a priori* an essential dehiscence and cleft [*brisure*].[18]

It is not a matter of denying that signatories have intentions but of situating those intentions. One way of doing this would be to take the unconscious, as Vincent Descombes has argued, "not as a phenomenon of the will but as a phenomenon of enunciation."[19] The thesis of the unconscious "makes sense only in relation to the subject of enunciation: he does not know what he says."[20] The unconscious is the excess of what one says over what one knows, or of what one says over what one wants to say. Either the speaker's intention is whatever content is present to consciousness at the moment of utterance, in which case it is variable and incomplete, unable to account for the illocutionary force of utterances, or else it is comprehensive and divided—conscious and unconscious—a structural intentionality which is never anywhere present and which includes implications that never, as we say, entered my mind. This latter notion of intention, marked by what Derrida calls an essential cleft or division, is indeed quite common. When questioned about the implications of an utterance, I may quite routinely include in my intention implications that had never occurred to me before I was questioned.

Either way, intention is perhaps best thought of as a product. To the extent one can ever "fully intend" what one's signature accomplishes, it is because one has read the document and one's signature as an iterable act, an act with certain consequences on any occasion when it is performed, and thus anticipates further explanations one might give if questioned on any point. Intentions are not a delimited content but open sets of discursive possibilities—what one will say in response to questions about an act.

The example of the signature thus presents us with the same structure we encountered in the case of other speech acts: (1) the dependence of meaning on conventional and contextual factors, but (2) the impossibility of exhausting contextual possibilities so as to specify the limits of illocutionary force, and thus (3) the impossibility of controlling effects of signification or the force of discourse by a theory, whether it appeal to intentions of subjects or to codes and contexts.

The view of meaning to which this leads is not simple: it entails, on the one hand, the contextual, conventional determination of meaning and, on the other hand, the impossibility of ever saturating or limiting context so as to control or rigorously determine the "true" meaning. It is thus possible, and even appropriate, to proclaim the indeterminacy of meaning—though the smug iconoclasm apparent in many such proclamations is irritating. On the other hand, it is necessary and appropriate to continue to interpret texts, classify speech acts, and generally elucidate as far as possible the conditions of signification. Though Austin demonstrates the collapse of his distinction between performative and constative, he does not for that reason abandon his attempt to discriminate various classes of performative. Even though one may have reason to believe, as Derrida says, that "the language of theory always leaves a residue that is neither formalizable nor idealizable in terms of that theory of language," this is no reason to stop work on theory.[21] In mathematics, for example, Gödel's demonstration of the incompleteness of metamathematics (the impossibility of constructing a theoretical system within which all true statements of number theory are theorems) does not lead mathematicians to abandon their work. The humanities, however, often seem touched with the belief that a theory which asserts the ultimate indeterminacy of meaning renders all effort pointless. The fact that such assertions emerge from essays that propose numerous particular determinations of meaning, specific interpretations of passages and texts, should indicate that we are dealing with a double, not a simple, view of meaning: if language always evades its conventions, it also depends on them.

NOTES

1. This is an excerpt from my book *On Deconstruction: Literary Theory in the 1970s*, published in 1982 by the Cornell University Press. 0028-6087/81/130015-16$1.00/0 Copyright© 1981 by *New Literary History*, The University of Virginia.

2. J. L. Austin, *How to Do Things with Words* (Cambridge, Mass., 1975), p. 1; hereafter cited in text as "*How to. . . .*"

3. John Lyons, *Semantics* II (Cambridge, 1977), p. 778.

4. Umberto Eco, *A Theory of Semiotics* (Bloomington, 1976), p. 7.

5. John Searle, "Reiterating the Differences: A Reply to Derrida," *Glyph* 1 (1977), pp. 204–5.

6. Jacques Derrida, *Limited Inc* (Baltimore, 1977) [supplement to *Glyph* 2], 39. English translation: "Limited Inc a b c . . . ," *Glyph* 2 (1977), p. 206.

7. Austin, *Philosophical Papers* (London, 1970), p. 27.

8. Shoshana Felman, in a fascinating discussion, casts Austin in the role of a Don Juan who seduces readers and disrupts all norms. She attempts to set aside Austin's exclusion of nonserious discourse by arguing that when Austin writes "I must not be joking, for example, or writing a poem" (in the example cited above), "cette phrase ne pourrait-elle pas être considérée elle-même comme une dénégation—comme une plaisanterie?" ["Could not this sentence itself be considered as a denial—as a joke?"], *Le Scandale du corps parlant: Don Juan* avec Austin, ou la séduction en deux langues (Paris, 1980), p. 188. This is a clever suggestion, part of a sustained attempt to attribute to Austin everything she has learned from Derrida—in order then to accuse Derrida of misreading Austin. But to treat the exclusion of jokes as a joke prevents one from explaining the logical economy of Austin's project, which can admit infelicities and exploit them so profitably only by excluding the fictional and the nonserious. This logic is what is at stake, not Austin's attitude or his liking for what Felman calls "le fun." Felman does argue convincingly, however, that by comparison with his successors, who see misfires and infelicities as events to be eliminated by a more rigorous idealization, Austin is a powerful defender of the irreducibility of the negative.

9. Searle, "Reiterating the Differences," p. 205.

10. Jacques Derrida, "Signature événement contexte," *Marges de la philosophie* (Paris, 1972), 389. English translation: "Signature Event Context," *Glyph* 1 (1977), pp. 191–92.

11. Searle accuses Derrida of confusing "no less than three separate and distinct phenomena: iterability, citationality, and parasitism." "There is a basic difference in that in parasitic discourse the expressions are being *used* and not *mentioned*"—a difference Derrida is said not to understand ("Reiterating the Differences," p. 206). But the distinction between *use* and *mention* is precisely one of the hierarchizations that Derrida's argument contests. The distinction seems clear and important in the classic examples: "Boston is populous" uses the word or expression *Boston*, while "*Boston* is disyllabic" does not use the expression but mentions it—mentions the word *Boston* by using an expression which is a metaname. Here the distinction seems important because it points to the difference between using a word to talk about a city and talking about a word. But when we turn to other examples of citation the problem becomes more complicated. If I write of a scholar, "Some of my colleagues think his work 'boring and incompetent' or 'pointless,' " what have I done? Have I used the expressions *boring and incompetent* and *pointless* as well as mentioned them? If we wish to preserve the distinction between use and mention here, we shall fall back on those notions of seriousness and of intention which Derrida claims are involved. I *use* the expressions insofar as I seriously intend the meanings of the sign sequences I utter; I mention them when I reiterate some of these signs (within quotation marks, for example) without committing myself to the meaning they convey. Mentioning, for Searle, would thus be parasitic upon use, and the distinction would separate the proper use of language, where I seriously intend the meaning of the signs I use, from a derivative reiteration that only mentions. We thus have a distinction—am I "seriously" applying the expressions *boring*, *incompetent*, and *pointless* or only mentioning them?—between two sorts of iteration, apparently based on intention, and Derrida is quite right to claim that *use/mention* is ultimately a hierarchy of the same sort as *serious/nonserious* and *speech/writing*. Each attempts to control language by characterizing distinctive aspects of its iterability as parasitic, derivative. A deconstructive reading would demonstrate that the hierarchy should be inverted and that *use* is but a special case of *mentioning*.

The distinction is still useful: among other things it helps us to describe how language subverts it. However much I may wish only to mention to a friend what others say about him, I effectively use these expressions, giving them meaning and force in my discourse. And no matter how wholeheartedly I may wish to "use" certain expressions, I find myself mentioning them: "I love you" is always something of a quotation, as many lovers have attested.

12. Derrida, *Limited Inc*, p. 61; "Limited Inc a b c . . . ," p. 231.

13. For discussion of this perspective, see Stanley Fish, *Is There a Text in This Class?* (Cambridge, 1980), 268–92 and 305–21; and esp. Susan Horton, *Interpreting Interpreting: Interpreting Dickens' "Dombey"* (Baltimore, 1979). In an excellent analysis of how interpretations are produced and justified, Horton argues that "each situation permits of innumerable acts of contextualizing" (p. 128) and that "what is responsible for those apparently infinite and infinitely variable interpretations of our texts, including *Dombey and Son*, is that everything else in that hermeneutical circle and not just the reader is in motion at the same time" (p. 17). Horton helped me to see that "interpretive conventions," on which Fish and I had tended to focus, should be seen as part of this boundless context. For another argument that breaks down the distinction between convention and context—but then draws the wrong conclusions—see Jay Schleusener, "Convention and the Context of Reading," *Critical Inquiry*, 6, No. 4 (Summer 1980), 669–80.

14. Searle, *Speech Acts: An Essay on the Philosophy of Language* (Cambridge, 1969), 59.

15. Derrida, *Limited Inc*, p. 47; "Limited Inc a b c . . . ," p. 215.

16. Derrida, "Signature événement contexte," p. 393; "Signature Event Context," p. 196.

17. "Signature événement contexte," pp. 391–92; "Signature Event Context," p. 194.

18. "Signature événement contexte," p. 389; "Signature Event Context," p. 192.

19. Vincent Descombes, *L'Inconscient malgré lui* (Paris, 1977), p. 85.

20. Descombes, p. 15.

21. Derrida, *Limited Inc*, p. 41; "Limited Inc a b c . . . ," p. 209. The first part of this sentence is missing from the French text of *Limited Inc*. A line of typescript has apparently been omitted from line 35 of p. 41 following "toujours."

14

Jacques Derrida
1930–

Jacques Derrida was born in Algiers and educated in France. He teaches the history of philosophy at the Ecole Normale Supérieure in Paris and teaches regularly in the United States. He is arguably one of the two or three most prominent living philosophers. While not a literary critic by training, his published work in philosophy, particularly his articulation and development of "deconstruction," has been tremendously influential on literary studies—"catalytic," as some have remarked—from the late 1960s through the present. In more recent years his influence has extended to other American studies such as theology, sociology, and the more general interdisciplinary area of "discourse theory." By some accounts Derrida has instigated a kind of revolution in the way literature is conceived in criticism and taught in university classrooms so that even those who disagree with him have responded to the impact of his work. He is a highly prolific writer on many different areas of study (including literature, art, psychology, linguistics, theater, theology, as well as philosophy). His books include: *Speech and Phenomena* (1967; trans. 1973); *Writing and Difference* (1967; trans. 1978); *Of Grammatology* (1967; trans. 1976); *Margins of Philosophy* (1972; trans. 1983); *Dissemination* (1972; trans. 1981); *Glas* (1974; trans. 1987); and *The Postcard* (1980; trans. 1987).

"Structure, Sign, and Play in the Discourses of the Human Sciences" is an early essay that Derrida presented at a conference on structuralism at Johns Hopkins University in 1966. It was his American debut right before the publication of three major works in 1967. *Writing and Difference* is a collection of essays (which included "Structure, Sign, and Play") beginning with a critique of structuralism but ranging over cultural phenomena as diverse as psychoanalysis and the theater of cruelty; *Speech and Phenomena* is a detailed critique of Husserl's phenomenology; and *Of Grammatology* is a critique of the structuralism of Saussure, Lévi-Strauss, and others by means of a close reading of Rousseau. In these works Derrida developed the deconstructive critique described in the Introduction to this section. Moreover, he critiques two philosophical positions—phenomenology and structuralism—that are diametrically opposed.

Here, in "Structure, Sign, and Play," he directs his critique specifically to the "structuralism" of Lévi-Strauss's structural anthropology. That structuralism, Derrida argues, is based on the tacit assumption, implicit in all conceptions of structure, of an opposition between the "structure" itself and a "center," which, as Derrida says, "was not only to orient, balance, and organize the structure—one cannot in fact conceive of an unorganized structure—but above all to make sure that the organizing principle of the structure would limit what we might call the *freeplay* of the structure." Such a center, however, is "not the center" because it is not "within" the "freeplay" of structurality. Structuralism, Derrida asserts, was the "rupture" and "disruption" that first became aware of the necessity of "freeplay" of structures, what Saussure, for instance, describes as the way signs, in the system or "structure" of language, can be understood as elements "each suggesting and opposing the others" (Section III). But structuralism failed, he implies, to explore "the desire for the center in the constitution of structure." Derrida explores that desire in Lévi-Strauss's work, noting the opposition within that work itself between the desire for the "freeplay" of "functional" explanation and, at the same time, a tacit desire for a center implicit in the privileging of nature over culture—"an ethic of nostalgia for origins, an ethic of archaic and natural innocence." Such privileging creates a "center"—the privileged position, in fact, *organizes* the argument of structuralism—even though structuralism itself imagined it reconceived structure. What results are "two interpretations of interpretation," one seeking grounded truth free from freeplay, the other affirming freeplay. Lévi-Strauss imagines he is following the second while he follows, willy nilly, the first. In this essay the "moves" of deconstruction described in the introduction are truncated. Structuralism itself makes the first move of reversing the value of the opposition between center and freeplay. Derrida makes the second "deconstructive" move of demonstrating that the opposition—reversed or not—can be seen to be a nonopposition, that "freeplay" and "center" are both "functional" (i.e., produced by freeplay) and organizing principles (i.e., "centers").

Structure, Sign, and Play in the Discourse of the Human Sciences[1]

Perhaps something has occurred in the history of the concept of structure that could be called an "event," if this loaded word did not entail a meaning which it is precisely the function of structural—or structuralist—thought to reduce or to suspect. But let me use the term "event" anyway, employing it with caution and as if in quotation marks. In this sense, this event will have the exterior form of a *rupture* and a *redoubling*.

It would be easy enough to show that the concept of structure and even the word "structure" itself are as old as the *epistèmè*—that is to say, as old as western science and western philosophy—and that their roots thrust deep into the soil of ordinary language, into whose deepest recesses the *epistèmè* plunges to gather them together once more, making them part of itself in a metaphorical displacement. Nevertheless, up until the event which I wish to mark out and define, structure—or rather the structurality of structure—although it has always been involved, has always been neutralized or reduced, and this by a process of giving it a center or referring it to a point of presence, a fixed origin. The function of this center was not only to orient, balance, and organize the structure–one cannot in fact conceive of an unorganized structure—but above all to make sure that the organizing principle of the structure would limit what we might call the *freeplay* of the structure. No doubt that by orienting and organizing the coherence of the system, the center of a structure permits the freeplay of its elements inside the total form. And even today the notion of a structure lacking any center represents the unthinkable itself.

Nevertheless, the center also closes off the freeplay it opens up and makes possible. *Qua* center, it is the point at which the substitution of contents, elements, or terms is no longer possible. At the center, the permutation or the transformation of elements (which may of course be structures enclosed within a structure) is forbidden. At least this permutation has always remained interdicted[2] (I use this word deliberately). Thus it has always been thought that the center, which is by definition unique, constituted that very thing within a structure which governs the structure, while escaping structurality. This is why classical thought concerning structure could say that the center is, paradoxically, *within* the structure and outside it. The center is at the center of the totality, and yet, since the center does not belong to the totality (is not part of the totality), the totality *has its center elsewhere*. The center is not the center. The concept of centered structure—although it represents coherence itself, the condition of the *epistèmè* as philosophy or science—is contradictorily coherent. And, as always, coherence in contradiction expresses the force of a desire. The concept of centered structure is in fact the concept of a freeplay based on a fundamental ground, a freeplay which is constituted upon a fundamental immobility and a reassuring certitude, which is itself beyond the reach of the freeplay. With this certitude anxiety can be mastered, for anxiety is invariably the result of a certain mode of being implicated in the game, of being caught by the game of being as it were from the very beginning at stake in the game.[3] From the basis of what we therefore call the center (and which, because it can be either inside or outside, is as readily called the origin as the end, as readily *archè as telos*), the repetitions, the substitutions, the transformations, and the permutations are always *taken* from a history of meaning [*sens*]—that is, a history, period—whose origin may always be revealed or whose end may always be anticipated in the form of presence. This is why one could perhaps say that the movement of any archeology, like that of any eschatology, is an accomplice of this reduction of the structurality of structure and always attempts to conceive of structure from the basis of a full presence which is out of play.

If this is so, the whole history of the concept of structure, before the rupture I spoke of, must be thought of as a series of substitutions of center for center, as a linked chain of determinations of the center. Successively, and in a regulated fashion, the center receives different forms or names. The history of metaphysics, like the history of the West, is the history of these metaphors and metonymies. Its matrix—if you will pardon me for demonstrating so little and for being so elliptical in order to bring me more quickly to my principal theme—*is the determination of being as presence in all the senses of this word*. It would be possible to show that all the names related to fundamentals, to principles, or to the center have always designated the constant of a presence—*eidos, archè, telos, energeia, ousia* (essence, existence, substance, subject) *aletheia*, transcendentality, consciousness, or conscience, God, man, and so forth.

The event I called a rupture, the disruption I alluded to at the beginning of this paper, would presumably have come about when the structurality of structure had to begin to be thought, that is to say, repeated, and this is why I said that this disruption was repetition in all of the senses of this word. From then on it became necessary to think the law which governed, as it were, the desire for the center in the constitution of structure and the process of signification prescribing its displacements and its substitutions for this law of the central presence—but a central presence which was never itself, which has always already been transported outside itself in its surrogate. The surrogate does not substitute itself for anything which has somehow pre-existed it. From then on it was probably necessary to begin to think that there was no center, that the center could not be thought in the form of a being-present, that the center had no natural locus, that it was not a fixed locus but a function, a sort of nonlocus in which an infinite number of sign-substitutions came into play. This moment was that in which language invaded the universal problematic; that in which, in the absence of a center or origin, everything became discourse—provided we can agree on this word—that is to say, when everything became a system where the central signified, the original or transcendental signified, is never absolutely present outside a system of differences. The absence of the transcendental signified extends the domain and the interplay of signification *ad infinitum*.

Where and how does this decentering, this notion of the structurality of structure, occur? It would be somewhat naïve to refer to an event, a doctrine, or an author in order to designate this occurrence. It is no doubt part of the totality of an era, our own, but still it has already begun to proclaim itself and begun to *work*. Nevertheless, if I wished to give some sort of indication by choosing one or two "names," and by recalling those authors in whose discourses this occurrence has most nearly maintained its most radical formulation, I would probably cite the Nietzschean critique of metaphysics, the critique of the concepts of being and truth, for which were substituted the concepts of play, interpretation, and sign (sign without truth present); the Freudian critique of self-presence, that is, the critique of consciousness, of the subject, of self-identity and of self-proximity or self-possession; and, more radically, the Heideggerean destruction of metaphysics, of onto-theology, of the determination of being as presence. But all these destructive discourses and all their analogues are trapped in a sort of circle. This circle is unique. It describes the form of the relationship between the history of metaphysics and the destruction of the history of metaphysics. There is no sense in doing without the concepts of the metaphysics in order to attack metaphysics. We have no language—no syntax and no lexicon—which is alien to this history; we cannot utter a single destructive proposition which has not already slipped into the form, the logic, and the implicit postulations of precisely what it seeks to contest. To pick out one example from many: the metaphysics of presence is attacked with the help of the concept of the sign. But from the moment anyone wishes this to show, as I suggested a moment ago, that there is no transcendental or privileged signified and that the domain or the interplay of signification has, henceforth, no limit, he ought to extend this refusal to the concept and to the word sign itself—which is precisely what cannot be done.

For the signification "sign" has always been comprehended and determined, in its sense, as sign-of, signifier referring to a signified, signifier different from its signified. If one erases the radical difference between signifier and signified, it is the word signifier itself which ought to be abandoned as a metaphysical concept. When Lévi-Strauss says in the preface to *The Raw and the Cooked*[4] that he has "sought to transcend the opposition between the sensible and the intelligible by placing [himself] from the very beginning at the level of signs," the necessity, the force, and the legitimacy of his act cannot make us forget that the concept of the sign cannot in itself surpass or bypass this opposition between the sensible and the intelligible. The concept of the sign is determined by this opposition: through and throughout the totality of its history and by its system. But we cannot do without the concept of the sign, we cannot give up this metaphysical complicity without also giving up the critique we are directing against this complicity, without the risk of erasing difference [altogether] in the self-identity of a signified reducing into itself its signifier, or, what amounts to the same thing, simply expelling it outside itself. For there are two heterogeneous ways of erasing the difference between the signifier and the signified: one, the classic way, consists in reducing or deriving the signifier, that is to say, ultimately in *submitting* the sign to thought; the other, the one we are using here against the first one, consists in putting into question the system in which the preceding reduction functioned: first and foremost, the opposition between the sensible and the intelligible. The *paradox* is that the metaphysical reduction of the sign needed the opposition it was reducing. The opposition is part of the system, along with the reduction. And what I am saying here about the sign can be extended to all the concepts and all the sentences of metaphysics, in particular to the discourse on "structure." But there are many ways of being caught in this circle. They are all more or less naïve, more or less empirical, more or less systematic, more or less close to the formulation or even to the formalization of this circle. It is these differences which explain the multiplicity of destructive discourses and the disagreement between those who make them. It was within concepts inherited from metaphysics that Nietzsche, Freud, and Heidegger worked, for example. Since these concepts are not elements or atoms and since they are taken from a syntax and a system, every particular borrowing drags along with it the whole of metaphysics. This is what allows these destroyers to destroy each other reciprocally—for example, Heidegger considering Nietzsche, with as much lucidity and rigor as bad faith and misconstruction, as the last metaphysician, the last "Platonist." One could do the same for Heidegger himself, for Freud, or for a number of others. And today no exercise is more widespread.

What is the relevance of this formal schéma when we turn to what are called the "human sciences"? One of them perhaps occupies a privileged place—ethnology. One can in fact assume that ethnology could have been born as a science only at the moment when a decentering had come about: at the moment when European culture—and, in consequence, the history of metaphysics and of its concepts—had been *dislocated*, driven from its locus, and forced to stop considering itself as the culture of reference. This moment is not first and foremost a moment of philosophical or scientific discourse, it is also a moment which is political, economic, technical, and so forth. One can say in total assurance that there is nothing fortuitous about the fact that the critique of ethnocentrism—the very condition of ethnology—should be systematically and historically contemporaneous with the destruction of the history of metaphysics. Both belong to a single and same era.

Ethnology—like any science—comes about within the element of discourse. And it is primarily a European science employing traditional concepts, however much it may struggle against them. Consequently, whether he wants to or not—and this does not depend on a decision on his part—the ethnologist accepts into his discourse the premises of ethnocentrism at the very moment when he is employed in denouncing them. This necessity is irreducible; it is not a historical contingency. We ought to consider very carefully all its implications. But if nobody can escape this necessity, and if no one is therefore responsible for giving in to it, however little, this does not mean that all the ways of giving in to it are of an equal pertinence. The quality and the fecundity of a discourse are perhaps measured by the critical rigor with which this relationship to the history of metaphysics and to inherited concepts is thought. Here it is a question of a critical relationship to the language of the human sciences and a question of a critical responsibility of the discourse. It is a question of putting expressly and systematically the problem of the status of a discourse which borrows from a heritage the resources necessary for the deconstruction of that heritage itself. A problem of *economy* and *strategy*.

If I now go on to employ an examination of the texts of Lévi-Strauss as an example, it is not only because of the privilege accorded to ethnology among the human sciences, nor yet because the thought of Lévi-Strauss weighs heavily on the contemporary theoretical situation. It is above all because a certain choice has made itself evident in the work of Lévi-Strauss and because a certain doctrine has been elaborated there, and precisely in a *more or less explicit manner*, in relation to this critique of language and to this critical language in the human sciences.

In order to follow this movement in the text of Lévi-Strauss, let me choose as one guiding thread among others the opposition between nature and culture. In spite of all its rejuvenations and its disguises, this opposition is congenital to philosophy. It is even older than Plato. It is at least as old as the Sophists. Since the statement of the opposition—*physis/nomos, physis/technè*—it has been passed on to us by a whole historical chain which opposes "nature" to the law, to education, to art, to technics—and also to liberty, to the arbitrary, to history, to society, to the mind, and so on. From the beginnings of his quest and from his first book, *The Elementary Structures of Kinship*,[5] Lévi-Strauss has felt at one and the same time the necessity of utilizing this opposition and the impossibility of making it acceptable. In the *Elementary Structures*, he begins from this axiom or definition: that belongs to nature which is *universal* and spontaneous, not depending on any particular culture or on any determinate norm. That belongs to culture, on the other hand, which depends on a system of norms regulating society and is therefore capable of *varying* from one social structure to another. These two definitions are of the traditional type. But, in the very first pages of the *Elementary Structures*, Lévi-Strauss, who has begun to give these concepts an acceptable standing, encounters what he calls a *scandal*, that is to say, something which no longer tolerates the nature/culture opposition he has accepted and which seems to require *at one and the same time* the predicates of nature and those of culture. This scandal is the *incest-prohibition*. The incest-prohibition is universal; in this sense one could call it natural. But it is also a prohibition, a system of norms and interdicts; in this sense one could call it cultural.

> Let us assume therefore that everything universal in man derives from the order of nature and is characterized by spontaneity, that everything which is subject to a norm belongs to culture and presents the attributes of the relative and the particular. We then find ourselves confronted by a fact, or rather an ensemble of facts, which, in the light of the preceding definitions, is not far from appearing as a scandal: the prohibition of incest presents without the least equivocation, and indissolubly linked together, the two characteristics in which we recognized the contradictory attributes of two exclusive orders. The prohibition of incest constitutes a rule, but a rule, alone of all the social rules, which possesses at the same time a universal character (p. 9).

Obviously there is no scandal except in the *interior* of a system of concepts sanctioning the difference between nature and culture. In beginning his work with the *factum* of the incest-prohibition, Lévi-Strauss thus puts himself in a position entailing that this difference, which has always been assumed to be self-evident, becomes obliterated or disputed. For, from the moment that the incest-prohibition can no longer be conceived within the nature/culture opposition, it can no longer be said that it is a scandalous fact, a nucleus of opacity within a network of transparent significations. The incest-prohibition is no longer a scandal one meets with or comes up against in the domain of traditional concepts; it is something which escapes these concepts and certainly precedes them—probably as the condition of their possibility. It could perhaps be said that the whole of philosophical conceptualization, systematically relating itself to the nature/culture opposition, is designed to leave in the domain of the unthinkable the very thing that makes this conceptualization possible: the origin of the prohibition of incest.

I have dealt too cursorily with this example, only one among so many others, but the example nevertheless reveals that language bears within itself the necessity of its own critique. This critique may be undertaken along two tracks, in two "manners." Once the limit of nature/culture opposition makes itself felt, one might want to question systematically and rigorously the history of these concepts. This is a first action. Such a systematic and historic questioning would be neither a philological nor a philosophical action in the classic sense of these words. Concerning oneself with the founding concepts of the whole history of philosophy, de-constituting them, is not to undertake the task of the philologist or of the classic historian of philosophy. In spite of appearances, it is probably the most daring way of making the beginnings of a step outside of philosophy. The step "outside philosophy" is much more difficult to conceive than is generally imagined by those who think they made it long ago with cavalier ease, and who are in general swallowed up in metaphysics by the whole body of the discourse that they claim to have disengaged from it.

In order to avoid the possibly sterilizing effect of the first way, the other choice—which I feel corresponds more nearly to the way chosen by Lévi-Strauss—consists in conserving in the field of empirical discovery all these old concepts, while at the same time exposing here and there their limits, treating them as tools which can still be of use. No longer is any truth-value attributed to them; there is a readiness to abandon them if necessary if other instruments should appear more useful. In the meantime, their relative efficacy is exploited, and they are employed to destroy the old machinery to which they belong and of which they themselves are pieces. Thus it is that the language of the human sciences criticizes *itself*. Lévi-Strauss thinks that in this way he can separate *method* from *truth*, the instruments of the method and the objective significations aimed at by it. One could almost say that this is the primary affirmation of Lévi-Strauss; in any event, the first words of the *Elementary Structures* are: "One begins to understand that the distinction between state of nature and state of society (we would be more apt to say today: state of nature and state of culture), while lacking any acceptable historical signification, presents a value which fully justifies its use by modern sociology: its value as a methodological instrument."

Lévi-Strauss will always remain faithful to this double intention: to preserve as an instrument that whose truth-value he criticizes.

On the one hand, he will continue in effect to contest the value of the nature/culture opposition. More than thirteen years after the *Elementary Structures, The Savage Mind*[6] faithfully echoes the text I have just quoted: "The opposition between nature and culture which I have previously insisted on seems today to offer a value which is above all methodological." And this methodological value is not affected by its "ontological" non-value (as could be said, if this notion were not suspect here): "It would not be enough to have absorbed particular humanities into a general humanity; this first enterprise prepares the way for others . . . which belong to the natural and exact sciences: to reintegrate culture into nature, and finally, to reintegrate life into the totality of its physiochemical conditions" (p. 327).

On the other hand, still in *The Savage Mind*, he presents as what he calls *bricolage*[7] what might be called the discourse of this method. The *bricoleur*, says Lévi-Strauss, is someone who uses "the means at hand," that is, the instruments he finds at his disposition around him, those which are already there, which had not been especially conceived with an eye to the operation for which they are to be used and to which one tries by trial and error to adapt them, not hesitating to change them whenever it appears necessary, or to try several of them at once, even if their form and their origin are heterogeneous—and so forth. There is therefore a critique of language in the form of *bricolage*, and it has even been possible to say that *bricolage* is the critical language itself. I am thinking in particular of the article by G. Genette, "Structuralisme et Critique littéraire," published in homage to Lévi-Strauss in a special issue of *L'Arc* (no. 26, 1965), where it is stated that the analysis of *bricolage* could "be applied almost word for word" to criticism, and especially to "literary criticism."[8]

If one calls *bricolage* the necessity of borrowing one's concepts from the text of a heritage which is more or less coherent or ruined, it must be said that every discourse is *bricoleur*. The engineer, whom Lévi-Strauss opposes to the *bricoleur*, should be the one to construct the totality of his language, syntax, and lexicon. In this sense the engineer is a myth. A subject who would supposedly be the absolute origin of his own discourse and would supposedly construct it "out of nothing," "out of whole cloth," would be the creator of the *verbe*, the *verbe* itself. The notion of the engineer who had supposedly broken with all forms of *bricolage* is therefore a theological idea; and since Lévi-Strauss tells us elsewhere that *bricolage* is mythopoetic, the odds are that the engineer is a myth produced by the *bricoleur*. From the moment that we cease to believe in such an engineer and in a discourse breaking with the received historical discourse, as soon as it is admitted that every finite discourse is bound by a certain *bricolage*, and that the engineer and the scientist are also species of *bricoleurs* then the very idea of *bricolage* is menaced and the difference in which it took on its meaning decomposes.

This brings out the second thread which might guide us in what is being unraveled here.

Lévi-Strauss describes *bricolage* not only as an intellectual activity but also as a mythopoetical activity. One reads in *The Savage Mind*, "Like *bricolage* on the technical level, mythical reflection can attain brilliant and unforeseen results on the intellectual level. Reciprocally, the mythopoetical character of *bricolage* has often been noted" (p. 26).

But the remarkable endeavor of Lévi-Strauss is not simply to put forward, notably in the most recent of his investigations, a structural science or knowledge of myths and of mythological activity. His endeavor also appears—I would say almost from the first—in the status which he accords to his own discourse on myths, to what he calls his "mythologicals." It is here that his discourse on the myth reflects on itself and criticizes itself. And this moment, this critical period, is evidently of concern to all the languages which share the field of the human sciences. What does Lévi-Strauss say of his "mythologicals"? It is here that we rediscover the mythopoetical virtue (power) of *bricolage*. In effect, what appears most fascinating in this critical search for a new status of the discourse is the stated abandonment of all reference to a center, to a *subject*, to a privileged *reference*, to an origin, or to an absolute *archè*. The theme of this decentering could be followed throughout the "Overture" to his last book, *The Raw and the Cooked*. I shall simply remark on a few key points.

1. From the very start, Lévi-Strauss recognizes that the Bororo myth which he employs in the book as the "reference-myth" does not merit this name and this treatment. The name is specious and the use of the myth improper. This myth deserves no more than any other its referential privilege:

   > In fact the Bororo myth which will from now on be designated by the name reference-myth is, as I shall try to show, nothing other than a more or less forced transformation of other myths originating either in the same society or in societies more or less far removed. It would therefore have been legitimate to choose as my point of departure any representative of the group whatsoever. From this point of view, the interest of the reference-myth does not depend on its typical character, but rather on its irregular position in the midst of a group (p. 10).

2. There is no unity or absolute source of the myth. The focus or the source of the myth are always shadows and virtualities which are elusive, unactualizable, and nonexistent in the first place. Everything begins with the structure, the configuration, the relationship. The discourse on this acentric structure, the myth, that is, cannot itself have an absolute subject or an absolute center. In order not to short change the form and the movement of the myth, that violence which consists in centering a language which is describing an acentric structure must be avoided. In this context, therefore, it is necessary to forego scientific or philosophical discourse, to renounce the *epistèmè* which absolutely requires, which is the absolute requirement that we go back to the source, to the center, to the founding basis, to the principle, and so on. In opposition to *epistèmic* discourse, structural discourse on myths—mythological discourse—must itself be *mythomorphic*. It must have the form of that of which it speaks. This is what Lévi-Strauss says in *The Raw and the Cooked*, from which I would now like to quote a long and remarkable passage:

   > In effect the study of myths poses a methodological problem by the fact that it cannot conform to the Cartesian principle of dividing the difficulty into as many parts as are necessary to resolve it. There exists no veritable end or term to mythical analysis, no secret unity which

> could be grasped at the end of the work of decomposition. The themes duplicate themselves to infinity. When we think we have disentangled them from each other and can hold them separate, it is only to realize that they are joining together again, in response to the attraction of unforeseen affinities. In consequence, the unity of the myth is only tendential and projective; it never reflects a state or a moment of the myth. An imaginary phenomenon implied by the endeavor to interpret, its role is to give a synthetic form to the myth and to impede its dissolution into the confusion of contraries. It could therefore be said that the science or knowledge of myths is an *anaclastic,* taking this ancient term in the widest sense authorized by its etymology, a science which admits into its definition the study of the reflected rays along with that of the broken ones. But, unlike philosophical reflection, which claims to go all the way back to its source, the reflections in question here concern rays without any other than a virtual focus. . . . In wanting to imitate the spontaneous movement of mythical thought, my enterprise, itself too brief and too long, has had to yield to its demands and respect its rhythm. Thus is this book, on myths itself and in its own way, a myth.

This statement is repeated a little farther on (p. 20): "Since myths themselves rest on second-order codes (the first-order codes being those in which language consists), this book thus offers the rough draft of a third-order code, destined to insure the reciprocal possibility of translation of several myths. This is why it would not be wrong to consider it a myth: the myth of mythology, as it were." It is by this absence of any real and fixed center of the mythical or mythological discourse that the musical model chosen by Lévi-Strauss for the composition of his book is apparently justified. The absence of a center is here the absence of a subject and the absence of an author: "The myth and the musical work thus appear as orchestra conductors whose listeners are the silent performers. If it be asked where the real focus of the work is to be found, it must be replied that its determination is impossible. Music and mythology bring man face to face with virtual objects whose shadow alone is actual. . . . Myths have no authors" (p. 25).

Thus it is at this point that ethnographic *bricolage* deliberately assumes its mythopoetic function. But by the same token, this function makes the philosophical or epistemological requirement of a center appear as mythological, that is to say, as a historical illusion.

Nevertheless, even if one yields to the necessity of what Lévi-Strauss has done, one cannot ignore its risks. If the mythological is mythomorphic, are all discourses on myths equivalent? Shall we have to abandon any epistemological requirement which permits us to distinguish between several qualities of discourse on the myth? A classic question, but inevitable. We cannot reply—and I do not believe Lévi-Strauss replies to it—as long as the problem of the relationships between the philosopheme or the theorem, on the one hand, and the mytheme or the mythopoem(e), on the other, has not been expressly posed. This is no small problem. For lack of expressly posing this problem, we condemn ourselves to transforming the claimed transgression of philosophy into an unperceived fault in the interior of the philosophical field. Empiricism would be the genus of which these faults would always be the species. Transphilosophical concepts would be transformed into philosophical naïvetés. One could give many examples to demonstrate this risk: the concepts of sign, history, truth, and so forth. What I want to emphasize is simply that the passage beyond philosophy does not consist in turning the page of philosophy (which usually comes down to philosophizing badly), but in continuing to read philosophers *in a cer-*

tain way. The risk I am speaking of is always assumed by Lévi-Strauss and it is the very price of his endeavor. I have said that empiricism is the matrix of all the faults menacing a discourse which continues, as with Lévi-Strauss in particular, to elect to be scientific. If we wanted to pose the problem of empiricism and *bricolage* in depth, we would probably end up very quickly with a number of propositions absolutely contradictory in relation to the status of discourse in structural ethnography. On the one hand, structuralism justly claims to be the critique of empiricism. But at the same time there is not a single book or study by Lévi-Strauss which does not offer itself as an empirical essay which can always be completed or invalidated by new information. The structural schemata are always proposed as hypotheses resulting from a finite quantity of information and which are subjected to the proof of experience. Numerous texts could be used to demonstrate this double postulation. Let us turn once again to the "Overture" of *The Raw and the Cooked,* where it seems clear that if this postulation is double, it is because it is a question here of a language on language:

> Critics who might take me to task for not having begun by making an exhaustive inventory of South American myths before analyzing them would be making a serious mistake about the nature and the role of these documents. The totality of the myths of a people is of the order of the discourse. Provided that this people does not become physically or morally extinct, this totality is never closed. Such a criticism would therefore be equivalent to reproaching a linguist with writing the grammar of a language without having recorded the totality of the words which have been uttered since that language came into existence and without knowing the verbal exchanges which will take place as long as the language continues to exist. Experience provides that an absurdly small number of sentences . . . allows the linguist to elaborate a grammar of the language he is studying. And even a partial grammar or an outline of a grammar represents valuable acquisitions in the case of unknown languages. Syntax does not wait until it has been possible to enumerate a theoretically unlimited series of events before becoming manifest, because syntax consists in the body of rules which presides over the generation of these events. And it is precisely a syntax of South American mythology that I wanted to outline. Should new texts appear to enrich the mythical discourse, then this will provide an opportunity to check or modify the way in which certain grammatical laws have been formulated, an opportunity to discard certain of them and an opportunity to discover new ones. But in no instance can the requirement of a total mythical discourse be raised as an objection. For we have just seen that such a requirement has no meaning (pp. 15–16).

Totalization is therefore defined at one time as *useless,* at another time as *impossible.* This is no doubt the result of the fact that there are two ways of conceiving the limit of totalization. And I assert once again that these two determinations coexist implicitly in the discourses of Lévi-Strauss. Totalization can be judged impossible in the classical style: one then refers to the empirical endeavor of a subject or of a finite discourse in a vain and breathless quest of an infinite richness which it can never master. There is too much, more than one can say. But nontotalization can also be determined in another way: not from the standpoint of the concept of finitude as assigning us to an empirical view, but from the standpoint of the concept of *freeplay.* If totalization no longer has any meaning, it is not because the infinity of a field cannot be covered by a finite glance or a finite discourse, but because the nature of the field —that is, language and a finite language— excludes totalization. This field is in fact that of *freeplay,* that is to say, a field of infinite substitutions in the closure of a finite ensemble. This field permits these infinite substitutions only because it is finite, that is to say, because instead of being an inexhaustible field, as in the classical hypothesis, instead of being too large, there is something missing from it: a center which arrests and founds the freeplay of substitutions. One could say—rigorously using that word whose scandalous signification is always obliterated in French—that this movement of the freeplay, permitted by the lack, the absence of a center or origin, is the movement of *supplementarity*. One cannot determine the center, the sign which *supplements*[9] it, which takes its place in its absence—because this sign adds itself, occurs in addition, over and above, comes as a *supplement*.[10] The movement of signification adds something, which results in the fact that there is always more, but this addition is a floating one because it comes to perform a vicarious function, to supplement a lack on the part of the signified. Although Lévi-Strauss in his use of the word supplementary never emphasizes as I am doing here the two directions of meaning which are so strangely compounded within it, it is not by chance that he uses this word twice in his "Introduction to the Work of Marcel Mauss,"[11] at the point where he is speaking of the "superabundance of signifier, in relation to the signifieds to which this superabundance can refer":

> In his endeavor to understand the world, man therefore always has at his disposition a surplus of signification (which he portions out amongst things according to the laws of symbolic thought—which it is the task of ethnologists and linguists to study). This distribution of a *supplementary* allowance [*ration* supplémentaire]—if it is permissible to put it that way—is absolutely necessary in order that on the whole the available signifier and the signified it aims at may remain in the relationship of complementarity which is the very condition of the use of symbolic thought (p. xlix).

(It could no doubt be demonstrated that this *ration supplémentaire* of signification is the origin of the *ratio* itself.) The word reappears a little farther on, after Lévi-Strauss has mentioned "this floating signifier, which is the servitude of all finite thought":

> In other words—and taking as our guide Mauss's precept that all social phenomena can be assimilated to language—we see in *mana, Wakau, oranda* and other notions of the same type, the conscious expression of a semantic function, whose role it is to permit symbolic thought to operate in spite of the contradiction which is proper to it. In this way are explained the apparently insoluble antinomies attached to this notion. . . . At one and the same time force and action, quality and state, substantive and verb; abstract and concrete, omnipresent and localized—*mana* is in effect all these things. But is it not precisely because it is none of these things that *mana* is a simple form, or more exactly, a symbol in the pure state, and therefore capable of becoming charged with any sort of symbolic content whatever? In the system of symbols constituted by all cosmologies, mana would simply be a *valeur symbolique zéro*, that is to say, a sign marking the necessity of a symbolic content *supplementary* [my italics] to that with which the signified is already loaded, but which can take on any value required, provided only that this value still remains part of the available reserve and is not, as phonologists put it, a group-term.

Lévi-Strauss adds the note:

> Linguists have already been led to formulate hypotheses of this type. For example: "A zero phoneme is opposed to all the other phonemes in French in that it entails no differential characters and no constant phonetic value. On the contrary, the proper function of the zero phoneme is to be opposed to phoneme absence." (R. Jakobson and J. Lutz, "Notes on the French Phonemic Pattern," *Word*, vol. 5, no. 2 [August, 1949], p. 155). Similarly, if we schematize the conception I am proposing here, it could almost be said that the function of notions like *mana* is to be opposed to the absence of signification, without entailing by itself any particular signification (p. 1 and note).

The superabundance of the signifier, its *supplementary* character, is thus the result of a finitude, that is to say, the result of a lack which must be *supplemented*.

It can now be understood why the concept of freeplay is important in Lévi-Strauss. His references to all sorts of games, notably to roulette, are very frequent, especially in his *Conversations*,[12] in *Race and History*,[13] and in *The Savage Mind*. This reference to the game or freeplay is always caught up in a tension.

It is in tension with history, first of all. This is a classical problem, objections to which are now well worn or used up. I shall simply indicate what seems to me the formality of the problem: by reducing history, Lévi-Strauss has treated as it deserves a concept which has always been in complicity with a teleological and eschatological metaphysics, in other words, paradoxically, in complicity with that philosophy of presence to which it was believed history could be opposed. The thematic of historicity, although it seems to be a somewhat late arrival in philosophy, has always been required by the determination of being as presence. With or without etymology, and in spite of the classic antagonism which opposes these significations throughout all of classical thought, it could be shown that the concept of *epistèmè* has always called forth that of *historia*, if history is always the unity of a becoming, as tradition of truth or development of science or knowledge oriented toward the appropriation of truth in presence and self-presence, toward knowledge in consciousness-of-self.[14] History has always been conceived as the movement of a resumption of history, a diversion between two presences. But if it is legitimate to suspect this concept of history, there is a risk, if it is reduced without an express statement of the problem I am indicating here, of falling back into an ahistoricism of a classical type, that is to say, in a determinate moment of the history of metaphysics. Such is the algebraic formality of the problem as I see it. More concretely, in the work of Lévi-Strauss it must be recognized that the respect for structurality, for the internal originality of the structure, compels a neutralization of time and history. For example, the appearance of a new structure, of an original system, always comes about—and this is the very condition of its structural specificity—by a rupture with its past, its origin, and its cause. One can therefore describe what is peculiar to the structural organization only by not taking into account, in the very moment of this description, its past conditions: by failing to pose the problem of the passage from one structure to another, by putting history into parentheses. In this "structuralist" moment, the concepts of chance and discontinuity are indispensable. And Lévi-Strauss does in fact often appeal to them as he does, for instance, for that structure of structures, language, of which he says in the "Introduction to the Work of Marcel Mauss" that it "could only have been born in one fell swoop":

> Whatever may have been the moment and the circumstances of its appearance in the scale of animal life, language could only have been born in one fell swoop. Things could not have set about signifying progressively. Following a transformation the study of which is not the concern of the social sciences, but rather of biology and psychology, a crossing over came about from a stage where nothing had a meaning to another where everything possessed it (p. xlvi).

This standpoint does not prevent Lévi-Strauss from recognizing the slowness, the process of maturing, the continuous toil of factual transformations, history (for example, in *Race and History*). But, in accordance with an act which was also Rousseau's and Husserl's, he must "brush aside all the facts" at the moment when he wishes to recapture the specificity of a structure. Like Rousseau, he must always conceive of the origin of a new structure on the model of catastrophe—an overturning of nature in nature, a natural interruption of the natural sequence, a brushing aside of nature.

Besides the tension of freeplay with history, there is also the tension of freeplay with presence. Freeplay is the disruption of presence. The presence of an element is always a signifying and substitutive reference inscribed in a system of differences and the movement of a chain. Freeplay is always an interplay of absence and presence, but if it is to be radically conceived, freeplay must be conceived of before the alternative of presence and absence; being must be conceived of as presence or absence beginning with the possibility of freeplay and not the other way around. If Lévi-Strauss, better than any other, has brought to light the freeplay of repetition and the repetition of freeplay, one no less perceives in his work a sort of ethic of presence, an ethic of nostalgia for origins, an ethic of archaic and natural innocence, of a purity of presence and self-presence in speech[15]—an ethic, nostalgia, and even remorse which he often presents as the motivation of the ethnological project when he moves toward archaic societies—exemplary societies in his eyes. These texts are well known.

As a turning toward the presence, lost or impossible, of the absent origin, this structuralist thematic of broken immediateness is thus the sad, *negative*, nostalgic, guilty, Rousseauist facet of the thinking of freeplay of which the Nietzschean *affirmation*—the joyous affirmation of the freeplay of the world and without truth, without origin, offered to an active interpretation—would be the other side. *This affirmation then determines the non-center otherwise than as loss of the center.* And it plays the game without security. For there is a sure freeplay: that which is limited to the *substitution of given and existing, present,* pieces. In absolute chance, affirmation also surrenders itself to genetic indetermination, to the *seminal* adventure of the trace.[16]

There are thus two interpretations of interpretation, of structure, of sign, of freeplay. The one seeks to decipher, dreams of deciphering, a truth or an origin which is free from freeplay and from the order of the sign, and lives like an exile the necessity of interpretation. The other, which is no longer turned toward the origin, affirms freeplay and tries to pass beyond man and humanism, the name man being the name of that being who, throughout the history of metaphysics or of ontotheology—in other words, through the history of all of his history—has dreamed of full presence, the reassuring foundation, the origin and the end of the game. The second interpretation of interpretation, to which Nietzsche showed us the way, does not seek in ethnography, as Lévi-Strauss wished, the "inspiration of a new humanism" (again from the "Introduction to the Work of Marcel Mauss").

There are more than enough indications today to suggest we might perceive that these two interpretations of interpretation—which are absolutely irreconcilable even if we live them simultaneously and reconcile them in an obscure economy—together share the field which we call, in such a problematic fashion, the human sciences.

For my part, although these two interpretations must acknowledge and accentuate their difference and define their irreducibility, I do not believe that today there is any question of *choosing*—in the first place because here we are in a region (let's say, provisionally, a region of historicity) where the category of choice seems particularly trivial; and in the second, because we must first try to conceive of the common ground, and the *différance* of this irreducible difference.[17] Here there is a sort of question, call it historical, of which we are only glimpsing today the *conception, the formation, the gestation, the labor*. I employ these words, I admit, with a glance toward the business of child-bearing—but also with a glance toward those who, in a company from which I do not exclude myself, turn their eyes away in the face of the as yet unnameable which is proclaiming itself and which can do so, as is necessary whenever a birth is in the offing, only under the species of the nonspecies, in the formless, mute, infant, and terrifying form of monstrosity.

DISCUSSION

Jean Hyppolite: I should simply like to ask Derrida, whose presentation and discussion I have admired, for some explanation of what is, no doubt, the technical point of departure of the presentation. That is, a question of the concept of the center of structure, or what a center might mean. When I take, for example, the structure of certain algebraic constructions [*ensembles*], where is the center? Is the center the knowledge of general rules which, after a fashion, allow us to understand the interplay of the elements? Or is the center certain elements which enjoy a particular privilege within the ensemble?

My question is, I think, relevant since one cannot think of the structure without the center, and the center itself is "destructured," is it not?—the center is not structured. I think we have a great deal to learn as we study the sciences of man; we have much to learn from the natural sciences. They are like an image of the problems which we, in turn, put to ourselves. With Einstein, for example, we see the end of a kind of privilege of empiric evidence. And in that connection we see a constant appear, a constant which is a combination of spacetime, which does not belong to any of the experimenters who live the experience, but which, in a way, dominates the whole construct; and this notion of the constant—is this the center? But natural science has gone much further. It no longer searches for the constant. It considers that there are events, somehow improbable, which bring about for a while a structure and an invariability. Is it that everything happens as though certain mutations, which don't come from any author or any hand, and which are, like the poor reading of a manuscript, realized [only] as a defect of a structure, simply exist as mutations? Is this the case? Is it a question of a structure which is in the nature of a genotype produced by chance from an improbable happening, of a meeting which involved a series of chemical molecules and which organized them in a certain way, creating a genotype which will be realized, and whose origin is lost in a mutation? Is that what you are tending toward? Because, for my part, I feel that I am going in that direction and that I find there the example—even when we are talking about a kind of end of history—of the integration of the historic; under the form of *event*, so long as it is improbable, at the very center of the realization of the structure, but a history which no longer has anything to do with eschatological history, a history which loses itself always in its own pursuit, since the origin is perpetually displaced. And you know that the language we are speaking today, *á propos* of language, is spoken about genotypes, and about information theory. Can this sign without sense, this perpetual turning back, be understood in the light of a kind of philosophy of nature in which nature will not only have realized a mutation, but will have realized a perpetual mutant: man? That is, a kind of error of transmission or of malformation would have created a being which is always malformed, whose adaptation is a perpetual aberration, and the problem of man would become part of a much larger field in which what you want to do, what you are in the process of doing, that is, the loss of the center—the fact that there is no privileged or original structure—could be seen under this very form to which man would be restored. Is this what you wanted to say, or were you getting at something else? That is my last question, and I apologize for having held the floor so long.

JACQUES DERRIDA: With the last part of your remarks, I can say that I agree fully—but you were asking a question. I was wondering myself if I know where I am going. So I would answer you by saying, first, that I am trying, precisely, to put myself at a point so that I do not know any longer where I am going. And, as to this loss of the center, I *refuse* to approach an idea of the "non-center" which would no longer be the tragedy of the loss of the center—this sadness is classical. And I don't mean to say that I thought of approaching an idea by which this loss of the center would be an affirmation.

As to what you said about the nature and the situation of man in the products of nature, I think that we have already discussed this together. I will assume entirely with you this partiality which you expressed—with the exception of your [choice of] words, and here the words are more than mere words, as always. That is to say, I cannot accept your precise formulation, although I am not prepared to offer a precise alternative. So, it being understood that I do not know where I am going, that the words which we are using do not satisfy me, with these reservations in mind, I am entirely in agreement with you.

Concerning the first part of your question, the Einsteinian constant is not a constant, is not a center. It is the very concept of variability—it is, finally, the concept of the game. In other words, it is not the concept of *something*—of a center starting from which an observer could master the field—but the very concept of the game which, after all, I was trying to elaborate.

HYPPOLITE:: It is a constant in the game?

DERRIDA: It is *the* constant of the game . . .

HYPPOLITE: It is the rule of the game.

DERRIDA: It is a rule of the game which does not govern the game; it is a rule of the game which does not dominate the game. Now, when the rule of the game is displaced by the game itself, we must find something other than the word *rule*. In what concerns algebra, then, I think that it is an example in which a group of significant figures, if you wish, or of signs, is deprived of a center. But we can consider algebra from two points of view. Either as the example or analogue of this absolutely de-centered game of which I have spoken; or we can try to consider algebra as a limited field of ideal objects, products in the Husserlian sense, beginning from a history, from a *Lebenswelt*, from a subject, etc., which constituted, created its ideal objects, and consequently we should always be able to make substitutions, by reactivating in it the origin—that of which the significants, seemingly lost, are the derivations. I think it is in this way that algebra was thought of classically. One could, perhaps, think of it otherwise as an image of the game. Or else one thinks of algebra as a field of ideal objects, produced by the activity of what we call a subject, or man, or history, and thus, we recover the possibility of algebra in the field of classical thought; or else we consider it as a disquieting mirror of a world which is algebraic through and through.

HYPPOLITE: What is a structure then? If I can't take the example of algebra anymore, how will you define a structure for me?—to see where the center is.

DERRIDA: The concept of structure itself—I say in passing—is no longer satisfactory to describe that game. How to define structure? Structure should be centered. But this center can be either thought, as it was classically, like a creator or being or a fixed and natural place; or also as a deficiency, let's say; or something which makes possible "freeplay," in the sense in which one speaks of the "jeu dans la machine," of the "jeu des pièces," and which receives—and this is what we call history—a series of determinations, of signifiers, which have no signifieds [signifiés] finally, which cannot become signifiers except as they begin from this deficiency. So, I think that what I have said can be understood as a criticism of structuralism, certainly.

RICHARD MACKSEY: I may be off-side [*hors jeu*] in trying to identify prematurely those players who can join your team in the critique of metaphysics represented by your tentative game-theory. Still, I was struck by the sympathy with which two contemporary figures might view that formidable prospect which you and Nietzsche invite us to contemplate. I am thinking, first, of the later career of Eugen Fink, a "reformed" phenomenologist with the peculiarly paradoxical relationship to Heidegger. Even as early as the colloquia at Krefeld and Royaumont he was prepared to argue the secondary status of the conceptual world, to see *Sein, Wahrheit*, and *Welt* as irreducibly part of a single, primal question. Certainly in his *Vor-Fragen* and in the last chapter of the Nietzsche book he advances a Zarathustrian notion of game as the step outside (or behind) philosophy. It is interesting to contrast his Nietzsche with Heidegger's; it seems to me that you would agree with him in reversing the latter's primacy of *Sein* over Seiendes, and thereby achieve some interesting consequences for the post-humanist critique to our announced topic, "les sciences humaines." For surely, in *Spiel als Weltsymbol* the presiding World-game is profoundly anterior and anonymous, anterior to the Platonic division of being and appearance and dispossessed of a human, personal center.

The other figure is that writer who has made the shifting center of his fictional poetics the narrative game in "the *unanimous* night," that architect and prisoner of labyrinths, the creator of Pierre Menard.

DERRIDA: You are thinking, no doubt, of Jorge Luis Borges.

CHARLES MORAZÉ: Just a remark. Concerning the dialogue of the past twenty years with Lévi-Strauss on the possibility of a grammar other than that of language—I have a great deal of admiration for what Lévi-Strauss has done in the order of a grammar of mythologies. I would like to point out that there is also a grammar of the event—that one can make a grammar of the event. It is more difficult to establish. I think that in the coming months, in the coming years, we will begin to learn how this grammar or rather this set of grammars of events can be constituted. And [this grammar] leads to results, may I say, anyway with regard to my personal experience, which are a little less pessimistic than those you have indicated.

LUCIEN GOLDMANN: I would like to say that I find that Derrida, with whose conclusions I do not agree, has a catalytic function in French cultural life, and for that reason I pay him homage. I said once that he brings to my mind that memory of when I arrived in France in '34. At that time there was a very strong royalist movement among the students and suddenly a group appeared which was equally in defense of royalism, but which demanded a real Merovingian king!

In this movement of negation of the subject or of the center, if you like, which Derrida defines remarkably, he is in the process of saying to all the people who represent this position, "But you contradict yourself; you never carry through to the end. Finally, in criticizing mythologies, if you deny the position, the existence, of the critic and the necessity of saying anything, you contradict yourself, because you are still M. Lévi-Strauss who says something and if you make a new mythology. . . ." Well, the criticism was remarkable and it's not worth taking it up again. But if I have noted the few words which were added to the text and which were of a destructive character, we could discuss that on the level of semiology. But I would like to ask Derrida a question: "Let us suppose that instead of discussing on the basis of a series of postulates toward which all contemporary currents, irrationalist as well as formalist, are oriented, you have before you a very different position, say the dialectical position. Quite simply, you think that science is something that men make, that history is not an error, that what you call theology is something acceptable, an attempt not to say that the world is ordered, that it is theological, but that the human being is one who places his stake on the possibility of giving a meaning to a word which will eventually, at some point, resist this meaning. And the origin or the fundamental of that which is before a typical state of dichotomy of which you speak (or in grammatology the action which registers before there is a meaning) is something which we are studying today, but which we cannot, which we don't even want to, penetrate from the inside, because it can be penetrated from the inside only in silence, while we want to understand it according to the logic which we have elaborated, with which we try somehow or other to go farther, not to discover a meaning hidden by some god, but to give a meaning to a world in which that is the function of man (without knowing, moreover, where man comes from—we can't be entirely consistent, because if the question is clear, we know, if we say that man comes from God, then somebody will ask "Where does God come from?" and if we say that man comes from nature, somebody will ask "Where does nature come from?" and so on). But we are on the inside and we are in this situation. Is this position before you, then, still contradictory?

Jan Kott: At one time this famous phrase of Mallarmé seemed to be very significant: "A throw of dice will never abolish chance." ["Un coup de dés n'abolira jamais le hasard,"] After this lesson you have given us, isn't it possible to say that: "And chance will never abolish the throw of dice!" ["Et le hasard n'abolira jamais le coup de dés."]

Derrida: I say "Yes" immediately to Mr. Kott. As to what Mr. Goldmann has said to me, I feel that he has isolated, in what I said, the aspect that he calls destructive. I believe, however, that I was quite explicit about the fact that nothing of what I said had a destructive meaning. Here or there I have used the word *déconstruction,* which has nothing to do with destruction. That is to say, it is simply a question of (and this is a necessity of criticism in the classical sense of the word) being alert to the implications, to the historical sedimentation of the language which we use—and that is not destruction. I believe in the necessity of scientific work in the classical sense, I believe in the necessity of everything which is being done and even of what you are doing, but I don't see why I should renounce or why anyone should renounce the radicality of a critical work under the pretext that it risks the sterilization of science, humanity, progress, the origin of meaning, etc. I believe that the risk of sterility and of sterilization has always been the price of lucidity. Concerning the initial anecdote, I take it rather badly, because it defines me as an ultra-royalist, or an "ultra," as they said in my native country not so long ago, whereas I have a much more humble, modest, and classical conception of what I am doing.

Concerning Mr. Morazé's allusion to the grammar of the event, there I must return his question, because I don't know what a grammar of the event can be.

SERGE DOUBROVSKY: You always speak of a *non-center*. How can you, within your own perspective, explain or at least understand what a perception is? For a perception is precisely the manner in which the world appears *centered* to me. And language you represent as flat or level. Now language is something else again. It is, as Merleau-Ponty said, a corporeal intentionality. And starting from this utilization of language, in as much as there is an intention of language, I inevitably find a center again. For it is not "One" who speaks, but "I." And even if you reduce the I, you are obliged to come across once again the concept of intentionality, which I believe is at the base of a whole thought, which, moreover, you do not deny. Therefore I ask how you reconcile it with your present attempts?

DERRIDA: First of all, I didn't say that there was no center, that we could get along without the center. I believe that the center is a function, not a being—a reality, but a function. And this function is absolutely indispensable. The subject is absolutely indispensable. I don't destroy the subject; I situate it. That is to say, I believe that at a certain level both of experience and of philosophical and scientific discourse one cannot get along without the notion of subject. It is a question of knowing where it comes from and how it functions. Therefore I keep the concept of center, which I explained was indispensable, as well as that of subject, and the whole system of concepts to which you have referred.

Since you mentioned intentionality, I simply try to see those who are founding the movement of intentionality—which cannot be conceived in the term intentionality. As to perception, I should say that once I recognized it as a necessary conservation. I was extremely conservative. Now I don't know what perception is and I don't believe that anything like perception exists. Perception is precisely a concept, a concept of an intuition or of a given originating from the thing itself, present itself in its meaning, independently from language, from the system of reference. And I believe that perception is interdependent with the concept of origin and of center and consequently whatever strikes at the metaphysics of which I have spoken strikes also at the very concept of perception. I don't believe that there is any perception.

Translated by Richard Macksey

NOTES

1. "La Structure, le signe et le jeu dans le discours des sciences humaines." The text which follows is a translation of the revised version of M. Derrida's communication. The word "jeu" is variously translated here as "play," "interplay," "game," and "stake," besides the normative translation "freeplay." All footnotes to this article are additions by the translator.

2. Interdite: "forbidden," "disconcerted," "confounded," "speechless."

3. ". . . qui naît toujours d'une certaine manière d'être impliqué dans le jeu, d'être pris au jeu, d'être comme être d'entrée de jeu dans le jeu."

4. *Le crut et le cuit* (Paris: Plon, 1964).

5. *Les structures élémentaires de la parenté* (Paris: Presses Universitaires de France, 1949).

6. *La pensée sauvage* (Paris: Plon, 1962).

7. A *bricoleur* is a jack-of-all trades, someone who potters about with odds-and-ends, who puts things together out of bits and pieces.

8. Reprinted in: G. Genette, *Figures* (Paris: Editions du Seuil, 1966), p. 145.

9. The point being that the word, both in English and French, means "to supply a deficiency," on the one hand, and "to supply something additional," on the other.

10. ". . . ce signe s'ajoute, vient en sus, en supplément."

11. "Introduction à l'oeuvre de Marcel Mauss," in: Marcel Mauss, *Sociologie et anthropologie* (Paris: Presses Universitaires de France, 1950).

12. Presumably: G. Charbonnier, *Entretiens avec Claude Lévi-Strauss* (Paris: Plon-Julliard, 1961).

13. *Race and History* (Paris: UNESCO Publications, 1958).

14. ". . . l'unité d'un devenir, comme tradition de la vérité dans la présence et la présence à soi, vers le savoir dans la conscience de soi."

15. ". . . de la présence à soi dans la parole."

16. "Tournée vers la présence, perdue ou impossible, de l'origine absente, cette thématique structuraliste de l'immédiateté rompue est donc la face triste, négative, nostalgique, coupable, rousseauiste, de la pensée du jeu dont *l'affirmation* nietzschéenne, l'affirmation joyeuse du jeu du monde et de l'innocence du devenir, l'affirmation d'un monde de signes sans faute, sans vérité, sans origine, offert à une interprétation active, serait l'autre face. Cette *affirmation* détermine alors le non-centre autrement que comme perte du centre. Et elle joue sans sécurité. Car il y a un jeu sûr: celui qui se limite à la substitution de piéces données et existantes, présentes. Dans le hasard absolu, l'affirmation se livre aussi à l'indétermination génétique, à l'aventure séminale de la trace."

17. From différer, in the sense of "to postpone," "put off," "defer." Elsewhere Derrida uses the word as a synonym for the German *Aufschub:* "Postponement," and relates it to the central Freudian concepts of *Verspätung, Nachträglichkeit,* and to the "détours to death" of *Beyond the Pleasure Principle* by Sigmund Freud (Standard Edition, ed. James Strachey, vol. XIX, London, 1961), Chap. V.

15

Paul de Man
1919–1983

Paul de Man was born in Antwerp and received a Ph.D. from Harvard University in 1960. At the time of his death he was Sterling Professor of French and comparative literature at Yale University. In the course of his academic career—especially in its last decade—he became a major intellectual force in American literary studies. In large part this was due to his early and articulate understanding of the importance of Continental philosophy to literary studies and the ease with which he moved between philosophy and literature and among English, French, and German texts. His major form was the philosophical-literary essay, written in a severe and difficult, yet rewarding style. All his books are collections of essays, including: *Blindness and Insight: Essays in the Rhetoric of Contemporary Criticism* (1971, rpt. 1983); *Allegories of Reading: Figural Language in Rousseau, Nietzsche, Rilke, and Proust* (1979); *The Rhetoric of Romanticism* (1984); and *The Resistance to Theory* (1986).

In important ways de Man's work most clearly articulated the literary implications of post-World War II Continental philosophy. In his early work he described a kind of Sartrean existential approach to literature, and later he turned to the phenomenological criticism occasioned by Husserl and Heidegger. But his major work is marked by the influence of Nietzsche and poststructuralist thought—especially that of Jacques Derrida—and, with his Yale colleagues J. Hillis Miller and Geoffrey Hartman, he helped to define a distinctively American brand of deconstructive literary criticism.

The following essay, "Semiology and Rhetoric" (1979), is part of this effort. In it de Man attempts to articulate and then render "undecidable" the difference between two seemingly incompatible yet self-evident ways of understanding language: language as rule-oriented "grammar" capable of being decoded so that its "unproblematic" meaning becomes clear; and language as "rhetoric," which "is a reading, not a decodage," and which consequently undermines the certainties grammar implies. "The grammatical model of the question becomes rhetorical," de Man asserts, "not when we have, on the one hand, a literal meaning and on the other hand a figural meaning, but when it is impossible to decide by grammatical or linguistic devices which of the two meanings (that can be entirely incompatible) prevails. Rhetoric radically suspends logic and opens up vertiginous possibilities of referential aberration." Here is a classic deconstructive gesture: through a rigorously logical argument and a rigorously close reading, de Man arrives at a conclusion that undermines (or deconstructs) the logic of its premises and procedures, not to demonstrate the preferability of one mode of understanding over another (of rhetoric over semiology, for instance), but to confront the reader with what de Man calls an "aporia," the simultaneous necessity and impossibility of choosing between incompatible options. His ultimate aim is to place the reader in a new relationship with the text, now conceived not as a source of authoritative information, but as a way of reconceiving "self-evident" truths.

Semiology and Rhetoric

To judge from various recent publications, the spirit of the times is not blowing in the direction of formalist and intrinsic criticism. We may no longer be hearing too much about relevance but we keep hearing a great deal about reference, about the nonverbal "outside" to which language refers, by which it is conditioned and upon which it acts. The stress falls not so much on the fictional status of literature—a property now perhaps somewhat too easily taken for granted—but on the interplay between these fictions and categories that are said to partake of reality, such as the self, man, society, "the artist, his culture and the human community," as one critic puts it. Hence the emphasis on hybrid texts considered to be partly literary and partly referential, on popular fictions deliberately aimed towards social and psychological gratification, on literary autobiography as a key to the understanding of the self, and so on. We speak as if, with the problems of literary form resolved once and forever, and with the techniques of structural analysis refined to near-perfection, we could now move "beyond formalism" towards the questions that really interest us and reap, at last, the fruits of the ascetic concentration on techniques that prepared us for this decisive step. With the internal law and order of literature well policed, we can now confidently devote ourselves to the foreign affairs, the external politics of literature. Not only do we feel able to do so, but we owe it to ourselves to take this step: our moral conscience would not allow us to do otherwise. Behind the assurance that valid interpretation is possible, behind the recent interest in writing and reading as potentially effective public speech acts, stands a highly respectable moral imperative that strives to reconcile the internal, formal, private structures of literary language with their external, referential, and public effects.

I want, for the moment, to consider briefly this tendency in itself, as an undeniable and recurrent historical fact, without regard for its truth or falseness or for its value as desirable or pernicious. It is a fact that this sort of thing happens, again and again, in literary studies. On the one hand, literature cannot merely be received as a definite unit of referential meaning that can be decoded without leaving a residue. The code is unusually conspicuous, complex, and enigmatic; it attracts an inordinate amount of attention to itself, and this attention has to acquire the rigor of a method. The structural moment of concentration on the code for its own sake cannot be avoided, and literature necessarily breeds its own formalism. Technical innovations in the methodical study of literature only occur when this kind of attention predominates. It can legitimately be said, for example, that, from a technical point of view, very little has happened in American criticism since the innovative works of New Criticism. There certainly have been numerous excellent books of criticism since, but in none of them have the techniques of description and interpretation evolved beyond the techniques of close reading established in the thirties and the forties. Formalism, it seems, is an all-absorbing and tyrannical muse; the hope that one can be at the same time technically original and discursively eloquent is not borne out by the history of literary criticism.

On the other hand—and this is the real mystery—no literary formalism, no matter how accurate and enriching in its analytic powers, is ever allowed to come into being without seeming reductive. When form is considered to be the external trappings of literary meaning or content, it seems superficial and expendable. The development of intrinsic, formalist criticism in the twentieth century has changed this model: form is now a solipsistic category of self-reflection, and the referential meaning is said to be extrinsic. The polarities of inside and outside have been reversed, but they are still the same polarities that are at play: internal meaning has become outside reference, and the outer form has become the intrinsic structure. A new version of reductiveness at once follows this reversal: formalism nowadays is mostly described in an imagery of imprisonment and claustrophobia: the "prison house of language," "the impasse of formalist criticism," etc. Like the grandmother in Proust's novel ceaselessly driving the young Marcel out into the garden, away from the unhealthy inwardness of his closeted reading, critics cry out for the fresh air of referential meaning. Thus, with the structure of the code so opaque, but the meaning so anxious to blot out the obstacle of form, no wonder that the reconciliation of form and meaning would be so attractive. The attraction of reconciliation is the elective breeding-ground of false models and metaphors; it accounts for the metaphorical model of literature as a kind of box that separates an inside from an outside, and the reader or critic as the person who opens the lid in order to release in the open what was secreted but inaccessible inside. It matters little whether we call the inside of the box the content or the form, the outside the meaning or the appearance. The recurrent debate opposing intrinsic to extrinsic criticism stands under the aegis of an inside/outside metaphor that is never being seriously questioned.

Metaphors are much more tenacious than facts, and I certainly don't expect to dislodge this age-old model in one short try. I merely wish to speculate on a different set of terms, perhaps less simple in their differential relationships than the strictly polar, binary opposition between inside and outside and therefore less likely to enter into the easy play of chiasmic reversals. I derive these terms (which are as old as the hills) pragmatically from the observation of developments and debates in recent critical methodology.

One of the most controversial among these developments coincides with a new approach to poetics or, as it is called in Germany, poetology, as a branch of general semiotics. In France, a semiology of literature comes about as the outcome of the long-deferred but all the more explosive encounter of the nimble French literary mind with the category of form. Semiology, as opposed to semantics, is the science or study of signs as signifiers; it does not ask what words mean but how they mean. Unlike American New Criticism, which derived the internalization of form from the practice of highly self-conscious modern writers, French semiology turned to linguistics for its model and adopted Saussure and Jakobson rather than Valéry or Proust for its masters. By an awareness of the arbitrariness of the sign (Saussure) and of literature as an autotelic statement "focused on the way it is expressed" (Jakobson) the entire question of meaning can be bracketed, thus freeing the critical discourse from the debilitating burden of paraphrase. The demystifying power of semiology, within the context of French historical and thematic criticism, has been considerable. It demonstrated that the perception of the literary dimensions of language is largely obscured if one submits uncritically to the authority of reference. It also revealed how tenaciously this authority continues to assert itself in a variety of disguises, ranging from the crudest ideology to the most refined forms of aesthetic and ethical judgment. It especially explodes the myth of semantic correspondence between sign and referent, the wishful hope of having it both ways, of being, to paraphrase Marx in the German Ideology, a formalist critic in the morning and a communal moralist in the afternoon, of serving both the technique of form and the substance of meaning. The results, in the practice of French criticism, have been as fruitful as they are irreversible. Perhaps for the first time since the late eighteenth century, French critics can come at least somewhat closer to the kind of linguistic awareness that never ceased to be operative in its poets and novelists and that forced all of them, including Sainte Beuve, to write their main works "contre Sainte Beuve." The distance was never so considerable in England and the United States, which does not mean, however, that we may be able, in this country, to dispense altogether with some preventive semiological hygiene.

One of the most striking characteristics of literary semiology as it is practiced today, in France and elsewhere, is the use of grammatical (especially syntactical) structures conjointly with rhetorical structures, without apparent awareness of a possible discrepancy between them. In their literary analyses, Barthes, Genette, Todorov, Greimas, and their disciples all simplify and regress from Jakobson in letting grammar and rhetoric function in perfect continuity, and in passing from grammatical to rhetorical structures without difficulty or interruption. Indeed, as the study of grammatical structures is refined in contemporary theories of generative, transformational, and distributive grammar, the study of tropes and of figures (which is how the term *rhetoric* is used here, and not in the derived sense of comment or of eloquence or persuasion) becomes a mere extension of grammatical models, a particular subset of syntactical relations. In the recent *Dictionnaire encyclopédique des sciences du langage*, Ducrot and Todorov write that rhetoric has always been satisfied with a paradigmatic view over words (words substituting for each other), without questioning their syntagmatic relationship (the contiguity of words to each other). There ought to be another perspective, complementary to the first, in which metaphor, for example, would not be defined as a substitution but as a particular type of combination. Research inspired by linguistics or, more narrowly, by syntactical studies, has begun to reveal this possibility—but it remains to be explored. Todorov, who calls one of his books a *Grammar of the Decameron*, rightly thinks of his own work and that of his associates as first explorations in the elaboration of a systematic grammar of literary modes, genres, and also of literary figures. Perhaps the most perceptive work to come out of this school, Genette's studies of figural modes, can be shown to be assimilations of rhetorical transformations or combinations to syntactical, grammatical patterns. Thus a recent study, now printed in *Figures III* and entitled *Metaphor and Metonymy in Proust*, shows the combined presence, in a wide and astute selection of passages, or paradigmatic, metaphorical figures with syntagmatic, metonymic structures. The combination of both is treaded descriptively and nondialectically without considering the possibility of logical tensions.

One can ask whether this reduction of figure to grammar is legitimate. The existence of grammatical structures, within and beyond the unit of the sentence, in literary texts is undeniable, and their description and classification are indispensable. The question remains if and how figures of rhetoric can be included in such a taxonomy. This question is at the core of the debate going on, in a wide variety of apparently unrelated forms, in contemporary poetics. But the historical picture of contemporary criticism is too confused to make the mapping out of such a topography a useful exercise. Not only are these questions mixed in and mixed up within particular groups or local trends, but they are often co-present, without apparent contradiction, within the work of a single author.

Neither is the theory of the question suitable for quick expository treatment. To distinguish the epistemology of grammar from the epistemology of rhetoric is a redoubtable task. On an entirely naïve level, we tend to conceive of grammatical systems as tending towards universality and as simply generative, i.e., as capable of deriving an infinity of versions from a single model (that may govern transformations as well as derivations) without the intervention of another model that would upset the first. We therefore think of the relationship between grammar and logic, the passage from grammar to propositions, as being relatively unproblematic: no true propositions are conceivable in the absence of grammatical consistency or of controlled deviation from a system of consistency no matter how complex. Grammar and logic stand to each other in a dyadic relationship of unsubverted support. In a logic of acts rather than of statements, as in Austin's theory of speech acts, that has had such a strong influence on recent American work in literary semiology, it is also possible to move between speech acts and grammar without difficulty. The performance of what is called illocutionary acts such as ordering, questioning, denying, assuming, etc., within the language is congruent with the grammatical structures of syntax in the corresponding imperative, interrogative, negative, optative sentences. "The rules for illocutionary acts," writes Richard Ohman in a recent paper, "determine whether performance of a given act is well-executed, in just the same way as *grammatical* rules determine whether the product of a locutionary act—a sentence—is well formed. . . . But whereas the rules of grammar concern the relationships among sound, syntax, and meaning, the rules of illocutionary acts concern relationships among people."[1] And since rhetoric is then conceived exclusively as persuasion, as actual action upon others (and not as an intralinguistic figure or trope), the continuity between the illocutionary realm of grammar and the perlocutionary realm of rhetoric is self-evident. It becomes the basis for a new rhetoric that, exactly as is the case for Todorov and Genette, would also be a new grammar.

Without engaging the substance of the question, it can be pointed out, without having to go beyond recent and American examples, and without calling upon the strength of an age-old tradition, that the continuity here assumed between grammar and rhetoric is not borne out by theoretical and philosophical speculation. Kenneth Burke mentions *deflection* (which he compares structurally to Freudian displacement), defined as "any slight bias or even unintended error," as the rhetorical basis of language, and deflection is then conceived as a dialectical subversion of the consistent link between sign and meaning that operates within grammatical patterns; hence Burke's well-known insistence on the distinction between grammar and rhetoric. Charles Sanders Peirce, who, with Nietzsche and Saussure, laid the philosophical foundation for modern semiology, stressed the distinction between grammar and rhetoric in his celebrated and so suggestively unfathomable definition of the sign. He insists, as is well known, on the necessary presence of a third element, called the interpretant, within any relationship that the sign entertains with its object. The sign is to be interpreted if we are to understand the idea it is to convey, and this is so because the sign is not the thing but a meaning derived from the thing by a process here called representation that is not simply generative, i.e., dependent on a univocal origin. The interpretation of the sign is not, for Peirce, a meaning but another sign; it is a reading, not a decodage, and this reading has, in its turn, to be interpreted into another sign, and so on *ad infinitum*. Peirce calls this process by means of which "one sign gives birth to another" pure rhetoric, as distinguished from pure grammar, which postulates the possibility of unproblematic, dyadic meaning, and pure logic, which postulates the possibility of the universal truth of meanings. Only if the sign engendered meaning in the same way that the object engenders the sign, that is, by representation, would there be no need to distinguish between grammar and rhetoric.

These remarks should indicate at least the existence and the difficulty of the question, a difficulty which puts its concise theoretical exposition beyond my powers. I must retreat therefore into a pragmatic discourse and try to illustrate the tension between grammar and rhetoric in a few specific textual examples. Let me begin by considering what is perhaps the most commonly known instance of an apparent symbiosis between a grammatical and a rhetorical structure, the so-called rhetorical question, in which the figure is conveyed directly by means of a syntactical device. I take the first example from the sub-literature of the mass media: asked by his wife whether he wants to have his bowling shoes laced over or laced under, Archie Bunker answers with a question: "What's the difference?" Being a reader of sublime simplicity, his wife replies by patiently explaining the difference between lacing over and lacing under, whatever this may be, but provokes only ire. "What's the difference" did not ask for difference but means instead "I don't give a damn what the difference is." The same grammatical pattern engenders two meanings that are mutually exclusive: the literal meaning asks for the concept (difference) whose existence is denied by the figurative meaning. As long as we are talking about bowling shoes, the consequences are relatively trivial; Archie Bunker, who is a great believer in the authority of origins (as long, of course, as they are the right origins) muddles along in a world where literal and figurative meanings get in each other's way, though not without discomforts. But suppose that it is a *de*-bunker rather than a "Bunker," and a de-bunker of the arche (or origin), an archie Debunker such as Nietzsche or Jacques Derrida for instance, who asks the question "What is the Difference"—and we cannot even tell from his grammar whether he "really" wants to know "what" difference is or is just telling us that we shouldn't even try to find out. Confronted with the question of the difference between grammar and rhetoric, grammar allows us to ask the question, but the sentence by means of which we ask it may deny the very possibility of asking. For what is the use of asking, I ask, when we cannot even authoritatively decide whether a question asks or doesn't ask?

The point is as follows. A perfectly

clear syntactical paradigm (the question) engenders a sentence that has at least two meanings, of which the one asserts and the other denies its own illocutionary mode. It is not so that there are simply two meanings, one literal and the other figural, and that we have to decide which one of these meanings is the right one in this particular situation. The confusion can only be cleared up by the intervention of an extratextual intention, such as Archie Bunker putting his wife straight; but the very anger he displays is indicative of more than impatience; it reveals his despair when confronted with a structure of linguistic meaning that he cannot control and that holds the discouraging prospect of an infinity of similar future confusions, all of them potentially catastrophic in their consequences. Nor is this intervention really a part of the mini-text constituted by the figure which holds our attention only as long as it remains suspended and unresolved. I follow the usage of common speech in calling this semiological enigma "rhetorical." The grammatical model of the question becomes rhetorical not when we have, on the one hand, a literal meaning and on the other hand a figural meaning, but when it is impossible to decide by grammatical or other linguistic devices which of the two meanings (that can be entirely incompatible) prevails. Rhetoric radically suspends logic and opens up vertiginous possibilities of referential aberration. And although it would perhaps be somewhat more remote from common usage, I would not hesitate to equate the rhetorical, figural potentiality of language with literature itself. I could point to a greater number of antecedents to this equation of literature with figure; the most recent reference would be to Monroe Beardsley's insistence in his contribution to the *Essays* to honor William Wimsatt, that literary language is characterized by being "distinctly above the norm in ratio of implicit [or, I would say rhetorical] to explicit meaning."[2]

Let me pursue the matter of the rhetorical question through one more example. Yeats's poem, "Among School Children" ends with the famous line: "How can we know the dancer from the dance?" Although there are some revealing inconsistencies within the commentaries, the line is usually interpreted as stating, with the increased emphasis of a rhetorical device, the potential unity between form and experience, between creator and creation. It could be said that it denies the discrepancy between the sign and the referent from which we started out. Many elements in the imagery and the dramatic development of the poem strengthen this traditional reading; without having to look any further than the immediately preceding lines, one finds powerful and consecrated images of the continuity from part to whole that makes synecdoche into the most seductive of metaphors: the organic beauty of the tree, stated in the parallel syntax of a similar rhetorical question, or the convergence, in the dance, of erotic desire with musical form:

> O chestnut-tree, great-rooted blossomer,
> Are you the leaf, the blossom or the bole?
> O body swayed to music. O brightening glance,
> How can we know the dancer from the dance?

A more extended reading, always assuming that the final line is to be read as a rhetorical question, reveals that the thematic and rhetorical grammar of the poem yields a consistent reading that extends from the first line to the last and that can account for all the details in the text. It is equally possible, however, to read the last line literally rather than figuratively, as asking with some urgency the question we asked earlier with the context of contemporary criticism: *not* that sign and referent are so exquisitely fitted to each other that all difference between them is at times blotted out but, rather, since the two essentially different elements, sign and meaning, are so intricately intertwined in the imagined "presence" that the poem addresses, how can we possibly make the distinctions that would shelter us from the error of identifying what cannot be identified? The clumsiness of the paraphrase reveals that it is not necessarily the literal reading which is simpler than the figurative one, as was the case in our first example; here, the figural reading, which assumes the question to be rhetorical, is perhaps naïve, whereas the literal reading leads to greater complication of theme and statement. For it turns out that the entire scheme set up by the first reading can be undermined, or deconstructed, in the terms of the second, in which the final line is read literally as meaning that, since the dancer and the dance are not the same, it might be useful, perhaps even desperately necessary—for the question can be given a ring of urgency, "Please tell me, how *can* I know the dancer from the dance"—to tell them apart. But this will replace the reading of each symbolic detail by a divergent interpretation. The oneness of trunk, leaf, and blossom, for example, that would have appealed to Goethe, would find itself replaced by the much less reassuring Tree of Life from the Mabinogion that appears in the poem "Vacillation," in which the fiery blossom and the earthly leaf are held together, as well as apart, by the crucified and castrated God Attis, of whose body it can hardly be said that it is "not bruised to pleasure soul." This hint should suffice to suggest that two entirely coherent but entirely incompatible readings can be made to hinge on one line, whose grammatical structure is devoid of ambiguity, but whose rhetorical mode turns the mood as well as the mode of the entire poem upside down. Neither can we say, as was already the case in the first example, that the poem simply has two meanings that exist side by side. The two readings have to engage each other in direct confrontation, for the one reading is precisely the error denounced by the other and has to be undone by it. Nor can we in any way make a valid decision as to which of the readings can be given priority over the other; none can exist in the other's absence. There can be no dance without a dancer, no sign without a referent. On the other hand, the authority of the meaning engendered by the grammatical structure is fully obscured by the duplicity of a figure that cries out for the differentiation that it conceals.

Yeats's poem is not explicitly "about" rhetorical questions but about images or metaphors, and about the possibility of convergence between experiences of consciousness such as memory or emotions—what the poem calls passion, piety, and affection—and entities accessible to the senses such as bodies, persons, or icons. We return to the inside/outside model from which we started out and which the poem puts into question by means of a syntactical device (the question) made to operate on a grammatical as well as on a rhetorical level. The couple grammar/rhetoric, certainly not a binary opposition since they in no way exclude each other, disrupts and confuses the neat antithesis of the inside/outside pattern. We can transfer this scheme to the act of reading and interpretation. By reading we get, as we say, *inside* a text that was first something alien to us and which we now make our own by an act of understanding. But this understanding becomes at once the representation of an extra-textual meaning; in Austin's terms, the illocutionary speech act becomes a perlocutionary actual act—in Frege's terms, *Bedeutung* becomes *Sinn*. Our recurrent question is whether this transformation is semantically controlled along grammatical or along rhetorical lines. Does the metaphor of reading really unite outer meaning with inner understanding, action with reflection, into one single totality? The assertion is powerfully and suggestively made in a passage from Proust that describes the experience of reading as such a union. It describes the young Marcel, near the beginning of Combray, hiding in the closed space of his room in order to read. The example differs from the earlier ones in that we are not dealing with a grammatical structure that also functions rhetorically but have instead the representation, the dramatization, in terms of the experience of a subject, of a rhetorical structure—just as, in many other passages, Proust dramatizes tropes by means of landscapes or descriptions of objects. The figure here dramatized is that of metaphor, an inside/outside correspondence as represented by the act of reading. The reading scene is the culmination of a series of actions taking place in enclosed spaces and leading up to the "dark coolness" of Marcel's room.

> I had stretched out on my bed, with a book, in my room which sheltered, tremblingly, its transparent and fragile coolness from the afternoon sun, behind the almost closed blinds through which a glimmer of daylight had nevertheless managed to push its yellow wings, remaining motionless between the wood and the glass, in a corner, poised like a butterfly. It was hardly light enough to read, and the sensation of the light's splendor was given me only by the noise of Camus . . . hammering dusty crates; resounding in the sonorous atmosphere that is peculiar to hot weather, they seemed to spark off scarlet stars; and also by the flies executing their little concert, the chamber music of summer: evocative not in the manner of a human tune that, heard perchance during the summer, afterwards reminds you of it but connected to summer by a more necessary link: born from beautiful days, resurrecting only when they return, containing some of their essence, it does not only awaken their image in our memory; it guarantees their return, their actual, persistent, unmediated presence.
>
> The dark coolness of my room related to the full sunlight of the street as the shadow relates to the ray of light, that is to say it was just as luminous and it gave my imagination the total spectacle of the summer, whereas my senses, if I had been on a walk, could only have enjoyed it by fragments; it matched my repose which (thanks to the adventures told by my book and stirring my tranquility) supported, like the quiet of a motionless hand in the middle of a running brook the shock and the motion of a torrent of activity. [*Swann's Way*. Paris: Pléiade, 1954, p. 83.]

For our present purpose, the most striking aspect of this passage is the juxtaposition of figural and metafigural language. It contains seductive metaphors that bring into play a variety of irresistible objects: chamber music, butterflies, stars, books, running brooks, etc., and it inscribes these objects within dazzling fire- and waterworks of figuration. But the passage also comments normatively on the best way to achieve such effects; in this sense, it is metafigural: it writes figuratively about figures. It contrasts two ways of evoking the natural experience of summer and unambiguously states its preference for one of these ways over the other: the "necessary link" that unites the buzzing of the flies to the summer makes it a much more effective symbol than the tune heard "perchance" during the summer. The preference is expressed by means of a distinction that corresponds to the difference between metaphor and metonymy, necessity and chance being a legitimate way to distinguish between analogy and contiguity. The inference of identity and totality that is constitutive of metaphor is lacking in the purely relational metonymic contact: an element of truth is involved in taking Achilles for a lion but none in taking Mr. Ford for a motor car. The passage is *about* the aesthetic superiority of metaphor over metonymy, but this aesthetic claim is made by means of categories that are the ontological ground of the metaphysical system that allows for the aesthetic to come into being as a category. The metaphor for summer (in this case, the synesthesia set off by the "chamber music" of the flies) guarantees a presence which, far from being contingent, is said to be essential, permanently recurrent and unmediated by linguistic representations or figurations. Finally, in the second part of the passage, the metaphor of presence not only appears as the ground of cognition but as the performance of an action, thus promising the reconciliation of the most disruptive of contradictions. By then, the investment in the power of metaphor is such that it may seem sacrilegious to put it in question.

Yet, it takes little perspicacity to show that the text does not practice what it preaches. A rhetorical reading of the passage reveals that the figural praxis and the metafigural theory do not converge and that the assertion of the mastery of metaphor over metonymy owes its persuasive power to the use of metonymic structures. I have carried out such an analysis in a somewhat more extended context . . . ; at this point, we are more concerned with the results than with the procedure. For the metaphysical categories of presence, essence, action, truth, and beauty do not remain unaffected by such a reading. This would become clear from an inclusive reading of Proust's novel or would become even more explicit in a language-conscious philosopher such as Nietzsche who, as a philosopher, has to be concerned with the epistemological consequences of the kind of rhetorical seductions exemplified by the Proust passage. It can be shown that the systematic critique of the main categories of metaphysics undertaken by Nietzsche in his late work, the critique of the concepts of causality, of the subject, of identity, of referential and revealed truth, etc., occurs along the same pattern of deconstruction that was operative in Proust's text; and it can also be shown that this pattern exactly corresponds to Nietzsche's description, in texts that precede *The Will to Power* by more than fifteen years, of the structure of the main rhetorical tropes. The key to this critique of metaphysics, which is itself a recurrent gesture throughout the history of thought, is the rhetorical model of the trope or, if one prefers to call it that, literature. It turns out that in these innocent-looking didactic exercises we are in fact playing for very sizeable stakes.

It is therefore all the more necessary to know what is linguistically involved in a rhetorically conscious reading of the type here undertaken on a brief fragment from a novel and extended by Nietzsche to the entire text of post-Hellenic thought. Our first examples dealing with the rhetorical questions were rhetorizations of grammar, figures generated by syntactical paradigms, whereas the Proust example could be better described as a grammatization of rhetoric. By passing from a paradigmatic structure based on substitution, such as metaphor, to a syntagmatic structure based on contingent association such as metonymy, the mechanical, repetitive aspect of grammatical forms is shown to be operative in a passage that seemed at first sight to celebrate the self-willed and autonomous inventiveness of a subject. Figures are assumed to be inventions, the products of a highly particularized individual talent, whereas no one can claim credit for the programmed pattern of grammar. Yet, our reading of the Proust passage shows that precisely when the highest claims are being made for the unifying power of metaphor, these very images rely in fact on the deceptive use of semi-automatic grammatical patterns. The deconstruction of metaphor and of all rhetorical patterns such as mimesis, paranomasis, or personification that use resemblance as a way to disguise differences, takes us back to the impersonal precision of grammar and of a semiology derived from grammatical patterns. Such a reading puts into question a whole series of concepts that underlie the value judgments of our critical discourse: the metaphors of primacy, of genetic history, and, most notably, of the autonomous power to will of the self.

There seems to be a difference, then, between what I called the rhetorization of grammar (as in the rhetorical question) and the grammatization of rhetoric, as in the readings of the type sketched out in the passage from Proust. The former end up in indetermination, in a suspended uncertainty that was unable to choose between two modes of reading, whereas the latter seems to reach a truth, albeit by the negative road of exposing an error, a false pretense. After the rhetorical reading of the Proust passage, we can no longer believe the assertion made in this passage about the intrinsic, metaphysical superiority of metaphor over metonymy. We seem to end up in a mood of negative assurance that is highly productive of critical discourse. The further text of Proust's novel, for example, responds perfectly to an extended application of this pattern: not only can similar gestures be repeated throughout the novel, at all the crucial articulations or all passages where large aesthetic and metaphysical claims are being made—the scenes of involuntary memory, the workshop of Elstir, the septette of Vinteuil, the convergence of author and narrator at the end of the novel—but a vast thematic and semiotic network is revealed that structures the entire narrative and that remained invisible to a reader caught in naïve metaphorical mystification. The whole of literature would respond in similar fashion, although the techniques and the patterns would have to vary considerably, of course, from author to author. But there is absolutely no reason why analyses of the kind here suggested for Proust would not be applicable, with proper modifications of technique, to Milton or to Dante or to Hölderlin. This will in fact be the task of literary criticism in the coming years.

It would seem that we are saying that criticism is the deconstruction of literature, the reduction to the rigors of grammar of rhetorical mystifications. And if we hold up Nietzsche as the philosopher of such a critical deconstruction, then the literary critic would become the philosopher's alley in his struggle with the poets. Criticism and literature would separate around the epistemological axis that distinguishes grammar from rhetoric. It is easy enough to see that this apparent glorification of the critic-philosopher in the name of truth is in fact a glorification of the poet as the primary source of this truth; if truth is the recognition of the systematic character of a certain kind of error, then it would be fully dependent on the prior existence of this error. Philosophers of science like Bachelard or Wittgenstein are notoriously dependent on the aberrations of the poets. We are back at our unanswered question: does the grammatization of rhetoric end up in negative certainty or does it, like the rhetorization of grammar, remain suspended in the ignorance of its own truth or falsehood?

Two concluding remarks should suffice to answer the question. First of all, it is not true that Proust's text can simply be reduced to the mystified assertion (the superiority of metaphor over metonymy) that our reading deconstructs. The reading is not "our" reading, since it uses only the linguistic elements provided by the text itself; the distinction between author and reader is one of the false distinctions that the reading makes evident. The deconstruction is not something we have added to the text but it constituted the text in the first place. A literary text simultaneously asserts and denies the authority of its own rhetorical mode, and by reading the text as we did we were only trying to come closer to being as rigorous a reader as the author had to be in order to write the sentence in the first place. Poetic writing is the most advanced and refined mode of deconstruction; it may differ from critical or discursive writing in the economy of its articulation, but not in kind.

But if we recognize the existence of such a moment as constitutive of all literary language, we have surreptitiously reintroduced the categories that this deconstruction was supposed to eliminate and that have merely been displaced. We have, for example, displaced the question of the self from the referent into the figure of the narrator, who then becomes the *signifié* of the passage. It becomes again possible to ask such naïve questions as what Proust's, or Marcel's, motives may have been in thus manipulating language: was he fooling himself, or was he represented as fooling himself and fooling us into believing that fiction and action are as easy to unite, by reading, as the passage asserts? The pathos of the entire section, which would have been more noticeable if the quotation had been a little more extended, the constant vacillation of the narrator between guilt and well-being, invites such questions. They are absurd questions, of course, since the reconciliation of fact and fiction occurs itself as a mere assertion made in a text, and is thus productive of more text at the moment when it asserts its decision to escape from textual confinement. But even if we free ourselves of all false questions of intent and rightfully reduce the narrator to the status of a mere grammatical pronoun, without which the narrative could not come into being, this subject remains endowed with a function that is not grammatical but rhetorical, in that it gives voice, so to speak, to a grammatical syntagm. The term *voice*, even when used in a grammatical terminology as when we speak of the passive or interrogative voice, is, of course, a metaphor inferring by analogy the intent of the subject from the structure of the predicate. In the case of the deconstructive discourse that we call literary, or rhetorical, or poetic, this creates a distinctive complication illustrated by the Proust passage. The reading revealed a first paradox: the passage valorizes metaphor as being the "right" literary figure, but then proceeds to constitute itself by means of the epistemologically incompatible figure of metonymy. The critical discourse reveals the presence of this delusion and affirms it as the irreversible mode of its truth. It cannot pause there however. For if we then ask the obvious and simple next question, whether the rhetorical mode of the text in question is that of metaphor or metonymy, it is impossible to give an answer. Individual metaphors, such as the chiaroscuro effect or the butterfly, are shown to be subordinate figures in a general clause whose syntax is metonymic; from this point of view, it seems that the rhetoric is superseded by a grammar that deconstructs it. But this metonymic clause has as its subject a voice whose relationship to this clause is again metaphorical. The narrator who tells us about the impossibility of metaphor is himself, or itself, a metaphor, the metaphor of a grammatical syntagm whose meaning is the denial of metaphor stated, by antiphrasis, as its priority. And this subject-metaphor is, in its turn, open to the kind of deconstruction to the second degree, the rhetorical deconstruction of psycholinguistics, in which the more advanced investigations of literature are presently engaged, against considerable resistance.

We end up, therefore, in the case of the rhetorical grammatization of semiology, just as in the grammatical rhetorization of illocutionary phrases, in the same state of suspended ignorance. Any question about the rhetorical mode of a literary text is always a rhetorical question which does not even know whether it is really questioning. The resulting pathos is an anxiety (or bliss, depending on one's momentary mood or individual temperament) of ignorance, not an anxiety of reference—as becomes thematically clear in Proust's novel when reading is dramatized, in the relationship between Marcel and Albertine, not as an emotive reaction to what language does, but as an emotive reaction to the impossibility of knowing what it might be up to. Literature as well as criticism—the difference between them being delusive—is condemned (or privileged) to be forever the most rigorous and, consequently, the most unreliable language in terms of which man names and transforms himself.

NOTES

1. "Speech, Literature, and the Space in Between," in *New Literary History*, 4 (Autumn 1972), 50.

2. "The Concept of Literature," in *Literary Theory and Structure: Essays in Honor of William K. Wimsatt*, ed. Frank Brady, John Palmer, and Martin Price (New Haven, 1973), 37.

16

Michel Foucault
1926–1984

Along with Jacques Derrida, Michel Foucault has become one of the most prominent European influences directing the pursuit of theory in recent American literary studies. Foucault's thought, however, has not been as readily integrated into literary criticism as have the ideas of Derrida and the "poststructuralist" work of Roland Barthes, Jacques Lacan, and Julia Kristeva (even though he has written on Gustave Flaubert, Maurice Blanchot, and Raymond Roussel). This difficulty of integration results from the specific concerns of his work. Unlike most "poststructuralists," Foucault is less concerned with language at the level of the sign and much more concerned with the relationship of language and social institutions, a relationship that he calls "discourse." To examine language at the level of discourse is to identify the institutional rules that make possible particular significations and, consequently, make possible particular forms of knowledge.

This concern with underlying rules that govern the production of knowledge is found in Foucault's early major work, in which he identifies the conditions that made possible the emergence and development of modern areas of knowledge and their corresponding institutions: the diagnosis of madness and the emergence of asylums (*Madness and Civilization*, 1961; trans. 1965), scientific medicine and the emergence of clinics (*Birth of the Clinic*, 1963; trans. 1973), and the emergence of the human sciences in 18th-century Europe (*The Order of Things*, 1966; trans. 1970). Though Foucault, in his later work, remained interested in the social conditions of knowledge, his focus shifted following the failed leftist uprising in Paris during May 1968. The failure of this uprising led Foucault to an analysis of the exercise of power through social practices, including uses of language, or "discursive practices." This shift of interest coincided with a prestigious appointment to the College de France in 1970. His inaugural lecture in this position, *The Discourse on Language* (1971; trans. 1972), set the agenda for future work by outlining the ways in which "in every society the production of discourse is at once controlled, selected, organized and redistributed according to a certain number of procedures. . . ." In *Discipline and Punish* (1975; trans. 1977), Foucault combined his interest in the emergence of social institutions (in this case, the rise of prisons in the early 19th-century) and the exercise of power through discipline, especially discipline of the body. This interest in the application of discipline through discursive and other practices continues in the last of Foucault's major work, the three volumes of *History of Sexuality* (1976, 1984; trans. 1978, 1986).

Foucault's thought, then, does not lend itself to commentaries on individual literary works as much as it directs us to view literature as a socially determined discursive practice. Also, Foucault's work has influenced several American critics to examine literary criticism (and its history) as a discursive practice. Foucault died in 1984.

"What Is an Author?" was first published in 1969; and, while it continues to probe the institutional forces that affect writing and knowledge (a project that he theorized in *The Archeology of Knowledge*, 1969; trans. 1972), it was the first worrk to reflect his new concern with the exercise of power. Foucault frames the essay by observing a contradiction in modern culture: in many ways our culture regards the author as unimportant (for example, formalist literary criticism and the structuralist approach to the human sciences), yet in our criticism we do not hesitate to use the names of authors. On the basis of this contradiction, Foucault sets the direction of his inquiry: "I am not certain that consequences derived from the disappearance or death of the author have been fully explored or that the importance of this event has been appreciated." Foucault, then, in posing the question, What is an author? is asking, In what ways do we use the notion of author? Foucault observes that we use the name of an author to do more than to refer to a person; instead, the notion of author, unlike the notion of writer, is used to *author*ize certain writings, to privilege those writings. Thus, by focusing on the notion of author, Foucault is able to raise the more general questions of what conditions and interests allow one writer to be regarded an "author" and another writer not. Also, Foucault uses this insight into the social/political nature of the notion of author to problematize the subjectivity of the writer, that is, to assert that a text is never the product of a unified consciousness (the author) but consists in several, socially determined roles, or "author-functions."

What Is an Author?

The coming into being of the notion of "author" constitutes the privileged moment of *individualization* in the history of ideas, knowledge, literature, philosophy, and the sciences. Even today, when we reconstruct the history of a concept, literary genre, or school of philosophy, such categories seem relatively weak, secondary, and superimposed scansions in comparison with the solid and fundamental unit of the author and the work.

I shall not offer here a sociohistorical analysis of the author's persona. Certainly it would be worth examining how the author became individualized in a culture like ours, what status he has been given, at what moment studies of authenticity and attribution began, in what kind of system of valorization the author was involved, at what point we began to recount the lives of authors rather than of heroes, and how this fundamental category of "the-man-

and-his-work criticism" began. For the moment, however, I want to deal solely with the relationship between text and author and with the manner in which the text points to this "figure" that, at least in appearance, is outside it and antecedes it.

Beckett nicely formulates the theme with which I would like to begin: " 'What does it matter who is speaking,' someone said, 'what does it matter who is speaking.' " In this indifference appears one of the fundamental ethical principles of contemporary writing (*écriture*). I say "ethical" because this indifference is not really a trait characterizing the manner in which one speaks and writes, but rather a kind of immanent rule, taken up over and over again, never fully applied, not designating writing as something completed, but dominating it as a practice. Since it is too familiar to require a lengthy analysis, this immanent rule can be adequately illustrated here by tracing two of its major themes.

First of all, we can say that today's writing has freed itself from the dimension of expression. Referring only to itself, but without being restricted to the confines of its interiority, writing is identified with its own unfolded exteriority. This means that it is an interplay of signs arranged less according to its signified content than according to the very nature of the signifier. Writing unfolds like a game (*jeu*) that invariably goes beyond its own rules and transgresses its limits. In writing, the point is not to manifest or exalt the act of writing, nor is it to pin a subject within language; it is, rather, a question of creating a space into which the writing subject constantly disappears.

The second theme, writing's relationship with death, is even more familiar. This link subverts an old tradition exemplified by the Greek epic, which was intended to perpetuate the immortality of the hero: if he was willing to die young, it was so that his life, consecrated and magnified by death, might pass into immortality; the narrative then redeemed this accepted death. In another way, the motivation, as well as the theme and the pretext of Arabian narratives—such as *The Thousand and One Nights*— was also the eluding of death: one spoke, telling stories into the early morning, in order to forestall death, to postpone the day of reckoning that would silence the narrator. Scheherazade's narrative is an effort, renewed each night, to keep death outside the circle of life.

Our culture has metamorphosed this idea of narrative, or writing, as something designed to ward off death. Writing has become linked to sacrifice, even to the sacrifice of life: it is now a voluntary effacement which does not need to be represented in books, since it is brought about in the writer's very existence. The work, which once had the duty of providing immortality, now possesses the right to kill, to be its author's murderer, as in the cases of Flaubert, Proust, and Kafka. That is not all, however: this relationship between writing and death is also manifested in the effacement of the writing subject's individual characteristics. Using all the contrivances that he set up between himself and what he writes, the writing subject cancels out the signs of his particular individuality. As a result, the mark of the writer is reduced to nothing more than the singularity of his absence; he must assume the role of the dead man in the game of writing.

None of this is recent; criticism and philosophy took note of the disappearance—or death—of the author some time ago. But the consequences of their discovery of it have not been sufficiently examined, nor has its import been accurately measured. A certain number of notions that are intended to replace the privileged position of the author actually seem to preserve that privilege and suppress the real meaning of his disappearance. I shall examine two of these notions, both of great importance today.

The first is the idea of the work. It is a very familiar thesis that the task of criticism is not to bring out the work's relationships with the author, nor to reconstruct through the text a thought or experience, but rather to analyze the work through its structure, its architecture, its intrinsic form, and the play of its internal relationships. At this point, however, a problem arises: What is a work? What is this curious unity which we designate as a work? Of what elements is it composed? Is it not what an author has written? Difficulties appear immediately. If an individual were not an author, could we say that what he wrote, said, left behind in his papers, or what has been collected of his remarks, could be called a "work"? When Sade was not considered an author, what was the status of his papers? Were they simply rolls of paper onto which he ceaselessly uncoiled his fantasies during his imprisonment?

Even when an individual has been accepted as an author, we must still ask whether everything that he wrote, said, or left behind is part of his work. The problem is both theoretical and technical. When undertaking the publication of Nietzsche's works, for example, where should one stop? Surely everything must be published, but what is "everything"? Everything that Nietzsche himself published, certainly. And what about the rough drafts for his works? Obviously. The plans for his aphorisms? Yes. What if, within a workbook filled with aphorisms, one finds a reference, the notation of a meeting or of an address, or a laundry list: Is it a work, or not? Why not? And so on, ad infinitum. How can one define a work amid the millions of traces left by someone after his death? A theory of the work does not exist, and the empirical task of those who naively undertake the editing of works often suffers in the absence of such a theory.

We could go even further: Does *The Thousand and One Nights* constitute a work? What about Clement of Alexandria's *Miscellanies* or Diogenes Laertius's *Lives*? A multitude of questions arises with regard to this notion of work. Consequently, it is not enough to declare that we should do without the writer (the author) and study the work itself. The word *work* and the unity that it designates are probably as problematic as the status of the author's individuality.

Another notion which has hindered us from taking full measure of the author's disappearance, blurring and concealing the moment of this effacement and subtly preserving the author's existence, is the notion of writing (*écriture*). When rigorously applied, this notion should allow us not only to circumvent references to the author, but also to situate his recent absence. The notion of writing, as currently employed, is concerned with neither the act of writing nor the indication—be it symptom or sign—of a meaning which someone might have wanted to express. We try, with great effort, to imagine the general condition of each text, the condition of both the space in which it is dispersed and the time in which it unfolds.

In current usage, however, the notion of writing seems to transpose the empirical characteristics of the author into a transcendental anonymity. We are content to efface the more visible mark of the author's empiricity by playing off, one against the other, two ways of characterizing writing, namely, the critical and the religious approaches. Giving writing a primal status seems to be a way of retranslating, in transcendental terms, both the theological affirmation of its sacred character and the critical affirmation of its creative character. To admit that writing is, because of the very history that it made possible, subject to the test of oblivion and repression, seems to represent, in transcendental terms, the religious principle of the hidden meaning (which requires interpretation) and the critical principle of implicit significations, silent determinations, and obscured contents (which gives rise to commentary). To imagine writing as absence seems to be a simple repetition, in transcendental terms, of both the religious principle of inalterable and yet never fulfilled tradition, and the aesthetic principle of the work's survival, its perpetuation beyond the author's death, and its enigmatic *excess* in relation to him.

This usage of the notion of writing runs the risk of maintaining the author's privileges under the protection of writing's *a priori* status: it keeps alive, in the gray light of neutralization, the interplay of those representations that formed a particular image of the author. The author's disappearance, which, since Mallarmé, has been a constantly recurring event, is subject to a series of transcendental barriers. There seems to be an important dividing line between those who believe that they can still locate today's discontinuities (*ruptures*) in the historico-transcendental tradition of the nineteenth century, and those who try to free themselves once and for all from that tradition.

It is not enough, however, to repeat the empty affirmation that the author has disappeared. For the same reason, it is not enough to keep repeating (after Nietzsche) that God and man have died a common death. Instead, we must locate the space left empty by the author's disappearance, follow the distribution of gaps and breaches, and watch for the openings that this disappearance uncovers.

First, we need to clarify briefly the problems arising from the use of the author's name. What is an author's name? How does it function? Far from offering a solution, I shall only indicate some of the difficulties that it presents.

The author's name is a proper name, and therefore it raises the problems common to all proper names. (Here I refer to Searle's analyses, among others.[1]) Obviously, one cannot turn a proper name into a pure and simple reference. It has other than indicative functions: more than an indication, a gesture, a finger pointed at someone, it is the equivalent of a description. When one says "Aristotle," one employs a word that is the equivalent of one, or a series, of definite descriptions, such as "the author of the *Analytics*," "the founder of ontology," and so forth. One cannot stop there, however, because a proper name does not have just one signification. When we discover that Rimbaud did not write *La Chasse spirituelle*, we cannot pretend that the meaning of this proper name, or that of the author, has been altered. The proper name and the author's name are situated between the two poles of description and designation: they must have a certain link with what they name, but one that is neither entirely in the mode of designation nor in that of description; it must be a *specific* link. However—and it is here that the particular difficulties of the author's name arise—the links between the proper name and the individual named and between the author's name and what it names are not isomorphic and do not function in the same way. There are several differences.

If, for example, Pierre Dupont does not have blue eyes, or was not born in Paris, or is not a doctor, the name Pierre Dupont will still always refer to the same person; such things do not modify the link of designation. The problems raised by the author's name are much more complex, however. If I discover that Shakespeare was not born in the house that we visit today, this is a modification which, obviously, will not alter the functioning of the author's name. But if we proved that Shakespeare did not write those sonnets which pass for his, that would constitute a significant change and affect the manner in which the author's name functions. If we proved that Shakespeare wrote Bacon's *Organon* by showing that the same author wrote both the works of Bacon and those of Shakespeare, that would be a third type of change which would entirely modify the functioning of the author's name. The author's name is not, therefore, just a proper name like the rest.

Many other facts point out the paradoxical singularity of the author's name. To say that Pierre Dupont does not exist is not at all the same as saying that Homer or Hermes Trismegistus did not exist. In the first case, it means that no one has the name Pierre Dupont; in the second, it means that several people were mixed together under one name, or that the true author had none of the traits traditionally ascribed to the personae of Homer or Hermes. To say that X's real name is actually Jacques Durand instead of Pierre Dupont is not the same as saying that Stendhal's name was Henri Beyle. One could also question the meaning and functioning of propositions like "Bourbaki is so-and-so, so-and-so, etc." and "Victor Eremita, Climacus, Anti-climacus, Frater Taciturnus, Constantine Constantius, all of these are Kierkegaard."

These differences may result from the fact that an author's name is not simply an element in a discourse (capable of being either subject or object, of being replaced by a pronoun, and the like); it performs a certain role with regard to narrative discourse, assuring a classificatory function. Such a name permits one to group together a certain number of texts, define them, differentiate them from and contrast them to others. In addition, it establishes a relationship among the texts. Hermes Trismegistus did not exist, nor did Hippocrates—in the sense that Balzac existed—but the fact that several texts have been placed under the same name indicates that there has been established among them a relationship of homogeneity, filiation, authentication of some texts by the use of others, reciprocal explication, or concomitant utilization. The author's name serves to characterize a certain mode of being of discourse: the fact that the discourse has an author's name, that one can say "this was written by so-and-so" or "so-and-so is its author," shows that this discourse is not ordinary everyday speech that merely comes and goes, not something that is immediately consumable. On the contrary, it is a speech that must be received in a certain mode and that, in a given culture, must receive a certain status.

It would seem that the author's name, unlike other proper names, does not pass from the interior of a discourse to the real and exterior individual who produced it; instead, the name seems always to be present, marking off the edges of the text, revealing, or at least characterizing, its mode of being. The author's name manifests the appearance of a certain discursive set and indicates the status of this discourse within a society and a culture. It has no legal status, nor is it located in the fiction of the work; rather, it is located in the break that founds a certain discursive construct and its very particular mode of being. As a result, we could say that in a civilization like our own there are a certain number of discourses that are endowed with the "author function," while others are deprived of it. A private letter may well have a signer—it does not have an author; a contract may well have a guarantor—it does not have an author. An anonymous text posted on a wall probably has a writer—but not an author. The author function is therefore characteristic of the mode of existence, circulation, and functioning of certain discourses within a society.

Let us analyze this "author function" as we have just described it. In our culture, how does one characterize a discourse containing the author function? In what way is this discourse different from other discourses? It we limit our remarks to the author of a book or a text, we can isolate four different characteristics.

First of all, discourses are objects of appropriation. The form of ownership from which they spring is of a rather particular type, one that has been codified for many years. We should note that, historically, this type of ownership has always been subsequent to what one might call penal appropriation. Texts, books, and discourses really began to have authors (other than mythical, "sacralized" and "sacralizing" figures) to the extent that authors became subject to punishment, that is, to the extent that discourses could be transgressive. In our culture (and doubtless in many others), discourse was not originally a product, a thing, a kind of goods; it was essentially an act—an act placed in the bipolar field of the sacred and the profane, the licit and the illicit, the religious and the blasphemous. Historically, it was a gesture fraught with risks before becoming goods caught up in a circuit of ownership.

Once a system of ownership for texts came into being, once strict rules concerning author's rights, author–publisher relations, rights of reproduction, and related matters were enacted—at the end of the eighteenth and the beginning of the nineteenth century—the possibility of transgression attached to the act of writing took on, more and more, the form of an imperative peculiar to literature. It is as if the author, beginning with the moment at which he was placed in the system of property that characterizes our society, compensated for the status that he thus acquired by rediscovering the old bipolar field of discourse, systematically practicing transgression and thereby restoring danger to a writing which was now guaranteed the benefits of ownership.

The author function does not affect all discourses in a universal and constant way, however. This is its second characteristic. In our civilization, it has not always been the same types of texts which have required attribution to an author. There was a time when the texts that we today call "literary" (narratives, stories, epics, tragedies, comedies) were accepted, put into circulation, and valorized without any question about the identity of their author; their anonymity caused no difficulties since their ancientness, whether real or imagined, was regarded as a sufficient guarantee of their status. On the other hand, those texts that we now would call scientific—those dealing with cosmology and the heavens, medicine and illnesses, natural sciences and geography—were accepted in the Middle Ages, and accepted as "true," only when marked with the name of their author. "Hippocrates said," "Pliny recounts," were not really formulas of an argument based on authority; they were the markers inserted in discourses that were supported to be received as statements of demonstrated truth.

A reversal occurred in the seventeenth or eighteenth century. Scientific discourses began to be received for themselves, in the anonymity of an established or always redemonstrable truth; their membership in a systematic ensemble, and not the reference to the individual who produced them, stood as their guarantee. The author function faded away, and the inventor's name served only to christen a theorem, proposition, particular effect, property, body, group of elements, or pathological syndrome. By the same token, literary discourses came to be accepted only when endowed with the author function. We now ask of each poetic or fictional text: From where does it come, who wrote it, when, under what circumstances, or beginning with what design? The meaning ascribed to it and the status or value accorded it depend on the manner in which we answer these questions. And if a text should be discovered in a state of anonymity—whether as a consequence of an accident or the author's explicit wish—the game becomes one of rediscovering the author. Since literary anonymity is not tolerable, we can accept it only in the guise of an enigma. As a result, the author function today plays an important role in our view of literary works. (These are obviously generalizations that would have to be refined insofar as recent critical practice is concerned.)

The third characteristic of this author function is that it does not develop spontaneously as the attribution of a discourse to an individual. It is, rather, the result of a complex operation which constructs a certain rational being that we call "author." Critics doubtless try to give this intelligible being a realistic status, by discerning, in the individual, a "deep" motive, a "creative" power, or a "design," the milieu in which writing originates. Nevertheless, these aspects of an individual which we designate as making him an author are only a projection, in more or less psychologizing terms, of the operations that we force texts to undergo, the connections that we make, the traits that we establish as pertinent, the continuities that we recognize, or the exclusions that we practice. All these operations vary according to periods and types of discourse. We do not construct a "philosophical author" as we do a "poet," just as, in the eighteenth century, one did not construct a novelist as we do today. Still, we can find through the ages certain constants in the rules of author construction.

It seems, for example, that the manner in which literary criticism once defined the author—or, rather, constructed the figure of the author beginning with existing texts and discourses—is directly derived from the manner in which Christian tradition authenticated (or rejected) the texts at its disposal. In order to "rediscover" an author in a work, modern criticism uses methods similar to those that Christian exegesis employed when trying to prove the value of a text by its author's saintliness. In *De viris illustribus,* Saint Jerome explains that homonymy is not sufficient to identify legitimately authors of more than one work: different individuals could have had the same name, or one man could have, illegitimately, borrowed another's patronymic. The name as an individual trademark is not enough when one works within a textual tradition.

How, then, can one attribute several discourses to one and the same author? How can one use the author function to determine if one is dealing with one or several individuals? Saint Jerome proposes four criteria: (1) if among several books attributed to an author one is inferior to the others, it must be withdrawn from the list of the author's works (the author is therefore defined as a constant level of value); (2) the same should be done if certain texts contradict the doctrine expounded in the author's other works (the author is thus defined as a field of conceptual or theoretical coherence); (3) one must also exclude works that are written in a different style, containing words and expressions not ordinarily found in the writer's production (the author is here conceived as a stylistic unity); (4) finally, passages quoting statements that were made or mentioning events that occurred after the author's death must be regarded as interpolated texts (the author is here seen as a historical figure at the crossroads of a certain number of events).

Modern literary criticism, even when—as is now customary—it is not concerned with questions of authentication, still defines the author the same way: the author provides the basis for explaining not only the presence of certain events in a work, but also their transformations, distortions, and diverse modifications (through his biography, the determination of his individual perspective, the analysis of his social position, and the revelation of his basic design). The author is also the principle of a certain unity of writing—all differences having to be resolved, at least in part, by the principles of evolution, maturation, or influence. The author also serves to neutralize the contradictions that may emerge in a series of texts: there must be—at a certain level of his thought or desire, of his consciousness or unconscious—a point where contradictions are resolved, where incompatible elements are at last tied together or organized around a fundamental or originating contradiction. Finally, the author is a particular source of expression that, in more or less completed forms, is manifested equally well, and with similar validity, in works, sketches, letters, fragments, and so on. Clearly, Saint Jerome's four criteria of authenticity (criteria which seem totally insufficient for today's exegetes) do define the four modalities according to which modern criticism brings the author function into play.

But the author function is not a pure and simple reconstruction made secondhand from a text given as passive material. The text always contains a certain number of signs referring to the author. These signs, well known to grammarians, are personal pronouns, adverbs of time and place, and verb conjugation. Such elements do not play the same role in discourses provided with the author function as in those lacking it. In the latter, such "shifters" refer to the real speaker and to the spatiotemporal coordinates of his discourse (although certain modifications can occur, as in the operation of relating discourses in the first person). In the former, however, their role is more complex and variable. Everyone knows that, in a novel narrated in the first person, neither the first-person pronoun nor the present indicative refers exactly either to the writer or to the moment in which he writes, but rather to an alter ego whose distance from the author varies, often changing in the course of the work. It would be just as wrong to equate the author with the real writer as to equate him with the fictitious speaker; the author function is carried out and operates in the scission itself, in this division and this distance.

One might object that this is a characteristic peculiar to novelistic or poetic discourse, a "game" in which only "quasi-discourses" participate. In fact, however, all discourses endowed with the author function do possess this plurality of self. The self that speaks in the preface to a treatise on mathematics—and that indicates the circumstances of the treatise's composition—is identical neither in its position nor in its functioning to the self that speaks in the course of a demonstration, and that appears in the form of "I conclude" or "I suppose." In the first case, the "I" refers to an individual without an equivalent who, in a determined place and time, completed a certain task; in the second, the "I" indicates an instance and a level of demonstration which any individual could perform provided that he accepted the same system of symbols, play of axioms, and set of previous demonstrations. We could also, in the same treatise, locate a third self, one that speaks to tell the work's meaning, the obstacles encountered, the results obtained, and the remaining problems; this self is situated in the field of already existing or yet-to-appear mathematical discourses. The author function is not assumed by the first of these selves at the expense of the other two, which would then be nothing more than a fictitious splitting in two of the first one. On the contrary, in these discourses the author function operates so as to effect the dispersion of these three simultaneous selves.

No doubt analysis could discover still

more characteristic traits of the author function. I will limit myself to these four, however, because they seem both the most visible and the most important. They can be summarized as follows: (1) the author function is linked to the juridical and institutional system that encompasses, determines, and articulates the universe of discourses; (2) it does not affect all discourses in the same way at all times and in all types of civilization; (3) it is not defined by the spontaneous attribution of a discourse to its producer, but rather by a series of specific and complex operations; (4) it does not refer purely and simply to a real individual, since it can give rise simultaneously to several selves, to several subjects—positions that can be occupied by different classes of individuals.

Up to this point I have unjustifiably limited my subject. Certainly the author function in painting, music, and other arts should have been discussed, but even supposing that we remain within the world of discourse, as I want to do, I seem to have given the term "author" much too narrow a meaning. I have discussed the author only in the limited sense of a person to whom the production of a text, a book, or a work can be legitimately attributed. It is easy to see that in the sphere of discourse one can be the author of much more than a book—one can be the author of a theory, tradition, or discipline in which other books and authors will in their turn find a place. These authors are in a position which we shall call "transdiscursive." This is a recurring phenomenon—certainly as old as our civilization. Homer, Aristotle, and the Church Fathers, as well as the first mathematicians and the originators of the Hippocratic tradition, all played this role.

Furthermore, in the course of the nineteenth century, there appeared in Europe another, more uncommon, kind of author, whom one should confuse with neither the "great" literary authors, nor the authors of religious texts, nor the founders of science. In a somewhat arbitrary way we shall call those who belong in this last group "founders of discursivity." They are unique in that they are not just the authors of their own works. They have produced something else: the possibilities and the rules for the formation of other texts. In this sense, they are very different, for example, from a novelist, who is, in fact, nothing more than the author of his own text. Freud is not just the author of *The Interpretation of Dreams* or *Jokes and Their Relation to the Unconscious;* Marx is not just the author of the *Communist Manifesto* or *Das Kapital:* they both have established an endless possibility of discourse.

Obviously, it is easy to object. One might say that it is not true that the author of a novel is only the author of his own text; in a sense, he also, provided that he acquires some "importance," governs and commands more than that. To take a very simple example, one could say that Ann Radcliffe not only wrote *The Castles of Athlin and Dunbayne* and several other novels, but also made possible the appearance of the Gothic horror novel at the beginning of the nineteenth century; in that respect, her author function exceeds her own work. But I think there is an answer to this objection. These founders of discursivity (I use Marx and Freud as examples, because I believe them to be both the first and the most important cases) make possible something altogether different from what a novelist makes possible. Ann Radcliffe's texts opened the way for a certain number of resemblances and analogies which have their model or principle in her work. The latter contains characteristic signs, figures, relationships, and structures which could be reused by others. In other words, to say that Ann Radcliffe founded the Gothic horror novel means that in the nineteenth-century Gothic novel one will find, as in Ann Radcliffe's works, the theme of the heroine caught in the trap of her own innocence, the hidden castle, the character of the black, cursed hero devoted to making the world expiate the evil done to him, and all the rest of it.

On the other hand, when I speak of Marx or Freud as founders of discursivity, I mean that they made possible not only a certain number of analogies, but also (and equally important) a certain number of differences. They have created a possibility for something other than their discourse, yet something belonging to what they founded. To say that Freud founded psychoanalysis does not (simply) mean that we find the concept of the libido or the technique of dream analysis in the works of Karl Abraham or Melanie Klein; it means that Freud made possible a certain number of divergences—with respect to his own texts, concepts, and hypotheses—that all arise from the psychoanalytic discourse itself.

This would seem to present a new difficulty, however: is the above not true, after all, of any founder of a science, or of any author who has introduced some important transformation into a science? After all, Galileo made possible not only those discourses that repeated the laws that he had formulated, but also statements very different from what he himself had said. If Cuvier is the founder of biology or Saussure the founder of linguistics, it is not because they were imitated, nor because people have since taken up again the concept of organism or sign; it is because Cuvier made possible, to a certain extent, a theory of evolution diametrically opposed to his own fixism; it is because Saussure made possible a generative grammar radically different from his structural analyses. Superficially, then, the initiation of discursive practices appears similar to the founding of any scientific endeavor.

Still, there is a difference, and a notable one. In the case of a science, the act that founds it is on an equal footing with its future transformations; this act becomes in some respects part of the set of modifications that it makes possible. Of course, this belonging can take several forms. In the future development of a science, the founding act may appear as little more than a particular instance of a more general phenomenon which unveils itself in the process. It can also turn out to be marred by intuition and empirical bias; one must then reformulate it, making it the object of a certain number of supplementary theoretical operations which establish it more rigorously, etc. Finally, it can seem to be a hasty generalization which must be limited, and whose restricted domain of validity must be retraced. In other words, the founding act of a science can always be reintroduced within the machinery of those transformations that derive from it.

In contrast, the initiation of a discursive practice is heterogeneous to its subsequent transformations. To expand a type of discursivity, such as psychoanalysis as founded by Freud, is not to give it a formal generality that it would not have permitted at the outset, but rather to open it up to a certain number of possible applications. To limit psychoanalysis as a type of discursivity is, in reality, to try to isolate in the founding act an eventually restricted number of propositions or statements to which, alone, one grants a founding value, and in relation to which certain concepts or theories accepted by Freud might be considered as derived, secondary, and accessory. In addition, one does not declare certain propositions in the work of these founders to be false: instead, when trying to seize the act of founding, one sets aside those statements that are not pertinent, either because they are deemed inessential, or because they are considered "prehistoric" and derived from another type of discursivity. In other words, unlike the founding of a science, the initiation of a discursive practice does not participate in its later transformations.

As a result, one defines a proposition's theoretical validity in relation to the work of the founders—while, in the case of Galileo and Newton, it is in relation to what physics or cosmology *is* (in its intrinsic structure and "normativity") that one affirms the validity of any proposition that those men may have put forth. To phrase it very schematically: the work of initiators of discursivity is not situated in the space that science defines; rather, it is the science or the discursivity which refers back to their work as primary coordinates.

In this way we can understand the inevitable necessity, within these fields of discursivity, for a "return to the origin." This return, which is part of the discursive field itself, never stops modifying it. The return is not a historical supplement which would be added to the discursivity, or merely an ornament; on the contrary, it constitutes an effective and necessary task of transforming the discursive practice itself. Reexamination of Galileo's text may well change our knowledge of the history of mechanics, but it will never be able to change mechanics itself. On the other hand, reexamining Freud's texts modifies psychoanalysis itself, just as a reexamination of Marx's would modify Marxism.

What I have just outlined regarding the initiation of discursive practices is, of course, very schematic; this is true, in particular, of the opposition that I have tried to draw between discursive initiation and scientific founding. It is not always easy to distinguish between the two; moreover, nothing proves that they are two mutually exclusive procedures. I have attempted the distinction for only one reason: to show that the author function, which is complex enough when one tries to situate it at the level of a book or a series of texts that carry a given signature, involves still more determining factors when one tries to analyze it in larger units, such as groups of works or entire disciplines.

To conclude, I would like to review the reasons why I attach a certain importance to what I have said.

First, there are theoretical reasons. On the one hand, an analysis in the direction that I have outlined might provide for an approach to a typology of discourse. It seems to me, at least at first glance, that such a typology cannot be constructed solely from the grammatical features, formal structures, and objects of discourse: more likely there exist properties or relationships peculiar to discourse (not reducible to the rules of grammar and logic), and one must use these to distinguish the major categories of discourse. The relationship (or nonrelationship) with an author, and the different forms this relationship takes, constitute—in a quite visible manner—one of these discursive properties.

On the other hand, I believe that one could find here an introduction to the historical analysis of discourse. Perhaps it is time to study discourses not only in terms of their expressive value or formal transformations, but according to their modes of existence. The modes of circulation, valorization, attribution, and appropriation of discourses vary with each culture and are modified within each. The manner in which they are articulated according to social relationships can be more readily understood, I believe, in the activity of the author function and in its modifications than in the themes or concepts that discourses set in motion.

It would seem that one could also, beginning with analyses of this type, reexamine the privileges of the subject. I realize that in undertaking the internal and architectonic analysis of a work (be it a literary text, philosophical system, or scientific work), in setting aside biographical and psychological references, one has already called back into question the absolute character and founding role of the subject. Still, perhaps one must return to this question, not in order to reestablish the theme of an originating subject, but to grasp the subject's points of insertion, modes of functioning, and system of dependencies. Doing so means overturning the traditional problem, no longer raising the questions: How can a free subject penetrate the substance of things and give it meaning? How can it activate the rules of a language from within and thus give rise to the designs which are properly its own? Instead, these questions will be raised: How, under what conditions, and in what forms can something like a subject appear in the order of discourse? What place can it occupy in each type of discourse, what functions can it assume, and by obeying what rules? In short, it is a matter of depriving the subject (or its substitute) of its role as originator, and of analyzing the subject as a variable and complex function of discourse.

Second, there are reasons dealing with the "ideological" status of the author. The question then becomes: How can one reduce the great peril, the great danger with which fiction threatens our world? The answer is: one can reduce it with the author. The author allows a limitation of the cancerous and dangerous proliferation of significations within a world where one is thrifty not only with one's resources and riches, but also with one's discourses and their significations. The author is the principle of thrift in the proliferation of meaning. As a result, we must entirely reverse the traditional idea of the author. We are accustomed, as we have seen earlier, to saying that the author is the genial creator of a work in which he deposits, with infinite wealth and generosity, an inexhaustible world of significations. We are used to thinking that the author is so different from all other men, and so transcendent with regard to all languages that, as soon as he speaks, meaning begins to proliferate, to proliferate indefinitely.

The truth is quite the contrary: the author is not an indefinite source of significations which fill a work; the author does not precede the works; he is a certain functional principle by which, in our culture, one limits, excludes, and chooses; in short, by which one impedes the free circulation, the free manipulation, the free composition, decomposition, and recomposition of fiction. In fact, if we are accustomed to presenting the author as a genius, as a perpetual surging of invention, it is because, in reality, we make him function in exactly the opposite fashion. One can say that the author is an ideological product, since we represent him as the opposite of his historically real function. (When a historically given function is represented in a figure that inverts it, one has an ideological production.) The author is therefore the ideological figure by which one marks the manner in which we fear the proliferation of meaning.

In saying this, I seem to call for a form of culture in which fiction would not be limited by the figure of the author. It would be pure romanticism, however, to imagine a culture in which the fictive would operate in an absolutely free state, in which fiction would be put at the disposal of everyone and would develop without passing through something like a necessary or constraining figure. Although, since the eighteenth century, the author has played the role of the regulator of the fictive, a role quite characteristic of our era of industrial and bourgeois society, of individualism and private property, still, given the historical modifications that are taking place, it does not seem necessary that the author function remain constant in form, complexity, and even in existence. I think that, as our society changes, at the very moment when it is in the process of changing, the author function will disappear, and in such a manner that fiction and its polysemous texts will once again function according to another mode, but still with a system of constraint—one which will no longer be the author, but which will have to be determined or, perhaps, experienced.

All discourses, whatever their status, form, value, and whatever the treatment to which they will be subjected, would then develop in the anonymity of a murmur. We would no longer hear the questions that have been rehashed for so long: Who really spoke? Is it really he and not someone else? With what authenticity or originality? And what part of his deepest self did he express in his discourse? Instead, there would be other questions, like these: What are the modes of existence of this discourse? Where has it been used, how can it circulate, and who can appropriate it for himself? What are the places in it where there is room for possible subjects? Who can assume these various subject functions? And behind all these questions, we would hear hardly anything but the stirring of an indifference: What difference does it make who is speaking?

Translated by Donald F. Bouchard and Sherry Simon

NOTES

1. John Searle, *Speech Acts: An Essay in the Philosophy of Language* (Cambridge, Eng.: Cambridge University Press, 1969), 162–74.

V

PSYCHOLOGY AND PSYCHOANALYSIS

Modern psychology has had a steady and deepening influence on criticism since the publication of Freud's *Interpretation of Dreams* in 1900. This influence ranges from early attempts by Ernest Jones, Marie Bonaparte, and Freud himself to apply psychological insights directly and "psychoanalyze" literature, to more recent attempts by poststructuralists and feminists to reimagine Freudian thought in relation to literary texts, language, female sexuality, and political power. Psychological criticism, thus, has taken many forms and continues to undergo radical and frequent reevaluation. Further, the incorporation of depth psychology—whether Jungian or Freudian—in literary studies is a characteristically modern development for at least two reasons. The more important is the possibility, inherent to psychological criticism, of interpreting disconnected or syncopated structures, the reading of disparate narrative details, for example, as part of a pattern—such as a "Great Mother" archetype, or an "Oedipus complex"—not suggested explicitly by the narrative itself. The second, closely connected reason is that psychology can show a literary text to have meaning of various kinds on several levels simultaneously. There could be, for instance, elements of an Oedipal complex in *Hamlet*'s overall dramatic structure and not confined by character make-up. This emphasis on the possibilities of fragmented form and on the potential for multiplicity of meaning strongly connects depth psychology and modernism generally.

A more fundamental connection with modern literary studies is the dialectical nature of psychological criticism: the attempt to relate a theory of mind to literary esthetics, narrative structure, a general system of literature, or the social and cultural context. This potential to connect with other areas, to change in productive ways, is responsible—more than anything else—for the strong continuing interest in the psychological understanding of literature throughout this century. Recently, in the work of Jacques Lacan and others on the Continent and the United States, the extension of psychoanalysis into the discourse on language, female sexuality, and power has made Freudian thought important in contemporary criticism. Thus, Jungian and Freudian psychological criticism contributed to the rise of modernism early in this century and, in the form of neo-Freudianism, is once again a vital force in contemporary discourse.

ARCHETYPAL CRITICISM

At mid-century there were two dominant formalist movements in American and European criticism: the New Criticism and *explication de texte*. Each approach prescribed a method of close reading and attempted to account for a variety of textual information, including imagery and image patterns, rhythm, sound, tone, and overall structure. Each method presented itself as potentially exhaustive, able to discover and catalogue *all* pertinent textual details in a manner approximating empirical observation in thoroughness and supposed objectivity. In the Anglo-American academy, however, the active development of the New Criticism came to an end in the late 1950s with the rise of archetypal criticism associated with the psychologist Carl Jung, which rapidly supplanted the New Criticism in practical influence and prestige. Archetypal criticism exploited certain aspects of the New Criticism (mainly, the deployment of paradox and irony) and then moved directly into areas that the New Criticism refused or failed to develop, particularly the relationship between literature and objects of study that exist "outside" the narrow formalist conception of literature. This included areas such as "mind," or personal psychology, history, culture, and even relations simultaneously "within" but transcending particular texts—what Northrop Frye specifically calls the "conceptual framework" of literature conceived as a "properly organized" intellectual discipline, the system of literature taken as more than "a huge aggregate or miscellaneous pile of creative efforts." (See "The Function of Criticism at the Present Time" in Section VIII.) On this issue, New Critics such as Cleanth Brooks, Wimsatt and Beardsley, John Crowe Ransom, Mark Schorer, and Joseph Frank were judged to be taking literary criticism outside of history—in a sense, outside of time—and advocating a practice unable to account for change in culture that affects literary form.

While approaches to archetypal criticism are varied, the central paradigm for interpretation is Jungian, even though Jung was Freud's close friend up through the 1920s, and even though psychoanalysis already contained its own theory of archetypes as evidenced in *Totem and Taboo.* Jung's primary focus, and the point on which he sought to divide from Freud, was his approach to the "collective unconscious," a realm of transpersonal imagery preserved and repeated throughout human experience. Belonging to the human race and also (at levels "below" consciousness) to individual people, the collective unconscious contains "archetypes," or fundamental patterns and forms of human experience, such as "mother," "rebirth," "spirit," and "trickster." Apprehendable only as fragments, or incomplete representations, the archetypes are like the light flickering on the walls of Plato's cave. Archetypal images, that is—never the totality of an archetype—are cast upon the screen of conscious thought, constituting informative patterns that are never quite unambiguous or completely unified.

In literary interpretation, archetypes show up in character, plot, and setting. Apparently unrelated textual elements as well as realistic, representational details form patterns suggestive of one or more of the archetypes. While sometimes sketchy and only minimally informative, these patterns, nonetheless, establish an archetypal orientation in the work and reflect what lies "beneath" the work's narrative and imagistic surface. In other words, archetypal interpretation organizes each literary text into (1) a narrative surface composed of images and (2) a textual "depth" where the connection with archetypes takes place. A full archetypal interpretation seeks to make explicit what is only implicit in the text's fragmented evocation of archetypes. An archetypal understanding of a text, in short, necessitates seeing how the appearance of suggestive details in a minimal sequence is, in reality, a disguised archetypal pattern.

The possibility of narrative progression in archetypal criticism is crucial for understanding archetypalism's ascendancy over the New Criticism. After all, the New Critical emphasis on imagery as the object of analysis depends on evidence drawn from poetry, particularly modernism's highly figurative, nonnarrative poetry. And as is often noted, the New Critics foundered on the difficulty of applying imagery and paradox/irony (essentially static and even pictorial in their avoidance of time) to fiction and its profoundly temporal dimension. Only late in the movement's development, during the late 1940s and 1950s, did Joseph Frank and Mark Schorer seek to recast the poetic image as "spatial form" and suggest "technique as [as a form of] discovery" in prose fiction. By contrast, archetypalism from its start attempted to define itself precisely in relation to a temporal order, that of the "monomyth" or "quest." As Erich Neumann and others have shown, the coherence of the archetypes rests precisely on their placement within a narrative development that moves from total narcissism toward the hero's individuation and relative autonomy, each stage in the quest being a further step toward independence from the Great Mother. This pattern is *monomythic* because it encompasses all possible human change and growth within a single story. Thus, the quest-narrative unites the repeatable form of each archetype with the principle of change dictated by the ongoing temporal development of a story itself. The potential circularity of merely locating self-defining archetypes in literature—wherein discoveries are dictated by foreknown patterns—is avoided through the necessity of accounting for the dynamic operation of narrative ("mythic") progression in particular cases.

Without question, the definitive archetypal approach to literature is presented in Frye's *Anatomy of Criticism* (1957), in which "The Function of Criticism at the Present Time," included in Section VIII, became the "Polemical Introduction." Frye was the most formidable archetypal critic to announce a decisive break, as he said, with the "ironic provincialism" and "delicate learning" of the New Criticism. Uncharacteristically disdainful in his appraisal of this literary school, Frye rejected what he considered the New Criticism's limited range and lack of sophistication. Also, the implicit religious—and "typological"—perspective of Frye's criticism conflicted with the implicit skepticism of the New Criticism. His harshest slap at the New Criticism was his choice of a title for the *Anatomy*'s first essay, "Historical Criticism: Theory of Modes," where with polemical bravado Frye is attempting to situate the archetypal project on the very historical terrain abandoned by the New Criticism. Frye proclaimed, in effect, that archetypal criticism's success would be precisely where the prior movement had failed. He then went on in "four essays" to erect the monomyth's structure over the whole of culture in a "proto-structuralist" reading of Western literature's archetypal development—from prehistoric and sacred "myth" to present-day "irony." In a remarkable elaboration of literary archetypes, Frye presented a comprehensive catalogue of literary forms (genre, sound, rhythm, tone, and so on) as part of his complex presentation of the archetypal paradigm. Implicit in his discussion is, in fact, a sense of the "development" of Western literature—his "Historical Criticism"—as Frye simultaneously suggested both an archetypal "conceptual framework" for criticism and an examination of the "history" of literature.

Throughout the 1960s, Frye's version of archetypalism influenced much theory and practical criticism, especially in Medieval-Renaissance studies. Gradually, however, Frye's approach came under attack from three directions: historical critics, structuralists, and feminists. Historicists like A. S. P. Woodhouse, Roy Harvey Pearce, and Lionel Trilling began to point out the failure of both the New Criticism and archetypalism in dealing with history except within narrow bounds. It can be argued, for example, that archetypalism develops an "historical" theory of modes (myth, romance, high mimetic, low mimetic, and irony) in order only to turn Western literature itself into a huge, static image or structure—an all-inclusive version of what Pound and others described as imagism, or history as image and as closed system. Whereas historical criticism should be able to analyze change, account for the as yet unmet and unthought, it is not clear that the archetypal progression of images adequately does this, or does anything more than impose an archetypal and static grid over literature as a substitute for historical understanding.

From a different angle, the Structuralists of the 1960s and 1970s argued with Frye's complicated but, in their view, often naive and overly rigid schema. In the first chapter of *The Fantastic*, for example, Tzvetan Todorov criticized Frye's tendency to analyze literature for "content," actual images (like a "tree" and "shore") in literature, when his professed aim was to examine literary structure as positioned beyond concrete examples. Todorov also noted, on the one hand, the formal rigidity of Frye's schema and, on the other, logical lapses in it—for example, the seasonal four-part structure of the "mythoi" as opposed to the five-part structure of his historical "modes."

Most devastating, though, is the feminist critique of Frye, which attacked the Jungian paradigm and the notion of the monomyth. As feminists pointed out, the archetypal hero is at base a male figure attempting to bring reconciliation with an "original" female (the Great Mother) and with a potential "anima" figure who is both the hero's ideal mate and his reward for success on the quest. This exclusively male paradigm assumes a male subject, and nowhere in Jung's thought, or Frye's, is there a serious attempt to reconceive a woman's experience outside of support for a man. Whereas some teachers and practical critics still employ archetypalism for specific ends, especially to create contexts for genre distinctions, the critiques of Frye—the archetypalist par excellence—have tended to halt the theoretical elaboration of archetypalism as a school of literary criticism. At the same time, it should be remembered that archetypalism also had particular value as a major critique of the New Criticism and, thus, at an early stage contributed to the reevaluation of formalism that is still very much in evidence today.

FREUDIAN CRITICISM

Psychoanalysis is the intellectual parent of archetypalism, but, as it happens, psychoanalytic criticism both precedes archetypalism in the first-generation Freudians beginning in the twenties and thirties and succeeds it in the more "recent" movement, the semiotic "return to Freud." Archetypal criticism, for all its virtues and power, and in spite of its criticism of the New Criticism, finally participates in a version of the positivist assumptions that govern American Formalism and the earlier criticism of Freudian ego psychologists (even if the positive "objects" of study are not independent texts but rather particular, transcendental archetypes). This can be seen, in fact, in Frye's attempt to develop a discipline of criticism as a social science in "The Function of Criticism at the Present Time." By contrast, the great strength of contemporary psychoanalytic criticism—contemporary Freudian criticism—is that it goes beyond some of the positivist assumptions of its master to use Freud's work to critique those assumptions and develop discursive modes (that is, self-consciously rhetorical modes) of reading.

It is common to note that critical movements develop through a kind of life cycle, eventually fade, and then may go on to stimulate new movements after them. With psychoanalysis, a first generation of Freudian criticism continued until the 1960s and included some of the better critical minds of the twentieth century: Ernest Jones, Marie Bonaparte, Frederick Crews, Edmund Wilson, Lionel Trilling, and others. This movement began to weaken at mid-century, as did Jungian criticism and the New Criticism, largely because of an inability to go beyond thematic ("therapeutic") comment to deal with literary structure. Then a new literary Freudianism, based initially on the suggestions made in Jacques Lacan's seminars, was reborn in France in the 1960s. The maturity of this new Freudian criticism can be gauged according to its usefulness as practical criticism—as interpretation. Since the mid-1970s, many "French Freud" readings of literature have appeared in Western Europe and the United States. Thus, psychoanalytic interpretation has a currency in contemporary practice that archetypal criticism does not.

It is helpful to remember that separating the old psychoanalytic criticism from the new is a real difference in Freudian theory between "ego-psychology" and structuralist, or semiotic, psychoanalysis. In the first the ego, or the self, can be seen as a little, interior person—autonomous as the texts for the New Critics—whose responsibility it is to negotiate between an id of insatiable appetites and a superego with standards of conduct impossible to meet. This ego, further, must negotiate between the internal world's id and superego and an external world of "reality," which continually blocks the ego from achieving its goals. In literary terms, this is the Freudianism of "substantial" meaning—that is, of literary "form" conceived as a positive "substance" on the model of the ego—text, character, plot, themes, symbols, etc., conceived as being common-sensically and inherently meaningful. From this viewpoint, in effect, the substantial ego is a model for literary texts (and for psychological archetypes) in that all are taken for granted as naturally and unquestionably meaningful.

In practice, "ego" psychology engenders literary criticism based on biographical sources and tends to see art as a "psychic bandage" made necessary, in Henry Lowenfeld's words, by "the coincidence of artistic talent and neurotic disposition." Literature, in this view, as Williams Barrett has said, is taken to be "the product of the personal being of its author." Literature is, therefore, the "natural" expression of the artist's or the human race's psychic life, and criticism's specific function is to illuminate the text's psychic content with a clarifying explanation. This approach casts psychoanalytic criticism, and by extension all criticism, in a secondary, subservient role (as if a parasite) to literature conceived as a vital host.

SEMIOTIC FREUD

In Jacques Lacan's elaboration of the semiotic, or "French," Freud the ego is no longer a central concept. In its place is what Lacan calls the "subject," the whole mechanism of conscious and unconscious operations. The subject is not a personal identity at all but a semiotic construct, a way of organizing and understanding the "discourse" that relates individual people to culture. Lacan specifically thinks of positions in language corresponding to family roles (father, mother, child), which are then conceived on the order of grammatical "persons," that is, markers for structural positions. (Lacan elaborates these roles in his discussion of the positions of the "glances" in his "Seminar on 'The Purloined Letter,' " included in this section.) The ego is but one "position"—

designated as the "speaking subject," or "I"—in discourse, and it has no controlling influence on the overall function of the discourse. This paradigm suggests a "semiotic" Freud in that neither the ego nor the "subject" is taken as naturally meaningful and possessed of an identity. The achieved effects of ego and subjectivity belong essentially to the linguistic operation Lacan calls the "discourse of the Other." The subject in this semiotic model is an "inscription" in unconscous discourse, a message, in effect, the unconscious sends to itself.

Such concepts as "inscription" and unconscious "discourse," and their systematic elaboration, are the characteristic concerns of a semiotic psychoanalysis. The schema of a "semiotic" Freud can even account for the phenomenon of ego-psychology in its supposed direct relationship of language and world—ego and reality. Lacan takes such a relationship, wherein the ego appears to confront the world directly, without the mediation of semiotic representation, as a narcissistic illusion and a phase of discourse called the "imaginary." The ego, in this view, is generated independently and without connection to the world. In sum, in ego psychology, Lacan asserts, the ego appears to be a totally integrated inner person who exists independent of the "world" for its constitution. In reality, this "imaginary" projection of the autonomous ego is a single moment in the "inscription" of—the operation that produces—the subject.

In this semiotic model of psychoanalysis the literary text is no longer the exclusive "object," the substance, of interpretation, but is read in conjunction with the Freudian text, not through it. Literature and psychoanalytic criticism, in this model, inform each other in textual interaction that is both a psychoanalytic reading of literature and a literary reading of psychoanalysis. The parasite/host relationship, in sum, becomes a dynamic series of reversals. Peter Brooks's reading of *Beyond the Pleasure Principle* (included here), for example, attempts to understand Freud's discussion of the "death instinct" in terms of a literary structure, what Brooks calls a "masterplot" that describes "a total scheme of how life proceeds from beginning to end." For Brooks, the literary and psychoanalytic texts inform each other creatively outside of the "therapeutic" application of psychoanalysis to literature.

This new Freudian criticism, based as it is on semiotics, has many connections to deconstructive criticism. Both attempt to dislodge a traditional mode of "ego-oriented" (what Derrida calls logocentric) reading and the interpretive system that underlies it. Lacan does this by critiquing the Western, generally Cartesian, notion of the "subject" as an autonomous observer—the objective nonparticipant who examines a world that stays forever separate from him. In the old model it is assumed that knowledge is continuous with, confined by, the subject's conscious experience. A literary text, for example, is often thought to "make sense" to the degree that it is "realistic," which usually means familiar and anticipatable. Further, the manifest representational figures—the images in the text—will be thought to compose the work's form, which will be taken for the text's "substance." By contrast, as Barbara Johnson and Jerry Flieger show in essays included here, the Lacanian text is not substantial, an absolute given in the process of reading, but differential, semiotic. The text, that is, is not a continuous, fixed form, or a "substance" but the manifestation of a dynamic operation. It is constituted semiotically with signifiers separated by gaps and radical inconsistencies and exists, in other words—as do the very signifiers that Lacan and Johnson emphasize—in relation to something it is not. As Lacan says in his seminar, the letter (or text) is "a pure signifier" determined by its *position* within discourse. And as Johnson says, "the letter, then, acts as a signifier *not* because its contents are lacking, but because its function is not dependent on the knowledge or nonknowledge of those contents. . . . It is not something with 'an *identity* to itself inaccessible to dismemberment' as Derrida interprets it; it is a *difference*."

In this sense, as Lacan explains, the signifier has "priority in relation to the signified." Textuality—in short—precedes and creates the matrix of meaning, and not vice versa. In fact, Lacan says, "we teach that the unconscious means that man is inhabited by [constituted by] the signifier." To be thus inhabited by the signifier, in Johnson's words, is to be "knotted" up, entangled in semiotic relations. "The letter as a signifier," as Johnson goes on, "is thus not a thing or the absence of a thing, nor a word or the absence of a word, nor an organ or the absence of an organ, but a *knot* in a structure where words, things and organs can neither be definably separated nor compatibly combined." Signifiers create "texts," and "knot" captures the etymological sense of the figural weaving that constitutes them. Lacan's vision of a text based on his contention that "the unconscious . . . is structured like a language" shows the deconstructed dimension, the problematic view of the text, in the "new" psychoanalysis.

The Lacanian text, therefore, tends to emphasize a large margin of "undecidability," or the degree to which a text escapes the conception of form altogether and is sustained—differentially signified—in the process of producing meaning. This version of the text emphasizes what Johnson calls textual rhetoric, the "circumlocutions" which—like the signifier and like the "frame of reference" itself—create the place of meaning.

Lacan's radical critique of the subject has made Freud newly useful for feminists and Marxists. Feminist critics such as Jane Gallop, Hélène Cixous, Julia Kristeva, and Shoshana Felman have found in the "French Freud" a potential for interpreting literary texts from other than a male (or "phallogocentric") perspective. Starting with Lacan, but often revising his critique of the subject, feminists have profitably read literary texts psychoanalytically. Likewise, Marxist critics such as Fredric Jameson, Louis Althusser, and Colin McCabe have used Lacan's figure of the split subject to integrate the political and the psychological critiques of literary texts. An important result of this project is the idea of a "political unconscious," an approach to power relations that uses Freud's model to analyze manifest and unconscious discourses. For both feminists and Marxists, Lacanian thought thus supports a deconstructive strategy for overturning the traditional Western subject and reinscribing (reimagining) the subject in a largely unconscious discourse. Lacan's is a difficult view of the text, but it is precisely the radicality—the deconstructive dimension—in the "new" psychoanalysis that has once more given Freud urgent importance in contemporary literary criticism.

The language of contemporary psychoanalysis, finally, may be the most difficult of all the contemporary discourses in that it attempts, as Johnson describes here, as much to create effects of "power" in itself—effects "on" and "within" the reader—as descriptions of meaning. (Shoshana Felman lucidly describes this use of language in "Psychoanalysis and Education" in Section VIII). In the terms examined in Section IV, it offers a language whose force is as "performative" as it is "constative," as much a theatricalization as a statement of truth. With this difficulty in mind, we have put together three essays that refer to one another in helpful ways. Lacan, for example, discusses Poe, semiotics, and psychoanalysis, whereas Barbara Johnson reads Poe, Lacan, and Derrida on Lacan-and-Poe. Flieger, then, does a feminist rereading of Freud, Lacan, and (implicitly) Derrida—with reference to Johnson. These essays appear in chronological order and will repay scrutiny most fully if read and reread as a group. These essays, finally, along with the one by Brooks, situate psychoanalysis among contemporary schools of theory in the same way we have tried to situate psychoanalytic criticism generally within the recent history of critical practice.

RELATED TEXTS IN *CONTEMPORARY LITERARY CRITICISM*

Ferdinand de Saussure, Selections from *Course in General Linguistics*
Roland Barthes, "The Structuralist Activity"
Fredric Jameson, "The Politics of Theory"
Hélène Cixous, "Castration or Decapitation?"
Shoshana Felman, "Psychoanalysis and Education: Teaching Terminable and Interminable"

FURTHER READING

Abraham, Nicolas, and Maria Torok, *Cryptonymie: Le Verbier de l'homme aux loups* (Paris: Aubier-Flammarion, 1976).

Barrett, Villiam, "Writers and Madness," in *Literature and Psychoanalysis.* Edith Kurzweil and William Phillips, ed. (New York: Columbia University Press, 1983).

Bellemin-Nöel, Jean, *Vers l'inconscient du texts* (Paris: Presses Universitaires de France, 1979).

Benvenuto, Rice, and Roger Kennedy, *Jacques Lacan* (New York: St. Martin's Press, 1986).

Bodkin, Maud, *Archetypal Patterns in Poetry* (New York: Vintage, 1958).

Brooks, Peter, "Fictions of the Wolfman: Freud and Narrative Understanding," in *Diacritics,* 9, No. 1 (1979), 72–83.

———, *Reading for the Plot* (New York: Knopf, 1984).

Campbell, Joseph, *The Hero with a Thousand Faces* (New York: Pantheon, 1949).

Caroll, David, "Freud and the Myth of Origins," in *New Literary History,* 6 (1975), 511–28.

Crews, Frederick C., *Out of My System* (New York: Oxford University Press, 1975).

———, ed., *Psychoanalysis and Literary Process* (Cambridge, Mass.: Winthrop, 1970).

———, *The Sins of the Fathers* (New York: Oxford University Press, 1966).

Davis, Robert Con, ed., special issue on "Psychoanalysis and Pedagogy," *College English,* 49, 6/7 (1987).

———, ed., *The Fictional Father: Lacanian Readings of the Text* (Amherst: University of Massachusetts Press, 1981).

———, ed., *Lacan and Narration: The Psychoanalytic Difference in Narrative Theory* (Baltimore: Johns Hopkins University Press, 1984).

Derrida, Jacques, *The Post Card,* trans. Alan Bass (Chicago: University of Chicago Press, 1987).

———, "Freud and the Scene of Writing," in his *Writing and Difference*, trans. Alan Bass (Chicago: University of Chicago Press, 1978), 196–231.

Felman, Shoshana, "Beyond Oedipus: The Specimen Story of Psychoanalysis," in *Lacan and Narration: The Psychoanalytic Difference in Narrative Theory*, ed. Robert Con Davis (Baltimore: Johns Hopkins University Press, 1984), 1021–53.

———, *The Literary Speech Act: Don Juan with J. L. Austin, or Seduction in Two Languages*, trans. Catherine Porter (Ithaca: Cornell University Press, 1983).

———, ed., *Literature and Psychoanalysis: The Question of Reading—Otherwise* (Baltimore: Johns Hopkins University Press, 1982).

Freud, Sigmund, *Totem and Taboo*, trans. A. A. Brill (New York: Moffat, Yard, 1918).

Frye, Northrop, *Anatomy of Criticism: Four Essays* (Princeton: Princeton University Press, 1957).

Gallop, Jane, *The Daughter's Seduction: Feminism and Psychoanalysis* (Ithaca: Cornell University Press, 1982).

———, *Reading Lacan* (Ithaca: Cornell University Press, 1985).

Hartman, Geoffrey H., "Psychoanalysis: The French Connection," in *Psychoanalysis and the Question of the Text*, ed. Geoffrey H. Hartman (Baltimore: Johns Hopkins University Press, 1978), 86–113.

Hertz, Neil, "Freud and the Sandman," in *Textual Strategies*, ed. Josué Harari (Ithaca: Cornell University Press, 1979), 296–321.

Hoffman, Frederick J., *Freudianism and the Literary Mind*, 2nd ed. (Baton Rouge: Louisiana State University Press, 1957).

Holland, Norman N., *The Dynamics of Literary Response* (New York: Oxford University Press, 1968).

———, *5 Readers Reading* (New Haven: Yale University Press, 1975).

———, *Poems in Persons* (New York: Norton, 1973).

Lacan, Jacques, *Ecrits: A Selection*, trans. Alan Sheridan (New York: Norton, 1977).

———, *Speech and Language in Psychoanalysis*, trans., notes, and commentary by Anthony G. Wilden (Baltimore: Johns Hopkins University Press, 1982).

———, and the École Freudienne, *Feminine Sexuality*, Juliet Mitchell and Jacqueline Rose, eds., trans. J. Rose (New York: Norton, 1982).

Lesser, Simon O., *Fiction and the Unconscious* (Boston: Beacon Press, 1957).

Lowenfeld, Henry, "Psychic Trauma and Productive Experience in the Artist," in Felman, ed., *Literature and Psychoanalysis* (see Barrett above).

MacCabe, Colin, ed., *The Talking Cure: Essays in Psychoanalysis and Language* (London: Macmillan, 1981).

MacCannell, Juliet, *Figuring Lacan* (Lincoln: University Nebraska Press, 1986).

Nagele, Rainer, *Reading After Freud* (New York: Columbia University Press, 1987).

Spivak, Gayatri Chakravorty, "The Letter as Cutting Edge," in *Yale French Studies*, 55/56 (1977), 208–26.

Trilling, Lionel, *Freud and the Crisis of Our Culture* (Boston: Beacon Press, 1955).

———, *The Liberal Imagination* (New York: Viking, 1951).

Wilson, Edmund, *The Triple Thinkers* (New York: Harcourt, Brace, 1938).

———, *The Wound and the Bow* (Boston: Houghton Mifflin, 1941).

Wright, Elizabeth, *Psychoanalytic Criticism: Theory in Practice* (London: Methuen, 1984).

17

Peter Brooks 1938–

Peter Brooks was born in New York and received his Ph.D. from Harvard University in 1965. He has taught at Yale University since 1965 and is currently a professor of French and comparative literature there. His writings include: *The Novel of Worldliness* (1969); *The Melodramatic Imagination* (1976); and *Reading for the Plot* (1984).

Brooks uses Freud's *Beyond the Pleasure Principle* as a model for reading and understanding narrative plot in his essay, "Freud's Masterplot." He draws parallels between Freud's discovery that a child will deliberately repeat an unpleasurable experience and sees repetition in narrative, which he equates with mastery, much as an individual asserts control over his own end by deliberately choosing that end. A primary example of this repetition in narrative is the death instinct; Brooks sees narrative as obituary (life acquires meaning only at and through death), and points to a major characteristic of narrative as proof that it parallels Freud's conclusion, "the aim of all life is death": narrative starts not at the beginning but the end. Repetition not only moves narrative to its final conclusion of the death instinct that works within it, but repetition also delays the final release of that ending by wandering off into various complex detours. These detours account for the development of narrative. Other parallels Brooks sees between Freud and narrative include the tension between beginnings and ends that demands the working out of the narrative plot; the temporality of narrative; and the way in which the functioning of the mental apparatus parallels the functioning of the text. Brooks's essay is a well-reasoned argument from the psychoanalytic perspective. His comments encourage reflection on narrative patterns and the underlying operations that give rise to those patterns.

Freud's Masterplot

As if they would confine th'
Interminable,
And tie him to his own prescript.

In one of his best essays in "narratology," where he is working toward a greater formalization of principles advanced by Vladimir Propp and Viktor Shklovsky, Tzvetan Todorov elaborates a model of narrative transformation whereby narrative plot (*le récit*) is constituted in the tension of two formal categories, difference and resemblance.[1] Transformation—a change in a predicate term common to beginning and end—represents a synthesis of difference and resemblance; it is, we might say, the same-but-different. Now "the same-but-different" is a common (and if inadequate, not altogether false) definition of metaphor. If Aristotle affirmed that the master of metaphor must have an eye for resemblances, modern treatments of the subject have affirmed equally the importance of difference included within the operation of resemblance, the chief value of the metaphor residing in its "tension." Narrative operates as metaphor in its affirmation of resemblance, in that it brings into relation different actions, combines them through perceived similarities (Todorov's common predicate term), appropriates them to a common plot, which implies the rejection of merely contingent (or unassimilable) incident or action. The plotting of meaning cannot do without metaphor, for meaning in plot is the structure of action in closed and legible wholes. Metaphor is in this sense totalizing. Yet it is equally apparent that the key figure of narrative must in some sense be not metaphor but metonymy: the figure of contiguity and combination, the figure of syntagmatic relations.[2] The description of narrative needs metonymy as the figure of movement, of linkage in the signifying chain, of the slippage of the signified under the signifier. That Jacques Lacan has equated metonymy and desire is of the utmost pertinence, since desire must be considered the very motor of narrative, its dynamic principle.

The problem with "the same-but-different" as a definition of narrative would be the implication of simultaneity and stasis in the formulation. The postulation of a static model indeed is the central deficiency of most formalist and structuralist work on narrative, which has sought to make manifest the structures of narrative in spatial and atemporal terms, as versions of Lévi-Strauss' "atemporal matrix structure."[3] Todorov is an exception in that, faithful to Propp, he recognizes the need to consider sequence and succession as well as the paradigmatic matrix. He supplements his definition with the remark: "Rather than a 'coin with two faces,' [transformation] is an operation in two directions: it affirms at once resemblance and difference; it puts time into motion and suspends it, in a single movement; it allows discourse to acquire a meaning without this meaning becoming pure information; in a word, it makes narrative possible and reveals its very definition."[4] The image of a double operation upon time has the value of returning us to the evident but frequently eluded fact that narrative meanings are developed in time, that any narrative partakes more or less of what Proust called "un jeu formidable . . . avec le Temps," and that this game of time is not merely in the world of reference (or in the *fabula*) but as well in the narrative, in the *sjužet*, be it only that the meanings developed by narrative *take time:* the time of reading.[5] If at the end of a narrative we can suspend time in a moment where past and present hold together in a metaphor which may be the very recognition which, said Aristotle, every good plot should bring, that moment does not abolish the movement, the slidings, the errors and partial recognitions of the middle. As Roland Barthes points out, in what so far must be counted our most satisfactory dynamic analysis of plot, the proairetic and hermeneutic codes—code of actions, code of enigmas and answers—are irreversible: their interpretation is determined linearly, in sequence, in one direction.[6]

Ultimately—Barthes writes elsewhere—the passion that animates us as readers of narrative is the passion for (of) meaning.[7] Since for Barthes meaning (in the "classical" or "readable" text) resides in full predication, completion of the codes in a "plenitude" of signification, this passion appears to be finally a desire for the end. It is at the end—for Barthes as for Aristotle—that recognition brings its illumination, which then can shed retrospective light. The function of the end, whether considered syntactically (as in Todorov and Barthes) or ethically (as in Aristotle) or as formal or cosmological closure (as in Barbara H. Smith or Frank Kermode) continues to fascinate and to baffle. One of the strongest statements of its determinative position in narrative plots comes in a passage from Sartre's *La Nausée* which bears qutotation once again. Roquentin is reflecting on the meaning of "adventure" and the difference between living and narrating. When you narrate, you appear to start with a beginning. You say, "It was a fine autumn evening in 1922. I was a notary's clerk in Marommes." But, says Roquentin:

> In reality you have started at the end. It was there, invisible and present, it is what gives these few words the pomp and value of a beginning. "I was out walking, I had left the town without realizing it, I was thinking about my money troubles." This sentence, taken simply for what it is, means that the man was absorbed, morose, a hundred miles from an adventure, exactly in a mood to let things happen without noticing them. But the end is there, transforming everything. For us, the man is already the hero of the story. His moroseness, his money troubles are much more precious than ours, they are all gilded by the light of future passions. And the story goes on in the reverse: instants have stopped piling themselves up in a haphazard way one on another, they are caught up by the end of the story which draws them and each one in its turn draws the instant preceding it: "It was night, the street was deserted." The sentence is thrown out negligently, it seems superfluous; but we don't let ourselves be duped, we put it aside: this is a piece of information whose value we will understand later on. And we feel that the hero has lived all the details of this night as annunciations, as promises, or even that he has lived only those that were promises, blind and deaf to all that did not herald adventure. We forget that the future wasn't yet there; the man was walking in a night without premonitions, which offered him in disorderly fashion its monotonous riches, and he did not choose.[8]

The beginning in fact presupposes the end. The very possibility of meaning plotted through time depends on the anticipated structuring force of the ending: the interminable would be the meaningless. We read the incidents of narration as "promises and annunciations" of final coherence: the metaphor reached through the chain of metonymies. As Roquentin further suggests, we read only those incidents and signs which can be construed as promise and annunciation, enchained toward a construction of significance—those signs which, as in the detective story, appear to be *clues* to the underlying intentionality of event.

The sense of beginning, then, is determined by the sense of an ending. And if we inquire further into the nature of the ending, we no doubt find that it eventually has to do with the human end, with death. In *Les Mots,* Sartre pushes further his reflection on ends. He describes how in order to escape contingency and the sense of being unjustified he had to imagine himself as one of the children in *L'Enfance des hommes illustres,* determined, as promise and annunciation, by what he would become for posterity. He began to live his life retrospectively, in terms of the death that alone would confer meaning and necessity on existence. As he succinctly puts it, "I became my own obituary."[9] All narration is obituary in that life acquires definable meaning only at, and through, death. In an independent but convergent argument, Walter Benjamin has claimed that life assumes transmissible form only at the moment of death. For Benjamin, this death is the very "authority" of narrative: we seek in fictions the knowledge of death, which in our own lives is denied to us. Death—

which may be figural but in the classic instances of the genre is so often literal—quickens meaning: it is the "flame," says Benjamin, at which we warm our "shivering" lives.[10]

We need to know more about this death-like ending which is nonetheless animating of meaning in relation to initiatory desire, and about how the interrelationship of the two determines, shapes, necessitates the middle—Barthes' "dilatory space" of retard, postponement—and the kinds of vacillation between illumination and blindness that we find there. If the end is recognition which retrospectively illuminates beginning and middle, it is not the exclusive truth of the text, which must include the processes along the way—the processes of "transformation"—in their metonymical complexity. If beginning is desire, and is ultimately desire for the end, between lies a process we feel to be necessary (plots, Aristotle tells us, must be of "a certain length") but whose relation to originating desire and to end remains problematic. It is here that Freud's most ambitious investigation of ends in relation to beginnings may be of help—and may suggest a contribution to a properly dynamic model of plot.

We undertake, then, to read *Beyond the Pleasure Principle* as an essay about the dynamic interrelationship of ends and beginnings, and the kind of processes that constitute the middle. The enterprise may find a general sort of legitimation in the fact that *Beyond the Pleasure Principle* is in some sense Freud's own masterplot, the text in which he most fully lays out a total scheme of how life proceeds from beginning to end, and how each individual life in its own way repeats the masterplot. Of Freud's various intentions in this text, the boldest—and most mysterious—may be to provide a theory of comprehension of the dynamic of the life-span, its necessary duration and its necessary end, hence, implicitly, a theory of the very narratability of life. In his pursuit of his "beyond," Freud is forced to follow the implications of argument—"to throw oneself into a line of thought and follow it wherever it leads," as he says late in the essay—to ends that he had not originally or consciously conceived.[11] *Beyond the Pleasure Principle* shows the very plotting of a masterplot made necessary by the structural demands of Freud's thought, and it is in this sense that we shall attempt to read it as a model for narrative plot.

Narrative always makes the implicit claim to be in a state of repetition, as a going over again of a ground already covered: a *sjužet* repeating the *fabula*, as the detective retraces the tracks of the criminal.[12] This claim to an act of repetition—"I sing," "I tell"—appears to be initiatory of narrative. It is equally initiatory of *Beyond the Pleasure Principle;* it is the first problem and clue that Freud confronts. Evidence of a "beyond" that does not fit neatly into the functioning of the pleasure principle comes first in the dreams of patients suffering from war neuroses, or from the traumatic neuroses of peace: dreams which return to the moment of trauma, to relive its pain in apparent contradiction of the wish-fulfillment theory of dreams. This "dark and dismal" example is superseded by an example from "normal" life, and we have the celebrated moment of child's play: the toy thrown away, the reel on the string thrown out of the crib and pulled back, to the alternate exclamation of *fort* and *da*. When he has established the equivalence between making the toy disappear and the child's mother's disappearance, Freud is faced with a set of possible interpretations. Why does the child repeat an unpleasurable experience? It may be answered that by staging his mother's disappearance and return, the child is compensating for his instinctual renunciation. Yet the child has also staged disappearance alone, without reappearance, as a game. This may make one want to argue that the essential experience involved is the movement from a passive to an active role in regard to his mother's disappearance, claiming mastery in a situation which he has been compelled to submit to.

Repetition as the movement from passivity to mastery reminds us of "The Theme of the Three Caskets," where Freud, considering Bassanio's choice of the lead casket in *The Merchant of Venice*—the correct choice in the suit of Portia—decides that the choice of the right maiden in man's literary play is also the choice of death; by this choice, he asserts an active mastery of what he must in fact endure. "Choice stands in the place of necessity, of destiny. In this way man overcomes death, which he has recognized intellectually."[13] If repetition is mastery, movement from the passive to the active; and if mastery is an assertion of control over what man must in fact submit to—choice, we might say, of an imposed end—we have already a suggestive comment on the grammar of plot, where repetition, taking us back again over the same ground, could have to do with the choice of ends.

But other possibilities suggest themselves to Freud at this point. The repetition of unpleasant experience—the mother's disappearance—might be explained by the motive of revenge, which would yield its own pleasure. The uncertainty which Freud faces here is whether repetition can be considered a primary event, independent of the pleasure principle, or whether there is always some direct yield of pleasure of another sort involved. The pursuit of this doubt takes Freud into the analytic experience, to his discovery of patients' need to repeat, rather than simply remember, repressed material; the need to reproduce and to "work through" painful material from the past as if it were present. The analyst can detect a "compulsion to repeat," ascribed to the unconscious repressed, particularly discernable in the transference, where it can take "ingenious" forms. The compulsion to repeat gives patients a sense of being fatefully subject to a "perpetual recurrence of the same thing"; it suggests to them pursuit by a daemonic power. We know also, from Freud's essay on "The Uncanny," that this feeling of the daemonic, arising from involuntary repetition, is a particular attribute of the literature of the uncanny.[14]

Thus in analytic work (as also in literary texts) there is slim but real evidence of a compulsion to repeat which can override the pleasure principle, and which seems "more primitive, more elementary, more instinctual than the pleasure principle which it overrides" (23). We might note at this point that the transference itself is a metaphor, a substitutive relationship for the patient's infantile experiences, and thus approximates the status of a text. Now repetition is so basic to our experience of literary texts that one is simultaneously tempted to say all and to say nothing on the subject. To state the matter baldly: rhyme, alliteration, assonance, meter, refrain, all the mnemonic elements of fictions and indeed most of its tropes are in some manner repetitions which take us back in the text, which allow the ear, the eye, the mind to make connections between different textual moments, to see past and present as related and as establishing a future which will be noticeable as some variation in the pattern. Todorov's "same but different" depends on repetition. If we think of the trebling characteristic of the folk tale, and of all formulaic literature, we may consider that the repetition by three constitutes the minimal repetition to the perception of series, which would make it the minimal intentional structure of action, the minimum plot. Narrative must ever present itself as a repetition of events that have already happened, and within this postulate of a generalized repetition it must make use of specific, perceptible repetitions in order to create plot, that is, to show us a significant interconnection of events. Event gains meaning by repeating (with variation) other events. Repetition is a *return* in the text, a doubling back. We cannot say whether this return is a return *to* or a return *of*: for instance, a return to origins or a return of the repressed. Repetition through this ambiguity appears to suspend temporal process, or rather, to subject it to an indeterminate shuttling or oscillation which binds different moments together as a middle which might turn forward or back. This inescapable middle is suggestive of the daemonic. The relation of narrative plot to story may indeed appear to partake of the daemonic, as a kind of tantalizing play with the primitive and the instinctual, the magic and the curse of reproduction or "representation." But in order to know more precisely the operations of repetition, we need to read further in Freud's text.

"What follows is speculation" (24). With this gesture, Freud, in the manner of Rousseau's dismissal of the facts in the *Discourse on the Origins of Inequality*, begins the fourth chapter and his sketch of the economic and energetic model of the mental apparatus: the system Pcpt-Cs and Ucs, the role of the outer layer as shield against excitations, and the definition of trauma as the breaching of the shield, producing a flood of stimuli which knocks the pleasure principle out of operation. Given this situation, the repetition of traumatic experiences in the dreams of neurotics can be seen to have the function of seeking retrospectively to master the flood of stimuli, to perform a mastery or binding of mobile energy through developing the anxiety whose omission was the cause of the traumatic neurosis. Thus the repetition compulsion is carrying out a task that must be accomplished *before* the dominance of the pleasure principle can begin. Repetition is hence a primary event, independent of the pleasure principle and more primitive. Freud now moves into an exploration of the theory of the instincts.[15] The instinctual is the realm of freely mobile, "unbound" energy: the "primary process," where energy seeks immediate discharge, where no postponement of gratification is tolerated. It appears that it must be "the task of the higher strata of the mental apparatus to bind the instinctual excitation reaching the primary process" before the pleasure principle can assert its dominance over the psychic economy (34-35). We may say that at this point in the essay we have moved from a postulate of repetition as the assertion of mastery (as in the passage from passivity to activity in the child's game) to a conception whereby repetition works as a process of *binding* toward the creation of an energetic constant-state situation which will permit the emergence of mastery, and the possibility of postponement.

That Freud at this point evokes once again the daemonic and the uncanny nature of repetition, and refers us not only to children's play but as well to their demand for exact repetition in storytelling, points our way back to literature. Repetition in all its literary manifestations may in fact work as a "binding," a binding of textual energies that allows them to be mastered by putting them into serviceable form within the energetic economy of the narrative. Serviceable form must in this case mean perceptible form: repetition, repeat, recall, symmetry, all these journeys back in the text, returns to and returns of, that allow us to bind one textual moment to another in terms of similarity or substitution rather than mere contiguity. Textual energy, all that is aroused into expectancy and possibility in a text—the term will need more definition, but corresponds well enough to our experience of reading—can become usable by plot only when it has been bound or formalized. It cannot otherwise be plotted in a course to significant discharge, which is what the pleasure principle is charged with doing. To speak of "binding" in a literary text is thus to speak of any of the formalizations (which, like binding, may be painful, retarding) that force us to recognize sameness within difference, or the very emergence of a *sjužet* from the material of *fabula*.

We need at present to follow Freud into his closer inquiry concerning the relation between the compulsion to repeat and the instinctual. The answer lies in "a universal attribute of instincts and perhaps of organic life in general," that "*an instinct is an urge inherent in organic life to restore an earlier state of things*" (36). Instincts, which we tend to think of as a drive toward change, may rather be an expression of "the conservative nature of living things." The organism has no wish to change; if its conditions remained the same, it would constantly repeat the very same course of life. Modifications are the effect of external stimuli, and these modifications are in turn stored up for further repetition, so that, while the instincts may give the appearance of tending toward change, they "are merely seeking to reach an ancient goal by paths alike old and new" (38). Hence Freud is able to proffer, with a certain bravado, the formulation: "*the aim of all life is death.*" We are given an evolutionary image of the organism in which the tension created by external influences has forced living substance to "diverge ever more widely from its original course of life and to make ever more complicated *détours* before reaching its aim of death" (38-49). In this view, the self-preservative instincts function to assure that the organism shall follow its own path to death, to ward off any ways of returning to the inorganic which are not immanent to the organism itself. In other words, "the organism wishes to die only in its own fashion." It must struggle against events (dangers) which would help it to achieve its goal too rapidly—by a kind of short-circuit.

We are here somewhere near the heart of Freud's masterplot for organic life, and it generates a certain analytic force in its superimposition on fictional plots. What operates in the text through repetition is the death instinct, the drive toward the end. Beyond and under the domination of the pleasure principle is this baseline of plot, its basic "pulsation," sensible or audible through the repetitions which take us back in the text. Repetition can take us both backwards and forwards because these terms have become reversible: the end is a time before the beginning. Between these two moments of quiescence, plot itself stands as a kind of divergence or deviance, a postponement in the discharge which leads back to the inanimate. For plot starts (must give the illusion of starting) from that moment at which story, or "life," is stimulated from quiescence into a state of narratability, into a tension, a kind of irritation, which demands narration. Any reflection on novelistic beginnings shows the beginning as an awakening, an arousal, the birth of an appetency, ambition, desire or intention.[16] To say this is of course to say—perhaps more pertinently—that beginnings are the arousal of an intention in reading, stimulation into a tension. (The specifically erotic nature of the tension of writing and its rehearsal in reading could be demonstrated through a number of exemplary texts, notably Rousseau's account, in *The Confessions*, of how his novel *La Nouvelle Héloïse* was born of a masturbatory reverie and its necessary fictions, or the very similar opening of Jean Genet's *Notre-Dame des fleurs;* but of course the sublimated forms of the tension are just as pertinent.) The ensuing narrative—the Aristotelean "middle"—is maintained in a state of tension, as a prolonged deviance from the quiescence of the "normal"—which is to say, the unnarratable—until it reaches the terminal quiescence of the end. The development of a narrative shows that the tension is maintained as an ever more complicated postponement or *détour* leading back to the goal of quiescence. As Sartre and Benjamin compellingly argued, the narrative must tend toward its end, seek illumination in its own death. Yet this must be the right death, the correct end. The complication of the *détour* is related to the danger of short-circuit: the danger of reaching the end too quickly, of achieving the im-proper death. The improper end indeed lurks throughout narrative, frequently as the wrong choice: choice of the wrong casket, misapprehension of the magical agent, false erotic object-choice. The development of the subplot in the classical novel usually suggests (as William Empson has intimated) a different solution to the problems worked through by the main plot, and often illustrates the danger of short-circuit.[17] The subplot stands as one means of warding off the danger of short-circuit, assuring that the main plot will continue through to the right end. The desire of the text (the desire of reading) is hence desire for the end, but desire for the end reached only through the at least minimally complicated *détour*, the intentional deviance, in tension, which is the plot of narrative.

Deviance, *détour*, an intention which is irritation: these are characteristics of the narratable, of "life" as it is the material of narrative, of *fabula* become *sjužet*. Plot is a kind of arabesque or squiggle toward the end. It is like Corporal Trim's arabesque with his stick, in *Tristram Shandy*, retraced by Balzac at the start of *La Peau de chagrin* to indicate the arbitrary, transgressive, gratuitous line of narrative, its deviance from the straight line, the shortest distance between beginning and end—which would be the collapse of one into the other, of life into immediate death. Freud's text will in a moment take us closer to understanding of the formal organization of this deviance toward the end. But it also at this point offers further suggestions about the beginning. For when he has identified both the death instincts and the life (sexual) instincts as conservative, tending toward the restoration of an earlier state of things, Freud feels obliged to deconstruct the will to believe in a human drive toward perfection, an impulsion forward and upward: a force which—he here quotes *Faust* as the classic text of man's forward striving—"*ungebändigt immer vorwärts dringt.*" The illusion of the striving toward perfection is to be explained by instinctual repression and the persisting tension of the repressed instinct, and the resulting difference between the pleasure of satisfaction *demanded* and that which is *achieved*, a difference which "provides the driving factor which will permit of no halting at any position attained" (36). This process of subtraction reappears in modified form in the work of Lacan, where it is the difference between *need* (the infant's need for the breast) and *demand* (which is always demand for recognition) that gives as its result *desire*, which is precisely the driving power, of plot certainly, since desire for Lacan is a metonymy, the forward movement of the signifying chain. If Roman Jakobson is able, in his celebrated essay, to associate the metonymic pole with prose fiction (particularly the nineteenth-century novel)—as the metaphoric pole is associated with lyric poetry—it would seem to be because the meanings peculiar to narrative inhere (or, as Lacan would say, "insist") in the metonymic chain, in the drive of desire toward meaning in time.[18]

The next-to-last chapter of *Beyond the Pleasure Principle* cannot here be rehearsed in detail. In brief, it leads Freud twice into the findings of biology, first on the track of the origins of death, to find out whether it is a necessary or merely a contingent alternative to interminability, then in pursuit of the origins of sexuality, to see whether it satisfies the description of the instinctual as conservative. Biology can offer no sure answer to either investigation, but it offers at least metaphorical confirmation of the necessary dualism of Freud's thought, and encouragement to reformulate his earlier opposition of ego instincts to sexual instincts as one between life instincts and death instincts, a shift in the grouping of oppositional forces which then allows him to reformulate the libidinal instincts themselves as the Eros "of the poets and philosophers" which holds all living things together, and which seeks to combine things in ever greater living wholes. Desire would then seem to be totalizing in intent, a process tending toward combination in new unities: metonymy in the search to become metaphor. But for the symmetry of Freud's opposition to be complete, he needs to be able to ascribe to Eros, as to the death instinct, the characteristic of a need to restore an earlier state of things. Since biology will not answer, Freud, in a remarkable gesture, turns toward myth, to come up with Plato's Androgyne, which precisely ascribes Eros to a search to recover a lost primal unity which was split asunder. Freud's apologetic tone in this last twist to his argument is partly disingenuous, for we detect a contentment to have formulated the forces of the human masterplot as "philosopher and poet." The apology is coupled with a reflection that much of the obscurity of the processes Freud has been considering "is merely due to our being obliged to operate with the scientific terms, that is to say with the figurative language, peculiar to psychology" (60). *Beyond the Pleasure Principle,* we are to understand, is not merely metapsychology, it is also mythopoesis, necessarily resembling "an equation with two unknown quantities" (57), or, we might say, a formal dynamic the terms of which are not substantial but purely relational. We perceive that *Beyond the Pleasure Principle* is itself a plot which has formulated that dynamic necessary to its own *détour.*

The last chapter of Freud's text recapitulates, but not without difference. He returns to the problem of the relationship between the instinctual processes of repetition and the dominance of the pleasure principle. One of the earliest and most important functions of the mental apparatus is to bind the instinctual impulses which impinge upon it, to convert freely mobile energy into a quiescent cathexis. This is a preparatory act on behalf of the pleasure principle, which permits its dominance. Sharpening his distinction between a *function* and a *tendency,* Freud argues that the pleasure principle is a "tendency operating in the service of a function whose business it is to free the mental apparatus entirely from excitation or to keep the amount of excitation in it constant or to keep it as low as possible" (62). This function is concerned "with the most universal endeavour of all living substance—namely to return to the quiescence of the inorganic world." Hence one can consider "binding" to be a preliminary function which prepares the excitation for its final elimination in the pleasure of discharge. In this manner, we could say that the repetition compulsion and the death instinct serve the pleasure principle; in a larger sense, the pleasure principle, keeping watch on the invasion of stimuli from without and especially from within, seeking their discharge, serves the death instinct, making sure that the organism is permitted to return to quiescence. The whole evolution of the mental apparatus appears as a taming of the instincts so that the pleasure principle—itself tamed, displaced—can appear to dominate in the complicated *détour* called life which leads back to death. In fact, Freud seems here at the very end to imply that the two antagonistic instincts serve one another in a dynamic interaction which is a perfect and self-regulatory economy which makes both end and *détour* perfectly necessary and interdependent. The organism must live in order to die in the proper manner, to die the right death. We must have the arabesque of plot in order to reach the end. We must have metonymy in order to reach metaphor.

We emerge from reading *Beyond the Pleasure Principle* with a dynamic model which effectively structures ends (death, quiescence, non-narratability) against beginnings (Eros, stimulation into tension, the desire of narrative) in a manner that necessitates the middle as *détour*, as struggle toward the end under the compulsion of imposed delay, as arabesque in the dilatory space of the text. We detect some illumination of the necessary distance between beginning and end, the drives which connect them but which prevent the one collapsing back into the other: the way in which metonymy and metaphor serve one another, the necessary temporality of the same-but-different which to Todorov constitutes the narrative transformation. The model suggests further that along the way of the path from beginning to end—in the middle—we have repetitions serving to bind the energy of the text in order to make its final discharge more effective. In fictional plots, these bindings are a system of repetitions which are returns to and returns of, confounding the movement forward to the end with a movement back to origins, reversing meaning within forward-moving time, serving to formalize the system of textual energies, offering the possibility (or the illusion) of "meaning" wrested from "life."

As a dynamic-energetic model of narrative plot, then, *Beyond the Pleasure Principle* gives an image of how "life," or the *fabula,* is stimulated into the condition of narrative, becomes *sjužet:* enters into a state of deviance and *détour* (ambition, quest, the pose of a mask) in which it is maintained for a certain time, through an at least minimally complex extravagance, before returning to the quiescence of the non-narratable. The energy generated by deviance, extravagance, excess—an energy which belongs to the textual hero's career and to the readers' expectation, his desire of and for the text—maintains the plot in its movement through the vacillating play of the middle, where repetition as binding works toward the generation of significance, toward recognition and the retrospective illumination which will allow us to grasp the text as total metaphor, but not therefore to discount the metonymies that have led to it. The desire of the text is ultimately the desire for the end, for that recognition which is the moment of the death of the reader in the text. Yet recognition cannot abolish textuality, does not annul the middle which, in its oscillation between blindness and recognition, between origin and endings, is the truth of the narrative text.

It is characteristic of textual energy in narrative that it should always be on the verge of premature discharge, of short-circuit. The reader experiences the fear—and excitation—of the improper end, which is symmetrical to—but far more immediate and present than—the fear of endlessness. The possibility of short-circuit can of course be represented in all manner of threats to the protagonist or to any of the functional logics which demand completion; it most commonly takes the form of temptation to the mistaken erotic object choice, who may be of the "Belle Dame sans merci" variety, or may be the too-perfect and hence annihilatory bride. Throughout the Romantic tradition, it is perhaps most notably the image of incest (of the fraternal-sororal variety) which hovers as the sign of a passion interdicted because its fulfillment would be too perfect, a discharge indistinguishable from death, the very cessation of narrative movement. Narrative is in a state of temptation to oversameness, and where we have no literal threat of incest (as in Chateaubriand, or Faulkner), lovers choose to turn the beloved into a soul-sister so that possession will be either impossible or mortal: Werther and Lotte, for instance, or, at the inception of the tradition, Rousseau's *La Nouvelle Héloïse*, where Saint-Preux's letter to Julie following their night of love begins: "Mourons, ô ma douce amie." Incest is only the exemplary version of a temptation of short-circuit from which the protagonist and the text must be led away, into *détour*, into the cure which prolongs narrative.

It may finally be in the logic of our argument that repetition speaks in the text of a return which ultimately subverts the very notion of beginning and end, suggesting that the idea of beginning presupposes the end, that the end is a time before the beginning, and hence that the interminable never can be finally bound in a plot. Analysis, Freud would eventually discover, is inherently interminable, since the dynamics of resistance and the transference can always generate new beginnings in relation to any possible end.[19] It is the role of fictional plots to impose an end which yet suggests a return, a new beginning: a rereading. A narrative, that is, wants at its end to refer us back to its middle, to the web of the text: to recapture us in its doomed energies.

One ought at this point to make a new beginning, and to sketch the possible operation of the model in the study of the plot of a fiction. One could, for instance, take Dickens' *Great Expectations*. One would have to show how the energy released in the text by its liminary "primal scene"—Pip's terrifying meeting with Magwitch in the graveyard—is subsequently bound in a number of desired but unsatisfactory ways (including Pip's "being bound" as apprentice, the "dream" plot of Satis House, the apparent intent of the "expectations"), and simultaneously in censored but ultimately more satisfying ways (through all the returns of the repressed identification of Pip and his convict). The most salient device of this novel's "middle" is literally the journey back—from London to Pip's home town—a repeated return to apparent origins which is also a return of the repressed, of what Pip calls "that old spell of my childhood." It would be interesting to demonstrate that each of Pip's choices in the novel, while consciously life-furthering, forward oriented, in fact leads back, to the insoluble question of origins, to the palindrome of his name, so that the end of the narrative—its "discharge"—appears as the image of a "life" cured of "plot," as celibate clerk for Clarrikers.

Pip's story, while ostensibly the search for progress, ascension, and metamorphosis, may after all be the narrative of an attempted homecoming: of the effort to reach an assertion of origin through ending, to find the same in the different, the time before in the time after. Most of the great nineteenth-century novels tell this same tale. Georg Lukács has called the novel "the literary form of the transcendent homelessness of the idea," and argued that it is in the discrepancy between idea and the organic that time, the process of duration, becomes constitutive of the novel as of no other genre:

> Only in the novel, whose very matter is seeking and failing to find the essence, is time posited together with the form: time is the resistance of the organic—which possesses a mere semblance of life—to the present meaning, the will of life to remain within its own completely enclosed immanence. . . . In the novel, meaning is separated from life, and hence the essential from

> the temporal; we might almost say that the entire inner action of the novel is nothing but a struggle against the power of time.[20]

The understanding of time, says Lukács, the transformation of the struggle against time into a process full of interest, is the work of memory—or more precisely, we could say with Freud, of "remembering, repeating, working through." Repetition, remembering, reenactment are the ways in which we replay time, so that it may not be lost. We are thus always trying to work back through time to that transcendent home, knowing of course that we cannot. All we can do is subvert or, perhaps better, pervert time: which is what narrative does.[21]

To forgo any true demonstration on a novel, and to bring a semblance of conclusion, we may return to the assertion, by Barthes and Todorov, that narrative is essentially the articulation of a set of verbs. These verbs are no doubt ultimately all versions of desire. Desire is the wish for the end, for fulfillment, but fulfillment delayed so that we can understand it in relation to origin, and to desire itself. The story of Scheherezade is doubtless the story of stories. This suggests that the tale as read is inhabited by the reader's desire, and that further analysis should be directed to that desire, not (in the manner of Norman Holland) his individual desire and its origins in his own personality, but his transindividual and intertextually determined desire as a reader. Because it concerns ends in relation to beginnings and the forces that animate the middle in between, Freud's model is suggestive of what a reader engages when he responds to plot. It images that engagement as essentially dynamic, an interaction with a system of energy which the reader activates. This in turn suggests why we can read *Beyond the Pleasure Principle* as a text concerning textuality, and conceive that there can be a psychoanalytic criticism of the text itself that does not become—as has usually been the case—a study of the psychogenesis of the text (the author's unconscious), the dynamics of literary response (the reader's unconscious), or the occult motivations of the characters (postulating an "unconscious" for them). It is rather the superimposition of the model of the functioning of the mental apparatus on the functioning of the text that offers the possibility of a psychoanalytic criticism. And here the superimposition of Freud's psychic masterplot on the plots of fiction seems a valid and useful maneuver. Plot mediates meanings with the contradictory human world of the eternal and the mortal. Freud's masterplot speaks of the temporality of desire, and speaks to our very desire for fictional plots.

NOTES

1. Tzvetan Todorov, "Les Transformations narratives," in *Poétique de la prose* (Paris: Seuil, 1971), p. 240. Todorov's terms *récit* and *histoire* correspond to the Russian Formalist distinction between *sjužet* and *fabula*. In English, we might use with the same sense of distinctions: narrative *plot* and *story*.

I wish at the outset of this essay to express my debt to two colleagues whose thinking has helped to clarify my own: Andrea Bertolini and David A. Miller. It is to the latter that I owe the term "the narratable."

2. See Roman Jakobson, "Two Types of Language and Two Types of Aphasic Disturbances," in Jakobson and Halle, *Fundamentals of Language* (The Hague: Mouton, 1956). Todorov in a later article adds to "transformation" the term "succession," and sees the pair as definitional of narrative. He discusses the possible equation of these terms with Jakobson's "metaphor" and "metonymy," to conclude that "the connection is possible but does not seem necessary." (Todorov, "The Two Principles of Narrative," *Diacritics*, Fall 1971, p. 42.) But there seem to be good reasons to maintain Jakobson's terms as "master tropes" referring to two aspects of virtually any text.

3. See Claude Lévi-Strauss, "La Structure et la forme," *Cahiers de L'Institut de science économique appliquée*, 99, série M, no. 7 (1960), p. 29. This term

is cited with approval by A.-J. Greimas in *Sémantique structurale* (Paris: Larousse, 1966) and Roland Barthes, in "Introduction à l'analyse structurale des récits," *Communications* 8 (1966).

4. Todorov, "Les Transformations narratives," *Poétique de la prose*, p. 240. Translations from the French, here and elsewhere, are my own.

5. Proust's phrase is cited by Gerard Genette in "Discours du récit," *Figures III* (Paris: Seuil, 1972), 182. Whereas Barthes maintains in "Introduction à l'analyse structurale des récits" that time belongs only to the referent of narrative, Genette gives attention to the time of reading and its necessary linearity. See pp. 77–78.

6. See Roland Barthes, *S/Z* (Paris: Seuil, 1970), 37.

7. "Introduction à l'analyse structurale des récits," p. 27.

8. Jean-Paul Sartre, *La Nausée* (Paris: Livre de Poche, 1957), 62–63.

9. Sartre, *Les Mots* (Paris: Gallimard, 1968), p. 171.

10. Walter Benjamin, "The Storyteller," in *Illuminations*, trans. Harry Zohn (New York: Schocken Books, 1969), 101.

11. Sigmund Freud, "Beyond the Pleasure Principle" (1920), in *The Standard Edition of the Complete Psychological Works of Sigmund Freud*, ed. James Strachey (London: Hogarth Press, 1955), 18, 59. Subsequent page references will be given between parentheses in the text.

12. J. Hillis Miller, in "Ariadne's Web" (unpublished manuscript), notes that the term *diegesis* suggests that narrative is a retracing of a journey already made. On the detective story, see Tzvetan Todorov, "Typologie du roman policier," *Poétique de la prose*, pp. 58–59.

13. Freud, "The Theme of the Three Caskets" (1913), *Standard Edition*, 12, 299.

14. See Freud, "The Uncanny" (*Das Unheimliche*) (1919), in *Standard Edition*, 17, 219–52.

15. I shall use the term "instinct" since it is the translation of *Trick* given throughout the *Standard Edition*. But we should realize that "instinct" is inadequate and somewhat misleading, since it loses the sense of "drive" associated with the word *Trieb*. The currently accepted French translation, *pulsion*, is more to our purposes: the model that interests me here might indeed be called "pulsional."

16. On the beginning as intention, see Edward Said, *Beginnings: Intention and Method* (New York: Basic Books, 1975). It occurs to me that the exemplary narrative beginning might be that of Kafka's *Metamorphosis:* waking up to find oneself transformed into a monstrous vermin.

17. See William Empson, "Double Plots," in *Some Versions of Pastoral* (New York: New Directions, 1960), 25–84.

18. See Jakobson, "Two Types of Language . . ." See, in Lacan's work, especially "Le Stade du miroir" and "L'Instance de la lettre dans l'inconscient," in *Écrits* (Paris: Seuil, 1966).

19. See Freud, "Analysis Terminable and Interminable" (1937), in *Standard Edition*, 23, 216–53.

20. Georg Lukács, *The Theory of the Novel*, trans. Anna Bostock (Cambridge. MIT Press, 1971), 122.

21. Genette discusses Proust's "perversion" of time in "Discours du récit," p. 182. "Remembering, Repeating, and Working Through" (*Erinnern, Wiederholen und Durcharbeiten*) (1914) is the subject of one of Freud's papers on technique. See *Standard Edition*, 12, 145–56.

18

Jacques Lacan
1901–1981

From his earliest writings, including his doctoral thesis (1932), Jacques Lacan expressed discontent with the limits of traditional psychoanalysis as practiced by rigid Freudians. After parting ways first with the French and then the international psychoanalytic establishment, in 1953 Lacan began weekly seminars attended by students, philosophers, and linguists. Along with his essays, most of which appear in his *Écrits* (1966; trans. 1977), these seminars provided Lacan with a field for his most important work. Lacan's intent was to reinterpret Freud, focusing especially on Freud's treatment of the unconscious, which communicates its formal structure through a specialized language. For Lacan, the true subject—of psychoanalysis and of discourse—is the unconscious rather than the ego; however, he did not reify the unconscious but viewed the idea of a unified subject as illusory, particularly in his 1936 lecture on the "mirror stage" of childhood development (revised and published in *Écrits*).

Like Lévi-Strauss, Foucault, Barthes, and Derrida, Lacan grounded his work in structural linguistics, particularly concentrating on the functions of signs. From this study, Lacan determined that the unconscious is "structured like language" and can reveal meaning only in the connections among signifiers. This linguistic model surfaced in Lacan's *Rome Discourse* (1953; trans. 1968), titled "The function and field of speech and language in psychoanalysis." His 1957 (trans. 1977) essay, "The instance of the letter, or reason since Freud," a Saussurian reading of the unconscious, emphasized the split between the signifier and signified by making the signifier the primary component of the schema, reversing the traditional Western notion of the primacy of the concept.

Lacan's seminar on Poe's "The Purloined Letter" (1956; trans. 1972) is as much an interpretation of Lacan himself as it is a reading of Poe. The story illustrates Lacan's interest in the interconnection of discourse and the psychoanalytic process, tracing as it does the displacement of the signifier—the purloined letter—which affects each of the story's characters in its path and "determines," as Lacan says here, "the subjects in their acts, in their destiny, in their refusals, in their blind spots, their end and fate. . . ." Poe's story, then, becomes a parable of the primacy of the linguistic sign in its control of the speaking subject. Lacan positioned this essay at the beginning of *Écrits* to illustrate the subject of the remaining essays, the law of the signifier. Like the letter in Poe's story, Lacan's style, with its use of metaphor, irony, and puns, refuses a systematic reading and demands that the reader follow the path of the signifier in order to read his text.

Seminar on "The Purloined Letter"

Und wenn es uns glückt,
Und wenn es sich schickt,
So sind es Gedanken.

Our inquiry has led us to the point of recognizing that the repetition automatism (*Wiederholungszwang*) finds its basis in what we have called the *insistence* of the signifying chain.[1] We have elaborated that notion itself as a correlate of the *ex-sistence* (or: eccentric place) in which we must necessarily locate the subject of the unconscious if we are to take Freud's discovery seriously.[2] As is known, it is in the realm of experience inaugurated by psychoanalysis that we may grasp along what imaginary lines the human organism, in the most intimate recesses of its being, manifests its capture in a *symbolic* dimension.[3]

The lesson of this seminar is intended to maintain that these imaginary incidences, far from representing the essence of our experience, reveal only what in it remains inconsistent unless they are related to the symbolic chain which binds and orients them.

We realize, of course, the importance of these imaginary impregnations (*Prägung*) in those partializations of the symbolic alternative which give the symbolic chain its appearance. But we maintain that it is the specific law of that chain which governs those psychoanalytic effects that are decisive for the subject: such as foreclosure (*Verwerfung*), repression (*Verdrängung*), denial (*Verneinung*) itself—specifying with appropriate emphasis that these effects follow so faithfully the displacement (*Entstellung*) of the signifier that imaginary factors, despite their inertia, figure only as shadows and reflections in the process.

But this emphasis would be lavished in vain, if it served, in your opinion, only to abstract a general type from phenomena whose particularity in our work would remain the essential thing for you, and whose original arrangement could be broken up only artificially.

Which is why we have decided to illustrate for you today the truth which may be drawn from that moment in Freud's thought under study—namely, that it is the symbolic order which is constitutive for the subject—by demonstrating in a story the decisive orientation which the subject receives from the itinerary of a signifier.

It is that truth, let us note, which makes the very existence of fiction possible. And in that case, a fable is as appropriate as any other narrative for bringing it to light—at the risk of having the fable's coherence put to the test in the process. Aside from that reservation, a fictive tale even has the advantage of manifesting symbolic necessity more purely to the extent that we may believe its conception arbitrary.

Which is why, without seeking any further, we have chosen our example from the very story in which the dialectic of the game of even or odd—from whose study we have but recently profited—occurs.[4] It is, no doubt, no accident that this tale revealed itself propitious to pursuing a course of inquiry which had already found support in it.

As you know, we are talking about the tale which Baudelaire translated under the title: *La lettre volé*. At first reading, we may distinguish a drama, its narration, and the conditions of that narration.

We see quickly enough, moreover, that these components are necessary and that they could not have escaped the intentions of whoever composed them.

The narration, in fact, doubles the drama with a commentary without which no *mise en scène* would be possible. Let us say that the action would remain, properly speaking, invisible from the pit—aside from the fact that the dialogue would be expressly and by dramatic necessity devoid of whatever meaning it might have for an audience: —in other words, nothing of the drama could be grasped, neither seen nor heard, without, dare we say, the twilighting which the narration, in each scene, casts on the point of view that one of the actors had while performing it.

There are two scenes, the first of which we shall straightway designate the primal scene, and by no means inadvertently, since the second may be considered its repetition in the very sense we are considering today.

The primal scene is thus performed, we are told, in the royal *boudoir*, so that we suspect that the person of the highest rank, called the "exalted personage," who is alone there when she receives a letter, is the Queen. This feeling is confirmed by the embarrassment into which she is plunged by the entry of the other exalted personage, of whom we have already been told prior to this account that the knowledge he might have of the letter in question would jeopardize for the lady nothing less than her honor and safety. Any doubt that he is in fact the King is promptly dissipated in the course of the scene which begins with the entry of the Minister D . . . At that moment, in fact, the Queen can do no better than to play on the King's inattentiveness by leaving the letter on the table "face down, address uppermost." It does not, however, escape the Minister's lynx eye, nor does he fail to notice the Queen's distress and thus to fathom her secret. From then on everything transpires like clockwork. After dealing in his customary manner with the business of the day, the Minister draws from his pocket a letter similar in appearance to the one in his view, and, having pretended to read it, he places it next to the other. A bit more conversation to amuse the royal company, whereupon, without flinching once, he seizes the embarrassing letter, making off with it, as the Queen, on whom none of his maneuver has been lost, remains unable to intervene for fear of attracting the attention of her royal spouse, close at her side at that very moment.

Everything might then have transpired unseen by a hypothetical spectator of an operation in which nobody falters, and whose *quotient* is that the Minister has filched from the Queen her letter and that—an even more important result than the first—the Queen knows that he now has it, and by no means innocently.

A *remainder* that no analyst will neglect, trained as he is to retain whatever is significant, without always knowing what to do with it: the letter, abandoned by the Minister, and which the Queen's hand is now free to roll into a ball.

Second scene: in the Minister's office. It is in his hotel, and we know—from the account the Prefect of police has given Dupin, whose specific genius for solving enigmas Poe introduces here for the second time—that the police, returning there as soon as the Minister's habitual, nightly absences allow them to, have searched the hotel and its surroundings from top to bottom for the last eighteen months. In vain,—although everyone can deduce from the situation that the Minister keeps the letter within reach.

Dupin calls on the Minister. The latter receives him with studied nonchalance, affecting in his conversation romantic *ennui*. Meanwhile Dupin, whom this pretense does not deceive, his eyes protected by green glasses, proceeds to inspect the premises. When his glance catches a rather crumpled piece of paper—apparently thrust carelessly in a division of an ugly pasteboard card-rack, hanging gaudily from the middle of the mantelpiece—he already knows that he's found what he's looking for. His conviction is re-enforced by the very details which seem to contradict the description he has of the stolen letter, with the exception of the format, which remains the same.

Whereupon he has but to withdraw, after "forgetting" his snuff-box on the table, in order to return the following day to reclaim it—armed with a facsimile of the letter in its present state. As an incident in the street, prepared for the proper moment, draws the Minister to the window, Dupin in turn seizes the opportunity to snatch the letter while substituting the imitation, and has only to maintain the appearances of a normal exit.

Here as well all has transpired, if not without noise, at least without all commotion. The quotient of the operation is that the Minister no longer has the letter, but, far from suspecting that Dupin is the culprit who has ravished it from him, knows nothing of it. Moreover, what he is left with is far from insignificant for what follows. We shall return to what brought Dupin to inscribe a message on his counterfeit letter. Whatever the case, the Minister, when he tries to make use of it, will be able to read these words, written so that he may recognize Dupin's hand: ". . . *Un dessein si funeste/ S'il n'est digne d'Atreé est digne de Thyeste,*" whose source, Dupin tells us, is Crébillon's *Atreé.*[5]

Need we emphasize the similarity of these two sequences? Yes, for the resemblance we have in mind is not a simple collection of traits chosen only in order to delete their difference. And it would not be enough to retain those common traits at the expense of the others for the slightest truth to result. It is rather the intersubjectivity in which the two actions are motivated that we wish to bring into relief, as well as the three terms through which it structures them.[6]

The special status of these terms results from their corresponding simultaneously to the three logical moments through which the decision is precipitated and the three places it assigns to the subjects among whom it constitutes a choice.

That decision is reached in a glance's time.[7] For the maneuvers which follow, however stealthily they prolong it, add nothing to that glance, nor does the deferring of the deed in the second scene break the unity of that moment.

This glance presupposes two others, which it embraces in its vision of the breach left in their fallacious complementarity, anticipating in it the occasion for larceny afforded by that exposure. Thus three moments, structuring three glances, borne by three subjects, incarnated each time by different characters.

The first is a glance that sees nothing: the King and the police.

The second, a glance which sees that the first sees nothing and deludes itself as to the secrecy of what it hides: the Queen, then the Minister.

The third sees that the first two glances leave what should be hidden exposed to whomever would seize it: the Minister, and finally Dupin.

In order to grasp in its unity the intersubjective complex thus described, we would willingly seek a model in the technique legendarily attributed to the ostrich attempting to shield itself from danger; for that technique might ultimately be qualified as political, divided as it here is among three partners: the second believing itself invisible because the first has its head stuck in the ground, and all the while letting the third calmly pluck its rear; we need only enrich its proverbial denomination by a letter, producing *la politique de l'autruiche,* for the ostrich itself to take on forever a new meaning.[8]

Given the intersubjective modulus of the repetitive action, it remains to recognize in it a *repetition automatism* in the sense that interest us in Freud's text.

The plurality of subjects, of course, can be no objection for those who are long accustomed to the perspectives summarized by our formula: *the unconscious is the discourse of the Other*.[9] And we will not recall now what the notion of the *immixture of subjects*, recently introduced in our re-analysis of the dream of Irma's injection, adds to the discussion.

What interests us today is the manner in which the subjects relay each other in their displacement during the intersubjective repetition.

We shall see that their displacement is determined by the place which a pure signifer—the purloined letter—comes to occupy in their trio. And that is what will confirm for us its status as repetition automatism.

It does not, however, seem excessive, before pursuing this line of inquiry, to ask whether the thrust of the tale and the interest we bring to it—to the extent that they coincide—do not lie elsewhere.

May we view as simply a rationalization (in our gruff jargon) the fact that the story is told to us as a police mystery?

In truth, we should be right in judging that fact highly dubious as soon as we note that everything which warrants such mystery concerning a crime or offense—its nature and motives, instruments and execution; the procedure used to discover the author, and the means employed to convict him—is carefully eliminated here at the start of each episode.

The act of deceit is, in fact, from the beginning as clearly known as the intrigues of the culprit and their effects on his victim. The problem, as exposed to us, is limited to the search for and restitution of the object of that deceit, and it seems rather intentional that the solution is already obtained when it is explained to us. Is *that* how we are kept in suspense? Whatever credit we may accord the conventions of a genre for provoking a specific interest in the reader, we should not forget that "the Dupin tale," this the second to appear, is a prototype, and that even if the genre were established in the first, it is still a little early for the author to play on a convention.[10]

It would, however, be equally excessive to reduce the whole thing to a fable whose moral would be that in order to shield from inquisitive eyes one of those correspondences whose secrecy is sometimes necessary to conjugal peace, it suffices to leave the crucial letters lying about on one's table, even though the meaningful side be turned face down. For that would be a hoax which, for our part, we would never recommend anyone try, lest he be gravely disappointed in his hopes.

Might there then be no mystery other than, concerning the Prefect, an incompetence issuing in failure—were it not perhaps, concerning Dupin, a certain dissonance we hesitate to acknowledge between, on the one hand, the admittedly penetrating, though, in their generality, not always quite relevant remarks with which he introduces us to his method and, on the other, the manner in which he in fact intervenes.

Were we to pursue this sense of mystification a bit further we might soon begin to wonder whether, from that initial scene which only the rank of the protagonists saves from vaudeville, to the fall into ridicule which seems to await the Minister at the end, it is not this impression that everyone is being duped which makes for our pleasure.

And we would be all the more inclined to think so in that we would recognize in that surmise, along with those of you who read us, the definition we once gave in passing of the modern hero, "whom ludicrous exploits exalt in circumstances of utter confusion."[11]

But are we ourselves not taken in by the imposing presence of the amateur detective, prototype of a latter-day swashbuckler, as yet safe from the insipidity of our contemporary *superman*?

A trick . . . sufficient for us to discern in this tale, on the contrary, so perfect a verisimilitude that it may be said that truth here reveals its fictive arrangement.

For such indeed is the direction in which the principles of that verisimilitude lead us. Entering into its strategy, we indeed perceive a new drama we may call complementary to the first, in so far as the latter was what is termed a play without words whereas the interest of the second plays on the properties of speech.[12]

If it is indeed clear that each of the two scenes of the real drama is narrated in the course of a different dialogue, it is only through access to those notions set forth in our teaching that one may recognize that it is not thus simply to augment the charm of the exposition, but that the dialogues themselves, in the opposite use they make of the powers of speech, take on a tension which makes of them a different drama, one which our vocabulary will distinguish from the first as persisting in the symbolic order.

The first dialogue—between the Prefect of police and Dupin—is played as between a deaf man and one who hears. That is, it presents the real complexity of what is ordinarily simplified, with the most confused results, in the notion of communication.

This example demonstrates indeed how an act of communication may give the impression at which theorists too often stop: of allowing in its transmission but a single meaning, as though the highly significant commentary into which he who understands integrates it, could, because unperceived by him who does not understand, be considered null.

It remains that if only the dialogue's meaning as a report is retained, its verisimilitude may appear to depend on a guarantee of exactitude. But here dialogue may be more fertile than it seems, if we demonstrate its tactics: as shall be seen by focusing on the recounting of our first scene.

For the double and even triple subjective filter through which that scene comes to us: a narration by Dupin's friend and associate (henceforth to be called the general narrator of the story)—of the account by which the Prefect reveals to Dupin—the report the Queen gave him of it, is not merely the consequence of a fortuitous arrangement.

If indeed the extremity to which the original narrator is reduced precludes her altering any of the events, it would be wrong to believe that the Prefect is empowered to lend her his voice in this case only by that lack of imagination on which he has, dare we say, the patent.

The fact that the message is thus retransmitted assures us of what may by no means be taken for granted: that it belongs to the dimension of language.

Those who are here know our remarks on the subject, specifically those illustrated by the counter case of the so-called language of bees: in which a linguist[13] can see only a simple signaling of the location of objects, in other words: only an imaginary function more differentiated than others.

We emphasize that such a form of communication is not absent in man, however evanescent a naturally given object may be for him, split as it is in its submission to symbols.

Something equivalent may no doubt be grasped in the communion established between two persons in their hatred of a common object: except that the meeting is possible only over a single object, defined by those traits in the individual each of the two resist.

But such communication is not transmissible in symbolic form. It may be maintained only in the relation with the object. In such a manner it may bring together an indefinite number of subjects in a common "ideal": the communication of one subject with another within the crowd thus constituted will nonetheless remain irreducibly mediated by an ineffable relation.[14]

This digression is not only a recollection of principles distantly addressed to those who impute to us a neglect of nonverbal communication: in determining the scope of what speech repeats, it prepares the question of what symptoms repeat.

Thus the indirect telling sifts out the linguistic dimension, and the general narrator, by duplicating it, "hypothetically" adds nothing to it. But its role in the second dialogue is entirely different.

For the latter will be opposed to the first like those poles we have distinguished elsewhere in language and which are opposed like word to speech.

Which is to say that a transition is made here from the domain of exactitude to the register of truth. Now that register, we dare think we needn't come back to this, is situated entirely elsewhere, strictly speaking at the very foundation of intersubjectivity. It is located there where the subject can grasp nothing but the very subjectivity which constitutes an Other as absolute. We shall be satisified here to indicate its place by evoking the dialogue which seems to us to merit its attribution as Jewish joke by that state of privation through which the relation of signifier to speech appears in the entreaty which brings the dialogue to a close: "Why are you lying to me?" one character shouts breathlessly. "Yes, why do you lie to me saying you're going to Cracow so I should believe you're going to Lemberg, when in reality you are going to Cracow?"[15]

We might be prompted to ask a similar question by the torrent of logical impasses, eristic enigmas, paradoxes and even jests presented to us as an introduction to Dupin's method if the fact that they were confided to us by a would-be disciple did not endow them with a new dimension through that act of delegation. Such is the unmistakable magic of legacies: the witness's fidelity is the cowl which blinds and lays to rest all criticism of his testimony.

What could be more convincing, moreover, than the gesture of laying one's cards face up on the table? So much so that we are momentarily persuaded that the magician has in fact demonstrated, as he promised, how his trick was performed, whereas he has only renewed it in still purer form: at which point we fathom the measure of the supremacy of the signifier in the subject.

Such is Dupin's maneuver when he starts with the story of the child prodigy who takes in all his friends at the game of even and odd with his trick of identifying with the opponent, concerning which we have nevertheless shown that it cannot reach the first level of theoretical elaboration, namely: intersubjective alternation, without immediately stumbling on the buttress of its recurrence.[16]

We are all the same treated—so much smoke in our eyes—to the names of La Rochefoucauld, La Bruyère, Machiavelli and Campanella, whose renown, by this time, would seem but futile when confronted with the child's prowess.

Followed by Chamfort, whose maxim that "it is a safe wager that every public idea, every accepted convention is foolish, since it suits the greatest number," will no doubt satisfy all who think they escape its law, that is, precisely, the greatest number. That Dupin accuses the French of deception for applying the word *analysis* to algebra will hardly threaten our pride since, moreover, the freeing of that term for other uses ought by no means to provoke a psychoanalyst to intervene and claim his rights. And there he goes making philological remarks which should positively delight any lovers of Latin: when he recalls without deigning to say any more that "*ambitus* doesn't mean ambition, *religio*, religion, *homines honesti*, honest men," who among you would not take pleasure in remembering . . . what those words mean to anyone familiar with Cicero and Lucretius. No doubt Poe is having a good time. . . .

But a suspicion occurs to us: might not this parade of erudition be destined to reveal to us the key words of our drama? Is not the magician repeating his trick before our eyes, without deceiving us this time about divulging his secret, but pressing his wager to the point of really explaining it to us without us seeing a thing. *That* would be the summit of the illusionist's art: through one of his fictive creations to *truly delude us*.

And is it not such effects which justify our referring, without malice, to a number of imaginary heroes as real characters?

As well, when we are open to hearing the way in which Martin Heidegger discloses to us in the word *aletheia* the play of truth, we rediscover a secret to which truth has always initiated her lovers, and through which they learn that it is in hiding that she offers herself to them *most truly*.

Thus even if Dupin's comments did not defy us so blatantly to believe in them, we should still have to make that attempt against the opposite temptation.

Let us track down [*dépistons*] his footprints there where they elude [*dépiste*] us.[17] And first of all in the criticism by which he explains the Prefect's lack of success. We already saw it surface in those furtive gibes the Prefect, in the first conversation, failed to heed, seeing in them only a pretext for hilarity. That it is, as Dupin insinuates, because a problem is too simple, indeed too evident, that it may appear obscure, will never have any more bearing for him than a vigorous rub of the rib cage.

Everything is arranged to induce in us a sense of the character's imbecility. Which is powerfully articulated by the fact that he and his confederates never conceive of anything beyond what an ordinary rogue might imagine for hiding an object—that is, precisely the all too well known series of extraordinary hiding places: which are promptly catalogued for us, from hidden desk drawers to removable table tops, from the detachable cushions of chairs to their hollowed-out legs, from the reverse side of mirrors to the "thickness" of book bindings.

After which, a moment of derision at the Prefect's error in deducing that because the Minister is a poet, he is not far from being mad, an error, it is argued, which would consist, but this is hardly negligible, simply in a false distribution of the middle term, since it is far from following from the fact that all madmen are poets.

Yes indeed. But we ourselves are left in the dark as to the poet's superiority in the art of concealment—even if he be a mathematician to boot—since our pursuit is suddenly thwarted, dragged as we are into a thicket of bad arguments directed against the reasoning of mathematicians, who never, so far as I know, showed such devotion to their formulae as to identify them with reason itself. At least, let us testify that unlike what seems to be Poe's experience, it occasionally befalls us—with our friend Riguet, whose presence here is a guarantee that our incursions into combinatory analysis are not leading us astray—to hazard such serious deviations (virtual blasphemies, according to Poe) as to cast into doubt that "x^2 plus px is perhaps not absolutely equal to q," without ever—here we give the lie to Poe—having had to fend off any unexpected attack.

Is not so much intelligence being exercised then simply to divert our own from what had been indicated earlier as given, namely, that the police have looked *everywhere*: which we were to understand—

vis-à-vis the area in which the police, not without reason, assumed the letter might be found—in terms of a (no doubt theoretical) exhaustion of space, but concerning which the tale's piquancy depends on our accepting it literally: the division of the entire volume into numbered "compartments," which was the principle governing the operation, being presented to us as so precise that "the fiftieth part of a line," it is said, could not escape the probing of the investigators. Have we not then the right to ask how it happened that the letter was not found *anywhere*, or rather to observe that all we have been told of a more far-ranging conception of concealment does not explain, in all rigor, that the letter escaped detection, since the area combed did in fact contain it, as Dupin's discovery eventually proves.

Must a letter then, of all objects, be endowed with the property of *nullibiety:* to use a term which the thesaurus known as Roget picks up from the semiotic utopia of Bishop Wilkins?[18]

It is evident ("a little *too* self-evident")[19] that between *letter* and *place* exist relations for which no French word has quite the extension of the English adjective: *odd. Bizarre,* by which Baudelaire regularly translates it, is only approximate. Let us say that these relations are . . . *singuliers,* for they are the very ones maintained with place by the *signifier.*

You realize, of course, that our intention is not to turn them into "subtle" relations, nor is our aim to confuse letter with spirit, even if we receive the former by pneumatic dispatch, and that we readily admit that one kills whereas the other quickens, insofar as the signifier—you perhaps begin to understand—materializes the agency of death.[20] But if it is first of all on the materiality of the signifier that we have insisted, that materiality is *odd* [*singulière*] in many ways, the first of which is not to admit partition. Cut a letter in small pieces, and it remains the letter it is—and this in a completely different sense than *Gestalttheorie* would account for which the dormant vitalism informing its notion of the whole.[21]

Language delivers its judgment to whomever knows how to hear it: through the usage of the article as partitive particle. It is there that spirit—if spirit be living meaning—appears, no less oddly, as more available for quantification than its letter. To begin with meaning itself, which bears our saying: a speech rich with meaning ["plein *de* signification"], just as we recognize a measure of intention ["*de* l'intention"] in an act, or deplore that there is no more love ["plus *d'amour*"]; or store up hatred ["*de la* haine"] and expend devotion ["*du* dévouement"], and so much infatuation ["tant *d*'infatuation"] is easily reconciled to the fact that there will always be ass ["*de la* cuisse"] for sale and brawling ["*du* ["*du* rififi"] among men.

But as for the letter—be it taken as typographical character, epistle, or what makes a man of letters—we will say that what is said is to be understood to the letter [*à la lettre*], that a *letter* [*une lettre*] awaits you at the post office, or even that you are acquainted with *letters* [*que vous* avez des lettres]—never that there is *letter* p*de la lettre*] anywhere, whatever the context, even to designate overdue mail.

For the signifier is a unit in its very uniqueness, being by nature symbol only of an absence. Which is why we cannot say of the purloined letter that, like other objects, it must be *or* not be in a particular place but that unlike them it will be *and* not be where it is, wherever it goes.[22]

Let us, in fact, look more closely at what happens to the police. We are spared nothing concerning the procedures used in searching the area submitted to their investigation: from the division of that space into compartments from which the slightest bulk could not escape detection, to needles probing upholstery, and, in the impossibility of sounding wood with a tap, to a microscope exposing the waste of any drilling at the surface of its hollow, indeed the infinitesimal gaping of the slightest abyss. As the network tightens to the point that, not satisfied with shaking the pages of books, the police take to counting them, do we not see space itself shed its leaves like a letter?

But the detectives have so immutable a notion of the real that they fail to notice that their search tends to transform it into its object. A trait by which they would be able to distinguish that object from all others.

This would no doubt be too much to ask them, not because of their lack of insight but rather because of ours. For their imbecility is neither of the individual nor the corporative variety; its source is subjective. It is the realist's imbecility, which does not pause to observe that nothing, however deep in the bowels of the earth a hand may seek to ensconce it, will ever be hidden there, since another hand can always retrieve it, and that what is hidden is never but what is *missing from its place*, as the call slip puts it when speaking of a volume lost in a library. And even if the book be on an adjacent shelf or in the next slot, it would be hidden there, however visibly it may appear. For it can *literally* be said that something is missing from its place only of what can change it: the symbolic. For the real, whatever upheaval we subject it to, is always in its place; it carries it glued to its heel, ignorant of what might exile it from it.

And, to return to our cops, who took the letter from the place where it was hidden, how could they have seized the letter? In what they turned between their fingers what did they hold but what *did not answer* to their description. "A letter, a litter": in Joyce's circle, they played on the homophony of the two words in English.[23] Nor does the seeming bit of refuse the police are now handling reveal its other nature for being but half torn. A different seal on a stamp of another color, the mark of a different handwriting in the superscription are here the most inviolable modes of concealment. And if they stop at the reverse side of the letter, on which, as is known, the recipient's address was written in that period, it is because the letter has for them no other side but its reverse.

What indeed might they find on its obverse? Its message, as is often said to our cybernetic joy? . . . But does it not occur to us that this message has already reached its recipient and has even been left with her, since the insignificant scrap of paper now represents it no less well than the original note.

If we could admit that a letter has completed its destiny after fulfilling its function, the ceremony of returning letters would be a less common close to the extinction of the fires of love's feasts. The signifier is not functional. And the mobilization of the elegant society whose frolics we are following would as well have no meaning if the letter itself were content with having one. For it would hardly be an adequate means of keeping it secret to inform a squad of cops of its existence.

We might even admit that the letter has an entirely different (if no more urgent) meaning for the Queen than the one understood by the Minister. The sequence of events would not be noticeably affected, not even if it were strictly incomprehensible to an uninformed reader.

For it is certainly not so for everybody, since, as the Prefect pompously assures us, to everyone's derision, "the disclosure of the document to a third person, who shall be nameless," (that name which leaps to the eye like the pig's tail twixt the teeth of old Ubu) "would bring in question the honor of a personage of most exalted station, indeed that the honor and peace of the illustrious personage are so jeopardized."

In that case, it is not only the meaning but the text of the message which it would be dangerous to place in circulation, and all the more so to the extent that it might appear harmless, since the risks of an indiscretion unintentionally committed by one of the letter's holders would thus be increased.

Nothing then can redeem the police's position, and nothing would be changed by improving their "culture." *Scripta manent:* in vain would they learn from a *de luxe*-edition humanism the proverbial lesson which *verba volant* concludes. May it but please heaven that writings remain, as is rather the case with spoken words: for the indelible debt of the latter impregnates our acts with its transferences.

Writings scatter to the winds blank checks in an insane charge.[24] And were they not such flying leaves, there would be no purloined letters.[25]

But what of it? For a purloined letter to exist, we may ask, to whom does a letter belong? We stressed a moment ago the oddity implicit in returning a letter to him who had but recently given wing to its burning pledge. And we generally deem unbecoming such premature publications as the one by which the Chevalier d'Éon put several of his correspondents in a rather pitiful position.

Might a letter on which the sender retains certain rights then not quite belong to the person to whom it is addressed? or might it be that the latter was never the real receiver?

Let's take a look: we shall find illumination in what at first seems to obscure matters: the fact that the tale leaves us in virtually total ignorance of the sender, no less than of the contents, of the letter. We are told only that the Minister immediately recognized the handwriting of the address and only incidentally, in a discussion of the Minister's camouflage, is it said that the original seal bore the ducal arms of the S . . . family. As for the letter's bearing, we know only the dangers it entails should it come into the hands of a specific third party, and that its possession has allowed the Minister to "wield, to a very dangerous extent, for political purposes," the power it assures him over the interested party. But all this tells us nothing of the message it conveys.

Love letter or conspiratorial letter, letter of betrayal or letter of mission, letter of summons or letter of distress, we are assured of but one thing: the Queen must not bring it to the knowledge of her lord and master.

Now these terms, far from bearing the nuance of discredit they have in *bourgeois* comedy, take on a certain prominence through allusion to her sovereign, to whom she is bound by pledge of faith, and doubly so, since her role as spouse does not relieve her of her duties as subject, but rather elevates her to the guardianship of what royalty according to law incarnates of power: and which is called legitimacy.

From then on, to whatever vicissitudes the Queen may choose to subject the letter, it remains that the letter is the symbol of a pact, and that, even should the recipient not assume the pact, the existence of the letter situates her in a symbolic chain foreign to the one which constitutes her faith. This incompatibility is proven by the fact that the possession of the letter is impossible to bring forward publicly as legitimate, and that in order to have that possession respected, the Queen can invoke but her right to privacy, whose privilege is based on the honor that possession violates.

For she who incarnates the figure of grace and sovereignty cannot welcome even a private communication without power being concerned, and she cannot avail herself of secrecy in relation to the sovereign without becoming clandestine.

From then on, the responsibility of the author of the letter takes second place to that of its holder: for the offense to majesty is compounded by *high treason*.

We say: the *holder* and not the *possessor*. For it becomes clear that the addressee's proprietorship of the letter may be no less debatable than that of anyone else into whose hands it comes, for nothing concerning the existence of the letter can return to good order without the person whose prerogatives it infringes upon having to pronounce judgment on it.

All of this, however, does not imply that because the letter's secrecy is indefensible, the betrayal of that secret would in any sense be honorable. The *honesti homines,* decent people, will not get off so easily. There is more than one *religio,* and it is not slated for tomorrow that sacred ties shall cease to rend us in two. As for *ambitus:* a detour, we see, is not always inspired by ambition. For if we are taking one here, by no means is it stolen (the word is apt), since, to lay our cards on the table, we have borrowed Baudelaire's title in order to stress not, as is incorrectly claimed, the conventional nature of the signifier, but rather its priority in relation to the signified. It remains, nevertheless, that Baudelaire, despite his devotion, betrayed Poe by translating as "le lettre volée" (the stolen letter) his title: the purloined letter, a title containing a word rare enough for us to find it easier to define its etymology than its usage.

To *purloin,* says the Oxford dictionary, is an Anglo-French word, that is: composed of the prefix pur-, found in *purpose, purchase, purport,* and of the Old French word: *loing, loigner, longé.* We recognize in the first element the Latin pro-, as opposed to *ante,* in so far as it presupposes a rear in front of which it is borne, possibly as its warrant, indeed even as its pledge (whereas *ante* goes forth to confront what it encounters). As for the second, an old French word: *loigner,* a verb attributing place *au loing* (or, still in use, *longé*), it does not mean *au loin* (far off), but *au long de* (alongside); it is a question then of *putting aside,* or, to invoke a familiar expression which plays on the two meanings: *mettre à gauche* (to put to the left; to put amiss).

Thus we are confirmed in our detour by the very object which draws us on into it: for we are quite simply dealing with a letter which has been diverted from its path; one whose course has been *prolonged* (etymologically, the word of the title), or, to revert to the language of the post office, a *letter in sufferance.*[26]

Here then, *simple and odd,* as we are told on the very first page, reduced to its simplest expression, is the singularity of the letter, which as the title indicates, is the *true subject* of the tale: since it can be diverted, it must have a course *which is proper to it:* the trait by which its incidence as signifier is affirmed. For we have learned to conceive of the signifier as sustaining itself only in a displacement comparable to that found in electric news strips or in the rotating memories of our machines-that-think-like men, this because of alternating operation which is its principle, requiring it to leave its place, even though it returns to it by a circular path.[27]

This is indeed what happens in the repetition automatism. What Freud teaches us in the text we are commenting on is that the subject must pass through the channels of the symbolic, but what is illustrated here is more gripping still: it is not only the subject, but the subjects, grasped in their intersubjectivity, who line up, in other words our ostriches, to whom we here return, and who, more docile than sheep, model their very being on the moment of the signifying chain which traverses them.

If what Freud discovered and rediscovers with a perpetually increasing sense of shock has a meaning, it is that the displacement of the signifier determines the subjects in their acts, in their destiny, in their refusals, in their blindnesses, in their end and in their fate, their innate gifts and social acquisitions notwithstanding, without regard for character or sex, and that, willingly or not, everything that might be considered the stuff of psychology, kit and caboodle, will follow the path of the signifier.

Here we are, in fact, yet again at the crossroads at which we had left our drama and its round with the question of the way in which the subjects replace each other in it. Our fable is so constructed as to show that it is the letter and its diversion which governs their entries and roles. If *it* be "in sufferance," *they* shall endure the pain. Should they pass beneath its shadow, they become its reflection. Falling in possession of the letter—admirable ambiguity of language—its meaning possesses them.

So we are shown by the hero of the drama in the repetition of the very situation which his daring brought to a head, a first time, to his triumph. If he now succumbs to it, it is because he has shifted to the second position in the triad in which he was initially third, as well as the thief —and this by virtue of the object of his theft.

For if it is, now as before, a question of protecting the letter from inquisitive eyes, he can do nothing but employ the same technique he himself has already foiled: leave it in the open? And we may properly doubt that he knows what he is thus doing, when we see him immediately captivated by a dual relationship in which we find all the traits of a mimetic lure or of an animal feigning death, and, trapped in the typically imaginary situation of seeing that he is not seen, misconstrue the real situation in which he is seen not seeing.

And what does he fail to see? Precisely the symbolic situation which he himself was so well able to see, and in which he is now seen seeing himself not being seen.

The Minister acts as a man who realizes that the police's search is his own defence, since we are told he allows them total access by his absences: he nonetheless fails to recognize that outside of that search he is no longer defended.

This is the very *autruicherie* whose artisan he was, if we may allow our monster to proliferate, but it cannot be by sheer stupidity that he now comes to be its dupe.[28]

For in playing the part of the one who hides, he is obliged to don the role of the Queen, and even the attributes of femininity and shadow, so propitious to the act of concealing.

Not that we are reducing the hoary couple of *Yin* and *Yang* to the elementary opposition of dark and light. For its precise use involves what is blinding in a flash of light, no less than the shimmering shadows exploit in order not to lose their prey.

Here sign and being, marvelously asunder, reveal which is victorious when they come into conflict. A man man enough to defy to the point of scorn a lady's fearsome ire undergoes to the point of metamorphosis the curse of the sign he has dispossessed her of.

For this sign is indeed that of woman, in so far as she invests her very being therein, founding it outside the law, which subsumes her nevertheless, originarily, in a position of signifier, nay, of fetish.[29] In order to be worthy of the power of that sign she has but to remain immobile in its shadow, thus finding, moreover, like the Queen, that simulation of mastery in inactivity that the Minister's "lynx eye" alone was able to penetrate.

This stolen sign—here then is man in its possession: sinister in that such possession may be sustained only through the honor it defies, cursed in calling him who sustains it to punishment or crime, each of which shatters his vassalage to the Law.

There must be in this sign a singular *noli me tangere* for its possession, like the

Socratic sting ray, to benumb its man to the point of making him fall into what appears clearly in his case to be a state of idleness.[30]

For in noting, as the narrator does as early as the first dialogue, that with the letter's use its power disappears, we perceive that this remark, strictly speaking, concerns precisely its use for ends of power—and at the same time that such a use is obligatory for the Minister.

To be unable to rid himself of it, the Minister indeed must not know what else to do with the letter. For that use places him in so total a dependence on the letter as such, that in the long run it no longer involves the letter at all.

We mean that for that use truly to involve the letter, the Minister, who, after all, would be so authorized by his service to his master the King, might present to the Queen respectful admonitions, even were he to assure their sequel by appropriate precautions—or initiate an action against the author of the letter, concerning whom, the fact that he remains outside the story's focus reveals the extent to which it is not guilt and blame which are in question here, but rather that sign of contradiction and scandal constituted by the letter, in the sense in which the Gospel says that it must come regardless of the anguish of whomever serves as its bearer,— or even submit the letter as even it alone concerns us; it suffices for us to know that the way in which he will have it issue in a Star Chamber for the Queen or the Minister's disgrace.

We will not know why the Minister does not resort to any of these uses, and it is fitting that we don't, since the effect of this non-use alone concerns us; it suffices for us to know that the way in which the letter was acquired would pose no obstacle to any of them.

For it is clear that if the use of the letter, independent of its meaning, is obligatory for the Minister, its use for ends of power can only be potential, since it cannot become actual without vanishing in the process,—but in that case the letter exists as a means of power only through the final assignations of the pure signifier, namely: by prolonging its diversion, making it reach whomever it may concern through a supplementary transfer, that is, by an additional act of treason whose effects the letter's gravity makes it difficult to predict,—or indeed by destroying the letter, the only sure means, as Dupin divulges at the start, of being rid of what is destined by nature to signify the annulment of what it signifies.

The ascendancy which the Minister derives from the situation is thus not a function of the letter, but, whether he knows it or not, of the role it constitutes for him. And the Prefect's remarks indeed present him as someone "who dares all things," which is commented upon significantly: "those unbecoming as well as those becoming a man," words whose pungency escapes Baudelaire when he translates: "ce qui est indigne d'un homme aussi bien que ce qui est digne de lui" (those unbecoming a man as well as those becoming him). For in its original form, the appraisal is far more appropriate to what might concern a woman.

This allows us to see the imaginary import of the character, that is, the narcissistic relation in which the Minister is engaged, this time, no doubt, without knowing it. It is indicated as well as early as the second page of the English text by one of the narrator's remarks, whose form is worth savoring: the Minister's ascendancy, we are told, "would depend upon the robber's knowledge of the loser's knowledge of the robber." Words whose importance the author underscores by having Dupin repeat them literally after the narration of the scene of the theft of the letter. Here again we may say that Baudelaire is imprecise in his language in having one ask, the other confirm, in these words: "Le voleur sait-il? . . ." (Does the robber know?), then: "Le voleur sait . . ."

(the robber knows). What? "que la personne volée connaît son voleur" (that the loser knows his robber).

For what matters to the robber is not only that the said person knows who robbed her, but rather with what kind of a robber she is dealing; for she believes him capable of anything, which should be understood as her having conferred upon him the position that no one is in fact capable of assuming, since it is imaginary, that of absolute master.

In truth, it is a position of absolute weakness, but not for the person of whom we are expected to believe so. The proof is not only that the Queen dares to call the police. For she is only conforming to her displacement to the next slot in the arrangement of the initial triad in trusting to the very blindness required to occupy that place: "No more sagacious agent could, I suppose," Dupin notes ironically, "be desired or even imagined." No, if she has taken that step, it is less out of being "driven to despair," as we are told, than in assuming the charge of an impatience best imputed to a specular mirage.

For the Minister is kept quite busy confining himself to the idleness which is presently his lot. The Minister, in point of fact, is not *altogether* mad.[31] That's a remark made by the Prefect, whose every word is gold: it is true that the gold of his words flows only for Dupin and will continue to flow to the amount of the fifty thousand francs worth it will cost him by the metal standard of the day, though not without leaving him a margin of profit. The Minister then is not *altogether* mad in his insane stagnation, and that is why he will behave according to the mode of neurosis. Like the man who withdrew to an island to forget, what? he forgot,—so the Minister, through not making use of the letter, comes to forget it. As is expressed by the persistence of his conduct. But the letter, no more than the neurotic's unconscious, does not forget him. It forgets him so little that it transforms him more and more in the image of her who offered it to his capture, so that he now will surrender it, following her example, to a similar capture.

The features of that transformation are noted, and in a form so characteristic in their apparent gratuitousness that they might validly be compared to the return of the repressed.

Thus we first learn that the Minister in turn has *turned the letter over,* not, of course, as in the Queen's hasty gesture, but, more assiduously, as one turns a garment inside out. So he must proceed, according to the methods of the day for folding and sealing a letter, in order to free the virgin space on which to inscribe a new address.[32]

That address becomes his own. Whether it be in his hand or another, it will appear in an extremely delicate feminine script, and, the seal changing from the red of passion to the black of its mirrors, he will imprint his stamp upon it. This oddity of a letter marked with the recipient's stamp is all the more striking in its conception, since, though forcefully articulated in the text, it is not even mentioned by Dupin in the discussion he devotes to the identification of the letter.

Whether that omission be intentional or involuntary, it will surprise in the economy of a work whose meticulous rigor is evident. But in either case it is significant that the letter which the Minister, in point of fact, addresses to himself is a letter from a woman: as though this were a phase he had to pass through out of natural affinity of the signifier.

Thus the aura of apathy, verging at times on an affectation of effeminacy; the display of an *ennui* bordering on disgust in his conversation; the mood the author of the philosophy of furniture[33] can elicit from virtually impalpable details (like that of the musical instrument on the table), everything seems intended for a character, all of whose utterances have revealed the most virile traits, to exude the oddest *odor di femina* when he appears.

Dupin does not fail to stress that this is an artifice, describing behind the bogus finery the vigilance of a beast of prey ready to spring. But that this is the very effect of the unconscious in the precise sense that we teach that the unconscious means that man is inhabited by the signifier: could we find a more beautiful image of it than the one Poe himself forges to help us appreciate Dupin's exploit? For with this aim in mind, he refers to those toponymical inscriptions which a geographical map, lest it remain mute, superimposes on its design, and which may become the object of a guessing game: who can find the name chosen by a partner?—noting immediately that the name most likely to foil a beginner will be one which, in large letters spaced out widely across the map, discloses, often without an eye pausing to notice it, the name of an entire country . . .

Just so does the purloined letter, like an immense female body, stretch out across the Minister's office when Dupin enters. But just so does he already expect to find it, and has only, with his eyes veiled by green lenses, to undress that huge body.

And that is why without needing any more than being able to listen in at the door of Professor Freud, he will go straight to the spot in which lies and lives what that body is designed to hide, in a gorgeous center caught in a glimpse, nay, to the very place seducers name Sant' Angelo's Castle in their innocent illusion of controlling the City from within it. Look! between the cheeks of the fireplace, there's the object already in reach of a hand the ravisher has but to extend . . . That question of deciding whether he seizes it above the mantelpiece as Baudelaire translates, or beneath it, as in the original text, may be abandoned without harm to the inferences of those whose profession is grilling.[34]

Were the effectiveness of symbols[35] to cease there, would it mean that the symbolic debt would as well be extinguished? Even if we could believe so, we would be advised of the contrary by two episodes which we may all the less dismiss as secondary in that they seem, at first sight, to clash with the rest of the work.

First of all, there's the business of Dupin's remuneration, which, far from being a closing *pirouette*, has been present from the beginning in the rather unselfconscious question he asks the Prefect about the amount of the reward promised him, and whose enormousness, the Prefect, however reticent he may be about the precise figure, does not dream of hiding from him, even returning later on to refer to its increase.

The fact that Dupin had been previously presented to us as a virtual pauper in his ethereal shelter ought rather to lead us to reflect on the deal he makes out of delivering the letter, promptly assured as it is by the check-book he produces. We do not regard it as negligible that the unequivocal hint through which he introduces the matter is a "story attributed to the character, as famous as it was excentric," Baudelaire tells us, of an English doctor named Abernethy, in which a rich miser, hoping to sponge upon him for a medical opinion, is sharply told not to take medicine, but to take advice.

Do we not in fact feel concerned with good reason when for Dupin what is perhaps at stake is his withdrawal from the symbolic circuit of the letter—we who become the emissaries of all the purloined letters which at least for a time remain in sufferance with us in the transference. And is it not the responsibility their transference entails which we neutralize by equating it with the signifier most destructive of all signification, namely: money.

But that's not all. The profit Dupin so

nimbly extracts from his exploit, if its purpose is to allow him to withdraw his stakes from the game, makes all the more paradoxical, even shocking, the partisan attack, the underhanded blow, he suddenly permits himself to launch against the Minister, whose insolent prestige, after all, would seem to have been sufficiently deflated by the trick Dupin has just played on him.

We have already quoted the atrocious lines Dupin claims he could not help dedicating, in his counterfeit letter, to the moment in which the Minister, enraged by the inevitable defiance of the Queen, will think he is demolishing her and will plunge into the abyss: *facilis descensus Averni*,[36] he waxes sententious, adding that the Minister cannot fail to recognize his handwriting, all of which, since depriving of any danger a merciless act of infamy; would seem, concerning a figure who is not without merit, a triumph without glory, and the rancor he invokes, stemming from an evil turn done him at Vienna (at the Congress?) only adds an additional bit of blackness to the whole.[37]

Let us consider, however, more closely this explosion of feeling, and more specifically the moment it occurs in a sequence of acts whose success depends on so cool a head.

It comes just after the moment in which the decisive act of identifying the letter having been accomplished, it may be said that Dupin already *has* the letter as much as if he had seized it, without, however, as yet being in a position to rid himself of it.

He is thus, in fact, fully a participant in the intersubjective triad, and, as such, in the median position previously occupied by the Queen and the Minister. Will he, in showing himself to be above it, reveal to us at the same time the author's intentions?

If he has succeeded in returning the letter to its proper course, it remains for him to make it arrive at its address. And that address is in the place previously occupied by the King, since it is there that it would re-enter the order of the Law.

As we have seen, neither the King nor the Police who replace him in that position were able to read the letter because that *place entailed blindness*.

Rex et augur, the legendary, archaic quality of the words seems to resound only to impress us with the absurdity of applying them to a man. And the figures of history, for some time now, hardly encourage us to do so. It is not natural for man to bear alone the weight of the highest of signifiers. And the place he occupies as soon as he dons it may be equally apt to become the symbol of the most outrageous imbecility.[38]

Let us say that the King here is invested with the equivocation natural to the sacred, with the imbecility which prizes none other than the Subject.[39]

That is what will give their meaning to the characters who will follow him in his place. Not that the police should be regarded as constitutionally illiterate, and we know the role of pikes planted on the *campus* in the birth of the State. But the police who exercise their functions here are plainly marked by the forms of liberalism, that is, by those imposed on them by masters on the whole indifferent to eliminating their indiscreet tendencies. Which is why on occasion words are not minced as to what is expected of them: "*Sutor ne ultra crepidam*, just take care of your crooks.[40] We'll even give you scientific means to do it with. That will help you not to think of truths you'd be better off leaving in the dark."[41]

We know that the relief which results from such prudent principles shall have lasted in history but a morning's time, that already the march of destiny is everywhere bringing back—a sequel to a just aspiration to freedom's reign—an interest in those who trouble it with their crimes, which occasionally goes so far as to forge

its proofs. It may even be observed that this practice, which was always well received to the extent that it was exercised only in favor of the greatest number, comes to be authenticated in public confessions of forgery by the very ones who might very well object to it: the most recent manifestation of the pre-eminence of the signifier over the subject.

It remains, nevertheless, that a police record has always been the object of a certain reserve, of which we have difficulty understanding that it amply transcends the guild of historians.

It is by dint of this vanishing credit that Dupin's intended delivery of the letter to the Prefect of police will diminish its import. What now remains of the signifier when, already relieved of its message for the Queen, it is now invalidated in its text as soon as it leaves the Minister's hands?

It remains for it now only to answer that very question, of what remains of a signifier when it has no more signification. But this is the same question asked of it by the person Dupin now finds in the spot marked by blindness.

For that is indeed the question which has led the Minister there, if he be the gambler as we are told and which his act sufficiently indicates. For the gambler's passion is nothing but that question asked of the signifier, figured by the *automaton* of chance.

"What are you, figure of the die I turn over in your encounter (*tychē*) with my fortune?[42] Nothing, if not that presence of death which makes of human life a reprieve obtained from morning to morning in the name of meanings whose sign is your crook. Thus did Scheherazade for a thousand and one nights, and thus have I done for eighteen months, suffering the ascendancy of this sign at the cost of a dizzying series of fraudulent turns at the game of even or odd."

So it is that Dupin, *from the place he now occupies*, cannot help feeling a rage of manifestly feminine nature against him who poses such a question. The prestigious image in which the poet's inventiveness and the mathematician's rigor joined up with the serenity of the dandy and the elegance of the cheat suddenly becomes, for the very person who invited us to savor it, the true *monstrum horrendum*, for such are his words, "an unprincipled man of genius."

It is here that the origin of that horror betrays itself, and he who experiences it has no need to declare himself (in a most unexpected manner) "a partisan of the lady" in order to reveal it to us: it is known that ladies detest calling principles into question, for their charms owe much to the mystery of the signifier.

Which is why Dupin will at last turn toward us the medusoid face of the signifier nothing but whose obverse anyone except the Queen has been able to read. The commonplace of the quotation is fitting for the oracle that face bears in its grimace, as is also its source in tragedy: ". . . *Un destin si funeste,/ S'il n'est digne d'Atrée, est digne de Thyeste.*"[43]

So runs the signifier's answer, above and beyond all significations: "You think you act when I stir you at the mercy of the bonds through which I knot your desires. Thus do they grow in force and multiply in objects, bringing you back to the fragmentation of your shattered childhood. So be it: such will be your feast until the return of the stone guest I shall be for you since you call me forth."

Or, to return to a more moderate tone, let us say, as in the quip with which—along with some of you who had followed us to the Zurich Congress last year—we rendered homage to the local password, the signifier's answer to whomever interrogates it is: "Eat your Dasein."

Is that then what awaits the Minister at a rendez-vous with destiny? Dupin assures us of it, but we have already learned not to be too credulous of his diversions.

No doubt the brazen creature is here reduced to the state of blindness which is man's in relation to the letters on the wall that dictate his destiny. But what effect, in calling him to confront them, may we expect from the sole provocations of the Queen, on a man like him? Love or hatred. The former is blind and will make him lay down his arms. The latter is lucid, but will awaken his suspicions. But if he is truly the gambler we are told he is, he will consult his cards a final time before laying them down and, upon reading his hand, will leave the table in time to avoid disgrace.[44]

Is that all, and shall we believe we have deciphered Dupin's real strategy above and beyond the imaginary tricks with which he was obliged to deceive us? No doubt, yes, for if "any point requiring reflection," as Dupin states at the start, is "examined to best purpose in the dark," we may now easily read its solution in broad daylight. It was already implicit and easy to derive from the title of our tale, according to the very formula we have long submitted to your discretion: in which the sender, we tell you, receives from the receiver his own message in reverse form. Thus it is that what the "purloined letter," nay, the "letter in sufferance" means is that a letter always arrives at its destination.

Translated by Jeffrey Mehlman

NOTES

1. The translation of repetition *automatism*—rather than *compulsion*—is indicative of Lacan's speculative effort to reinterpret Freudian "overdetermination" in terms of the laws of probability. (Chance is *automaton*, a "cause not revealed to human thought," in Aristotle's *Physics*.) Whence the importance assumed by the Minister's passion for gambling later in Lacan's analysis. Cf. *Ecrits*, pp. 41–61). *Trans. note.*

2. Cf. Heidegger, *Vom Wesen dar Wahrheit.* Freedom, in this essay, is perceived as an "exposure." *Dasein* ex-sists, stands out "into the disclosure of what is." It is *Dasein's* "ex-sistent insistence" which preserves the disclosure of beings. *Trans. note.*

3. For the meanings Lacan attributes to the terms *imaginary* and *symbolic,* see entries from the *Vocabulaire de la Psychanalyse* (Laplanche and Pontalis) *Trans. note.*

4. Lacan's analysis of the guessing game in Poe's tale entails demonstrating the insufficiency of an *imaginary* identification with the opponent as opposed to the *symbolic* process of an identification with his "reasoning." See *Ecrits,* p. 59. *Trans. note.*

5. "So infamous a scheme,/ If not worthy of Atreus, is worthy of Thyestes." The lines from Atreus's monologue in Act V, Scene V of Crébillon's play refer to his plan to avenge himself by serving his brother the blood of the latter's own son to drink. *Trans. note.*

6. This intersubjective setting which coordinates three terms is plainly the Oedipal situation. The illusory security of the initial *dyad* (King and Queen in the first sequence) will be shattered by the introduction of a *third* term. *Trans. note.*

7. The necessary reference here may be found in "Le Temps logique et l'Assertion de la certitude anticipée," *Ecrits,* p. 197.

8. *La politique de l'autruiche* condenses ostrich (*autruche*), other people (*autrui*), and (the politics of) Austria (*Autriche*). *Trans. note.*

9. Such would be the crux of the Oedipus complex: the assumption of adesire which is originally another's, and which, in its displacements, is perpetually other than "itself." *Trans. note.*

10. The first "Dupin tale" was "The Murders in the Rue Morgue." *Trans note.*

11. Cf. "Fonction et champ de la parole et du langage" in *Ecrits.* Translated by A. Wilden, *The Language of the Self* (Baltimore, 1968).

12. The complete understanding of what follows presupposes a rereading of the short and easily available text of "The Purloined Letter."

13. Cf. Emile Benveniste, "Communication animale et langage humain," *Diogène,* No. 1, and our address in Rome, *Ecrits,* p. 178.

14. For the notion of *ego ideal,* see Freud, *Group Psychology and the Analysis of the Ego. Trans. note.*

15. Freud comments on this joke in *Jokes and Their Relation to the Unconscious,* New York, 1960, p. 115: "But the more serious substance of the joke is

what determines the truth. . . . Is it the truth if we describe things as they are without troubling to consider how our hearer will understand what we say? . . . I think that jokes of that kind are sufficiently different from the rest to be given a special position: What they are attacking is not a person or an institution but the certainty of our knowledge itself, one of our speculative possessions." Lacan's text may be regarded as a commentary on Freud's statement, an examination of the corrosive effect of the demands of an intersubjective communicative situation on any naive notion of "truth." *Trans. note.*

16. Cf. *Ecrits*, p. 58. "But what will happen at the following step (of the game) when the opponent, realizing that I am sufficiently clever to follow him in his move, will show his own cleverness by realizing that it is by playing the fool that he has the best chance to deceive me? From then on my reasoning is invalidated, since it can only be repeated in an indefinite oscillation . . ."

17. We should like to present again to M. Benveniste the question of the antithetical sense of (primal or other) words after the magisterial rectification he brought to the erroneous philological path on which Freud engaged it (cf. *La Psychanalyse*, vol. 1, pp. 5–16). For we think that the problem remains intact once the instance of the signifier has been evolved. Bloch and Von Wartburg date at 1875 the first appearance of the meaning of the verb *dépister* in the second use we make of it in our sentence.

18. The very one to which Jorge Luis Borges, in works which harmonize so well with the phylum of our subject, has accorded an importance which others have reduced to its proper proportions. Cf. *Les Temps modernes*, June–July 1955, pp. 235–36 and Oct. 1955, pp. 574–75.

19. Underlined by the author.

20. The reference is to the "death instinct," whose "death," we should note, lies entirely in its diacritical opposition to the "life" of a naive vitalism or naturalism. As such, it may be compared with the logical moment in Lévi-Strauss's thought whereby "nature" exceeds, supplements, and symbolizes itself: the prohibition of incest. *Trans. note.*

21. This is so true that philosophers, in those hackneyed examples with which they argue on the basis of the single and the multiple, will not use to the same purpose a simple sheet of white paper ripped in the middle and a broken circle, indeed a shattered vase, not to mention a cut worm.

22. Cf. Saussure, *Cours de linguistique générale*, Paris, 1969, p. 166: "The preceding amounts to saying that *in language there are only differences*. Even more: a difference presupposes in general positive terms between which it is established, but in language there are only differences *without positive terms*." *Trans. note.* [See essay # 9 above.]

23. Cf. *Our Examination Round his Factification for Incamination of Work in Progress*, Shakespeare & Co., 12 rue de l'Odéon, Paris, 1929.

24. The original sentence presents an exemplary difficulty in translation: "Les écrits emportent au vent les traites en blanc d'une cavalerie folle." The bland (bank) drafts (or transfers) are not delivered to their rightful recipients (the sense of *de cavalerie, de complaisance*). That is: in analysis, one finds absurd symbolic debts being paid to the "wrong" persons. At the same time, the mad, driven quality of the payment is latent in *traite*, which might also refer to the day's trip of an insane cavalry. In our translation, we have displaced the "switch-word"—joining the financial and equestrian series—from *traite* to *charge*. *Trans. note.*

25. *Flying leaves* (also fly-sheets) and *purloined letters*—*feuilles volantes* and *lettres volées*—employ different meanings of the same word in French. *Trans. note.*

26. We revive this archaism (for the French: *lettre en souffrance*). The sense is a letter held up in the course of delivery. In French, of course, *en souffrance* means in a state of suffering as well. *Trans. note.*

27. See *Ecrits*, p. 59: ". . . it is not unthinkable that a modern computer, by discovering the sentence which modulates without his knowing it and over a long period of time the choices of a subject, would win beyond any normal proportion at the game of even and odd . . ."

28. *Autruicherie* condenses, in addition to the previous terms, deception (tricherie). Do we not find in Lacan's proliferating "monster" something of the *proton pseudos*, the "first lie" of Freud's 1895 *Project*: the persistent illusion which seems to structure the mental life of the patient? *Trans. note.*

29. The fetish, as replacement for the missing maternal phallus, at once masks and reveals the scandal of sexual difference. As such it is the analytic object *par excellence*. The female temptation to exhibitionism, understood as a desire to *be* the (maternal) phallus, is thus tantamount to being a fetish. *Trans. note.*

30. See Plato's *Meno*: "Socrates, . . . at this moment I feel you are exercising magic and witchcraft upon me and positively laying me under your spell until I am just a mass of helplessness. If I may be flippant, I think that not only in outward appearance but in other respects as well you are like the flat sting ray that one meets in the sea. Whenever anyone

comes into contact with it, it numbs him, and that is the sort of thing you are doing to me now . . . *Trans. note.*

31. Baudelaire translates Poe's "*altogether* a fool" as "*absolument* fou." In opting for Baudelaire, Lacan is enabled to allude to the realm of psychosis. *Trans. note.*

32. We felt obliged to demonstrate the procedure to an audience with a letter from the period concerning M. de Chateaubriand and his search for a secretary. We were amused to find that M. de Chateaubriand completed the first version of his recently restored memoirs in the very month of November 1841 in which the purloined letter appeared in *Chamber's Journal.* Might M. de Chateaubriand's devotion to the power he decries and the honor which that devotion bespeaks in him (*the gift* had not yet been invented), place him in the category to which we will later see the Minister assigned: among men of genius with or without principles?

33. Poe is the author of an essay with this title.

34. And even to the cook herself.—J. L.

The paragraph might be read as follows: analysis, in its violation of the imaginary integrity of the ego, finds its fantasmatic equivalent in rape (or castration, as in the passage analyzed in the previous essay). But whether that "rape" takes place from in front or from behind (above or below the mantelpiece) is, in fact, a question of interest for policemen and not analysts. Implicit in the statement is an attack on those who have become wed to the ideology of "maturational development" (libidinal stages et al.) in Freud (i.e., the ego psychologists). *Trans. note.*

35. The allusion is to Lévi-Strauss's article of the same title ("L'efficacité symbolique") in *L'Anthropologie structurale. Trans. note.*

36. Virgil's line reads: *facilis descensus Averno.*

37. Cf. Corneille, *Le Cid* (II, 2): "A vaincre sans péril, on triomphe sans gloire." (To vanquish without danger is to triumph without glory). *Trans. note.*

38. We recall the witty couplet attributed before his fall to the most recent in date to have rallied Candide's meeting in Venice:

> "Il n'est plus aujourd'hui que cinq rois sur la terre,
> Les quatre rois des cartes et le roi d'Angleterre."

(There are only five kings left on earth: four kings of cards and the king of England).

39. For the antithesis of the "sacred," see Freud's "The Antithetical Sense of Primal Words." The idiom *tenir à* in this sentence means both to prize and to be a function of. The two senses—King and/as Subject—are implicit in Freud's frequent allusions to "His Majesty the Ego." *Trans. note.*

40. From Pliny, 35, 10, 35: "A cobbler not beyond his sole . . ." *Trans. note.*

41. This proposal was openly presented by a noble Lord speaking to the Upper Chamber in which his dignity earned him a place.

42. We note the fundamental opposition Aristotle makes between the two terms recalled here in the conceptual analysis of change he gives in his *Physics.* Many discussions would be illuminated by a knowledge of it.

43. Lacan misquotes Crébillon (as well as Poe and Baudelaire) here by writing *destin* (destiny) instead of *dessein* (scheme). As a result he is free to pursue his remarkable development on the tragic Don Juan ("multiply in objects . . . stone guest). *Trans. note.*

44. Thus nothing shall (have) happen(ed)—the final turn in Lacan's theatre of lack. Yet within the simplicity of that empty present the most violent of (pre-)Oedipal dramas—Atreus, Thyestes—shall silently have played itself out. *Trans. note.*

19

Barbara Johnson
1947–

Barbara Johnson is a professor of comparative literature and French at Harvard University. Her work includes theoretical work and criticism of a wide range of writers such as Mallarmé and Zora Neale Hurston. Johnson received her Ph.D. from Yale in 1977, the same year she published "The Frame of Reference." Other words include *Défigurations du langage poetique* (1979), *The Critical Difference* (1980), the translation of Derrida's *Dissemination* (1981), and *A World of Difference* (1987). She edited *The Pedagogical Imperative: Teaching as a Literary Genre* (1982) in which Shoshana Felman's essay "Psychoanalysis and Education" (Section VIII) first appeared.

Johnson's numerous essays prove that the nature of language subverts the intention of the speaker or writer to achieve a position of authority. Like Paul de Man, Johnson deconstructs the effects of power in a given text by showing how language, in its effects, works to destabilize the supposed position of an author. In the following essay, she "un-knots" the intertextual/sexual play of language in Derrida's reading of Lacan's reading of Poe's "The Purloined Letter." Joining with Lacan and Derrida to form a symbolic order analogous to that of the characters in "The Purloined Letter," Johnson demonstrates how meaning is modified by each successive reader—as language performs (or "enacts") each reader (character)—creating a chain of meaning that both expands and turns back upon itself. In her reading of Derrida's text, she uncovers added meaning within the diversions, contradictions, incompatibilities, and ellipses which "stand as the challenge, the enigma, the despair, and the delight both of the lover and of the reader of literature." As she analyzes the effects of Derrida's deconstructive reading of the effects of Lacan's reading of this crime story, she comes to a denouement by returning to Poe's letter. This movement is fitting for "The Frame of Reference," for just as the purloined letter "poses the question of its own rhetorical status," so too does Johnson acknowledge her own self-subversion. In effect, she stops writing where Poe's narrator begins, with an "infinitely regressing reference to previous writings."

The Frame of Reference: Poe, Lacan, Derrida

THE PURLOINED PREFACE

A literary text that both analyzes itself and shows that it actually has neither a self nor any neutral metalanguage with which to do the analyzing, calls out irresistibly for analysis. When that call is answered by two eminent French thinkers whose readings emit their own equally paradoxical call-to-analysis, the resulting triptych, in the context of the question of the act-of-reading (-literature), places its would-be reader in a vertiginously insecure position.

The three texts in question are Edgar Allan Poe's short story "The Purloined Letter," Jacques Lacan's "Seminar on The Purloined Letter" and Jacques Derrida's reading of Lacan's reading of Poe, "The Purveyor of Truth" ("Le Facteur de la Vérité").[1] In all three texts, it is the *act of analysis* which seems to occupy the center of the discursive stage, and the *act of analysis of the act of analysis* which in some way disrupts that centrality. In the resulting asymmetrical, abyssal structure, no analysis—including this one—can intervene without transforming and repeating other elements in the sequence, which is thus not a stable sequence, but which nevertheless produces certain regular effects. It is the functioning of this regularity, and the structure of these effects, which will provide the basis for the present study.

The subversion of any possibility of a position of analytical mastery occurs in many ways. Here, the very fact that we are dealing with *three* texts is in no way certain. Poe's story not only fits into a triptych of its own, but is riddled with a constant, peculiar kind of intertextuality (the epigraph from Seneca which is not from Seneca, the lines from Crébillon's *Atrée* which serve as Dupin's signature, etc.). Lacan's text not only presents itself backwards (its introduction following its conclusion), but it never finishes presenting itself ("*Ouverture de ce recueil,*" "*Présentation de la suite,*" "*Présentation*" to the *Points* edition). And Derrida's text is not only preceded by several years of annunciatory marginalia and footnotes but is itself structured by its own deferment, its *différance* (cf. the repetition of such expressions as "mais nous n'en sommes pas encore là" ["but we are getting ahead of ourselves"], etc.). In addition, an unusually high degree of apparent digressiveness characterizes these texts, to the point of making the reader wonder whether there is really any true subject matter there at all. It is as though any attempt to follow the path of the purloined letter is automatically purloined from itself. Which is, as we shall see, just what the letter has always already been saying.

Any attempt to do "justice" to three such complex texts is obviously out of the question. But in each of these readings of the act of analysis the very question being asked is, What is the nature of such "justice"? It can hardly be an accident that the debate proliferates around a *crime* story—a robbery and its undoing. Somewhere in each of these texts, the economy of justice cannot be avoided. For in spite of the absence of mastery, there is no lack of effects of power.

As the reader goes on with this series of prefatory remarks, he may begin to see how contagious the deferment of the subject of the purloined letter can be. But the problem of how to present these three texts is all the more redoubtable since each of them both presents itself and the others, and clearly shows the fallacies inherent in any type of "presentation" of a text. It is small comfort that such fallacies are not only inevitable but also *constitutive* of any act of reading—also demonstrated by each of the texts—since the resulting injustices, however unavoidable in general, always appear corrigible in detail. Which is why the sequence continues.

The question of how to present to the reader a text too extensive to quote in its entirety has long been one of the underlying problems of literary criticism. Since a shorter version of the text must somehow be produced, two solutions constantly recur: paraphrase and quotation. Although these tactics are seldom if ever used in isolation, the specific configuration of their combinations and permutations determines to a large extent the "plot" of the critical narrative to which they give rise. The first act of our own narrative, then, will consist of an analysis of the strategic effects of the use of paraphrase versus quotation in each of the three texts in question.

ROUND ROBBIN'

Round robin: 1) A tournament in which each contestant is matched against every other contestant. 2) A petition or protest on which the signatures are arranged in the form of a circle in order to conceal the order of signing. 3) A letter sent among members of a group, often with comments added by each person in turn. 4) An extended sequence.

—American Heritage Dictionary

In 1845, Edgar Allan Poe published the third of his three detective stories, "The Purloined Letter," in a collective volume entitled—ironically, considering all the robberies in the story—*The Gift: A Christmas, New Year, and Birthday Present.* "The Purloined Letter" is a first-person narration of two scenes in which dialogues occur among the narrator, his friend C. Auguste Dupin, and, initially, the Prefect of the Parisian police. The two scenes are separated by an indication of the passage of a month's time. In each of the two dialogues, reported to us verbatim by the narrator, one of the other two characters tells the story of a robbery. In the first scene, it is the Prefect of Police who repeats the Queen's eyewitness account of the Minister's theft of a letter addressed to her; in the second scene, it is Dupin who narrates his own theft of the same letter from the Minister, who had meanwhile readdressed it to himself. In a paragraph placed between these two "crime" stories, the narrator himself narrates a wordless scene in which the letter changes hands again before his eyes, passing from Dupin—not without the latter's having addressed not the letter but a check to himself—to the Prefect (who will pocket the remainder of the reward) and thence, presumably, back to the Queen.

By appearing to repeat to us faithfully every word in both dialogues, the narrator would seem to have resorted exclusively to direct quotation in presenting his story. Even when paraphrase could have been expected—in the description of the exact procedures employed by the police in searching unsuccessfully for the letter, for example,—we are spared none of the details. Thus it is all the more surprising to find that there *is* one little point at which direct quotation of the Prefect's words gives way to paraphrase. This point, however brief, is of no small importance, as we shall see. It occurs in the concluding paragraph of the first scene:

> "I have no better advice to give you," said Dupin. "You have, of course, an accurate description of the letter?"
>
> "Oh, yes!"—And here the Prefect, producing a memorandum-book, proceeded to read aloud a minute account of the internal, and especially of the external, appearance of the missing document. Soon after finishing the perusal of this description, he took his departure, more entirely depressed in spirits than I had ever known the good gentleman before. (Poe, Pp. 206–7)

What is paraphrased is thus the description of the letter the story is about. And, whereas it is generally supposed that the function of paraphrase is to strip off the form of a speech in order to give us only its contents, here the use of paraphrase does the very opposite: it withholds the contents of the Prefect's remarks, giving us only their form. And what is swallowed up in this ellipsis is nothing less than the contents of the letter itself. The fact that the letter's message is never revealed, which will serve as the basis for Lacan's reading of the story, is thus negatively made explicit by the functioning of Poe's text itself, through what Derrida might have called a repression of the written word (a suppression of what is written in the memorandum-book—and in the letter). And the question of the strategic use of paraphrase versus quotation begins to invade the literary text as well as the critical narrative.

Lacan's presentation of Poe's text involves the paraphrase, or plot summary, of the two thefts as they are told to the narrator by the Prefect and by Dupin. Since Derrida, in his critique of Lacan, chooses to quote Lacan's paraphrase, we can combine all the tactics involved by, in our turn, quoting Derrida's quotation of Lacan's paraphrase of Poe's quoted narrations.[2]

> There are two scenes, the first of which we shall straightway designate the primal scene, and by no means inadvertently, since the second may be considered its repetition in the very sense we are considering today.
>
> The primal scene is thus performed, we are told [by neither Poe, nor the scriptor, nor the narrator, but by G, the Prefect of Police who is *mis en scène* by all those involved in the dialogues—J. D.[3]] in the royal *boudoir*, so that we suspect that the person of the highest rank, called the "exalted personage," who is alone there when she receives a letter, is the Queen. This feeling is confirmed by the embarrassment into which she is plunged by the entry of the other exalted personage, of whom we have already been told [again by G—J. D.] prior to this account that the knowledge he might have of the letter in question would jeopardize for the lady nothing less than her honor and safety. Any doubt that he is in fact the King is promptly dissipated in the course of the scene which begins with the entry of Minister D. . . . At that moment, in fact, the Queen can do no better than to play on the King's inattentiveness by leaving the letter on the table "face down, address uppermost." It does not, however, escape the Minister's lynx eye, nor does he fail to notice the Queen's distress and thus to fathom her secret. From then on everything transpires like clockwork. After dealing in his customary manner with the business of the day, the Minister draws from his pocket a letter similar in appearance to the one in his view, and having pretended to read it, places it next to the other. A bit more conversation to amuse the royal company, whereupon, without flinching once, he seizes the embarrassing letter, making off with it, as the Queen, on whom none of his maneuver has been lost, remains unable to intervene for fear of attracting the attention of her royal spouse, close at her side at that very moment.
>
> Everything might then have transpired unseen by a hypothetical spectator of an operation in which nobody falters, and whose *quotient* is that the Minister has filched from the Queen her letter and that—an even more important result than the first—the Queen knows that he now has it, and by no means innocently.
>
> A *remainder* that no analyst will neglect, trained as he is to retain whatever is significant, without always knowing what to do with it: the letter, abandoned by the Minister, and which the Queen's hand is now free to roll into a ball.

Second scene: in the Minister's office. It is in his hotel, and we know—from the account the Prefect of Police has given Dupin, whose specific genius for solving enigmas Poe introduces here for the second time—that the police, returning there as soon as the Minister's habitual nightly absences allow them to, have searched the hotel and its surroundings from top to bottom for the last eighteen months. In vain—although everyone can deduce from the situation that the Minister keeps the letter within reach.

Dupin calls on the Minister. The latter receives him with studied nonchalance, affecting in his conversation romantic *ennui*. Meanwhile Dupin, whom this pretence does not deceive, his eyes protected by green glasses, proceeds to inspect the premises. When his glance catches a rather crumbled piece of paper—apparently thrust carelessly in a division of an ugly pasteboard card-rack, hanging gaudily from the middle of the mantelpiece—he already knows that he's found what he's looking for. His conviction is reinforced by the very details which seem to contradict the description he has of the stolen letter, with the exception of the format, which remains the same.

Whereupon he has but to withdraw, after "forgetting" his snuff-box on the table, in order to return the following day to reclaim it—armed with a facsimile of the letter in its present state. As an incident in the street, prepared for the proper moment, draws the Minister to the window, Dupin in turn seizes the opportunity to seize the letter while substituting the imitation, and has only to maintain the appearances of a normal exit.

Here as well all has transpired, if not without noise, at least without all commotion. The quotient of the operation is that the Minister no longer has the letter, but, far from suspecting Dupin is the culprit who has ravished it from him, knows nothing of it. Moreover, what he is left with is far from insignificant for what follows. We shall return to what brought Dupin to inscribe a message on his counterfeit letter. Whatever the case, the Minister, when he tries to make use of it, will be able to read these words, written so that he may recognize Dupin's hand: ". . . Un dessein si funeste/S'il n'est digne d'Atrée est digne de Thyeste,"[4] whose source, Dupin tells us, is Crébillon's *Atrée*.

Need we emphasize the similarity of those two sequences? Yes, for the resemblance we have in mind is not a simple collection of traits chosen only in order to delete their difference. And it would not be enough to retain those common traits at the expense of the others for the slightest truth to result. It is rather the intersubjectivity in which the two actions are motivated that we wish to bring into relief, as well as the three terms through which it structures them.

The special status of these terms results from their corresponding simultaneously to the three logical moments through which the decision is precipitated and the three places it assigns to the subjects among whom it constitutes a choice.

That decision is reached in a glance's time. For the maneuvers which follow, however stealthily they prolong it, add nothing to that glance, nor does the deferring of the deed in the second scene break the unity of that moment.

This glance presupposes two others, which it embraces in its vision of the breach left in their fallacious complementarity, anticipating in it the occasion for larceny afforded by that exposure. Thus three moments, structuring three glances, borne by three subjects, incarnated each time by different characters.

The first is a glance that sees nothing: the King and the police.

The second, a glance which sees that the first sees nothing and deludes itself as to the secrecy of what it hides: the Queen, then the Minister.

The third sees that the first two glances leave what should be hidden exposed to whoever would seize it: the Minister and finally Dupin.

In order to grasp in its unity the intersubjective complex thus described, we would willingly seek a model in the technique legendarily attributed to the ostrich attempting to shield itself from danger; for that technique might ultimately be qualified as political, divided as it here is among three partners: the second believing itself invisible because the first has its head stuck in the ground, and all the while letting the third calmly pluck its rear; we need only enrich its proverbial denomination by a letter, producing *la politique de l'autruiche,*[5] for the ostrich itself to take on forever a new meaning.

Given the intersubjective modulus of the repetitive action, it remains to recognize in it a *repetition automatism* in the sense that interests us in Freud's text. (SPL, pp. 41–44; PT, pp. 54–57)

Thus, it is neither the character of the individual subjects, nor the contents of the letter, but the position of the letter within the group which decides what each person will do next. Because the letter does not function as a unit of meaning (a *signified*) but as that which produces certain effects (a *signifier*), Lacan reads the story as an illustration of "the truth which may be drawn from that moment in Freud's thought under study—namely, that it is the symbolic order which is constitutive for the subject—by demonstrating . . . the decisive orientation which the subject receives from the itinerary of a signifier" (SPL, p. 40). The letter acts like a signifier to the extent that its function in the story does not require that its meaning be revealed: "the letter was able to produce its effects *within* the story: on the actors in the tale, including the narrator, as well as *outside* the story: on us, the readers, and also on its author, without anyone's ever bothering to worry about what it meant" (not translated in SPL; *Ecrits*, p. 57, translation and emphasis mine). "The Purloined Letter" thus becomes for Lacan a kind of *allegory of the signifier.*

Derrida's critique of Lacan's reading does not dispute the validity of the allegorical interpretation on its own terms, but questions its implicit presuppositions and its modus operandi. Derrida aims his objections at two kinds of target: (1) what Lacan puts into the letter and (2) what Lacan leaves out of the text.

1. *What Lacan puts into the letter.* While asserting that the letter's meaning is lacking, Lacan, according to Derrida, makes this lack into *the* meaning of the letter. But Derrida does not stop there. He goes on to assert that what Lacan means by that lack is the truth of lack-as-castration-as-truth: "The truth of the purloined letter is the truth itself. . . . What is veiled/unveiled in this case is a hole, a non-being [non-étant]; the truth of being [l'être], as non-being. Truth is 'woman' as veiled/unveiled castration" (PT, pp. 60–61). Lacan himself, however, never uses the word *castration* in the text of the original "Seminar." That it is suggested is indisputable, but Derrida, by filling in what *Lacan* left blank, is repeating the same gesture of blank-filling for which he criticizes Lacan.
2. *What Lacan leaves out of the text.* This objection is itself double: on the one hand, Derrida criticizes Lacan for neglecting to consider "The Purloined Letter" in connection with the other two stories in what Derrida calls Poe's "Dupin Trilogy." And on the other hand, according to Derrida, at the very moment Lacan is reading the story as an allegory of the signifier, he is being blind to the disseminating power of the signifier in the *text* of the allegory, in what Derrida calls the "scene of writing." To cut out part of a text's frame of reference as though it did not exist and to reduce a complex textual functioning to a single meaning are serious blots indeed in the annals of literary criticism. Therefore it is all the more noticeable that Derrida's own reading of Lacan's text repeats the crimes of which he accuses it: on the one hand, Derrida makes no mention of Lacan's long development on the relation between symbolic determination and random series. And on the other hand, Derrida dismisses Lacan's "style" as a mere ornament, veiling, for a time, an unequivocal message: "Lacan's 'style,' moreover, was such that for a long time it would hinder and delay all access to a *unique* content or a single unequivocal meaning determinable beyond the writing itself" (PT, p. 40). Derrida's

> repetition of the very gestures he is criticizing does not in itself invalidate his criticism of their effects, but it does problematize his statement condemning their existence.

What kind of logic is it that thus seems to turn one-upmanship into inevitable one-downmanship?

It is the very logic of the purloined letter.

ODD COUPLES

> *Je tiens la reine!*
> *O sûr châtiment . . .*
> —Mallarmé, "L'aprés-mid d'un faune"

> *L'ascendant que le ministre tire de la situation ne tient donc pas à la lettre, mais, qu'il le sache ou non, au personnage qu'elle lui constitue.*
> —Lacan, SPL.

We have just seen how Derrida, in his effort to right (write) Lacan's wrongs, can, on a certain level, only repeat them, and how the rectification of a previous injustice somehow irresistibly dictates the filling in of a blank which then becomes the new injustice. In fact, the act of clinching one's triumph by filling in a blank is already prescribed in all its details within Poe's story, in Dupin's unwillingness to "leave the interior blank" (Poe, p. 219) in the facsimile he has left for the Minister, in place of the purloined letter he, Dupin, has just repossessed by means of a precise repetition of the act of robbery he is undoing. What is written in the blank is a quotation-as-signature, which curiously resembles Derrida's initialed interventions in the passages he quotes from Lacan, a resemblance on which Derrida is undoubtedly playing. And the text of the quotation transcribed by Dupin describes the structure of rectification-as-repetition-of-the-crime which has led to its being transcribed in the first place:

> —Un dessein si funeste,
> S'il n'est digne d'Atrée, est digne de Thyeste.

Atreus, whose wife had long ago been seduced by Thyestes, is about to make Thyestes eat (literally) the fruit of that illicit union, his son Plisthenes. The avenger's plot may not be worthy of him, says Atreus, but his brother Thyestes deserves it. What the addressee of the violence is going to get is simply his own message backwards. It is this vengeful anger that, as both Lacan and Derrida show, places Dupin as one of the "ostriches" in the "triad." Not content simply to return the letter to its "rightful" destination, Dupin jumps into the fray as the wronged victim himself, by recalling an "evil turn" the minister once did him in Vienna and for which he is now, personally, taking his revenge.

Correction must thus posit a previous pretextual, pre-textual crime that will justify its excesses. Any degree of violence is permissible in the act of getting even ("To be *even* with him," says Dupin, "I complained of my weak eyes" [Poe, p. 216, emphasis mine]). And Dupin's backward revision of the story repeats itself in his readers as well. The existence of the same kind of prior aggression on Lacan's part is posited by Derrida in a long footnote in his book *Positions*, in which he outlines what will later develop into *Le Facteur de la Vérité:* "In the texts I have published up to now, the absence of reference to Lacan is indeed almost total. That is *justified* not only by the *acts of aggression* in the form of, or with the intention of, reappropriation which, ever since *De la grammatologie* appeared in *Critique* (1965) (and even earlier, I am told) Lacan has multiplied . . . " (emphasis mine). The priority of aggression is doubled by the aggressiveness of priority: "At the time of my first publications, Lacan's *Ecrits* had not yet been collected and published. . . ."[6] And Lacan, in turn, mentions in his *Presentation* to the "Points" edition of his *Ecrits:* "what I properly call the instance of the letter *before any grammatology*"[7] (emphasis mine). The rivalry over something neither man will credit the other with possessing, the retrospective revision of the origins of both their resemblances and their differences, thus spirals backward and forward in an indeterminable pattern of cancellation and duplication. If it thus becomes impossible to determine "who started it" (or even whether "it" was started by either one of them), it is also impossible to know who is ahead or even whose "turn" it is—which is what makes the business of getting even so *odd*.

This type of oscillation between two terms, considered as totalities in binary opposition, is studied by Lacan in connection with Poe's story of the eight-year-old prodigy who succeeded in winning, far beyond his due, at the game of even and odd. The game consists of guessing whether the number of marbles an opponent is holding is even or odd. The schoolboy explains his success by his identification with the physical characteristics of his opponent, from which he deduces the opponent's degree of intelligence and its corresponding line of reasoning. What Lacan shows, in the part of his seminar which Derrida neglects, is that the mere identification with the opponent as an image of totality is not sufficient to insure success—and in no way explains Dupin's actual strategy—since, from the moment the opponent becomes aware of it, he can then play on his own appearance and dissociate it from the reasoning that is presumed to go with it. (This is, indeed, what occurs in the encounter between Dupin and the Minister: the Minister's feigned nonchalance is a true vigilance but a blinded vision, whereas Dupin's feigned blindness ["weak eyes"] is a vigilant act of lucidity, later to succumb to its own form of blindness.) From then on, says Lacan, the reasoning "can only repeat itself in an indefinite oscillation" (*Ecrits*, p. 58, translation mine). And Lacan reports that, in his own classroom tests of the schoolboy's technique, it was almost inevitable that each player begin to feel he was losing his marbles.[8]

But if the complexities of these texts could be reduced to a mere combat between ostriches, a mere game of heads and tails played out in order to determine a "winner," they would have very little theoretical interest. It is, on the contrary, the way in which each mastermind avoids simply becoming the butt of his own joke that displaces the opposition in unpredictable ways and transforms the textual encounter into a source of insight. For if the very possibility of meeting the opponent on a common ground, without which no contact is possible, implies a certain symmetry, a sameness, a repetition of the error that the encounter is designed to correct, any true avoidance of that error entails a nonmeeting or incompatibility between the two forces. If to hit the target is in a way to become the target, then to miss the target is perhaps to hit it elsewhere. It is not how Lacan and Derrida meet each other but how they miss each other that opens up a space for interpretation.

Clearly, what is at stake here has something to do with the status of the number *2*. If the face-off between two opponents or polar opposites always simultaneously backfires and misfires, it can only be because *2* is an extremely "odd" number. On the one hand, as a specular illusion of symmetry or metaphor, it can be either narcissistically reassuring (the image of the other as a reinforcement of my identity) or absolutely devastating (the other whose existence can totally cancel me out). This is what Lacan calls the "*imaginary* duality." It is characterized by its absoluteness, its independence from any accident or contingency that might subvert the unity of the terms in question, whether in their opposition or in their fusion. To this, Lacan opposes the *symbolic*, which is the entrance of difference or otherness or temporality into the idea of identity—it is not something that befalls the imaginary duality, but something that has always already inhabited it, something that subverts not the symmetry of the imaginary couple, but the possibility of the independent unity of any one term whatsoever. It is the impossibility not of the number *2* but of the number *1*—which, paradoxically enough, turns out to lead to the number 3.

If *3* is what makes *2* into the impossibility of *1*, is there any inherent increase in lucidity in passing from a couple to a triangle? Is a triangle in any way more "true" than a couple?

It is Derrida's contention that, for psychoanalysis, the answer to that question is yes. The triangle becomes the magical, Oedipal figure that explains the functioning of human desire. The child's original imaginary dual unity with the mother is subverted by the law of the father as that which prohibits incest under threat of castration. The child has "simply" to "assume castration" as the necessity of substitution in the object of his desire (the object of desire becoming the locus of substitution and the focus of repetition), after which the child's desire becomes "normalized." Derrida's criticism of the "triangles" or "triads" in Lacan's reading of Poe is based on the assumption that Lacan's use of triangularity stems from this psychoanalytical myth.

Derrida's criticism takes two routes, both of them numerical:

1. The structure of "The Purloined Letter" cannot be reduced to a triangle unless the narrator is eliminated. The elimination of the narrator is a blatant and highly revealing result of the way "psychoanalysis" does violence to literature in order to find its own schemes. What psychoanalysis sees as a triangle is therefore really a quadrangle, and that fourth side is the point from which literature problematizes the very possibility of a triangle. Therefore: *3* = *4*.
2. Duality as such cannot be dismissed or simply absorbed into a triangular structure. "The Purloined Letter" is traversed by an uncanny capacity for doubling and subdividing. The narrator and Dupin are doubles of each other, and Dupin himself is first introduced as a "Bi-Part Soul" (Poe, p. 107), a sort of Dupin Duplex, "the creative and the resolvent." The Minister, D——, has a brother for whom it is possible to mistake him, and from whom he is to be distinguished because of his doubleness (poet and mathematician). Thus the Minister and Dupin become doubles of each other through the fact of their both being already double, in addition to their other points of resemblance, including their names. "The 'Seminar'," writes Derrida,

> mercilessly forecloses this problematic of the double and of *Unheimlichkeit*—no doubt considering that it is confined to the imaginary, to the dual relationship which must be kept rigorously separate from the symbolic and the triangular. . . . All the "uncanny" relations of duplicity, limitlessly deployed in a dual structure, find themselves omitted or marginalized [in the "Seminar"]. . . . What is thus kept under surveillance and control is the Uncanny itself, and the frantic anxiety which can be provoked, with no hope of reappropriation, enclosure, or truth, by the infinite play from simulacrum to simulacrum, from double to double. (omitted in PT; FV, P. 124, translation mine).

Thus the triangle's angles are always already bisected, and *3* = (a factor of) *2*.

In the game of odd versus even, then, it would seem that Derrida is playing evens (*4* or *2*) against Lacan's odds (*3*). But somehow the numbers *2* and *4* have become uncannily odd, while the number *3* has been evened off into a reassuring symmetry. How did this happen, and what are the consequences for an interpretation of "The Purloined Letter"?

Before any answer to this question can be envisaged, several remarks should be made here to problematize the terms of Derrida's critique:

1. If the narrator and Dupin are a strictly dual pair whose relationship is in no way mediated by a third term in any Oedipal sense, how is one to explain the fact that their original meeting was brought about by their potential rivalry over the same object: "the accident of our both being in search of the *same* very rare and very remarkable volume" (emphasis mine). Whether or not they ever found it, or can share it, is this not a triangular relationship?
2. Although Lacan's reading of "The Purloined Letter" divides the story into triadic structures, his model for (inter-)subjectivity, the so-called schema L, which is developed in that part of the "Seminar's" introduction glossed over by Derrida, is indisputably quadrangular. In order to read Lacan's repeating triads as a triangular, Oedipal model of the subject instead of as a mere structure of repetition, Derrida must therefore lop off one corner of the schema L in the same way as he accuses Lacan of lopping off a corner of Poe's text—and Derrida does this by lopping off that corner of Lacan's text in which the quadrangular schema L is developed.

But can what is at stake here really be reduced to a mere numbers game?

Let us approach the problem from another angle, by asking two more questions:

1. What is the relation between a divided unity and a duality? Are the two *2*'s synonymous? Is a "Bi-Part Soul," for example, actually composed of two wholes? Or is it possible to conceive of a division which would not lead to two separate parts, but only to a problematization of the idea of unity? This would class what Derrida calls "duality" not in Lacan's "imaginary," but in Lacan's "symbolic."
2. If the doubles are forever redividing or multiplying, does the number *2* really apply? If $1 = 2$, how can $2 = 1 + 1$? If what is uncanny about the doubles is that they never stop doubling up, would the number *2* still be uncanny if it did stop at a truly dual symmetry? Is it not the very limitlessness of the process of the dissemination of unity, rather than the existence of any one duality, which Derrida is talking about here?

Clearly, in these questions, the very notion of a number becomes problematic, and the argument on the basis of numbers can no longer be read literally. If Derrida opposes doubled quadrangles to Lacan's triangles, it is not because he wants to turn Oedipus into an octopus.

To what, then, does the critique of triangularity apply?

The problem with psychoanalytical triangularity, in Derrida's eyes, is not that it contains the wrong number of terms, but that it presupposes the possibility of a successful dialectical mediation and harmonious normalization, or *Aufhebung*, of desire. The three terms in the Oedipal triad enter into an opposition whose resolution resembles the synthetic moment of a Hegelian dialectic. The process centers on the phallus as the locus of the question of sexual difference; when the observation of the mother's lack of a penis is joined with the father's threat of castration as the punishment for incest, the child passes from the alternative (thesis vs. antithesis; presence vs. absence of penis) to the synthesis (the phallus as a sign of the fact that the child can only enter into the circuit of desire by assuming castration as the phallus's simultaneous presence and absence; that is, by assuming the fact that both the subject and the object of desire will always be substitutes for something that was never really present). In Lacan's article "La signification du phallus," which Derrida quotes, this process is evoked in specifically Hegelian terms:

> All these remarks still do nothing but veil the fact that it [the phallus] cannot play its role except veiled, that is to say as itself sign of the latency with which anything signifiable is stricken as soon as it is raised (*aufgehoben*) to the function of signifier.
>
> The phallus is the signifier of this *Aufhebung* itself which it inaugurates (initiates) by its disappearance. (*Ecrits,* P. 692; PT, P. 98.)

"It would appear," comments Derrida, "that the Hegelian movement of *Aufhebung* is here reversed since the latter sublates [relève] the sensory signifier in the ideal signified" (PT, p. 98). But then, according to Derrida, Lacan's privileging of the spoken over the written word annuls this reversal, reappropriates all possibility of uncontainable otherness, and brings the whole thing back within the bounds of the type of "logocentrism" that has been the focus of Derrida's entire deconstructive enterprise.

The question of whether or not Lacan's privileging of the voice is strictly logocentric in Derrida's sense is an extremely complex one with which we cannot hope to deal adequately here.[9] But what does all this have to do with "The Purloined Letter"?

In an attempt to answer this question, let us examine how Derrida deduces from Lacan's text that, for Lacan, the letter is a symbol of the (mother's) phallus. Since Lacan never uses the word *phallus* in the "Seminar," this is already an interpretation on Derrida's part, and quite an astute one at that, with which Lacan, as a later reader of his own "Seminar," implicitly agrees by placing the word *castrated*—which had not been used in the original text—in his "Points" *Presentation*. The disagreement between Derrida and Lacan thus arises not over the *validity* of the equation "letter = phallus," but over its *meaning*.

How, then, does Derrida derive this equation from Lacan's text? The deduction follows four basic lines of reasoning, all of which will be dealt with in greater detail later in the present essay:

1. The letter "belongs" to the Queen as a substitute for the phallus she does not have. It feminizes (castrates) each of its successive holders and is eventually returned to her as its rightful owner.
2. Poe's description of the position of the letter in the Minister's apartment, expanded upon by the figurative dimensions of Lacan's text, suggests an analogy between the shape of the fireplace from the center of whose mantelpiece the letter is found hanging and that point on a woman's anatomy from which the phallus is missing.
3. The letter, says Lacan, cannot be divided: "But if it is first of all on the materiality of the signifier that we have insisted, that materiality is *odd* [singulière] in many ways, the first of which is not to admit partition" (SPL, p. 53). This indivisibility, says Derrida, is odd indeed, but becomes comprehensible if it is seen as an *idealization* of the phallus, whose integrity is necessary for the edification of the entire psychoanalytical system. With the phallus

safely idealized and located in the voice, the so-called signifier acquires the "unique, living, non-mutilable integrity" of the self-present spoken word, unequivocally pinned down to and by the *signified*. "Had the phallus been per (mal)-chance divisible or reduced to the status of a partial object, the whole edification would have crumbled down, and this is what has to be avoided at all cost" (PT, pp. 96–97).

4. And finally, if Poe's story "illustrates" the "truth," the last words of the "Seminar" proper seem to reaffirm that truth in no uncertain terms: "Thus it is that what the 'purloined letter,' nay the 'letter in sufferance' means is that *a letter always arrives at its destination*" (SPL, p. 72, emphasis mine). Now, since it is unlikely that Lacan is talking about the efficiency of the postal service, he must, according to Derrida, be affirming the possibility of unequivocal meaning, the eventual reappropriation of the message, its total equivalence with itself. And since the "truth" Poe's story illustrates is, in Derrida's eyes, the truth of veiled/unveiled castration and of the transcendental identity of the phallus as the lack that makes the system work, this final sentence in Lacan's "Seminar" seems to affirm both the absolute truth of psychoanalytical theories and the absolute decipherability of the literary text. Poe's message will have been totally, unequivocally understood and explained by the psychoanalytical myth. "The hermeneutic discovery of meaning (truth), the deciphering (that of Dupin and that of the "Seminar"), arrives itself at its destination" (PT, p. 66).

Thus, the law of the phallus seems to imply a reappropriating return to the place of true ownership, an indivisible identity functioning beyond the possibility of disintegration or unrecoverable loss, and a totally self-present, unequivocal meaning or truth.

The problem with this type of system, counters Derrida, is that it cannot account for the possibility of sheer accident, irreversible loss, unreappropriable residues, and infinite divisibility, which are necessary and inevitable in the system's very elaboration. In order for the circuit of the letter to end up confirming the law of the phallus, it must begin by transgressing it; the letter is a sign of high treason. Phallogocentrism mercilessly represses the uncontrollable multiplicity of ambiguities, the disseminating play of *writing*, which irreducibly transgresses any unequivocal meaning. "Not that the letter never arrives at its destination, but part of its structure is that it is always capable of not arriving there. . . . Here dissemination threatens the law of the signifier and of castration as a contract of truth. Dissemination mutilates the unity of the signifier, that is, of the phallus" (PT, p. 66).

In contrast to Lacan's "Seminar," then, Derrida's text would seem to be setting itself up as a "Disseminar."

From the foregoing remarks, it can easily be seen that the disseminal criticism of Lacan's apparent reduction of the literary text to an unequivocal message depends for its force upon the presupposition of unambiguousness in Lacan's text. And indeed, the statement that a letter always reaches its destination seems straightforward enough. But when the statement is reinserted into its context, things become palpably less certain:

> Is that all, and shall we believe we have deciphered Dupin's real strategy above and beyond the imaginary tricks upon which he was obliged to deceive us? No doubt, yes, for if "any point requiring reflection," as Dupin states at the start, is "examined to best purpose in the dark," we may now easily read its solution in broad daylight. It was

> already implicit and easy to derive from the title of our tale, according to the very formula we have long submitted to your discretion: in which the sender, we tell you, receives from the receiver his own message in reverse form. Thus it is that what the "purloined letter," nay, the "letter in sufferance" means is that a letter always arrives at its destination. (SPL, p. 72.)

The meaning of this last sentence is problematized not so much by its own ambiguity as by a series of reversals in the preceding sentences. If the "best" examination takes place in darkness, what does "reading in broad daylight" imply? Could it not be taken as an affirmation not of actual lucidity but of delusions of lucidity? Could it not then move the "yes, no doubt" as an answer, not to the question, Have we deciphered? but to the question, Shall we *believe* we have deciphered? And if this is possible, does it not empty the final affirmation of all unequivocality, leaving it to stand with the *force* of an assertion, without any definite content? And if the sender receives from the receiver his own message backward, who is the sender here, who the receiver, and what is the message? It is not even clear what the expression "the purloined letter" refers to: Poe's text? the letter it talks about? or simply the expression "the purloined letter"?

We will take another look at this passage later, but for the moment its ambiguities seem sufficient to problematize, if not subvert, the presupposition of univocality that is the very foundation on which Derrida has edified his interpretation.

But surely such an oversimplification on Derrida's part does not result from mere blindness, oversight, or error. As Paul de Man says of Derrida's similar treatment of Rousseau, "the pattern is too interesting not to be deliberate."[10] Derrida being the sharp-eyed reader that he is, his consistent forcing of Lacan's statements into systems and patterns from which they are actually trying to escape must correspond to some strategic necessity different from the attentiveness to the letter of the text which characterizes Derrida's way of reading Poe. And in fact, the more one works with Derrida's analysis, the more convinced one becomes that although the critique of what Derrida calls psychoanalysis is entirely justified, it does not quite apply to what Lacan's text is actually saying. Derrida argues, in effect, not against Lacan's *text* but against Lacan's *power*—or rather, against "Lacan" as the apparent cause of certain effects of power in French discourse today. Whatever Lacan's text may *say*, it functions, according to Derrida, as if it said what *he* says it says. The statement that a letter always reaches its destination may be totally undecipherable, but its assertive force is taken all the more seriously as a sign that Lacan himself has everything all figured out. Such an assertion, in fact, gives him an appearance of mastery like that of the Minister in the eyes of the letterless Queen. "The ascendancy which the Minister derives from the situation," explains Lacan, "is attached not to the letter but to the character it makes him into."

Thus Derrida's seemingly "blind" reading, whose vagaries we shall be following here, is not a mistake, but the positioning of what can be called the "average reading" of Lacan's text—the true object of Derrida's deconstruction. Since Lacan's text is read as if it said what Derrida says it says, its actual textual functioning is irrelevant to the agonistic arena in which Derrida's analysis takes place and which is suggested by the very first word of the epigraph: *ils* (they):

> They thank him for the grand truths he has just proclaimed,—for they have discovered (o verifier of what cannot be verified) that everything he said was absolutely true; even though, at first, these honest souls admit, they might have suspected that it could have

> been a simple fiction . . . (PT, P. 31; translation mine.)

The fact that this quotation from Baudelaire refers to Poe and not Lacan does not completely erase the impression that the unidentified "him" in its first sentence is the "Purveyor of Truth" of the title. The evils of Lacan's analysis of Poe are thus located less in the letter of the text than in the gullible readers, the "braves gens" who are taken in by it. Lacan's ills are really *ils*.

If Derrida's reading of Lacan's reading of Poe is actually the deconstruction of a reading whose status is difficult to determine, does this mean that Lacan's text is completely innocent of the misdemeanors of which it is accused? If Lacan can be shown to be opposed to the same kind of logocentric error that Derrida opposes, does that mean that they are both really saying the same thing? These are questions that must be left, at least for the moment, hanging.

But the structure of Derrida's transference of guilt from a certain reading of Lacan onto Lacan's text is not indifferent in itself, in the context of what, after all, started out as a relatively simple crime story. For what it amounts to is nothing less than a *frame*.

THE FRAME OF REFERENCE

> *Elle, défunte* nue *en le miroir, encor*
> Que, dans l'oubli fermé par le cadre,
> *se fixe*
> *De scintillations sitôt le septuor.*
>
> —Mallarmé, "Sonnet en X"

If Derrida is thus framing Lacan for an interpretative malpractice of which he himself is, at least in part, the author, what can this frame teach us about the nature of the act of reading, in the context of the question of literature and psychoanalysis?

Interestingly enough, one of the major crimes for which Derrida frames Lacan is the psychoanalytical reading's elimination of the literary text's *frame*. That frame here consists not only of the two stories that precede "The Purloined Letter" but also of the stratum of narration through which the stories are told, and, "beyond" it, of the text's entire functioning as *écriture:*

> Without breathing a word about it, Lacan excludes the textual fiction within which he isolates the so-called "general narration." Such an operation is facilitated, too obviously facilitated, by the fact that the narration covers the entire surface of the fiction entitled "The Purloined Letter." But *that* is the fiction. There is an invisible but structurally irreducible frame around the narration. Where does it begin? With the first letter of the title? With the epigraph from Seneca? With the words, "At Paris, just after dark . . ."? It is more complicated than that and will require reconsideration. Such complication suffices to point out everything that is misunderstood about the structure of the text once the frame is ignored. Within this invisible or neutralized frame, Lacan takes the borderless narration and makes another subdivision, once again leaving aside the frame. He cuts out two dialogues from within the frame of the narration itself, which form the narrated history, i.e. the content of a representation, the internal meaning of a story, the all-enframed which demands our complete attention, mobilizes all the psychoanalytical schemes—Oedipal, as it happens—and draws all the effort of decipherment towards its center. What is missing here is an elaboration of the problem of the frame, the signature and the *parergon*. This lack allows us to reconstruct the scene of the signifier as a signified (an ever inevitable process in the logic of the sign), writing as the written, the text as discourse or more precisely as an "intersubjective" dialogue (there is nothing fortuitous in the fact that the Seminar discusses only the two *dialogues* in "The Purloined Letter"). (PT, pp. 52–53, translation modified.)

It is well known that "The Purloined Letter" belongs to what Baudelaire called a "kind of trilogy," along with "The Murders in the Rue Morgue" and "The Mystery of

Marie Rogêt." About this Dupin trilogy, the Seminar does not breathe a word; not only does Lacan lift out the narrated triangles (the "real drama") in order to center the narration around them and make them carry the weight of the interpretation (the letter's destination), but he also lifts one third of the Dupin cycle out of an ensemble discarded as if it were a natural, invisible frame. (Not translated in PT; FV, p. 123; translation mine.)

In framing with such violence, in cutting a fourth side of the narrated figure itself in order to see only triangles, a certain complication, perhaps a complication of the Oedipal structure, is eluded, a complication which makes itself felt in the scene of writing. (PT, p. 54; translation entirely modified.)

It would seem, then, that Lacan is guilty of several sins of omission: the omission of the narrator, the nondialogue parts of the story, the other stories in the trilogy. But does this criticism amount to a mere plea for the inclusion of what has been excluded? No; the problem is not simply quantitative. What has been excluded is not homogeneous to what has been included. Lacan, says Derrida, misses the specifically literary dimension of Poe's text by treating it as a "real drama," a story like the stories a psychoanalyst hears every day from his patients. What has been left out is literature itself.

Does this mean that the frame is what makes a text literary? In an issue of *New Literary History* devoted to the question "What is literature?" (and totally unrelated to the debate concerning the purloined letter) one of the contributors comes to this very conclusion: "Literature is language . . . but it is language around which we have drawn a *frame*, a frame that indicates a decision to regard with a particular self-consciousness the resources language has always possessed"[11] (emphasis mine).

Such a view of literature, however, implies that a text is literary because it remains inside certain definite borders; it is a many-faceted object, perhaps, but still, it is an object. That this is not quite what Derrida has in mind becomes clear from the following remarks:

By overlooking the narrator's position, the narrator's involvement in the content of what he seems to be recounting, one omits from the scene of writing anything going beyond the two triangular scenes.

And first of all one omits that what is in question—with no possible access route or border—is a scene of writing whose boundaries crumble off into an abyss. From the simulacrum of an overture, of a "first word," the narrator, in narrating himself, advances a few positions which carry the unity of the "tale" into an endless drifting-off course: a textual drifting not at all taken into account in the Seminar. (PT, pp. 100–101; translation modified.)

These reminders, of which countless other examples could be given, alert us to the effects of the frame, and of the paradoxes in the parergonal logic. Our purpose is not to prove that "The Purloined Letter" functions within a frame (omitted by the Seminar, which can thus be assured of its triangular interior by an active, surreptitious limitation starting from a metalinguistic overview), but to prove that the structure of the framing effects is such that no totalization of the border is even possible. Frames are always framed: thus, by part of their content. Pieces without a whole, "divisions" without a totality—this is what thwarts the dream of a letter without division, allergic to division. (PT, p. 99; translation slightly modified.)

Here the argument seems to reverse the previous objection; Lacan has eliminated not the frame but the unframability of the literary text. But what Derrida calls "parergonal logic" is paradoxical precisely because both of these incompatible (but not totally contradictory) arguments are equally valid. The total inclusion of the frame is both mandatory and impossible. The frame thus becomes not the borderline between the inside and the outside, but precisely what subverts the applicability of the inside/outside polarity to the act of interpretation.

The frame is, in fact, one of a series of paradoxical "borderline cases"—along with the tympanum and the hymen—through which Derrida has recently been studying the limits of spatial logic as it relates to intelligibility. Lacan, too, has been seeking to displace the Euclidean model of understanding (comprehension, for example, means spatial inclusion) by inventing a "new geometry" by means of the logic of knots. The relation between these two attempts to break out of spatial logic has yet to be articulated, but some measure of the difficulties involved may be derived from the fact that *to break out of* is still a spatial metaphor. The urgency of these undertakings cannot, however, be overestimated, since the logic of metaphysics, of politics, of belief, and of knowledge itself is based on the imposition of definable objective frontiers and outlines whose possibility and/or justifiability are here being put in question. If "comprehension" is the framing of something whose limits are undeterminable, how can we know what we are comprehending? The play on the spatial and the criminal senses of the word *frame* with which we began this section may thus not be as gratuitous as it seemed. And indeed, the question of the fallacies inherent in a Euclidean model of intelligibility, far from being a tangential theoretical consideration here, is central to the very plot of "The Purloined Letter" itself. For it is precisely the notion of space as finite and homogeneous that underlies the Prefect's method of investigation: "I presume you know," he explains, "that, to a properly trained police-agent, such a thing as a 'secret' drawer is impossible. Any man is a dolt who permits a 'secret' drawer to escape him in a search of this kind. The thing is *so* plain. There is a certain amount of bulk—of space—to be accounted for in every cabinet. Then we have accurate rules. The fiftieth part of a line could not escape us" (Poe, p. 204). The assumption that what is not seen must be hidden—an assumption Lacan calls the "realist's imbecillity"—is based on a falsely objective notion of the act of *seeing*. The polarity "hidden/exposed" cannot alone account for the police's *not* finding the letter—which was entirely exposed, inside out—let alone for Dupin's finding it. A "subjective" element must be added, which subverts the geometrical model of understanding through the interference of the polarity "blindness/sight" with the polarity "hidden/exposed." The same problematic is raised by the story of "The Emperor's New Clothes," which Derrida cites as an example of psychoanalysis' failure to go beyond the polarity "hidden/exposed" (in Freud's account). We will return to the letter's "place" later on in this essay, but it is already clear that the "range" of any investigation is located not in geometrical space, but in its implicit notion of what "seeing" is.

What enables Derrida to problematize the literary text's frame is, as we have seen, what he calls "the scene of writing." By this he means two things.

1. *The textual signifier's resistance to being totally transformed into a signified.* In spite of Lacan's attentiveness to the path of the letter in Poe's story as an illustration of the functioning of a signifier, says Derrida, the psychoanalytical reading is still blind to the functioning of the signifier in the narration itself. In reading "The Purloined Letter" as an allegory of the signifier, Lacan, according to Derrida, has made the "signifier" into the story's truth: "The displacement of the signifier is analyzed as a signified, as the recounted object in a short story" (PT, p. 48). Whereas, counters Derrida, it is precisely the textual signifier that resists being thus totalized into meaning, leaving an irreducible residue: "The rest, the remnant, would be 'The Pur-

loined Letter,' the text that bears this title, and whose place, like the once more invisible large letters on the map, is not where one was expecting to find it, in the enclosed content of the 'real drama' or in the hidden and sealed interior of Poe's story, but in and as the open letter, the very open letter which fiction is" (PT, p. 64).

2. *The actual writings*—the books, libraries, quotations, and previous tales that surround "The Purloined Letter" with a frame of (literary) references. The story begins in "a little back library, or book-closet" (Poe, p. 199), where the narrator is mulling over a previous conversation on the subject of the two previous instances of Dupin's detective work as told in Poe's two previous tales, the first of which recounted the original meeting between Dupin and the narrator—in a library, of course, where both were in search of the same rare book. The story's beginning is thus an infinitely regressing reference to previous writings. And therefore, says Derrida, "nothing begins. Simply a drifting or a disorientation from which one never moves away" (PT, p. 101). Dupin, himself, is in fact a walking library; books are his "sole luxuries," and the narrator is "astonished" at "the vast extent of his reading" (Poe, p. 106). Even Dupin's last, most seemingly personal words—the venomous lines he leaves in his substitute letter to the Minister—are a quotation, whose transcription and proper authorship are the last things the story tells us. "But," concludes Derrida, "beyond the quotation marks that surround the entire story, Dupin is obliged to quote this last word in quotation marks, to recount his signature: that is what I wrote to him and how I signed it. What is a signature within quotation marks? Then, within these quotation marks, the seal itself is a quotation within quotation marks. This remnant is still literature" (PT, pp. 112–13).

It is by means of these two extra dimensions that Derrida intends to show the crumbling, abyssal, nontotalizable edges of the story's frame. Both of these objections, however, are in themselves more problematic and double-edged than they appear. Let us begin with the second. "Literature" in Derrida's demonstration is indeed clearly the beginning, middle, and end—and even the interior—of the purloined letter. But how was this conclusion reached? To a large extent, by listing the books, libraries, and other writings recounted in the story. That is, by following the theme—and not the functioning—of "writing" within "the content of a representation." But if Dupin's signing with a quotation, for example, is for Derrida a sign that "this remnant is still literature," does this not indicate that "literature" has become not the signifier but the signified in the story? If the play of the signifier is really to be followed, does it not play beyond the range of the *seme* "writing"? And if Derrida criticizes Lacan for making the "signifier" into the story's signified, is Derrida not here transforming "writing" into "the written" in much the same way? What Derrida calls "the reconstruction of the scene of the signifier as a signified" seems indeed to be "an inevitable process" in the logic of reading the purloined letter.

Derrida, of course, implicitly counters this objection by protesting—twice—that the textual drifting for which Lacan does not account should not be considered "the *real subject* of the tale," but rather the "remarkable ellipsis" of any subject (PT, p. 102). But the question of the seemingly inevitable slipping from the signifier to the signified still remains, and not as an objection to the logic of the frame, but as its fundamental question. For if the "paradoxes of parergonal logic" are such that the frame is always being framed by part of its contents, it is this very slippage between signifier and signified, *acted out* by both Derrida and Lacan against their intentions, which best illustrates those paradoxes. Derrida's justification of his framing of the "Lacan" he is reading as neither being limited to the "Seminar" nor as including Lacan's later work, itself obeys the contradictory logic of the frame. On the one hand, Derrida will study that part of Lacan's work which seems to embody a system of truth even though other writings might put that system in question, and on the other hand this same part of Lacan's work, says Derrida, will probably some day be called the work of the "young Lacan" by "academics eager to divide up *what cannot be divided*" (PT, p. 82, translation modified). Whatever Derrida actually thinks he is doing here, his contradictory way of explaining it obeys the paradoxes of parergonal logic so perfectly that this self-subversion may have even been deliberate.

If the question of the frame thus problematizes the object of any interpretation by setting it at an angle or fold (*pli*) with itself, then Derrida's analysis errs not in opposing this paradoxical functioning to Lacan's allegorical reading, but in not following the consequences of its own insight far enough. For example, if it is the frame that makes it impossible for us to know where to begin and when to stop, why does Derrida stop within the limits of the Dupin trilogy? And if the purpose of studying "writing" is to sow an uncanny uncertainty about our position in the abyss, is not the disseminal library Derrida describes still in a way just a bit too comfortable?

"The Purloined Letter," says Derrida, is signed "literature." What does this mean, if not that the letter's contents—the only ones we are allowed to see—are in another text? That the locus of the letter's meaning is not in the letter, but somewhere else? That the context of that meaning is the way in which its context is lacking, both through the explicit designation of a proper origin (Crébillon's *Atrée*) *outside* the text and through a substitutive structure from letter to letter, from text to text, and from brother to brother, *within* the text, such that the expressions *outside* and *within* have ceased to be clearly definable? But until we have actually opened that other text, we cannot know the modality of the precise otherness of the abyss to itself, the way in which the story's edges do not simply crumble away.

In order to escape the reduction of the "library" to its thematic presence as a *sign* of writing, let us therefore pull some of the books off the shelves and see what they contain. This is a track neither Lacan nor Derrida has taken, but we will soon see how it in some way enfolds them both.

First of all, the name *Dupin* itself, according to Poe scholars, comes out of Poe's interior library: from the pages of a volume called *Sketches of Conspicuous Living Characters of France* (Philadelphia: Lea & Blanchard, 1841), which Poe reviewed for *Graham's Magazine* during the same month his first Dupin story appeared. André-Marie-Jean-Jacques Dupin, a minor French statesman, is there described as himself a walking library: "To judge from his writings, Dupin must be a perfect living encyclopedia. From Homer to Rousseau, from the Bible to the civil code, from the laws of the twelve tables to the Koran, he has read every thing, retained every thing . . ." (p. 224). Detective Dupin's "origin" is thus multiply bookish. He is a reader whose writer read his name in a book describing a writer as a reader—a reader whose nature can only be described in writing, in fact, as irreducibly double: "He is the personage for whom the painters of political portraits, make the most enormous consumption of antithesis. In the same picture, he will be drawn as both great and little, courageous and timid, trivial and dignified, disinterested and mercenary, restive and pliable, obstinate and fickle, white and black; there is no understanding it" (p. 210). And the writing that serves as the vehicle of this description of written descriptions of double Dupin is itself double: a translation, by a Mr. Walsh, of a series of articles by a Frenchman whose name is not even known to the translator but who is said to call himself "an *homme de rien*, a nobody" (p. 2). "Nobody" thus becomes the proper name of the original author in the series.[12]

But the author of the last word in "The Purloined Letter" is clearly *not* nobody. It is not even Poe; it is Crébillon. When read as the context from which Dupin's letter to the Minister has been purloined, Crébillon's *Atrée* is remarkable not simply because it tells the story of revenge as a symmetrical repetition of the original crime, but because it does so precisely by means of a purloined letter. A *letter* informs King Atreus of the extent of his betrayal and serves as an instrument of his revenge; the King himself has purloined the letter—written by the Queen to her lover, Thyestes, just before her death. The letter reveals that Plisthenes, whom everyone believes to be Atreus's son, is really the son of his brother Thyestes. Having kept the letter and its message secret for twenty years, Atreus plans to force Plisthenes, unaware of his true parentage, to commit patricide. Thwarted in this plan by Plisthenes's refusal to kill the father of his beloved, Theodamia, who is, unknown to him, his sister, Atreus is forced to produce the letter, reunite the illicit family, and transfer his revenge from Plisthenes's patricide to Thyestes's infantophagy. A Queen betraying a King, a letter representing that betrayal being purloined for purposes of power, an eventual return of that letter to its addressee, accompanied by an act of revenge which duplicates the original crime—"The Purloined Letter" as a story of repetition is itself a repetition of the story from which it purloins its last words. The Freudian "truth" of the repetition compulsion is not simply illustrated *in* the story; it is illustrated *by* the story. The story obeys the very law it conveys; it is framed by its own content. And thus "The Purloined Letter" no longer simply repeats its own "primal scene": what it repeats is nothing less than a previous story of repetition. The "last word" names the place where the "nonfirstness" of the "first word" repeats itself.

This is not the only instance of the folding-in of the frame of references upon the purloined letter's interior. Another allusion, somewhat more hidden, is contained in the description of the Minister as someone "who dares all things, those unbecoming as well as those becoming a man" (Poe, p. 201). These words echo Macbeth's protestation to his ambitious wife: "I dare do all that may become a man./Who dares do more is none" (1,7). The reference to *Macbeth* substantiates Lacan's reading of the description of the Minister as pointing toward femininity; it is indeed Lady Macbeth who dares to do what is unbecoming a man. And what is Lady Macbeth doing when we first catch sight of her? She is reading a letter. Not a purloined letter, perhaps, but one that contains the ambiguous letter of destiny, committing Macbeth to the murder of the King, whose place Macbeth will take and whose fate he will inevitably share. Kings seem to be unable to remain unscathed in the face of a letter—Atreus betrayed by his wife's letter to his brother; Duncan betrayed by Macbeth's letter to Lady Macbeth; Macbeth himself betrayed by his own confidence in his ability to read the letter of his Fate; and of course, the King in "The Purloined Letter," whose power is betrayed by his not even knowing about the existence of the letter that betrays him.

The questions raised by all these texts together are legion. What is a man? Who is the child's father? What is the relation between incest, murder, and the death of a child? What is a king? How can we read the letter of our destiny? What is seeing? The crossroads where these stories come together seems to point to the story of what occurred at another crossroads: the tragedy of Oedipus the King. We seem to have returned to our starting point, then, except for one thing: it is no longer "The Purloined Letter" that repeats the story of Oedipus, but the story of Oedipus that repeats all the letters purloined from "The Purloined Letter" 's abyssal interior.

But the letter does not stop there. For the very Oedipal reading that Derrida attributes to Lacan is itself, according to Derrida, a purloined letter—purloined by Lacan from Marie Bonaparte's psychobiographical study of the life and works of Edgar Allan Poe: "At the moment when the Seminar, like Dupin, finds the letter where it is to be found, between the legs of the woman, the deciphering of the enigma is anchored in truth. . . . Why then does it find, at the same time that it finds truth, the same meaning and the same topos as Bonaparte when, leaping over the text, she proposes a psycho-biographical analysis of 'The Purloined Letter'?" (PT, p. 66). In that analysis, Bonaparte sees Dupin's restitution of the letter to the Queen as the return of the missing maternal penis to the mother. The letter's hiding place in the Minister's apartment, moreover, is "almost an anatomical chart" of the female body—which leads Bonaparte to note that Baudelaire's translation of "hung from a little brass knob just beneath the middle of the mantelpiece" as "suspendu à un petit bouton de cuivre—au dessus du manteau de la cheminée" ("*above* the mantelpiece") is "completely wrong" (quoted in PT, p. 68). Bonaparte's frame of reference—the female body—cannot tolerate this error of translation.

A note that Lacan drops on the subject of the letter's position enables Derrida to frame Lacan for neglecting to mention his references: "The question of deciding," says Lacan, "whether he [Dupin] seizes it [the letter] above the mantelpiece as Baudelaire translates, or beneath it, as in the original text, may be abandoned without harm to the inferences of those whose profession is grilling [aux inférences de la cuisine]." Lacan's note: "And even to the cook herself" (SPL, pp. 66–67). In this cavalier treatment of Bonaparte as the "cook," Lacan thus "makes clear" to Derrida "that Lacan had read Bonaparte, although the Seminar never alludes to her. As an author so careful about debts and priorities, he could have acknowledged an irruption that orients his entire interpretation, namely, the process of rephallization as the proper course of the letter, the 'return of the letter' restored to its 'destination' after having been found between the legs of the mantelpiece" (PT, p. 68). The interpretation of the letter (as the phallus that must be returned to the mother) must itself be returned to the "mother" from whom it has been purloined—Marie Bonaparte. Derrida thus follows precisely the logic he objects to in Lacan, the logic of rectification and correction: "to return the letter to its proper course, supposing that its trajectory is a line, is to correct a deviation, to rectify a divergence, to recall a direction, an authentic line" (PT, p. 65). But the mere fact that Derrida's critique repeats the same logic he denounces is in itself less interesting than the fact that this rectification presupposes another, which puts its very foundations in question. For when Lacan says that the question of the exact position of the letter "may be abandoned without harm" to the grillers, Derrida protests, "Without harm? On the contrary, the harm would be decisive, within the Seminar itself: *on* the mantelpiece, the letter could not have been 'between the cheeks of the fireplace,' 'between the legs of the fireplace' " (PT, p. 69). Derrida must thus correct Lacan's text, eliminate its apparent contradiction, in order to return the letter of interpretation to its rightful owner. And all this in order to criticize Lacan's enterprise as one of rectification and circular return. If "rectification" as such is to be criticized, it is difficult to determine where it begins and where it ends. In rectifying Lacan's text in order to make it fit into the logic of rectification, Derrida thus problematizes the very status of the object of his criticism.

But if the correction of Lacan's text is itself a mutilation that requires correction, how *are* we to interpret the contradiction between Lacan's description of the Minister's apartment as "an immense female body" (SPL, p. 66) and his statement that the letter's exact location does not matter? This, it seems to me, is the crux of the divergence between Derrida's and Lacan's interpretation of what the equation "letter = phallus" means.

For Bonaparte, it was precisely the analogy between the fireplace and the female body which led to the letter's phallic function. The phallus was considered as a real, anatomical referent serving as the model for a figurative representation. Bonaparte's frame of reference was thus *reference* itself.

For Derrida, on the other hand, the phallus's frame of reference is "psychoanalytical theory" 's way of preserving the phallus's referential status in the act of negating it. In commenting on Lacan's discussion of "The Meaning of the Phallus," Derrida writes:

> Phallogocentrism is one thing. And what is called man and what is called woman might be subject to it. The more so, we are reminded, since the phallus is neither a phantasy ("imaginary effect") nor an object ("partial, internal, good, bad"), even less the organ, penis or clitoris, which it symbolizes (*Ecrits*, p. 690). Androcentrism ought therefore to be something else.
>
> Yet what is going on? The entire phallogocentrism is articulated from the starting-point of a determinate *situation* (let us give this word its full impact) in which the phallus is the mother's desire inasmuch as she does not have it. An (individual, perceptual, local, cultural, historical, etc.) situation on the basis of which is developed something called a "sexual theory": in it the phallus is not the organ, penis or clitoris, which it symbolizes; but it does to a larger extent and in the first place symbolize the penis. . . ." This consequence had to be traced in order to recognize the meaning [the direction, *sens*] of the purloined letter in the "course *which is proper to it.*" (PT, pp. 98–99).

Thus, says Derrida, the very nonreferentiality of the phallus, in the final analysis, insures that the penis is its referent.

Before trying to determine the applicability of this summary to Lacan's actual statements in "The Meaning of the Phallus"—not to mention in the "Seminar"—let us follow its consequences further in Derrida's critique. From the very first words of "The Purveyor of Truth," psychoanalysis is implicitly being criticized for being capable of finding only itself wherever it looks: "Psychoanalysis, supposing, finds itself" (PT, p. 31, translation mine). In whatever it turns its attention to, psychoanalysis seems to recognize nothing but its own (Oedipal) schemes. Dupin finds the letter because "he knows that the letter finally *finds itself* where it must *be found* in order to return circularly and adequately to its proper place. This proper place, known to Dupin and to the psychoanalyst who intermittently takes his place, is the place of castration" (PT, p. 60; translation modified). The psychoanalyst's act, then, is one of mere *recognition* of the expected, a recognition that Derrida finds explicitly stated as such by Lacan in the underlined words he quotes from the "Seminar": "Just so does the purloined letter, like an immense female body, stretch out across the Minister's office when Dupin enters. But just so does he already *expect to find it* [emphasis mine—J.D.] and has only, with his eyes veiled by green lenses, to undress that huge body" (PT, pp. 61–62; emphasis and brackets in original).

But if recognition is a form of blindness, a form of violence to the otherness of the object, it would seem that, by eliminating Lacan's suggestion of a possible complication of the phallic scheme, and by lying in wait between the brackets of the fireplace to catch the psychoanalyst at his own game, Derrida, too, is "recognizing" rather than reading. He recognizes, as he himself says, a certain classical conception of psychoanalysis: "From the beginning," writes Derrida early in his study, "*we recognize* the classical landscape of applied psychoanalysis" (PT, p. 45; emphasis mine). It would seem that the theoretical frame of reference which governs recognition is a constitutive element in the blindness of any interpretative insight. That frame of reference allows the analyst to frame the author of the text he is reading for practices whose locus is simultaneously beyond the letter of the text and behind the vision of its reader. The reader is framed by his own frame, but he is not even in possession of his own guilt, since it is that which prevents his vision from coinciding with itself. Just as the author of a criminal frame transfers guilt from himself to another by leaving *signs* that he hopes will be read as insufficiently erased traces or referents left by the other, the author of any critique is himself framed by his own frame of the other, no matter how guilty or innocent the other may be.

What is at stake here is therefore the question of the relation between referentiality and interpretation. And here we find an interesting twist: while criticizing Lacan's notion of the phallus as being too referential, Derrida goes on to use referential logic against it. This comes up in connection with the letter's famous "materiality," which Derrida finds so odd. "It would be hard to exaggerate here the scope of this proposition on the indivisibility of the letter, or rather on its identity to itself inaccessible to dismemberment . . . as well as on the so-called materiality of the signifier (the letter) intolerant to partition. But where does this idea come from? A torn-up letter may be purely and simply destroyed, it happens . . ." (PT, pp. 86–87; translation modified). The so-called materiality of the signifier, says Derrida, is nothing but an *idealization*.

But what if the signifier were precisely what put the polarity "materiality/ideality" in question? Has it not become obvious that neither Lacan's description ("Tear a letter into little pieces, it remains the letter that it is") nor Derrida's description ("A torn-up letter may be purely and simply destroyed, it happens . . .") can be read literally? Somehow, a rhetorical fold (pli) in the text is there to trip us up whichever way we turn. Especially since the expression "it happens" (*ça arrive*) uses the very word on which the controversy over the letter's *arrival* at its destination turns.

Our study of the readings of "The Purloined Letter" has thus brought us to the point where the word *letter* no longer has any literality.

But what is a letter that has no literality?

A "PLI" FOR UNDERSTANDING

I pull in resolution, and begin
To doubt the equivocation of the fiend
That lies like truth.

—Macbeth

"*Why do you lie to me saying you're going to Cracow so I should believe*

you're going to Lemberg, when in reality you are *going to Cracow?"*
—Joke quoted by Lacan after Freud

The letter, then, poses the question of its own rhetorical status. It moves rhetorically through the two long, minute studies in which it is presumed to be the literal object of analysis, without having any literality. Instead of simply being explained by those analyses, the rhetoric of the letter problematizes the very rhetorical mode of analytical discourse. And if *literal* means "to the letter," the literal becomes the most problematically figurative mode of all.

As the locus of rhetorical displacement, the letter made its very entrance into Poe's story by "traumatizing" the Prefect's discourse about it. After a series of paradoxes and pleas for absolute secrecy, the Prefect describes the problem created by the letter with a proliferation of *periphrases* which the narrator dubs "the cant of diplomacy":

> "Well, then; I have received personal information, from a very high quarter, that a certain document of the last importance has been purloined from the royal apartments. The individual who purloined it is known; this beyond a doubt; he was seen to take it. It is known, also, that it still remains in his possession."
>
> "How is this known?" asked Dupin.
>
> "It is clearly inferred," replied the Prefect, "from the nature of the document, and from the non-appearance of certain results which would at once arise from its passing *out* of the robber's possession—that is to say, from his employing it as he must design in the end to employ it."
>
> "Be a little more explicit," I said.
>
> "Well, I may venture so far as to say that the paper gives its holder a certain power in a certain quarter where such power is immensely valuable." The Prefect was fond of the cant of diplomacy. (Poe, P. 200.)

The letter thus enters the discourse of Poe's story as a rhetorical fold that actually hides nothing, since, although *we* never find out what was written in the letter, presumably the Queen, the Minister, Dupin, the Prefect—who all held the letter in their hands—and even the narrator, who heard what the Prefect read from his memorandum-book, *did*. The way in which the letter dictates a series of circumlocutions, then, resembles the way in which the path of the letter dictates the characters' circumvolutions—not that the letter's contents *must* remain hidden, but that the question of whether or not they are revealed is immaterial to the displacement the letter governs. The character and actions of each of the letter's holders are determined by the rhetorical spot it puts them in *whether or not* that spot can be read by the subjects it displaces.

The letter, then, acts as a signifier *not* because its contents are lacking, but because its function is not dependent on the knowledge or nonknowledge of those contents. Therefore, by saying that the letter cannot be divided Lacan does not mean that the phallus must remain intact, but that the phallus, the letter, and the signifier *are not substances*. The letter cannot be divided because it only functions *as* a division. It is not something with "an *identity* to itself inaccessible to dismemberment" (PT, pp. 86–87, emphasis mine) as Derrida interprets it; it is a *difference*. It is known only in its effects. The signifier is an articulation in a chain, not an identifiable unit. It cannot be known in itself because it is capable of "sustaining itself *only* in a displacement" (SPL, p. 59; emphasis mine). It is localized, but only as the nongeneralizable locus of a differential relationship. Derrida, in fact, enacts this law of the signifier in the very act of opposing it:

> Perhaps only one letter need be changed, maybe even less than a letter in the expression: "missing from its place" [*manaque à sa place*]. Perhaps we need only introduce a written "a," i.e. without accent, in order to bring out that if the lack *has* its place [*le*

> *manque a sa place*] in this atomistic topology of the signifier, that is, if it occupies therein a specific place of definite contours, the order would remain undisturbed. (PT, p. 45.)

While thus criticizing the hypostasis of a lack—the letter as the substance of an absence (which is not what Lacan is saying)—Derrida is illustrating what Lacan *is* saying about both the materiality and the localizability of the signifier as the mark of difference by operating on the letter as a material locus of differentiation: by removing the little signifier "`," an accent mark which has no meaning in itself.[13]

The question of the nature of the "lack," however, brings us back to the complexities of the meaning and place of the "phallus." For while it is quite easy to show the signifier as a "difference" rather than a "lack," the question becomes much trickier in relation to the phallus. There would seem to be no ambiguity in Lacan's statement that "clinical observation shows us that this test through the desire of the Other is not decisive insofar as the subject thereby learns whether or not he himself has a real phallus, but insofar as he learns *that the mother does not*" (*Ecrits*, p. 693; translation and emphasis mine). The theory seems to imply that at some point in human sexuality, a referential moment is unbypassable: the observation that the mother does not have a penis is necessary. And therefore it would seem that the "lack" is localizable as the substance of an absence or a hole. To borrow a joke from Geoffrey Hartman's discussion of certain solutionless detective stories, if the purloined letter is the mother's phallus, "instead of a whodunit we get a whodonut, a story with a hole in it."[14]

But even on this referential level, is the object of observation really a lack? Is it not instead an interpretation—an interpretation ("castration") not of a lack but of a *difference*? If what is observed is irreducibly anatomical, what is anatomy here but the irreducibility of difference? Even on the most elementary level, the phallus is a sign of sexuality as difference, and not as the presence or absence of this or that organ.

But Lacan defines the phallus in a much more complicated way. For if the woman is defined as "giving in a love-relation that which she does not have," the definition of what the woman does not have is not limited to the penis. At another point in the discussion, Lacan refers to "the gift of what one does not have" as "love" (*Ecrits*, p. 691). Is "love" here a mere synonym for the phallus? Perhaps; but only if we modify the definition of the phallus. Love, in Lacan's terminology, is what is in question in the "request for love" ("demande d'amour"), which is "unconditional," the "demand for a presence or an absence" (*Ecrits*, p. 691). This "demande" is not only a reference to "what the Other doesn't have," however. It is also language. And language is what alienates human desire such that "it is from the place of the Other that the subject's message is emitted" (*Ecrits*, p. 690). The "demande" is thus a request for the unconditional presence or absence not of an organ but of the Other in answer to the question asked by the subject from the place of the Other. But this "demande" is not yet the definition of "desire." Desire is what is left of the "demande" when all possible satisfaction of "real" needs has been subtracted from it. "Desire is neither the appetite for satisfaction, nor the demand for love, but the difference which results from the subtraction of the first from the second, the very phenomenon of their split [*Spaltung*]" (*Ecrits*, p. 691). And if the phallus as a signifier, according to Lacan, "gives the *ratio* of desire," the definition of the phallus can no longer bear a simple relation either to the body or to language, because it is that which prevents both the body and language from being simple: "The phallus is the privileged signifier of that mark where logos is joined together with the advent of desire" (*Ecrits*, p. 692; all translations in this paragraph mine).

The important word in this definition is *joined*. For if language (alienation of needs through the place of the Other) and desire (the remainder that is left after the subtraction of the satisfaction of real needs from absolute demand) are neither totally separable from each other nor related in the same way to their own division, the phallus is the signifier of the articulation between two very problematic chains. But what is a signifier in this context? "A signifier," says Lacan, "is what represents a subject for another signifier." A signifier represents, then, and what it represents is a subject. But it only does so for another signifier. What does the expression "for another signifier" mean, if not that the distinction between subject and signifier posed in the first part of the definition is being subverted in the second? "Subject" and "signifier" are coimplicated in a definition that is unable either to separate them totally or to fuse them completely. There are three positions in the definition, two of which are occupied by the same word, but that word is differentiated from itself in the course of the definition—because it begins to take the place of the *other* word. The signifier for which the other signifier represents a subject thus acts like a subject because it is the place where the representation is "understood." The signifier, then, situates the place of something like a reader. And the reader becomes the place where representation would be understood if there were any such thing as a place beyond representation; the place where representation is inscribed as an infinite chain of substitutions whether or not there is any place from which it can be understood.

The letter as a signifier is thus not a thing or the absence of a thing, not a word or the absence of a word, not an organ or the absence of an organ, but a *knot* in a structure where words, things, and organs can neither be definably separated nor compatibly combined. This is why the exact representational position of the letter in the Minister's apartment both matters and does not matter. It matters to the extent that sexual anatomical difference creates an irreducible dissymmetry to be accounted for in every human subject. But it does not matter to the extent that the letter is not hidden in geometrical space, where the police are looking for it, or in anatomical space, where a literal understanding of psychoanalysis might look for it. It is located "in" a *symbolic* structure, a structure that can only be perceived in its effects, and whose effects are perceived as repetition. Dupin finds the letter "in" the symbolic order not because he knows where to look, but because he knows *what to repeat*. Dupin's "analysis" is the repetition of the scene that led to the necessity of analysis. It is not an interpretation or an insight, but an act—an act of untying the knot in the structure by the repetition of the act of tying it. The word *analyze*, in fact, etymologically means "untie," a meaning on which Poe plays in his prefatory remarks on the nature of analysis as "that moral activity which disentangles" (Poe, p. 102). The analyst does not intervene by giving meaning, but by effecting a *dénouement*.

But if the act of (psycho-)analysis has no identity apart from its status as a repetition of the structure it seeks to analyze (to untie), then Derrida's remarks against psychoanalysis as being always already *mise en abyme* in the text it studies and as being only capable of finding *itself*, are not objections to psychoanalysis but a profound insight into its very essence. Psychoanalysis is, in fact, itself the primal scene it seeks: it is the first occurrence of what has been repeating itself in the patient without ever having occurred. Psychoanalysis is not the interpretation of repetition; it is the repetition of a *trauma of interpretation*—called "castration" or "parental coitus" or "the Oedipus complex" or even "sexuality"—the traumatic deferred interpretation not *of* an event, but *as* an event that never took place as such. The "primal scene" is not a scene but an interpretative infelicity whose result was to situate the interpreter in an intolerable position. And psychoanalysis is the reconstruction of that interpretative infelicity not as its interpretation, but as its first and last act. Psychoanalysis has content only insofar as it repeats the discontent of what never took place.

But, as Dupin reminds us, "there is such a thing as being too profound. Truth is not always in a well. In fact, as regards the more important knowledge, I do believe that she is invariably superficial" (Poe, p. 119). Have we not here been looking beyond Lacan's signifier instead of at it? When Lacan insists on the "materiality of the signifier" that does not "admit partition," what is *his* way of explaining it? Simply that the word *letter* is never used with a partitive article: you can have "some mail" but not "some letter."

> Language delivers its judgment to whoever knows how to hear it: through the usage of the article as partitive particle. It is there that the spirit—if spirit be living meaning—appears, no less oddly, as more available for quantification than the letter. To begin with meaning itself, which bears our saying: a speech rich with meaning ["plein *de* signification"], just as we recognize a measure of intention ["*de* l'intention"] in an act, or deplore that there is no more love ["plus *d'amour*]; or store up hatred ["*de la* haine"] and expend devotion ["*du* dévouement"], and so much infatuation ["tant *d'*infatuation"] is easily reconciled to the fact that there will always be ass ["*de la* cuisse"] for sale and brawling ["*du* rififi"] among men.
>
> But as for the letter—be it taken as typographical character, epistle, or what makes a man of letters—we will say that what is said is to be understood to the *letter* [*à la lettre*], that *a letter* [*une lettre*] awaits you at the post office, or even that you are acquainted with letters [*que vous avez des lettres*]—never that there is *letter* [*de la lettre*] anywhere, whatever the context, even to designate overdue mail. (SPL, pp. 53–54.)

If this passage is particularly resistant to the translation, that is because its message is in the "superficial" play of the signifier. Like the large letters on the map which are so obvious as to be invisible, Lacan's textual signifier has gone unnoticed in the search for the signified, "signifier."

But the question of translation in connection with a message so obvious that it goes unseen is not an accident here. For in his discussion of Dupin's statement that " 'analysis' conveys 'algebra' about as much as, in Latin, '*ambitus*' implies 'ambition,' '*religio*,' religion, or '*homines honesti*' a set of '*honorable* men' " (Poe, p. 212), Lacan asks:

> Might not this parade of erudition be destined to reveal to us the key words of our drama?[15] Is not the magician repeating his trick before our eyes, without deceiving us this time about divulging his secret, but pressing his wager to the point of really explaining it to us without us seeing a thing. *That* would be the summit of the illusionist's art: through one of his fictive creations to *truly delude us*. (SPL, pp. 50–51.)

But the trick does not end here. For has Lacan himself not slipped into the paragraph on the quantification of the letter a parade of "key words" for his reading of the situation? "Full of meaning," "intention," "hatred," "love," "infatuation," "devotion," "ass for sale," and "brawling among men"—all of these words occur as the possible "signifieds" of "The Purloined Letter" in the "Seminar." But if the key words of a reading of the story thus occur only in the mode of a play of the signifier, the *difference* between "signifier" and "signified" in Lacan's text, as well as in Poe's, has been effectively subverted. What the reader finally reads when he deciphers the signifying surface of the map of his misreading is: "You have been fooled." And in this discussion of "being fooled" Lacan, far from excluding the narrator, situates him in the dynamic functioning of the text, as a reader *en abyme* duped by Dupin's trick explanations of his technique; a reader who, however, unconscious of the nonsequiturs he is repeating, is so much in awe of his subject that his admiration blinds us to the tricky functioning of what he so faithfully transmits.

To be fooled by a text implies that the text is not constative but performative, and that the reader is in fact one of its effects. The text's "truth" puts the status of the reader in question, "performs" him as its "address." Thus "truth" is not what the fiction reveals as a nudity behind a veil. When Derrida calls Lacan's statement that "truth inhabits fiction" an unequivocal expression or revelation of the truth of truth (PT, p. 46), he is simply not seeing the performative perversity of the rest of the sentence in which that "statement" occurs: "It is up to the reader to give the letter . . . what he will find as its last word: its destination. That is, Poe's message deciphered and coming back from him, the reader, from the fact that, in reading it, he is able to say of himself that he is not more feigned than truth when it inhabits fiction" (*Ecrits*, p. 10; translation mine). The play between truth and fiction, reader and text, message and feint, has become impossible to unravel into an "unequivocal" meaning.

We have thus come back to the question of the letter's destination and of the meaning of the enigmatic "last words" of Lacan's "Seminar." "The sender," writes Lacan, "receives from the receiver his own message in reverse form. Thus it is that what the 'purloined letter,' nay, the 'letter in sufferance' means is that a letter always arrives at its destination" (SPL, p. 72). The reversibility of the direction of the letter's movement between sender and receiver has now come to stand for the fact, underlined by Derrida as if it were an *objection* to Lacan, that there is no position from which the letter's message can be read as an object: "no neutralization is possible, no general point of view" (PT, p. 106). This is the same "discovery" that psychoanalysis makes—that the analyst is involved (through transference) in the very "object" of his analysis.

Everyone who has held the letter—or even beheld it—including the narrator, has ended up having the letter addressed to him as its destination. The reader is comprehended by the letter; there is no place from which he can stand back and observe it. Not that the letter's meaning is subjective rather than objective, but that the letter is precisely that which subverts the polarity "subjective/objective," that which makes subjectivity into something whose position in a structure is situated by an object's passage through it. The letter's destination is thus *wherever it is read:* the place it assigns to its reader as his own partiality. Its destination is not a place, decided a priori by the sender, because the receiver is the sender, and the receiver is whoever receives the letter, including nobody. When Derrida says that a letter can miss its destination and be disseminated, he reads "destination" as a place that pre-exists the letter's movement. But if, as Lacan shows, the letter's destination is not its literal addressee, nor even whoever possesses it, but whoever is possessed by it, then the very disagreement over the meaning of "reaching the destination" is an *illustration* of the nonobjective nature of that "destination." The rhetoric of Derrida's differentiation of his own point of view from Lacan's enacts that law:

> Thanks to castration, the phallus always stays in its place in the transcendental to-

> pology we spoke of earlier. It is indivisible and indestructible there, like the letter which takes its place. And that is why the *interested* presupposition, never proved, of the letter's materiality as indivisibility was indispensable to this restricted economy, this circulation of property.
>
> The difference I am *interested* in here is that, a formula to be read however one wishes, the lack has no place of its own in dissemination. (PT, P. 63; translation modified, emphasis mine.)

The play of "interest" in this expression of difference is too interesting not to be deliberate. The opposition between the "phallus" and "dissemination" is not between two theoretical objects but between two interested positions. And if sender and receiver are merely the two poles of a reversible message, then Lacan's very substitution of *destin* for *dessein* in the Crébillon quotation—a misquotation that Derrida finds revealing enough to end his analysis upon—*is*, in fact, the quotation's message. The sender (dessein) and the receiver (destin) of the violence which passes between Atreus and Thyestes are equally subject to the violence the letter *is*.

The reflexivity between receiver and sender is, however, not an expression of symmetry in itself, but only an evocation of the interdependence of the two terms, of the *question* of symmetry as a *problem* in the transferential structure of all reading. As soon as accident or exteriority or time or repetition enters into that reflexivity—that is to say, from the beginning—"Otherness" becomes in a way the letter's sender. The message I am reading may be either my own (narcissistic) message backward or the way in which that message is always traversed by its own otherness to itself or by the narcissistic message of the other. In any case, the letter is in a way the materialization of my death. And once these various possibilities are granted, none of them can function in isolation. The question of the letter's origin and destination can no longer be asked as such. And whether this is because it involves two, three or four terms must remain undecidable.

The sentence "a letter always arrives at its destination" can thus either be simply pleonastic or variously paradoxical; it can mean "the only message I can read is the one I send," "wherever the letter is, is its destination," "when a letter is read, it reads the reader," "the repressed always returns," "I exist only as a reader of the other," "the letter has no destination," and "we all die." It is not any one of these readings, but all of them and others in their incompatibility, which repeat the letter in its way of reading the act of reading. Far from giving us the "Seminar" 's final truth, these last words enact the impossibility of any ultimate analytical metalanguage.

If it at first seemed possible to say that Derrida was opposing the unsystematizable to the systematized, "chance" to psychoanalytical "determinism," or the "undecidable" to the "destination," the positions of these oppositions seem now to be reversed; Lacan's apparently unequivocal ending says only its own dissemination, while "dissemination" has erected itself into a kind of "last word." But these oppositions are themselves misreadings of the dynamic functioning of what is at stake here. For if the letter is what dictates the rhetorical indetermination of any theoretical discourse about it, then the oscillation between unequivocal statements of undecidability and ambiguous assertions of decidability is one of the letter's inevitable effects. For example, the "indestructibility of desire," which could be considered a psychoanalytical belief in the return of the *same*, turns out to name repetition as the repetition not of sameness but of *otherness*, resulting in the dissemination of the subject. And "symbolic determination" is not opposed to "chance": it is what emerges as the *syntax* of chance.[16] But "chance," out of which springs that which repeats, cannot in any way be "known," since "knowing" is one of its effects. We can therefore never be sure whether or not "chance" itself exists at all. "Undecidability" can no more be used as a last word than "destination." "Car," said Mallarmé, "il y a et il n'y a pas de hasard." The "undeterminable" is not opposed to the determinable; "dissemination" is not opposed to repetition. If we could be sure of the difference between the determinable and the undeterminable, the undeterminable would be comprehended within the determinable. What is undecidable is whether a thing is decidable or not.

As a final fold in the letter's performance of its reader, it should perhaps be noted that, in this discussion of the letter as what prevents me from knowing whether Lacan and Derrida are really saying the same thing or only enacting their own differences from themselves, my own theoretical "frame of reference" is precisely, to a very large extent, the writings of Lacan and Derrida. The frame is thus framed again by part of its content; the sender again receives his own message backward from the receiver. And the true otherness of the purloined letter of literature has perhaps still in no way been accounted for.

NOTES

1. Edgar Allan Poe, *Great Tales and Poems of Edgar Allan Poe* (New York: Pocket Library, 1951); hereafter designated as "Poe." Jacques Lacan, *Ecrits* (Paris: Seuil, 1966); quotations in English are taken, unless otherwise indicated, from the partial translation in *Yale French Studies* 48 (*French Freud*), 1973; hereafter designated as "SPL." Jacques Derrida, published in French in *Poétique* 21 (1975) and, somewhat reduced in *Yale French Studies* 52 (*Graphesis*), 1975; unless otherwise indicated, references are to the English version, hereafter designated as "PT."

2. Such a concatenation could jokingly be called, after the nursery rhyme, "This is the text that Jacques built." But in fact, it is precisely this kind of sequence or chain that is in question here.

3. We will speak about this bracketed signature later; for the time being, it stands as a sign that Derrida's signature has indeed been added to our round robin.

4. "So infamous a scheme/If not worthy of Atreus, is worthy of Thyestes."

5. *La politique de l'autruiche* combines the policy of the ostrich (*autruche*), others (*autrui*) and Austria (*Autriche*).

6. Jacques Derrida, *Positions* (Paris: Minuit, 1972), pp. 112–13; translation is my own; Ibid., p. 113.

7. Jacques Lacan, *Ecrits* (Paris: Seuil ["Points"], 1966), p. 11; translation is my own.

8. Cf. Lacan's description in *Ecrits*, p. 60, of the "effect of disorientation, or even of great anxiety," provoked by these exercises.

9. Some idea of the possibilities for misunderstanding inherent in this question can be gathered from the following: In order to show that psychoanalysis *represses* "writing" in a logocentric way, Derrida quotes Lacan's statement against tape recorders: "But precisely because it comes to him through an alienated form, even a retransmission of his own recorded discourse, be it from the mouth of his own doctor, cannot have the same effects as psychoanalytical interlocution." This Derrida regards as a *condemnation* of the "simulacrum," a "disqualification of recording or of repetition in the name of the living and present word." But what does Lacan actually *say*? Simply that a tape recording *does not have the same effects* as psychoanalytical interlocution. Does the fact that psychoanalysis is a technique based on verbal interlocution automatically reduce it to a logocentric error? Is it not equally possible to regard what Lacan calls "full speech" as being *full* of precisely what Derrida calls "*writing*"?

10. Paul de Man, *Blindness and Insight* (London: Oxford University Press, 1971), p. 140.

11. Stanley E. Fish, "How Ordinary is Ordinary Language?," *New Literary History*, 5, (1973) 52.

12. In a final twist to this *mise en abyme* of writing, the words "by L. L. de Loménie" have been penciled into the Yale library's copy of this book under the title in a meticulous nineteenth-century hand, as the book's "*supplément d'origine*."

13. It is perhaps not by chance that the question here arises of whether or not to put the accent on the letter *a*. The letter *a* is perhaps the purloined letter

par excellence in the writings of all three authors: Lacan's "objet *a*," Derrida's "différance," and Edgar Poe's middle initial, *A*, taken from his foster father, John Allan.

14. Geoffrey Hartman, "Literature High and Low: the Case of the Mystery Story," *The Fate of Reading* (Chicago: University of Chicago Press, 1975): 206.

15. *Ambitus* means "detour"; *religio*, "sacred bond"; *homines honesti*, "decent men." Lacan expands upon these words as the "key words" of the story by saying: "All of this . . . does not imply that because the letter's secrecy is indefensible, the betrayal of that secret would in any sense be honorable. The *honesti homines*, decent people, will not get off so easily. There is more than one *religio*, and it is not slated for tomorrow that sacred ties shall cease to rend us in two. As for *ambitus:* a detour, we see, is not always inspired by ambition" (SPL, p. 58).

16. This is what the mathematical model in the "Introduction" of the "Seminar" clearly shows; beginning with a totally arbitrary binary series, a syntax of regularity emerges from the simple application of a law of combination to the series. When it is objected that that syntax *is not*, unless the subject *remembers* the series, Lacan responds in *Ecrits*, p. 43: "That is just what is in question here: it is less out of anything real . . . than precisely out of *what never was*, that what repeats itself springs"; translation mine. Memory could thus be considered not as a *condition* of repetition, but as one of its syntactic effects. What we call a random series is, in fact, already an *interpretation*, not a given; it is not a materialization of chance itself, but only of something which obeys our conception of the laws of probability.

20

Jerry Aline Flieger
1947–

Jerry Aline Flieger teaches French literature, women's studies, and critical theory at Rutgers University. She is interested in gender questions in literature, particularly how the new French feminism has influenced theories of textuality and narrative. She has published widely on psychoanalytic and modern criticism in such journals as Diacritics, SubStance,French Forum, and MLN. Her book on the comic mode in contemporary French literature will soon be published.

In "The Purloined Punchline" (1983) Flieger uses Freud's well-known theory of jokes as a model for the literary text, particularly the theory as it recounts "the transmission of sexual desire in a socio-linguistic circuit." Flieger's ultimate concern is the way in which women may find themselves in language and "whether 'she,' as subject, can speak or write" from a Freudian viewpoint. Her own view of Freudian theory is drawn from a radical psychoanalysis, particularly the rereading of Freud by Jacques Lacan and feminists such as Luce Irigaray and Michele Montrelay. For Flieger, Lacan's work addresses "narrative, a theory of narrative, and a theory of human intersubjectivity and sexuality *as* narrative." Like many other feminists, Flieger probes language and literature *with* Lacan but wishes to modify psychoanalytic discourse in light of the experience of women as language users.

The Purloined Punchline: Joke as Textual Paradigm

> *"Freud, the very name's a laugh . . . the most hilarious leap in the holy farce of history."*
>
> —Jacques Lacan, "A Love Letter"[1]

THE CLUE IN FULL VIEW

Freud clearly loved nothing more than a good story, except perhaps a good laugh. From Dora to Moses, from Oedipus to the Jewish marriage broker, Freud's cast of characters plays out the human drama in suspenseful narratives spiced with anecdote and warmed with wit. Little wonder, then, that some of Freud's most provocative insights concern the twin esthetic mysteries dear to his heart: the writer's magic (which he calls "the poet's secret") and the joker's art.

In his own "return to Freud," Lacan has followed the master story-teller's example. For Lacan's own artful use of pun, allusion, and narrative technique creates a performative theoretical discourse which reenacts the plot of intersubjective desire which it analyzes. Lacan's work thus tends to speak to questions of narrative and textuality in an oblique manner, by example. In order to elaborate a Lacanian theory of narrative, one needs to decipher the clues in Lacan's own sometimes turgid and hermetic text.

In one of the best examples of Lacan's narrative craft—the much discussed "Seminar on 'The Purloined Letter' "[2]—Lacan passes on a useful lesson learned from Poe's arch-sleuth, Dupin: the best clues, he tells us, are always at once marginal and obvious ("Perhaps a little *too* self-evident," *S.P.L.*, p. 53). One such marginal yet obvious clue to Lacan's own difficult work, it seems to me, may be found in the first volume of *Écrits* (Paris: Editions du Seuil, 1966), in which Lacan alludes in passing to Freud's seminal text on joke theory:

> For, however neglected by our interest—and for good reason—*Jokes and their Relation to the Unconscious*[3] remains the most unchallengeable of Freud's works because it is the most transparent, in which the effect of the Unconscious is revealed to us in its most subtle confines. (*Écrits, I*, p. 148, my translation)

What are we to make of this puzzling statement of simultaneous homage and disparagement? Why does Lacan *marginalize* Freud's text ("however neglected by our interest—and for good reason—") at the same time that he insists on its "transparency" and its centrality as "the most unchallengeable of Freud's works"? Perhaps like the purloined letter of Poe's detective tale, which has been hidden in plain sight, Freud's work may be a *somewhat too evident* clue to understanding Lacan's own version of the Freudian master narrative. For if Freud's transparent text is clearly about what it promises to be—"Jokes and their Relation to the Unconscious"—it is also about the transmission of sexual desire in a sociolinguistic circuit. In addition, it may be read as a model story, a paradigm tracing the possibilities of narrative itself. Indeed, such a reading of Freud's "transparent" essay on the joking process as an "evident" clue to the functioning of textual processes seems to suggest that Lacan's own punchline—the discovery that everything human is textual, caught in an intersubjective narrative web—has been purloined from Freud. Yet in returning this punchline or message to its initiator, we find that it has been transcribed in Lacan's hand, and that this transcription will in turn permit us to rethink the joking process itself, so that it no longer appears as a guarantor of identity or as a cementer of the social bond, but rather as a symptom motivated by the same pre-text of desire which gives rise to the literary text.

In order to reread the Freudian paradigm in Lacanian terms, with an eye to formulating a Lacanian theory of literary narrative, I want to trace the following chain of metonymic equivalences: subjectivity as intersubjectivity; intersubjectivity as narrative/text; text as "feminine" symptom; femininity as (form of) subjectivity. This chain may be described as *metonymic* because in Lacan's view of intersubjectivity as a kind of text, each of these processes or phenomena is an overlapping link which leads inevitably to the next. And this metonymic chain in turn describes a circular itinerary or plot, in which the final point—which visits that question, perplexing to Freud and to Lacan alike, of the nature of femininity—returns to the point of departure, a questioning of the role of the subject not only in the creation of the literary text, but in the forming of the larger human plot or text. For the question of feminine subjectivity—and of whether "she," as subject, can speak or write—is a central one in Lacan's work, and it is a question which must be addressed in reading that work as (at one and the same time) a narrative, theory *of* narrative, and a theory of human intersubjectivity and sexuality *as* narrative.

I. SUBJECTIVITY AS INTERSUBJECTIVITY

> *Generally speaking, a tendentious joke calls for three people: in addition to the one who makes the joke, there must be a second who is taken as the object of the hostile or sexual aggressiveness, and a third in whom the joke's aim of producing pleasure is fulfilled.*
>
> —Freud, *Jokes and their Relation to the Unconscious*, p. 100

A Classic Plot

In the third section of the essay on jokes ("The Purposes of Jokes"), Freud tells the story of the origin of joking itself: the joker-protagonist overcomes a series of adverse circumstances and enjoys a happy ending of sorts ("Jokes make possible the satisfaction of an instinct—whether lustful or hostile—in the face of an obstacle which stands in its way," p. 101). Thus the happy ending, the satisfaction of a lustful or hostile instinct, is achieved only by the circumlocution afforded by the joking process ("Jokes circumvent the obstacle and in that way draw pleasure from a source which the obstacle had made inaccessible," p. 101). The scenario of the development of the obscene joke, which Freud uses as the paradigm for all tendentious joking, unfolds like a classic boy-meets-girl narrative, complicated by an equally classic love triangle.

PART I: BOY MEETS GIRL. "The one who makes the joke" (p. 100) encounters a desirable "object," gets ideas, and makes them known in "wooing talk" which he hopes "will yield at once to sexual action" (pp. 98–99). The first in a series of detours from direct satisfaction of "a lustful instinct" is thus necessitated by the obstacle of social convention: wooing must precede action. Now if the wooing proves unsuccessful—if the object resists because she is offended or inhibited—the frustrated wooer "turns positively hostile and cruel" and begins to express himself in "smut" or "sexually explicit speech" (pp. 98–100). A second detour from direct satisfaction is thus experienced, since the sexually exciting speech becomes an aim in itself ("sexual aggressiveness . . . pauses at the evocation of excitement and derives pleasure from the signs of it in the woman," p. 99). PART II: BOY LOSES GIRL. As if the woman's inhibition did not pose problems enough for the wooer's design, enter a second male—a potential rival and a decidedly importune third party ("The ideal case of resistance of this kind on the woman's part occurs if another man is present at the same time—a third person—for in that case an immediate surrender is as good as out of the question," p. 99). Alas, even if girl wants boy, the implicit rivalry—a kind of shorthand for the whole corpus of societal laws and prohibitions governing sexuality—interrupts the natural course of events. PART III: JOKE CONQUERS ALL. But, never fear, boy does get girl, by "exposing her in the obscene joke" and enjoying the spectacle of her embarrassment ("By making our enemy small, inferior, despicable, or comic, we achieve in a roundabout way the enjoyment of overcoming him," p. 103). Thus "boy" gets satisfaction only in the sense that one "gets" a joke, by effecting an imaginary exposure, humiliation or put-down which is clearly both voyeuristic and exhibitionist in character: the hapless woman, Freud tells us, has now been exposed before a listener who has "been bribed by the effortless satisfaction of his own libido" (p. 100). The pleasure game is played out between poles one and three, joker and listener, at the expense of pole two (who is often so offended as to leave the room, Freud tells us, "feeling ashamed"). In the Freudian scenario, the locker room joys of male bonding have replaced the original aim of seduction, since the joker actually "calls on the originally interfering third party as his ally" (p. 100). EPILOGUE: BOY GETS BOY? Indeed, "boy" wins the attention and complicity of his rival-turned-accomplice in this plot, and the complicit listener in turn receives a free entertainment, the "effortless satisfaction of his own libido." Pole three, the listener-voyeur, seems to enjoy the happiest ending of anyone in this narrative of obstructed and deflected desire.

But the freeloading listener does not escape unscathed. Elsewhere, Freud points out the aggressive nature of the capture of the listener's attention by the device of ideational mimetics (pp. 192–193). If the listener gets pleasure from the joke process, it is only because he is taken in by the joke itself, caught unawares by the punchline. Boy must capture boy by an expert delivery, or the joking transaction will fail. Indeed, in a later elaboration on the technique of nonsense humor, Freud points out the pleasure which the joker takes in "misleading and annoying his hearer" who "damps down his annoyance" by resolving "to tell the joke himself later on" (p. 139, n.) to the next victim in the joking chain. Thus the joking triangle is always a quadrilateral of sorts, a social chain in which the imaginary capture of both the joke's object (pole two) and its listener (pole three) is perpetuated with a changing cast of players. Even though the joke *seems* to function as a tool for establishing community (between one and three) and for allowing the ego of the victorious joker to triumph over adversity by circumventing obstacles to satisfaction, the joking process nonetheless turns out to be as double-edged as its punchline. For the joking process is a circuit in which no one's identity remains uncontaminated by exposure to the Other's desire. In the case of the joker himself, the joke betrays an incapacity to fulfill the original design, except in imagination (boy never really gets girl, after all); while in the case of the butt of the joke, the process signifies vulnerability to humiliation or exposure. As for the listener of the joke, the transaction entails being taken in by the joker's bribe of pleasure, and being "used" to arouse the joker's pleasure (Freud: "I am making use of him to arouse my own laughter," p. 156); the listener, moreover, is subsequently *compelled* to pass this stigma of pleasure along to the next unsuspecting victim in the chain. As Freud insists, "a joke *must* be told to someone else . . . something *remains over* which seeks, by communicating the idea, to bring the unknown process of constructing a joke to a conclusion" (p. 143, my emphasis).

More Love Stories

Freud of course wrote *Jokes* early in his career (the first edition was published in 1905), but he returned to it again and again, both by allusion to the original theory and by repetition of the master-plot in a number of other avatars. Version number two is another shady story of love, aggressivity, and renunciation, even more classic than the first.

The subject of Freud's second love story is Oedipus; the desired object his mother.[4] In the classic myth, of course, boy does indeed get girl, by simply eliminating the paternal rival. The bad joke is thus pulled on the subject by the Father/Fate, who reveals the punchline—"your girl is your mother"—too late to allow Oedipus to avert the tragic short-circuit, the incestuous bond. Significantly, Freud points out the importance of the dramatic device of surprise in this revelation.[5] We might say, then, that the sudden revelation of the mystery, after the subject's prolonged and circuitous voyage towards a veiled truth, functions like a punchline of sorts, depending on the same sort of "bewilderment and illumination" (*J.R.U.*, pp. 11–14) which produces the impact of the joke. (It is also an instance of "the rediscovery of something familiar"—all too familiar in the case of Oedipus—discussed in the fourth section of *Jokes*.) The shock of the revealed truth does of course finally obstruct the "wooing talk," undoing the incestuous bond which should never have been consummated in the first place, and reestablishing paternal legitimacy. But once the incest has been committed, it is too late to establish the comic bond (the understanding and complicity between male rivals, poles one and three of the joking paradigm), for the happy ending relies on a series of deflections and a play of "almosts."

Freud's own retelling of the Oedipal myth, however—the postulation of a normal outcome to the Oedipal phase in human development[6]—reinstates the happy ending of the joke paradigm: the subject identifies with the rival father, renounces the impossible love, and chooses a substitute love object to ensure the long-circuiting of his desire. Similarly, in the joking scenario, the illumination at joke's end is no longer the exposure of a tragic crime, but the unveiling of some other forbidden (but less menacing) "truth." (Freud repeatedly reminds us that the joke always has something forbidden to say, and that the primary function of the joke-work is thus to disguise the joke's point—until its revelation in the punchline—and to soften its punch by "wrapping" it in acceptable form [p. 132]). The comic long-circuit is thus necessarily a theatrical one, a drama of disguise and façade, which requires at least three layers of layering. First, it must veil its own point, in order to surprise the listener at joke's end. Second, it wraps the point in taste and good humor, in order not to offend the listener at the (always partial) unveiling. Finally, as the superimposition of the Oedipal triangle on the joking process suggests, the joke cloaks the primal urges of love and aggressivity which found all human creativity (does not Freud insist that all noninnocent jokes are "hostile or obscene"? p. 97). Indeed, Freud's own comic retelling of the Oedipal myth is already a creative textual process: Freud effects a weaving of motive and action in which the fundamental impulse (towards the short-circuit of incest, a death-like quiescence of desire) always remains disguised, perhaps even to the master story-teller himself.

Story as Creative Play

To the reader acquainted with Freud's own account of the creation of narrative (in the 1908 essay "Creative Writers and Daydreaming," *S.E.*, 9, 143), all of this talk of disguise and façade will seeem uncannily familiar. For Freud's own *Poetics* insists on the role of veiling (*Verkleidung*) in the creative process: the writer softens his own daydreams—themselves already "veiled" versions of the selfsame hostile and erotic impulses which motivate the joking process—by "changes and disguises" (*S.E.*, 9, 153). In other words, in order for the writer to satisfy his own wish, he must display his "object" to a voyeur (the reader), but only after an appropriate veiling has taken place. Like the joker, who says something forbidden in an acceptable way, the writer stages a tasteful strip tease, consummating his own pleasure by establishing a bond with the reader. The writing triangle, when superimposed on the first two, emerges as yet another circuitous retelling of the masterplot of human desire, in which the final

2
desired female-butt of joke
Jocasta-Mother
Writer's "daydream" object-character

1	3
desiring subject-joker	intruder-accomplice-joke hearer
Oedipus-Child	Laius-Father
writer-dreamer	reader

union is one of social complicity rather than a short-circuit of illicit libido. The joking triangle may be overdetermined as shown above.

Interestingly, both of Freud's major esthetic treatises—the essay on writers and writing, and the work on jokes—insist on the relation of creative activity to child's play, first as a source of pleasure entailing the rebellion against logic and propriety, and second as the initial social process by which the child gains mastery over reality, replaying unpleasant experiences to his own liking. In *Beyond the Pleasure Principle* (1920), a third work which holds clues crucial to an understanding of the Freudian esthetic (*S.E.*, 18, 23), child's play is described as two different manifestations of the compulsion to repeat.

In the first of the scenes described by Freud, the often-discussed "*Fort-Da*" game of Freud's grandchild, the child compensates for the absence of the real object (the Mother, who presumably has been "taken out" by the Father) by casting away and retrieving the substitute objects, his toys, in a kind of yo-yo repetition which *he* controls absolutely. Like the writer or the joker, the desiring child comes to terms with privation or frustration with a creative solution which affords him a compensation for the satisfaction denied by the interference of the third party (the Father who initiates him into social contract or comic bond to which all human beings are subject).

In Freud's second version of the play situation, the social interaction is not implied (with other actors in the wings) but explicit: the child repeats an unpleasant experience (a visit to the family doctor, for instance) by playing at it later on with a playmate (*S.E.*, 18, 11). Only in the repeat performance, the usually younger or smaller playmate is forced to be the patient, the *object* of the experiment. The mechanism by which the child moves from a passive to an active role, mastering reality, is thus strikingly similar to that by which the joke's hearer gains vengeance on the teller by repeating the joke to the next victim (see above). Freud's own repetition of the original boy meets girl anecdote, then—replayed as "boy meets adversary/doctor"—reveals that desire may be experienced not only as an impulse to possession of a libidinal object but also as an impulse to domination or mastery. Frustration of either aspect of desire, the hostile or the erotic, seems to inflict a stigma of sorts, activating a compelling urge to pass the experience along, by sharing (or inflicting?) the pleasure.

Enter Lacan, who hears the joke of human intersubjectivity from Freud, and captivated in his turn, resolves to retell it with his own inflection, insisting on the "Imaginary" nature of all happy endings.

II. INTERSUBJECTIVITY AS TEXT

This is precisely where the Oedipus complex [. . .] may be said to mark the limits that our discipline assigns to subjectivity [. . . .] The primordial Law is revealed clearly enough as identical to an order of Language.

—Lacan, *Écrits*, I, p. 156

Joke as "Imaginary" Capture

In his very useful translation and study of Lacan's "The Function of Language in Psychoanalysis,"[7] Anthony Wilden emphasizes two vectors of Lacan's Imaginary order (pp. 155–177), as that enthrallment with a fellow being which is first manifest in the mirror stage of human development (the vector of aggressivity of capture, aiming at the incorporation of the image of the other); and the vector of identification with the other as a fellow being, an alter ego or like self (pp. 166–168). Laplanche and Pontalis have pointed out (in *Le vocabulaire de la psychanalyse* [Paris: P.U.F., 1967]) that Lacan also uses the term Imaginary to designate a type of understanding or logic which is "essentially predisposed to delusion" and in which resemblance and identification play a major role, enabling the subject to maintain certain illusions about his *own* identify or "image." (Lacan concedes that some such "delusions" are necessary to the maintenance of mental health.)

Now according to Freud's explanation of the joking process as a kind of defense mechanism against the obstacles to desire posed by reality, the joking reaction would seem to qualify as one of those patterns of Imaginary behavior which function as a support of the subject's self-image. For, as we have seen, the mirage of the joker's identity as victor in the joking transaction is a Lacanian *méconnaissance* of sorts, supported by mechanisms of mimetic capture and identification (see above). Similarly, Freud's view of the *writer's* activity seems to suggest that the creation of a literary text is a related Imaginary transaction, since it depends both on the writer's identification with his object (the hero of his narrative) and the reader's identification with the writer's desire, "misrecognized" as that of the novel's protagonist, thanks to the technique of disguise or veiling.

But of course Lacan's insistence on the illusory nature of all Imaginary triumphs suggests that the transparency of Freud's masterplot masks a more complicated story. For it is equally possible to argue that the joking process functions in the Symbolic register, both because of its Oedipal sub-plot, emphasizing the third term, and because of its reliance on the Symbolic order of language to effect a resolution of the Oedipal rivalry.[8] In other words, one could argue that the Symbolic register, identified by Lacan with paternal Law, designates the domination of the pleasure principle by the reality principle.[9] The human subject's encounter with "real" obstacles, ensured by the very existence of an Oedipal third term, initiates all creative response. This is the punchline of Freud's master anecdote, as retold by Lacan (and relaying, as the old joke says, "some good news and some bad news"): the Symbolic reign of Law both deprives and enables, frustrating the subject's desire and offering the possibility of creative recompense.

"The Unconscious Is Structured Like a Language"

Lacan's purloined punchline then, concerns the inevitability of the encounter of every human subject with an excessive circuit of desire, and declares the primacy of the Symbolic order in this *Unconscious* intersubjective system. In an important essay on Lacan and Lévi-Strauss, Jeffrey Mehlman defines this intersubjective linguistic Unconscious as "a third domain, neither self nor other, but the system of communicative relations by which both are necessarily constituted and in which they are alienated" ("The Floating Signifier: from Lévi-Strauss to Lacan," in *Yale French Studies*, 48 [1972], p. 17). In other words, if the "Unconscious is structured like a language," to cite Lacan's celebrated formula, it is because as the locus of intersubjective involvement, the Unconscious is the very condition of language.

Once again, we may look to Freud's "transparent" text of joking for an "evident" clue to understanding Lacan's doctrine. For the main point of *Jokes* is that the joke-work (condensation and displacement) is grounded in primary process. The paradigm of desiring intersubjectivity is written in the very language of the Unconscious itself.

Now for Lacan, condensation and displacement, the fundamental modes of primary process, are associated with metaphor and metonymy, the fundamental modes of language. Borrowing from Roman Jakobson, Lacan defines these functions as the two intersecting axes of language: metaphor corresponds with the vertical axis of selection (the "paradigmatic" axis in Jakobson's system), while metonymy corresponds with the horizontal axis of combination (Jakobson's "syntagmatic" axis).[10] Metaphor, moreover, as the substitution of one word *for* another, is associated in Lacan's system with the process of repression, which excludes the original term from the spoken or conscious discourse; while metonymy, as the linking of one word *to* another, is associated with the excessive chain of desire which acts like the motor of language, driving the signifying chain forward into meaningful combinations.[11]

Thus for Lacan the metaphoric and metonymic structures are themselves metaphors for intersubjectivity (the trope of metaphor representing the function of repression in which the conscious/unconscious split ["*Spaltung*"] occurs; the trope of metonymy representing the social community of interrelated subjects). Or it might be more accurate to say that both figures function as synecdoches for the system of language to which they belong; for in Lacan's theory, metaphor and metonymy seem to function as "parts which represent the whole," moments in language which illustrate and reenact the functioning of the whole system as a desiring circuit of interrelated subjects.

The Art of Procrastination

In a fascinating essay on *Beyond the Pleasure Principle* ("Freud's Masterplot," *Yale French Studies*, 55/56 [1977]) Peter Brooks has described the interworkings of metaphor and metonymy as the motor of narrative plot. Brooks argues that an oscillation between a kind of horizontal drive toward the ending of the story and a vertical blockage achieved by all the repetitions or doubling back in the text provides a kind of "grammar of plot, where repetition, taking us back again over the same ground, could have to do with the choice of ends" (p. 286). In other words, the rhythm of narrative plot is a comic rhythm, a movement of starts and stops which defers the final imaginary solution. When one views the narrative process through the transparent theory of the joking process—as a play of blockage (metaphor) and forward movement (metonymy)—one perceives that the work of fiction, like the living subject who creates it, is motivated by energies which must be bound or contained by metaphoric repetition so that the narrative (to borrow a phrase from Freud) may "die in its own way."

In "Desire and the Interpretation of Desire in *Hamlet*" (translated in *Yale French Studies*, 55/56 [1977], p. 11), Lacan describes the circuitous nature of the plot of Shakespeare's famous tale in similar terms, emphasizing the role of the hero as a procrastinator, an idler who is forced to feign madness "in order to follow the winding paths that lead him to the completion of his act" (p. 13). In this story of detours and deliberately missed opportunities, Hamlet's desire seems to be engendered by a privation: the absence of the slain father. Lacan points out that the plot is prolonged by a series of missed appointments (pp. 41–44) which are emblematic of the failure of the desiring subject to attain his goal or to possess the object of his desire. But what, exactly, *is* Hamlet's "objective"? If one reads *Hamlet* in terms of the Freudian masterplot (the Oedipal-joking-writing triangular circuit), it becomes clear that the missing and desired object is not the dead father, but the guilty mother (and her alter-ego Ophelia, the sister-figure who is tainted by Hamlet's desire). The missed appointment to which Lacan refers, then, could be read as Hamlet's failure to consummate the incestuous union, that infantile short-circuit which is also the original temptation in the joking circuit. The forbidden incest, furthermore, may itself be read as a metaphoric stand-in, "veiling" the final satisfaction of death (return to the womb = return to the tomb).

One might say, then, that the missed appointment upon which Lacan focuses functions as a kind of comic obstacle, allowing the play to go on in a prolonged detour from its fatal and tragic conclusion. Yet Hamlet's procrastination has its own double meaning: If, on the one hand, it is an avoidance of the incestuous "Imaginary" solution, the short-circuit of desire, it is at the same time an avoidance of compliance with the Symbolic Law. In other words, Hamlet's postponement is hesitation between complicity with the maternal incest (which as a guilty onlooker, the son "enjoys" vicariously) and compliance with the paternal demand for vengeance. Of course, just as in the case of Oedipus, it is already too late for Hamlet to establish a comic bond with the interfering third party: the father who could save him is dead, and Hamlet is in effect a co-conspirator in the crime of incest, because of his guilty silence. The choice for Hamlet, then, is not "to be or not to be," but how long to prolong being, whether to opt for the pleasure-death of incest or the punishment-death to which he is sentenced by his Father's Law, whether to go to death by the long or the short route. Hamlet's final act, of course, is a sacrifice to the Symbolic, a coming to terms with the Law. The play ends in that fatal duel scene, wherein Hamlet "demands satisfaction," and finds it, in death. When the comic possibility is finally relinquished, so is the fiction itself: the play comes to its timely end, after its dalliance with impossible comic detours. From Lacan's reading of *Hamlet*, then, we may perceive that the destiny of plot parallels and repeats that of the human subject, caught in a text of sexual and linguistic intersubjectivity. Narrative or plot thus replays the human comedy itself: in a perverse gesture of deflection from goal, each of us plays a comic role of dalliance en route to the final scene of the intersubjective play in which we are cast.

III. TEXT AS (FEMININE) SYMPTOM

> "*The symptom is a* metaphor . . . *just as desire is a metonymy.*"
>
> —Lacan, "The Instance of the Letter in the Unconscious"

> "*For this sign is indeed that of the woman.*"
>
> —Lacan, "Seminar on 'The Purloined Letter' "

Narrative as Perversion

In Freud's *Three Essays on the Theory of Sexuality* (*S.E.*, 7, 125), a clear distinction is drawn between two types of sexual aberration. Writing that perversion is the *negative* of neurosis, Freud insists that any perversion—including the specific perversion of fetishism which denies the observed fact of the castration of the desired female object—both displaces and satisfies sexual desire with an object which has been substituted for the original unattainable one. (Or, as Lacan would have it, the new object takes the place of what the subject is deprived of.) In neurosis, on the other hand, the desire is not displaced but is repressed into the Unconscious, leaving the neurotic symptom to signify what it has replaced. Transcoding Freud's theory into linguistic terms, Lacan has maintained that the neurotic symptom is metaphoric in nature, because it replaces the original repressed sexual meaning with a non-sexual term. (Both hysteria—which is the result of unsatisfied desire—and obsession—the result of impossible desire—are thus metaphoric functions for Lacan.)[12] In the essay on *Hamlet*, moreover, Lacan differentiates between the metaphoric neurosis and the metonymic perversion in terms of the presence or absence of the subject in the symptomatic behavior: whereas the subject experiences a gratification of sorts in the perverse solution to desire, in the neurotic or hysteric solution the "real" subject is barred or silenced, repressed into the unconscious chain. (This is perhaps another way of framing Freud's assertion that the hysteric is not capable of recounting her own history, without the intervention of the analyst.) In any case, Lacan's theory emphasizes the symptomatic nature of both metaphor and metonymy as responses to obstructions of desire.

In addition to defining perversion as the negative of neurosis (in the *Three Essays* cited above), Freud emphasizes that perversion is a derailment of sorts, a sidetracking by which desire is deflected from its original biological aim.[13] (Similarly, Lacan refers to metonymy as a "derailment of instinct," insisting on the fetishistic nature of the metonymic displacement [*Écrits*, I, pp. 277–278]). In the introduction to his work on jokes, written at the same time as the *Three Essays on a Theory of Sexuality*, Freud defines the term esthetic as an "attitude towards an object . . . characterized by the condition that we do not ask anything of the object, *especially no satisfaction of our vital needs*" (*J.R.U.*, pp. 10–11, my emphasis). Readers like Peter Brooks and Jeffrey Mehlman [14] have not failed to point out the implication in Freud's companion definitions of the *perverse* and the *esthetic*: by Freud's own logic, esthetic processes—including joking and textual/literary activity—may be considered "perverse," since they depend on deflection and deferral of desire, which is sidetracked from its original goal in order to produce a pleasure clearly dissociated from "the satisfaction of vital needs." Yet in a Lacanian reading, this view of esthetic processes as both perverse and excessive need not imply a divorce from the mundanities of real life (as does, for instance, the Kantian view of the esthetic as that which is unsullied by utilitarian concerns or goals), since for Lacan the literary work must be understood as a function of the subject's involvement in a social web of Others.

Now insofar as metaphoric "repression" results from an encounter with the restraining and censoring agent of Law, it might be associated with the Symbolic register. Metonymy, on the other hand, might be associated with the Imaginary register, both because it seems to offer a satisfactory ending with a substitute object (happy endings are always suspect for Lacan) and because it is associated with a denial or misrecognition of the obstacles or privations to which the human subject is exposed (as in the denial of castration by the fetishist, for example). The interworking of these two orders or registers—in the joking process as in the literary text—stands as evidence that the Imaginary and the Symbolic modes are not successive stages of human development so much as coextensive principles of intersubjective experience.

The emphasis on one or the other of these functions in the literary process, however, will inevitably be reflected in one's critical perspective.[15] For depending upon which register is perceived as the dominant one in the esthetic act of writing, the reader will either see the literary process as an exercise of identification with a poet of superior vision (the artist as seer or Legislator of Mankind); or s/he will view the literary process as an intersubjective (Symbolic) circuit which traps both author and reader in an ongoing "end-game" played according to the rules of farce. In the second perspective, the Imaginary confidence in the literary process as a cure for desire is considered to be illusory, for the text is read as a symptom of the inexhaustibility of the desire which generates it.

The Gender of Symptom

> *A man man enough to defy to the point of scorn a lady's fearsome ire undergoes the curse of the sign he has dispossessed her of.*
>
> —Lacan, "Seminar on 'The Purloined Letter' "

If Lacan himself may be considered to have written a "transparent" text—containing an "evident" clue concerning the intersubjective nature of the textual process—it is doubtless the "Seminar on 'The Purloined Letter,' " which comments on desire as a metonymic process, transmissible symptom in a social chain. In the Seminar, the desire of each of the players results not merely from privation, the absence of the object of satisfaction (the purloined letter): it also results from contact with other desiring agents, and as such, functions as a contractable social contagion. Even to enter the game is to function as an object oneself, in a curious kind of relay where the letter is passed from hand to hand. In a dazzling display of wit, Lacan describes this game as a play of a group of ostriches ("*l'autruicherie*"), each of whom imagines himself secure, head in the sand, even as he is plucked bare from behind.[16] This circuit of desire obeys the inexorable logic of farce, summed up in the pithy (and somewhat untranslatable) French aphorism "*à trompeur, trompeur et demie.*" For in this game of rogues and dupes, each Dupin is duped in turn; each rogue is assured of his comeuppance at the hands of a more clever scoundrel, "a rogue and a half."

Now the notion of the *gender* of the symptom of desire is central to Lacan's Seminar on Poe. Indeed, for Lacan as for Freud, femininity seems to be a stigma (of castration? or passivity?), a symptom signifying a vulnerability or privation which may be passed from player to player. Throughout Freud's work, the question of the relation between symptom and gender —a question which underlies not only the "boy meets girl" formulation of the joking scenario, but also the classification of the disorder of paranoia as "male" and the disorder of hysteria as "female"—is complicated by Freud's own hesitation between two views of sexuality. In some of his works, Freud seems to argue for a natural and gender-specific sexuality—as in his early formulation of symmetrical Oedipal phases for boys and girls, with each sex attracted to the opposite sex— while in other works (primarily in the *Three Essays* on sexuality discussed above), he seems to assume a natural bisexuality, whereby both sexes, as possessors of a "male" libido, are initially attracted to the maternal love object. According to this view, femininity is an acquired trait which the girl child learns to accept reluctantly, after the discovery of her anatomical "deficiency."[17] In any case, Freud consistently associates the gender "male" with an active and armed state, and "female" with a passive and disarmed condition.

The notion of femininity as transmissible stigma and the corollary notion of the feminizing effect of entry into the desiring circuit are both crucial considerations for that "frame" of discussions on Poe's celebrated story (Johnson on Derrida on Lacan on Poe)[18] to which I wish to return in concluding this essay. The gender-related facts of the case *appear* "evident" (perhaps too evident?): the original victim in the desiring circuit (the Queen) is archetypically female; and she is clearly "violated" by the theft of the incriminating letter. Like pole two in the original joking circuit, her (guilty) sexuality is "exposed" to (and by) the Minister's male gaze. But once again, the "evidence" may be misleading: even this initial act of violation, apparently perpetrated by male on female, is marked by ambiguity of gender, owing to the phallic nature of the letter which the Queen-as-Ruler initially possesses. (Derrida, of course, has argued that Lacan's reading is phallocentric, agreeing with Marie Bonaparte that the purloined letter signifies the clitoris rather than the phallus, based on its anatomical position in the Minister's room.) In Lacan's reading, the Queen seems to begin in the "male" position of power and possession, and is only subsequently feminized as a result of the castrating act of the Minister. And as the plot thickens, so does the ambiguity: the male ravisher, now holding the phallic sign of power, has moved to an exposed position where he is vulnerable to attack by the next "duper," Dupin. This explains Lacan's characterization of the letter as a curse, a kind of "hot potato" destined to be passed on, and which inevitably causes its holder to get burned, as the next object of the next trick. In this curious game of tag, the player is never so feminine as when it is "his" turn to be "it," when s/he is *possessed* of the phallic object (and not when "she" is castrated or deprived of the phallus, as psychoanalytic convention would have it). As Barbara Johnson points out, the curious message of the purloined letter is that "femininity" seems to be a position or locus: anyone may be on the spot the butt of the joke. (Indeed, we have seen that in the joking paradigm one is feminine if "she" has something the other wants—attention, love, maternal breast—and thus the feminine "object" is the holder of a certain ambiguous power over the desiring subject.) The ambiguity of the "on the spot" position of the letter's holder may be described as follows: one is stigmatized and objectified by the very power that defines her/him as agent. (The person who is "it," after all, is galvanized to action by this stigma, compelled to act.) This is the paradoxical gist of farcical logic: *à trompeur, trompeur et demie.*

The logic of farce also seems to inform the Lacanian concept of desire as excess (the surplus of demand over need),[19] since Lacan insists that the pur-loined letter is not only stolen but "pro-longed" in its "excessive" journey. In Lacan's reading, the purloined letter is above all else a chain letter whose accruing returns are assured (*à trompeur, trompeur et demie*), and which thus provides a punchline of sorts to the archetypal nonsense joke. Why does the chicken cross the road, if not to come home to roost?

LITERARY TRICKERY

Thus Lacan's retelling of Freud's masterplot clears up several points in the too transparent "boy meets girl" scenario. In Lacan's version, for instance, it becomes obvious that the supposedly distinct and gender-identified roles of the joking triangle are not only often exchangeable but are actually coincidental or superimposed: each player is active *and* passive, desiring *and* desired, giver *and* receiver, not only successively but simultaneously. Since one only receives the punchline (like the purloined letter) in order to give it away, the notions of "active" and "passive" lose their specificity, as do the corollary notions of "male" and "female" gender.

Lacan's version of Freud's masterplot also clearly reveals the fetishistic nature of the desiring circuit. In Lacan's narrative, each successive theft is concealed in the replacement of the missing object by something similar which veils its absence, a simulacrum of the original letter. The sleight of hand is all important: the ravisher *must* put something in the place of the stolen letter, so that the victim will remain unaware of the trick, for a time at least. In this case, then, the feminine position (of dupe) is that of a fetishist whose attention is fixed on a substitute for the missing object of desire.[20] In this way, Poe's theft reproduces the technique of the joking exchange, which also depends on a sleight of hand, a displacement of the listener's attention until the final unveiling of the punchline. Of course the listener is a willing victim in this entertainment, since he voluntarily lends his attention to the joker-trickster who has lured his "victim" with the promise of pleasure.

Similarly, the literary text "passifies" its reader-receiver by a bribe of pleausre, enlisting the reader's cooperation in a pleasure-circuit which would otherwise remain incomplete. But just as in the joking transaction, which depends on the art of the joker's technique (or delivery) in order to produce its effect, the textual transaction depends on the writer's art, and thus places the artist himself "on the spot." For if his art fails, if we fail to enjoy his text (like a joke fallen flat), the writer's very identity as poet–craftsman is shattered. His "image" is always constituted by an Imaginary bargain—the willing suspension of disbelief—which entails the reader-spectator's acceptance of a literary code different from that governing everyday communication. The completed pleasure circuit of the text, whether narrative or poetic, relies on a tenuous agreement to grant the writer a certain pose of enchantment, and to accept the "bribe of forepleasure" which veils and softens egotistical material. The textual exchange, like the joking exchange, is a power-play on the part of the subject, initiated (paradoxically) by privation or impotence. It is thus an Imaginary satisfaction enabled by the Symbolic Law (the "truth" of the renunciation which the substitute satisfaction "veils"). The joking/literary transaction is, then, the negative of the analytic transaction—yet another triangular drama, but one in which the analyst plays two of the three roles ("object" and listener). And in this particular triangle, the analyst must *refuse* the "bribe" of pleasure, adopting a posture of scepticism vis-à-vis the truth of the subject's discourse, in order to break the Imaginary bond between subject and object (the transference). If the analyst *fails* to refuse to get involved, he will of course prejudice the result of the therapy, as is evinced, for instance, by Freud's celebrated failure with Dora.[21] (This recalls Freud's assertion that if the hearer becomes emotionally involved with the topic of the joke, his sympathetic reaction will jeopardize the joke's effect or impact.)

What each of these instances of the desiring circuit finally underscores is that the Imaginary and the Symbolic are not distinct developmental phases in human life, but interacting registers of a continuing intersubjective discourse. Indeed, the joking paradigm demonstrates how an interplay of recognition and misrecognition, bewilderment and illumination, passivity and activity, establishes the essential plot or rhythm of all creative endeavor. This recognition (of the interworking of Imaginary and Symbolic registers) is accentuated in many contemporary texts, which—rather than insisting on writing as a triumph of "activity," a display of masculine mastery—have opted to emphasize the desire which motivates the textplay. This is perhaps the sense of the poststructuralist emphasis on the *écriture féminine*, and on *écriture* as "féminine": the stigma of femininity as symptom becomes the privileged metaphor for the writer's own situation in desire.

IV. FEMININITY AS SUBJECTIVITY (CAN "SHE" WRITE?)

And what does this experience, precisely, teach us about the phallus, if not that it makes a joke of phallicism?

—Moustafa Safouan, "Feminine Sexuality in Psychoanalytic Doctrine"[22]

Our circular itinerary has visited several questions—the comic nature of intersubjectivity, intersubjectivity as text, text as play of metaphoric and metonymic symptom, symptom as "femininity"—and has arrived at a puzzling punchline. In Lacan's version of Freud's transparent master narrative, the closing line seems to read (comically) neither BOY GETS GIRL nor even BOY GETS BOY but BOY *IS* GIRL. For Lacan, the role of "second"—the objective locus in the master paradigm—is a role which we all play in turn.

But if Lacan's lesson for the subject (pole one, the joker/writer) is that he too may be "female," it still remains unclear whether the obverse is also true: can "she" assume subjectivity? Can the "shifter" "I" shift genders?[23] Can "she" become the agent of desire, the active pole, the joker? What happens if "she" refuses to mediate the (Male) comic bond?[24] In terms of Freud's original scenario, what happens if "she," however offended by the male conspirators, refuses to leave the room, feeling ashamed?[25] In other words, what does a woman want? The question, first posed by Freud, reverberates throughout Lacan's work, and leads inevitably to a second inquiry: What is Woman? Can "she" want anything at all?[26]

Indeed, in his later work, Lacan not only speculates about the femininity of metaphoric symptom (as veiling or masquerade) and of metonymic desire (as a perverse circuit which castrates its participants), but he also comes to posit "Woman" herself as symptom of the male system which her myth sustains ("the Woman does not exist").[27] As Jacqueline Rose and Juliet Mitchell have pointed out in their introductory notes to Lacan's essays in *Feminine Sexuality* (New York and London: W.W. Norton, 1982), there has been a lively debate as to whether Lacan's position may be considered to be a *feminist* critique of the structures of patriarchy, refuting an Imaginary notion of "The Woman," or merely the latest patriarchal strategy for relegating femininity to the idealist and absolute category of "Otherness," in which Woman is destined to function as a predicate to the male subject.

For while Lacan appears to espouse the Freudian notion of bisexuality, refuting the notion of pre-given gender, he nonetheless insists on defining femininity as a linguistically determined locus (Rose: "Woman is excluded by the nature of words, meaning that the definition poses her as exclusion. . . . Within the phallic definition, the woman is constituted as 'not all' in so far as the phallic function rests on an exception—the 'not'—which is assigned to her" [*Feminine Sexuality*, p. 49]). Thus Lacan insists on assigning woman to an objective role—the role of the excluded term—even while he insists that that exclusion is linguistically rather than biologically determined. Indeed, Lacan's exile of the feminine subject from language is reminiscent of Freud's theory of the feminine hysteric as a "blocked" speaker whose symptoms include lying (the misuse of language) and pantomime (the non-use of language). Freud refers to the hysteric's discourse as "an unnavigable river whose stream is choked by masses of rock," and thus suggests that it is the analyst's function to steer a course through the shoals of "her" obstructed discourse.[28]

Lacan is again following Freud's lead by insisting on woman's position as object—or even as absence—in the linguistic system. Even though he insists that this position is not inherent, but is rather a position *conferred* by language ("woman is not inferior, she is subjugated" [Lacan] *F.S.*, p. 45), Lacan nonetheless insists on the insoluble character of the feminine linguistic dilemma (Rose: "All speaking beings must line themselves up on one side or other of this division of gender, but anyone can cross over and inscribe themselves on the opposite side from that to which they are anatomically destined," *F.S.*, p. 49). One could argue that by placing the phallus at the center of the signifying system, Lacan has assured the predicative status of woman, and has also effectively canceled the possibility of finding an anwer to the question which persists throughout his later work ("what does a woman want?"). For as long as woman cannot speak, as long as she is excluded from the subjective roles in the desiring triangle (poles one and three, joker and future joker), she is condemned to her role as "wanted woman," the *object* in the hunt for the feminine subject.

Other Voices

Feminist theorists have not failed to point out the ideological problems inherent in Lacan's definition of femininity as acquired (or required?) linguistic trait, persisting in a critique of phallocentrism by pointing out the hidden agenda which informs the grounding of libido (or speech itself) in the male body. Luce Irigaray, for example, argues that the metaphorization of female sexuality (by which the clitoris is represented in terms of the phallus) *represses* the feminine term in its specificity, replacing it by the male term (of which it becomes a deficient copy).[29]

Similarly, Gayatri Spivak has emphasized the ideological functions of this repression of feminine sexuality. In a recent essay, she has pointed out that the threatening aspect of feminine sexuality, the "scandal" that must be repressed, is the biological fact that woman's pleasure is excessive, insofar as it functions "perversely" in its independence from reproductive process ("French Feminism in an International Frame," *YFS*, 62 [1981], pp. 154–184). In the same volume of *Yale French Studies*, Naomi Schor raises the related issue of the gender of theory. (For Freud, of course, the paranoid-theorist is essentially male; the female paranoid is considered an aberration.)[30] Schor points out that female theorizing seems to be grounded in the body, even in Freud's account, and that this is the source of its "feminine" specificity. This argument is reminiscent of Kristeva's characterization of feminine writing as a kind of *jouissance*, a pleasure grounded in the heterogeneity of a pre-Oedipal semiotic mode.[31] But as Schor herself argues, any such emphasis on the grounding of theory in the female body is in fact "a risky enterprise" (p. 215), since any valorization of the essential and biologically unique aspects of femininity may reinforce the conclusion that biology is destiny.[32]

Of course, Lacanian theory represents the antithesis of this essentialist view, because it maintains that gender is a linguistic rather than a biological distinction. Even more importantly, the notion of subjectivity itself is problematized by Lacan in a way which has profound consequences for his theory of femininity and feminine sexuality. In her introduction to the essays in *Feminine Sexuality*, Jacqueline Rose sums up Lacan's rebuttal to feminist objections concerning the male orientation of psychoanalytic theory:

> He [argues] that failure to recognize the interdependency of these two concerns in Freud's work—the theory of subjectivity and femininity together—has led psychoanalysts into an ideologically loaded mistake, that is, an attempt to resolve the difficulties of Freud's account of femininity by aiming to resolve the difficulty of femininity itself. For by restoring the woman to her place and identity (which, they argue, Freud out of "prejudice" failed to see), they have missed Freud's corresponding stress on the division and precariousness of human subjectivity itself. . . . Re-opening the debate on feminine sexuality must start, therefore, with the link between sexuality and the unconscious. . . . For Lacan, the unconscious undermines the subject from any position of certainty . . . and *simultaneously* reveals the fictional nature of the sexual category to which every human subject is nonetheless assigned. (*Feminine Sexuality*, p. 29).

In other words, Lacanian theory exposes the privilege of the (male) primary signifier as an Imaginary construct: the phallus is precisely what no one "himself" ever has. Yet the effect of this theory, as we have seen, is to lead "woman" back to her place (Rose: "The question is what a woman is in this account always stalls on the crucial acknowledgment that there is absolutely no guarantee that she *is* at all. But if she takes up her place according to the process described, then her sexuality will betray, necessarily, the impasses of its history," *F.S.*, p. 43.). Thus if she agrees to exist at all, "woman" must take up her impossible place on the Other side of the divide.

There are of course many feminist theorists—among them Kristeva, Schor, Spivak, Alice Jardine—who have taken a position on feminine sexuality which lies somewhere between the extremes of the essentialist biological view and the non-essentialist linguistic view espoused by Lacan (a view which threatens to do away with "woman" altogether). These theorists generally do posit an essential difference between male and female sexuality/subjectivity, and they tend to concur that this difference is grounded in the body, rather than in a purely linguistic or symbolic determination.[33] For Naomi Schor, however, a theory of feminine subjectivity must reconsider the givens of linguistic theory. Schor proposes supplementing the Lacanian theory on metaphor and metonymy—which she sees as reflections of a masculinist perspective on sexuality and subjectivity—with a theory of synechdoche, which she considers to be a uniquely feminine trope.[34] Gayatri Spivak and Alice Jardine both insist that the search for an authentic feminine subjectivity must be grounded in the "Real" (to use Lacan's term for the third register of human experience), that is, in a critique of the assumptions and attidues of partriarchy. Their studies attempt to retain the radical thrust of Lacan's reevaluation of subjectivity without reentering that impasse by which woman becomes only locus or socio-linguistic construct.

"Return to Freud"

Now it is ironic that Lacan's later work, which continually poses the question of the nature of femininity, seems to have lost sight of that important clue to the enigma hidden in Freud's "transparent" essay on the joking process. Before describing the "boy meets girl" scenario which enacts the fundamental narrative of desire, Freud makes a few seemingly marginal, and deceptively obvious, remarks about the nature of sexuality in general:

> It can only help to clarify things if at this point we go back to the fundamental facts. A desire to see the organs peculiar to each sex exposed is one of the original components of our libido. It may itself be a substitute for something earlier and go back to a hypothetical primary desire to touch the sexual

> parts. . . . The libido for looking and touching is present in everyone in two forms, active and passive, male and female; and, according to the preponderance of the sexual character, one form or the other predominates. (*J.R.U.*, p. 98).

Now this characterization of sexuality clearly manifests the bias which persists throughout Freud's work: the identification of active with male and passive with female. But Freud's own joking scenario reveals that the terms active and passive are ambiguous at best, and are coextensive with all three loci of the joking triangle. In this "pre-text" to the joking discussion, moreover, it is the common nature of human sexual experience, be it male or female, which is emphasized: *all* sexuality is first manifest as an active voyeurism or corollary exhibitionism. Freud goes on to suggest that the differences may be culturally determined, maintaining that the female's urge to exhibitionism is "buried under the imposing *reactive* function of sexual modesty" (p. 98). The final sentence of this passage further reinforces the emphasis on cultural variables as determinants of female sexual expression: "I need only hint at the elasticity and variability in the amount of exhibitionism which women are permitted to retain in accordance with differing convention and circumstances" (p. 98). "Convention" permitting, women seem as likely as men to engage in active exhibitionism, the primal expression of libido.

The essential point, furthermore, of Freud's allusion to the commonality of human sexual experience seems to be that it is entirely possible to regard the masculine and the feminine as *different* sexualities without entering into the Lacanian impasse, using that perception of difference to authorize an exclusion of either gender from the creative role of "subject." It would seem, ironically, that Freud's own most "transparent" formulation of the origins of human sexuality is ultimately more compatible with the feminist view—of the *specificity* but not the *essentiality* of "Femininity"—than is that of Lacan. For Freud at least seems to imply, perhaps unwittingly, that even if the female experience of subjectivity is not *identical* to the male experience, owing to sexual difference, there is nevertheless enough common ground on the subjective side of the linguistic divide to accommodate male and female subjects alike. This is perhaps the most important lesson to be gleaned from the "evident" clues in the joking paradigm (with the help of Freud's "Minister" Lacan): if man and woman do exist on opposite sides of a linguistic divide, as Lacan would have it, neither side necessarily initiates the creative activity by which we may attempt to scale the wall.

Lacan has placed a telling epigraph at the head of the third section of "The Function of Language in Psychoanalysis," the same essay in which he alludes to Freud's essay on jokes:

> Between man and love,
> There is woman.
> Between man and woman,
> There is a world.
> Between man and the world,
> There is a Wall.
>
> —*Antoine Tudal, in* Paris in the Year 2000
> (*Écrits, I, p. 170, my translation*)

Like the aphorism which describes the farcical circuit of the joking paradigm as well as the intersubjective workings of the literary text (*à trompeur, trompeur et demie*), Lacan's cryptic epigraph contains some good news and some bad news. For if the Wall of desire as emblem of Law is an unavoidable part of our intersubjective experience, Lacan's "return to Freud" suggests that the graffiti which will inevitably appear on the Wall may be read as a comic response to the Symbolic barrier of Law. And as the work of feminist writers and theorists attests, "she" writes on the Wall as well.

NOTES

1. *Seminar XX* (1972–3), in *Feminine Sexuality*, eds. Juliet Mitchell and Jacqueline Rose (New York and London: W.W. Norton, 1982), 157.

2. Translated in *Yale French Studies*, No. 48 (1976), 39–72. (Hereafter referred to as *S.P.L.*) [Essay #18 above.]

3. James Strachey, trans., *Standard Edition of the Complete Works of Sigmund Freud* (hereafter referred to as *S.E.*), 8 (New York and London: W.W. Norton).

4. For Freud's treatment of *Oedipus Rex*, and his account of the Oedipal complex, see *The Interpretation of Dreams* (1900), *S.E.*, 4–5; and the *Introductory Lectures on Psycho-analysis* (1916–17), S.E., 15–16.

5. See Section V of the *Interpretation of Dreams* for Freud's discussion of the dramatic technique of *Oedipus Rex*.

6. See "The Dissolution of the Oedipus Complex" (1924), *S.E.*, 19, 173.

7. Anthony Wilden, *The Language of the Self* (New York: Dell Publishing, 1975).

8. For a discussion of Lacan's Symbolic register, see Wilden, ibid., pp. 249–270.

9. Freud, "Two Principles of Mental Functioning," *S.E.*, 12, 215.

10. Roman Jakobson, "Two Aspects of Language and Two Types of Aphasic Disturbances," in *Fundamentals of Language* (The Hague: Mouton, 1956), 55–82.

11. In "L'Instance de la lettre dans l'inconscient," *Écrits*, I, p. 274, Lacan elaborates on Saussure's linguistic theory, recasting the formula S/s to represent the figures of metaphor and metonymy.

12. Lacan on *Hamlet*, op. cit., p. 17.

13. In "L'Instance de la lettre dans l'inconscient" (*Écrits*, I, p. 278), Lacan calls metonymy the "derailing of instinct . . . eternally extended towards the desire of something else" ("*le désir d' autre chose*").

14. See Jeffrey Mehlman, "How to Read Freud on Jokes: the Critic as *Schadchen*," *New Literary History*, 6, No. 2 (Winter 1975), 439–61.

15. See, for instance, Fredric Jameson's "Imaginary and Symbolic in Lacan: Marxism, Psychoanalytic Criticism, and the Problem of the Subject," *Yale French Studies* 55/56 (1977), pp. 338–95.

16. *S.P.L.*, *Écrits*, I, p. 24.

17. "Some Psychological Consequences of the Anatomical Distinction Between the Sexes" (1925), *S.E.*, 19, 243.

18. See Barbara Johnson's "The Frame of Reference: Poe, Lacan, Derrida," *Yale French Studies* 55/56 (1977), p. 457. [Essay #19 above.]

19. For Lacan's distinction between need, demand, and desire, see Wilden's discussion on pp. 185–92 in *The Language of the Self*.

20. See Freud's "Fetishism" (1927), *S.E.*, 21, 149.

21. For a series of essays on Freud's "Fragment of an Analysis of a Case of Hysteria" (1905), *S.E.*, 7, 3 see *Diacritics*, 13, No. 1 (Spring 1983), "A Fine Romance: Freud and Dora."

22. In *Feminine Sexuality*, p. 134.

23. For a discussion of pronouns as "shifters," see Wilden, op. cit., pp. 179–185.

24. René Girard's concept of mediated desire, for instance, centers on the relation between the two male terms in the Oedipal triangle. For a critique of this perspective, see Toril Moi's "The Missing Mother: the Oedipal Rivalries of René Girard," *Diacritics*, 12, No. 2 (Summer 1982), 21–31.

25. In this context, see Jane Gallop's "Why Does Freud Giggle when the Women Leave the Room?"—paper read at the *Women and Humor* section of the NEMLA Conference, Hartford, Conn., March 1979.

26. For a discussion of Lacan's definition of Woman, see Moustafa Safouan's "Feminine Sexuality in Psychoanalytic Doctrine," in *Feminine Sexuality* (cited above), pp. 132–36.

27. For Lacan on The Woman, see Rose's Introduction to *Feminine Sexuality*, p. 48.

28. Cited from Sharon Willis, "A Symptomatic Narrative," *Diacritics*, 13, No. 1 (Spring 1983), 48.

29. Ibid., p. 51.

30. Freud's theory of paranoia is the subject of Naomi Schor's "Female Paranoia: The Case for Psychoanalytic Feminist Criticism," *Yale French Studies*, 62 (1981), 204–219.

31. Julia Kristéva, *Desire in Language*, ed. Leon S. Roudiez (New York: Columbia University Press, 1980).

32. In the same issue of *Yale French Studies*, Gayatri Spivak voices similar reservations, about the "essentialist" view of radical feminists (p. 181).

33. See, for example, Spivak's aforementioned piece in *Feminist Readings: French Texts/American Contexts*, *Yale French Studies*, 62 (1981), pp. 154–84, and Alice Jardine's "Pre-Texts for the Transatlantic Feminist," in the same issue of *YFS*, pp. 220–236.

34. For Schor, synechdoche "represents" clitoral sexuality, as a "part for the whole" feminine sexual process (*YFS*, 62, p. 219).

VI

MARXISM AND NEW HISTORICISM

The historical approach to literary criticism has traditionally sought to accomplish three goals. The first is to cast light on and clarify the text itself. This may mean establishing the date of composition and the authoritative text (in regard to manuscripts or spurious editions) as well as identifying a text's references to history—specific allusions to actual people, political events, economic developments, and so on. This effort locates the text as an historical phenomenon—and it includes the "source study" that Stephen Greenblatt describes in "Shakespeare and the Exorcists," in this section, what he calls "the elephants' graveyard of literary history." The second goal is to describe the author as an artist with a significant past and a predisposition to write in a certain manner. This is the goal of most literary biography and tends to range over a broad area of intellectual, cultural, and esthetic concerns, including the "symptomatic" (highly person-oriented) reading of literature that dominated the work of Freudian ego-psychology described in the introduction to Section V. It is "history" in the sense of being a single author's history of "life and work." The third goal is to grasp a literary work as it reflects the historical forces that shaped it initially, to understand how an historical moment produced a particular work of literary art. This projects the historical process itself as a kind of ultimate author, both the origin and composer of any work.

Successful historical criticism—criticism that accomplishes all three goals—endeavors, as Hippolyte Taine said, to recover "from the monuments of literature, a knowledge of the manner in which men thought and felt centuries ago." Taine's approach to historical criticism, known today as the "traditional" approach, thus defines literary interpretation on a *genetic* model, as an explanation of how a work's genesis in a historical situation (where specific causes are manifested) brings the work into being as a distinct esthetic object. From this viewpoint, the literary critic necessarily studies history directly, since the literary text is an object produced by the operation of history. Indeed, since history produces or determines literature, the study of literature must first be a study of history, the virtual master text. In several senses at least, although this is contrary to Aristotle's opinion, history is superior to literature in that it shapes literature and determines its nature. Such traditional historical study Stephen Greenblatt defines as "old" historicism as against a "new historicism," the "old" being "the dominant historical scholarship of the past." In the "Introduction" to *The Forms of Power and the Power of Forms in the Renaissance*, he says that the "old" kind "tends to be monological; that is, it is concerned with discovering a single political vision, usually identical to that said to be held by the entire literate class or indeed the entire population." As such, he argues, "this vision can serve as a stable point of reference, beyond contingency, to which literary interpretation can securely refer. Literature is conceived to mirror the period's beliefs, but to mirror them, as it were, from a safe distance." Greenblatt refers specifically to traditional literary scholarship, but he is also voicing the traditional Marxist distinction between the "historical" economic base of social relationships—the modes of production at a given historical moment—and the superstructure of ideology, beliefs, and assumptions embodied in art, intellectual "world-views" and other consciously or unconsciously held "ideas."

MARXIST CRITICISM

Modern historical criticism has tended to veer away from the "old" historicism as it disrupts both the hierarchy of history as superior to literature and the distance between the two. Instead of viewing history as the determining context for literature, critics like Georg Lukacs and Raymond Williams throughout the twentieth century have reconceived history as a field of discourse in which literature and criticism make their own impact as political forces and, in effect, participate in an historical dialectic. In this Marxist view of literary criticism, the critic is a member of an intellectual proletariat who promotes cultural revolution through a political commitment in literary studies. Lukacs, for example, fulfilled this social commitment by attempting to "lay bare" the "devices" of literature that can lead us to see the ideological orientation of a work. In the case of modernist literature, particularly James Joyce's *Ulysses,* Lukacs demonstrated the dehumanizing and fragmenting effect of capitalist culture and, further, showed how a modernist novel can promote the acceptance of underlying social principles and values. As Lukacs says of Franz Kafka, the "mood of total impotence, of paralysis in the face of the unintelligible power of circumstances, informs" the modernists' world view and expresses bourgeois ideology. Fredric Jameson, in *The Political Unconscious,* attempts to modify this extreme view of modernism by isolating the "utopian vocation" in modernist discourse, its "mission . . . to restore at least a symbolic experience of libidinal gratification." Patrocinio Schweickart uses Jameson's concept and offers a helpful example of the dialectical relationship between the negative and positive elements of modernism in "Reading Ourselves" in Section III of this book.

Raymond Williams, likewise, investigates vast areas of modern culture in the attempt to understand subtle coercion in the promotion of capitalist ideology. Typical of Williams is his groundbreaking analysis of "country and city" in English literature—that is, ideology (values articulated in actual use) based on the opposition of ideal pastoral and pragmatic urban values. Such an "opposition" is governed, above all, by the "contradictions" that inhabit all social life. As Williams notes in "Base and Superstructure in Marxist Cultural Theory" in this section, "it is indeed one of the central propositions of Marx's sense of history that there are deep contradictions in the relationships of production and in the consequent social relationships." The economic "base" of a society, as manifested in the "relations of production," he goes on, determine that society's "superstructure"—its arts and ideology—as a "consequence" of the base. Here Williams articulates the central tenet of Marxist literary criticism: that literature and art are *social practices* that cannot be separated "from other kinds of social practice, in such a way as to make them subject to quite special and distinct laws. They may have quite specific features as practices, but they cannot be separated from the general social process." In the words of Etienne Balibar and Pierre Macherey, literature "does not 'fall from the heavens,' the product of a mysterious 'creation,' but is the product of social practice (rather a particular social practice); neither is it an 'imaginary' activity, albeit it produces imaginary effects, but inescapably part of a material process."

Other Marxist critics make the same assumption. There is, Bakhtin/Volosinov writes in "Discourse in Life and Discourse in Art," a "social essence of art." "Verbal discourse," this essay asserts, "is a social event; it is not self-contained in the sense of some abstract linguistic quantity, nor can it be derived psychologically from the speaker's subjective consciousness taken in isolation." Rather, the extraverbal—the "historical"—situation enters into verbal discourse including literary discourse "as an essential constitutive part of the structure of its import." Thus, the audience—the "listener"—is not, as Ong suggests, simply a function of a text, but rather the listener "has *his own independent place* in the event of artistic creation." In this way a Marxist rhetoric is quite different from that of Ong. Rather than stabilizing the position of the reader, creating a normative reader, as Ong advances that literature does in "The Writer's Audience Is Always a Fiction" (Section II), Terry Eagleton argues here (following the theatrical practice of Bertolt Brecht) that the rhetorical function of literature is precisely to *destabilize* the reader, to create an "alienation effect"—not unrelated to the "defamiliarization" of Russian Formalism—that allows the reader or audience to reconceive his or her position as situated within a particular social structure. Alienation, Eagleton argues, "hollows out the imaginary plenitude of everyday actions, deconstructing them into their social determinants and inscribing within them the conditions of their making." Art, then, at least as Brecht conceived it, can make one notice what is artificial in the seemingly "natural," to ask the "crude" question of what ends particular discursive practices serve rather than "refined" questions that assume the stability and permanence of those practices. This, Eagleton argues, is the significance of Brecht's slogan, "plumpes Denken"—think crudely.

In this way contemporary Marxist work situates criticism as it does literature. In *Literary Theory* Terry Eagleton argues "that the history of modern literary theory is part of the political and ideological history of our epoch," and many contemporary critics—including Jameson, Williams, Eagleton, Gayatri Spivak, Edward Said, and most of the feminist critics represented in this book—share a strong sense of criticism as a historically situated activity that deeply involves the critic, so that the critic cannot stand apart from the text being read and interpreted but can only choose to recognize his or her own effect on the text. Any literary theory, as Eagleton says, in use is either "indissociably bound up with political beliefs and ideological values"—or not. Brecht's "crude" thinking highlights performance and power rather than meaning and knowledge. It reminds the reader that the "superstructure" of knowledge and meaning has a crude material base. And it reminds the critic that even the most "disinterested" contemplation of meaning and art—even the most esoteric criticism—is situated in a social and political world and, for that reason, is a more or less "crude" activity with social and political consequences that can never achieve the purity of "disinterestedness."

But contemporary Marxist approaches to literature situate criticism in another way as well: they demand that criticism become more overtly political, that it attempt, as Marx said, not simply to interpret but to change the world. This sense of the need for commitment (defined more expansively than Jean Paul Sartre's idea of the subordination of literature to the "higher" political commitment) and the political responsibility of the literary critic pervades the work of these critics and much of contemporary literary criticism carried out from an historical viewpoint. The stance is clear in Williams's (implicitly "utopian") assertion that human practices are "inexhaustible" and consequently one can always imagine and work for a world better than our present world. "No mode of production," he writes, "and therefore no dominant society or order of society, and therefore no dominant culture, in reality exhausts the full range of human practice, human energy, human intention." This stance is evident in Eagleton's description of the function of rhetoric and in Frank Lentricchia's definition of criticism in *Criticism and Social Change* as "the production of knowledge to the ends of power and, maybe, of social change." "The activity that a Marxist literary intellectual preeminently engages in—should engage in—" Lentricchia goes on, "is the activity of interpretation . . . which does not passively 'see,' as Burke put it, but constructs a point of view in its engagement with textual events, and in so constructing produces an image of history as social struggle, of, say, class struggle." "This sort of interpretation," he concludes, "will above all else attempt to displace traditional interpretations which cover up the political work of culture."

In his literary criticism, Fredric Jameson has consistently pursued such politically oriented cultural work—what he calls in "The Politics of Theory" the disengagment of the "seeds of the future" from the present "both through analysis and through political praxis." What distinguishes Jameson—and makes it difficult to present a "selection" from his work—is the range of his vision. He has consistently attempted to discover the usefulness, in a Marxist sense of "usefulness," of contemporary literary theory. *The Political Unconscious*, for instance, uses Freudian, structuralist, and poststructuralist concepts in its "political work of culture." In his various discussions of "postmodernism" Jameson brings the same range of methods and interest to bear in a Marxist analysis. He attempts to present a sophisticated analysis of the relationship between the base and superstructure regarding the specific cultural phenomenon of "postmodernism." Rather than seeing it as an isolated cultural phenomenon, or a mere symptom of the so-called "postindustrial" society, Jameson tries in a number of essays, including "The Politics of Theory," reprinted here, to show how postmodernism is related to and serves the economic order, how "what is most often conducted as an aesthetic debate" about the nature of "postmodernism" in fact, defines "political positions." Thus the "logical" positions on postmodernism "can always be shown to articulate visions of history" and can, in fact, be related to "moments of the capitalism from which it emerged." In this way Jameson analyzes the ideology of late capitalism, the way it implies the "ahistorical" nature of its cultural artifacts ranging from architecture to pop art, from literature to television, in terms he takes up from a range of modern critics and social theorists such as Lyotard, Habermas, Jencks, and many others. But the point of his analysis—isolating, as he calls it in another postmodern essay, the "schizophrenic" element of postmodern culture—is not simply to interpret culture, but to situate it in relation to its historical "base." Its point is to present an analysis of the social forces that govern consciousness and, consequently, govern action. It is, as it was for Marx, to create a situation from which to imagine the world different from the existing social and political institutions—to change the world.

NEW HISTORICISM

In Jameson, especially, with his wide-ranging use of contemporary critical methods to help define the "cultural practice" (as Williams articulates it) he pursues, we can see contemporary historical criticism moving even further away from the traditional hierarchy of history over literature. It does so, at least in part, as Eagleton suggests in his use of the term "deconstruction" in his description of rhetoric in "Brecht and Rhetoric," under the sway of Continental philosopher-critics—particularly the French—who have begun to redraw the boundaries of history as a discipline. Michel Foucault, in particular, has been influential in his view of history as "discursive practice," what it is possible to say in one era as opposed to another. Thus, in "What Is an Author?" (Section IV) he says that "the author's name manifests the apperance of a certain discursive set and indicates the status of this discourse within a society and a culture." Such discursive practices are, as Williams says, "hegemonic" in their effect, both creating and created by "a whole body of practices and expectations." Hans Robert Jauss, Hans-Georg Gadamer, and Eugene Vance, likewise, have suggested new ways of understanding *history as a language*. In this section, for example, Stephen Greenblatt asserts that "history cannot be divorced from textuality, and all texts can be compelled to confront the crisis of undecidability revealed in the literary text." In general, this conception of history abandons any notion of history as direct mimesis, any belief in history as a mere imitation of events in the world—history as a reflection of an activity happening "out there." Hayden White, especially, tends to view history as itself a narrative, a narrated sequence marked by inexplicable gaps or ruptures. The sequence of history itself elaborates relationships that belong to an "episteme," not a mode of thought that characterizes an age (as in the "old" historicism), but the discursive limits on what can be thought (i.e., "discursivized") at any particular moment, so that history as a discipline necessarily traces ruptures rather than continuities, empty spaces of thought within and between epistemes.

This is an intentionally problematic view of history, nearly a contradiction in historical terms, in which historicity, as Foucault said in *The Order of Things*, "in its very fabric, makes possible the necessity of an origin which must be both internal and foreign to it." Rather than proposing an integrated story about the world, this model suggests that history is fundamentally comprehensible as a way, or ways, of knowing the world, as successive forms of discourse. Therefore, insofar as history comes out of an "origin" that is "foreign to it," history is "thinking the Other," a sequential elaboration of the lacunae in experience. Foucault is quick to caution the historian that these gaps in history are not lacunae "that must be filled." They are "nothing more," he explained, "and nothing less, than the unfolding of a space in which it is once more possible to think." Fundamentally, then, history in this new view is a continual renewal of the grids for thinking and constitutes an epistemological posture (a way of knowing—an "episteme") toward the world. This definition of history would hold true for the histories we write as well as for the immediate sense we have of history as reality, even its personal impact. Thus, the new "textual" sense of history, difficult and sometimes forbidding in its terminology, has done much to encourage literary critics both to view history as a species of language and to look beyond formalist esthetics in order to read literature in the context of power relations and ever wider and deeper contexts of culture.

The current view of history as a "discourse" indeed reverses the hierarchy of history over literature. Now history, like literature, is seen as a product of language, and both represent themselves as formed in a sequence of gaps, as a narrative discourse. If in this way fundamentally a breached narrative, history in its constitution is virtually indistinguishable from literature. This is not to say that history is "made up"—"fictitious" or "mythical" in the derogatory sense—and, thus, rendered trivial. On the contrary, the reality of history in this new view is as "real" (as intractable and even as potentially "hurtful") as it ever was. The new awareness, rather, is that history, like a fictional narrative, exists in a dialogue with something "foreign" or "other" to it that can never be contained or controlled by the historian. In this view, instead of being a more or less accurate story about something that already exists, history is now a knowing that is a making that never quite makes what was intended. Alternatively, we can try to make of history a process of repetition, as T. S. Eliot imagined, so that what was valuable in the past is continually regained ("made new") through poetry in a kind of cultural retrieval mechanism. Or we can make of history an apocalyptic promise to be fulfilled in time, as Northrop Frye in *Anatomy of Criticism*—and, indeed, the Bible—envisioned it. And we can project history as a series of irrational ruptures, as Friedrich Nietzsche and Foucault imagined it. But whether as repetition, apocalypse, or rupture, history is not an order in the world that simply is copied but an order of encounter with the world that Heidegger called Dasein—"being-in-the-world," a conception of making and participating with the world all at once.

One result of this reconception of history and the historicity of literature has been the emergence of a movement in literary criticism that has come to be called "new historicism," a term recently coined by Stephen Greenblatt in a special issue of the journal *Genre*. New Historicism attempts to situate literary works, as Marxist criticism does, within an historical matrix, but it does not necessarily define that matrix as a relationship between a base and superstructure. Rather, following Foucault (in some of its adherents), it describes both history and literature in terms that eschew universalizing and transcendental descriptions and draws upon, instead, the "discursive" presuppositions we have been describing. As Greenblatt says in "Shakespeare and the Exorcists," "for me the study of literature is the study of contingent, particular, intended, and historically embedded works." This is a conception of literature as not being "autonomous, separable from its cultural context and hence divorced from the social, ideological, and material matrix in which all art is produced and consumed." Joined by the work of Jonathan Goldberg, Louis Montrose, Leonard Tennenhouse, and others Greenblatt has produced a significant rereading of Renaissance literature in terms of a sense that, in Tennenhouse's words, "the history of a culture is a history of all its products, literature being just one such product, social organization another, the legal apparatus yet another, and so on." Tennenhouse argues, further, that "one is forced to make an artificial distinction among cultural texts between those which are literary and those which are political in the effort to demonstrate how, in sharing common themes and a common teleology, they actually comprised a seamless discourse." This project of articulating what Greenblatt calls "cultural poetics" has not been limited to Renaissance studies. Nancy Armstrong has "historicized" (in the sense we are discussing) feminist readings of nineteenth-century culture. Similar work for other periods in literary history is going on, and what they all attempt to do (as does Marxist criticism) is to read in literature what Greenblatt calls "a deeper and unexpressed institutional exchange."

In this project, then, the "new historicism" shares a good deal with Marxist literary criticism—in fact, some critics have argued that it is a part of Marxist criticism. Whether or not this is so—and certainly self-consciously Marxist readers like Jameson give more emphasis to the relation between the period of literary history they examine and the political situation of the present than does Greenblatt—nevertheless, both Marxism and new historicism recognize

in literary texts, as Catherine Belsey says, "not 'knowledge' but ideology itself in all its inconsistency and partiality." In doing so, they situate literary criticism in a larger framework of cultural criticism, what Eagleton called (in a passage quoted in the Introduction to Section II) "rhetoric" and "discourse theory." Such theory above all attempts to understand literature as historically situated practices that encompass power as much as knowledge.

RELATED TEXTS IN *CONTEMPORARY LITERARY CRITICISM*

Viktor Shklovsky, "Art as Technique"
Patrocinio Schweickart, "Reading Ourselves: Toward a Feminist Theory of Reading"
Michel Foucault, "What Is an Author?"
Gayatri Spivak, "Imperialism and Sexual Difference"
Edward Said, "Reflections on American 'Left' Literary Criticism"
Henry Louis Gates, Jr., "The Blackness of Blackness: A Critique of the Sign and the Signifying Monkey"

FURTHER READING

Adorno, Theodor W., *Prisms,* trans. Samuel Weber and Shierry Weber (Cambridge: MIT Press, 1983).

Armstrong, Nancy, *Desire and Domestic Fiction* (New York: Oxford University Press, 1987).

Auerbach, Erich, *Mimesis: The Representation of Reality in Western Literature,* trans. Willard Trask (Princeton, N.J.: Princeton University Press, 1953).

Balibar, Etienne, and Pierre Macherey, "On Literature as an Ideological Form," trans. Ian McLeod, John Whitehead, and Ann Wordsworth, in *Untying the Text,* ed. Robert Young (Boston: Routledge, 1981), pp. 79–99.

Belsey, Catherine, *Critical Practice* (London: Methuen, 1980).

Benjamin, Walter, *Illuminations* (New York: Schocken, 1970).

Bowers, Fredson, *Textual and Literary Criticism* (New York: Cambridge University Press, 1959).

Coward, Rosalind, and John Ellis, *Language and Materialism: Developments in Semiology and the Theory of the Subject* (London: Routledge and Kegan Paul, 1977).

Eagleton, Terry, *Criticism and Ideology* (New York: Schocken, 1978).

______, *Literary Theory: An Introduction* (Minneapolis: University of Minnesota Press, 1983).

______, *Marxism and Literary Criticism* (Berkeley: University of California Press, 1976).

Foucault, Michel, *Language, Counter-Memory, Practice,* trans. Donald F. Bouchard (Ithaca: Cornell University Press, 1977).

______, *Madness and Civilization,* trans. Richard Howard (New York: Pantheon, 1965).

______, *The Order of Things* (New York: Pantheon, 1972).

Goldmann, Lucien, *The Hidden God*, trans. Philip Thody (New York: Humanities Press, 1976).

Greenblatt, Stephen, "Introduction," *The Forms of Power and the Powers of Form in The Renaissance, Genre* 15 (1982), 3–6.

Hicks, Granville, *The Great Tradition* (New York: Macmillan, 1933; rev. 1935).

James, C. Vaughan, *Soviet Socialist Realism: Origins and Theory* (New York: Macmillan, 1973).

Jameson, Fredric, *Marxism and Form: Twentieth-Century Dialectical Theories of Literature* (Princeton: Princeton University Press, 1971).

______, *The Political Unconscious: Narrative as a Socially Symbolic Act* (Ithaca: Cornell University Press, 1981).

______, *The Prison-House of Language: A Critical Account of Structuralism and Russian Formalism* (Princeton, N.J.: Princeton University Press, 1972).

Jay, Martin, *The Dialectical Imagination: A History of the Frankfurt School* (Boston: Little Brown, 1973).

Lentricchia, Frank, *Criticism and Social Change* (Chicago: University of Chicago Press, 1983).

Lukacs, Georg, *The Historical Novel* (London: Merlin Press, 1962).

______, *Realism in Our Time* (New York: Harper Torchbooks, 1971).

Macherey, Pierre, *A Theory of Literary Production*, trans. G. Wall (London: Routledge and Kegan Paul, 1978).

Merod, Jim, *The Political Responsibility of the Critic* (Ithaca: Cornell University Press, 1987).

Robertson, D. W., Jr., "Historical Criticism," in *English Institute Essays: 1950*, ed. Alan S. Downer (New York: Columbia University Press, 1951), 3–31.

Tennenhouse, Leonard, "Representing Power: *Measure for Measure* in its Time," in Greenblatt, pp. 139–56.

Sartre, Jean-Paul, *What is Literature?* (New York: Philosophical Library, 1949).

Wellek, René, "Literary Theory, Criticism, and History," in *Sewanee Review*, 68 (1960), 1–19.

White, Hayden, *Metahistory: The Historical Imagination in Nineteenth-Century Europe* (Baltimore: Johns Hopkins University Press, 1973).

______, *Tropics of Discourse: Essays in Cultural Criticism* (Baltimore: Johns Hopkins University Press, 1978).

Willett, John, ed., *Brecht on Theatre* (London: Methuen, 1964).

Williams, Raymond, *Marxism and Literature* (New York: Oxford University Press, 1977).

______, *Problems in Materialism and Culture* (New York: Schocken, 1981).

Wimsatt, W. K., Jr., "History and Criticism: A Problematic Relationship," in *PMLA*, 66 (1951), 21–31.

21

Raymond Williams
1921–1988

Raymond Williams was a professor of drama at Jesus College, Cambridge. Among his nearly twenty published books are: *Culture and Society, 1780–1950* (1958); *The Long Revolution (1961); Drama from Ibsen to Brecht* (1969); *The English Novel from Dickens to Lawrence* (1970); *The Country and the City* (1973); *Keywords* (1976); *Marxism and Literature* (1977); *Politics and Letters* (interviews, 1979); *Problems in Materialism and Culture* (1981); *Culture* (1981); *The Sociology of Culture* (1982); *Writing in Society* (1983); and four novels, published between 1960 and 1979.

Williams may be the most important British Marxist literary critic and theoretician of culture since World War II. With the publication of *Culture and Society* in 1958 Williams single-handedly changed the image of Marxist literary criticism in the English-speaking world from simplistic notions of culture as economically determined and rigid demands for political orthodoxy to a subtle and complex understanding of all writers and all writing as embedded in specific, concrete relations, all writing as responses to real situations. His impressive body of work spanning the next three decades has continued to demonstrate his keen awareness and understanding of the deep sociology of culture. From close readings of both canonical and mass cultural works to more general, theoretical essays on culture, he seeks always to convince us of the shaping power of social and economic practices and institutions, and of the significant function and effects of cultural practice within the larger social context.

"Base and Superstructure in Marxist Cultural Theory" is drawn from his selected essays, *Problems in Materialism and Culture*. It appeared originally in *New Left Review* in 1973. Much of the essay appeared as well in *Marxism and Literature* in 1977. In this essay, Williams is grappling with the central issue for Marxist theory of the *determination* of culture (and consciousness) by human social existence. He is at pains here to refute the "straw man" of vulgar Marxist economic determinism, in which culture is seen as some simple, direct "reflection" of economic forces. At the same time he uses Antonio Gramsci's notion of "hegemony" to argue for the validity of a subtle and carefully argued Marxist position with regard to the real power of dominant political and economic forces in cultural as in other aspects of life. Another key aspect of this influential essay is Williams's formulation—which he develops further in *Marxism and Literature*—with regard to dominant, residual, and emergent strains, which always exist in varying strengths and different configurations, and in differing relations to one another, at any given moment in any culture, with an equally universal struggle, within emergent cultural practices and formations, between the alternative and the oppositional. This schema has been widely taken up by other Marxist critics (see, for example, Fredric Jameson's various essays on postmodernism), and provides an extremely useful analytical tool. Williams's work in the sociology of culture has laid the groundwork for much of the most important contemporary work in the area of cultural studies.

Base and Superstructure in Marxist Cultural Theory

Any modern approach to a Marxist theory of culture must begin by considering the proposition of a determining base and a determined superstructure. From a strictly theoretical point of view this is not, in fact, where we might choose to begin. It would be in many ways preferable if we could begin from a proposition which originally was equally central, equally authentic: namely the proposition that social being determines consciousness. It is not that the two propositions necessarily deny each other or are in contradiction. But the proposition of base and superstructure, with its figurative element, with its suggestion of a fixed and definite spatial relationship, constitutes, at least in certain hands, a very specialized and at times unacceptable version of the other proposition. Yet in the transition from Marx to Marxism, and in the development of mainstream Marxism itself, the proposition of the determining base and the determined superstructure has been commonly held to be the key to Marxist cultural analysis.

It is important, as we try to analyse this proposition, to be aware that the term of relationship which is involved, that is to say "determines," is of great linguistic and theoretical complexity. The language of determination and even more of determinism was inherited from idealist and especially theological accounts of the world and man. It is significant that it is in one of his familiar inversions, his contradictions of received propositions, that Marx uses the word which becomes, in English translation, "determines" (the usual but not invariable German word is *bestimmen*). He is opposing an ideology that had been insistent on the power of certain forces outside man, or, in its secular version, on an abstract determining consciousness. Marx's own proposition explicitly denies this, and puts the origin of determination in men's own activities. Nevertheless, the particular history and continuity of the term serves to remind us that there are, within ordinary use—and this is true of most of the major European languages—quite different possible meanings and implications of the word "determine." There is, on the one hand, from its theological inheritance, the notion of an external cause which totally predicts or prefigures, indeed totally controls a subsequent activity. But there is also, from the experience of social practice, a notion of determination as setting limits, exerting pressures.[1]

Now there is clearly a difference between a process of setting limits and exerting pressures, whether by some external force or by the internal laws of a particular development, and that other process in which a subsequent content is essentially prefigured, predicted and controlled by a preexisting external force. Yet it is fair to say, looking at many applications of Marxist cultural analysis, that it is the second sense, the notion of prefiguration, prediction or control, which has often explicitly or implicitly been used.

SUPERSTRUCTURE: QUALIFICATIONS AND AMENDMENTS

The term of relationship is then the first thing that we have to examine in this proposition, but we have to do this by going on to look at the related terms themselves. "Superstructure" (*Überbau*) has had most attention. In common usage, after Marx, it acquired a main sense of a unitary "area" within which all cultural and ideological activities could be placed. But already in Marx himself, in the later correspondence of Engels, and at many points in the subsequent Marxist tradition, qualifications were made about the determined character of certain superstructural activities. The first kind of qualification had to do with delays in time, with complications, and with certain indirect or relatively distant relationships. The simplest notion of a superstructure, which is still by no means entirely abandoned, had been the reflection, the imitation or the reproduction of the reality of the base in the superstructure in a more or less direct way. Positivist notions of reflection and reproduction of course directly supported this. But since in many real cultural activities this relationship cannot be found, or cannot be found without effort or even violence to the material or practice being studied, the notion was introduced of delays in time, the famous lags; of various technical complications; and of indirectness, in which certain kinds of activity in the cultural sphere—philosophy, for example—were situated at a greater distance from the primary economic activities. That was the first stage of qualification of the notion of superstructure: in effect, an operational qualification. The second stage was related but more fundamental, in that the process of the relationship itself was more substantially looked at. This was the kind of reconsideration which gave rise to the modern notion of "mediation," in which something more than simple reflection or reproduction—indeed something radically different from either reflection or reproduction—actively occurs. In the later twentieth century there is the notion of "homologous structures," where there may be no direct or easily apparent similarity, and certainly nothing like reflection or reproduction, between the superstructural process and the reality of the base, but in which there is an essential homology or correspondence of structures, which can be discovered by analysis. This is not the same notion as "mediation," but it is the same kind of amendment in that the relationship between the base and the superstructure is not supposed to be direct, nor simply operationally subject to lags and complications and indirectnesses, but that of its nature it is not direct reproduction.

These qualifications and amendments are important. But it seems to me that what has not been looked at with equal care is the received notion of the "base" (*Basis, Grundlage*). And indeed I would argue that the base is the more important concept to look at if we are to understand the realities of cultural process. In many uses of the proposition of base and superstructure, as a matter of verbal habit, "the base" has come to be considered virtually as an object, or in less crude cases, it has been considered in essentially uniform and usually static ways. "The base" is the real social existence of man. "The base" is the real relations of production corresponding to a stage of development of the material productive forces. "The base" is a mode of production at a particular stage of its development. We make and repeat propositions of this kind, but the usage is then very different from Marx's emphasis on productive activities, in particular structural relations, constituting the foundation of all other activities. For while a particular stage of the development of production can be discovered and made precise by analysis, it is never in practice either uniform or static. It is indeed one of the central propositions of Marx's sense of history that there are deep contradictions in the relationships of production and in the consequent social relationships. There is therefore the continual possibility of the dynamic variation of these forces. Moreover, when these forces are considered, as Marx always considers them, as the specific activities and relationships of real men, they mean something very much more active, more complicated and more contradictory than the developed metaphorical notion of "the base" could possibly allow us to realize.

THE BASE AND THE PRODUCTIVE FORCES

So we have to say that when we talk of "the base," we are talking of a process and not a state. And we cannot ascribe to that process certain fixed properties for subsequent translation to the variable processes of the superstructure. Most people who have wanted to make the ordinary proposition more reasonable have concentrated on refining the notion of superstructure. But I would say that each term of the proposition has to be revalued in a particular direction. We have to revalue "determination" towards the setting of limits and the exertion of pressure, and away from a predicted, prefigured and controlled content. We have to revalue "superstructure" towards a related range of cultural practices, and away from a reflected, reproduced or specifically dependent content. And, crucially, we have to revalue "the base" away from the notion of a fixed economic or technological abstraction, and towards the specific activities of men in real social and economic relationships, containing fundamental contradictions and variations and therefore always in a state of dynamic process.

It is worth observing one further implication behind the customary definitions. "The base" has come to include, especially in certain twentieth-century developments, a strong and limiting sense of basic industry. The emphasis on heavy industry, even, has played a certain cultural role. And this raises a more general problem, for we find ourselves forced to look again at the ordinary notion of "productive forces." Clearly what we are examining in the base is primary productive forces. Yet some very crucial distinctions have to be made here. It is true that in his analysis of capitalist production Marx considered "productive work" in a very particular and specialized sense corresponding to that mode of production. There is a difficult passage in the *Grundrisse* in which he argues that while the man who makes a piano is a productive worker, there is a real question whether the man who distributes the piano is also a productive worker; but he probably is, since he contributes to the realization of surplus value. Yet when it comes to the man who plays the piano, whether to himself or to others, there is no question: he is not a productive worker at all. So piano-maker is base, but pianist superstructure. As a way of considering cultural activity, and incidentally the economics of modern cultural activity, this is very clearly a dead-end. But for any theoretical clarification it is crucial to recognize that Marx was there engaged in an analysis of a particular kind of production, that is capitalist commodity production. Within his analysis of this mode, he had to give to the notion of "productive labour" and "productive forces" a specialized sense of primary work on materials in a form which produced commodities. But this has narrowed remarkably, and in a cultural context very damagingly, from his more central notion of *productive forces,* in which, to give just brief reminders, the most important thing a worker ever produces is himself, himself in the fact that kind of labour, or the broader historical emphasis of men producing themselves, themselves and their history. Now when we talk of the base, and of primary productive forces, it matters very much whether we are referring, as in one degenerate form of this proposition became habitual, to primary production within the terms of capitalist economic relationships, or to the primary production of society itself, and of men themselves, the material production and reproduction of real life. If we have the broad sense of productive forces, we look at the whole question of the base differently, and we are then less tempted to dismiss as superstructural, and in that sense as merely secondary, certain vital productive social forces, which are in the broad sense, from the beginning, basic.

USES OF TOTALITY

Yet, because of the difficulties of the ordinary proposition of base and superstructure, there was an alternative and very important development, an emphasis primarily associated with Lukács, on a social "totality." The totality of social practices was opposed to this layered notion of base and a consequent superstructure. This concept of a totality of practices is compatible with the notion of social being determining consciousness, but it does not necessarily interpret this process in terms of a base and a superstructure. Now the language of totality has become common, and it is indeed in many ways more acceptable than the notion of base and superstructure. But with one very important reservation. It is very easy for the notion of totality to empty of its essential content the original Marxist proposition. For if we come to say that society is composed of a large number of social practices which form a concrete social whole, and if we give to each practice a certain specific recognition, adding only that they interact, relate and combine in very complicated ways, we are at one level much more obviously talking about reality, but we are at another level withdrawing from the claim that there is any process of determination. And this I, for one, would be very unwilling to do. Indeed, the key question to ask about any notion of totality in cultural theory is this: whether the notion of totality includes the notion of intention.

If totality is simply concrete, if it is simply the recognition of a large variety of miscellaneous and contemporaneous practices, then it is essentially empty of any content that could be called Marxist. Intention, the notion of intention, restores the key question, or rather the key emphasis. For while it is true that any society is a complex whole of such practices, it is also true that any society has a specific organization, a specific structure, and that the principles of this organization and structure can be seen as directly related to certain social intentions, intentions by which we define the society, intentions which in all our experience have been the rule of a particular class. One of the unexpected consequences of the crudeness of the base/superstructure model has been the too easy acceptance of models which appear less crude—models of totality or of a complex whole—but which exclude the facts of social intention, the class character of a particular society and so on.

And this reminds us of how much we lose if we abandon the superstructural emphasis altogether. Thus I have great difficulty in seeing processes of art and thought as superstructural in the sense of the formula as it is commonly used. But in many areas of social and political thought—certain kinds of ratifying theory, certain kinds of law, certain kinds of institution, which after all in Marx's original formulations were very much part of the superstructure—in all that kind of social apparatus, and in a decisive area of political and ideological activity and construction, if we fail to see a superstructural element we fail to recognize reality at all. These laws, constitutions, theories, ideologies, which are so often claimed as natural, or as having universal validity or significance, simply have to be seen as expressing and ratifying the domination of a particular class. Indeed the difficulty of revising the formula of base and superstructure has had much to do with the perception of many militants—who have to fight such institutions and notions as well as fighting economic battles—that if these institutions and their ideologies are not perceived as having that kind of dependent and ratifying relationship, if their claims to universal validity or legitimacy are not denied and fought, then the class character of the society can no longer be seen. And this has been the effect of some versions of totality as the description of cultural process. Indeed I think we can properly use the notion of totality only when we combine it with that other crucial Marxist concept of "hegemony."

THE COMPLEXITY OF HEGEMONY

It is Gramsci's great contribution to have emphasized hegemony, and also to have understood it at a depth which is, I think, rare. For hegemony supposes the existence of something which is truly total, which is not merely secondary or superstructural, like the weak sense of ideology, but which is lived at such a depth, which saturates the society to such an extent, and which, as Gramsci put it, even constitutes the substance and limit of common sense for most people under its sway, that it corresponds to the reality of social experience very much more clearly than any notions derived from the formula of base and superstructure. For if ideology were merely some abstract, imposed set of notions, if our social and political and cultural ideas and assumptions and habits were merely the result of specific manipulation, of a kind of overt training which might be simply ended or withdrawn, then the society would be very much easier to move and to change than in practice it has ever been or is. This notion of hegemony as deeply saturating the consciousness of a society seems to me to be fundamental. And hegemony has the advantage over general notions of totality, that it at the same time emphasizes the facts of domination.

Yet there are times when I hear discussions of hegemony and feel that it too, as a concept, is being dragged back to the relatively simple, uniform and static notion which "superstructure" in ordinary use had become. Indeed I think that we have to give a very complex account of hegemony if we are talking about any real social formation. Above all we have to give an account which allows for its elements of real and constant change. We have to emphasize that hegemony is not singular; indeed that its own internal structures are highly complex, and have continually to be renewed, recreated and defended; and by the same token, that they can be continually challenged and in certain respects modified. That is why instead of speaking simply of "the hegemony," "a hegemony," I would propose a model which allows for this kind of variation and contradiction, its sets of alternatives and its processes of change.

For one thing that is evident in some of

the best Marxist cultural analysis is that it is very much more at home in what one might call *epochal* questions than in what one has to call *historical* questions. That is to say, it is usually very much better at distinguishing the large features of different epochs of society, as commonly between feudal and bourgeois, than at distinguishing between different phases of bourgeois society, and different moments within these phases: that true historical process which demands a much greater precision and delicacy of analysis than the always striking epochal analysis which is concerned with main lineaments and features.

The theoretical model which I have been trying to work with is this. I would say first that in any society, in any particular period, there is a central system of practices, meanings and values, which we can properly call dominant and effective. This implies no presumption about its value. All I am saying is that it is central. Indeed I would call it a corporate system, but this might be confusing, since Gramsci uses "corporate" to mean the subordinate as opposed to the general and dominant elemtns of hegemony. In any case what I have in mind is the central, effective and dominant system of meanings and values, which are not merely abstract but which are organized and lived. That is why hegemony is not to be understood at the level of mere opinion or mere manipulation. It is a whole body of practices and expectations; our assignments of energy, our ordinary understanding of the nature of man and of his world. It is a set of meanings and values which as they are experienced as practices appear as reciprocally confirming. It thus constitutes a sense of reality for most people in the society, a sense of absolute because experienced reality beyond which it is very difficult for most members of the society to move, in most areas of their lives. But this is not, except in the operation of a moment of abstract analysis, in any sense a static system. On the contrary we can only understand an effective and dominant culture if we understand the real social process on which it depends: I mean the process of incorporation. The modes of incorporation are of great social significance. The educational institutions are usually the main agencies of the transmission of an effective dominant culture, and this is now a major economic as well as a cultural activity; indeed it is both in the same moment. Moreover, at a philosophical level, at the true level of theory and at the level of the history of various practices, there is a process which I call the *selective tradition:* that which, within the terms of an effective dominant culture, is always passed off as "*the* tradition," "*the* significant past." But always the selectivity is the point; the way in which from a whole possible area of past and present, certain meanings and practices are chosen for emphasis, certain other meanings and practices are neglected and excluded. Even more crucially, some of these meanings and practices are reinterpreted, diluted, or put into forms which support or at least do not contradict other elements within the effective dominant culture. The processes of education; the processes of a much wider social training within institutions like the family; the practical definitions and organization of work; the selective tradition at an intellectual and theoretical level: all these forces are involved in a continual making and remaking of an effective dominant culture, and on them, as experienced, as built into our living, its reality depends. If what we learn there were merely an imposed ideology, or if it were only the isolable meanings and practices of the ruling class, or of a section of the ruling class, which gets imposed on others, occupying merely the top of our minds, it would be—and one would be glad—a very much easier thing to overthrow.

It is not only the depths to which this

process reaches, selecting and organizing and interpreting our experience. It is also that it is continually active and adjusting; it isn't just the past, the dry husks of ideology which we can more easily discard. And this can only be so, in a complex society, if it is something more substantial and more flexible than any abstract imposed ideology. Thus we have to recognize the alternative meanings and values, the alternative opinions and attitudes, even some alternative senses of the world, which can be accommodated and tolerated within a particular effective and dominant culture. This has been much under-emphasized in our notions of a superstucture, and even in some notions of hegemony. And the under-emphasis opens the way for retreat to an indifferent complexity. In the practice of politics, for example, there are certain truly incorporated modes of what are nevertheless, within those terms, real oppositions, that are felt and fought out. Their existence within the incorporation is recognizable by the fact that, whatever the degree of internal conflict or internal variation, they do not in practice go beyond the limits of the central effective and dominant definitions. This is true, for example, of the practice of parliamentary politics, though its internal oppositions are real. It is true about a whole range of practices and arguments, in any real society, which can by no means be reduced to an ideological cover, but which can nevertheless be properly analysed as in my sense corporate, if we find that, whatever the degree of internal controversy and variation, they do not in the end exceed the limits of the central corporate definitions.

But if we are to say this, we have to think again about the sources of that which is not corporate; of those practices, experiences, meanings, values which are not part of the effective dominant culture. We can express this in two ways. There is clearly something that we can call alternative to the effective dominant culture, and there is something else that we can call oppositional, in a true sense. The degree of existence of these alternative and oppositional forms is itself a matter of constant historical variation in real circumstances. In certain societies it is possible to find areas of social life in which quite real alternatives are at least left alone. (If they are made available, of course, they are part of the corporate organization.) The existence of the possibility of opposition, and of its articulation, its degree of openness, and so on, again depends on very precise social and political forces. The facts of alternative and oppositional forms of social life and culture, in relation to the effective and dominant culture, have then to be recognized as subject to historical variation, and as having sources which are very significant as a fact about the dominant culture itself.

RESIDUAL AND EMERGENT CULTURES

I have next to introduce a further distinction, between *residual* and *emergent* forms, both of alternative and of oppositional culture. By "residual" I mean that some experiences, meanings and values, which cannot be verified or cannot be expressed in terms of the dominant culture, are nevertheless lived and practised on the basis of the residue—cultural as well as social—of some previous social formation. There is a real case of this in certain religious values, by contrast with the very evident incorporation of most religious meanings and values into the dominant system. The same is true, in a culture like Britain, of certain notions derived from a rural past, which have a very significant popularity. A residual culture is usually at some distance from the effective dominant culture, but one has to recognize that, in real cultural activities, it may get incorporated into it. This is because some part of it, some version of it—and especially if the residue is from some major area of the past—will in many cases have had to be incorporated if the effective dominant culture is to make sense in those areas. It is also because at certain points a dominant culture cannot allow too much of this kind of practice and experience outside itself, at least without risk. Thus the pressures are real, but certain genuinely residual meanings and practices in some important cases survive.

By "emergent" I mean, first, that new meanings and values, new practices, new significances and experiences, are continually being created. But there is then a much earlier attempt to incorporate them, just because they are part—and yet not a defined part—of effective contemporary practice. Indeed it is significant in our own period how very early this attempt is, how alert the dominant culture now is to anything that can be seen as emergent. We have then to see, first, as it were a temporal relation between a dominant culture and on the one hand a residual and on the other hand an emergent culture. But we can only understand this if we can make distinctions, that usually require very precise analysis, between residual-incorporated and residual not incorporated, and between emergent-incorporated and emergent not incorporated. It is an important fact about any particular society, how far it reaches into the whole range of human practices and experiences in an attempt at incorporation. It may be true of some earlier phases of bourgeois society, for example, that there were some areas of experience which it was willing to dispense with, which it was prepared to assign as the sphere of private or artistic life, and as being no particular business of society or the state. This went along with certain kinds of political tolerance, even if the reality of that tolerance was malign neglect. But I am sure it is true of the society that has come into existence since the last war, that progressively, because of developments in the social character of labour, in the social character of communications, and in the social character of decision, it extends much further than ever before in capitalist society into certain hitherto resigned areas of experience and practice and meaning. Thus the effective decision, as to whether a practice is alternative or oppositional, is often now made within a very much narrower scope. There is a simple theoretical distinction between alternative and oppositional, that is to say between someone who simply finds a different way to live and wishes to be left alone with it, and someone who finds a different way to live and wants to change the society in its light. This is usually the difference between individual and small-group solutions to social crisis and those solutions which properly belong to political and ultimately revolutionary practice. But it is often a very narrow line, in reality, between alternative and oppositional. A meaning or a practice may be tolerated as a deviation, and yet still be seen only as another particular way to live. But as the necessary area of effective dominance extends, the same meanings and practices can be seen by the dominant culture, not merely as disregarding or despising it, but as challenging it.

Now it is crucial to any Marxist theory of culture that it can give an adequate explanation of the sources of these practices and meanings. We can understand, from an ordinary historical approach, at least some of the sources of residual meanings and practices. These are the results of earlier social formations, in which certain real meanings and values were generated. In the subsequent default of a particular phase of a dominant culture, there is then a reaching back to those meanings and values which were created in real societies in the past, and which still seem to have some significance because they represent areas of human experience, aspiration and achievement, which the dominant culture under-values or opposes, or even cannot recognize. But our hardest task, theoretically, is to find a non-metaphysical and non-subjectivist explanation of emergent cultural practice. Moreoever, part of our answer to this question bears on the process of persistence of residual practices.

CLASS AND HUMAN PRACTICE

We have indeed one source to hand from the central body of Marxist theory. We have the formation of a new class, the coming to consciousness of a new class. This remains, without doubt, quite centrally important. Of course, in itself, this process of formation complicates any simple model of base and superstructure. It also complicates some of the ordinary versions of hegemony, although it was Gramsci's whole purpose to see and to create by organization that hegemony of a proletarian kind which would be capable of challenging the bourgeois hegemony. We have then one central source of new practice, in the emergence of a new class. But we have also to recognize certain other kinds of source, and in cultural practice some of these are very important. I would say that we can recognize them on the basis of this proposition: that no mode of production, and therefore no dominant society or order of society, and therefore no dominant culture, in reality exhausts the full range of human practice, human energy, human intention (this range is not the inventory of some original "human nature" but, on the contrary, is that extraordinary range of variations, both practised and imagined, of which human beings are and have shown themselves to be capable). Indeed it seems to me that this emphasis is not merely a negative proposition, allowing us to account for certain things which happen outside the dominant mode. On the contrary, it is a fact about the modes of domination that they select from and consequently exclude the full range of actual and possible human practice. The difficulties of human practice outside or against the dominant mode are, of course, real. It depends very much whether it is in an area in which the dominant class and the dominant culture have an interest and a stake. If the interest and the stake are explicit, many new practices will be reached for, and if possible incorporated, or else extirpated with extraordinary vigour. But in certain areas, there will be in certain periods practices and meanings which are not reached for. There will be areas of practice and meaning which, almost by definition from its own limited character, or in its profound deformation, the dominant culture is unable in any real terms to recognize. This gives us a bearing on the observable difference between, for example, the practices of a capitalist state and a state like the contemporary Soviet Union in relation to writers. Since from the whole Marxist tradition literature was seen as an important activity, indeed a crucial activity, the Soviet state is very much sharper in investigating areas where different versions of practice, different meanings and values, are being attempted and expressed. In capitalist practice, if the thing is not making a profit, or if it is not being widely circulated, then it can for some time be overlooked, at least while it remains alternative. When it becomes oppositional in an explicit way, it does, of course, get approached or attacked.

I am saying then that in relation to the full range of human practice at any one time, the dominant mode is a conscious selection and organization. At least in its fully formed state it is conscious. But there are always sources of actual human practice which it neglects or excludes. And these can be different in quality from the developing and articulate interests of a rising class. They can include, for example, alternative perceptions of others, in immediate personal relationships, or new perceptions of material and media, in art and science, and within certain limits these new perceptions can be practised. The relations between the two kinds of source—the emerging class and either the dominatively excluded or the more generally new practices—are by no means necessarily contradictory. At times they can be very close, and on the relations between them much in political practice depends. But culturally and as a matter of theory the areas can be seen as distinct.

Now if we go back to the cultural question in its most usual form—what are the relations between art and society, or literature and society?—in the light of the preceding discussion, we have to say first that there are no relations between literature and society in that abstracted way. The literature is there from the beginning as a practice in the society. Indeed until it and all other practices are present, the society cannot be seen as fully formed. A society is not fully available for analysis until each of its practices is included. But if we make that emphasis we must make a corresponding emphasis: that we cannot separate literature and art from other kinds of social practice, in such a way as to make them subject to quite special and distinct laws. They may have quite specific features as practices, but they cannot be separated from the general social process. Indeed one way of emphasizing this is to say, to insist, that literature is not restricted to operating in any one of the sectors I have been seeking to describe in this model. It would be easy to say, it is a familiar rhetoric, that literature operates in the emergent cultural sector, that it represents the new feelings, the new meanings, the new values. We might persuade ourselves of this theoretically, by abstract argument, but when we read much literature, over the whole range, without the sleight-of-hand of calling Literature only that which we have already selected as embodying certain meanings and values at a certain scale of intensity, we are bound to recognize that the act of writing, the practices of discourse in writing and speech, the making of novels and poems and plays and theories, all this activity takes place in all areas of the culture.

Literature appears by no means only in the emergent sector, which is always, in fact, quite rare. A great deal of writing is of a residual kind, and this has been deeply true of much English literature in the last half-century. Some of its fundamental meanings and values have belonged to the cultural achievements of long-past stages of society. So widespread is this fact, and the habits of mind it supports, that in many minds "literature" and "the past" acquire a certain identity, and it is then said that there is now no literature: all that glory is over. Yet most writing, in any period, including our own, is a form of contribution to the effective dominant culture. Indeed many of the specific qualities of literature—its capacity to embody and enact and perform certain meanings and values, or to create in single particular ways what would be otherwise merely general truths—enable it to fulfill this effective function with great power. To literature, of course, we must add the visual arts and music, and in our own society the powerful arts of film and of broadcasting. But the general theoretical point should be clear. If we are looking for the relations between literature and society, we cannot either separate out this one practice from a formed body of other practices, nor when we have identified a particular practice can we give it a uniform, static and ahistorical relation to some abstract social formation. The arts of writing and the arts of creation and performance, over their whole range, are parts of the cultural process in all the different ways, the different sectors, that I have been seeking to describe. They contribute to the effective dominant culture and are a central articulation of it. They embody residual meanings and values, not all of which are incorporated, though many are. They express also and significantly some emergent practices and meanings, yet some of these may eventually be incorporated, as they reach people and begin to move them. Thus it was very evident in the sixties, in some of the emergent arts of performance, that the dominant culture reached out to transform, or seek to transform, them. In this process, of course, the dominant culture itself changes, not in its central formation, but in many of its articulated features. But then in a modern society it must always change in this way, if it is to remain dominant, if it is still to be felt as in real ways central in all our many activities and interests.

CRITICAL THEORY AS CONSUMPTION

What then are the implications of this general analysis for the analysis of particular works of art? This is the question towards which most discussion of cultural theory seems to be directed: the discovery of a method, perhaps even a methodology, through which particular works of art can be understood and described. I would not myself agree that this is the central use of cultural theory, but let us for a moment consider it. What seems to me very striking is that nearly all forms of contemporary critical theory are theories of *consumption*. That is to say, they are concerned with understanding an object in such a way that it can profitably or correctly be consumed. The earliest stage of consumption theory was the theory of "taste," where the link between the practice and the theory was direct in the metaphor. From taste there came the more elevated notion of "sensibility," in which it was the consumption by sensibility of elevated or insightful works that was held to be the essential practice of reading, and critical activity was then a function of this sensibility. There were then more developed theories, in the 1920s with I. A. Richards, and later in New Criticism, in which the effects of consumption were studied directly. The language of the work of art as object then became more overt. "What effect does this work ('the poem' as it was ordinarily described) have on me?" Or, "what impact does it have on me?" as it was later to be put in a much wider area of communication studies. Naturally enough, the notion of the work of art as *object*, as *text*, as an isolated artifact, became central in all these later consumption theories. It was not only that the practices of *production* were then overlooked, though this fused with the notion that most important literature anyway was from the past. The real social conditions of production were in any case neglected because they were believed to be at best secondary. The true relationship was seen always as between the taste, the sensibility or the training of the reader and this isolated work, this object "as in itself it really is," as most people came to put it. But the notion of the work of art as object had a further large theoretical effect. If you ask questions about the work of art seen as object, they may include questions about the components of its production. Now, as it happened, there was a use of the formula of base and superstructure which was precisely in line with this. The components of a work of art were the real activities of the base, and you could study the object to discover these components. Sometimes you even studied the components and then projected the object. But in any case the relationship that was looked for was one between an object and its components. But this was not only true of Marxist suppositions of a base and a superstructure. It was true also of various kinds of psychological theory, whether in the form of archetypes, or the images of the collective unconscious, or the myths and symbols which were seen as the *components* of particular works of art. Or again there was biography, or psychobiography and its like, where the components were in the man's life and the work of art was an object in which components of this kind were discovered. Even in some of the more rigorous forms of New Criticism and of structuralist criticism, this essential procedure of regarding the work as an object which has to be reduced to its components, even if later it may be reconstituted, came to persist.

OBJECTS AND PRACTICES

Now I think the true crisis in cultural theory, in our own time, is between this view of the work of art as object and the alternative view of art as a practice. Of course it is at once argued that the work of art *is* an object: that various works have survived from the past, particular sculptures, particular paintings, particular buildings, and these are objects. This is of course true, but the same way of thinking is applied to works which have no such singular existence. There is no *Hamlet*, no *Brothers Karamazov*, no *Wuthering Heights*, in the sense that there is a particular great painting. There is no *Fifth Symphony*, there is no work in the whole area of music and dance and performance, which is an object in any way comparable to those works in the visual arts which have survived. And yet the habit of treating all such works as objects has persisted because this is a basic theoretical and practical presupposition. But in literature (especially in drama), in music and in a very wide area of the performing arts, what we permanently have are not objects but *notations*. These notations have then to be interpreted in an active way, according to the particular conventions. But indeed this is true over an even wider field. The relationship between the making of a work of art and its reception is always active, and subject to conventions, which in themselves are forms of (changing) social organization and relationship, and this is radically different from the production and consumption of an object. It is indeed an activity and a practice, and in its accessible forms, although it may in some arts have the character of a singular object, it is still only accessible through active perception and interpretation. This makes the case of notation, in arts like drama and literature and music, only a special case of a much wider truth. What this can show us here about the practice of analysis is that we have to break from the common procedure of isolating the object and then discovering its components. On the contrary we have to discover the nature of a practice and then its conditions.

Often these two procedures may in part resemble each other, but in many other cases they are of radically different kinds, and I would conclude with an observation on the way this distinction bears on the Marxist tradition of the relation between primary economic and social practices, and cultural practices. If we suppose that what is produced in cultural practice is a series of objects, we shall, as in most current forms of sociological-critical procedure, set about discovering their components. Within a Marxist emphasis these components will be from what we have been in the habit of calling the base. We then isolate certain features which we can so to say recognize *in component form*, or we ask what processes of transformation or mediation these components have gone through before they arrived in this accessible state.

But I am saying that we should look not for the components of a product but for the conditions of a practice. When we find ourselves looking at a particular work, or group of works, often realizing, as we do so, their essential community as well as their irreducible individuality, we should find ourselves attending first to the reality of their practice and the conditions of the practice as it was then executed. And from this I think we ask essentially different questions. Take for example the way in which an object—"a text"—is related to a genre, in orthodox criticism. We identify it by certain leading features, we then assign it to a larger category, the genre, and then we may find the components of the genre in a particular social history (although in some variants of criticism not even that is done, and the genre is supposed to be some permanent category of the mind).

It is not that way of proceeding that is now required. The recognition of the relation of a collective mode and an individual project—and these are the only categories that we can initially presume—is a recognition of related practices. That is to say, the irreducibly individual projects that particular works are, may come in experience and in analysis to show resemblances which allow us to group them into collective modes. These are by no means always genres. They may exist as resemblances within and across genres. They may be the practice of a group in a period, rather than the practice of a phase in a genre. But as we discover the nature of a particular practice, and the nature of the relation between an individual project and a collective mode, we find that we are analysing, as two forms of the same process, both its active composition and its conditions of composition, and in either direction this is a complex of extending active relationships. This means, of course, that we have no built-in procedure of the kind which is indicated by the fixed character of an object. We have the principles of the relations of practices, within a discoverably intentional organization, and we have the available hypotheses of dominant, residual and emergent. But what we are actively seeking is the true practice which has been alienated to an object, and the true conditions of practice—whether as literary conventions or as social relationships—which have been alienated to components or to mere background.

As a general proposition this is only an emphasis, but it seems to me to suggest at once the point of break and the point of departure, in practical and theoretical work, within an active and self-renewing Marxist cultural tradition.

NOTES

1.. For a further discussion of the range of meanings in "determine" see *Keywords*, London 1976, pp. 87–91.

22

Mikhail Bakhtin/ V. N. Vološinov 1895–1975

Mikhail Bakhtin's greatest periods of productivity—the 1920s and 1930s—were troubled first by the effects of the Russian civil war and revolution and then by the repressive Stalin regime. During the 1920s, three books and several articles were published under the names of his friends; these include *The Formal Method in Literary Scholarship; Freudianism: A Critical Sketch; Marxism and the Philosophy of Language;* "Beyond the Social"; "Contemporary Vitalism"; and "Discourse in Life and Discourse in Art." In 1946 and 1949, the State Accrediting Bureau rejected his 1940 dissertation, "Rabelais and Folk culture of the Middle Ages and Renaissance," and it remained unpublished until 1965. Since that time it has gone through several editions in Japanese, German, and English.

Bakhtin's early work was devoted to developing a philosophy of language grounded in the interplay of communication. Bakhtin first defined the utterance as a dialogic process, involving both the speaker or writer and the implied or actual listener or reader, in his "Problems of Dostoevsky's Art" (1929). In the dialogic process, the importance of context becomes crucial to understanding the meaning of an utterance. Language, like all art, Bakhtin defined as an "exchange" or clash of values between a work and its audience. This definition of language, a "sociological poetics," views language as both determining and determined by the historical components of particular utterances. Consequently, it rejects both the formalism that treats a text as a static, purely linguistic object and the "vulgar" Marxism that would define a text as determined entirely by its creator and reader.

Bakhtin's first attempt to define a theory of the utterance appeared in "Discourse in Life and Discourse in Art" (1926) published under V. N. Volosinov's name but attributed by most scholars to Bakhtin. Bakhtin asserts here that context, including nonverbal elements, is an integral component rather than external to utterance. Artistic form, he concludes, is largely influenced by extra-artistic reality. In the course of his discussion, Bakhtin attacks the traditional sociological method of studying art. The Marxist terminology is used to enter into dialogue with the Marxist sociologies of literature; but Bakhtin uses this terminology to propose a brand of analysis more radical than that of the Marxists in its definition of language as an "event" in which both linguistic and social elements predetermine one another in a struggle toward textual meaning.

Discourse in Life and Discourse in Art (Concerning Sociological Poetics)

I

In the study of literature, the sociological method has been applied almost exclusively for treating historical questions while remaining virtually untouched with regard to the problems of so-called *theoretical poetics*—that whole area of issues involving artistic form and its various factors, style, and so forth.

A fallacious view, but one adhered to even by certain Marxists, has it that the sociological method becomes legitimate only at that point where poetic form acquires added complexity through the ideological factor (the content) and begins to develop historically in conditions of external social reality. Form in and of itself, according to this view, possesses its own special, not sociological but specifically artistic, nature and system of governance.

Such a view fundamentally contradicts the very bases of the Marxist method—its monism and its historicity. The consequence of this and similar views is that form and content, theory and history, are rent asunder.

But we cannot dismiss these fallacious views without further, more detailed inquiry; they are too characteristic for the whole of the modern study of the arts.

The most patent and consistent development of the point of view in question appeared recently in a work by Professor P. N. Sakulin.[1] Sakulin distinguishes two dimensions in literature and its history: the immanent and the causal. The immanent "artistic core" of literature possesses special structure and governance peculiar to itself alone; so endowed, it is capable of autonomous evolutionary development "by nature." But in the process of this development, literature becomes subject to the "causal" influence of the extraartistic social milieu. With the "immanent core" of literature, its structure and autonomous evolution, the sociologist can have nothing to do—those topics fall within the exclusive competence of theoretical and historical poetics and their special methods.[2] The sociological method can successfully study only the causal interaction between literature and its surrounding extraartistic social milieu. Moreover, immanent (nonsociological) analysis of the essence of literature, including its intrinsic, autonomous governance, must precede sociological analysis.[3]

Of course, no Marxist sociologist could agree with such an assertion. Nevertheless, it has to be admitted that sociology, up to the present moment, has dealt almost exclusively with concrete issues in history of literature and has not made a single serious attempt to utilize its methods in the study of the so-called "immanent" structure of a work of art. That structure has, in plain fact, been relegated to the province of aesthetic or psychological or other methods that have nothing in common with sociology.

To verify this fact we need only examine any modern work on poetics or even on the theory of art study in general. We will not find a trace of any application of sociological categories. Art is treated as if it were nonsociological "by nature" just exactly as is the physical or chemical structure of a body. Most West European and Russian scholars of the arts make precisely this claim regarding literature and art as a whole, and on this basis persistently defend the study of art as a special discipline against sociological approaches of any kind.

They motivate this claim of theirs in

approximately the following way. Every item that becomes the object of supply and demand, that is, that becomes a commodity, is subject, as concerns its value and its circulation within human society, to the governing socioeconomic laws. Let us suppose that we know those laws very well; still, despite that fact, we shall understand exactly nothing about the physical and chemical structure of the item in question. On the contrary, the study of commodities is itself in need of preliminary physical and chemical analysis of the given commodity. And the only persons competent to perform such analysis are physicists and chemists with the help of the specific methods of their fields. In the opinion of these art scholars, art stands in an analogous position. Art, too, once it becomes a social factor and becomes subject to the influence of other, likewise social, factors, takes its place, of course, within the overall system of sociological governance—but from that governance we shall never be able to derive art's *aesthetic essence*, just as we cannot derive the chemical formula for this or that commodity from the governing economic laws of commodity circulation. What art study and theoretical poetics are supposed to do is to seek such a formula for a work of art—one that is *specific* to art and independent of sociology.

This conception of the essence of art is, as we have said, fundamentally in contradiction with the bases of Marxism. To be sure, you will never find a chemical formula by the sociological method, but a scientific "formula" for any domain of *ideology* can be found, and can only be found, by the methods of sociology. All the other—"immanent"—methods are heavily involved in subjectivism and have been unable, to the present day, to break free of the fruitless controversy of opinions and points of view and, therefore, are least of all capable of finding anything even remotely resembling the rigorous and exact formulas of chemistry. Neither, of course, can the Marxist method claim to provide such a "formula"; the rigor and exactness of the natural sciences are impossible within the domain of ideological study due to the very nature of what it studies. But the closest approximation to genuine scientificness in the study of ideological creativity has become possible for the first time thanks to the sociological method in its Marxist conception. Physical and chemical bodies or substances exist outside human society as well as within it, but all products of ideological creativity arise in and for human society. Social definitions are not applicable from outside, as is the case with bodies and substances in nature—*ideological formations are intrinsically, immanently sociological*. No one is likely to dispute that point with respect to political and juridical forms—what possible nonsociological, immanent property could be found in them? The most subtle formal nuances of a law or of a political system are all equally amenable to the sociological method and only to it. But exactly the same thing is true for other ideological forms. They are all *sociological through and through*, even though their structure, mutable and complex as it is, lends itself to exact analysis only with enormous difficulty.

Art, too, is just as immanently social; the extraartistic social milieu, affecting art from outside, finds direct, intrinsic response within it. This is not a case of one foreign element affecting another but of one social formation affecting another social formation. The *aesthetic*, just as the juridical or the cognitive, is *only a variety of the social*. Theory of art, consequently, can only be a sociology of art.[4] No "immanent" tasks are left in its province.

II

If sociological analysis is to be properly and productively applied to the theory of art (poetics in particular), then two fallacious views that severely narrow the scope of art by operating exclusively with certain isolated factors must be rejected.

The first view can be defined as the *fetishization of the artistic work artifact.* This fetishism is the prevailing attitude in the study of art at the present time. The field of investigation is restricted to the work of art itself, which is analyzed in such a way as if everything in art were exhausted by it alone. The creator of the work and the work's contemplators remain outside the field of investigation.

The second point of view, conversely, restricts itself to the study of the psyche of the creator or of the contemplator (more often than not, it simply equates the two). For it, all art is exhausted by the experiences of the person doing the contemplating or doing the creating.

Thus, for the one point of view the object of study is only the structure of the work artifact, while for the other it is only the individual psyche of the creator or contemplator.

The first point of view advances the material to the forefront of aesthetic investigation. Form, understood very narrowly as the form of the material—that which organizes it into a single unified and complete artifact—becomes the main and very nearly exclusive object of study.

A variety of the first point of view is the so-called formal method. For the formal method, a poetic work is verbal material organized by form in some particular way. Moreover, it takes *the verbal* not as a sociological phenomenon but from an abstract linguistic point of view. That it should adopt just such a point of view is quite understandable: Verbal discourse, taken in the broader sense as a phenomenon of cultural communication, ceases to be something self-contained and can no longer be understood independently of the social situation that engenders it.

The first point of view cannot be consistently followed out to the end. The problem is that if one remains within the confines of the artifact aspect of art, there is no way of indicating even such things as the boundaries of the material or which of its features have artistic significance. The material in and of itself directly merges with the extraartistic milieu surrounding it and has an infinite number of aspects and definitions—in terms of mathematics, physics, chemistry, and so forth as well as of linguistics. However far we go in analyzing all the properties of the material and all the possible combinations of those properties, we shall never be able to find their aesthetic significance unless we slip in the contraband of another point of view that does not belong within the framework of analysis of the material. Similarly, however far we go in analyzing the chemical structure of a body or substance, we shall never understand its value and significance as a commodity unless we draw economics into the picture.

The attempt of the second view to find the aesthetic in the individual psyche of the creator or contemplator is equally vain. To continue our economic analogy, we might say that such a thing is similar to the attempt to analyze the individual psyche of a proletarian in order thereby to disclose the objective production relations that determine his position in society.

In the final analysis, both points of view are guilty of the same fault: *They attempt to discover the whole in the part,* that is, they take the structure of a part, abstractly divorced from the whole, and claim it as the structure of the whole. Meanwhile, "the artistic" in its total integrity is not located in the artifact and not located in the separately considered psyches of creator and contemplator; it encompasses all three of these factors. It is a *special form of interrelationship between creator and contemplator fixed in a work of art.*

This *artistic communication* stems from the basis common to it and other social forms, but, at the same time, it retains, as do all other forms, its own uniqueness; it is a special type of communication, possessing a form of its own peculiar to itself. *To understand this special form of social communication realized and fixed in the material of a work of art—that precisely is the task of sociological poetics.*

A work of art, viewed outside this communication and independently of it, is simply a physical artifact or an exercise in linguistics. It becomes art only in the process of the interaction between creator and contemplator, as the essential factor in this interaction. Everything in the material of a work of art that cannot be drawn into the communication between creator and contemplator, that cannot become the "medium," the means of their communication, cannot be the recipient of artistic value, either.

Those methods that ignore the social essence of art and attempt to find its nature and distinguishing features only in the organization of the work artifact are in actuality obliged to project the social interrelationship of creator and contemplator into various aspects of the material and into various devices for structuring the material. In exactly the same way, psychological aesthetics projects the same social relations into the individual psyche of the perceiver. This projection distorts the integrity of these interrelationships and gives a false picture of both the material and the psyche.

Aesthetic communication, fixed in a work of art, is, as we have already said, entirely unique and irreducible to other types of ideological communication such as the political, the juridical, the moral, and so on. If political communication establishes corresponding institutions and, at the same time, juridical forms, aesthetic communication organizes only a work of art. If the latter rejects this task and begins to aim at creating even the most transitory of political organizations or any other ideological form, then by that very fact it ceases to be aesthetic communication and relinquishes its unique character. *What characterizes aesthetic communication is the fact that it is wholly absorbed in the creation of a work of art, and in its continuous re-creations in the co-creation of contemplators, and does not require any other kind of objectification.* But, needless to say, this unique form of communication does not exist *in isolation;* it participates in the unitary flow of social life, it reflects the common economic basis, and it engages in interaction and exchange with other forms of communication.

The purpose of the present study is to try to reach an understanding of the poetic utterance as a form of this special, verbally implemented aesthetic communication. But in order to do so, we must first analyze in detail certain aspects of verbal utterances outside the realm of art—utterances in the *speech of everyday life and behavior,* for in such speech are already embedded the bases, the potentialities of artistic form. Moreover, the social essence of verbal discourse stands out here in sharper relief and the connection between an utterance and the surrounding social milieu lends itself more easily to analysis.

III

In life, verbal discourse is clearly not self-sufficient. It arises out of an extraverbal pragmatic situation and maintains the closest possible connection with that situation. Moreover, such discourse is directly informed by life itself and cannot be divorced from life without losing its import.

The kind of characterizations and evaluations of pragmatic, behavioral utterances we are likely to make are such things as: "that's a lie," "that's the truth," "that's a daring thing to say," "you can't say that," and so on and so forth.

All these and similar evaluations, whatever the criteria that govern them (ethical, cognitive, political, or other), take in a good deal more than what is enclosed within the strictly verbal (linguistic) factors of the utterance. *Together with the verbal factors, they also take in the extraverbal situation of the utterance.* These judgments and evaluations refer to a certain whole wherein the verbal discourse directly engages an event in life and merges with that event, forming an indissoluble unity. The verbal discourse itself, taken in isolation as a purely linguistic phenomenon, cannot, of course, be true or false, daring or diffident.

How does verbal discourse in life relate to the extraverbal situation that has engendered it? Let us analyze this matter, using an intentionally simplified example for the purpose.

Two people are sitting in a room. They are both silent. Then one of them says, "Well!" The other does not respond.

For us, as outsiders, this entire "conversation" is utterly incomprehensible. Taken in isolation, the utterance "Well!" is empty and unintelligible. Nevertheless, this peculiar colloquy of two persons, consisting of only one—although, to be sure, one expressively intoned—word, does make perfect sense, is fully meaningful and complete.

In order to disclose the sense and meaning of this colloquy, we must analyze it. But what is it exactly that we can subject to analysis? Whatever pains we take with the purely verbal part of the utterance, however subtly we define the phonetic, morphological, and semantic factors of the word *well,* we shall still not come a single step closer to an understanding of the whole sense of the colloquy.

Let us suppose that the intonation with which this word was pronounced is known to us: indignation and reproach moderated by a certain amount of humor. This intonation somewhat fills in the semantic void of the adverb *well* but still does not reveal the meaning of the whole.

What is it we lack, then? We lack the "extraverbal context" that made the word *well* a meaningful locution for the listener. This *extraverbal context* of the utterance is comprised of three factors: (1) the *common spatial purview* of the interlocutors (the unity of the visible—in this case, the room, the window, and so on), (2) the interlocutors' *common knowledge and understanding of the situation,* and (3) their *common evaluation* of that situation.

At the time the colloquy took place, both interlocutors *looked up* at the window and *saw* that it had begun to snow; both *knew* that it was already May and that it was high time for spring to come; finally, *both* were *sick and tired* of the protracted winter—*they both were looking forward* to spring and *both were bitterly disappointed* by the late snowfall. On this "jointly seen" (snowflakes outside the window), "jointly known" (the time of year—May) and "unanimously evaluated" (winter wearied of, spring looked forward to)—on all this the utterance *directly depends,* all this is seized in its actual, living import—is its very sustenance. And yet all this remains without verbal specification or articulation. The snowflakes remain outside the window; the date, on the page of a calendar; the evaluation, in the psyche of the speaker; and nevertheless, all this is *assumed* in the word *well.*

Now that we have been let in on the "assumed," that is, now that we know the *shared spatial and ideational purview,* the whole sense of the utterance "Well!" is perfectly clear to us and we also understand its intonation.

How does the extraverbal purview relate to the verbal discourse, how does the said relate to the unsaid?

First of all, it is perfectly obvious that, in the given case, the discourse does not at all reflect the extraverbal situation in the way a mirror reflects an object. Rather, the discourse here *resolves the situation*, bringing it to an *evaluative conclusion*, as it were. Far more often, behavioral utterances actively continue and develop a situation, adumbrate a plan for future action, and organize that action. But for us it is another aspect of the behavioral utterance that is of special importance: Whatever kind it be, the behavioral utterance always joins the participants in the situation together as *co-participants* who know, understand, and evaluate the situation in like manner. *The utterance*, consequently, *depends on their real, material appurtenance to one and the same segment of being and gives this material commonness ideological expression and further ideological development.*

Thus, the extraverbal situation is far from being merely the external cause of an utterance—it does not operate on the utterance from outside, as if it were a mechanical force. Rather, *the situation enters into the utterance as an essential constitutive part of the structure of its import.* Consequently, a behavioral utterance as a meaningful whole is comprised of two parts: (1) the part realized or actualized in words and (2) the assumed part. On this basis, the behavioral utterance can be likened to the enthymeme.[5]

However, it is an enthymeme of a special order. The very term enthymeme (literally translated from the Greek, something located in the heart or mind) sounds a bit too psychological. One might be led to think of the situation as something in the mind of the speaker on the order of a subjective-psychical act (a thought, idea, feeling). But that is not the case. The individual and subjective are backgrounded here by *the social and objective.* What *I* know, see, want, love, and so on cannot be assumed. Only what all of us speakers know, see, love, recognize—only those points on which we are all united can become the assumed part of an utterance. Furthermore, this fundamentally social phenomenon is completely objective; it consists, above all, of *the material unity of world that enters the speakers' purview* (in our example, the room, the snow outside the window, and so on) and *of the unity of the real conditions of life* that *generate a community of value judgments*—the speakers' belonging to the same family, profession, class, or other social group, and their belonging to the same time period (the speakers are, after all, contemporaries). Assumed value judgments are, therefore, not individual emotions but regular and essential social acts. *Individual* emotions can come into play only as overtones accompanying the *basic tone of social evaluation.* "I" can realize itself verbally only on the basis of "we."

Thus, every utterance in the business of life is an objective social enthymeme. It is something like a "password" known only to those who belong to the same social purview. The distinguishing characteristic of behavioral utterances consists precisely in the fact that they make myriad connections with the extraverbal context of life and, once severed from that context, lose almost all their import—a person ignorant of the immediate pragmatic context will not understand these utterances.

This immediate context may be of varying scope. In our example, the context is extremely narrow: It is *circumscribed by the room and the moment of occurrence,* and the utterance makes an intelligible statement only for the two persons involved. However, the unified purview on which an utterance depends can expand in both space and time: *The "assumed" may be that of the family, clan, nation, class and may encompass days or years or whole epochs.* The wider the overall purview and its corresponding social group, the more *constant* the assumed factors in an utterance become.

When the assumed real purview of an utterance is narrow, when, as in our example, it coincides with the actual purview of two people sitting in the same room and seeing the same thing, then even the most momentary change within that purview can become the assumed. Where the purview is wider, the utterance can operate only on the basis of constant, stable factors in life and substantive, fundamental social evaluations.

Especially great importance, in this case, belongs to assumed evaluations. The fact is that all the basic social evaluations that stem directly from the distinctive characteristics of the given social group's economic being are usually not articulated: They have entered the flesh and blood of all representatives of the group; they organize behavior and actions; they have merged, as it were, with the objects and phenomena to which they correspond, and for that reason they are in no need of special verbal formulation. We seem to perceive the value of a thing together with its being as one of its qualities, we seem, for instance, to sense, along with its warmth and light, the sun's value for us, as well. All the phenomena that surround us are similarly merged with value judgments. If a value judgment is in actual fact conditioned by the being of a given community, it becomes a matter of dogmatic belief, something taken for granted and not subject to discussion. On the contrary, whenever some basic value judgment is verbalized and justified, we may be certain that it has already become dubious, has separated from its referent, has ceased to organize life, and, consequently, has lost its connection with the existential conditions of the given group.

A healthy social value judgment remains within life and from that position organizes the very form of an utterance and its intonation, but it does not at all aim to find suitable expression in the content side of discourse. Once a value judgment shifts from formal factors to content, we may be sure that a reevaluation is in the offing. Thus, a viable value judgment exists wholly without incorporation into the content of discourse and is not derivable therefrom; instead, it determines the *very selection of the verbal material and the form of the verbal whole*. It finds its purest expression in intonation. Intonation establishes a firm link between verbal discourse and the extraverbal context—genuine, living intonation moves verbal discourse beyond the border of the verbal, so to speak.

Let us stop to consider in somewhat greater detail the connection between intonation and the pragmatic context of life in the example utterance we have been using. This will allow us to make a number of important observations about the social nature of intonation.

IV

First of all, we must emphasize that the word *well*—a word virtually empty semantically—cannot to any extent predetermine intonation through its own content. Any intonation—joyful, sorrowful, contemptuous, and so on—can freely and easily operate in this word; it all depends on the context in which the word appears. In our example, the context determining the intonation used (indignant-reproachful but moderated by humor) is provided entirely by the extraverbal situation that we have already analyzed, since, in this instance, there is no immediate verbal context. We might say in advance that even were such an immediate verbal context present and even, moreover, if that context were entirely sufficient from all other points of view, the intonation would still take us beyond its confines. Intonation can be thoroughly understood only when one is in touch with the assumed value judgments of the given social group, whatever the scope of that group might be. *Intonation always lies on the border of the verbal and the nonverbal, the said and the unsaid.* In intonation, discourse comes directly into contact with life. And it is in intonation above all that the speaker comes into contact with the listener or listeners—intonation is social par excellence. It is especially sensitive to all the vibrations in the social atmosphere surrounding the speaker.

The intonation in our example stemmed from the interlocutors' shared yearning for spring and shared disgruntlement over the protracted winter. This commonness of evaluations assumed between them supplied the basis for the intonation, the basis for the distinctness and certitude of its major tonality. Given an atmosphere of sympathy, the intonation could freely undergo deployment and differentiation within the range of the major tone. But if there were no such firmly dependable "choral support," the intonation would have gone in a different direction and taken on different tones—perhaps those of provocation or annoyance with the listener, or perhaps the intonation would simply have contracted and been reduced to the minimum. When a person anticipates the disagreement of his interlocutor or, at any rate, is uncertain or doubtful of his agreement, he intones his words differently. We shall see later that not only intonation but the whole formal structure of speech depends to a significant degree on what the relation of the utterance is to the assumed community of values belonging to the social milieu wherein the discourse figures. A creatively productive, assured, and rich intonation is possible only on the basis of presupposed "choral support." Where such support is lacking, the voice falters and its intonational richness is reduced, as happens, for instance, when a person laughing suddenly realizes that he is laughing alone—his laughter either ceases or degenerates, becomes forced, loses its assurance and clarity and its ability to generate joking and amusing talk. *The commonness of assumed basic value judgments constitutes the canvas upon which living human speech embroiders the designs of intonation.*

Intonation's set toward possible sympathy, toward "choral support," does not exhaust its social nature. It is only one side of intonation—the side turned toward the listener. But intonation contains yet another extremely important factor for the sociology of discourse.

If we scrutinize the intonation of our example, we will notice that it has one "mysterious" feature requiring special explanation.

In point of fact, the intonation of the word *well* voiced not only passive dissatisfaction with an occurring event (the snowfall) but also active indignation and reproach. To whom is this reproach addressed? Clearly not to the listener but to somebody else. This tack of the intonational movement patently makes an opening in the situation for a *third participant.* Who is this third participant? Who is the recipient of the reproach? The snow? Nature? Fate, perhaps?

Of course, in our simplified example of a behavioral utterance the third participant—the "hero" of this verbal production—has not yet assumed full and definitive shape; the intonation has demarcated a definite place for the hero but his semantic equivalent has not been supplied and he remains nameless. Intonation has established an active attitude toward the referent, toward the object of the utterance, an attitude of a kind verging on *apostrophe* to that object as the incarnate, living culprit, while the listener—

the second participant—is, as it were, called in *as witness and ally.*

Almost any example of live intonation in emotionally charged behavioral speech proceeds as if it addressed, behind inanimate objects and phenomena, animate participants and agents in life; in other words, it has an inherent *tendency toward personification.* If the intonation is not held in check, as in our example, by a certain amount of irony, then it becomes the source of the mythological image, the incantation, the prayer, as was the case in the earliest stages of culture. In our case, however, we have to do with an extremely important phenomenon of language creativity—*the intonational metaphor:* The intonation of the utterance "Well!" makes the word sound as if it were reproaching the living culprit of the late snowfall—winter. We have in our example an instance of *pure* intonational metaphor wholly confined within the intonation; but latent within it, in cradle, so to speak, there exists the possibility of the usual *semantic metaphor.* Were this possibility to be realized, the word *well* would expand into some such metaphorical expression as: "What a *stubborn winter! It just won't give up,* though goodness knows it's time!" But this possibility, inherent in the intonation, remained unrealized and the utterance made do with the almost semantically inert adverb *well.*

It should be noted that the intonation in behavioral speech, on the whole, is a great deal more metaphorical than the words used: The aboriginal myth-making spirit seems to have remained alive in it. Intonation makes it sound as if the world surrounding the speaker were still full of animate forces—it threatens and rails against or adores and cherishes inanimate objects and phenomena, whereas the usual metaphors of colloquial speech for the most part have been effaced and the words become semantically spare and prosaic.

Close kinship unites the intonational metaphor with the *gesticulatory metaphor* (indeed, words were themselves originally lingual gestures constituting one component of a complex, omnicorporeal gesture)—the term "gesture" being understood here in a broad sense including miming as facial gesticulation. Gesture, just as intonation, requires the choral support of surrounding persons; only in an atmosphere of sympathy is free and assured gesture possible. Furthermore, and again just as intonation, gesture makes an opening in the situation and introduces a third participant—the hero. Gesture always has latent within itself the germ of attack or defence, of threat or caress, with the contemplator and listener relegated to the role of ally or witness. Often, the "hero" is merely some inanimate thing, some occurrence or circumstance in life. How often we shake our fist at "someone" in a fit of temper or simply scowl at empty space, and there is literally nothing we cannot smile at—the sun, trees, thoughts.

A point that must constantly be kept in mind (something that psychological aesthetics often forgets to do) is this: *Intonation and gesture are active and objective by tendency.* They not only express the passive mental state of the speaker but also always have embedded in them a living, forceful relation with the external world and with the social milieu—enemies, friends, allies. When a person intones and gesticulates, he assumes an active social position with respect to certain specific values, and this position is conditioned by the very bases of his social being. It is precisely this objective and sociological, and not subjective and psychological, aspect of intonation and gesture that should interest theorists of the various relevant arts, inasmuch as it is here that reside forces in the arts that are responsible for aesthetic creativity and that devise and organize artistic form.

As we see then, every instance of intonation is oriented *in two directions*: with respect to the listener as ally or witness and with respect to the object of the utterance as the third, living participant whom the intonation scolds or caresses, denigrates or magnifies. *This double social orientation is what determines all aspects of intonation and makes it intelligible.* And this very same thing is true for all the other factors of verbal utterances: They are all organized and in every way given shape in the same process of the speaker's *double orientation*; this social origin is only most easily detectable in intonation since it is the verbal factor of greatest sensitivity, elasticity, and freedom.

Thus, as we now have a right to claim, *any locution actually said aloud or written down for intelligible communication* (i.e., anything but words merely reposing in a dictionary) *is the expression and product of the social interaction of three participants: the speaker* (author), *the listener* (reader), and *the topic* (the *who or what*) *of speech* (the hero). Verbal discourse is a social event; it is not self-contained in the sense of some abstract linguistic quantity, nor can it be derived psychologically from the speaker's subjective consciousness taken in isolation. Therefore, both the formal linguistic approach and the psychological approach equally miss the mark: The concrete, sociological essence of verbal discourse, that which alone can make it true or false, banal or distinguished, necessary or unnecessary, remains beyond the ken and reach of both these points of view. Needless to say, it is also this very same "social soul" of verbal discourse that makes it beautiful or ugly, that is, that makes it artistically meaningful, as well. To be sure, once subordinated to the basic and more concrete sociological approach, both abstract points of view—the formal linguistic and the psychological—retain their value. Their collaboration is even absolutely indispensable; but separately, each by itself in isolation, they are inert.

The concrete utterance (and not the linguistic abstraction) is born, lives, and dies in the process of social interaction between the participants of the utterance. Its form and meaning are determined basically by the form and character of this interaction. When we cut the utterance off from the real grounds that nurture it, we lose the key to its form as well as to its import—all we have left is an abstract linguistic shell or an equally abstract semantic scheme (the banal "idea of the work" with which earlier theorists and historians of literature dealt)—two abstractions that are not mutually joinable because there are no concrete grounds for their organic synthesis.

It remains for us now only to sum up our short analysis of utterance in life and of those *artistic potentials, those rudiments of future form and content*, that we have detected in it.

The meaning and import of an utterance in life (of whatever particular kind that utterance may be) do not coincide with the purely verbal composition of the utterance. Articulated words are impregnated with assumed and unarticulated qualities. What are called the "understanding" and "evaluation" of an utterance (agreement or disagreement) always encompass the extraverbal pragmatic situation together with the verbal discourse proper. Life, therefore, does not affect an utterance from without; it penetrates and exerts an influence on an utterance from within, as that unity and commonness of being surrounding the speakers and that unity and commonness of essential social value judgments issuing from that being without all of which no intelligible utterance is possible. Intonation lies on the border between life and the verbal aspect of the utterance; it, as it were, pumps energy from a life situation into the verbal discourse, it endows everything linguistically stable with living historical momentum and uniqueness. Finally, the utterance reflects the social interaction of the speaker, listener, and hero as the product and fixation in verbal material of the act of living communication among them.

Verbal discourse is like a "*scenario*" of a certain event. A viable understanding of the whole import of discourse must *reproduce* this event of the mutual relationship between speakers, must, as it were, "reenact" it, with the person wishing to understand taking upon himself the role of the listener. But in order to carry out that role, he must distinctly understand the positions of the other two participants, as well.

For the linguistic point of view, neither this event nor its living participants exist, of course; the linguistic point of view deals with abstract, bare words and their equally abstract components (phonetic, morphological, and so on). Therefore, the *total import of discourse* and *its ideological value*—the cognitive, political, aesthetic, or other—are inaccessible to it. Just as there cannot be a linguistic logic or a linguistic politics, so there cannot be a linguistic poetics.

V

In what way does an artistic verbal utterance—a complete work of poetic art—differ from an utterance in the business of life?

It is immediately obvious that discourse in art neither is nor can be so closely dependent on all the factors of the extraverbal context, on all that is seen and known, as in life. A poetic work cannot rely on objects and events in the immediate milieu as things "understood," without making even the slightest allusion to them in the verbal part of the utterance. In this regard, a great deal more is demanded of discourse in literature: Much that could remain outside the utterance in life must find verbal representation. Nothing must be left unsaid in a poetic work from the pragmatic-referential point of view.

Does it follow from this that in literature the speaker, listener, and hero come in contact for the first time, knowing nothing about one another, having no purview in common, and are, therefore, bereft of anything on which they can jointly rely or hold assumptions about? Certain writers on these topics are inclined to think so.

But in actuality a poetic work, too, is closely enmeshed in the unarticulated context of life. If it were true that author, listener, and hero, as abstract persons, come into contact for the first time devoid of any unifying purview and that the words used are taken as from a dictionary, then it is hardly likely that even a nonpoetic work would result, and certainly not a poetic one. Science does to some degree approach this extreme—a scientific definition has a minimum of the "assumed"; but it would be possible to prove that even science cannot do entirely without the assumed.

In literature, assumed value judgments play a role of particular importance. We might say that *a poetic work is a powerful condenser of unarticulated social evaluations*—each word is saturated with them. *It is these social evaluations that organize form as their direct expression.*

Value judgments, first of all, determine the author's *selection of words* and the reception of that selection (the coselection) by the listener. The poet, after all, selects words not from the dictionary but from the context of life where words have been steeped in and become permeated with value judgments. Thus, he selects the value judgments associated with the words and does so, moreover, from the standpoint of the incarnated bearers of those value judgments. It can be said that the poet constantly works in conjunction with his listener's sympathy or antipathy, agreement or disagreement. Furthermore, evaluation is operative also with regard to the object of the utterance—the hero. The simple selection of an epithet or a metaphor is already an active evaluative act with orientation in both directions—toward the listener and toward the hero. *Listener and hero are constant participants in the creative event,* which does not for a single instant cease to be an event of living communication involving all three.

The problem of sociological poetics would be resolved if each factor of form could be explained as the active expression of evaluation in these two directions—toward the listener and toward the object of utterance, the hero.[6] But at the present time the data are too insufficient for such a task to be carried out. All that can be done is to map out at least the preliminary steps leading toward that goal.

The formalistic aesthetics of the present day defines artistic forms as *the form of the material.* If this point of view be carried out consistently, content must necessarily be ignored, since no room is left for it in the poetic work; at best, it may be regarded as a factor of the material and in that way, indirectly, be organized by artistic form in its direct bearing on the material.[7]

So understood, form loses its active evaluative character and becomes merely a stimulus of passive feelings of pleasure in the perceiver.

It goes without saying that form is realized with the help of the material—it is fixed in material; but by virtue of *its significance* it exceeds the material. *The meaning, the import of form has to do not with the material but with the content.* So, for instance, the form of a statue may be said to be not the form of the marble but the form of the human body, with the added qualification that the form "heroicizes" the human depicted or "dotes upon" him or, perhaps, denigrates him (the caricature style in the plastic arts); that is, the form expresses some specific evaluation of the object depicted.

The evaluative significance of form is especially obvious in verse. Rhythm and other formal elements of verse overtly express a certain active attitude toward the object depicted: The form celebrates or laments or ridicules that object.

Psychological aesthetics calls this the "emotional factor" of form. But it is not the psychological side of the matter that is important for us, not the identity of the psychical forces that take part in the creation of form and the cocreative perception of form. What is important is the significance of these experiences, their active role, their bearing on content. Through the agency of artistic form the creator takes up *an active position with respect to content.* The form in and of itself need not necessarily be pleasurable (the hedonistic explanation of form is absurd); what it must be is *a convincing evaluation* of the content. So, for instance, while the form of "the enemy" might even be repulsive, the positive state, the pleasure that the contemplator derives in the end, is a consequence of the fact that the form is *appropriate to the enemy* and that it is *technically perfect* in its realization through the agency of the material. It is in these two aspects that form should be studied: with respect to content, as its ideological evaluation, and with respect to the material, as the technical realization of that evaluation.

The ideological evaluation expressed through form is not at all supposed to transpose into content as a maxim or a proposition of a moral, political, or other kind. The evaluation should remain in the rhythm, *in the very evaluative impetus* of the epithet or metaphor, *in the manner of the unfolding* of the depicted event; it is supposed to be realized by the formal means of the material only. But, at the same time, while not transposing into content, the form must not lose its connection with content, its correlation with it, otherwise it becomes a technical experiment devoid of any real artistic import.

The general definition of style that classical and neoclassical poetics had advanced, together with the basic division of style into "high" and "low," aptly brings out precisely this active evaluative nature of artistic form. The structure of form is indeed *hierarchical,* and in this respect it comes close to political and juridical gradations. Form similarly creates, in an artistically configured content, a complex system of hierarchical interrelations: Each of its elements—an epithet or a metaphor, for instance—either raises the designatum to a higher degree or lowers it or equalizes it. The selection of a hero or an event determines from the very outset the general level of the form and the admissibility of this or that particular set of configurating devices. And this basic requirement of *stylistic suitability* has in *view the evaluative-hierarchical suitability of form and content.* They must be *equally adequate* for one another. The selection of content and the selection of form constitute one and the same act establishing the creator's basic position; and in that act one and the same social evaluation finds expression.

VI

Sociological analysis can take its starting point only, of course, from the purely verbal, linguistic makeup of a work, but it must not and cannot confine itself within those limits, as linguistic poetics does. Artistic contemplation via the reading of a poetic work does, to be sure, start from the grapheme (the visual image of written or printed words), but at the very instant of perception this visual image gives way to and is very nearly obliterated by other verbal factors—articulation, sound image, intonation, meaning—and these factors eventually take us beyond the border of the verbal altogether. And so it can be said that *the purely linguistic factor of a work is to the artistic whole as the grapheme is to the verbal whole.* In poetry, as in life, verbal discourse is a *"scenario" of an event.* Competent artistic perception reenacts it, sensitively surmising from the words and the forms of their organization the specific, living interrelations of the author with the world he depicts and entering into those interrelations as a third participant (the listener's role). Where linguistic analysis sees only words and the interrelations of their abstract factors (phonetic, morphological, syntactic, and so on), there, for living artistic perception and for concrete sociological analysis, relations among *people* stand revealed, relations merely reflected and fixed in verbal material. Verbal discourse is the skeleton that takes on living flesh only in the process of creative perception—consequently, only in the process of living social communication.

In what follows here we shall attempt to provide a brief and preliminary sketch of the essential factors in the interrelationships of the participants in an artistic event—those factors that determine the broad and basic lines of poetic style as a social phenomenon. Any further detailing of these factors would, of course, go beyond the scope of the present essay.

The author, hero, and listener that we have been talking about all this time are to be understood not as entities outside the artistic event but only as entities of the very perception of an artistic work, entities that are essential constitutive factors of the work. They are the living forces that determine form and style and are distinctly detectable by any competent contemplator. This means that all those definitions that a historian of literature and society might apply to the author and his heroes—the author's biography, the precise qualifications of heroes in chronological and sociological terms and so on—are excluded here: They do not enter directly into the structure of the work but remain outside it. The listener, too, is taken here as the listener whom the author himself takes into account, the one toward whom the work is oriented and who, consequently, intrinsically determines the work's structure. Therefore, we do not at all mean the actual people who in fact made up the reading public of the author in question.

The first form-determining factor of content is the *evaluative rank* of the depicted event and its agent—the hero (whether named or not), taken in strict correlation with the rank of the creator and contemplator. Here we have to do, just as in legal or political life, with a *two-sided relationship;* master-slave, ruler-subject, comrade-comrade, and the like.

The basic stylistic tone of an utterance is therefore determined above all by who is talked about and what his relation is to the speaker—whether he is higher or lower than or equal to him on the scale of the social hierarchy. King, father, brother, slave, comrade, and so on, as heroes of an utterance, also determine its formal structure. And this *specific hierarchical weight* of the hero is determined, in its turn, by that unarticulated context of basic evaluations in which a poetic work, too, participates. Just as the "intonational metaphor" in our example utterance from life established an organic relationship with the object of the utterance, so also all elements of the style of a poetic work are permeated with the author's evaluative attitude toward content and express his basic social position. Let us stress once again that we have in mind here not those ideological evaluations that are incorporated into the content of a work in the form of judgments or conclusions but that deeper, more ingrained kind of *evaluation via form* that finds expression in the very manner in which the artistic material is viewed and deployed.

Certain languages, Japanese in particular, possess a rich and varied store of special lexical and grammatical forms to be used in strict accordance with the rank of the hero of the utterance (language etiquette).[8]

We might say that what is still a *matter of grammar* for the Japanese has already become for us a *matter of style.* The most important stylistic components of the heroic epic, the tragedy, the ode, and so forth are determined precisely by the hierarchical status of the object of the utterance with respect to the speaker.

It should not be supposed that this hierarchical interdefinition of creator and hero has been eliminated from modern literature. It has been made more complex and does not reflect the contemporary sociopolitical hierarchy with the same degree of distinctness as, say, classicism did in its time—but *the very principle of change of style in accordance with change in the social value of the hero of the utterance* certainly remains in force as before. After all, it is not his personal enemy that the poet hates, not his personal friend that his form treats with love and tenderness, not the events from his private life that he rejoices or sorrows over. Even if a poet has in fact borrowed his passion in good measure from the circumstances of his own private life, still, he must *socialize* that passion and, consequently, elaborate the event with which it corresponds to the level of *social significance.*

The second style-determining factor in the interrelationship between hero and creator is *the degree of their proximity* to one another. All languages possess direct grammatical means of expression for this aspect: first, second, and third persons and variable sentence structure in accordance with the person of the subject ("I" or "you" or "he"). The form of a proposition about a third person, the form of an address to a second person, the form of an utterance about oneself (and their modifications) are already different in terms of grammar. Thus, here *the very structure of the language reflects the event of the speakers' interrelationship.*

Certain languages have purely grammatical forms capable of conveying with even greater flexibility the nuances of the speakers' social interrelationship and the various degrees of their proximity. From this angle, the so-called "inclusive" and "exclusive" forms of the plural in certain languages present a case of special interest. For example, if a speaker using the form *we* has the listener in mind and includes him in the subject of the proposition, then he uses one form, whereas if he means himself and some other person (*we* in the sense of *I* and *he*), he uses a different form. Such is the use of the dual in certain Australian languages, for instance. There, too, are found two special forms of the trial: one meaning *I and you and he;* the other, *I and he and he* (with *you*—the listener—excluded).[9]

In European languages these and similar interrelationships between speakers have no special grammatical expression. The character of these languages is more abstract and not so capable of reflecting the situation of utterance via grammatical structure. However, interrelationships between speakers do find expression in these languages—and expression of far greater subtletly and diversity—*in the style and intonation of utterances.* Here the social situation of creativity finds thoroughgoing reflection in a work by means of purely artistic devices.

The form of a poetic work is determined, therefore, in many of its factors by *how the author perceives his hero*—the hero who serves as the organizing center of the utterance. The form of *objective narration,* the form of *address of apostrophe* (prayer, hymn, certain lyric forms), the form of *self-expression* (confession, autobiography, lyric avowal—an important form of the love lyric) are determined precisely by the *degree of proximity between author and hero.*

Both the factors we have indicated—the hierarchical value of the hero and the degree of his proximity to the author—are as yet insufficient, taken independently and in isolation, for the determination of artistic form. The fact is that a third participant is constantly in play as well—the listener, whose presence affects the interrelationship of the other two (creator and hero).

The interrelationship of author and hero never, after all, actually is an intimate relationship of two; all the while form makes provision for the third participant—the listener—who exerts crucial influence on all the other factors of the work.

In what way can the listener determine the style of a poetic utterance? Here, too, we must distinguish two basic factors: first, the listener's proximity to the author and, second, his relation to the hero. Nothing is more perilous for aesthetics than to ignore the autonomous role of the listener. A very commonly held opinion has it that the listener is to be regarded as equal to the author, excepting the latter's technical performance, and that the position of a competent listener is supposed to be a simple reproduction of the author's position. In actual fact this is not so. Indeed, the opposite may sooner be said to be true: The listener never equals the author. The listener has *his own independent place* in the event of artistic creation; he must occupy a special, and, what is more, a *two-sided* position in it—with respect to the author and with respect to the hero—and it is this position that has determinative effect on the style of an utterance.

How does the author sense his listener? In our example of an utterance in the business of life, we have seen to what degree the presumed agreement or disagreement of the listener shaped an utterance. Exactly the same is true regarding all factors of form. To put it figuratively, the listener normally stands *side by side* with the author as his ally, but this classical positioning of the listener is by no means always the case.

Sometimes the listener begins to lean toward the hero of the utterance. The most unmistakable and typical expression of this is the polemical style that aligns the hero and the listener together. Satire, too, can involve the listener as someone calculated to be close to the hero ridiculed and not to the ridiculing author. This constitutes a sort of *inclusive form of ridicule* distinctly different from the exclusive form where the listener is in solidarity with the jeering author. In romanticism, an interesting phenomenon can be observed where the author *concludes an alliance,* as it were, *with his hero against the listener* (Friedrich Schlegel's *Lucinda* and, in Russian literature, *Hero of Our Time* to some extent).

Of very special character and interest for analysis is the author's sense of his listener in the forms of the confession and the autobiography. All shades of feeling from humble reverence before the listener, as before a veritable judge, to contemptuous distrust and hostility can have determinative effect on the style of a confession or an autobiography. Extremely interesting material for the illustration of this contention can be found in the works of Dostoevskij. The confessional style of Ippolit's "article" (*The Idiot*) is determined by an almost extreme degree of contemptuous distrust and hostility directed toward all who are to hear this dying confession. Similar tones, but somewhat softened, determine the style of *Notes from Underground*. The style of "Stavrogin's Confession" (*The Possessed*) displays far greater trust in the listener and acknowledgments of his rights, although here too, from time to time, a feeling almost of hatred for the listener erupts, which is what is responsible for the jaggedness of its style. Playing the fool, as a special form of utterance, one, to be sure, lying on the periphery of the artistic, is determined above all by an extremely complex and tangled conflict of the speaker with the listener.

A form especially sensitive to the position of the listener is the lyric. The underlying condition for lyric intonation is *the absolute certainty of the listener's sympathy*. Should any doubt on this score creep into the lyric situation, the style of the lyric changes drastically. This conflict with the listener finds its most egregious expression in so-called lyric irony (Heine, and in modern poetry, Laforgue, Annenskij, and others). The form of irony in general is conditioned by a social conflict: It is the encounter in one voice of two incarnate value judgments and their interference with one another.

In modern aesthetics a special, so-called juridical theory of tragedy was proposed, a theory amounting essentially to the attempt to conceive of *the structure of a tragedy as the structure of a trial in court.*[10]

The interrelationship of hero and chorus, on the one side, and the overall position of the listener, on the other, do indeed, to a degree, lend themselves to juridical interpretation. But of course this can only be meant as *an analogy*. The important common feature of tragedy—indeed of any work of art—and judicial process comes down merely to the existence of "sides," that is, the occupying by the several participants of *different positions*. The terms, so widespread in literary terminology, that define the poet as "judge," "exposer," "witness," "defender," and even "executioner" (the

phraseology for "scourging satire"—Juvenal, Barbier, Nekrasov, and others), and associated definitions for heroes and listeners, reveal by way of analogy, the same social base of poetry. At all events, author, hero, and listener nowhere merge together into one indifferent mass—they occupy *autonomous positions,* they are indeed "sides," the sides not of a judicial process but of an artistic event with specific social structure the "protocol" of which is the work of art.

It would not be amiss at this point to stress once again that we have in mind, and have had in mind all this time, the listener as an immanent participant in the artistic event who has determinative effect on the form of the work from within. This listener, on a par with the author and the hero, is an essential, intrinsic factor of the work and does not at all coincide with the so-called reading public, located outside the work, whose artistic tastes and demands can be consciously taken into account. Such a conscious account is incapable of direct and profound effect on artistic form in the process of its living creation. What is more, if this conscious account of the reading public does come to occupy a position of any importance in a poet's creativity, that creativity inevitably loses its artistic purity and degrades to a lower social level.

This external account bespeaks the poet's loss of *his immanent listener,* his divorce from the *social whole* and *intrinsically,* aside from all abstract considerations, has the capability of determining *his value judgments* and the artistic form of his poetic utterances,which form is the expression of those crucial social value judgments. The more a poet is cut off from the social unity of his group, the more likely he is to take into account the *external* demands of a *particular reading public.* Only a social group alien to the poet can determine his creative work from outside. One's *own* group needs no such external definition: It exists in the poet's voice, in the basic tone and intonations of that voice—whether the poet himself intends this or not.

The poet acquires his words and learns to intone them *over the course of his entire life* in the process of his every-sided contact with his environment. The poet begins to use those words and intonations already in the *inner speech* with the help of which he thinks and becomes conscious of himself, even when he does not produce utterances. It is naive to suppose that one can assimilate as one's own *an external speech that runs counter to one's inner speech,* that is, runs counter to one's whole inner verbal manner of being aware of oneself and the world. Even if it is possible to create such a thing for some pragmatic occasion, still, as something cut off from all sources of sustenance, it will be devoid of any artistic productiveness. A poet's style is engendered from *the style of his inner speech,* which does not lend itself to control, and his inner speech is itself the product of his entire social life. "Style is the man," they say; but we might say: Style is at least two persons or, more accurately, one person plus his social group in the form of its authoritative representative, the listener—the constant participant in a person's inner and outward speech.

The fact of the matter is that no conscious act of any degree of distinctness can do without inner speech, without words and intonations—without evaluations, and, consequently, every conscious act is already a social act, an act of communication. Even the most intimate self-awareness is an attempt to translate oneself into the common code, to take stock of another's point of view, and, consequently, entails orientation toward a possible listener. This listener may be only the bearer of the value judgments of the social group to which the "conscious" person belongs. In this regard, consciousness, provided that we do not lose sight of its content, is *not just a psychological phenomenon* but also, and above all, an *ideological phenomenon, a product of social intercourse*. This constant *coparticipant* in all our conscious acts determines not only the content of consciousness but also—and this is the main point for us—the very *selection* of the content, the selection of what precisely we become conscious of, and thus determines also those *evaluations* which permeate consciousness and which psychology usually calls the "emotional tone" of consciousness. It is precisely from this constant participant in all our conscious acts that the listener who determines artistic form is engendered.

There is nothing more perilous than to conceive of this subtle social structure of verbal creativity as analogous with the conscious and cynical speculations of the bourgeois publisher who "calculates the prospects of the book market," and to apply to the characterization of the immanent structure of a work categories of the "supply-demand" type. Alas, all too many "sociologists" are likely to identify the creative writer's service to society with the vocation of the enterprising publisher.

Under the conditions of the bourgeois economy, the book market does, of course, "regulate" writers, but this is not in any way to be identified with the regulative role of the listener as a constant structural element in artistic creativity. For a historian of the literature of the capitalist era, the market is a very important factor, but for theoretical poetics, which studies the basic ideological structure of art, that external factor is irrelevant. However, even in the historical study of literature the history of the book market must not be confused with the history of literature.

VII

All the form-determining factors of an artistic utterance that we have analyzed—(1) the hierarchical value of the hero or event serving as the content of the utterance, (2) the degree of the latter's proximity to the author, and (3) the listener and his interrelationship with the author, on the one side, and the hero, on the other—all those factors are *the contact points between the social forces of extraartistic reality and verbal art*. Thanks precisely to that kind of *intrinsically social structure* which artistic creation possesses, it is *open on all sides to the influence of other domains of life*. Other ideological spheres, prominently including the sociopolitical order and the economy, have determinative effect on verbal art not merely from outside but with direct bearing upon its intrinsic structural elements. And, conversely, the artistic interaction of author, listener, and hero may exert its influence on other domains of social intercourse.

Full and thoroughgoing elucidation of questions as to who the typical heroes of literature at some particular period are, what the typical formal orientation of the author toward them is, what the interrelationships of the author and hero with the listener are in the whole of an artistic creation—elucidation of such questions presupposes thoroughgoing analysis of the economic and ideological conditions of the time.

But these concrete historical issues exceed the scope of theoretical poetics which, however, still does include one other important task. Up to now we have been concerned only with those factors which determine form in its relation to content, that is, form as the embodied social evaluation of precisely that content, and we have ascertained that every factor of form is a product of social interaction. But we also pointed out that form must be understood from another angle, as well—as form realized with the help of *specific material*. This opens up a whole long series of questions connected with *the technical aspect of form*.

Of course, *these technical questions can be separated out from questions of the sociology of form only in abstract terms; in actuality* it is impossible to divorce the *artistic* import of some device, say, a metaphor that relates to content and expresses the formal evaluation of it (i.e., the metaphor degrades the object or raises it to a higher rank), from *the purely linguistic* specification of that device.

The extraverbal import of a metaphor—a regrouping of values—and its *linguistic covering*—a semantic shift—are merely different points of view on one and the same real phenomenon. But the second point of view is subordinate to the first: A poet uses a metaphor in order to regroup values and not for the sake of a linguistic exercise.

All questions of form can be taken in relation with material—in the given case, in relation with language in its linguistic conception. Technical analysis will then amount to the question as to *which linguistic means are used for the realization of the socioartistic purpose of the form.* But if that purpose is not known, if its import is not elucidated in advance, technical analysis will be absurd.

Technical questions of form, of course, go beyond the scope of the task we have set ourself here. Moreover, their treatment would require an incomparably more diversified and elaborated analysis of the socioartistic aspect of verbal art. Here we have been able to provide only a brief sketch of the basic directions such as analysis must take.

If we have succeeded in demonstrating even the mere possibility of a sociological approach to the immanent structure of poetic form, we may consider our task to have been fulfilled.

Translated by I. R. Titunik

NOTES

1. P. N. Sakulin, *Sociologičeskij metod v literaturovedenii* [The Sociological Method in the Study of Literature] (1925).

2. "Elements of poetic form (sound, word, image, rhythm, composition, genre), poetic thematics, artistic style in totality—all these things are studied, as preliminary matters, with the help of methods that have been worked out by theoretical poetics, grounded in psychology, aesthetics, and linguistics, and that are now practiced in particular by the so-called formal method." Ibid., p. 27.

3. "Viewing literature as a social phenomenon, we inevitably arrive at the question of its causal conditioning. For us this is a matter of sociological causality. Only at the present time has the historian of literature received the right to assume the position of a sociologist and to pose 'why' questions so as to include literary facts within the general process of the social life of some particular period and so as to, thereupon, define the place of literature in the whole movement of history. It is at this point that the sociological method, as applied to history of literature, becomes a historical-sociological method.

In the first, immanent stage, a work was conceived of as an artistic value and not in its social and historical meaning." Ibid., pp. 27, 28.

4. We make a distinction between theory and history of art only as a matter of a technical division of labor. There cannot be any methodological breach between them. Historical categories are of course applicable in absolutely all the fields of the humanities, whether they be historical or theoretical ones.

5. The enthymeme is a form of syllogism one of whose premises is not expressed but assumed. For example: "Socrates is a man, therefore he is mortal." The assumed premise: "All men are mortal."

6. We ignore technical questions of form here but will have something to say on this topic later.

7. The point of view of V. M. Žirmunskij.

8. See W. Humboldt, *Kawi-Werk*, No. 2:335, and Hoffman, *Japan. Sprachlehre*, p. 75.

9. See Matthews, *Aboriginal Languages of Victoria*. Also, Humboldt, *Kawi-Werk*.

10. For the most interesting development of this point of view, see Hermann Cohen, *Ästhetik des reinen Gefühls*, vol. 2.

23

Terry Eagleton
1943–

Terry Eagleton was educated at Cambridge University (where he studied under Raymond Williams) and since 1969 has been a fellow and tutor at Wadham College, Oxford University. His books include: *Shakespeare and Society* (1967); *The Body as Language: Outlines of a "New Left" Theology* (1970); *Exiles and Emigrés: Studies in Modern Literature* (1970); *Myths of Power: A Marxist Study of the Brontës* (1976); *Criticism and Ideology* (1978); *Walter Benjamin, or Towards A Revolutionary Criticism* (1981); *The Rape of Clarissa: Writing, Sexuality and Class Struggle in Samuel Richardson* (1982); *Literary Theory: An Introduction* (1983); *The Function of Criticism, From the Spectator to Post-Structuralism* (1984); and *Against the Grain* (1986).

Eagleton may be the most prominent among the younger generation of Marxist literary critics in the English-speaking world. His work is subtle and sophisticated but also highly partisan and polemical in tone. Like Fredric Jameson, Eagleton shows the influence of French poststructuralist thinkers, especially Lacan and Derrida, and the Marxists, Althusser and Machery. As one of his titles suggests, his work also draws on Walter Benjamin. Eagleton's work in cultural theory brings together Frankfort school Marxism of the 1930s, recent and contemporary theories of discourse which have their root in Saussure and the formalists, and the tradition of philosophical linguistics, especially Wittgenstein.

Eagleton's *Literary Theory: An Introduction* has been very successful and has made his position well-known and influential among American students of literature and theory. As another title suggests, Eagleton's main concern is with the *function* of literature, of theory, and of culture as a whole. In the canonical texts of British literature, in critical and theoretical texts, and in the institutional practices of academic intellectuals in our society, Eagleton seeks always to demonstrate, to elucidate, the effect of "ideology," which he defines as the link or nexus between discourse and power. Like Edward Said, Eagleton insists on the shaping presence of politics and power in both academic and high cultural institutions and practices—"against the grain" of a prevalent modern ideology which would insist on the autonomy of art and thought.

"Brecht and Rhetoric" is one of Eagleton's "selected essays" collected in *Against the Grain*. It originally appeared in *New Literary History* in 1982. In this highly condensed essay Eagleton establishes convincingly the kinship between the modernist Marxism of Brecht (and Benjamin) and "left" deconstruction. Eagleton argues that in

Brecht we have a prototype for the deconstruction through theory of the illusions of individualism and selfhood. Thus does Eagleton join his Marxist project to the poststructuralist critique of the subject. The self-reflexive, critical position Eagleton advocates—the position toward the self and the subject that is the result or effect of Brechtian theatre—links his work to that of Jameson, Said, and other contemporary oppositional critics.

Two explanatory notes may prove helpful: when Eagleton speaks early on of "alienated acting" and the "A-effect" he is referring to a notion at the heart of Brechtian dramaturgy. The word in German is *Verfremdung*, or the "V-effect." The referent is Brecht's idea that there should be a deliberate separation or space between the actor and the role or the words he says. This is part of a larger goal of destroying the illusion of reality in the theater (Brecht's notion is akin to the "making strange" of the Russian formalists). And when Eagleton refers to "a piece of *Plumpes Denken*" he refers to Brecht's famous injunction to "think crudely!"—not to get so involved with the complexities of theoretical argument that we lose sight of class conflict, exploitation, and oppression.

Brecht and Rhetoric

In a notorious comment, J. L. Austin once wrote that "a performative utterance will, for example, be *in a peculiar way* hollow or void if said by an actor on a stage."[1] Perhaps Austin only ever attended amateur theatricals. Bertolt Brecht approved of amateur acting, since the occasional flatness and hollowness of its utterances seemed to him an unwitting form of alienation effect. For Brecht, the whole point of acting was that it should be in a peculiar sense hollow or void. Alienated acting hollows out the imaginary plenitude of everyday actions, deconstructing them into their social determinants and inscribing within them the conditions of their making. The "void" of alienated acting is a kind of Derridean "spacing," rendering a piece of stage business exterior to itself, sliding a hiatus between actor and action and thus, it is hoped, dismantling the ideological self-identity of our routine social behaviour. The actor, Walter Benjamin remarked in "What Is Epic Theatre?" "must be able to space his gestures as the compositor produces spaced type."[2] The dramatic gesture, by miming routine behaviour in contrivedly hollow ways, represents it in all its lack, in its suppression of material conditions and historical possibilities, and thus represents an absence which it at the same time produces. What the stage action represents is the routine action as differenced through the former's non-self-identity, which nevertheless remains self-identical—recognizable—enough to do all this representing rather than merely to "reflect" a "given" non-identity in the world. A certain structure of presence must, in other words, be preserved: "verisimilitude" between stage and society can be disrupted only if it is posited. Brecht was particularly keen on encouraging his actors to observe and reproduce actions precisely, for without such an element of presence and recognition the absencing of the A-effect would be non-productively rather than productively empty. The internal structure of the effect is one of presence and absence together, or rather a problematic contention of the two in which the distinction between "representation" and "non-representation" is itself thrown into question. The stage action must be self-identical enough to represent as non-self-identical an apparently self-identical world, but in that very act puts its own self-identity into question. This self-cancelling or self-transcending of the theatrical signifier becomes a political metaphor: if political society were to know itself in its difference, there would be no need for this kind of representational theatre. It is because political society does not recognize itself as a *production* that it must be *represented* as such, which (since the concept of production itself overturns classical notions of representation) is bound to result in a self-contradictory aesthetic. It is not surprising that Brecht never seems able to make up his mind about the political value of representation. The A-effect, however, turns this contradiction to fruitful use, positing and subverting simultaneously; as a "supplement" to social reality it posits its solid anterior existence *and* unmasks it as crippledly incomplete.

Another way of putting this is to claim that Brechtian theatre deconstructs social processes into rhetoric, which is to say reveals them as social *practices*. "Rhetoric" here means grasping language and action in the context of the politico-discursive conditions inscribed within them, and Brecht's term for this is *Gest*. To view things gestically is to catch the gist in terms of the gesture, or rather to position oneself at the point where the one German word hovers indeterminately between the two English ones. *Gest* denotes the curve of intentionality, the class of socially typical performative utterances, to which in a piece of *plumpes Denken* the complexities of action or discourse may be reduced. An unpublished fragment by Brecht headed "representation of sentences in a new encyclopaedia" would suggest that he thought all sentences, not just obviously performative ones like theatrical speech, could and should be treated in this way:

1. Who is the sentence of use to?
2. Who does it claim to be of use to?
3. What does it call for?
4. What practical action corresponds to it?
5. What sort of sentences result from it? What sort of sentences support it?
6. In what situation is it spoken? By whom?[3]

All discourse is gestic or rhetorical, but some—dramatic discourse—is more rhetorical than the rest. It *needs* to be, since its task is to reveal the repressed rhetoricity of non-theatrical utterances, a revelation which is for Brecht ineluctably materialist because it involves contextualizing what is said or done in terms of its institutional conditions. The function of theatre is to show that all the world's a stage.

But if all language is performative, what becomes of representation? Brecht's answer to this, briefly, is that what representations represent are performatives. The theatre simply lays bare the process by which we come to grasp "constative" utterances in the first place only by an act of "theatrical" miming. In a piece significantly entitled "Two Essays on Unprofessional Acting," Brecht writes:

> One easily forgets that human education proceeds along highly theatrical lines. In a quite theatrical manner the child is taught how to behave; logical arguments only come

> later. When such-and-such occurs, it is told (or sees), one must laugh. It joins in when there is laughter, without knowing why; if asked why it is laughing it is wholly confused. In the same way it joins in shedding tears, not only weeping because the grown-ups do so but also feeling genuine sorrow. This can be seen at funerals, whose meaning escapes children entirely. These are theatrical events which form the character. The human being copies gestures, miming, tones of voice. And weeping arises from sorrow, but sorrow also arises from weeping.[4]

Rhetoric, in other words, precedes logic: grasping propositions is only possible by participating in specific forms of social life. As children we get the gist by miming the gesture, grow into "appropriate" feelings by performing the behaviours criterial of them. Only later will logic bury rhetoric, the gesture be surreptitiously slid beneath the gist. What utterances "represent" is not referents but practices, including other utterances: "gestures, miming, tones of voice." As with the A-effect, then, Brecht's focus is at once representational and anti-representational, mimetic and performative together. The child grows towards representational meaning by redoubling rhetoric, miming a miming, performing a performative; indeed when Brecht writes (perhaps by a slide of the signifier) of the child *copying miming,* he suggests the possibility of performing the performing of a performance.

The child, one might say, begins as an amateur or Brechtian actor, performing what he does not yet truly feel, and by dint of doing so ends up as a professional or Aristotelian one, fully at one with his forms of life. The aim of Brechtian theory, then, must be to reverse this unhappy process and regress us to a childlike condition once more, make us all amateurs again. The child and the Marxist move in opposite directions but meet in the middle: the child's understanding is at first purely practical, the effect of a spontaneous involvement with forms of life, and only later crystallizes out into a logical or representational system.[5] The Marxist is confronted by that (ideo)logical system and has to work his or her way back to the practical conditions it now suppresses, rewriting it as a piece of rhetoric or mode of social performance. We forget that we have to learn our emotions through sharing in forms of social behaviour, that feelings are social institutions; in the theatre we can re-enact our childhood at a conscious level, observe new forms of behaviour and so develop the forms of subjectivity appropriate to them. In both theatre and childhood, meaning is not "representational" but the effect of representation, the consequence of a certain practical miming. Mimesis is what precedes and encircles meaning, the material conditions for the emergence of logical thought. In the end, child and materialist will come out at the same point: "I now see thinking just as a way of behaving," says the Actor in the *Messingkauf Dialogues,* "and behaving socially at that. It's something that the whole body takes part in, with all its senses."

To "act" is to go through the motions of behavior without really feeling it, lacking the appropriate experiences. Acting is a kind of fraud; and flagrantly "fraudulent" acting, of an amateur or alienated kind, returns us self-consciously to the fictive formation of the self, re-opens that gap or lag between our action and its appropriate inwardness which was there in the first place as a consequence of our desiring the desire of the Other. Children are allegorists, confusedly hunting the elusive meaning of behaviour; adults are symbolists, unable to dissociate action and significance. Amateur actors, like political revolutionaries, are those who find the conventions hard to grasp and perform them badly, having never recovered from their childhood puzzlement.

Such puzzlement is perhaps what we call "theory." The child is an incorrigible theoretician, forever urging the most impossibly fundamental questions. The form of a philosophical question, Wittgenstein remarks, is "I don't know my way around"; and since this is literally true of the child, it is driven to pose questions which are not answerable simply in rhetorical terms ("The meaning of this action is this") but which press perversely on to interrogate the whole form of social life which might generate such particular meanings in the first place. Theory is in this sense the logical refuge of those puzzled or naive enough not to find simply rhetorical answers adequate, or who want to widen the boundaries of what mature minds take to be adequate rhetorical explanations. The revolutionary questioner sees the world with the astonishment of a child ("Where does capitalism come from, Mummy?"), and refuses to be fobbed off by the adults' customary Wittgensteinian justifications of their practices: "This is just what we *do*, dear." He or she accepts that all justification is in this sense rhetorical, an appeal to existing practices and conventions, but does not see why one should not do something else for a change. The theoretical question is as utterly estranged as the metaphysician's traditional wonderment about why there is anything at all, rather than just nothing. Why do we have all *these* practices, utterances and institutions, rather than some others?

Since such a question is not of course simply requesting historical information, it is rhetorical in its turn—both in the sense that it implies its own answer (we *shouldn't* rest happy with such practices), and in the sense that like the discourses it addresses it is therefore animated by malice, scorn, insecurity, hostility, the will to reject. If the child's questions are naive, the revolutionary's are *faux naif*. "I don't know my way around" implies, "What the hell is all this?" The theoretical question, then, is as much a performative as the languages it challenges; it is just that it tries to view those other languages in a new way, as Brecht reported that it was only by reading Marx that he was able to understand his own plays. Theory begins to take hold once one realizes that the adults don't know their way around either, even if they *act* as though they do. They act as well as they do precisely because they can no longer see, and so question, the conventions by which they behave. The task of theory is to breed bad actors, of which Brecht's remarks about the A-effect is one small model.

Just as Marxism can be seen as a morality in the properly classical rather than narrowly fashionable sense, concerned with as many as possible of the factors (and not just interpersonal ones) which condition the quality of human behaviour, so "theory" can be seen as rhetorical study in its broadest and richest sense, reckoning in modes of production as well as conventions of promising. Where theory is most importantly performative, however, is in the practical difference it makes to our routine rhetorics. "Lamenting by means of sounds, or better still words," says the Philosopher in the *Messingkauf Dialogues*, "is a vast liberation, because it means that the sufferer is beginning to produce something. He's already mixing his sorrow with an account of the blows he has received; he's already making something out of the utterly devastating. Observation has set in." If the child's trek from rhetoric to logic is part of the problem, the sufferer's transition from screaming to explaining is part of the solution. When lamenting becomes propositional it is transformed: it becomes, like theory, a way of encompassing a situation rather than being its victim. To give an account of one's sorrow even as one grieves; to act and, in alienated style, to observe oneself acting: this is the dialectical feat which, for quite different reasons, neither child nor logician can achieve, and which is central at once to Brecht's dramaturgy and to his politics.

NOTES

1. J. L. Austin, *How to Do Things with Words*, Cambridge, Mass. 1975, p. 21.

2. Walter Benjamin, *Understanding Brecht*, London 1973, p. 19.

3. *Brecht on Theatre: The Development of an Aesthetic*, translated by John Willett, London 1964, p. 106.

4. Ibid., p. 152.

5. Walter Benjamin admired the way in which, in children, cognition was tied to action, and found in their behaviour a "language of gestures" more basic than conceptual discourse. For Benjamin as for Brecht, children's behaviour was essentially mimetic, a matter of forging bizarre correspondences of the kind that the revolutionary theorist must also generate. See, for this neglected aspect of Benjamin's thought, Susan Buck-Morss, "Walter Benjamin: Revolutionary Writer (11)," *New Left Review* 129, September–October 1981.

24

Fredric Jameson 1934–

Educated at Haverford College, Yale University, and the Universities of Aix, Munich and Berlin, Fredric Jameson has taught at many major American universities, including Harvard and Yale, and is now on the faculty of Duke University. His major monographs include: *Marxism and Form: Twentieth Century Dialectical Theories of Literature* (1971); *The Prison House of Language: A Critical Account of Structuralism and Russian Formalism* (1972); *The Political Unconscious: Narrative as a Socially Symbolic Act* (1981), and two studies of individual authors, *Sartre: The Origins of a Style* (1961), and *Fables of Aggression: Wyndham Lewis, the Modernist as Fascist* (1979). In addition to such books, Jameson has published throughout his career many articles that have been very important and influential, though they have not yet been collected together in book form. His "Metacommentary" in the *PMLA* in 1971 was a major contribution to the rise in the American academy and intellectual life generally of what we today call "theory." "Imaginary and Symbolic in Lacan: Marxism, Psychoanalytical Criticism, and the Problem of the Subject," (*Yale French Studies*, 55/56, 1977) constitutes a major contribution to a central issue in contemporary theory. His most important work of recent years is probably the three articles on postmodernism—all published in 1984—of which "The Politics of Theory" is one. The other two are "Periodizing the 60's," in a special double issue of *Social Text, The 60's Without Apology*, and "Postmodernism, or the Cultural Logic of Late Capitalism," in *New Left Review*, No. 146.

What has made Jameson one of the most influential critics and theorists writing today is a dialectical thrust that has characterized his work from *Marxism and Form* through the postmodernism articles: all of his work can be seen as a continuing meditation on the base-superstructure debate, the terms of which are laid out so clearly by Raymond Williams in this volume. As the title of *Marxism and Form* emphasizes, Jameson has sought from the outset to disengage Marxist criticism and theory from the simplistic concern with *content* that has sometimes characterized the critical practice of "vulgar" Marxism, with its simple strict economic determinism, where the economic base "causes" culture, without mediations. Jameson has continued this project throughout his career, as exemplified by the brilliantly complex formal analyses of Conrad and Balzac in *The Political Unconscious*. At the same time he has occupied a dialectical position exactly opposite to that one, obeying Brecht's injunction to "Think crudely"; he has continued to insist on the key importance of causal base-superstructure relations, as indicated by the title of "Postmodernism, or the Cultural Logic of Late Capitalism," where the direct article and the appositional "or" insist on the truth and significance of the central Marxist assumption (in *The Prison House of Language* Jameson calls it Marx's "ever-scandalous assertion") of the social constitution of culture, and the cultural constitution of "the subject."

The last few pages of "The Politics of Theory" are perhaps the most important. There Jameson joins this essay to the central concerns of the other two postmodernism essays. In the long paragraph following the schematic diagram of the positions on postmodernism he has been discussing, he sums up in a phrase a central purpose of his entire career; a historical and dialectical analysis of "a present of time and of history in which we ourselves exist and struggle," while in the last sentence of that paragraph is a description of his postmodernism project as a whole.

When he uses the term "Utopian" a few paragraphs later it is in the positive sense of the term as it is employed by Walter Benjamin and others in the Frankfort school—to indicate the necessity of using the historical imagination to see the future as fundamentally different from the present. Jameson's view of the present is increasingly dark; one of the theses of the postmodernism articles is that a nearly total world capitalist system has penetrated and occupied hitherto uncolonized areas of reality, including even the unconscious mind, with terrible results. But Jameson's dialectic insists also on optimism; when he gives "History" its capital "H" in the last word of this essay (the first two words of *The Political Unconscious* are "Always historicize"), he is deliberately employing the totalizing Hegelian vocabulary so denounced in contemporary criticism by Paul de Man and others. He is "thinking crudely" in order both to argue that "history is what hurts"—the Marxist tenet that exploitation and oppression have predominated in history—and to insist that the imperative to struggle for change that inevitably flows from such a view of the present and the past is made all the more urgent by the Utopian possibilities of a fundamentally altered future.

The Politics of Theory: Ideological Positions in the Postmodernism Debate

The problem of postmodernism—how its fundamental characteristics are to be described, whether it even exists in the first place, whether the very *concept* is of any use, or is, on the contrary, a mystification—this problem is at one and the same time an aesthetic and a political one. The various positions which can logically be taken on it, whatever terms they are couched in, can always be shown to articulate visions of history, in which the evaluation of the social moment in which we live today is the object of an essentially political affirmation or repudiation. Indeed, the very enabling premise of the debate turns on an initial, strategic, presupposition about our social system: to grant some historic originality to a postmodernist culture is also implicitly to affirm some radical structural difference between what is sometimes called consumer society and earlier moments of the capitalism from which it emerged.

The various logical possibilities, however, are necessarily linked with the taking of a position on that other issue inscribed in the very designation "postmodernism" itself, namely, the evaluation of what must now be called high or classical modernism itself. Indeed, when we make some initial inventory of the varied cultural artifacts that might plausibly be characterized as postmodern, the temptation is strong to seek the "family resemblance" of such heterogeneous styles and products, not in themselves, but in some common high modernist impulse and aesthetic against which they all, in one way or another, stand in reaction.

The seemingly irreducible variety of the postmodern can be observed fully as problematically within the individual media (of arts) as between them: what affinities, besides some overall generational reaction, to establish between the elaborate false sentences and syntactic mimesis of John Ashbery and the much simpler talk poetry that began to emerge in the early 1960s in protest against the New Critical aesthetic of complex ironic style? Both register, no doubt in very different ways indeed, the institutionalization of high modernism in this same period, the shift from an oppositional to a hegemonic position of the classics of modernism, the latter's conquest of the university, the museum, the art gallery network and the foundations, the assimilation, in other words, of the various high modernisms, into the "canon" and the subsequent attenuation of everything in them felt by our grandparents to be shocking, scandalous, ugly, dissonant, immoral and antisocial.

The same heterogeneity can be detected in the visual arts, between the inaugural reaction against the last high modernist school in painting—Abstract Expressionism—in the work of Andy Warhol and so-called pop art, and such quite distinct aesthetics as those of conceptual art, photorealism and the current New Figuration or neo-Expressionism. It can be witnessed in film, not merely between experimental and commercial production, but also within the former itself, where Godard's "break" with the classical filmic modernism of the great "auteurs" (Hitchcock, Bergman, Fellini, Kurasawa) generates a series of stylistic reactions against itself in the 1970s, and is also accompanied by a rich new development of experimental video (a new medium inspired by, but significantly and structurally distinct from, experimental film). In music also, the inaugural moment of John Cage now seems far enough from such later syntheses of classical and popular styles in composers like Phil Glass and Terry Riley, as well as from punk and New Wave rock of the type of The Clash, The Talking Heads and The Gang of Four, themselves significantly distinct from disco or glitter rock. (In film or in rock, however, a certain historical logic can be reintroduced by the hypothesis that such newer media recapitulate the evolutionary stages or breaks between realism, modernism and postmodernism, in a compressed time span, such that the Beatles and the Stones occupy the high modernist moment embodied by the "auteurs" of 1950s and 1960s art films.)

In narrative proper, the dominant conception of a dissolution of linear narrative, a repudiation of representation, and a "revolutionary" break with the (repressive) ideology of storytelling generally, does not seem adequate to encapsulate such very different work as that of Burroughs, but also of Pynchon and Ishmael Reed; of Beckett, but also of the French *nouveau roman* and its own sequels, and of the "non-fiction novel" as well, and the New Narrative. Meanwhile, a significantly distinct aesthetic has seemed to emerge both in commercial film and in the novel with the production of what may be called nostalgia art (or *la mode rétro*).

But it is evidently architecture which is the privileged terrain of struggle of postmodernism and the most strategic field in which this concept has been debated and its consequences explored. Nowhere else has the "death of modernism" been felt so intensely, or pronounced more stridently; nowhere else have the theoretical and practical stakes in the debate been articulated more programmatically. Of a burgeoning literature on the subject, Robert Venturi's *Learning from Las Vegas* (1971), a series of discussions by Christopher Jencks, and Pier Paolo Portoghesi's Biennale presentation, *After Modern Architecture,* may be cited as usefully illuminating the central issues in the attack on the architectural high modernism of the International Style (Le Corbusier, Wright, Mies): namely, the bankruptcy of the monumental (buildings which, as Venturi puts it, are really *sculptures*), the failure of its protopolitical or Utopian program (the transformation of all of social life by way of the transformation of space), its elitism including the authoritarianism of the charismatic leader, and finally its virtual destruction of the older city fabric by a proliferation of glass boxes and of high rises that, disjoining themselves from their immediate contexts, turn these last into the degraded public space of an urban no-man's-land.

Still, architectural postmodernism is itself no unified or monolithic period style, but spans a whole gamut of allusions to styles of the past, such that within it can be distinguished a baroque postmodernism (say, Michael Graves), a rococo postmodernism (Charles Moore or Venturi), a classical and a neoclassical postmodernism (Rossi and De Porzemparc respectively), and perhaps even a Mannerist and a Romantic variety, not to speak of a High Modernist postmodernism itself. This complacent play of historical allusion and stylistic pastiche (termed "historicism" in the architectural literature) is a central feature of postmodernism more generally.

Yet the architectural debates have the merit of making the political resonance of these seemingly aesthetic issues inescapable, and allowing it to be detectable in the sometimes more coded or veiled discussions in the other arts. On the whole, four general positions on postmodernism may be disengaged from the variety of recent pronouncements on the subject; yet even this relatively neat scheme or *combinatoire* is further complicated by one's impression that each of these possibilities is susceptible of either a politically progressive or a politically reactionary expression (speaking now from a Marxist or more generally left perspective).

One can, for example, salute the arrival of postmodernism from an essentially anti-modernist standpoint.[1] A somewhat earlier generation of theorists (most notably Ihab Hassan) seems already to have done something like this when they dealt with the postmodernist aesthetic in terms of a more properly post-structuralist thematics (the *Tel quel* attack on the ideology of representation, the Heideggerian or Derridean "end of Western metaphysics"): here what is often not yet called postmodernism (see the Utopian prophecy at the end of Foucault's *The Order of Things*) is saluted as the coming of a whole new way of thinking and being in the world. But since Hassan's celebration also includes a number of the more extreme monuments of high modernism (Joyce, Mallarmé), this would be a relatively more ambiguous stance, were it not for the accompanying celebration of a new information high technology which marks the affinity between such evocations and the political thesis of a properly *postindustrial society*.

All of which is largely disambiguated in Tom Wolfe's *From Bauhaus to Our House*, an otherwise undistinguished book report on the recent architectural debates by a writer whose own New Journalism itself constitutes one of the varieties of postmodernism. What is interesting and symptomatic about this book is however the absence of any Utopian celebration of the postmodern and—far more strikingly—the passionate hatred of the Modern that breathes through the otherwise obligatory camp sarcasm of the rhetoric; and this is not a new, but a dated and archaic passion. It is as though the original horror of the first middle class spectators of the very emergence of the Modern itself—the first Corbusiers, as white as the first freshly built cathedrals of the 12th century, the first scandalous Picasso heads, with two eyes on one profile like a flounder, the stunning "obscurity" of the first editions of *Ulysses* or *The Waste Land*: as though this disgust of the original philistines, Spiessbürger, bourgeois or Main Street Babbitry, had suddenly come back to life, infusing the newer critiques of modernism with an ideologically very different spirit, whose effect is on the whole to reawaken in the reader an equally archaic sympathy with the protopolitical, Utopian, anti-middle-class impulses of a now extinct high modernism itself. Wolfe's diatribe thus offers a stunning example of the way in which a reasoned and contemporary, theoretical repudiation of the modern—much of whose progressive force springs from a new sense of the urban and a now considerable experience of the destruction of older forms of communal and urban life in the name of a high modernist orthodoxy—can be handily reappropriated and pressed into the service of an explicitly reactionary cultural politics.

These positions—anti-modern, pro-postmodern—then find their opposite number and structural inversion in a group of counter-statements whose aim is to discredit the shoddiness and irresponsibility of the postmodern in general by way of a reaffirmation of the authentic impulse of a high modernist tradition still considered to be alive and vital. Hilton Kramer's twin manifestoes in the inaugural issue of his new journal, *The New Criterion*, articulate these views with force, contrasting the moral responsibility of the "masterpieces" and monuments of classical modernism with the fundamental irresponsibility and superficiality of a postmodernism associated with camp and with the "facetiousness" of which the Wolfe style is a ripe and obvious example.

What is more paradoxical is that politically Wolfe and Kramer have much in common; and there would seem to be a certain inconsistency in the way in which Kramer must seek to eradicate from the "high seriousness" of the classics of the modern their fundamentally anti-middle-class stance and the protopolitical passion which informs the repudiation, by the great modernists, of Victorian taboos and family life, of commodification, and of the increasing asphyxiation of a desacralizing capitalism, from Ibsen to Lawrence, from Van Gogh to Jackson Pollock. Kramer's ingenious attempt to assimilate this ostensibly anti-bourgeois stance of the great modernists to a "loyal opposition" secretly nourished, by way of foundations and grants, by the bourgeoisie itself—while most unconvincing indeed—is surely itself enabled by the contradictions of the cultural politics of modernism proper, whose negations depend on the

persistence of what they repudiate and entertain—when they do not, very rarely indeed (as in Brecht), attain some genuine political self-consciousness—a symbiotic relationship with capital.

It is, however, easier to understand Kramer's move here when the political project of *The New Criterion* is clarified: for the mission of the journal is clearly to eradicate the 1960s and what remains of that legacy, to consign that whole period to the kind of oblivion which the 1950s was able to devise for the 1930s, or the 1920s for the rich political culture of the pre-World-War-I era. *The New Criterion* therefore inscribes itself in the effort, ongoing and at work everywhere today, to construct some new conservative cultural counter-revolution, whose terms range from the aesthetic to the ultimate defense of the family and of religion. It is therefore paradoxical that this essentially political project should explicitly deplore the omnipresence of politics in contemporary culture—an infection largely spread during the 1960s, but which Kramer holds responsible for the moral imbecility of the postmodernism of our own period.

The problem with the operation—an obviously indispensable one from the conservative viewpoint—is that for whatever reason its paper-money rhetoric does not seem to have been backed by the solid gold of state power, as was the case with McCarthyism or in the period of the Palmer raids. The failure of the Vietnam War seems, at least for the moment, to have made the naked exercise of repressive power impossible,[2] and endowed the 1960s with a persistence in collective memory and experience which it was not given to the traditions of the 1930s or the pre-World-War-I period to know. Kramer's "cultural revolution" therefore tends most often to lapse into a feebler and sentimental nostalgia for the 1950s and the Eisenhower era.

It will not be surprising, in the light of what has been shown for an earlier set of positions on modernism and postmodernism, that in spite of the openly conservative ideology of this second evaluation of the contemporary cultural scene, the latter can also be appropriated for what is surely a far more progressive line on the subject. We are indebted to Jürgen Habermas[3] for this dramatic reversal and rearticulation of what remains the affirmation of the supreme value of the Modern and the repudiation of the theory, as well as the practice, of postmodernism. For Habermas, however, the vice of postmodernism consists very centrally in its politically reactionary function, as the attempt everywhere to discredit a modernist impulse Habermas himself associates with the bourgeois Enlightenment and with the latter's still universalizing and Utopian spirit. With Adorno himself, Habermas seeks to rescue and to recommemorate what both see as the essentially negative, critical and Utopian power of the great high modernisms. On the other hand, his attempt to associate these last with the spirit of the 18th century Enlightenment marks a decisive break indeed with Adorno and Horkheimer's somber *Dialectic of Enlightenment*, in which the scientific ethos of the *philosophes* is dramatized as a misguided will to power and domination over nature, and their own desacralizing program as the first stage in the development of a sheerly instrumentalizing world view which will lead straight to Auschwitz. This very striking divergence can be accounted for by Habermas' own vision of history, which seeks to maintain the promise of "liberalism" and the essentially Utopian content of the first, universalizing bourgeois ideology (equality, civil rights, humanitarianism, free speech and open media) over against the failure of those ideals to be realized in the development of capital itself.

As for the aesthetic terms of the debate, however, it will not be adequate to respond to Habermas' resuscitation of the modern by some mere empirical certification of the latter's extinction. We need to take into account the possibility that the national situation in which Habermas thinks and writes is rather different from our own: McCarthyism and repression are, for one thing, realities in the Federal Republic today, and the intellectual intimidation of the Left and the silencing of a left culture (largely associated, by the West German right, with "terrorism") has been on the whole a far more successful operation than elsewhere in the West.[4] The triumph of a new McCarthyism and of the culture of the Spiessbürger and the philistine suggests the possibility that in this particular national situation Habermas may well be right, and the older forms of high modernism may still retain something of the subversive power which they have lost elsewhere. In that case, a postmodernism which seeks to enfeeble and to undermine that power may well also merit his ideological diagnosis in a local way, even though the assessment remains ungeneralizable.

Both of the previous positions—antimodern/propostmodern, and promodern/antipostmodern—are characterized by an acceptance of the new term which is tantamount to an agreement on the fundamental nature of some decisive "break" between the modern and the postmodern moments, however these last are evaluated. There remain, however, two final logical possibilities both of which depend on the repudiation of any conception of such a historical break and which therefore, implicitly or explicitly, call into question the usefulness of the very category of postmodernism. As for the works associated with the latter, they will then be assimilated back into classical modernism proper, so that the "postmodern" becomes little more than the form taken by the authentically modern in our own period, and a mere dialectical intensification of the old modernist impulse towards innovation. (I must here omit yet another series of debates, largely academic, in which the very continuity of modernism as it is here reaffirmed is itself called into question by some vaster sense of the profound continuity of Romanticism itself, from the late 18th century on, of which both the modern and the postmodern will be seen as mere organic stages.)

The two final positions on the subject thus logically prove to be a positive and negative assessment respectively of a postmodernism now assimilated back into the high modernist tradition. Jean-Francois Lyotard[5] thus proposes that his own vital commitment to the new and the emergent, to a contemporary or postcontemporary cultural production now widely characterized as "postmodern," be grasped as part and parcel of a reaffirmation of the authentic older high modernisms very much in Adorno's spirit. The ingenious twist or swerve in his own proposal involves the proposition that something called "post-modernism" does not *follow* high modernism proper, as the latter's waste product, but rather very precisely *precedes* and prepares it, so that the contemporary postmodernisms all around us may be seen as the promise of the return and the reinvention, the triumphant reappearance, of some new high modernism endowed with all its older power and with fresh life. This is a prophetic stance, whose analyses turn on the anti-representational thrust of modernism and postmodernism; Lyotard's aesthetic positions, however, cannot be adequately evaluated in aesthetic terms, since what informs them is an essentially social and political conception of a new social system beyond classical capitalism (our old friend, "postindustrial society"): the vision of a regenerated modernism is in that sense inseparable from a certain prophetic faith in the possibilities and the promise of the new society itself in full emergence.

The negative inversion of this position will then clearly involve an ideological repudiation of modernism of a type which might conceivably range from Lukács' older analysis of modernist forms as the replication of the reification of capitalist social life all the way to some of the more articulated critiques of high modernism of the present day. What distinguishes this final position from the antimodernisms already outlined above is, however, that it does not speak from the security of an affirmation of some new postmodernist culture, but rather sees even the latter itself as a mere degeneration of the already stigmatized impulses of high modernism proper. This particular position, perhaps the bleakest of all and the most implacably negative, can be vividly confronted in the works of the Venetian architecture historian Manfredo Tafuri, whose extensive analyses[6] constitute a powerful indictment of what we have termed the "protopolitical" impulses in high modernism (the "Utopian" substitution of cultural politics for politics proper, the vocation to transform the world by transforming its forms, space or language). Tafuri is however no less harsh in his anatomy of the negative, demystifying, "critical" vocation of the various modernisms, whose function he reads as a kind of Hegelian "ruse of History," whereby the instrumentalizing and desacralizing tendencies of capital itself are ultimately realized through just such demolition work by the thinkers and artists of the modern movement. Their "anticapitalism" therefore ends up laying the basis for the "total" bureaucratic organization and control of late capitalism, and it is only logical that Tafuri should conclude by positing the impossibility of any radical transformation of culture before a radical transformation of social relations themselves.

The political ambivalence demonstrated in the earlier two positions seems to me to be maintained here, but *within* the positions of both of these very complex thinkers. Unlike many of the previously mentioned theorists, Tafuri and Lyotard are both explicitly political figures, with an overt commitment to the values of an older revolutionary tradition. It is clear, for example, that Lyotard's embattled endorsement of the supreme value of aesthetic innovation is to be understood as the figure for a certain kind of revolutionary stance; while Tafuri's whole conceptual framework is largely consistent with the classical Marxist tradition. Yet both are also, implicitly, and more openly at certain strategic moments, rewritable in terms of a post-Marxism which at length becomes indistinguishable from anti-Marxism proper. Lyotard has for example very frequently sought to distinguish his "revolutionary" aesthetic from the older ideals of political revolution, which he sees as either being Stalinist, or as archaic and incompatible with the conditions of the new postindustrial social order; while Tafuri's apocalyptic notion of the total social revolution implies a conception of the "total system" of capitalism which, in a period of depoliticization and reaction, is only too fatally destined for the kind of discouragement which has so often led Marxists to a renunciation of the political altogether (Adorno and Merleau-Ponty come to mind, along with many of the ex-Trotskyists of the 1930s and 1940s and the ex-Maoists of the 1960s and 1970s).

The combination scheme outlined above can now be schematically represented as follows; the plus and minus signs designating the politically progressive or reactionary functions of the positions in question:

	ANTI-MODERNIST	PRO-MODERNIST
PRO-POSTMODERNIST	Wolfe – Jencks +	Lyotard {+ –
ANTI-POSTMODERNIST	Tafuri {– +	Kramer – Habermas +

With these remarks we come full circle and may now return to the more positive potential political content of the first position in question, and in particular to the question of a certain *populist* impulse in postmodernism which it has been the merit of Charles Jencks (but also of Venturi and others) to have underscored—a question which will also allow us to deal a little more adequately with the absolute pessimism of Tafuri's Marxism itself. What must first be observed, however, is that most of the political positions which we have found to inform what is most often conducted as an aesthetic debate are in reality moralizing ones, which seek to develop final judgments on the phenomenon of postmodernism, whether the latter is stigmatized as corrupt or on the other hand saluted as a culturally and aesthetically healthy and positive form of innovation. But a genuinely historical and dialectical analysis of such phenomena—particularly when it is a matter of a present of time and of history in which we ourselves exist and struggle—cannot afford the impoverished luxury of such absolute moralizing judgments: the dialectic is "beyond good and evil" in the sense of some easy taking of sides, whence the glacial and inhuman spirit of its historical vision (something that already disturbed contemporaries about Hegel's original system). The point is that we are *within* the culture of postmodernism to the point where its facile repudiation is as impossible as any equally facile celebration of it is complacent and corrupt. Ideological judgment on postmodernism today necessarily implies, one would think, a judgment on ourselves as well as on the artifacts in question; nor can an entire historical period, such as our own, be grasped in any adequate way by means of global moral judgments or their somewhat degraded equivalent, pop-psychological diagnosis (such as those of Lasch's *Culture of Narcissism*). On the classical Marxian view, the seeds of the future already exist within the present and must be conceptually disengaged from it, both through analysis and through political praxis (the workers of the Paris Commune, Marx once remarked in a striking phrase, "*have no ideals to realize*"; they merely sought to disengage emergent forms of new social relations from the older capitalist social relations in which the former had already begun to stir). In place of the temptation either to denounce the complacencies of postmodernism as some final symptom of decadence, or to salute the new forms as the harbingers of a new technological and technocratic Utopia, it seems more appropriate to assess the new cultural production within the working hypothesis of a general modification of culture itself within the social restructuration of late capitalism as a system.[7]

As for emergence, however, Jencks' assertion that postmodern architecture distinguishes itself from that of high modernism through its populist priorities,[8] may serve as the starting point for some more general discussion. What is meant, in the specifically architectural context, is that where the now more classical high modernist space of a Corbusier or a Wright sought to differentiate itself radically from the fallen city fabric in which it appears—its forms thus dependent on an act of radical disjunction from its spatial context (the great *pilotis* dramatizing separation from the ground and safeguarding the *Novum* of the new space)—postmodernist buildings on the contrary celebrate their insertion into the heterogeneous fabric of the commercial strip and the motel and fast-food landscape of the post-superhighway American city. Meanwhile a play of allusion and formal echoes ("historicism") secures the kinship of these new art buildings with the surrounding commercial icons and spaces, thereby renouncing the high modernist claim to radical difference and innovation.

Whether this undoubtedly significant feature of the newer architecture is to be characterized as *populist* must remain an open question: since it would seem essential to distinguish the emergent forms of a new commercial culture—beginning with advertisements and spreading on to formal *packaging* of all kinds, from products to buildings and not excluding artistic commodities such as television shows (the "logo") and bestsellers and films—from the older kinds of folk and genuinely "popular" culture which flourished when the older social classes of a peasantry and an urban *artisanat* still existed and which, from the mid-19th century on, have gradually been colonized and extinguished by commodification and the market system.

What can at least be admitted is the more universal presence of this particular feature, which appears more unambiguously in the other arts as an effacement of the older distinction between high and so-called mass culture, a distinction on which modernism depended for its specificity, its Utopian function consisting at least in part in the securing of a realm of authentic experience over against the surrounding environment of philistinism, of schlock and kitsch, of commodification and of Reader's Digest culture. Indeed, it can be argued that the emergence of high modernism is itself contemporaneous with the first great expansion of a recognizable mass culture (Zola may be taken as the marker for the last coexistence of the art novel and the bestseller to be within a single text).

It is now this constitutive differentiation which seems on the point of disappearing: we have already mentioned the way in which, in music, after Schönberg and even after Cage, the two antithetical traditions of the "classical" and the "popular" once again begin to merge. In a more general way, it seems clear that the artists of the "postmodern" period have been fascinated precisely by the whole new object world, not merely of the Las Vegas strip, but also of the late show and the grade-B Hollywood film, of so-called paraliterature with its airport paperback categories of the gothic and the romance, the popular biography, the murder mystery and the science-fiction or fantasy novel (in such a way that the older generic categories discredited by modernism seem on the point of living an unexpected

reappearance). In the visual arts, the renewal of photography as a significant medium in its own right and also as the "plane of substance" in pop art or photorealism is a crucial symptom of the same process. At any rate, it becomes minimally obvious that the newer artists no longer "quote" the materials, the fragments and motifs, of a mass or popular culture, as Joyce (and Flaubert) began to do, or Mahler; they somehow incorporate them to the point where many of our older critical and evaluative categories (founded precisely on the radical differentiation of modernist and mass culture) no longer seem functional.

But if this is the case, then it seems at least possible that what wears the mask and makes the gestures of "populism" in the various postmodernist apologias and manifestoes is in reality a mere reflex and symptom of a (to be sure momentous) cultural mutation, in which what used to be stigmatized as mass or commercial culture is now received into the precincts of a new and enlarged cultural realm. In any case, one would expect a term drawn from the typology of political ideologies to undergo basic semantic readjustments when its initial referent (that Popular-front class coalition of workers, peasants and petty bourgeois generally called "the people") has disappeared.

Perhaps, however, this is not so new a story after all: one remembers, indeed, Freud's delight at discovering an obscure tribal culture, which alone among the multitudinous traditions of dream-analysis on the earth had managed to hit on the notion that all dreams had hidden sexual meanings—except for sexual dreams, which meant something else! So also it would seem in the postmodernist debate, and the depoliticized bureaucratic society to which it corresponds, where all seemingly cultural positions turn out to be symbolic forms of political moralizing, except for the single overtly political note, which suggests a slippage from politics back into culture again. I have the feeling that the only adequate way out of this vicious circle, besides praxis itself, is a historical and dialectical view which seeks to grasp the present as History.

NOTES

1. The following analysis does not seem to me applicable to the work of the *boundary two* group, who early on appropriated the term "postmodernism" in the rather different sense of a critique of establishment "modernist" thought.

2. Written in spring, 1982.

3. See his "Modernity—An Incomplete Project," in Hal Foster, ed., *The Anti-Aesthetic* (Port Townsend, Washington: Bay Press, 1983), pp. 3–15. The essay was first published in *New German Critique*, 22 (Winter 1981), 3–14, under the different title "Modernity versus Postmodernity."

4. The specific politics associated with the "Greens" would seem to constitute a reaction to this situation, rather than an exception from it.

5. See "Answering the Questions: What Is Postmodernism?" in J. F. Lyotard, *The Postmodern Condition* (Minneapolis: University of Minnesota Press, 1984), pp. 71–82; the book itself focusses primarily on science and epistemology rather than on culture.

6. See in particular *Architecture and Utopia* (Cambridge: MIT Press, 1976) and *Modern Architecture*, with Francesco Dal Co (New York: Abrams, 1979); and also my "Architecture and the Critique of Ideology," in *ReVisions: Papers in Architectural Theory and Criticism*, 1, No. 1 (Winter 1984).

7. I have tried to do this in "Postmodernism, Or, The Cultural Logic of Late Capitalism," *New Left Review*, 146 (July–August 1984), 53–92; my contribution to *The Anti-Aesthetic*, op. cit., is a fragment of this definitive version.

8. See, for example, Charles Jencks, *Late-Modern Architecture* (New York: Rizzoli, 1980); Jencks here however shifts his usage of the term from the designation for a cultural dominant or period style to the name for one aesthetic movement among others.

25

Stephen J. Greenblatt
1943–

Stephen J. Greenblatt teaches at the University of California at Berkeley. He is important to the study of the English Renaissance, having published *Sir Walter Raleigh: The Renaissance Man and his Roles* (1973), *Renaissance Self-Fashioning* (1980), and edited *The Forms of Power and the Power of Forms in the Renaissance* (1982). In addition, Greenblatt serves as co-editor of *Representations*, a journal published by the University of California.

He is associated with a school of criticism known as "new historicism," a term he introduced in a special issue of *Genre* in 1982. The new historicism distinguishes itself from older historicism by not thinking of history as a "background" to literature but, rather, by conceiving of both history and literature as "textual"—as made up by particular texts—which are, as he says in the introduction to the *Genre* special issue, "fields of force, places of dissension and shifting interests, occasions for the jostling of orthodox and subversive impulses." "Shakespeare and the Exorcists" is an excellent example of the new historicism. Greenblatt brings together Samuel Harsnett's book *A Declaration of Egregious Popish Impostures*, written in 1603, and *King Lear* to show how Shakespeare "converges exorcism and theater." "*King Lear*'s relation to Harsnett's book," Greenblatt writes, "is essentially one of reiteration, a reiteration that signals a deeper and unexpressed institutional exchange." In his discussion Greenblatt aligns himself with the textualism of deconstruction as well as the historicism of Marxism to offer a fine sense of the power of Shakespeare's play.

Shakespeare and the Exorcists

Between the spring of 1585 and the summer of 1586, a group of English Catholic priests led by the Jesuit William Weston, alias Father Edmunds, conducted a series of spectacular exorcisms, principally in the house of a recusant gentleman, Sir George Peckham of Denham, Buckinghamshire. The priests were outlaws—by an Act of 1585 the mere presence in England of a Jesuit or seminary priest constituted high treason—and those who sheltered them were guilty of a felony, punishable by death. Yet the exorcisms, though clandestine, drew large crowds, almost certainly in the hundreds, and must have been common knowledge to hundreds more. In 1603, long after the arrest and punishment of those involved,

Samuel Harsnett, then chaplain to the Bishop of London, wrote a detailed account of the cases, based upon sworn statements taken from four of the demoniacs and one of the priests. It has been recognized since the eighteenth century that Shakespeare was reading Harsnett's book, *A Declaration of Egregious Popish Impostures*, as he was writing *King Lear*.[1]

My concern is with the relation between these two texts, and I want to suggest that our understanding of this relation is greatly enhanced by the theoretical ferment that has affected (some would say afflicted) literary studies during the past decade. This claim may arouse scepticism on several counts. Source study is, as we all know, the elephants' graveyard of literary history. My own work, moreover, has consistently failed to make the move that can redeem, on these occasions, such unpromising beginnings: the move from a local problem to a universal, encompassing, and abstract problematic within which the initial concerns are situated. For me the study of the literary is the study of contingent, particular, intended, and historically embedded works; if theory inevitably involves the desire to escape from contingency into a higher realm, a realm in which signs are purified of the slime of history, then this paper is written *against* theory.[2]

But I am not convinced that theory necessarily drives toward the abstract purity of autonomous signification, and, even when it does, its influence upon the study of literature may be quite distinct from its own designs. Indeed, I believe that the most important effect of contemporary theory upon the practice of literary criticism, and certainly upon *my* practice, is to subvert the tendency to think of aesthetic representation as ultimately autonomous, separable from its cultural context and hence divorced from the social, ideological, and material matrix in which all art is produced and consumed. This subversion is true not only of Marxist theory explicitly engaged in polemics against literary autonomy, but also of deconstructionist theory, even at its most hermetic and abstract. For the undecidability that deconstruction repeatedly discovers in literary signification also calls into question the boundaries between the literary and the nonliterary. The intention to produce a work of literature does not guarantee an autonomous text, since the signifiers always exceed and thus undermine intention. This constant exceeding (which is the paradoxical expression of an endless deferral of meaning) forces the collapse of all stable oppositions, or rather compels interpretation to acknowledge that one position is always infected with traces of its radical antithesis.[3] Insofar as the absolute disjunction of the literary and the nonliterary had been the root assumption of mainstream Anglo-American criticism in the mid-twentieth century, deconstruction emerged as a liberating challenge, a salutary return of the literary text to the condition of all other texts and a simultaneous assault on the positivist certitude of the nonliterary, the privileged realm of historical fact. History cannot be divorced from textuality, and all texts can be compelled to confront the crisis of undecidability revealed in the literary text. Hence history loses its epistemological innocence, while literature loses an isolation that had come to seem more a prison than a privilege.

The problem with this theoretical liberation, in my view, is that it is forced, by definition, to discount the specific, institutional interests served both by local episodes of undecidability and contradiction and by the powerful if conceptually imperfect differentiation between the literary and the nonliterary. Deconstruction is occasionally attacked as if it were a satanic doctrine, but I sometimes think that it is not satanic enough; as John Wesley wrote to his brother, "If I have any

fear, it is not of falling into hell, but of falling into nothing."[4] Deconstructionist readings lead too readily and predictably to the void; in actual literary practice the perplexities into which one is led are not moments of pure, untrammeled *aporia* but localized strategies in particular historical encounters. Similarly, it is important to expose the theoretical untenability of the conventional boundaries between facts and artifacts, but the particular terms of this boundary at a specific time and place cannot simply be discarded. On the contrary, as I will try to demonstrate in some detail, these impure terms that mark the difference between the literary and the nonliterary are the currency in crucial institutional negotiations and exchange. This institutional economy is one of the central concerns of the critical method that I have called cultural poetics.

Let us return to Samuel Harsnett. The relation between *King Lear* and *A Declaration of Egregious Popish Impostures* has, as I have remarked, been known for centuries, but the knowledge has remained almost entirely inert, locked in the conventional pieties of source study. From Harsnett, we are told, Shakespeare borrowed the names of the foul fiends by whom Edgar, in his disguise as the Bedlam beggar Poor Tom, claims to be possessed. From Harsnett, too, the playwright derived some of the language of madness, several of the attributes of hell, and a substantial number of colorful adjectives. These and other possible borrowings have been carefully catalogued, but the question of their significance has been not only unanswered but unasked.[5] Until recently, the prevailing model for the study of literary sources, a model in effect parceled out between the old historicism and the new criticism, blocked such a question. As a freestanding, self-sufficient, disinterested art-work produced by a solitary genius, *King Lear* has only an accidental relation to its sources: they provide a glimpse of the "raw material" that the artist fashioned. In so far as this "material" is taken seriously at all, it is as part of the work's "historical background," a phrase that reduces history to a decorative setting or a convenient, well-lighted pigeonhole. But once the differentiations upon which this model is based begin to crumble, then source study is compelled to change its character: history cannot simply be set against literary texts as either stable antithesis or stable background, and the protective isolation of those texts gives way to a sense of their interaction with other texts and hence to the permeability of their boundaries. "When I play with my cat," writes Montaigne, "who knows if I am not a pastime to her more than she is to me?"[6] When Shakespeare borrows from Harsnett, who knows if Harsnett has not already, in a deep sense, borrowed from Shakespeare's theater what Shakespeare borrows back? Whose interests are served by the borrowing? And is there a larger cultural text produced by the exchange?

Such questions do not lead, for me at least, to the *O altitudo!* of radical indeterminacy. They lead rather to an exploration of the institutional strategies in which both *King Lear* and Harsnett's *Declaration* are embedded. These strategies, I suggest, are part of an intense and sustained struggle in late sixteenth- and early seventeenth-century England to redefine the central values of society. Such a redefinition entailed a transformation of the prevailing standards of judgment and action, a rethinking of the conceptual categories by which the ruling élites constructed their world, and which they attempted to impose upon the majority of the population. At the heart of this struggle, which had as its outcome a murderous civil war, was the definition of the sacred, a definition that directly involved secular as well as religious institutions, since the legitimacy of the state rested explicitly upon its claim to a measure of sacredness. What is the sacred? Who defines and polices its boundaries? How can society distinguish between legitimate and illegitimate claims to sacred authority? In early modern England, rivalry among elites competing for the major share of authority was characteristically expressed not only in parliamentary factions but in bitter struggles over religious doctrine and practice.

Harsnett's *Declaration* is a weapon in one such struggle, the attempt by the established and state-supported Church of England to eliminate competing religious authorities by wiping out pockets of rivalrous charisma. Charisma, in Edward Shil's phrase, is "awe-arousing centrality,"[7] the sense of breaking through the routine into the realm of the "extraordinary," and hence the sense of making direct contact with the ultimate, vital sources of legitimacy, authority, and sacredness. Exorcism was for centuries one of the supreme manifestations in Latin Christianity of this charisma; "in the healing of the possessed," Peter Brown writes, "the *præsentia* of the saints was held to be registered with unfailing accuracy, and their ideal power, their *potentia*, shown most fully and in the most reassuring manner."[8] Reassuring, that is, not only or even primarily to the demoniac, but to the community of believers who bore witness to the ritual and indeed, through their tears and prayers and thanksgiving, participated in it. For unlike sorcery, which occurred most frequently in the dark corners of the land, in remote rural hamlets and isolated cottages, demonic possession seems largely an urban phenomenon. The devil depended upon an audience, as did the charismatic healer: the great exorcisms of the late middle ages and early Renaissance took place at the heart of cities, in cathedrals packed with spectators. They were, as voluminous contemporary accounts declare, moving testimonials to the power of the true faith. But in Protestant England of the late sixteenth century, neither the *præsentia* nor the *potentia* of the exorcist was any longer reassuring to religious authorities, and the Anglican Church had no desire to treat the urban masses to a spectacle whose edifying value had been called into question. Even relatively small assemblies, gathered far from the cities in the obscurity of private houses, had come to represent a threat.

In the *Declaration*, Harsnett specifically attacks exorcism as practiced by Jesuits, but he had earlier leveled the same charges at the Puritan exorcist John Darrell.[9] And he does so not, as we might expect, to claim a monopoly on the practice for the Anglican Church, but to expose exorcism itself as a fraud. On behalf of established religious and secular authority, Harsnett wishes, in effect, to cap permanently the great rushing geysers of charisma released in rituals of exorcism. Spiritual *potentia* will henceforth be distributed with greater moderation and control through the whole of the Anglican hierarchy, a hierarchy at whose pinnacle is placed the sole legitimate possessor of absolute charismatic authority, the monarch, supreme head of the Church in England.

The arguments that Harsnett marshalls against exorcism have a rationalistic cast that may mislead us, for despite appearances we are not dealing with an Enlightenment attempt to construct a rational faith. Harsnett denies the presence of the demonic in those whom Father Edmunds claimed to exorcize, but finds it in the exorcists themselves:

> And who was the deuil, the brocher, herald, and perswader of these vnutterable treasons, but Weston [*alias* Edmunds] the Iesuit, the chief plotter, and . . . all the holy Couey of the twelue deuilish comedians in their seueral turnes: for there was neither deuil, nor vrchin, nor Elfe, but themselues.[10]

Hence, writes Harsnett, the "Dialogue between *Edmunds*, & the deuil" was in reality a dialogue between "the deuil *Edmunds*, and *Edmunds* the deuil, for he played both parts himself."[11]

This strategy—the reinscription of evil onto the professed enemies of evil—is one of the characteristic operations of religious authority in the early modern period, and has its secular analogues in more recent history when famous revolutionaries are paraded forth to be tried as counter-revolutionaries. The paradigmatic Renaissance instance is the case of the *benandanti*, analyzed brilliantly by the historian Carlo Ginzburg.[12] The *benandanti* were members of a northern Italian folk cult who believed that their spirits went forth seasonally to battle with fennel stalks against their enemies, the witches. If the *benandanti* triumphed, their victory assured the peasants of good harvests; if they lost, the witches would be free to work their mischief. The Inquisition first became interested in the practice in the late sixteenth century; after conducting a series of lengthy inquiries, the Holy Office determined that the cult was demonic, and in subsequent interrogations attempted, with some success, to persuade the witch-fighting *benandanti* that they were themselves witches.

Harsnett does not hope to persuade exorcists that they are devils; he wishes to expose their fraudulence and relies upon the state to punish them. But he is not willing to abandon the demonic altogether, and it hovers in his work, half-accusation, half-metaphor, whenever he refers to Father Edmunds or the Pope. Satan served too important a function to be cast off lightly by the early seventeenth-century clerical establishment. The same state Church that sponsored the attacks on superstition in the *Declaration of Egregious Popish Impostures* continued to cooperate, if less enthusiastically than before, in the ferocious prosecutions of witches. These prosecutions significantly were handled by the secular judicial apparatus—witchcraft was a criminal offense like aggravated assault or murder—and hence reinforced rather than rivaled the bureaucratic control of authority. The eruption of the demonic into the human world was not denied altogether, but the problem was to be processed through the proper, secular channels. In cases of witchcraft, the devil was defeated in the courts through the simple expedient of hanging his human agents and not, as in cases of possession, compelled by a spectacular spiritual counterforce to speak out and depart.

Witchcraft, then, was distinct from possession, and though Harsnett himself is skeptical about accusations of witchcraft, his principal purpose is to expose a nexus of chicanery and delusion in the practice of exorcism.[13] By doing so he hopes to drive the practice out of society's central zone, to deprive it of its prestige and discredit its apparent efficacy. In late antiquity, as Peter Brown has demonstrated, exorcism was based upon the model of the Roman judicial system: the exorcist conducted a formal *quæstio* in which the demon, under torture, was forced to confess the truth.[14] Now, after more than a millennium, this power would once again be vested solely in the state.

Harsnett's efforts, backed by his powerful superiors, did seriously restrict the practice of exorcism. Canon 72 of the new Church Canons of 1604 ruled that henceforth no minister, unless he had the special permission of his bishop, was to attempt "upon any pretense whatsoever, whether of possession or obsession, by fasting and prayer, to cast out any devil or devils, under pain of the imputation of imposture or cozenage and deposition from the minstery."[15] Since special permission was rarely if ever granted, exorcism had, in effect, been officially halted. But it proved easier to drive exorcism from the center to the periphery than to strip it entirely of its power. Exorcism had been a process of reintegration as well as a manifestation of authority; as the ethnographer Shirokogorov observed of the shamans of Siberia, exorcists could "master" harmful spirits and restore "psychic equilibrium" to whole communities as well as to individuals.[16] The pronouncements of English bishops could not suddenly banish from the land inner demons who stood, as Peter Brown puts it, "for the intangible emotional undertones of ambiguous situations and for the uncertain motives of refractory individuals."[17] The possessed gave voice to the rage, anxiety, and sexual frustration that built up particularly easily in the authoritarian, patriarchal, impoverished, and plague-ridden world of early modern England. The Anglicans attempted to dismantle a corrupt and inadequate therapy without effecting a new and successful cure. In the absence of exorcism, Harsnett could only offer the possessed the very slender reed of Jacobean medicine; if the recently deciphered journal of the Buckinghamshire physician, Richard Napier, is at all representative, doctors in the period struggled to treat a substantial number of cases of possession.[18] But for Harsnett the problem does not really exist, for he argues that the great majority of cases of possession are either fraudulent or subtly called into existence by the ritual designed to treat them. Eliminate the cure and you eliminate the disease. He is forced to concede that at some distant time possession and exorcism were authentic, for, after all, Jesus himself had driven a legion of unclean spirits out of a possessed man and into the Gadarene swine (Mark 5:1–19); but the age of miracles has passed, and corporeal possession by demons is no longer possible. The spirit abroad is "the spirit of illusion."[19] Whether they profess to be Catholics or Calvinists does not matter; all modern exorcists practice the same time-honored trade: "the feate of iugling and deluding the people by counterfeyt miracles."[20] Exorcists sometimes contend, acknowledged Harsnett, that the casting out of devils is not a miracle but a wonder—"*mirandum & non miraculum*"—but "both tearmes spring from one roote of wonder or maruell: an effect which a thing strangely done doth procure in the minds of the beholders, as being aboue the reach of nature and reason."[21]

The significance of exorcism, then, lies not in any intrinsic quality of the ritual nor in the precise character of the marks of possession: it lies entirely in the impression made upon the spectators. It may appear that the exorcist and the possessed are utterly absorbed in their terrifying confrontation, but in the midst of the sound and fury—"crying, gnashing of teeth, wallowing, foaming, extraordinarie and supernaturall strength, and supernaturall knowledge"[22]—the real object of the performers' attention is the crowd of beholders.

To counter these effects, Harsnett needed an analytical tool that would enable him to demystify exorcism, to show his readers why the ritual could be so empty and yet so powerful, why beholders could be induced to believe that they were witnessing the ultimate confrontation of good and evil, why a few miserable shifts could produce the experience of horror and wonder. He finds that tool in *theater*.

In the most powerful artistic practice of his age, Harsnett claims to reveal the analytical key to disclosing the degradation of the ancient spiritual practice: exorcisms are stage plays fashioned by cunning clerical dramatists and performed by actors skilled in improvisation. Harsnett first used this theatrical analysis in his attack on Darrell, but it was not until three years later, in his polemic against the Jesuit exorcists, that he worked out its implica-

tions in detail.[23] In the account presented in the *Declaration of Egregious Popish Impostures*, some of the participants are self-conscious professionals, like Father Edmunds and his cohorts; others (mostly impressionable young serving women and unstable, down-at-heel young gentlemen) are amateurs cunningly drawn into the demonic stage business. Those selected to play the possessed are in effect taught their roles without realizing at first that they *are* roles.

The priests begin by talking conspicuously about the way successful exorcisms abroad had taken place, and describing in lurid detail the precise symptoms of the possessed. They then await occasions upon which to improvise: a serving man, "beeing pinched with penurie, & hunger, did lie but a night, or two, abroad in the fieldes, and beeing a melancholicke person, was scared with lightning, and thunder, that happened in the night, & loe, an euident signe, that the man was possessed"[24]; a dissolute young gentleman "had a spice of the *Hysterica passio*" or, as it is popularly called, "the Moother,"[25] and that too is a sign of possession. An inflamed toe, a pain in the side, a fright taken from the sudden leaping of a cat, a fall in the kitchen, an intense depression following the loss of a beloved child—all are occasions for the priests to step forward and detect the awful presence of the demonic, whereupon the young "scholers," as Harsnett wryly terms the naive performers, "*frame* themselues iumpe and fit vnto the Priests humors, to mop, mow, iest, raile, raue, roare, commend & discommend, and as the priests would haue them, vpon fitting occasions (according to the differences of times, places, and commers in) in all things to play the deuils accordinglie."[26]

The theatricality of exorcism, to which the *Declaration* insistently calls attention, has been repeatedly noted by modern ethnographers who do not share Harsnett's reforming zeal or his sense of outrage. In an illuminating study of possession among the Ethiopians of Gondar, Michel Leiris notes that the healer carefully instructs the *zar*, or spirit, who has seized upon someone, how to behave: the types of cries appropriate to the occasion, the expected violent contortions, the "decorum," as Harsnett would put it, of the trance state.[27] The treatment is in effect an initiation into the performance of the symptoms, which are then cured precisely because they conform to the stereotype of the healing process. One must not conclude, writes Leiris, that there are no "real"—that is, sincerely experienced—cases of possession, for many of the patients (principally young women and slaves) seem genuinely ill, but at the same time there are no cases that are exempt from artifice.[28] Between authentic possession, spontaneous and involuntary, and inauthentic possession, simulated to provide a show or extract some material or moral benefit, there are so many subtle shadings that it is impossible to draw a firm boundary.[29] Possession in Gondar *is* theater, but theater that cannot confess its own theatrical nature, for this is not "theater played" (*théâtre joué*) but "theater lived" (*théâtre vécu*), lived not only by the spirit-haunted actor but by the audience. Those who witness a possession may at any moment be themselves possessed, and even if they are untouched by the *zar*, they remain participants rather than passive spectators. For the theatrical performance is not shielded from them by an impermeable membrane; possession is extraordinary but not marginal, a heightened but not separate state. In possession, writes Leiris, the collective life itself takes the form of theater.[30]

Precisely those qualities that fascinate and charm the ethnographer disgust the embattled Harsnett: where the former can write of "authentic" possession, in the unspoken assurance that none of his readers actually believes in the existence of "*zars*," the latter, granted no such assurance and culturally threatened by the alternative vision of reality, struggles to prove that possession is by definition inauthentic; where the former sees a complex ritual integrated into the social process, the latter sees "a *Stygian* comedy to make silly people afraid";[31] where the former sees the theatrical expression of collective life, the latter sees the theatrical promotion of specific and malevolent institutional interests. And where Leiris's central point is that possession is a theater that does not confess its own theatricality, Harsnett's concern is to enforce precisely such a confession: the last 102 pages of the *Declaration of Egregious Popish Impostures* reprint the "severall Examinations, and confessions of the parties pretended to be possessed, and dispossessed by *Weston* the Iesuit, and his adherents: set downe word for worde as they were taken vpon oath before her Maiesties Commissioners for causes Ecclesiasticall."[32] These transcripts prove, according to Harsnett, that the solemn ceremony of exorcism is a "play of sacred miracles," a "wonderful pageant," a "deuil Theater."[33]

The force of this confession, for Harsnett, is to demolish exorcism. Theater is not the disinterested expression of the popular spirit, but the indelible mark of falsity, tawdriness, and rhetorical manipulation. And these sinister qualities are rendered diabolical by that which so appeals to Leiris: exorcism's cunning concealment of its own theatricality. The spectators do not know that they are responding to a powerful if sleazy tragicomedy; hence their tears and joy, their transports of "commiseration and compassion,"[34] are rendered up, not to a troupe of acknowledged players, but to seditious Puritans or to the supremely dangerous Catholic Church. The theatrical seduction is not, for Harsnett, merely a Jesuitical strategy; it is the essence of the Church itself: Catholicism is a "Mimick superstition."[35]

Harsnett's response is to try to compel the Church to become the theater, just as Catholic clerical garments—the copes and albs and amices and stoles that were the glories of medieval textile crafts—were sold during the Reformation to the players. When an actor in a history play took the part of an English bishop, he could conceivably have worn the actual robes of the character he was representing. Far more is involved here than thrift: the transmigration of a single ecclesiastical cloak from the vestry to the wardrobe may stand as an emblem of the more complex and elusive institutional exchanges that are my subject: a sacred sign, designed to be displayed before a crowd of men and women, is emptied, made negotiable, traded from one institution to another. Such exchanges are rarely so tangible; they are not usually registered in inventories, not often sealed with a cash payment. Nonetheless they occur constantly, for it is precisely through the process of institutional negotiation and exchange that differentiated expressive systems, distinct cultural discourses, are fashioned. We may term such fashioning cultural poesis; the sale of clerical garments is an instance of the ideological labor that such poesis entails. What happens when the piece of cloth is passed from the church to the playhouse? A consecrated object is reclassified, assigned a cash value, transferred from a sacred to a profane setting, deemed suitable to be staged. The theater company is willing to pay for the object not because it contributes to naturalistic representation but because it still bears a symbolic value, however attenuated. On the bare Elizabethan stage, costumes were particularly important—companies were willing to pay more for a good costume than for a good play—and that importance in turn reflected culture's fetishistic obsession with clothes as a mark of status and degree. And if for the theater the acquisition of clerical garments was a significant appropriation of symbolic power, why would the Church part with that power? Because selling Catholic vestments to the players was a form of symbolic aggression: a vivid, wry reminder that Catholicism, as Harsnett puts it, is "the Pope's playhouse."[36]

This blend of appropriation and aggression is similarly at work in the transfer of possession and exorcism from sacred to profane representation. Hence the *Declaration* take pains to identify exorcism not merely with "the theatrical"—a category that scarcely exists for Harsnett—but with the actual theater; at issue is not so much a metaphorical concept as a functioning institution. For if Harsnett can drive exorcism into the theater—if he can show that the stately houses in which the rituals were performed were playhouses, that the sacred garments were what he calls a "lousie holy wardrop,"[37] that the terrifying writhings were simulations, that the uncanny signs and wonders were contemptible stage tricks, that the devils were the "cassiered woodden-beated" Vices from medieval drama,[38] and that the exorcists were "vagabond players, that coast from Towne to Towne"[39]—then the ceremony and everything for which it stands will, as far as he is concerned, be emptied out. And, with this emptying out, Harsnett will have driven exorcism from the center of the periphery—in the case of London, quite literally to the periphery, where increasingly stringent urban regulation had already driven the public playhouses.

It is in this symbolically charged zone of pollution, disease, and licentious entertainment that Harsnett seeks to situate the practice of exorcism.[40] What had once occurred in solemn glory at the very center of the city would now be staged alongside the culture's other vulgar spectacles and illusions. Indeed the sense of the theater's tawdriness, marginality, and emptiness—the sense that everything the players touch is thereby rendered hollow—underlies Harsnett's analysis not only of exorcism but of the entire Catholic Church. Demonic possession is a particularly attractive cornerstone for such an analysis, not only because of its histrionic intensity but because the theater itself is by its very nature bound up with possession. Harsnett did not have to believe that the cult of Dionysus out of which the Greek drama evolved was a cult of possession; even the ordinary and familiar theater of his own time depended upon the apparent transformation of the actor into the voice, the actions, and the face of another.

With his characteristic opportunism and artistic self-consciousness, Shakespeare in his first known play, *The Comedy of Errors* (1950), was already toying with the connection between theater, illusion, and spurious possession. Antipholus of Syracuse, accosted by his twin's mistress, imagines that he is encountering the devil: "Satan avoid I charge thee tempt me not" (IV.iii.46). The Ephesian Antipholus's wife, Adriana, dismayed by the apparently and behavior of her husband, imagines that the devil has possessed him, and she dutifully calls in an exorcist: "Good Doctor Pinch, you are a conjurer;/Establish him in his true sense again" (IV.iv.45–6). Pinch begins the solemn ritual:

> I charge thee, Satan, hous'd within this man,
> To yield possession to my holy prayers,
> And to thy state of darkness hie thee straight;
> I conjure thee by all the saints in heaven.
> *(IV.iv.52–5)*

only to be interrupted with a box on the ears from the outraged husband: "Peace, doting wizard, peace; I am not mad." For the exorcist, such denials only confirm the presence of an evil spirit: "the fiend is strong within him" (IV.iv.105). At the scene's end, Antipholus is dragged away to be "bound and laid in some dark room."

The false presumption of demonic possession in *The Comedy of Errors* is not the result of deception; it is an instance of what one of Shakespeare's sources calls a "suppose"—an attempt to make sense of a series of bizarre actions gleefully generated by the comedy's screwball coincidences. Exorcism is the kind of straw people clutch at when the world seems to have gone mad. In *Twelfth Night*, written some ten years later, Shakespeare's view of exorcism, though still comic, has darkened. Possession now is not a mistaken "suppose" but a fraud, a malicious practical joke played upon Malvolio. "Pray God he be not bewitched" (III.iv.102), Maria piously intones at the sight of the cross-gartered, leering gull, and when he is out of earshot Fabian laughs, "If this were played upon a stage now, I could condemn it as an improbable fiction" (III.iv.128–9).[41] The theatrical self-consciousness is intensified when Feste the clown is brought in to conduct a mock-exorcism; "I would I were the first that ever dissembled in such a gown" (IV.ii.5–6), he remarks sententiously as he disguises himself as Sir Topas the curate. If the gibe had a specific reference for the play's original audience, it would be to the Puritan Darrell who had only recently been convicted of dissembling in the exorcism of William Sommers of Nottingham. Now, the scene would suggest, the tables are being turned on the self-righteous fanatic. "Good Sir Topas," pleads Malvolio, "do not think I am mad. They have laid me here in hideous darkness." "Fie, thou dishonest Satan!" Feste replies. "I call thee by the most modest terms, for I am one of those gentle ones that will use the devil himself with courtesy" (IV.ii.29–34).

By 1600 then Shakespeare had clearly marked out possession and exorcism as frauds, so much so that in *All's Well That Ends Well*, a few years later, he could casually use the term "exorcist" as a synonym for illusion-monger: "Is there no exorcist/Beguiles the truer office of mine eyes?" cries the King of France when Helena, whom he thought dead, appears before him: "Is't real that I see?" (V.iii.298–300). When in 1603 Harsnett was whipping exorcism toward the theater, Shakespeare was already at the entrance to the Globe to welcome it.

Given Harsnett's frequent expressions of the "anti-theatrical prejudice," this welcome may seem strange, but in fact nothing in the *Declaration of Egregious Popish Impostures* necessarily implies hostility to the theater as a professional institution. It was Darrell, and not Harsnett, who represented an implacable threat to the theater, for where the Anglican polemicist saw the theatrical in the demonic the Puritan polemicist saw the demonic in the theatrical: "The Devil," wrote Stephen Gosson, "is the efficient cause of plays."[42] Harsnett's work attacks a form of theater that pretends that it is not entertainment but sober reality; hence his polemic virtually depends upon the existence of an officially designated commercial theater, marked off openly from all other forms and ceremonies of public life precisely by virtue of its freely acknowledged fictionality. Where there is no pretense to truth, there can be no *imposture:* it is this argument that permits so ontologically anxious a figure as Sir Philip Sidney to defend poetry—"Now for the poet, he nothing affirms, and therefore never lieth."[43]

In this spirit Puck playfully defends *A Midsummer Night's Dream:*

> If we shadows have offended,
> Think but this, and all is mended,
> That you have but slumber'd here
> While these visions did appear.

And this weak and idle theme,
No more yielding but a dream.
(V.i.409–14)

With a similarly frank admission of illusion Shakespeare can open the theater to Harsnett's polemic. Indeed, as if Harsnett's momentum carried *him* into the theater along with the fraud he hotly pursues, Shakespeare in *King Lear* stages not only exorcism, but Harsnett *on* exorcism:

> Five fiends have been in poor Tom at once; as Oberdicut, of lust; Hoberdidance, prince of dumbness; Mahu, of stealing; Modo, of murder; Flibbertigibbet, of mopping and mowing; who since possesses chambermaids and waiting-women.[44] (IV.i.57–62)

Those in the audience who had read Harsnett's book or heard of the notorious Buckinghamshire exorcisms would recognize in Edgar's lines an odd, joking allusion to the chambermaids, Sara and Friswood Williams, and the waiting woman, Ann Smith, principal actors in Father Edmund's "Devil Theater." The humor of the anachronism here is akin to the Fool's earlier quip, "This prophecy Merlin shall make; for I live before his time" (Ill.ii.95–6); both are bursts of a cheeky self-consciousness that dares deliberately to violate the historical setting in order to remind the audience of the play's conspicuous doubleness, its simultaneous distance and contemporaneity.

A *Declaration of Egregious Popish Impostures* supplies Shakespeare not only with an uncanny anachronism but with the model for Edgar's histrionic disguise. For it is not the *authenticity* of the demonology that the playwright finds in Harsnett—the usual reason for authorial recourse to a specialized source (as, for example, to a military or legal handbook)—but rather the inauthenticity of a theatrical role. Shakespeare appropriates for Edgar, then, a documented fraud, complete with an impressive collection of what the *Declaration* calls "uncouth non-significant names"[45] that have been made up to sound exotic and that carry with them a faint but ineradicable odor of spuriousness.

In Sidney's *Arcadia,* which provided the outline of the Gloucester subplot, the good son, having escaped his father's misguided attempt to kill him, becomes a soldier in another land and quickly distinguishes himself. Shakespeare insists not only on Edgar's perilous fall from his father's favor but upon his marginalization: Edgar becomes the possessed Poor Tom, the outcast with no possibility of working his way back in toward the center. "My neighbours," writes John Bunyan in the 1660s, "were amazed at this my great conversion from prodigious profaneness to something like a moral life; and truly so well they might for this my conversion was as great as for a Tom of Bethlem to become a sober man."[46] Of course, Edgar is only a pretend Tom o'Bedlam and hence can return to the community when it is safe to do so; but the force of Harsnett's argument is to make mimed possession even more marginal and desperate than the real thing.

Indeed, Edgar's desperation is bound up with the stress of "counterfeiting," a stress he has already noted in the presence of the mad and ruined Lear and now, in the lines I have just quoted, feels still more intensely in the presence of his blinded and ruined father. He is struggling with the urge to stop playing or, as he puts it, with the feeling that he "cannot daub it further" (IV.i.51). Why he does not simply reveal himself to Gloucester at this point is entirely unclear. "And yet I must" is all he says of his continued disguise, as he recites the catalog of devils and leads his despairing father off to Dover Cliff.[47]

The subsequent episode—Gloucester's suicide attempt—deepens the play's brooding upon spurious exorcism. "It is a good *decorum* in a Comedie," writes

Harsnett, "To giue us emptie names for things, and to tell us of strange Monsters within, where there be none";[48] so too the "Miracle-minter," Father Edmunds, and his fellow exorcists manipulate their impressionable gulls: "The priests doe report often in their patients hearing the dreadful formes, similitudes, and shapes, that the deuils vse to depart in out of those possessed bodies . . . : and this they tell with so graue a countenance, pathetical termes, and accomodate action, as it leaues a very deepe impression in the memory, and fancie of their actors."[49] Thus by the power of theatrical suggestion, the anxious subjects on whom the priests work their charms come to believe that they too have witnessed the devil depart in grotesque form from their own bodies, whereupon the priests turn their eyes heavenward and give thanks to the Blessed Virgin. In much the same manner Edgar persuades Gloucester that he stands on a high cliff, and then, after his credulous father has flung himself forward, Edgar switches roles and pretends that he is a bystander who has seen a demon depart from the old man:

As I stood here below methought his eyes
Were two full moons; he had a thousand
    noses,
Horns whelk'd and wav'd like the enridged
    sea:
It was some fiend; therefore, thou happy
    father,
Think that the clearest Gods, who make
    them honours
Of men's impossibilities, have preserved
    thee.

(IV.vi.69–74)

Edgar tries to create in Gloucester an experience of awe and wonder so intense that it can shatter his suicidal despair and restore his faith in the benevolence of the gods: "Thy life's a miracle," he tells his father.[50] For Shakespeare, as for Harsnett, this miracle-minting is the product of specifically histrionic manipulations; the scene at Dover is simultaneously a disenchanted analysis of religious and of theatrical illusions. Walking about on a perfectly flat stage, Edgar does to Gloucester what the theater usually does to the audience: he persuades his father to discount the evidence of his senses—"Methinks the ground is even"—and to accept a palpable fiction: "Horrible steep." But the audience at a play, of course, never absolutely accepts such fictions: we enjoy being brazenly lied to, we welcome for the sake of pleasure what we know to be untrue, but we withhold from the theater the simple assent that we grant to everyday reality. And we enact this withholding when, depending on the staging, either we refuse to believe that Gloucester is on a cliff above Dover beach or we realize that what we thought was a cliff (in the convention of theatrical representation) is in reality flat ground.

Hence, in the midst of Shakespeare's demonstration of the convergence of exorcism and theater, we return to the difference that enables *King Lear* to borrow comfortably from Harsnett: the theater elicits from us complicity rather than belief. Demonic possession is responsibly marked out for the audience as a theatrical fraud, designed to gull the unsuspecting: monsters such as the fiend with the thousand noses are illusions most easily imposed on the old, the blind, and the despairing; evil comes not from the mysterious otherworld of demons but from this world, the world of court and family intrigue. In *King Lear* there are no ghosts, as there are in *Richard III, Julius Caesar*, or *Hamlet;* no witches, as in *Macbeth;* no mysterious music of departing demons, as in *Antony and Cleopatra*.

King Lear is haunted by a sense of rituals and beliefs that are no longer efficacious, that have been *emptied out*. The characters appeal again and again to the pagan gods, but the gods remain utterly silent.[51] Nothing answers to human questions but human voices; nothing breeds about the heart but human desires; nothing inspires awe or terror but human suffering and human depravity. For all the invocation of the gods in *King Lear,* it is quite clear that there are no devils.

Edgar is no more possessed than the sanest of us, and we can see for ourselves that there was no demon standing by Gloucester's side. Likewise Lear's madness does not have a supernatural origin: it is linked, as in Harsnett, to *hysterica passio,* exposure to the elements, and extreme anguish, and its cure comes at the hands not of an exorcist but of a doctor. His prescription involves neither religious rituals (as in Catholicism) nor fasting and prayer (as in Puritanism), but tranquillized sleep:

> Our foster-nurse of nature is repose,
> The which he lacks; that to provoke in him,
> Are many simples operative, whose power
> Will close the eye of anguish.
>
> (IV.iv.12–15)[52]

King Lear's relation to Harsnett's book, then, is essentially one of reiteration, a reiteration that signals a deeper and unexpressed institutional exchange. The official church dismantles and cedes to the players the powerful mechanisms of an unwanted and dangerous charisma; in return, the players confirm the charge that those mechanisms are theatrical and hence illusory. The material structure of Elizabethan and Jacobean public theaters heightened this confirmation, since, unlike medieval drama with its fuller integration into society, Shakespeare's drama took place in carefully demarcated playgrounds. *King Lear* offers then a double corroboration of Harsnett's arguments: within the play, Edgar's possession is clearly designated as a fiction, while the play itself is bounded by the institutional signs of fictionality: the wooden walls of the play space, payment for admission, known actors playing the parts, applause, the dances that followed the performance.

The theatrical confirmation of the official position is neither superficial nor unstable. And yet, I want now to suggest, Harsnett's arguments are alienated from themselves when they make their appearance on the Shakespearean stage. This alienation may be set in the context of a more general observation: the closer Shakespeare seems to a source, the more faithfully he reproduces it on stage, the more devastating and decisive his transformation of it. Let us take, for a small, initial instance, Shakespeare's borrowing from Harsnett of the unusual adjective "corky"—i.e. sapless, dry, withered. The word appears in the *Declaration* in the course of a sardonic explanation of why, despite the canonists' declaration that only old women are to be exorcized, Father Edmunds and his crew have a particular fondness for tying in a chair and exorcizing young women. Along with more graphic sexual innuendoes, Harsnett observes that the theatrical role of a demoniac requires "certain actions, motions, distortions, writhings, tumblings, and turbulent passions . . . not to be performed but by suppleness of sinewes. . . . It would (I feare mee) pose all the cunning Exorcists, that are this day to be found, to teach an old corkie woman to writhe, tumble, curvet, and fetch her morice gamboles."[53]

Now Shakespeare's eye was caught by the word "corkie," and he reproduces it in a reference to old Gloucester. But what had been a flourish of Harsnett's typically bullying comic style becomes part of the horror of an almost unendurable scene, a scene of torture that begins when Cornwall orders his servant to take the captive Gloucester and "Bind fast his corky arms" (III.vii.29). The note of bullying humor is still present in the word, but it is present in the character of the torturer.

This one-word instance of repetition as transvaluation may suggest in the tiniest compass what happens to Harsnett's work in the course of *Lear*. The *Declaration's* arguments are loyally reiterated but in a curiously divided form. The voice of skepticism is assimilated to Cornwall, to Goneril, and above all to Edmund, whose "naturalism" is exposed as the argument of the younger and illegitimate son bent on displacing his legitimate older brother and eventually on destroying his father. The fraudulent possession and exorcism are given to the legitimate Edgar, who is forced to such shifts by the nightmarish persecution directed against him. Edgar adopts the role of Poor Tom not out of a corrupt will to deceive, but out of a commendable desire to survive. Modu, Mabu, and the rest are fakes, exactly as Harsnett said they were, but they are the venial sins of a will to endure. And even "venial sins" is too strong: they are the clever inventions that enable a decent and unjustly persecuted man to live. Similarly, there is no grotesque monster standing on the cliff with Gloucester—there isn't even any cliff—but Edgar, himself hunted down like an animal, is trying desperately to save his father from suicidal despair.

All of this has an odd and unsettling resemblance to the situation of the Jesuits in England, if viewed from an unofficial perspective. The resemblance does not necessarily resolve itself into an allegory in which Catholicism is revealed to be the persecuted, legitimate elder brother forced to defend himself by means of theatrical illusions against the cold persecution of his skeptical bastard brother Protestantism. But the possibility of such a radical undermining of the orthodox position exists, and not merely in the cool light of our own historical distance. In 1610 a company of traveling players in Yorkshire included *King Lear* and *Pericles* in a repertoire that included a "St Christopher Play" whose performance came to the attention of the Star Chamber. The plays were performed in the manor house of a recusant couple, Sir John and Lady Julyan Yorke, and the players themselves and their organizer, Sir Richard Cholmeley, were denounced for recusancy by their Puritan neighbor, Sir Posthumus Hoby.[54] It is difficult to resist the conclusion that someone in Stuart Yorkshire believed that, despite its apparent staging of a fraudulent possession, *King Lear* was not hostile, was strangely sympathetic even, to the situation of persecuted Catholics. At the very least, we may suggest, the current of sympathy is enough to undermine the intended effect of Harsnett's *Declaration:* an intensified adherence to the central system of official values. In Shakespeare, the realization that demonic possession is a theatrical imposture leads not to a clarification—the clear-eyed satisfaction of the man who refuses to be gulled—but to a deeper uncertainty, a loss of moorings, in the face of evil.

"Let them anatomize Regan," Lear raves, "see what breeds about her heart. Is there any cause in nature that makes these hard hearts?" (III.vi.74–6). We know that there is no cause *beyond* nature; the voices of evil in the play—"Thou, Nature, art my goddess"; "What need one?"; "Bind fast his corky arms"—come from the unpossessed. Does it make it any better to know this? Is it a relief to understand that the evil was not visited upon the characters by demonic agents but released from the structure of the family and the state by Lear himself?

Edgar's pretended demonic possession, by ironic contrast, is of the homiletic variety; the devil compels him to acts of self-punishment, the desperate masochism of the very poor, but not to acts of viciousness. On the contrary, like the demoniacs in Harsnett's contemptuous account who praise the Mass and the Catholic Church, Poor Tom gives a highly moral performance:

> Take heed o'th'foul fiend. Obey thy parents; keep thy word justly; swear not; commit not with man's sworn spouse; set not thy sweet heart on proud array. Tom's a-cold. (III.iv.78–81)

Is it a relief to know that Edgar is only miming this little sermon?

All attempts by the characters to explain or relieve their sufferings through the invocation of transcendent forces are baffled. Gloucester's belief in the influence of "These late eclipses in the sun and moon" (I.ii.100) is decisively dismissed, even if the spokesman for the dismissal is the villainous Edmund. Lear's almost constant appeals to the gods

> O Heavens,
> If you do love old men, if your sweet sway
> Allow obedience, if you yourselves are old,
> Make it your cause; send down and take my
> part!
>
> *(II.iv.187–90)*

are constantly left unanswered. The storm in the play seems to several characters to be of more than natural intensity, and Lear above all tries desperately to make it *mean* something (a symbol of his daughters' ingratitude, a punishment for evil, a sign from the gods of the impending universal judgment); but the thunder refuses to speak. When Albany calls Goneril a "devil" and a "fiend" (IV.ii.59,66), we know that he is not identifying her as a supernatural being—it is impossible, in this play, to witness the eruption of the denizens of hell into the human world—just as we know that Albany's prayer for "visible spirits" to be sent down by the heavens "to tame these vilde offences" (IV.ii.46–7) will be unanswered.

In *King Lear*, as Harsnett says of the Catholic Church, "neither God, Angel, nor devil can be gotten to speake."[55] For Harsnett this silence betokens a liberation from lies; we have learned, as the last sentence of his tract puts it, "to loath these despicable Impostures and returne vnto the truth."[56] But for Shakespeare the silence leads to the desolation of the play's close:

> Lend me a looking-glass;
> If that her breath will mist or stain the stone,
> Why, then she lives.
>
> *(V.iii.260–2)*

The lines give voice to a hope by which the audience has been repeatedly tantalized: a hope that Cordelia will not die, that the play will build toward a revelation powerful enough to justify Lear's atrocious suffering, that we are in the midst of what the Italians called a *tragedia di fin lieto*, that is, a play where the villains absorb the tragic punishment while the good are wondrously restored.[57] Shakespeare in effect invokes the conventions of this genre, only to insist with appalling finality that Cordelia is "dead as earth."

In the wake of Lear's first attempt to see some signs of life in Cordelia, Kent asks, "Is this the promis'd end?" Edgar echoes the question, "Or image of that horror?" And Albany says, "Fall and cease." By itself Kent's question has an oddly literary quality, as if he were remarking on the end of the play, either wondering what kind of ending this is or implicitly objecting to the disastrous turn of events. Edgar's response suggests that the "end" is the end of the world, the Last Judgment, here experienced not as a "promise"—the punishment of the wicked, the reward of the good—but as a "horror." But, like Kent, Edgar is not certain about what he is seeing: his question suggests that he may be witnessing not the end itself but a possible "image" of it, while Albany's enigmatic "Fall and cease" empties even that image of significance. The theatrical means that might have produced a "counterfeit miracle" out of this moment are abjured; there will be no imposture, no histrionic revelation of the supernatural.

Lear repeats this miserable emptying out of the redemptive hope in his next lines:

> This feather stirs; she lives! if it be so,
> It is a chance which does redeem all
> sorrows
> That ever I have felt.
>
> *(V.iii.264–6)*

Deeply moved by the sight of the mad king, a nameless gentleman had earlier remarked, "Thou hast one daughter,/who redeems nature from the general curse/ Which twain have brought her to" (IV.vi.202–4). Now, in Lear's words, this vision of universal redemption through Cordelia is glimpsed again, intensified by the king's own conscious investment in it. What would it mean to "redeem" Lear's sorrows? To buy them back from the chaos and brute meaninglessness they now seem to signify, to reward the king with a gift so great that it outweighs the sum of misery in his entire long life, to reinterpret his pain as the necessary preparation—the price to be paid—for a consummate bliss. In the theater such reinterpretation would be represented by a spectacular turn in the plot—a surprise unmasking, a sudden reversal of fortunes, a resurrection—and this dramatic redemption, however secularized, would almost invariably recall the consummation devoutly wished by centuries of Christian believers. This consummation had in fact been represented again and again in medieval resurrection plays which offered the spectators ocular proof that Christ had risen.[58] Despite the pre-Christian setting of Shakespeare's play, Lear's craving for just such proof—"This feather stirs; she lives!"—would seem to evoke precisely this theatrical and religious tradition, only in order to reveal itself, in C. L. Barber's acute phrase, as "post-Christian."[59] *If it be so:* Lear's sorrows are not redeemed; nothing can turn them into joy, but the forlorn hope of an impossible redemption persists, drained of its institutional and doctrinal significance, empty and vain, cut off even from a theatrical realization but, like the dream of exorcism, ineradicable.

The close of *King Lear* in effect acknowledges that it can never satisfy this dream, but the acknowledgment must not obscure the fact that the play itself has generated the craving for such satisfaction. That is, Shakespeare does not simply inherit and make use of an anthropological given; rather, at the moment when the official religious and secular institutions were, for their own reasons, abjuring the rituals they themselves had once fostered, Shakespeare's theater moves to appropriate this function. On stage the ritual is effectively contained in the ways we have examined, but Shakespeare intensifies as theatrical experience the need for exorcism, and his demystification of the practice is not identical in its interests to Harsnett's.

Harsnett's polemic is directed toward a bracing anger against the lying agents of the Catholic Church and a loyal adherence to the true, established Church of England. He writes as a representative of that true Church, and this institutional identity is reinforced by the secular institutional imprimatur on the confessions that are appended to the text. The joint religious and secular apparatus works to strip away imposture and discover the hidden reality which is, Harsnett says, the theater. Shakespeare's play dutifully reiterates this discovery: when Lear thinks he has found in Poor Tom "the thing itself," "unaccommodated man," he has in fact found a man playing a theatrical role. But if false religion is theater, and if the difference between true and false religion is the presence of theater, what happens when this difference is enacted in the theater?

What happens, as we have already begun to see, is that the official position is *emptied out,* even as it is loyally confirmed. This "emptying out" bears a certain resemblance to Brecht's "alienation effect," and still more to Althusser and Macherey's "internal distantiation." But the most fruitful terms for describing the felt difference between Shakespeare's art and the religious ideology to which it gives voice are to be found, I think, within the theological system to which Harsnett adhered. What is the status of the Law, asks Hooker, after the coming of Christ? Clearly the Saviour effected the "evacuation of the Law of Moses." But did that abolition mean "that the very name of Altar, of Priest, of Sacrifice itself, should be banished out of the world"? No, replies Hooker, even after evacuation, "the words which were do continue; the only difference is, that whereas before they had a literal, they now have a metaphorical use, and are as so many notes of remembrance unto us, that what they did signify in the letter is accomplished in the truth."[60] Both exorcism and Harsnett's own attack on exorcism undergo a comparable process of evacuation and transformed reiteration in *King Lear*. Whereas before they had a literal, they now have a literary use, and are as so many notes of remembrance unto us, that what they did signify in the letter is accomplished—with a drastic swerve from the sacred to the secular—in the theater.

Edgar's possession is a theatrical performance, exactly in Harsnett's terms, but there is no saving institution, purged of theater, against which it may be set, nor is there a demonic institution which the performance may be shown to serve. On the contrary, Edgar's miming is a response to a free-floating, contagious evil more terrible than anything Harsnett would allow. For Harsnett the wicked are corrupt individuals in the service of a corrupt Church; in *King Lear* there are neither individuals nor institutions adequate to contain the released and enacted wickedness; the force of evil in the play is larger than any local habitation or name. In this sense, Shakespeare's tragedy reconstitutes as theater the demonic principle demystified by Harsnett. Edgar's fraudulent, histrionic performance is a response to this principle: evacuated rituals, drained of their original meaning, are preferable to no rituals at all.

Shakespeare does not counsel, in effect, that one accept as true the fraudulent institution for the sake of the dream of a cure—the argument of the Grand Inquisitor. He writes for the greater glory and profit of the theater, a fraudulent institution that never pretends to be anything but fraudulent, an institution that calls forth what is not, that signifies absence, that transforms the literal into the metaphorical, that evacuates everything it represents. By doing so the theater makes for itself the hollow round space within which it survives. The force of *King Lear* is to make us love the theater, to seek out its satisfactions, to serve its interests, to confer upon it a place of its own, to grant it life by permitting it to reproduce itself over generations. Shakespeare's theater has outlived the institutions to which it paid homage, has lived to pay homage to other, competing institutions which in turn it seems to represent and empty out. This complex, limited institutional independence, this marginal and impure autonomy, arises not out of an inherent, formal self-reflexiveness but out of the ideological matrix in which Shakespeare's theater is created and recreated.

There are, of course, further institutional strategies that lie beyond a love for the theater. In a move that Ben Jonson rather than Shakespeare seems to have anticipated, the theater itself comes to be emptied out in the interests of reading. In the argument made famous by Charles Lamb and Coleridge, and reiterated by

Bradley, theatricality must be discarded to achieve absorption, and Shakespeare's imagination yields forth its sublime power not to a spectator but to one who, like Keats, sits down to reread *King Lear*. Where institutions like the King's Men had been thought to generate their texts, now texts like *King Lear* appear to generate their institutions. The commercial contingency of the theater gives way to the philosophical necessity of literature.

Why has our culture embraced *King Lear's* massive display of mimed suffering and fraudulent exorcism? Because the judicial torture and expulsion of evil have for centuries been bound up with the display of power at the center of society. Because we no longer believe in the magical ceremonies through which devils were once made to speak and were driven out of the bodies of the possessed. Because the play recuperates and intensifies our need for these ceremonies, even though we do not believe in them, and performs them, carefully marked out for us as frauds, for our continued consumption. Because, with our full complicity, Shakespeare's company and scores of companies that followed have catered profitably to our desire for spectacular impostures.

And also, perhaps, because the Harsnetts of the world would free us from the oppression of false belief only in order to reclaim us more firmly for the official state Church, and the "solution"—confirmed by the rechristening, as it were, of the devil as the Pope—is hateful. Hence we embrace an alternative that seems to confirm the official line and thereby to take its place in the central system of values, yet that works at the same time to unsettle all official lines.[61] Shakespeare's theater empties out the center that it represents, and in its cruelty—Edmund, Goneril, Regan, Cornwall, Gloucester, Cordelia, Lear: all dead as earth—paradoxically creates in us the intimation of a fullness that we can only savor in the conviction of its irremediable loss:

> we that are young
> Shall never see so much, nor live so long.

APPENDIX

Hooker, *Laws of Ecclesiastical Polity:*

> "They which honour the Law as an image of the wisdom of God himself, are notwithstanding to know that the same had an end in Christ. But what? Was the Law so abolished with Christ, that after his ascension the office of Priests became immediately wicked, and the very name hateful, as importing the exercise of an ungodly function? No, as long as the glory of the Temple continued, and till the time of that final desolation was accomplished, the very Christian Jews did continue with their sacrifices and other parts of legal service. That very Law therefore which our Saviour was to abolish, did not so *soon* become unlawful to be observed as some imagine; nor was it afterwards unlawful *so far*, that the very name of Altar, of Priest, of Sacrifice itself, should be banished out of the world. For though God do now hate sacrifice, whether it be heathenish or Jewish, so that we cannot have the same things which they had but with impiety; yet unless there be some greater let than the only evacuation of the Law of Moses, the names themselves may (I hope) be retained without sin, in respect of that proportion which things established by our Saviour have unto them which by him are abrogated. And so throughout all the writings of the ancient Fathers we see that the words which were do continue; the only difference is, that whereas before they had a literal, they now have a metaphorical use, and are as so many notes of remembrance unto us, that what they did signify in the letter is accomplished in the truth. And as no man can deprive the Church of this liberty, to use names whereunto the Law was accustomed, so neither are we generally forbidden the use of things which the Law hath; though it neither command us any particular rite, as it did the Jews a number, and the weightiest which it did command them are unto us in the Gospel prohibited." (IV.xi.10)

NOTES

1. Samuel Harsnett, *A Declaration of Egregious Popish Impostures* (London, 1603). Harsnett's influence is noted in Lewis Theobald's edition of Shakespeare, first published in 1733. On the clandestine exorcisms I am particularly indebted to D. P. Walker, *Unclean Spirits: Possession and Exorcism in France and England in the Late Sixteenth and Early Seventeenth Centuries* (Philadelphia, 1981). *King Lear* is quoted from the New Arden text, ed. Kenneth Muir (London, 1972). All other quotations from Shakespeare are taken from the Arden editions.

2. For extended arguments for and against theory, see Walter Michaels and Steven Knapp, "Against theory" (*Critical Inquiry*, 8 (1982), 723–42), and the ensuing controversy in *Critical Inquiry*, 9 (1983), 725–800.

3. I am indebted to an important critique of Marxist and deconstructive literary theory by D. A. Miller, "Discipline in different voices: bureaucracy, police, family and *Bleak House*" (*Representations*, 1 (1983), 59–89).

4. John Wesley, ed. Albert C. Outlet (New York, 1964), 82.

5. A major exception, with conclusions different from my own, has just been published: John L. Murphy, *Darkness and Devils: Exorcism and "King Lear"* (Athens, Ohio, 1984). Murphy's fascinating study, which he kindly allowed me to read in galleys after hearing the present paper delivered as a lecture, argues that exorcism is an aspect of clandestine political and religious resistance to Queen Elizabeth's rule. See also, for interesting reflections, William Elton, *"King Lear" and the Gods* (San Marino, 1966). For useful accounts of Harsnett's relation to Lear, see Geoffrey Bullough, ed., *Narrative and Dramatic Sources of Shakespeare* (London, 1975), 7, 299–302; Kenneth Muir, "Samuel Harsnett and King Lear" (*Review of English Studies*, 2 (1951), 11–21); Kenneth Muir, ed., *King Lear* (London, 1972), 239–42.

6. Michel de Montaigne, "Apology for Raymond Sebond," in *Complete Essays*, trans. Donald Frame (Stanford, 1948), 331.

7. Edward Shils, *Center and Periphery: Essays in Macrosociology* (Chicago, 1975), 3. My account of institutional strategies is indebted to Shils.

8. Peter Brown, *The Cult of the Saints: Its Rise and Function in Latin Christianity* (Chicago, 1981), 107.

9. Samuel Harsnett, *A Discovery of the Fraudulent Practices of John Darrel* (London, 1599).

10. Harsnett, *Declaration*, 154–55.

11. Ibid., 86.

12. Carlo Ginzburg, *I benandanti: Recerche sulla stregoneria e sui culti agrari tra Cinquecento e Seicento* (Turin, 1966).

13. For Harsnett's comments on witchcraft, see *Declaration*, 135–56. The relation between demonic possession and witchcraft is extremely complex. John Darrell evidently had frequent recourse, in the midst of his exorcisms, to accusations of witchcraft whose evidence was precisely the demonic possessions; Harsnett remarks wryly that "Of all the partes of the tragicall Comedie acted between him and Somers, there was no one Scene in it, wherein M. *Darrell* did with more courage & boldness acte his part, then in this of the discouerie of witches" (*Discovery*, 142). There is a helpful discussion of possession and witchcraft, along with an important account of Harsnett and Darrell, in Keith Thomas, *Religion and the Decline of Magic* (London, 1971).

14. Brown, op. cit., 109–11.

15. Thomas, op. cit., 485.

16. S. M. Shirokogorov, *The Psycho-Mental Complex of the Tungus* (Peking and London, 1935), 265.

17. Brown, op. cit., 110.

18. Michael MacDonald, *Mystical Bedlam* (Cambridge, 1981).

19. Harsnett, *Declaration*, A_3^r.

20. Harsnett, *Discovery*, A_2^r.

21. Ibid., A_4^{r-v}.

22. Ibid., 29.

23. D. P. Walker suggests that the attack on the Jesuits is a screen for an attack on the more politically sensitive nonconformists; in early seventeenth-century England, when in doubt it was safer to attack a Catholic.

24. Harsnett, *Declaration*, 24.

25. Ibid., 25. See Edmund Jorden, *A Briefe Discourse of a Disease Called the Suffocation of the Mother* (London, 1603).

26. Harsnett, *Declaration*, 38.

27. Michel Leiris, *La Possession et ses aspects théâtraux chez les Ethiopiens de Gondar* (Paris, 1958).

28. Ibid., 27–8.

29. Ibid., 94–5.

30. Ibid., 96.

31. Harsnett, *Declaration*, 69.

32. Ibid., 172.

33. Ibid., 2, 106.

34. Ibid., 74.

35. Ibid., 20. This argument has the curious effect of identifying all exorcisms, including those conducted by nonconformist preachers, with the Pope. On attacks on the Catholic Church as a theater, see Jonas Barish, *The Antitheatrical Prejudice* (Berkeley, 1981), 66–131 *passim*.

36. Harsnett, *Discovery*, A_3^r.

37. Ibid., 78.

38. Ibid., 114–15.

39. Ibid., 149.

40. Harsnett was not, of course, alone. See, for example, John Gee: "The Jesuits being or having Actors of such dexterity, I see no reason but that they should set up a company for themselves, which surely will put down The Fortune, Red-Bull, Cockpit, and Globe" (*New Shreds of the Old Snare* (London, 1624)). I owe this reference, along with powerful reflections on the significance of the public theater's physical marginality, to Steven Mullaney.

41. This sentiment could serve as the epigraph to both of Harsnett's books on exorcism; it is the root perception from which most of Harsnett's rhetoric grows.

42. Stephen Gosson, *Plays Confuted in Five Actions* (London, c. 1582), cited in E. K. Chambers, *The Elizabethan Stage* (Oxford, 1923), 215.

43. Philip Sidney, *The Defense of Poesie* (1583), in *Literary Criticism: Plato to Dryden*, ed. Allan H. Gilbert (Detroit, 1962), 439.

44. These lines were included in the Quarto but omitted from the Folio. For the tangled textual history, see Michael J. Warren, "Quarto and Folio *King Lear*, and the interpretation of Albany and Edgar," in David Bevington and Jay L. Halio, eds., *Shakespeare: Pattern of Excelling Nature* (Newark, Del., 1978), 95–107; Steven Urkowitz, *Shakespeare's Revision of "King Lear"* (Princeton, 1980); and Gary Taylor, "The war in King Lear" (*Shakespeare Survey*, 33 (1980), 27–34). Presumably, by the time the Folio appeared, the point of the allusion to Harsnett would have been lost, and the lines were dropped.

45. Harsnett, *Declaration*, 46.

46. John Bunyan, *Grace Abounding to the Chief of Sinners*, ed. Roger Sharrock (Oxford, 1966), 15.

47. Edgar's later explanation—that he feared for his father's ability to sustain the shock of an encounter—is, like so many explanations in *King Lear*, too little, too late. On this characteristic belatedness as an element of the play's greatness, see Stephen Booth, *"King Lear," "Macbeth," Indefinition, and Tragedy* (New Haven, 1983).

48. Harsnett, *Declaration*, 142.

49. Ibid., 142–3.

50. On the production of "counterfeit miracles" in order to arouse awe and wonder, see especially Harsnett, *Discovery*, "Epistle to the reader."

51. Words, signs, gestures that claim to be in touch with super-reality, with absolute goodness and absolute evil, are exposed as vacant—illusions manipulated by the clever and imposed upon the gullible.

52. This is, in effect, Edmund Jorden's prescription for cases such as Lear's.

53. Harsnett, *Declaration*, 23.

54. On the Yorkshire performance, see Murphy, op. cit., 93–118.

55. Harsnett, *Declaration*, 169.

56. Ibid., 171.

57. In willing this disenchantment against the evidence of our senses, we pay tribute to the theater. Harsnett has been twisted around to make this tribute possible.

58. O. B. Hardison, Jr., *Christian Rite and Christian Drama in the Middle Ages: Essays in the Origin and Early History of Modern Drama* (Baltimore, 1965), esp. 220–52.

59. C. L. Barber, "The family in Shakespeare's development: tragedy and sacredness," in *Representing Shakespeare: New Psychoanalytic Essays*, ed. Murray M. Schwartz and Coppelia Kahn (Baltimore, 1980). 196.

60. Hooker, *Laws of Ecclesiastical Polity*, IV.xi.10. This truth, which is the triumph of the metaphorical over the literal, confers upon the Church the liberty to use certain names and rites, even though they have been abolished. For the entire passage from Hooker, see Appendix. I am indebted for the reference to Richard Hooker to John Coolidge.

61. Roland Barthes, *Mythologies*, trans. Annette Lavers (New York, 1972), 135.

VII

FEMINISM

A survey of recent feminist literary criticism reveals a wide variety of approaches being developed with remarkable intensity. This high interest is characteristic of the early stages of a "movement"—or better, a "reorientation." Evident in this reorientation is the urgency to understand literature from a female viewpoint that has already led many literary critics and teachers to rethink their assumptions and practices. Such a "reorientation," as Elaine Showalter argues in "Towards a Feminist Poetics," takes the form of reading from the specific viewpoint of a woman. Showalter cites Irving Howe when he describes Michael Henchard's selling of his wife and daughter at the beginning of *The Mayor of Casterbridge*. Howe asserts that to "shake loose from" and "discard" his wife "through the public sale of her body to a stranger" wrings a "second change out of life." Showalter notes that "a woman . . . will have a different experience of this scene," and that only the training in "androcentric" reading, as Patrocinio Schweickart describes it in Section II, has obscured this difference. As Schweickart notes, "the feminist inquiry into the activity of reading begins with the realization that the literary canon is androcentric, and this has a profoundly damaging effect on women readers." In this way, the "reorientation" effected by the feminist inquiry into reading and literature suggests that all readings are not the same and that "texts" are not endowed with transcendental ("constative") meanings. Rather, reading is historically and socially situated.

This situation is clear if we contrast the survey of feminist literary criticism Showalter presents in "Feminist Criticism in the Wilderness" in this section with J. Hillis Miller's essay in Section VIII, "The Search for Grounds in Literary Study." Both critics isolate four approaches to the criticism they are describing. Showalter is describing feminist criticism and Miller is describing criticism in general. Miller describes (1) a societal or social ground, "the more or less hidden social or ideological pressures which impose themselves on literature"; (2) a psychological ground, "the more or less hidden psychic pressures which impose themselves on a work of literature"; (3) a linguistic ground, "the more or less hidden rhetorical pressures, or pressures from . . . language itself as such"; and, finally, (4) an almost inarticulable ground which Miller calls "properly religious, metaphysical, or ontological, though hardly in a traditional or conventional way." In a similar way, Showalter describes "theories of women's writing [which] presently make use of four models of difference: biological, linguistic, psychoanalytic, and cultural." In these two catalogues, three of the four categories coincide even though the order of their presentation—explicitly important for Showalter and, at least, implicitly important for Miller—is different. Both Miller and Showalter note that literature and criticism can be studied from the viewpoints of language, psychology, and social or cultural life. Showalter's first category, or position, the biology of gender difference, is occupied in Miller's discussion with the religious, ontological approach to literature. In a way, of course, "biology," the physical aspect of existence, is parallel to "ontology," the study of "being," but it is so only by a remarkable feat of abstraction. And this is the point: where Miller is most abstract Showalter is most concrete; where Miller gropes for a language that can hardly articulate the transcendental, strange "situation" of "man" (meaning humankind)—namely, "something encountered in our relations to other people, especially relations involving love, betrayal, and the ultimate betrayal by the other of our love for him or her, the death of the other"—Showalter surveys literal and metaphorical articulations of the physical difference between men and women in "feminist criticism which itself tries to be biological, to write from the critic's body, . . . [criticism which is] intimate, confessional, often innovative in style and form." Rather than abstract "grounds," Showalter presents concrete models of difference, approaches that situate the act of reading and criticism in particular linguistic, psychological, and cultural contexts.

Both Miller and Showalter are describing different schools of criticism presented in this book. Miller is describing all species of Marxist criticism in his discussion of social and ideological pressures examined by criticism. He describes psychological and psychoanalytic criticism in his second category; he describes the structuralist grounding of literary study in linguistics in his next category; and in his final category he describes the global, "metaphysical" vision of the antimetaphysics of poststructuralism and deconstruction. Feminist approaches also draw from at least four areas of contemporary critical thought, and we have attempted to include examples of all of them in this collection. Hélène Cixous's essay in this section, "Castration or Decapitation?" draws on both biology and psychoanalysis in her description of Little Red Riding Hood as "a little clitoris" in her psychoanalytically informed discussion, but even here she discusses the great opposition between Nature and Culture introduced by Lévi-Strauss (and discussed in Section III by Kristeva) and examines the relations between hysterical silence—the loss of speech—and female decapitation. In the same way, Schweikart's essay in Section II examines the linguistic strategies of literature from a feminist viewpoint, and again that orientation encompasses biological, psychological, and cultural concerns within its rhetorical approach. Flieger's examination of Freud and Lacan in Section V—while offering a feminist reading of contemporary psychoanalytic criticism—highlights the questions of sexual difference, linguistic strategies, and cultural understanding within that framework. A good example of the interweaving of approaches is the essay by Kristeva in Section III (discussed at some length in that section's introduction). Kristeva weaves together different discourses—a discourse of the maternal body and a discourse of cultural history—to articulate the multifaceted relationship between the experience of womanhood and biology, language, psychology, and culture.

Moreover, other essays in this book explicitly address wider social and cultural questions from the reorientation of feminist criticism. Shoshana Felman's discussion of teaching and psychoanalysis and Lillian Robinson's rethinking of the literary canon are essays from Section VIII of this book—the next section which, following from the interdisciplinary direction of feminist studies, attempts to describe the profound effect contemporary literary criticism has had as a mode of "cultural studies" (including feminist studies) on the question of literary studies: what literary studies do, how they do it, and in relation to what values. And the essays of this section, as we will examine, also focus on such larger cultural questions in relation to more specific readings of literature and criticism. Literary "feminism," in short, comprises the set of issues in various disciplines pertinent to women's experience, and to this experience a feminist perspective brings both substantiation and elaborated understanding. In this way, feminism implicitly challenges literary theory to confront the difficult task of assimilating the findings of an expanding sphere of interdisciplinary inquiry. To the degree that this challenge has already been accepted, a significant "historical compromise" is taking shape, an acceptance of a power shift from male to female and a decisive reorientation in literary studies that will be far-reaching. It may well be that the future of literary studies is being decided as current feminist theory and criticism are being written.

FEMINIST LITERARY CRITICISM

Modern feminist criticism is deeply indebted to the work of two writers, Virginia Woolf and Simone de Beauvoir. Their criticism exemplifies the strength as well as the challenge of literary feminism in its determination to go two ways at once: (1) toward a feminist social critique, or an analysis of women attempting to write in a patriarchal culture, and (2) toward the development of a feminist esthetic, or an explanation of how writing by women manifests a *distinctively* female discourse. Woolf displays this dual awareness in *A Room of One's Own* (1924) when she describes female writing as shaped primarily by its subject and less by the "shadow across the page" (the imposition of ego) characteristic of male discourse. Woolf suggests a model of textual alinearity and plasticity (female) versus hegemony and rigidity (male) that guides her critique of women as displaced socially in relation to the "shadow" that the ego of the privileged male casts starkly across Western culture. Woolf's "room of one's own," a female domain, simultaneously incorporates the interiority of female discourse and the social sanctuary within which a woman may realize her potential. The successful articulation of these two dimensions in the same metaphor is a lasting achievement of Woolf's vision.

Woolf's deployment of a metaphorical "room," however, did not fully relate the two realms of male and female within a feminist critique without losing cohesion in the divided focus. Simone de Beauvoir in *The Second Sex* (1949), for example, criticized patriarchal culture and analyzed the marginal position of women in society and the arts. More intently than Woolf, de Beauvoir described a male-dominated social discourse within which particular misogynist practices occur. Tending toward a Marxist analysis—and anticipating Shulamith Firestone to some extent—de Beauvoir identified a base of political and economic oppression of women with a kind of "superstructure" of sexist literature and art. In a useful analysis of the mechanism of sexism, de Beauvoir found reflections of socioeconomic injustices in what she saw as fundamentally imitative modes of literature (literature conceived as "reflecting" a social reality). While her work illustrates the double focus also evident in Woolf's criticism, it tended to dismiss literary production per se as a strict reflection (mimesis) of social and ideological schemes. This analysis yielded valuable insights into cultural sexism generally, but it contributed little to understanding a feminine esthetic, or a sense of what a woman's writing is fundamentally—the activity of a woman in writing.

De Beauvoir and Woolf mark out the terrain of feminist literary criticism from social critique to feminist esthetic and discourse. Elaine Showalter follows suit with her idea (most fully articulated in "Towards a Feminist Poetics," but also discussed in "Feminist Criticism in the Wilderness") of two "distinct varieties" of feminist criticism as directed toward either the *woman as reader* or *the woman as writer.* The first focuses on the significance of sexual codes ("woman-as-sign") in an historical and political context. This is socially oriented criticism with strong reflections of de Beauvoir's critique. The second focuses on the four categories of gender difference we have already discussed. This second focus is close to Woolf's concern and is the area of feminism that Showalter christened *gynocritics* (in "Towards a Feminist Poetics")—"a female framework for the analysis of women's literature" beginning "at the point when we free ourselves from the linear absolutes of male literary history." Resulting from gynocritics' discovery, in Showalter's words, "the lost continent of the female tradition has risen like Atlantis from the sea of English literature."

Showalter's survey of feminist criticism in "Feminist Criticism in the Wilderness"—the title of which echoes Geoffrey Hartman's survey of contemporary criticism in *Criticism in the Wilderness* (1980), a study which fails, as Showalter notes, to examine any women writers—asserts, in its most global understanding, the situation of woman within culture rather than outside of it. That is, this essay surveys feminist criticism and cultural studies, as Showalter explicitly says, to define a woman's discourse, what a woman wants, as Flieger notes in her psychoanalytic discussion. Cixous also attempts such a definition, yet her mode is closer to the performative critiques we have included in every section of this book—in Shklovsky, Fish, Kristeva, Foucault, Greenblatt, and Flieger herself—than Showalter's wide-ranging schematization of feminist studies. In this, Cixous combines the categories of woman as reader and as writer in a wide-ranging literary practice that, as Annette Kuhn has noted, is what Cixous herself calls a "woman-text," "a return of the repressed feminine that with its energetic, joyful, and transgressive 'flying in language and making it fly' dislocates the repressive structures of phallologocentrism." "Cixous's own work," Kuhn continues, offers a practice of writing "that aims to do this by posing plurality against unity; multitudes of meanings against single, fixed meanings; diffuseness against instrumentality; openness against closure." This discourse is what Rachel Blau DuPlessis calls "situational," "a both/and vision born of shifts, contraries, negations, contradictions; linked to personal vulnerability and need."

The difficulty of such "female" discourse is formidable. When Jacques Derrida, for example, discusses the "dissemination" of writing under the figure "hymen," he intends to describe a feminine dimension of all writing wherein "meaning" is not unified but inevitably scattered and "lost" along discontinuous and irregular channels. This version of writing with female authority (under the "hymen") is quite distinct from the "phallic" continuity of male writing with its emphasis on exclusion and a linear decorum. The real difficulty of such conceptions—Woolf's, Cixous's, Derrida's, and others as well—is unavoidable precisely because as we attempt to reconceive writing, we are trying to reconceive humans in relation to the world. Such difficulty is not merely what George Steiner calls a "tactical" problem, or language deployed strategically to jar us from old perceptual patterns. Rather, the difficulty of feminist criticism may go deeper, to what Steiner calls the "ontological" level (some feminists would say "biological" here), the raising of "questions," as Steiner says, "about the nature of human speech [and] about the status of significance." In other words, this is an inquiry that forces us to reconceive the very concepts and relations of "self" and "world." The resolution of this "difficulty" of feminist criticism would be a grand enterprise, indeed—a "field" theory, an explanation of the whole range of gender's impact on literature, virtually an ultimate correction of all the world's errors and mysteries (a "healing," as Nietzsche said, of the "eternal wound of existence"). Moreover, to the extent that feminist literary criticism attempts to encompass the entire sexual dialectic, the dimensions of Woolf's "room of one's own" and all that lies within its walls, feminism presses on the very questions about private and public life, culture and power, female and male that demand attention in contemporary thought. Feminism's ultimate goal, in this way, would be to insist on recasting all relationships, the world itself.

A less ambitious project, of course, is the recasting of literary studies, and Sandra M. Gilbert offers a remarkable "recasting" of traditional literary study in "Life's Empty Pack: Notes Towards a Literary Daughteronomy." In many ways this essay consolidates the advances in reading that feminist criticism has made since the publication of Kate Millett's *Sexual Politics* in 1970. Gilbert begins her essay by implicitly defining, in its "unprecedented situation," the function of feminist criticism at the present time: "For the first time all of us, men and women alike, can look back on nearly two centuries of powerful literary ancestresses." For the first time at the present time, Gilbert argues, the questions that feminism has fought to make legitimate can be addressed as a matter of course and within the context of contemporary literary critics—Harold Bloom and his examination of the literary tradition, Freud and Lacan and their examinations of family constellations, Lévi-Strauss and his discussion of exchange and incest, and the host of literary critics, men and women, cited in the course of this thematic and literary-historical discussion of the relationship between fathers and daughters in George Eliot, Edith Wharton, and society in general. Thus, Gilbert writes, what the Oedipus complex and its relationship to language "means for the boy . . . has been elaborately and famously explored by both Freud and Lacan (and also, in a different way, by Lévi-Strauss). What it means for the girl is much less clearly understood." The understanding she pursues is situated fully within the "mainstream" of literary criticism: an understanding of "the conundrum of the empty pack which *until recently* has confronted every woman writer."

The "empty pack," or lack of a heritage, that is the inheritance of the female child, Gilbert implies, is not quite so empty as it has been, and one evidence of such change is her essay itself, exploring the theme of female inheritance—the role of the female child—in society. Part of the new, "unprecedented" situation is articulated in the structure of her essay. It examines Eliot's *Silas Marner* and Wharton's *Summer*, examining the narrative and thematic relationships between these books. But the last section of the essay moves on to larger cultural questions—to "sociological" questions that explicitly link this essay with the concerns (but not the methods or assumptions) of the "sociological" criticism of Burke and Bakhtin/Volosinov in Sections II and VI. Here Gilbert explicitly examines the nature of "father-daughter desire" in families and society and implicitly suggests that the very examination of such questions—their legitimization—is a consolidating achievement of feminist literary criticism.

FEMINISM AND CULTURAL CRITIQUE

The last essay we have included in this section, Gayatri Chakravorty Spivak's "Imperialism and Sexual Difference," attempts to situate the very practice of feminist criticism within the context of middle-class academic life in the

Western world. To do so Spivak places, as many of the essays of this book do, feminist practice within the context of New Critical formalism and structuralist and poststructuralist developments in her reading of a poem by Baudelaire. But then she enlarges that context to a short novel by Kipling that describes and articulates feminism in relation to British imperialism in India and, finally, to an internal memo of the East India Company which governed India. In each instance she shows the "blindness"—the colonial tendency to universalize a particular situation into the human situation. Thus, she writes, "even as we feminist critics discover the troping error of the masculist truth-claim to universality or academic objectivity, we perform the lie of constituting a truth of global sisterhood where the model remains . . . European." She notes, in particular, the "post-romantic concept of irony" articulated by one of her students, which springs "from the imposition of her own historical and voluntarist" position with "U.S. academic feminism as a 'universal' model of the 'natural' reactions of the female psyche." Such a practice, Spivak says, carries with it a "*structural* effect" of colonialism and imperialism as marked as that of the East India Company.

Spivak articulates a critique of feminism informed by the advances that structuralism, poststructuralism, Marxism, and feminism itself have brought to the examination of literature and discourse in general. In fact, Spivak examines literature and discourse in general—critical discourse, political discourse, and philosophic discourse—and interprets them as discursive practices. Her critique is particularly fitting just as is Gilbert's consolidation of biological, linguistic, psychological, and cultural feminist criticism in reading the "powerful literary ancestresses." That is, together they delineate the outlines of feminism in contemporary literary criticism and demonstrate the reconception—the reorientation—of literary studies as cultural criticism and critique.

RELATED TEXTS IN *CONTEMPORARY LITERARY CRITICISM*

Shoshana Felman, "Psychoanalysis and Education"
Jerry Flieger, "The Purloined Punchline: Joke as Textual Paradigm"
Julia Kristeva, "Stabat Mater"
Jacques Lacan, "Seminar on the 'Purloined Letter' "
Lillian Robinson, "Treason Our Text: Feminist Challenge to the Literary Canon"
Patrocinio Schweickart, "Reading Ourselves: Toward a Feminist Theory of Reading"

FURTHER READING

Cixous, Hélène, "La fiction et les fantomes," in *Poetique*, 10 (1972), 199–216.

_____, "The Laugh of the Medusa," in *Signs*, 1 (1976), 875–93.

_____, and Catherine Clement, *The Newly Born Woman*, trans. Betsy Wing (Minneapolis: University of Minnesota Press, 1986).

Conley, Verena Andermatt, *Hélène Cixous: Writing the Feminine* (Lincoln: University of Nebraska Press, 1984).

Daly, Mary, *Beyond God the Father: Towards a Philosophy of Women's Liberation* (Boston: Beacon Press, 1973).

——, *Gyn/Ecology* (Boston: Beacon Press, 1978).

——, "The Transformation of Silence into Language and Action," in *Sinister Wisdom*, 6 (1978).

Davis, Robert Con, "Woman as Oppositional Reader: Cixous on Discourse," forthcoming in *Papers in Language and Literature*.

de Beauvoir, Simone, *The Second Sex*, trans. H. M. Parshley (New York: Knopf, 1953).

Dinnerstein, Dorothy, *The Mermaid and the Minotaur: Sexual Arrangements and Human Malaise* (New York: Harper & Row, 1976).

Donovan, Josephine, ed., *Feminist Literary Criticism* (Lexington: University of Kentucky Press, 1975).

DuPlessis, Rachel Blau, "For the Etruscans," in *The New Feminist Criticism*, ed. Elaine Showalter (New York: Pantheon Books, 1985), pp. 271–91.

Edwards, Lee, and Arlyn Diamond, eds., *The Authority of Experience: Essays in Feminist Criticism* (Amherst: University of Massachusetts Press, 1977).

Eisenstein, Hester, and Alice Jardine, eds., *The Future of Difference* (Boston: G. K. Hall, 1980).

Ellman, Mary, *Thinking About Women* (New York: Harcourt, Brace, 1978).

Felman, Shoshana, "Rereading Femininity," in *Yale French Studies*, 62 (1981), 19–44.

——, "Women and Madness: The Critical Phallacy." *Diacritics*, 5, No. 4 (1975), 2–10.

Finke, Laurie, "The Rhetoric of Marginality: Why I Do Feminist Theory," in *Tulsa Studies in Women's Literature*, 5, 2 (1986), 251–72.

Gilbert, Sandra M., and Susan Gubar, *The Madwoman in the Attic* (New Haven: Yale University Press, 1979).

——, *No Man's Land: The Place of the Woman Writer in the Twentieth Century*, vol. I (New Haven and London: Yale University Press, 1988).

Irigaray, Luce, *This Sex Which Is Not One*, trans. Catherine Porter (Ithaca: Cornell University Press, 1985; orig. 1977).

——, *Speculum of the Other Woman*, trans. Gillian C. Gill (Ithaca: Cornell University Press, 1985; orig. 1974).

Jacobus, Mary, ed., *Women Writing and Writing About Women* (London: Croom Helm, 1979).

Jardine, Alice, *Gynesis: Configurations of Woman and Modernity* (Ithaca: Cornell University Press, 1985).

Kamuf, Peggy, "Writing Like a Woman," in *Woman and Language in Literature and Society*, ed. Sally McConnell-Ginet et al. (New York: Praeger, 1980), 284–99.

Kofman, Sarah, "Freud's Suspension of the Mother," in *Enclitic*, 4, No. 2 (1980), 17–28.

——, "The Narcissistic Woman: Freud and Girard," in *Diacritics*, 10, No. 3 (1980), 36–45.

Kolodny, Annette, "Some Notes on Defining a 'Feminist Literary Criticism,' " *Critical Inquiry*, 2 (1975), 75–92.

Kuhn, Annette, "Introduction to Hélène Cixous's 'Castration or Decapitation?'" *Signs*, 7 (1981), 36–40.

McConnell-Ginet, Sally, et al., eds., *Women and Language in Literature and Society* (New York: Praeger, 1980).

Marks, Elaine, "Women and Literature in France," in *Signs*, 3 (1978), 832–42.

———, and Isabelle Courtivron, eds., *New French Feminisms: An Anthology* (Amherst: University of Massachusetts Press, 1980).

Millett, Kate, *Sexual Politics* (Garden City, N.Y.: Doubleday, 1970).

Moi, Toril, *Sexual/Textual Politics: Feminist Literary Theory* (London: Methuen, 1985).

Montrelay, Michele, "Inquiry into Femininity," trans. Parveen Adams, *m/f*, 1 (1978), 83–101.

Pratt, Annis, *Archetypal Patterns in Women's Fiction* (Bloomington: Indiana University Press, 1981).

Showalter, Elaine, *A Literature of Their Own: British Women Novelists from Bronte to Lessing* (Princeton, N.J.: Princeton University Press, 1977).

———, ed. *The New Feminist Criticism* (New York: Pantheon Books, 1985).

Spivak, Gayatri Chakravorty, *In Other Worlds* (New York and London: Methuen, 1987).

Woolf, Virginia, *Collected Essays* (London: Hogarth, 1966).

———, *A Room of One's Own* (New York: Harcourt Brace Jovanovich, 1981).

26

Elaine Showalter
1941—

Born in Cambridge, Massachusetts, Elaine Showalter received an M.A. from Brandeis University and a Ph.D from the University of California at Davis. She has taught at Rutgers University and now teaches at Princeton University. She has edited such volumes as *Women's Liberation and Literature; Female Studies IV; Women's Studies;* and *Signs: Journal of Women, Culture and Society.* In 1977 she published *A Literature of Their Own: British Women Novelists from Brontë to Lessing.* Most recently she has edited *The New Feminist Criticism* (1985).

In "Feminist Criticism in the Wilderness," Showalter asks the question: "What is *the difference* in women's writing?" It is a question with exhilarating possibilities and, once posed, by herself and other feminist writers, it began the "shift from an androcentric to a gynocentric feminist criticism." Revisionist readings of the male canon can therefore no longer contain the momentum of women's criticism. In this essay, she analyzes four theoretical models that explore this difference: biological, linguistic, psychoanalytic, and cultural. These models are sequential, with each being subsumed and enhanced by the one following. Thus, the cultural model provides "a more complete and satisfying way to talk about the specificity and difference of women's writing." Showalter, then, begins the work of providing a ground for feminist criticism, a ground that is not "the serenely undifferentiated universality of texts but the tumultuous and intriguing wilderness of difference itself."

Feminist Criticism in the Wilderness

PLURALISM AND THE FEMINIST CRITIQUE

Women have no wilderness in them,
They are provident instead
Content in the tight hot cell of their hearts
To eat dusty bread.

Louise Bogan, "Women"

In a splendidly witty dialogue of 1975, Carolyn Heilbrun and Catharine Stimpson identified two poles of feminist literary criticism. The first of these modes, righteous, angry, and admonitory, they compared to the Old Testament, "looking for the sins and errors of the past." The second mode, disinterested and seeking "the grace of imagination," they compared to the New Testament. Both are necessary, they concluded, for only the Jeremiahs of ideology can lead us out of the "Egypt of female servitude" to the promised land of humanism.[1] Matthew Arnold also thought that literary critics might perish in the wilderness before they reached the promised land of disinterestedness; Heilbrun and Stimpson were neo-Arnoldian as befitted members of the Columbia and Barnard faculties. But if, in the 1980s, feminist literary critics are still wandering in the wilderness, we are in good company; for, as Geoffrey Hartman tells us, *all* criticism is in the wilderness.[2] Feminist critics may be startled to find ourselves in this band of theoretical pioneers, since in the American literary tradition the wilderness has been an exclusively masculine domain. Yet between feminist ideology and the liberal ideal of disinterestedness lies the wilderness of theory, which we too must make our home.

Until very recently, feminist criticism has not had a theoretical basis; it has been an empirical orphan in the theoretical storm. In 1975, I was persuaded that no theoretical manifesto could adequately account for the varied methodologies and ideologies which called themselves feminist reading or writing.[3] By the next year, Annette Kolodny had added her observation that feminist literary criticism appeared "more like a set of interchangeable strategies than any coherent school or shared goal orientation."[4] Since then, the expressed goals have not been notably unified. Black critics protest the "massive silence" of feminist criticism about black and Third-World women writers and call for a black feminist aesthetic that would deal with both racial and sexual politics. Marxist feminists wish to focus on class along with gender as a crucial determinant of literary production.[5] Literary historians want to uncover a lost tradition. Critics trained in deconstructionist methodologies wish to "synthesize a literary criticism that is both textual and feminist."[6] Freudian and Lacanian critics want to theorize about women's relationship to language and signification.

An early obstacle to constructing a theoretical framework for feminist criticism was the unwillingness of many women to limit or bound an expressive and dynamic enterprise. The openness of feminist criticism appealed particularly to Americans who perceived the structuralist, post-structuralist, and deconstructionist debates of the 1970s as arid and falsely objective, the epitome of a pernicious masculine discourse from which many feminists wished to escape. Recalling in *A Room of One's Own* how she had been prohibited from entering the university library, the symbolic sanctuary of the male *logos*, Virginia Woolf wisely observed that while it is "unpleasant to be locked out . . . it is worse, perhaps, to be locked in." Advocates of the antitheoretical position traced their descent from Woolf and from other feminist visionaries, such as Mary Daly, Adrienne Rich, and Marguerite Duras, who had satirized the sterile narcissism of male scholarship and celebrated women's fortunate exclusion from its patriarchal methodolatry. Thus for some, feminist criticism was an act of resistance to theory, a confrontation with existing canons and judgments, what Josephine Donovan calls "a mode of negation within a fundamental dialectic." As Judith Fetterley declared in her book, *The Resisting Reader*, feminist criticism has been characterized by "a resistance to codification and a refusal to have its parameters prematurely set." I have discussed elsewhere, with considerable sympathy, the suspicion of monolithic systems and the rejection of scientism in literary study that many feminist critics have voiced. While scientific criticism struggled to purge itself of the subjective, feminist criticism reasserted the authority of experience.[7]

Yet it now appears that what looked like a theoretical impasse was actually an evolutionary phase. The ethics of awakening have been succeeded, at least in the universities, by a second stage characterized by anxiety about the isolation of feminist criticism from a critical community increasingly theoretical in its interests and indifferent to women's writing. The question of how feminist criticism should define itself with relation to the new critical theories and theorists has occasioned sharp debate in Europe and the United States. Nina Auerbach has noted the absence of dialogue and asks whether feminist criticism itself must accept responsibility:

> Feminist critics seem particularly reluctant to define themselves to the uninitiated. There is a sense in which our sisterhood has become too powerful; as a school, our belief in ourself is so potent that we decline communication with the networks of power and respectability we say we want to change.[8]

But rather than declining communication with these networks, feminist criticism has indeed spoken directly to them, in their own media: *PMLA, Diacritics, Glyph, Tel Quel, New Literary History,* and *Critical Inquiry*. For the feminist critic seeking clarification, the proliferation of communiqués may itself prove confusing

There are two distinct modes of feminist criticism, and to conflate them (as most commentators do) is to remain permanently bemused by their theoretical potentialities. The first mode is ideological; it is concerned with the feminist as *reader,* and it offers feminist readings of texts which consider the images and stereotypes of women in literature, the omissions and misconceptions about women in criticism, and woman-assign in semiotic systems. This is not all feminist reading can do; it can be a liberating intellectual act, as Adrienne Rich proposes:

> A radical critique of literature, feminist in its impulse, would take the work first of all as a clue to how we live, how we have been living, how we have been led to imagine ourselves, how our language has trapped as well as liberated us, how the very act of naming has been till now a male prerogative, and how we can begin to see and name—and therefore live—afresh.[9]

This invigorating encounter with literature, which I will call *feminist reading* or the *feminist critique,* is in essence a mode of interpretation, one of many which any complex text will accommodate and permit. It is very difficult to propose theoretical coherence in an activity which by its nature is so eclectic and wide-ranging, although as a critical practice feminist reading has certainly been very influential. But in the free play of the interpretive field, the feminist critique can only compete with alternative readings, all of which have the built-in obsolescence of Buicks, cast away as newer readings take their place. As Kolodny, the most sophisticated theorist of feminist interpretation, has conceded:

> All the feminist is asserting, then, is her own equivalent right to liberate new (and perhaps different) significances from these same texts; and, at the same time, her right to choose which features of a text she takes as relevant because she is, after all, asking new and different questions of it. In the process, she claims neither definitiveness nor structural completeness for her different readings and reading systems, but only their usefulness in recognizing the particular achievements of woman-as-author and their applicability in conscientiously decoding woman-as-sign.

Rather than being discouraged by these limited objectives, Kolodny found them the happy cause of the "playful pluralism" of feminist critical theory, a pluralism which she believes to be "the only critical stance consistent with the current status of the larger women's movement."[10] Her feminist critic dances adroitly through the theoretical minefield.

Keenly aware of the political issues involved and presenting brilliant arguments, Kolodny nonetheless fails to convince me that feminist criticism must altogether abandon its hope "of establishing some basic conceptual model." If we see our critical job as interpretation and reinterpretation, we must be content with pluralism as our critical stance. But if we wish to ask questions about the process and the contexts of writing, if we genuinely wish to define ourselves to the uninitiated, we cannot rule out the prospect of theoretical consensus at this early stage.

All feminist criticism is in some sense revisionist, questioning the adequacy of accepted conceptual structures, and indeed most contemporary American criticism claims to be revisionist too. The most exciting and comprehensive case for this "revisionary imperative" is made by Sandra Gilbert: at its most ambitious, she asserts, feminist criticism "wants to decode and demystify all the disguised questions and answers that have always shadowed the connections between textuality and sexuality, genre and gender, psychosexual identity and cultural authority."[11] But in practice, the revisionary feminist critique is redressing a grievance and is built upon existing models. No one would deny that feminist criticism has affinities to other contemporary critical practices and methodologies and that the best work is also the most fully informed. Nonetheless, the feminist obsession with correcting, modifying, supplementing, revising, humanizing, or even attacking male critical theory keeps us dependent upon it and retards our progress in solving our own theoretical problems. What I mean here by "male critical theory" is a concept of creativity, literary history, or literary interpretation based entirely on male experience and put forward as universal. So long as we look to androcentric models for our most basic principles—even if we revise them by adding the feminist frame of reference—we are learning nothing new. And when the process is so one-sided, when male critics boast of their ignorance of feminist criticism, it is disheartening to find feminist critics still anxious for approval from the "white fathers" who will not listen or reply. Some feminist critics have taken upon themselves a revisionism which becomes a kind of homage; they have made Lacan the ladies' man of *Diacritics* and have forced Pierre Macherey into those dark alleys of the psyche where Engels feared to tread. According to Christiane Makward, the problem is even more serious in France than in the United States. "If neo-feminist thought in France seems to have ground to a halt," she writes, "it is because it has continued to feed on the discourse of the masters."[12]

It is time for feminist criticism to decide whether between religion and revision we can claim any firm theoretical ground of our own. In calling for a feminist criticism that is genuinely women centered, independent, and intellectually coherent, I do not mean to endorse the separatist fantasies of radical feminist visionaries or to exclude from our critical practice a variety of intellectual tools. But we need to ask much more searchingly what we want to know and how we can find answers to the questions that come from *our* experience. I do not think that feminist criticism can find a usable past in the androcentric critical tradition. It has more to learn from women's studies than from English studies, more to learn from international feminist theory than from another seminar on the masters. It must find its own subject, its own system, its own theory, and its

asking: what we want to know? and how to find answers

own voice. As Rich writes of Emily Dickinson, in her poem "I Am in Danger —Sir—," we must choose to have the argument out at last on our own premises.

DEFINING THE FEMININE: GYNOCRITICS AND THE WOMAN'S TEXT

> *A woman's writing is always feminine; it cannot help being feminine; at its best it is most feminine; the only difficulty lies in defining what we mean by feminine.*
>
> Virginia Woolf

> *It is impossible to define a feminine practice of writing, and this is an impossibility that will remain, for this practice will never be theorized, enclosed, encoded—which doesn't mean that it doesn't exist.*
>
> Hélène Cixous, "The Laugh of the Medusa"

In the past decade, I believe, this process of defining the feminine has started to take place. Feminist criticism has gradually shifted its center from revisionary readings to a sustained investigation of literature by women. The second mode of feminist criticism engendered by this process is the study of women *as writers*, and its subjects are the history, styles, themes, genres, and structures of writing by women; the psychodynamics of female creativity; the trajectory of the individual or collective female career; and the evolution and laws of a female literary tradition. No English term exists for such a specialized critical discourse, and so I have invented the term "gynocritics." Unlike the feminist critique, gynocritics offers many theoretical opportunities. To see women's writing as our primary subject forces us to make the leap to a new conceptual vantage point and to redefine the nature of the theoretical problem before us. It is no longer the ideological dilemma of reconciling revisionary pluralisms but the essential question of difference. How can we constitute women as a distinct literary group? What is *the difference* of women's writing?

Patricia Meyer Spacks, I think, was the first academic critic to notice this shift from an androcentric to a gynocentric feminist criticism. In *The Female Imagination* (1975), she pointed out that few feminist theorists had concerned themselves with women's writing. Simone de Beauvoir's treatment of women writers in *The Second Sex* "always suggests an a priori tendency to take them less seriously than their masculine counterparts"; Mary Ellmann, in *Thinking about Women*, characterized women's literary success as escape from the categories of womanhood; and, according to Spacks, Kate Millett, in *Sexual Politics*, "has little interest in woman imaginative writers."[13] Spacks' wide-ranging study inaugurated a new period of feminist literary history and criticism which asked, again and again, how women's writing had been different, how womanhood itself shaped women's creative expression. In such books as Ellen Moers's *Literary Women* (1976), my *A Literature of Their Own* (1977), Nina Baym's *Woman's Fiction* (1978), Sandra Gilbert and Susan Gubar's *The Madwoman in the Attic* (1979), and Margaret Homans's *Women Writers and Poetic Identity* (1980), and in hundreds of essays and papers, women's writing asserted itself as the central project of feminist literary study.

This shift in emphasis has also taken place in European feminist criticism. To date, most commentary on French feminist critical discourse has stressed its fundamental dissimilarity from the empirical American orientation, its unfamiliar intellectual grounding in linguistics, Marxism, neo-Freudian and Lacanian psychoanalysis, and Derridean deconstruction. Despite these differences, however, the new French feminisms have much in common with radical American feminist theories in terms of intellectual affiliations and rhetorical energies. The concept of *écriture féminine*, the inscription of the female body and female difference in language and text, is a significant theoretical formulation in French feminist criticism, although it describes a Utopian possibility rather than a literary practice. Hélène Cixous, one of the leading advocates of *écriture féminine*, has admitted that, with only a few exceptions, "there has not yet been any writing that inscribes femininity," and Nancy Miller explains that *écriture féminine* "privileges a textuality of the avant-garde, a literary production of the late twentieth century, and it is therefore fundamentally a hope, if not a blueprint, for the future."[14] Nonetheless, the concept of *écriture féminine* provides a way of talking about women's writing which reasserts the *value* of the feminine and identifies the theoretical project of feminist criticism as the analysis of difference. In recent years, the translations of important work by Julia Kristeva, Cixous, and Luce Irigaray and the excellent collection *New French Feminisms* have made French criticism much more accessible to American feminist scholars.[15]

English feminist criticism, which incorporates French feminist and Marxist theory but is more traditionally oriented to textual interpretation, is also moving toward a focus on women's writing.[16] The emphasis in each country falls somewhat differently: English feminist criticism, essentially Marxist, stresses oppression; French feminist criticism, essentially psychoanalytic, stresses repression; American feminist criticism, essentially textual, stresses expression. All, however, have become gynocentric. All are struggling to find a terminology that can rescue the feminine from its stereotypical associations with inferiority.

Defining the unique difference of women's writing, as Woolf and Cixous have warned, must present a slippery and demanding task. Is difference a matter of style? Genre? Experience? Or is it produced by the reading process, as some textual critics would maintain? Spacks calls the difference of women's writing a "delicate divergency," testifying to the subtle and elusive nature of the feminine practice of writing. Yet the delicate divergency of the woman's text challenges us to respond with equal delicacy and precision to the small but crucial deviations, the cumulative weightings of experience and exclusion, that have marked the history of women's writing. Before we can chart this history, we must uncover it, patiently and scrupulously; our theories must be firmly grounded in reading and research. But we have the opportunity, through gynocritics, to learn something solid, enduring, and real about the relation of women to literary culture.

Theories of women's writing presently make use of four models of difference: biological, linguistic, psychoanalytic, and cultural. Each is an effort to define and differentiate the qualities of the woman writer and the woman's text; each model also represents a school of gynocentric feminist criticism with its own favorite texts, styles, and methods. They overlap but are roughly sequential in that each incorporates the one before. I shall try now to sort out the various terminologies and assumptions of these four models of difference and evaluate their usefulness.

WOMEN'S WRITING AND WOMAN'S BODY

More body, hence more writing.
Cixous, "The Laugh of the Medusa"

Organic or biological criticism is the most extreme statement of gender difference, of a text indelibly marked by the body:

anatomy is textuality. Biological criticism is also one of the most sibylline and perplexing theoretical formulations of feminist criticism. Simply to invoke anatomy risks a return to the crude essentialism, the phallic and ovarian theories of art, that oppressed women in the past. Victorian physicians believed that women's physiological functions diverted about twenty percent of their creative energy from brain activity. Victorian anthropologists believed that the frontal lobes of the male brain were heavier and more developed than female lobes and thus that women were inferior in intelligence.

While feminist criticism rejects the attribution of literal biological inferiority, some theorists seem to have accepted the *metaphorical* implications of female biological difference in writing. In *The Madwoman in the Attic*, for example, Gilbert and Gubar structure their analysis of women's writing around metaphors of literary paternity. "In patriarchal western culture," they maintain, ". . .the text's author is a father, a progenitor, a procreator, an aesthetic patriarch whose pen is an instrument of generative power like his penis." Lacking phallic authority, they go on to suggest, women's writing is profoundly marked by the anxieties of this difference: "If the pen is a metaphorical penis, from what organ can females generate texts?"[17]

To this rhetorical question Gilbert and Gubar offer no reply; but it is a serious question of much feminist theoretical discourse. Those critics who, like myself, would protest the fundamental analogy might reply that women generate texts from the brain or that the word-processor, with its compactly coded microchips, its inputs and outputs, is a metaphorical womb. The metaphor of literary paternity, as Auerbach has pointed out in her review of *The Madwoman*, ignores "an equally timeless and, for me, even more oppressive metaphorical equation between literary creativity and childbirth."[18] Certainly metaphors of literary *maternity* predominated in the eighteenth and nineteenth centuries; the process of literary creation is analogically much more similar to gestation, labor, and delivery than it is to insemination. Describing Thackeray's plan for *Henry Esmond*, for example, Douglas Jerrold jovially remarked, "You have heard, I suppose, that Thackeray is big with twenty parts, and unless he is wrong in his time, expects the first installment at Christmas."[19] (If to write is metaphorically to give birth, from what organ can males generate texts?)

Some radical feminist critics, primarily in France but also in the United States, insist that we must read these metaphors as more than playful; that we must seriously rethink and redefine biological differentiation and its relation to women's writing. They argue that "women's writing proceeds from the body, that our sexual differentiation is also our source."[20] In *Of Woman Born*, Rich explains her belief that

> female biology . . . has far more radical implications than we have yet come to appreciate. Patriarchal thought has limited female biology to its own narrow specifications. The feminist vision has recoiled from female biology for these reasons; it will, I believe, come to view our physicality as a resource rather than a destiny. In order to live a fully human life, we require not only *control* of our bodies . . . we must touch the unity and resonance of our physicality, the corporeal ground of our intelligence.[21]

Feminist criticism written in the biological perspective generally stresses the importance of the body as a source of imagery. Alicia Ostriker, for example, argues that contemporary American women poets use a franker, more pervasive anatomical imagery than their male counterparts and that this insistent body language refuses the spurious transcendence that comes at the price of denying the flesh. In a fascinating essay on Whitman and Dickinson, Terence Diggory shows that physical nakedness, so potent a poetic symbol of authenticity for Whitman and other male poets, had very different connotations for Dickinson and her successors, who associated nakedness with the objectified or sexually exploited female nude and who chose instead protective images of the armored self.[22]

Feminist criticism which itself tries to be biological, to write from the critic's body, has been intimate, confessional, often innovative in style and form. Rachel Blau DuPlessis's "Washing Blood," the introduction to a special issue of *Feminist Studies* on the subject of motherhood, proceeds, in short lyrical paragraphs, to describe her own experience in adopting a child, to recount her dreams and nightmares, and to meditate upon the "healing unification of body and mind based not only on the lived experiences of motherhood as a social institution . . . but also on a biological power speaking through us."[23] Such criticism makes itself defiantly vulnerable, virtually bares its throat to the knife, since our professional taboos against self-revelation are so strong. When it succeeds, however, it achieves the power and the dignity of art. Its existence is an implicit rebuke to women critics who continue to write, according to Rich, "from somewhere outside their female bodies." In comparison to this flowing confessional criticism, the tight-lipped Olympian intelligence of such texts as Elizabeth Hardwick's *Seduction and Betrayal* or Susan Sontag's *Illness as Metaphor* can seem arid and strained.

Yet in its obsessions with the "corporeal ground of our intelligence," feminist biocriticism can also become cruelly prescriptive. There is a sense in which the exhibition of bloody wounds becomes an initiation ritual quite separate and disconnected from critical insight. And as the editors of the journal *Questions féministes* point out, "it is . . . dangerous to place the body at the center of a search for female identity. . . . The themes of otherness and of the Body merge together, because the most visible difference between men and women, and the only one we know for sure to be permanent . . . is indeed the difference in body. This difference has been used as a pretext to 'justify' full power of one sex over the other" (trans. Yvonne Rochette-Ozzello, *NFF*, p. 218). The study of biological imagery in women's writing is useful and important as long as we understand that factors other than anatomy are involved in it. Ideas about the body are fundamental to understanding how women conceptualize their situation in society; but there can be no expression of the body which is unmediated by linguistic, social, and literary structures. The difference of woman's literary practice, therefore, must be sought (in Miller's words) in "the body of her writing and not the writing of her body."[24]

WOMEN'S WRITING AND WOMEN'S LANGUAGE

> *The women say, the language you speak poisons your glottis tongue palate lips. They say, the language you speak is made up of words that are killing you. They say, the language you speak is made up of signs that rightly speaking designate what men have appropriated.*
>
> Monique Wittig, *Les Guérillères*

Linguistic and textual theories of women's writing ask whether men and women use language differently; whether sex differences in language use can be theorized in terms of biology, socialization, or culture; whether women can create new languages of their own; and whether speaking, reading, and writing are all gender marked. American, French, and British feminist critics have all drawn attention to the philosophical, linguistic, and practical problems of women's use of language, and the debate over language is one of the most exciting areas in gynocritics. Poets and writers have led the attack on what Rich calls "the oppressor's language," a language sometimes criticized as sexist, sometimes as abstract. But the problem goes well beyond reformist efforts to purge language of its sexist aspects. As Nelly Furman explains, "It is through the medium of language that we define and categorize areas of difference and similarity, which in turn allow us to comprehend the world around us. Male-centered categorizations predominate in American English and subtly shape our understanding and perception of reality; this is why attention is increasingly directed to the inherently oppressive aspects for women of a male-constructed language system."[25] According to Carolyn Burke, the language system is at the center of French feminist theory:

> The central issue in much recent women's writing in France is to find and use an appropriate female language. Language is the place to begin: a *prise de conscience* must be followed by a *prise de la parole*. . . . In this view, the very forms of the dominant mode of discourse show the mark of the dominant masculine ideology. Hence, when a woman writes or speaks herself into existence, she is forced to speak in something like a foreign tongue, a language with which she may be personally uncomfortable.[26]

Many French feminists advocate a revolutionary linguism, an oral break from the dictatorship of patriarchal speech. Annie Leclerc, in *Parole de femme*, calls on women "to invent a language that is not oppressive, a language that does not leave speechless but that loosens the tongue" (trans. Courtivron, *NFF*, p. 179). Chantal Chawaf, in an essay on "La chair linguistique," connects biofeminism and linguism in the view that women's language and a genuinely feminine practice of writing will articulate the body:

> In order to reconnect the book with the body and with pleasure, we must disintellectualize writing. . . . And this language, as it develops, will not degenerate and dry up, will not go back to the fleshless academicism, the stereotypical and servile discourses that we reject.
>
> . . . Feminine language must, by its very nature, work on life passionately, scientifically, poetically, politically in order to make it invulnerable. [Trans. Rochette-Ozzello, *NFF*, pp. 177–78]

But scholars who want a women's language that *is* intellectual and theoretical, that works *inside* the academy, are faced with what seems like an impossible paradox, as Xavière Gauthier has lamented: "As long as women remain silent, they will be outside the historical process. But, if they begin to speak and write *as men do*, they will enter history subdued and alienated; it is a history that, logically speaking, their speech should disrupt" (trans. Marilyn A. August, *NFF*, pp. 162–63). What we need, Mary Jacobus has proposed, is a women's writing that works within "male" discourse but works "ceaselessly to deconstruct it: to write what cannot be written," and according to Shoshana Felman, "the challenge facing the woman today is nothing less than to 'reinvent' language, . . . to speak not only against, but outside of the specular phallogocentric structure, to establish a discourse the status of which would no longer be defined by the phallacy of masculine meaning."[27]

Beyond rhetoric, what can linguistic, historical, and anthropological research tell us about the prospects for a women's language? First of all, the concept of a women's language is not original with feminist criticism; it is very ancient and appears frequently in folklore and myth. In such myths, the essence of women's language is its secrecy; what is really being described is the male fantasy of the enigmatic nature of the feminine. Herodotus, for example, reported that the Amazons were able linguists who easily mastered the languages of their male antagonists, although men could never learn the women's tongue. In *The White Goddess,* Robert Graves romantically argues that a women's language existed in a matriarchal stage of prehistory; after a great battle of the sexes, the matriarchy was overthrown and the women's language went underground, to survive in the mysterious cults of Eleusis and Corinth and the witch covens of Western Europe. Travelers and missionaries in the seventeenth and eighteenth centuries brought back accounts of "women's languages" among American Indians, Africans, and Asians (the differences in linguistic structure they reported were usually superficial). There is some ethnographic evidence that in certain cultures women have evolved a private form of communication out of their need to resist the silence imposed upon them in public life. In ecstatic religions, for example, women, more frequently than men, speak in tongues, a phenomenon attributed by anthropologists to their relative inarticulateness in formal religious discourse. But such ritualized and unintelligible female "languages" are scarcely cause for rejoicing; indeed, it was because witches were suspected of esoteric knowledge and possessed speech that they were burned.[28]

From a political perspective, there are interesting parallels between the feminist problem of a women's language and the recurring "language issue" in the general history of decolonization. After a revolution, a new state must decide which language to make official: the language that is "psychologically immediate," that allows "the kind of force that speaking one's mother tongue permits"; or the language that "is an avenue to the wider community of modern culture," a community to whose movements of thought only "foreign" languages can give access.[29] The language issue in feminist criticism has emerged, in a sense, after our revolution, and it reveals the tensions in the women's movement between those who would stay outside the academic establishments and the institutions of criticism and those who would enter and even conquer them.

The advocacy of a women's language is thus a political gesture that also carries tremendous emotional force. But despite its unifying appeal, the concept of a women's language is riddled with difficulties. Unlike Welsh, Breton, Swahili, or Amharic, that is, languages of minority or colonized groups, there is no mother tongue, no genderlect spoken by the female population in a society, which differs significantly from the dominant language. English and American linguists agree that "there is absolutely no evidence that would suggest the sexes are preprogrammed to develop structurally different linguistic systems." Furthermore, the many specific differences in male and female speech, intonation, and language use that have been identified cannot be explained in terms of "two separate sex-specific languages" but need to be considered instead in terms of styles, strategies, and contexts of linguistic performance.[30] Efforts at quantitative analysis of language in texts by men or women, such as Mary Hiatt's computerized study of contemporary fiction, *The Way Women Write* (1977), can easily be attacked for treating words apart from their meanings and purposes. At a higher level, analyses which look for "feminine style" in the repetition of stylistic devices, image patterns, and syntax in women's writing tend to confuse innate forms with the overdetermined results of literary choice. Language and style are never raw and instinctual but are always the products of innumerable factors, of genre, tradition, memory, and context.

The appropriate task for feminist criticism, I believe, is to concentrate on women's access to language, on the available lexical range from which words can be selected, on the ideological and cultural determinants of expression. The problem is not that language is insufficient to express women's consciousness but that women have been denied the full resources of language and have been forced into silence, euphemism, or circumlocution. In a series of drafts for a lecture on women's writing (drafts which she discarded or suppressed), Woolf protested against the censorship which cut off female access to language. Comparing herself to Joyce, Woolf noted the differences between their verbal territories: "Now men are shocked if a woman says what she feels (as Joyce does). Yet literature which is always pulling down blinds is not literature. All that we have ought to be expressed—mind and body—a process of incredible difficulty and danger."[31]

"All that we have ought to be expressed—mind and body." Rather than wishing to limit women's linguistic range, we must fight to open and extend it. The holes in discourse, the blanks and gaps and silences, are not the spaces where female consciousness reveals itself but the blinds of a "prison-house of language." Women's literature is still haunted by the ghosts of repressed language, and until we have exorcised those ghosts, it ought not to be in language that we base our theory of difference.

WOMEN'S WRITING AND WOMAN'S PSYCHE

Psychoanalytically oriented feminist criticism locates the difference of women's writing in the author's psyche and in the relation of gender to the creative process. It incorporates the biological and linguistic models of gender difference in a theory of the female psyche or self, shaped by the body, by the development of language, and by sex-role socialization. Here too there are many difficulties to overcome; the Freudian model requires constant revision to make it gynocentric. In one grotesque early example of Freudian reductivism, Theodor Reik suggested that women have fewer writing blocks than men because their bodies are constructed to facilitate release: "Writing, as Freud told us at the end of his life, is connected with urinating, which physiologically is easier for a woman—they have a wider bladder."[32] Generally, however, psychoanalytic criticism has focused not on the capacious bladder (could this be the organ from which females generate texts?) but on the absent phallus. Penis envy, the castration complex, and the Oedipal phase have become the Freudian coordinates defining women's relationship to language, fantasy, and culture. Currently the French psychoanalytic school dominated by Lacan has extended castration into a total metaphor for female literary and linguistic disadvantage. Lacan theorizes that the acquisition of language and the entry into its symbolic order occurs at the Oedipal phase in which the child accepts his or her gender identity. This stage requires an acceptance of the phallus as a privileged signification and a consequent female displacement, as Cora Kaplan has explained:

> The phallus as a signifier has a central, crucial position in language, for if language embodies the patriarchal law of the culture, its basic meanings refer to the recurring process by which sexual difference and subjectivity are acquired. . . . Thus the little girl's access to the Symbolic, i.e., to language and its laws, is always negative and/or mediated by introsubjective relation to a

> third term, for it is characterized by an identification with lack.[33]

In psychoanalytic terms, "lack" has traditionally been associated with the feminine, although Lac(k)anian critics can now make their statements linguistically. Many feminists believe that psychoanalysis could become a powerful tool for literary criticism, and recently there has been a renewed interest in Freudian theory. But feminist criticism based in Freudian or post-Freudian psychoanalysis must continually struggle with the problem of feminine disadvantage and lack. In *The Madwoman in the Attic*, Gilbert and Gubar carry out a feminist revision of Harold Bloom's Oedipal model of literary history as a conflict between fathers and sons and accept the essential psychoanalytic definition of the woman artist as displaced, disinherited, and excluded. In their view, the nature and "difference" of women's writing lies in its troubled and even tormented relationship to female identity; the woman writer experiences her own gender as "a painful obstacle or even a debilitating inadequacy." The nineteenth-century woman writer inscribed her own sickness, her madness, her anorexia, her agoraphobia, and her paralysis in her texts; and although Gilbert and Gubar are dealing specifically with the nineteenth century, the range of their allusion and quotation suggests a more general thesis:

> Thus the loneliness of the female artist, her feelings of alienation from male predecessors coupled with her need for sisterly precursors and successors, her urgent sense of her need for a female audience together with her fear of the antagonism of male readers, her culturally conditioned timidity about self-dramatization, her dread of the patriarchal authority of art, her anxiety about the impropriety of female invention—all these phenomena of "inferiorization" mark the woman writer's struggle for artistic self-definition and differentiate her efforts at self-creation from those of her male counterpart.[34]

In "Emphasis Added," Miller takes another approach to the problem of negativity in psychoanalytic criticism. Her strategy is to expand Freud's view of female creativity and to show how criticism of women's texts has frequently been unfair because it has been based in Freudian expectations. In his essay "The Relation of the Poet to Daydreaming" (1908), Freud maintained that the unsatisfied dreams and desires of women are chiefly erotic; these are the desires that shape the plots of women's fiction. In contrast, the dominant fantasies behind men's plots are egoistic and ambitious as well as erotic. Miller shows how women's plots have been granted or denied credibility in terms of their conformity to this phallocentric model and that a gynocentric reading reveals a repressed egoistic/ambitious fantasy in women's writing as well as in men's. Women's novels which are centrally concerned with fantasies of romantic love belong to the category disdained by George Eliot and other serious women writers as "silly novels"; the smaller number of women's novels which inscribe a fantasy of power imagine a world for women outside of love, a world, however, made impossible by social boundaries.

There has also been some interesting feminist literary criticism based on alternatives to Freudian psychoanalytic theory: Annis Pratt's Jungian history of female archetypes, Barbara Rigney's Laingian study of the divided self in in women's fiction, and Ann Douglas's Ericksonian analysis of inner space in nineteenth-century women's writing.[35] And for the past few years, critics have been thinking about the possibilities of a new feminist psychoanalysis that does *not* revise Freud but instead emphasizes the development and construction of gender identities.

The most dramatic and promising new work in feminist psychoanalysis looks at the pre-Oedipal phase and at the process of psychosexual differentiation. Nancy Chodorow's *The Reproduction of Mothering: Psychoanalysis and the Sociology of Gender* (1978) has had an enormous influence on women's studies. Chodorow revises traditional psychoanalytic concepts of differentiation, the process by which the child comes to perceive the self as separate and to develop ego and body boundaries. Since differentiation takes place in relation to the mother (the primary caretaker), attitudes toward the mother "emerge in the earliest differentiation of the self"; the mother, who is a woman, becomes and remains for children of both genders the other, or object."[36] The child develops core gender identity concomitantly with differentiation, but the process is not the same for boys and girls. A boy must learn his gender identity negatively as being not-female, and this difference requires continual reinforcement. In contrast, a girl's core gender identity is positive and built upon sameness, continuity, and identification with the mother. Women's difficulties with feminine identity come after the Oedipal phase, in which male power and cultural hegemony give sex differences a transformed value. Chodorow's work suggests that shared parenting, the involvement of men as primary caretakers of children, will have a profound effect on our sense of sex difference, gender identity, and sexual preference.

But what is the significance of feminist psychoanalysis for literary criticism? One thematic carry-over has been a critical interest in the mother-daughter configuration as a source of female creativity.[37] Elizabeth Abel's bold investigation of female friendship in contemporary women's novels uses Chodorow's theory to show how not only the relationships of women characters but also the relationship of women writers to each other are determined by the psychodynamics of female bonding. Abel too confronts Bloom's paradigm of literary history, but unlike Gilbert and Gubar she sees a "triadic female pattern" in which the Oedipal relation to the male tradition is balanced by the woman writer's pre-Oedipal relation to the female tradition. "As the dynamics of female friendship differ from those of male," Abel concludes, "the dynamics of female literary influence also diverge and deserve a theory of influence attuned to female psychology and to women's dual position in literary history."[38]

Like Gilbert, Gubar, and Miller, Abel brings together women's texts from a variety of national literatures, choosing to emphasize "the constancy of certain emotional dynamics depicted in diverse cultural situations." Yet the privileging of gender implies not only the constancy but also the immutability of these dynamics. Although psychoanalytically based models of feminist criticism can now offer us remarkable and persuasive readings of individual texts and can highlight extraordinary similarities between women writing in a variety of cultural circumstances, they cannot explain historical change, ethnic difference, or the shaping force of generic and economic factors. To consider these issues, we must go beyond psychoanalysis to a more flexible and comprehensive model of women's writing which places it in the maximum context of culture.

WOMEN'S WRITING AND WOMEN'S CULTURE

> *I consider women's literature as a specific category, not because of biology, but because it is, in a sense, the literature of the colonized.*
>
> Christiane Rochefort, "The Privilege of Consciousness"

A theory based on a model of women's culture can provide, I believe, a more complete and satisfying way to talk about the specificity and difference of women's writing than theories based in biology, linguistics, or psychoanalysis. Indeed, a theory of culture incorporates ideas about women's body, language, and psyche but interprets them in relation to the social contexts in which they occur. The ways in which women conceptualize their bodies and their sexual and reproductive functions are intricately linked to their cultural environments. The female psyche can be studied as the product or construction of cultural forces. Language, too, comes back into the picture, as we consider the social dimensions and determinants of language use, the shaping of linguistic behavior by cultural ideals. A cultural theory acknowledges that there are important differences between women as writers: class, race, nationality, and history are literary determinants as significant as gender. Nonetheless, women's culture forms a collective experience within the cultural whole, an experience that binds women writers to each other over time and space. It is in the emphasis on the binding force of women's culture that this approach differs from Marxist theories of cultural hegemony.

Hypotheses of women's culture have been developed over the last decade primarily by anthropologists, sociologists, and social historians in order to get away from masculine systems, hierarchies, and values and to get at the primary and self-defined nature of female cultural experience. In the field of women's history, the concept of women's culture is still controversial, although there is agreement on its significance as a theoretical formulation. Gerda Lerner explains the importance of examining women's experience in its own terms:

> Women have been left out of history not because of the evil conspiracies of men in general or male historians in particular, but because we have considered history only in male-centered terms. We have missed women and their activities, because we have asked questions of history which are inappropriate to women. To rectify this, and to light up areas of historical darkness we must, for a time, focus on a *woman-centered* inquiry, considering the possibility of the existence of a female culture *within* the general culture shared by men and women. History must include an account of the female experience over time and should include the development of feminist consciousness as an essential aspect of women's past. This is the primary task of women's history. The central question it raises is: What would history be like if it were seen through the eyes of women and ordered by values they define?[39]

In defining female culture, historians distinguish between the roles, activities, tastes, and behaviors prescribed and considered appropriate for women and those activities, behaviors, and functions actually generated out of women's lives. In the late-eighteenth and nineteenth centuries, the term "woman's sphere" expressed the Victorian and Jacksonian vision of separate roles for men and women, with little or no overlap and with women subordinate. Woman's sphere was defined and maintained by men, but women frequently internalized its precepts in the American "cult of true womanhood" and the English "feminine ideal." Women's culture, however, redefines women's "activities and goals from a woman-centered point of view. . . . The term implies an assertion of equality and an awareness of sisterhood, the communality of women." Women's culture refers to "the broad-based communality of values, institutions, relationships, and methods of communication" unifying nineteenth-century female experience, a culture nonetheless with significant variants by class and ethnic group (*MFP*, pp. 52, 54).

Some feminist historians have accepted the model of separate spheres and have seen the movement from woman's sphere to women's culture to women's-rights activism as the consecutive stages of an evolutionary political process. Others see a more complex and perpetual negotiation taking place between women's culture and the general culture. As Lerner has argued:

> It is important to understand that "woman's culture" is not and should not be seen as a subculture. It is hardly possible for the majority to live in a subculture. . . . Women live their social existence within the general culture and, whenever they are confined by patriarchal restraint or segregation into separateness (which always has subordination as its purpose), they transform this restraint into complementarity (asserting the importance of woman's function, even its "superiority") and redefine it. Thus, women live a duality—as members of the general culture and as partakers of women's culture. [*MFP*, p. 52]

Lerner's views are similar to those of some cultural anthropologists. A particularly stimulating analysis of female culture has been carried out by two Oxford anthropologists, Shirley and Edwin Ardener. The Ardeners have tried to outline a model of women's culture which is not historically limited and to provide a terminology for its characteristics. Two essays by Edwin Ardener, "Belief and the Problem of Women" (1972) and "The 'Problem' Revisited" (1975), suggest that women constitute a *muted group*, the boundaries of whose culture and reality overlap, but are not wholly contained by, the *dominant (male) group*. A model of the cultural situation of women is crucial to understanding both how they are perceived by the dominant group and how they perceive themselves and others. Both historians and anthropologists emphasize the incompleteness of androcentric models of history and culture and the inadequacy of such models for the analysis of female experience. In the past, female experience which could not be accommodated by androcentric models was treated as deviant or simply ignored. Observation from an exterior point of view could never be the same as comprehension from within. Ardener's model also has many connections to and implications for current feminist literary theory, since the concepts of perception, silence, and silencing are so central to discussions of women's participation in literary culture.[40]

By the term "muted," Ardener suggests problems both of language and of power. Both muted and dominant groups generate beliefs or ordering ideas of social reality at the unconscious level, but dominant groups control the forms or structures in which consciousness can be articulated. Thus muted groups must mediate their beliefs through the allowable forms of dominant structures. Another way of putting this would be to say that all language is the language of the dominant order, and women, if they speak at all, must speak through it. How then, Ardener asks, "does the symbolic weight of that other mass of persons express itself?" In his view, women's beliefs find expression through ritual and art, expressions which can be deciphered by the ethnographer, either female or male, who is willing to make the effort to perceive beyond the screens of the dominant structure.[41]

Let us now look at Ardener's diagram of the relationship of the dominant and the muted group:

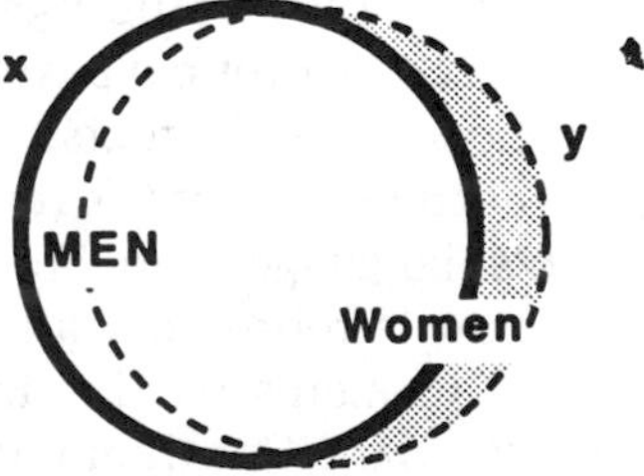

Unlike the Victorian model of complementary spheres, Ardener's groups are represented by intersecting circles. Much of muted circle Y falls within the boundaries of dominant circle X; there is also a crescent of Y which is outside the dominant boundary and therefore (in Ardener's terminology) "wild." We can think of the "wild zone" of women's culture spatially, experientially, or metaphysically. Spatially it stands for an area which is literally no-man's-land, a place forbidden to men, which corresponds to the zone in X which is off limits to women. Experientially it stands for the aspects of the female life-style which are outside of and unlike those of men; again, there is a corresponding zone of male experience alien to women. But if we think of the wild zone metaphysically, or in terms of consciousness, it has no corresponding male space since all of male consciousness is within the circle of the dominant structure and thus accessible to or structured by language. In this sense, the "wild" is always imaginary; from the male point of view, it may simply be the projection of the unconscious. In terms of cultural anthropology, women know what the male crescent is like, even if they have never seen it, because it becomes the subject of legend (like the wilderness). But men do not know what is in the wild.

For some feminist critics, the wild zone, or "female space," must be the address of a genuinely women-centered criticism, theory, and art, whose shared project is to bring into being the symbolic weight of female consciousness, to make the invisible visible, to make the silent speak. French feminist critics would like to make the wild zone the theoretical base of women's difference. In their texts, the wild zone becomes the place for the revolutionary women's language, the language of everything that is repressed, and for the revolutionary women's writing in "white ink." It is the Dark Continent in which Cixous's laughing Medusa and Wittig's *guérillères* reside. Through voluntary entry into the wild zone, other feminist critics tell us, a woman can write her way out of the "cramped confines of patriarchal space."[42] The images of this journey are now familiar in feminist quest fictions and in essays about them. The writer/heroine, often guided by another woman, travels to the "mother country" of liberated desire and female authenticity; crossing to the other side of the mirror, like Alice in Wonderland, is often a symbol of the passage.

Many forms of American radical feminism also romantically assert that women are closer to nature, to the environment, to a matriarchal principle at once biological and ecological. Mary Daly's *Gyn/Ecology* and Margaret Atwood's novel *Surfacing* are texts which create this feminist mythology. In English and American literature, women writers have often imagined Amazon Utopias, cities or countries situated in the wild zone or on its border: Elizabeth Gaskell's gentle *Cranford* is probably an Amazon Utopia; so is Charlotte Perkins Gilman's *Herland* or, take a recent example, Joanna Russ's *Whileaway*. A few years ago, the feminist publishing house Daughters, Inc. tried to create a business version of the Amazon Utopia; as Lois Gould reported in the *New York Times Magazine* (2 January 1977), "They believe they are building the working models for the critical next stage of feminism: full independence from the control and influence of "male-dominated" institutions—the news media, the health, education, and legal systems, the art, theater, and literary worlds, the banks."

These fantasies of an idyllic enclave represent a phenomenon which feminist criticism must recognize in the history of women's writing. But we must also understand that there can be no writing or criticism totally outside of the dominant structure; no publication is fully independent from the economic and political pressures of the male-dominated society. The concept of a woman's text in the wild zone is a playful abstraction: in the reality to which we must address ourselves as critics, women's writing is a "double-voiced discourse" that always embodies the social, literary, and cultural heritages of both the muted and the dominant.[43] And insofar as most feminist critics are also women writing, this precarious heritage is one we share; every step that feminist criticism takes toward defining women's writing is a step toward self-understanding as well; every account of a female literary culture and a female literary tradition has parallel significance for our own place in critical history and critical tradition.

Women writing are not, then, *inside* and *outside* of the male tradition; they are inside two traditions simultaneously, "undercurrents," in Ellen Moers's metaphor, of the mainstream. To mix metaphors again, the literary estate of women, as Myra Jehlen says, "suggests . . . a more fluid imagery of interacting juxtapositions, the point of which would be to represent not so much the territory, as its defining borders. Indeed, the female territory might well be envisioned as one long border, and independence for women, not as a separate country, but as open access to the sea." As Jehlen goes on to explain, an aggressive feminist criticism must poise itself on this border and must see women's writing in its changing historical and cultural relation to that other body of texts identified by feminist criticism not simply as literature but as "men's writing."[44]

The difference of women's writing, then, can only be understood in terms of this complex and historically grounded cultural relation. An important aspect of Ardener's model is that there are muted groups other than women; a dominant structure may determine many muted structures. A black American woman poet, for example, would have her literary identity formed by the dominant (white male) tradition, by a muted women's culture, and by a muted black culture. She would be affected by both sexual and racial politics in a combination unique to her case; at the same time, as Barbara Smith points out, she shares an experience specific to her group: "Black women writers constitute an identifiable literary tradition . . . thematically, stylistically, aesthetically, and conceptually. Black women writers manifest common approaches to the act of creating literature as a direct result of the specific political, social, and economic experience they have been obliged to share."[45] Thus the first task of a gynocentric criticism must be to plot the precise cultural locus of female literary identity and to describe the forces that intersect an individual woman writer's cultural field. A gynocentric criticism would also situate women writers with respect to the variables of literary culture, such as modes of production and distribution, relations of author and audience, relations of high to popular art, and hierarchies of genre.

Insofar as our concepts of literary periodization are based on men's writing, women's writing must be forcibly assimilated to an irrelevant grid; we discuss a Renaissance which is not a renaissance for women, a Romantic period in which women played very little part, a modernism with which women conflict. At the same time, the ongoing history of women's writing has been suppressed, leaving large and mysterious gaps in accounts of the development of genre. Gynocentric criticism is already well on the way to providing us with another perspective on literary history. Margaret Anne Doody, for example, suggests that "the period between the death of Richardson and the appearance of the novels of Scott and Austen" which has "been regarded as a dead period, a dull blank" is in fact the period in which late eighteenth-century women writers were developing "the paradigm for women's fiction of the nineteenth century—something hardly less than the paradigm of the nineteenth-century novel itself."[46] There has also been a feminist rehabilitation of the female gothic, a mutation of a popular genre once believed marginal but now seen as part of the great tradition of the novel.[47] In American literature, the pioneering work of Ann Douglas, Nina Baym, and Jane Tompkins, among others, has given us a new view of the power of women's fiction to feminize nineteenth-century American culture.[48] And feminist critics have made us aware that Woolf belonged to a tradition other than modernism and that this tradition surfaces in her work precisely in those places where criticism has hitherto found obscurities, evasions, implausibilities, and imperfections.[49]

Our current theories of literary influence also need to be tested in terms of women's writing. If a man's text, as Bloom and Edward Said have maintained, is fathered, then a woman's text is not only mothered but parented; it confronts both paternal and maternal precursors and must deal with the problems and advantages of both lines of inheritance. Woolf says in *A Room of One's Own* that "a woman writing thinks back through her mothers." But a woman writing unavoidably thinks back through her fathers as well; only male writers can forget or mute half of their parentage. The dominant culture need not consider the muted, except to rail against "the woman's part" in itself. Thus we need more subtle and supple accounts of influence, not just to explain women's writing but also to understand how men's writing has resisted the acknowledgment of female precursors.

We must first go beyond the assumption that women writers either imitate their male predecessors or revise them and that this simple dualism is adequate to describe the influences on the woman's text. I. A. Richards once commented that the influence of G. E. Moore had had an enormous negative impact on his work: "I feel like an obverse of him. Where there's a hole in him, there's a bulge in me."[50] Too often women's place in literary tradition is translated into the crude topography of hole and bulge, with Milton, Byron, or Emerson the bulging bogeys on one side and women's literature from Aphra Behn to Adrienne Rich a pocked moon surface of revisionary lacunae on the other. One of the great advantages of the women's-culture model is that it shows how the female tradition can be a positive source of strength and solidarity as well as a negative source of powerlessness; it can generate its own experiences and symbols which are not simply the obverse of the male tradition.

How can a cultural model of women's writing help us to read a woman's text? One implication of this model is that women's fiction can be read as a double-voiced discourse, containing a "dominant" and a "muted" story, what Gilbert and Gubar call a "palimpsest." I have described it elsewhere as an object/field problem in which we must keep two alternative oscillating texts simultaneously in view: "In the purest feminist literary criticism we are . . . presented with a radical alteration of our vision, a demand that we see meaning in what has previously been empty space. The orthodox plot recedes, and another plot, hitherto submerged in the anonymity of the background, stands out in bold relief like a thumbprint." Miller too sees "another text" in women's fiction, "more or less muted from novel to novel" but "always there to be read."[51]

Another interpretative strategy for feminist criticism might be the contextual analysis that the cultural anthropologist Clifford Geertz calls "thick description." Geertz calls for descriptions that seek to understand the meaning of cultural phenomena and products by "sorting out the structures of signification . . . and determining their social ground and import."[52] A genuinely "thick" description of women's writing would insist upon gender and upon a female literary tradition among the multiple strata that make up the force of meaning in a text. No description, we must concede, could ever be thick enough to account for all the factors that go into the work of art. But we could work toward completeness, even as an unattainable ideal.

In suggesting that a cultural model of women's writing has considerable usefulness for the enterprise of feminist criticism, I don't mean to replace psychoanalysis with cultural anthropology as the answer to all our theoretical problems or to enthrone Ardener and Geertz as the new white fathers in place of Freud, Lacan, and Bloom. No theory, however suggestive, can be a substitute for the close and extensive knowledge of women's texts which constitutes our essential subject. Cultural anthropology and social history can perhaps offer us a terminology and a diagram of women's cultural situation. But feminist critics must use this concept in relation to what women actually write, not in relation to a theoretical, political, metaphoric, or visionary ideal of what women ought to write.

I began by recalling that a few years ago feminist critics thought we were on a pilgrimage to the promised land in which gender would lose its power, in which all texts would be sexless and equal, like angels. But the more precisely we understand the specificity of women's writing not as a transient by-product of sexism but as a fundamental and continually determining reality, the more clearly we realize that we have misperceived our destination. We may never reach the promised land at all; for when feminist critics see our task as the study of women's writing, we realize that the land promised to us is not the serenely undifferentiated universality of texts but the tumultuous and intriguing wilderness of difference itself.

NOTES

1. Carolyn G. Heilbrun and Catharine R. Stimpson, "Theories of Feminist Criticism: A Dialogue," in *Feminist Literary Criticism*, ed. Josephine Donovan (Lexington: University Press of Kentucky, 1975), 64. I also discuss this distinction in my "Toward a Feminist Poetics," in *The New Feminist Criticism*, ed. Elaine Showalter (New York: Pantheon Books, 1985), pp. 125–143; a number of the ideas in the first part of the present essay are raised more briefly in the earlier piece.

2. No women critics are discussed in Geoffrey Hartman's *Criticism in the Wilderness: The Study of Literature Today* (New Haven, Yale University Press, 1980), but he does describe a feminine spirit called "the Muse of Criticism": "more a governess than a Muse, the stern daughter of books no longer read under trees and in the fields" (p. 175).

3. See my "Literary Criticism," Review Essay, *Signs*, 1 (Winter 1975), 435–60.

4. Annette Kolodny, "Literary Criticism," Review Essay, *Signs*, 2 (Winter 1976), 420.

5. On black criticism, see Barbara Smith, "Toward a Black Feminist Criticism," in *The New Feminist Criticism*, pp. 168–85, and Mary Helen Washington, "New Lives and New Letters: Black Women Writers at the End of the Seventies," *College English*, 43 (January 1981): 1–11. On Marxist criticism, see the Marxist-Feminist Literature Collective's "Women's Writing," *Ideology and Consciousness*, 3 (Spring 1978), 27–48, a collectively written analysis of several nineteenth-century women's novels which gives equal weight to gender, class, and literary production as textual determinants.

6. Margaret Homans, *Women Writers and Poetic Identity: Dorothy Wordsworth, Emily Brontë, and Emily Dickinson* (Princeton, N.J.: Princeton University Press, 1980), 10.

7. Josephine Donovan, "Afterward: Critical Revision," *Feminist Literary Criticism*, p. 74. Judith Fetterley, *The Resisting Reader: A Feminist Approach to American Fiction* (Bloomington: Indiana University Press, 1978), viii. See my "Toward a Feminist Poetics," pp. 125–43. *The Authority of Experience* is the title of an anthology edited by Arlyn Diamond and Lee R. Edwards (Amherst: University of Massachusetts Press, 1977).

8. Nina Auerbach, "Feminist Criticism Reviewed," in *Gender and Literary Voice*, ed. Janet Todd (New York: Holmes & Meier, 1980), 258.

9. Adrienne Rich, "When We Dead Awaken: Writing as Re-Vision," in *On Lies, Secrets, and Silence* (New York: W.W. Norton, 1979), 35.

10. Annette Kolodny, "Dancing through the Minefield: Some Observations on the Theory, Practice, and Politics of a Feminist Literary Criticism," in *The New Feminist Criticism*, pp. 144–67. The complete theoretical case for a feminist hermeneutics is outlined in Kolodny's essays, including "Some Notes on Defining a 'Feminist Literary Criticism,' " *Critical Inquiry*, 2 (Autumn 1975): 75–92; "A Map for Rereading; or, Gender and the Interpretation of Literary Texts," in *The New Feminist Criticism*, pp. 46–62; and "The Theory of Feminist Criticism" (paper delivered at the National Center for the Humanities Conference on Feminist Criticism, Research Triangle Park, N.C., March 1981).

11. Sandra M. Gilbert, "What Do Feminist Critics Want? A Postcard from the Volcano," in *The New Feminist Criticism*, p. 36.

12. Christiane Makward, "To Be or Not to Be. . . . A Feminist Speaker," in *The Future of Difference*, ed. Hester Eisenstein and Alice Jardine (Boston: G.K. Hall, 1980), p. 102. On Lacan, see Jane Gallop, "The Ladies' Man," *Diacritics*, 6 (Winter 1976): 28–34; on Macherey, see the Marxist-Feminist Literature Collective's "Women's Writing."

13. Patricia Meyer Spacks, *The Female Imagination* (New York: Alfred A. Knopf, 1975), 19, 32.

14. Hélène Cixous, "The Laugh of the Medusa," trans. Keith and Paula Cohen, *Signs*, 1 (Summer 1976): 878. Nancy K. Miller, "Emphasis Added: Plots and Plausibilities in Women's Fiction," in *The New Feminist Criticism*, pp. 339–60.

15. For an overview, see Domna C. Stanton, "Language and Revolution: The Franco-American Dis-Connection," in Eisenstein and Jardine, *Future of Difference*, pp. 73–87, and Elaine Marks and Isabelle de Courtivron, eds., *New French Feminisms* (Amherst: University of Massachusetts Press, 1979); all further references to *New French Feminisms*, abbreviated *NFF*, will hereafter be included with translator's name parenthetically in the text.

16. Two major works are the manifesto of the Marxist-Feminist Literature Collective, "Women's Writing," and the papers from the Oxford University lectures on women and literature, Mary Jacobus, ed., *Women Writing and Writing about Women* (New York: Barnes & Noble Imports, 1979).

17. Sandra M. Gilbert and Susan Gubar, *The Madwoman in the Attic: The Woman Writer and the Nineteenth-Century Literary Imagination* (New Haven: Yale University Press, 1979), 6–7.

18. Nina Auerbach, review of *Madwoman*, *Victorian Studies*, 23 (Summer 1980): 506.

19. Douglas Jerrold, quoted in Kathleen Tillotson, *Novels of the Eighteen-Forties* (London: Oxford University Press, 1961), 39 n. James Joyce imagined the creator as female and literary creation as a process of gestation; see Richard Ellmann, *James Joyce: A Biography* (London: Oxford University Press, 1959), 306–8.

20. Carolyn C. Burke, "Report from Paris: Women's Writing and the Women's Movement," *Signs*, 3 (Summer 1978), 851.

21. Adrienne Rich, *Of Woman Born: Motherhood as Experience and Institution* (New York: W.W. Norton, 1976), 62. Biofeminist criticism has been influential in other disciplines as well: e.g., art critics, such as Judy Chicago and Lucy Lippard, have suggested that women artists are compelled to use a uterine or vaginal iconography of centralized focus, curved lines, and tactile or sensuous forms. See Lippard, *From the Center: Feminist Essays on Women's Art* (New York: E.P. Dutton, 1976).

22. See Alicia Ostriker, "Body Language: Imagery of the Body in Women's Poetry," in *The State of the Language*, ed. Leonard Michaels and Christopher Ricks (Berkeley: University of California Press, 1980), 247–63, and Terence Diggory, "Armoured Women, Naked Men: Dickinson, Whitman, and Their Successors," in *Shakespeare's Sisters: Feminist Essays on Women Poets*, ed. Sandra M. Gilbert and Susan Gubar (Bloomington: Indiana University Press, 1979), 135–50.

23. Rachel Blau DuPlessis, "Washing Blood," *Feminist Studies*, 4 (June 1978), 10. The entire issue is an important document of feminist criticism.

24. Nancy K. Miller, "Women's Autobiography in France: For a Dialectics of Identification," in *Women and Language in Literature and Society*, ed. Sally McConnell-Ginet, Ruth Borker, and Nelly Furman (New York: Praeger, 1980), 271.

25. Nelly Furman, "The Study of Women and Language: Comment on Vol. 3, No. 3," *Signs*, 4 (Autumn 1978), 182.

26. Burke, "Report from Paris," p. 844.

27. Jacobus, "The Difference of View," in *Women's Writing and Writing about Women*, pp. 12–13. Shoshana Felman, "Women and Madness: The Critical Phallacy," *Diacritics*, 5 (Winter 1975), 10.

28. On women's language, see Sarah B. Pomeroy, *Goddesses, Whores, Wives, and Slaves: Women in Classical Antiquity* (New York: Schocken Books,

1976), 24; Sally McConnell-Ginet, "Linguistics and the Feminist Challenge," in *Women and Language,* p. 14; and Ioan M. Lewis, *Ecstatic Religion* (1971), cited in Shirley Ardener, ed., *Perceiving Women* (New York: Halsted Press, 1978), 50.

29. Clifford Geertz, *The Interpretation of Cultures* (New York: Basic Books, 1973), 241–42.

30. McConnell-Ginet, "Linguistics and the Feminist Challenge," pp. 13, 16.

31. Virginia Woolf, "Speech, Manuscript Notes," *The Pargiters: The Novel-Essay Portion of the Years 1882–1941,* ed. Mitchell A. Leaska (New York: New York Public Library, 1977), 164.

32. Quoted in Erika Freeman, *Insights: Conversations with Theodor Reik* (Englewood Cliffs, N.J.: Prentice-Hall, 1971), 166. Reik goes on, "But what the hell, writing! The great task of a woman is to bring a child into the world."

33. Cora Kaplan, "Language and Gender," unpublished paper, University of Sussex, 1977, p. 3.

34. Gilbert and Gubar, *Madwoman in the Attic,* p. 50.

35. See Annis Pratt, "The New Feminist Criticisms," in *Beyond Intellectual Sexism: A New Woman, a New Reality,* ed. Joan I. Roberts (New York: Longman, 1976); Barbara H. Rigney, *Madness and Sexual Politics in the Feminist Novel: Studies in Brontë, Woolf, Lessing, and Atwood* (Madison: University of Wisconsin Press, 1978); and Ann Douglas, "Mrs. Sigourney and the Sensibility of the Inner Space," *New England Quarterly,* 45 (June 1972), 163–81.

36. Nancy Chodorow, "Gender, Relation, and Difference in Psychoanalytic Perspective," in Eisenstein and Jardine, *Future of Difference,* p. 11. See also Chodorow et al., "On *The Reproduction of Mothering:* A Methodological Debate," *Signs,* 6 (Spring 1981), 482–514.

37. See, e.g., *The Lost Tradition: Mothers and Daughters in Literature,* ed. Cathy M. Davidson and E. M. Broner (New York: Frederick Ungar, 1980); this work is more engaged with myths and images of matrilineage than with redefining female identity.

38. Elizabeth Abel, "(E)Merging Identities: The Dynamics of Female Friendship in Contemporary Fiction by Women," *Signs,* 6 (Spring 1981), 434.

39. Gerda Lerner, "The Challenge of Women's History," *The Majority Finds Its Past: Placing Women in History* (New York: Oxford University Press, 1979); all further references to this book, abbreviated *MFP,* will hereafter be included parenthetically in the text.

40. See, e.g., Tillie Olsen, *Silences* (New York: Delacorte Press, 1978); Sheila Rowbotham, *Woman's Consciousness, Man's World* (New York: Penguin Books, 1974), 31–37; and Marcia Landy, "The Silent Woman: Towards a Feminist Critique," in Diamond and Edwards, *Authority of Experience* (n. 7 above), 16–27.

41. Edwin Ardener, "Belief and the Problem of Women," in S. Ardener, *Perceiving Women* (note 28 above), p. 3.

42. Mari McCarty, "Possessing Female Space: 'The Tender Shoot,' " *Women's Studies,* 8 (1981): 368.

43. Susan Lanser and Evelyn Torton Beck, "[Why] Are There No Great Women Critics? And What Difference Does It Make?" in *The Prism of Sex: Essays in the Sociology of Knowledge,* ed. Beck and Julia A. Sherman (Madison: University of Wisconsin Press, 1979), 86.

44. Myra Jehlen, "Archimedes and the Paradox of Feminist Criticism," *Signs,* 6 (Fall 1981), 582.

45. Smith, "Black Feminist Criticism," in *The New Feminist Criticism,* 168–85. See also Gloria T. Hull, "Afro-American Women Poets: A Bio-Critical Survey," in Gilbert and Gubar, *Shakespeare's Sisters,* pp. 165–82, and Elaine Marks, "Lesbian Intertextuality," in *Homosexualities and French Literature,* ed. Marks and George Stambolian (Ithaca: Cornell University Press, 1979).

46. Margaret Anne Doody, "George Eliot and the Eighteenth-Century Novel," *Nineteenth-Century Fiction,* 35 (December 1980), 267–68.

47. See, e.g., Judith Wilt, *Ghosts of the Gothic: Austen, Eliot, and Lawrence* (Princeton, N.J.: Princeton University Press, 1980).

48. See Ann Douglas, *The Feminization of American Culture* (New York: Alfred A. Knopf, 1977); Nina Baym, *Woman's Fiction: A Guide to Novels by and about Women in America, 1820–1870* (Ithaca: Cornell University Press, 1978); and Jane P. Tompkins, "Sentimental Power: *Uncle Tom's Cabin* and the Politics of Literary History," in *The New Feminist Criticism,* pp. 81–104.

49. See, e.g., the analysis of Woolf in Sandra M. Gilbert, "Costumes of the Mind: Transvestism as Metaphor in Modern Literature," *Critical Inquiry,* 7 (Winter 1980), 391–417.

50. I. A. Richards, quoted in John Paul Russo, "A Study in Influence: The Moore-Richards Paradigm," *Critical Inquiry,* 5 (Summer 1979), 687.

51. Showalter, "Literary Criticism," p. 435; Miller, "Emphasis Added: Plots and Plausibilities in Women's Fiction," in *The New Feminist Criticism,* pp. 339–60. To take one example, whereas *Jane Eyre* had always been read in relation to an implied "dominant" fictional and social mode and had thus been

perceived as flawed, feminist readings foreground its muted symbolic strategies and explore its credibility and coherence in its own terms. Feminist critics revise views like those of Richard Chase, who describes Rochester as castrated, thus implying that Jane's neurosis is penis envy, and G. Armour Craig, who sees the novel as Jane's struggle for superiority, to see Jane instead as healthy within her own system, that is, a *women's* society. See Chase, "The Brontës; or, Myth Domesticated," in *Jane Eyre* (New York: W.W. Norton, 1971), 462–71; Craig, "The Unpoetic Compromise: On the Relation between Private Vision and Social Order in Nineteenth-Century English Fiction," in *Self and Society*, ed. Mark Schorer (New York, 1956), 30–41; Nancy Pell, "Resistance, Rebellion, and Marriage: The Economics of *Jane Eyre*," *Nineteenth-Century Fiction*, 31 (March 1977), 397–420; Helene Moglen, *Charlotte Brontë: The Self Conceived* (New York: W.W. Norton, 1977); Adrienne Rich, "*Jane Eyre*: The Temptations of a Motherless Woman," *MS*, October 1973; and Maurianne Adams, "*Jane Eyre*: Woman's Estate," in Diamond and Edwards, *Authority of Experience*, pp. 137–59.

52. Geertz, *Interpretation of Cultures*, p. 9.

27

Hélène Cixous
1937–

Essayist, dramatist, and literary critic, Hélène Cixous has contributed a substantial body of scholarship illuminating the relationship between language and culture. More specifically, her concerns have centered on the numerous ways that the politics of language determine the roles assigned to women. She is the co-founder of the review *Poétique*, and her more recent writings include *La Bataille d'Arcachon* and *Entre l'Ecriture* (Within Writing). Many of her earlier writings, such as *The Newly-Born Woman* (1975; trans. 1986) and *Inside* (1969; trans. 1986), for which Cixous was awarded the Prix Medicis in 1969, have been translated into English, and, thus, the sphere of Cixous's influence on intellectual thought continues to expand. A professor at the University of Paris VIII at Vincennes, Cixous has been highly sought as a lecturer throughout the United States and Canada.

In the following essay, decapitation of the female represents the effect of a masculine economy imposed on woman. This economy, motivated by fear and loss, finds its corrective in appropriation. In decapitating woman, man appropriates her head; deprived of both her intellect and her voice, woman falls silent. Cixous traces the cultural process by which silent mourning functions as a diminished replacement for the sounds of womanly joy. In "Castration or Decapitation?" Cixous rejects the language of withholding and loss that have determined feminine experience and offers an alternative economy predicated on fullness and unceasing giving. The feminine economy "takes up the challenge of loss" and releases the feminine text from sublimation. The metaphor of the gift signifies the impulse of the feminine economy as well as the act that restores woman's head and allows the sound of "endless laughter" to echo across the pages of her writing once more.

Castration or Decapitation?

On sexual difference: Let's start with these small points. One day Zeus and Hera, the ultimate couple, in the course of one of their intermittent and thoroughgoing disagreements—which today would be of the greatest interest to psychoanalysts—called on Tiresias to arbitrate. Tiresias, the blind seer who had enjoyed the uncommon fortune of having lived seven years as a woman and seven years as a man.

He was gifted with second sight. Second sight in a sense other than we might usually understand it: it isn't simply that as a prophet he could see into the future. He could also see it from both sides: from the side of the male and from the side of the female.

The subject of the disagreement was the question of sexual pleasure: "Of man and woman, who enjoys the greater pleasure?" Obviously neither Zeus nor Hera could answer this without giving their *own* answer, which they saw would be inadequate, since the ancients made fewer assumptions than we do about the possibility of making such identifications. So it came about that Tiresias was sought, as the only person who could know "which of the two." And Tiresias answered: "If sexual pleasure could be divided up into ten parts, nine of them would be the woman's." Nine. It's no coincidence that Tiresias makes another appearance in none other than the oedipal scene. It was Tiresias who, at Oedipus's command, reminded Oedipus that blindness was his master, and Tiresias who, so they say, "made the scales fall from his eyes" and showed Oedipus who he really was. We should note that these things are all linked together and bear some relation to the question "What is woman for man?"

It reminds me of a little Chinese story. Every detail of this story counts. I've borrowed it from a very serious text, Sun Tse's manual of strategy, which is a kind of handbook for the warrior. This is the anecdote. The king commanded General Sun Tse: "You who are a great strategist and claim to be able to train anybody in the arts of war. . . . take my wives (all one hundred and eighty of them!) and make soldiers out of them." We don't know why the king conceived this desire—it's the one thing we don't know. . . . it remains precisely "un-(re)countable" or unaccountable in the story. But it is a king's wish, after all.

So Sun Tse had the women arranged in two rows, each headed by one of the two favorite wives, and then taught them the language of the drumbeat. It was very simple: two beats—right, three beats—left, four beats—about turn or backward march. But instead of learning the code very quickly, the ladies started laughing and chattering and paying no attention to the lesson, and Sun Tse, the master, repeated the lesson several times over. But the more he spoke, the more the women fell about laughing, upon which Sun Tse put his code to the test. It is said in this code that should women fall about laughing instead of becoming soldiers, their actions might be deemed mutinous, and the code has ordained that cases of mutiny call for the death penalty. So the women were condemned to death. This bothered the king somewhat: a hundred and eighty wives are a lot to lose! He didn't want his wives put to death. But Sun Tse replied that since he was put in charge of making soldiers out of the women, he would carry out the order: Sun Tse was a man of absolute principle. And in any case there's an order even more "royal" than that of the king himself: the Absolute Law. . . . One does not go back on an order. He therefore acted according to the code and with his saber beheaded the two women commanders. They were replaced and the exercise started again, and as if they had never done anything except practice the art of war, the women turned right, left, and about in silence and with never a single mistake.

It's hard to imagine a more perfect example of a particular relationship between two economies: a masculine economy and a feminine economy, in which the masculine is governed by a rule that keeps time with two beats, three beats, four beats, with pipe and drum, exactly as it should be. An order that works by inculcation, by education: it's always a question of education. An education that consists of trying to make a soldier of the feminine by force, the force history keeps reserved for woman, the "capital" force that is effectively decapitation. Women have no choice other than to be decapitated, and in any case the moral is that if they don't actually lose their heads by the sword, *they only keep them on condition that they lose them*—lose them, that is, to complete silence, turned into automatons.

It's a question of submitting feminine disorder, its laughter, its inability to take the drumbeats seriously, to the threat of decapitation. If man operates under the threat of castration, if masculinity is culturally ordered by the castration complex, it might be said that the backlash, the return, on women of this castration anxiety is its displacement as decapitation, execution, of woman, as loss of her head.

We are led to pose the woman question to history in quite elementary forms like, "Where is she? Is there any such thing as woman?" At worst, many women wonder whether they even exist. They feel they don't exist and wonder if there has ever been a place for them. I am speaking of woman's place, *from* woman's place, if she takes (a) place.

In *La Jeune Née*[1] I made use of a story that seemed to me particularly expressive of woman's place: the story of Sleeping Beauty. Woman, if you look for her, has a strong chance of always being found in one position: in bed. In bed and asleep—"laid (out)." She is always to be found on or in a bed: Sleeping Beauty is lifted from her bed by a man because, as we all know, women don't wake up by themselves: man has to intervene, you understand. She is lifted up by the man who will lay her in her next bed so that she may be confined to bed ever after, just as the fairy tales say.

And so her trajectory is from bed to bed: one bed to another, where she can dream all the more. There are some extraordinary analyses by Kierkegaard on women's "existence"—or that part of it set aside for her by culture—in which he says he sees her as sleeper. She sleeps, he says, and first love dreams her and then she dreams of love. From dream to dream, and always in second position. In some stories, though, she can be found standing up, but not for long. Take Little Red Riding Hood as an example: it will not, I imagine, be lost on you that the "red riding hood" in question is a little clitoris. Little Red Riding Hood basically gets up to some mischief: she's the little female sex that tries to play a bit and sets out with her little pot of butter and her little jar of honey. What is interesting is that it's her mother who gives them to her and sends her on an excursion that's tempting precisely because it's forbidden: Little Red Riding Hood leaves one house, mommy's house, not to go out into the big wide world but to go from one house to another by the shortest route possible: to make haste, in other words, from the mother to the other. The other in this case is grandmother, whom he might imagine as taking the place of the "Great Mother," because there are great men but no great women: there are Grand-Mothers instead. And grandmothers are always wicked: she is the bad mother who always shuts the daughter in whenever the daughter might by chance want to live or take pleasure. So she'll always be carrying her little pot of butter and her little jar of honey to grandmother, who is there as jealousy . . . the jealousy of the woman who can't let her daughter go.

But in spite of all this Little Red Riding Hood makes her little detour, does what women should never do, travels through her own forest. She allows herself the forbidden . . . and pays dearly for it: she goes back to bed, in grandmother's stomach. The Wolf is grandmother, and all women recognize the Big Bad Wolf! We know that always lying in wait for us somewhere in some big bed is a Big Bad

Wolf. The Big Bad Wolf represents, with his big teeth, his big eyes, and his grandmother's looks, that great Superego that threatens all the little female red riding hoods who try to go out and explore their forest without the psychoanalyst's permission. So, between two houses, between two beds, she is laid, ever caught in her chain of metaphors, metaphors that organize culture . . . ever her moon to the masculine sun, nature to culture, concavity to masculine convexity, matter to form, immobility/inertia to the march of progress, terrain trod by the masculine footstep, vessel. . . . While man is obviously the active, the upright, the productive . . . and besides, that's how it happens in History.

This opposition to woman cuts endlessly across all the oppositions that order culture. It's the classic opposition, dualist and hierarchical. Man/Woman automatically means great/small, superior/inferior . . . means high or low, means Nature/History, means transformation/inertia. In fact, every theory of culture, every theory of society, the whole conglomeration of symbolic systems—everything, that is, that's spoken, everything that's organized as discourse, art, religion, the family, language, everything that seizes us, everything that acts on us—it is all ordered around hierarchical oppositions that come back to the man/woman opposition, an opposition that can only be sustained by means of a difference posed by cultural discourse as "natural," the difference between activity and passivity. It always works this way, and the opposition is founded in the *couple*. A couple posed in opposition, in tension, in conflict . . . a couple engaged in a kind of war in which death is always at work—and I keep emphasizing the importance of the opposition as *couple*, because all this isn't just about one word; rather everything turns on the Word: everything is the Word and only the Word. To be aware of the couple, that it's the couple that makes it all work, is also to point to the fact that it's on the couple that we have to work if we are to deconstruct and transform culture. The couple as terrain, as space of cultural struggle, but also as terrain, as space demanding, insisting on, a complete transformation in the relation of one to the other. And so work still has to be done on the couple . . . on the question, for example, of what a completely different couple relationship would be like, what a love that was more than merely a cover for, a veil of, war would be like.

I said it turns on the Word: we must take culture at its word, as it takes us into its Word, into its tongue. You'll understand why I think that no political reflection can dispense with reflection on language, with work on language. For as soon as we exist, we are born into language and language speaks (to) us, dictates its law, a law of death: it lays down its familial model, lays down its conjugal model, and even at the moment of uttering a sentence, admitting a notion of "being," a question of being, an ontology, we are already seized by a certain kind of masculine desire, the desire that mobilizes philosophical discourse. As soon as the question "What is it?" is posed, from the moment a question is put, as soon as a reply is sought, *we are already caught up in masculine interrogation*. I say "masculine interrogation": as we say so-and-so was interrogated by the police. And this interrogation precisely involves the work of signification: "What is it? Where is it?" A work of meaning, "This means that," the predicative distribution that always at the same time orders the constitution of meaning. And while meaning is being constituted, it only gets constituted in a movement in which one of the terms of the couple is destroyed in favor of the other.

"Look for the lady," as they say in the stories. . . . "Cherchez la femme"—we always know that means: you'll find her in bed. Another question that's posed in History, rather a strange question, a typical male question, is: "What do women want?" The Freudian question, of course. In his work on desire, Freud asks somewhere, or rather doesn't ask, leaves hanging in the air, the question "What do women want?" Let's talk a bit about this desire and about why/how the question "What do women want?" gets put, how it's both posed and left hanging in the air by philosophical discourse, by analytic discourse (analytic discourse being only one province of philosophical discourse), and how it is posed, let us say, by the Big Bad Wolf and the Grand-Mother.

"What does she want?" Little Red Riding Hood knew quite well what she wanted, but Freud's question is not what it seems: it's a rhetorical question. To pose the question "What do women want?" is to pose it already as answer, as from a man who isn't expecting any answer, because the answer is "She wants nothing. . . ." "What does she want? . . . Nothing!" Nothing because she is passive. The only thing man can do is offer the question "What could she want, she who wants nothing?" Or in other words: "Without me, what could she want?"

Old Lacan takes up the slogan "What does she want?" when he says, "A woman cannot speak of her pleasure." Most interesting! It's all there, a woman *cannot*, is unable, hasn't the power. Not to mention "speaking": it's exactly this that she's forever deprived of. Unable to speak of pleasure = no pleasure, no desire: power, desire, speaking, pleasure, none of these is for woman. And as a quick reminder of how this works in theoretical discourse, one question: you are aware, of course, that for Freud/Lacan, woman is said to be "outside the Symbolic": outside the Symbolic, that is outside language, the place of the Law, excluded from any possible relationship with culture and the cultural order. And she is outside the Symbolic because she lacks any relation to the phallus, because she does not enjoy what orders masculinity—the castration complex. Woman does not have the advantage of the castration complex—it's reserved solely for the little boy. The phallus, in Lacanian parlance also called the "transcendental signifier," transcendental precisely as primary organizer of the structure of subjectivity, is what, for psychoanalysis, inscribes its effects, its effects of castration and resistance to castration and hence the very organization of language, as unconscious relations, and so it is the phallus that is said to constitute the a priori condition of all symbolic functioning. This has important implications as far as the body is concerned: the body is not sexed, does not recognize itself as, say, female or male without having gone through the castration complex.

What psychoanalysis points to as defining woman is that she lacks lack. She lacks lack? Curious to put it in so contradictory, so extremely paradoxical, a manner: she lacks lack. To say she lacks lack is also, after all, to say she doesn't miss lack . . . since she doesn't miss the lack of lack. Yes, they say, but the point is "she lacks The Lack," The Lack, lack of the Phallus. And so, supposedly, she misses the great lack, so that without man she would be indefinite, indefinable, nonsexed, unable to recognize herself: outside the Symbolic. But fortunately there is man: he who comes . . . Prince Charming. And it's man who teaches woman (because man is always the Master as well), who teaches her to be aware of lack, to be aware of absence, aware of death. It's man who will finally order woman, "set her to rights," by teaching her that without man she could "misrecognize." He will teach her the Law of the Father. Something of the order of: "Without me, without me—the Absolute—Father (the father is always that much more absolute the more he is improbable, dubious)—without me you wouldn't exist, I'll show you." Without him she'd remain in a state of distressing and distressed undifferentiation, unbordered, unorganized, "unpoliced" by the phallus . . . incoherent, chaotic, and embedded in the Imaginary in her ignorance of the Law of the Signifier. Without him she would in all probability not be contained by the threat of death, might even, perhaps, believe herself eternal, immortal. Without him she would be deprived of sexuality. And it might be said that man works very actively to produce "his woman." Take for example *Le Ravissement de Lol V. Stein,*[2] and you will witness the moment when man can finally say "his" woman, "my" woman. It is that moment when he has taught her to be aware of Death. So man *makes,* he makes (up) his woman, not without being himself seized up and drawn into the dialectical movement that this sort of thing sets in play. We might say that the Absolute Woman, in culture, the woman who really represents femininity most effectively . . . who is closest to femininity as *prey* to masculinity, is actually the hysteric. . . . he makes her image for her!

The hysteric is a divine spirit that is always at the edge, the turning point, of making. She is one who does not make herself . . . she does not make herself but she does make the other. It is said that the hysteric "makes-believe" the father, plays the father, "makes-believe" the master. Plays, makes up, makes-believe: she makes-believe she is a woman, unmakes-believe too . . . plays at desire, plays the father . . . turns herself into him, unmakes him at the same time. Anyway, without the hysteric, there's no father . . . without the hysteric, no master, no analyst, no analysis! She's the *unorganizable* feminine construct, whose power of producing the other is a power that never returns to her. She is really a wellspring nourishing the other for eternity, yet not drawing back from the other . . . not recognizing herself in the images the other may or may not give her. She is given images that don't belong to her, and she forces herself, as we've all done, to resemble them.

And so in the face of this person who lacks lack, who does not miss lack of lack, we have the construct that is infinitely easier to analyze, to put in place—manhood, flaunting its metaphors like banners through history. You know those metaphors: they are most effective. It's always clearly a question of war, of battle. If there is no battle, it's replaced by the stake of battle: strategy. Man is strategy, is reckoning . . . "how to win" with the least possible loss, at the lowest possible cost. Throughout literature masculine figures all say the same thing: "I'm reckoning" what to do to win. Take Don Juan and you have the whole masculine economy getting together to "give women just what it takes to keep them in bed" then swiftly taking back the investment, then reinvesting, etc., so that nothing ever gets given, everything gets taken back, while in the process the greatest possible dividend of pleasure is taken. Consumption without payment, of course.

Let's take an example other than Don Juan, one clearly pushed to the point of paroxysm . . . Kafka. It was Kafka who said there was one struggle that terrified him beyond all others (he was an embattled man, but his battle was with death—in this sense he was a man greater than the rest): but in matters concerning women his was a struggle that terrified him (death did not). He said the struggle with women ended up in bed: this was his greatest fear. If you know a little about Kafka's life you should know that in his complete integrity, his absolute honesty, he attempted to live through this awful anguish in his relationships with women, in the struggle whose only outcome is bed, by working . . . finally to produce a neurosis of quite extraordinary beauty and terror consisting of a life-and-death relationship with a woman, but at the greatest possible distance. As close as possible and as distanced as possible. He would be betrothed, passionately desire a marriage which he feared above all else, and keep putting off the wedding by endless unconscious maneuvers . . . by a pattern of repeated breakups that took him right to his deathbed, the very deathbed he'd always wanted—a bed, that is, in which he could finally be alone with death. This work of keeping women at a distance while at the same time drawing them to him shows up strikingly in his diary, again because Kafka was honest enough to reveal everything, to say everything. He wrote in little columns, putting debits on the left and credits on the right . . . all the reasons I absolutely must marry, all the reasons I absolutely must not. This tension points to the spirit of male/female relationships in a way it isn't normally revealed, because what is normally revealed is actually a decoy . . . all those words about love, etc. All that is always just a cover for hatred nourished by the fear of death: woman, for man, is death. This is actually the castration complex at its most effective: giving is really dicing with death.

Giving: there you have a basic problem, which is that masculinity is always associated—in the unconscious, which is after all what makes the whole economy function—with debt. Freud, in deciphering the latent antagonisms between parents and children, shows very well the extent to which the family is founded, as far as the little boy is concerned, on a fearful debt. The child *owes* his parents his life and his problem is exactly to *repay* them: nothing is more dangerous than obligation. Obligation is submission to the enormous weight of the other's generosity, is being threatened by a blessing . . . and a blessing is always an evil when it comes from someone else. For the moment you receive something you are effectively "open" to the other, and if you are a man you have only one wish, and that is hastily to return the gift, to break the circuit of an exchange that could have no end . . . to be nobody's child, to owe no one a thing.

And so debt, what is always expressed in religions by laws like "a tooth for a tooth," "a gift for a gift," "an eye for an eye," is a system of absolute equivalence . . . of no inequality, for inequality is always interpreted by the masculine as a difference of strength, and thus as a threat. This economy is ruled by price: there's a price to pay, life is dear, the price of life has to be paid. And here lies a difficulty in connection with love, in that, at coming, love starts escaping the system of equivalence in all sorts of ways. It's very hard to give back something you can't pin down. What's so frightening in relations between male and female at the moment of coming (*au niveau de la jouissance*) is the possibility that there might be more on one side than on the other and the Symbolic finds it really tough to know who wins and who loses, who gives more in a relationship of this sort. The memory of debt and the fear of having to recognize one's debt rise up straightaway. But the refusal to know is nonetheless ambivalent in its implications, for not knowing is threatening while at the same time (and this is where the castration complex comes in) it reinforces the desire to know. So in the end woman, in man's desire, stands in the place of not knowing, the place of mystery. In this sense she is no good, but at the same time she is good because it's this mystery that leads man to keep overcoming, dominating, subduing, putting his manhood to the test, against the mystery he has to keep forcing back.

And so they want to keep woman in the place of mystery, consign her to mystery, as they say "keep her in her place," keep her at a distance: she's always not quite there . . . but no one knows exactly where she is. She is kept in place in a quite characteristic way—coming back to Oedipus, the place of one who is too often forgotten,[3] the place of the sphinx . . . she's kept in the place of what we might call the "watch-bitch" (*chienne chanteuse*). That is to say, she is outside the city, at the edge of the city—the city is man, ruled by masculine law—and there she is. In what way is she there? She is there not recognizing: the sphinx doesn't recognize herself, she it is who poses questions, just as it's man who holds the answer and furthermore, as you know, his answer is completely worthy of him: "Man," simple answer . . . but it says everything. "Watch-bitch," the sphinx was called: she's an animal and she sings out. She sings out because women do . . . they do utter a little, but they don't speak. Always keep in mind the distinction between speaking and talking. It is said, in philosophical texts, that women's weapon is the word, because they talk, talk endlessly, chatter, overflow with sound, mouth-sound: but they don't actually *speak*, they have nothing to say. They always inhabit the place of silence, or at most make it echo with their singing. And neither is to their benefit, for they remain outside knowledge.

Silence: silence is the mark of hysteria. The great hysterics have lost speech, they are aphonic, and at times have lost more than speech: they are pushed to the point of choking, nothing gets through. They are decapitated, their tongues are cut off and what talks isn't heard because it's the body that talks, and man doesn't hear the body. In the end, the woman pushed to hysteria is the woman who disturbs and is nothing but disturbance. The master dotes on disturbance right from the moment he can subdue it and call it up at his command. Conversely the hysteric is the woman who cannot not ask the master what he wants her to want: she wants nothing, truly she wants nothing. She wants . . . she wants to want. But what is it she wants to want? So she goes to school: she asks the master: "What should I want?" and "What do you want me to want, so that I might want it?" Which is what happens in analysis.

Let's imagine that all this functioned otherwise, that it could function otherwise. We'd first have to imagine resistance to masculine desire conducted by woman as hysteric, as distracted. We'd first have to imagine her ceasing to support with her body what I call the realm of the proper. The realm of the proper in the sense of the general cultural heterosocial establishment in which man's reign is held to be proper: proper may be the opposite of improper, and also of unfitting, just as black and white are opposites. Etymologically, the "proper" is "property," that which is not separable from me. Property is proximity, nearness: we must love our neighbors, those close to us, as ourselves: we must draw close to the other so that we may love him/her, because we love ourselves most of all. The realm of the proper, culture, functions by the appropriation articulated, set into play, by man's classic fear of seeing himself expropriated, seeing himself deprived . . . by his refusal to be deprived, in a state of separation, by his fear of losing the prerogative, fear whose response is all of History. Everything must return to the masculine. "Return": the economy is founded on a system of returns. If a man spends and is spent, it's on condition that his power returns. If a man should go out, if he should go out to the other, it's always done according to the Hegelian model, the model of the master-slave dialectic.

Woman would then have to start by resisting the movement of reappropriation that rules the whole economy, by being party no longer to the masculine return, but by proposing instead a desire no longer caught up in the death struggle, no longer implicated in the reservation and reckoning of the masculine economy, but breaking with the reckoning that "I never lose anything except to win a bit more" . . . so as to put aside all negativeness and bring out a positiveness which might be called the living other, the rescued other, the other unthreatened by destruction. Women have it in them to organize this regeneration, this vitalization of the other, of otherness in its entirety. They have it in them to affirm the difference, *their* difference, such that nothing can destroy that difference, rather that it might be affirmed, affirmed to the point of strangeness. So much so that when sexual difference, when the preservation or dissolution of sexual difference, is touched on, the whole problem of destroying the strange, destroying all the forms of racism, all the exclusions, all those instances of outlaw and genocide that recur through History, is also touched on. If women were to set themselves to transform History, it can safely be said that every aspect of History would be completely altered. Instead of being made by man, History's task would be to make woman, to produce her. And it's at this point that work by women themselves on women might be brought into play, which would benefit not only women but all humanity.

But first she would have to *speak*, start speaking, stop saying that she has nothing to say! Stop learning in school that women are created to listen, to believe, to make no discoveries. Dare to speak her piece about giving, the possibility of a giving that doesn't take away, but *gives*. Speak of her pleasure and, God knows, she has something to say about that, so that she gets to unblock a sexuality that's just as much feminine as masculine, "dephallocentralize" the body, relieve man of his phallus, return him to an erogenous field and a libido that isn't stupidly organized round that monument, but appears shifting, diffused, taking on all the others of oneself. Very difficult: first we have to get rid of the systems of censorship that bear down on every attempt to speak in the feminine. We have to get rid of and also explain what all knowledge brings with it as its burden of power: to show in what ways, culturally, knowledge is the accomplice of power: that whoever stands in the place of knowledge is always getting a dividend of power: show that all thinking until now has been ruled by this dividend, this surplus value of power that comes back to him who knows. Take the philosophers, take their position of mastery, and you'll see that there is not a soul who dares to make an advance in thought, into the as-yet-unthought, without shuddering at the idea that he is under the surveillance of the ancestors, the grandfathers, the tyrants of the concept, without thinking that there behind your back is always the famous Name-of-the-Father, who knows whether or not you're writing whatever it is you have to write without any spelling mistakes.

Now, I think that what women will have to do and what they will do, right from the moment they venture to speak what they have to say, will of necessity bring about a shift in metalanguage. And I think we're completely crushed, especially in places like universities, by the highly repressive operations of metalanguage, the operations, that is, of the commentary on the commentary, the code, the operation that sees to it that the moment women open their mouths—women more often than men—they are immediately asked in whose name and from what theoretical standpoint they are speaking, who is their master and where they are coming from: they have, in short, to salute . . . and show their identity papers. There's work to be done against *class*, against categorization, against classification—classes. "Doing classes" in France means doing military service.

There's work to be done against military service, against all schools, against the pervasive masculine urge to judge, diagnose, digest, name . . . not so much in the sense of the loving precision of poetic naming as in that of the repressive censorship of philosophical nomination/conceptualization.

Women who write have for the most part until now considered themselves to be writing not as women but as writers. Such women may declare that sexual difference means nothing, that there's no attributable difference between masculine and feminine writing. . . . What does it mean to "take no position"? When someone says "I'm not political" we all know what that means! It's just another way of saying: "My politics are someone else's!" And it's exactly the case with writing! Most women are like this: they do someone else's—man's—writing, and in their innocence sustain it and give it voice, and end up producing writing that's in effect masculine. Great care must be taken in working on feminine writing not to get trapped by names: to be signed with a woman's name doesn't necessarily make a piece of writing feminine. It could quite well be masculine writing, and conversely, the fact that a piece of writing is signed with a man's name does not in itself exclude femininity. It's rare, but you can sometimes find femininity in writings signed by men: it does happen.

Which texts appear to be woman-texts and are recognized as such today, what can this mean, how might they be read?[4] In my opinion, the writing being done now that I see emerging around me won't only be of the kinds that exist in print today, though they will always be with us, but will be something else as well. In particular we ought to be prepared for what I call the "affirmation of the difference," not a kind of wake about the corpse of the mummified woman, nor a fantasy of woman's decapitation, but something different: a step forward, an adventure, an exploration of woman's powers: of her power, her potency, her ever-dreaded strength, of the regions of femininity. Things are starting to be written, things that will constitute a feminine Imaginary, the site, that is, of identifications of an ego no longer given over to an image defined by the masculine ("like the woman I love, I mean a dead woman"), but rather inventing forms for women on the march, or as I prefer to fantasize, "in flight," so that instead of lying down, women will go forward by leaps in search of themselves.

There is work to be done on female sexual pleasure and on the production of an unconscious that would no longer be the classic unconscious. The unconscious is always cultural and when it talks it tells you your old stories, it tells you the old stories you've heard before because it consists of the repressed of culture. But it's also always shaped by the forceful return of a libido that doesn't give up that easily, and also by what is strange, what is outside culture, by a language which is a savage tongue that can make itself understood quite well. This is why, I think, *political* and not just literary work is started as soon as writing gets done by women that goes beyond the bounds of censorship, reading, the gaze, the masculine command, in that cheeky risk taking women can get into when they set out into the unknown to look for themselves.

This is how I would define a feminine textual body: as a *female libidinal economy*, a regime, energies, a system of spending not necessarily carved out by culture. A feminine textual body is recognized by the fact that it is always endless, without ending: there's no closure, it doesn't stop, and it's this that very often makes the feminine text difficult to read. For we've learned to read books that basically pose the word "end." But this one doesn't finish, a feminine text goes on and on and at a certain moment the volume comes to an end but the writing continues and for the reader this means being thrust into the void. These are texts that work on the beginning but not on the origin. The origin is a masculine myth: I always want to know where I come from. The question "Where do children come from?" is basically a masculine, much more than a feminine, question. The quest for origins, illustrated by Oedipus, doesn't haunt a feminine unconscious. Rather it's the beginning, or beginnings, the manner of beginning, not promptly with the phallus in order to close with the phallus, but starting on all sides at once, that makes a feminine writing. A feminine text starts on all sides at once, starts twenty times, thirty times, over.

The question a woman's text asks is the question of giving—"What does this writing give?" "How does it give?" And talking about nonorigin and beginnings, you might say it "gives a send-off" (*donne le départ*). Let's take the expression "giving a send-off" in a metaphorical sense: giving a send-off is generally giving the *signal* to depart. I think it's more than giving the departure signal, it's really giving, making a *gift* of, departure, allowing departure, allowing breaks, "parts," partings, separations . . . from this we break with the return-to-self, with the specular relations ruling the coherence, the identification, of the individual. When a woman writes in nonrepression she passes on her others, her abundance of non-ego/s in a way that destroys the form of the family structure, so that it is defamilialized, can no longer be thought in terms of the attribution of roles within a social cell: what takes place is an endless circulation of desire from one body to another, above and across sexual difference, outside those relations of power and regeneration constituted by the family. I believe regeneration leaps, age leaps, time leaps. . . . A woman-text gets across a detachment, a kind of disengagement, not the detachment that is immediately taken back, but a real capacity to lose hold and let go. This takes the metaphorical form of wandering, excess, risk of the unreckonable: no reckoning, a feminine text can't be predicted, isn't predictable, isn't knowable and is therefore very disturbing. It can't be anticipated, and I believe femininity is written outside anticipation: it really is the text of the unforeseeable.

Let's look not at syntax but at fantasy, at the unconscious: all the feminine texts I've read are very close to the voice, very close to the flesh of language, much more so than masculine texts . . . perhaps because there's something in them that's freely given, perhaps because they don't rush into meaning, but are straightway at the threshold of feeling. There's *tactility* in the feminine text, there's touch, and this touch passes through the ear. Writing in the feminine is passing on what is cut out by the Symbolic, the voice of the mother, passing on what is most archaic. The most archaic force that touches a body is one that enters by the ear and reaches the most intimate point. This innermost touch always echoes in a woman-text. So the movement, the movement of the text, doesn't trace a straight line. I see it as an outpouring . . . which can appear in primitive or elementary texts as a fantasy of blood, of menstrual flow, etc., but which I prefer to see as vomiting, as "throwing up," "disgorging." And I'd link this with a basic structure of property relations defined by mourning.

Man cannot live without resigning himself to loss. He has to mourn. It's his way of withstanding castration. He goes through castration, that is, and by sublimation incorporates the lost object. Mourning, resigning oneself to loss, means not losing. When you've lost something and the loss is a dangerous one, you refuse to admit that something of your self might be lost in the lost object. So you "mourn," you make haste to recover the investment made in the lost object. But I believe women *do not mourn*, and this is where their pain lies! When you've mourned, it's all over after a year, there's no more suffering. Woman, though, does not mourn, does not resign herself to loss. She basically *takes up the challenge of loss* in order to go on living: she lives it, gives it life, is capable of unsparing loss. She does not hold onto loss, she loses without holding onto loss. This makes her writing a body that overflows, disgorges, vomiting as opposed to masculine incorporation. . . . She loses, and doubtless it would be to the death were it not for the intervention of those basic movements of a feminine unconscious (this is how I would define *feminine sublimation*) which provide the capacity of passing above it all by means of a form of oblivion which is not the oblivion of burial or interment but the oblivion of *acceptance*. This is taking loss, seizing it, living it. Leaping. This goes with not withholding: she does not withhold. She does not withhold, hence the impression of constant return evoked by this lack of withholding. It's like a kind of open memory that ceaselessly makes way. And in the end, she will write this not-withholding, this not-writing: she writes of not-writing, not-happening. . . . She crosses limits: she is neither outside nor in, whereas the masculine would try to "bring the outside in, if possible."[5]

And finally this open and bewildering prospect goes hand in hand with a certain kind of laughter. Culturally speaking, women have wept a great deal, but once the tears are shed, there will be endless laughter instead. Laughter that breaks out, overflows, a humor no one would expect to find in women—which is nonetheless surely their greatest strength because it's a humor that sees man much further away than he has ever been seen. Laughter that shakes the last chapter of my text *LA*,[6] "she who laughs last." And her first laugh is at herself.

Translated by Annette Kuhn

NOTES

This article first appeared as "Le Sexe ou la tête?" in *Les Cahiers du GRIF*, no. 13 (1976), pp. 5–15. The text was transcribed from a conversation between Hélène Cixous and the editors of *Les Cahiers du GRIF* which took place in Brussels during 1975. The present translation follows the published transcript with two exceptions (signaled in nn. 4 and 5) and is published with the permission of Hélène Cixous. The approach and arguments are developed in Cixous's more recent work. See, e.g., *Vivre l'orange* (Paris: Editions des femmes, 1979), written in French and English, and *Illa* (Paris: Editions des femmes, 1980). Thanks are due to Elaine Marks for suggesting this translation of the title, to Keith Cohen for advice on specific points of translation, and to Chris Holmlund for bibliographical assistance. *Trans. note.*

1. Hélène Cixous and Catherine Clément, *La Jeune Née* (Paris: October 18, 1975). *Trans. note.*

2. Marguerite Duras, *Le Ravissement de Lol V. Stein* (Paris: Gallimard, 1964). There are two English translations of this work: *The Ravishing of Lol V. Stein*, trans. Richard Seaver (New York: Grove Press, 1966), and *The Rapture of Lol V. Stein*, trans. Eileen Ellenbogen (London: Hamish Hamilton, 1967). *Trans. note.*

3. "La place de celle qu'on oublie en français trop souvent parce qu'on dit 'sphinx' au lieu de 'sphinge' ": That is, the French form of the word would suggest that the sphinx is male, whereas the sphinx of the oedipal myth is in fact female. *Trans. note.*

4. There follows in the original a passage in which several categories of women's writing existing at the time (1975) are listed and discussed. These include: " 'the little girl's story,' where the little girl is getting even for a bad childhood," "texts of a return to a woman's own body," and texts which were a critical success, "ones about madwomen, deranged, sick women." The passage is omitted here, at the author's request, on the grounds that such a categorization is outdated, and that the situation with regard to women's writing is very much different now than it was five or six years ago. *Trans. note.*

5. The following passage, deleted from the main body of the text, is regarded by the author as expressing a position tangential to the central interest of her work, which has to do with homosexuality: "And it's this being 'neither out nor in,' being 'beyond the outside/inside opposition' that permits the play of 'bisexuality.' Female sexuality is always at some point bisexual. Bisexual doesn't mean, as many people think, that she can make love with both a man and a woman, it doesn't mean she has two partners, even if it can at times mean this. Bisexuality on an unconscious level is the possibility of extending into the other, of being in such a relation with the other that *I* move into the other without destroying the other: that I will look for the other where s/he is without trying to bring everything back to myself." *Trans. note.*

6. Hélène Cixous, *LA*, (Paris: Gallimard, 1976). *Trans. note.*

28

Sandra Gilbert
1936–

Sandra M. Gilbert holds an M.A. from New York University and a Ph.D. from Columbia University. A writer of fiction and poetry as well as of literary criticism, she has taught English at a number of institutions, including Indiana University and the University of California at Davis. Currently on the faculty at Princeton University, she is one of the dominant voices in American feminist criticism. She is the co-author with Susan Gubar of the groundbreaking *The Madwoman in the Attic* (1979) and of the newly published *No Man's Land: The Place of the Woman Writer in the Twentieth Century* (1988). Also with Susan Gubar, Sandra Gilbert edited *Shakespeare's Sisters: Feminist Essays on Women Poets,* as well as the pioneering *Norton Anthology of Literature by Women* (1985).

In "Life's Empty Pack: Notes Toward a Literary Daughteronomy," Gilbert draws on Freudian and Lacanian psychoanalytic theory. Lévi-Strauss's work in anthropology, and recent feminist theory to argue that "a prescription for father-daughter incest lies at the heart of female psychosexual development in patriarchal society." Gilbert locates this determining paradigm in George Eliot's culturally central *Silas Marner,* as well as in *Summer,* a revisionary tale by Edith Wharton, and "Allerleirauh," a Grimm's fairy tale. Gilbert's concern is not simply to identify the myth she defines as so chillingly pervasive: she argues that no woman writer can ever fully extricate herself from this myth, for the message inscribed by her literary foremothers is that the daughter must give herself to the father. Gilbert's feminist analysis thus indicates that patriarchal values control even the most rebellious (and creative) of women. The "mother tongue" teaches submission to the Father's Law.

Life's Empty Pack: Notes Toward A Literary Daughteronomy

No mother gave me birth. Therefore
the father's claim
And male supremacy in all
things . . .
. . . wins my whole heart's loyalty.

—Athene, in Aeschylus, *The Eumenides*

If underneath the water
You comb your golden hair
With a golden comb, my daughter,
Oh would that I were there!
—Christina Rossetti, "Father and Lover"

Sad and weary I go back to you, my cold father, my cold mad father, my cold mad feary father . . . I rush, my only, into your arms.
—Anna Livia Plurabelle, in James Joyce, *Finnegans Wake*

O father, all by yourself
You are pithy and historical as the
Roman Forum.
—Sylvia Plath, "The Colossus"

For the first time all of us, men and women alike, can look back on nearly two centuries of powerful literary ancestresses. Aside from the specifically literary-historical implications of such a phenomenon—an issue that Susan Gubar and I have addressed elsewhere[1]—what effects has this unprecedented situation had? In particular, what paradigms of female sexuality have strong female precursors passed on to other women writers? These are questions I want to begin to address here—specifically, by exploring an aspect of female psychosexual development. A dark, indeed problematic, pattern emerges when we juxtapose the accounts of female maturation and obligation that are offered by theorists like Sigmund Freud and Claude Lévi-Strauss with the meaning that George Eliot's frequently studied *Silas Marner* may have had for the women who are in a sense that powerful literary mother's aesthetic daughters.

I choose Eliot as my paradigm of the female precursor because, as Virginia Woolf put it, she was "the first woman of the age," a thinker who became, in one historian's words, a "Man of Ideas," her official importance sanctioned by the biography Woolf's own father dutifully produced for the English Men of Letters Series.[2] At the same time, however, I see Eliot as paradigmatic because her very power—the success that made her into what we call a "precursor"—evidently disquieted so many of her female contemporaries and descendants. As Elaine Showalter reminds us, "most nineteenth-century women novelists seem to have found [Eliot] a troubling and demoralizing competitor, one who had created an image of the woman artist they could never equal." "George Eliot *looks* awful. Her picture frightens me!" exclaims a character in Elizabeth Robins' novel *George Mandeville's Husband*.[3] Even Eliot's most fervent female admirers, moreover, express ambivalence toward her in the rhetoric through which they try to come to terms with her. Two of these notable Eliotian heiresses are Emily Dickinson and Edith Wharton. Both offer commentaries curiously haunted by ambiguities, and though these commentaries are ostensibly about the writer's life story, they provide a dramatic set of metaphors that can help us interpret the messages these literary daughters extracted from such an apparently "legendary" story as *Silas Marner*.[4]

In 1883, after having waited with great anxiety to receive a copy of the Eliot biography written by John Walter Cross, the novelist's husband in the last year of her life, Dickinson wrote a thank-you note to the Boston publisher Thomas Niles, in which she succinctly mythologizes the career of her English precursor. "The Life of Marian Evans had much I never knew," she begins. "A Doom of Fruit without the Bloom, like the Niger Fig," and a poem follows this strange introduction.

Her Losses make our Gains ashamed—
She bore Life's empty Pack
As gallantly as if the East
Were swinging at her Back.
Life's empty Pack is heaviest,
As every Porter knows—

In vain to punish Honey—
It only sweeter grows.[5]

"A Doom of Fruit without the Bloom." "Life's empty Pack." "In vain to punish Honey." These are striking but mysterious phrases. Where do they come from, and what do they mean?

Several remarks by Wharton, though almost equally paradoxical, begin to provide some clarification. Reviewing Leslie Stephen's English Men of Letters Series volume on Eliot, Wharton writes that "unconsciously, perhaps, [the Victorian novelist] began to use her books as a vehicle of rehabilitation, a means, not of defending her own course, but of proclaiming, with increasing urgency and emphasis, her allegiance to the law she appeared to have violated." Earlier in her essay, Wharton offers a metaphorical, almost Dickinsonian statement of what she means by "the law": "The stern daughter of the voice of God," she writes, "stands ever at the side of Romola and Dorothea, of Lydgate and Maggie, and lifts even Mr. Farebrother and poor Gwendolyn to heights of momentary heroism."[6]

Putting statements like these together with Woolf's sense of Eliot's success and centrality, we can begin to see why the author of *Silas Marner* was both a paradigmatic and a problematic female precursor. Metaphorically speaking, such a conflation of reactions suggests that Eliot represents the conundrum of the empty pack which until recently has confronted every woman writer. Specifically, this conundrum is the riddle of daughterhood, a figurative empty pack with which—as it has seemed to many women artists—not just every powerful literary mother but every literal mother presents her daughter. For such artists, the terror of the female precursor is not that she is an emblem of power but, rather, that when she achieves her greatest strength, her power becomes self-subverting: in the moment of psychic transformation that is the moment of creativity, the literary mother, even more than the literal one, becomes the "stern daughter of the voice of God" who paradoxically proclaims her "allegiance to the law" she herself appears to have violated.

As such a preceptor, the literary mother necessarily speaks both of and for the father, reminding her female child that she is not and cannot be his inheritor: like her mother and like Eliot's Dorothea, the daughter must inexorably become a "foundress of nothing."[7] For human culture, says the literary mother, is bound by rules which make it possible for a woman to speak but which oblige her to speak of her own powerlessness, since such rules might seem to constitute what Jacques Lacan calls the "Law of the Father," the law that means culture is by definition both patriarchal and phallocentric and must therefore transmit the empty pack of disinheritance to every daughter.[8] Not surprisingly, then, even while the literary daughter, like the literal one, desires the matrilineal legitimation incarnated in her precursor/mother, she fears her literary mother: the more fully the mother represents culture, the more inexorably she tells the daughter that she cannot have a mother because she has been signed with and assigned to the Law of the Father.[9] Like Eliot, who aspired to be a "really cultured woman," this "culture-mother" uses her knowledge, as Eliot advised in her scornful essay "Silly Novels by Lady Novelists," "to form a right estimate of herself"—that is, to put herself (and, by implication, her daughters) in the "right" place.[10]

This speculation rests of course on syntheses of Freud and Lévi-Strauss that psychoanalytic thinkers like Lacan and Juliet Mitchell have lately produced. Concentrating on the Oedipus complex, such writers have argued that every child enters the language-defined system of kinship exchange that we call "culture" by learning that he or she cannot remain permanently in the state of nature signified by the embrace of the mother; instead, the child must be assigned a social place denoted by the name (and the Law) of the Father, the potent symbol of human order who disrupts the blissful mother-child dyad. What this means for the boy—a temporary frustration of desire coupled with the promise of an ultimate accession to power—has been elaborately and famously explored by both Freud and Lacan (and also, in a different way, by Lévi-Strauss). What it means for the girl is much less clearly understood; hence, in meditating on the empty pack of daughterhood, I am necessarily improvising both literary and psychoanalytic theory. But my task will, I hope, be made possible by Eliot's status as paradigmatic female precursor, or symbolic culture-mother, and made plausible by the juxtaposition of one of Eliot's texts, *Silas Marner*, with what we might call a revisionary daughter-text, Wharton's *Summer*.

A definition of Eliot as renunciatory culture-mother may seem an odd preface to a discussion of *Silas Marner* since, of all her novels, this richly constructed work is the one in which the empty pack of daughterhood appears fullest, the honey of femininity most unpunished. I want to argue, however, that this "legendary tale," whose status as a schoolroom classic makes it almost as much a textbook as a novel, examines the relationship between woman's fate and the structure of society in order to explicate the meaning of the empty pack of daughterhood. More specifically, this story of an adoptive father, an orphan daughter, and a dead mother broods on events that are actually or symbolically situated on the margins or boundaries of society, where culture must enter into a dialectical struggle with nature, in order to show how the young female human animal is converted into the human daughter, wife, and mother. Finally, then, this fictionalized "daughteronomy" becomes a female myth of origin narrated by a severe literary mother who uses the vehicle of a half-allegorical family romance to urge acquiescence in the Law of the Father.

If *Silas Marner* is not obviously a story about the empty pack of daughterhood, it is plainly, of course, a "legendary tale" about a wanderer with a heavy yet empty pack. In fact, it is through the image of the packman that the story, in Eliot's own words, "came *across* my other plans by a sudden inspiration"—and, clearly, her vision of this burdened outsider is a revision of the Romantic wanderer who haunts the borders of society, seeking a local habitation and a name.[11] I would argue further, though, that Eliot's depiction of Silas Marner's alienation begins to explain Ruby Redinger's sense that the author of this "fluid and metamorphic" story "is" both Eppie, the redemptive daughter, and Silas, the redeemed father. For in examining the outcast weaver's marginality, this novelist of the "hidden life" examines also her own female disinheritance and marginality.[12]

Almost everything that we learn about Silas and the tribe of pack-bearing wanderers he represents tends to reinforce our sense that he belongs in what anthropologists call a "liminal zone."[13] Pallid, undersized, alien-looking, he is one of the figures ordinary country folk see at the edges of time and place—"on the upland, dark against the early winter sunset," "far away among the lanes, or deep in the bosom of the hills." As a weaver, moreover, he is associated with those transformations that take place on the borders of culture—activities that seem to partake "of the nature of conjuring."[14] Again, he is liminal because, both shortsighted and cataleptic, he cannot participate meaningfully in the social world. That he dwells on the edge of Raveloe, near the disused Stone-pits, and never strolls "into the village to drink a pint at [the local pub called] the Rainbow" further emphasizes his alienation, as does the story of his Job-like punishment when the casting of lots in Lantern Yard "convicted" him of a theft he had not committed (*SM*, 1. 1). Finally, his obsessive hoarding, in which gold is drained of all economic signification, reduces the currency of society to absurdity, further emphasizing his alienation.

Considering all these deprivations and denials of social meaning, it is no wonder that this wanderer's pack seems to be heavy with emptiness. Psychologically, moreover, it is no wonder that Eliot in some sense "is" the Silas whom we first encounter at the Stone-pits, if only because through him she examines the liminality that Marian Evans experienced in fact and Maggie Tulliver in fiction. Her own metaphors frequently remind us, furthermore, that just as he weaves textiles, she "weaves" texts—and at the time his story "thrust itself" into the loom of her art, her texts were turning to gold as surely (and as problematically) as his textiles did.[15] In addition, as the man without a place, Silas carries with him the dispossession that she herself had experienced as part of the empty pack of daughterhood. Perhaps, indeed, it is because he shares to some extent in what Sherry Ortner has seen as woman's liminal estate that Silas is often associated not only with the particulars of Marian Evans' femaleness but also with a number of socially defined female characteristics, including a domestic expertise which causes him, in the words of one Raveloer, to be "partly as handy as a woman" (*SM*, 1. 14).[16]

Paradoxically, however, it is his handily maternal rearing of Eppie that redeems Silas as a *man* even while his transformation from outcast to parent reflects a similar but more troubled metamorphosis that Marian Evans was herself undergoing at the time she wrote the novel. Significantly, at the moment the plot of *Silas Marner* began to "unfold" in her mind, George Eliot was becoming a "mother" to George Henry Lewes' children. But where her ambiguous status as "mother" of "a great boy of eighteen . . . as well as two other boys, almost as tall" isolated her further from the society that had cast her out, Silas' status as father of a golden-haired daughter definitively integrates him into a community that had previously thought him diabolic.[17] His transformations of role and rank, therefore, suggest at least one kind of redemption a fallen literary woman might want to imagine for herself: becoming a father.

Silas' redemptive fatherhood, which originates at Christmastime, is prepared for by Eliot's long meditation on the weaver's relationship to his gold, perhaps the most compelling passage of psychological analysis in the novel and the one that most brilliantly propounds the terms of the submerged metaphor that is to govern the book's dramatic action. For the miser, as I noted earlier, what would ordinarily be a kind of language that links members of society is empty of signification and therefore not only meaningless but dead-ended. Halted, static, even regressive, the currency does not flow: nothing goes out into the world, and therefore nothing returns.[18] Silas' history is thus a history without a story because it is without characters—without, that is, both persons and signifiers. Yet its terror consists not merely in the absence of meaning but in the presence of empty matter: the shining purposeless heaps of coins which "had become too large for the iron pot to hold them" (*SM*, 1. 2). It is this mass of lifeless matter that must be imprinted with vital signification if the outcast weaver is to be resurrected and redeemed. And ultimately, indeed, Silas' transformation from fall to fatherhood is symbolized, in a kind of upside-down myth of Midas, by the metamorphosis of his meaningless gold into a living and meaningful child, a child whose Christmas coming marks her as symbolically divine but whose function as divine daughter rather than sacred son is to signify, rather than to replace, the power of her newly created father.

To make way for Eppie, who is his gold made meaningful, Silas must first, of course, be separated from his meaningless gold. What is surely most important about this loss, however, is that the absence of the gold forces the miser to confront the absence that his gold represented. In addition, if we think of this blank, this empty pack, in relation to the Christmas myth for which Eliot is preparing us, we can see that Silas' dark night of the soul is the long dark night of the winter solstice, when dead matter must be kindled and dead flesh made Word if culture is to survive. That "the invisible wand of catalepsy" momentarily freezes the weaver in his open doorway on the crucial New Year's Eve that is to lead to his resurrection merely emphasizes this point. His posture is that of the helpless virgin who awaits annunciation "like a graven image . . . powerless to resist either the good or evil that might enter there" (*SM*, 1. 12).

Because it depends on drastic role reversals, however, Eliot's deliberate parody of the Christmas story suggests that she is half-consciously using the basic outlines of a central culture myth to meditate not on the traditionally sanctified relationship of Holy Mother and Divine Son but on another, equally crucial, bond—that of Holy Father and Divine Daughter. In doing so, she clarifies for herself and for her readers the key differences between sonship and daughterhood. For when the divine child is a son he is, as the Christian story tells us, an active spiritual agent for his mother. To put the matter in a Freudian or Lacanian way, he is the "Phallus" for her, an image of sociocultural as well as sexual power.[19] But when the divine child is a daughter, or so the story of Silas Marner tells us, she is a treasure, a gift the father is given so that he can give it to others, thereby weaving himself into the texture of society. To put the matter in a Lévi-Straussian way, she is the currency whose exchange constitutes society, a point Eliot stunningly anticipated in her submerged metaphor of the girl who is not only as good as but better than gold because her very existence is a pot of gold not at the end but at the beginning of the Rainbow covenant between man and man.

This last allusion is, of course, a reference to the central notion of *The Elementary Structures of Kinship*, in which Lévi-Strauss argues that both the social order, which distinguishes culture from nature, and the incest taboo, which universally manifests the social order, are based upon the exchange of women.[20] In this anthropological view, a daughter is a treasure whose potential passage from man to man insures psychological and social well-being: if the very structure of a patrilineage guarantees that ultimately, inexorably, a man's son will *take* his place and his name, it also promises that a daughter will never be such a usurper since she is an instrument—rather than an agent—of culture. In fact, because she is the father's wealth, his treasure, she is what he *has*, for better or worse.

That Silas christens his Christmas child "Hephzibah" dramatizes this point even while it begins to weave him deeply into the common life of "Bible names" and knit him back into his own past (*SM*, 1. 14). "Hephzibah," or "Eppie," was the name of both Silas' mother and his sister: in gaining a new Hephzibah, he has regained the treasure of all his female kin. Even more significantly, the name itself, drawn from Isaiah, refers to the title Zion will be given after the coming of the

Messiah. Literally translated as "my delight is in her," "Hephzibah" magically signifies both a promised land and a redeemed land (see Isa. 62:4 and 5). Diffusely female, this delightful land incarnates the treasure that is possessed and exchanged by male citizens, and therefore it represents the culture that is created by the covenant between man and man as well as between God and man. A philological fact upon which Eliot herself once meditated enriches further such an association. According to an etymology given by the *Oxford English Dictionary* and based upon Grimm's law, the Anglo-Saxon word "daughter" can be traced back to the Indo-European root *dhugh*, meaning "to milk." Hence, this daughter named Hephzibah is not only milkmaid but milk giver, she who nurtures as well as she who is nurtured—for, as defined by the Law and reinforced by the lexicon of the Father, a daughter *is* the promised land of milk and honey, the gift of wealth that God the Father gives to every human father.[21]

Most of these points are made quite explicit in the concern with weddings that permeates *Silas Marner*, a concern which surfaces in the famous conversation that happens to be taking place at the Rainbow Tavern just when Silas is discovering the loss of his gold. Old Mr. Macey, the parish clerk, is recounting the story of the Lammeter marriage, a ceremony in which the minister got his phrases oddly turned around. The tale asks the question, "Is't the meanin' or the words as makes folks fast i' wedlock?" and answers that "it's neither the meaning nor the words—its the regester does it—that's the glue" (*SM*, 1. 16). But of course, as we learn by the end of *Silas Marner*, it is the very idea of the wedding itself, the having and giving of the daughter, that is the glue.[22] For as Silas and Eppie, Aaron and Dollie parade through Raveloe on their way back to Silas' enlarged cottage after Eppie's marriage to Aaron, the harmony of the bridal party contrasts strikingly with our memory of Silas' former isolation. In marrying Aaron, Silas' daughter has married Silas—married him both to the world and to herself.[23] What had been the "shrunken rivulet" of his love has flowed into a larger current and a dearer currency, a treasure he has given so that it can return to him. And it has returned: "O father," says Eppie, just as if she had married *him*, "What a pretty home ours is" (*SM*, "Conclusion"). Unlike that other Romantic wanderer, the Ancient Mariner, Silas Marner is a member of the wedding. But then, the Ancient Mariner never got the Christian Christmas gift of a daughter.

How does the gift feel about herself, however? What does it mean to Eppie to mean all this for Silas? Certainly Eliot had long been concerned with the social significance and cultural possibilities of daughterhood. Both *The Mill on the Floss*—the novel that precedes *Silas Marner*—and *Romola*—the one that follows it—are elaborate examinations of the structural inadequacies of a daughter's estate. As for Marian Evans, moreover, her real life had persistently confronted her with the problematic nature of daughterhood and its corollary condition, sisterhood. As biographers have shown, her feelings for her own father were ambivalent not only during his lifetime but throughout hers; yet his superegoistic legacy pervaded other relationships she formed. When she was in her early twenties, for instance, she became a dutiful disciple to the Casaubon-like Dr. Brabant, who "punningly baptized her *Deutera* because she was to be a second daughter to him."[24] And even when she was a middle-aged woman, she remembered her older brother Isaac as a kind of miniature father, "a Like unlike, a Self that self restrains," observing wistfully that "were another childhood-world my share,/I would be born a little sister there."[25] Since "Eppie" was the name of Silas' little sister, it seems likely that, in being "born" again to the mild weaver, Marian Evans did in fiction if not in fact re-create herself as both daughter and little sister.

Certainly Eppie's protestations of daughterly devotion suggest that she is in some sense a born-again daughter. "I should have no delight i' life any more if I was forced to go away from my father," she tells Nancy and Godfrey Cass (*SM*, 2. 19). Like the Marian Evans who became "Deutera," Eppie is not so much a second daughter as twice a daughter—a doubly daughterly daughter. As such a "Deutera," she is the golden girl whose being reiterates those cultural commandments Moses set forth for the second time in Deuteronomy. Thus, although scrupulous Nancy Lammeter Cass has often been seen as articulating Eliot's moral position on the key events of this novel, it is really the more impulsive Eppie who is the conscience of the book.

This becomes clearest when Nancy argues that "there's a duty you owe to your lawful father." Eppie's instant reply, with its counterclaim that "I can't feel as I've got any father but one," expresses a more accurate understanding of the idea of fatherhood (*SM*, 2. 19). For in repudiating *God-free* Cass, who is only by chance (*casus*) her natural father, and affirming Silas Marner, who is by choice her cultural father, Eppie rejects the lawless father in favor of the lawful one, indicating her clear awareness that fatherhood itself is both *a* social construct (or, in Stephen Dedalus' words, "a legal fiction") and *the* social construct that constructs society.[26] Having achieved and acted on this analysis, she is rewarded with a domestic happiness which seems to prove Dickinson's contention that it is "vain to punish Honey,/It only sweeter grows." At the same time, in speaking such a law, this creature of milk and honey initiates the reeducation and redemption of Godfrey Cass: the cultural code of Deuteronomy speaks through her, suggesting that, even if she is a Christmas child, she is as much a daughter of the Old Testament as of the New, of the first telling of the law as of its second telling.[27]

Happy and dutiful as she is, however, Eppie is not perfectly contented, for she has a small fund of anxiety that is pledged to her other parent—her lost mother. This intermittent sadness, which manifests itself as a preoccupation with her mother's wedding ring, directs our attention to a strange disruption at the center of *Silas Marner*: the history of Eppie's dead mother. On the surface, of course, the ring that Silas has saved for his adopted daughter is an aptly ironic symbol of that repressed plot, since there never was any bond beyond an artificial one between Molly Farren and Godfrey Cass, the lawless father "of whom [the ring] was the symbol." But Eppie's frequent ruminations on the questions of "how her mother looked, whom she was like, and how [Silas] had found her against the furze bush" suggest that there is something more problematic than a traditional bad marriage at issue here (*SM*, 2. 16). As so often in this "legendary tale," what seems like a moral point also offers an eerily accurate account of what Freud sees as the inexorable psychosexual growth and entry of the daughter into a culture shaped by the codes of the father. "Our insight into [the pre-Oedipus] phase in the little girl's development comes to us as a surprise, comparable . . . with . . . the discovery of the Minoan-Mycenaean civilization behind that of Greece," remarks Freud, explaining that "everything connected with this first mother-attachment has . . . seemed to me . . . lost in a past so dim and shadowy . . . that it seemed as if it had undergone some specially inexorable repression."[28]

Indeed, Molly Farren *has* undergone a "specially inexorable repression" in this novel. Three or four pages of a single chapter are devoted to her, though her damned and doomed wanderings in the snow strikingly recapitulate the lengthier wanderings of fallen women like Hetty Sorel and Maggie Tulliver. I suggest that Eliot attempts this drastic condensation precisely because *Silas Marner,* in allowing her to speak symbolically about the meaning of daughterhood, also allowed her to speak in even more resonant symbols about the significance of motherhood. What she said was what she saw: that it is better to be a daughter than a mother and better still to be a father than a daughter. For when the Deuteronomy of culture formulates the incest laws that lie at the center of human society, that severe code tells the son: "You may not have your mother; you may not kill your father." But when it is translated into a "Daughteronomy" preached for the growing girl, it says: "You must bury your mother; you must give yourself to your father."[29] Since the daughter has inherited an empty pack and cannot *be* a father, she has no choice but to be *for* the father—to be his treasure, his land, his voice.

Yet, as Eliot shows, the growing girl is haunted by her own difficult passage from mother to father, haunted by the primal scene in the snow when she was forced to turn away from the body of the mother, the emblem of nature which can give only so much and no more, and seek the hearth of the father, the emblem of culture that must compensate for nature's inadequacies.[30] This moment is frozen into the center of *Silas Marner* like the dead figure of Molly Farren Cass, whose final posture of self-abandonment brings about Eppie's "effort to regain the pillowing arm and bosom; but mammy's ear was deaf, and the pillow seemed to be slipping away backward" (*SM,* 1. 12). Indeed, for women the myth that governs personality may be based on such a moment, a confrontation of the dead mother that is as enduring and horrifying to daughters as Freud (in *Totem and Taboo*) claimed the nightmare of the dead father was to sons. Finally, the garden that Eppie and Silas plant at the end of the novel memorializes this moment. " 'Father,' " says the girl "in a tone of gentle gravity . . . , 'we shall take the furze bush into the garden' "—for it was against the bush that Molly died (*SM,* 2. 16). Now, fenced in by the garden of the law, the once "straggling" bush will become a symbol of nature made meaningful, controlled and confined by culture (*SM,* 1. 12).

In the end, then, it is Silas Marner, the meek weaver of Raveloe, who inherits the milk and honey of the earth, for he has affirmed the Law of the Father that weaves kin and kindness together. Not coincidentally, when Silas' adopted daughter's engagement to Aaron knits him definitively into the world, Dunstan Cass' skeleton is uncovered and the gold is restored: since Silas has been willing to give his treasure to another, his treasure is given back to him. The intricate web of nemesis and apotheosis that Eliot has woven around Silas reminds us, moreover, that the very name "Raveloe" preserves two conflicting meanings along with an allegorical pun on the word "law." According to *Webster's,* to "ravel" means both to "entangle" or "make intricate" and to "unravel" or "disentangle." And indeed, in this "legendary" domain the nots and knots of the law are unraveled—untangled and clarified—in an exemplary manner, even while the *Ravel* or entanglement of the *Law* weaves people together with Rainbow threads of custom and ceremony.

Finally, too, all is for the best in this domain because this tale of ravelings and unravelings has been told both by and about a daughter of wisdom. Indeed, though Silas as Job is, of course, no Jove and the daughter of his single parenthood is no Minerva, the structure of the relationship between innocently wise Eppie and her lawful father repeats the structure of the relationship between the goddess of wisdom and her law-giving father, just as the frozen burial of Molly Farren Cass affirms the fateful judgment of *The Oresteia* that the mother "is not the true parent of the child/Which is called hers."[31] In Hélène Cixous' wry words, there is "no need for mother—provided that there is something of the maternal: and it is the father then who acts as—is—the mother."[32] With no Eumenides in sight, the redeemed land of Raveloe belongs to fathers and daughters. It is no wonder that Wharton begins her revisionary *Summer* with Charity Royall, an angry transformation of Eppie, trapped in a library ruled by a plaster bust of Minerva.

Writing to Wharton in 1912 about *The Reef*, perhaps the most Jamesian of her novels, Henry James thought of Eliot and suggested that his friend's revisionary clarification of Eliot's message was so radical that the American writer had made herself, metaphorically speaking, into her English culture-mother's primordial precursor. "There used to be little notes in you that were like fine benevolent fingermarks of the good George Eliot—the echo of much reading of that excellent woman," he told Wharton. "But now you are like a lost and recovered 'ancient' whom *she* might have got a reading of (especially were he a Greek) and of whom in *her* texture some weaker reflection were to show."[33] In fact, James' remarks were more prophetic than analytic, for if the not altogether successful *Reef* was quasi-Jamesian rather than proto-Eliotian, the brilliantly coherent *Summer* does surface the *Ur*-myth, and specifically the dark "Daughteronomy," on which *Silas Marner* is based.

It may seem odd to argue that *Summer*, a sexy story of an illicit love affair, has anything in common with Eliot's pedagogically respectable *Silas Marner*. Yet, like *Silas Marner*, *Summer* is a family romance which also incorporates a female *Bildungsroman*, the account of a daughter's growth to maturity. As in *Silas Marner*, too, both the covert symbolic romance and the overt educational *roman* are resolved through the relationship between an adopted daughter and a man who seems to act as both her father and her mother. Again, like *Silas Marner*, *Summer* broods on the winter of civilization's discontent and the summer of reproduction; in doing so, moreover, Wharton's romance, like Eliot's fable, explores events that are situated on the margins of society, where culture must enter into a dialectical struggle with nature in order to transform "raw" female reality into "cooked" feminine sex roles.[34] In addition, as a corollary of this exploration, *Summer*, like *Silas Marner*, traces the redemption that the father achieves through his possession of the daughter. Finally, therefore, the two novels illuminate each other with striking reciprocity: in the conciliatory coziness with which it evades desire, *Silas Marner* is the story Wharton might have liked to tell, while in the relentless rigor with which it renounces desire, *Summer* is the tale Eliot may have feared to confront.

As James' remark about her "ancient" quality implied, Wharton had begun to become a fierce mythologist by the time she wrote this short novel; in particular, she had started to read Joseph Conrad, whose grasp of archaic symbolism she much admired and imported into *Summer*, strengthening her implicit reading of *Silas Marner* with a quest plot that mimics the psychic journey at the heart of his *Heart of Darkness*. Thus, as my epigraph from Sylvia Plath's poem "The Colossus" is meant to suggest, "a blue sky out of the Oresteia" does arch over *Summer*, infusing and illuminating every detail of a mythic narrative that revolves around three figures: a father who "all by [himself is] pithy and historical as the Roman Forum," a daughter who marries the "winter of [his] year" as helplessly as Aeschylus' Electra or Plath's "Electra on Azalea Path" marries the shadow of Agamemnon, and a dead mother who must be as definitively consigned to barren ground as Clytemnestra or the Eumenides.[35] Appropriately enough, therefore, *Summer* begins as its heroine, teenage Charity Royall, walks down the main street of the New England village of North Dormer to her part-time job in a library presided over by a plaster cast of "sheep-nosed" Minerva,[36] the divine daddy's girl who resolved *The Oresteia* by ruling in favor of "the father's claim/And male supremacy in all things." A representative of nature bewildered by culture, Charity is a sort of foundling who, we learn, was "brought down" from a nearby mountain (always mysteriously called "the Mountain," with an ominous capital *M*) when she was very little, an origin which places her among the "humblest of the humble even in North Dormer, where to come from the Mountain was the worst disgrace." At the same time, however, both her job as librarian and the odd fact that she keeps the lace she is making "wound about the buckram back of a disintegrated copy of 'The Lamplighter' " significantly qualify her humbleness (*S*, pp. 22, 14). For, like Eliot's Eppie and like Gerty, the heroine of Maria Cummins' 1854 best-seller, Wharton's Charity is the ward of a solitary older man who dotes on and delights in her youth, her dependence.[37]

Where both Eliot's Silas Marner and Cummins' Trueman Flint are sympathetic men almost from the first, however, Charity's guardian is an equivocal figure, and his difference begins to reveal the secret dynamics such apparently divergent works as Cummins' and Eliot's novels share with Wharton's. For Lawyer Royall, says the narrator of *Summer*, "ruled in North Dormer; and Charity ruled in lawyer Royall's house. . . . But she knew her power, knew what it was made of, and hated it." *Lawyer* Royall: so far as we know, this "magnificent monument of a man" has no other name (*S*, pp. 23, 27). Indeed, as Charity's father/guardian/suitor and (eventually) husband, he is, ultimately, no more than the role his professional title and allegorical surname together denote: a regal law-giver, a mythologized superego whose occupation links him with the library and with culture, that is, with the complex realm of patriarchal history that both puzzles and imprisons the wild child he is trying to make into a desirable daughter/bride.

Even while he is a "towering" public man, however, Lawyer Royall is a notably pathetic private man. From the first, Wharton deconstructs the colossus of the father to make explicit the ways in which this paradigmatic patriarch is as dependent on his Charity as Silas Marner was on his Eppie or, indeed, as Agamemnon was on Iphigenia or Electra, Oedipus on Antigone and Ismene, or the biblical Jephthah on his (nameless) daughter. To begin with, we learn that Charity had long ago perceived Lawyer Royall as "too lonesome" for her to go away to school (*S*, p. 26); later, more dramatically, we discover that his "lonesomeness" manifested itself in an abortive attempt to rape her. Finally, we are told that it was this episode which drove the girl to try to establish her independence by taking her deathly job in the library. But, of course, this attempt at escape, as in some Sophoclean case history, simply impels her even more inexorably toward her fate.

For it is in "Minerva's" library that Charity meets her lover-to-be, a handsome architect named Lucius Harney—a far more glamorously equivocal representative of culture than the aging Lawyer Royall. Townbred, easy with books, this dashing young man is culture's heir; at the same time, he is a golden boy whose "lusciousness," as Andrea Hammer has observed, links him to nature, even seems to make him nature's emissary—and that is why *he* is an equivocal figure. Young, sensual, magnetic, he is frequently associated with the grass, the sky, the "flaming breath" of summer; indeed, he and Charity conduct their affair while he is "camping" halfway up the Mountain in a little abandoned house surrounded by a fallen fence, "crowding grasses," and rosebushes that have "run wild" (*S*, p. 166).[38] That he is often connected in Charity's mind with her mysterious Mountain relative Liff Hyatt, whose initials echo his, seems at first to suggest, moreover, that, like Liff, Lucius is a brother figure—and his earliest advances *are* described as "more fraternal than lover-like" (*S*, p. 95).[39] Yet, just as Eppie Marner's marriage to the brother figure Aaron also marries her definitively to her father, Silas, so Charity's apparently illegitimate romance with Lucius Harney moves her inexorably into the arms of Lawyer Royall, and this not just because it is Lawyer Royall who marries her to "rescue" her from unwed motherhood but because it eventually becomes plain that even Lucius Harney's desire for her is entangled in feelings of rivalrous identification with the patriarchally "majestic" lawyer (see *S*, p. 191).

For Charity, in every sense of that word, must be given to the father. And, as *Summer's* denouement finally makes clear, even while Lucius Harney has seemed to act against the patriarchal Royall, he has also acted *for* the lawyer, appearing as if by magic in the library to deflower Charity and impregnate her so that she is at last ready for the marriage to her guardian that she had earlier persistently refused. Indeed, it is arguable that throughout the affair in which he seems to have functioned as nature's emissary by drawing the girl into the wilderness of her own sexuality, Harney has really performed as culture's messenger and, specifically, as a vivid and vital "Phallus" whose glamour seduces the daughter into the social architecture from which she would otherwise have tried to flee. For in patriarchal marriage, says Wharton's plot, the brother/equal inevitably turns into the father/ruler. Not surprisingly, therefore, when Charity and Lawyer Royall start on their journey toward the allegorically named town of *Nettle*ton, where the girl's sexual initiation began and where she is finally going to be married to her legal guardian, Charity briefly imagines that she is "sitting beside her lover with the leafy arch of summer bending over them." But "this illusion [is] faint and transitory" because it implies a deceptive liberty of desire (*S*, p. 273). As Wharton reluctantly observed, the daughter's summer of erotic content blooms only to prepare her for what Dickinson called "a Doom of Fruit without the Bloom"—an autumn and winter of civilized discontent in which, like her precursor, the first Mrs. Royall, she will be "sad and timid and weak" (*S*, p. 24). As in Wharton's pornographic "Beatrice Palmato" fragment—a more melodramatic tale of father-daughter incest which makes overt some of the psychodynamics that even in *Summer* are only covert—the symbolic father will "reap [the] fruit" borne from the son/lover's deflowering of the daughter.[40]

Charity does, however, make one last frantic effort to flee the wintry prison house of culture that is closing around her, and that is in her wild pilgrimage up the Mountain in search of her mother. As the girl's affair with Lucius Harney has progressed, she has become increasingly concerned about her origins and begun to try, the way Eppie did in *Silas Marner*, to explain to herself what it means both to have and to be a mother. Finally, when she realizes she is pregnant, she also understands that there is "something in her blood that [makes] the Mountain the only answer to her questioning," and in an astonishing episode, which includes some of the most fiercely imagined scenes in American fiction, she journeys toward the originary heart of darkness where she will find and lose her mother (*S*, p. 236).

Appropriately enough, Charity's mother's name is *Mary* Hyatt. Equally appropriately, Charity arrives in the outlaw community on the Mountain only to discover that the woman has just died. It is as if the very idea of the daughter's quest must necessarily kill her female progenitor, not only to emphasize the unavailability of female power but also to underscore the Oresteian dictum that "The mother is not the true parent of the child/ Which is called hers. She is [merely] a nurse who tends the growth/Of young seed planted by its true parent, the male."[41] Worse still, this anti–Virgin Mary is not only dead, she is horrifyingly dead, dead "like a dead dog in a ditch," "lips parted in a frozen gasp above . . . broken teeth," one leg drawn up under a torn skirt and the other "swollen glistening leg" flung out, "bare to the knee," in a death paroxysm that parodies the paroxysm of birth and suggests the nausea of nakedness in which the flesh of the mother expels and repels the flesh of the child (*S*, pp. 250, 248). As Mr. Miles, the clergyman who ascends the Mountain only for funerals, prepares to bury the woman's uncoffined body in frozen ground, nameless and indistinguishable squatters, Charity's undefinable relatives, squabble over the pitiful furnishings in the shanty where Mary Hyatt died on a mattress on the floor. Nothing, they say, was hers: "She never had no bed"; "And the stove warn't hers." Nor does the reading of the Bible, the Book of patriarchal Law, offer any hope of redemption for the dead woman. When Mr. Miles intones "yet in my flesh shall I see God," Charity thinks of "the gaping mouth and stony eyes [and] glistening leg," and when he proposes that Jesus Christ shall change this "vile body that it may be like unto His glorious body," a last spadeful of earth falls heavily "on the vile body of Mary Hyatt" (*S*, pp. 251, 255).

Where women poets from Elizabeth Barrett Browning and Emily Dickinson transformed mothers into "multitudinous mountains sitting in/[A] magic circle, with [a] mutual touch/Electric," and "Sweet Mountains" into "Strong Madonnas," Wharton, like her culture-mother George Eliot, saw the mother as blind, deaf, and stony and the maternal Mountain as a place of mourning.[42] As if Eliot anticipated the French feminist psychoanalyst Christiane Olivier's contention that the mirror which man holds toward woman "contains only the image of a dead woman" and, more specifically, a dead Jocasta, the morbid moment of Molly Farren Cass' death in the snow and her daughter Eppie's discovery that "mammy's ear was deaf" is—as we saw—frozen into the center of *Silas Marner.*[43] Similarly, frozen into the center of *Summer* is the moment of Mary Hyatt's burial in the snow and her daughter Charity's mortifying discovery that there is no salvation from or for her mother's "vile body."

Neither is there salvation or even significant charity for Charity from other women in the novel. To be sure, one of the girl's unnamed relatives—Liff Hyatt's mother—lets her spend the night on a mattress on the floor "as her dead mother's body had lain," but as that simile suggests, such an act of kindness only promises to induct Charity into the "passive promiscuity" lived by the matriarchal horde on the Mountain, a life entirely outside the comforts and controls of culture, a life in which the mother—possessionless and unpossessed—is "glad to have the child go" (*S*, pp. 258, 260). As for the other women, the semisenile figure of Verena Marsh, the Royalls' housekeeper, "with her old deaf-looking eyes" foreshadows the blind deaf stony figure of Charity's mother; the "fallen" Julia Hawes and her impoverished sister Ally, together with the "indestructible" Annabel Balch, reemphasize women's dependence on male legal and financial protection; and the pseudomotherly abortionist, Dr. Merkel, suggests that a daughter who wants to live apart from the father must kill her baby or else, like Mary Hyatt, be "cut down" and killed by the "savage misery" of a life apart from culture (*S*, pp. 155, 254, 259).

Taken together, therefore, the decisions and destinies of all these women italicize Charity's own perception that "in the established order of things as she [knows] them, [there is] no place for her individual adventure." In fact, the pregnancy that signals her transformation from girl to woman, from daughter to mother, has so severely depersonalized her that she feels herself "a mere speck in the lonely circle of the sky." Like dead Mary Hyatt, she has nothing and is nothing but a vessel for her child; thus the impersonal biological imperative of the coming life is, as Wharton brilliantly puts it, "like a load that [holds] her down, and yet like a hand that pull[s] her to her feet" (*S*, pp. 235, 264, 265). The annunciation of summer, Charity discovers, inexorably entails the renunciation that is winter, a divestment of desire that definitively prepares her for her final turn toward the rescuing father. Fated to move from father to library to lover to father, she goes to Nettleton and marries her guardian. And by now even the Romantic nature she had experienced with her lover has been transmuted into culture—that is, into a set of cultural artifacts: an engraving of a couple in a boat that decorates her bridal chamber, and a pin set with a lake blue gem which implies that in the bloomless winter of her maturity the lake itself must turn to stone.

But if a stone is all Charity has, Charity is what Lawyer Royall has, an emblem of redemption that he needs as much as Silas Marner needs "his" Eppie. For if, as Freud argues, the girl arrives at "the ultimate normal feminine attitude in which she takes her father as love-object" only after "a lengthy process of [symbolically castrating] development" ("FS," p. 199) which, in Helene Deutsch's words, "drive[s]" her "into her constitutionally predetermined passive role," then the daughter's desire for the father must be understood to be, like Charity's need for Lawyer Royall, constructed by a patriarchal order that forces her to renounce what might be more "natural" desires—for lover/brother, for mother, for self.[44] But as the ambiguous allegory of Charity's name suggests, the father's desire for the daughter is inevitable, a desire not only to give but to receive charity. Standing outside the girl's room after proposing to her (and being rejected) for the second time, Lawyer Royall seems to understand this: "His hand on the door knob[,] 'Charity!' he plead[s]" (*S*, p. 119). For not only is the "daughter" a milk-giving creature, a suitably diminished and dependent mother, she is also, as a living manifestation of the father's wealth, the charity to which he is culturally entitled.

Finally, therefore, from Charity's point of view, *Summer* is very much a novel about both renunciation and resignation. When her last hope for escape is buried with her mother, she must resign herself, or, rather, reassign herself, to her symbolic father.[45] After her marriage she will be Charity Royall Royall, a name whose redundancy emphasizes the proprietorial power by which her guardian/husband commands her loyalty. But from Lawyer Royall's point of view or, for that matter, from Lucius Harney's, *Summer* is a novel about assignment—that is, about the roles of cultural authority to which men are assigned and about the women who are assigned—marked out, given over—to them to signify that authority. No wonder, then, that Lawyer Royall's first gesture after his marriage to Charity is to give his new bride the munificent sum of forty dollars to buy clothes so that, like an illustration from Thorstein Veblen's *Theory of the Leisure Class,* she will prove his wealth by "beating" all the other girls "hollow" (*S,* p. 285). "Of course, *he's* the book," said Wharton enigmatically about Lawyer Royall.[46] Consciously, she no doubt meant that he is the novel's most complex personality—indeed, its only Jamesian adult—and therefore the only character whose redemption is worth tracing in detail. But, less consciously, she might have meant that, as law-giving patriarch, he is the "book" in which Charity's fate must be inscribed; for it is, after all, the text of his desire that determines the destiny of hers.

Apart from fictions like *Silas Marner* and *Summer,* what evidence have we that father-daughter incest is a culturally constructed paradigm of female desire? Equally to the point, what proof is there that the father may need, even desire, the daughter at least as much as she needs him? Though psychoanalytic and sociological replies to both these questions have been disputed, many answers have been offered, particularly in recent years. From Phyllis Chesler to Judith Lewis Herman, for instance, feminist theorists have argued that in a patriarchal culture women are encouraged by society, in Chesler's words, "to commit incest as a way of life." "As opposed to marrying our fathers, we marry men like our fathers." Chesler declares, "men who are older than us, [and] have more money [and] more power [and are taller]." Similarly, in her study of literal father-daughter incest, Herman claims that "overt incest represents only the furthest point on a continuum—an exaggeration of patriarchal family norms, but not a departure from them."[47] Less extravagantly but along the same lines, Nancy Chodorow has observed, following Talcott Parsons, that "father-daughter incest does not threaten a daughter [with a return to infantile dependency] in the same way" in which "mother-son incest . . . threatens a son," so that "mother-son and mother-*daughter* [not father-daughter] incest are the major threats to the formation of new families (as well as to the male-dominant family)."[48]

Nor are any of these views incompatible with Freud's own belief that what he called the "female Oedipus complex"—the process through which the little girl relinquishes her earliest mother-attachment and transfers her affection to her father—is both the end result of an extraordinarily difficult procedure and, as he puts it, a "positive" development. Only by a "very circuitous path," he admits in his late essay "Female Sexuality" (1931), does the girl "arrive at the ultimate normal feminine attitude in which she takes her father as love-object." And because *her* Oedipus complex (unlike the boy's) represents the "final result of a lengthy process . . . it escapes the strong hostile influences which, in men, tend to its destruction"—that is, because the female Oedipus complex is not destroyed but created by the "castration complex" (which signifies the recognition of sexual difference), many women, in Freud's view, never surmount the female Oedipus complex at all and perhaps never should ("FS," p. 199).

As the researches of Judith Herman and Lisa Hirschman have shown, however, and as Deutsch argued, the desire of the father for the daughter is frequently complicitous, even essential in constructing the desire for him that she manifests in the "positive" female Oedipus complex. Proposing a theory of what has come to be called "reciprocal role learning," Deutsch suggested in *The Psychology of Women* that the father functions "as a seducer, with whose help the girl's aggressive instinctual components are transformed into masochistic ones."[49] Recent investigators have suggested that girls do "learn to behave in a feminine fashion through complementing the masculine behavior of their fathers." Tellingly, though, "there is no evidence that reciprocal role learning is of any significance in the development of masculinity."[50] In other words, boys are not encouraged to learn to be boys by responding with precocious virility to seductive behavior by their mothers. This last point, however, leads to my second question—What proof is there that the father needs the daughter at least as much as she needs him?—and to a related query—Why *should* the father desire the daughter? If men have not developed masculinity through reciprocal role learning with mothers, why should they interact "reciprocally" with their daughters? I have extrapolated from my readings of *Silas Marner* and *Summer* the idea that the father needs the daughter because she is a suitably diminished "milk giver," a miniaturized version of the mother whom patriarchal culture absolutely forbids him to desire. Beyond the often ambiguous configurations that shape literary texts like Eliot's and Wharton's, there is considerable evidence that this is so.

The empirical investigations of Herman and Hirschman, for instance, have yielded crucial information: in studying surveys of "white, predominantly middle-class, urban, educated women," these clinical psychologists discovered that "between four and twelve percent of all women reported a sexual experience with a relative, and one woman in one hundred reported a sexual experience with her father or stepfather." Examining individual incest cases, moreover, they learned that, often because of a wife's illness, absence, or alleged frigidity, a father had transferred his affections to his daughter in an attempt "to continue to receive female nurturance." More generally, they observed that "in the father's fantasy life, the daughter becomes the source of all the father's infantile longings for nurturance and care. He thinks of her first as the idealized childhood bride or sweetheart, and finally as the all-good, all-giving mother." Reasoning both from anthropological studies and from the Bible, they conclude that "in patriarchal societies [where] the rights of ownership and exchange of women within the family are vested primarily in the father[, t]hese rights find their most complete expression in the father's relationship with his daughter" because—of all female relatives—"the daughter belongs to the father alone." They then cite a key passage from Leviticus in which, while forbidding sexual union with every other female blood relative or in-law, "the patriarchal God sees fit to pass over father-daughter incest in silence."[51]

Freud's theories of psychoanalysis began, of course, with the hypothesis that just such incest was the root cause of the hysteria manifested by the female patients he and Josef Breuer treated in the 1890s. But traditional interpretations of the history of psychoanalysis propose that, as Diane Sadoff puts it, "Freud realized that his female patients' stories of remembered paternal seduction did not necessarily report reality and may have reported fantasy [so that] the scene of paternal seduction retroactively seeks to represent and solve a major enigma confronting the daughter: the origin or upsurge of her sexuality."[52] In fact, explains O. Mannoni, "the theory of trauma, of the seduction by the father . . . served as [Freud's] defense against knowledge of the Oedipus complex."[53] Even the feminist theorist Juliet Mitchell acquiesces in this view, observing that "the fact that, as Freud himself was well aware, *actual* paternal seduction or rape occurs not infrequently, has nothing to do with the essential concepts of psychoanalysis" (which are, after all, founded on the hypothesis of filial rather than paternal desire) (*PF*, p. 9). Yet, interestingly enough, we have from the Father of Psychoanalysis himself strikingly direct evidence of the reality of paternal desire.

In May 1897, shortly before abandoning his theory that hysteria was caused by paternal seduction or rape, Freud had a dream about "feeling over-affectionately towards" his oldest daughter, Mathilde. "The dream," he wrote to his friend Wilhelm Fliess, "of course fulfills my wish to pin down a father as the originator of neurosis and put an end to my persistent doubts."[54] Yet, on the one hand, the experience clearly troubled him, while, on the other hand, it does seem to have functioned as a screen for what troubled him even more: the sequence of dreams and memories Freud recorded in the letters of spring–summer 1897 shows that many of the psychic events he examined as part of the self-analysis he was conducting at this time had to do with desires for or anxieties about mature women—his mother or figures for her. The sequence culminated in his crucial speculation that "(between the ages of two and two-and-a-half) libido towards *matrem* was aroused" at a time when he "had the opportunity of seeing her *nudam*."[55] Embedded in this dramatic series of reveries in his equally dramatic decision that though "in every case [of female hysteria] blame was laid on perverse acts by the father . . . it was hardly credible that perverted acts against children were so general," a decision that, despite its negative implications for a career he had been building on theories about paternal seduction, left him feeling inexplicably exhilarated.[56]

Careful analysis of these materials suggests that Freud's brilliant self-interrogations both reveal and conceal a slippage in his thinking. His no doubt accurate discovery of feelings for his mother is quite unaccountably associated with the notion, which he later repudiated, that his female patients would naturally have had equivalent desires for their *fathers*. That even as he surfaced his own Oedipal wishes, he may have disguised them (for instance, reporting awful dreams about an ugly elderly nurse who washed him in "reddish water") implies his own *resistance* to these wishes, however, a resistance also expressed in his dream of Mathilde. As Mitchell observes, even "Freud . . . found it more acceptable to be the father than the incest-desiring or rival-castrating son—as do most men" (*PF*, p. 75). Thus the theory of paternal seduction appropriately led to Freud's understanding of the son's desire for the mother, of which the father's desire for the daughter is a belated but more socially acceptable transformation. Nevertheless, the father's desire for the daughter was not so acceptable to Freud that he could persist in his "wish to pin down a father as the originator of neurosis."[57] Rather, having admitted his own filial desire, he seems to have wished to "pin down" daughters as equivalent sources of desire. Yet as his later formulations of female psychosexual development were to suggest, erotic feelings of daughters for fathers symmetrical with those of sons for mothers were not necessarily implicit in the accounts of paternal seduction that he called his patients' "fantasies." In fact, as recent reports about the unpublished portions of his letters to Fliess, along with analyses of the alterations and evasions in *Studies on Hysteria* have suggested, Freud himself was, in Mitchell's phrase, "well aware" that many of these patients were not fantasizing, that they actually had been seduced or in some sense seductively manipulated by their fathers or by father figures. Their "hysteria" may therefore have constituted not a rejection of their own desire but a refusal of the paternal demands that not only their own families but also their culture defined as psychologically "right."[58] Even so early in his career, in other words, Freud's fruitful transformation of speculations about father-daughter seduction into a theory about son-mother incest, with its corollary evasion of a theory of father-daughter desire, expresses his proleptic awareness that he would eventually have to construct a far more complicated model of female psychosexual development in order to trace the girl's "circuitous path" to what he was to define as mature (heterosexual) femininity.

That path, with its obstacles, its terrors, and its refusals, is the road studied in *Silas Marner* and *Summer*—in *Silas Marner*'s exploration of the powers the daughter gives the father and in *Summer*'s examination of the powers the father takes away from the daughter. But of course countless other literary texts—written by both men and women—focus on the submerged paradigm of father-daughter incest that shapes the plots and possibilities inscribed in these novels. From *The Oresteia*'s repudiation and repression of the matriarchal Furies and its concomitant aggrandizement of Athene, the dutiful father's daughter, to *Oedipus at Colonus*' praise of Antigone and Ismene, the two loyal daughters who have been their father's sole guardians in the blinded exile to which his incestuous marriage with his mother condemned him, Greek literature consistently valorizes such a paradigm. That Oedipus' daughters, in particular, functioned as their father's "eyes" reminds us, moreover, that "the word for daughter in Greek is *Kore*, the literal meaning of which is pupil of the eye."[59] Similarly, the violent obliteration of the mother in these works and many others recalls one version of the story of Athene's origin: after raping Metis the Titaness, the father-god *swallowed her*, having heard that, though she was now pregnant with a daughter, she would bear a son who would depose him if she had another child; then, "in due time . . . seized by a raging headache," he himself gave birth to Athene, who "sprang fully armed" from his skull.[60] In just the way that Antigone and Ismene properly replace Jocasta as Oedipus' helpmeets—indeed, as the "eyes" who, according to Freud, would signify his continuing sexual potency—so Athene supplants Metis as Zeus' true child/bride.

To be sure, these archaic texts enact the prescriptions and proscriptions of patriarchal culture with exceptional clarity; yet such imperatives also underlie a surprising number of other, later works, ranging from Shakespeare's *King Lear* to Percy Bysshe Shelley's *Cenci*, from Mary Shelley's *Mathilda* to Christina Stead's *Man Who Loved Children*, from some of Sylvia Plath's and Anne Sexton's most striking poems to Toni Morrison's *Bluest Eye*. Whereas the stories of such heroines as Antigone and her later, more angelically Victorian avatar Eppie Marner—the creation of a novelist long haunted by Antigone—had recounted the daughter's acquiescence in her filial destiny, however, these works, like Wharton's *Summer*, record her ambivalence toward a fate in which, as Beatrice Cenci cries, "all things" terrifyingly transform themselves into "my father's spirit,/His eye, his voice, his touch surrounding me."[61] Specifically, in each of these works a father more or less explicitly desires a daughter. His incestuous demands may be literal or they may be figurative, but in either case the heroine experiences them as both inexorable and stifling. Thus, in each work the girl struggles with more or less passion to escape, arguing that "I love your Majesty according to my bond, no more, no less." And in almost all these works, she discovers, finally, just what the nature of that bond is: no more, no less, than—on the one hand—death or—on the other hand—a surrender to the boundless authority of paternal desire that governs the lives of mothers and daughters in what Adrienne Rich has called "the kingdom of the sons" and the fathers.[62] Indeed, in the few works (for instance, Plath's "Daddy" and Stead's *Man Who Loved Children*) where the daughter neither dies nor acquiesces, she becomes a murderess and an outlaw.

Reducing the plot, as fairy tales so often do, to its most essential psychic outline, a narrative recorded by the brothers Grimm provides a resonant summary of the father-daughter "story" I have been exploring here. The fairy tale "Allerleirauh" (which means "many different kinds of fur") introduces us to a king whose dying wife has made him promise not to remarry unless he can find a new bride who is as beautiful as she is and who has "just such golden hair as I have."[63] Grief-stricken, the king keeps his word until one day he looks at his growing daughter, sees that she is "just as beautiful as her dead mother, and ha[s] the same golden hair," "suddenly [feels] a violent love for her," and resolves to marry *her*. Shocked, the daughter tries to escape by setting him impossible tasks—she asks for three magical dresses and "a mantle of a thousand different kinds of fur"—but when he fulfills her requests, she has no choice but to run away. Taking her three dressses and three tiny domestic treasures, she wraps herself in her fur mantle and escapes to a great forest. There she is asleep in a hollow tree when "the King to whom this forest belong[s]" passes through with some huntsmen who capture her, thinking she is "a wondrous beast." When she tells them she is simply a poor orphan child, they bring her to this king's palace, where they set her to work, like Cinderella, in the kitchen ("A," pp. 327, 328).[64]

Of course, however, the king at this palace soon manages to discover her identity. He gives a series of three feasts, at each of which she appears in one of her magic dresses; he admires the soup she cooks while she is disguised in her furry Cinderella garb; and he finally manages to tear off her protective mantle, revealing her magic dress and her golden hair so that, in the words of the story, "she [can] no longer hide herself," and the pair are wed soon after this epiphany ("A," p. 331). Like such texts as *Summer*, *Mathilda*, and *The Cenci*, then, this tale records the case history of a daughter who tries to escape paternal desire, and like the heroines of many such works (for instance, Charity Royall journeying to the Mountain), the "fair princess" who becomes "Allerleirauh" flees from culture (her father's palace) to nature (the great wood), trying to transform herself into a creature of nature (a "hairy animal") rather than acquiesce in the extreme demands culture is making upon her ("A," pp. 329, 330).[65] Like a number of the other protagonists of these stories and case histories, however, Allerleirauh cannot altogether abandon the imperatives her culture has impressed upon her: she brings with her the three magical dresses and the three domestic tokens which will eventually reveal her identity and knit her back into society. Like countless other heroines in such tales, moreover, she is motherless, a fact which, the story emphasizes, has brought about the seductive paternal persecution she is trying to evade. Finally, like that of so many of these heroines—perhaps most notably *Silas Marner*'s Eppie—her function as a "treasure" to both kings is manifested by the golden hair that she is at last unable to conceal.

That there are in fact two kings in "Allerleirauh" may at first seem to controvert my argument that this tale offers us a paradigm of the prescription for father-daughter incest that lies at the heart of female psychosexual development in patriarchal society. Not just the princess but also the first king's courtiers, after all, express dismay at his desire to marry his daughter. In addition, the second king is distinguished from the first by a restrictive clause: he is not "the king, who owns this forest"—that is, the king from whose palace Allerleirauh has just fled—but, rather, "the king who owns this forest." Yet structurally and psychologically, if not grammatically, the two kings are one: paternal figures from both of whom the "fair princess" tries to escape, though not, perhaps, with equal vigor. In fact, for all practical purposes, the distinction between the two is best expressed by a single comma, the linguistic mark that marks the difference between illegitimate and legitimate incest, a difference Allerleirauh herself involuntarily acknowledges by the ambivalence with which at one moment she decks herself in glorious apparel and then, soon after, retreats into her old life as a wild child.

To be sure, given such ambivalence, some readers might see this tale simply as an account of the advances and retreats through which an adolescent girl comes to terms with her own mature desires. At the same time, however, what gives the tale a good deal of its force is the fatality it shares with subtler works like *Silas Marner* and *Summer*—specifically, a fatality provided by the *mother's* complicity in her dauther's destiny. For it is, after all, Allerleirauh's mother who has set the girl's story going with her admonition to the father that he must marry only a bride as beautiful as she. Lost to the daughter, like Molly Farren Cass and Mary Hyatt, she nevertheless rules her daughter's life with the injunctions of the culture-mother: "You must bury your mother, you must give yourself to your father." In such novels as *Silas Marner* and *Summer*, the authors themselves replace her, splitting the maternal function between the ignominy of the dead mother and the qualified triumph of the male-identified maternal authority. But in all these stories, as even in more apparently rebellious works, the text itself discovers no viable alternative to filial resignation. Certainly, paradigmatic culture-mothers like Eliot and Wharton do not suggest (at least not in works like *Silas Marner* and *Summer*) that the daughter has any choice but that of acquiescence.[66] Though the "empty Pack" of daughteronomy may be heavy, as Dickinson saw perhaps more clearly than they, it is vain to "punish" the cultural "Honey" it manufactures; for the daughter who understands her duty and her destiny, such honey "only sweeter" grows. Under "a blue sky out of the Oresteia," Eppie Marner, Charity Royall, and the fair princess Allerleirauh, along with many others, and each in her own way, obey the implicit command of patriarchal society and marry the winter of the Father's year.

NOTES

This essay was researched and written with the assistance of grants from the Rockefeller and Guggenheim foundations, to both of which I am very grateful. In addition, I have profited greatly from criticisms and suggestions offered by many friends and colleagues including (as always) Susan Gubar and Elliot Gilbert, as well as Andrea Hammer, Susan Lurie, Elyse Blankley, Peter Hays, Suzanne Graver, and Michael Wolfe. Finally, I have learned much from audiences at a number of institutions where this paper was "tried out" in various forms, among them helpful and incisive respondents at the Rutgers University, George Eliot Centenary Conference, and at Harvard University, the University of Colorado, the University of Washington, Yale University, the University of Southern California, and Princeton University.

1. See Sandra M. Gilbert and Susan Gubar, "Tradition and the Female Talent," *Proceedings of the Northeastern University Center for Literary Studies*, 2 (1984), and " 'Forward Into the Past': The Complex Female Affiliation Complex," in *Historical Studies in Literary Criticism*, ed. Jerome J. McGann (Madison, Wis., 1985).

2. Virginia Woolf to Lady Robert Cecil [21 Jan.? 1919] (no. 1010), *The Letters of Virginia Woolf*, ed. Nigel Nicolson and Joanne Trautmann, 6 vols. (New York, 1975–80), 2:322; the historian Shelton Rothblatt called George Eliot a "Man of Ideas" (paper

delivered at the George Eliot Centenary Conference, Rutgers University, Sept. 1980); and see Leslie Stephen, *George Eliot*, English Men of Letters Series (London and New York, 1902).

3. Elaine Showalter, *A Literature of Their Own: British Women Novelists from Brontë to Lessing* (Princeton, N.J., 1977), p. 108; Elizabeth Robins, *George Mandeville's Husband*, quoted in *A Literature of Their Own*, p. 109.

4. Eliot had said that *Silas Marner* "came to me first of all, quite suddenly, as a sort of legendary tale" (Eliot to John Blackwood, 24 Feb. 1861, quoted in Gordon S. Haight, *George Eliot: A Biography* [New York, 1968], p. 341).

5. Emily Dickinson to Thomas Niles, Apr. 1883 (no. 814), *The Letters of Emily Dickinson*, ed. Thomas H. Johnson, 3 vols. (Cambridge, Mass., 1965), 3:769–70; and see Dickinson, *The Complete Poems of Emily Dickinson*, ed. Johnson (Boston, 1960), no. 1562, p. 650.

6. Edith Wharton, review of *George Eliot* by Stephen, *Bookman*, 15 (May 1902), 251, 250.

7. Eliot, "Prelude," *Middlemarch*, ed. W. J. Harvey (Harmondsworth, 1965), p. 26.

8. Jacques Lacan, "On a Question Preliminary to Any Possible Treatment of Psychosis," *Ecrits: A Selection*, trans. Alan Sheridan (New York, 1977), 199. Anika Lemaire succinctly summarizes this Lacanian position:

> Society and its structures are always present in the form of the family institution and the father, the representative of the law of society into which he will introduce his child by forbidding dual union with the mother (the register of the imaginary, of nature). By identifying with the father, the child receives a name and a place in the family constellation; restored to himself, he discovers that he is to be made in and by a world of Culture, language and civilization. [*Jacques Lacan*, trans. David Macey (London, 1977), p. 92]

Elsewhere, Lacan observes: "That the woman should be inscribed in an order of exchange of which she is the object, is what makes for the fundamentally conflictual, and, I would say, insoluble character of her position: the symbolic order literally submits her, it transcends her" (Lacan, "Seminar 2" [1954–55], quoted in Jacqueline Rose, intro. to *Feminine Sexuality: Jaques Lacan and the "école freudienne,"* ed. Juliet Mitchell and Rose, trans. Rose [New York, 1983], p. 45).

9. For female "anxiety of authorship" and women's corollary need for matrilineal legitimation, see Gilbert and Gubar, *The Madwoman in the Attic: The Woman Writer and the Nineteenth Century Literary Imagination* (New Haven, Conn., 1979), chap. 2.

10. Eliot, "Silly Novels by Lady Novelists," *The Writings of George Eliot*, 25 vols. (Boston and New York, 1907–8), 22:209. In a study of Eliot's stance toward paternal authority, Diane F. Sadoff makes a point similar to this one, nothing that Eliot seeks "to usurp [paternal authority] as the discourse of a male narrator, the authority of a male author" (*Monsters of Affection: Dickens, Eliot, and Brontë on Fatherhood* [Baltimore, 1982], p. 3).

11. Eliot to Blackwood, 12 Jan. 1861, quoted in Ruby V. Redinger, *George Eliot: The Emergent Self* (New York, 1975), 436. As Susan Gubar has suggested to me, the resonant image of the "packman" may be associated with the figure of Bob Jakin in *The Mill on the Floss* (which Eliot had just completed), the itinerant pack-bearing peddler who brings Maggie Tulliver a number of books, the most crucial of which is Thomas à Kempis' treatise on Christian renunciation (so that its subject metaphorically associates it with Silas Marner's pack full of emptiness).

12. Redinger, *George Eliot*, p. 439; Eliot, "Finale," *Middlemarch*, p. 896.

13. For "liminal zone," see Victor Turner, "Passages, Margins, and Poverty: Religious Symbols of Communitas," *Dramas, Fields, and Metaphors: Symbolic Action in Human Society* (Ithaca, 1974), 231–71, and "Betwixt and Between: The Liminal Period in *Rites de Passage*," *The Forest of Symbols: Aspects of Ndembu Ritual* (Ithaca, 1967), 93–111.

14. Eliot, *Silas Marner: The Weaver of Raveloe*, ed. Q. D. Leavis (Harmondsworth, 1967), pt. 1, chap. 1, pp. 51, 52; all further references to this work, abbreviated *SM*, will be included in the text, with only part and chapter numbers (or chapter title) for the convenience of those using other editions.

15. Eliot herself consciously exploits the text-textile analogy in *Silas Marner*, referring to the "tale" of cloth Silas weaves and letting Silas accuse William Dane of having "woven a plot" against him (*SM*, 1. 2, 1). For discussions of her more general use of webs, weaving, and spinning as metaphors, see Gilbert and Gubar, *The Madwoman in the Attic*, pp. 522–28; Reva Stump, *Movement and Vision in George Eliot's Novels* (Seattle, 1959), pp. 172–214; and J. Hillis Miller, "Optic and Semiotic in *Middlemarch*," in *The Worlds of Victorian Fiction*, ed. Jerome H. Buckley (Cambridge, Mass., 1975), 125–45. On Eliot's own tendency to avarice—an inclination that, at least in the view of Blackwood, her publisher, became problematic just at the time she was composing *Silas Marner*—see Lawrence Jay Dessner, "The

Autobiographical Matrix of *Silas Marner*," *Studies in the Novel*, 11 (Fall 1979), 258–59.

16. See Sherry B. Ortner, "Is Female to Male as Nature Is to Culture?," in *Women, Culture, and Society*, ed. Michelle Zimbalist Rosaldo and Louise Lamphere (Stanford, Calif., 1974), 67–87. In connection with Silas' "female" qualities, it is interesting that the villagers respond to his herbal knowledge by trying to make him take the place of "the Wise Woman," a role he at first vigorously resists (see *SM*, 1. 2).

17. Eliot, quoted in Haight, *George Eliot*, p. 336. U. C. Knoepflmacher has pointed out that Silas, like Shakespeare's Pericles, will become "another passive Job . . . redeemed through the miraculous gift of a daughter" (*George Eliot's Early Novels: The Limits of Reality* [Berkeley and Los Angeles, 1968], 229).

18. In a psychoanalytic study of Eliot's work, Laura Comer Emery points out "the connection of [Silas'] guineas" to a solipsistic "anality" (*George Eliot's Creative Conflict: The Other Side of Silence* [Berkeley and Los Angeles, 1976], 62, 63).

19. See Sigmund Freud's observation that, as the girl enters the Oedipal stage, her "libido slips into a new position by means—there is no other way of putting it—of the equation 'penis = child.' She gives up her wish for a penis and puts in place of it a wish for a child" ("Some Psychological Consequences of the Anatomical Distinction between the Sexes" [1925], trans. James Strachey, *Sexuality and the Psychology of Love*, ed. Philip Rieff [New York, 1963], p. 191). On the special qualities of a boy-child, see Nancy Chodorow, *The Reproduction of Mothering: Psychoanalysis and the Sociology of Gender* (Berkeley and Los Angeles, 1978), 107, 131–32.

20. See Claude Lévi-Strauss: "Even with regard to our own society, where marriage appears to be a contract between persons, . . . the relationship of reciprocity which is the basis of marriage is not established between men and women, but between men by means of women, who are merely the occasion of this relationship" (*The Elementary Structures of Kinship*, trans. James Harle Bell, John Richard von Sturmer, and Rodney Needham, ed. Needham [Boston, 1969], 115–166).

21. See Eliot, *A Writer's Notebook, 1854–1879, and Uncollected Writings*, ed. Joseph Wiesenfarth (Charlottesville, Va., 1981), p. 98, where Eliot looks at Grimm's law, which traces the evolution of *dhugh* into "daughter." The theme of the daughter as treasure is, in addition, one that Eliot might have picked up from Honoré de Balzac's *Eugénie Grandet* (1833), novel which treats the relationship of a miserly father and a "treasured" only daughter far more cynically than *Silas Marner* does; also, in an unpublished discussion of *Romola*, Robin Sheets has proposed to analyze this theme.

22. It is arguable that the very name "George Eliot" represents Marian Evans' own concern with this question. Unable legally to marry the man to whom she felt herself to be married, she still wanted, like a dutiful wife, to "take" his name. Since George Henry Lewes' surname was not available to her—his first "wife" had preempted it—she had to content herself with his Christian name. In this way, though she was ostensibly a lawbreaker, she was able symbolically to signal that even "so substantive and rare a creature" as Marian Evans had been properly (if only partially) "absorbed into the life of another," as, according to the laws of her society, every woman ought to be (Eliot, "Finale," *Middlemarch*, p. 894).

23. Emery cbserves that at the end of *Silas Marner* "it is almost as though Eppie and her father were being married" (*George Eliot's Creative Conflict*, p. 70). Similarly, Sadoff suggests that Eliot "portrays . . . daughterly desire as fabled fantasy in *Silas Marner* and *Felix Holt*," adding in a general analysis of the (father-daughter) "scene of seduction" that "the story the daughter relates about this scene, this moment in her history, symbolizes the emergence of her sexuality expressed as desire for her father and represents her attempt to solve this enigma of childhood history" (*Monsters of Affection*, pp. 78, 104). Although Sadoff cites an early, unpublished version of my "Life's Empty Pack" essay as making some of the same points she makes, we differ radically in our interpretation of the meaning that the female Oedipus complex has for Eliot and other culture-mothers. Sadoff takes as a given the "emergence" of female sexuality and its inevitable expression as "daughterly desire"; I am interested in the coercive cultural construction of "daughterly desire," a point Mitchell emphasizes when she remarks that "the father, so crucial for the development of femininity, and the men that follow him, so essential for the preservation of 'normal' womanhood, are only secondary figures, for pride of place as love-object is taken by the mother—for both sexes [so that] in a sense, the father is only second-best anyway" (*Psychoanalysis and Feminism* [New York, 1975], p. 111; all further references to this work, abbreviated *PF*, will be included in the text).

24. Haight, *George Eliot*, p. 49.

25. Eliot, "Brother and Sister," *The Poems of George Eliot* (New York, n.d.), pp. 356, 357.

26. James Joyce, *Ulysses* (New York, 1934), p. 205; on the significance of the name "Cass," see Knoepflmacher, *George Eliot's Early Novels*, p. 239.

27. Because of her metonymic as well as coincidental connection with the gold stolen by Godfrey Cass' brother Dunstan, Eppie represents the law in yet another way, reinforcing our sense that its curses as well as its blessings cannot be averted. The place in society that Silas' false brother, William *Dane*, stole from him is ironically restored to him through an act of theft perpetrated by Godfrey's false brother, *Dunstan* Cass. Though he has tried to flee culture on the horse Wildfire, moreover, Dunstan falls inexorably into the Stone-pits of damnation—the abyss the law has prepared for him. Similarly, his God-free brother, who tries to flee his cultural responsibility as father, loses not one but all children and inherits an empty house, a mere shell or box (a "case," so to speak) devoid of meaning because devoid both of sons who can carry on its name and daughters who can link it into society. Even his refusal to be his prodigal brother's keeper eventually brings about Godfrey's nemesis, for it is the discovery of Dunstan's skeleton in the Stone-pits that causes this rejecting father to make his rejected proposal to Eppie. In all these cases, essentially, the machinations of murderous brothers dramatize failures of just those Mosaic Laws of the Father which should make transactions between man and man both orderly and faithful.

28. Freud, "Female Sexuality" [1931], trans. Joan Riviere, *Sexuality and the Psychology of Love*, p. 195; all further references to this work, abbreviated "FS," will be included in the text.

29. According to Freud, the Oedipus complex means for the girl an attachment to the father which parallels the boy's attachment to his mother; but for the girl, her attachment to the father is a "positive" phenomenon that succeeds an earlier "negative" phase in which she experiences the same "first mother-attachment" that the boy feels. When the girl learns that her mother has not "given" her a penis, however—i.e., in Lacan's sense, that the mother has not given her the power represented by the "Phallus"—she turns in disgust and despair to the father, the one who has the phallus and may therefore be able to give her some of its power (see Freud, "FS," pp. 195, 199, and passim, and "Some Psychological Consequences of the Anatomical Distinction between the Sexes"). Interestingly, in this regard, Sadoff observes that a pattern of the displaced mother occurs throughout Eliot's novels and serves the story of father-daughter seduction" (*Monsters of Affection*, p. 69).

30. Observing that "a boy's repression of his Oedipal maternal attachment (and his preoedipal dependence) seems to be more complete than a girl's"—in part, no doubt, because the boy can look forward to a future in which he will "have" at least a figure of the mother, Chodorow quotes Alice Balint's assertion that "the amicable loosening of the bond between daughter and mother is one of the most difficult tasks of education" (*The Reproduction of Mothering*, p. 130.)

31. Aeschylus, *The Eumenides, The Oresteian Trilogy*, trans. Philip Vellacott (Harmondsworth, 1959), p. 169; this is Apollo's argument.

32. Hélène Cixous, "Sorties," trans. Ann Liddle, in *New French Feminisms: An Anthology*, ed. Elaine Marks and Isabelle de Courtivron (Amherst, Mass., 1980), p. 92.

33. Henry James to Wharton, Dec. 1912, quoted in Millicent Bell, *Edith Wharton and Henry James: The Story of Their Friendship* (New York, 1965), 274.

34. On the analogy between nature ("raw") and culture ("cooked"), see Lévi-Strauss, *Introduction to a Science of Mythology*, vol. 1, *The Raw and the Cooked* (New York, 1969).

35. Sylvia Plath, "The Colossus," *The Collected Poems*, ed. Ted Hughes (New York, 1981), p. 129; "The Beekeeper's Daughter," *Collected Poems*, p. 118; and see "Electra on Azalea Path," pp. 116–17.

36. Wharton, *Summer* [with an intro. by Cynthia Griffin Wolff] (New York, 1980), p. 44; all further references to this work, abbreviated *S*, will be included in the text.

37. See Maria Cummins, *The Lamplighter* (Boston, 1854); a major best-seller in its day, it tells the story of orphaned Gerty's daughterly devotion to the adoptive father, Trueman Flint, who rescued her from poverty and starvation. For a discussion of the book's appeal in its day, see Nina Baym, *Woman's Fiction: A guide to Novels by and about Women in America, 1820–1870* (Ithaca, N.Y., 1978), pp. 164–69.

38. Andrea Hammer's remark was made in an unpublished paper on *Summer*. Wolff notes that Charity Royall's feelings for Lucius Harney are "explicitly sexual" and her view of him "inescapably phallic" (intro. to *Summer*, p. xi).

39. It is possible that in recounting Charity's desire for Lucius Harney, Wharton is recording nostalgic details of her affair with Morton Fullerton (see R. W. B. Lewis, *Edith Wharton: A Biography* [New York, 1975], pp. 203–328). In addition, by implying that Charity at first experiences her passion for Lucius Harney as a desire for a brotherly equal, she may be meditating on Fullerton's long erotic relationship with his cousin Katherine, who had been brought up to believe she was his half-sister (see pp. 200–203). Further resonance might have been added to the relationship by the brother-sister romance of Siegmund and Sieglinde in Richard Wagner's *Die Walküre*, a work Wharton surely knew.

40. Wharton, "Beatrice Palmato," in Lewis, *Edith Wharton*, p. 548; and see pp. 544–48. For a related analysis of father-daughter incest in *Summer* and "Beatrice Palmato," see Elizabeth Ammons' suggestion that *Summer* is "Wharton's bluntest criticism of the patriarchal sexual economy" and her ensuing discussion of the two texts (*Edith Wharton's Argument and America* [Athens, Ga., 1980], p. 133; and see pp. 133–43). I agree with many points on Ammons' reading of *Summer* but do not believe that Wharton was consciously "criticizing" the "patriarchal sexual economy"; rather, like Eliot, she was transcribing a myth that nonjudgmentally (if painfully) "explains" woman's position in patriarchal culture.

41. Aeschylus, *The Eumenides*, p. 169; and see Lewis, *Edith Wharton*, p. 397.

42. Elizabeth Barrett Browning, *Aurora Leigh*, *"Aurora Leigh" and Other Poems* (London, 1978), bk. 1, l. 622–23, p. 57; Dickinson, *Complete Poems*, no. 722, p. 354. For a more general discussion of maternal images in the works of Barrett Browning, see Gilbert, "From *Patria* to *Matria*: Elizabeth Barrett Browning's *Risorgimento*," *PMLA* 99 (Mar. 1984): 194–211; for a discussion of Dickinson's use of such imagery, see Gilbert and Gubar, *The Madwoman in the Attic*, pp. 642–50.

43. Christiane Olivier, *Les Enfants de Jocaste: L'Empreinte de la mère* (Paris, 1980), p. 149; my translation ("Or dans [le miroir tendu par l'homme] la femme ne voit pas son image mais celle que l'homme a d'elle. Jocaste a imprime au coeur de l'homme sa trace indelebile car ce miroir ne contient que l'image d'une femme 'morte' ").

44. Helen Deutsch, *The Psychology of Women: A Psychoanalytic Interpretation*, 2 vols. (New York, 1944–45), 1:252.

45. In his essay "Fathers and Daughters," the psychoanalyst Joseph H. Smith makes a similar case for the inevitability of what I am calling "resignation" in women; see "Fathers and Daughters," *Man and World: An International Philosophical Review*, 13 (1980): esp. 391 and 395. For a different formulation of the same point, see Freud, "Analysis Terminable and Interminable" [1937], trans. Riviere, *Therapy and Technique*, ed. Rieff (New York, 1963), esp. pp. 268–71. Freud's n. 14, a quotation from Sandor Ferenczi, is particularly telling in this regard: "In every male patient the sign that his castration-anxiety has been mastered . . . is a sense of equality of rights with the analyst; and every female patient . . . must have . . . become able to *submit without bitterness* to thinking in terms of her feminine role" (p. 270 n. 14; italics mine).

46. Wharton, quoted in Wolff, intro. to *Summer*, p. xv.

47. Phyllis Chesler, "Rape and Psychotherapy," in *Rape: The First Sourcebook for Women*, ed. Noreen Connell and Cassandra Wilson (New York, 1974), p. 76; Judith Lewis Herman, with Lisa Hirschman, *Father-Daughter Incest* (Cambridge, Mass., 1981), p. 110.

48. Chodorow, *The Reproduction of Mothering*, p. 132. Chodorow also notes that "sociologist Robert Winch reports that marked attachment to the opposite gender parent retards courtship progress for male college students and accelerates it for females" (p. 133); thus, the father-daughter bond is actually "healthful" for women while the mother-son bond is "unhealthy" for men.

49. Deutsch, *The Psychology of Women*, 1:252.

50. Michael E. Lamb, Margaret Tresch Owen, and Lindsay Chase-Lansdale, "The Father-Daughter Relationship: Past, Present, and Future," in *Becoming Female: Perspectives on Development*, ed. Claire B. Kopp, in collaboration with Martha Kirkpatrick (New York, 1979), 94.

51. Herman, with Hirschman, *Father-Daughter Incest*, pp. 12, 87, 60, 61.

52. Sadoff, *Monsters of Affection*, p. 68.

53. O. Mannoni, *Freud*, trans. Renaud Bruce (New York, 1971), p. 45.

54. Freud to Wilhelm Fliess, 31 May 1897 (no. 64), *The Origins of Psycho-Analysis: Letters to Wilhelm Fliess, Drafts and Notes: 1887–1902*, ed. Marie Bonaparte, Anna Freud, and Ernst Kris, trans. Eric Mosbacher and Strachey (New York, 1977), p. 206.

55. Freud to Fliess, 3 Oct. 1897 (no. 70), *Origins*, p. 219; and see the dreams and memories reported on pp. 215–25.

56. Freud to Fliess, 21 Sept. 1897 (no. 69), *Origins*, pp. 215–16.

57. An article in *Newsweek* in 1981 reported interviews with a number of scholars who speculated, on the basis of recently discovered documents relating to the Freud family and unpublished portions of the letters to Fliess, that Freud's anxiety about his own father "prevented him from recognizing the primal guilt of Laius"—that is, of all fathers (David Gelman, "Finding the Hidden Freud," *Newsweek*, 30 Nov. 1981, p. 67; and see pp. 64–70).

58. As Kris points out in a footnote to the Fliess letters, Freud later observed that seduction "still retains a certain aetiological importance, and I still consider that some of the psychological views expressed [in the first theory] meet the case" (*Origins*, p. 271 n. 1). Herman declares that "Freud falsified his incest cases," that he named uncles instead of fathers as seducers in several instances, because he wanted to exercise "discretion" (*Father-Daughter Incest*, p. 9). The *Newsweek* article asserts that "in

unpublished passages of the Fliess letters [Freud] continued to describe cases of sexual brutality by fathers" ("Finding the Hidden Freud," p. 67). In a pioneering essay on this subject, Robert Seidenberg and Evangelos Papathomopoulos discuss the pressures put on late-Victorian daughters by ill or tyrannical fathers and the implications of those pressures for *Studies on Hysteria* (see "Daughters Who Tend Their Fathers: A Literary Survey," *Psychoanalytic Study of Society*, 2 [1962], esp. 135–39).

59. Seidenberg and Papathomopoulos, "Daughters Who Tend Their Fathers," p. 150. They observe, in addition, that "the word, *Kore*, is also used to designate the female figures who act as supports, the Caryatids of the Holy Temples" (p. 150).

60. Robert Graves, quoted in ibid., p. 151.

61. Percy Bysshe Shelley, *The Cenci*, *Poetical Works*, ed. Thomas Hutchinson (New York, 1967), act 5, sc. 4, 11. 60–61, p. 332. For discussions of Eliot's views of Antigone, see Gilbert and Gubar, *The Madwoman in the Attic*, p. 494, and Redinger, *George Eliot*, pp. 314–15 and 325; both these analyses emphasize the rebellious heroine of *Antigone*, but, significantly, Eliot had the eponymous heroine of *Romola* sit for a portrait of Antigone at Colonus—the dutiful daughter.

62. Adrienne Rich, "Sibling Mysteries," *The Dream of a Common Language: Poems, 1974–1977* (New York, 1978), p. 49.

63. "Allerleirauh," *The Complete Grimm's Fairy Tales*, trans. Margaret Hunt and James Stern, rev. ed. (New York, 1972), pp. 326–27; all further references to this work, abbreviated "A," will be included in the text.

64. In a brief discussion of this tale, Herman argues that "Allerleirauh" is a version of "Cinderella"; see *Father-Daughter Incest*, p. 2. Even more interestingly, the folklorist Alan Dundes argues a connection between the plot of this story ("tale type 923, Love Like Salt"), "Cinderella," and *King Lear*, although he claims—as perhaps Sadoff would—that this basic plot functions as "*a projection of incestuous desires on the part of the daughter*" (" 'To Love My Father All': A Psychoanalytic Study of the Folktale Source of *King Lear*," *Southern Folklore Quarterly*, 40 [Sept.–Dec. 1976]: 355, 360; italics his).

65. Psychologically speaking, in fact, Allerleirauh's flight could even be compared to the seizures of hysteria suffered by so many of Freud's and Josef Breuer's patients, daddy's girls who sought to escape the imprisonment of the father by rejecting not only the modes and manners but also the language of "his" culture and speaking instead through a more "natural" body language.

66. To be sure, in, e.g., *Romola* and *Middlemarch* and in, e.g., *The Age of Innocence*, Eliot and Wharton, respectively, embed fantasies of female, and sometimes even matriarchal autonomy, fantasies which clearly function as covertly compensatory gestures toward liberation from the father-daughter scripts elaborated in works like *Silas Marner* and *Summer*.

29

Gayatri Chakravorty Spivak 1942–

Born in Calcutta, Gayatri Chakravorty Spivak taught at the Universities of Iowa and Texas before assuming her current position at the University of Pittsburgh. Known for her feminist and Marxist perspectives, she has been instrumental in extracting the issues contained under the rubric "marginality" and bringing them to the forefront of critical discussion. Spivak translated Jacques Derrida's *Of Grammatology* (1976), and she has recently published a collection of critical essays entitled *In Other Worlds: Essays in Cultural Politics* (1987).

In "Imperialism and Sexual Difference," Spivak identifies the cultural norm of white maleness as a political trope. She argues, however, that whatever is taken as the "norm" is never neutral or universal, but rather governed by the specific requirements and limitations of a particular class or society. Thus feminism, she suggests, has begun to take Western, postromantic experiences as the "norm" of female experience. Spivak recognizes that the refusal to make the fundamental connections between "imperialistic disciplinary practice" and feminism constitutes a dangerous blindness, and so she considers a proposal for elucidating the problems inherent in the intersection of imperialism and feminism. She alerts feminist criticism to the self-blinding that occurs when it mistakes a trope for truth and defines itself against the political trope "sanctioned" by imperialism. In this essay, Spivak works toward a critical strategy that will effectively evaluate imperialism and hold it accountable for its assignations of marginality.

Imperialism and Sexual Difference

Feminist criticism can be a force in changing the discipline. To do so, however, it must recognize that it is complicitous with the institution within which it seeks its space. That slow labour might transform it from opposition to critique.

Let me describe a certain area of this complicity in a theoretical and a historical way:

My theoretical model is taken from Paul de Man. De Man suggests that a critical philosopher initially discovers that the basis of a truth claim is no more than a trope. In the case of academic feminism the discovery is that to take the privileged male of the white race as a norm for universal humanity is no more than a politically interested figuration. It is a trope that passes itself off as truth, and claims that woman or the racial other is merely a kind of troping of that truth of man—in the sense that they must be understood *as* unlike (non-identical with) it and yet *with* reference to it. In so far as it participates in this discovery, even the most "essentialist" feminism or race-analysis is engaged in a tropological deconstruction.[1] De Man goes on to suggest, however, that even as it establishes the truth of this discovery, the critical philosopher's text begins to perform the problems inherent in the very institution of epistemological production, of the production, in other words, of any "truth" at all. By this logic, varieties of feminist theory and practice must reckon with the possibility that, like any other discursive practice, they are marked and constituted by, even as they constitute, the field of their production. If much of what I write here seems to apply as much to the general operations of imperialist disciplinary practice as to feminism, it is because I wish to point at the dangers of not acknowledging the connections between the two.

(These problems—that "truths" can only be shored up by strategic exclusions, by declaring opposition where there is complicity, by denying the possibility of randomness, by proclaiming a provisional origin or point of departure as ground—are the substance of deconstructive concerns. The price of the insight into the tropological nature of a truth-claim is the blindness of truth-telling.)[2]

My historical caveat is, in sum, that feminism within the social relations and institutions of the metropolis has something like a relationship with the fight for individualism in the upwardly class-mobile bourgeois cultural politics of the European nineteenth century. Thus, even as we feminist critics discover the troping error of the masculist truth-claim to universality or academic objectivity, we perform the lie of constituting a truth of global sisterhood where the mesmerizing model remains male and female sparring partners of generalizable or universalizable sexuality who are the chief protagonists in that European contest. In order to claim sexual difference where it makes a difference, global sisterhood must receive this articulation even if the sisters in question are Asian, African, Arab.[3]

I will attempt to consolidate my general points by way of readings of three masculist texts: *Le cygne* by Baudelaire, "William the Conqueror" by Kipling, and a discussion paper laid before a secret meeting of the Court of Directors of the East India Company. The first two—a lyric of justly celebrated subtlety and a "popular" narrative of imperialist sentiments—can both be made to offer us a mirror of our performance of certain imperialist ideological structures even as we deconstruct the tropological error of masculism. The third, mere minutes of a meeting, shows the affinity between those structures and some of racism's crude presuppositions.

Baudelaire's stunning poem begins "*Andromaque, je pense à vous*" (Andromache, I think of you). The poet transforms the "truth" of the memory of a cityscape to the allegorical troping of literary history and a metaphor for his consuming melancholy. The woman in the case, Queen Andromache, is no more than the poet's object, not only brought forth into textual existence by the magisterial "I think of you," not only celebrated as Homer's good heroine beside the erring Helen, not only used to establish the classic continuity of the brotherhood of European poetry—celebrating women from Homer through Virgil and Racine now to Baudelaire—but utilized thus by way of the careful invocation of a woman mourning a husband. As if this is not enough, the boldly obvious pun in the title (in French *cygne* sounds like both sign and swan) gives her the status of sign rather than subject from the very start. Yet this emptying out—by phonocentric convention a sign means something other than itself whereas a person is self-proximate, even self-identical—is accompanied by the usual gestures of hyperbolic admiration. By the time the "real" swan appears, its figuration as sign is not secure precisely because the word *cygne* happens, properly or literally, to mean swan. It is as if, by being the sign of the poet's prowess, Queen Andromache is more of a swan than the swan itself. It now begins to seem possible that, in the world of Baudelaire's poem, sign-status is not necessarily less fortunate than person-status, or indeed that, in *Le cygne*, personhood might not be operated by the laws of everyday phonocentrism—the privileging of voice-consciousness over any system of mere signs.[4] Yet, as I have argued elsewhere, at whatever remove from phonocentrism we throw the dice, and however phonocentrism is critiqued, the ontic differential between the poet-operating-as-controlling-subject and the woman-manipulated-as-sign will not disappear.[5]

Once this is granted, we are free to notice the power of Andromache within the syntactic and metaphoric logic of the poem. The memory of the real city (given in the simple declarative of reportage) is put under the spell of the reflection of the mythic Andromache (metonymically represented by her griefs) in the false river of her own tears (a quadruple representation) by the force of the *jadis* (once), repeated strategically:

Ce petit fleuve,
Pauvre et triste miroir où jadis resplendit
L'immense majesté de vos douleures de veuve

(That narrow stream, poor and sad mirror that *once* resplended with the immense majesty of your window's grief)[6]

l. 1–3; emphasis mine

and, "Là s'étalait *jadis* une ménagerie" (a menagerie once sprawled just there; 1. 13; emphasis mine). If Andromache is forever present in every reading of the poem by the poet's magisterial act of thought, the real swan, as it is introduced after the spell-binding *jadis,* is controlled by the absolute past, stronger than the preterite in English: "je vis" (I saw; l. 14).

Thus Andromache is the condition of the emergence of the image of the swan. But she is also its effect, for when the poet most specifies her by her kinship inscriptions, she is compared metonymically to the swan in the words "vil bétail" (vile cattle; the word has connotations of breeding-cattle which would relate interestingly in making Andromache the condition and effect of the fertilization of Baudelaire's memory as well.)

Unlike the description of the predicament of the Woman as Queen in the Great Tradition, that of the poet's predicament is not made to shuttle rhetorically between the status of condition and effect. Lines 29–33 ("Paris change . . . une image m'opprime"—Paris is changing . . .an image oppresses me) stand on their own. In fact we cannot be sure what image oppresses the poet; he keeps the secret. The delicate paratactic gesture of the colon with which the next movement opens: "Je pense à mon grand cygne" (I think of my grand swan, 1. 34) certainly draws the reader into thinking that the image is that of the swan. But is it not possible that this obsessed, oppressed, and melancholic speaker should turn to a dear memory to escape from the oppression of an image? Certainly a T. S. Eliot would claim affinity with Baudelaire on the issue of an "escape from personality" into "a medium . . . in which impressions and experiences combine in peculiar and unexpected ways."[7] Since parataxis, even more than the rhetorical question, will allow this indeterminacy, it seems fair to expect the deliberate syntactic logic of the poem to harbour it.

The point I am making, then, is that, whatever the spectacular manipulative mechanics of Andromache as fertilizer might be, in *Le cygne* the poet-speaker retains a syntactically impregnable house and a rhetorically enigmatic "subjectivity."

At the end of the poem, the "à" (of) of "penser à" (think of) seems to change function and become a dedicatory "to" toward many crowded lonely people until the text seems to disappear in the vague inconsequence of "bien d'autres encor" (and many others). Although Andromache does not appear, her singular control (as a memory-sign framed by the poet's apostrophe) over the production of the poem is reasserted by force of contrast. She remains the only "thou" in the poem. But she is also caught in the second person of the only apostrophe which is not quite one: "I *think* of you." The poet's self-deconstruction is made possible by the metaphor of the powerful woman.

This is the outline of a reading that shows that not only the power but even the self-undermining of the man may be operated by the troping of the woman. I considered it an important moment in my education when I learned to read the homoerotic Great Tradition in this way.[8] I thought it a not insignificant supplement to theorizing about feminine subjectivity and retrieving woman as object of investigation, two more justifiably important activities within feminist literary criticism in the U.S. The price of learning such a tropological deconstruction of masculism, however, was the performance of a blindness to the other woman in the text.

Introducing the list of nameless people at the end of the poem, there stands a nameless woman moving her feet in the mud, who is distinguished by nothing but colour, a derisive name for her ethnicity: "Je pense à la négresse" (I think of the negress, l. 42).[9] Here the object of thought is clearly in the third person. Indeed, this blurred figure with her fixed and haggard eye is almost "naturalized" or "de-personified." (By contrast, the "natural" swan, looking up as, per Ovid, only man does, may be seen as "personified.") The negress is an image not of semiosis but of what de Man has called "the stutter, the piétinement" (her only named action in the poem) "of aimless enumeration."[10] The swan is gifted with speech. "Eau, quand donc pleuvras-tu? quand tonneras-tu, foudre?" (O water, when will you rain down? O lightning, when will you rage? l. 23–24) the poet had heard him say. This woman is mute. Andromache begins the poem and usurps the first half of the second section, which Baudelaire brings to an end by addressing her again by name, and specifying her, through intricate echoes of Virgil, as Hector's widow and Helenus' wife. Her geography is not only implicit in her history. In a metaphoric gender-switch, the *false* river Simois created by her tears had, to begin with, fertilized his memory of the intricate cartography of the changeful city of Paris, itself implausibly shadowed by the name of Homer's hero: "Ce Simois menteur qui par vos pleurs grandit,/ A fécondé soudain ma mémoire fertile memory, l. 4–5). Against all this labyrinthine specificity and exchange between male and female is juxtaposed the immense vagueness of the negress' geography, etched in no more than three words: "la superbe Afrique" (superb Africa, l. 44).
words: "la superbe Afrique" (superb Africa, l. 44).

Indeed, if Andromache is the over-specified condition of emergence of the title-image (the swan), the only possible function of the negress would be to mark the indeterminate moment when specificity is dissolved at the poem's end.

In the longer work of which this essay is a part, I have developed the idea of reading by interception of the text as it flies from implied sender to implied receiver by animating the perspective of the "native informant," roughly as follows:

The clearing of a subject-position in order to speak or write is unavoidable. One way to reckon with this bind is an interminable preoccupation with the (autobiographical) self. If we are interested in a third-worldist criticism, however, we might want to acknowledge that access to autobiography, for whole groups of people, has only been possible through the dominant mediation of an investigator or field-worker. The "autobiographies" of such people have not entered the post-Enlightenment European "subjective" tradition of autobiography. They have gone, rather, to provide "objective evidence" for the "sciences" of anthropology and ethnolinguistics. "Oral history," coming of age in the sixties, tried to efface or at least minimize the role of the investigator. Much third-worldist feminist work has taken on this task of the effacement of the investigator in works typically entitled—"Women Speak." This brief account reveals the various alibis that the dominant subject-position gives itself as it constructs the subordinate as other. The curious "objectified" subject-position of this other is what, following the language of anthropology and linguistics, I call the position of the "native informant." In order to produce a critique of imperialism, I suggest the invention of a reading-subject's perspective that would occupy or cathect the representative space or blank presupposed by the dominant text. The space will remain specific to the dominant text which presupposes it and yet, since this is not a space of the critic's autobiography as a marginal, it must be foregrounded as a historically representative space. The other must always be constituted by way of consolidating the self. This method will at least make the problems visible, and the efforts at hedging the problems provisionally accessible to the reader.

Such a reading is, strictly speaking, inappropriate to the text. Yet deconstructive approaches have been suggesting for the last two decades that every reading is an upheaval para-sitical to the text.[11] Here, I use the resources of deconstruction "in the service of reading" to develop a strategy rather than a theory of reading that might be a critique of imperialism.

If to develop such a perspective we look at the naming of the negress as negress, we uncover a curious tale. She might of course "be" Jeanne Duval, Baudelaire's famous Afro-European mistress. But there is another, textual, clue as well. Lines 41–44 of *Le cygne* uses two lines from another poem by Baudelaire titled *A une malabaraise* (To A Malabar Woman):[12] "L'oeil pensif, et suivant, dans nos sales brouillards,/ Des cocotiers absents les fantomes épars" (Eyes pensive, pursuing in our dirty fogs, the vanished ghosts of absent palm trees, l. 27–28). The "original" of the negress in *Le cygne* is a textual palimpsest of the "original" of the agonist of *A une malabaraise*, one of two women Baudelaire encountered in Mauritius and the island of Réunion respectively. Who are these "malabarians"?

Malabar is the name of the southernmost stretch of the south-west coast of India. The islands of Mauritius and Réunion, terrains of military colonial exchange between France and Britain, have a sizeable population of Indian origin as a result of the British import of Indian indentured labour. These people are not necessarily, not even largely, from India's Malabar coast. Their naming is like "American Indian" or "turkey cock," products of hegemonic false cartography. At the time of Baudelaire's writing, the treatment of these unfortunate people was so harsh by the French colonists, that the British imperial authorities finally prohibited further emigration of labourers from India (1882). It is this vague woman, encountered on either one of the two colonial possessions, mis-named by white convention, that Baudelaire shifts and mis-places, for the poem's exigency, on an imagined native place as generalized as "Africa."

Under the principles of New Criticism, it is not permitted to introduce such "extraneous" considerations into a reading of the poem. Some deconstructive readings allow us to see the writing of a life (auto-bio-graphy) as a text imbricated in the production of literature or the discourse of the human sciences.[13] I am using that permission to suggest here that, whereas Baudelaire, inscribing himself as poet within the tradition of European poetry, is meticulous about the specificity of that tradition, the inscription of himself as an admirer of negresses can only be deciphered by guesswork outside of the boundaries of the poem. It is seemingly irrelevant to the poem's proper functioning. And it is mired in a conventionally sanctioned carelessness about identities. I am suggesting further that, if we recognize the lineaments of domination in the first case and ignore the foreclosure of the second, we are, in part, Baudelaire's accomplice.

Indeed, there are at least three ways of ignoring the inscription of the "negress." First, by asserting, as did a U.S. woman student in my class, that perhaps Baudelaire meant to focus on her predicament as being exiled without history and geography. Lisa Jardine has correctly described this as "recovering some concealed radical message from ostensibly reactionary writing."[14] Secondly, by bringing in precisely the details about Jeanne Duval or the elusive *malabaraise*, without attending to the way the negress is displayed in the poem. Thirdly, and this troubles me most, by suggesting as Edward Ahearn has done, that the negress is somehow Baudelaire's dark double.[15] These readings, as they deconstruct an error, themselves perform a lie.

There is an element of chance in these three texts being put together in one essay. I discovered the scandal in Baudelaire's poem because I wanted to teach some Baudelaire (because Walter Benjamin had written on him) in a course combining theory and history in practical criticism; one could not bypass reactions to the age of revolution. The story by Kipling I discovered in a volume loaned by a white but politically correct South African friend in response to a desperate need for bedtime reading; there was a certain historical irony in *The Penguin Book of English Short Stories* passing between a South African and an Indian as a text to lull her into sleep. The East India Company minutes I found at the India Office Library in London while "looking for something else." What was striking to me was that in such a random trio of texts I should find the double standard that troubles me under the auspices of feminist literary criticism in my workplace.

Writing in the 1890s, Kipling is attempting to create a species of New Woman in his short story "William the Conqueror"; and, in the attempt, he reveals most of the shortcomings of a benevolent masculism.[16] William is the name of the female protagonist. By implying archly that her conquest of the heart of the male protagonist is to be compared to the Norman Conquest of England, is Kipling producing a proleptic parody of "the personal is political"? We cannot know. If, however, in pondering this trivial question we overlook the fact that, under cover of the romance, the conquest of India is being effaced and re-inscribed as a historically appropriate event rather than anything that could in fact be called a "conquest," we are, once again, applying the double standard.

Kipling's New Woman is distinctly unbeautiful. "Her face was white as bone, and in the centre of her forehead was a big silvery scar the size of a shilling—the mark of a Delhi sore."[17] She does the most unfeminine thing of travelling by dreadful train across horrid India in the company of men to tend the poor bestial Indians in the throes of the Madras famine of 1876–78. I think Kipling is ironic (again, somewhat archly, but that is his tone) about the traffic in British girls in the colonies. In recompense, to treat "William" differently, he makes her almost a man. She "look[s] more like a boy than ever" (WC, 229), and her brother admits that "she's as clever as a man, confound her" (WC, 235). In the end, however, Kipling shows that a woman's a woman for all that, and she conquers, as women will, through love. "Life with men who had a great deal of work to do, and very little time to do it in, had taught her the wisdom of effacing as well as of fending for herself" (WC 236). And she nurtures sentiments appropriate to a true "men's woman": "That [to make fun of a girl]'s different. . . . She was only a girl, and she hadn't done anything except walk like a quail, and she *does*. But it isn't fair to make fun of a man" (WC, 257).

Kipling does not write about sexual difference subtly. I will point at one more detail to indicate the kind of function it performs in his text. In the interest of creating a "different" kind of romance, Kipling gives to his hero some soft and "feminine" qualities. The protagonists come together in love when he teaches her how to milk goats to feed starving Indian babies. But this possible effeminacy is forestalled by a proper objective correlative from classical pastoral with Biblical overtones: "One waiting at the tent door behind, with new eyes, a young man, beautiful as Paris, a god in a halo of golden dust, walking slowly at the head of his flocks, while at his knee ran small naked Cupids" (WC, 249). Before we dismiss this as Victorian kitsch—some critics find the passage admirable—we should note that this is the story's icon for imperialism *in loco parentis*.[18] That is made painfully clear a few pages later: "She dreamed for the twentieth time of the god in the golden dust, and woke refreshed to feed loathsome black children" (WC, 261; "Kipling's attitude to children, with its special tenderness and understanding . . .");[19] at any rate, love flourishes and, at the end of the story, at the noble festival of Christmas, "drawing closer to Scott . . . it was William who wiped her eyes," even as some men of the Club sang "Glad tidings of great joy I bring/To you and all mankind" (WC, 274). It is one of the clichés of imperialism that the settlement of the colonies is part of these glad tidings.

There is a lot of self-conscious "local colour" in the story. At first glance, then, it might seem as if the complaint about Baudelaire, that he denies the negress her proper and specific space, cannot be entertained here. And it is of course correct that Kipling is a chronicler of "Indian life." Let us therefore pause a moment on Kipling's technique of specifying India.[20]

"Is it officially declared yet?" are the first words of the text. Narrative logic throws a good deal of weight on the answer to this question. Indeed, the first movement of narrative energy in "William the Conqueror" seems to be a demonstration of how an affirmative answer to this question might be shaped. Slowly the reader comes to sense that the "it" in question is the precise descriptive substantive: Famine, and that the affirmative answer to the initial question is in a shape of benevolent imperialism: "the operation of the Famine Code" (WC, 223): the exasperated yet heroic British tending the incompetent, unreasonable, and childish south Indians. The panoramic heterogeneity of the people and landscape of southern India is offered in declaration of and apposition to the monolithic rubric: Famine.

The narrative purpose of "Famine"—

the container of the specificity of south India—is instrumental. When it has served to promote love between the two human (that is, British) actors, the rubric is dissolved, the declaration undone: "And so Love ran about the camp unrebuked in broad daylight, while men picked up the pieces and put them neatly away of the Famine in the Eight Districts" (WC, 204).

The action moves back to Northwest India, where it began. Here is an account of that move:

> The large open names of the home towns were good to listen to. Umballa, Ludhiana, Phillour, Jullundur, they rang like marriage bells in her ears, and William felt deeply and truly sorry for all strangers and outsiders—visitors, tourists, and those fresh-caught for the service of the country (WC, 273).

These sonorous place-names are in Punjab. We have left Madras behind as we have left "Famine" behind. The mention of "home" and "outside" is not a specification of India at all, but rather the disappearance of India if defined as the habitation of Indians. The description of William and Scott's "homecoming" to the North leaves the distinct impression that the North is more British—India has receded here. This is how the roll of names I quote above is introduced:

> The South of Pagodas and palm-trees, the over-populated Hindu South, was done with. Here was the land she knew, and before her lay the good life she understood, among folk of her own caste and mind. They were picking them up at almost every station now—men and women coming in for the Christmas Week, with racquets, with fox-terriers and saddles. . . . Scott would stroll up to William's window, and murmur: "Good enough, isn't it?" and William would answer with sighs of pure delight: "Good enough, indeed" (WC, 272).

Thus the incantation of the names, far from being a composition of place, is precisely the combination of effacement of specificity and appropriation that one might call violation. It starts early on in a benign way, as we encounter the hero putting on evening clothes: "Scott moved leisurely to his room, and changed into *the evening-dress of the season and the country*; spotless white linen from head to foot, with a broad silk cummerbund" (WC, 225; italics mine). "The dress of the season and country" sutures nature and culture and inscribes nature appropriately. Thus "home" and "outside" become terms of a distinction between the old and the new British in India. The words "Punjabi" and "Madrassi" are consistently used for the British who "serve" in those parts of India. The word "native," which is supposed to mean "autochthonous," is paradoxically re-inscribed as an unindividuated para-humanity that cannot aspire to a proper habitation.

Kipling uses many Hindusthani words in his text—pidgin Hindusthani, barbaric to the native speaker, devoid of syntactic connections, always infelicitous, almost always incorrect. The narrative practice sanctions this usage and establishes it as "correct," without, of course, any translation. This is British pidgin, originating in a decision that Hindusthani is a language of servants not worth mastering "correctly"; this is the version of the language that is established textually as "correct." By contrast, the Hindusthani speech of the Indian servants is painstakingly translated into archaic and awkward English. The servants' occasional forays into English are mocked in phonetic transcription. Let us call this ensemble of moves—in effect a mark of perceiving a language as subordinate—translation-as-violation. And let us contrast this to a high European moment in the discussion of translation as such.

Walter Benjamin wrote as follows on the topic of translation from classical Greek into German: "Instead of making itself similar to the meaning . . . the translation must rather, lovingly and in detail, in its own language, form itself according to the manner of meaning in the original, to make both recognizable as broken parts of the greater language." This passage quite logically assumes that the language one translates from is structurally the language of authority rather than subordination. Commenting on this passage de Man writes:

> The faithful translation, which is always literal, how can it also be free? It can only be free if it reveals the instability of the original, and if it reveals that instability as the linguistic tension between trope and meaning. Pure language is perhaps more present in the translation than in the original, but in the mode of trope.[21]

The distant model of this magisterial discourse on translation is the European Renaissance, when a tremendous activity of translation from texts of classical antiquity helped shape hegemonic Europe's image of itself. (German cultural self-representation, in the eighteenth and nineteenth centuries, of non-participation in the Renaissance, gives the specifically German speculations on the problem of translation a particular poignancy.) When, however, the violence of imperialism straddles a subject-language, translation can become a species of violation. Freedom-in-troping arguments from the European Renaissance do not apply to the translation-as-violation in Kipling's text.

I have been arguing that the tropological deconstruction of masculism does not exempt us from performing the lie of imperialism. The last time I taught "William the Conqueror," I included David Arnold's recent essay on the Madras famine as required reading. (Some of the documentation provided in the essay puts the noble-whites-helping-incompetent-blacks scenario into question.)[22] The class was taken up by the analysis of the taming-of-the-tomboy routine between the two white protagonists. Toward the end of the hour I deflected the discussion to a moment in Arnold's essay, which quotes a Tamil sexual-role-reversal doggerel sung by peasant women to make the drought end: "A wonder has taken place, O Lord! The male is grinding millet and the female is ploughing fields./Is not your heart moved with pity, O God!/ The widow Brahmani is ploughing the field."[23] In order to think of this folk-ritual as potentially efficacious and evocative of chaos in an ordered universe, the women must, of course, have taken seriously a patriarchal division of sexual labour. What little time was left in the class was taken up with a young woman's insistence that the peasant women must have been singing the doggerel ironically. In the total ignorance of history and subject-constitution, this insistence on a post-romantic concept of irony no doubt sprang from the imposition of her own historical and voluntarist constitution within the second wave of U.S. academic feminism as a "universal" model of the "natural" reactions of the female psyche.[24] This too is an example of translation-as-violation.

The structure of translation-as-violation describes certain tendencies within third-worldist literary pedagogy more directly. It is of course part of my general argument that, unless third-worldist feminist criticism develops a vigilance against such tendencies, it cannot help but participate in them. As follows:

Our own mania for "third world literature" anthologies, when the teacher or critic often has no sense of the original languages, or of the subject-constitution of the social and gendered agents in question (and therefore the student cannot sense this as a loss), participates more in the logic of translation-as-violation than in the ideal of translation as freedom-in-troping. What is at play there is a phenomenon that can be called "sanctioned ignorance."

Let us look briefly at the document from the East India Company. (Although a commercial company, between the end of the eighteenth and the middle of the nineteenth centuries, the East India Company governed its possessions in India. We are therefore reading about the employment of Indians in their own government.) The language here is so explicit that not much analytical effort is required. Let me tabulate the points I would emphasize. This document reflects an attempt, in the interests of efficiency, to revise racial discrimination based on chromatism, the visible difference in skin colour. (Chromatism seems to me to have something like a hold on the official philosophy of U.S. anti-racist feminism. When it is not "third world women," the buzz-word is "women of colour." This leads to absurdities. Japanese women, for instance, have to be re-defined as "third world." Hispanics must be seen as "women of colour." And post-colonial female subjects, women of the indigenous elite of Asia, Africa, Arabia, obvious examples of the production of Ariel—if Prospero is the imperial master—are invited to masquerade as Caliban in the margins.)[25]

The standards being applied in the document to legitimate racial discrimination show that both the native male and the native female are clearly inferior to the European female. Indeed, as in "William the Conqueror" and the classroom reaction to it, sexual difference comes into play only in the white arena. The concept of legitimacy in the union of the sexes only comes into being with the introduction of the European. And, even as Caliban is defined out, it is only the produced Ariel who is allowed into the arena; the final requirement for the acceptable half-caste is a "European liberal education."

Here, then, are extracts from the document itself:

> The chairman laid before [a Secret Court of the Directors of the Hon'ble Company Held on 6th March, 1822] a Paper signed by Himself and the Deputy Chairman submitting several suggestions in view to an exposition and practical illustration of the Standing Order of 1791 which provides "That no person the son of a Native Indian shall be appointed to employment in the Civil, Military, or Marine Service of the Company."[26]

Here are the passages on chromatism and the acceptability of the European female:

> It may be *fairly* deduced, that the *complexion* of those Persons was in view of the Court a serious objection to their admission. . . . The next object of consideration is the offspring of a connection between a European and a half-caste; and *it appears a matter of indifference whether the European blood be on the Male or the Female side.* The Candidates for admission to the Company's service, who have been of this class of persons, have since 1791 been subjected to the examination of one of the Committees of the Direction; and if they have exhibited signs of Native origin in their colour or otherwise, have been accepted or rejected by the Committee according to the degree in which their hue appeared objectionable or unobjectionable. These rejections . . . have produced some anomalies. One Brother has been accepted, another rejected. Europeans whose parents were both European, have been on the brink of Rejection for their dark complexion. . . . Discrepancies have arisen from the different views entertained by the Committee (italics mine).

In the interest of the efficient management of these anomalies and absurdities, the following criteria are offered. Here we will encounter native intercourse implicitly placed outside of legitimacy as such; and the clinching requirement of a "European liberal education":

> It is submitted
> That the Sons of aboriginal Natives of India and of the Countries to the Eastward of

> Native Portugese Indians, of Native West Indians, and of Africans of either sex, who are the Offspring of a connection of such Natives with Europeans, be invariably held ineligible. . . . That the Descendants from aboriginal Native Indians in the second and succeeding generations shall be held eligible . . . on production of certain Certificates . . . that the grandfather or grandmother of the Candidate . . . was bona fide an European . . . that the father or mother of the Candidate was bona fide an European. A Certificate of Marriage of the father and mother of the candidate. The Baptismal Certificate of the Candidate. A certificate from the Master or Masters of some reputable seminary or seminaries in the United Kingdom of Great Britain and Ireland that the Candidate has had the benefit of a liberal Education under his or her tuition for a period of six years. . . . The inconveniences which might arise from the indiscriminate or unconditional admission into the Company's service of the Descendants of aboriginal Native Indians in the second or succeeding generations will be obviated . . . by the stipulated qualification of *legitimate birth* and liberal European education (italics mine).

To repeat, this distasteful document describes the efficient articulation of the right of access to a white world administering the black. Because I think that this point cannot be too strongly made, I have put it forth as Exhibit C in my argument that much so-called cross-cultural disciplinary practice, even when "feminist," reproduces and forecloses colonialist structures: sanctioned ignorance, and a refusal of subject-status and therefore "human"-ness; that an unexamined chromatism is not only no solution but belongs to the repertory of colonialist axiomatics. On the face of it, the document seems infinitely more brutal and malevolent than anything that might happen in the house of feminist criticism. But mere benevolence will not remove the possibility that the *structural* effect of limited access to the norm can be shared by two such disparate phenomena.

When versions of my general argument are presented to academic Women's Resource Groups and the like, sympathy seems instantaneous. Yet, because of the presence of the double standard, the difference in the quality or level of generosity of discourse and allocation that engage the First and the Third Worlds remains striking. This discrepancy is also to be observed within curricular planning. In the distribution of resources, feminist literary criticism celebrates the heroines of the First World in a singular and individualist, and the collective presence of women elsewhere in a pluralized and inchoate fashion. These tendencies are not covered over by our campus battles for affirmative action on behalf of "women of colour." Such battles should, of course, be fought with our full participation. But they are ad hoc sexist activities that should be distinguished from a specifically "feminist" enterprise. In the absence of persistent vigilance, there is no guarantee that an upwardly mobile woman of colour in the U.S. academy would not participate in the structure I have outlined—at least to the extent of conflating the problems of ethnic domination in the United States with the problem of exploitation across the international division of labour; just as many in Britain tend to confuse it with problems of Immigration Law.[27] It may be painful to reckon that this, too, is a case of the certified half-caste's limited access to the norm. It is almost as if the problem of racism within feminism can qualify as such only when resident or aspiring to be resident in the First World.

Indeed, those of us who ask for these standards are becoming marginalized or tokenized within mainstream feminism. We are deeply interested in the tropological deconstruction of masculist universalism. But when questions of the inscription of feminine subject-effects arise we do not want to be caught within the institutional performance of the imperialist lie. We know the "correction" of a performative deconstruction is to point at another troping, and thus to another errant performance, that the critique must be persistent. We want the chance of an entry into the vertiginous process. And this can perhaps begin to happen if, in terms of disciplinary standards, you grant the thoroughly stratified larger theatre of the Third World, the stage of so-called de-colonization, equal rights of historical, geographical, linguistic specificity and theoretical sophistication.

NOTES

I am grateful to David Bathrick for a critical reading of the manuscript.

1. For a handy definition of essentialism, see Barry Hindess and Paul Q. Hirst, *Pre-capitalist Modes of Production* (London: Routledge, 1975), 9; for a discussion of essentialism in the feminist context, see Toril Moi, *Sexual/Textual Politics: Feminist Literary Theory* (New York: Methuen, 1985), 154 and passim. For a brief critique, see Spivak, "Criticism, Feminism and the Institution," *Thesis Eleven*, 10/11 (1984–95).

2. The references to these concerns are to be found pervasively in Paul de Man's later and Jacques Derrida's earlier work. For specific references, see de Man, *Allegories of Reading: Figural Language in Rousseau, Nietzsche, Rilke, and Proust* (New Haven: Yale University Press, 1979), 205, 208–9, 236, 253; and Derrida, "Limited inc: abc," *Glyph* 2 (1977). For a practical reconsideration, see Spivak, "Sex and History in *The Prelude* (1805), Books Nine to Thirteen," *TSLL* 23: 3 (Fall, 1981), 325.

3. Because the Latin American countries have had a more direct and long-standing relationship with U.S. imperialis, the relationship and demands are more informed and specific even when oppressive.

4. For the dubious value of the truth of personhood in Baudelaire, see Paul de Man, *Blindness and Insight: Essays in the Rhetoric of Contemporary Criticism* (2nd ed., Minneapolis: University of Minnesota Press, 1983), 35 and *The Rhetoric of Romanticism* (New York: Columbia University Press, 1984), 243.

5. See Spivak, "Displacement and the Discourse of Woman," in *Displacement: Derrida and After*, ed. Mark Krupnick (Bloomington: Indiana University Press, 1983), 184–186.

6. Charles Baudelaire, *Baudelaire*, trans. Francis Scarfe (Baltimore: Penguin, 1961), 209. I have modified the translation when necessary and indicated line numbers in the text.

7. T. S. Eliot, "Tradition and the Individual Talent," in *the Sacred Wood: Essays On Poetry and Criticism*, 7th ed. (London: Methuen, 1967), 58, 56.

8. For a more extensive account of this, see Spivak, "Finding Feminist Readings: Dante-Yeats," in *American Criticism in the Poststructuralist Age*, ed. Ira Konigsberg (Ann Arbor: University of Michigan Press, 1981).

9. I will consider later the question of Jeanne Duval, Baudelaire's Afro-European mistress. Here let me say that I am concerned with the deployment of the figure of the negress in the text. Of Duval, Baudelaire had written in his suicide note at age twenty four: she "is the only woman I have ever loved—she has nothing" (Baudelaire, *Correspondence générale*, ed. Jacques Crépet, Paris: Louis Conrad, 1947, vol. 1, p. 72; translation mine). Even if one were to read the poem as no more than a direct biographical transcript, one might wonder at the historical irony that produces such a hierarchized presentation of the only beloved woman.

10. De Man, *Romanticism*, 254.

11. I have discussed this at greater length in "Revolutions that As Yet Have No Model: Derrida's Limited Inc.," *Diacritics*, 10: 4 (Winter, 1980).

12. Baudelaire, *Les Fleurs du mal*, ed. Antoine Adam (Paris: Garnier, 1961), 382.

13. For the most spectacular examples of this, see Derrida's treatment of Hegel in *Glas* (Paris: Galilée, 1974) and of Freud in *La Carte postale* (Paris: Flammanon, 1981).

14. Lisa Jardine, "Girl Talk" (see above).

15. Edward Ahearn, "Black Woman, White Poet: Exile and Exploitation in Baudelaire's Jeanne Duval Poems," *FR*, 51 (1976). Andrew Bush, in a brilliant essay titled "Le cygne" or "El cisne": the History of a Misreading," *Comp Lit Studies*, 17: 4 (Dec. 1980), completely reduces the asymmetrical deployment of the two women through a perfunctory continuist approach which disregards the rhetorical texture of the poem. Bush can thus speak of "the condition of exile, suffered variously by Andromache, the negress, the abandoned sailors, and the poet himself, all of whom are represented in the central images of the swan" (419). He traces the male line of Baudelaire's poetic brotherhood adding Proust and Reuben Darío to the stars I have already mentioned.

He emends the opening words of "Le cygne," to . . . "*Andromaque* [Racine's play], je pense à vous!" (422). Via Harold Bloom's notion of "the anxiety of influence," Bush goes on to a consideration of Baudelaire's oedipal problems: "An only child to a dead father and a mother who, by remarriage, betrays the son, as he believes. Baudelaire would have us read Virgil, where he, a belated and corrupted Astyanax, is rewriting Racine" (423). Edward W. Kaplan, in "Baudelaire's Portrait of the Poet as Widow: three Poèmes en Prose and 'Le Cygne,'" *Symposium*, 34: 3 (Fall 1980), takes the male desire to appropriate the womb and the feminine in general as fulfilled in the declaration. Here too the rhetorical texture of the poem is ignored. "Baudelaire identifies here with bereaved women . . . as widow he is the exile," and finally, he "imitates the mother and creates" (245, 246).

16. "It was a story about 'a new sort of woman,'" wrote Carrie [Rudyard's wife], and "she turned out stunningly . . . She is presented in the round, as no earlier of Kipling's heroines had been" (Charles Carrington, *Rudyard Kipling: His Life and Work*, London: Macmillan, 1955, 223, 224). But even such a temperate "feminist" gesture has been quickly misunderstood. The protagonist has been described as "a hard-riding young lady with a preference for men of action" (Stephen Lucius Gwynn, "The Madness of Mr. Kipling," in *Kipling: The Critical Heritage*, ed. Roger Lancelot Green, London: Routledge, 1971, 213).

17. Rudyard Kipling, *The Writings in Prose and Verse* (New York: Scribner's, 1913), Vol. 31:1, 227. Hereafter cited in text as WC.

18. For favourable assessments of this passage, see *Kipling*, ed. Green, 213 and Carrington, *Rudyard Kipling*, 224.

19. Kingsley Amis, *Rudyard Kipling and His World* (New York: Scribners, 1975), 25.

20. I am not considering the vexed question of Kipling's "imperialism" here. I am looking rather at the fact that sexual difference becomes relevant in this text only in terms of the colonizer. It is, however, worth pointing at a poignant piece of evidence of the effects of imperialism. Almost all the Western critics I have read, many of them (such as T. S. Eliot, George Orwell, Lionel Trilling, Randall Jarrell) conveniently collected in *Kipling*, ed. Green, and *Kipling and the Critics*, ed. Eliot L. Gilbert (New York: New York University Press, 1965), speak of the formative impact of Kipling's stories and novels upon their boyhood. Compare the following remark by a Bengali writer to that collective testimony: "I read Kipling's *Jungle Book* first at the age of ten in an East Bengal village, but never read anything else by him for fear of being hurt by his racial arrogance" (Nirad C. Chaudhuri, "The Wolf Without A Pack," *TLS*, Oct. 6, 1978); the above is a memory; it is followed in Chaudhuri's piece by a judgment, reflecting so-called decolonization and the disavowal of the economic, with which I cannot agree.

21. Both the Benjamin and the de Man passages are to be found in Paul de Man, "Conclusion": Walter Benjamin's "The Task of the Translator": Messenger Lecture, Cornell University, March 4, 1983, *YFS*, 69 (1985), 44.

22. David Arnold, "Famine in Peasant Consciousness and Peasant Action: Madras 1876–8," in *Subaltern Studies: Writings on South Asian History and Society*, ed. Ranajit Guha (Delhi: Oxford University Press, 1984). In this context, the representative assertion by Orwell, that Kipling's account of "nineteenth century Anglo-India" is "the best . . . picture we have" ("Rudyard Kipling," in *Kipling and the Critics*, ed. Gilbert, 82), must be understood to mean the best account of typical British self-representations of what India was about.

23. Arnold, "Famine," 73.

24. For considerations of a (sexed) subject-constitution outside of the discourse on psychoanalysis and counter-psychoanalysis, see Spivak, "Can the Subaltern Speak? Considerations of Widow-Sacrifice," *Wedge*, 7 (1985).

25. This distinction is taken from Roberto Fernandez Retamár, "Caliban: Notes Towards A Discussion of Culture in Our America," trans. Lynn Garafola et al., *Massachusetts Review*, 15 (Winer-Spring, 1979).

26. L/P & S/1/2 Minutes of the Secret Court of Directors 1784–1858.

27. A text that puts us on guard against such conflations in the British context by frequently taking the geopolitical context into account is *Worlds Apart: Women under Immigration and Nationality Law*, eds. Jacqueline Bhabha et al. (London: Pluto Press, 1985).

VIII

ETHICS, PROFESSION, CANON

Contemporary literary criticism, as we hope the essays and introductions in this book demonstrate, has participated in enormous intellectual reorientations—extraordinary transformations in the study of literature—in the last twenty-five years. These reorientations have raised questions concerning the basic assumptions of literary study and literary criticism. As Edward Said notes in "Reflections on American 'Left' Literary Criticism" in this section, "never before in the history of American literary culture has there been such widespread and such serious, sometimes technical, and frequently contentious discussion of issues in literary criticism." These issues include examination of the responsibilities of literary studies, the institutions that define the nature and govern the practices of literary study, and the specific constitution of the objects of serious literary culture—how particular texts come to be considered part of the literary and, even, the critical canon. The answers to the questions of what literary criticism is supposed to do, how it goes about doing its business, and what, precisely, it does these things to are no longer considered self-evident. The "reorientation" in literary criticism—really, the examination or, as Hillis Miller describes it, the "interrogation" of the assumptions that govern the study of literature—is now the subject of widespread debate. Said calls this "oppositional debate without real opposition," but even if he is correct in this assessment, even if the debate constitutes what Richard Rorty calls "crosstalk" in which the participants share none of the same assumptions, the debate itself, nevertheless, is important in relation to the responsibilities, institutionalizations, and objects of literary study. Even if the "debate" is between radically different conceptions of language and literature (such as the different conceptions of "decidability" that de Man presents in "Semiology and Rhetoric," Section IV, the "grammatical" distinction between literal and figurative meaning versus the "rhetorical" situation of being unable to decide), nevertheless the debate questions assumptions that for a long time in critical studies were simply taken to be true. The current debate in contemporary literary criticism within the cultural studies discussed in the general introduction makes these assumptions something to be examined.

ETHICS

The issue of a critic's responsibility, and that of criticism generally, is quickly moving to the center of contemporary literary studies. In *The Ethics of Reading*, Hillis Miller argues that "the ethical moment in the act of reading . . . faces in two directions." In one direction, he argues, it is a response to literary works themselves, responsible and responsive. In the other, it leads to action in social, political, and institutional realms. Criticism, then, has responsibility to texts and authors but also to students and colleagues, and to society at large, to the larger "culture" of which it is a part. Said addresses cultural responsibility, just as other critics in this section focus upon other aspects of critical responsibility. In fact, the first three essays all address this question, and they do so in precisely the kind of polemical debate Said describes in the conflict between "the new subculture of theoretical opposition" and the "old traditions fighting back with appeals to humanism, tact, good sense, and the like."

Northrop Frye joins this debate in "The Function of Criticism at the Present Time" (which he later revised as the "Polemical Introduction" to *Anatomy of Criticism*) and takes exception to the traditional view that criticism is subservient to literature, "a parasitic form of literary expression," a "jackal" of other disciplines simply trying, in M. H. Abram's words, to understand the meaning of authors through "our ordinary skill and tact at language," "our ordinary realm of experience in speaking, hearing, reading, and understanding language." For Frye, literature—and the responsibility to literature—is not "ordinary"; rather, literature is extraordinary precisely because while criticism "can talk, all the arts are dumb." That is, for Frye the responsibility of criticism is to texts and, more widely, to literature as a human institution. The first thing a critic must do, he says, "is to read literature"; but the next thing is to create a conceptual "framework" in which to understand what literature "means as a whole." "Just as mathematics exists in a mathematical universe which is at the circumference of the common field of experience," he writes, "so literature exists in a verbal universe, which is not a commentary on life or reality, but contains life and reality in a system of verbal relationships." This position is indeed polemical, and it is directed at reorienting criticism, changing it from an examination of great works of literature in their particularity—the "autonomous" works that New Criticism examines or the author's vision, what "*he* meant," as Abrams articulates it in his version of "pluralism"—to a systematic and "scientific" exploration of the conditions that allow "literature" to come into existence. But most grandly, Frye would create a responsible discipline of criticism in which nothing escapes being considered "critically," that is, in which "life and reality"—what Frye calls at the end of his essay "culture"—are understood within a framework of verbal relations. Such relations, for Frye, are neither simply linguistic, nor are they conventionally social or individually psychological. Rather, they are "anagogic," as he says in the *Anatomy*, encompassing and articulating an abstract and ultimate sense of the human imagination conceived in terms of archetypes (see the introduction to Section V).

The most important point here, however, is Frye's felt need to redefine and reorient the practice of criticism at the present time. Doing so in the essay included here (1949), he addressed—somewhat prophetically—all the questions this section is attempting to delineate. He asks about the responsibility of criticism, what institutional forms would best realize that responsibility, and what definition of "literature" is entailed—either as a cause or as a result—in relation to this responsibility. Frye defines criticism as a discipline that articulates the human imagination as it is realized in literary works. To do this he posits the necessity of institutionalizing a "conceptual framework" for literary studies analogous to the conceptual framework instituted by the physical and social sciences. And, finally, he suggests that such a framework will *define* the nature of particular literary works—will, in fact, define the literary canon (allowing us, in his example, to identify the genre of *Gulliver's Travels*). In a way, Frye's essay could stand at the beginning of this entire critical collection just as it stands at the beginning of the general introduction—his work, as Frank Lentricchia has argued, has created a conceptual framework that has helped define literary studies in the last thirty years. But equally important, his work—in its very polemic—helps to reorient literary studies in terms of cultural studies, or what Eagleton calls "discourse theory." It imagines a framework of discourse—a "frame of reference"—in which all sorts of verbal activities find their significance and relationship—their responsibility—toward other aspects of human life.

Still, Frye's essay is "polemical" because it answers directly different assumptions about the nature of literature and literary study. One set of such assumptions, as we have mentioned, is the basis of Abrams's self-proclaimed "pluralist" view of literary studies. Abrams assumes that the responsibility of the critic is towards the author of literary texts and to the "ordinary" usages—what Swift calls the "common forms"—of language and life. Literature in Abrams's view consists of a given number of autonomous "written texts" whose meaning is governed by the intentions of their authors. Such texts do not form a system (such as Frye's archetypal system or the linguistically modeled system of structuralism), and the job of the critic is merely to trace their "history" and recover their meaning. In this description of criticism, however, literature, in Frye's words, "appears as a huge aggregate or miscellaneous pile of creative efforts," the understanding of which can only be discovered in its chronology. According to Abrams, however, at stake in this version of literature and criticism "is the validity of the premises and procedures of the entire body of traditional inquiries in the human sciences." Abrams's definitions are common-sensical and fully traditional. They do not question what Lillian Robinson calls "the apparently systematic neglect of women's experience in the literary canon," nor do they create the possibility of reconsidering, as Robinson says, "whether the great monuments are really so great, after all." In other words, for Abrams the rationale for inclusion in the canon—what makes a literary work great—is self-evident and needs no discussion.

It is precisely the examination of the self-evident that governs J. Hillis Miller's inquiry in "The Search for Grounds in Literary Study." Miller begins from a viewpoint directly at odds with the unexamined assumption of the value of "traditional inquiries in the human sciences." Miller describes four basic assumptions that govern modes of inquiry in the "human sciences" (which we discussed in the introduction to Section VII). These assumptions, or "grounds," make understanding possible by "grounding" the infinite "play" of the discourse of the human sciences Derrida describes in Section IV, discourses that correspond to various schools of contemporary criticism described in this book. One such ground Miller describes is social, which reduces the play of meanings to articulations of more or less explicit social forces: the Marxist "base," Foucauldian "power," feminist "phallologocentrism," or most generally Burke's (and Bakhtin/Volosinov's) definition of language and literature as "equipment for living" with other people. A second ground is language itself, which reduces the play of meanings to the linguistic forms and structures that govern meaning in the linguistic methods of structuralist criticism. A third ground Miller describes is psychology, which reduces the play of meanings to the conscious and unconscious intentions of the subject of discourse, Abrams's self-evident understanding of literature, but it also governs the varieties of contemporary psychoanalytic criticism. The final ground Miller describes is, as he says, "properly religious, metaphysical, or ontological, though hardly in a traditional or conventional way." This ground, in Miller's argument, is the basis of Derrida's unconventional metaphysics, which, as Greenblatt points out, leads a critic like de Man, though perhaps not Derrida or Miller, "too readily and predictably to the void." Like the anagogics of Frye's vision of literature as a "verbal universe," it grounds particular articulations in an overriding vision of the whole of "discourse" or cultural life.

The point of Miller's discussion, however, is ethical. He—like Said, Gerald Graff, and many others writing today—wants to test these assumptions against the tasks they are set to perform. Most globally, he wants to test "literature" itself against the "entire body of traditional inquiries in the human sciences" Abrams (as well as the Arnoldians Miller cites in his essay) stakes on literary study. To this end he describes the "imperialism" of each of the grounds he describes, their tendency to reduce and dismiss all other explanations—that is, to make each ground, in turn, a "base" to the superstructure and epiphenomena of other discursive formations. Along with this tendency he also describes the blind and almost hysterical resistance contemporary versions of these grounds—Marxist, structuralist, psychoanalytic, and deconstructive—have encountered in polemics that have reduced Said's "old traditions fighting back" to an extraordinary loss of self-control and tact.

Both of these aspects of grounding gestures—the "self-evident" ability to account for everything by their adherents and the equally self-evident dismissal by those who do not subscribe to them—have ethical implications. They define the responsibility of criticism according to the larger aspects of human life. When the study of literature is reducible to the study of language, then criticism becomes "scientific" and "object" in relation to other cultural formations. It ceases to traffic in the cultural values Miller is describing and turns its attention to the linguistic conditions that allow such values to arise. Further, if the study of literature is reducible to the study of psychology, then criticism becomes either a symtomatics, diagnosing particular authors or even particular eras in terms of "health," or, more usually, "disease," or it becomes a model for understanding based upon more or less autonomous subjects. But in either case it also ceases to traffic in cultural values and turns its attention to individual ("psychologized") values.

If the study of literature is reducible to the study of society, then criticism becomes a program for social action—what Lentricchia calls "the production of knowledge to the ends of power." In this case, the study of literature recognizes cultural values, but those values themselves are only defined collectively and socially and, like the other grounding gestures, leave out or "marginalize" (as "false consciousness," "ideology," "self-interest," and other such terms) what it cannot describe as "basic." Finally, if the study of literature is expandible to one anagogics or another, it leads, "too readily and predictably," as Greenblatt says in Section VI, to one or another vision of the world—to the deconstructive "void"—in Greenblatt's terms—or to "a transfiguration of the scene which leaves it nevertheless the same," as Miller says. This study of literature could also lead to a conception of poetry as existing impersonally in "the mind of Europe" which is "much more important" than the poet's own private mind—and only accessible, as Eliot says, to "those who have personality and emotions [and consequently] know what it means to want to escape from these things."

Both imperialism and resistance, then, are acts that call for ethical judgment. Based on particular "grounds" of literary study, they account for only so much, while claiming—in Raymond William's terms in Section

VI—"to exhaust the full range of human practice, human energy, human intention (. . . that extraordinary range of variations, both practised and imagined, of which human beings are and have shown themselves to be capable)." And the job for ethics, in John Dewey's traditional terms, is to deal "with conduct in its entirety, with reference . . . to what makes it conduct, its *ends*, its real meaning." Its job, in Julia Kristeva's more contemporary terms, is no longer its "coercive, customary manner of ensuring the cohesiveness of a particular group." Now, she continues, "ethics crops up wherever a code (mores, social contract) must be shattered in order to give way to the free play of negativity, need, desire, pleasure, and jouissance, before being put together again." In both cases—of the "old" traditional humanism and the "new subculture of theoretical opposition" Said describes in the contemporary debate—the issue can be and is being understood in terms of the ethics of the profession.

PROFESSION

In that the reorientation in criticism described in this book has ethical implications, it also has—and perhaps more strikingly—professional implications for what we do as students, teachers, and scholars. Frye notes in "The Function of Criticism at the Present Time" the arbitrary and unsystematic nature of the institutionalization of literary studies in American higher education. He says, for instance, that the idea of "English literature . . . ought not to make any sense at all to a literary critic," and even "the phrase 'history of English literature' ought to mean nothing at all." Earlier, Kenneth Burke in "Literature as Equipment for Living" (Section II) had mockingly described the outrage his rhetorical and "sociological" understanding of literature would occasion in "those persons who take the division of faculties in our universities to be an exact replica of the way in which God himself divided up the universe." And recently in the wake of various critical debates there has been much interest in the history of literary studies as a discipline. Jonathan Culler in *Framing the Sign: Criticism and Its Institutions* (1988) traces the history and function of contemporary criticism, and Gerald Graff in *Professing Literature* (1987) traces the institutionalization of English studies—in actual English departments—in the last hundred years. Graff describes how the structure of literary studies into chronological periods has served institutional, "departmental," interests rather than—or at least along with—the interests of knowledge and learning by creating a situation which avoided "the need for instructors to debate aims and methods." They have had no need to define and critique exactly what they were doing. In the same way, Robert Scholes has examined "the notions of institution, genre, and language" as examples of "powerful tools of thought, whose interrelatedness has only recently become apparent. . . . This new perception," he goes on, ". . . is leading many scholars to reconsider the dimension of their academic disciplines, as they rediscover the very objects of their study." Miller's essay, as we have seen, is just such a reconsideration, and his debate with Abrams—and Said's wider situating of that debate within professional ethics and responsibilities—is part of the larger reorientation of literary studies occasioned by a range of contemporary conerns.

One such concern, represented here in Shoshana Felman's "Psychoanalysis and Education: Teaching Terminable and Interminable," is with the nature and role of teaching. Felman's argument links her pedagogical concerns with Miller's ethical concerns; "teaching," she says, "like analysis, does not deal so much with *lack* of knowledge as with *resistances* to knowledge." In other words, like so many contributors to this volume—like all the essays of this section—Felman is attempting to situate the practice of pedagogy, that is, to "reorient" it in relation to the interpersonal relationships of power that discourse conveys along with its "knowledge." Felman attempts to explore and analyze the relationships between knowledge and ignorance—between teacher and student—in a way suggestive of structuralism's reconsideration of language effects as opposed to the unconscious structures that allow language to function. Parallel to both is poststructuralism's reconsideration of the "constative" and "performative" forces of discourse, all of which duplicates Marxism's reconsideration of base and superstructure, the relationship between apparently "transcendental," "timeless" ideas, beliefs, and feelings about the world and the historically situated material base that gives rise to those ideas. Along the same line is feminism's reconsideration of the sex-based differences and the social practices—or "ideology"—those differences give rise to. All of this is parallel, finally, to Miller's discussion of the grounds of contemporary ethical debate.

Similarly, Felman traces the relationship between knowledge and ignorance in teaching and psychoanalysis in ways that shed light on the rethinking of the profession and discipline of English studies more generally. Teaching, psychoanalysis teaches us, must learn to learn from ignorance. Ignorance, she argues, is not simply the absence of knowledge, but a resistance to knowledge that *"itself can teach us something."* The aim of teaching "is not the transmission of ready-made knowledge; it is rather the creation of a new *condition* of knowledge." According to Jacques Lacan, the analyst—and implicitly the teacher—does not possess what the patient, or the student, wants to know. The analyst's "competence, insists Lacan, lies in 'what I would call *textual knowledge,*' " which is, Felman says, "the very stuff the literature teacher is supposed to deal in—. . . knowledge of the functioning of language, of symbolic structures, of the signifier, knowledge at once derived from—and directed towards—interpretation."

In this reorienting of what the teacher does, knowledge, Felman argues, "cannot be *exchanged,* it has to be *used,*" just as the purloined letter in Poe's tale and Lacan's "Seminar" (Section V) can only be used. This is also the reorientation in English studies from a model of the "transmission" of great, independent works of art, to the study of the conditions and realization of discourse in its myriad forms—psychological, social, linguistic, anagogic. Teaching uncovers the conditions of knowledge, and it functions as much by performative "utterances" as it does by constative statements. "Misinterpretations of the psychoanalytical critique of pedagogy," Felman argues, "refer exclusively to Lacan's or Freud's explicit *statements* about pedagogy, and thus fail to see the illocutionary force, the didactic function of the *utterance* as opposd to the mere content of the statement." If it "is not a purely cognitive, informative experience," she goes on, but also an emotional, "transferential" one, then English studies must expand and restructure itself to emphasize the functioning of language, of symbolic structures, of signification—knowledge at once derived from and directed toward interpretation. This reorientation of English studies, then, is an orientation toward the cultural studies we examined in the general introduction to *Contemporary Literary Criticism*. It is a reorientation that includes the various grounds—the various schools of criticism—of the study of contemporary criticism itself.

CANON

This reorientation toward cultural studies may sound to some very like the "pluralism" (associated with Wayne Booth, M. H. Abrams, and others) we mentioned earlier in this introduction. If this is so, then one could object: "it's all well and good to describe but not to make ethical choices, to define teaching as both cognitive and emotional, to say there are many ways to organize the discipline of English studies, but the fact is such a 'pluralism' simply demonstrates complicity with a repressive social order" (as Lentricchia says), or an "inability to look into things all the way down to the bottom" (as Miller says). Such "pluralism" could also be "mystified apprehension of the effects [which] linguistic relationships occasion as substantialized 'objects' in the world" (as Greimas says). Pluralism may also embody the "psychological resistance to the truth" (as Freud often seems to imply). The fact is, as each of these positions argue, sooner or later ethical and political choices must be made.

In teaching, for example, an ethical choice is made each time texts are ordered for a course, just as for this text we—as editors—have made choices concerning the essays to be included. Lillian Robinson argues this point in "Treason Our Text: Feminist Challenges to the Literary Canon": "when we turn from the construction of pantheons, which have no *prescribed* number of places, to the construction of course syllabi, then something does have to be eliminated each time something else is added, and here ideologies [Miller's "grounds"], aesthetic and extra-aesthetic, do necessarily come into play." What is to be taught? What is the object of English studies? Robinson argues—as do Schweickart and Showalter—that, in one way or another, female writing "humanizes" male critical theory and the canon. Whether this is an esthetic or extra-aesthetic ground is not altogether clear.

But Sandra Gilbert in "Life's Empty Pack: Notes Toward a Literary Daughteronomy" (Section VII) and Henry Louis Gates, Jr., in "The Blackness of Blackness: A Critique of the Sign and the Signifying Monkey" (in this section) both argue, on clearly aesthetic *and* critical grounds, for the canonical inclusion of female and black literature. Gilbert follows Freud and Lacan in rewriting a feminist literary history, while Gates follows structuralist and postructuralist "signifying" and "signification" in situating black literature in relation to itself and to a critical canon. "The Signifying Monkey," he says, ". . . seems to dwell in this space between two linguistic domains," standard American English and "American Negro usage." Gates's suggestion is that contemporary black literature and criticism uses "*signifying* as the slave's trope, the trope of tropes . . . a trope that subsumes other rhetorical tropes, including metaphor, metonymy, synecdoche and irony." This practice defines the themes and techniques of postmodern literary practice much the way New Criticism used Modernist texts to define and justify its critical formulations.

Critical practice, in this sense, is always canonical. It always forms canons. Just as Stanley Fish argues that interpretive strategies condition and determine the so-called "facts" of discourse (Section II), so the practices of criticism help to determine the objects of study. The "signify'n" Gates describes, like the critical practice that allows him to see its significance, produces—as he says—"a critique of traditional notions of closure in interpretation." The strongest of those notions, like the "restrictive institution" we are hardly aware of "until we come into conflict with it," Robinson describes as the institution of the literary canon, determine the professional and canonical domain of literary and cultural studies, and their examination and interrogation form part of an "ethics" of literary study. For this reason these notions are subject to the various critiques of contemporary criticism. Moreover, the ethical responsibility of English studies as an institution lies in asking precisely the kinds of questions and pursuing the issues we have discussed here. English studies, and cultural studies generally, have been subject to the invigorating debates we have been outlining, debates that have engulfed and transformed the study of literature in recent years.

RELATED TEXTS IN *CONTEMPORARY LITERARY CRITICISM*

Mikhail Bakhtin/V.N. Vološinov, "Discourse in Life and Discourse in Art"
Kenneth Burke, "Literature as Equipment for Living"
Jacques Derrida, "Structure, Sign, and Play in the Discourse of the Human Sciences"
Michel Foucault, "What Is an Author?"
Fredric Jameson, "The Politics of Theory"
Patrocinio P. Schweickart, "Reading Ourselves: Toward a Feminist Theory of Reading"
Raymond Williams, "Base and Superstructure in Marxist Cultural Theory"

REFERENCES

Bové, Paul A., *Intellectuals in Power: A Genealogy of Critical Humanism* (New York: Columbia University Press, 1986).

Culler, Jonathan, *Framing the Sign: Criticism and Its Institutions* (Norman: University of Oklahoma Press, 1988).

Davis, Robert Con, guest editor, "Psychoanalysis and Pedagogy," double special issue of *College English*, 49, 6/7 (1987).

Dewey, John, *Outlines of a Critical Theory of Ethics*, in *Early Works*, Vol. 3, 1889–1892, ed. Jo Ann Boydaton (Carbondale: Southern Illinois University Press, 1969).

Graff, Gerald, *Professing Literature* (Chicago: University of Chicago Press, 1987).

Grafton, Anthony, and Lisa Jardine, *From Humanism to the Humanities* (Cambridge: Harvard University Press, 1987).

Kirsteva, Julia, "The Ethics of Linguistics," in *Desire in Language*, trans. Thomas Gora, Alice Jardine, Leon Roudiez (New York: Columbia University Press, 1980).

Merod, Jim, *The Political Responsibility of the Critic* (Ithaca: Cornell University Press, 1987).

Miller, J. Hillis, *The Ethics of Reading* (New York: Columbia University Press, 1986).

Rorty, Richard, *Consequences of Pragmatism* (Minneapolis: University of Minnesota Press, 1982).

Schleifer, Ronald and James Comas, "The Ethics of Publishing," *The Eighteenth Century: Theory and Interpretation*, 29 (1988).

Scholes, Robert, *Textual Power* (New Haven and London: Yale University Press, 1985).

30

Northrop Frye
1912–

Northrop Frye's most acclaimed work is *Anatomy of Criticism* (1957), in which he introduced his systematic approach to literature. Among his other works are *The Well-Tempered Critic* (1963); *The Critical Path: An Essay on the Social Context of Literary Criticism* (1971); and *The Stubborn Structure: Essays on Criticism and Society* (1970). He also authored two books on Shakespeare: *Fools of Time: Studies in Shakespearean Tragedy* (1967) and *A Natural Perspective* (1965). His two in-depth studies of Romanticism are *Fearful Symmetry: A Study of William Blake* (1947) and *A Study of English Romanticism* (1968).

In his work Frye offers a concise, fully developed, and systematic approach to the study of literature. Unlike the preceding theories of formalism (which concentrate on the individual work) and historicism (emphasizing the author as creator), his method identifies the whole of literature as a culturally structured entity consisting of the entire canon of poems, dramas, and prose. Frye uses a mythological model to illustrate the morphology of literature: it consists of birth (melodrama), zenith (comedy), death (tragedy), and darkness (ironic literature).

In "The Function of Criticism at the Present Time," Frye considers it the responsibility of the critic to systematize the previously unorganized study of literature. As the shaper of intellectual tradition, the critic must organize the material within a critical framework that follows the natural contours of literature. Before criticism can exist as an organized system, it must thoroughly—even scientifically— classify reconsidering the all-too-frequent use of unsupported value judgments by many writers. To truly understand literature, says Frye, requires seeing it as a system of word-symbols, not unlike mathematics, which must be considered as part of its greater structure, separate from the world that gave rise to the ideas it depicts.

The Function of Criticism at the Present Time

The subject-matter of literary criticism is an art, and criticism is presumably an art too. This sounds as though criticism were a parasitic form of literary expression, an art based on pre-existing art, a second-hand imitation of creative power. The conception of the critic as a creator *manque* is very popular, especially among artists. Yet the critic has specific jobs to do which the experience of literature has proved to be less ignoble. One obvious function of criticism is to mediate between the artist and his public. Art that tries to do without criticism is apt to get involved in either of two fallacies. One is the attempt to reach the public directly through "popular" art, the assumption being that criticism is artificial and public taste natural. Below this is a further assumption about natural taste which goes back to Rousseau. The opposite fallacy is the conception of art as a mystery, an initiation into an esoteric community. Here criticism is restricted to masonic signs of occult understanding, to significant exclamations and gestures and oblique cryptic comments. This fallacy is like the other one in assuming a rough correlation between the merit of art and the degree of public response to it, though the correlation it assumes is inverse. But art of this kind is cut off from society as a whole, not so much because it retreats from life—the usual charge against it—as because it rejects criticism.

On the other hand, a public that attempts to do without criticism, and asserts that it knows what it likes, brutalizes the arts. Rejection of criticism from the point of view of the public, or its guardians, is involved in all forms of censorship. Art is a continuously emancipating factor in society, and the critic, whose job it is to get as many people in contact with the best that has been and is being thought and said, is, at least ideally, the pioneer of education and the shaper of cultural tradition. There is no immediate correlation either way between the merits of art and its general reception. Shakespeare was more popular than Webster, but not because he was a greater dramatist; W. H. Auden is less popular than Edgar Guest, but not because he is a better poet. But after the critic has been at work for a while, some positive correlation may begin to take shape. Most of Shakespeare's current popularity is due to critical publicity.

Why does criticism have to exist? The best and shortest answer is that it can talk, and all the arts are dumb. In painting, sculpture, or music it is easy enough to see that the art shows forth, and cannot *say* anything. And, although it sounds like a frantic paradox to say that the poet is inarticulate or speechless, literary works also are, for the critic, mute complexes of facts, like the data of science. Poetry is a *disinterested* use of words: it does not address a reader directly. When it does so, we feel that the poet has a certain distrust in the capacity of readers and critics to interpret his meaning without assistance, and has therefore stopped creating a poem and begun to talk. It is not merely tradition that impels a poet to invoke a Muse and protest that his utterance is involuntary. Nor is it mere paradox that causes Mr. MacLeish, in his famous "Ars Poetica," to apply the words "mute," "dumb," and "wordless" to a poem. The poet, as Mill saw in a wonderful flash of critical insight, is not heard, but overheard. The first assumption of criticism, and the assumption on which the autonomy of criticism rests, is not that the poet does not know what he is talking about, but that he cannot talk about what he knows, any more than the painter or composer can.

The poet may of course have some critical ability of his own, and so interpret his own work; but the Dante who writes a commentary on the first canto of the *Paradiso is merely one more of Dante's* critics. What he says has a peculiar interest, but not a peculiar authority. Poets are too often the most unreliable judges of the value or even the meaning of what they have written. When Ibsen maintains that *Emperor and Galilean* is his greatest play and that certain episodes in *Peer Gynt* are not allegorical, one can only say that Ibsen is an indifferent critic of Ibsen. Wordsworth's Preface to the *Lyrical Ballads* is a remarkable document, but as a piece of Wordsworthian criticism nobody would give it more than about a B plus. Critics of Shakespeare are often supposed to be ridiculed by the assertion that if Shakespeare were to come back from the dead he would not be able to understand their criticism and would accuse them of reading far more meaning into his work than he intended. This, though pure hypothesis, is likely enough: we have very little evidence of Shakespeare's interest in criticism, either of himself or of anyone else. But all that this means is that Shakespeare, though a great dramatist, was not also the greatest Shakespearean critic. Why should he be?

The notion that the poet is necessarily his own best interpreter is indissolubly linked with the conception of the critic as a parasite or jackal of literature. Once we admit that he has a specific field of activity, and that he has autonomy within that field, we are forced to concede that criticism deals with literature in terms of a specific conceptual framework. This framework is not that of literature itself, for this is the parasite theory again, but neither is it something outside literature, for in that case the autonomy of criticism would again disappear, and the whole subject would be assimilated to something else.

Here, however, we have arrived at another conception of criticism which is different from the one we started with. This autonomous organizing of literature may be criticism, but it is not the activity of mediating between the artist and his public which we at first ascribed to criticism. There is one kind of critic, evidently, who faces the public and another who is still as completely involved in literary values as the poet himself. We may call this latter type the critic proper, and the former the critical reader. It may sound like quibbling to imply such a distinction, but actually the whole question of whether the critic has a real function, independent both of the artist at his most explicit and of the public at its most discriminating, is involved in it.

Our present-day critical traditions are rooted in the age of Hazlitt and Arnold and Sainte-Beuve, who were, in terms of our distinction, critical readers. They represented, not another conceptual framework within literature, but the reading public at its most expert and judicious. They conceived it to be the task of a critic to exemplify how a man of taste uses and evaluates literature, and thus how literature is to be absorbed into society. The nineteenth century has bequeathed to us the conception of the *causerie*, the man of taste's reflections on works of literature, as the normal form of critical expression. I give one example of the difference between a critic and a critical reader which amounts to a head-on collision. In one of his curious, brilliant, scatter-brained footnotes to *Munera Pulveris*, John Ruskin says:

> Of Shakspeare's names I will afterwards speak at more length; they are curiously—often barbarously—mixed out of various traditions and languages. Three of the clearest in meaning have been already noticed. Desdemona—"*δυσδαιμονία*" *miserable fortune*—is also plain enough. Othello is, I believe, "the careful"; all the calamity of the tragedy arising from the single flaw and error in his magnificently collected strength. Ophelia, "serviceableness," the true, lost wife of Hamlet, is marked as having a Greek name by that of her brother, Laertes; and its signification is once exquisitely alluded to in that brother's last word of her, where her gentle preciousness is opposed to the uselessness of the churlish clergy: "*A ministering* angel shall my sister be, when thou liest howling."

On this passage Matthew Arnold comments as follows:

> Now, really, what a piece of extravagance all that is! I will not say that the meaning of Shakspeare's names (I put aside the question as to the correctness of Mr. Ruskin's etymologies) has no effect at all, may be entirely lost sight of; but to give it that degree of prominence is to throw the reins to one's whim, to forget all moderation and proportion, to lose the balance of one's mind altogether. It is to show in one's criticism, to the highest excess, the note or provinciality.

Ruskin is a critic, perhaps the only important one that the Victorian age produced, and, whether he is right or wrong, what he is attempting is genuine criticism. He is trying to interpret Shakespeare in terms of a conceptual framework which belongs to the critic alone, and yet relates itself to the plays alone. Arnold is perfectly right in feeling that this is not the sort of material that the public critic can directly use. But he does not suspect the existence of criticism as we have defined it above. Here it is Arnold who is the provincial. Ruskin has learned his trade from the great iconological tradition which comes down through classical and biblical scholarship into Dante and Spenser, both of whom he knew how to read, and which is incorporated in the medieval cathedrals he had pored over in such detail. Arnold is assuming, as a universal law of nature, certain "plain sense" critical assumptions which were hardly heard of before Dryden's time and which can assuredly not survive the age of Freud and Jung and Frazer and Cassirer. What emerges from this is that the critic and critical reader are each better off when they know of one another's existence, and perhaps best off when their work forms different aspects of the same thing.

However, the *causerie* does not, or at least need not, involve any fallacy in the theory of criticism itself. The same cannot be said of the reaction against the *causerie* which has produced the leading twentieth-century substitute for criticism. This is the integrated system of religious, philosophical, and political ideas which takes in, as a matter of course, a critical attitude to literature. Thus Mr. Eliot defines his outlook as classical in literature, royalist in politics, anglo-catholic in religion; and it is clear that the third of these has been the spark-plug, the motivating power that drives the other two. Mr. Allen Tate describes his own critical attitude as "reactionary" in a sense intended to include political and philosophical overtones, and the same is true of Hulme's *Speculations*, which are primarily political speculations. Mr. Yvor Winters collects his criticism under the title "In Defence of Reason." What earthly business, one may inquire, has a literary critic to defend reason? He might as well be defending virtue. And so we could go through the list of Marxist, Thomist, Kierkegaardian, Freudian, Jungian, Spenglerian, or existential critics, all determined to substitute a critical attitude for criticism, all proposing, not to find a conceptual framework for criticism within literature, but to attach criticism to one of a miscellany of frameworks outside it.

The axioms and postulates of criticism have to grow out of the art that the critic is dealing with. The first thing that the literary critic has to do is to read literature, to make an inductive survey of his own field and let his critical principles shape themselves solely out of his knowledge of that field. Critical principles cannot be taken over ready-made from theology, philosophy, politics, science, or any combination of these. Further, an inductive survey of his own field is equally essential for the critic of painting or of music, and so each art has its own criticism. Aesthetics, or the consideration of art as a whole, is not a form of criticism but a branch of philosophy. I state all this as dogma, but I think the experience of literature bears me out. To subordinate criticism to a critical attitude is to stereotype certain values in literature which can be related to the extra-literary source of the value-judgment. Mr. Eliot does not mean to say that Dante is a greater poet than Shakespeare or perhaps even Milton; yet he imposes on literature an extra-literary schematism, a sort of religio-political colour-filter, which makes Dante leap into prominence, shows Milton up as dark and faulty, and largely obliterates the outlines of Shakespeare. All that the genuine critic can do with this colour-filter is to murmur politely that it shows things in a new light and is indeed a most stimulating contribution to criticism.

If it is insisted that we cannot criticize literature until we have acquired a coherent philosophy of criticism with its centre of gravity in something else, the existence of criticism as a separate subject is still being denied. But there is one possibility further. If criticism exists, it must be, we have said, an examination of literature in terms of a conceptual framework derivable from an inductive survey of the literary field. The word "inductive" suggests some sort of scientific procedure. What if criticism is a science as well as an art? The writing of history is an art, but no one doubts that scientific principles are involved in the historian's treatment of evidence, and that the presence of this scientific element is what distinguishes history from legend. Is it also a scientific element in criticism which distinguishes it from *causerie* on the one hand, and the superimposed critical attitude on the other? For just as the presence of science changes the character of a subject from the casual to the causal, from the random and intuitive to the systematic, so it also safeguards the integrity of a subject from external invasions. So we may find in science a means of strengthening the fences of criticism against enclosure movements coming not only from religion and philosophy, but from the other sciences as well.

If criticism is a science, it is clearly a social science, which means that it should waste no time in trying to assimilate its methods to those of the natural sciences. Like psychology, it is directly concerned with the human mind, and will only confuse itself with statistical methodologies. I understand that there is a Ph.D. thesis somewhere that displays a list of Hardy's novels in the order of the percentages of gloom that they contain, but one does not feel that that sort of procedure should be encouraged. Yet as the field is narrowed to the social sciences the distinctions must be kept equally sharp. Thus there can be no such thing as a sociological "approach" to literature. There is no reason why a sociologist should not work exclusively on literary material, but if he does he should pay no attention to literary values. In his field Horatio Alger and the writer of the Elsie books are more important than Hawthorne or Melville, and a single issue of the *Ladies' Home Journal* is worth all of Henry James. The literary critic using sociological data is similarly under no obligation to respect sociological values.

It seems absurd to say that there *may* be a scientific element in criticism when there are dozens of learned journals based on the assumption that there is, and thousands of scholars engaged in a scientific procedure related to literary criticism. Either literary criticism is a science, or all these highly trained and intelligent people are wasting their time on a pseudoscience, one to be ranked with phrenology and election forecasting. Yet one is forced to wonder whether scholars as a whole are consciously aware that the assumptions on which their work is based are scientific ones. In the growing complication of secondary sources which constitutes literary scholarship, one misses, for the most part, that sense of systematic progressive consolidation which belongs to a science. Research begins in what is known as "background," and one would expect it, as it goes on, to organize the foreground as well. The digging up of relevant information about a poet should lead to a steady consolidating progress in the criticism of his poetry. One feels a certain failure of nerve in coming out of the background into the foreground, and research seems to prefer to become centrifugal, moving away from the works of art into more and more research projects. I have noticed this particularly in two fields in which I am interested, Blake and Spenser. For every critic of Spenser who is interested in knowing what, say, the fourth book of *The Faerie Queene* actually means as a whole, there are dozens who are interested primarily in how Spenser used Chaucer, Malory, and Ariosto in putting it together. So far as I know there is no book devoted to an analysis of *The Faerie Queene* itself, though there are any number on its sources, and, of course, background. As for Blake, I have read a whole shelf of books on his poetry by critics who did not know what any of his major poems meant. The better ones were distinguishable only by the fact that they did not boast of their ignorance.

The reason for this is that research is ancillary to criticism, but the critic to whom the researcher should entrust his materials hardly exists. What passes for criticism is mainly the work of critical readers or spokesmen of various critical attitudes, and these make, in general, a random and haphazard use of scholarship. Such criticism is therefore often regarded by the researcher as a subjective and regressive dilettantism, interesting in its place, but not real work. On the other hand, the critical reader is apt to treat the researcher as Hamlet did the grave-digger, ignoring everything he throws out except an odd skull that he can pick up and moralize about. Yet unless research consolidates into a criticism which preserves the scientific and systematic element in research, the literary scholar will be debarred by his choice of profession from ever making an immediately significant contribution to culture. The absence of direction in research is, naturally, clearest on the very lowest levels of all, where it is only a spasmodic laying of unfertilized eggs in order to avoid an administrative axe. Here the research is characterized by a kind of desperate tentativeness, an implied hope that some synthesizing critical Messiah of the future will find it useful. A philologist can show the relationship of even the most minute study of dialect to his subject as a whole, because philology is a properly organized science. But the researcher who collects all a poet's references to the sea or God or beautiful women does not know who will find this useful or in what ways it could be used, because he has no theory of imagery.

I am not, obviously, saying that literary scholarship at present is doing the wrong thing or should be doing something else: I am saying that it should be possible to get a clearer and more systematic comprehension of what it is doing. Most literary scholarship could be described as prior criticism (the so-called "lower" criticism of biblical scholarship), the editing of texts and the collecting of relevant facts. Of the posterior (or "higher") criticism that is obviously the final cause of this work we have as yet no theory, no tradition, and above all no systematic organization. We have, of course, a good deal of the thing itself. There is even some good posterior criticism of Spenser, though most of it was written in the eighteenth century. And in every age the great scholar will do the right thing by the instinct of genius. But genius is rare, and scholarship is not.

Sciences normally begin in a state of naïve induction: they come immediately in contact with phenomena and take the things to be explained as their immediate data. Thus physics began by taking the immediate sensations of experience, classified as hot, cold, moist, and dry, as fundamental principles. Eventually physics turned inside out, and discovered that its real function was to explain what heat and moisture were. History began as chronicle; but the difference between the old chronicler and the modern historian is that to the chronicler the events he recorded were also the structure of history, whereas the historian sees these events as historical phenomena, to be explained in terms of a conceptual framework different in shape from them. Similarly each modern science has had to take what Bacon calls (though in another context) an inductive leap, occupying a new vantage ground from which it could see its former principles as new things to be explained. As long as astronomers regarded the movements of heavenly bodies as the *structure* of astronomy, they were compelled to regard their own point of view as fixed. Once they thought of movement as itself an explainable phenomenon, a mathematical theory of movement became the conceptual framework, and so the way was cleared for the heliocentric solar system and the law of gravitation. As long as biology thought of animal and vegetable forms of life as constituting its subject, the different branches of biology were largely efforts of cataloguing. As soon as it was the existence of forms of life themselves that had to be explained, the theory of evolution and the conceptions of protoplasm and the cell poured into biology and completely revitalized it.

It occurs to me that literary criticism is now in such a state of naïve induction as we find in a primitive science. Its materials, the masterpieces of literature, are not yet regarded as phenomena to be explained in terms of a conceptual framework which criticism alone possesses. They are still regarded as somehow constituting the framework or form of criticism as well. I suggest that it is time for criticism to leap to a new ground from which it can discover what the organizing or containing forms of its conceptual framework are. And no one can examine the present containing forms of criticism without being depressed by an overwhelming sense of unreality. Let me give one example.

In confronting any work of literature, one obvious containing form is the genre to which it belongs. And criticism, incredible as it may seem, has as yet no coherent conception of genres. The very word sticks out in an English sentence as the unpronounceable and alien thing it is. In poetry, the common-sense Greek division by methods of performance, which distinguishes poetry as lyric, epic, or dramatic according to whether it is sung, spoken, or shown forth, survives vestigially. On the whole it does not fit the facts of Western poetry, though in Joyce's *Portrait* there is an interesting and suggestive attempt made to re-define the terms. So, apart from a drama which belongs equally to prose, a handful of epics recognizable as such only because they are classical imitations, and a number of long poems also called epics because they are long, we are reduced to the ignoble and slovenly practice of calling almost the whole of poetry "lyric" because the Greeks had no other word for it. The Greeks did not need to develop a classification of prose forms: we do, but have never done so. The circulating-library distinction between fiction and non-fiction, between books which are about things admitted not to be true and books which are about everything else, is apparently satisfactory to us. Asked what the forms of prose fiction are, the literary critic can only say, "well, er—the novel." Asked what form of prose fiction *Gulliver's Travels,* which is clearly not a novel, belongs to, there is not one critic in a hundred who could give a definite answer, and not one in a thousand who would regard the answer (which happens to be "Menippean satire") as essential to the critical treatment of the book. Asked what he is working on, the critic will invariably say that he is working on Donne, or Shelley's thought, or the period from 1640 to 1660, or give some other answer which implies that history, or philosophy, or literature itself, constitutes the structural basis of criticism. It would never occur to any critic to say, for instance, "I am working on the theory of genres." If he actually were interested in this, he would say that he was working on a "general" topic; and the work he would do would probably show the marks of naïve induction: that is, it would be an effort to classify and pigeon-hole instead of clarifying the tradition of the genre.

If we do not know how to handle even the genre, the most obvious of all critical conceptions, it is hardly likely that subtler instruments will be better understood. In any work of literature the characteristics of the language it is written in form an essential critical conception. To the philologist, literature is a function of language, its works linguistic documents, and to the philologist the phrase "English literature" makes sense. It ought not to make any sense at all to a literary critic. For while the philologist sees English literature as illustrating the organic growth of the English language, the literary critic can only see it as the miscellaneous pile of literary works that happened to get written in English. (I say in English, not in England, for the part of "English literature" that was written in Latin or Norman French has a way of dropping unobtrusively into other departments.) Language is an important secondary aspect of literature, but when magnified into a primary basis of classification it becomes absurdly arbitrary.

Critics, of course, maintain that they know this, and that they keep the linguistic categories only for convenience. But theoretical fictions have a way of becoming practical assumptions, and in no time the meaningless convenience of "English literature" expands into the meaningless inconvenience of the "history of English literature." Now, again, the historian must necessarily regard literature as an historical product and its works as historical documents. It is also quite true that the time a work was written in forms an essential critical conception. But again, to the literary critic, as such, the phrase "history of English literature" ought to mean nothing at all. If he doubts this, let him try writing one, and he will find himself confronted by an insoluble problem of form, or rather by an indissoluble amorphousness. The "history" part of his project is an abstract history, a bald chronicle of names and dates and works and influences, deprived of all the real historical interest that a real historian would give it, however much enlivened with discussions of "background." This chronicle is periodically interrupted by conventional judgments of value lugged in from another world, which confuse the history and yet are nothing by themselves. The *form* of literary history has not been discovered, and probably does not exist, and every successful one has been either a textbook or a *tour de force*. Linear time is not an exact enough category to catch literature, and all writers whatever are subtly belittled by a purely historical treatment.

Biography, a branch of history, presents a similar fallacy to the critic, for the biographer turns to a different job and a different kind of book when he turns to criticism. Again, the man who wrote the poem is one of the legitimate containing forms of criticism. But here we have to distinguish the poet *qua* poet, whose work is a single imaginative body, from the poet as man, who is something else altogether. The latter involves us in what is known as the personal heresy, or rather the heroic fallacy. For a biographer, poetry is an emanation of a personality; for the literary critic it is not, and the problem is to detach it from the personality and consider it on impersonal merits. The no man's land between biography and criticism, the process by which a poet's impressions of his environment are transmuted into poetry, has to be viewed by biographer and critic from opposite points of view. The process is too complex ever to be completely unified, Lowes's *Road to Xanadu* being the kind of exception that goes a long way to prove the rule. In Johnson's *Lives of the Poets* a biographical narrative is followed by a critical analysis, and the break between them is so sharp that it is represented in the text by a space.

In all these cases, the same principle recurs. The critic is surrounded by biography, history, philosophy, and language. No one doubts that he has to familiarize himself with these subjects. But is his job only to be the jackal of the historian, the philologist, and the biographer, or can he use these subjects in his own way? If he is not to sell out to all his neighbours in turn, what is distinctive about his approach to the poet's life, the time when he lived, and the language he wrote? To ask this is to raise one of the problems involved in the whole question of what the containing forms of literature are as they take their place in the conceptual framework of criticism. This confronts me with the challenge to make my criticism of criticism constructive. All I have space to do is to outline what I think the first major steps should be.

We have to see what literature is, and try to distinguish the category of literature among all the books there are in the world. I do not know that criticism has made any serious effort to determine what literature is. Next, as discussed above, we should examine the containing forms of criticism, including the poet's life, his historical context, his language, and his thought, to see whether the critic can impose a unified critical form on these things, without giving place to or turning into a biographer, an historian, a philologist, or a philosopher. Next, we should establish the broad distinctions, such as that between prose and poetry, which are preparatory to working out a comprehensive theory of genres. I do not know that critics have clearly explained what the difference between prose and poetry, for instance, really is. Then we should try to see whether the critic, like his neighbours the historian and the philosopher, lives in his own universe. To the historian there is nothing that cannot be considered historically; to the philosopher nothing that cannot be considered philosophically. Does the critic aspire to contain all things in criticism, and so swallow history and philosophy in his own synthesis, or must he be forever the historian's and philosopher's pupil? If I have shown up Arnold in a poor light, I should say that he is the only one I know who suggests that criticism can be, like history and philosophy, a total attitude to experience. And finally, since criticism may obviously deal with anything in a poem from its superficial texture to its ultimate significance, the question arises whether there are different levels of meaning in literature, and, if so, whether they can be defined and classified.

It follows that arriving at value-judgments is not, as it is so often said to be, part of the immediate tactic of criticism. Criticism is not well enough organized as yet to know what the factors of value in a critical judgment are. For instance, as was indicated above in connection with Blake and Spenser, the question of the quality of a poet's thinking as revealed in the integration of his argument is an essential factor in a value-judgment, but many poets are exhaustively discussed in terms of value without this factor being considered. Contemporary judgments of value come mainly from either the critical reader or from the spokesman of a critical attitude. That is, they must be on the whole either unorganized and tentative, or over-organized and irrelevant. For no one can jump directly from research to a value-judgment. I give one melancholy instance. I recently read a study of the sources of mythological allusions in some of the romantic poets, which showed that for the second part of *Faust* Goethe had used a miscellany of cribs, some of dubious authenticity. "I have now, I hope," said the author triumphantly at the end of his investigation, "given sufficient proof that the second part of *Faust* is not a great work of art." I do not deny the ultimate importance of the value-judgment. I would even consider the suggestion that the value-judgment is precisely what distinguishes the social from the natural science. But the more important it is, the more careful we should be about getting it solidly established.

What literature is may perhaps best be understood by an analogy. We shall have to labour the analogy, but that is due mainly to the novelty of the idea here presented. Mathematics appears to begin in the counting and measuring of objects, as a numerical commentary on the world. But the mathematician does not think of his subject as the counting and measuring of physical objects at all. For him it is an autonomous language, and there is a point at which it becomes in a measure independent of that common field of experience which we think of as the physical world, or as existence, or as reality, according to our mood. Many of its terms, such as irrational numbers, have no direct connection with the common field of experience, but depend for their meaning solely on the interrelations of the subject itself. Irrational numbers in mathematics may be compared to prepositions in verbal languages, which, unlike nouns and verbs, have no external symbolic reference. When we distinguish pure from applied mathematics, we are thinking of the former as a disinterested conception of numerical relationships, concerned more and more with its inner integrity, and less and less with its reference to external criteria.

Where, in that case, is pure mathematics going? We may gain a hint from the final chapter of Sir James Jeans' *Mysterious Universe*, which I choose because it shows some of the characteristics of the imaginative leap to a new conceptual framework already mentioned. There, the author speaks of the failure of physical cosmology in the nineteenth century to conceive of the universe as ultimately mechanical, and suggests that a mathematical approach to it may have better luck. The universe cannot be a machine, but it may be an interlocking set of mathematical formulas. What this means is surely that pure mathematics exists in a mathematical universe which is no longer a commentary on an "outside" world, but contains that world within itself. Mathematics is at first a form of understanding an objective world regarded as its content, but in the end it conceives of the content as being itself mathematical in form, so that when the conception of the mathematical universe is reached, form and content become the same thing.

Jeans was a mathematician, and thought of his mathematical universe as *the* universe. Doubtless it is, but it does not follow that the only way of conceiving it is mathematical. For we think also of literature at first as a commentary on an external "life" or "reality." But just as in mathematics we have to go from three apples to three, and from a square field to a square, so in reading Jane Austen we have to go from the faithful reflection of English society to the novel, and pass from literature as symbol to literature as an autonomous language. And just as mathematics exists in a mathematical universe which is at the circumference of the common field of experience, so literature exists in a verbal universe, which is not a commentary on life or reality, but contains life and reality in a system of verbal relationships. This conception of a verbal universe, in which life and reality are inside literature, and not outside it and being described or represented or approached or symbolized by it, seems to me the first postulate of a properly organized criticism.

It is vulgar for the critic to think of literature as a tiny palace of art looking out upon an inconceivably gigantic "life." "Life" should be for the critic only the seed-plot of literature, a vast mass of potential literary forms, only a few of which will grow up into the greater world of the verbal universe. Similar universes exist for all the arts. "We make to ourselves picture of facts," says Wittgenstein, but by pictures he means representative illustrations, which are not pictures. Pictures as pictures are themselves facts, and exist only in a pictorial universe. It is easy enough to say that while the stars in their courses may form the subject of a poem, they will still remain the stars in their courses, forever outside poetry. But this is pure regression to the common field of experience, and nothing more; for the more strenuously we try to conceive the stars in their courses in non-literary ways, the more assuredly we shall fall into the idioms and conventions of some other mental universe. The conception of a constant external reality acts as a kind of censor principle in the arts. Painting has been much bedevilled by it, and much of the freakishness of modern painting is clearly due to the energy of its revolt against the representational fallacy. Music on the other hand has remained fairly free of it: at least no one, so far as I know, insists that it is flying in the face of common sense for music to do anything but reproduce the sounds heard in external nature. In literature the chief function of representationalism is to neutralize its opposing fallacy of an "inner" or subjective reality.

These different universes are presumably different ways of conceiving the same universe. What we call the common field of experience is a provisional means of unifying them on the level of sense-perception, and it is natural to infer a higher unity, a sort of beatification of common sense. But it is not easy to find any human language capable of reaching such exalted heights. If it is true, as is being increasingly asserted, that metaphysics is a system of verbal constructions with no direct reference to external criteria by means of which its truth or falsehood may be tested, it follows that metaphysics forms part of the verbal universe. Theology postulates an ultimate reality in God, but it does not assume that man is capable of describing it in his own terms, nor does it claim to be itself such a description. In any case, if we assert this final unity too quickly we may injure the integrity of the different means of approaching it. It does not help a poet much to tell him that the function of literature is to empty itself into an ocean of superverbal significance, when the nature of that significance is unknown.

Pure mathematics, we have said, does not relate itself directly to the common field of experience, but indirectly, not to avoid it, but with the ultimate design of swallowing it. It thus presents the appearance of a series of hypothetical possibilities. It by-passes the confirmation from without which is the goal of applied mathematics, and seeks it only from within: its conclusions are related primarily to its own premises. Literature also proceeds by hypothetical possibilities. The poet, said Sidney, never affirmeth. He never says "this is so"; he says "let there be such a situation," and poetic truth, the validity of his conclusion, is to be tested primarily by its coherence with his original postulate. Of course, there is applied literature, just as there is applied mathematics, which we test historically, by its lifelikeness, or philosophically, by the cogency of its propositions. Literature, like mathematics, is constantly useful, a word which means having a continuing relationship to the common field of experience. But pure literature, like pure mathematics, is disinterested, or useless: it contains its own meaning. Any attempt to determine the category of literature must start with a distinction between the verbal form which is primarily itself and the verbal form which is primarily related to something else. The former is a complex verbal fact, the latter a complex of verbal symbols.

We have to use the mathematical analogy once more before we leave it. Literature is, of course, dependent on the haphazard and unpredictable appearance of creative genius. So actually is mathematics, but we hardly notice this because in mathematics a steady consolidating process goes on, and the work of its geniuses is absorbed in the evolving and expanding patern of the mathematical universe. Literature being as yet unorganized by criticism, it still appears as a huge aggregate or miscellaneous pile of creative efforts. The only organizing principle so far discovered in it is chronology, and when we see the miscellaneous pile strung out along a chronological line, some coherence is given to it by the linear factors in tradition. We can trace an epic tradition by virtue of the fact that Virgil succeeded Homer, Dante Virgil, and Milton Dante. But, as already suggested, this is very far from being the best we can do. Criticism has still to develop a theory of literature which will see this aggregate within a verbal universe, as forms integrated within a total form. An epic, besides occurring at a certain point in time, is also something of a definitive statement of the poet's imaginative experience, whereas a lyric is usually a more fragmentary one. This suggests the image of a kind of radiating circle of literary experience in which the lyric is nearer to a periphery and the epic nearer to a centre. It is only an image, but the notion that literature, like any other form of knowledge, possesses a centre and a circumference seems reasonable enough.

If so, then literature is a single body, a vast organically growing form, and, though of course works of art do not improve, yet it may be possible for criticism to see literature as showing a progressive evolution in time, of a kind rather like what Newman postulates for Catholic dogma. One could collect remarks by the dozen from various critics, many of them quite misleading, to show that they are dimly aware, on some level of consciousness, of the possibility of a critical progress toward a total comprehension of literature which no critical history gives any hint of. When Mr. Eliot says that the whole tradition of Western poetry from Homer down ought to exist simultaneously in the poet's mind, the adverb suggests a transcending by criticism of the tyranny of historical categories. I even think that the consolidation of literature by criticism into the verbal universe was one of the things that Matthew Arnold meant by culture. To begin this process seems to me the function of criticism at the present time.

31

M. H. Abrams
1912–

Meyer Howard Abrams was born in Long Branch, New Jersey. He attended Harvard University and Cambridge University and received a Ph.D. from Harvard in 1940. He has lectured and taught at many American universities and is currently Class of 1916 Professor at Cornell University. Abrams is a distinguished critic and historian of nineteenth-century literature, particularly the British romantic movement. His books include: *The Milk of Paradise* (1970); *The Mirror and the Lamp* (1953); *A Glossary of Literary Terms* (1971); *Natural Supernaturalism* (1971); and (as editor) the *Norton Anthology of English Literature*.

M. H. Abrams is closely identified with what is called "pluralism" in contemporary criticism. That is, like Wayne C. Booth, he imagines the diversity of contemporary critical positions to constitute a potentially reconcilable whole, a harmonious assortment of differences that may be described from a dispassionate and more or less objective stance. In "The Deconstructive Angel" (1977), for example, Abrams says that bringing "diverse points of view, with diverse results" on a subject is necessary to understanding literary and cultural history. He also says, however, that the deconstructive criticism in the 1970s "goes beyond the limits of pluralism." Specifically, he notes J. Hillis Miller's "challenging review" of his own *Natural Supernaturalism* and Booth's response to Miller. Abrams then examines Derrida's notion of writing, which Miller draws on, as *écriture*—a concept that radically challenges the possibility of pluralism. Abrams objects that Derrida "puts out of play, before the game [of writing literary history] even begins, every source of norms, controls, or indicators which, in the ordinary use and experience of language, set a limit to what we can mean and what we can be understood to mean." Abrams's forceful discussion ends with his critical refusal "to substitute the rules of the deconstructive enterprise for our ordinary skill and tact at language . . . ," the very "skill" that enables the objective stance that Abrams values.

The Deconstructive Angel

DEMOGORGON.—*If the Abysm*
Could vomit forth its secrets:—but a voice
Is wanting . . .

Shelley, *Prometheus Unbound*

We have been instructed these days to be wary of words like "origin," "center," and "end," but I will venture to say that this session had its origin in the dialogue between Wayne Booth and myself which centered on the rationale of the historical procedures in my book, *Natural Supernaturalism*. Hillis Miller had, in all innocence, written a review of that book; he was cited and answered by Booth, then recited and re-answered by me, and so was sucked into the vortex of our exchange to make it now a dialogue of three. And given the demonstrated skill of our chairman in fomenting debates, who can predict how many others will be drawn into the vortex before it comes to an end?

I shall take this occasion to explore the crucial issue that was raised by Hillis Miller in his challenging review. I agreed with Wayne Booth that pluralism—the bringing to bear on a subject of diverse points of view, with diverse results—is not only valid, but necessary to our understanding of literary and cultural history: in such pursuits the convergence of diverse points of view is the only way to achieve a vision in depth. I also said, however, that Miller's radical statement, in his review, of the principles of what he calls deconstructive interpretation goes beyond the limits of pluralism, by making impossible anything that we would account as literary and cultural history.[1] The issue would hardly be worth pursuing on this public platform if it were only a question of the soundness of the historical claims in a single book. But Miller considered *Natural Supernaturalism* as an example "in the grand tradition of modern humanistic scholarship, the tradition of Curtius, Auerbach, Lovejoy, C. S. Lewis,"[2] and he made it clear that what is at stake is the validity of the premises and procedures of the entire body of traditional inquiries in the human sciences. And that is patently a matter important enough to warrant our discussion.

Let me put as curtly as I can the essential, though usually implicit, premises that I share with traditional historians of Western culture, which Miller puts in question and undertakes to subvert:

1. The basic materials of history are written texts; and the authors who wrote these texts (with some off-center exceptions) exploited the possibilities and norms of their inherited language to say something determinate, and assumed that competent readers, insofar as these shared their own linguistic skills, would be able to understand what they said.
2. The historian is indeed for the most part able to interpret not only what the passages that he cites might mean now, but also what their writers meant when they wrote them. Typically, the historian puts his interpretation in language which is partly his author's and partly his own; if it is sound, this interpretation approximates, closely enough for the purpose at hand, what the author meant.
3. The historian presents his interpretation to the public in the expectation that the expert reader's interpretation of a passage will approximate his own and so confirm the "objectivity" of his interpretation. The worldly-wise author expects that some of his interpre-

> tations will turn out to be mistaken, but such errors, if limited in scope, will not seriously affect the soundness of his overall history. If, however, the bulk of his interpretations are misreadings, his book is not to be accounted a history but an historical fiction.

Notice that I am speaking here of linguistic interpretation, not of what is confusingly called "historical interpretation"—that is, the categories, topics, and conceptual and explanatory patterns that the historian brings to his investigation of texts, which serve to shape the story within which passages of texts, with their linguistic meanings, serve as instances and evidence. The differences among these organizing categories, topics, and patterns effect the diversity in the stories that different historians tell, and which a pluralist theory finds acceptable. Undeniably, the linguistic meanings of the passages cited are in some degree responsive to differences in the perspective that a historian brings to bear on them; but the linguistic meanings are also in considerable degree recalcitrant to alterations in perspective, and the historian's fidelity to these meanings, without his manipulating and twisting them to fit his preconceptions, serves as a prime criterion of the soundness of the story that he undertakes to tell.

One other preliminary matter: I don't claim that my interpretation of the passages I cite exhausts everything that these passages mean. In his review, Hillis Miller says that "a literary or philosophical text, for Abrams, has a single unequivocal meaning 'corresponding' to the various entities it 'represents' in a more or less straightforward mirroring." I don't know how I gave Miller the impression that my "theory of language is implicitly mimetic," a "straightforward mirror" of the reality it reflects,[3] except on the assumption he seems to share with Derrida, and which seems to me obviously mistaken, that all views of language which are not in the deconstructive mode are mimetic views. My view of language, as it happens, is by and large functional and pragmatic: language, whether spoken or written, is the use of a great variety of speech-acts to accomplish a great diversity of human purposes; only one of these many purposes is to assert something about a state of affairs; and such a linguistic assertion does not mirror, but serves to direct attention to selected aspects of that state of affairs.

At any rate, I think it is quite true that many of the passages I cite are equivocal and multiplex in meaning. All I claim—all that any traditional historian needs to claim—is that, whatever else the author also meant, he meant, at a sufficient approximation, at least *this*, and that the "this" that I specify is sufficient to the story I undertake to tell. Other historians, having chosen to tell a different story, may in their interpretation identify different aspects of the meanings conveyed by the same passage.

That brings me to the crux of my disagreement with Hillis Miller. His central contention is not simply that I am sometimes, or always, wrong in my interpretation, but instead that I—like other traditional historians—can never be right in my interpretation. For Miller assents to Nietzsche's challenge of "the concept of 'rightness' in interpretation," and to Nietzsche's assertion that "the same text authorizes innumerable interpretations (*Auslegungen*): there is no 'correct' interpretation."[4] Nietzsche's views of interpretation, as Miller says, are relevant to the recent deconstructive theorists, including Jacques Derrida and himself, who have "reinterpreted Nietzsche" or have written "directly or indirectly under his aegis." He goes on to quote a number of statements from Nietzsche's *The Will to Power* to the effect, as Miller puts it, "that reading is never the objective identifying of a sense but the importation of meaning into a text which has no meaning 'in itself.'" For example: "Ultimately, man finds in things nothing but what he himself has imported into them." "In fact interpretation is itself a means of becoming master of something."[5] On the face of it, such sweeping deconstructive claims might suggest those of Lewis Carroll's linguistic philosopher, who asserted that meaning is imported into a text by the interpreter's will to power:

> "The question is," said Alice, "whether you *can* make words mean so many different things."
> "The question is," said Humpty Dumpty, "which is to be master—that's all."

But of course I don't at all believe that such deconstructive claims are, in Humpty Dumpty fashion, simply dogmatic assertions. Instead, they are conclusions which are derived from particular linguistic premises. I want, in the time remaining, to present what I make out to be the elected linguistic premises, first of Jacques Derrida, then of Hillis Miller, in the confidence that if I misinterpret these theories, my errors will soon be challenged and corrected. Let me eliminate suspense by saying at the beginning that I don't think that their radically skeptical conclusions from these premises are wrong. On the contrary, I believe that their conclusions are right—in fact, they are *infallibly* right, and that's where the trouble lies.

I

It is often said that Derrida and those who follow his lead subordinate all inquiries to a prior inquiry into language. This is true enough, but not specific enough, for it does not distinguish Derrida's work from what Richard Rorty calls "the linguistic turn"[6] which characterizes modern Anglo-American philosophy and also a great part of Anglo-American literary criticism, including the "New Criticism," of the last half-century. What is distinctive about Derrida is first that, like other French structuralists, he shifts his inquiry from language to *écriture,* the written or printed text; and second that he conceives a text in an extraordinarily limited fashion.

Derrida's initial and decisive strategy is to disestablish the priority, in traditional views of language, of speech over writing. By priority I mean the use of oral discourse as the conceptual model from which to derive the semantic and other features of written language and of language in general. And Derrida's shift of elementary reference is to a written text which consists of what we find when we look at it—to "un texte déjà écrit, noir sur blanc."[7] In the dazzling play of Derrida's expositions, his ultimate recourse is to these black marks on white paper as the sole things that are actually present in reading, and so are not fictitious constructs, illusions, phantasms; the visual features of these black-on-blanks he expands in multiple dimensions of elaborately figurative significance, only to contract them again, at telling moments, to their elemental status. The only things that are patently there when we look at the text are "marks" that are demarcated, and separated into groups, by "blanks"; there are also "spaces," "margins," and the "repetitions" and "differences" that we find when we compare individual marks and groups of marks. By his rhetorical mastery Derrida solicits us to follow him in his move to these new premises, and to allow ourselves to be locked into them. This move is from what he calls the closed "logocentric" model of all traditional or "classical" views of language (which, he maintains, is based on the illusion of a Platonic or Christian transcendent being or presence, serving as the origin and guarantor of meanings) to what I shall call his own graphocentric model, in which the sole presences are marks-on-blanks.

By this bold move Derrida puts out of play, before the game even begins, every source of norms, controls, or indicators which, in the ordinary use and experience of language, set a limit to what we can mean and what we can be understood to mean. Since the only givens are already-existing marks, "déjà écrit," we are denied recourse to a speaking or writing subject, or ego, or cogito, or consciousness, and so to any possible agency for the intention of meaning something ("vouloir dire"); all such agencies are relegated to the status of fictions generated by language, readily dissolved by deconstructive analysis. By this move he leaves us no place for referring to how we learn to speak, understand, or read language, and how, by interaction with more competent users and by our own developing experience with language, we come to recognize and correct our mistakes in speaking or understanding. The author is translated by Derrida (when he's not speaking in the momentary shorthand of traditional fictions) to a status as one more mark among other marks, placed at the head or the end of a text or set of texts, which are denominated as "bodies of work identified according to the 'proper name' of a signature."[8] Even syntax, the organization of words into a significant sentence, is given no role in determining the meanings of component words, for according to the graphocentric model, when we look at a page we see no organization but only a "chain" of grouped marks, a sequence of individual signs.

It is the notion of "the sign" that allows Derrida a limited opening-out of his premises. For he brings to a text the knowledge that the marks on a page are not random markings, but signs, and that a sign has a dual aspect as signifier and signified, signal and concept, or mark-with-meaning. But these meanings, when we look at a page, are not there, either as physical or mental presences. To account for significance, Derrida turns to a highly specialized and elaborated use of Saussure's notion that the identity either of the sound or of the signification of a sign does not consist in a positive attribute, but in a negative (or relational) attribute—this is, its "difference," or differentiability, from other sounds and other significations within a particular linguistic system.[9] This notion of difference is readily available to Derrida, because inspection of the printed page shows that some marks and sets of marks repeat each other, but that others differ from each other. In Derrida's theory "difference"—not "the difference between a and b and c . . ." but simply "difference" in itself—supplements the static elements of a text with an essential operative term, and as such (somewhat in the fashion of the term "negativity" in the dialectic of Hegel) it performs prodigies. For "difference" puts into motion the incessant play (*jeu*) of signification that goes on within the seeming immobility of the marks on the printed page.

To account for what is distinctive in the signification of a sign, Derrida puts forward the term "trace," which he says is not a presence, though it functions as a kind of "simulacrum" of a signified presence. Any signification that difference has activated in a signifier in the past remains active as a "trace" in the present instance as it will in the future,[10] and the "sedimentation" of traces which a signifier has accumulated constitutes the diversity in the play of its present significations. This trace is an elusive aspect of a text which is not, yet functions as though it were; it plays a role without being "present"; it "appears/disappears"; "in presenting itself it effaces itself."[11] Any attempt to define or interpret the significance of a sign or chain of signs consists in nothing more than the interpreter's putting in its place another sign or chain of signs, "sign-substitutions," whose self-effacing traces merely defer laterally, from substitution to substitution, the fixed and present meaning (or the signified "presence") we vainly pursue. The promise that the trace seems to offer of a presence on which the play of signification can come to rest in a determinate reference is thus never realizable, but incessantly deferred, put off, delayed. Derrida coins what in French is the portmanteau term *différance* (spelled *-ance*, and fusing the notions of differing and deferring) to indicate the endless play of generated significances, in which the reference is interminably postponed.[12] The conclusion, as Derrida puts it, is that "the central signified, the originating or transcendental signified" is revealed to be "never absolutely present outside a system of differences," and this "absence of an ultimate signified extends the domain and play of signification to infinity."[13]

What Derrida's conclusion comes to is that no sign or chain of signs can have a determinate meaning. But it seems to me that Derrida reaches this conclusion by a process which, in its own way, is no less dependent on an origin, ground, and end, and which is no less remorselessly "teleological," than the most rigorous of the metaphysical systems that he uses his conclusions to deconstruct. His origin and ground are his graphocentric premises, the closed chamber of texts for which he invites us to abandon our ordinary realm of experience in speaking, hearing, reading, and understanding language. And from such a beginning we move to a foregone conclusion. For Derrida's chamber of texts is a sealed echo-chamber in which meanings are reduced to a ceaseless echolalia, a vertical and lateral reverberation from sign to sign of ghostly nonpresences emanating from no voice, intended by no one, referring to nothing, bombinating in a void.

For the mirage of traditional interpretation, which vainly undertakes to determine what an author meant, Derrida proposes the alternative that we deliver ourselves over to a free participation in the infinite free-play of signification opened out by the signs in a text. And on this cheerless prospect of language and the cultural enterprise in ruins Derrida bids us to try to gaze, not with a Rousseauistic nostalgia for a lost security as to meaning which we never in fact possessed, but instead with "a Nietzschean *affirmation*, the joyous affirmation of the play of the world and of the innocence of becoming, the affirmation of a world of signs without error [*faute*], without truth, without origin, which is offered to an active interpretation. . . . And it plays without security. . . . In absolute chance, affirmation also surrenders itself to *genetic* indeterminancy, to the *seminal* chanciness [*aventure*] of the trace."[14] The graphocentric premises eventuate in what is patently a metaphysics, a world-view of the free and unceasing play of *différance* which (since we can only glimpse this world by striking free of language, which inescapably implicates the entire metaphysics of presence that this view replaces) we are not able even to name. Derrida's vision is thus, as he puts it, of an "as yet unnamable something which cannot announce itself except . . . under the species of a non-species, under the formless form, mute, infant, and terrifying, of monstrosity."[15]

II

Hillis Miller sets up an apt distinction between two classes of current structuralist critics, the "canny critics" and the "uncanny critics." The canny critics cling still to the possibility of "a structuralist-inspired criticism as a rational and rationalizable activity, with agreed-upon rules of procedure, given facts, and measurable results." The uncanny critics have renounced such a nostalgia for impossible certainties.[16] And as himself an uncanny critic, Miller's persistent enterprise is to get us to share, in each of the diverse works that he criticizes, its self-deconstructive revelation that in default of any possible origin, ground, presence, or end, it is an interminable free-play of indeterminable meanings.

Like Derrida, Miller sets up as his given the written text, "innocent black marks on a page"[17] which are endowed with traces, or vestiges of meaning; he then employs a variety of strategies that maximize the number and diversity of the possible meanings while minimizing any factors that might limit their free-play. It is worthwhile to note briefly two of those strategies.

For one thing Miller applies the terms "interpretation" and "meaning" in an extremely capacious way, so as to conflate linguistic utterance or writing with any metaphysical representation of theory or of "fact" about the physical world. These diverse realms are treated equivalently as "texts" which are "read" or "interpreted." He thus leaves no room for taking into account that language, unlike the physical world, is a cultural institution that developed expressly in order to mean something and to convey what is meant to members of a community who have learned how to use and interpret language. And within the realm of explicitly verbal texts, Miller allows for no distinction with regard to the kinds of norms that may obtain or may not obtain for the "interpretation" of the entire corpus of an individual author's writings, or of a single work in its totality, or of a particular passage, sentence, or word within that work. As a critical pluralist, I would agree that there are a diversity of sound (though not equally adequate) interpretations of the play *King Lear*, yet I claim to know precisely what Lear meant when he said, "Pray you undo this button."

A second strategy is related to Derrida's treatment of the "trace." Like Derrida, Miller excludes by his elected premises any control or limitation of signification by reference to the uses of a word or phrase that are current at the time an author writes, or to an author's intention, or to the verbal or generic context in which a word occurs. Any word within a given text—or at least any "key word," as he calls it, that he picks out for special scrutiny—can thus be claimed to signify any and all of the diverse things it has signified in the varied forms that the signifier has assumed through its recorded history; and not only in a particular language, such as English or French, but back through its etymology in Latin and Greek all the way to its postulated Indo-European root. Whenever and by whomever and in whatever context a printed word is used, therefore, the limits of what it can be said to mean in that use are set only by what the interpreter can find in historical and etymological dictionaries, supplemented by any further information that the interpreter's own erudition can provide. Hence Miller's persistent recourse to etymology—and even to the significance of the shapes of the printed letters in the altering form of a word—in expounding the texts to which he turns his critical attention.[18]

Endowed thus with the sedimented meanings accumulated over its total history, but stripped of any norms for selecting some of these and rejecting others, a key word—like the larger passage or total text of which the word is an element—becomes (in the phrase Miller cites from Mallarmé) a *suspens vibratoire*,[19] a vibratory suspension of equally likely meanings, and these are bound to include "incompatible" or "irreconcilable" or "contradictory" meanings. The conclusion from these views Miller formulates in a variety of ways: a key word, or a passage, or a text, since it is a ceaseless play of anomalous meanings, is "indeterminable," "undecipherable," "unreadable," "undecidable."[20] Or more bluntly: "All reading is misreading." "Any reading can be shown to be a misreading on evidence drawn from the text itself." But in misreading a text, the interpreter is merely repeating what the text itself has done before him, for "any literary text, with more or less explicitness or clarity, already reads or misreads itself."[21] To say that this concept of interpretation cuts the ground out from under the kind of history I undertook to write is to take a very parochial view of what is involved; for what it comes to is that no text, in part or whole, can mean anything in particular, and that we can never say just what anyone means by anything he writes.

But if all interpretation is misinterpretation, and if all criticism (like all history) of texts can engage only with a critic's own misconstruction, why bother to carry on the activities of interpretation and criticism? Hillis Miller poses this question more than once. He presents his answers in terms of his favorite analogues for the interpretive activity, which he explores with an unflagging resourcefulness. These analogues figure the text we read as a Cretan labyrinth, and also as the texture of a spider's web; the two figures, he points out, have been fused in earlier conflations in the myth of Ariadne's thread, by which Theseus retraces the windings of the labyrinth, and of Arachne's thread, with which she spins her web.[22] Here is one of Miller's answers to the question, why pursue the critical enterprise?

> Pater's writings, like those of other major authors in the Occidental tradition, are at once open to interpretation and ultimately indecipherable, unreadable. His texts lead the critic deeper and deeper into a labyrinth until he confronts a final aporia. This does not mean, however, that the reader must give up from the beginning the attempt to understand Pater. Only by going all the way into the labyrinth, following the thread of a given clue, can the critic reach the blind alley, vacant of any Minotaur, that impasse which is the end point of interpretation.[23]

Now, I make bold to claim that I understand Miller's passage, and that what it says, in part, is that the deconstructive critic's act of interpretation has a beginning and an end; that it begins as an intentional, goal-oriented quest; and that this quest is to end in an impasse.

The reaching of the interpretive aporia or impasse precipitates what Miller calls "the uncanny moment"—the moment in which the critic, thinking to deconstruct the text, finds that he has simply participated in the ceaseless play of the text as a self-deconstructive artifact. Here is another of Miller's statements, in which he describes both his own and Derrida's procedure:

> Deconstruction as a mode of interpretation works by a careful and circumspect entering of each textual labyrinth. . . . The deconstructive critic seeks to find, by this process of retracing, the element in the system studied which is alogical, the thread in the text in question which will unravel it all, or the loose stone which will pull down the whole building. The deconstruction, rather, annihilates the ground on which the building stands by showing that the text has already annihilated that ground, knowingly or unknowingly. Deconstruction is not a dismantling of the structure of a text but a demonstration that it has already dismantled itself.[24]

The uncanny moment in interpretation, as Miller phrases it elsewhere, is a sudden "*mise en abyme*" in which the bottom drops away and, in the endless regress of the self-baffling free-play of meanings in the very signs which both reveal an abyss and, by naming it, cover it over, we catch a glimpse of the abyss itself in a "vertigo of the underlying nothingness."[25]

The "deconstructive critic," Miller has said, "*seeks* to find" the alogical element in a text, the thread which, when pulled, will unravel the whole texture. Given the game Miller has set up, with its graphocentric premises and freedom of interpretive maneuver, the infallible rule of the deconstructive quest is, "Seek and ye shall find." The deconstructive method works, because it can't help working; it is a can't-fail enterprise; there is no complex passage of verse or prose which could possibly serve as a counter-instance to test its validity or limits. And the uncanny critic, whatever the variousness and distinctiveness of the texts to which he applies his strategies, is bound to find that they all reduce to one thing and one thing only. In Miller's own words: each deconstructive reading, "performed on any literary, philosophical, or critical text . . . reaches, in the particular way the given text allows it, the 'same' moment of an aporia. . . . The reading comes back again and again, with different texts, to the 'same' impasse."[26]

It is of no avail to point out that such criticism has nothing whatever to do with our common experience of the uniqueness, the rich variety, and the passionate human concerns in works of literature, philosophy, or criticism—these matters which are among the linguistic illusions that the criticism dismantles. There are, I want to emphasize, rich rewards in reading Miller, as in reading Derrida, which include a delight in his resourceful play of mind and language and the many and striking insights yielded by his wide reading and by his sharp eye for unsuspected congruities and differences in our heritage of literary and philosophical writings. But these rewards are yielded by the way, and that way is always to the ultimate experience of vertigo, the uncanny *frisson* at teetering with him on the brink of the abyss; and even the shock of this discovery is soon dulled by its expected and invariable recurrence.

I shall cite a final passage to exemplify the deft and inventive play of Miller's rhetoric, punning, and figuration, which give his formulations of the *mise en abyme* a charm that is hard to resist. In it he imposes his fused analogues of labyrinth and web and abyss on the black-on-blanks which constitute the elemental given of the deconstructive premises:

> Far from providing a benign escape from the maze, Ariadne's thread makes the labyrinth, is the labyrinth. The interpretation or solving of the puzzles of the textual web only adds more filaments to the web. One can never escape from the labyrinth because the activity of escaping makes more labyrinth, the thread of a linear narrative or story. Criticism is the production of more thread to embroider the texture or textile already there. This thread is like a filament of ink which flows from the pen of the writer, keeping him in the web but suspending him also over the chasm, the blank page that thin line hides.[27]

To interpret: Hillis Miller, suspended by the labyrinthine lines of a textual web over the abyss that those black lines demarcate on the blank page, busies himself to unravel the web that keeps him from plunging into the blank-abyss, but finds he can do so only by an act of writing which spins a further web of lines, equally vulnerable to deconstruction, but only by another movement of the pen that will trace still another inky net over the ever-receding abyss. As Miller remarks, I suppose ruefully, at the end of the passage I quoted, "In one version of Ariadne's story she is said to have hanged herself with her thread in despair after being abandoned by Theseus."

III

What is one to say in response to this abysmal vision of the textual world of literature, philosophy, and all the other achievements of mankind in the medium of language? There is, I think, only one adequate response, and that is the one that William Blake made to the Angel in *The Marriage of Heaven and Hell*. After they had groped their way down a "winding cavern," the Angel revealed to Blake a ghastly vision of hell as an "infinite Abyss"; in it was "the sun, black but shining," around which were "fiery tracks on which revolv'd vast spiders." But no sooner, says Blake, had "my friend the Angel" departed, "then this appearance was no more, but I found myself sitting on a pleasant bank beside a river by moon light, hearing a harper who sung to a harp." The Angel, "surprised asked me how I escaped? I answered: 'All that we saw was owing to your metaphysics.' "

As a deconstructive Angel, Hillis Miller, I am happy to say, is not serious about deconstruction, in Hegel's sense of "serious"; that is, he does not entirely and consistently commit himself to the consequences of his premises. He is in fact, fortunately for us, a double agent who plays the game of language by two very different sets of rules. One of the games he plays is that of a deconstructive critic of literary texts. The other is the game he will play in a minute or two when he steps out of his graphocentric premises onto this platform and begins to talk to us.

I shall hazard a prediction as to what Miller will do then. He will have determinate things to say and will masterfully exploit the resources of language to express these things clearly and forcibly, addressing himself to us in the confidence that we, to the degree that we have mastered the constitutive norms of this kind of discourse, will approximate what he means. He will show no inordinate theoretical difficulties about beginning his discourse or conducting it through its middle to an end. What he says will manifest, by immediate inference, a thinking subject or ego and a distinctive and continuant ethos, so that those of you who, like myself, know and admire his recent writings will be surprised and delighted by particularities of what he says, but will correctly anticipate both its general tenor and its highly distinctive style and manner of proceeding. What he says, furthermore, will manifest a feeling as well as thinking subject; and unless it possesses a superhuman forbearance, this subject will express some natural irritation that I, an old friend, should so obtusely have misinterpreted what he has said in print about his critical intentions.

Before coming here, Miller worked his thoughts (which involved inner speech) into the form of writing. On this platform, he will proceed to convert this writing to speech; and it is safe to say—since our chairman is himself a double agent, editor of a critical journal as well as organizer of this symposium—that soon his speech will be reconverted to writing and presented to the public. This substitution of *écriture* for *parole* will certainly make a difference, but not an absolute difference; what Miller says here, that is, will not jump an ontological gap to the printed page, shedding on the way all the features that made it intelligible as discourse. For each of his readers will be able to reconvert the black-on-blanks back into speech, which he will hear in his mind's ear; he will perceive the words not simply as marks nor as sounds, but as already invested with meaning; also, by immediate inference, he will be aware in his reading of an intelligent subject, very similar to the one we will infer while listening to him here, who organizes the well-formed and significant sentences and marshals the argument conveyed by the text.

There is no linguistic or any other law

we can appeal to that will prevent a deconstructive critic from bringing his graphocentric procedures to bear on the printed version of Hillis Miller's discourse—or of mine, or of Wayne Booth's—and if he does, he will infallibly be able to translate the text into a vertiginous *mise en abyme*. But those of us who stubbornly refuse to substitute the rules of the deconstructive enterprise for our ordinary skill and tact at language will find that we are able to understand this text very well. In many ways, in fact, we will understand it better than while hearing it in the mode of oral discourse, for the institution of print will render the fleeting words of his speech by a durable graphic correlate which will enable us to take our own and not the speaker's time in attending to it, as well as to re-read it, to collocate, and to ponder until we are satisfied that we have approximated the author's meaning.

After Hillis Miller and I have pondered in this way over the text of the other's discourse, we will probably, as experience in such matters indicates, continue essentially to disagree. By this I mean that neither of us is apt to find the other's reasons so compelling as to get him to change his own interpretive premises and aims. But in the process, each will have come to see more clearly what the other's reasons are for doing what he does, and no doubt come to discover that some of these reasons are indeed good reasons in that, however short of being compelling, they have a bearing on the issue in question. In brief, insofar as we set ourselves, in the old-fashioned way, to make out what the other means by what he says, I am confident that we shall come to a better mutual understanding. After all, without that confidence that we can use language to say what we mean and can interpret language so as to determine what was meant, there is no rationale for the dialogue in which we are now engaged.

NOTES

1. "Rationality and Imagination in Cultural History: A Reply to Wayne Booth," *Critical Inquiry*, 2 (Spring 1976), 456–60.

2. "Tradition and Difference," *Diacritics*, 2 (Winter 1972), 6.

3. Ibid., pp. 10–11.

4. Ibid., pp. 8, 12.

5. Ibid.

6. Richard Rorty, ed., *The Linguistic Turn* (Chicago and London, 1967).

7. Jacques Derrida, "La Double séance," in *La Dissémination* (Paris, 1972), 203.

8. Derrida, "La Mythologie blanche: la métaphore dans le texte philosophique," in *Marges de la philosophie* (Paris, 1972), 304. Translations throughout are my own.

9. Ferdinand de Saussure, *Course in General Linguistics*, trans. Wade Baskin (New York, 1959), pp. 117–21.

10. Derrida, "La Différance," in *Marges de la philosophie*, pp. 12–14, 25.

11. Ibid., pp. 23–24.

12. In the traditional or "classical" theory of signs, as Derrida describes the view that he dismantles, the sign is taken to be a "deferred presence . . . the circulation of signs defers the moment in which we will be able to encounter the thing itself, to get hold of it, consume or expend it, touch it, see it, have a present intuition of it" (ibid., p. 9). See also "Hors livre" in *La Dissémination*, pp. 10–11.

13. Derrida, "La Structure, le signe et le jeu dans le discours des sciences humaines," in *L'Écriture et la différence* (Paris, 1967), 411.

14. Ibid, p. 427. Derrida adds that this "interpretation of interpretation," which "affirms free-play . . . tries to pass beyond man and humanism. . . ." On the coming "monstrosity," see also *De la grammatologie* (Paris, 1967), 14.

15. Derrida, "La Structure, le signe," p. 428. "We possess no language . . . which is alien to this history; we cannot express a single destructive proposition which will not already have slipped into the form, the logic, and the implicit postulates of that very thing that it seeks to oppose." "Each limited borrowing drags along with it all of metaphysics" (pp. 412–13).

16. J. Hillis Miller, "Stevens' Rock and Criticism as Cure, II," *The Georgia Review*, 30 (Summer 1976), 335–36.

17. Miller, "Walter Pater: A Partial Portrait," *Daedalus*, 105 (Winter 1976), 107.

18. See, for example, his unfolding of the meanings of "cure" and "absurd" in "Stevens' Rock and Criticism as Cure," I, *The Georgia Review*, 30 (Spring 1976), 6–11. For his analysis of significance in the altering shapes, through history, of the printed form of a word see his exposition of *abyme*, ibid., p. 11; also his exposition of the letter *x* in "Ariadne's Thread: Repetition and the Narrative Line," *Critical Inquiry*, 3 (Autumn 1976), 75–76.

19. "Tradition and Difference," p. 12.

20. See, e.g., "Stevens' Rock," I, pp. 9–11; "Walter Pater," p. 111.

21. "Walter Pater," p. 98; "Stevens' Rock, II," p. 333.

22. "Ariadne's Thread," p. 66.

23. "Walter Pater," p. 112.

24. "Stevens' Rock, II," p. 341. See also "Walter Pater," p. 101, and "Ariadne's Thread," p. 74.

25. "Stevens' Rock," I, pp. 11–12. The unnamable abyss which Miller glimpses has its parallel in the unnamable and terrifying monstrosity which Derrida glimpses; see above, p. 433.

26. "Deconstructing the Deconstructors," *Diacritics*, 5 (Summer 1975), 30.

27. "Stevens' Rock, II." p. 337.

32

J. Hillis Miller
1928–

J. Hillis Miller, a distinguished critic and scholar, received a Ph.D. from Harvard University in 1951. He taught for more than two decades at Johns Hopkins University and fourteen years at Yale University. He is now Distinguished Professor of English and Comparative Literature at the University of California, Irvine. At Yale with Geoffrey Hartman and Paul de Man, Miller had been vital in introducing Continental literary studies and philosophy to the Anglo-American academic community, practicing versions of deconstructive and Poststructuralist criticism. Miller's work has always been at the forefront of critical discourse in the United States; in fact, his career—including a Formalist dissertation, books that approach texts from a phenomenological perspective, and his present work in deconstructive criticism—epitomizes postwar American literary studies. His major works include: *Charles Dickens: The World of his Novels* (1958); *The Disappearance of God* (1963); *The Poets of Reality: Six Twentieth-Century Writers* (1965); *The Form of Victorian Fiction* (1968); *Thomas Hardy: Distance and Desire* (1970); *Fiction and Repetition* (1982); *The Linguistic Moment* (1985); and *The Ethics of Reading* (1987).

The most striking aspect of Miller's work is his lucid faithfulness to the literary or critical texts he examines in the context of the most profound questions of the experience of those texts. Throughout his career, Miller has sought in many ways for such a "metaphysical" reading of literature, but never without maintaining a close sense of the literary texts themselves. As he wrote in *Fiction and Repetition*, "A theory is all too easy to refute or deny, but a reading can be controverted only by going through the difficult task of rereading the work in question and proposing an alternative reading."

In "The Search for Grounds in Literary Study" (1985) Miller specifically returns to Matthew Arnold in the kind of rereading he is calling for. In this essay he is attempting to do several things simultaneously. First of all, he is trying to account for the *experience* of reading, to make sense of—or at least to describe—the strange uncanny experience reading sometimes gives rise to. Second, he is trying to articulate the unconscious assumptions that govern critical writing: he argues that there are four "grounds" upon which to base reading—linguistic, social, psychological, and ontological or metaphysical—and that various critics and schools of critics assume one or the other of these. Moreover, these grounds have two striking qualities: first, they are "imperialist," by which Miller means they tend to reduce all understanding to their own base; and second, they each occasion remarkable resistance, almost hysterical denial (in the Freudian sense of the word) way beyond proportion. A third aim of this essay is to question the larger "ground" of literary study, to ask why it is that literature, since Arnold's time, has been "burdened" with the weight of carrying and maintaining cultural values. For Miller, this is not a necessary aspect of literature, and one can, indeed, question why so many people have seen this as a function of literature. Finally, Miller is also providing a method of criticism, what he calls the "scrupulously slow reading" that Nietzsche speaks of in his call "back to the texts!"

The Search for Grounds in Literary Study

You ask me in what I think or have thought you going wrong: in this: that you would never take your assiette as something determined final and unchangeable for you and proceed to work away on the basis of that: but were always poking and patching and cobbling at the assiette itself—

(Matthew Arnold, *Letters to Clough*)[1]

. . . perhaps one is a philologist still, that is to say, a teacher of slow reading [ein Lehrer des langsamen Lesens].

(Friedrich Nietzsche, "Preface" to *Daybreak*)[2]

An important passage in George Eliot's *Daniel Deronda* (1876) speaks of the liability of the heroine, Gwendolen Harleth, to sudden, inexplicable fits of hysterical terror or of "spiritual dread." She has these fits when faced with open spaces: "Solitude in any wide scene impressed her with an undefined feeling of immeasurable existence aloof from her, in the midst of which she was helplessly incapable of asserting herself."[3]

A strange little paragraph by Maurice Blanchot entitled "Une scène primitive," "A Primitive Scene," and published just a century later, in 1976, describes a "similar" "experience," ascribed this time to a child of seven or eight standing at the window and looking at a wintry urban or suburban scene outside:

> Ce qu'il voit, le jardin, les arbres d'hiver, le mur d'une maison; tandis qu'il voit, sans doute à la manière d'un enfant, son espace de jeu, il se lasse et lenterment regarde en haut vers le ciel ordinaire, avec les nuages, la lumière grise, le jour terne et sans lointain. Ce qui se passe ensuite: le ciel, le *même* ciel, soudain ouvert, noir absolument et vide absolument, révélant (comme par la vitre brisée) une telle absence que tout s'y est depuis toujours et à jamais perdu, au point que s'y affirme et s'y dissipe le savoir vertigineux que rien est ce qu'il y a, et d'abord rien au-delà.

> [What he saw, the garden, the winter trees, the wall of a house; while he looked, no doubt in the way a child does, at his play area, he got bored and slowly looked higher toward the ordinary sky, with the clouds, the grey light, the day flat and without distance. What happened then: the sky, the *same* sky, suddenly opened, black absolutely and empty absolutely, revealing (as if the window had been broken) such an absence that everything is since forever and for forever lost, to the point at which there was affirmed and dispersed there the vertiginous knowledge that nothing is what there is there, and especially nothing beyond.][4]

"Rien est ce qu'il y a, et d'abord rien au-delà": nothing is what there is there, and first of all nothing beyond. As in the case of Wallace Stevens's "The Snow Man," where the listener and watcher in the snow, "nothing himself, beholds/ Nothing that is not there and the nothing that is,"[5] the devastating experience of a transfiguration of the scene which leaves it nevertheless exactly the same, the *same* sky, is the confrontation of a nothing which somehow is, has being, and which absorbs into itself any beyond or transcendence. In this primitive scene, original and originating, for Blanchot's child, or possibly even for Blanchot as a child, the sky definitely does not open to reveal heavenly light or choirs of angels singing "Glory, glory, glory." If the effect on Gwendolen Harleth in Eliot's novel of confronting open space in solitude is sometimes hysterical outbursts, the effect on Blanchot's child of an opening of the sky which does not open is seemingly endless tears of a "ravaging joy [joie ravagéant]."

I take these details from *Daniel Deronda* and from Blanchot's little scene, quite arbitrarily, or almost quite arbitrarily, as parables for the terror or dread readers may experience when they confront a text which seems irreducibly strange, inexplicable, perhaps even mad, for example Blanchot's *Death Sentence* [*L'arrêt de mort*]. As long as we have not identified the law by which the text can be made reasonable, explicable, it is as if we have come face to face with an immeasurable existence aloof from us, perhaps malign, perhaps benign, in any case something we have not yet mastered and assimilated into what we already know. It is as if the sky had opened, while still remaining the same sky, for are not those words there on the page familiar and ordinary words, words in our own language or mother tongue, words whose meaning we know? And yet they have suddenly opened and become terrifying, inexplicable. On the one hand, our task as readers is to transfer to reading Henry James's injunction to the observer of life, the novice writer: "Try to be one of those on whom nothing is lost." A good reader, that is, especially notices oddnesses, gaps, anacoluthons, non sequiturs, apparently irrelevant details, in short, all the marks of the inexplicable, all the marks of the unaccountable, perhaps of the mad, in a text. On the other hand, the reader's task is to reduce the inexplicable to the explicable, to find its reason, its law, its ground, to make the mad sane. The task of the reader, it will be seen, is not too different from the task of the psychoanalyst.

Current criticism tends to propose one or another of the three following grounds on the basis of which the anomalies of literature may be made lawful, the unaccountable accountable: society, the more or less hidden social or ideological pressures which impose themselves on literature and reveal themselves in oddnesses; individual psychology, the more or less hidden psychic pressures which impose themselves on a work of literature and make it odd, unaccountable; language, the more or less hidden rhetorical pressures, or pressures from some torsion within language itself as such, which impose themselves on the writer and make it impossible for his work to maintain itself as an absolutely lucid and reasonable account.

The stories or *récits* of Maurice Blanchot, as well as his criticism, propose a fourth possibility. Though this possibility is, in the case of Blanchot at least, exceedingly difficult to name in so many words, and though the whole task of the reader of Blanchot could be defined as a (perhaps impossible) attempt to make this definition clear to oneself or to others, it can be said that this fourth possibility for the disturber of narrative sanity and coherence, a disruptive energy neither society nor individual psychology nor language itself, is properly religious, metaphysical, or ontological, though hardly in a traditional or conventional way. To borrow a mode of locution familiar to readers of Blanchot it is an ontology without ontology. Nor is it to be defined simply as a species of negative theology. Blanchot gives to this "something" that enters into the words or between the words the names, among others, of it [*il*]; the thing [*la chose*]; dying [*mourir*]; the neutral [*le neutre*]; the non-presence of the eternal return [*le retour éternel*]; writing [*écrire*]; the thought [*la pensée*]; the truth [*la verité*]; the other of the other [*l'autre de l'autre*]; meaning something encountered in our relations to other people, especially relations involving love, betrayal, and that ultimate betrayal by the other of our love for him or her, the death of the other. To list these names in this way cannot possibly convey very much, except possibly, in their multiplicity and incoherence, a glimpse of the inadequacy of any one of them and of the fact that all of them must in one way or another be figurative rather than literal. What sort of "thing" is it which cannot be pinned down and labelled with one single name, so that all names for it are improper, whether proper or generic? All Blanchot's writing is a patient, continual, long-maintained attempt to answer this question, the question posed by the experience recorded in "A Primitive Scene."

Two further features may be identified of my four proposed modes of rationalizing or accounting for or finding grounds for the irrational or unaccountable in any literary account.

The first feature seems obvious enough, though it is evaded often enough to need emphasizing. This is the exclusivity or imperialism of any one of the four. Each has a mode of explanation or of grounding the anomalous in literature demands to exercise sovereign control over the others, to make the others find their ground in *it*. You cannot have all four at once or even any two of them without ultimately grounding, or rather without having already implicitly grounded, all but one in the single regal ur-explanation. Psychological explanations tend to see linguistic, religious, or social explanations as ultimately finding *their* cause in individual human psychology. Social explanations see human psychology, language, and religion as epiphenomena of underlying and determining social forces, the "real" conditions of class, production, consumption, exchange. Linguistic explanations tend to imply or even openly to assert that society, psychology, and religion are "all language," generated by language in the first place and ultimately to be explained by features of language. Metaphysical explanations see society, psychology, and language as secondary, peripheral. Each of these modes of grounding explanation asserts that it is the true "principle of reason," the true *Satz vom Grund*, the others bogus, an abyss not a ground. Each asserts a jealous will to power over the others.

The second feature of these four modes of explaining oddnesses in literature is the strong resistance each of them seems to generate in those to whom they are proposed. The resistance, for example, to Sigmund Freud's assertion of a universal unconscious sexual etiology for neurosis is notorious, and that resistance has by no means subsided. In Marxist theory, for example that of Louis Althusser in *For Marx*, "ideology" is the name given to the imaginary structures, whereby men and women resist facing directly the real economic and social conditions of their existence. "Ideology, then," says Althusser, "is the expression of the relation between men and their 'world,' that is, the (overdetermined) unity of the real relation and the imaginary relation between them and their real conditions of existence."[6] There is a tremendous resistance to totalizing explanations which say, "It's all language," the resistance encountered, for example, by structuralism, semiotics, and by misunderstandings of so-called "deconstruction" today. Many people, finally, seem able to live on from day to day and year to year, even as readers of literature, without seeing religious or metaphysical questions as having any sort of force or subtance. It is not the case that man is everywhere and universally a religious or metaphysical animal. George Eliot, speaking still of Gwendolen, describes eloquently the latter's resistance to two of my sovereign principles of grounding:

> She had no permanent consciousness of other fetters, or of more spiritual restraints, having always disliked whatever was presented to her under the name of religion, in the same way that some people dislike arithmetic and accounts: it had raised no other emotion in her, no alarm, no longing; so that the question whether she believed it had not occurred to her, any more than it had occurred to her to inquire into the conditions of colonial property and banking, on which, as she had had many opportunities of knowing, the family fortune was dependent. (pp. 89–90)

Why this resistance to looking into things, including works of literature, all the way down to the bottom is so strong and so universal I shall not attempt here to explain. Perhaps it is inexplicable. Perhaps it is a general consensus that, as Conrad's Winnie Verloc in *The Secret Agent* puts it, "life doesn't stand much looking into."[7] It might be better not to know.

Is it legitimate to seek in literature a serious concern for such serious topics, to see works of literature as in one way or another interrogations of the ground, taking ground in the sense of a sustaining metaphysical foundation outside language, outside nature, and outside the human mind? The role granted to poetry or to "literature" within our culture and in particular within our colleges and universities today is curiously contradictory. The contradiction is an historical inheritance going back at least to Kant and to eighteenth-century aesthetic theory or "critical philosophy." The tradition comes down from the enlightenment through Romantic literary theory and later by way of such figures as Matthew Arnold (crucial to the development of the "humanities" in American higher education) to the New Criticism and the academic humanism of our own day. On the one hand the enjoyment of poetry is supposed to be the "disinterested" aesthetic contemplation of beautiful or sublime organic forms made of words. It is supposed to be "value free," without contamination by use of the poem for any cognitive, practical, ethical, or political purposes. Such appropriations, it is said, are a misuse of poetry. According to this aestheticizing assumption one ought to be able to read Dante and Milton, for example, or Aeschylus and Shelley, without raising either the question of the truth or falsity of their philosophical and religious beliefs, or the question of the practical consequences of acting on those beliefs. Cleanth Brooks, for example, in a recent essay vigorously reaffirming the tenets of the New Criticism, presents *Paradise Lost* as a case in point: "Milton tells us in the opening lines of *Paradise Lost* that his purpose is to 'justify the ways of God to men,' and there is no reason to doubt that this was what he hoped to do. But what we actually have in the poem is a wonderful interconnected story of events in heaven and hell and upon earth, with grand and awesome scenes brilliantly painted and with heroic actions dramatically rendered. In short, generations of readers have found that the grandeur of the poem far exceeds any direct statement of theological views. The point is underscored by the fact that some readers who reject

Milton's theology altogether nevertheless regard *Paradise Lost* as a great poem."[8]

On the other hand, literature has been weighted down in our culture with the burden of carrying from generation to generation the whole freight of the values of that culture, what Matthew Arnold called "the best that is known and thought in the world."[9] Cleanth Brooks elsewhere in his essay also reiterates this traditional assumption about literature. Walter Jackson Bate, in a recent polemical essay, sees specialization, including the New Criticism's specialization of close reading, as greatly weakening the humanities generally and departments of English in particular. Bate regrets the good old days (from 1930 to 1950) when departments of English taught everything under the sun but reading as such, in a modern reincarnation of the Renaissance ideal of *litterae humaniores*. The literature components of the humanities in our colleges and universities, and departments of English in particular, have with a good conscience undertaken, after hurrying through a soupçon of rhetoric and poetics, to teach theology, metaphysics, psychology, ethics, politics, social and intellectual history, even the history of science and natural history, in short, "Allerleiwissenschaft," like Carlyle's Professor Diogenes Teufelsdröck.[10]

The implicit reasoning behind this apparently blatant contradiction may not be all that difficult to grasp, though the reasoning will only restate the contradiction. It is just because, and only because, works of literature are stable, self-contained, value-free objects of disinterested aesthetic contemplation that they can be trustworthy vehicles of the immense weight of values they carry from generation to generation uncontaminated by the distortions of gross reality. Just because the values are enshrined in works of literature, uninvested, not collecting interest, not put out to vulgar practical use, they remain pure, not used up, still free to be reappropriated for whatever use we may want to make of them. Has not Kant in the third critique, the *Critique of Judgment*, once and for all set works of art as reliable and indispensable middle member (*Mittelglied*), between cognition (pure reason, theory, the subject of the first critique) and ethics (practical reason, praxis, ethics, the subject of the second critique)? And has not Kant defined beauty, as embodied for example in a poem, as "the symbol of morality [*Symbol der Sittlichkeit*]"?[11] Both Bate and René Wellek, the latter in another outspoken polemical essay with the nice title of "Destroying Literary Studies," invoke Kant, or rather their understanding of Kant, as having settled these matters once and for all, as if there were no more need to worry about them, and as if our understanding of Kant, or rather theirs, could safely be taken for granted: ". . . Why not," asks Bate, "turn to David Hume, the greatest skeptic in the history of thought . . . and then turn to Kant, by whom so much of this is answered?" (p. 52); "One can doubt the very existence of aesthetic experience," says Wellek, "and refuse to recognize the distinctions, clearly formulated in Immanuel Kant's *Critique of Judgment*, between the good, the true, the useful, and the beautiful."[12] So much is at stake here that it is probably a good idea to go back and read Kant for ourselves, no easy task to be sure, in order to be certain that he says what Bate and Wellek say he says.

When Matthew Arnold, the founding father, so to speak, of the American concept of the humanities, praises the virtues of disinterested contemplation, he is being faithful to the Kantian inheritance, no doubt by way of its somewhat vulgarizing distortions in Schiller. It was, and is, by no means necessary to have read Kant to be a Kantian of sorts. Arnold's full formulaic definition of criticism, in "The Function of Criticism at the Present Time"

(1864), is "a disinterested endeavour to learn and propagate the best that is known and thought in the world."[13] He speaks elsewhere in the same essay of the "disinterested love of a free play of the mind on all subjects, for its own sake."[14] When Arnold, in a well-known statement in "The Study of Poetry" (1880) which has echoed down the decades as the implicit credo of many American departments of English, says: "The future of poetry is immense, because in poetry, where it is worthy of its high destinies, our race, as time goes on, will find an ever surer and surer stay," he goes on to make it clear that poetry is a "stay" just because it is detached from the question of its truth or falsity as fact. Poetry can therefore replace religion when the fact fails religion. Poetry is cut off from such questions, sequestered in a realm of disinterested fiction. Just for this reason poetry is a "stay," a firm resting place when all else gives way, like a building without a solid foundation. "There is not a creed which is not shaken," says Arnold in his melancholy litany, "not an accredited dogma which is not shown to be questionable, not a received tradition which does not threaten to dissolve. Our religion has materialized itself in the fact, in the supposed fact; it has attached its emotion to the fact, and now the fact is failing it. But for poetry the idea is everything; the rest is a world of illusion, of divine illusion. Poetry attaches its emotion to the idea; the idea *is* the fact."[15] The image here is that of a self-sustaining linguistic fiction or illusion which holds itself up by a kind of intrinsic magic of levitation over the abyss, like an aerial floating bridge over chaos, as long as one does not poke and patch at the assiette. This bridge or platform may therefore hold up also the ideas the poem contains and the readers who sustain themselves by these ideas.

Arnold had this double or even triple notion of the staying power of poetry already in mind when, in 1848 or 1849, many years before writing "The Study of Poetry," he wrote to Arthur Hugh Clough: "Those who cannot read G[ree]k sh[ou]ld read nothing but Milton and parts of Wordsworth: the state should see to it. . . ."[16] Most Freshman and Sophomore courses in American colleges and universities in "Major English Authors" are still conceived in the spirit of Arnold's categorical dictum. The uplifting moral value of reading Milton and parts of Wordsworth, so important that it should be enforced by the highest civil authority, is initially stylistic. Arnold opposes the solemn, elevated, composing "grand" style of Homer, or, failing that, of Milton and parts of Wordsworth, to the "confused multitudinousness" (ibid.) of Browning, Keats, and Tennyson, the Romantics and Victorians generally, excepting that part of Wordsworth. The occasion of Arnold's letter to Clough is the devastating effect on him of reading Keats's letters: "What a brute you were to tell me to read Keats's Letters. However it is over now: and reflexion resumes her power over agitation" (p. 96). From Keats Arnold turns to the Greeks, to Milton, and to those parts of Wordsworth to subdue his inner agitation as well as to protect himself from the agitation without.

Only secondary to the sustaining effect of the grand style as such are the "ideas" expressed in that style. A writer, says Arnold, "must begin with an Idea of the world in order not to be prevailed over by the world's multitudinousness" (ibid., p. 97). The Idea, so to speak, is the style, or the style is the Idea, since the grand style is nothing but the notion of composure, elevation, coherence, objectivity, that is, just the characteristics of the grand style. This combination of grand elevated style and presupposed, preconceived, or preposited grand comprehensive Idea of the world (never mind whether it is empirically verifiable) not only composes and elevates the mind but also fences it off from the confused multitudinousness outside and the danger therefore of confused multitudinousness within. The latter, Arnold, in the "Preface" of 1853, calls "the dialogue of the mind with itself."[17] He associates it especially with the modern spirit, and fears it more than anything else. It is the dissolution of the mind's objectivity, calm, and unity with itself. This composing, lifting up, and fencing out through literature takes place, to borrow from one of the authors Arnold tells us exclusively to read, as God organizes chaos in the work of creation, or as Milton, at the beginning of *Paradise Lost*, prays that his interior chaos, likened to the unformed Abyss, may be illuminated, elevated, impregnated, and grounded by the Holy Spirit or heavenly muse: "Thou from the first/Was present, and with mighty wings outspread/Dove-like satst brooding on the vast Abyss/And madst it pregnant: What in me is dark/Illumine, what is low raise and support" (*Paradise Lost*, I, 19–23).

It is only a step from Kant's image in paragraph 59 of the *Critique of Judgment* of art or poetry as *hypotyposis* [*Hypotypose*], indirect symbols of intuitions for which there is no direct expression,[18] to Hegel's assertion that sublime poetry, like parable, fable, and apologue, is characterized by the non-adequation and dissimilarity between symbol and symbolized, what he calls the *Sichnichtentsprechen beider*, the noncorrespondence of the two.[19] It is only another step beyond that to I. A. Richards' assertion, in *Principles of Literary Criticism*, with some help from Jeremy Bentham's theory of fictions, that the function of poetry is to produce an equilibrium among painfully conflicting impulses and thereby to provide fictive solutions to real psychological problems. Another step in this sequence (which is not even a progression, radicalizing or deepening, but a movement in place), takes us to Wallace Stevens's resonant formulation in the *Adagia* of what all these writers in somewhat different ways are saying: "The final belief is to believe in a fiction, which you know to be a fiction, there being nothing else. The exquisite truth is to know that it is a fiction and that you believe in it willingly."[20]

Proof that Matthew Arnold still plays an indispensable role within this sequence as the presumed base for a conservative humanism is a forceful recent article by Eugene Goodheart, "Arnold at the Present Time," with accompanying essays and responses by George Levine, Morris Dickstein, and Stuart M. Tave.[21] As is not surprising, the oppositions among these essays come down to a question of how one reads Arnold. If Goodheart grossly misrepresents "deconstruction" and the sort of "criticism as critique" I advocate (which is not surprising), he is also a bad reader or a non-reader of Arnold. Goodheart takes for granted the traditional misreading of Arnold which has been necessary to make him, as Goodheart puts it, "the inspiration of humanistic study in England and America" (p. 451). Levine, Dickstein, and Tave are, it happens, far better and more searching readers of Arnold. Adjudication of differences here is of course possible only by a response to that call, "Back to the texts!," which must be performed again and again in literary study. Nothing previous critics have said can be taken for granted, however authoritative it may seem. Each reader must do again for himself the laborious task of a scrupulous slow reading, trying to find out what the texts actually say rather than imposing on them what she or he wants them to say or wishes they said. Advances in literary study are not made by the free invention of new conceptual or historical schemes (which always turn out to be old ones anew in any case), but by that grappling with the texts which always has to be done over once more by each new reader. In the case of Arnold the poetry and prose must be read together, not assumed to be discontinuous units or an early negative stage and a late affirmative stage negating the earlier negation. Far from offering a firm "assiette" to the sort of humanism Goodheart advocates, such a careful reading of Arnold will reveal him to be a nihilist writer through and through, nihilist in the precise sense in which Nietzsche or Heidegger defines the term: as a specifically historical designation of the moment within the development of Western metaphysics when the highest values devalue themselves and come to nothing as their transcendent base dissolves:[22] "There is not a creed which is not shaken, not an accredited dogma which is not shown to be questionable, not a received tradition which does not threaten to dissolve." "I am nothing and very probably never shall be anything," said Arnold in one of the letters to Clough.[23]

A house built on sand, in this case a humanistic tradition built on the shaky foundation of a misreading of Matthew Arnold, cannot stand firmly. To put this another way, the affirmations of Goodheart, Bate, Wellek, and others like them participate inevitably in the historical movement of nihilism ("the history of the next two centuries," Nietzsche called it)[24] which they contest. Most of all they do this in the act itself of contestation. "The question arises," says Heidegger in the section on nihilism in his *Nietzsche*, "whether the innermost essence of nihilism and the power of its dominion do not consist precisely in considering the nothing merely as a nullity [*nur für etwas Nichtiges*], considering nihilism as an apotheosis of the merely vacuous [*der blossen Leere*], as a negation [*eine Verneinung*] that can be set to rights at once by an energetic affirmation."[25]

In a brilliant essay on "The Principle of Reason: The University in the Eyes of its Pupils,"[26] Jacques Derrida identifies the way the modern university and the study of literature within it are based on the domination of the Leibnizian principle of reason, what in German is called "der Satz vom Grund," the notion that everything can and should be accounted for, *Omnis veritatis reddi ratio potest,* that nothing is without reason, *nihil est sine ratione.* Following Nietzsche and Heidegger, Derrida also argues that so-called nihilism is an historical moment which is "completely symmetrical to, thus dependent on, the principle of reason" (p. 15). Nihilism arises naturally and inevitably during a period, the era of technology, when the principle of universal accountability holds sway in the organization of society and of the universities accountable to that society. "For the principle of reason," says Derrida, "may have obscurantist and nihilist effects. They can be seen more or less everywhere, in Europe and America among those who believe they are defending philosophy, literature, and the humanities against these new modes of questioning that are also a new relation to language and tradition, a new affirmation, and new ways of taking responsibility. We can easily see on which side obscurantism and nihilism are lurking when on occasion great professors or representatives of prestigious institutions lose all sense of proportion and control; on such occasions they forget their principles that they claim to defend in their work and suddenly begin to heap insults, to say whatever comes into their heads on the subject of texts that they obviously have never opened or that they have encountered through a mediocre journalism that in other circumstances they would pretend to scorn" (p. 15). Obviously much is at stake here, and we must go carefully, looking before and after, testing the ground carefully, taking nothing for granted.

If such a tremendous burden is being

placed on literature throughout all the period from Kant to academic humanists of our own day like Bate and Goodheart, it is of crucial importance to be sure that literature is able to bear the weight, or that it is a suitable instrument to perform its function. The question is too grave for its answer to be left untested. To raise the question of the weight-bearing capacities of the medium of poetry is of course not the only thing criticism can do or ought to do, but I claim it is one all-important task of literary study. The question in question here is not of the thematic content of or the assertions made by works of literature but of the weight-bearing characteristics of the medium of literature, that is, of language. It is a question of what the language of poetry is and does. Is it indeed solid enough and trustworthy enough to serve, according to the metaphor Kant proposes at the end of the introduction to the *Critique of Judgment*, as the fundamentally necessary bridge passing back and forth between pure cognition and moral action, between *theoria* and *praxis*? "The realm of the natural concept under the one legislation," says Kant, "and that of the concept of freedom under the other are entirely removed [*gänzlich abgesondert*] from all mutual influence [*wechselseitigen Einfluss*] which they might have on one another (each according to its fundamental laws) by the great gulf [*die grosse Kluft*] that separates the supersensible from phenomena [*das Übersinnliche von den Erscheinungen*]. The concept of freedom determines nothing in respect of the theoretical cognition of nature, and the internal concept determines nothing in respect of the practical laws of freedom. So far, then, it is not possible to throw a bridge from the one realm to the other [*eine Brücke von einem Gebiete zu dem andern hinüber zu schlagen*]."[27]

Art or the aesthetic experience is the only candidate for a possible bridge. The whole of the *Critique of Judgment* is written to test out the solidity, so to speak, of the planks by which this indispensable bridge from the realm of knowledge to the realm of moral action might be built, across the great gulf that separates them. If the "beauty" of the work of art is the sensible symbol of morality, it is, on the other hand, the sensible embodiment of the pure idea, what Hegel was to call, in a famous formulation, and in echo of Kant's word *Erscheinungen*, "the sensible shining forth of the idea [*das sinnliche 'scheinen' der Idee*]."[88] As Hegel elsewhere puts it, "art occupies the intermediate ground between the purely sensory and pure thought [*steht in der 'Mitte' zwischen der umittelbaren Sinnlichkeit und dem ideellen Gedanken*]" (Ibid., I, 60, my trans.). Whether Kant or Hegel establish satisfactorily the solidity of this ground, its adequacy as a bridge, is another question, one that a full reading of Kant's third *Kritik* and of Hegel's *Ästhetik* would be necessary to answer. That the answer is affirmative does not go without saying, nor of course that it is negative either. Others are at work on this task of re-reading Kant and Hegel.

The sort of interrogation for which I am calling is neither a work of "pure theory" nor a work of pure praxis, a series of explications. It is something between those two or preparatory to them, a clearing of the ground and an attempt to sink foundations. It is "criticism" in the fundamental sense of "critique," discriminating testing out, in this case a testing out of the medium of which the bridge between theory and practice is made. If criticism as critique is between theory and practice, it is also neither to be identified with hermeneutics, or the search for intentional meaning, on the one side, nor with poetics, or the theory of how texts have meaning, on the other side, though it is closely related to the latter. Critique, however, is a testing of the grounding of language in this or that particular text, not in the abstract or in abstraction from any particular case.

If this sort of investigation of the weight-bearing features of language is often an object of suspicion these days from the point of view of a certain traditional humanism, the humanism of *litterae humaniores*, it is also under attack from the other direction, from the point of view of those who see the central work of literary study as the reinsertion of the work of literature within its social context. The reproaches from the opposite political directions are strangely similar or symmetrical. They often come to the same thing or are couched in the same words. It is as if there were an unconscious alliance of the left and the right to suppress something which is the bad conscience of both a conservative humanism and a "radical" politicizing or sociologizing of the study of literature. A specific problematic is associated with the latter move, which attempts to put literature under the law of economy, under the laws of economic change and social power. I shall examine this problematic in detail elsewhere,[29] but it may be said here that the most resolute attempts to bracket linguistic considerations in the study of literature, to take the language of literature for granted and shift from the study of the relations of word with word to the study of the relations of words with things or with subjectivities, will only lead back in the end to the study of language. Any conceivable encounter with things or with subjectivities in literature or in discourse about literature must already have represented things and subjects in words, numbers, or other signs. Any conceivable representation of the relations of words to things, powers, persons, modes of production and exchange, juridical or political systems (or whatever name the presumably non-linguistic may be given) will turn out to be one or another figure of speech. As such, it will require a rhetorical interpretation, such as that given by Marx in *Capital* and in the *Grundrisse*. Among such figures are that of mimesis, mirroring reflection or representation. This turns out to be a species of metaphor. Another such figure is that of part to whole, work to surrounding and determining milieu, text to context, container to thing contained. This relation is one variety or another of synecdoche or of metonymy. Another figure of the relation of text to social context is that of anamorphosis or of ideology, which is a species of affirmation by denial, abnegation, what Freud called *Verneinung*. Sociologists of literature still all too often do no more than set some social fact side by side with some citation from a literary work and assert that the latter reflects the former, or is accounted for by it, or is determined by it, or is an intrinsic part of it, or is grounded in it. It is just in this place, in the interpretation of this asserted liaison, that the work of rhetorical analysis is indispensable. The necessary dialogue between those practicing poetics or rhetoric and sociologists of literature has scarcely begun. Conservative humanists and "radical" sociologists of literature have this at least in common: both tend to suppress, displace, or replace what I call the linguistic moment in literature.[30] Here too, however, denegation is affirmation. The covering over always leaves traces behind, tracks which may be followed back to those questions about language I am raising.

Kant, once more, in the "Preface" to the *Critique of Judgment* has admirably formulated the necessity of this work of critique: "For if such a system is one day to be completed [*einmal zu Stande kommen soll*] under the general name of metaphysic . . . , the soil for the ediface [*den Boden zu diesem Gebaude*] must be explored by critique [*die Kritik*] as deep down as the foundation [*die erste Grundlage*] of the faculty of principles independent of experience, in order that it may sink in no part [*damit es nicht an irgend einem Teile sinke*], for this would inevitably bring about the downfall [*Einsturz*] of the whole" (Eng. 4; Ger. 74–75). Elsewhere, in the *Critique of Pure Reason*, the same metaphor has already been posited as the foundation of the edifice of pure thought: "But though the following out of these considerations is what gives to philosophy its peculiar dignity, we must meantime occupy ourselves with a less resplendent [*nicht so glänzenden*], but still meritorious task, namely, to level the ground, and to render it sufficiently secure for moral edifices of these majestic dimensions [*den Boden zu jenen majestätischen sittlichen Gebäuden eben und baufest zu machen*]. For this ground has been honeycombed by subterranean workings [*allerlei Maulwurfsgänge*: all sorts of mole tunnels: Smith's translation effaces the figure] which reason, in its confident but fruitless search for hidden treasures has carried out in all directions, and which threaten the security of the superstructures [*und die jenes Bauwerk unsicher machen*]."[31]

Which is critique? Is it groundbreaking to be distinguished from mole-tunnelling and a repair of it, as the second quotation claims, or is critique, as the first quotation affirms, the work of tunnelling itself, the underground search for bedrock which in that process hollows out the soil? Does this contradiction in Kant's formulations not have something to do with the fact that Kant uses a metaphor from art, or to put this another way, throws out a little artwork of his own in the form of an architectural metaphor, in order to define the work of criticism which is supposed to be a testing out of the very instrument of bridging of which the definition makes use? This is an example of a *mise en abyme* in the technical sense of placing within the larger sign system a miniature image of that larger one, a smaller one potentially within that, and so on, in a filling in and covering over of the abyss, gulf, or *Kluft* which is at the same time an opening of the abyss. Such a simultaneous opening and covering over is the regular law of the *mise en abyme*.

Have I not, finally, by an intrinsic and unavoidable necessity, done the same thing as Kant, with my images of bridges, tunnels, bedrock, pathways, and so on, and with my strategy of borrowing citations from Arnold, Kant, and the rest to describe obliquely my own enterprise? This somersaulting, self-constructing, self-undermining form of language, the throwing out of a bridge where no firm bedrock exists, in place of the bedrock, is a fundamental feature of what I call critique. Groundlevelling, it appears, becomes inevitably tunnelling down in search of bedrock, as, to quote Milton again, beneath the lowest deep a lower deep still opens.

I end by drawing several conclusions from what I have said, and by briefly relating what I have said to the question of genre. The first conclusion is a reiteration of my assertion that the stakes are so large in the present quarrels among students of literature that we must go slowly and circumspectly, testing the ground carefully and taking nothing for granted, returning once more to those founding texts of our modern tradition of literary study and reading them anew with patience and care. To put this another way, the teaching of philology, of that "slow reading" or *langsamen Lesen* for which Nietzsche calls, is still a fundamental responsibility of the humanities, at no time more needed than today. Second conclusion: Disagreements among students of literature can often be traced to often more covert disagreements about the presupposed ground of literature—whether that ground is assumed to be society, the self, language, or the "thing." One of these four presuppositions may be taken so for granted by a given critic that he is not even aware that it determines all his procedures and strategies of interpretation. Much will be gained by bringing the fundamental causes of these disagreements into the open. Third conclusion: Though the intellectual activity of ground-testing and of testing out the very idea of the ground or of the principle of reason, through slow reading, has a long and venerable tradition under the names of philology and of critical philosophy, nevertheless such testing has a peculiar role in the university. It is likely to seem subversive, threatening, outside the pale of what is a legitimate activity within the university, if research within the university, including research and teaching in the humanities, is all under the sovereign and unquestioned rule of the principle of reason. Nevertheless, moving forward to the necessary new affirmation and the new taking of responsibility for the humanities and within the humanities depends now, as it alway has, on allowing that interrogation to take place.

This new taking of responsibility for language and literature, for the language of literature, which I am calling critique, has, finally, important implications for genre theory or for generic criticism. What I have said would imply not that generic classifications or distinctions and the use of these as a guide to interpretation and evaluation are illegitimate, without grounds, but that they are in a certain sense superficial. They do not go all the way to the ground, and the choice of a ground (or being chosen by one) may be more decisive for literary interpretation than generic distinctions and even determine those generic distinctions and their import. It is only on the grounds of a commitment to language, society, the self, or the "it," one or another of these, that generic distinctions make sense and have force. The choice of a ground determines both the definition of each genre and the implicit or explicit hierarchy among them. It is possible, it makes sense, to say "This is a lyric poem," or "This is a novel," and to proceed on the basis of that to follow certain interpretative procedures and ultimately to say, "This is a good lyric poem," or "This is a bad novel." Nevertheless, it is possible and makes sense to do these things only on the grounds of a prior commitment, perhaps one entirely implicit or even unthought, to founding assumptions about the ultimate ground on which all these genres are erected as so many different dwelling places or cultural forms for the human spirit to live in and use.

Beyond that, it might be added that what I am calling critique, in its double emphasis on rhetoric as the study of tropes, on the one hand, in a work of whatever genre, and, on the other hand, on the way any work of literature, of whatever genre, tells a story with beginning, middle, end, and underlying *logos* or *Grund* and at the same time interrupts or deconstructs that story—this double emphasis tends to break down generic distinctions and to recognize, for example, the fundamental role of tropes in novels, the way any lyric poem tells a story and can be interpreted as a narrative, or the way a work of philosophy may be read in terms of its tropological patterns or in terms of the story it tells. Much important criticism today goes against the grain of traditional generic distinctions, while at the same time perpetuating them in new ways in relation to one or another of my four grounds, just as many important works of recent primary literature do not fit easily into any one generic pigeon-hole.

NOTES

1. *The Letters of Matthew Arnold to Arthur Hugh Clough*, ed. H. F. Lowry (London and New York: Oxford University Press, 1932), 130.

2. Friedrich Nietzsche, *Daybreak: Thoughts on the*

Prejudices of Morality, trans. R. J. Hollingdale (Cambridge: Cambridge University Press, 1982), 5, trans. slightly altered; German: Freidrich Nietzsche, *Morgenröte*, "Vorrede," *Werke in Drei Bänden*, ed. Karl Schlecta, I (Munich: Carl Hanser Verlag, 1966), 1016. Further citations will be from these editions.

3. George Eliot, *Daniel Deronda*, I, *Works*, Cabinet Edition (Edinburgh and London: William Blackwood and Sons, n. d.), chap. 6, p. 90. Further references will be to this volume of this edition.

4. In *Première Livraison* (1976), my trans.

5. Wallace Stevens, *The Collected Poems* (New York: Alfred A. Knopf, 1954), 10.

6. Louis Althusser, *For Marx*, trans. Ben Brewster (New York: Vintage Books, 1970), pp. 233–34.

7. Joseph Conrad, *The Secret Agent* (Garden City, N.Y.: Doubleday, Page, 1925), xiii.

8. Cleanth Brooks, "The Primacy of the Author," *The Missouri Review*, 6 (1982), 162.

9. Matthew Arnold, "The Function of Criticism at the Present Time," *Lectures and Essays in Criticism, The Complete Prose Works*, ed. R. H. Super, III (Ann Arbor: The University of Michigan Press, 1962), 270.

10. See Walter Jackson Bate, "The Crisis in English Studies," *Harvard Magazine*, 85, No. 1, (1982), 46–53, esp. pp. 46–47. For a vigorous reply to Bate's essay see Paul de Man, "The Return to Philology," *The Times Literary Supplement*, No. 4, 158 (Friday, December 10, 1982), 1355–56.

11. Immanuel Kant, paragraph 59, "Of Beauty as the Symbol of Morality," *Critique of Judgment*, trans. J. H. Bernard (New York: Hafner Publishing Company, 1951), p. 196; German: *Kritik der Urteilskraft, Werkausgabe*, ed. Wilhelm Weischedel, X (Frankfurt am Main: Suhrkamp Verlag, 1979), 294.

12. René Wellek, "Destroying Literary Studies," *The New Criterion* (December 1983), 2.

13. Matthew Arnold, "The Function of Criticism at the Present Time," p. 282.

14. Ibid., p. 268.

15. Matthew Arnold, "The Study of Poetry," *English Literature and Irish Politics, The Complete Prose Works*, ed. R. H. Super, IX (Ann Arbor: The University of Michigan Press, 1973), 161.

16. *Letters to Clough*, p. 97.

17. Matthew Arnold, *Poems*, ed. Kenneth Allott (London: Longmans, Green and Co. Ltd., 1965), p. 591.

18. See Kant, *Critique of Judgment*, eds. cit.: Eng., pp. 197–98; Ger., pp. 295–297.

19. G. W. F. von Hegel, *Aesthetics: Lectures on Fine Art*, trans. T. M. Knox, I (New York: Oxford University Press, 1975), 378; *Vorlesungen über die Ästhetik*, I (Frankfurt am Main: Surhkamp, 1970), 486.

20. Wallace Stevens, *Opus Posthumous* (New York: Alfred A. Knopf, 1957), p. 163.

21. "The Function of Matthew Arnold at the Present Time," *Critical Inquiry*, 9 (1983), 451–516. Goodheart's essay, "Arnold at the Present Time," is on pp. 451–68.

22. See Freidrich Nietzsche, "European Nihilism," *The Will to Power*, trans. Walter Kaufmann and R. J. Hollingdale (New York: Vintage Books, 1968), pp. 5–82. These notes are dispersed in chronological order with the other notes traditionally making up *Der Wille zur Macht* in Nietzsche, "Aus dem Nachlass der Achtzigerjahre," *Werke in Drei Bänden*, III, 415–925. See also Martin Heidegger, "Nihilism," *Nietzsche*, trans. Frank A. Capuzzi, IV (San Francisco: Harper & Row, 1982); German: *Nietzsche*, II (Pfullingen: Verlag Günther Neske, 1961), 31–256; 335–98.

23. *Letters to Clough*, p. 135.

24. *The Will to Power*, p. 3.

25. Heidegger, "Nihilism," *Nietzsche*, IV, 21; German: *Nietzsche*, II, 53.

26. Trans. Catherine Porter and Edward P. Morris, *Diacritics*, 13 (1983), 3–20.

27. Kant, *Critique of Judgment*, Eng., p. 32; Ger., p. 106.

28. Hegel, *Ästhetik*, I, 151, my trans.

29. In "Economy," in *Penelope's Web: On the External Relations of Narrative*, forthcoming.

30. A book on nineteenth and twentieth-century poetry with that title is forthcoming from Princeton University Press.

31. Immanuel Kant, *Critique of Pure Reason*, trans. Norman Kemp Smith (New York: St. Martin's Press, 1965), pp. 313–14; German: *Kritik der reinen Vernunft*, A (1781), p. 319; B (1787), pp. 375–76, *Werkausgabe*, ed. cit., III, 325–26. For a discussion of the image of the mole in Kant, Hegel, and Nietzsche see David Farrell Krell, "*Der Maulwurf: Die philosophische Wühlarbeit bei Kant, Hegel und Nietzsche*/The Mole: Philosophic Burrowings in Kant, Hegel, and Nietzsche," *Boundary*, 2, 9 and 10 (Spring/Fall, 1981), 155–79.

33

Edward W. Said
1935–

By birth, upbringing, and education, Edward W. Said is both exile and cosmopolitan. He is a native Palestinian who was born in Jerusalem in 1935 into that city's Arab-Anglican minority; and he has lived most of his life outside Palestine, attending colonial British public schools Cairo as well as their counterparts, private U.S. schools, including the Princeton. Currently, Said is Parr Professor of English and Comparative Literature at Columbia University. He is—perhaps quite understandably—the foremost proponent of a secular, or practical, literary criticism that is fundamentally antitheoretical in its determination of the text's unavoidable locus of "being-in-the-world." In addition to his scholarly work, Said writes with a clear and profound eloquence on life in exile ("The Mind of Winter," *Harper's*, September 1984) and serves in the Palestine National Council, the Palestinian parliament-in-exile. Thus, Said is the Sartrean ideal of the writer *engagé*, and, like Sartre, committed to a conception of prose as meaningful discourse between writer and reader that is necessarily worldly/political. However, Said has not assumed Sartre's theoretical baggage, acknowledging both Foucault and Chomsky as significant influences. In addition, he is pointedly non-Derridean, perceiving Derrida's theoretical commitments as a reinstitution of the literary work of art as an esthetic object devoid of the particulars of identification.

From 1966, beginning with *Joseph Conrad and the Fiction of Autobiography*, his first book, until 1983 and publication of *The World, the Text, and the Critic*, of which the following essay is a chapter, Said's work has been particularly impressive for its clarity and for the implicit wholeness of its development and integration within his personal history as exile. The Conrad study was a noncausal account of the relationship of Conrad's letters to his shorter fiction. *Beginnings* (1975) addressed the significance of a text's beginning for the determination of its similarities and dissimilarities with other texts, and discussed contrasts between Foucault and Derrida. *Orientalism* (1978) identified inherent power relations in the discourse of nineteenth and twentieth century oriental studies. *The World, the Text, and the Critic* builds upon and expands the significance of these previous works. The result is that Said, as no previous scholar-critic has before, effectively counters the ahistorical Structuralist and Poststructuralist approaches to the criticism of literary works of art and corrects the ahistoricism found so limiting in the New Criticism.

In the essay that follows, "Reflections on American 'Left' Criticism," Said addresses those particulars by discussing at length their absence from the discourse of American literary criticism. He begins by writing "that the oppositional manner of new New Criticism does not accurately represent its ideas and practice, which, after all is said and done, further solidify and guarantee the social structure and the culture that produced them." Literary critics and theoreticians have divided themselves into right- and left-wing positions, but, despite what it says of its oppositional role, the left-wing position—its work remaining within the academic tradition—along with other positions in contemporary American literary criticism reconfirm New Criticism's isolation of the literary work of art from its historical and social context. Insofar as the literary work of art contributes to culture, such isolation is, according to Said, untenable. With reference to this isolation, Said cites de Man and like critics who "direct their attention to the impossibility of political and social responsibility," quoting de Man's assertion that "philosophical knowledge can only come into being when it is turned back upon itself." Countering this position, Said discusses Gramsci's observations of how culture serves the authority of the state, and writes that the contemporary literary critic/theoretician should address the intentional roles of literary works of art through an understanding of the cultural affiliations of these works. This address, in general, does not occur within the American academy.

Reflections on American 'Left' Literary Criticism

Never before in the history of American literary culture has there been such widespread and such serious, sometimes technical, and frequently contentious discussion of issues in literary criticism. Every critic or teacher of literature is affected by the discussion. Still, there is no automatic agreement on what the main or even the important issues are in the critical hurly-burly. It is probably true, for example, that even though many of the critical schools (among others, semiotics, hermeneutics, Marxism, deconstruction) continue to have their strict apostles, the critical atmosphere is a mixed one, with everyone more or less in touch with most of the reigning methods, schools, and disciplines. Nevertheless it is almost certain that no one underestimates the sociological as well as the intellectual importance of the large division separating adherents of what may be called new New Criticism from those of the old or traditional criticism. Not all critics are polarized by this often invidious division. But what is remarkable, I think, is that in debates between the sides there is a marked willingness to take positions simplifying and exaggerating not only one's opponent but one's own team, so to speak. A deconstructionist speaking *sub specie aeternitatis* for vanguard criticism makes us feel that a challenge to Western thought itself is being portended when he or she analyzes some lines by Rousseau, Freud, or Pater; conversely, critics who believe themselves to be pronouncing in the name of sanity, decency, and the family when they discuss the ideas of what humanism is all about denigrate even their own work unintentionally by appearing to simplify the formidable codes of academic scholarship that make intelligible what they do as scholars.

Without thinking through all of the aspects of this large opposition, we cannot properly hope to know in detail what really goes on in literary criticism and theory today, although we can speak accurately of certain patterns common both to criticism and to the history, society, and culture that produced it. One of my points will be that if the fierce polemics between, say, M. H. Abrams and J. Hillis Miller, or between Gerald Graff and the so-called Yale School, or between *Boundary 2*, *Glyph*, and *Diacritics* and other little magazines, seem to present clear theoretical demarcations between old or right-wing positions and new or left-wing positions, the divergence on both sides of the controversy between the rhetoric of theory and the actualities of practice is very nearly the same. This is of course always true in polemics: we argue in theory for what in practice we never do, and we do the same kind of thing with regard to what we oppose. Nonetheless we find that a new criticism adopting a position of opposition to what is considered to be established or conservative academic scholarship consciously takes on the function of the left wing in politics and argues *as if* for the radicalization of thought, practice, and perhaps even of society by means not so much of what it does and produces, but by means of what it says about itself and its opponents. True, there are important actual achievements to which it can point with pride. There are genuinely original, even revolutionary works of critical theory and interpretation, and these have been surrounded by a whole rhetorical armor of apology, attack, and extended programmatic elaboration: Harold Bloom's work and the repeated arguments about it come immediately to mind. But in the main Bloom's work and what it has produced in the way of anger and praise on theoretical grounds remain solidly within the tradition of academic criticism. The texts, authors, and periods have stayed inside a recognizable and commonly agreed-upon canon, even if the words and phrases used to describe them vary considerably depending on whether you are for or against Bloom.

To such a thesis there is first the response that I, in my own turn, am being a reductionist and, second, that criticism is perforce restricted to the academy and banned—not only by virtue of its own politeness—from the street. Both objections are justified in part. But what I am trying to say (with almost embarrassing generality) is that the oppositional manner of new New Criticism does not accurately represent its ideas and practice, which, after all is said and done, further solidify and guarantee the social structure and the culture that produced them. Deconstruction, for example, is practiced as if Western culture were being dismantled; semiotic analysis argues that its work amounts to a scientific and hence social revolution in the sciences of man. The examples can be multiplied, but I think what I am saying will be readily understood. There is oppositional debate without real opposition. In this setting, even Marxism has often been accommodated to the wild exigencies of rhetoric while surrendering its true radical prerogatives.

All of this is a long way of explaining why in my title the word *Left* is enclosed in skeptical quotation marks. Also, I find the transition from the notion of the Left in politics to the Left in literary criticism a difficult one to make. Of course there is opposition between Abrams and Derrida or Miller, but can we say with assurance that what is at stake, which seems at most to be a question of whose superstructural visions are better, matches the apparent violence of the disagreement? Both new and old critics have been content to confine themselves to the academic matter of literature, to the existing institutions for teaching and employing students of literature, to the often ridiculous and always self-flattering notion that their debates have a supremely important bearing upon crucial interests affecting humankind. In accepting these confinements the putative Left, no less than the Right, is very far from playing a genuinely political role. Indeed, what distinguishes the present situation is, on the one hand, a greater isolation than ever before in recent American cultural history of the literary critics from the major intellectual, political, moral, and ethical issues of the day and, on the other hand, a rhetoric, a pose, a posture (let us at last be candid) claiming not so much to represent as *to be* the afflictions entailed by true adversarial politics. A visitor from another world would surely be perplexed were he to overhear a so-called old critic calling the new critics dangerous. What, this visitor would ask, are they dangers to? The state? The mind? Authority?

A quick glance at recent intellectual history reveals the story pretty well. No one would have any trouble finding a Left in American culture between the twenties and the fifties, as Daniel Aaron's book *Writers on the Left* will immediately testify. Certainly it is true that during those decades intellectual debate in this country was preeminently conducted in political language having a direct connection with actual politics. The careers of such men as Randolph Bourne and Joseph Freeman, for instance, are inextricable from the problems of war or nonintervention, class conflict, Stalinism or Trotskyism. If we feel that what these writers wrote lacked the sophistication of the criticism of their contemporaries—Eliot, Valéry, Richards, Empson—we also feel that their awareness of literature as literature (that is, literature as something more than ideological construct) was impressively strong. In the work of the best of them, say the Edmund Wilson of *To the Finland Station*, there is a fairly high order of intellect and scholarship, as well as considerable political sophistication and historical engagement, neither of which rarely comes through as untreated propaganda or as what we have come to call vulgar Marxism. When, in this rather large and amorphous period that I designate simply as "recent cultural history," a major critic in the academy would seek to place her- or himself responsibly in the world, we might get an essay such as F. O. Matthiessen's "The Responsibilities of the Critic," originally written in 1949. Matthiessen makes no pretense at being a Marxist, but he does make it very clear that the critic of literature must be concerned with the material with which Marxism deals along with "the works of art of our own time." The essay's controlling metaphor is an horticultural one: criticism can become "a kind of closed garden" unless the critic realizes "that the land beyond the garden's walls is more fertile, and that the responsibilities of the critic lie in making renewed contact with the soil." Not only does this mean that critics are to acquaint themselves with "the economic foundations underlying any cultural superstructure." It means

> that we in the universities cannot afford to turn our backs . . . upon the world . . . The proper place for the thinker, as William James conceived it, was at the central point where a battle is being fought. It is impossible for us to take that metaphor with the

> lightness that he could. Everywhere we turn in these few fateful years since the first atom bomb dropped on Hiroshima we seem menaced by such vast forces that we may well feel that we advance at our peril. But even greater peril would threaten us if those whose prime responsibility as critics is to keep open the life-giving communications between art and society should waver in their obligations to provide ever fresh thought for our own society.[1]

There is an unmistakable implication in these remarks that the vast menacing forces of post-Hiroshima history can be kept at bay and comprehended by the critic's "fresh thought." We might easily smile at Matthiessen's naiveté here, since today very few critics consider their work to be pitted directly against these or any other brute historical forces. Moreover, as any reader of Paul de Man can tell you, the language of crisis is endemic to criticism, but, he would warn, unless language in such situations turns back upon itself, there is more likely to be mystification and falseness than knowledge or real criticism. To Matthiessen, then, literature and criticism are nourished by the very same experiences out of which economics, material history, and social conflict are generated. Such a proposition, in all its seemingly unproblematic ontological simplicity, is most unlikely to reappear today, when what de Man calls "the fallen world of our facticity" is considered to be matched ironically by a literature whose language "is the only form of language free from the fallacy of unmediated expression." And yet Matthiessen's achievement as a critic was a considerable one; books such as his *American Renaissance* reveal neither a deluded *schone Seele* nor a crude sociologist of knowledge. The problem is to see how he spoke so passionately and politically of the critic's responsibilities and why, twenty-odd years later, critics like de Man (whose current influence is very estimable) direct their attention to the impossibility of political and social responsibility.

For de Man, "philosophical knowledge can only come into being when it is turned back upon itself." This is another way of saying that anyone using language as a means for communicating knowledge is liable to fall into the trap of believing that his or her authority as possessor and communicator of knowledge is not bound by language, which in fact is only language and not immediate facticity. Literature, on the other hand, is basically about demystification and, according to de Man, "poetic language names this void [the presence of nothingness, supposedly denoted by the words of a literary composition whose essential task is to refer only to itself and to be ironically aware of so doing] with ever-renewed understanding and, like Rousseau's longing, it never tires of naming it again." Such an insight allows de Man to assert that in its endless naming and renaming of the void, literature is most emphatically itself, never more strongly than when literature seems to be suppressed in order that mere knowledge might be allowed to appear. Thus:

> When modern critics think they are demystifying literature, they are in fact being demystified by it, but since this necessarily occurs in the form of a crisis, they are blind to what takes place within themselves. At the moment that they claim to do away with literature, literature is everywhere; what they call anthropology, linguistics, psychoanalysis is nothing but literature reappearing, like Hydra's head, in the very spot where it had supposedly been suppressed. The human mind will go through amazing feats of distortion to avoid facing "the nothingness of human matters."[2]

Unlike Derrida, for whose work he was later to show considerable affinity, de Man is less interested in the force and productivity of human distortion (what Derrida calls *l'impensé*) than he is in its continuing and repeated performance, its insistence as insistence so to speak. This is why corrosive irony is really de Man's central concern as a critic: he is always interested in showing that when critics or poets believe themselves to be stating something, they are really revealing—critics unwittingly, poets wittingly—the impossible premises of stating anything at all, the so-called aporias of thought to which de Man believes all great literature always returns. Yet these intellectual hobbles on the possibility of statement have not inhibited de Man from stating and restating them on the numerous occasions when, more ably than most other critics, he analyzes a piece of literature. I would hesitate to call de Man a polemicist, but insofar as he exhorts critics to do one thing rather than another, I would say that he tells them to avoid talking as if historical scholarship, for example, could ever get beyond and talk seriously about literature. Why? Because if great literature is already demystified, scholarship could never tell us anything essential about it that the literature itself had not previously predicted. The most that can happen is that the critic is demystified, which amounts to saying that he acknowledges literature's prior demystification of itself.

I have no wish to use de Man as a general representative of what is being done these days in literary criticism: his work is too important, his talents too extraordinary for merely representative status. But I think that he can be regarded as exemplifying an intellectual current opposing, in no very explicit way, what customarily is the norm in academic literary studies. The literary work for him stands in a position of almost unconditional superiority over historical facticity not by virtue of its power but by virtue of its admitted powerlessness; its originality resides in the premise that it has disarmed itself "from the start," as if by having said in advance that it had no illusions about itself and its fictions it directly accedes to the realm of acceptable form. These ideas of course express a major tendency in all symbolist art, a tendency made considerably interesting by every variety of twentieth-century critical formalism: to paraphrase a famous remark by Mallarmé, underlying it is the notion that, if the world exists at all, it must have ended up in or as a book, and once in a book then the world is left behind forever. Literature, in short, expresses only itself (this is a maximalist position; the minimalist view is that literature is "about" nothing): its world is a formal one, and its relationship to quotidian reality can only be understood, as de Man implies, by means either of negation or of a radically ironic theory, as severe as it is consistent, whose workings depend on the opposite propositions that, if the world is not a book, then too the book is not the world. These are perhaps not as unexceptionable as they may seem, especially if we remember the extent to which most criticism since Aristotle has admitted of a certain amount of an often surreptitious and unadmitted mimetic bias.

But de Man's criticism garners some of its justified authority because de Man has been a pioneer of European "metaphysical criticism," as some people like to call it. Here we rush headlong into the sociological and historical actuality that contemporary "left" or oppositional criticism in America is heavily influenced by European, especially French, criticism. One could give a number of reasons for the dramatic change in language and tone that came over the American critical scene during the late 1960s, and I do not intend here to spend much time doing so. But it is fair to say that among the effects of European criticism on our critical vocabulary and positions was a sense that the primacy of "English studies" in the literary field had come to an end. Most of the literary criticism dominating the academy, indeed even the world of journalism, was based on the achievements of British and American modernist writers, and a feeling too that assumptions of national primacy—in all senses of that phrase—ought to dominate criticism. The believers in this area include Arnold at the beginning, later Leavis, Empson, Richards, and most of the southern New Critics. I do not mean to say that these were provincial or local-minded men, but that for them everything outside the Anglo-Saxon world had to bend around to Anglo-Saxon ends. Even T. S. Eliot, much the most international critic of the period until the early 1960s, saw in European poets like Dante, Virgil, and Goethe the vindication of such Anglo-Saxon values as monarchy, an unbroken nonrevolutionary tradition, and the idea of a national religion. Thus the intellectual hegemony of Eliot, Leavis, Richards, and the New Critics coincides not only with the work of masters like Joyce, Eliot himself, Stevens, and Lawrence, but also with the serious and autonomous development of literary studies in the university, a development that in time became synonymous with "English" as subject, language, and attitude.

At its very best "English" had Lionel Trilling, W. A. Wimsatt, Reuben Brower, and a small handful of others as its prominent, deeply intelligent and humane, and very diverse defenders. But it was challenged—well before the French efflorescence—in two ways, one internal to it, the other external. Internally "English" produced only an implicit ideology, and no easily communicable methods. There are complex reasons for this, and anyone attempting to describe the situation that prevailed would have to go into such matters as the revulsion from Stalinism, the Cold War, the circumvention of theory, and the paradoxical unmediated, ahistorical association of values, commitment, and even ideas with "style." What I am most interested in here is what, generally speaking, they produced intellectually: a type of criticism based principally on endless refinement. In the sudden mood of competition and expansion that followed Sputnik, there were the various national-security language programs funded by NDEA, and then there was "English," which refined, without essentially adding to, our "strength" as a nation. The dissertation model was not the carefully researched historical monograph but the sensitive essay; students of English became adjuncts to, and felt themselves, at a very far point away from what was important. The role of English was at best an instrumental one (this clearly was what Richard Ohmann and Louis Kampf were reacting to in the late sixties), although its practitioners like Trilling, Abrams, and Wimsatt were looked to as nonideological reassurances that style, humanism, and values really mattered. The net result of all this was an endemic flaccidity in English studies, for how far could one go in these circumstances along the road of mere refinement?

As an instance of how brilliant and resourceful literary refinement could become there was Northrop Frye, whose meteoric theoretical ascendancy over the whole field of English studies in the fifties and sixties can partly be accounted for by the climate of refinement (which he dignified and intensified in his *Anatomy*) and the prevailing historical-theoretical vacuum. As an instance of how dull and enervating it all was, there was a huge agglomeration of various literary industries (Joyce, Conrad, Pound, Eliot) that had never even pretended to be a coherent part of the general march toward knowledge. In a unique and perhaps puzzling way then, literary modernity was associated first not with the present but with an immediate past, which was endlessly validated and revalidated; second, with the production of a virtually unassimilable secondary elaboration of a body of writings universally accepted as primary. The point to be made is that this body of secondary elaborations—like de Man's literary texts—was demystified from the start. It too pretended to no illusion about itself; it was secondary, harmless, and ideologically neutral, except within the internal confines of the more and more professionalized profession.

The second challenge to "English" was external. Here I have found it useful to employ the concept, seriously alluded to first by George Steiner, of extraterritoriality. Again there are many things to be mentioned in this connection, and again I must be summary and selective. There was the greatly expanded paperback book market and with it the dramatic increase in the number of translations from foreign languages; there was the gradual impression upon "English" of such outside fields as psychoanalysis, sociology, and anthropology; there was the decentering effect (under NDEA auspices by the way) of comparative literature and with it the weighty prestige of genuinely extraterritorial critics like Auerbach, Curtius, and Spitzer; and finally there was what now seems to have been a genuinely fortuitous intervention in our literary scene of ongoing European criticism, first through residents like de Man and Georges Poulet, then through more and more frequent visitors from abroad. It is important to mention at this juncture that Marxism became an intellectual presence to be reckoned with in this context of external challenge of importation from abroad. So far as I have been able to tell, the kind of Marxism practiced or announced in university literary departments owes very little to the American radical movement that ended with the McCarthy period. The new Marxism came to this country partly as a result of the interest in French criticism and later the Frankfurt School, partly because of the general wave of antiwar agitation on the campuses. It did so in the form of sudden discovery and just as sudden application to literary problems. Its main weaknesses were the comparative absence of a continuous native Marxist theoretical tradition or culture to back it up and its relative isolation from any concrete political struggle.

Between them, the internal and external challenges to English studies were decisive—but only in very limited ways. This is a crucial thing to understand. During the great upheavals of the sixties the academic literary establishment, which had for years been accustomed to being a factory for turning out refined minds and essays, responded to the times with a demand for instant relevance. In fact this meant only that the teaching and scholarship of literature should occasionally show us how literary masterpieces were relevant to contemporary reality, that in reading Swift or Shakespeare we could "understand" man's inhumanity to man or how evil apartheid is. I have little hesitation in saying that the much-vaunted Modern Language Association revolution brought only cosmetic changes, and these changes testified not to the will for change in various well-intentioned scholars, but rather to the depth and resilience of an ideology of refinement that had effectively absorbed even this new and potentially violent challenge. True, there was an extraordinary, not to say alarming, tendency to overkill in the oppositional rhetoric of the late sixties and early seventies. The vocabulary became suddenly more "technical" and self-consciously "difficult"; the Barthes-Piccard controversy was relived and even reproduced in many journals, congresses, and departments; and it became *de rigeur*—indeed profitable for many of us—to aspire to the condition of "literary theorists," a position in departmental rosters virtually unthinkable a scant ten years before. There was a peculiar search for interdisciplinary projects, programs, "minds," and gimmicks, all of this accentuating the extent to which one could not discuss a Donne poem without also referring to Jakobson, perhaps even to European Latinity, and at least to metaphor and metonymy. On the one hand, therefore, you had the appearance of a genuine new subculture of theoretical opposition to the old nationalist literary traditions institutionalized in the academy, and, on the other, you had those old traditions fighting back with appeals to humanism, tact, good sense, and the like. The question is whether in these instances Tweedledum and Tweedledee were really all that different from each other, and whether either had produced work that justified both the oppositional rhetoric of the one or the strong moral defensiveness of the other.

I am only concerned, however, with the "Left" side of the controversy, and my real beginning point is a pair of observations about what the Left has not produced. Consider, first, that in American literary studies there has not in the past quarter century been enough work of major historical scholarship that can be called "revisionist." I use this last adjective to indicate some parallel with what has gone on in American historical studies, in the work of Williams, Alperovitz, Kolko, and many others. For there to be effective interpretation in what is, after all is said and done, a historical discipline, there must also be effective history, effective archival work, effective involvement in the actual material of history. Certainly the individual work of literature exists to a considerable extent by virtue of its formal structures, and it articulates itself by means of a formal energy, intention, capacity, or will. But it does not exist only by those, nor can it be apprehended and understood only formally. And yet for the most part literary studies have been dominated, even in their Marxist variety, by a relative absence of the historical dimension. Historical research on the Left has been neutralized by the notion that interpretation is based ultimately on method or rhetoric, as if either of those two defined the separate competency and dignity of the literary theorist. Moreover, the whole concern with oppositional knowledge (that is, a knowledge that exists essentially to challenge and change received ideas, entrenched institutions, questionable values) has succumbed to the passivity of ahistorical refinement upon what is already given, acceptable, and above all already defined. One looks everywhere and finds few alternatives to the attitude that argues how, for instance, *Our Mutual Friend* can be understood better and better the more you see it in itself as more and more of a novel, which is the more you study it as a finer and finer illustration of a precisely reticulated theory of narrative fiction, whose conditions of readability and whose force depend on formal grammars, generative abstractions, and innate structures. There is a certain element of parody in my description, but some accuracy too.

The second observation is the other side of the coin, that literary studies on the Left, far from producing work to challenge or revise prevailing values, institutions, and definitions, have in fact gone too long a way in confirming them. In many ways this is a more serious matter.

No society known to human history has ever existed which has not been governed by power and authority, and, as Gramsci says repeatedly, every society can be divided into interlocking classes of rulers and ruled. There is nothing static about these basic conceptions, since if we consider society to be a dynamic distribution of power and positions we will also be able to regard the categories of rulers and ruled as a highly complex and highly changeable pair of categories. To use only

Gramsci's terminology for the moment, we can divide society into emergent and traditional classes, into civil and political sectors, into subaltern and dominant, hegemonic and authoritative powers. Yet standing over and above all this activity is at least an idea, or set of ideas, and at most a group of agencies of authority, which gain their power from the State. The central reality of power and authority in Western history, at least since the period from the end of feudalism on, is the presence of the State, and I think we would have to say that to understand not only power but authority—which is a more interesting and various idea than power—we must also understand the way in which any authority in modern society is derived to some degree from the presence of the State.

To a great extent culture, cultural formations, and intellectuals exist by virtue of a very interesting network of relationships with the State's almost absolute power. About this set of relationships I must say immediately that all contemporary Left criticism of the sort I have been discussing is for the most part stunningly silent. There are a few exceptions to this. Foucault is one, and Ohmann, and Poulantzas; one is hard put to name others whose criticism is directly concerned with the matter. Quite the contrary, nearly everyone producing literary or cultural studies makes no allowance for the truth that all intellectual or cultural work occurs somewhere, at some time, on some very precisely mapped-out and permissible terrain, which is ultimately contained by the State. Feminist critics have opened this question part of the way, but they have not gone the whole distance. If it is true that, according to an art-for-art's-sake theory, the world of culture and aesthetic production subsists on its own, away from the encroachments of the State and authority, then we must still be prepared to show that independence was gained and, more important, how it is maintained. In other words, the relationship between aesthetics and state authority obtains in the case both of direct dependence and of the much less likely one of complete independence.

The sense I now have of taking on far too huge an area of historical experience is intensified by the realization that cultural, theoretical, or critical discourse today provides me with no vocabulary, no conceptual or documentary language, much less a concrete body of specific analyses, to make myself clear. For the most part our critical ethos is formed by a pernicious analytic of blind demarcation by which, for example, imagination is separated from thought, culture from power, history from form, texts from everything that is *hors texte*, and so forth. In addition we misuse the idea of what method is, and we have fallen into the trap of believing that method is sovereign and can be systematic without also acknowledging that method is always part of some larger ensemble of relationships headed and moved by authority and power. For if the body of objects we study—the corpus formed by works of literature—belongs to, gains coherence from, and in a sense emanates out of the concepts of nation, nationality, and even of race, there is very little in contemporary critical discourse making these actualities possible as subjects of discussion. I do not intend to advocate a kind of reductive critical language whose bottom-line rationale is the endlessly affirmed thesis that "it's all political," whatever in that context one means by *it*, *all*, or *political*. Rather what I have in mind is the kind of analytic pluralism proposed by Gramsci for dealing with historical-cultural blocks, for seeing culture and art as belonging not to some free-floating ether or to some rigidly governed domain or iron determinism, but to some large intellectual endeavor—systems and currents of thought—connected in complex ways to doing things, to accomplishing certain things, to force, to social class and economic production, to diffusing ideas, values, and world pictures. If we agree with Gramsci that one cannot freely reduce religion, culture, or art to unity and coherence, then we will go along with the following theses for humanistic research and study:

> What must . . . be explained is how it happens that in all periods there co-exist many systems and currents of philosophic thought, how these currents are born, how they are diffused, and why in the process of diffusion they fracture along certain lines and in certain directions. The fact of this process goes to show how necessary it is to order in a systematic, coherent and critical fashion one's own intuitions of life and the world, and to determine exactly what is to be understood by the word "systematic," so that it is not taken in the pedantic and academic sense. But this elaboration must be, and can only be, performed in the context of the history of philosophy, for it is this history which shows how thought has been elaborated over the centuries and what a collective effort has gone into the present method of thought which has subsumed and absorbed all this past history, including all its follies and mistakes. Nor should those mistakes themselves be neglected, for, although made in the past and since corrected, one cannot be sure that they will not be reproduced in the present and once again require correcting.[3]

I have quoted the last sentence not because I agree with it, but because it expresses the didactic seriousness with which Gramsci believed all historical research should be conducted. But his main point of course is the suggestive insight that thought is produced so that actions can be accomplished, that it is diffused in order to be effective, persuasive, forceful, and that a great deal of thought elaborates on what is a relatively small number of principal, directive ideas. The concept of elaboration is crucial here. By elaboration Gramsci means two seemingly contradictory but actually complementary things. First, to elaborate means to refine, to work out (*e-laborare*) some prior or more powerful idea, to perpetuate a world view. Second, to elaborate means something more qualitatively positive, the proposition that culture itself or thought or art is a highly complex and quasi-autonomous extension of political reality and, given the extraordinary importance attached by Gramsci to intellectuals, culture, and philosophy, it has a density, complexity, and historical-semantic value that is so strong as to make politics possible. Elaboration is the ensemble of patterns making it feasible for society to maintain itself. Far from denigrating elaboration to the status of ornament, Gramsci makes it the very reason for the strength of what he calls civil society, which in the industrial West plays a role no less important than that of political society. Thus elaboration is the central cultural activity and, whether or not one views it as little more than intellectual propaganda for ruling-class interests, it is the material making a society a society. In other words, elaboration is a great part of the social web of which George Eliot spoke in her late novels. Gramsci's insight is to have recognized that subordination, fracturing, diffusing, reproducing, as much as producing, creating, forcing, guiding, are all necessary aspects of elaboration.

One could even go so far to say that culture—elaboration—is what gives the State something to govern and yet, as Gramsci is everywhere careful to note, cultural activity is neither uniform nor mindlessly homogeneous. The real depth in the strength of the modern Western State is the strength and depth of its culture, and culture's strength is its variety, its heterogenous plurality. This view distinguishes Gramsci from nearly every other important Marxist thinker of his period. He loses sight neither of the great central facts of power, and how they flow through a whole network of agencies operating by rational consent, nor of the detail—diffuse, quotidian, unsystematic, thick—from which inevitably power draws its sustenance, on which power depends for its daily bread. Well before Foucault, Gramsci had grasped the idea that culture serves authority, and ultimately the national State, not because it represses and coerces but because it is affirmative, positive, and persuasive. Culture is productive, Gramsci says, and this—much more than the monopoly of coercion held by the State—is what makes a national Western society strong, difficult for the revolutionary to conquer. Consequently the intellectual is not really analogous to the police force, nor is the artist merely a propagandist for wealthy factory owners. Culture is a separately capitalized endeavor, which is really to say that its relationship to authority and power is far from nonexistent. For we must be able to see culture as historical force possessing its own configurations, ones that intertwine with those in the socioeconomic sphere and that finally bear on the State as a State. Thus elaboration's meaning is not only that it is there, furnishing the material out of which society makes itself a going enterprise, but that like everything else in the world of nations, elaboration aspires to the condition of hegemony, with intellectuals playing the role of what Gramsci calls "experts in legitimation."

Because I consider them essential, I have pulled these ideas out of Gramsci to serve as a point of comparison with the historical and political ideas now propagated by oppositional or avant-garde literary theory. What I have been calling contemporary "Left" criticism is vitally concerned with various problems stemming from authority: such problematics as that of the return to Marx, Freud, and Saussure, the issue of influence and intertextuality, the questions of *l'impensé* and the undecideable in deconstructive criticism, ideology as a factor in literary creation and dissemination. Yet hardly anywhere in all this does one encounter a serious study of what authority is, either with reference to the way authority is carried historically and circumstantially from the State down into a society saturated with authority or with reference to the actual workings of culture, the role of intellectuals, institutions, and establishments. Furthermore, if the language of magazines like *Critical Inquiry*, *Glyph*, and *Diacritics* is brimming with sentiments of depth, radicality, and insight, there is rarely a paragraph expended on what in the way of ideas, values, and engagement is being urged. Nor, for that matter, does one often stumble on a serious attempt made to characterize what historically (and not rhetorically) it is that advanced critics are supposed to be opposing. Our impression is that the young critic has a well-developed political sense; yet close examination of this sense reveals a haphazard anecdotal content enriched neither by much knowledge of what politics and political issues are all about nor by any very developed awareness that politics is something more than liking or disliking some intellectual orthodoxy now holding sway over a department of literature.

Considering its potential, oppositional Left criticism contributes very little to intellectual debate in the culture today. Our bankruptcy on the once glamorous question of human rights alone is enough to strip us of our title to humanism, and as for dealing with the subtle distinction between authoritarianism and totalitarianism, we are not even willing to analyze these terms semantically, much less politically. Yet I do not wish to downgrade the period of almost Renaissance brilliance through which technical criticism has passed in the last few decades. We can gratefully acknowledge that and at the same time add that it has been a period characterized by a willingness to accept the isolation of literature and literary studies away from the world. It has also been a period during which very few of us have examined the reasons for this confinement, even while most of us have tacitly accepted, even celebrated, the State and its silent rule over culture—without so much, during the Vietnam and post-Vietnam period, as a polite murmur.

My disappointment at this stems from a conviction that it is our technical skill as critics and intellectuals that the culture has wanted to neutralize, and if we have cooperated in this project, perhaps unconsciously, it is because that is where the money has been. In our rhetorical enthusiasm for buzz words like scandal, rupture, transgression, and discontinuity, it has not occurred to us to be concerned with the relations of power at work in history and society, even as we have assumed that a text's textuality is a matter endlessly to be explored as something concerning other texts, vaguely denoted conspiracies, fraudulent genealogies entirely made up of books stripped of their history and force. The underlying assumption is that texts are radically homogeneous, the converse of which is the extraordinarily Laputan idea that to a certain extent everything can be regarded as a text. The result so far as critical practice is concerned is that rhetorical individualism in criticism and in the texts studied by the critic is cultivated for its own sake, with the further result that writing is seen as deliberately aiming for alienation—the critic from other critics, from readers, from the work studied.

The compelling irony of this depressing isolation, given the way we (as part of the secular priesthood of what Bakunin called "the era of scientific intelligence") are viewed by our political leaders, is almost staggering. A 1975 Trilateral Commission publication, *The Crisis of Democracy*, surveyed the post-1960s era with some degree of concern over the masses' sense of their political demands and aspirations; this has produced a problem of what the authors call "governability," since it is clear that the population at large is no longer so docile as it once was.[4] To this situation, then, the class of intellectuals contributes two things that derive directly from the two kinds of intellectuals contemporary democratic societies now produce. On the one hand are technocratic and policy-oriented, so-called responsible intellectuals; on the other, politically dangerous, value-oriented "traditional" intellectuals. The second group is where, by any reasonable standard, we are supposed to be, for it is the members of this group that supposedly "devote themselves to the derogation of leadership, the challenging of authority, and the unmasking and delegitimation of established institutions." The irony is, however, that literary critics, by virtue of their studious indifference to the world they live in and to the values by which their work engages history, do not see themselves as a threat to anything, except possibly to each other. Certainly they are as governable as they have always been since state worship became fashionable, and certainly their passive devotion to masterpieces, culture, texts, and structures posited simply in their own "texts" as functioning yet finished enterprises, poses no threat to authority or to values kept in circulation and managed by the technocratic managers.

But in more specific terms, what actually is the role of modern critical consciousness, of oppositional criticism? The relevant background, in very schematic terms, is as follows. As Raymond Williams has shown, words like *culture* and *society* acquire a concrete, explicit significance only in the period after the French Revolution. Before that, European culture as a whole identified itself positively as being different from non-European regions and cultures, which for the most part were given a negative value. Yet during the nineteenth century the idea of culture acquired an affirmatively nationalist cast, with the result that figures like Matthew Arnold make an active identification between culture and the state. It is the case with cultural or aesthetic activity that the possibilities and circumstances of its production get their authority by virtue of what I have called affiliation, that implicit network of peculiarly cultural associations between forms, statements, and other aesthetic elaborations on the one hand and, on the other, institutions, agencies, classes, and amorphous social forces. Affiliation is a loose enough word both to suggest the kinds of cultural ensembles Gramsci discusses in the passage I quoted earlier, as well as to allow us to retain the essential concept of *hegemony* guiding cultural and broadly intellectual activity, or elaboration, as a whole.

Let me try to suggest the general importance of this notion to contemporary critical activity. In the first place, as a general interpretive principle affiliation mitigates somewhat the facile theories of homology and filiation, which have created the homogeneously utopian domain of texts connected serially, seamlessly, and immediately only with other texts. By contrast affiliation is what enables text to maintain itself as a text, and this is covered by a range of circumstances: status of the author, historical moment, conditions of publication, diffusion and reception, values drawn upon, values and ideas assumed, a framework of consensually held tacit assumptions, presumed background, and so on and on. In the second place, to study affiliation is to study and to recreate the bonds between texts and the world, bonds that specialization and the institutions of literature have all but completely effaced. Every text is an act of will to some extent, but what has not been very much studied is the degree to which texts are made permissible. To recreate the affiliative network is therefore to make visible, to give materiality back to, the strands holding the text to society, author, and culture. In the third place, affiliation releases a text from its isolation and imposes upon the scholar or critic the presentational problem of historically recreating or reconstructing the possibilities from which the text arose. Here is the place for intentional analysis and for the effort to place a text in homological, dialogical, or antithetical relationships with other texts, classes, and institutions.

None of this interest in affiliation—both as a principle of critical research and as an aspect of cultural process itself—is worth very much unless, first, it is actively generated out of genuine historical research (and I mean that critics are to feel themselves making discoveries, making unknown things known) and, second, it is ultimately fixed for its goals upon understanding, analyzing, and contending with the management of power and authority within the culture. Let me put it this way: we are humanists because there is something called humanism, legitimated by the culture, given a positive value by it. What we must be interested in directly is the historical process by which the central core of humanist ideology has produced literary specialists, who have construed their domain as restricted to something called literature whose components (including "literarity") have been given epistemological, moral, and ontological priority. In acting entirely within this domain, then, the literary critic effectively confirms the culture and the society enforcing those restrictions; this confirmation acts to strengthen the civil and political societies whose fabric is the culture itself. What is created as a result is what can reasonably be called a liberal consensus: the formal, restricted analysis of literary-aesthetic works validates the culture, the culture validates the humanist, the humanist the critic, and the whole enterprise the State. Thus authority is maintained by virtue of the cultural process, and anything more than refining power is denied the refining critic. By the same token, it has been true that "literature" as a cultural agency has become more and more blind to its actual complicities with power. That is the situation we need to comprehend.

Consider how this situation was formed during the nineteenth century by cultural discourse: one thinks immediately of people like Arnold, Mill, Newman, Carlyle, Ruskin. The very possibility of culture is based on the notion of refinement. Arnold's thesis that culture is the best that is thought or said gives this notion its most compact form. Culture is an instrument for identifying, selecting, and affirming certain "good" things, forms, practices, or ideas over others and in so doing culture transmits, diffuses, partitions, teaches, presents, propagates, persuades, and above all it creates and recreates itself as specialized apparatus for doing all those things. Most interestingly, I think, culture becomes the opportunity for a refracted verbal enterprise whose relationship to the State is always understated and, if the solecism is permitted, *understood*. The realistic novel plays a major role in this enterprise, for it is the novel—as it becomes ever more "novel" in the work of James, Hardy, and Joyce—that organizes reality and knowledge in such a way as to make them susceptible to systematic verbal reincarnation. The novel's realistic bodying forth of a world is to provide representational or representative norms selected from among many possibilities. Thus the novel acts to include, state, affirm, normalize, and naturalize some things, values, and ideas, but not others. Yet none of these can be seen, directly perceived, in the novel itself, and it has been the singular mission of most contemporary formalist critics today to make sure that the novel's remarkably precise articulation of its own selectivity appears simply either as a fact of nature or as a given ontological formalism, and not as the result of sociocultural process. For to see the novel as cooperating with society in order to reject, what Gareth Steadman Jones has called outcast populations, is also to see how the great aesthetic achievements of the novel—in Dickens, Eliot, Hardy—result from a technique for representing and appropriating objects, people, settings, and values in affiliation with specific historical and social norms of knowledge, behavior, and physical beauty.

In the widest perspective, the novel, and with it dominant currents in modern Occidental culture, is not only selective and affirmative but centralizing and powerful. Apologists for the novel continue to assert the novel's accuracy, freedom of representation, and such; the implication of this is that the culture's opportunities for expression are unlimited. What such ideas mask, mystify, is precisely the network binding writers to the State and to a world-wide "metropolitan" imperialism that, at the moment they were writing, furnished them in the novelistic techniques of narration and description with implicit models of accumulation, discipline, and normalization. What we must ask is why so few "great" novelists deal directly with the major social and economic outside facts of their existence—colonialism and imperialism—and why, too, critics of the novel have continued to honor this remarkable silence. With what is the novel, and for that matter most modern cultural discourse, affiliated, whether in the language of affirmation or in the structure of accumulation, denial, repression, and mediation that characterizes major aesthetic form? How is the cultural edifice constructed so as to limit the imagination in some ways, enlarge it in others? How is imagination connected with the dreams, constructions, and ambitions of official knowledge, with executive knowledge, with administrative knowledge? What is the community of interests that produces Conrad and C. L. Temple's *The Native Races and Their Rulers*? To what degree has culture collaborated in the worst excesses of the State, from its imperial wars and colonial settlements to its self-justifying institutions of anithuman repression, racial hatred, economic and behavioral manipulation?

Nothing in what I have been trying to say rapidly here implies mediating or reducing the specific density of individual cultural artifacts to the impersonal forces supposedly responsible for producing them. The study of cultural affiliation necessitates an acute understanding of the specificity of objects and, even more important, of their intentional roles, neither of which can be given their proper due by reductionism or by positivistic refinement. I would guess that Williams' term *cultural materialism* suits the methodological attitude I am trying to describe. In the main American literary criticism can afford to shed its partly self-imposed and socially legislated isolation, at least with reference to history and society. There is a whole world manipulated not only by so-called reasons of state but by every variety of ahistorical consumerism, whose ethnocentrism and mendacity promise the impoverishment and oppression of most of the globe. What is lacking in contemporary oppositional criticism is not only the kind of perspective found in Joseph Needham's civilizational approach to culture and society, but some sense of involvement in the affiliative processes that go on, whether we acknowledge them or not, all around us. But, as I have been saying over and over, these are matters to do with knowledge, not refinement. I suspect that the most urgent question to be asked now is if we still have the luxury of choice between the two.

NOTES

1. *The Responsibilities of the Critic: Essays and Reviews by F. O. Matthiessen*, selected by John Rackliffe (New York: Oxford University Press, 1952), p. 9.

2. Paul de Man, *Blindness and Insight: Essays in the Rhetoric of Contemporary Civilization* (New York: Oxford University Press, 1971), p. 18.

3. Antonio Gramsci, *The Prison Notebooks: Selections*, trans. and ed. Quintin Hoare and Geoffrey Nowell Smith (New York: International Publishers, 1971), p. 327.

4. M. J. Crozier, S. P. Huntington, and J. Watanuki, *The Crisis of Democracy: Report on the Governability of Democracies to the Trilateral Commission* (New York: New York University Press, 1975).

34

Shoshana Felman
1942–

Shoshana Felman is the Thomas E. Donnelley Professor of French and Comparative Literature at Yale University. She is a leading exponent of psychoanalytic literary criticism. Her lucid explications of the theories of Jacques Lacan and, through Lacan, of Freud, and her practical applications of those theories to the study of literature have helped make the practice of psychoanalytic literary criticism accessible to a wide audience. Felman's work includes *La "Folie" dans l'oeuvre romanesques de Stendhal* (1971), *The Literary Speech Act: Don Juan with Austin* (1980; trans. 1983), *Madness and Writing* (1978; trans. 1985), and *Jacques Lacan and the Adventure of Insight* (1987). She also edited *Literature and Psychoanalysis* (1982).

In "Psychoanalysis and Education: Teaching Terminable and Interminable," Felman discusses what she calls the "radical impossibility of teaching." With close attention to the writings of Freud and Lacan, she demonstrates the similarities between the relationships of teacher and student and analyst and analysand, indicating the ways in which psychoanalytic methodology may be used as a tool to facilitate the learning process. That is, she argues that there is a parallel between the analysand's "repression" or "resistance" in psychotherapy and students' "ignorance." Teaching, like psychoanalysis, must "deal not so much with *lack* of knowledge as with *resistances* to knowledge"; the teacher, like the analyst, must learn not to "*exchange*" knowledge with students but to "*use*" his or her knowledge to help students discover (or rediscover) their own. Psychoanalytic methods are, in Felman's view, especially applicable to the teaching of literature; literature, like the recovering analysand and the brighter student, "*knows it knows, but does not know the meaning of its knowledge*—it does not know *what* it knows."

Psychoanalysis and Education: Teaching Terminable and Interminable

In memory of Jacques Lacan

> *Meno:* Can you tell me, Socrates, if virtue can be taught? Or is it not teachable but the result of practice, or is it neither of these, but men possess it by nature?
>
> *Socrates:* . . . You must think me happy indeed if you think I know whether virtue can be taught . . . I am so far from knowing whether virtue can be taught or not that I do not even have any knowledge of what virtue itself is.
>
> ....
>
> *Meno:* Yes, Socrates, but how do you mean that we do not learn, but that what we call learning is recollection? Can you teach me how this is so?
>
> *Socrates:* . . . Meno, you are a rascal. Here you are asking me to give you my "teaching," I who claim that there is no such thing as teaching, only recollection.
>
> —Plato, *Meno*[1]

THE MEASURE OF A TASK

Socrates, that extraordinary teacher who taught humanity what pedagogy is, and whose name personifies the birth of pedagogics as a science, inaugurates his teaching practice, paradoxically enough, by asserting not just his own ignorance, but the radical impossibility of teaching.

Another extraordinarily effective pedagogue, another one of humanity's great teachers, Freud, repeats, in his own way, the same conviction that teaching is a fundamentally impossible profession. "None of the applications of psychoanalysis," he writes, "has excited so much interest and aroused so many hopes . . . as its use in the theory and practice of education . . .":

> My personal share in this application of psychoanalysis has been very slight. At an early stage I had accepted the *bon mot* which lays it down that there are three impossible professions—educating, healing, governing—and I was already fully occupied with the second of them.[2]

In a later text—indeed the very last one that he wrote—Freud recapitulates this paradoxical conviction which time and experience seem to have only reinforced, confirmed:

> It almost looks as if analysis were the third of those "impossible" professions in which one can be sure beforehand of achieving unsatisfying results. The other two, which have been known much longer, are education and government. [Standard, XXIII, 248]

If teaching is impossible—as Freud and Socrates both point out—what are we teachers doing? How should we understand—and carry out—our task? And why is it precisely two of the most effective teachers ever to appear in the intellectual history of mankind, who regard the task of teaching as impossible? Indeed, is not their radical enunciation of the impossibility of teaching itself actively engaged in teaching, itself part of the lesson they bequeath us? And if so, what can be learnt from the fact that it is impossible to teach?

What can the impossibility of teaching teach us?

As much as Socrates, Freud has instituted, among other things, a revolutionary pedagogy. It is my contention—which I will here attempt to elucidate and demonstrate—that it is precisely in giving us unprecedented insight into the impossibility of teaching, that psychoanalysis has opened up unprecedented teaching possibilities, renewing both the questions and the practice of education.

This pedagogical renewal was not, however, systematically thought out by Freud himself, or systematically articulated by any of his followers; nor have its thrust and scope been to date fully assimilated or fully grasped, let alone utilized, exploited in the classroom. The only truly different pedagogy to have practically emerged from what might be called the psychoanalytic lesson is the thoroughly original teaching-style of Jacques Lacan, Freud's French disciple and interpreter. If Lacan is, as I would argue, Freud's best student—that is, the most radical effect of the insights of Freud's teaching—perhaps his teaching practice might give us a clue to the newness of the psychoanalytic lesson about lessons, and help us thus define both the actual and, more importantly, the potential contribution of psychoanalysis to pedagogy.

WHAT IS A CRITIQUE OF PEDAGOGY?

Lacan's relationship with pedagogy has, however, been itself—like that of Freud—mostly oversimplified, misunderstood, reduced. The reason for the usual misinterpretations of both Lacan's and Freud's pedagogical contribution lies in a misunderstanding of the critical position taken by psychoanalysis with respect to traditional methods and assumptions of education. Lacan's well-known critique of what he has pejoratively termed "academic discourse" (*le discours universitaire*) situates "the radical vice" in "the transmission of knowledge." "A Master of Arts," writes Lacan ironically, "as well as other titles, protect the secret of a substantialized knowledge."[3] Lacan thus blames "the narrow-minded horizon of pedagogues" for having "reduced" the "strong notion" of "teaching"[4] to a "functional apprenticeship" (E 445).

Whereas Lacan's pedagogical critique is focused on grown-up training—on academic education and the ways it handles and structures knowledge, Freud's pedagogical critique is mainly concerned with children's education and the ways it handles and structures repression. "Let us make ourselves clear," writes Freud, "as to what the first task of education is":

> The child must learn to control his instincts. It is impossible to give him liberty to carry out all his impulses without restriction . . . Accordingly, *education must inhibit, forbid and suppress*[5] and this is abundantly seen in all periods of history. But we have learnt from analysis that precisely this suppression of instincts involves the risk of neurotic illness. . . . Thus education has to find its way between the Scylla of non-interference and the Charybdis of frustration. . . . An optimum must be discovered which will enable education to achieve the most and damage the least. . . . A moment's reflection tells us that hitherto education has fulfilled its task very badly and has done children great damage. [Standard, XXII, 149]

Thus, in its most massive statements and in its polemical pronouncements, psychoanalysis, in Freud as well as in Lacan—although with different emphases—is first and foremost *a critique of pedagogy*. The legacy of this critique has been, however, misconstrued and greatly oversimplified, in that the critical stance has been understood—in both Lacan's and Freud's case—as a desire to escape the pedagogical imperative: a desire—whether possible or impossible—to do away with pedagogy altogether. "Psychoanalysis," writes Anna Freud, "whenever it has come into contact with pedagogy, has always expressed the wish to *limit education*. Psychoanalysis has brought before us the quite definite danger arising from education."[6]

The illocutionary force of the psychoanalytical (pedagogical) critique of pedagogy has thus been reduced, either to a simple negativity, or to a simple positivity, of that critique. Those who, in an oversimplification of the Freudian lesson, equate the psychoanalytic critical stance with a simple positivity, give consequently positive advice to educators, in an attempt to conceive of more liberal methods for raising children—methods allowing "to each stage in the child's life the right proportion of instinct-gratification and instinct-restriction."[7] Those who, on the other hand, in an oversimplification of the Lacanian lesson, equate the psychoanalytical critical stance with a simple negativity, see in psychoanalysis "literally an inverse pedagogy": "the analytic process is in effect a kind of reverse pedagogy, which aims at undoing what has been established by education."[8] In the title of a recent book on the relationship of Freud to pedagogy, Freud is thus defined as "The Anti-Pedagogue."[9] This one-sidedly negative interpretation of the relation of psychoanalysis to pedagogy fails to see that every true pedagogue is in effect an anti-pedagogue, not just because every pedagogy has historically emerged as a critique of pedagogy (Socrates: "There's a chance, Meno, that we, you as well as me . . . have been inadequately educated, you by Gorgias, I by Prodicus"[10]), but because, in one way or another, every pedagogy stems from its confrontation with the impossibility of teaching (Socrates: "You see, Meno, that I am not teaching . . . anything, but all I do is question . . ."[11]). The reductive conception of "Freud: The Anti-Pedagogue" thus fails to see that there is no such thing as an anti-pedagogue: an anti-pedagogue is *the* pedagogue par excellence. Such a conception overlooks, indeed, and fails to reckon with, Freud's own stupendous pedagogical performance, and its relevance to his declarations about pedagogy.

The trouble, both with the positivisitic and with the negativistic misinterpretations of the psychoanalytical critique of pedagogy, is that they refer exclusively to Lacan's or Freud's explicit *statements* about pedagogy, and thus fail to see the illocutionary force, the didactic function of the *utterance* as opposed to the mere content of the statement. They fail to see, in other words, the pedagogical situation —the pedagogical dynamic in which statements function not as simple truths but as performative speech-*acts*. Invariably, all existing psychoanalytically-inspired theories of pedagogy fail to address the question of the pedagogical speech-act of Freud himself, or of Lacan himself: what can be learnt about pedagogy not just from their theories (which only fragmentarily and indirectly deal with the issue of education) but from their way of *teaching* it, from their own practice as teachers, from their own pedagogical performance.

Lacan refers explicitly to what he calls the psychoanalyst's "mission of teaching" (E 241, N 34 TM),[12] and speaks of his own teaching—the bi-monthly seminar he gave for forty years—as a vocation, "a function . . . to which I have truly devoted my entire life" (S-XI, 7, N 1).[13] Unlike Lacan, Freud addresses the issue of teaching more indirectly, rather by refusing to associate his person with it:

> But there is one topic which I cannot pass over so easily—*not, however, because I understand particularly much about it* or have contributed very much to it. Quite the contrary: *I have scarcely concerned myself with it at all*. I must mention it because it is so exceedingly important, so rich in hopes for

> the future, perhaps the most important of all the activities of analysis. What I am thinking of is the application of psychoanalysis to education. [Standard, XXII, 146]

This statement thus promotes pedagogy to the rank of "perhaps the most important of all the activities of analysis" only on the basis of Freud's denial of his own personal involvement with it. However, this very statement, this very denial is itself engaged in a dramatic pedagogical performance; it itself is part of an imaginary "lecture," significantly written in the form of an academic public address and of a dialogue with students—a pedagogic dialogue imaginarily conducted by a Freud who, in reality terminally ill and having undergone an operation for mouth-cancer, is no longer capable of speech:

> My *Introductory Lectures on Psychoanalysis* were delivered . . . in a lecture room of the Vienna Psychiatric Clinic before an audience gathered from all the Faculties of the University. . . .
>
> These new lectures, unlike the former ones, have never been delivered. My age had in the meantime absolved me from the obligation of giving expression to my membership in the University (which was in any case a peripheral one) by delivering lectures; and a surgical operation had made speaking in public impossible for me. If, therefore, I once more take my place in the lecture room during the remarks that follow, it is only by an artifice of the imagination; it may help me not to forget to bear the reader in mind as I enter more deeply into my subject. . . . Like their predecessors, [these lectures] are addressed to the multitude of educated people to whom we may perhaps attribute a benevolent, even though cautious, interest in the characteristics and discoveries of the young science. This time once again it has been my chief aim to make no sacrifice to an appearance of being simple, complete or rounded-off, not to disguise problems and not to deny the existence of gaps and uncertainties. [Standard, XXII, 5–6]

No other such coincidence of fiction and reality, biography and theory, could better dramatize Freud's absolutely fundamental pedagogic gesture. What better image could there be for the pedagogue in spite of himself, the pedagogue in spite of everything—the dying teacher whose imminent death, like that of Socrates, only confirms that he is a born teacher—than this pathetic figure, this living allegory of the speechless speaker, of the teacher's teaching out of—through—the very radical impossibility of teaching?

Pedagogy in psychoanalysis is thus not just a theme: it is a rhetoric. It is not just a statement: it is an utterance. It is not just a meaning: it is action; an action which itself may very well, at times, belie the stated meaning, the didactic *thesis*, the theoretical assertion. It is essential to become aware of this complexity of the relationship of pedagogy and psychoanalysis, in order to begin to think out what the psychoanalytic teaching about teaching might well be.

Discussing "The Teaching of Psychoanalysis in Universities," Freud writes: "it will be enough if [the student] learns something *about* psychoanalysis and something *from* it" (Standard, XVII, 173). To learn "something *from* psychoanalysis" is a very different thing than to learn "something *about* it:" it means that psychoanalysis is not a simple *object* of the teaching, but its *subject*. In his essay, "Psychoanalysis and Its Teaching," Lacan underlines the same ambiguity, the same dynamic complexity, indicating that the true object of psychoanalysis, the object of his teaching, can only be that mode of learning which institutes psychoanalysis itself as subject—as the purveyor of the act of teaching. "How can what psychoanalysis teaches us be taught?," he asks (E 439).

As myself both a student of psychoanalysis and a teacher, I would here like to suggest that the lesson to be learnt about pedagogy from psychoanalysis is less that of "the *application* of psychoanalysis to pedagogy" than that of the *implication* of psychoanalysis in pedagogy and of pedagogy in psychoanalysis. Attentive, thus, both to the pedagogical speech-act of Freud and to the teaching-practice of Lacan, I would like to address the question of teaching as itself a psychoanalytic question. Reckoning not just with the pedagogical thematics *in* psychoanalysis, but with the pedagogical rhetoric *of* psychoanalysis, not just with what psychoanalysis says *about* teachers but with psychoanalysis *itself as teacher,* I will attempt to analyze the ways in which—modifying the conception of what *learning* is and of what *teaching* is—psychoanalysis has shifted pedagogy by radically displacing our very modes of intelligibility.

ANALYTICAL APPRENTICESHIP

Freud conceives of the process of a psychoanalytic therapy as a learning process —an apprenticeship whose epistemological validity far exceeds the contingent singularity of the therapeutic situation:

> Psychoanalysis sets out to explain . . . uncanny disorders; it engages in careful and laborious investigations . . . until at length it can speak thus to the ego:
>
> ". . . A part of the activity of your own mind has been withdrawn from your knowledge and from the command of your will . . . you are using one part of your force to fight the other part . . . A great deal more must constantly be going on in your mind than can be known to your consciousness. Come, *let yourself be taught* . . . ! What is in your mind does not coincide with what you are conscious of; whether something is going on in your mind and whether you hear of it, are two different things. In the ordinary way, I will admit, the intelligence which reaches your consciousness is enough for your needs; and *you may cherish the illusion that you learn of all the more important things.* But in some cases, as in that of an instinctual conflict . . . your intelligence service breaks down . . . In every case, the news that reaches your consciousness is incomplete and often not to be relied on. . . . Turn your eyes inward, . . . *learn first to know yourself!* . . .
>
> It is thus that *psychoanalysis has sought to educate the ego.* [Standard, XVII, 142–143]

Psychoanalysis is thus a pedagogical experience: as a process which gives access to new knowledge hitherto denied to consciousness, it affords what might be called a lesson in cognition (and in miscognition), an epistemological instruction.

Psychoanalysis institutes, in this way, a unique and radically original mode of learning: original not just in its procedures, but in the fact that it gives access to information unavailable through any other mode of learning—unprecedented information, hitherto *unlearnable.* "We learnt," writes Freud, "a quantity of things which could not have been learnt except through analysis" (Standard, XXII, 147).

This new mode of investigation and of learning has, however, a very different temporality than the conventional linear—cumulative and progressive—temporality of learning, as it has traditionally been conceived by pedagogical theory and practice. Proceeding not through linear progression, but through breakthroughs, leaps, discontinuities, regressions, and deferred action, the analytic learning-process puts indeed in question the traditional pedagogical belief in intellectual perfectibility, the progressistic view of learning as a simple one-way road from ignorance to knowledge.

It is in effect the very concept of both ignorance and knowledge—the understanding of what "to know" and "not to know" may really mean—that psychoanalysis has modified, renewed. And it is precisely the originality of this renewal which is central to Lacan's thought, to

Lacan's specific way of understanding the cultural, pedagogical and epistemological revolution implied by the discovery of the unconscious.

KNOWLEDGE

Western pedagogy can be said to culminate in Hegel's philosophical didacticism: the Hegelian concept of "absolute knowledge"—which for Hegel defines at once the potential aim and the actual end of dialectics, of philosophy—is in effect what pedagogy has always aimed at as its ideal: the exhaustion—through methodical investigation—of all there is to know; the absolute completion—termination—of apprenticeship. Complete and totally appropriate knowledge will become—in all senses of the word—a *mastery*. "In the Hegelian perspective," writes Lacan, "the completed discourse" is "an instrument of power, the scepter and the property of those who know" (S-II, 91). "What is at stake in absolute knowledge is the fact that discourse closes back upon itself, that it is entirely in agreement with itself" (S-II, 91).

But the unconscious, in Lacan's conception, is precisely the discovery that human discourse can by definition never be entirely in agreement with itself, entirely identical to its knowledge of itself, since, as the vehicle of unconscious knowledge, it is constitutively the material locus of a signifying difference from itself.

What, indeed, is the unconscious, if not a kind of *unmeant knowledge* which escapes intentionality and meaning, a knowledge which is spoken by the language of the subject (spoken, for instance, by his "slips" or by his dreams), but which the subject cannot recognize, assume as *his*, appropriate; a speaking knowledge which is nonetheless denied to the speaker's knowledge? In Lacan's own terms, the unconscious is "knowledge which can't tolerate one's knowing that one knows" (Seminar, Feb. 19, 1974; unpublished). "Analysis appears on the scene to announce that there is *knowledge which does not know itself*, knowledge which is supported by the signifier as such" (S-XX, 88). "It is from a place which differs from any capture by a subject that a knowledge is surrendered, since that knowledge offers itself only to the subject's slips—to his misprision" (*Scilicet* I, 38).[14] "The discovery of the unconscious . . . is that the implications of meaning infinitely exceed the signs manipulated by the individual" (S-II, 150). "As far as signs are concerned, man is always mobilizing many more of them than he knows" (S-II, 150).

If this is so, there can constitutively be no such thing as absolute knowledge: absolute knowledge is knowledge that has exhausted its own articulation; but articulated knowledge is by definition what cannot exhaust its own self-knowledge. For knowledge to be spoken, linguistically articulated, it would constitutively have to be supported by the ignorance carried by language, the ignorance of the *excess of signs* that of necessity its language—its articulation—"mobilizes." Thus, human knowledge is, by definition, that which is *untotalizable*, that which rules out any possibility of totalizing what it knows or of eradicating its own ignorance.

The epistemological principle of the irreducibility of ignorance which stems from the unconscious, receives an unexpected confirmation from modern science, to which Lacan is equally attentive in his attempt to give the theory of the unconscious its contemporary scientific measure. The scientific a-totality of knowledge is acknowledged by modern mathematics, in set theory (Cantor: "the set of all sets in a universe does not constitute a set"); in contemporary physics, it is the crux of what is known as "the uncertainty principle" of Heisenberg:

> This is what the Heisenberg principle amounts to. When it is possible to locate, to define precisely one of the points of the system, it is impossible to formulate the others. When the place of electrons is discussed . . . it is no longer possible to know anything about . . . their speed. And inversely . . . [S-II, 281]

From the striking and instructive coincidence between the revolutionary findings of psychoanalysis and the new theoretical orientation of modern physics, Lacan derives the following epistemological insight—the following pathbreaking pedagogical principle:

> Until further notice, we can say that *the elements do not answer in the place where they are interrogated.* Or more exactly, as soon as they are interrogated somewhere, it is impossible to grasp them in their totality. [S-II, 281]

IGNORANCE

Ignorance is thus no longer simply *opposed* to knowledge: it is itself a radical condition, an integral part of the very *structure* of knowledge. But what does ignorance consist of, in this new epistemological and pedagogical conception?

If ignorance is to be equated with the a-totality of the unconscious, it can be said to be a kind of forgetting—of forgetfulness: while learning is obviously, among other things, remembering and memorizing ("all learning is recollection," says Socrates), ignorance is linked to what is *not remembered*, what will not be memorized. But what will not be memorized is tied up with repression, with the imperative to forget—the imperative to exclude from consciousness, to not admit to knowledge. Ignorance, in other words, is not a passive state of absence—a simple lack of information: it is an active dynamic of negation, an active refusal of information. Freud writes:

> It is a long superseded idea . . . that the patient suffers from a sort of ignorance, and that if one removes this ignorance by giving him information (about the causal connection of his illness with his life, about his experiences in childhood, and so on) he is bound to recover. The pathological factor is not his ignorance in itself, but the root of this ignorance in his *inner resistances*; it was they who first called this ignorance into being, and they still maintain it now. The task of the treatment lies in combating these resistances. [Standard, XI, 225]

Teaching, like analysis, has to deal not so much with *lack* of knowledge as with *resistances* to knowledge. Ignorance, suggests Lacan, is a "passion." Inasmuch as traditional pedagogy postulated a desire for knowledge, an analytically informed pedagogy has to reckon with "the passion for ignorance" (S-XX, 110). Ignorance, in other words is nothing other than a *desire to ignore*: its nature is less cognitive than performative; as in the case of Sophocles' nuanced representation of the ignorance of Oedipus, it is not a simple lack of information but the incapacity—or the refusal—to acknowledge *one's own implication* in the information.

The new pedagogical lesson of psychoanalysis is not subsumed, however, by the revelation of the dynamic nature—and of the irreducibility—of ignorance. The truly revolutionary insight—the truly revolutionary *pedagogy* discovered by Freud—consists in showing the ways in which, however irreducible, *ignorance itself can teach us something*—become itself *instructive*. This is, indeed, the crucial lesson that Lacan has learnt from Freud:

> It is necessary, says Freud, to interpret the phenomenon of doubt as an integral part of the message. [S-II, 155]

> The forgetting of the dream is . . . itself part of the dream. [S-II, 154]

> The message is not forgotten in just any manner. . . . A censorship is an intention. Freud's argumentation properly reverses the burden of the proof—"In these elements that you cite in objection to me, the memory lapses and the various degradations of the dream, I continue to see a meaning, and even an additional meaning. When the phenomenon of forgetting intervenes, it interests me all the more . . . *These negative phenomena, I add them to the interpretation of the meaning, I recognize that they too have the function of a message.* Freud discovers this dimension . . . What interests Freud . . . [is] *the message as an interrupted discourse,* and which insists. [S-II, 153]

The pedagogical question crucial to Lacan's own teaching will thus be: *Where does it resist?* Where does a text (or a signifier in a patient's conduct) precisely make no sense, that is, *resist interpretation?* Where does what I see—and what I read—resist my understanding? Where is the *ignorance*—the resistance to knowledge—located? And what can I thus *learn* from the locus of that ignorance? How can I interpret *out of* the dynamic ignorance I analytically encounter, both in others and in myself? How can I turn ignorance into an instrument of teaching?

> . . . Teaching [says Lacan] is something rather problematic. . . . As an American poet has pointed out, no one has ever seen a professor who has fallen short of the task because of ignorance . . .
>
> One always knows enough in order to occupy the minutes during which one exposes oneself in the position of the one who knows. . . .
>
> This makes me think that there is no true teaching other than the teaching which succeeds in provoking in those who listen an insistence—this desire to know which can only emerge when they themselves have *taken the measure of ignorance as such*—of ignorance inasmuch as it is, as such, fertile—in the one who teaches as well. [S-II, 242]

THE USE OF THAT WHICH CANNOT BE EXCHANGED

Teaching, thus, is not the transmission of ready-made knowledge, it is rather the creation of a new *condition* of knowledge—the creation of an original learning-disposition. "What I teach you," says Lacan, "does nothing other than express the *condition* thanks to which what Freud says is possible" (S-II, 368). The lesson, then, does not "teach" Freud: it teaches the "condition" which make it *possible to learn* Freud—the condition which makes possible Freud's teaching. What is this condition?

In analysis, what sets in motion the psychoanalytical apprenticeship is the peculiar pedagogical structure of the analytic situation. The analysand speaks to the analyst, whom he endows with the authority of the one who possesses knowledge—knowledge of what is precisely lacking in the analysand's own knowledge. The analyst, however, knows nothing of the sort. His only competence, insists Lacan, lies in "what I would call *textual knowledge,* so as to oppose it to the referential notion which only masks it" (*Scilicet* I, 21). Textual knowledge—the very stuff the literature teacher is supposed to deal in—is knowledge of the functioning of language, of symbolic structures, of the signifier, knowledge at once derived from—and directed towards—interpretation.

But such knowledge cannot be acquired (or possessed) once and for all: each case, each text, has its own specific, singular symbolic functioning, and requires thus a different—an original—interpretation. The analysts, says Lacan, are "those who share this knowledge only at the price, on the condition of their *not being able to exchange it*" (*Scilicet* I, 59). Analytic (textual) knowledge cannot be *exchanged,* it has to be *used*—and used in each case differently, according to the singularity of the case, according to the specificity of the text. Textual (or analytic) knowledge is, in other words, that peculiarly specific knowledge which, unlike any commodity, is subsumed by its *use* value, having no exchange value whatsoever.[15] Analysis has thus no use for ready-made interpretations, for knowledge given in advance. Lacan insists on "the insistence with which Freud recommends to us to approach each new case as if we had never learnt anything from his first interpretations" (*Scilicet*, I, 20). "What the analyst must know," concludes Lacan, "is how to ignore what he knows."

DIALOGIC LEARNING, OR THE ANALYTICAL STRUCTURE OF INSIGHT

Each case is thus, for the analyst as well as for the patient, a new apprenticeship. "If it's true that our knowledge comes to the rescue of the patient's ignorance, it is not less true that, for our part, we, too, are plunged in ignorance" (S-I, 78). While the analysand is obviously ignorant of his own unconscious, the analyst is doubly ignorant: pedagogically ignorant of his suspended (given) knowledge; actually ignorant of the very knowledge the analysand presumes him to possess of his own (the analysand's) unconscious: knowledge of the very knowledge he—the patient—lacks. In what way does knowledge, then, emerge in and from the analytic situation?

Through the analytic dialogue the analyst, indeed, has first to learn where to situate the ignorance: where his own textual knowledge is *resisted*. It is, however, out of this resistance, out of the patient's active ignorance, out of the patient's speech which says much more than it itself knows, that the analyst will come to *learn* the *patient's own* unconscious *knowledge*, that knowledge which is inaccessible to itself because it cannot tolerate knowing that it knows; and it is the signifiers of this constitutively a-reflexive knowledge coming from the patient that the analyst *returns* to the patient from his different vantage point, from his non-reflexive, asymmetrical position as an Other. Contrary to the traditional pedagogical dynamic, in which the teacher's question is addressed to an answer from the other—from the student—which is totally reflexive, and expected, "the true Other" says Lacan, "is the Other who gives the answer one does not expect" (S-II, 288). Coming from the Other, knowledge is, by definition, that which comes as a surprise, that which is constitutively the return of a difference:

> TEIRESIAS: . . . *You* are the land's pollution.
> OEDIPUS: How shamelessly you started up this taunt! How do you think you will escape?
> TEIRESIAS: . . . I have escaped; the truth is what I cherish and that's my strength.
> OEDIPUS: And *who has taught you* truth? Not your profession surely!
> TEIRESIAS: *You have taught me*, for you have made me speak against my will.
> OEDIPUS: Speak what? Tell me again that I may *learn* it better.
> TEIRESIAS: Did you not understand before or would you provoke me into speaking?
> OEDIPUS: *I did not grasp it, not so to call it known*. Say it again.
> TEIRESIAS: I say you are the murderer of the king whose murderer you seek.[16]

As Teiresias—so as to be able to articulate the truth—must have been *"taught"* not by "his profession" but *by Oedipus*, so the analyst precisely must be *taught* by the analysand's unconscious. It is by structurally occupying the position of the analysand's unconscious, and by thus making himself a *student of the patient's knowledge*, that the analyst becomes the patient's teacher—makes the patient learn what would otherwise remain forever inaccessible to him.

For teaching to be realized, for knowledge to be learnt, the position of alterity is therefore indispensable: knowledge is what is already there, but always in the Other. Knowledge, in other words, is not a *substance* but a structural dynamic: it is not *contained* by any individual but comes about out of the mutual apprenticeship between two partially unconscious speeches which both say more than they know. Dialogue is thus the radical condition of learning and of knowledge, the analytically constitutive condition through which ignorance becomes structurally informative; knowledge is essentially, irreducibly dialogic. "No knowledge," writes Lacan, "can be supported or transported by one alone" (*Scilicet* I, 59).

Like the analyst, the teacher, in Lacan's eyes, cannot in turn be, alone, a *master* of the knowledge which he teaches. Lacan transposes the radicality of analytic dialogue—as a newly understood structure of insight—into the pedagogical situation. This is not simply to say that he encourages "exchange" and calls for students' interventions—as many other teachers do. Much more profoundly and radically, he attempts to *learn from the students his own knowledge*. It is the following original pedagogical appeal that he can thus address to the audience of his seminar:

> It seems to me I should quite naturally be the point of convergence of the questions that may occur to you.
>
> Let everybody tell me, in his own way, *his idea of what I am driving at*. How, for him, is opened up—or closed—or how already he resists, the question as I pose it . . . (S-II, 242)

THE SUBJECT PRESUMED TO KNOW

This pedagogical approach, which makes no claim to total knowledge, which does not even claim to be in possession of its own knowledge, is, of course, quite different from the usual pedagogical pose of mastery, different from the image of the self-sufficient, self-possessed proprietor of knowledge, in which pedagogy has traditionally featured the authoritative figure of the teacher. This figure of infallible human authority implicity likened to a God, that is, both modeled on and guaranteed by divine *omniscience*, is based on an illusion: the illusion of a consciousness transparent to itself. "It is the case of the unconscious," writes Lacan, "that it abolishes the postulate of the subject presumed to know" (*Scilicet* I, 46).

Abolishing a postulate, however, doesn't mean abolishing an illusion: while psychoanalysis uncovers the mirage inherent in the function of the subject presumed to know, it also shows the prestige and the affective charge of that mirage to be constitutively irreducible, to be indeed most crucial to, determinant of, the emotional dynamic of all discursive human interactions, of all human relationships founded on sustained interlocution. The psychoanalytical account of the functioning of this dynamic is the most directly palpable, the most explicit lesson psychoanalysis has taught us about teaching.

In a brief and peculiarly introspective essay called "Some Reflections on Schoolboy Psychology," the already aging Freud nostalgically probes into his own "schoolboy psychology," the affect of which even time and intellectual achievements have not entirely extinguished. "As little as ten years ago," writes Freud, "you may have had moments at which you suddenly felt quite young again":

> As you walked through the streets of Vienna—already a grey-beard and weighed down by all the cares of family life—you might come unexpectedly on some well-preserved, elderly gentleman, and would greet him humbly almost, because you had

> recognized him as one of your former schoolmasters. But afterwards, you would stop and reflect: "Was that really he? or only someone deceptively like him? How youthful he looks! And how old you yourself have grown! . . . *Can it be possible that the men who used to stand for us as types of adulthood were so little older than we* were?" [Standard, XIII, 241]

Commenting on "my emotion at meeting my old schoolmaster," Freud goes on to give an analytical account of the emotional dynamic of the pedagogical situation:

> It is hard to decide whether what affected us more . . . was our concern with the sciences that we were taught or with . . . our teachers . . . In many of us *the path to the sciences led only through our teachers*. . . .
>
> We courted them and turned our backs on them, we imagined sympathies and antipathies which probably had no existence . . .
>
> . . . *psychoanalysis has taught us* that the individual's emotional attitudes to other people . . . are . . . established at an unexpectedly early age . . . The people to whom [the child] is in this way fixed are his parents . . . His later acquaintances are . . . obliged to *take over a kind of emotional heritage*; they encounter sympathies and antipathies to the production of which they themselves have contributed little . . .
>
> These men [the teachers] became our *substitute fathers*. That was why, even though they were still quite young, *they struck us as so mature and so unattainably adult. We transferred* to them *the respect and expectations attaching to the omniscient father of our childhood*, and then we began to treat them as we treated our own fathers at home. We confronted them with the *ambivalence* that we had acquired in our own families and with its help we struggled with them as we had been in the habit of struggling with our fathers . . . [Standard, XIII, 242–44]

This phenomenon of the compulsive unconscious reproduction of an archaic emotional pattern, which Freud called "transference" and which he saw both as the energetic spring and as the interpretive key to the psychoanalytic situation, is further thought out by Lacan as what accounts for the functioning of authority in general: as essential, thus, not just to any pedagogic situation but to the problematics of knowledge as such. "As soon as there is somewhere a subject presumed to know, there is transference," writes Lacan (S-XI, 210).

Since "transference is the acting out of the reality of the unconscious" (S-XI, 150, 240, N 174, 267), teaching is not a purely cognitive, informative experience, it is also an emotional, erotical experience. "I deemed it necessary," insists Lacan, "to support the idea of transference, as indistinguishable from love, with the formula of the subject presumed to know. I cannot fail to underline the new resonance with which this notion of knowledge is endowed. The person in whom I presume knowledge to exist, thereby acquires my love" (S-XX, 64). "The question of love is thus linked to the question of kowledge" (S-XX, 84). "Transference *is* love . . . I insist: it is love directed toward, addressed to, knowledge" (*Scilicet* V, 16).

"Of this subject presumed to know, who," asks Lacan, "can believe himself to be entirely invested?—That is not the question. The question, first and foremost, for each subject, is how to situate *the place from which he himself addresses* the subject presumed to know?" (S-XX, 211) Insofar as knowledge is itself *a structure of address*, cognition is always both motivated and obscured by love; theory, both guided and misguided by an implicit transferential structure.

ANALYTIC PEDAGOGY, OR DIDACTIC PSYCHOANALYSIS: THE INTERMINABLE TASK

In human relationships, sympathies and antipathies usually provoke—and call for—a similar emotional response in the person they are addressed to. Transference on "the subject presumed to know"—the analyst or the teacher—may provoke a counter-transference on the latter's part. The analytic or the pedagogical situation may thus degenerate into an imaginary mirror-game of love and hate, where each of the participants would unconsciously enact past conflicts and emotions, unwarranted by the current situation and disruptive with respect to the real issues, unsettling the topical stakes of analysis or education.

In order to avoid this typical degeneration, Freud conceived of the necessity of a preliminary psychoanalytic training of "the subjects presumed to know," a practical didactic training through their own analysis which, giving them insight into their own transferential structure, would later help them understand the students' or the patients' transferential mechanisms and, more importantly, keep under control their own—avoid being entrapped in counter-transference. "The only appropriate preparation for the profession of educator," suggests Freud, "is a thorough psycho-analytic training . . . The analysis of teachers and educators seems to be a more efficacious prophylactic measure than the analysis of children themselves" (Standard, XXII, 150).

While this preliminary training [which has come to be known as "didactic psychoanalysis") is, however, only a recommendation on Freud's part as far as teachers are concerned, it is an absolute requirement and precondition for the habilitation—and qualification—of the psychoanalyst. In his last and therefore, in a sense, testamentary essay, "Analysis Terminable and Interminable," Freud writes:

> Among the factors which influence the prospects of analytic treatment and add to its difficulties in the same manner as the resistances, must be reckoned not only the nature of the patient's ego but the individuality of the analyst.
>
> It cannot be disputed that *analysts . . . have not invariably come up to the standard* of psychical normality *to which they wish to educate their patients.* Opponents of analysis often point to this fact with scorn and use it as an argument to show the uselessness of analytic exertions. We might reject this criticism as making unjustifiable demands. *Analysts are people who have learnt to practice a particular art*; alongside of this, they may be allowed to be *human beings like anyone else.* After all, nobody maintains that a physician is incapable of treating internal diseases if his own internal organs are not sound; on the contrary, it may be argued that there are certain advantages in a man who is himself threatened with tuberculosis specializing in the treatment of persons suffering from that disease. . . .
>
> It is reasonable, [however,] . . . to expect of an analyst, as part of his qualifications, a considerable degree of mental normality and correctness. In addition, he must possess some kind of superiority, so that in certain analytic situations he can *act as a model for his patient* and in others *as a teacher.* And finally, we must not forget that the analytic relationship is based on a love of truth—that is, on a recognition of reality—and that it precludes any kind of sham or deceit. . . .
>
> It almost looks as if analysis were the third of those 'impossible' professions . . . *Where is the poor wretch to acquire the ideal qualifications* which he will need in his profession? *The answer is, in an analysis of himself,* with which his preparation for his future activity begins. For practical reasons this analysis can only be short and incomplete. . . . It has accomplished its purpose if it gives *the learner* a firm conviction of the existence of the unconscious, if it enables him . . . to perceive in himself things which would otherwise be incredible to him, and if it shows him a first example of the technique . . . in analytic work. *This alone would not suffice for his instruction; but we reckon on the stimuli he has received in his own analysis not ceasing when it ends* and *on the process of remodelling the ego continuing* spontaneously in the analysed subject and making use of all subsequent experiences in this newly-acquired sense. This does in fact happen, and *in so far as it happens, it makes* the analysed subject qualified to be an analyst. [Standard, XXIII, 247–49]

Nowhere else does Freud describe as keenly *the revolutionary radicality of the very nature of the teaching* to be (practically and theoretically) derived from the originality of the psychoanalytical experience. The analysand is qualified to be an analyst as of the point at which he understands his own analysis to be inherently unfinished, incomplete, as of the point, that is, at which he settles into his own didactic analysis—or his own analytical apprenticeship—as fundamentally interminable. It is, in other words, as of the moment the student recognizes that *learning has no term,* that he can himself become a teacher, assume the position of the teacher. But the position of the teacher is itself the position of *the one who learns,* of the one who *teaches* nothing other than *the way he learns.* The subject of teaching is interminably—a student; the subject of teaching is interminably—a learning. This is the most radical, perhaps the most far-reaching insight psychoanalysis can give us into pedagogy.

Freud pushes this original understanding of what pedagogy is to its logical limit. Speaking of the "defensive" tendency of psychoanalysts "to divert the implications and demands of analysis from themselves (probably by directing them on to other people)"—of the analysts' tendency, that is, *"to withdraw from the critical and corrective influence of analysis,"* as well as of the temptation of power threatening them in the very exercise of their profession, Freud enjoins:

> Every analyst should periodically—at intervals of five years or so—submit himself to analysis once more, without feeling ashamed of taking this step. This would mean, then, that not only the therapeutic analysis of patients[17] but *his own analysis would change from a terminable into an interminable task.* [Standard, XXIII, 249]

Of all Freud's followers, Lacan alone has picked up on the radicality of Freud's pedagogical concern with didactic psychoanalysis, not just as a subsidiary technical, pragmatic question (how should analysts be trained?), but as a major theoretical concern, as a major pedagogical investigation crucial to the very innovation, to the very revolutionary core of psychoanalytic insight. The highly peculiar and surprising style of Lacan's own teaching-practice is, indeed, an answer to, a follow-up on, Freud's ultimate suggestion—in Lacan's words—"to make psychoanalysis and education (training) collapse into each other" (E 459).

This is the thrust of Lacan's original endeavor both as psychoanalyst and as teacher: "in the field of psychoanalysis," he writes, "what is necessary is the restoration of the identical status of didactic psychoanalysis and of the teaching of psychoanalysis, in their common scientific opening" (E 236).

As a result of this conception, Lacan considers not just the practical analyses which he—as analyst—directs, but his own public teaching, his own seminar—primarily directed towards the (psychoanalytical) training of analysts—as partaking of didactic psychoanalysis, as itself, thus, analytically didactic and didactically analytical, in a new and radical way.

"How can what psychoanalysis teaches us be taught?" (E 439)—Only by continuing, in one's own teaching, one's own interminable didactic analysis. Lacan has willingly transformed himself into the *analysand* of his Seminar[18] so as to teach, precisely, psychoanalysis *as* teaching, and teaching *as* psychoanalysis.

Psychoanalysis as teaching, and teaching as psychoanalysis, radically subvert the demarcation-line, the clear-cut opposition between the analyst and the analysand, between the teacher and the student (or the learner)—showing that what counts, in both cases, is precisely the transition, the struggle-filled *passage* from one position to the other. But the passage is itself interminable; it can never be crossed once and for all: "The psychoanalytic act has but to falter slightly, and it is the analyst who becomes the analysand" (*Scilicet* I, 47). Lacan denounces, thus, "the reactionary principle" of the professional belief in "the duality of the one who suffers and the one who cures," in "the opposition between the one who knows and the one who does not know. . . . The most corrupting of comforts is intellectual comfort, just as one's *worst* corruption is the belief that one is *better*" (E 403).

Lacan's well-known polemical and controversial stance—his *critique of psychoanalysis*—itself partakes, then, of his understanding of the pedagogical imperative of didactic psychoanalysis. Lacan's original endeavor is to submit *the whole discipline of psychoanalysis* to what Freud called "the critical and corrective influence of analysis" (Standard, XXIII, 249). Lacan, in other words, is the first to understand that the psychoanalytic discipline is an unprecedented one in that its *teaching* does not just reflect upon itself, but turns back upon itself so as to *subvert itself*, and truly *teaches* only insofar as it subverts itself. Psychoanalytic teaching is pedagogically unique in that it is inherently, interminably, self-critical. Lacan's amazing pedagogical performance thus sets forth the unparalleled example of a teaching whose fecundity is tied up, paradoxically enough, with the inexhaustibility—the interminability—of its *self-critical potential*.

From didactic analysis, Lacan derives, indeed, a whole new theoretical (didactic) mode of *self-subversive self-reflection*.

> A question suddenly arises . . . : in the case of the knowledge yielded solely to the subject's mistake, what kind of subject could ever be in a position to know it in advance? (*Scilicet* I, 38)
>
> Retain at least what this text, which I have tossed out in your direction, bears witness to: my enterprise does not go beyond the act in which it is caught, and, therefore, its only chance lies in its being mistaken. (*Scilicet* I, 41)
>
> This lesson seems to be one that should not have been forgotten, had not psychoanalysis precisely taught us that it is, as such, forgettable. [E 232]

Always submitting analysis itself to the instruction of an unexpected analytic turn of the screw, to the surprise of an additional reflexive turn, of an additional self-subversive ironic twist, didactic analysis becomes for Lacan what might be called a *style*: a teaching style which has become at once a life-style and a writing-style: "the ironic style of calling into question the very foundations of the discipline" (E 238).

> Any return to Freud founding a teaching worthy of the name will occur only on that pathway where truth . . . becomes manifest in the revolutions of culture. That pathway is the only training we can claim to transmit to those who follow us. It is called—a style. (E 458)

Didactic analysis is thus invested by Lacan not simply with the practical, pragmatic value, but with the theoretical significance—the allegorical instruction—of a paradigm: a paradigm, precisely, of the interminability, not just of teaching (learning) and of analyzing (being analyzed), but of the very act of thinking, theorizing: of teaching, analyzing, thinking, theorizing, in such a way as to make psychoanalysis "what it has never ceased to be: an act that is yet to come" (*Scilicet* I, 9).

TEACHING AS A LITERARY GENRE

Among so many other things, Lacan and Freud thus teach us teaching, teach us—in a radically new way—what it might mean to teach. Their lesson, and their pedagogical performance, profoundly renew at once the meaning and the status of the very act of teaching.

If they are both such extraordinary teachers, it is—I would suggest—because they both are, above all, quite extraordinary learners. In Freud's case, I would argue, the extraordinary teaching stems from Freud's original—unique—position as a student; in Lacan's case, the extraordinary teaching stems from Lacan's original—unique—position as disciple.

"One might feel tempted," writes Freud, "to agree with the philosophers and the psychiatrists and like them, rule out the problem of dream-interpretation as a purely fanciful task. *But I have been taught better*" (Standard, IV, 100).

By whom has Freud been taught—taught better than by "the judgement of the prevalent science of today," better than by established scholarly authorities of philosophy and psychiatry? Freud has been taught *by dreams* themselves: his own, and those of others; Freud has been taught by his own patients: "*My patients* . . . told me their dreams and so *taught me* . . .—" (Standard, VI, 100–101).

Having thus been taught by dreams, as well as by his patients, that—contrary to the established scholarly opinion—dreams do have meaning, Freud is further taught by a literary text:

> This discovery is confirmed by a legend that has come down to us from antiquity. . . .
>
> While the poet . . . brings to light the guilt of Oedipus, he is at the same time compelling us to recognize our own inner minds . . .
>
> Like Oedipus, we live in ignorance of these wishes . . . and after their revelation, we may all of us well seek to close our eyes to the scenes of our childhood. [Standard, VI, 261–263]

"But I have been taught better." What is unique about Freud's position as a student—as a learner—is that he learns from, or puts in the position of his teacher, the least authoritative sources of information that can be imagined: that he knows how to derive a teaching, or a lesson, from the very unreliability—the very *non-authority*—of literature, of dreams, of patients. For the first time in the history of learning, Freud, in other words, has recourse—scientific recourse—to a knowledge which is not authoritative, which is not that of a master, a knowledge which does not know what it knows, and is thus *not in possession of itself*.

Such, precisely, is the very essence of literary knowledge. "I went to the poets," says Socrates; ". . . I took them some of the most elaborate passages in their own writings, and asked them what was the meaning of them—thinking that they would teach me something. Will you believe me? I am almost ashamed to confess the truth, but I must say that there is hardly a person present who would not have talked better about their poetry than they did themselves. Then I knew that *not by wisdom do poets write poetry, but by a sort of genius or inspiration*; they are like diviners or soothsayers who also *say many fine things, but do not understand the meaning of them*. The poets appeared to me to be much in the same case."[19] From a philosophical perspective, knowledge is mastery—that which is in mastery of its own meaning. Unlike Hegelian philosophy, which *believes it knows all that there is to know*; unlike Socratic (or contemporary post-Nietzschean) philosophy, which *believes it knows it does not know*—literature, for its part, *knows it knows, but does not know the meaning of its knowledge*—does not know *what* it knows.

For the first time, then, Freud gives authority to the instruction—to the teaching—of a knowledge which does not know its own meaning, to a knowledge (that of dreams, of patients, of Greek tragedy) which we might define as literary: knowledge that is not in mastery of itself.

Of all Freud's students and disciples, Lacan alone has understood and emphasized the *radical* significance of Freud's indebtedness to literature: the role played by *literary knowledge* not just in the historical constitution of psychoanalysis, but in the very actuality of the psychoanalytic act, of the psychoanalytic (ongoing) *work* of learning and of teaching. Lacan alone has understood and pointed out the ways in which Freud's teaching—in all senses of the word—is not accidentally, but radically and fundamentally, a *literary* teaching. Speaking of "the training of the analysts of the future," Lacan thus writes:

> One has only to turn the pages of his works for it to become abundantly clear that Freud regarded a study . . . of the resonances . . . of literature and of the significations involved in works of art as necessary to an understanding of the text of our experience. Indeed, Freud himself is a striking instance of his own belief: he derived his inspiration, his ways of thinking and his technical weapons, from just such a study. But he also regarded it as a necessary condition in any teaching of psychoanalysis. [E 435, N 144]
>
> This [new] technique [of interpretation] would require for its teaching as well as for its learning a profound assimilation of the resources of a language, and especially of those that are concretely realized in its poetic texts. It is well known that Freud was in this position in relation to German literature, which, by virtue of an incomparable translation, can be said to include Shakespeare's plays. Every one of his works bears witness to this, and to the continual recourse he had to it, no less in his technique than in his discovery. [E 295, N 83]
>
> The psychoanalytic experience has rediscovered in man the imperative of the Word as the law that has formed him in its image. It manipulates the poetic function of language to give to his desire its symbolic mediation. [E 322, N 106]
>
> Freud had, eminently, this feel for meaning, which accounts for the fact that any of his works, *The Three Caskets*, for instance, gives the reader the impression that it is written by a soothsayer, that it is guided by that kind of meaning which is of the order of poetic inspiration. [S-II, 353]

It is in this sense, among others, that Lacan can be regarded as Freud's best student: Lacan is the sole Freudian who has sought to learn from Freud how to learn Freud: Lacan is "taught" by Freud in much the same way Freud is "taught" by dreams; Lacan reads Freud in much the same way Freud reads *Oedipus the King*, specifically seeking in the text its *literary knowledge*. From Freud as teacher, suggests Lacan, we should learn to derive that kind of *literary teaching* he himself derived in an unprecedented way from literary texts. Freud's text should thus itself be read as a poetic text:

> . . . the notion of the death instinct involves a basic irony, since its meaning has to be sought in the conjunction of two contrary terms: instinct . . . being the law that governs . . . a cycle of behavior whose goal is the accomplishment of a vital function; and death appearing first of all as the destruction of life. . . .
>
> This notion must be approached through its resonances in what I shall call *the poetics of the Freudian corpus*, the first way of access to the penetration of its meaning, and the essential dimension, from the origins of the work to the apogee marked in it by this notion, for an understanding of its dialectical repercussions. [E 316–17, N 101–02]

It is here, in conjunction with Lacan's way of relating to Freud's literary teaching and of learning from Freud's literary knowledge, that we touch upon the historical uniqueness of Lacan's position as disciple, and can thus attempt to understand the way in which this pedagogically unique discipleship accounts for Lacan's astounding originality as a teacher.

"As Plato pointed out long ago," says Lacan, "it is not at all necessary that the poet know what he is doing, in fact, it is preferable that he not know. That is what gives a primordial value to what he does. We can only bow our heads before it" (Seminar, April 9, 1974, unpublished). Although apparently Lacan seems to espouse Plato's position, his real pedagogical stance is, in more than one way, at the antipodes of that of Plato; and not just because he bows his head to poets, whereas Plato casts them out of the Republic. If Freud himself, indeed, bears witness, in his text, to some poetic—literary—knowledge, it is to the extent that, like the poets, he, too, cannot exhaust the meaning of his text—he too partakes of the poetic ignorance of his own knowledge. Unlike Plato who, from his position as an admiring disciple, reports Socrates' assertion of his ignorance without—it might be assumed—really believing in the *non-ironic truth* of that assertion ("For the hearers," says Socrates, "always imagine that I myself possess the wisdom I find wanting in others"),[20] Lacan can be said to be the first disciple in the whole history of pedagogy and of culture who *does indeed believe in the ignorance of his teacher—of his master*. Paradoxically enough, this is why he can be said to be, precisely, Freud's best student: a student of Freud's own revolutionary way of learning, of Freud's own unique position as the unprecedented student of unauthorized, unmastered knowledge. "The truth of the subject," says Lacan, "even when he is the position of a master, is not in himself" (S-XI, 10).

> [Freud's] texts, to which for the past . . . years I have devoted a two-hour seminar every Wednesday . . . without having covered a quarter of the total, . . . , have given me, and those who have attended my seminars, the surprise of genuine discoveries. These discoveries, which range from concepts that have remained unused to clinical details uncovered by our exploration, demonstrate *how far the field investigated by Freud extended beyond the avenues that he left us to tend*, and how little his observation, which sometimes gives an impression of exhaustiveness, was the slave of what he had to demonstrate. Who . . . has not been moved by this research in action, whether in "The Interpretation of Dreams," "The Wolf Man," or "Beyond the Pleasure Principle?" [E 404, N 117, TM]

Commenting on *The Interpretation of Dreams*, Lacan situates in Freud's text the discoverer's own transferential structure—Freud's own unconscious structure of address:

> What polarizes at that moment Freud's discourse, what organizes the whole of Freud's existence, is the conversation with Fliess. . . . It is in this dialogue that Freud's self-analysis is realized . . . This vast speech addressed to Fliess will later become the whole written work of Freud.
>
> The conversation of Freud with Fliess, this fundamental discourse, which at that moment is unconscious, is the essential dynamic element [of *The Interpretation of Dreams*]. Why is it unconscious at the moment? Because its significance goes far beyond what both of them, as individuals, can consciously apprehend or understand of it at the moment. As individuals, they are nothing other, after all, than two little erudites, who are in the process of exchanging rather weird ideas.
>
> The discovery of the unconscious, in the full dimension with which it is revealed at the very moment of its historical emergence, is that the scope, the implications of meaning go far beyond the signs manipulated by the individual. As far as signs are concerned, man is always mobilizing many more of them than he knows. [S-II, 150]

It is to the extent that Lacan precisely teaches us to read in Freud's text (in its textual excess) the signifiers of Freud's ignorance—his ignorance of his own knowledge—that Lacan can be considered Freud's best reader, as well as the most compelling teacher of the Freudian pedagogical imperative: the imperative to learn from and through the insight which does not know its own meaning, from and through the knowledge which is not entirely in mastery—in possession—of itself.

This unprecedented *literary* lesson, which Lacan derives from Freud's revolutionary way of learning and in the light of which he learns Freud, is transformed, in Lacan's own work, into a deliberately literary style of teaching. While—as a subject of praise or controversy—the originality of Lacan's eminently literary, eminently "poetic" style has become a stylistic *cause célèbre* often commented upon, what has not been understood is the extent to which this style—this poetic theory or theoretical poetry—is *pedagogically* poetic: poetic in such a way as to raise, through every answer that it gives, the literary question of its non-mastery of itself. In pushing its own thought beyond the limit of its self-possession, beyond the limitations of its own capacity for mastery; in passing on understanding which does not fully understand what it understands; in *teaching*, thus, *with blindness*—with and through the very blindness of its literary knowledge, of insights not entirely transparent to themselves—Lacan's unprecedented theoretically *poetic pedagogy* always implicitly opens up onto the infinitely literary, infinitely *teaching* question: What is the "navel"[21] of my own theoretical dream of understanding? What is the specificity of my incomprehension? What is the riddle which I in effect here pose under the guise of knowledge?

> "But what was it that Zarathustra once said to you? That poets lie too much? But Zarathustra too is a poet. Do you believe that in saying this he spoke the truth? Why do you believe that?"
>
> The disciple answered, "I believe in Zarathustra." But Zarathustra shook his head and smiled.[22]
>
> Any return to Freud founding a teaching worthy of the name will occur only on that pathway where truth . . . becomes manifest in the revolutions of culture. That pathway is the only training we can claim to transmit to those who follow us. It is called—a style. [E 458][23]

NOTES

1. Plato, *Meno*, 70 a, 71 a, 82 a. Translated by G. M. A. Grube (Indianapolis: Hackett Publishing Company, 1980), 3, 14 (translation modified).

2. *The Complete Psychological Works of Sigmund Freud*, translated from the German under the general editorship of James Strachey (London: The Hogarth Press and the Institute of Psychoanalysis), volume XIX, p. 273. Hereafter, this edition will be referred to as "Standard," followed by volume number (in roman numerals) and page number (in arabic numerals).

3. Jacques Lacan, *Ecrits* (Paris: Seuil, 1966), 233, my translation. Henceforth I will be using the abbreviations: "E" (followed by page number)—for this original French edition of the *Ecrits*, and "N" (followed by page number) for the corresponding Norton edition of the English translation (*Ecrits: A Selection*, translated by Alan Sheridan, New York: Norton, 1977). When the reference to the French edition of the *Ecrits* (E) is not followed by a reference to the Norton English edition (N), the passage quoted (as in this case) is in my translation and has not been included in the "Selection" of the Norton edition.

4. Which for Lacan involves "the relationship of the individual to language": E 445.

5. Italics mine. As a rule, in the quoted passages, italics are mine unless otherwise indicated.

6. Anna Freud, *Psychoanalysis for Teachers and Parents*, trans. Barbara Low (Boston: Beacon press, 1960), 95–6.

7. Ibid., p. 105.

8. Catherine Millot, interview in *l'Âne, le magasine freudien*, No. 1, April–May 1981, p. 19.

9. Catherine Millot, *Freud Anti-Pedagogue* (Paris: Bibliothèque d'Ornicar?, 1979).

10. Plato, *Meno*, 96 d, op. cit., p. 28 (translation modified).

11. Ibid., 82 e, p. 15.

12. The abbreviation "TM"—"translation modified"—will signal my alterations of the official English translation of the work in question.

13. The abbreviation S-XI (followed by page number) refers to Jacques Lacan, *Le Séminaire, livre XI, Les Quatre concepts fondamentaux de la psychanalyse* (Paris: Seuil, 1973). The following abbreviation "N" (followed by page number) refers to the

corresponding English edition: *The Four Fundamental Concepts of Psychoanalysis,* edited by Jacques-Alain Miller, translated by Alan Sheridan (New York: Norton, 1978).

As for the rest of Lacan's Seminars which have appeared in book form, the following abbreviations will be used:

S-I (followed by page number), for: J. Lacan, *Le Séminaire, livre I: Les Ecrits techniques de Freud* (Paris: Seuil, 1975);

S-II (followed by page number), for: J. Lacan, *Le Séminaire, livre II: le Moi dans la théorie de Freud et dans la technique de la psychanalyse* (Paris: Seuil, 1978);

S–XX (followed by page number), for: J. Lacan, *Le Séminaire, livre XX: Encore* (Paris: Seuil, 1975).

All quoted passages from these (as yet untranslated) Seminars are here in my translation.

14. Abbreviated for Lacan's texts published in *Scilicet: Tu peux savoir ce qu'en pense l'école freudienne de Paris* (Paris: Seuil). The roman numeral stands for the issue number (followed by page number). Number I appeared in 1968.

15. As soon as analytic knowledge *is* exchanged, it ceases to be knowledge and becomes opinion, prejudice, presumption: "the sum of prejudices that every knowledge contains, and that each of us transports . . . Knowledge is always, somewhere, only one's belief that one knows" (*S-II*, 56).

16. Sophocles, *Oedipus the King,* trans. David Grene, in *Sophocles I,* (Chicago & London: The University of Chicago Press, 1954), 25–6.

17. The therapeutic analysis of patients is "interminable" to the extent that repression can never be totally lifted, only displaced. Cf. Freud's letter to Fliess, dated April 16, 1900: " 'E's career as a patient has at last come to an end . . . His riddle is *almost* completely solved, his condition is excellent . . . At the moment a residue of his symptoms remains. I am beginning to understand that the apparently interminable nature of the treatment is something determined by law and is dependent on the transference." Hence, Freud speaks of "the asymptotic termination of treatment." (Standard, XXIII, 215) Freud's italics.

18. The occasional master's pose—however mystifying to the audience—invariably exhibits itself as a parodic symptom of the analysand.

19. Plato *Apology,* 22 a–c, in *Dialogues of Plato,* Jowett translation, edited by J. D. Kaplan (New York: Washington Square Press, Pocket Books, 1973), 12.

20. Plato, *Apology,* 22 a–c, op. cit., p. 12.

21. "There is," writes Freud, "at least one spot in every dream at which it is unplumbable—a navel, as it were, that is its point of contact with the unknown" (Standard, IV, 111).

22. Nietzsche, *Thus Spoke Zarathustra,* translated by Walter Kaufmann (TM), in *The Portable Nietzsche* (New York: the Viking Press, 1971), 239, "On Poets."

23. The present essay is a chapter from my forthcoming book: *Psychoanalysis in Contemporary Culture: Jacques Lacan and the Adventure of Insight.*

The news of Lacan's death (on September 9, 1981) reached me as I was writing the section here entitled "The Interminable Task." The sadness caused by the cessation of a life as rich in insight and as generous in instruction, was thus accompanied by an ironic twist which itself felt like a typical Lacanian turn, one of the ironies of his teaching: teaching terminable and interminable . . . Few deaths, indeed, have been as deeply inscribed as a lesson in a teaching, as Lacan's, who always taught the implications of the Master's death. "Were I to go away," he said, some time ago, "tell yourselves that it is in order to at last be truly Other."

I have deliberately chosen not to change, and to pursue, the grammatical present tense which I was using to describe Lacan's teaching: since his life has ceased to be, teaching is, indeed, all the more present, all the more alive, all the more interminably "what it has never ceased to be: an act that is yet to come."

35

Lillian S. Robinson
1941–

Lillian S. Robinson is NEH Visiting Professor at Albright College and is an affiliated scholar at the Stanford University Center for Research on Women. Her works include Sex, *Class and Culture* (1978), an abbreviated version of the argument she posits in her published dissertation *Monstrous Regiment: The Lady Knight in Sixteenth Century Epic* (1985). She co-authored *Feminist Scholarship: Kindling in the Groves of Academe* (1985).

Robinson is a valuable recorder of feminist movement in the field of literary studies. In co-authoring *Feminist Scholarship* with Ellen Dubois, Gail Kelly, Elizabeth Kennedy, and Carolyn Korsmeyer, Robinson took part in a collective process that embodies the spirit of feminist movement. No doubt the accommodation necessary to the shared goal of that project has influenced Robinson's scholarly point of view, resulting in a systematic and balanced account of feminist critics' contribution, challenge, and areas of concentration in "Treason Our Text." The treason of which she speaks constitutes movement to "humanize the canon," not to challenge its existence but to call into question the criteria that "themselves intrinsically exclude or tend to exclude women." That treason seeks not to eliminate any "greats" from the canon but to "make room" for "another literary reality, which, joined with the existing canon, will come closer to telling the (poetic) truth" of Western culture. As she presents an overview of the fundamental work of recovering the female tradition in the work of Patricia Meyer Spacks, Louise Bernikow, Ellen Moers, Elaine Showalter, Sandra Gilbert and Susan Gubar, and Judith Lowder Newton, it becomes clear that feminist treason arises not from opposition to a male canon but, as Mary Daly observes, from the fact that feminist critics have withdrawn the focus of their scholarly attention from that male center and applied themselves to what Robinson calls "an alternative complex" in women's literature. Treason, to this point, is male-defined. Robinson concludes, however, by calling for a return to "confrontation with 'the' canon, examining it as a source of ideas, themes, motifs, and myths about the two sexes," and, she has made clear, about ethnic voices. As feminist critics have appropriated the term, "Treason" has indeed become "Our Text."

Treason our Text
Feminist Challenges to the Literary Canon

> *Successful plots have often had gunpowder in them. Feminist critics have gone so far as to take treason to the canon as our text.*[1]
>
> Jane Marcus

THE LOFTY SEAT OF CANONIZED BARDS (POLLOK, 1872)

As with many other restrictive institutions, we are hardly aware of it until we come into conflict with it; the elements of the literary canon are simply absorbed by the apprentice scholar and critic in the normal course of graduate education, without anyone's ever seeming to inculcate or defend them. Appeal, were any necessary, would be to the other meaning of "canon," that is, to established standards of judgment and of taste. Not that either definition is presented as rigid and immutable—far from it, for lectures in literary history are full of wry references to a benighted though hardly distant past when, say, the metaphysical poets were insufficiently appreciated or Vachel Lindsay was the most modern poet recognized in American literature. Whence the acknowledgment of a subjective dimension, sometimes generalized as "sensibility," to the category of taste. Sweeping modifications in the canon are said to occur because of changes in collective sensibility, but individual admissions and elevations from "minor" to "major" status tend to be achieved by successful critical promotion, which is to say, demonstration that a particular author does meet generally accepted criteria of excellence.

The results, moreover, are nowhere codified: they are neither set down in a single place, nor are they absolutely uniform. In the visual arts and in music, the cold realities of patronage, purchase, presentation in private and public collections, or performance on concert programs create the conditions for a work's canonical status or lack of it. No equivalent set of institutional arrangements exists for literature, however. The fact of publication and even the feat of remaining in print for generations, which are at least analogous to the ways in which pictures and music are displayed, are not the same sort of indicators; they represent less of an investment and hence less general acceptance of their canonicity. In the circumstances, it may seem somewhat of an exaggeration to speak of "the" literary canon, almost paranoid to call it an institution, downright hysterical to characterize that institution as restrictive. The whole business is so much more informal, after all, than any of these terms implies, the concomitant processes so much more gentlemanly. Surely, it is more like a gentlemen's agreement than a repressive instrument—isn't it?

But a gentleman is inescapably—that is, by definition—a member of a privileged class and of the male sex. From this perspective, it is probably quite accurate to think of the canon as an entirely gentlemanly artifact, considering how few works by nonmembers of that class and sex make it into the informal agglomeration of course syllabi, anthologies, and widely commented-upon "standard authors" that constitutes the canon as it is generally understood. For, beyond their availability on bookshelves, it is through the teaching and study—one might even say the habitual teaching and study—of certain works that they become institutionalized as canonical literature. Within that broad canon, moreover, those admitted but read only in advanced courses, commented upon only by more or less narrow specialists, are subjected to the further tyranny of "major" versus "minor."

For more than a decade now, feminist scholars have been protesting the apparently systematic neglect of women's experience in the literary canon, neglect that takes the form of distorting and misreading the few recognized female writers and excluding the others. Moreover, the argument runs, the predominantly male authors in the canon show us the female character and relations between the sexes in a way that both reflects and contributes to sexist ideology—an aspect of these classic works about which the critical tradition remained silent for generations. The feminist challenge, although intrinsically (and, to my mind, refreshingly) polemical, has not been simply a reiterated attack, but a series of suggested alternatives to the male-dominated membership and attitudes of the accepted canon. In this essay, I propose to examine these feminist alternatives, assess their impact on the standard canon, and propose some directions for further work. Although my emphasis in each section is on the substance of the challenge, the underlying polemic is, I believe, abundantly clear.

THE PRESENCE OF CANONIZED FOREFATHERS (BURKE, 1790)

Start with the Great Books, the traditional desert-island ones, the foundation of courses in the Western humanistic tradition. No women authors, of course, at all, but within the works thus canonized, certain monumental female images: Helen, Penelope, and Clytemnestra, Beatrice and the Dark Lady of the Sonnets, Bérénice, Cunégonde, and Margarete. The list of interesting female characters is enlarged if we shift to the Survey of English Literature and its classic texts; here, moreover, there is the possible inclusion of a female author or even several, at least as the course's implicit "historical background" ticks through and past the Industrial Revolution. It is a possibility that is not always honored in the observance. "*Beowulf* to Virginia Woolf" is a pleasant enough joke, but though lots of surveys begin with the Anglo-Saxon epic, not all that many conclude with *Mrs. Dalloway*. Even in the nineteenth century, the pace and the necessity of mass omissions may mean leaving out Austen, one of the Brontës, or Eliot. The analogous overview of American literary masterpieces, despite the relative brevity and modernity of the period considered, is likely to yield a similarly all-male pantheon; Emily Dickinson may be admitted—but not necessarily—and no one else even comes close.[2] Here again, the male-authored canon contributes to the body of information, stereotype, inference, and surmise about the female sex that is generally in the culture.

Once this state of affairs has been exposed, there are two possible approaches for feminist criticism. It can emphasize alternative readings of the tradition, readings that reinterpret women's character, motivations, and actions and that identify and challenge sexist ideology. Or it can concentrate on gaining admission to the canon for literature by women writers. Both sorts of work are being pursued, although, to the extent that feminist criticism has defined itself as a subfield of literary studies—as distinguished from an approach or method—it has tended to concentrate on writing by women.

In fact, however, the current wave of feminist theory began as criticism of certain key texts, both literary and paraliterary, in the dominant culture. Kate

Millett, Eva Figes, Elizabeth Janeway, Germaine Greer, and Carolyn Heilbrun all use the techniques of essentially literary analysis on the social forms and forces surrounding those texts.[3] The texts themselves may be regarded as "canonical" in the sense that all have had significant impact on the culture as a whole, although the target being addressed is not literature or its canon.

In criticism that is more strictly literary in its scope, much attention has been concentrated on male writers in the American tradition. Books like Annette Kolodny's *The Lay of the Land* and Judith Fetterley's *The Resisting Reader* have no systematic, comprehensive equivalent in the criticism of British or European literature.[4] Both of these studies identify masculine values and imagery in a wide range of writings, as well as the alienation that is their consequence for women, men, and society as a whole. In a similar vein, Mary Ellmann's *Thinking About Women* examines ramifications of the tradition of "phallic criticism" as applied to writers of both sexes.[5] These books have in common with one another and with overarching theoretical manifestos like *Sexual Politics* a sense of having been betrayed by a culture that was supposed to be elevating, liberating, and one's own.

By contrast, feminist work devoted to that part of the Western tradition which is neither American nor contemporary is likelier to be more evenhanded. "Feminist critics," declare Lenz, Greene, and Neely in introducing their collection of essays on Shakespeare, "recognize that the greatest artists do not necessarily duplicate in their art the orthodoxies of their culture; they may exploit them to create character or intensify conflict, they may struggle with, criticize, or transcend them."[6] From this perspective, Milton may come in for some censure, Shakespeare and Chaucer for both praise and blame, but the clear intention of a feminist approach to these classic authors is to enrich our understanding of what is going on in the texts, as well as how—for better, for worse, or for both—they have shaped our own literary and social ideas.[7] At its angriest, none of this reinterpretation offers a fundamental challenge to the canon *as canon*; although it posits new values, it never suggests that, in the light of those values, we ought to reconsider whether the great monuments are really so great, after all.

SUCH IS ALL THE WORLDE HATHE CONFIRMED AND AGREED UPON, THAT IT IS AUTHENTIQUE AND CANONICAL (T. WILSON, 1553).

In an evolutionary model of feminist studies in literature, work on male authors is often characterized as "early," implicitly primitive, whereas scholarship on female authors is the later development, enabling us to see women—the writers themselves and the women they write about—as active agents rather than passive images or victims. This implicit characterization of studies addressed to male writers is as inaccurate as the notion of an inexorable evolution. In fact, as the very definition of feminist criticism has come increasingly to mean scholarship and criticism devoted to women writers, work on the male tradition has continued. By this point, there has been a study of the female characters or the views on the woman question of every major—perhaps every known—author in Anglo-American, French, Russian, Spanish, Italian, German, and Scandinavian literature.[8]

Nonetheless, it is an undeniable fact that most feminist criticism focuses on women writers, so that the feminist efforts to humanize the canon have usually meant bringing a woman's point of view to bear by incorporating works by women into the established canon. The least threatening way to do so is to follow the accustomed pattern of making the case for individual writers one by one. The case here consists in showing that an already recognized woman author has been denied her rightful place, presumably because of the general devaluation of female efforts and subjects. More often than not, such work involves showing that a woman already securely established in the canon belongs in the first rather than the second rank. The biographical and critical efforts of R. W. B. Lewis and Cynthia Griffin Wolff, for example, have attempted to enhance Edith Wharton's reputation in this way.[9] Obviously, no challenge is presented to the particular notions of literary quality, timelessness, universality, and other qualities that constitute the rationale for canonicity. The underlying argument, rather, is that consistency, fidelity to those values, requires recognition of at least the few best and best-known women writers. Equally obviously, this approach does not call the notion of the canon itself into question.

WE ACKNOWLEDGE IT CANONLIKE, BUT NOT CANONICALL (BISHOP BARLOW, 1601).

Many feminist critics reject the method of case-by-case demonstration. The wholesale consignment of women's concerns and productions to a grim area bounded by triviality and obscurity cannot be compensated for by tokenism. True equity can be attained, they argue, only by opening up the canon to a much larger number of female voices. This is an endeavor that eventually brings basic aesthetic questions to the fore.

Initially, however, the demand for wider representation of female authors is substantiated by an extraordinary effort of intellectual reappropriation. The emergence of feminist literary study has been characterized, at the base, by scholarship devoted to the discovery, republication, and reappraisal of "lost" or undervalued writers and their work. From Rebecca Harding Davis and Kate Chopin through Zora Neale Hurston and Mina Loy to Meridel LeSueur and Rebecca West, reputations have been reborn or remade and a female counter-canon has come into being, out of components that were largely unavailable even a dozen years ago.[10]

In addition to constituting a feminist alternative to the male-dominated tradition, these authors also have a claim to representation in "the" canon. From this perspective, the work of recovery itself makes one sort of *prima facie* case, giving the lie to the assumption, where it has existed, that aside from a few names that are household words—differentially appreciated, but certainly well known—there simply has not been much serious literature by women. Before any aesthetic arguments have been advanced either for or against the admission of such works to the general canon, the new literary scholarship on women has demonstrated that the pool of potential applicants is far larger than anyone has hitherto suspected.

WOULD AUGUSTINE, IF HE HELD ALL THE BOOKS TO HAVE AN EQUAL RIGHT TO CANONICITY . . . HAVE PREFERRED SOME TO OTHERS? (W. FITZGERALD, TRANS. WHITAKER, 1849)

But the aesthetic issues cannot be forestalled for very long. We need to understand whether the claim is being made that many of the newly recovered or validated texts by women meet existing criteria or, on the other hand, that those criteria themselves intrinsically exclude or tend to exclude women and hence should be modified or replaced. If this polarity is not, in fact, applicable to the process, what are the grounds for presenting a large number of new female candidates for (as it were) canonization?

The problem is epitomized in Nina Baym's introduction to her study of American women's fiction between 1820 and 1870:

> Reexamination of this fiction may well show it to lack the esthetic, intellectual and moral complexity and artistry that we demand of great literature. I confess frankly that, although I have found much to interest me in these books, I have not unearthed a forgotten Jane Austen or George Eliot or hit upon the one novel that I would propose to set alongside *The Scarlet Letter*. Yet I cannot avoid the belief that "purely" literary criteria, as they have been employed to identify the best American works, have inevitably had a bias in favor of things male—in favor of, say, a whaling ship, rather than a sewing circle as a symbol of the human community. . . . While not claiming any literary greatness for any of the novels . . . in this study, I would like at least to begin to correct such a bias by taking their content seriously. And it is time, perhaps—though this task lies outside my scope here—to reexamine the grounds upon which certain hallowed American classics have been called great.[11]

Now, if students of literature may be allowed to confess to one Great Unreadable among the Great Books, my own *bête noire* has always been the white whale; I have always felt I was missing something in *Moby Dick* that is clearly there for many readers and that is there for me when I read, say, Aeschylus or Austen. So I find Baym's strictures congenial, at first reading. Yet the contradictory nature of the position is also evident on the face of it. Am I or am I not being invited to construct a (feminist) aesthetic rationale for my impatience with *Moby Dick*? Do Baym and the current of thought she represents accept "esthetic, intellectual and moral complexity and artistry" as the grounds of greatness, or are they challenging those values as well?

As Myra Jehlen points out most lucidly, this attractive position will not bear close analysis: "[Baym] is having it both ways, admitting the artistic limitations of the women's fiction . . . and at the same time denying the validity of the rulers that measure these limitations, disdaining any ambition to reorder the literary canon and, on second thought, challenging the canon after all, or rather challenging not the canon itself but the grounds for its selection."[12] Jehlen understates the case, however, in calling the duality a paradox, which is, after all, an intentionally created and essentially rhetorical phenomenon. What is involved here is more like the *agony* of feminist criticism, for it is the champions of women's literature who are torn between defending the quality of their discoveries and radically redefining literary quality itself.

Those who are concerned with the canon as a pragmatic instrument rather than a powerful abstraction—the compilers of more equitable anthologies or course syllabi, for example—have opted for an uneasy compromise. The literature by women that they seek—as well as that by members of excluded racial and ethnic groups and by working people in general—conforms as closely as possible to the traditional canons of taste and judgment. Not that it reads like such literature as far as content and viewpoint are concerned, but the same words about artistic intent and achievement may be applied without absurdity. At the same time, the rationale for a new syllabus or anthology relies on a very different criterion: that of truth to the culture being represented, the *whole* culture and not the creation of an almost entirely male white elite. Again, no one seems to be proposing—aloud—the elimination of *Moby Dick* or *The Scarlet Letter*, just squeezing them over somewhat to make room for another literary reality, which, joined with the existing canon, will come closer to telling the (poetic) truth.

The effect is pluralist, at best, and the epistemological assumptions underlying the search for a more fully representative literature are strictly empiricist: by including the perspective of women (who are, after all, half-the-population), we will know more about the culture as it actually was. No one suggests that there might be something in this literature itself that challenges the values and even the validity of the previously all-male tradition. There is no reason why the canon need speak with one voice or as one man on the fundamental questions of human experience. Indeed, even as an elite white male voice, it can hardly be said to do so. Yet a commentator like Baym has only to say "it is time, perhaps . . . to reexamine the grounds," *while not proceeding to do so*, for feminists to be accused of wishing to throw out the entire received culture. The argument could be more usefully joined, perhaps, if there *were* a current within feminist criticism that went beyond insistence on representation to consideration of precisely how inclusion of women's writing alters our view of the tradition. Or even one that suggested some radical surgery on the list of male authors usually represented.

After all, when we turn from the construction of pantheons, which have no *prescribed* number of places, to the construction of course syllabi, then something does have to be eliminated each time something else is added, and here ideologies, aesthetic and extra-aesthetic, do necessarily come into play. Is the canon and hence the syllabus based on it to be regarded as the compendium of excellence or as the record of cultural history? For there comes a point when the proponent of making the canon recognize the achievement of both sexes has to put up or shut up; either a given woman writer is good enough to replace some male writer on the prescribed reading list or she is not. If she is not, then either she should replace him anyway, in the name of telling the truth about the culture, or she should not, in the (unexamined) name of excellence. This is the debate that will have to be engaged and that has so far been broached only in the most "exclusionary" of terms. It is ironic that in American literature, where attacks on the male tradition have been most bitter and the reclamation of women writers so spectacular, the appeal has still been only to pluralism, generosity, and guilt. It is populism without the politics of populism.

TO CANONIZE YOUR OWNE WRITERS (POLIMANTERIA, 1595).

Although I referred earlier to a feminist counter-canon, it is only in certain rather restricted contexts that literature by women has in fact been explicitly placed "counter" to the dominant canon. Generally speaking, feminist scholars have been more concerned with establishing the existence, power, and significance of a specifically female tradition. Such a possibility is adumbrated in the title of Patricia Meyer Spacks's *The Female Imagination*; however, this book's overview of selected themes and stages in the female life-cycle as treated by some women writers neither broaches nor (obviously) suggests an answer to the question of whether there is a female imagination and what characterizes it.[13]

Somewhat earlier, in her anthology of British and American women poets, Louise Bernikow had made a more positive assertion of a continuity and connection subsisting among them.[14] She leaves it to the poems, however, to forge their own links, and, in a collection that boldly and incisively crosses boundaries between published and unpublished writing, literary and anonymous authorship, "high" art, folk art, and music, it is not easy for the reader to identify what the editor believes it is that makes women's poetry specifically *"women's."*

Ellen Moers centers her argument for a (transhistorical) female tradition upon the concept of "heroinism," a quality shared by women writers over time with the female characters they created.[15] Moers also points out another kind of continuity, documenting the way that women writers have read, commented on, and been influenced by the writings of other women who were their predecessors or contemporaries. There is also an unacknowledged continuity between the writer and her female reader. Elaine Showalter conceives the female tradition, embodied particularly in the domestic and sensational fiction of the nineteenth century, as being carried out through a kind of subversive conspiracy between author and audience.[16] Showalter is at her best in discussing this minor "women's fiction." Indeed, without ever making a case for popular genres as serious literature, she bases her arguments about a tradition more solidly on them than on acknowledged major figures like Virginia Woolf. By contrast, Sandra Gilbert and Susan Gubar focus almost exclusively on key literary figures, bringing women writers and their subjects together through the theme of perceived female aberration—in the act of literary creation itself, as well as in the behavior of the created persons or personae.[17]

Moers's vision of a continuity based on "heroism" finds an echo in later feminist criticism that posits a discrete, perhaps even autonomous "women's culture." The idea of such a culture has been developed by social historians studying the "homosocial" world of nineteenth-century women.[18] It is a view that underlies, for example, Nina Auerbach's study of relationships among women in selected novels, where strong, supportive ties among mothers, daughters, sisters, and female friends not only constitute the real history in which certain women are conceived as living but function as a normative element as well.[19] That is, fiction in which positive relations subsist to nourish the heroine comes off much better, from Auerbach's point of view, than fiction in which such relations do not exist.

In contrast, Judith Lowder Newton sees the heroines of women's fiction as active, rather than passive, precisely because they do live in a man's world, not an autonomous female one.[20] Defining their power as "ability" rather than "control," she perceives "both a preoccupation with power and subtle power strategies" being exercised by the women in novels by Fanny Burney, Jane Austen, Charlotte Brontë, and George Eliot. Understood in this way, the female tradition, whether or not it in fact reflects and fosters a "culture" of its own, provides an alternative complex of possibilities for women, to be set beside the pits and pedestals offered by all too much of the Great Tradition.

CANONIZE SUCH A MULTIFARIOUS GENEALOGIE OF COMMENTS (NASHE, 1593).

Historians like Smith-Rosenberg and Cott are careful to specify that their generalizations extend only to white middle- and upper-class women of the nineteenth century. Although literary scholars are equally scrupulous about the national and temporal boundaries of their subject, they tend to use the gender term comprehensively. In this way, conclusions about "women's fiction" or "female consciousness" have been drawn or jumped to from considering a body of work whose authors are all white and comparatively privileged. Of the critical studies I have mentioned, only Bernikow's anthology, *The World Split Open,* brings labor songs, black women's blues lyrics, and anonymous ballads into conjunction with poems that were written for publication by professional writers, both black and white. The other books, which build an extensive case for a female tradition that Bernikow only suggests, delineate their subject in such a way as to exclude not only black and working-class authors but any notion that race and class might be relevant categories in the definition and apprehension of "women's literature." Similarly, even for discussions of writers who were known to be lesbians, this aspect of the female tradition often remains unacknowledged; worse yet, some of the books that develop the idea of a female tradition are openly homophobic, employing the word "lesbian" only pejoratively.[21]

Black and lesbian scholars, however, have directed much less energy to polemics against the feminist "mainstream" than to concrete, positive work on the literature itself. Recovery and reinterpretation of a wealth of unknown or undervalued texts has suggested the existence of both a black women's tradition and a lesbian tradition. In a clear parallel with the relationship between women's literature in general and the male-dominated tradition, both are by definition part of women's literature, but they are also distinct from and independent of it.

There are important differences, however, between these two traditions and the critical effort surrounding them. Black feminist criticism has the task of demonstrating that, in the face of all the obstacles a racist and sexist society has been able to erect, there is a continuity of black women who have written and written well. It is a matter of gaining recognition for the quality of the writing itself and respect for its principal subject, the lives and consciousness of black women. Black women's literature is also an element of black literature as a whole, where the recognized voices have usually been male. A triple imperative is therefore at work: establishing a discrete and significant black female tradition, then situating it within black literature and (along with the rest of that literature) within the common American literary heritage.[22] So far, unfortunately, each step toward integration has met with continuing exclusion. A black women's tradition has been recovered and revaluated chiefly through the efforts of black feminist scholars. Only some of that work has been accepted as part of either a racially mixed women's literature or a two-sex black literature. As for the gatekeepers of American literature in general, how many of them are willing to swing open the portals even for Zora Neale Hurston or Paule Marshall? How many have heard of them?

The issue of "inclusion," moreover, brings up questions that echo those raised by opening the male-dominated canon to women. How do generalizations about women's literature "as a whole" change when the work of black women is not merely added to but fully incorporated into that tradition? How does our sense of black literary history change? And what implications do these changes have for reconsideration of the American canon?

Whereas many white literary scholars continue to behave as if there were no major black woman writers, most are prepared to admit that certain well-known white writers were lesbians for all or part of their lives. The problem is getting beyond a position that says either "so *that's* what was wrong with her!" or, alternatively, "it doesn't matter who she slept with—we're talking about literature." Much lesbian feminist criticism has addressed theoretical questions about *which* literature is actually part of the lesbian tradition, all writing by lesbians, for example, or all writing by women about women's relations with one another. Questions of class and race enter here as well, both in their own guise and in the by now familiar form of "aesthetic standards." Who speaks for the lesbian community: the highly educated experimentalist with an unearned income or the naturalist working-class autobiographer? Or are both the *same kind* of foremother, reflecting the community's range of cultural identities and resistance?[23]

A CHEAPER WAY OF CANON-MAKING IN A CORNER (BAXTER, 1639).

It is not only members of included social groups, however, who have challenged the fundamentally elite nature of the existing canon. "Elite" is a literary as well as a social category. It is possible to argue for taking all texts seriously as texts without arguments based on social oppression or cultural exclusion, and popular genres have therefore been studied as part of the female literary tradition. Feminists are not in agreement as to whether domestic and sentimental fiction, the female Gothic, the women's sensational novel functioned as instruments of expression, repression, or subversion, but they have successfully revived interest in the question as a legitimate cultural issue.[24] It is no longer automatically assumed that literature addressed to the mass female audience is necessarily bad because it is sentimental, or for that matter, sentimental because it is addressed to that audience. Feminist criticism has examined without embarrassment an entire literature that was previously dismissed solely because it was popular with women and affirmed standards and values associated with femininity. And proponents of the "continuous tradition" and "women's culture" positions have insisted that this material be placed beside women's "high" art as part of the articulated and organic female tradition.

This point of view remains controversial within the orbit of women's studies, but the real problems start when it comes into contact with the universe of canon formation. Permission may have been given the contemporary critic to approach a wide range of texts, transcending and even ignoring the traditional canon. But in a context where the ground of struggle—highly contested, moreover—concerns Edith Wharton's advancement to somewhat more major status, fundamental assumptions have changed very little. Can Hawthorne's "d___d mob of scribbling women" *really* be invading the realms so long sanctified by Hawthorne himself and his brother geniuses? Is this what feminist criticism or even feminist cultural history means? Is it—to apply some outmoded and deceptively simple categories—a good development or a bad one? If these questions have not been raised, it is because women's literature and the female tradition tend to be evoked as an autonomous cultural experience, not impinging on the rest of literary history.

WISDOME UNDER A RAGGED COATE IS SELDOME CANONICALL (CROSSE, 1603).

Whether dealing with popular genres or high art, commentary on the female tradition usually has been based on work that was published at some time and was produced by professional writers. But feminist scholarship has also pushed back the boundaries of literature in other directions, considering a wide range of forms and styles in which women's writing—especially that of women who did not perceive themselves as writers—appears. In this way, women's letters, diaries, journals, autobiographies, oral histories, and private poetry have come under critical scrutiny as evidence of women's consciousness *and expression*.

Generally speaking, feminist criticism

has been quite open to such material, recognizing that the very conditions that gave many women the impetus to write made it impossible for their culture to define them as writers. This acceptance has expanded our sense of possible forms and voices, but it has not challenged our received sense of appropriate style. What it amounts to is that if a woman writing in isolation and with no public audience in view nonetheless had "good"—that is, canonical—models, we are impressed with the strength of her text when she applies what she has assimilated about writing to her own experiences as a woman. If, however, her literary models were chosen from the same popular literature that some critics are now beginning to recognize as part of the female tradition, then she has not got hold of an expressive instrument that empowers her.

At the Modern Language Association meeting in 1976, I included in my paper the entire two-page autobiography of a participant in the Summer Schools for Women Workers held at Bryn Mawr in the first decades of the century. It is a circumstantial narrative in which events from the melancholy to the melodramatic are accumulated in a serviceable, somewhat hackneyed style. The anonymous "Seamer on Men's Underwear" had a unique sense of herself both as an individual and as a member of the working class. But was she a writer? Part of the audience was as moved as I was by the narrative, but the majority was outraged at the piece's failure to meet the criteria—particularly, the "complexity" criteria—of good art.

When I developed my remarks for publication, I wrote about the problems of dealing with an author who is trying too hard to write elegantly, and attempted to make the case that clichés or sentimentality need not be signals of meretricious prose and that ultimately it is honest writing for which criticism should be looking.[25] Nowadays, I would also address the question of the female tradition, the role of popular fiction within it, and the influence of that fiction on its audience. It seems to me that, if we accept the work of the professional "scribbling woman," we have also to accept its literary consequences, not drawing the line at the place where that literature may have been the force that enabled an otherwise inarticulate segment of the population to grasp a means of expression and communication.

Once again, the arena is the female tradition itself. If we are thinking in terms of canon formation, it is the alternative canon. Until the aesthetic arguments can be fully worked out in the feminist context, it will be impossible to argue, in the general marketplace of literary ideas, that the novels of Henry James ought to give place—a *little* place, even—to the diaries of his sister Alice. At this point, I suspect most of our male colleagues would consider such a request, even in the name of Alice James, much less the Seamer on Men's Underwear, little more than a form of "reverse discrimination"—a concept to which some of them are already overly attached. It is up to feminist scholars, when we determine that this is indeed the right course to pursue, to demonstrate that such an inclusion would constitute a genuinely affirmative action for all of us.

The development of feminist literary criticism and scholarship has already proceeded through a number of identifiable stages. Its pace is more reminiscent of the survey course than of the slow processes of canon formation and revision, and it has been more successful in defining and sticking to its own intellectual turf, the female counter-canon, than in gaining general canonical recognition for Edith Wharton, Fanny Fern, or the female diarists of the Westward Expansion. In one sense, the more coherent our sense of the female tradition is, the stronger will be our eventual case. Yet the longer we wait, the more comfortable the women's literature ghetto—separate, apparently autonomous, and far from equal—may begin to feel.

At the same time, I believe the challenge cannot come only by means of the patent value of the work of women. We must pursue the questions certain of us have raised and retreated from as to the eternal verity of the received standards of greatness or even goodness. And, while not abandoning our newfound female tradition, we have to return to confrontation with "the" canon, examining it as a source of ideas, themes, motifs, and myths about the two sexes. The point in so doing is not to label and hence dismiss even the most sexist literary classics, but to enable all of us to apprehend them, finally, in all their human dimensions.

NOTES

1. Jane Marcus, "Gunpowder Treason and Plot," talk delivered at the School of Criticism and Theory, Northwestern University, colloquium "The Challenge of Feminist Criticism," November 1981. Seeking authority for the sort of creature a literary canon might be, I turned, like many another, to the *Oxford English Dictionary*. The tags that head up the several sections of this essay are a by-product of that effort rather than of any more exact and laborious scholarship.

2. In a survey of 50 introductory courses in American literature offered at 25 U.S. colleges and universities, Emily Dickinson's name appeared more often than that of any other woman writer: 20 times. This frequency puts her in a fairly respectable twelfth place. Among the 61 most frequently taught authors, only 7 others are women; Edith Wharton and Kate Chopin are each mentioned 8 times, Sarah Orne Jewett and Anne Bradstreet 6 each, Flannery O'Connor 4 times, Willa Cather and Mary Wilkins Freeman each 3 times. The same list includes 5 black authors, all of them male. Responses from other institutions received too late for compilation only confirmed these findings. See Paul Lauter, "A Small Survey of Introductory Courses in American Literature," *Women's Studies Quarterly*, 9 (Winter 1981), 12. In another study, 99 professors of English responded to a survey asking which works of American literature published since 1941 they thought should be considered classics and which books should be taught to college students. The work mentioned by the most respondents (59 citations) was Ralph Ellison's *Invisible Man*. No other work by a black appears among the top 20 that constitute the published list of results. Number 19, *The Complete Stories of Flannery O'Connor*, is the only work on this list by a woman. (*Chronicle of Higher Education*, September 29, 1982.) For British literature, the feminist claim is not that Austen, the Brontës, Eliot, and Woolf are habitually omitted, but rather that they are by no means always included in courses that, like the survey I taught at Columbia some years ago, had room for a single nineteenth-century novel. I know, however, of no systematic study of course offerings in this area more recent than Elaine Showalter's "Women in the Literary Curriculum," *College English*, 32 (May 32 1971), 855–62.

3. Kate Millett, *Sexual Politics* (Garden City, N.Y.: Doubleday, 1970); Eva Figes, *Patriarchal Attitudes* (New York: Stein & Day, 1970); Elizabeth Janeway, *Man's World, Woman's Place: A Study in Social Mythology* (New York: William Morrow, 1971); Germaine Greer, *The Female Eunuch* (New York: McGraw-Hill, 1971); Carolyn G. Heilbrun, *Toward a Recognition of Androgyny* (New York: Harper & Row, 1974). The phenomenon these studies represent is discussed at greater length in a study of which I am a co-author; see Ellen Carol DuBois, Gail Paradise Kelly, Elizabeth Lapovsky Kennedy, Carolyn W. Korsmeyer, and Lillian S. Robinson, *Feminist Scholarship: Kindling in the Groves of Academe* (Urbana: University of Illinois Press, 1985).

4. Annette Kolodny, *The Lay of the Land: Metaphor as Experience and History in American Life and Letters* (Chapel Hill: University of North Carolina Press, 1975); Judith Fetterley, *The Resisting Reader: A Feminist Approach to American Fiction* (Bloomington: Indiana University Press, 1978).

5. Mary Ellmann, *Thinking About Women* (New York: Harcourt, Brace & World, 1968).

6. Carolyn Ruth Swift Lenz, Gayle Greene, and Carol Thomas Neely, eds. *The Woman's Part: Feminist Criticism of Shakespeare* (Urbana: University of Illinois Press, 1980), p. 4. In this vein, see also Juliet Dusinberre, *Shakespeare and the Nature of Woman* (London: Macmillan, 1975); Irene G. Dash, *Wooing, Wedding, and Power: Women in Shakespeare's Plays* (New York: Columbia University Press, 1981).

7. Sandra M. Gilbert, "Patriarchal Poetics and the Woman Reader: Reflections on Milton's Bogey," *PMLA*, 93 (May 1978), 368–82. The articles on

Chaucer and Shakespeare in *The Authority of Experience: Essays in Feminist Criticism*, ed. Arlyn Diamond and Lee R. Edwards (Amherst: University of Massachusetts Press, 1977), reflect the complementary tendency.

8. As I learned when surveying fifteen years' worth of *Dissertation Abstracts* and MLA programs, much of this work has taken the form of theses or conference papers rather than books and journal articles.

9. See R. W. B. Lewis, *Edith Wharton: A Biography* (New York: Harper & Row, 1975); Cynthia Griffin Wolff, *A Feast of Words: The Triumph of Edith Wharton* (New York: Oxford University Press, 1977); see also Marlene Springer, *Edith Wharton and Kate Chopin: A Reference Guide* (Boston: G. K. Hall, 1976).

10. See, for instance, Rebecca Harding Davis, *Life in the Iron Mills* (Old Westbury, N.Y.: Feminist Press, 1972), with a biographical and critical Afterword by Tillie Olsen; Kate Chopin, *The Complete Works*, ed. Per Seyersted (Baton Rouge: Louisiana State University Press, 1969); Alice Walker, "In Search of Zora Neale Hurston," *Ms.*, March 1975, pp. 74–75; Robert Hemenway, *Zora Neale Hurston* (Urbana: University of Illinois Press, 1978): Zora Neale Hurston, *I Love Myself When I Am Laughing and Also When I Am Looking Mean and Impressive* (Old Westbury: Feminist Press, 1979), with introductory material by Alice Walker and Mary Helen Washington; Carolyn G. Burke, "Becoming Mina Loy," *Women's Studies*, 7 (1979), 136–50; Meridel LeSueur, *Ripening* (Old Westbury: Feminist Press, 1981); on LeSueur, see also Mary McAnally, ed., *We Sing Our Struggle: A Tribute to Us All* (Tulsa, Okla.: Cardinal Press, 1982); *The Young Rebecca: Writings of Rebecca West, 1911–1917*, selected and introduced by Jane Marcus (New York: Viking Press, 1982).

The examples cited are all from the nineteenth and twentieth centuries. Valuable work has also been done on women writers before the Industrial Revolution. See Joan Goulianos, ed., *By a Woman Writt: Literature from Six Centuries by and About Women* (Indianapolis: Bobbs-Merrill, 1973); Mary R. Mahl and Helene Koon, eds., *The Female Spectator: English Women Writers before 1800* (Bloomington: Indiana University Press, 1977).

11. Nina Baym, *Women's Fiction: A Guide to Novels By and About Women in America, 1820–70* (Ithaca: Cornell University Press, 1978), 14–15.

12. Myra Jehlen, "Archimedes and the Paradox of Feminist Criticism," *Signs*, 6 (Summer 1981), 592.

13. Patricia Meyer Spacks, *The Female Imagination* (New York: Alfred A. Knopf, 1975).

14. *The World Split Open: Four Centuries of Women Poets In England and America, 1552–1950*, ed. and intro. Louise Bernikow (New York: Vintage Books, 1974).

15. Ellen Moers, *Literary Women: The Great Writers* (Garden City, N.Y.; Doubleday, 1976).

16. Elaine Showalter, *A Literature of Their Own: British Women Novelists from Brontë to Lessing* (Princeton, N.J.: Princeton University Press, 1977).

17. Sandra M. Gilbert and Susan Gubar, *The Madwoman in the Attic: The Woman Writer and the Nineteenth-Century Literary Imagination* (New Haven: Yale University Press, 1979).

18. Carroll-Smith Rosenberg, "The Female World of Love and Ritual: Relations Between Women in Nineteenth-Century America," *Signs*, 1 (Fall 1975), 1–30; Nancy F. Cott, *The Bonds of Womanhood: "Woman's Sphere" in New England, 1780–1830* (New Haven: Yale University Press, 1977).

19. Nina Auerbach, *Communities of Women: An Idea in Fiction* (Cambridge: Harvard University Press, 1979). see also Janet M. Todd, *Women's Friendship in Literature* (New York: Columbia University Press, 1980); Louise Bernikow, *Among Women* (New York: Crown, 1980).

20. Judith Lowder Newton, *Women, Power, and Subversion: Social Strategies in British Fiction* (Athens: University of Georgia Press, 1981).

21. On the failings of feminist criticism with respect to black and lesbian writers, see Barbara Smith, "Toward a Black Feminist Criticism," in *The New Feminist Criticism*, ed. Elaine Showalter (New York: Pantheon Books, 1985), pp. 168–85; Mary Helen Washington, "New Lives and New Letters: Black Women Writers at the End of the Seventies," *College English*, 43 (January 1981), 1–11; Bonnie Zimmerman, "What Has Never Been: An Overview of Lesbian Feminist Literary Criticism," in *The New Feminist Criticism*, pp. 200–24.

22. See, e.g., Smith, "Toward a Black Feminist Criticism"; Barbara Christian, *Black Women Novelists: The Development of a Tradition, 1892–1976* (Westport, Conn.: Greenwood Press, 1980); Erlene Stetson, ed., *Black Sister: Poetry by Black American Women, 1764–1980* (Bloomington: Indiana University Press, 1981) and its forthcoming sequel; Gloria Hull, "Black Women Poets from Wheatley to Walker," in *Sturdy Black Bridges: Visions of Black Women in Literature*, ed. Roseann P. Bell et al. (Garden City, N.Y.: Anchor Books, 1979); Mary Helen Washington, "Introduction: In Pursuit of Our Own History," *Midnight Birds: Stories of Contemporary Black Women Writers* (Garden City, N.Y.: Anchor Books, 1980); the essays and bibliographies in *But Some of Us Are Brave: Black Women's*

Studies, ed. Gloria Hull, Patricia Bell Scott, and Barbara Smith (Old Westbury: Feminist Press, 1982).

23. See Zimmerman, "What Has Never Been"; Adrienne Rich, "Jane Eyre: Trials of a Motherless Girl," *Lies, Secrets, and Silence: Selected Prose, 1966–1978* (New York: W. W. Norton, 1979); Lillian Faderman, *Surpassing the Love of Men: Romantic Friendship and Love Between Women from the Renaissance to the Present* (New York: William Morrow, 1981); the literary essays in *Lesbian Studies*, ed. Margaret Cruikshank (Old Westbury: Feminist Press, 1982).

24. Some examples on different sides of the question are: Ann Douglas, *The Feminization of American Culture* (New York: Alfred A. Knopf, 1976); Elaine Showalter, *A Literature of Their Own* and her article "Dinah Mulock Craik and the Tactics of Sentiment: A Case Study in Victorian Female Authorship," *Feminist Studies*, 2 (May 1975): 5–23; Katherine Ellis, "Paradise Lost: The Limits of Domesticity in the Nineteenth-Century Novel," *Feminist Studies*, 2 (May 1975): 55–65.

25. Lillian S. Robinson, "Working/Women/Writing," *Sex, Class, and Culture* (Bloomington: Indiana University Press, 1978), 252.

36

Henry Louis Gates, Jr. 1950–

Henry Louis Gates, Jr., is professor of English at Cornell University and a leading scholar and literary critic in the field of contemporary black literature and literary theory. Educated at Yale and later at Cambridge, Gates has received numerous awards, including the prestigious MacArthur Prize Fellowship (1981–86) and the Afro-American teaching prize (1983). He is editor of *The Classic Slave Narratives* (1983) and *Black Literature and Literary Theory* (1984) and author of *Figures in Black* (1987) and *The Signifying Monkey: A Theory of Afro-American Literary Criticism* (1988).

"The Blackness of Blackness: A Critique of the Sign and the Signifying Monkey" traces the emergence of the vernacular black usage of "signifyin' " as an expression of cultural identification, which, as it happens, is homonymous with the Structuralist and Poststructuralist term "signifying." With this connection, Gates traces the history and evolution of "signifyin' " from a pan-African mythical heritage involving the antics of the "signifying monkey" as a paradigm for analyzing different modes of discourse within contemporary black art, music, and literature. Moreover, following this figurative lead, he offers a short history of twentieth-century literature, tracing the movement from realism (Richard Wright), to modernism (Ralph Ellison), to postmodernism (Ishmael Reed). Here, then, Gates is pursuing a wide number of threads: he is offering a literary history, a semiotic ("signifying") analysis, a cultural history, and an attempt to situate black literature and culture within the context of a larger American "culture." Finally, we suspect, basing all this on a homonym, he might very well be "signifyin' " on all these enterprises.

The "Blackness of Blackness": A Critique of the Sign and Signifying Monkey

"Signification is the nigger's
occupation."

—Traditional[1]

"Be careful what you do,
Or Mumbo-Jumbo, God of the Congo,
And all of the other
Gods of the Congo,
Mumbo-Jumbo will hoo-doo you,
Mumbo-Jumbo will hoo-doo you,
Mumbo-Jumbo will hoo-doo you."

—Vachel Lindsay, "The Congo"

I need not trace here the history of the concept of signification. Since Ferdinand de Saussure, at least, signification has become a crucial aspect of contemporary theory. It is curious to me that this neologism in the Western tradition is a homonym of a term in the black vernacular tradition that is approximately two centuries old. Tales of the Signifying Monkey had their origins in slavery; hundreds of these tales have been recorded since the nineteenth century. In black music, Jazz Gillum, Count Basie, Oscar Peterson, Oscar Brown, Jr., Little Willie Dixon, Nat King Cole, Otis Redding, Wilson Pickett, and Johnny Otis—among others—have recorded songs called either "The Signifying Monkey" or, simply, "signifyin(g)." My theory of interpretation, arrived at from within the black cultural matrix, is a theory of formal revision; it is tropological; it is often characterized by pastiche; and, most crucially, it turns on repetition of formal structures, and their difference. Signification is a theory of reading that arises from Afro-American culture; learning how "to signify" is often part of our adolescent education. I had to step outside my culture, had to defamiliarize the concept by translating it into a new mode of discourse, before I could see its potential in critical theory.[2]

1. SIGNIFYIN(G): DEFINITIONS

Perhaps only Tar Baby is as enigmatic and compelling a figure from Afro-American mythic discourse as is that oxymoron, the Signifying Monkey.[3] The ironic reversal of a received racist image of the black as simianlike, the Signifying Monkey—he who dwells at the margins of discourse, ever punning, ever troping, ever embodying the ambiguities of language—is our trope for repetition and revision, indeed, is our trope of chiasmus itself, repeating and simultaneously reversing in one deft, discursive act. If Vico and Burke, or Nietzsche, Paul de Man, and Harold Bloom, are correct in identifying "master tropes," then we might think of these as the "master's tropes," and of *signifying* as the slave's trope, the trope of tropes, as Bloom characterizes metalepsis, "a trope-reversing trope, a figure of a figure." Signifying is a trope that subsumes other rhetorical tropes, including metaphor, metonymy, synecdoche, and irony (the "master" tropes), and also hyperbole, litotes, and metalepsis (Bloom's supplement to Burke). To this list, we could easily add aporia, chiasmus, and catachresis, all of which are used in the ritual of signifying.

The black tradition has its own subdivisions of signifying, which we could readily identify with the typology of figures received from classical and medieval rhetoric, as Bloom has done with his "map of misprision." In black discourse "signifying" means modes of figuration itself. When one signifies, as Kimberly W. Benston puns, one "tropes-a-dope." The black rhetorical tropes subsumed under signifying would include "marking," "loud-talking," "specifying," "testifying," "calling out" (of one's name), "sounding," "rapping," and "playing the dozens."[4]

Let us consider received definitions of the act of signifying and of black mythology's archetypal signifier, the Signifying Monkey. The Signifying Monkey is a trickster figure, of the order of the trickster figure of Yoruba mythology, Ès̀ù-Ẹlẹgbára in Nigeria, and Legba among the Fon in Dahomey, whose New World figurations —Exú in Brazil, Echu-Elegua in Cuba, Papa Legba in the pantheon of the *loa* of *Vaudou* in Haiti, and Papa La Bas in the *loa* of Hoodoo in the United States—speak eloquently of the unbroken arc of metaphysical presuppositions and patterns of figuration shared through space and time among black cultures in West

Africa, South America, the Caribbean, and the United States. These trickster figures, aspects of Èṣù, are primarily *mediators:* as tricksters they are mediators and their mediations are tricks.[5]

The versions of Èṣù are all messengers of the gods: he interprets the will of the gods to man; he carries the desires of man to the gods. He is known as the divine linguist, the keeper of *àse* ("logos") with which Olódùmarè created the universe. Èṣù of guardian of the crossroads, master of style and the stylus, phallic god of generation and fecundity, master of the mystical barrier that separates the divine from the profane world. In Yoruba mythology, Èṣù always limps, because his legs are of different lengths: one is anchored in the realm of the gods, the other rests in the human world. The closest Western relative of Èṣù is Hermes, of course; and, just as Hermes' role as interpreter lent his name readily to "hermeneutics," the study of the process of interpretation, so too the figure of Èṣù can stand, for the critic of comparative black literature, as our metaphor for the act of interpretation itself. In African and Latin American mythologies, Èṣù is said to have taught Ifa how to read the signs formed by the sixteen sacred palm nuts which, when manipulated, configure into "the signature of an Odù," 256 of which comprise the corpus of *Ifá* divination. The Ọpọ́n Ifá, the carved wooden divination tray used in the art of interpretation, is said to contain at the center of its upper perimeter a carved image of Èṣù, meant to signify his relation to the act of interpretation, which we can translate either as *ìtúmọ̀* ("to untie or unknot knowledge") or as *yípadà* ("to turn around" or "to translate"). That which we call "close reading," the Yoruba call *Ọ̀dá fá* ("reading the signs"). Above all else, Èṣù is the Black Interpreter, the Yoruba god of indeterminacy, the sheer plurality of meaning, or *àriyẹ̀muyẹ̀* ("that which no sooner is held than slips through one's fingers"). As Hermes is to hermeneutics, Èṣù is to *Èṣù-'túfunààlò* ("bringing out the interstices of the riddle").[6]

The Èṣù figures, among the Yoruba systems of thought in Dahomey and Nigeria, in Brazil and in Cuba, in Haiti and in New Orleans are divine: they are gods who function in sacred myths as do characters in a narrative. Èṣù's functional equivalent in Afro-American profane discourse is the Signifying Monkey, a figure who seems to be distinctly Afro-American, probably derived from Cuban mythology which generally depicts Echu-Elegua and a monkey at his side.[7] Unlike his Pan-African Èṣù cousins, the Signifying Monkey exists in the discourse of mythology not primarily as a character in a narrative but rather as a vehicle for narration itself. It is from this corpus of mythological narratives that signifying derives. The Afro-American rhetorical strategy of signifying is a rhetorical practice unengaged in information giving. Signifying turns on the play and chain of signifiers, and not on some supposedly transcendent signified. Alan Dundes suggests that the origins of signifying could "lie in African rhetoric." As anthropologists demonstrate, the Signifying Monkey is often called "the signifier," he who wreaks havoc upon "the signified." One is "signified upon" by the signifier. The Signifying Monkey is indeed the "signifier as such," in Julia Kristeva's phrase, "a presence that precedes the signification of object or emotion."[8]

Scholars have for some time commented upon the peculiar use of the word "signifying" in black discourse. Though sharing some connotations with the standard English-language word, "signifying" has its own definitions in black discourse. Roger D. Abrahams defines it this way:

> Signifying seems to be a Negro term, in use if not in origin. It can mean any of a number of things; in the case of the toast about the

> signifying monkey, it certainly refers to the trickster's ability to talk with great innuendo, to carp, cajole, needle, and lie. It can mean in other instances the propensity to talk around a subject, never quite coming to the point. It can mean making fun of a person or situation. Also it can denote speaking with the hands and eyes, and in this respect encompasses a whole complex of expressions and gestures. Thus it is signifying to stir up a fight between neighbors by telling stores; it is signifying to make fun of a policeman by parodying his motions behind his back; it is signifying to ask for a piece of cake by saying, "My brother needs a piece of cake."[9]

Essentially, Abrahams concludes, signifying is a "*technique* of indirect argument or persuasion," "a language of implication," "to imply, goad, beg, boast, by *indirect* verbal or gestural means." "The name 'signifying,'" he concludes, "shows the monkey to be a trickster, signifying being the language of trickery, that set of words or gestures achieving Hamlet's 'direction through indirection.'" The Monkey, in short, is not only "a master of technique," as Abrahams concludes, he *is* technique, or style, or the *literariness* of literary language; he is the great Signifier. In this sense, one does not signify something; rather, one signifies in *some way*.[10]

There are thousands of "toasts" of the Signifying Monkey, most of which commence with a variant of the following formulaic lines:

> Deep down in the jungle so they say
> There's a signifying monkey down the
> way,
> There hadn't been no disturbin' in
> the jungle for quite a bit,
> For up jumped the monkey in the
> tree one day and laughed,
> "I guess I'll start some shit."[11]

Endings, too, tend toward the formulaic, as in:

> Monkey, said the Lion,
> Beat to his unbooted knees,
> You and all your signifying children
> Better stay up in them trees.
> Which is why today
> Monkey does his signifying
> *A-way-up* out of the way.[12]

In the narrative poems, the Signifying Monkey invariably "repeats" to his friend, the Lion, some insult purportedly generated by their mutual friend, the Elephant. The Lion, indignant and outraged, demands an apology from the Elephant, who refuses and then trounces the Lion. The Lion, realizing that his mistake was to take the Monkey literally, returns to trounce the Monkey. Although anthropologists and sociolinguists have succeeded in establishing a fair sample of texts featuring the Signifying Monkey, they have been less successful at establishing a consensus of definitions of black "signifying."

In addition to Abrahams' definitions of "signifying," those by Thomas Kochman, Claudia Mitchell-Kernan, Geneva Smitherman, Zora Neale Hurston, and Ralph Ellison are of particular interest here for what they reveal about the nature of Afro-American narrative parody.[13] I shall attempt to explicate Afro-American narrative parody and then to employ it in reading Ishmael Reed's third novel, *Mumbo Jumbo*, as a signifying pastiche of the Afro-American narrative tradition itself. Kochman argues that signifying depends upon the signifier *repeating* what someone else has said about a third person in order to *reverse* the status of a relationship heretofore harmonious; signifying can also be employed to *reverse* or *undermine* pretense or even one's opinion about one's own status. This use of repetition and reversal (chiasmus) constitutes an implicit parody of a subject's own complicity in illusion. Mitchell-Kernan, in perhaps the most thorough study of the concept, compares the etymology of "signifying" in black usage with usages from standard English: "What is unique in Black English usage is the way in which signifying is extended to cover a range of meanings and events which are not covered in its Standard English usage. In the Black community it is possible to say, 'He is signifying' and 'Stop signifying'—sentences which would be anomalous elsewhere."[14] Mitchell-Kernan points to the ironic, or dialectic, relation between "identical" terms in standard and black English which have vastly different meanings:

> The Black concept of *signifying* incorporates essentially a folk notion that dictionary entries for words are not always sufficient for interpreting meanings or messages, or that meaning goes beyond such interpretations. Complimentary remarks may be delivered in a left-handed fashion. A particular utterance may be an insult in one context and not another. What pretends to be informative may intend to be persuasive. The hearer is thus constrained to attend to all potential meaning carrying symbolic systems in speech events—the total universe of discourse. ["Sig," p. 314]

This is an excellent instance of the nature of signifying. Mitchell-Kernan refines these definitions somewhat by suggesting that the Signifying Monkey is able to signify upon the Lion only because the Lion does not understand the nature of the Monkey's discourse: "There seems something of symbolic relevance from the perspective of language in this poem. The monkey and the lion do not speak the same language; the lion is not able to interpret the monkey's use of language" ("Sig," p. 323). The Monkey speaks *figuratively,* in a symbolic code; the Lion interprets or "reads" *literally* and suffers the consequences of his folly, which is a reversal of his status as King of the Jungle. The Monkey rarely acts in these narrative poems; he simply speaks. As the signifier, he determines the actions of the signified—the hapless Lion and the puzzled Elephant.

As Mitchell-Kernan and Hurston attest, signifying is not a gender-specific rhetorical game, despite the frequent use, in the "masculine" versions, of expletives that connote intimate relations with one's mother. Hurston, in *Mules and Men* (1935), and Mitchell-Kernan, in her perceptive "Signifying, Loud-talking, and Marking," are the first scholars to record and explicate female signifying rituals. Hurston is the first author of the tradition to represent signifying itself as a vehicle of liberation for an oppressed woman, and as a rhetorical strategy in the narration of fiction.[15]

Hurston, whose definitions of the term in *Mules and Men* is one of the earliest in the linguistic literature, has made *Their Eyes Were Watching God* (1937) into a paradigmatic signifying text, for this novel resolves that implicit tension between the literal and the figurative contained in standard English usages of the term "signifying." *Their Eyes* represents the black trope of signifying both as thematic matter and as a rhetorical strategy of the novel itself. Janie, the protagonist, gains her voice, as it were, in her husband's store not only by engaging with the assembled men in the ritual of signifying (which her husband had expressly forbidden her to do) but also by openly *signifying upon* her husband's impotency. His image wounded fatally, he soon dies of a displaced "kidney" failure. Janie "kills" her husband, rhetorically. Moreover, Hurston's masterful use of free indirect discourse (*style indirect libre*) allows her to signify upon the tension between the two voices of Jean Toomer's *Cane* (1923) by adding to direct and indirect speech a strategy through which she can privilege the black oral tradition, which Toomer had found to be problematic, and dying. The text of *Their Eyes,* therefore, is itself a signifying structure, a structure of intertextual revision, because it revises key tropes and rhetorical strategies received from such precursory texts as Toomer's *Cane* and W. E. B. Du Bois' *The Quest of the Silver Fleece* (1911).

Afro-American literary history is characterized by such *tertiary* formal revision, by which I mean its authors seem to revise at least two antecedent texts, often taken from different generations or periods within the tradition. Hurston's opening of *Their Eyes* is a masterful revision of *Narrative* (1845), Frederick Douglass' apostrophe to the ships at Chesapeake Bay; *Their Eyes* also revises the trope of the swamp in Du Bois' *Quest*, as well as the relation of character to setting in Toomer's *Cane*. The example of Ellison is even richer: *Invisible Man* (1952) revises Richard Wright's *Native Son* (1940) and *Black Boy* (1945), along with Du Bois' *The Souls of Black Folk* (1903) and Toomer's *Cane* (but it also revises Melville's *Confidence-Man* and Joyce's *Portrait of the Artist as a Young Man*, among others). Reed, in *Mumbo Jumbo* (1972), revises Hurston, Wright, and Ellison.[16] It is clear that black writers read and critique other black texts as an act of rhetorical self-definition. Our literary tradition exists because of these precisely chartable formal literary relationships, relationships of signifying.

The key aspect of signifying for Mitchell-Kernan is "its indirect intent or metaphorical reference," a rhetorical indirection which she says is "almost purely stylistic": its art characteristics remain foregrounded. By "indirection," Mitchell-Kernan means that

> the correct semantic (referential interpretation) or signification of the utterance cannot be arrived at by a consideration of the dictionary meaning of the lexical items involved and the syntactic rules for their combination alone. The apparent significance of the message differs from its real significance. The apaprent meaning of the sentence signifies its actual meaning. ["Sig," p. 325]

This rhetorical naming by indirection is, of course, central to our notions of figuration, troping, and parody. This parody of forms, or pastiche, is in evidence when one writer repeats another's structure by one of several means, including a fairly exact repetition of a given narrative or rhetorical structure, filled incongruously with a ludicrous or incrongruent content. T. Thomas Fortune's "The Black Man's Burden" is an excellent example of this form of pastiche, signifying as it does upon Rudyard Kipling's "The White Man's Burden":

> What is the Black Man's Burden,
> Ye hypocrites and vile,
> Ye whited sepulchres
> From th' Amazon to the Nile?
> What is the Black Man's Burden,
> Ye Gentile parasites,
> Who crush and rob your brother
> Of his manhood and his rights?

Dante Gabriel Rossetti's "Uncle Ned," a dialect verse parody of Harriet Beecher Stowe's *Uncle Tom's Cabin*, provides a second example:

> Him tale dribble on and on
> widout a break,
> Till you hab no eyes for to see;
> When I reach Chapter 4 I
> had got a headache;
> So I had to let Chapter 4 be.

Another kind of formal parody suggests a given structure precisely by failing to coincide with it—that is, suggests it by dissemblance. Repeating a form and then inverting it through a process of variation is central to jazz—a stellar example is John Coltrane's rendition of "My Favorite Things," compared to Julie Andrews' vapid version. Resemblance, thus, can be evoked cleverly by dissemblance. Aristophanes' *Frogs*, which parodies the styles of both Aeschylus and Euripides; Cervantes' relationship to the fiction of knight-errantry; Fielding's parody in *Jo-*

seph Andrews, of the Richardsonian novel of sentiment; and Lewis Carroll's double parody in "Hiawatha's Photographing," which draws upon Longfellow's rhythms to parody the convention of the family photograph, all come readily to mind.

Ellison defines the parody aspect of signifying in several ways which I will bring to bear on my discussion below of the formal parody strategies at work in Reed's *Mumbo Jumbo*. In his complex short story "And Hickman Arrives" (1960), Ellison's narrator defines "signifying":

> And the two men [Daddy Hickman and Deacon Wilhite] standing side by side, the one large and dark, the other slim and light brown; the other reverends rowed behind them, their faces staring grim with engrossed attention to the reading of the Word; like judges in their carved, high-backed chairs. And the two voices beginning their call and countercall as Daddy Hickman began spelling out the text which Deacon Wilhite read, playing variations on the verses just as he did with his trombone when he really felt like signifying on a tune the choir was singing.[17]

Following this introduction, the two ministers demonstrate this "signifying," which in turn signifies upon the antiphonal structure of the Afro-American sermon. Ellison's parody of form here is of the same order as Richard Pryor's parody of that sermonic structure *and* Stevie Wonder's "Living for the City," which he effects by speaking the lyrics of Wonder's song in the form of and with the intonation peculiar to the Afro-American sermon in his "reading" of "The Book of Wonder." Pryor's parody is a signification of the second order, revealing simultaneously the received structure of the sermon (by its presence, demystified here by its incongruous content), the structure of Wonder's music (by the absence of its form and the presence of its lyrics), and the complex, yet direct, formal relationship between both the black sermon and Wonder's music specifically, and black sacred and secular narrative forms generally.

Ellison defines "signifying" in other ways as well. In his essay on Charlie Parker, "On Bird, Bird-Watching, and Jazz" (1962), Ellison defines the satirical aspect of signifying as one aspect of riffing in jazz.

> But what kind of bird was Parker? Back during the thirties members of the old Blue Devils Orchestra celebrated a certain robin by playing a lugubrious little tune called "They Picked Poor Robin." It was a jazz community joke, musically an extended "signifying riff" or melodic naming of a recurrent human situation, and was played to satirize some betrayal of faith or loss of love observed from the bandstand.[18]

Here, again, the parody is twofold, involving a formal parody of the melody of "They Picked Poor Robin" as well as a ritual naming, and therefore a troping, of an action "observed from the bandstand."

Ellison, of course, is our Great Signifier, naming things by indirection and troping throughout his works. In his well-known review of LeRoi Jones' *Blues People*, Ellison defines "signifying" in yet a third sense, then signifies upon Jones' reading of Afro-American cultural history, which he argues is misdirected and wrongheaded: "The tremendous burden of sociology which Jones would place upon this body of music," writes Ellison, "is enough to give even the blues the blues." Ellison writes that Lydia Maria Child's title, *An Appeal in Favor of that Class of Americans Called Africans*,

> sounds like a fine bit of contemporary ironic *signifying*—"signifying" here meaning, in the unwritten dictionary of American Negro usage, "rhetorical understatements." It tells

> us much of the thinking of her opposition, and it reminds us that as late as the 1890s, a time when Negro composers, singers, dancers and comedians dominated the American musical stage, popular Negro songs (including James Weldon Johnson's "Under the Bamboo Tree," now immortalized by T. S. Eliot) were commonly referred to as "Ethiopian Airs."[19]

Ellison's stress upon "the unwritten dictionary of American Negro usage" reminds us of the problem of definitions, of signification itself, when one is translating between two languages. The Signifying Monkey, perhaps appropriately, seems to dwell in this space between two linguistic domains. One wonders, incidentally, about this Afro-American figure and a possible French connection between *signe* ("sign") and *singe* ("monkey").

Ellison's definition of the relation that his works bear to those of Wright constitutes a definition of "narrative signification," "pastiche," or "critical parody," although Ellison employs none of these terms. His explanation of what might be called "implicit formal criticism," however, comprises what is sometimes called "troping" and offers a profound definition of "critical signification" itself.

> I felt no need [writes Ellison] to attack what I considered the limitations of [Wright's] vision because I was quite impressed by what he had achieved. And in this, although I saw with the black vision of Ham, I was, I suppose, as pious as Shem and Japheth. Still I would write my own books and they would be in themselves, implicitly, criticisms of Wright's; just as all novels of a given historical moment form an argument over the nature of reality and are, to an extent, criticisms each of the other.[20]

Ellison in his fictions signifies upon Wright by parodying Wright's literary structures through repetition and difference. The complexities of the parodying I can readily suggest. The play of language, the signifying, starts with the titles: Wright's *Native Son* and *Black Boy*, titles connoting race, self, and presence, Ellison tropes with *Invisible Man*, invisibility an ironic response, of absence, to the would-be presence of "blacks" and "natives," while "man" suggests a more mature and stronger status than either "son" or "boy." Wright's distinctive version of naturalism Ellison signifies upon with a complex rendering of modernism: Wright's reacting protagonist, voiceless to the last, Ellison signifies upon with a nameless protagonist. Ellison's protagonist is nothing but voice, since it is he who shapes, edits, and narrates his own tale, thereby combining action with the representation of action to define "reality" by its representation. This unity of presence and representation is perhaps Ellison's most subtle reversal of Wright's theory of the novel as exemplified in *Native Son*. Bigger's voicelessness and powerlessness to act (as opposed to react) signify an absence, despite the metaphor of presence found in the novel's title; the reverse obtains in *Invisible Man*, where the absence implied by invisibility is undermined by the presence of the narrator as the narrator of his own text.

There are other aspects of critical parody at play here, too, one of the funniest being Jack's glass eye plopping into his water glass before him. This is functionally equivalent to the action of Wright's protagonist in "The Man Who Lived Underground" as he stumbles over the body of a dead baby, deep down in the sewer. It is precisely at this point in the narrative that we know Fred Daniels to be "dead, baby," in the heavy-handed way that Wright's naturalism was self-consciously "symbolic." If Daniels' fate is signified by the objects over which he stumbles in the darkness of the sewer, Ellison signifies upon Wright's novella by repeating this underground scene of discovery, but having his protagonist burn the bits of paper through which he had allowed himself to be defined by others. By explicitly repeating and reversing key figures of Wright's fictions, and by implicitly defining in the process of narration a sophisticated form more akin to Hurston's *Their Eyes Were Watching God,* Ellison exposed naturalism as merely a hardened conventional representation of "the Negro problem," and perhaps part of "the Negro problem" itself. I cannot emphasize enough the major import of this narrative gesture to the subsequent development of black narrative forms. Ellison recorded a new way of seeing and defined both a new manner of representation and its relation to the concept of presence.

The formal relationship that Ellison bears to Wright, Reed bears to both, though principally to Ellison. Not surprisingly, Ellison has formulated this type of complex and inherently polemical intertextual relationshp of formal signifying. In a refutation of Irving Howe's critique of his work Ellison states: "I agree with Howe that protest is an element of all art, though it does not necessarily take the form of speaking for a political or social program. It might appear in a novel as a *technical assault against the styles* which have gone before."[21] This form of critical parody, of repetition and inversion, is what I define to be "critical signification," or "formal signifying," and is my metaphor for literary history.

I intend here to elicit the tertiary relationship in *Mumbo Jumbo* of Reed's signifying post-modernism to Wright's naturalism and Ellison's modernism. The set of intertextual relations that I chart through formal signification is related to what Mikhail Bakhtin labels "double-voiced" discourse, which he subdivides into parodic narration and the hidden or internal polemic. These two types of double-voiced discourse can merge, as they do in *Mumbo Jumbo.* In hidden polemic

> the other speech act remains outside the bounds of the author's speech, but is implied or alluded to in that speech. The other speech act is not reproduced with a new intention, but shapes the author's speech while remaining outside its boundaries. Such is the nature of discourse in hidden polemic. . . .
>
> In hidden polemic the author's discourse is oriented toward its referential object, as is any other discourse, but at the same time each assertion about that object is constructed in such a way that, besides its referential meaning, the author's discourse brings a polemical attack to bear against another speech act, another assertion, on the same topic. Here one utterance focused on its referential object clashes with another utterance on the grounds of the referent itself. That other utterance is not reproduced; it is understood only in its import.[22]

Ellison's definition of the formal relationship his works bear to Wright's is a salient example of the hidden polemic: Ellison's texts clash with Wright's "on the grounds of the referent itself." "As a result," Bakhtin continues, "the latter begins to influence the author's speech from within." In this double-voiced relationship, one speech act determines the internal structure of another, the second effecting the "voice" of the first by absence, by difference.

Much of the Afro-American literary tradition can, in a real sense, be read as successive attempts to create a new narrative space for representing the recurring referent of Afro-American literature—the so-called black experience. Certainly, this is the way we read the relation of Sterling Brown's regionalism to Toomer's lyricism, Hurston's lyricism to Wright's naturalism, and, equally, Ellison's modernism to Wright's naturalism. This set of relationships can be illustrated by the schematic representation on page 638, which I intend only to be suggestive.[23]

These relationships are reciprocal because we are free to read in critical time machines, to read backwards. The direct relation most important to my own theory

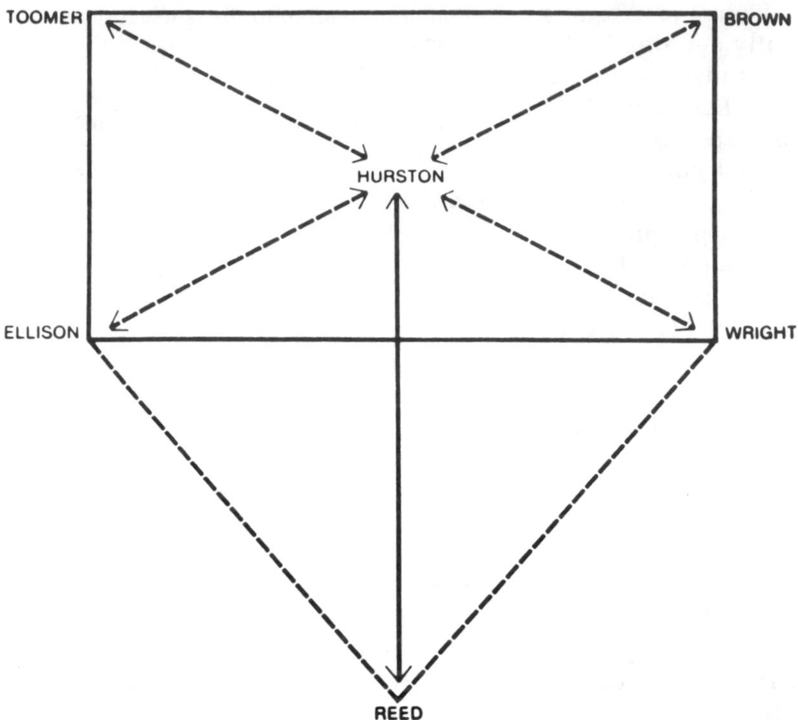

of reading is that solid black line connecting Reed with Hurston. While Reed and Hurston seem to relish the play of the tradition, Reed's work seems to be a magnificently conceived play *on* the tradition. Both Hurston and Reed have written myths of Moses, both draw upon black sacred and secular mythic discourse as metaphorical and metaphysical systems, both write self-reflexive texts which comment upon the nature of writing itself, both make use of the frame to bracket their narratives-within-a-narrative, and both are authors of fictions which I characterize as "speakerly texts." Speakerly texts privilege the representation of the speaking black voice, of what the Russian Formalists called *skaz* and which Hurston and Reed have called "an oral book, a talking book" (a figure which occurs, remarkably enough, in five of the first six slave narratives in the black tradition).[24]

Reed's relation to these authors in the tradition is double-voiced at all points, since he seems to be especially concerned with employing satire to utilize literature in what Northrop Frye calls "a special function of analysis, of breaking up the lumber of stereotypes, fossilized beliefs, superstitious terrors, crank theories, pedantic dogmatisms, oppressive fashions, and all other things that impede the free movement . . . of society."[25] Reed, of course, seems to be most concerned with the "free movement" of writing itself. In his work, parody and hidden polemic overlap, in a process Bakhtin describes as follows: "When parody becomes aware of substantial resistance, a certain forcefulness and profundity in the speech act it parodies, it takes on a new dimension of complexity via the tones of the hidden polemic. . . . A process of inner dialogization takes place within the parodic speech act."[26]

This "inner dialogization" can have

curious implications, the most interesting, perhaps, being what Bakhtin describes as "the splitting of double-voiced discourse into two speech acts, into the two entirely separate and autonomous voices." The clearest evidence that Reed is signifying in *Mumbo Jumbo* through parody-as-hidden-polemic is his use of these two autonomous narrative voices. Reed employs these two voices in the manner of, and renders them through, foregrounding, to parody the two simultaneous stories of detective narration (that of the present and that of the past) in a narrative flow that moves hurriedly from cause to effect. In *Mumbo Jumbo*, however, the narrative of the past bears an ironic relation to the narrative of the present, because it comments not only upon the other narrative but upon the nature of *its writing itself*. Frye describes this, in another context, as "the constant tendency to self-parody in satiric rhetoric which prevents even the process of writing itself from becoming an oversimplified convention or ideal."[27] Reed's rhetorical strategy assumes the form of the relation between the text and the criticism of that text, which serves as discourse upon that text.

2. TALKING TEXTS: SIGNIFYING REVISIONS

Consult the text!

—Ralph Ellison, *Shadow and Act*[28]

With these definitions of narrative parody and critical signification as a frame, let me turn directly to Reed's *Mumbo Jumbo*. A close reading of Reed's works suggests strongly his concerns with the received form of the novel, with the precise rhetorical shape of the Afro-American literary tradition, and with the relation that the Afro-American tradition bears to the Western tradition.[29] Reed's concerns, as exemplified in his narrative forms, seem to be twofold: (1) the relation his own art bears to his black literary precursors, including Hurston, Wright, Ellison, and James Baldwin; and (2) the process of willing-into-being a rhetorical structure, a literary language, replete with its own figures and tropes, but one that allows the black writer to posit a structure of feeling that simultaneously critiques both the metaphysical presuppositions inherent in Western ideas and forms of writing and the metaphorical system in which the "blackness" of the writer and his experience have been valorized as a "natural" absence. In six demanding novels, Reed has criticized, through signifying, what he perceives to be the conventional structures of feeling that he has received from the Afro-American tradition. He has proceeded almost as if the sheer process of the analysis can clear a narrative space for the next generation of writers as decidedly as Ellison's narrative response to Wright and naturalism cleared a space for Leon Forrest, Toni Morrison, Alice Walker, James Alan McPherson, and especially for Reed himself.

By undertaking the difficult and subtle art of pastiche, Reed criticizes the Afro-American idealism of a transcendent black subject, integral and whole, self-sufficient, and plentiful, the "always already" black signified, available for literary representation in received Western forms as would be the water dippered from a deep and dark well. Water can be poured into glasses or cups or canisters, but it remains water just the same. Put simply, Reed's fictions argue that the so-called black experience cannot be thought of as a fluid content to be poured into received and static containers. For Reed, it is the signifier that both shapes and defines any discrete signified—and it is the signifiers of the Afro-American tradition with whom Reed is concerned.

Reed's first novel lends credence to this

sort of reading and also serves to create a set of generic expectations for reading the rest of his works. *The Free-Lance Pallbearers* is, above all else, a parody of the confessional mode which is the fundamental, undergirding convention of Afro-American narrative, received, elaborated upon, and transmitted in a chartable heritage from Briton Hammon's captivity narrative of 1760, through the antebellum slave narratives, to black autobiography, and into black fiction, especially the fictions of Hurston, Wright, Baldwin, and Ellison.[30] The narrative of Reed's Bukka Doopeyduk is a pastiche of the classic black narrative of the questing protagonist's "journey into the heart of whiteness"; but it parodies that narrative form by turning it inside out, exposing the character of the originals and thereby defining their formulaic closures and disclosures. Doopeyduk's tale ends with his own crucifixion; as the narrator of his own story, therefore, Doopeyduk articulates, literally, from among the dead, an irony implicit in all confessional and autobiographical modes, in which any author is forced by definition to imagine him or herself to be dead. More specifically, Reed signifies upon *Black Boy* and *Go Tell It on the Mountain* in a foregrounded critique which can be read as an epigraph to the novel: "read growing up in soulsville first of three installments—or what it means to be a backstage darky."[31] Reed foregrounds the "scat-singing voice" that introduces the novel against the "other" voice of Doopeyduk, whose "second" voice narrates the novel's plot. Here, Reed parodies both Hurston's use of free indirect discourse in *Their Eyes Were Watching God* and Ellison's use in *Invisible Man* of the foregrounded voice in the prologue and epilogue that frame his nameless protagonists' picaresque account of his own narrative. In his second novel, *Yellow Back Radio Broke-Down*, Reed more fully, and successfully, critiques both realism and modernism. The exchange between Bo Shmo and the Loop Garoo Kid is telling:

> It was Bo Shmo and the neo-social realist gang. They rode to this spot from their hideout in the hills. Bo Shmo leaned in his saddle and scowled at Loop, whom he considered a deliberate attempt to be obscure. A buffoon an outsider and frequenter of sideshows. . . .
>
> The trouble with you Loop is that you're too abstract, the part time autocrat monarchist and guru finally said. Crazy dada nigger that's what you are. You are given to fantasy and are off in matters of detail. Far out esoteric bullshit is where you're at. Why in those suffering books that I write about my old neighborhood and how hard it was every gumdrop machine is in place while your work is a blur and a doodle. I'll bet you can't create the difference between a German and a redskin.
>
> What's your beef with me Bo Shmo, what if I write circuses? No one says a novel has to be one thing. It can be anything it wants to be, a vaudeville show, the six o'clock news, the mumblings of wild men saddled by demons.
>
> All art must be for the end of liberating the masses. A landscape is only good when it shows the oppressor hanging from a tree.
>
> Right on! Right on, Bo, the henchmen chorused.
>
> Did you receive that in a vision or was it revealed to you?[32]

At several points in his first two novels, then, Reed deliberately reflects upon the history of the black tradition's debate over the nature and purpose of art.

Reed's third novel, *Mumbo Jumbo*, is a novel about writing itself—not only in the figurative sense of the post-modern, self-reflexive text but also in a literal sense: "So Jes Grew is seeking its words. Its text. For what good is a liturgy without a text?"[33] *Mumbo Jumbo* is both a book about texts and a book of texts, a composite narrative composed of sub-texts, pre-texts, post-texts, and narratives-within-narratives. It is both a definition of Afro-American culture and its deflation. "The Big Lie concerning Afro-American culture," *Mumbo Jumbo*'s dust jacket states, "is that it lacks a tradition." The "Big Truth" of the novel, on the other hand, is that this very tradition is as rife with hardened convention and presupposition as is the rest of the Western tradition. Even this cryptic riddle of Jes Grew and its Text parodies Ellison: *Invisible Man*'s plot is set in motion with a riddle, while the themes of the relation between words and texts echo a key passage from Ellison's short story "And Hickman Arrives": "Good. Don't talk like I talk; talk like I *say* talk. Words are your business, boy. Not just *the* Word. Words are everything. The key to the Rock, the answer to the Question."[34]

Reed's signifying on tradition begins with his book's title. "Mumbo jumbo" is the received and ethnocentric Western designation for the rituals of black religions as well as for all black languages themselves. A vulgarized Western "translation" of a Swahili phrase, *mambo, jambo,* "mumbo jumbo," according to *Webster's Third New International Dictionary,* connotes "language that is unnecessarily involved and difficult to understand: GIBBERISH." The *Oxford English Dictionary* cites its etymology as "of unknown origin," implicitly serving here as the signified on which Reed's title signifies, recalling the myth of Topsy in *Uncle Tom's Cabin* who, with no antecedents, "jes' grew"—a phrase with which James Weldon Johnson characterizes the creative process of black sacred music. *Mumbo Jumbo,* then, signifies upon Western etymology, abusive Western practices of deflation through misnaming, and Johnson's specious, albeit persistent, designation of black creativity as anonymous.

But there is even more parody in this title. Whereas Ellison tropes the myth of presence in Wright's titles of *Native Son* and *Black Boy* through his title of *Invisible Man,* Reed parodies all three titles by employing as his title the English-language parody of *black language itself.* Although the etymology of "mumbo jumbo" has been problematic for Western lexicographers, any Swahili speaker knows that the phrase derives from the common greeting *jambo* and its plural, *mambo,* which loosely translated mean "What's happening?" Reed is also echoing, and signifying upon, Vachel Lindsay's ironic poem, "The Congo," which so (fatally) influenced the Harlem Renaissance poets, as Charles T. Davis has shown.[35] From its title on, *Mumbo Jumbo* serves as a critique of black and Western literary forms and conventions, and of the complex relations between the two.

On the book's cover, which Reed designed (with Allen Weinberg), repeated and reversed images of a crouching, sensuous Josephine Baker are superimposed upon a rose.[36] Counterposed to this image is a medallion depicting a horse with two riders. These signs, the rose and the medallion, adumbrate the two central oppositions of the novel's complicated plot. The rose and the double image of Baker together form a cryptic *vé vé.* A *vé vé* is a key sign in Haitian *Vaudou,* a sign drawn on the ground with sand, cornmeal, flour, and coffee to represent the *loas.* The *loas* are the deities comprising the pantheon of *Vaudou* gods. The rose is a sign of Erzulie, goddess of love, as are the images of Baker, who became the French goddess of love in the late 1920s, in the Parisian version of the Jazz Age. The doubled image, as if mirrored, is meant to suggest the divine crossroads, where human beings meet their fate. At its center presides the *loa* Legba (Èṣù), guardian of the divine crossroads, messenger of the gods, the figure representing the interpreter and interpretation itself, the muse or *loa* of the critic. Legba is master of that mystical barrier separating the divine from the profane world. This complex yet cryptic *vé vé* is meant both to placate Legba himself and to summon his attention and integrity in a double act of criticism and interpretation: that of Reed in the process of his representation of the tradition, to be found between the covers of the book, and of the critic's interpretation of Reed's figured interpretation.

Located outside of the *vé vé*, as counterpoint, placed almost off the cover itself, is the medallion, the sign of the Knights Templar, representing the heart of the Western tradition. The opposition between the *vé vé* and the medallion represents two distinct warring forces, two mutually exclusive modes of reading. Already we are in the realm of doubles, but not the binary realm; rather, we are in the realm of doubled doubles. ("Doubled doubles" are central figures in Yoruba mythology, as is Èṣù.) Not only are two distinct and conflicting metaphysical systems here represented and invoked, but Reed's cover also serves as an overture to the critique of dualism and binary opposition which gives a major thrust to the text of *Mumbo Jumbo*. Reed parodies this dualism, which he thinks is exemplified in Ellison's *Invisible Man,* not just in *Mumbo Jumbo* but also in another text, in his poem "Dualism: in ralph ellison's invisible man."

This critique of dualism is implicit in *Mumbo Jumbo*'s central *speaking* character, PaPa LaBas. I emphasize "speaking" here because the novel's central character, of course, is Jes Grew itself, which never speaks and is never seen in its "abstract essence," only in discrete manifestations, or "outbreaks." Jes Grew is the supraforce which sets the text of *Mumbo Jumbo* in motion, as Jes Grew and Reed seek their texts, as all characters and events define themselves against this omnipresent, compelling force. Jes Grew, here, is a clever and subtle parody of similar forces invoked in the black novel of naturalism, most notably in Wright's *Native Son*.

Unlike Jes Grew, PaPa LaBas does indeed speak. He is the chief detective in hard-and-fast pursuit of both Jes Grew and its Text. PaPa LaBas' name is a conflation of two of the several names of Èṣù, the Pan-African trickster. Called "Papa Legba" as his Haitian honorific and invoked through the phrase "eh là-bas" in New Orleans jazz recordings of the 1920s and 1930s, PaPa LaBas is the Afro-American trickster figure from black sacred tradition. His surname, of course, is French for "over there," and his presence unites "over there" (Africa) with "right here." He is indeed the messenger of the gods, the divine Pan-African interpreter, pursuing, in the language of the text, "The Work," which is not only *Vaudou* but also the very work (and play) of art itself. PaPa LaBas is the figure of the critic, in search of the text, decoding its telltale signs in the process. Even the four syllables of his name recall *Mumbo Jumbo*'s play of doubles. Chief sign reader, LaBas also in a sense is a sign himself. Indeed, PaPa LaBas' incessant and ingenious search for the Text of Jes Grew, culminating as it does in his recitation and revision of the myth of Thoth's gift of writing to civilization, constitutes an argument against the privileging in black discourse of what Reed elsewhere terms "the so-called oral tradition" in favor of the primacy and priority of the written text. It is a brief for the permanence of the written text, for the need of criticism, for which LaBas' myth of origins also accounts ("Guides were initiated into the Book of Thoth, the 1st anthology written by the 1st choreographer" [*MJ*, p. 164]).

Let us examine the text of *Mumbo Jumbo* as a text-book, complete with illustrations, footnotes, and a bibliography. A prologue, an epilogue, and an appended "Partial Bibliography" frame the text-proper, again in a parody of Ellison's framing devices in *Invisible Man*. (Reed supplements Ellison's epilogue with the bibliography, parodying the device both by its repeated presence and by the subsequent asymmetry of *Mumbo Jumbo*). This documentary scheme of notes, illustrations, and bibliography parodies the documentary conventions of black realism and naturalism, as does Reed's recurrent use of lists and catalogs. These "separate" items Reed fails to separate with any sort of punctuation, thereby directing attention to their presence as literary conventions rather than as sources of information, particularly about the "black experience." Reed's text also includes dictionary definitions, epigraphs, epigrams, anagrams, photoduplicated type from other texts, newspaper clips and headlines, signs (such as those that hang on doors), invitations to parties, telegrams, "Situation Reports" (which come "from the 8-tubed Radio" [*MJ*, p. 32]), yin-yang symbols, quotations from other texts, poems, cartoons, drawings of mythic beasts, handbills, photographs, book jacket copy, charts and graphs, playing cards, a representation of a Greek vase, and a four-page handwritten letter, among even other items. Just as our word "satire" derives from *satura*, "hash," so Reed's form of satire is a version of "gumbo," a parody of form itself.[37]

Reed here parodies and underscores our notions of intertextuality, present in all texts. *Mumbo Jumbo* is the great black inter-text, replete with intra-texts referring to one another within the text of *Mumbo Jumbo* and also referring outside of themselves to all those other named texts, as well as to those texts unnamed but invoked through concealed reference, repetition, and reversal. The "Partial Bibliography" is Reed's most brilliant stroke, since its unconcealed presence (along with the text's other undigested texts) parodies both the scholar's appeal to authority and all studied attempts to conceal literary antecedents and influence. All texts, claims *Mumbo Jumbo*, are inter-texts, full of intra-texts. Our notions of originality, Reed's critique suggests, are more related to convention and material relationships than to some supposedly transcendent truth. Reed lays bare that mode of concealment and the illusion of unity which characterize modernist texts. Coming as it does after the epilogue, Reed's "Partial Bibliography" is an implicit parody of Ellison's ideas of craft and technique in the novel and suggests an image of Ellison's nameless protagonist, buried in his well-lighted hole, eating vanilla ice cream smothered by sloe gin, making annotations for his sequel to *Invisible Man*. The device, moreover, mimics the fictions of documentation and history which claim to order the ways societies live. The presence of the bibliography also recalls Ellison's remarks about the complex relationship between the "writer's experience" and the writer's experiences with books.

Reed's parodic use of intertextuality demonstrates that *Mumbo Jumbo* is a post-modern text. But what is its parody of the Jazz Age and the Harlem Renaissance about, and for whom do the characters stand? Reed's novel is situated in the 1920s because, as the text explains, the Harlem Renaissance was the first full-scale, patronized attempt to capture the essence of Jes Grew in discrete *literary* texts. Jes Grew had made its first appearance in the 1890s, when "the Dance" swept the country. Indeed, James Weldon Johnson appropriated the phrase "jes' grew" to refer to the composition of the musical texts of Ragtime, which depended upon signifying riffs to transform black secular, and often vulgar, songs into formal, repeatable compositions. Ellison makes essentially the same statement about the 1890s by suggesting that signifying is implicit in the common designation of this music as "Ethiopian Airs." Ellison's pun could well serve as still another signified upon which *Mumbo Jumbo* signifies. The power of Jes Grew was allowed to peter out in the 1890s, Reed argues, because it found no literary texts to contain, define, interpret, and thereby will it to subsequent black cultures.

Although the Harlem Renaissance did succeed in the creation of numerous texts of art and criticism, most critics agree that it failed to find its voice, which lay muffled beneath the deadweight of Romantic convention, which most black writers seemed not to question but to adopt eagerly. This is essentially the same critique rendered by Wallace Thurman in his *Infants of the Spring* (1932), a satirical novel about the Harlem Renaissance, written by one of its most thoughtful literary critics. Few of Reed's characters stand for historical personages; most are figures for types. Hinckle Von Vampton, however, suggests Carl Van Vechten, but his first name, from the German *hinken* ("to limp"), could suggest the German engraver Hermann Knackfuss, whose name translates as "a person with a clubfoot."[38] Abdul Sufi Hamid recalls a host of Black Muslims, most notably Duse Mohamed Ali, editor of the *African Times and Orient Review*, as well as Elijah Muhammad's shadowy mentor, W. D. Fard. The key figures in the action of the plot, however, are the Atonist Path and its military wing, the Wallflower Order, on one hand, and the Neo-HooDoo detectives, headed by PaPa LaBas, and its "military" wing, the *Mu'tafikah*, on the other. "Wallflower Order" is a two-term pun on "Ivy League," while *Mu'tafikah* puns on a twelve-letter word which signifies chaos. Also, "mu" is the twelfth letter of the Greek alphabet, suggesting "the dozens," which forms a subdivision of the black ritual of signifying; the *Mu'tafikah* play the dozens on Western art museums. The painter Knackfuss created a heliogravure from Wilhelm H's allegorical drawing of the European authority to go to war against the Chinese. This heliogravure, *Völker Europas, wahrt eure heiligsten Güter* (People of Europe, protect that which is most holy to you), was completed in 1895. It appears in *Mumbo Jumbo* as part of a chapter in which members of the Wallflower Order plot against the *Mu'tafikah* (see *MJ*, p. 155). The pun on "Knackfuss" and *hinken* is wonderfully consistent with Reed's multiple puns on the "Wallflower Order" and "Atonist."

"Atonist" signifies multiply here. "One who atones" is an Atonist; a follower of Aton, Pharoah Akhnaton's Supreme Being who "reappears" as Jehovah, is an Atonist; but also one who lacks physiological tone, especially of a contractile organ, is an Atonist. On a wall at Atonist headquarters are the Order's symbols:

> the Flaming Disc, the #1 and the creed—
>
> *Look at them! Just look at them! throwing their hips this way, that way* while I, my muscles, stone, the marrow of my spine, plaster, *my back supported by decorated paper, stand here as goofy as a Dumb Dora. Lord, if I can't dance, no one shall* [*MJ*, p. 65; original in italics, emphasis mine]

The Atonists and the Jes Grew Carriers ("J.G.C.s") reenact allegorically a primal, recurring battle between the forces of light and the forces of darkness, between forces of the Left Hand and forces of the Right Hand, between the descendants of Set and the descendants of Osiris, all symbolized in Knackfuss' heliogravure.

We learn of this war in *Mumbo Jumbo*'s marvelous parody of the scene of recognition so fundamental to the structure of detective fiction, which occurs in the library of a black-owned villa at Irvington-on-Hudson, called Villa Lewaro, "an anagram," the text tells us, "upon the Hostess' name, by famed tenor Enrico Caruso" (*MJ*, p. 156). Actually, "Lewaro" is an anagram for "we oral." This recognition scene in which PaPa LaBas and his sidekick, Black Herman, arrest Hinckle Von Vampton and his sidekick, Hubert "Safecracker" Gould, parodies its counterpart in the detective novel by its exaggerated frame. When forced to explain the charges against Von Vampton and Gould, LaBas replies, "Well if you must know, it all began 1000s of years ago in Egypt, according to a high up member in the Haitian aristocracy" (*MJ*, p. 160). He then proceeds to narrate, before an assembled company of hundreds, the myth of Set and Osiris and its key subtext, the myth of the introduction of writing in Egypt by the god Thoth. The parody involved here is the length of the recapitulation of facts—of the decoded signs—which LaBas narrates in a thirty-one-page chapter, the longest in the book (see *MJ* pp. 161–91). The myth, of course, recapitulates the action of the novel up to this point of the narrative, but by an *allegorical* representation through mythic discourse. By fits and turns, we realize that Von Vampton and the Wallflower Order are the descendants of Set, by way of the story of Moses and Jethro and the birth of the Knights Templar in A.D. 1118. Von Vampton, we learn, was the Templar librarian, who found the sacred Book of Thoth, "the 1st anthology written by the 1st choreographer," which is Jes Grew's sacred Text (*MJ*, p. 164). In the twentieth century, Von Vampton subdivided the Book of Thoth into fourteen sections, just as Set had dismembered his brother Osiris' body into fourteen segments. The fourteen sections of the anthology he mailed anonymously to fourteen black people, who are manipulated into mailing its parts to each other in a repeating circle, in the manner of a "chain book" (*MJ*, p. 69). Abdul Sufi Hamid, one of these fourteen who, we learn, are unwitting Jes Grew Carriers, calls in the other thirteen chapters of the anthology, reassembles the Text, and even translates the Book of Thoth from the hieroglyphics. Sensing its restored Text, Jes Grew surfaces in New Orleans, as it had in the 1890s with the birth of Ragtime, and heads toward New York. Ignorant of the existence or nature of Jes Grew and of the true nature of the sacred Text, Abdul destroys the Book, and then, when he refuses to reveal its location, is murdered by the Wallflower Order. LaBas, Von Vampton's arch foe, master of HooDoo, devout follower of Jes Grew ("PaPa LaBas carries Jes Grew in him like most other folk carry genes" [*MJ*, p. 23]), chief decoder of signs, recapitulates this complex story, in elaborate detail, to the assembled guests at Villa Lewaro, thereby repeating, through the recited myth, the figures of *Mumbo Jumbo's* own plot, functioning as what Reed calls "the shimmering Etheric Double of the 1920s. The thing that gives it its summary" (*MJ*, p. 20). Despite numerous murders and even the arrests of Von Vampton and Gould and their repatriation to Haiti for trial by the *loas* of *Vaudou*, neither the mystery of the nature of Jes Grew nor the identity of its Text is ever resolved. The epilogue presents PaPa LaBas in the 1960s, delivering his annual lecture to a college audience on the Harlem Renaissance and its unconsummated Jes Grew passion.

But just as we can define orders of multiple substitution and signification for Reed's types and caricatures, as is true of allegory generally (e.g., Von Vampton/Van Vechten, *hinken*/Knackfuss), so too we can find many levels of meaning which could provide a closure to the text. The first decade of readers of *Mumbo Jumbo* have attempted, with great energy, to find one-to-one correlations, decoding its allegorical structure by finding analogues between, for example, the Harlem Renaissance and the Black Arts Movement. As interesting as such parallel universes are, however, I am more concerned here with *Mumbo Jumbo*'s status as a rhetorical structure, as a mode of narration, and with relating this mode of narration to a critique of traditional notions of closure in interpretation. Reed's most subtle achievement in *Mumbo Jumbo* is to parody, to signify upon, the notions of closure implicit in the key texts of the Afro-American canon. *Mumbo Jumbo,* in contrast to that canon, is a novel that figures and glorifies *indeterminacy.* In this sense, *Mumbo Jumbo* stands as a profound critique and elaboration upon the convention of closure, and its metaphysical implications, in the black novel. In its stead, Reed posits the notion of aesthetic *play*: the play of the tradition, the play on the tradition, the sheer play of indeterminacy itself.

3. INDETERMINACY AND THE TEXT OF BLACKNESS

The text of *Mumbo Jumbo* is framed by devices characteristic of film narration. The prologue, situated in New Orleans, functions as a "false start" of the action: five pages of narration are followed by a second title page, a second copyright and acknowledgment page, and a second set of epigraphs, the first of which concludes the prologue. This prologue functions like the prologue of a film, with the title and credits appearing next, before the action continues. The novel's final words are "Freeze frame" (*MJ,* p. 218). The relative fluidity of the narrative structure of film, compared with that of conventional prose narrative, announces here an emphasis upon figural multiplicity rather than singular referential correspondence, an emphasis that Reed recapitulates throughout the text by an imaginative play of doubles. The play of doubles extends from the title and the double-Erzulie image of Baker on the novel's cover ("Erzulie" means "love of mirrors" [*MJ,* p. 162]) to the double beginning implicit in every prologue, through all sorts of double images scattered in the text (such as the "two heads" of PaPa LaBas [see *MJ,* pp. 25, 45] and the frequently repeated arabic numerals 4 and 22), all the way to the double ending of the novel implied by its epilogue and "Partial Bibliography." The double beginning and double ending frame the text of *Mumbo Jumbo,* a book of doubles, from its title on.

These thematic aspects of doubleness represent only its most obvious form of doubling; the novel's narrative structure, a brilliant elaboration upon that of the detective novel, is itself a rather complex doubling. Reed refers to this principle of "structuration" as "a doubleness, not just of language, but the idea of a double-image on form. A mystery-mystery, *Erzulie-Erzulie.*"[39] In *Mumbo Jumbo,* form and content, theme and structure, all are ordered upon this figure of the double; doubling is Reed's "figure in the carpet." The form the narration takes in *Mumbo Jumbo* replicates the tension of the two stories which grounds the form of the detective novel, defined by Tzvetan Todorov as "the missing story of the crime, and the presented story of the investigation, the role justification of which is to make us discover the first story." Todorov describes three forms of detective fiction—the whodunit, the *série noire* (the thriller, exemplified by Chester Himes' *For Love of Imabelle*), and the suspense novel, which combines the narrative features of the first two.[40] Let us consider Todorov's typology in relation to the narrative structure of *Mumbo Jumbo.*

The whodunit comprises two stories: the story of the crime and the story of the investigation. The first story, that of the crime, has ended by the time the second story, that of the investigation of the crime, begins. In the story of the investigation, the characters "do not act, they learn." The whodunit's structure, as in Agatha Christie's *Murder on the Orient*

Express, is often framed by a prologue and an epilogue, "that is, the discovery of the crime and the discovery of the killer" (*PP*, p. 45). The second story functions as an explanation not just of the investigation but also of how the book came to be written; indeed, "it is precisely the story of that very book" (*PP*, p. 45). As Todorov concludes, these two stories are the same as those which the Russian Formalists isolated in every narrative, that of the *fable* (story) and that of the *subject* (or plot): "The story is what has happened in life, the plot is the way the author presents it to us" (*PP*, p. 45). "Story," here, describes the reality represented, while "plot" describes the mode of narration, the literary convention and devices, used to represent. A detective novel merely renders these two principles of narrative *present* simultaneously. The story of the crime is a story of an absence since the crime of the whodunit has occurred before the narrative begins; the second story, therefore, "serves only as mediator between the reader and the story of the crime" (*PP*, p. 46). This second story, the plot, generally depends upon temporal inversions and subjective, shifting points of view. These two conventions figure prominently in the narrative structure of *Mumbo Jumbo*.

Todorov's second type of detective fiction, the *série noire*, or thriller, combines the two stories into one, suppressing the first and vitalizing the second. Whereas the whodunit proceeds from effect to cause, the thriller proceeds from cause to effect: the novel reveals at its outset the causes of the crime, the *données* (in *Mumbo Jumbo*, the Wallflower Order, the dialogue of whose members occupies 60 percent of the prologue), and the narration sustains itself through sheer suspense, through the reader's expectation of what will happen next. Although *Mumbo Jumbo*'s narrative strategy proceeds through the use of suspense, its two stories, as it were, are not fused; accordingly, neither of these categories fully describe it.

Mumbo Jumbo imitates and signifies upon the narrative strategy of the third type of detective novel, the suspense novel. According to Todorov, its defining principles are these: "it keeps the mystery of the whodunit and also the two stories, that of the past and that of the present; but it refuses to reduce the second to a simple detection of the truth" (*PP*, p. 50). What *has* happened is only just as important to sustaining interest as what *shall* happen; the second story, then, the story of the present, is the focus of interest. Reed draws upon this type of narrative as his rhetorical structure in *Mumbo Jumbo*, with one important exception. We do find the two-stories structure intact. What's more, the mystery presented at the outset of the text, the double mystery of the suppression of both Jes Grew *and* its Text (neither of which is ever revealed nor their mysteries solved in the standard sense of the genre) is relayed through the dialogue of the *données*. This means that the movement of the narration is from cause to effect, from the New Orleans branch of the Wallflower Order and their plans to "decode this coon mumbo jumbo" (*MJ*, p. 4) through their attempts to kill its Text and thereby dissipate its force. The detective of the tale, PaPa LaBas, moreover, is integrated solidly into the action and universe of the other characters, risking his life and systematically discovering the murdered corpses of his friends and colleagues as he proceeds to decode the signs of the mystery's solution, in the manner of "the vulnerable detective," which Todorov identifies as a subtype of the suspense novel (*PP*, p. 51).

In these ways, the structure of *Mumbo Jumbo* conforms to that of the suspense novel. The crucial exception to the typology, however, whereby Reed is able to parody even the mode of the two stories themselves and transform the structure into a self-reflecting text or allegory upon the nature of writing itself, is *Mumbo Jumbo*'s device of drawing upon the story of the past *to reflect upon, analyze, and philosophize about* the story of the present. The story of the present is narrated from the limited but multiple points of view of the characters who people its sub-plots and sub-mysteries; the story of the past, however, is narrated in an omniscient voice, which "reads" the story of the present, in the manner of a literary critic close reading a primary text. *Mumbo Jumbo*'s double narrative, then, its narrative-within-a-narrative, is an allegory of the act of reading itself. Reed uses this second mode of ironic omniscient narration to signify upon the nature of the novel in general but especially upon Afro-American naturalism and modernism.

The mystery type of narrative discourse is characterized by plot inversions, which, of course, function as temporal inversions. Before discussing Reed's use of the narrative-within-a-narrative and its relation to the sort of indeterminacy the text seems to be upholding, it would be useful to chart his use of inversion as impediment. The summary of the *fable*, the essential causal-temporal relationships of the work which I have sketched in part 2 above, is somewhat misleading, for the novel can be related in summary fashion only *after* we have read it. In the reading process we confront a collection of mysteries, mysteries-within-mysteries, all of which are resolved eventually except for the first two. We can list the following mysteries which unfold in this order as the *subject*, or the plot:[41]

1. The mystery of Jes Grew ("the Thing").	These are basic mysteries. They frame the plot and remain unresolved.
2. The mystery of its Text.	
3. The mystery of the Wallflower Order's history and its relation to that of the Knights Templar.	The mystery of the identity of these medieval orders, Jes Grew's antagonists, runs the length of the novel and is resolved only in the recognition scene at Villa Lewaro. Figured as antithetical dance metaphors.
4. The *Mu'tafikah*'s raids on American art museums, especially the North Wing of the Center of Art Detention.	This partial mystery is resolved, but disastrously for LaBas' forces. It creates a series of imbalances between Earline and Berbelang, and between Berbelang and PaPa LaBas, which function as structural parts to the tension between the Wallflower Order and the Knights Templar.
5. Installation of the anti–Jes Grew President Warren Harding and mystery of his complex racial heritage.	Plot impediments.
6. The mystery of the Talking Android.	
7. Gang wars between Buddy Jackson and Schlitz, "the Sarge of Yorktown."	
8. Mystery of the	Resolved midway;

	U.S. Marine invasion of Haiti.	allows for ironic denouncement.
9.	Mystery of PaPa LaBas' identity and Mumbo Jumbo Kathedral.	Resolved in epilogue.
10.	Woodrow Wilson Jefferson and the mystery of the Talking Android.	Plot impediments; resolved, but ambiguously. Explanations resort to fantastic element.
11.	Staged mystery of "Charlotte's (Isis) Pick" (Doctor Peter Pick).	
12.	Hinckle Von Vampton's identity.	This mystery is resolved and in the process resolves the mysteries of the Wallflower Order and the Atonist Path.
13.	Mystery of the fourteen J.G.C.s and the sacred anthology.	This resolves mystery 2, but only partially, superficially.
14.	The mystery of Abdul Sufi Hamid's murder and his riddle, "Epigram on American-Egyptian Cotton."	These mysteries function in a curious way, seemingly to resolve the mystery of Jes Grew's Text.
15.	Berbelang's murder and betrayal of the *Mu'tafikah* by Thor Wintergreen. Charlotte's murder.	Plot impediments.
16.	Earline's possession by Erzulie and Yemanjá *loas*; Doctor Peter Pick's disappearance.	
17.	Mystery of *The Black Plume* and Benoit Battraville, and the ring of the Dark Tower.	VooDoo/HooDoo exposition. Resolves Knights Templar mystery. Leads to capture of Von Vampton.

Most of these interwoven mysteries impede the plot in the manner of detective fiction by depicting, as does jazz, several simultaneous actions whose relationship is not apparent. These mysteries run parallel throughout the novel, only to be resolved in the scene of recognition in the library at the Villa Lewaro, where PaPa LaBas presents his decoded evidence through his elaborate recasting of the myth of Osiris and Set. This allegory recapitulates, combines, and decodes the novel's several simultaneous sub-plots and also traces the novel's complex character interrelationships from ancient Egypt up to the very moment of LaBas' narration. The narration leads to the arrest of Gould and Von Vampton, but also to the anti-discovery of the sacred Book of Thoth, the would-be Text of Jes Grew. Recast myths serve the same function of plot impediment for the purpose of repeating the novel's events through metaphorical substitution in two other places: these are the allegories of Faust and of the *houngan*, Ti Bouton (see *MJ*, pp. 90–92, 132–39). These recast myths serve as the play of doubles, consistent with the "double-image on form," which Reed sought to realize, and are implicit in the nature of allegory itself.

Plot impediment can be created in ways other than through temporal inversion; local-color description does as well. Local color, of course, came to be a standard feature in the social novel; in the Afro-American narrative, realism-as-local-color is perhaps the most consistent aspect of black rhetorical strategy from the slave narratives to *Invisible Man*. Reed uses and simultaneously parodies the convention of local color as plot impediment by employing unpunctuated lists and categories throughout the text, as seen in the novel's first paragraph:

> A True Sport, the Mayor of New Orleans, spiffy in his patent-leather brown and white shoes, his plaid suit, the Rudolph Valentino parted-down-the-middle hair style, sits in his office. Sprawled upon his knees is Zuzu, local doo-wack-a-doo and voo-do-dee-odo-fizgig. A slatternly floozy, her green, sequined dress quivers. [*MJ*, p. 3]

The following sentence exemplifies Reed's undifferentiated catalogs: "The dazzling parodying punning mischievous pre-Joycean style-play of your Cakewalking your Calinda your Minstrelsy give-and-take of the ultra-absurd" (*MJ*, p. 152). Viktor Šklovskj says that the mystery novel was drawn upon formally by the social novel; Reed's use of devices from the detective novel, then, to parody the black social novel reverses this process, appropriately and ironically enough.[42]

I have discussed how the tension of the two stories generally operates in the types of detective fiction. Reed's play of doubles assumes its most subtle form in his clever rhetorical strategy of using these two narratives, the story of the past and the story of the present. It is useful to think of these two as the narrative of *understanding* and the narrative of *truth*. The narrative of understanding is the presented narrative of the investigation of a mystery, in which a detective (reader) interprets or decodes "clues." Once these signs are sufficiently decoded, this narrative of understanding reconstitutes the missing story of the crime, which we can think of as the narrative of truth. The presented narrative, then, is implicitly a story of another, absent story and hence functions as an internal allegory.

The nature of this narrative of the investigation in *Mumbo Jumbo* can be easily characterized: the narrative remains close to the action with local-color description and dialogue as its two central aspects; character-as-description and extensive catalogs propel the narrative forward; the narrative remains essentially in the present tense, and the point of view is both in the third person and limited, as it must be if the reader's understanding of the nature of the mystery is to remain impeded until the novel's detective decodes all the clues, assembles all the suspects, interprets the signs, and reveals the truth of the mystery. The detective makes his arrests, and then everyone left eats dinner.

Mumbo Jumbo's prologue opens in this narrative mode of the story of the present. Near the end of the prologue, however, a second narrative mode intrudes. It is separated from the first narrative by spacing and is further foregrounded by italic type (see *MJ*, p. 6). It not only interprets and comments upon characters and actions in the first story but does so in a third-person omniscient mode. In other words, it *reads* its counterpart narrative, of which it is a negation. Following its italic type are three other sorts of sub-texts which comprise crucial aspects of this second, antithetical narration of past, present, and future: a black-and-white photograph of people dancing; an epigraph on the nature of the "second line," written by Louis Armstrong; and an etymology of the phrase "mumbo jumbo," taken from the *American Heritage Dictionary*. That which the characters ponder or "misunderstand" this foregrounded antithetical narration reads "correctly" for the reader.

> *But they did not understand that the Jes Grew epidemic was unlike physical*

> *plagues. Actually Jes Grew was an anti-plague. Some plagues caused the body to waste away; Jes Grew enlivened the host. . . . So Jes Grew is seeking its word. Its text. For what good is a liturgy without a text? In the 1890s the text was not available and Jes Grew was out there all alone. Perhaps the 1920s will also be a false alarm and Jes Grew will evaporate as quickly as it appeared again broken-hearted and double-crossed (++). [MJ,* p. 6]

This second, anti, narration consists of all of *Mumbo Jumbo*'s motley sub-texts which are not included in its first narration. Whereas the first story adheres to the present, the second roams remarkably freely through space and time, between myth and "history," humorously employing the device of anachronism. It is discontinuous and fragmentary, not linear like its counterpart; it never contains dialogue, it contains all of the text's abstractions.

All of the novel's sub-texts (illustrations, excerpts from other texts, Situation Reports, etc.) are parts of this second narration, which we might think of as an extended discourse on the history of Jes Grew. The only mysteries this antithetical narration does not address are the text's first two mysteries—what exactly Jes Grew is and what precisely its Text is. After chapter 8, the foregrounding of italics tends to disappear, for the narration manages to bracket or frame itself, functioning almost as the interior monologue of the first narrative mode. While the first story remains firmly in the tradition of the presented detective story, the second turns that convention inside out, functioning as an ironic double, a reversed mirror image like the cryptic *vé vé* on the novel's cover.

This second mode of narration allows for the "allegorical double" of *Mumbo Jumbo*. As many critics have gone to great lengths to demonstrate, *Mumbo Jumbo* is a thematic allegory of the Black Arts Movement of the 1960s rendered through causal connections with the Harlem Renaissance of the 1920s. A more interesting allegory, however, is that found in the antithetical narrative, which is a discourse on the history and nature of writing itself, especially that of the Afro-American literary tradition. *Mumbo Jumbo*, then, is a text that directs attention to its own writing, to its status as a text, related to other texts which it signifies upon. Its second narration reads its first, as does discourse upon a text. It is Reed reading Reed and the tradition. A formal metaphor for Reed's mode of writing is perhaps the bebop mode of jazz, as exemplified in that great reedist, Charlie Parker, who sometimes played a chord on the alto saxophone, then repeated and reversed the same chord to hear, if I understand him correctly, what he had just played. Parker is a recurring figure in Reed's works: "Parker, the houngan (a word derived from *n'gana gana*) for whom there was no master adept enough to award him the Asson, is born" (*MJ*, p. 16).[43] Just as Jes Grew, the novel's central "character," in searching for its Text is seeking to actualize a desire, to "find its Speaking or strangle upon its own ineloquence," so too is the search for a text replicated and referred to throughout the second, signifying narration (*MJ*, p. 34).

What is the status of this desired Text? How are we to read Reed? Jes Grew's desire would be actualized only by finding its Text. *Mumbo Jumbo*'s parodic use of the presented story of the detective novel states this desire; the solution of the novel's central mystery would be for Jes Grew to find its Text. This Text, PaPa LaBas' allegorical narrative at the Villa Lewaro tells us, is in fact the vast and terrible Text of Blackness itself, "always already" there: "the Book of Thoth, the sacred Work . . . of the Black Birdman, an assistant to Osiris. (If anyone thinks this is 'mystifying the past' [the narrative intrudes] kindly check out your local bird book and you will find the sacred Ibis' Ornithological name to be *Threskiornis aethiopicus*)" (*MJ*, p. 188). The irony of the mystery structure evident in *Mumbo Jumbo* is that this Text, Jes Grew's object of desire, is "defined" only by its absence; it is never seen, or found. At the climax of LaBas' amusingly detailed and long recapitulation of his process of reading the signs of the mystery (as well as the history of the dissemination of the Text itself), LaBas instructs his assistant, T Malice, to unveil the Text:

> Go get the Book T!
>
> T Malice goes out to the car and returns with a huge gleaming box covered with snakes and scorpions shaped of sparkling gems.
>
> The ladies intake their breath at such a gorgeous display. On the top can be seen the Knights Templar seal; 2 Knights riding Beaseauh, the Templars' piebald horse. T Malice places the box down in the center of the floor and removes the 1st box, an iron box, and the 2nd box, which is bronze and shines so that they have to turn the ceiling lights down. And within this box is a sycamore box and under the sycamore, ebony, and under this ivory, then silver and finally gold and then . . . empty!! [*MJ*, p. 196]

The nature of the Text remains undetermined, and indeed, indeterminate, as it was at the novel's beginning. Once the signs of its presence have been read, the Text disappears, in what must be the most humorous anticlimax in the whole of Afro-American fiction.

We can read this anticlimax against the notion of indeterminacy. Geoffrey H. Hartman defines the function of indeterminacy as "a bar separating understanding and truth."[44] The "bar" in *Mumbo Jumbo* is signified by that unbridgeable white space that separates the first narrative mode from the second, the narrative of truth. *Mumbo Jumbo* is a novel about indeterminacy in interpretation itself. The text repeats this theme again and again. In addition to the two narrative voices, the Atonist Path and its Wallflower Order are criticized severely for a foolish emphasis upon unity, upon the number 1, upon what the novel calls "point." One of the three symbols of the Atonist Order is "the #1" (*MJ*, p. 65). Their leader is called "Hierophant 1" (*MJ*, p. 63). A "hierophant," of course, is an expositor. The Atonists are defined in the antithetical narrative as they who seek to interpret the world through one interpretation: "To some if you owned your own mind you were indeed sick but when you possessed an Atonist mind you were healthy. A mind which sought to interpret the world by using a single loa. Somewhat like filling a milk bottle with an ocean" (*MJ*, p. 24). The novel defines the nature of this urge for the reduction of unity:

> 1st they intimidate the intellectuals by condemning work arising out of their own experience as being 1-dimensional, enraged, non-objective, preoccupied with hate and not universal, universal being a word coopted by the Catholic Church when the Atonists took over Rome, as a way of measuring every 1 by their deals. [*MJ*, p. 133]

One is an Atonist, the novel maintains consistently, who attempts to tie the sheer plurality of signification to one, determinate meaning.

In contrast is the spirit of Jes Grew and PaPa LaBas. As I have shown, the name "LaBas" is derived from Ẹ̀ṣù-Ẹlẹ́gbára. The Yoruba call Ẹ́ṣú the god of indeterminacy (*àriyẹ̀muyẹ̀*) and of uncertainty. PaPa LaBas, in contradistinction to Hierophant 1, has not one but two heads, like the face of the sign: "PaPa LaBas, noonday HooDoo, fugitve-hermit, obeah-man, botanist, animal impersonator, 2-headed man, You-Name-It" (*MJ*, p. 45). Moreover, he functions, as the detective of Jes Grew, as a decoder, as a sign reader, the man who cracked *de* code, by using his two heads: "Evidence? Woman, I dream about it, I feel it, I use my 2 heads. My Knockings" (*MJ*, p. 25). LaBas is the critic, engaged in The Work, the work of art, refusing to reduce it to a "point":

> People in the 60s said they couldn't follow him. (In Santa Cruz the students walked out.) What's your point? they asked in Seattle whose central point, the Space Needle, is invisible from time to time. What are you driving at? they would say in Detroit in the 1950s. In the 40s he haunted the stacks of a ghost library. [*MJ*, p. 218]

While arguing ironically with Abdul Sufi Hamid, the Black Muslim who subsequently burns the Book of Thoth, LaBas critiques Abdul's "black aesthetic" in terms identical to his critique of the Atonists:

> Where does that leave the ancient Vodun aesthetic: pantheistic, becoming, 1 which bountifully permits 1000s of spirits, as many as the imagination can hold. Infinite Spirits and Gods. So many that it would take a book larger than the Koran and the Bible, the Tibetan Book of the Dead and all of the holy books in the world to list, and still room would have to be made for more. [*MJ*, p. 35; see also Abdul's letter to LaBas, *MJ*, pp. 200–203]

It is indeterminacy, the sheer plurality of meaning, the very play of the signifier itself, which *Mumbo Jumbo* celebrates. *Mumbo Jumbo* addresses the *play* of the black literary tradition and, as a parody, is a *play* upon that same tradition. Its central character, Jes Grew, cannot be reduced by the Atonists, as they complain: "It's nothing we can bring into focus or categorize; once we call it 1 thing it forms into something else" (*MJ*, p. 4). Just as LaBas the detective is the text's figure for indeterminacy (paradoxically because he is a detective), so too is Jes Grew's "nature" indeterminate: its Text is never a presence, and it disappears when its Text disappears, as surely as does Charlotte when Doctor Peter Pick recites, during his reverse-minstrel plantation routine, an incantation from PaPa LaBas' *Blue Back: A Speller* (see *MJ*, pp. 104–5, 199).

Even the idea of one transcendent subject, Jes Grew's Text, the Text of Blackness itself, *Mumbo Jumbo* criticizes. When the poet, Nathan Brown, asks the Haitian *houngan* Benoit Battraville how to catch Jes Grew, Benoit replies: "don't ask me how to catch Jes Grew. Ask Louis Armstrong, Bessie Smith, your poets, your painters, your musicians, ask them how to catch it" (*MJ*, p. 152). Jes Grew also manifests itself in more curious forms:

> The Rhyming Fool who sits in Re-mote Mississippi and talks "crazy" for hours. The dazzling parodying punning mischievous pre-Joycean style-play of your Cakewalking your Calinda your Minstrelsy give-and-take of the ultra-absurd. Ask the people who put wax paper over combs and breathe through them. In other words, Nathan, I am saying Open-Up-To-Right-Here and then you will have something coming from your experience that the whole world will admire and need. [*MJ*, p. 152]

Jes Grew's Text, in other words, is not a transcendent signified but must be *produced* in a dynamic process and manifested in discrete forms, as in black music and black speech acts: "The Blues is a Jes Grew, as James Weldon Johnson surmised. Jazz was a Jes Grew which followed the Jes Grew of Ragtime. Slang is Jes Grew too," PaPa LaBas tells his 1960s audience in his annual lecture on the Harlem Renaissance (*MJ*, p. 214).

"Is this the end of Jes Grew?" the narrative questions when we learn that its Text does not exist. "Jes Grew has no end and no beginning," the text replies (*MJ*, p. 204). The echoes here are intentional: Reed echoes Ellison, or, rather, Ellison's echo of T. S. Eliot. "In my end is my beginning," writes Eliot in "East Coker,"

"In my beginning is my end." The "end," writes Ellison, "is in the beginning and lies far ahead."[45] Reed signifies upon Ellison's gesture of closure here, and that of the entire Afro-American literary tradition, by positing an open-endedness of interpretation, of the play of signifiers, just as his and Ellison's works both signify upon the idea of the transcendent signified of the black tradition, the Text of Blackness itself.

The tradition's classic text on the "Blackness of Blackness" is found in the prologue of *Invisible Man*:

> "Brothers and sisters, my text this morning is the 'Blackness of Blackness.'"
> And a congregation of voices answered:
> "That blackness is most black, brother, most black . . ."
> "In the beginning . . ."
> "At the very start," they cried.
> ". . . there was blackness . . ."
> "Preach it . . ."
> ". . . and the sun . . ."
> "The sun, Lawd . . ."
> ". . . was bloody red . . ."
> "Red . . ."
> "Now black is . . ." the preacher shouted.
> "Bloody . . ."
> "I said black is . . ."
> "Preach it, brother . . ."
> ". . . an' black ain't . . ."
> "Red, Lawd, red: He said it's red!"
> "Amen, brother . . ."
> "Black will git you . . ."
> "Yes, it will . . ."
> ". . . an' black won't . . ."
> "Naw, it won't!"
> "It do . . ."
> "It do, Lawd . . ."
> ". . . an' it don't."
> "Halleluiah . . ."
> ". . . It'll put you, glory, glory, Oh my Lawd, in the WHALE'S BELLY."
> "Preach it, dear brother . . ."
> ". . . an' make you tempt . . ."
> "Good God a-mighty!"
> "Old Aunt Nelly!"
> "Black will make you . . ."
> "Black . . ."
> ". . . or black will un-make you."
> "Ain't it the truth, Lawd?" [*IM*, pp. 12–13]

This sermon signifies on Melville's passage in *Moby-Dick* on "the blackness of darkness" and on the sign of blackness, as represented by the algorithm $\frac{\text{signified}}{\text{signifier}}$[46]. As Ellison's text states, "black is" and "black ain't," "It do, Lawd," "an' it don't." Ellison parodies here the notion of essence, of the supposedly natural relation between the symbol and the symbolized. The vast and terrible Text of Blackness, we realize, has no essence; rather, it is signified into being by a signifier. The trope of blackness in Western discourse has signified absence at least since Plato. Plato, in the *Phaedrus*, recounts the myth of Theuth (*Mumbo Jumbo*'s "Thoth") and the introduction of writing into Egypt. Along the way, Plato has Socrates draw upon the figure of blackness as a metaphor for one of the three divisions of the soul, that of "badness": "The other is crooked of frame, a massive jumble of a creature, with thick short neck, snub nose, black skin, and gray eyes; hot-blooded, consorting with wantonness and vainglory; shaggy of ear, deaf, and hard to control with whip and goad."[47] Reed's use of the myth of Thoth is, of course, not accidental or arbitrary: he repeats and inverts Plato's dialogue, salient point for salient point, even down to Socrates' discourse on the excesses of the dance, which is a theme of *Mumbo Jumbo*.[48] It is not too much to say that *Mumbo Jumbo* is one grand signifying riff on the *Phaedrus*, parodying it through the hidden polemic.

Both Ellison and Reed, then, critique the received idea of blackness as a negative essence, as a natural, transcendent signified; but implicit in such a critique is an equally thorough critique of blackness as a *presence*, which is merely another transcendent signified. Such a critique, therefore, is a critique of the structure of the sign itself and constitutes a profound critique. The Black Arts Movement's grand gesture was to make of the trope of blackness a trope of presence. That movement willed it to be, however, a transcendent presence. Ellison's "text for today," "the 'Blackness of Blackness' " (*IM*, p. 12), analyzes this gesture, just as surely as does Reed's Text of Blackness, the "sacred Book of Thoth." In literature, blackness is *produced* in the text only through a complex process of signification. There can be no transcendent blackness, for it cannot and does not exist beyond manifestations of it in specific figures. Put simply, Jes Grew cannot conjure its texts; "texts," in the broadest sense of this term (Parker's music, Ellison's fictions, Romare Bearden's collages, etc.), conjure Jes Grew.

Reed has, in *Mumbo Jumbo*, signified upon Ellison's critique of the central presupposition of the Afro-American literary tradition, by drawing upon Ellison's trope as a central theme of the plot of *Mumbo Jumbo* and by making explicit Ellison's implicit critique of the nature of the sign itself, of a transcendent signified, an essence, which supposedly exists prior to its figuration. Their formal relationship can only be suggested by the relation of modernism to post-modernism, two overworked terms. Blackness exists, but "only" as a function of its signifiers. Reed's open-ended structure, and his stress on the indeterminacy of the text, demands that we, as critics, in the act of reading, *produce* a text's signifying structure. For Reed, as for his great precursor, Ellison, figuration is indeed the "nigger's occupation."

4. CODA: THE WARP AND THE WOOF

Reed's signifying relation to Ellison is exemplified in his poem, "Dualism: in ralph ellison's invisible man":

> i am outside of
> history. i wish
> i had some peanuts, it
> looks hungry there in
> its cage.
>
> i am inside of
> history. its
> hungrier than i
> thot.[49]

The figure of history, here, is the Signifying Monkey; the poem signifies upon that repeated trope of dualism figured initially in black discourse in Du Bois' essay "Of Our Spiritual Strivings," which forms the first chapter of *The Souls of Black Folk*. The dualism parodied by Reed's poem is that represented in the epilogue of *Invisible Man*: "Now I know men are different and that all life is divided and that only in division is there true health" (*IM*, p. 499). For Reed, this belief in the "reality" of dualism spells death. Ellison, here, had refigured Du Bois' trope:

> After the Egyptian and Indian, the Greek and Roman, the Teuton and Mongolian, the Negro is a sort of seventh son, born with a veil, and gifted with second-sight in this American world,—a world which yields him no true self-consciousness, but only lets him see himself through the revelation of the other world. It is a peculiar sensation, this double-consciousness, this sense of always looking at one's self through the eyes of others, of measuring one's soul by the tape of a world that looks on in amused contempt and pity. One ever feels his two-ness,—an American, a Negro; two souls, two thoughts, two unreconciled strivings; two warring ideals in one dark body, whose dogged strength alone keeps it from being torn asunder.
>
> The history of the American Negro is the history of this strife,—this longing to attain self-conscious manhood, to merge his double self into a better and truer self. In this merging he wishes neither of the older selves to be lost.[50]

Reed's poem parodies, profoundly, both the figure of the black as outsider and the figure of the divided self. For, he tells us, even these are only tropes, figures of speech, rhetorical constructs like "double-consciousness," and not some preordained reality or thing. To read these figures literally, Reed tells us, to be duped by figuration, just like the signified Lion. Reed has secured his place in the canon precisely by his critique of the received, repeated tropes peculiar to that very canon. His works are the grand works of critical signification.

NOTES

1. Quoted in Roger D. Abrahams, *Deep Down in the Jungle . . . : Negro Narrative Folklore from the Streets of Philadelphia* (Chicago, 1970), p. 53.

2. The present essay is extracted from my larger work *The Signifying Monkey: Towards a Theory of Literary History*, forthcoming.

3. On Tar Baby, see Ralph Ellison, "Hidden Man and Complex Fate: A Writer's Experience in the United States." *Shadow and Act* (New York, 1964), p. 147, and Toni Morrison, *Tar Baby* (New York, 1981). On the black as quasi-simian, see Jean Bodin, *Method for the Easy Comprehension of History*, trans. Beatrice Reynolds (1945; New York, 1966), p. 105; Aristotle *Historia Animalium* 606b; Thomas Herbert, *Some Years Travels* (London, 1677), pp. 16–17; and John Locke, *An Essay Concerning Human Understanding*, 8th ed., 2 vols. (London, 1721), 2:53.

4. Geneva Smitherman defines these and other black tropes and then traces their use in several black texts. Smitherman's work, like that of Claudia Mitchell-Kernan and Abrahams, is especially significant for literary theory. See Smitherman, *Talkin and Testifyin: The Language of Black America* (Boston, 1977), 101–66. See also nn. 13 and 14 below.

5. On versions of Èṣù, see Robert Farris Thompson, *Black Gods and Kings* (1971; Bloomington, Ind., 1976), Chap. 4, 1–12, and *Flash of the Spirit* (New York, 1983); Pierre Verger, *Notes sur le culte des Orisa et Vodun* (Dakar, 1957); Joan Westcott, "The Sculpture and Myths of Eshu-Elegba, The Yoruba Trickster," *Africa*, 32 (Oct. 1962), 336–54; Leo Frobenius, *The Voice of Africa*, 2 vols. (London, 1913); Melville J. and Frances Herskovits, *Dahomean Narrative* (Evanston, Ill., 1958); Wande Abimbola, *Sixteen Great Poems of Ifa* (New York, 1975); William R. Bascom, *Ifa Divination: Communication between Gods and Men in West Africa* (Bloomington, Ind., 1969); Ayodele Ogundipe, "Esu Elegbara: The Yoruba God of Chance and Uncertainty," 2 vols. (Ph.D. diss., Indiana Univ., 1978); E. Bolaji Idowu, *Olódùmarè, God in Yoruba Belief* (London, 1962), pp. 80–85; and Robert Pelton, *The Trickster in West Africa* (Los Angeles, 1980).

6. On Èsù and indeterminacy, see Robert Plant Armstrong. *The Powers of Presence: Consciousness, Myth, and Affecting Presence* (Philadelphia, 1981), p. 4. See ibid., p. 43, for a drawing of the *Opón Ifá*, and Thompson, *Black Gods and Kings*, chap. 5.

7. On Èsù and the Monkey, see Lydia Cabrerra, *El Monte: Notes sobre las religiones, la magia, las supersticiones y el folklore de los negros criollos y el pueblo de Cuba* (Miami, 1975), p. 84, and Alberto de Pozo, *Oricha* (Miami, 1982), p. 1. On the Signifying Monkey, see Abrahams, *Deep Down in the Jungle*, pp. 51–53, 66, 113–19, 142–47, 153–56, and esp. 264; Bruce Jackson, comp., *"Get Your Ass in the Water and Swim Like Me": Narrative Poetry from Black Oral Tradition* (Cambridge, Mass., 1974), pp. 161–80; Daryl Cumber Dance, *Shuckin; and Jivin': Folklore from Contemporary Black Americans* (Bloomington, Ind., 1978), pp. 197–99; Dennis Wepman, Ronald B. Newman, and Murray B. Binderman, comps., *The Life: The Lore and Folk Poetry of the Black Hustler* (Philadelphia, 1976), pp. 21–29; Lawrence W. Levine, *Black Culture and Black Consciousness: Afro-American Folk Thought from Slavery to Freedom* (New York, 1977), pp. 346, 378–80, 438; and Richard M. Dorson, comp., *American Negro Folktales* (New York, 1967), pp. 98–99.

8. Julia Kristeva, *Desire in Language: A Semiotic Approach to Literature and Art*, ed. Leon S. Roudiez, trans. Thomas Gora, Alice Jardine, and Roudiez (New York, 1980), p. 31.

9. Abrahams, *Deep Down in the Jungle*, pp. 51–52. See also Abrahams, " 'Playing the Dozens,' " *Journal of American Folklore*, 75 (July–Sept. 1962), 209–20; "The Changing Concept of the Negro Hero," in *The Golden Log*, ed. Mody C. Boatright, Wilson M. Hudson, and Allen Maxwell, Publications of the Texas Folklore Society, No. 31 (Dallas, 1962), pp. 125–34; and *Talking Black* (Rowley, Mass., 1976).

10. Abrahams, *Deep Down in the Jungle*, pp. 52, 264, 66, 67; emphasis mine. Abrahams' awareness of the need to define uniquely black significations is exemplary; as early as 1964, when he published the first edition of *Deep Down in the Jungle*, he saw fit to add a glossary, as an appendix of "Unusual Terms and Expressions," a title which unfortunately suggests the social scientist's apologia.

11. Ibid., p. 113. In the second line of the stanza, "motherfucker" is often substituted for "monkey."

12. "The Signifying Monkey" in *The Book of Negro Folklore*, ed. Langston Hughes and Anna Bontemps (New York, 1958), pp. 365–66.

13. On signifying as a rhetorical trope, see Thomas Kockman, ed., *Rappin' and Stylin' Out: Communication in Urban Black America* (Urbana, Ill., 1972), and " 'Rappin' in the Black Ghetto," *Transaction*, 6 (Feb. 1969), 32; Smitherman, *Talkin and Testifyin*, pp. 101–67; Alan Dundes, ed., *Mother Wit from the Laughing Barrel* (Englewood Cliffs, N.J., 1973), p. 310; and Ethel M. Albert, " 'Rhetoric,' 'Logic,' and 'Poetics' in Burundi: Culture Patterning of Speech Behavior," in *The Ethnography of Communication*, ed. John J. Gumperz and Dell Hymes, *American Anthropologist*, 66 pt. 2 (Dec. 1964), 35–54. One example of signifying can be gleaned from an anecdote: While writing this essay, I asked a colleague, Dwight Andrews, if as a child he had heard of the Signifying Monkey. "Why, no," he replied intently, "I never heard of the Signifying Monkey until I came to Yale and read about him in a book." I had been signified upon. If I had responded to Mr. Andrews, "I know what you mean; your Momma read to me from that same book the last time I was in Detroit," I would have signified upon him in return.

14. Mitchell-Kernan, "Signifying," in *Mother Wit from the Laughing Barrel*, p. 313; all further references to this work, abbreviated "Sig," will be included parenthetically in the text. See also her "Signifying, Loud-talking, and Marking," in *Rappin' and Stylin' Out*, pp. 315–35.

15. See Mitchell-Kernan, "Signifying, Loud-talking, and Marking," pp. 315–35. For Zora Neale Hurston's definition of "signifying," see *Mules and Men: Negro Folktales and Voodoo Practices in the South* (1935; New York, 1970), p. 161.

16. For a definitive study of revision and its relation to ideas of modernism, see Kimberly W. Benston, *Afro-American Modernism*, forthcoming. Benston's reading of Hurston's revision of Frederick Douglass has heavily informed my own.

17. Ellison, "And Hickman Arrives," in *Black Writers of America: A Comprehensive Anthology*, ed. Richard Barksdale and Kenneth Kinnamon (New York, 1972), p. 704.

18. Ellison, "On Bird, Bird-Watching, and Jazz," *Shadow and Act*, p. 231.

19. Ellison, "Blues People," *Shadow and Act*, pp. 249–50.

20. Ellison, "The World and the Jug," *Shadow and Act*, p. 117.

21. Ibid., p. 137; emphasis mine.

21. Mixhail Baxtin [Mikhail Bakhtin], "Discourse Typology in Prose," in *Readings in Russian Poetics: Formalist and Structuralist Views*, ed. Ladislav Matejka and Krystyna Pomorska (Cambridge, Mass., 1971), p. 187; see also pp. 176–96.

23. The use of interlocking triangles as a metaphor for the intertextual relationships of the tradition is not meant to suggest any form of concrete, inflexible reality. On the contrary, it is a systematic metaphor, as René Girard puts it, "systematically pursued":

> The triangle is no *Gestalt*. The real structures are intersubjective. They cannot be localized anywhere; *the triangle has no reality whatever; it is a systematic metaphor, systematically pursued.* Because changes in size and shape do not destroy the identity of this figure, as we will see later, the diversity as well as the unity of the works can be simultaneously illustrated. The purpose and limitations of this structural geometry may become clearer through a reference to "structural models." The triangle is a model of a sort, or rather a whole family of models. But these models are not "mechanical" like those of Claude Lévi-Strauss. They always allude to the mystery, transparent yet opaque, of human relations. All types of structural thinking assume that human reality is intelligible; it is a *logos* and, as such, *it is an incipient logic, or it degrades itself into a logic.* It can thus be systematized, at least up to a point, however unsystematic, irrational, and chaotic it may appear even to those, or rather especially to those who operate the system. [René Girard, *Deceit, Desire, and the Novel: Self and Other in Literary Structure*, trans. Yvonne Freccero (Baltimore, 1965), pp. 2–3; emphasis mine]

24. For Ishmael Reed on "a talking book," see "Ishmael Reed: A Self Interview," *Black World*, 23 (June 1974), 25. For the slave narratives in which this figure appears, see James Albert Ukawsaw Gronniosaw, *A Narrative of the Most Remarkable Particulars of the Life of James Albert Ukawsaw Gronniosaw, An African Prince* (Bath, 1770); John Marrant, *Narrative of the Lord's Wonderful Dealings with John Marrant, A Black* (London, 1785); Ottabah Cugoano, *Thoughts and Sentiments on the Evil and Wicked Traffic of the Slavery and Commerce of the Human Species* (London, 1787); Olaudah Equiano, *The Interesting Narrative of the Life of Olaudah Equiano, or Gustavus Vassa. The African, Written by Himself* (London, 1789); and John Jea, *The Life and Sufferings of John Jea, An African Preacher* (Swansea, 1806).

25. Northrop Frye, *Anatomy of Criticism: Four Essays* (Princeton, N.J., 1957), p. 233.

26. Baxtin [Bakhtin], "Discourse Typology in Prose," p. 190.

27. Frye, *Anatomy of Criticism*, p. 234.

28. Ellison, "The World and the Jug," p. 140.

29. See Reed, *The Free-Lance Pallbearers* (Garden City, N.Y., 1967), *Yellow Back Radio Broke-Down* (Garden City, N.Y., 1969), *Mumbo Jumbo* (Garden City, N.Y., 1972), *The Last Days of Louisiana Red* (New York, 1974), *Flight to Canada* (New York, 1976), and *The Terrible Twos* (New York, 1982).

30. See Neil Schmitz, "Neo-HooDoo: The Experimental Fiction of Ishmael Reed," *Twentieth Century Literature*, 20 (Apr. 1974), 126–28. Schmitz's splendid reading is, I believe, the first to discuss this salient aspect of Reed's rhetorical strategy. This paragraph is heavily indebted to Schmitz's essay.

31. Reed, *The Free-Lance Pallbearers*, p. 107.

32. Reed, *Yellow Back Radio Broke-Down*, pp. 34–36. For an excellent close reading of *Yellow Back Radio Broke-Down*, see Michel Fabre, "Postmodern Rhetoric in Ishmael Reed's *Yellow Back Radio Broke-Down*," in *The Afro-American Novel since 1960*, ed. Peter Bruck and Wolfgand Karrer (Amsterdam, 1982), pp. 167–88.

33. Reed, *Mumbo Jumbo*, p. 6; all further references to this work, abbreviated *MJ*, will be included parenthetically in the text.

34. Ellison, "And Hickman Arrives," p. 701.

35. See Charles T. Davis, *Black is the Color of the Cosmos: Essays on Black Literature and Culture, 1942–1981*, ed. Henry Louis Gates, Jr. (New York, 1982), pp. 167–233.

36. My reading of the imagery on Reed's cover was inspired by a conversation with Thompson.

37. On Reed's definition of "gombo" (gumbo), see his "The Neo-HooDoo Aesthetic," *Conjure: Selected Poems, 1963–1970* (Amherst, Mass., 1972), p. 26.

38. This clever observation is James A. Snead's, for whose Yale seminar on parody I wrote the first draft of this essay.

39. Reed, interview by Calvin Curtis, 29 Jan. 1979.

40. Tzvetan Todorov, "The Two Principles of Narrative," trans. Philip E. Lewis, *Diacritics* 1 (Fall 1971):
41. See his *The Poetics of Prose*, trans. Richard Howard (Ithaca, 1977), pp. 42–52; all further references to this work, abbreviated *PP*, will be included parenthetically in the text.

41. For a wonderfully useful discussion of *fabula* ("fable") and *sjužet* ("subject"), see Victor Šklovskij, "The Mystery Novel: Dickens' *Little Dorrit*," in *Readings in Russian Poetics*, pp. 220–226. On use of typology, see p. 222.

42. See Šklovskij, "The Mystery Novel," pp. 222, 226.

43. A *houngan* is a priest of *Vaudou*. On *Vaudou*, see Jean Price-Mars, *Ainsi parla l'Oncle* (Port-au-Prince, 1928) and Alfred Metraux, *Le Vodou haitien* (Paris, 1958).

44. Geoffrey H. Hartman, *Criticism in the Wilderness: The Study of Literature Today* (New Haven, Conn., 1980), p. 272.

45. Ellison, *Invisible Man* (New York, 1952), p. 9; all further references to this work, abbreviated *IM*, will be included parenthetically in the text.

46. Melville's passage from *Moby-Dick* reads: "It seemed the great Black Parliament sitting in Tophet. A hundred black faces turned round in their rows to peer; and beyond, a black Angel of Doom was beating a book in a pulpit. It was a negro church; and the preacher's text was about the blackness of darkness, and the weeping and wailing and teeth-gnashing there. Ha, Ishmael, muttered I, backing out, Wretched entertainment at the sign of 'The Trap' " (*Moby-Dick* [1851; New York, 1967], p. 18). This curious figure also appears in James Pike's *The Prostrate State: South Carolina under Negro Government* (New York, 1874), p. 62.

47. Plato *Phaedrus* 253d–254a. For the myth of Theuth, see 274c–275b.

48. See ibid., 259b–259e.

49. Reed, "Dualism: in ralph ellison's invisible man," *Conjure*, p. 50.

50. W. E. B. Du Bois, *The Souls of Black Folk: Essays and Sketches* (1903; New York, 1961), pp. 16–17.

Acknowledgments (continued)

"Brecht and Rhetoric," by Terry Eagleton from *Against the Grain*, pp. 167–172. Copyright © 1986 by Verso. Reprinted by permission of Terry Eagleton.

"The Politics of Theory: Ideological Positions in the Postmodernism Debate," by Fredric Jameson from *New German Critique*, 33, pp. 53–65. Copyright © 1984 by Cornell University. Reprinted by permission of Cornell University.

"Shakespeare and the Exorcist," by Stephen Greenblatt from *Shakespeare and the Question of Theory*, pp. 163–187, edited by Patricia Parker and Geoffrey Hartman. New York: Methven, 1985. Copyright © 1985 by Stephen Greenblatt. Reprinted by permission of the author.

"Feminist Criticism in the Wilderness," by Elaine Showalter from *Critical Inquiry*, No. 8, pp. 243–270. Copyright ©1981 by the University of Chicago Press. Reprinted by permission of the University of Chicago Press.

"Castration or Decapitation," by Hélène Cixous from *Signs* 7.11, pp. 41–55, translated by Annette Kuhn. Copyright © 1981 by the University of Chicago Press. Reprinted by permission of the University of Chicago Press.

"Life's Empty Pack: Notes toward a Literary Daughteronomy," by Sandra Gilbert from *Critical Inquiry* 11.3, pp. 355–384. Copyright © 1985 by the University of Chicago Press. Reprinted by permission of the University of Chicago Press.

"Imperialism and Sexual Difference," by Gayatri Chakravorty Spivak from *Sexual Difference*, pp. 225–240. edited by Robert Young, *Oxford Literary Review* 8. Copyright © 1986 by the Oxford Literary Review. Reprinted by permission of the Oxford Literary Review.

"The Function of Criticism at the Present Time," by Northrop Frye from *Our Sense of Identity*, pp. 247–265, edited by Malcolm Ross. Copyright © 1954 by Northrop Frye. Reprinted by permission of the author.

"The Deconstructive Angel," by M.H. Abrams from *Critical Inquiry* 3, pp. 425–438. Copyright © 1977 by the University of Chicago Press. Reprinted by permission of the University of Chicago Press.

"The Grounds of Literary Study," by J. Hillis Miller from *Rhetoric and Form: Deconstruction at Yale*, pp. 19–36, edited by Robert Con Davis and Ronald Schleifer. Copyright © 1984 by the University of Oklahoma Press. Reprinted by permission of the University of Oklahoma Press.

"Reflections on American 'Left' Literary Criticism," reprinted by permission of the publishers from *The World, the Text, and the Critic*, by Edward W. Said, Cambridge, Massachusetts: Harvard University Press. Copyright © 1979, 1983 by Edward W. Said.

"Psychoanalysis and Education: Teaching Terminable and Interminable," by Shoshana Felman from *Yale French Studies*, 63, pp. 21–44. Copyright © 1982 by Yale University Press. Reprinted by permission of Yale University Press.

"Treason Our Text: Feminist Challenges to the Literary Canon," by Lillian S. Robinson from *Tulsa Studies in Women's Literature*, Vol. 2, No. 1, pp. 105–121. Copyright © 1983 by Tulsa Studies in Women's Literature. Reprinted by permission of the publisher.

"The 'Blackness of Blackness': A Critique of the Sign and the Signifying Monkey," by Henry Louis Gates, Jr., from *Black Literature and Literary Theory*, pp. 285–321. Copyright © 1984 by Henry Louis Gates, Jr. Reprinted by permission of Brandt & Brandt Literary Agents, Inc.

Index